Miller & Levine Biology

CORE EDITION

Kenneth R. Miller, Ph.D.

Professor of Biology, Brown University
Providence, Rhode Island

Joseph S. Levine, Ph.D.

Science Writer and Producer
Concord, Massachusetts

PEARSON

Boston, Massachusetts • Chandler, Arizona • Glenview, Illinois • Upper Saddle River, New Jersey

Print Components

Student Core Edition

Teacher's Core Edition

Study Workbook A

Study Workbook A, Teacher's Edition

Study Workbook B: Reading Foundations

Study Workbook B: Reading Foundations,
  Teacher's Edition

Laboratory Manual A

Laboratory Manual A, Teacher's Edition

Laboratory Manual B: Skill Foundations

Laboratory Manual B: Skill Foundations,
  Teacher's Edition

Probeware Lab Manual

Assessment Resources

Transparencies

Technology Components

Biology.com

Untamed Science® Video Series: BioAdventures DVD

Classroom Resources DVD-ROM

ExamView® CD-ROM

Virtual BioLab DVD-ROM with Lab Manual

English Language Learners

Teacher's ELL Handbook

Multilingual Glossary

Spanish Components

Spanish Student Edition (with online Spanish audio)

Spanish Teacher's Guide

Spanish Study Workbook

Photographs Every effort has been made to secure permission and provide appropriate credit for photographic material. The publisher deeply regrets any omission and pledges to correct errors called to its attention in subsequent editions. Unless otherwise acknowledged, all photographs are the property of Pearson Education, Inc.

Credits appear on pages C–1 to C–2, which constitute an extension of this copyright page. Select images were replaced in 2011 to meet contractual obligations.

ISBN-13: 978-0-13-368506-0

ISBN-10: 0-13-368506-3

5 6 7 8 9 10   V057   15 14 13 12 11

About the Authors

Kenneth R. Miller grew up in Rahway, New Jersey, attended the local public schools, and graduated from Rahway High School in 1966. Miller attended Brown University on a scholarship and graduated with honors. He was awarded a National Defense Education Act fellowship for graduate study, and earned his Ph.D. in Biology at the University of Colorado. Miller is professor of Biology at Brown University in Providence, Rhode Island, where he teaches courses in general biology and cell biology.

Miller's research specialty is the structure of biological membranes. He has published more than 70 research papers in journals such as *Cell, Nature,* and *Scientific American.* He has also written the popular trade books *Finding Darwin's God* and *Only a Theory.* He is a fellow of the American Association for the Advancement of Science.

Miller lives with his wife, Jody, on a small farm in Rehoboth, Massachusetts. He is the father of two daughters, one a wildlife biologist and the other a high-school history teacher. He swims competitively in the masters' swimming program and umpires high school and collegiate softball.

Joseph S. Levine was born in Mount Vernon, New York, where he attended public schools. He earned a B.S. in Biology at Tufts University, a master's degree from the Boston University Marine Program, and a Ph.D. at Harvard University. His research has been published in scientific journals ranging from *Science* to *Scientific American,* and in several academic books. He has taught introductory biology, ecology, marine biology, neurobiology, and coral reef biology at Boston College and in the Boston University Marine Program. He has also co-taught a field biology course for high-school teachers entitled "Rainforests and Reefs" at the Organization for Tropical Studies in Costa Rica.

After receiving a Macy Fellowship in Science Broadcast Journalism at WGBH-TV, Levine dedicated himself to improving public understanding of science. His popular scientific writing has appeared in five trade books and in magazines such as *Smithsonian, GEO,* and *Natural History.* He has produced science features for National Public Radio and has designed exhibit programs for state aquarium projects in Texas, New Jersey, and Florida. Since 1987, Levine has served as scientific advisor at WGBH, where he worked on NOVA programs including *Judgment Day,* and on projects including the OMNI-MAX films *Cocos: Island of Sharks* and *Coral Reef Adventure.* He also served as science editor for the PBS series *The Secret of Life* and *The Evolution Project.*

Levine and his family live in Concord, Massachusetts, a short distance from Thoreau's Walden Pond.

Miller & Levine Biology: Core Edition

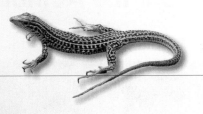

The Core Edition of *Miller & Levine Biology* is the perfect option for a classroom looking for a concise textbook that is light on the book bag. Accompanied by robust digital support on Biology.com, the Core Edition covers the following standards-based units:

- The Nature of Life
- Ecology
- Cells
- Genetics
- Evolution

For classrooms that are looking for units covering Plants, Animals, and the Human Body, the full textbook is available on Biology.com with all 8 units.

A Blended Approach

The Core Edition provides full intergration of textbook and technology into a dynamic program that allows for complete content coverage while allowing Biology.com to bring biology alive in your classroom. By providing a comprehensive mix of inquiry, engaging visuals, reading support, and comprehensive assessments, the Core Edition combines the power of print and technology to give you the content and support you need.

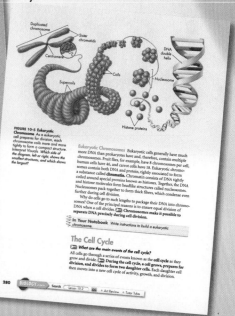

iv

Biology.com

After logging into the student center on Biology.com, you can access your Interactive Textbook with audio as well as a wealth of activities that pick up art content directly from the textbook to create a seamless transition from print to online.

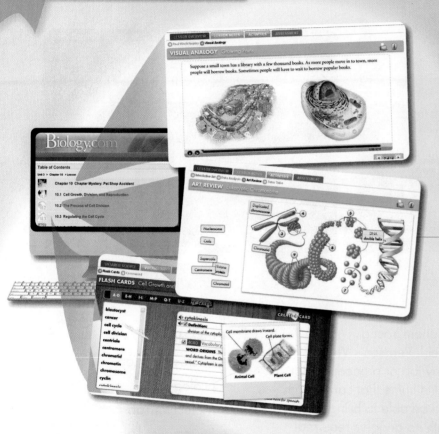

Your assets on Biology.com include: In Your Notebook, Visual Analogies, Interactive Art, Data Analysis, Chapter Mystery with Untamed Science, Flashcards, Asessments and much more.

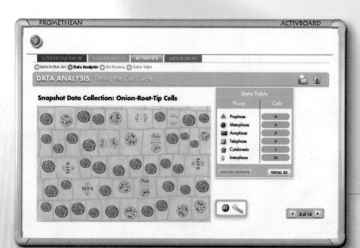

The Core Edition of Miller & Levine Biology brings biology to life in your classroom by combining the power of print and technology to give you the content and support you need.

Premium Online Learning on Biology.com PLUS

Looking for more digital support? Access to Biology.com comes included with your textbook, but there's even more premium content available on Biology.com PLUS. Explore biology in a virtual environment through a Pearson exclusive—Virtual BioLab. Keep yourself informed on the latest developments in the world of biology and interact with your authors through monthly author updates. Both available only on Biology.com PLUS.

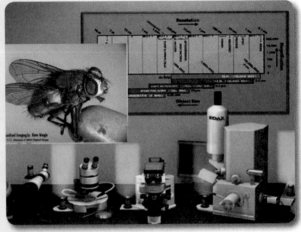

Virtual BioLab

Developed in conjunction with Brigham Young University Professor Brian Woodfield, Pearson's Virtual BioLab program helps you with any lab or procedure that can be performed in a real lab—and some that can't! With Virtual BioLab, your classroom will be able to bring your lab experience to a new level—with no goggles required!

Labs include:

- Genetics Lab
- Microscopy Lab
- Ecology Lab
- Molecular Lab
- Systematics Lab

Monthly Author Updates

Keep up-to-date with the latest developments in Biology with Monthly Author updates from Ken and Joe.

Updates include:

- Articles and Presentations from Ken and Joe on the latest current events in Biology

- Podcasts of Ken and Joe so you can get information directly from the authors' mouths

- News feeds to external Biology websites available via RSS feed.

Visit PearsonSchool.com to learn more on how you can access Biology.com PLUS!

Consultants/Reviewers

Grant Wiggins, Ed.D. is a co-author of the *Understanding by Design Handbook*. His approach to instructional design provides teachers with a disciplined way of thinking about curriculum design, assessment, and instruction that moves teaching from covering the content to ensuring understanding.

The Association for Supervision of Curriculum Development (ASCD), publisher of the "Understanding by Design Handbook" co-authored by Grant Wiggins and registered owner of the trademark "Understanding by Design", has not authorized, approved or sponsored this work and is in no way affiliated with Pearson or its products.

Big idea Big Ideas are one of the core components of the Understanding by Design approach in *Miller & Levine Biology.* These Big Ideas, such as Science as a Way of Knowing and the Cellular Basis of Life, establish a conceptual framework for the program. In the Student Edition, look for opportunities throughout each chapter to link back to the Big Ideas. And, since the Understanding by Design methodology is by nature a teaching tool, see the Teacher's Edition for additional applications of this philosophy.

Jim Cummins is Professor and Canada Research Chair in the Curriculum, Teaching and Learning department at the Ontario Institute for Studies in Education at the University of Toronto. His research focuses on literacy development in multilingual schools and the role of technology in promoting language and literacy development.

Program materials for *Miller & Levine Biology* incorporate research-based essential principles using Dr. Cummins's Into/Through/Beyond structure. You will find ample support for ELL instruction in the Teacher's Edition, Teacher's ELL Handbook, the Multilingual Glossary, as well as the Spanish components offered with this program.

Content Reviewers

Lily Chen
Associate Professor
Department of Biology
San Francisco State University
San Francisco, CA

Elizabeth Coolidge-Stolz, MD
Medical/Life Science Writer/Editor
North Reading, MA

Elizabeth A. De Stasio, Ph.D.
Raymond H. Herzog
Professor of Science
Associate Professor of Biology
Lawrence University
Appleton, WI

Jennifer C. Drew, Ph.D.
Lecturer/Scientist
University of Florida
Kennedy Space Center, FL

Donna H. Duckworth, Ph.D.
Professor Emeritus
College of Medicine
University of Florida
Gainesville, FL

Alan Gishlick, Ph.D.
Assistant Professor
Gustavus Adolphus College
St. Peter, MN

Deborah L. Gumucio, Ph.D.
Professor
Department of Cell and
Developmental Biology
University of Michigan
Ann Arbor, MI

Janet Lanza, Ph.D.
Professor of Biology
University of Arkansas
at Little Rock
Little Rock, AR

Charles F. Lytle, Ph.D.
Professor of Zoology
North Carolina State University
Raleigh, NC

Martha Newsome, DDS
Adjunct Instructor of Biology
Cy-Fair College, Fairbanks Center
Houston, TX

Jan A. Pechenik, Ph.D.
Professor of Biology
Tufts University
Medford, MA

Imara Y. Perera, Ph.D.
Research Assistant, Professor
Department of Plant Biology
North Carolina State University
Raleigh, NC

Daniel M. Raben, Ph.D.
Professor
Department of Biological
Chemistry
Johns Hopkins University
Baltimore, MD

Megan Rokop, Ph.D.
Educational Outreach Program
Director
Broad Institute of MIT and
Harvard
Cambridge, MA

Gerald P. Sanders
Former Biology Instructor
Grossmont College
Julian, CA

Ronald Sass, Ph.D.
Professor Emeritus
Rice University
Houston, TX

Linda Silveria, Ph.D.
Professor
University of Redlands
Redlands, CA

Richard K. Stucky, Ph.D.
Curator of Paleontology and
Evolution
Denver Museum of Nature and
Science
Denver, CO

Robert Thornton, Ph.D.
Senior Lecturer Emeritus
Department of Plant Biology
College of Biological Sciences
University of California at Davis
Davis, CA

Edward J. Zalisko, Ph.D.
Professor of Biology
Blackburn College
Carlinville, IL

ESL Lecturer

**Nancy Vincent Montgomery,
Ed.D.**
Southern Methodist University
Dallas, TX

High-School Reviewers

Christine Bill
Sayreville War Memorial High
School
Parlin, NJ

Jean T. (Caye) Boone
Central Gwinnett High School
Lawrenceville, GA

Samuel J. Clifford, Ph.D.
Biology Teacher
Round Rock High School
Round Rock, TX

Jennifer Collins, M.A.
South County Secondary School
Lorton, VA

Roy Connor, M.S.
Science Department Head
Muncie Central High School
Muncie, IN

Norm Dahm, Jr.
Belleville East High School
Belleville, IL

Cora Nadine Dickson
Science Department Chair
Jersey Village High School
Cypress Fairbanks ISD
Houston, TX

Dennis M. Dudley
Science Department Chair/
Teacher
Shaler Area High School
Pittsburgh, PA

Mary K. Dulko
Sharon High School
Sharon, MA

Erica Everett, M.A.T., M.Ed.
Science Department Chair
Manchester-Essex Regional High
School
Manchester, MA

Heather M. Gannon
Elisabeth Ann Johnson High
School
Mt. Morris, MI

Virginia Glasscock
Science Teacher
California High School
Whittier, CA

Ruth Gleicher
Biology Teacher
Niles West High School
Skokie, IL

Lance Goodlock
Biology Teacher/Science
Department Chairperson
Sturgis High School
Sturgis, MI

W. Tony Heiting, Ph.D.
State Science Supervisor (retired)
Iowa Department of Education
Panora, IA

Patricia Anne Johnson, M.S.
Biology Teacher
Ridgewood High School
Ridgewood, NJ

Judith Decherd Jones, M.A.T.
NBCT AYA Science
East Chapel Hill High School
Chapel Hill, NC

Shellie Jones
Science Teacher
California High School
Whittier, CA

Michelle Lauria, M.A.T.
Biology Teacher
Hopkinton High School
Hopkinton, MA

Kimberly Lewis
Science Department Chair
Wellston High School
Wellston, OH

Consultants *(continued)*

Lenora Lewis
Teacher
Creekview High School
Canton, GA

JoAnn Lindell-Overton, M.Ed.
Supervisor of Secondary Science
Chesapeake Public Schools
Chesapeake, VA

Lender Luse
H.W. Byers High School
Holly Springs, MS

Molly J. Markey, Ph.D.
Science Teacher
Newton Country Day School of the Sacred Heart
Newton, MA

Rebecca McLelland-Crawley
Biological Sciences Teacher
Piscataway, NJ

Mark L. Mettert, M.S. Ed.
Science Department Chair
New Haven High School
New Haven, IN

Jane Parker
Lewisville High School North
Lewisville, TX

Ian Pearce
Educator
Austin, TX

Jim Peters
Science Resource Teacher
Carroll County Public Schools
Westminster, MD

Michelle Phillips, M.A.T.
Secondary Science: Education
Science Teacher
Jordan High School
Durham, NC

Randy E. Phillips
Science Teacher/Department Chair
Green Bay East High School
Green Bay, WI

Nancy Richey
Educator
Longmont, CO

Linda Roberson
Department Chairman
Jenks Freshman Academy
Jenks, OK

Sharon D. Spencer
Assistant Principal
Bronx Center for Science and Math
Bronx, NY

Stephen David Wright, M.S.
Biology Teacher
Montgomery County Public Schools
Columbia, MD

Alan W. Zimroth, M.S.
Science Teacher/Department Chairperson
Hialeah-Miami Lakes High School
Hialeah, FL

Contents

UNIT 1   The Nature of Life   1–60

1 The Science of Biology **2**

> **Big idea** What role does science play in the study of life?

1.1   What Is Science? 4
- Art in Motion: Experimental Design
- Art Review: Revising Hypotheses
- InterActive Art: Redi and Pasteur's Experiment

1.2   Science in Context. 10

1.3   Studying Life. 17
- Data Analysis: Adventures in Measurement

CHAPTER MYSTERY *Height by Prescription*

● Go Digital: Biology.com

2 The Chemistry of Life **32**

> **Big idea** What are the basic chemical principles that affect living things?

2.1   The Nature of Matter 34
- Art Review: Ionic and Covalent Bonding

2.2   Properties of Water 40
- Art in Motion: A Salt Solution
- Data Analysis: Acid Rain and Freshwater Habitats

2.3   Carbon Compounds 45

2.4   Chemical Reactions and Enzymes 50
- Visual Analogy: Lock and Key

CHAPTER MYSTERY *The Ghostly Fish*

Unit 1 Project **60**

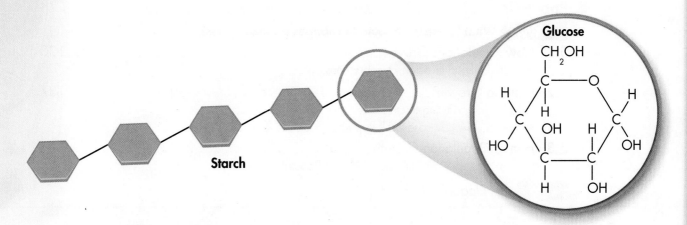

Starch

Glucose

CH_2OH

BIOLOGY.com ● Go Digital. See what awaits you at Biology.com.

3 The Biosphere **62**

Big idea How do living and nonliving parts of the Earth interact and affect the survival of organisms?

3.1 **What Is Ecology?** 64
  - Art in Motion: Levels of Organization
  - Data Analysis: Counting on Nature

3.2 **Energy, Producers, and Consumers** 69
  - Art Review: Producers and Consumers
  - Tutor Tube: Producers and Consumers

3.3 **Energy Flow in Ecosystems** 73
  - Visual Analogy: Earth's Recycling Center

3.4 **Cycles of Matter** 79
  - InterActive Art: The Water Cycle
  - Visual Analogy: Interlocking Nutrient Cycles

  CHAPTER MYSTERY *Changes in the Bay*

4 Ecosystems and Communities **94**

Big idea How do abiotic and biotic factors shape ecosystems?

4.1 **Climate** 96
  - Visual Analogy: The Greenhouse Effect

4.2 **Niches and Community Interactions** 99
  - Data Analysis: The Intertidal Zone

4.3 **Succession** 106
  - Art in Motion: Primary and Secondary Succession

4.4 **Biomes** 110

4.5 **Aquatic Ecosystems** .117
  - Art Review: Ocean Zones

  CHAPTER MYSTERY *The Wolf Effect*

5 Populations **128**

Big idea What factors contribute to changes in populations?

5.1 **How Populations Grow** 130
  - Data Analysis: Invasion of Zebra Mussels

5.2 **Limits to Growth** 137
  - Art Review: Limiting Factors
  - InterActive Art: Moose-Wolf Populations on Isle Royale

5.3 **Human Population Growth** 142
  - Art in Motion: Age Structure of World Population

  CHAPTER MYSTERY *A Plague of Rabbits*

BIOLOGY.com ▸ • Go Digital. See what awaits you at Biology.com.

6 Humans in the Biosphere **152**

Big idea How have human activities shaped local and global ecology?

6.1 A Changing Landscape 154
6.2 Using Resources Wisely 158
    ● Art in Motion: Biological Magnification
6.3 Biodiversity 166
    ● Art Review: Threats to Biodiversity
    ● Data Analysis: Measuring Biodiversity
6.4 Meeting Ecological Challenges 173
    ● Visual Analogy: Ecological Footprints
CHAPTER MYSTERY *Moving the Moai*

Unit 2 Project **186**

UNIT 3 Cells   187–304

7 Cell Structure and Function **188**

Big idea How are cell structures adapted to their functions?

7.1 Life Is Cellular 190
7.2 Cell Structure 196
    ● Art Review: Plant and Animal Cells
    ● Tutor Tube: Plants Have Mitochondria Too
    ● Visual Analogy: The Cell as a Living Factory
7.3 Cell Transport 208
    ● Art in Motion: Active Transport
    ● InterActive Art: Diffusion and Osmosis
7.4 Homeostasis and Cells 214
    ● Data Analysis: Maximizing Mitochondria
CHAPTER MYSTERY *Death by...Water?*

    ● Go Digital: Biology.com

8 Photosynthesis **224**

Big idea How do plants and other organisms capture energy from the sun?

8.1 Energy and Life 226
    ● Visual Analogy: ATP as a Charged Battery
8.2 Photosynthesis: An Overview 230
    ● InterActive Art: Photosynthesis
    ● Tutor Tube: Sorting Out Light-Independent and Dependent Reactions
    ● Visual Analogy: Carrying Electrons
    ● Data Analysis: Shedding Light on Marine Algae
8.3 The Process of Photosynthesis 235
    ● Art in Motion: Light-Dependent Reactions
    ● Art Review: The Calvin Cycle
CHAPTER MYSTERY *Out of Thin Air?*

BIOLOGY.com   ● Go Digital. See what awaits you at Biology.com.

9 Cellular Respiration and Fermentation **248**

Big idea ▶ How do organisms obtain energy?

9.1 Cellular Respiration: An Overview 250
  • Art in Motion: Opposite Processes: Respiration and Photosynthesis

9.2 The Process of Cellular Respiration 254
  • Art Review: Electron Transport and ATP Synthesis
  • Tutor Tube: Oxygen as the Acceptor of Cellular Respiration Waste
  • InterActive Art: Cellular Respiration and Fermentation

9.3 Fermentation 262
  • Data Analysis: Lactic Acid and Athletes

CHAPTER MYSTERY *Diving Without a Breath*

10 Cell Growth and Division **272**

Big idea ▶ How does a cell produce a new cell?

10.1 Cell Growth, Division, and Reproduction 274
10.2 The Process of Cell Division 279
  • Visual Analogy: Growing Pains
10.3 Regulating the Cell Cycle 286
  • InterActive Art: Mitosis
  • Data Analysis: Timing the Cell Cycle
  • Art Review: Eukaryotic Chromosome
  • Tutor Tube: Unraveling Chromosome Vocabulary
10.4 Cell Differentiation 292
  • Art in Motion: Growth of Cancer Cells

CHAPTER MYSTERY *Pet Shop Accident*

Unit 3 Project **304**

UNIT 4 Genetics   305–446

11 Introduction to Genetics **306**

Big idea ▶ How does cellular information pass from one generation to another?

11.1 The Work of Gregor Mendel 308
11.2 Applying Mendel's Principles 313
  • InterActive Art: Punnett Squares
11.3 Other Patterns of Inheritance 319
  • Art Review: Types of Dominance
11.4 Meiosis 323
  • Art in Motion: Meiosis
  • Tutor Tube: Connecting Punnett Squares to Meiosis
  • Data Analysis: Gene Location and Crossing-Over

CHAPTER MYSTERY *Green Parakeets*

BIOLOGY.com • Go Digital. See what awaits you at Biology.com.

12 DNA 336

Big idea ▶ What is the structure of DNA, and how does it function in genetic inheritance?

12.1 Identifying the Substance of Genes 338
   ● Art in Motion: Hershey-Chase Experiment
   ● Visual Analogy: The Main Functions of DNA and Books

12.2 The Structure of DNA 344
   ● Data Analysis: Tracking Illegal Whaling
   ● Tutor Tube: Memory Tricks for Base Pairing

12.3 DNA Replication 350
   ● Art Review: Differences in DNA Replication
   ● InterActive Art: DNA Replication

CHAPTER MYSTERY *UV Light*

13 RNA and Protein Synthesis 360

Big idea ▶ How does information flow from the cell nucleus to direct the synthesis of proteins in the cytoplasm?

13.1 RNA 362
   ● Art in Motion: RNA Processing
   ● Visual Analogy: Master Plans and Blueprints

13.2 Ribosomes and Protein Synthesis 366
   ● InterActive Art: Transcription and Translation
   ● Tutor Tube: Why Are Proteins so Important?

13.3 Mutations 372
   ● Art Review: Chromosomal Mutations & Point Mutations

13.4 Gene Regulation and Expression 377
   ● Data Analysis: A Complicated Operon

CHAPTER MYSTERY *Mouse-Eyed Fly*

14 Human Heredity 390

Big idea ▶ How can we use genetics to study human inheritance?

14.1 Human Chromosomes 392
   ● Art Review: A Human Karyotype
   ● InterActive Art: Pedigrees
   ● Tutor Tube: Skipping a Generation
   ● Data Analysis: Blood Types and Cholera

14.2 Human Genetic Disorders 398
   ● Art in Motion: Nondisjunction Disorders

14.3 Studying the Human Genome 403

CHAPTER MYSTERY *The Crooked Cell*

● Go Digital: Biology.com

BIOLOGY.com ▶ ● Go Digital. See what awaits you at Biology.com.

xv

15 Genetic Engineering **416**

Big idea How and why do scientists manipulate DNA in living cells?

15.1 Selective Breeding. 418
15.2 Recombinant DNA 421
● Art in Motion: Plasmid DNA Transformation
15.3 Applications of Genetic Engineering .428
● Art Review: Identifying Individuals
15.4 Ethics and Impacts of Biotechnology 436
● Data Analysis: Genetic Engineering for Nutrition
CHAPTER MYSTERY *A Case of Mistaken Identity*

Unit 4 Project **446**

UNIT 5 Evolution   447–570

16 Darwin's Theory of Evolution **448**

Big idea What is natural selection?

16.1 Darwin's Voyage of Discovery 450
16.2 Ideas that Shaped Darwin's Thinking. 454
● Art in Motion: The Ladder of Life
16.3 Darwin Presents His Case 460
● Data Analysis: Natural Selection
16.4 Evidence of Evolution. 465
● Art Review: Homologous and Analogous
● Visual Analogy: Finch Beak Tools
CHAPTER MYSTERY *Such Varied Honeycreepers*

17 Evolution of Populations **480**

Big idea How can populations evolve to form new species?

17.1 Genes and Variation 482
● Art Review: Frequency and Dominance
17.2 Evolution as Genetic Change in Populations. 487
● Art in Motion: Natural Selection
17.3 The Process of Speciation. 494
● Data Analysis: Galápagos Finches: Evolution in Action
● Tutor Tube: Organizing the Vocabulary of Speciation
17.4 Molecular Evolution. 498
CHAPTER MYSTERY *Epidemic*

● Go Digital: Biology.com

● Go Digital. See what awaits you at Biology.com.

18 Classification 508

Big idea What is the goal of biologists who classify living things?

18.1 Finding Order in Diversity 510
- Art in Motion: Using a Dichotomous Key

18.2 Modern Evolutionary Classification 516
- InterActive Art: Cladograms

18.3 Building the Tree of Life 523
- Art Review: Three Domains
- Data Analysis: Lonesome George

CHAPTER MYSTERY *Grin and Bear It*

19 History of Life 536

Big idea How do fossils help biologists understand the history of life on Earth?

19.1 The Fossil Record 538
- Art in Motion: Fossil Formation
- Visual Analogy: Geologic Time as a Clock

19.2 Patterns and Processes of Evolution 546
- Data Analysis: Explaining Extinctions

19.3 Earth's Early History 553
- Art Review: Conditions on the Early Earth

CHAPTER MYSTERY *Murder in the Permian*

Unit 5 Project 570

BIOLOGY.com | The full text book content for Units 6–8

You have Units 1–5 in this Core Edition textbook, but if you're looking for some extra coverage on Plants, Animals, and the Human Body — the full textbook is available on Biology.com with all 8 Units.

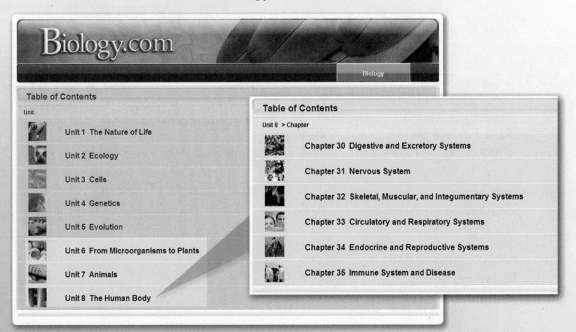

Biology.com

Table of Contents

Unit
- Unit 1 The Nature of Life
- Unit 2 Ecology
- Unit 3 Cells
- Unit 4 Genetics
- Unit 5 Evolution
- Unit 6 From Microorganisms to Plants
- Unit 7 Animals
- Unit 8 The Human Body

Table of Contents

Unit 8 > Chapter
- Chapter 30 Digestive and Excretory Systems
- Chapter 31 Nervous System
- Chapter 32 Skeletal, Muscular, and Integumentary Systems
- Chapter 33 Circulatory and Respiratory Systems
- Chapter 34 Endocrine and Reproductive Systems
- Chapter 35 Immune System and Disease

Bacteria . . . . DOL•6

Archaea . . . . DOL•8

Protists . . . . DOL•10

Fungi . . . . DOL•16

Plants . . . . DOL•20

Animals . . . . DOL•30

Appendix A: Science Skills
   Data Tables and Graphs A–1
   Reading Diagrams A–3
   Basic Process Skills A–4
   Organizing Information A–6

Appendix B: Lab Skills
   Conducting an Experiment . . . A–8
   The Metric System A–10
   Safety Symbols A–11
   Science Safety Rules A–12
   Use of the Microscope A–14

Appendix C: Technology & Design . . . A–16

Appendix D: Math Skills A–18

Appendix E: Periodic Table A–24

English/Spanish Glossary G–1

Index I–1

Credits C–1

Labs and Activities

Quick Lab

Replicating Procedures. 13
Model an Ionic Compound. 36
Acidic and Basic Foods 43
How Do Abiotic Factors Affect
   Different Plant Species?. 67
How Do Different Types
   of Consumers Interact? 72
Successful Succession?. 108
How Does Competition Affect Growth? 138
Reduce, Reuse, Recycle 155
What Is a Cell?. 193
Making a Model of a Cell 203
What Waste Material Is Produced
   During Photosynthesis? 234
How Does Exercise Affect Disposal of
   Wastes From Cellular Respiration? 264
Modeling the Relationship Between
   Surface Area and Volume 275
Mitosis in Action. 283
Classroom Variation 311
How Are Dimples Inherited?. 315
Modeling DNA Replication 352
How Does a Cell Interpret Codons?. 367
Modeling Mutations 374
How Is Colorblindness Transmitted?. 395
Modeling Restriction Enzymes. 405
Inserting Genetic Markers 425
Survey Biotechnology Opinions 438
Darwin's Voyage 451
Variation in Peppers 457
Classifying Fruits. 513
Constructing a Cladogram 520
Modeling Half-Life. 541

Design Your Own Lab

Temperature and Enzymes 54
Acid Rain and Seeds 180
Regeneration in Planaria 298
Dichotomous Keys. 530

Forensics Lab

Using DNA to Identify Human Remains 410
Using DNA to Solve Crimes 440
Using Index Fossils 564

Real-World Lab

The Effect of Fertilizer on Algae 88
Abiotic Factors and Plant Selection 122
Comparing Fermentation Rates of Sugars. 266

Skills Lab

Using a Microscope to Estimate Size 26
The Growth Cycle of Yeast 146
Detecting Diffusion 218
Plant Pigments and Photosynthesis. 242
Modeling Meiosis. 330
Extracting DNA 354
From DNA to Protein Synthesis 384
Amino Acid Sequences: Indicators of Evolution. . . 474
Competing for Resources 502

Analyzing Data

What's in a Diet? 20
Comparing Fatty Acids 48
The 10 Percent Rule. 77
Predator-Prey Dynamics 102
Which Biome? 115
Multiplying Rabbits 135
American Air Pollution Trends. 164
Saving the Golden Lion Tamarin 172
Mitochondria Distribution in the Mouse 216
Rates of Photosynthesis 240
You Are What You Eat. 251
The Rise and Fall of Cyclins 288
Cellular Differentiation of *C. elegans*. 294
Human Blood Types. 320
Calculating Haploid and Diploid Numbers. 327
Base Percentages 345
The Discovery of RNA Interference 381
The Geography of Malaria 400
Genetically Modified Crops in the
     United States. 429
Molecular Homology in *Hoxc8* 470
Allele Frequency 491
Fishes in Two Lakes 500
Comparing the Domains 524
Extinctions Through Time 548
Comparing Atmospheres 556

Features

Visual Analogies

Unlocking Enzymes 53
Earth's Recycling Center. 74
The Matter Mill 79
Interlocking Nutrients. 86
The Greenhouse Effect 97
Ecological Footprints 173
The Cell as a Living Factory 196
ATP as a Charged Battery 227
Carrying Electrons. 232
Growing Pains 276
The Main Functions of DNA 342

Master Plans and Blueprints 363
Finch Beak Tools 472
Geologic Time as a Clock 543

Technology & Biology

A Nature-Inspired Adhesive 39
Global Ecology from Space 87
Fluorescence Microscopy 291
Artificial Life? 435
Bar-Coding Life. 529

Biology & History

Understanding Photosynthesis. 229
Discovering the Role of DNA 349
Origins of Evolutionary Thought 459

Careers & Biology

Marine Biologist, Park Ranger,
     Wildlife Photographer 105
Laboratory Technician, Microscopist, Pathologist. . 195
Forensic Scientist, Plant Breeder,
     Population Geneticist 322
Fossil Preparator, Museum Guide, Paleontologist . . 559

Biology & Society

Who Should Fund Product Safety Studies? 16
What Can Be Done About Invasive Mussels? 136
Should Creatine Supplements Be Regulated? 261
Are Laws Protecting Genetic Privacy Necessary? . 402
Should Antibiotic Use Be Restricted? 493

Dear Student:

Welcome to our world—the endlessly fascinating world of biology.

*I can guess what some of you are thinking right now. "Fascinating? Yeah, right. Totally."
Well, give us—and biology—a chance to show you that the study of the natural world really
is more exciting, more fascinating, and more important to you personally than you've ever
realized. In fact, biology is more important to our daily lives today than it has ever been.*

*Why? Three words: "We are one." This isn't meant in a "touchy-feely" or "New Age" way.
"We" includes all forms of life on Earth. And "are one" means that all of us are tied together
more tightly, in more different ways, than anyone imagined until recently.*

*Both our "hardware" (body structures) and our "software" (genetic instructions and
biochemical processes that program body functions) are incredibly similar to those of all
other living things. Genetic instructions in our bodies are written in the same universal code
as instructions in bacteria and palm trees. As biologists "read" and study that code, they
find astonishingly similar processes in all of us. That's why medical researchers can learn
about human diseases that may strike you or your family by studying not only apes and
pigs and mice, but even yeasts. We are one on the molecular level.*

*All organisms interact with one another and with the environment to weave our planet's
web of life. Organisms make rain forests and coral reefs, prairies and swamps—and farms
and cities. We interact, too, with the winds and ocean currents that tie our planet together.
Human activity is changing local and global environments in ways that we still don't
understand … and that affect our ability to produce food and protect ourselves from
diseases. We are one ecologically with the rest of life on Earth.*

*All organisms evolve over time, adapting to their surroundings. If humans alter the
environment, other organisms respond to that change. When we use antibiotics against
bacteria, they develop resistance to our drugs. If we use pesticides against insects, they
become immune to our poisons. We are one in our ability to evolve over time.*

*Those are the kinds of connections you
will find in this book. Microscopic.
Enormous. Amusing. Threatening. But
always fascinating. That's why—no
matter where you start off in your
attitude about biology—we think you
are in for some surprises!*

Sincerely,

Joe Levine

Dear Student,

Biology is one of the subjects you're going to study this year, but I hope you'll realize from the very first pages of this book that biology is a lot more than just a "subject." Biology is what makes an eagle fly, a flower bloom, or a caterpillar turn into a butterfly. It's the study of ourselves—of how our bodies grow and change and respond to the outside world, and it's the study of our planet, a world transformed by the actions of living things. Of course, you might have known some of this already. But there's something more—you might call it a "secret" that makes biology unique.

That secret is that you've come along at just the right time. In all of human history, there has never been a moment like the present, a time when we stood so close to the threshold of answering the most fundamental questions about the nature of life. You belong to the first generation of students who can read the human genome almost as your parents might have read a book or a newspaper. You are the first students who will grow up in a world that has a chance to use that information for the benefit of humanity, and you are the very first to bear the burden of using that knowledge wisely.

If all of this seems like heavy stuff, it is. But there is another reason we wrote this book, and we hope that is not a secret at all. Science is fun! Biologists aren't a bunch of serious, grim-faced, middle-aged folks in lab coats who think of nothing but work. In fact, most of the people we know in science would tell you honestly, with broad grins on their faces, that they have the best jobs in the world. They would say there's nothing that compares to the excitement of doing scientific work, and that the beauty and variety of life make every day a new adventure.

We agree, and we hope that you'll keep something in mind as you begin the study of biology. You don't need a lab coat or a degree or a laboratory to be a scientist. What you do need is an inquiring mind, the patience to look at nature carefully, and the willingness to figure things out. We've filled this book with some of the latest and most important discoveries about living things, but we hope we've also filled it with something else: our wonder, our amazement, and our sheer delight in the variety of life itself. Come on in, and enjoy the journey!

Sincerely,

Ken Miller

The Nature of Life

Chapters

1 The Science of Biology
2 The Chemistry of Life

INTRODUCE the

Big ideas

- **Science as a Way of Knowing**
- **Matter and Energy**

66Science is 'a way of knowing'— a way of explaining the natural world through observations, questions, and experiments. But science isn't just dry old data, pressed between pages of this book like prom flowers in a school yearbook. Science is a living adventure story, aimed at understanding humans and the world around us. That story begins with the relationship between the matter that forms our bodies and the energy that powers life's processes.99

Joe Levine

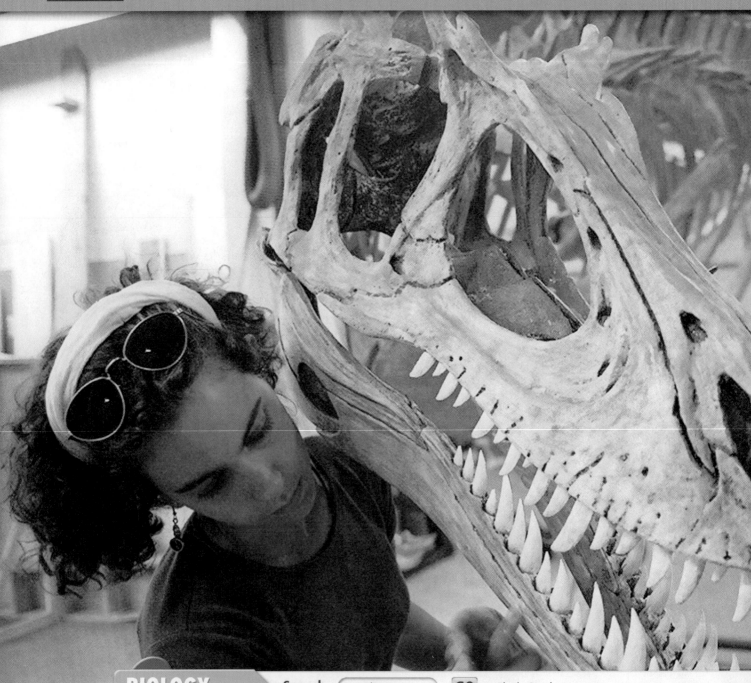

1

The Science of Biology

Science as a Way of Knowing

Q: What role does science play in the study of life?

INSIDE:

- 1.1 What Is Science?
- 1.2 Science in Context
- 1.3 Studying Life

These paleontologists—biologists who study ancient life—are working to reconstruct the skeleton of Carcharodontosaurus, a giant dinosaur that lived over 90 million years ago. By using scientific skills such as observation and inference, scientists can learn how ancient animals lived. The huge teeth of this dinosaur are sharp and serrated like a knife, suited for eating meat—a lot of it!

- Untamed Science Video - Chapter Mystery

CHAPTER MYSTERY

HEIGHT BY PRESCRIPTION

A doctor injects a chemical into the body of an eight-year-old boy named David. This healthy boy shows no signs of disease. The "condition" for which he is being treated is quite common— David is short for his age. The medication he is taking is human growth hormone, or HGH.

HGH, together with genes and diet, controls growth during childhood. People who produce little or no HGH are abnormally short and may have other related health problems. But David has normal HGH levels. He is short simply because his parents are both healthy, short people.

But if David isn't sick, why does his doctor prescribe HGH? Where does medicinal HGH come from? Is it safe? What does this case say about science and society? As you read this chapter, look for clues about the nature of science, the role of technology in our modern world, and the relationship between science and society. Then, solve the mystery.

Never Stop Exploring Your World.
Finding the solution to the growth hormone mystery is only the beginning. Take a video field trip with the ecogeeks of Untamed Science to see where this mystery leads.

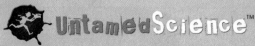

1.1 What Is Science?

Key Questions

🔑 What are the goals of science?

🔑 What procedures are at the core of scientific methodology?

Vocabulary

science • observation • inference • hypothesis • controlled experiment • independent variable • dependent variable • control group • data

Taking Notes

Flowchart As you read, create a flowchart showing the steps scientists use to answer questions about the natural world.

THINK ABOUT IT One day long ago, someone looked around and wondered: Where did plants and animals come from? How did I come to be? Since then, humans have tried to answer those questions in different ways. Some ways of explaining the world have stayed the same over time. Science, however, is always changing.

What Science Is and Is Not

🔑 What are the goals of science?

This book contains lots of facts and ideas about living things. Many of those facts are important, and you will be tested on them! But you shouldn't think that biology, or any science, is just a collection of never-changing facts. For one thing, you can be sure that some "facts" presented in this book will change soon—if they haven't changed already. What's more, science is not a collection of unchanging beliefs about the world. Scientific ideas are open to testing, discussion, and revision. So, some ideas presented in this book will also change.

These statements may puzzle you. If "facts" and ideas in science change, why should you bother learning them? And if science is neither a list of facts nor a collection of unchanging beliefs, what is it?

FIGURE 1-1 Studying the Natural World How do whales communicate? How far do they travel? How are they affected by environmental changes? These are questions whale researchers can use science to answer.

Science as a Way of Knowing **Science** is an organized way of gathering and analyzing evidence about the natural world. It is a way of observing, a way of thinking, and "a way of knowing" about the world. In other words, science is a *process,* not a "thing." The word *science* also refers to the body of knowledge that scientific studies have gathered over the years.

Several features make science different from other human endeavors. First, science deals only with the natural world. Scientific endeavors never concern, in any way, supernatural phenomena of any kind. Second, scientists collect and organize information in an orderly way, looking for patterns and connections among events. Third, scientists propose explanations that are based on evidence, not belief. Then they test those explanations with more evidence.

The Goals of Science The scientific way of knowing includes the view that the physical universe is a system composed of parts and processes that interact. From a scientific perspective, all objects in the universe, and all interactions among those objects, are governed by universal natural laws. The same natural laws apply whether the objects or events are large or small.

Aristotle and other Greek philosophers were among the first to try to view the universe in this way. They aimed to explain the world around them in terms of events and processes they could observe. Modern scientists continue that tradition. **One goal of science is to provide natural explanations for events in the natural world. Science also aims to use those explanations to understand patterns in nature and to make useful predictions about natural events.**

Science, Change, and Uncertainty Over the centuries, scientists have gathered an enormous amount of information about the natural world. Scientific knowledge helps us cure diseases, place satellites in orbit, and send instantaneous electronic communications. Yet, despite all we know, much of nature remains a mystery. It is a mystery because science never stands still; almost every major scientific discovery raises more questions than it answers. Often, research yields surprises that point future studies in new and unexpected directions. This constant change doesn't mean science has failed. On the contrary, it shows that science continues to advance.

That's why learning about science means more than just understanding what we know. It also means understanding what we don't know. You may be surprised to hear this, but science rarely "proves" anything in absolute terms. Scientists aim for the best understanding of the natural world that current methods can reveal. Uncertainty is part of the scientific process and part of what makes science exciting! Happily, as you'll learn in later chapters, science has allowed us to build enough understanding to make useful predictions about the natural world.

FIGURE 1–2 Science in Action These marine scientists are recording information as they study whales in Alaska.

BUILD Vocabulary

WORD ORIGINS The word science derives from the Latin word *scientia,* which means "knowledge." Science represents knowledge that has been gathered over time.

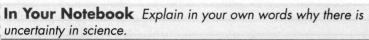

In Your Notebook *Explain in your own words why there is uncertainty in science.*

Scientific Methodology: The Heart of Science

🔑 **What procedures are at the core of scientific methodology?**

You might think that science is a mysterious process, used only by certain people under special circumstances. But that's not true, because you use scientific thinking all the time. Suppose your family's car won't start. What do you do? You use what you know about cars to come up with ideas to test. At first, you might think the battery is dead. So you test that idea by turning the key in the ignition. If the starter motor works but the engine doesn't start, you reject the dead-battery idea. You might guess next that the car is out of gas. A glance at the fuel gauge tests that idea. Again and again, you apply scientific thinking until the problem is solved—or until you run out of ideas and call a mechanic!

Scientists approach research in pretty much the same way. There isn't any single, cut-and-dried "scientific method." There is, however, a general style of investigation that we can call scientific methodology. 🔑 **Scientific methodology involves observing and asking questions, making inferences and forming hypotheses, conducting controlled experiments, collecting and analyzing data, and drawing conclusions.** Figure 1–3 shows how one research team used scientific methodology in its study of New England salt marshes.

Observing and Asking Questions Scientific investigations begin with **observation,** the act of noticing and describing events or processes in a careful, orderly way. Of course, scientific observation involves more than just looking at things. A good scientist can, as the philosopher Arthur Schopenhauer put it, "Think something that nobody has thought yet, while looking at something that everybody sees." That kind of observation leads to questions that no one has asked before.

FIGURE 1-3 Salt Marsh Experiment Salt marshes are coastal environments often found where rivers meet the sea. Researchers made an interesting observation on the way marsh grasses grow. Then, they applied scientific methodology to answer questions that arose from their observation.

OBSERVING AND ASKING QUESTIONS

Researchers observed that marsh grass grows taller in some places than others. This observation led to a question: *Why do marsh grasses grow to different heights in different places?*

INFERRING AND HYPOTHESIZING

The researchers inferred that something limits grass growth in some places. It could be any environmental factor—temperature, sunlight, water, or nutrients. Based on their knowledge of salt marshes, they proposed a hypothesis: *Marsh grass growth is limited by available nitrogen.*

Inferring and Forming a Hypothesis After posing questions, scientists use further observations to make inferences. An **inference** is a logical interpretation based on what scientists already know. Inference, combined with a creative imagination, can lead to a hypothesis. A **hypothesis** is a scientific explanation for a set of observations that can be tested in ways that support or reject it.

Designing Controlled Experiments Testing a scientific hypothesis often involves designing an experiment that keeps track of various factors that can change, or variables. Examples of variables include temperature, light, time, and availability of nutrients. Whenever possible, a hypothesis should be tested by an experiment in which only one variable is changed. All other variables should be kept unchanged, or controlled. This type of experiment is called a **controlled experiment.**

▶ *Controlling Variables* Why is it important to control variables? The reason is that if several variables are changed in the experiment, researchers can't easily tell which variable is responsible for any results they observe. The variable that is deliberately changed is called the **independent variable** (also called the manipulated variable). The variable that is observed and that changes in response to the independent variable is called the **dependent variable** (also called the responding variable).

▶ *Control and Experimental Groups* Typically, an experiment is divided into control and experimental groups. A **control group** is exposed to the same conditions as the experimental group except for one independent variable. Scientists always try to reproduce or replicate their observations. Therefore, they set up several sets of control and experimental groups, rather than just a single pair.

 In Your Notebook *What is the difference between an observation and an inference? List three examples of each.*

DESIGNING CONTROLLED EXPERIMENTS

Control Group — No nitrogen added

Experimental Group — Nitrogen added

The researchers selected similar plots of marsh grass. All plots had similar plant density, soil type, input of freshwater, and height above average tide level. The plots were divided into control and experimental groups.

The researchers added nitrogen fertilizer (the independent variable) to the experimental plots. They then observed the growth of marsh grass (the dependent variable) in both experimental and control plots.

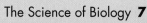

Collecting and Analyzing Data Scientists make detailed records of experimental observations, gathering information called **data.** There are two main types of data. Quantitative data are numbers obtained by counting or measuring. In the marsh grass experiment, quantitative data could include the number of plants per plot, the length, width, and weight of each blade of grass, and so on. Qualitative data are descriptive and involve characteristics that cannot usually be counted. Qualitative data in the marsh grass experiment might include notes about foreign objects in the sample plots or information on whether the grass was growing upright or sideways.

▶ *Research Tools* Scientists choose appropriate tools for collecting and analyzing data. The tools may range from simple devices such as metersticks and calculators to sophisticated equipment such as machines that measure nitrogen content in plants and soil. Charts and graphs are also tools that help scientists organize their data. In the past, data were recorded by hand, often in notebooks or personal journals. Today, researchers typically enter data into computers, which make organizing and analyzing data easier. Many kinds of data are now gathered directly by computer-controlled equipment.

▶ *Sources of Error* Researchers must be careful to avoid errors in data collection and analysis. Tools used to measure the size and weight of marsh grasses, for example, have limited accuracy. Data analysis and sample size must be chosen carefully. In medical studies, for example, both experimental and control groups should be quite large. Why? Because there is always variation among individuals in control and experimental groups. The larger the sample size, the more reliably researchers can analyze that variation and evaluate the differences between experimental and control groups.

MYSTERY CLUE

Describe a controlled experiment that can be designed to test the hypothesis that extra HGH helps children grow taller. What ethical issues can you imagine in actually carrying out such a study?

FIGURE 1–3 Continued

COLLECTING AND ANALYZING DATA

Control Group

Experimental Group

The researchers sampled all the plots throughout the growing season. They measured growth rates and plant sizes, and analyzed the chemical composition of living leaves.

DRAWING CONCLUSIONS

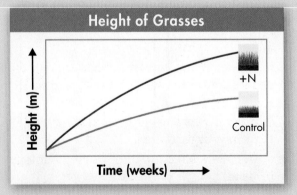

Height of Grasses

Height (m)

Time (weeks)

+N

Control

Data from all plots were compared and evaluated by statistical tests. Data analysis confirmed that marsh grasses in experimental plots with additional nitrogen did, in fact, grow taller and larger than controls. The hypothesis and its predictions were supported.

Drawing Conclusions Scientists use experimental data as evidence to support, refute, or revise the hypothesis being tested, and to draw a valid conclusion. Hypotheses are often not fully supported or refuted by one set of experiments. Rather, new data may indicate that the researchers have the right general idea but are wrong about a few particulars. In that case, the original hypothesis is reevaluated and revised; new predictions are made, and new experiments are designed. Those new experiments might suggest changes in the experimental treatment or better control of more variables. As shown in **Figure 1–4,** many circuits around this loop are often necessary before a final hypothesis is supported and conclusions can be drawn.

When Experiments Are Not Possible It is not always possible to test a hypothesis with an experiment. In some of these cases, researchers devise hypotheses that can be tested by observations. Animal behavior researchers, for example, might want to learn how animal groups interact in the wild. Investigating this kind of natural behavior requires field observations that disturb the animals as little as possible. When researchers analyze data from these observations, they may devise hypotheses that can be tested in different ways.

Sometimes, ethics prevents certain types of experiments—especially on human subjects. Medical researchers who suspect that a chemical causes cancer, for example, would not intentionally expose people to it! Instead, they search for volunteers who have already been exposed to the chemical. For controls, they study people who have not been exposed to the chemical. The researchers still try to control as many variables as possible. For example, they might exclude volunteers who have serious health problems or known genetic conditions. Medical researchers always try to study large groups of subjects so that individual genetic differences do not produce misleading results.

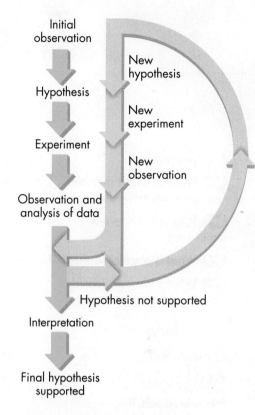

FIGURE 1–4 Revising Hypotheses During the course of an investigation, hypotheses may have to be revised and experiments redone several times.

1.1 Assessment

Review Key Concepts 🔑

1. a. Review What is science?

b. Explain What kinds of understandings does science contribute about the natural world?

c. Form an Opinion Do you think that scientists will ever run out of things to study? Explain your reasoning.

2. a. Review What does scientific methodology involve?

b. Explain Why are hypotheses so important to controlled experiments?

WRITE ABOUT SCIENCE

Creative Writing

3. A few hundred years ago, observations seemed to indicate that some living things could just suddenly appear: maggots showed up on meat; mice were found on grain; and beetles turned up on cow dung. Those observations led to the incorrect idea of spontaneous generation—the notion that life could arise from nonliving matter. Write a paragraph for a history magazine evaluating the spontaneous generation hypothesis. Why did it seem logical at the time? What evidence was overlooked or ignored?

1.2 Science in Context

THINK ABOUT IT Scientific methodology is the heart of science. But that vital "heart" is only part of the full "body" of science. Science and scientists operate in the context of the scientific community and society at large.

Exploration and Discovery: Where Ideas Come From

🔑 **What scientific attitudes help generate new ideas?**

Scientific methodology is closely linked to exploration and discovery, as shown in **Figure 1–5**. Recall that scientific methodology starts with observations and questions. But where do those observations and questions come from in the first place? They may be inspired by scientific attitudes, practical problems, and new technology.

Scientific Attitudes Good scientists share scientific attitudes, or habits of mind, that lead them to exploration and discovery. 🔑 **Curiosity, skepticism, open-mindedness, and creativity help scientists generate new ideas.**

▶ *Curiosity* A curious researcher, for example, may look at a salt marsh and immediately ask, "What's that plant? Why is it growing here?" Often, results from previous studies also spark curiosity and lead to new questions.

▶ *Skepticism* Good scientists are skeptics, which means that they question existing ideas and hypotheses, and they refuse to accept explanations without evidence. Scientists who disagree with hypotheses design experiments to test them. Supporters of hypotheses also undertake rigorous testing of their ideas to confirm them and to address any valid questions raised.

▶ *Open-Mindedness* Scientists must remain open-minded, meaning that they are willing to accept different ideas that may not agree with their hypothesis.

▶ *Creativity* Researchers also need to think creatively to design experiments that yield accurate data.

Key Questions

🔑 *What scientific attitudes help generate new ideas?*

🔑 *Why is peer review important?*

🔑 *What is a scientific theory?*

🔑 *What is the relationship between science and society?*

Vocabulary

theory • bias

Taking Notes

Preview Visuals Before you read, study **Figure 1–10.** As you read, use the figure to describe the role science plays in society.

FIGURE 1–5 The Process of Science As the arrows indicate, the different aspects of science are interconnected—making the process of science dynamic, flexible, and unpredictable.

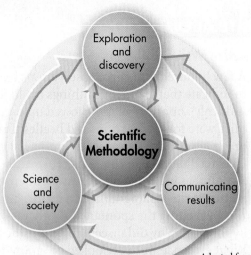

Adapted from *Understanding Science,*
UC Berkeley, Museum of Paleontology

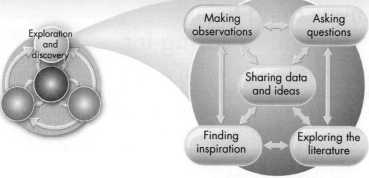

Making observations ⟷ Asking questions

Sharing data and ideas

Finding inspiration ⟷ Exploring the literature

Exploration and discovery

Curiosity
Surprising observation
Personal motivation
Practical problem
New technology

Adapted from *Understanding Science,*
UC Berkeley, Museum of Paleontology

FIGURE 1–6 Exploration and Discovery Ideas in science can arise in many ways—from simple curiosity or from the need to solve a particular problem. Scientists often begin investigations by making observations, asking questions, talking with colleagues, and reading about previous experiments.

Practical Problems Sometimes, ideas for scientific investigations arise from practical problems. Salt marshes, for example, play vital roles in the lives of many ecologically and commercially important organisms, as you will learn in the next unit. Yet they are under intense pressure from industrial and housing development. Should marshes be protected from development? If new houses or farms are located near salt marshes, can they be designed to protect the marshes? These practical questions and issues inspire scientific questions, hypotheses, and experiments.

The Role of Technology Technology, science, and society are closely linked. Discoveries in one field of science may lead to new technologies. Those technologies, in turn, enable scientists in other fields to ask new questions or to gather data in new ways. For example, the development of new portable, remote data-collecting equipment enables field researchers to monitor environmental conditions around the clock, in several locations at once. This capability allows researchers to pose and test new hypotheses. Technological advances can also have big impacts on daily life. In the field of genetics and biotechnology, for instance, it is now possible to mass-produce complex substances—such as vitamins, antibiotics, and hormones—that before were only available naturally.

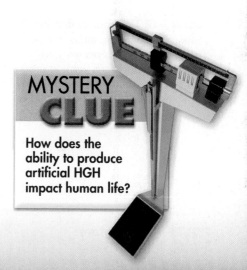

MYSTERY CLUE

How does the ability to produce artificial HGH impact human life?

In Your Notebook *Describe a situation where you were skeptical of a "fact" you had seen or heard.*

FIGURE 1–7 Ideas From Practical Problems
People living on a strip of land like this one in Murrells Inlet, South Carolina, may face flooding and other problems.
Pose Questions *What are some scientific questions that can arise from a situation like this one?*

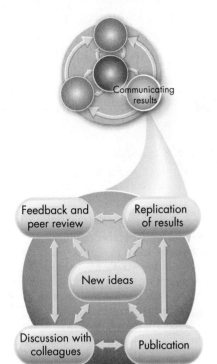

Adapted from *Understanding Science*,
UC Berkeley, Museum of Paleontology

FIGURE 1–8 Communicating Results
Communication is an important part
of science. Scientists review and
evaluate one another's work to ensure
accuracy. Results from one study may
lead to new ideas and further studies.

**FIGURE 1–9 Mangrove
Swamp** In tropical areas,
mangrove swamps serve as
the ecological equivalents
of temperate salt marshes.
The results of the salt marsh
experiment suggest that nitrogen
might be a limiting nutrient for
mangroves and other plants in
these similar habitats.
Design an Experiment *How
would you test this hypothesis?*

Communicating Results:
Reviewing and Sharing Ideas

Why is peer review important?

Data collection and analysis can be a long process. Scientists may focus
intensely on a single study for months or even years. Then, the exciting time comes when researchers communicate their experiments and
observations to the scientific community. Communication and sharing of ideas are vital to modern science.

Peer Review Scientists share their findings with the scientific community by publishing articles that have undergone peer review. In
peer review, scientific papers are reviewed by anonymous, independent experts. **Publishing peer-reviewed articles in scientific
journals allows researchers to share ideas and to test and evaluate
each other's work.** Scientific articles are like high-powered versions of
your high school lab reports. They contain details about experimental
conditions, controls, data, analysis, and conclusions. Reviewers read
them looking for oversights, unfair influences, fraud, or mistakes in
techniques or reasoning. They provide expert assessment of the work
to ensure that the highest standards of quality are met. Peer review
does not guarantee that a piece of work is correct, but it does certify
that the work meets standards set by the scientific community.

Sharing Knowledge and New Ideas Once research has been published, it enters the dynamic marketplace of scientific ideas, as shown
in **Figure 1–8.** How do new findings fit into existing scientific understanding? Perhaps they spark new questions. For example, the finding that growth of salt marsh grasses is limited by available nitrogen
suggests other hypotheses: Is the growth of other plants in the same
habitat also limited by nitrogen? What about the growth of different
plants in similar environments, such as the mangrove swamp shown
in **Figure 1–9?** Each of these logical and important questions leads to
new hypotheses that must be independently confirmed by controlled
experiments.

In Your Notebook *Predict what might happen if an article is
published without undergoing peer review.*

Replicating Procedures

❶ Working with a partner behind a screen, assemble ten blocks into an unusual structure. Write directions that others can use to replicate that structure without seeing it.

❷ Exchange directions with another team. Replicate the team's structure by following its directions.

❸ Compare each replicated structure to the original. Identify which parts of the directions were clear and accurate, and which were unclear or misleading.

Analyze and Conclude

1. Evaluate How could you have written better directions?

2. Infer Why is it important that scientists write procedures that can be replicated?

Scientific Theories

🔑 **What is a scientific theory?**

Evidence from many scientific studies may support several related hypotheses in a way that inspires researchers to propose a scientific **theory** that ties those hypotheses together. As you read this book, you will often come across terms that will be new to you because they are used only in science. But the word *theory* is used both in science and in everyday life. It is important to understand that the meaning you give the word *theory* in daily life is very different from its meaning in science. When you say, "I have a theory," you may mean, "I have a hunch." When a friend says, "That's just a theory" she may mean, "People aren't too certain about that idea." In those same situations, a scientist would probably use the word *hypothesis.* But when scientists talk about gravitational theory or evolutionary theory, they mean something very different from *hunch* or *hypothesis.*

🔑 **In science, the word *theory* applies to a well-tested explanation that unifies a broad range of observations and hypotheses and that enables scientists to make accurate predictions about new situations.** Charles Darwin's early observations and hypotheses about change over time in nature, for example, grew and expanded for years before he collected them into a theory of evolution by natural selection. Today, evolutionary theory is the central organizing principle of all biological and biomedical science. It makes such a wide range of predictions about organisms—from bacteria to whales to humans—that it is mentioned throughout this book.

A useful theory that has been thoroughly tested and supported by many lines of evidence may become the **dominant** view among the majority of scientists, but no theory is considered absolute truth. Science is always changing; as new evidence is uncovered, a theory may be revised or replaced by a more useful explanation.

BUILD Vocabulary

ACADEMIC WORDS A scientific **theory** describes a well-tested explanation for a range of phenomena. Scientific theories are different from scientific laws and it is important to understand that theories do not *become* laws. Laws, such as ideal gas laws in chemistry or Newton's laws of motion, are concise, specific descriptions of how some aspect of the natural world is expected to behave in a certain situation. In contrast, scientific theories, such as cell theory or the theory of evolution, are more dynamic and complex. Scientific theories encompass a greater number of ideas and hypotheses than laws, and are constantly fine-tuned through the process of science.

Science and Society

What is the relationship between science and society?

Make a list of health-related things that you need to understand to protect your life and the lives of others close to you. Your list may include drugs and alcohol, smoking and lung disease, AIDS, cancer, and heart disease. Other topics focus on social issues and the environment. How much of the information in your genes should be kept private? Should communities produce electricity using fossil fuels, nuclear power, solar power, wind power, or hydroelectric dams? How should chemical wastes be disposed of?

All these questions require scientific information to answer, and many have inspired important research. But none of these questions can be answered by science alone. These questions involve the society in which we live, our economy, and our laws and moral principles. **Using science involves understanding its context in society and its limitations. Figure 1–10** shows the role science plays in society.

Science, Ethics, and Morality When scientists explain "why" something happens, their explanation involves only natural phenomena. Pure science does not include ethical or moral viewpoints. For example, biologists try to explain in scientific terms what life is, how life operates, and how life has changed over time. But science cannot answer questions about why life exists or what the meaning of life is.

Similarly, science can tell us how technology and scientific knowledge can be applied but not whether it should be applied in particular ways. Remember these limitations when you study and evaluate science.

Avoiding Bias The way that science is applied in society can be affected by bias. A **bias** is a particular preference or point of view that is personal, rather than scientific. Examples of biases include personal taste, preferences for someone or something, and societal standards of beauty.

Science aims to be objective, but scientists are human, too. They have likes, dislikes, and occasional biases. So, it shouldn't surprise you to discover that scientific data can be misinterpreted or misapplied by scientists who want to prove a particular point. Recommendations made by scientists with personal biases may or may not be in the public interest. But if enough of us understand science, we can help make certain that science is applied in ways that benefit humanity.

FIGURE 1-10 Science and Society Science both influences society and is influenced by society. The researcher below tests shellfish for toxins that can poison humans. **Form an Opinion** *Should shellfish be routinely screened for toxins?*

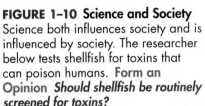

Develop technology — Address societal issues

Build knowledge — Inform policy

Satisfy curiosity — Solve everyday problems

Science and society

Adapted from *Understanding Science,*
UC Berkeley, Museum of Paleontology

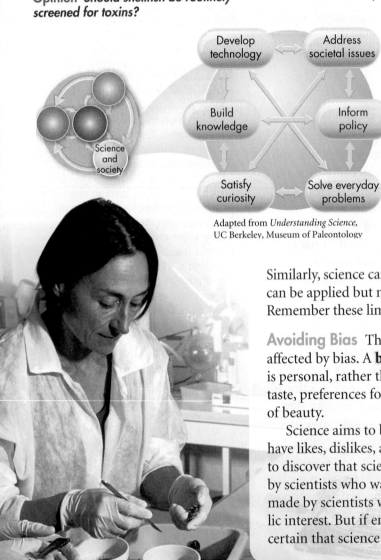

Understanding and Using Science Science will keep changing as long as humans keep wondering about nature. We invite you to join us in that wonder and exploration as you read this book. Think of this text, not as an encyclopedia, but as a "user's guide" to the study of life. Don't just memorize today's scientific facts and ideas. And please don't *believe* them! Instead, try to *understand* how scientists developed those ideas. Try to see the thinking behind experiments we describe. Try to pose the kinds of questions scientists ask.

If you learn to think as scientists think, you will understand the process of science and be comfortable in a world that will keep changing throughout your life. Understanding science will help you make complex decisions that also involve cultural customs, values, and ethical standards.

Furthermore, understanding biology will help you realize that we humans can predict the consequences of our actions and take an active role in directing our future and that of our planet. In our society, scientists make recommendations about big public policy decisions, but they don't make the decisions. Who makes the decisions? Citizens of our democracy do. In a few years, you will be able to exercise the rights of a voting citizen, influencing public policy by the ballots you cast and the messages you send public officials. That's why it is important that you understand how science works and appreciate both the power and the limitations of science.

FIGURE 1–11 Using Science in Everyday Life These student volunteers are planting mangrove saplings as part of a mangrove restoration project.

1.2 Assessment

Review Key Concepts

1. a. Review List the attitudes that lead scientists to explore and discover.

b. Explain What does it mean to describe a scientist as skeptical? Why is skepticism an important quality in a scientist?

2. a. Review What is peer review?

b. Apply Concepts An advertisement claims that studies of a new sports drink show it boosts energy. You discover that none of the study results have been peer-reviewed. What would you tell consumers who are considering buying this product?

3. a. Review What is a scientific theory?

b. Compare and Contrast How does use of the word *theory* differ in science and in daily life?

4. a. Review How is the use of science related to its context in society?

b. Explain Describe some of the limitations of science.

c. Apply Concepts A study shows that a new pesticide is safe for use on food crops. The researcher who conducted the study works for the pesticide company. What potential biases may have affected the study?

Apply the Big idea

Science as a Way of Knowing

5. Explain in your own words why science is considered a "way of knowing."

Biology & Society

Who Should Fund Product Safety Studies?

Biology plays a major role in the research, development, and production of food, medicine, and other consumer items. Companies that make these items profit by selling reliable and useful products in the marketplace. For example, the plastics industry provides countless products for everyday use.

But sometimes questions arise concerning product safety. Bisphenol-A (BPA), for instance, is a chemical found in hard plastics. Those plastics are used to make baby bottles, reusable water bottles, and the linings of many food and soft drink cans. Is BPA safe? This type of question can be posed as a scientific hypothesis to be tested. But who does the testing? Who funds the studies and analyzes the results?

Ideally, independent scientists test products for safety and usefulness. That way, the people who gather and analyze data can remain objective—they have nothing to gain by exaggerating the positive effects of products and nothing to lose by stating any risks. However, scientists are often hired by private companies to develop or test their products.

Often, test results are clear: A product is safe or it isn't. Based on these results, the Food and Drug Administration (FDA) or another government agency makes recommendations to protect and promote public health. Sometimes, though, results are tough to interpret.

More than 100 studies have been done on BPA—some funded by the government, some funded by the plastics industry. Most of the independent studies found that low doses of BPA could have negative health effects on laboratory animals. A few studies, mostly funded by the plastics industry, concluded that BPA is safe. In this case, the FDA ultimately declared BPA to be safe. When the issue of BPA safety hit the mass media, government investigations began. So, who should sponsor product safety studies?

The Viewpoints

Independent Organizations Should Fund Safety Studies

Scientists performing safety studies should have no affiliation with private industries, because conflict of interest seems unavoidable. A company, such as a BPA manufacturer, would naturally benefit if its product is declared to be safe. Rather, safety tests should be funded by independent organizations such as universities and government agencies, which should be as independent as possible. This way, recommendations for public health can remain free of biases.

Private Industries Should Fund Safety Studies

There are an awful lot of products out there! Who would pay scientists to test all those products? There are simply too many potentially useful and valuable products being developed by private industry for the government to keep track of and test adequately with public funds. It is in a company's best interest to produce safe products, so it would be inclined to maintain high standards and perform rigorous tests.

Research and Decide

1. Analyze the Viewpoints To make an informed decision, research the current status of the controversy over BPA by using the Internet and other resources. Compare this situation with the history of safety studies on cigarette smoke and the chemical Teflon.

2. Form an Opinion Should private industries be able to pay scientists to perform their product safety studies? How would you deal with the issue of potential bias in interpreting results?

1.3 Studying Life

THINK ABOUT IT Think about important and exciting news stories you've seen or heard. Bird flu spreads around the world, killing thousands of birds and threatening a human epidemic. Users of certain illegal drugs experience permanent damage to their brains and other parts of their nervous systems. Reports surface about efforts to clone human cells to grow new organs to replace those lost to disease or injury. These and many other stories involve biology—the science that employs scientific methodology to study living things. (The Greek word *bios* means "life," and *-logy* means "study of.")

Characteristics of Living Things

🔑 What characteristics do all living things share?

Biology is the study of life. But what is life? What distinguishes living things from nonliving matter? Surprisingly, it isn't as simple as you might think to describe what makes something alive. No single characteristic is enough to describe a living thing. Also, some nonliving things share one or more traits with organisms. For example, a firefly and fire both give off light, and each moves in its own way. Mechanical toys, automobiles, and clouds (which are not alive) move around, while mushrooms and trees (which are alive) stay in one spot. To make matters more complicated, some things, such as viruses, exist at the border between organisms and nonliving things.

Despite these difficulties, we can list characteristics that most living things have in common. 🔑 **Living things are made up of basic units called cells, are based on a universal genetic code, obtain and use materials and energy, grow and develop, reproduce, respond to their environment, maintain a stable internal environment, and change over time.**

FIGURE 1–12 Is It Alive? The fish are clearly alive, but what about the colorful structure above them? Is it alive? As a matter of fact, it is. The antlerlike structure is actually a marine animal called elkhorn coral. Corals show all the characteristics common to living things.

Key Questions

🔑 What characteristics do all living things share?

🔑 What are the central themes of biology?

🔑 How do different fields of biology differ in their approach to studying life?

🔑 How is the metric system important in science?

Vocabulary

biology • DNA • stimulus • sexual reproduction • asexual reproduction • homeostasis • metabolism • biosphere

Taking Notes

Concept Map As you read, draw a concept map showing the big ideas in biology.

VISUAL SUMMARY

THE CHARACTERISTICS OF LIVING THINGS

FIGURE 1-13 Apple trees share certain characteristics with other living things. **Compare and Contrast** *How are the apple tree and the grass growing below similar? How are they different?*

Living things are based on a universal genetic code. All organisms store the complex information they need to live, grow, and reproduce in a genetic code written in a molecule called **DNA**. That information is copied and passed from parent to offspring. With a few minor variations, life's genetic code is almost identical in every organism on Earth.

◄ *The growth, form, and structure of an apple tree are determined by information in its DNA.*

Living things grow and develop. Every organism has a particular pattern of growth and development. During development, a single fertilized egg divides again and again. As these cells divide, they differentiate, which means they begin to look different from one another and to perform different functions.

◄ *An apple tree develops from a tiny seed.*

Living things respond to their environment. Organisms detect and respond to stimuli from their environment. A **stimulus** is a signal to which an organism responds.

▼ *Some plants can produce unsavory chemicals to ward off caterpillars that feed on their leaves.*

Living things reproduce. All organisms reproduce, which means that they produce new similar organisms. Most plants and animals engage in sexual reproduction. In **sexual reproduction,** cells from two parents unite to form the first cell of a new organism. Other organisms reproduce through **asexual reproduction,** in which a single organism produces offspring identical to itself.

▶ *Beautiful blossoms are part of the apple tree's cycle of sexual reproduction.*

Living things maintain a stable internal environment. All organisms need to keep their internal environment relatively stable, even when external conditions change dramatically. This condition is called **homeostasis.**

◀ *These specialized cells help leaves regulate gases that enter and leave the plant.* SEM 1200×

Living things obtain and use material and energy. All organisms must take in materials and energy to grow, develop, and reproduce. The combination of chemical reactions through which an organism builds up or breaks down materials is called **metabolism.**

▶ *Various metabolic reactions occur in leaves.*

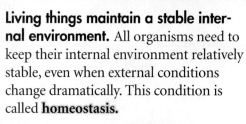

Living things are made up of cells.
Organisms are composed of one or more cells—the smallest units considered fully alive. Cells can grow, respond to their surroundings, and reproduce. Despite their small size, cells are complex and highly organized.

▲ *A single branch of an apple tree contains millions of cells.* LM 250×

Taken as a group, living things evolve.
Over generations, groups of organisms evolve, or change over time. Evolutionary change links all forms of life to a common origin more than 3.5 billion years ago. Evidence of this shared history is found in all aspects of living and fossil organisms, from physical features to structures of proteins to sequences of information in DNA.

▶ *Signs of one of the first land plants, Cooksonia, are preserved in rock over 400 million years old.*

Analyzing Data

What's in a Diet?

The circle graph shows the diet of the siamang gibbon, a type of ape found in the rainforests of Southeast Asia.

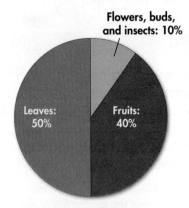

Flowers, buds, and insects: 10%

Leaves: 50%

Fruits: 40%

Analyze and Conclude

1. Interpret Graphs Which plant parts do siamangs rely on most as a source of their matter and energy?

2. Predict How would siamangs be affected if the rainforests they live in were cut down?

Big Ideas in Biology

🔑 What are the central themes of biology?

The units of this book seem to cover different subjects. But we'll let you in on a secret: That's not how biology works. All biological sciences are tied together by themes and methods of study that cut across disciplines. These "big ideas" overlap and interlock, and crop up again and again throughout the book. You'll also notice that several of these big ideas overlap with the characteristics of life or the nature of science.

🔑 **The study of biology revolves around several interlocking big ideas: The cellular basis of life; information and heredity; matter and energy; growth, development, and reproduction; homeostasis; evolution; structure and function; unity and diversity of life; interdependence in nature; and science as a way of knowing.**

Big idea ▶ Cellular Basis of Life Living things are made of cells. Many living things consist of only a single cell; they are called unicellular organisms. Plants and animals are multicellular. Cells in multicellular organisms display many different sizes, shapes, and functions. The human body contains 200 or more different cell types.

Big idea ▶ Information and Heredity Living things are based on a universal genetic code. The information coded in DNA forms an unbroken chain that stretches back roughly 3.5 billion years. Yet, the DNA inside your cells right now can influence your future—your risk of getting cancer, the amount of cholesterol in your blood, and the color of your children's hair.

Big idea ▶ Matter and Energy Living things obtain and use material and energy. Life requires matter that serves as nutrients to build body structures, and energy that fuels life's processes. Some organisms, such as plants, obtain energy from sunlight and take up nutrients from air, water, and soil. Other organisms, including most animals, eat plants or other animals to obtain both nutrients and energy. The need for matter and energy link all living things on Earth in a web of interdependent relationships.

Big idea ▶ Growth, Development, and Reproduction All living things reproduce. Newly produced individuals are virtually always smaller than adults, so they grow and develop as they mature. During growth and development, generalized cells typically become more and more different and specialized for particular functions. Specialized cells build tissues, such as brains, muscles, and digestive organs, that serve various functions.

Big idea ▶ Homeostasis Living things maintain a relatively stable internal environment, a process known as homeostasis. For most organisms, any breakdown of homeostasis may have serious or even fatal consequences.

 In Your Notebook *Describe what happens at the cellular level as a baby grows and develops.*

Big idea Evolution Taken as a group, living things evolve. Evolutionary change links all forms of life to a common origin more than 3.5 billion years ago. Evidence of this shared history is found in all aspects of living and fossil organisms, from physical features to structures of proteins to sequences of information in DNA. Evolutionary theory is the central organizing principle of all biological and biomedical sciences.

Big idea Structure and Function Each major group of organisms has evolved its own particular body part "tool kit,"—a collection of structures that have evolved in ways that make particular functions possible. From capturing food to digesting it, and from reproducing to breathing, organisms use structures that have evolved into different forms as species have adapted to life in different environments. The structures of wings, for example, enable birds and insects to fly. The structures of legs enable horses to gallop and kangaroos to hop.

Big idea Unity and Diversity of Life Although life takes an almost unbelievable variety of forms, all living things are fundamentally similar at the molecular level. All organisms are composed of a common set of carbon-based molecules, store information in a common genetic code, and use proteins to build their structures and carry out their functions. One great contribution of evolutionary theory is that it explains both this unity of life and its diversity.

Big idea Interdependence in Nature All forms of life on Earth are connected into a **biosphere,** which literally means "living planet." Within the biosphere, organisms are linked to one another and to the land, water, and air around them. Relationships between organisms and their environments depend on the cycling of matter and the flow of energy. Human life and the economies of human societies also require matter and energy, so human life depends directly on nature.

Big idea Science as a Way of Knowing Science is not a list of facts, but "a way of knowing." The job of science is to use observations, questions, and experiments to explain the natural world in terms of natural forces and events. Successful scientific research reveals rules and patterns that can explain and predict at least some events in nature. Science enables us to take actions that affect events in the world around us. To make certain that scientific knowledge is used for the benefit of society, all of us must understand the nature of science—its strengths, its limitations, and its interactions with our culture.

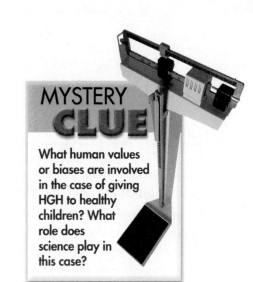

MYSTERY CLUE

What human values or biases are involved in the case of giving HGH to healthy children? What role does science play in this case?

FIGURE 1–14 Different But Similar
The colorful keel-billed toucan is clearly different from the plant on which it perches. Yet, the two organisms are fundamentally similar at the molecular level. Unity and diversity of life is an important theme in biology.

Fields of Biology

🔑 *How do different fields of biology differ in their approach to studying life?*

Living systems range from groups of molecules that make up cells to collections of organisms that make up the biosphere. 🔑 **Biology includes many overlapping fields that use different tools to study life from the level of molecules to the entire planet.** Here's a peek into a few of the smallest and largest branches of biology.

Global Ecology Life on Earth is shaped by weather patterns and processes in the atmosphere so large that we are just beginning to understand them. We are also learning that activities of living organisms—including humans—profoundly affect both the atmosphere and climate. Humans now move more matter and use more energy than any other multicellular species on Earth. Global ecological studies, aided by satellite technology and supercomputers, are enabling us to learn about our global impact, which affects all life on Earth.

▲ *An ecologist studies lichens on Douglas fir. Many lichens are extremely sensitive to nitrogen- and sulfur-based air pollution. Thus, researchers often monitor lichens in efforts to study the effects of air pollution on forest health.*

Biotechnology This field, created by the molecular revolution, is based on our ability to "edit" and rewrite the genetic code—in a sense, redesigning the living world to order. We may soon learn to correct or replace damaged genes that cause inherited diseases. Other research seeks to genetically engineer bacteria to clean up toxic wastes. Biotechnology also raises enormous ethical, legal, and social questions. Dare we tamper with the fundamental biological information that makes us human?

▶ *A plant biologist analyzes genetically modified rice plants.*

Building the Tree of Life Biologists have discovered and identified roughly 1.8 million different kinds of living organisms. That may seem like an incredible number, but researchers estimate that somewhere between 2 and 100 million more forms of life are waiting to be discovered around the globe—from caves deep beneath the surface, to tropical rainforests, to coral reefs and the depths of the sea. Identifying and cataloguing all these life forms is enough work by itself, but biologists aim to do much more. They want to combine the latest genetic information with computer technology to organize all living things into a single universal "Tree of All Life"— and put the results on the Web in a form that anyone can access.

▶ *Paleontologists study the fossilized bones of dinosaurs.*

Ecology and Evolution of Infectious Diseases HIV, bird flu, and drug-resistant bacteria seem to have appeared out of nowhere, but the science behind their stories shows that relationships between hosts and pathogens are dynamic and constantly changing. Organisms that cause human disease have their own ecology, which involves our bodies, medicines we take, and our interactions with each other and the environment. Over time, disease-causing organisms engage in an "evolutionary arms race" with humans that creates constant challenges to public health around the world. Understanding these interactions is crucial to safeguarding our future.

▶ *A wildlife biologist studies a group of wild gelada baboons. Pathogens in wild animal populations may evolve in ways that enable them to infect humans.*

Genomics and Molecular Biology These fields focus on studies of DNA and other molecules inside cells. The "molecular revolution" of the 1980s created the field of genomics, which is now looking at the entire sets of DNA code contained in a wide range of organisms. Ever-more-powerful computer analyses enable researchers to compare vast databases of genetic information in a fascinating search for keys to the mysteries of growth, development, aging, cancer, and the history of life on Earth.

▶ *A molecular biologist analyzes a DNA sequence.*

23

Performing Biological Investigations

🗝 *How is the metric system important in science?*

During your study of biology, you will have the opportunity to perform scientific investigations. Biologists, like other scientists, rely on a common system of measurement and practice safety procedures when conducting studies. As you study and experiment, you will become familiar with scientific measurement and safety procedures.

Scientific Measurement Because researchers need to replicate one another's experiments, and because many experiments involve gathering quantitative data, scientists need a common system of measurement. 🗝 **Most scientists use the metric system when collecting data and performing experiments.** The metric system is a decimal system of measurement whose units are based on certain physical standards and are scaled on multiples of 10. A revised version of the original metric system is called the International System of Units, or SI. The abbreviation *SI* comes from the French *Le Système International d'Unités*.

Because the metric system is based on multiples of 10, it is easy to use. Notice in **Figure 1–15** how the basic unit of length, the meter, can be multiplied or divided to measure objects and distances much larger or smaller than a meter. The same process can be used when measuring volume and mass. You can learn more about the metric system in Appendix B.

BUILD Vocabulary

PREFIXES The SI prefix *milli-* means "thousandth." Therefore, 1 millimeter is one-thousandth of a meter, and 1 milligram is one-thousandth of a gram.

Common Metric Units

Length	Mass
1 meter (m) = 100 centimeters (cm) 1 meter = 1000 millimeters (mm) 1000 meters = 1 kilometer (km)	1 kilogram (kg) = 1000 grams (g) 1 gram = 1000 milligrams (mg) 1000 kilograms = 1 metric ton (t)

Volume	Temperature
1 liter (L) = 1000 milliliters (mL) 1 liter = 1000 cubic centimeters (cm³)	0°C = freezing point of water 100°C = boiling point of water

FIGURE 1–15 The Metric System Scientists usually use the metric system in their work. This system is easy to use because it is based on multiples of 10. In the photo, biologists in Alaska weigh a small polar bear. **Predict** *What unit of measurement would you use to express the bear's mass?*

Safety Scientists working in a laboratory or in the field are trained to use safe procedures when carrying out investigations. Laboratory work may involve flames or heating elements, electricity, chemicals, hot liquids, sharp instruments, and breakable glassware. Laboratory work and fieldwork may involve contact with living or dead organisms—not just potentially poisonous plants and venomous animals but also disease-carrying mosquitoes and water contaminated with dangerous microorganisms.

Whenever you work in your biology laboratory, you must follow safe practices as well. Careful preparation is the key to staying safe during scientific activities. Before performing any activity in this course, study the safety rules in Appendix B. Before you start each activity, read all the steps and make sure that you understand the entire procedure, including any safety precautions.

The single most important safety rule is to always follow your teacher's instructions and directions in this textbook. Any time you are in doubt about any part of an activity, ask your teacher for an explanation. And because you may come in contact with organisms you cannot see, it is essential that you wash your hands thoroughly after every scientific activity. Remember that you are responsible for your own safety and that of your teacher and classmates. If you are handling live animals, you are responsible for their safety too.

FIGURE 1–16 Science Safety
Wearing appropriate protective gear is important while working in a laboratory.

1.3 Assessment

Review Key Concepts 🔑

1. a. Review List the characteristics that define life.

b. Applying Concepts Suppose you feel hungry, so you reach for a plum you see in a fruit bowl. Explain how both external and internal stimuli are involved in your action.

2. a. Review What are the themes in biology that come up again and again?

b. Predict Suppose you discover a new organism. What would you expect to see if you studied it under a microscope?

3. a. Review At what levels do biologists study life?

b. Classify A researcher studies why frogs are disappearing in the wild. What field of biology does the research fall into?

4. a. Review Why do scientists use a common system of measurement?

b. Relate Cause and Effect Suppose two scientists are trying to perform an experiment that involves dangerous chemicals. How might their safety be affected by not using a common measurement?

PRACTICE PROBLEM

5. In an experiment, you need 250 grams of potting soil for each of 10 plant samples. How many kilograms of soil in total do you need?
MATH

Skills Lab

Pre-Lab: Using a Microscope to Estimate Size

Problem How can you use a microscope to estimate the size of an object?

Materials compound microscope, transparent 15-cm plastic ruler, prepared slide of plant root or stem, prepared slide of bacteria

Lab Manual Chapter 1 Lab

Skills Focus Observe, Measure, Calculate, Predict

Connect to the **Big idea** Science provides a way of knowing the world. The use of technology to gather data is a central part of modern science. In biology, the compound microscope is a vital tool. With a microscope, you can observe objects that are too tiny to see with the unaided eye. These objects include cells, which are the basis for all life.

In this lab, you will explore another important use of the microscope. You will use the microscope to estimate the size of cells.

Background Questions

a. Explain How did the invention of the microscope help scientists know the natural world?

b. Explain How can a microscope help a scientist use scientific methodology?

c. Infer List one important fact about life that scientists would not know without microscopes. *Hint:* Review the characteristics of living things.

Pre-Lab Questions

Preview the procedure in the lab manual.

1. Review Which lens provides more magnification— a low-power lens or a high-power lens? Which lens provides the larger field of view?

2. Use Analogies A photographer may take wide views and close-ups of the same scene. How are these views similar to the low-power and high-power lenses on a microscope? What is an advantage of each view?

3. Calculate Eight cells fit across a field of view of 160 μm. What is the width of each cell? MATH

4. Predict Which cell do you think will be larger, the plant cell or the bacterial cell? Give a reason for your answer.

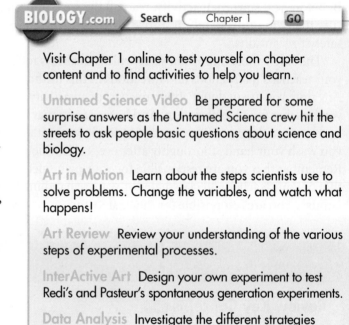

BIOLOGY.com   Search (Chapter 1)   GO

Visit Chapter 1 online to test yourself on chapter content and to find activities to help you learn.

Untamed Science Video Be prepared for some surprise answers as the Untamed Science crew hit the streets to ask people basic questions about science and biology.

Art in Motion Learn about the steps scientists use to solve problems. Change the variables, and watch what happens!

Art Review Review your understanding of the various steps of experimental processes.

InterActive Art Design your own experiment to test Redi's and Pasteur's spontaneous generation experiments.

Data Analysis Investigate the different strategies scientists use for measurement.

1 Study Guide

By applying scientific methodology, biologists can find answers to questions that arise in the study of life.

1.1 What Is Science?

🔑 One goal of science is to provide natural explanations for events in the natural world. Science also aims to use those explanations to understand patterns in nature and to make useful predictions about natural events.

🔑 Scientific methodology involves observing and asking questions, making inferences and forming hypotheses, conducting controlled experiments, collecting and analyzing data, and drawing conclusions.

science (5)
observation (6)
inference (7)
hypothesis (7)
controlled experiment (7)

independent variable (7)
dependent variable (7)
control group (7)
data (8)

1.2 Science in Context

🔑 Curiosity, skepticism, open-mindedness, and creativity help scientists generate new ideas.

🔑 Publishing peer-reviewed articles in scientific journals allows researchers to share ideas and to test and evaluate each other's work.

🔑 In science, the word *theory* applies to a well-tested explanation that unifies a broad range of observations and hypotheses and that enables scientists to make accurate predictions about new situations.

🔑 Using science involves understanding its context in society and its limitations.

theory (13)
bias (14)

1.3 Studying Life

🔑 Living things are made up of units called cells, are based on a universal genetic code, obtain and use materials and energy, grow and develop, reproduce, respond to their environment, maintain a stable internal environment, and change over time.

🔑 The study of biology revolves around several interlocking big ideas: the cellular basis of life; information and heredity; matter and energy; growth, development, and reproduction; homeostasis; evolution; structure and function; unity and diversity of life; interdependence in nature; and science as a way of knowing.

🔑 Biology includes many overlapping fields that use different tools to study life from the level of molecules to the entire planet.

🔑 Most scientists use the metric system when collecting data and performing experiments.

biology (17)
DNA (18)
stimulus (18)
sexual reproduction (19)

asexual reproduction (19)
homeostasis (19)
metabolism (19)
biosphere (21)

Think Visually Using the information in this chapter, complete the following concept map:

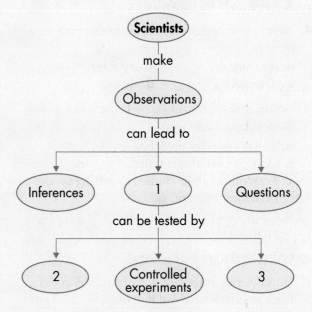

Scientists

make

Observations

can lead to

Inferences · 1 · Questions

can be tested by

2 · Controlled experiments · 3

1 Assessment

Understand Key Concepts

1. Which of the following statements about the image shown below is NOT an observation?
   a. The insect has three legs on the left side.
   b. The insect has a pattern on its back.
   c. The insect's pattern shows that it is poisonous.
   d. The insect is green, white, and black.

2. The statement "The worm is 2 centimeters long" is a(n)
   a. observation.   c. inference.
   b. theory.   d. hypothesis.

3. An inference is
   a. the same as an observation.
   b. a logical interpretation of an observation.
   c. a statement involving numbers.
   d. a way to avoid bias.

4. To be useful in science, a hypothesis must be
   a. measurable.   c. testable.
   b. observable.   d. correct.

5. Which of the following statements about a controlled experiment is true?
   a. All the variables must be kept the same.
   b. Only one variable is tested at a time.
   c. Everything can be studied by setting up a controlled experiment.
   d. Controlled experiments cannot be performed on living things.

6. What are the goals of science?

7. How does an observation about an object differ from an inference about that object?

8. How does a hypothesis help scientists understand the natural world?

9. Why does it make sense for scientists to test just one variable at a time in an experiment?

10. Distinguish between an experimental group and a control group.

11. What steps are involved in drawing a conclusion?

12. How can a graph of data be more informative than a table of the same data?

Think Critically

13. **Design an Experiment** Suggest an experiment that would show whether one food is better than another at speeding an animal's growth.

14. **Control Variables** Explain why you cannot draw a conclusion about the effect of one variable in an investigation when the other key variables are not controlled.

Understand Key Concepts

15. A skeptical attitude in science
    a. prevents scientists from accepting new ideas.
    b. encourages scientists to readily accept new ideas.
    c. means a new idea will only be accepted if it is backed by evidence.
    d. is unimportant.

16. The purpose of peer review in science is to ensure that
    a. all scientific research is funded.
    b. the results of experiments are correct.
    c. all scientific results are published.
    d. published results meet standards set by the scientific community.

17. A scientific theory is
    a. the same as a hypothesis.
    b. a well-tested explanation that unifies a broad range of observations.
    c. the same as the conclusion of an experiment.
    d. the first step in a controlled experiment.

18. Why are scientific theories useful?

19. Why aren't theories considered absolute truths?

Think Critically

20. Evaluate Why is it misleading to describe science as a collection of facts?

21. Propose a Solution How would having a scientific attitude help you in everyday activities, for example, in trying to learn a new skill?

22. Conduct Peer Review If you were one of the anonymous reviewers of a paper submitted for publication, what criteria would you use to determine whether or not the paper should be published?

1.3 Studying Life

Understand Key Concepts

23. The process in which two cells from different parents unite to produce the first cell of a new organism is called
   a. homeostasis.
   b. development.
   c. asexual reproduction.
   d. sexual reproduction.

24. The process by which organisms keep their internal conditions relatively stable is called
   a. metabolism.
   b. a genome.
   c. evolution.
   d. homeostasis.

25. How are unicellular and multicellular organisms alike? How are they different?

26. Give an example of changes that take place as cells in a multicellular organism differentiate.

27. List three examples of stimuli that a bird responds to.

Think Critically

28. Measure Use a ruler to find the precise length and width of this book in millimeters.

29. Interpret Visuals Each of the following safety symbols might appear in a laboratory activity in this book. Describe what each symbol stands for. (*Hint:* Refer to Appendix B.)

solve the CHAPTER MYSTERY

HEIGHT BY PRESCRIPTION

Although scientific studies have not proved that HGH treatment significantly increases adult height, they do suggest that extra HGH may help some short kids grow taller sooner. Parents who learn about this possibility may want treatment for their children. David's doctor prescribed HGH to avoid criticism for not presenting it as an option.

This situation is new. Many years ago, HGH was available only from cadavers, and it was prescribed only for people with severe medical problems. Then, genetic engineering made it possible to mass-produce safe, artificial HGH for medical use—safe medicine for sick people.

However, many people who are shorter than average often face prejudice in our society. This led drug companies to begin marketing HGH to parents of healthy, short kids. The message: "Help your child grow taller!"

As David's case illustrates, science has the powerful potential to change lives, but new scientific knowledge and advances may raise more questions than they answer. Just because science makes something *possible*, does that mean it's *right* to do it? This question is difficult to answer. When considering how science should be applied, we must consider both its limitations and its context in society.

1. Relate Cause and Effect Search the Internet for the latest data on HGH treatment of healthy children. What effect does early HGH treatment have on adult height?

2. Predict HGH was among the first products of the biotechnology revolution. Many more are in the pipeline. As products become available that could change other inherited traits, what challenges await society?

3. Connect to the Big idea Why would it be important for scientists to communicate clearly the results of HGH studies? How might parents benefit by understanding the science behind the results?

Use Science Graphics

The following graphs show the size of four different populations over a period of time. Use the graphs to answer questions 30–32.

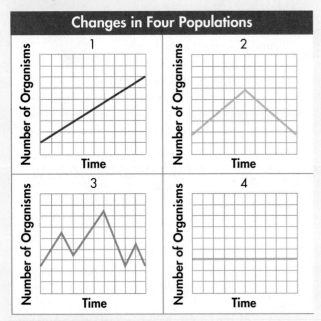

Changes in Four Populations

30. **Analyze Data** Write a sentence summarizing what each graph shows.

31. **Interpret Graphs** Before any of the graphs could be used to make direct comparisons among the populations, what additional information would be necessary?

32. **Compare and Contrast** Graphs of completely different events can have the same appearance. Select one of the graphs and explain how the shape of the graph could apply to a different set of events.

Write About Science

33. **Explanation** Suppose you have a pet cat and want to determine which type of cat food it prefers. Write an explanation of how you could use scientific methodology to determine the answer. (*Hint:* Before you start writing, list the steps you might take, and then arrange them in order beginning with the first step.)

34. **Assess the Big idea** Many people add fertilizer to their house and garden plants. Make a hypothesis about whether you think fertilizers really help plants grow. Next, design an experiment to test your hypothesis. Include in your plan what variable you will test and what variables you will control.

A researcher studied two groups of fruit flies: Population A was kept in a 0.5 L container; Population B was kept in a 1 L container.

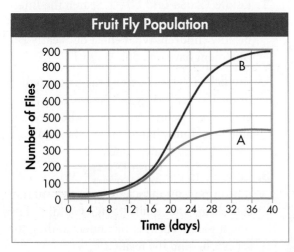

Fruit Fly Population

35. **Interpret Graphs** The independent variable in the controlled experiment was the
   a. number of flies.
   b. number of groups studied.
   c. number of days.
   d. size of the containers.

36. **Infer** Which of the following is a logical inference based on the content of the graph?
   a. The flies in Group B were healthier than those in Group A.
   b. A fly population with more available space will grow larger than a population with less space.
   c. If Group B was observed for 40 more days, the size of the population would double.
   d. In 40 more days, the size of both populations would decrease at the same rate.

Standardized Test Prep

Multiple Choice

1. To ensure that a scientific work is free of bias and meets standards set by the scientific community, a research group's work is peer reviewed by
   A anonymous scientific experts.
   B the general public.
   C the researchers' friends.
   D lawmakers.

2. Which of the following characteristics is NOT shared by both a horse and the grass it eats?
   A uses energy
   B response to stimulus
   C movement from place to place
   D stable internal environment

3. Which of the following statements about a scientific theory is NOT true?
   A It has the same meaning in science as it does in daily life.
   B It enables scientists to make accurate predictions about new situations.
   C Scientific theories tie many hypotheses together.
   D It is based on a large body of evidence.

4. A bird-watcher sees an unusual bird at a feeder. He takes careful notes on the bird's color, shape, and other physical features and then goes to a reference book to see if he can identify the species. What aspect of scientific thinking is most apparent in this situation?
   A observation
   B inference
   C hypothesis formation
   D controlled experimentation

5. Unlike sexual reproduction, asexual reproduction involves
   A two cells.   C one parent.
   B two parents.   D one nonliving thing.

6. One meter is equal to
   A 1000 millimeters.
   B 1 millimeter.
   C 10 kilometers.
   D 1 milliliter.

Questions 7–8

Once a month, a pet owner recorded the mass of her puppy in a table. When the puppy was 3 months old, she started to feed it a "special puppy food" she saw advertised on TV.

Change in a Puppy's Mass Over Time		
Age (months)	Mass at Start of Month (kg)	Change in Mass per Month (kg)
2	5	—
3	8	+3
4	13	+5

7. According to the table, which statement is true?
   A The puppy's mass increased at the same rate for each month shown.
   B The puppy's mass was less than 5 kg at the start of the new diet.
   C The puppy gained 5 kg between age 3 and 4 months.
   D The puppy had gained 13 kg as a result of the new diet.

8. All of the following statements about the pet owner's study are true EXCEPT
   A The owner used the metric system.
   B The owner recorded data.
   C The owner could graph the data.
   D The owner conducted a controlled experiment.

Open-Ended Response

9. Explain how a controlled experiment works.

If You Have Trouble With . . .								
Question	1	2	3	4	5	6	7	8	9
See Lesson	1.2	1.3	1.2	1.1	1.3	1.3	1.1	1.1	1.1

2 The Chemistry of Life

Matter and Energy

Q: What are the basic chemical principles that affect living things?

INSIDE:

- **2.1 The Nature of Matter**
- **2.2 Properties of Water**
- **2.3 Carbon Compounds**
- **2.4 Chemical Reactions and Enzymes**

Water is locked in ice in the Svalbard islands of Norway—home to the polar bear. Even in such an extreme environment, organisms are able to obtain the matter and energy they need to survive.

CHAPTER MYSTERY

THE GHOSTLY FISH

Most fish, just like you and other vertebrates, have red blood. Red blood cells carry oxygen, a gas essential for life. The cells' red color comes from an oxygen-binding protein called hemoglobin.

But a very small number of fish don't have such cells. Their blood is clear—almost transparent. Because they live in cold antarctic waters and have a ghostly appearance, they are nicknamed "ice fish." How do these animals manage to survive without red blood cells?

As you read this chapter, look for clues to help you explain the ice fish's unusual feature. Think about the chemistry that might be involved. Then, solve the mystery.

Never Stop Exploring Your World.
Finding the solution to the fishy mystery is only the beginning. Take a video field trip with the ecogeeks of Untamed Science to see where this mystery leads.

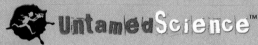

2.1 The Nature of Matter

Key Questions

🔑 What three subatomic particles make up atoms?

🔑 How are all of the isotopes of an element similar?

🔑 In what ways do compounds differ from their component elements?

🔑 What are the main types of chemical bonds?

Vocabulary

atom • nucleus • electron • element • isotope • compound • ionic bond • ion • covalent bond • molecule • van der Waals forces

Taking Notes

Outline Before you read, make an outline of the major headings in the lesson. As you read, fill in main ideas and supporting details under each head.

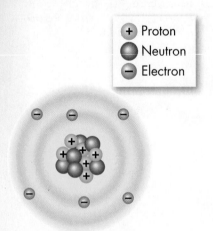

FIGURE 2–1 A Carbon Atom

THINK ABOUT IT What are you made of? Just as buildings are made from bricks, steel, glass, and wood, living things are made from chemical compounds. But it doesn't stop there. When you breathe, eat, or drink, your body uses the substances in air, food, and water to carry out chemical reactions that keep you alive. If the first task of an architect is to understand building materials, then what would be the first job of a biologist? Clearly, it is to understand the chemistry of life.

Atoms

🔑 **What three subatomic particles make up atoms?**

The study of chemistry begins with the basic unit of matter, the **atom.** The concept of the atom came first from the Greek philosopher Democritus, nearly 2500 years ago. Democritus asked a simple question: If you take an object like a stick of chalk and break it in half, are both halves still chalk? The answer, of course, is yes. But what happens if you break it in half again and again and again? Can you continue to divide without limit, or does there come a point at which you cannot divide the fragment of chalk without changing it into something else? Democritus thought that there had to be a limit. He called the smallest fragment the atom, from the Greek word *atomos,* which means "unable to be cut."

Atoms are incredibly small. Placed side by side, 100 million atoms would make a row only about 1 centimeter long—about the width of your little finger! Despite its extremely small size, an atom contains subatomic particles that are even smaller. **Figure 2–1** shows the subatomic particles in a carbon atom. 🔑 **The subatomic particles that make up atoms are protons, neutrons, and electrons.**

Protons and Neutrons Protons and neutrons have about the same mass. However, protons are positively charged particles (+) and neutrons carry no charge at all. Strong forces bind protons and neutrons together to form the **nucleus,** at the center of the atom.

Electrons The **electron** is a negatively charged particle (−) with only 1/1840 the mass of a proton. Electrons are in constant motion in the space surrounding the nucleus. They are attracted to the positively charged nucleus but remain outside the nucleus because of the energy of their motion. Because atoms have equal numbers of electrons and protons, their positive and negative charges balance out, and atoms themselves are electrically neutral.

Elements and Isotopes

🔑 *How are all of the isotopes of an element similar?*

A chemical **element** is a pure substance that consists entirely of one type of atom. More than 100 elements are known, but only about two dozen are commonly found in living organisms. Elements are represented by one- or two-letter symbols. C, for example, stands for carbon, H for hydrogen, Na for sodium, and Hg for mercury. The number of protons in the nucleus of an element is called its atomic number. Carbon's atomic number is 6, meaning that each atom of carbon has six protons and, consequently, six electrons. See Appendix E, The Periodic Table, which shows the elements.

Isotopes Atoms of an element may have different numbers of neutrons. For example, although all atoms of carbon have six protons, some have six neutrons, some seven, and a few have eight. Atoms of the same element that differ in the number of neutrons they contain are known as **isotopes.** The total number of protons and neutrons in the nucleus of an atom is called its mass number. Isotopes are identified by their mass numbers. **Figure 2–3** shows the subatomic composition of carbon-12, carbon-13, and carbon-14 atoms. The weighted average of the masses of an element's isotopes is called its atomic mass. "Weighted" means that the abundance of each isotope in nature is considered when the average is calculated. 🔑 **Because they have the same number of electrons, all isotopes of an element have the same chemical properties.**

FIGURE 2–2 Droplets of Mercury
Mercury, a silvery-white metallic element, is liquid at room temperature and forms droplets. It is extremely poisonous.

Isotopes of Carbon

Isotope	Number of Protons	Number of Electrons	Number of Neutrons
Carbon–12 (nonradioactive)	6	6	6
Carbon–13 (nonradioactive)	6	6	7
Carbon–14 (radioactive)	6	6	8

FIGURE 2–3 Carbon Isotopes
Isotopes of carbon all have 6 protons but different numbers of neutrons—6, 7, or 8. They are identified by the total number of protons and neutrons in the nucleus: carbon–12, carbon–13, and carbon–14. **Classify** *Which isotope of carbon is radioactive?*

Radioactive Isotopes Some isotopes are radioactive, meaning that their nuclei are unstable and break down at a constant rate over time. The radiation these isotopes give off can be dangerous, but radioactive isotopes have a number of important scientific and practical uses.

Geologists can determine the ages of rocks and fossils by analyzing the isotopes found in them. Radiation from certain isotopes can be used to detect and treat cancer and to kill bacteria that cause food to spoil. Radioactive isotopes can also be used as labels or "tracers" to follow the movements of substances within organisms.

In Your Notebook *Draw a diagram of a helium atom, which has an atomic number of 2.*

Chemical Compounds

In what ways do compounds differ from their component elements?

In nature, most elements are found combined with other elements in compounds. A chemical **compound** is a substance formed by the chemical combination of two or more elements in definite proportions. Scientists show the composition of compounds by a kind of shorthand known as a chemical formula. Water, which contains two atoms of hydrogen for each atom of oxygen, has the chemical formula H_2O. The formula for table salt, NaCl, indicates that the elements that make up table salt—sodium and chlorine—combine in a 1 : 1 ratio.

The physical and chemical properties of a compound are usually very different from those of the elements from which it is formed. For example, hydrogen and oxygen, which are gases at room temperature, can combine explosively and form liquid water. Sodium is a silver-colored metal that is soft enough to cut with a knife. It reacts explosively with water. Chlorine is very reactive, too. It is a poisonous, yellow-greenish gas that was used in battles during World War I. Sodium chloride, table salt, is a white solid that dissolves easily in water. As you know, sodium chloride is not poisonous. In fact, it is essential for the survival of most living things.

Chemical Bonds

What are the main types of chemical bonds?

The atoms in compounds are held together by various types of chemical bonds. Much of chemistry is devoted to understanding how and when chemical bonds form. Bond formation involves the electrons that surround each atomic nucleus. The electrons that are available to form bonds are called valence electrons. **The main types of chemical bonds are ionic bonds and covalent bonds.**

Quick Lab
GUIDED INQUIRY

Model an Ionic Compound

❶ You will be assigned to represent either a sodium atom or a chlorine atom.

❷ Obtain the appropriate number of popcorn kernels to represent your electrons.

❸ Find a partner with whom you can form the ionic compound sodium chloride—table salt.

❹ In table salt, the closely packed sodium and chloride ions form an orderly structure called a crystal. With all your classmates, work as a class to model a sodium chloride crystal.

Analyze and Conclude

1. Relate Cause and Effect Describe the exchange of popcorn kernels (electrons) that took place as you formed the ionic bond. What electrical charges resulted from the exchange?

2. Use Models How were the "ions" arranged in the model of the crystal? Why did you and your classmates choose this arrangement?

A. Ionic Bonding

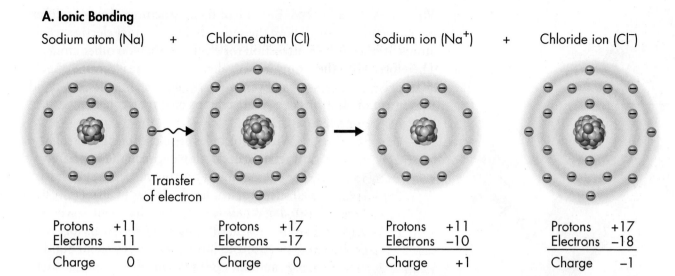

| Sodium atom (Na) | + | Chlorine atom (Cl) | | Sodium ion (Na⁺) | + | Chloride ion (Cl⁻) |

Transfer of electron

Protons	+11	Protons	+17	Protons	+11	Protons	+17
Electrons	−11	Electrons	−17	Electrons	−10	Electrons	−18
Charge	0	Charge	0	Charge	+1	Charge	−1

Ionic Bonds An **ionic bond** is formed when one or more electrons are transferred from one atom to another. Recall that atoms are electrically neutral because they have equal numbers of protons and electrons. An atom that loses electrons becomes positively charged. An atom that gains electrons has a negative charge. These positively and negatively charged atoms are known as **ions.**

Figure 2–4A shows how ionic bonds form between sodium and chlorine in table salt. A sodium atom easily loses its one valence electron and becomes a sodium ion (Na⁺). A chlorine atom easily gains an electron and becomes a chloride ion (Cl⁻). In a salt crystal, there are trillions of sodium and chloride ions. These oppositely charged ions have a strong attraction, forming an ionic bond.

Covalent Bonds Sometimes electrons are shared by atoms instead of being transferred. What does it mean to share electrons? It means that the moving electrons actually travel about the nuclei of both atoms, forming a **covalent bond.** When the atoms share two electrons, the bond is called a single covalent bond. Sometimes the atoms share four electrons and form a double bond. In a few cases, atoms can share six electrons, forming a triple bond. The structure that results when atoms are joined together by covalent bonds is called a molecule. The **molecule** is the smallest unit of most compounds. The diagram of a water molecule in **Figure 2–4B** shows that each hydrogen atom is joined to water's lone oxygen atom by a single covalent bond. When atoms of the same element join together, they also form a molecule. Oxygen molecules in the air you breathe consist of two oxygen atoms joined by covalent bonds.

In Your Notebook *In your own words, describe the differences between ionic and covalent bonds.*

B. Covalent Bonding

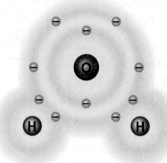

Water molecule (H_2O)

FIGURE 2–4 Ionic Bonding and Covalent Bonding A. The compound sodium chloride forms when sodium loses its valence electron to chlorine. **B.** In a water molecule, each hydrogen atom shares two electrons with the oxygen atom.

MYSTERY CLUE

Fish do not break water molecules into their component atoms to obtain oxygen. Rather, they use oxygen gas dissolved in the water. How are the atoms in an oxygen molecule (O_2) joined together?

Van der Waals Forces Because of their structures, atoms of different elements do not all have the same ability to attract electrons. Some atoms have a stronger attraction for electrons than do other atoms. Therefore, when the atoms in a covalent bond share electrons, the sharing is not always equal. Even when the sharing is equal, the rapid movement of electrons can create regions on a molecule that have a tiny positive or negative charge.

When molecules are close together, a slight attraction can develop between the oppositely charged regions of nearby molecules. Chemists call such intermolecular forces of attraction **van der Waals forces,** after the scientist who discovered them. Although van der Waals forces are not as strong as ionic bonds or covalent bonds, they can hold molecules together, especially when the molecules are large.

ZOOMING IN

VAN DER WAALS FORCES AT WORK

FIGURE 2–5 The underside of each foot on this Tokay gecko is covered by millions of tiny hairlike projections. The projections themselves are made of even finer fibers, creating more surface area for "sticking" to surfaces at the molecular level. This allows geckos to scurry up walls and across ceilings.

SEM 950×

2.1 Assessment

Review Key Concepts 🔑

1. a. Review Describe the structure of an atom.

 b. Infer An atom of calcium contains 20 protons. How many electrons does it have?

2. a. Review Why do all isotopes of an element have the same chemical properties?

 b. Compare and Contrast Compare the structure of carbon–12 and carbon–14.

3. a. Review What is a compound?

 b. Apply Concepts Water (H_2O) and hydrogen peroxide (H_2O_2) both consists of hydrogen and oxygen atoms. Explain why they have different chemical and physical properties.

4. a. Review What are two types of bonds that hold the atoms within a compound together?

 b. Classify A potassium atom easily loses its one valence electron. What type of bond will it form with a chlorine atom?

Apply the Big idea

Matter and Energy

5. Why do you think it is important that biologists have a good understanding of chemistry?

Technology & BIOLOGY

A Nature-Inspired Adhesive

People who keep geckos as pets have always marveled at the way these little lizards can climb up vertical surfaces, even smooth glass walls, and then hang on by a single toe despite the pull of gravity. How do they do it? No, they do not have some sort of glue on their feet and they don't have suction cups. Incredibly, they use van der Waals forces.

A gecko foot is covered by as many as half a million tiny hairlike projections. Each projection is further divided into hundreds of tiny, flat-surfaced fibers. This design allows the gecko's foot to come in contact with an extremely large area of the wall at the molecular level. Van der Waals forces form between molecules on the surface of the gecko's foot and molecules on the surface of the wall. This allows the gecko to actually balance the pull of gravity.

If it works for the gecko, why not for us? That's the thinking of researchers at the Massachusetts Institute of Technology, who have now used the same principle to produce a bandage. This new bandage is held to tissue by van der Waals forces alone. Special materials make it possible for the new bandage to work even on moist surfaces, which means that it may be used to reseal internal tissues after surgery. By learning a trick or two from the gecko, scientists may have found a way to help heal wounds, and even save lives in the process.

WRITING Suppose you are a doctor reviewing this new bandage for its potential applications. In what ways might you use such a bandage? Present your ideas as a list.

SEM 12,000×

The surface of the new bandage mimics the surface of the gecko foot at the microscopic level.

2.2 Properties of Water

Key Questions

🔑 How does the structure of water contribute to its unique properties?

🔑 How does water's polarity influence its properties as a solvent?

🔑 Why is it important for cells to buffer solutions against rapid changes in pH?

Vocabulary

hydrogen bond • cohesion • adhesion • mixture • solution • solute • solvent • suspension • pH scale • acid • base • buffer

Taking Notes

Venn Diagram As you read, draw a Venn diagram showing the differences between solutions and suspensions and the properties that they share.

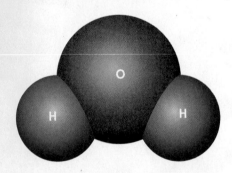

FIGURE 2–6 A Water Molecule
A water molecule is polar because there is an uneven distribution of electrons between the oxygen and hydrogen atoms. The negative pole is near the oxygen atom and the positive pole is between the hydrogen atoms.

THINK ABOUT IT Looking back at our beautiful planet, an astronaut in space said that if other beings have seen the Earth, they must surely call it "the blue planet." He referred, of course, to the oceans of water that cover nearly three fourths of Earth's surface. The very presence of liquid water tells a scientist that life may also be present on such a planet. Why should this be so? Why should life itself be connected so strongly to something so ordinary that we often take it for granted? The answers to those questions suggest that there is something very special about water and the role it plays in living things.

The Water Molecule

🔑 **How does the structure of water contribute to its unique properties?**

Water is one of the few compounds found in a liquid state over most of the Earth's surface. Like other molecules, water (H_2O) is neutral. The positive charges on its 10 protons balance out the negative charges on its 10 electrons. However, there is more to the story.

Polarity With 8 protons, water's oxygen nucleus attracts electrons more strongly than the single protons of water's two hydrogen nuclei. As a result, water's shared electrons are more likely to be found near the oxygen nucleus. Because the oxygen nucleus is at one end of the molecule, as shown in **Figure 2–6**, water has a partial negative charge on one end, and a partial positive charge on the other.

A molecule in which the charges are unevenly distributed is said to be "polar," because the molecule is a bit like a magnet with two poles. The partial charges on a polar molecule are written in parentheses, (–) or (+), to show that they are weaker than the charges on ions such as Na^+ and Cl^-.

Hydrogen Bonding Because of their partial positive and negative charges, polar molecules such as water can attract each other. The attraction between a hydrogen atom with a partial positive charge and another atom with a partial negative charge is known as a **hydrogen bond.** The most common partially negative atoms involved in hydrogen bonding are oxygen, nitrogen, and fluorine.

Hydrogen bonds are not as strong as covalent or ionic bonds, but they give one of life's most important molecules many of its unique characteristics. 🔑 **Because water is a polar molecule, it is able to form multiple hydrogen bonds, which account for many of water's special properties.** These include the fact that water expands slightly upon freezing, making ice less dense than liquid water. Hydrogen bonding also explains water's ability to dissolve so many other substances, a property essential in living cells.

▶*Cohesion* **Cohesion** is an attraction between molecules of the same substance. Because a single water molecule may be involved in as many as four hydrogen bonds at the same time, water is extremely cohesive. Cohesion causes water molecules to be drawn together, which is why drops of water form beads on a smooth surface. Cohesion also produces surface tension, explaining why some insects and spiders can walk on a pond's surface, as shown in **Figure 2–7.**

▶*Adhesion* On the other hand, **adhesion** is an attraction between molecules of different substances. Have you ever been told to read the volume in a graduated cylinder at eye level? As shown in **Figure 2–8,** the surface of the water in the graduated cylinder dips slightly in the center because the adhesion between water molecules and glass molecules is stronger than the cohesion between water molecules. Adhesion between water and glass also causes water to rise in a narrow tube against the force of gravity. This effect is called capillary action. Capillary action is one of the forces that draws water out of the roots of a plant and up into its stems and leaves. Cohesion holds the column of water together as it rises.

▶*Heat Capacity* Another result of the multiple hydrogen bonds between water molecules is that it takes a large amount of heat energy to cause those molecules to move faster, which raises the temperature of the water. Therefore, water's heat capacity, the amount of heat energy required to increase its temperature, is relatively high. This allows large bodies of water, such as oceans and lakes, to absorb large amounts of heat with only small changes in temperature. The organisms living within are thus protected from drastic changes in temperature. At the cellular level, water absorbs the heat produced by cell processes, regulating the temperature of the cell.

In Your Notebook *Draw a diagram of a meniscus. Label where cohesion and adhesion occur.*

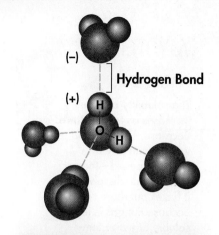

FIGURE 2–7 Hydrogen Bonding and Cohesion Each molecule of water can form multiple hydrogen bonds with other water molecules. The strong attraction between water molecules produces a force sometimes called "surface tension," which can support very lightweight objects, such as this raft spider. **Apply Concepts** *Why are water molecules attracted to one another?*

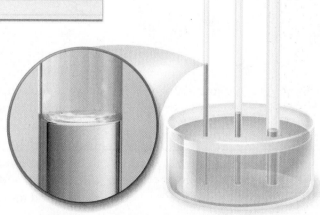

FIGURE 2–8 Adhesion Adhesion between water and glass molecules is responsible for causing the water in these columns to rise. The surface of the water in the glass column dips slightly in the center, forming a curve called a meniscus.

Solutions and Suspensions

How does water's polarity influence its properties as a solvent?

Water is not always pure; it is often found as part of a mixture. A **mixture** is a material composed of two or more elements or compounds that are physically mixed together but not chemically combined. Salt and pepper stirred together constitute a mixture. So do sugar and sand. Earth's atmosphere is a mixture of nitrogen, oxygen, carbon dioxide, and other gases. Living things are in part composed of mixtures involving water. Two types of mixtures that can be made with water are solutions and suspensions.

Solutions If a crystal of table salt is placed in a glass of warm water, sodium and chloride ions on the surface of the crystal are attracted to the polar water molecules. Ions break away from the crystal and are surrounded by water molecules, as illustrated in **Figure 2–9.** The ions gradually become dispersed in the water, forming a type of mixture called a solution. All the components of a **solution** are evenly distributed throughout the solution. In a saltwater solution, table salt is the **solute**—the substance that is dissolved. Water is the **solvent**—the substance in which the solute dissolves. **Water's polarity gives it the ability to dissolve both ionic compounds and other polar molecules.**

Water easily dissolves salts, sugars, minerals, gases, and even other solvents such as alcohol. Without exaggeration, water is the greatest solvent on Earth. But even water has limits. When a given amount of water has dissolved all of the solute it can, the solution is said to be saturated.

FIGURE 2–9 A Salt Solution When an ionic compound such as sodium chloride is placed in water, water molecules surround and separate the positive and negative ions. *Interpret Visuals What happens to the sodium ions and chloride ions in the solution?*

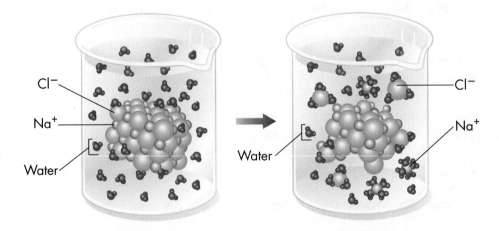

Suspensions Some materials do not dissolve when placed in water, but separate into pieces so small that they do not settle out. The movement of water molecules keeps the small particles suspended. Such mixtures of water and nondissolved material are known as **suspensions.** Some of the most important biological fluids are both solutions and suspensions. The blood that circulates through your body is mostly water. The water in the blood contains many dissolved compounds. However, blood also contains cells and other undissolved particles that remain in suspension as the blood moves through the body.

Acids, Bases, and pH

Why is it important for cells to buffer solutions against rapid changes in pH?

Water molecules sometimes split apart to form ions. This reaction can be summarized by a chemical equation in which double arrows are used to show that the reaction can occur in either direction.

$$H_2O \;\rightleftharpoons\; H^+ \;+\; OH^-$$

$$\text{water} \;\rightleftharpoons\; \text{hydrogen ion} \;+\; \text{hydroxide ion}$$

How often does this happen? In pure water, about 1 water molecule in 550 million splits to form ions in this way. Because the number of positive hydrogen ions produced is equal to the number of negative hydroxide ions produced, pure water is neutral.

The pH Scale Chemists devised a measurement system called the **pH scale** to indicate the concentration of H^+ ions in solution. As **Figure 2–10** shows, the pH scale ranges from 0 to 14. At a pH of 7, the concentration of H^+ ions and OH^- ions is equal. Pure water has a pH of 7. Solutions with a pH below 7 are called acidic because they have more H^+ ions than OH^- ions. The lower the pH, the greater the acidity. Solutions with a pH above 7 are called basic because they have more OH^- ions than H^+ ions. The higher the pH, the more basic the solution. Each step on the pH scale represents a factor of 10. For example, a liter of a solution with a pH of 4 has 10 times as many H^+ ions as a liter of a solution with a pH of 5.

In Your Notebook *Order these items in order of increasing acidity: soap, lemon juice, milk, acid rain.*

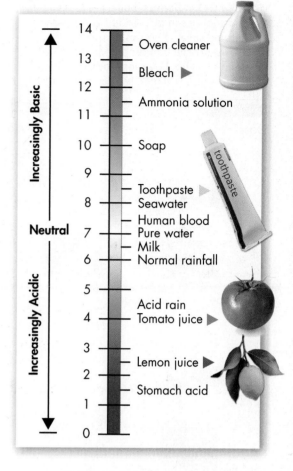

FIGURE 2–10 The pH Scale The concentration of H^+ ions determines whether solutions are acidic or basic. The most acidic material on this pH scale is stomach acid. The most basic material on this scale is oven cleaner.

Quick Lab
GUIDED INQUIRY

Acidic and Basic Foods

❶ Predict whether the food samples provided are acidic or basic.

❷ Tear off a 2-inch piece of pH paper for each sample you will test. Place these pieces on a paper towel.

❸ Construct a data table in which you will record the name and pH of each food sample.

❹ Use a scalpel to cut a piece off each solid. **CAUTION:** *Be careful not to cut yourself. Do not eat the food.* Touch the cut surface of each sample to a square of pH paper. Use a dropper pipette to place a drop of any liquid sample on a square of pH paper. Record the pH of each sample in your data table.

Analyze and Conclude

1. Analyze Data Were most of the samples acidic or basic?

2. Evaluate Was your prediction correct?

FIGURE 2–11 Buffers Buffers help prevent drastic changes in pH. Adding acid to an unbuffered solution causes the pH of the unbuffered solution to drop. If the solution contains a buffer, however, adding the acid will cause only a slight change in pH.

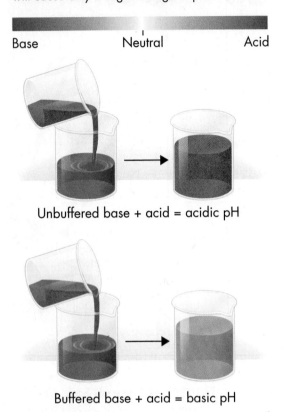

Base　　　　Neutral　　　　Acid

Unbuffered base + acid = acidic pH

Buffered base + acid = basic pH

Acids Where do all those extra H^+ ions in a low-pH solution come from? They come from acids. An **acid** is any compound that forms H^+ ions in solution. Acidic solutions contain higher concentrations of H^+ ions than pure water and have pH values below 7. Strong acids tend to have pH values that range from 1 to 3. The hydrochloric acid (HCl) produced by the stomach to help digest food is a strong acid.

Bases A **base** is a compound that produces hydroxide (OH^-) ions in solution. Basic, or alkaline, solutions contain lower concentrations of H^+ ions than pure water and have pH values above 7. Strong bases, such as the lye (commonly NaOH) used in soapmaking, tend to have pH values ranging from 11 to 14.

Buffers The pH of the fluids within most cells in the human body must generally be kept between 6.5 and 7.5. If the pH is lower or higher, it will affect the chemical reactions that take place within the cells. Thus, controlling pH is important for maintaining homeostasis. One of the ways that organisms control pH is through dissolved compounds called buffers. **Buffers** are weak acids or bases that can react with strong acids or bases to prevent sharp, sudden changes in pH. Blood, for example, has a normal pH of 7.4. Sudden changes in blood pH are usually prevented by a number of chemical buffers, such as bicarbonate and phosphate ions. ⊶ **Buffers dissolved in life's fluids play an important role in maintaining homeostasis in organisms.**

2.2 Assessment

Review Key Concepts ⊶

1. a. Review What does it mean when a molecule is said to be "polar"?

b. Explain How do hydrogen bonds between water molecules occur?

c. Use Models Use the structure of a water molecule to explain why it is polar.

2. a. Review Why is water such a good solvent?

b. Compare and Contrast What is the difference between a solution and a suspension?

3. a. Review What is an acid? What is a base?

b. Explain The acid hydrogen fluoride (HF) can be dissolved in pure water. Will the pH of the solution be greater or less than 7?

c. Infer During exercise, many chemical changes occur in the body, including a drop in blood pH, which can be very serious. How is the body able to cope with such changes?

WRITE ABOUT SCIENCE

Creative Writing

4. Suppose you are a writer for a natural history magazine for children. This month's issue will feature insects. Write a paragraph explaining why some bugs, such as the water strider, can walk on water.

2.3 Carbon Compounds

THINK ABOUT IT In the early 1800s, many chemists called the compounds created by organisms "organic," believing they were fundamentally different from compounds in nonliving things. Today we understand that the principles governing the chemistry of living and nonliving things are the same, but the term "organic chemistry" is still around. Today, organic chemistry means the study of compounds that contain bonds between carbon atoms, while inorganic chemistry is the study of all other compounds.

The Chemistry of Carbon

🔑 **What elements does carbon bond with to make up life's molecules?**

Why is carbon so interesting that a whole branch of chemistry should be set aside just to study carbon compounds? There are two reasons for this. First, carbon atoms have four valence electrons, allowing them to form strong covalent bonds with many other elements. 🔑 **Carbon can bond with many elements, including hydrogen, oxygen, phosphorus, sulfur, and nitrogen to form the molecules of life.** Living organisms are made up of molecules that consist of carbon and these other elements.

Even more important, one carbon atom can bond to another, which gives carbon the ability to form chains that are almost unlimited in length. These carbon-carbon bonds can be single, double, or triple covalent bonds. Chains of carbon atoms can even close up on themselves to form rings, as shown in **Figure 2–12**. Carbon has the ability to form millions of different large and complex structures. No other element even comes close to matching carbon's versatility.

Key Questions

🔑 *What elements does carbon bond with to make up life's molecules?*

🔑 *What are the functions of each of the four groups of macromolecules?*

Vocabulary

monomer • polymer • carbohydrate • monosaccharide • lipid • nucleic acid • nucleotide • protein • amino acid

Taking Notes

Compare/Contrast Table As you read, make a table that compares and contrasts the four groups of organic compounds.

FIGURE 2–12 Carbon Structures Carbon can form single, double, or triple bonds with other carbon atoms. Each line between atoms in a molecular drawing represents one covalent bond. **Observing** *How many covalent bonds are there between the two carbon atoms in acetylene?*

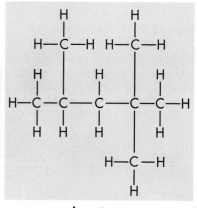

| Methane | Acetylene | Butadiene | Benzene | Isooctane |

🔑 **What are the functions of each of the four groups of macromolecules?**

Many of the organic compounds in living cells are so large that they are known as macromolecules, which means "giant molecules." Macromolecules are made from thousands or even hundreds of thousands of smaller molecules.

Most macromolecules are formed by a process known as polymerization (pah lih mur ih ZAY shun), in which large compounds are built by joining smaller ones together. The smaller units, or **monomers,** join together to form **polymers.** The monomers in a polymer may be identical, like the links on a metal watch band; or the monomers may be different, like the beads in a multicolored necklace. **Figure 2–13** illustrates the process of polymerization.

Biochemists sort the macromolecules found in living things into groups based on their chemical composition. The four major groups of macromolecules found in living things are carbohydrates, lipids, nucleic acids, and proteins. As you read about these molecules, compare their structures and functions.

Carbohydrates **Carbohydrates** are compounds made up of carbon, hydrogen, and oxygen atoms, usually in a ratio of 1:2:1. 🔑 **Living things use carbohydrates as their main source of energy. Plants, some animals, and other organisms also use carbohydrates for structural purposes.** The breakdown of sugars, such as glucose, supplies immediate energy for cell activities. Many organisms store extra sugar as complex carbohydrates known as starches. As shown in **Figure 2–14,** the monomers in starch polymers are sugar molecules.

▶ *Simple Sugars* Single sugar molecules are also known as **monosaccharides** (mahn oh SAK uh rydz). Besides glucose, monosaccharides include galactose, which is a component of milk, and fructose, which is found in many fruits. Ordinary table sugar, sucrose, consists of glucose and fructose. Sucrose is a disaccharide, a compound made by joining two simple sugars together.

WORD ORIGINS Monomer comes from the Greek words *monos,* meaning "single," and *meros,* meaning "part." *Monomer* means "single part." The prefix *poly-* comes from the Greek word *polus,* meaning "many," so **polymer** means "many parts."

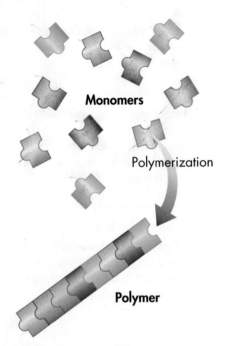

Monomers

Polymerization

Polymer

FIGURE 2–13 Polymerization When monomers join together, they form polymers. **Using Analogies** *How are monomers similar to links in a chain?*

FIGURE 2–14 Carbohydrates Starches form when sugars join together in a long chain. Each time two glucose molecules are joined together, a molecule of water (H_2O) is released when the covalent bond is formed.

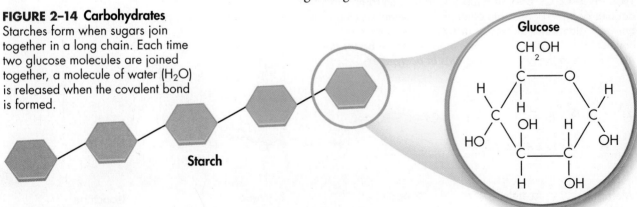

Starch

Glucose

CH$_2$OH

► *Complex Carbohydrates* The large macromolecules formed from monosaccharides are known as polysaccharides. Many animals store excess sugar in a polysaccharide called glycogen, which is sometimes called "animal starch." When the level of glucose in your blood runs low, glycogen is broken down into glucose, which is then released into the blood. The glycogen stored in your muscles supplies the energy for muscle contraction and, thus, for movement.

Plants use a slightly different polysaccharide, called starch, to store excess sugar. Plants also make another important polysaccharide called cellulose. Tough, flexible cellulose fibers give plants much of their strength and rigidity. Cellulose is the major component of both wood and paper, so you are actually looking at cellulose as you read these words!

Lipids Lipids are a large and varied group of biological molecules that are generally not soluble in water. **Lipids** are made mostly from carbon and hydrogen atoms. The common categories of lipids are fats, oils, and waxes. ⚷ **Lipids can be used to store energy. Some lipids are important parts of biological membranes and waterproof coverings.** Steroids synthesized by the body are lipids as well. Many steroids, such as hormones, serve as chemical messengers.

Many lipids are formed when a glycerol molecule combines with compounds called fatty acids, as shown in **Figure 2–15.** If each carbon atom in a lipid's fatty acid chains is joined to another carbon atom by a single bond, the lipid is said to be saturated. The term *saturated* is used because the fatty acids contain the maximum possible number of hydrogen atoms.

If there is at least one carbon-carbon double bond in a fatty acid, the fatty acid is said to be unsaturated. Lipids whose fatty acids contain more than one double bond are said to be polyunsaturated. If the terms *saturated* and *polyunsaturated* seem familiar, you have probably seen them on food package labels. Lipids that contain unsaturated fatty acids, such as olive oil, tend to be liquid at room temperature. Other cooking oils, such as corn oil, sesame oil, canola oil, and peanut oil, contain polyunsaturated lipids.

〰️ **In Your Notebook** *Compare and contrast saturated and unsaturated fats.*

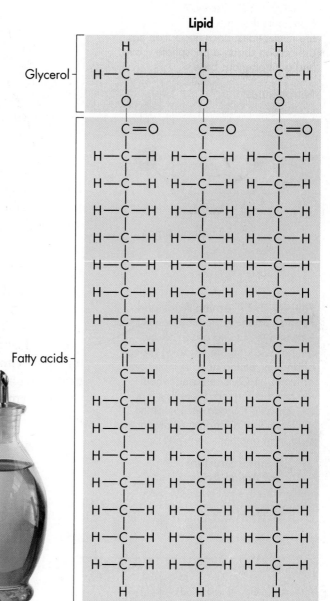

FIGURE 2–15 Lipids Lipid molecules are made up of glycerol and fatty acids. Liquid lipids, such as olive oil, contain mainly unsaturated fatty acids.

Analyzing Data

Comparing Fatty Acids

The table compares four different fatty acids. Although they all have the same number of carbon atoms, their properties vary.

1. Interpret Data Which of the four fatty acids is saturated? Which are unsaturated?

2. Observe How does melting point change as the number of carbon-carbon double bonds increases?

Effect of Carbon Bonds on Melting Point			
Fatty Acid	Number of Carbons	Number of Double Bonds	Melting Point (°C)
Stearic acid	18	0	69.6
Oleic acid	18	1	14
Linoleic acid	18	2	−5
Linolenic acid	18	3	−11

3. Infer If room temperature is 25°C, which fatty acid is a solid at room temperature? Which is liquid at room temperature?

FIGURE 2–16 Nucleic Acids The monomers that make up a nucleic acid are nucleotides. Each nucleotide has a 5-carbon sugar, a phosphate group, and a nitrogenous base.

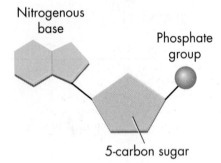

Nitrogenous base

Phosphate group

5-carbon sugar

FIGURE 2–17 Amino Acids and Peptide Bonding Peptide bonds form between the amino group of one amino acid and the carboxyl group of another amino acid. A molecule of water (H_2O) is released when the bond is formed. Note that it is the variable R-group section of the molecule that distinguishes one amino acid from another.

Nucleic Acids **Nucleic acids** are macromolecules containing hydrogen, oxygen, nitrogen, carbon, and phosphorus. Nucleic acids are polymers assembled from individual monomers known as nucleotides. **Nucleotides** consist of three parts: a 5-carbon sugar, a phosphate group ($-PO_4$), and a nitrogenous base, as shown in **Figure 2–16**. Some nucleotides, including the compound known as adenosine triphosphate (ATP), play important roles in capturing and transferring chemical energy. Individual nucleotides can be joined by covalent bonds to form a polynucleotide, or nucleic acid.

🔑 **Nucleic acids store and transmit hereditary, or genetic, information.** There are two kinds of nucleic acids: ribonucleic acid (RNA) and deoxyribonucleic acid (DNA). As their names indicate, RNA contains the sugar ribose and DNA contains the sugar deoxyribose.

Protein **Proteins** are macromolecules that contain nitrogen as well as carbon, hydrogen, and oxygen. Proteins are polymers of molecules called amino acids, shown in **Figure 2–17**. **Amino acids** are compounds with an amino group ($-NH_2$) on one end and a carboxyl group ($-COOH$) on the other end. Covalent bonds called peptide bonds link amino acids together to form a polypeptide. A protein is a functional molecule built from one or more polypeptides. 🔑 **Some proteins control the rate of reactions and regulate cell processes. Others form important cellular structures, while still others transport substances into or out of cells or help to fight disease.**

General Structure of Amino Acids

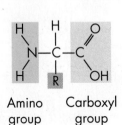

Amino group   Carboxyl group

Formation of Peptide Bond

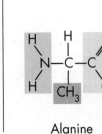 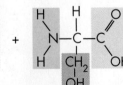

Alanine   Serine   Peptide bond

▶ **Structure and Function** More than 20 different amino acids are found in nature. All amino acids are identical in the regions where they may be joined together by covalent bonds. This uniformity allows any amino acid to be joined to any other amino acid—by bonding an amino group to a carboxyl group. Proteins are among the most diverse macromolecules. The reason is that amino acids differ from each other in a side chain called the R-group, which have a range of different properties. Some R-groups are acidic and some are basic. Some are polar, some are nonpolar, and some even contain large ring structures.

▶ **Levels of Organization** Amino acids are assembled into polypeptide chains according to instructions coded in DNA. To help understand these large molecules, scientists describe proteins as having four levels of structure. A protein's primary structure is the sequence of its amino acids. Secondary structure is the folding or coiling of the polypeptide chain. Tertiary structure is the complete, three-dimensional arrangement of a polypeptide chain. Proteins with more than one chain are said to have a fourth level of structure, describing the way in which the different polypeptides are arranged with respect to each other. **Figure 2–18** shows these four levels of structure in hemoglobin, a protein found in red blood cells that helps to transport oxygen in the bloodstream. The shape of a protein is maintained by a variety of forces, including ionic and covalent bonds, as well as van der Waals forces and hydrogen bonds. In the next lesson, you will learn why a protein's shape is so important.

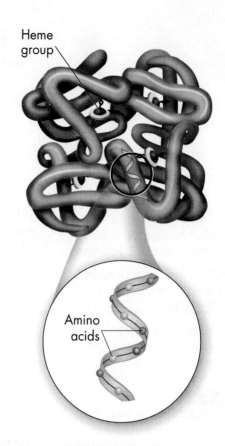

Heme group

Amino acids

FIGURE 2–18 Protein Structure
The protein hemoglobin consists of four subunits. The iron-containing heme group in the center of each subunit gives hemoglobin its red color. An oxygen molecule binds tightly to each heme molecule. **Interpret Visuals** *How many levels of organization does hemoglobin have?*

2.3 Assessment

Review Key Concepts 🔑

1. a. Review What are the major elements of life?

b. Relate Cause and Effect What properties of carbon explain carbon's ability to form different large and complex structures?

2. a. Review Name four groups of organic compounds found in living things.

b. Explain Describe at least one function of each group of organic compound.

c. Infer Why are proteins considered polymers but lipids not?

VISUAL THINKING

3. A structural formula shows how the atoms in a compound are arranged.

CH₂OH   H   OH

HO   O   O

OH   H   OH   H

H   H   H   O   H

H   OH   CH₂OH

a. Observe What atoms constitute the compound above?

b. Classify What class of macromolecule does the compound belong to?

2.4 Chemical Reactions and Enzymes

Key Questions

🔑 What happens to chemical bonds during chemical reactions?

🔑 How do energy changes affect whether a chemical reaction will occur?

🔑 What role do enzymes play in living things and what affects their function?

Vocabulary

chemical reaction • reactant • product • activation energy • catalyst • enzyme • substrate

Taking Notes

Concept Map As you read, make a concept map that shows the relationship among the vocabulary terms in this lesson.

THINK ABOUT IT Living things, as you have seen, are made up of chemical compounds—some simple and some complex. But chemistry isn't just what life is made of—chemistry is also what life does. Everything that happens in an organism—its growth, its interaction with the environment, its reproduction, and even its movement—is based on chemical reactions.

Chemical Reactions

🔑 **What happens to chemical bonds during chemical reactions?**

A **chemical reaction** is a process that changes, or transforms, one set of chemicals into another. An important scientific principle is that mass and energy are conserved during chemical transformations. This is also true for chemical reactions that occur in living organisms. Some chemical reactions occur slowly, such as the combination of iron and oxygen to form an iron oxide called rust. Other reactions occur quickly. The elements or compounds that enter into a chemical reaction are known as **reactants.** The elements or compounds produced by a chemical reaction are known as **products.** 🔑 **Chemical reactions involve changes in the chemical bonds that join atoms in compounds.** An important chemical reaction in your bloodstream that enables carbon dioxide to be removed from the body is shown in **Figure 2–19.**

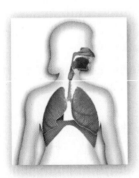

FIGURE 2–19 Carbon Dioxide in the Bloodstream As it enters the blood, carbon dioxide reacts with water to produce carbonic acid (H_2CO_3), which is highly soluble. This reaction enables the blood to carry carbon dioxide to the lungs. In the lungs, the reaction is reversed and produces carbon dioxide gas, which you exhale.

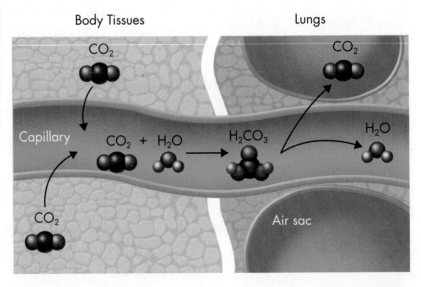

Energy in Reactions

How do energy changes affect whether a chemical reaction will occur?

Energy is released or absorbed whenever chemical bonds are formed or broken. This means that chemical reactions also involve changes in energy.

Energy Changes Some chemical reactions release energy, and other reactions absorb it. Energy changes are one of the most important factors in determining whether a chemical reaction will occur. **Chemical reactions that release energy often occur on their own, or spontaneously. Chemical reactions that absorb energy will not occur without a source of energy.** An example of an energy-releasing reaction is the burning of hydrogen gas, in which hydrogen reacts with oxygen to produce water vapor.

$$2H_2 + O_2 \longrightarrow 2H_2O$$

The energy is released in the form of heat, and sometimes—when hydrogen gas explodes—light and sound.

The reverse reaction, in which water is changed into hydrogen and oxygen gas, absorbs so much energy that it generally doesn't occur by itself. In fact, the only practical way to reverse the reaction is to pass an electrical current through water to decompose water into hydrogen gas and oxygen gas. Thus, in one direction the reaction produces energy, and in the other direction the reaction requires energy.

Energy Sources In order to stay alive, organisms need to carry out reactions that require energy. Because matter and energy are conserved in chemical reactions, every organism must have a source of energy to carry out chemical reactions. Plants get that energy by trapping and storing the energy from sunlight in energy-rich compounds. Animals get their energy when they consume plants or other animals. Humans release the energy needed to grow tall, to breathe, to think, and even to dream through the chemical reactions that occur when we metabolize, or break down, digested food.

Activation Energy Chemical reactions that release energy do not always occur spontaneously. That's a good thing because if they did, the pages of this book might burst into flames. The cellulose in paper burns in the presence of oxygen and releases heat and light. However, paper burns only if you light it with a match, which supplies enough energy to get the reaction started. Chemists call the energy that is needed to get a reaction started the **activation energy.** As **Figure 2–20** shows, activation energy is involved in chemical reactions regardless of whether the overall chemical reaction releases energy or absorbs energy.

FIGURE 2–20 Activation Energy The peak of each graph represents the energy needed for the reaction to go forward. The difference between this required energy and the energy of the reactants is the activation energy. *Interpret Graphs How do the energy of the reactants and products differ between an energy-absorbing reaction and an energy-releasing reaction?*

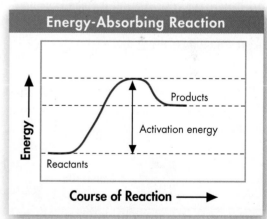

Energy-Absorbing Reaction

Energy

Products

Activation energy

Reactants

Course of Reaction →

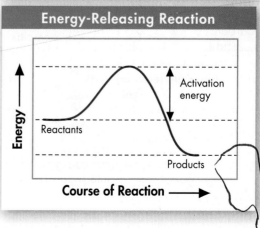

Energy-Releasing Reaction

Energy

Activation energy

Reactants

Products

Course of Reaction →

FIGURE 2–21 Effect of Enzymes
Notice how the addition of an enzyme lowers the activation energy in this reaction. The enzyme speeds up the reaction.

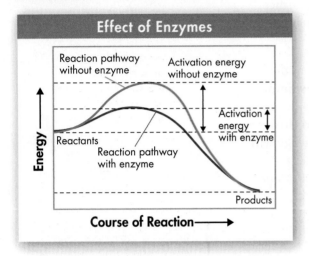

Effect of Enzymes

Reaction pathway without enzyme

Activation energy without enzyme

Activation energy with enzyme

Reactants

Reaction pathway with enzyme

Products

Energy →

Course of Reaction →

FIGURE 2–22 An Enzyme-Catalyzed
Reaction The enzyme carbonic anhydrase converts the substrates carbon dioxide and water into carbonic acid (H_2CO_3).
Predicting *What happens to the carbonic anhydrase after the products are released?*

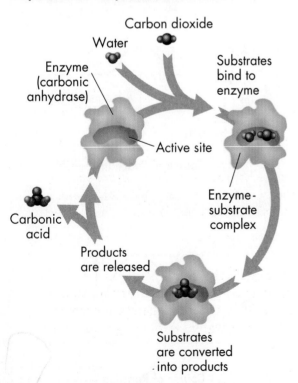

Carbon dioxide

Water

Enzyme (carbonic anhydrase)

Active site

Substrates bind to enzyme

Enzyme-substrate complex

Carbonic acid

Products are released

Substrates are converted into products

Enzymes

🔑 *What role do enzymes play in living things and what affects their function?*

Some chemical reactions that make life possible are too slow or have activation energies that are too high to make them practical for living tissue. These chemical reactions are made possible by a process that would make any chemist proud—cells make catalysts. A **catalyst** is a substance that speeds up the rate of a chemical reaction. Catalysts work by lowering a reaction's activation energy.

Nature's Catalysts **Enzymes** are proteins that act as biological catalysts. 🔑 **Enzymes speed up chemical reactions that take place in cells.** Like other catalysts, enzymes act by lowering the activation energies, as illustrated by the graph in **Figure 2–21.** Lowering the activation energy has a dramatic effect on how quickly the reaction is completed. How big an effect does it have? Consider the reaction in which carbon dioxide combines with water to produce carbonic acid.

$$CO_2 + H_2O \longrightarrow H_2CO_3$$

Left to itself, this reaction is so slow that carbon dioxide might build up in the body faster than the bloodstream could remove it. Your bloodstream contains an enzyme called carbonic anhydrase that speeds up the reaction by a factor of 10 million. With carbonic anhydrase on the job, the reaction takes place immediately and carbon dioxide is removed from the blood quickly.

Enzymes are very specific, generally catalyzing only one chemical reaction. For this reason, part of an enzyme's name is usually derived from the reaction it catalyzes. Carbonic anhydrase gets its name because it also catalyzes the reverse reaction that removes water from carbonic acid.

The Enzyme-Substrate Complex How do enzymes do their jobs? For a chemical reaction to take place, the reactants must collide with enough energy so that existing bonds will be broken and new bonds will be formed. If the reactants do not have enough energy, they will be unchanged after the collision.

Enzymes provide a site where reactants can be brought together to react. Such a site reduces the energy needed for reaction. The reactants of enzyme-catalyzed reactions are known as **substrates. Figure 2–22** provides an example of an enzyme-catalyzed reaction.

The substrates bind to a site on the enzyme called the active site. The active site and the substrates have complementary shapes. The fit is so precise that the active site and substrates are often compared to a lock and key, as shown in **Figure 2–23**.

Regulation of Enzyme Activity Enzymes play essential roles in controlling chemical pathways, making materials that cells need, releasing energy, and transferring information. Because they are catalysts for reactions, enzymes can be affected by any variable that influences a chemical reaction. 🗝 **Temperature, pH, and regulatory molecules can affect the activity of enzymes.**

Many enzymes are affected by changes in temperature. Not surprisingly, those enzymes produced by human cells generally work best at temperatures close to 37°C, the normal temperature of the human body. Enzymes work best at certain ionic conditions and pH values. For example, the stomach enzyme pepsin, which begins protein digestion, works best under acidic conditions. In addition, the activities of most enzymes are regulated by molecules that carry chemical signals within cells, switching enzymes "on" or "off" as needed.

MYSTERY CLUE

The chemical reactions of living things, including those that require oxygen, occur more slowly at low temperatures. How would frigid antarctic waters affect the ice fish's need for oxygen?

VISUAL ANALOGY

UNLOCKING ENZYMES

FIGURE 2–23 This space-filling model shows how a substrate binds to an active site on an enzyme. The fit between an enzyme and its substrates is so specific it is often compared to a lock and key.

2.4 Assessment

Review Key Concepts 🗝

1. a. Review What happens to chemical bonds during chemical reactions?

b. Apply Concepts Why is the melting of ice not a chemical reaction?

2. a. Review What is activation energy?

b. Compare and Contrast Describe the difference between a reaction that occurs spontaneously and one that does not.

3. a. Review What are enzymes?

b. Explain Explain how enzymes work, including the role of the enzyme-substrate complex.

c. Use Analogies A change in pH can change the shape of a protein. How might a change in pH affect the function of an enzyme such as carbonic anhydrase? (*Hint:* Think about the analogy of the lock and key.)

VISUAL THINKING

4. Make a model that demonstrates the fit between an enzyme and its substrate. Show your model to a friend or family member and explain how enzymes work using your model.

Design Your Own Lab

GUIDED INQUIRY

Pre-Lab: Temperature and Enzymes

Problem How does temperature affect the rate of an enzyme-catalyzed reaction?

Materials raw liver, forceps, petri dish, dropper pipette, 1% hydrogen peroxide solution, 25-mL graduated cylinder, 50-mL beakers, puréed liver, filter paper disks, paper towels, timer or clock with a second hand, water baths, thermometers, beaker tongs

Lab Manual Chapter 2 Lab

Skills Focus Form a Hypothesis, Design an Experiment, Measure, Interpret Graphs

Connect to the **Big idea** Many chemical reactions in living organisms could not take place without enzymes. Enzymes catalyze the reactions that release energy from nutrients. They also catalyze the synthesis of the complex molecules that organisms need to grow and stay healthy. One factor that affects the action of enzymes is temperature. Think about why people store some foods in a refrigerator. The cold temperature limits the ability of enzymes to break down, or spoil, those foods.

Do high temperatures have the opposite effect on enzymes? Do they become more and more active as the temperature rises? In this lab, you will investigate the effect of temperature on an enzyme-catalyzed reaction.

Background Questions

a. Review Why do many reactions that occur in cells require enzymes? How do enzymes speed up chemical reactions?

b. Review Name three variables that can affect enzyme activity.

c. Use Analogies Use eggs and a frying pan on a stove as an analogy for reactants and an enzyme. Use the control knob on the stove burner as an analogy for how a variable can affect the action of an enzyme.

Pre-Lab Questions

Preview the procedure in the lab manual.

1. Relate Cause and Effect How will you know that a chemical reaction is taking place in Part A? How will you know in Part B?

2. Control Variables In Part B of the lab, which variable will you manipulate? Which variable is the dependent variable?

3. Relate Cause and Effect How is the time required for the filter-paper disk to float related to the activity of the enzyme?

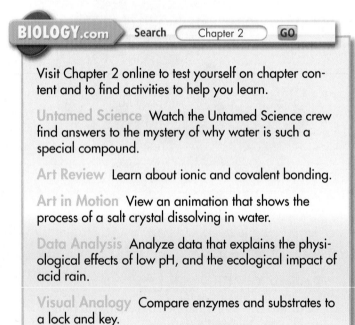

BIOLOGY.com   Search   Chapter 2   GO

Visit Chapter 2 online to test yourself on chapter content and to find activities to help you learn.

Untamed Science Watch the Untamed Science crew find answers to the mystery of why water is such a special compound.

Art Review Learn about ionic and covalent bonding.

Art in Motion View an animation that shows the process of a salt crystal dissolving in water.

Data Analysis Analyze data that explains the physiological effects of low pH, and the ecological impact of acid rain.

Visual Analogy Compare enzymes and substrates to a lock and key.

2 Study Guide

Big idea ▶ Matter and Energy

Chemical bonds join together the molecules and compounds of life. Water and carbon compounds play essential roles in organisms, which carry out chemical reactions in their daily life processes.

2.1 The Nature of Matter

🔑 The subatomic particles that make up atoms are protons, neutrons, and electrons.

🔑 All isotopes of an element have the same chemical properties, because they have the same number of electrons.

🔑 The physical and chemical properties of a compound are usually very different from those of the elements from which it is formed.

🔑 The main types of chemical bonds are ionic bonds and covalent bonds.

atom (34)	ionic bond (37)
nucleus (34)	ion (37)
electron (34)	covalent bond (37)
element (35)	molecule (37)
isotope (35)	van der Waals forces (38)
compound (36)	

2.2 Properties of Water

🔑 Water is a polar molecule. Therefore, it is able to form multiple hydrogen bonds, which account for many of its special properties.

🔑 Water's polarity gives it the ability to dissolve both ionic compounds and other polar molecules.

🔑 Buffers play an important role in maintaining homeostasis in organisms.

hydrogen bond (41)	solution (42)	pH scale (43)
cohesion (41)	solute (42)	acid (44)
adhesion (41)	solvent (42)	base (44)
mixture (42)	suspension (42)	buffer (44)

2.3 Carbon Compounds

🔑 Carbon can bond with many elements, including hydrogen, oxygen, phosphorus, sulfur, and nitrogen to form the molecules of life.

🔑 Living things use carbohydrates as their main source of energy. Plants, some animals, and other organisms also use carbohydrates for structural purposes.

🔑 Lipids can be used to store energy. Some lipids are important parts of biological membranes and waterproof coverings.

🔑 Nucleic acids store and transmit hereditary, or genetic, information.

🔑 Some proteins control the rate of reactions and regulate cell processes. Some proteins build tissues such as bone and muscle. Others transport materials or help to fight disease.

monomer (46)	nucleic acid (48)
polymer (46)	nucleotide (48)
carbohydrate (46)	protein (48)
monosaccharide (46)	amino acid (48)
lipid (47)	

2.4 Chemical Reactions and Enzymes

🔑 Chemical reactions always involve changes in the chemical bonds that join atoms in compounds.

🔑 Chemical reactions that release energy often occur spontaneously. Chemical reactions that absorb energy will not occur without a source of energy.

🔑 Enzymes speed up chemical reactions that take place in cells.

🔑 Temperature, pH, and regulatory molecules can affect the activity of enzymes.

chemical reaction (50)	catalyst (52)
reactant (50)	enzyme (52)
product (50)	substrate (52)
activation energy (51)	

Think Visually Create a table in which you compare the structures and functions of the following macromolecules: carbohydrates, lipids, proteins, and nucleic acids.

2 Assessment

Understand Key Concepts

1. The positively charged particle in an atom is called the
   a. neutron.   c. proton.
   b. ion.   d. electron.

2. Two or more different atoms are combined in definite proportions in any
   a. symbol.   c. element.
   b. isotope.   d. compound.

3. A covalent bond is formed by the
   a. transfer of electrons.
   b. sharing of electrons.
   c. gaining of electrons.
   d. losing of electrons.

4. Explain the relationship among atoms, elements, and compounds.

5. What is a radioactive isotope? Describe two scientific uses of radioactive isotopes.

6. Describe how the atoms in a compound are held together.

7. Distinguish among single, double, and triple covalent bonds.

Think Critically

8. **Use Models** Make a diagram like the one in **Figure 2–4** to show how chlorine and hydrogen form from the compound hydrogen chloride, HCl.

9. **Calculate** A nanometer (nm) is one billionth of a meter (1 nm = 10^{-9} m). If 100 million atoms make a row 1 cm in length, what is the diameter of one atom in nanometers? MATH

Understand Key Concepts

10. When you shake sugar and sand together in a test tube, you cause them to form a
    a. compound.   c. solution.
    b. mixture.   d. suspension.

11. A compound that produces hydrogen ions in solution is a(n)
    a. salt.   c. base.
    b. acid.   d. polymer.

12. Compared to most other substances, a great deal of heat is needed to raise the temperature of water by a given amount. This is because water
    a. is an acid.
    b. readily forms solutions.
    c. has a high heat capacity.
    b. acts as a buffer.

13. Explain the properties of cohesion and adhesion. Give an example of each property.

14. What is the relationship among solutions, solutes, and solvents?

15. How are acids and bases different? How do their pH values differ?

Think Critically

16. **Propose a Solution** Silica is a hard, glassy material that does not dissolve in water. Suppose sodium chloride is accidentally mixed with silica. Describe a way to remove the sodium chloride.

17. **Predict** As part of the digestive process, the human stomach produces hydrochloric acid, HCl. Sometimes excess acid causes discomfort. In such a case, a person might take an antacid such as magnesium hydroxide, $Mg(OH)_2$. Explain how this substance can reduce the amount of acid in the stomach.

Understand Key Concepts

18. What does the following formula represent?

    a. a sugar   c. an amino acid
    b. a starch   d. a fatty acid

19. Proteins are polymers formed from
    a. lipids.   c. amino acids.
    b. carbohydrates.   d. nucleic acids.

20. Explain the relationship between monomers and polymers, using polysaccharides as an example.

21. Identify three major roles of proteins.

22. Describe the parts of a nucleotide.

Think Critically

23. **Design an Experiment** Suggest one or two simple experiments to determine whether a solid white substance is a lipid or a carbohydrate. What evidence would you need to support each hypothesis?

24. **Infer** Explain what the name "carbohydrate" might indicate about the chemical composition of sugars.

2.4 Chemical Reactions and Enzymes

Understand Key Concepts

25. An enzyme speeds up a reaction by
    a. lowering the activation energy.
    b. raising the activation energy.
    c. releasing energy.
    d. absorbing energy.

26. In a chemical reaction, a reactant binds to an enzyme at a region known as the
    a. catalyst.   **c.** substrate.
    b. product.   **d.** active site.

27. Describe the two types of energy changes that can occur in a chemical reaction.

28. What relationship exists between an enzyme and a catalyst?

29. Describe some factors that may influence enzyme activity.

Think Critically

30. **Infer** Why is it important that energy-releasing reactions take place in living organisms?

31. **Predict** Changing the temperature or pH can change an enzyme's shape. Describe how changing the temperature or pH might affect the function of an enzyme.

32. **Use Analogies** Explain why a lock and key are used to describe the way an enzyme works. Describe any ways in which the analogy is not perfect.

solve the CHAPTER MYSTERY

THE GHOSTLY FISH

The oxygen-binding abilities of hemoglobin enable the blood of most fish to carry nearly 50 times the oxygen it would without the protein. The ghostly white appearance of the antarctic ice fish results from its clear blood—blood without hemoglobin. Ice fish, however, are able to survive without hemoglobin because of the properties of water at low temperatures.

Oxygen from the air dissolves in seawater, providing the oxygen that fish need to survive. Fish absorb dissolved oxygen directly through their gills, where it passes into their bloodstream. The solubility of oxygen is much greater at low temperatures. Therefore, the icy cold antarctic waters are particularly rich in oxygen.

The large, well-developed gills and scaleless skin of ice fishes allow them to absorb oxygen efficiently from the water. Compared to red-blooded fishes, ice fishes have a higher blood volume, thinner blood, and larger hearts. So, their blood can carry more dissolved oxygen and the large hearts can pump the thinner blood through the body faster. These and other physical features, combined with the chemistry of oxygen in water at low temperatures, enable ice fish to survive where many other organisms cannot.

1. **Relate Cause and Effect** Ice fish produce antifreeze proteins to keep their blood from freezing; their body temperature stays below 0°C. How does low body temperature affect the blood's ability to carry dissolved oxygen?

2. **Infer** People living at high altitudes generally have more hemoglobin in their blood than people living at sea level. Why do you think this is so?

3. **Predict** If the antarctic oceans were to warm up, how might this affect ice fish?

4. **Connect to the** Big idea The chemical reactions in all living things slow down at low temperatures. Since some of the most important reactions in our body require oxygen, how would low temperatures affect the ice fish's need for oxygen?

Use Science Graphics

The following graph shows the total amount of product from a chemical reaction performed at three different temperatures. The same enzyme was involved in each case. Use the graph to answer questions 33–35.

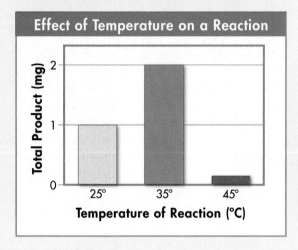

Effect of Temperature on a Reaction

33. Interpret Graphs At which temperature was the greatest amount of product formed?

34. Draw Conclusions Describe the results of each reaction. How can you explain these results?

35. Predict A student performs the same chemical reaction at 30°C. Approximately how much product can she expect to obtain?

Write About Science

36. Explanation Write a paragraph that includes the following: **(a)** a description of the four major classes of organic compounds found in living things, and **(b)** a description of how these organic compounds are used by the human body.

37. Assess the Big idea What properties of carbon allow it to play such a major role in the chemistry of living things?

Analyzing Data

A student measured the pH of water from a small pond at several intervals throughout the day. Use the graph to answer questions 38 and 39.

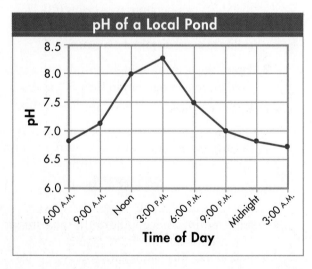

pH of a Local Pond

38. Interpret Graphs At what time of day is the pond most acidic?
  a. between noon and 6:00 P.M.
  b. at noon
  c. between midnight and 6:00 A.M.
  d. at 6:00 P.M.

39. Form a Hypothesis Which of the following is the most reasonable hypothesis based on the results obtained?
  a. Pond water maintains constant pH throughout the day.
  b. pH rises with increasing daylight and falls with decreasing daylight.
  c. Living things cannot survive in this pond because enzymes will be destroyed.
  d. pH is higher at night than during the day.

Standardized Test Prep

Multiple Choice

1. The elements or compounds that enter into a chemical reaction are called

  A products.   **C** active sites.

  B catalysts.   **D** reactants.

2. Chemical bonds that involve the total transfer of electrons from one atom or group of atoms to another are called

  A covalent bonds.

  B ionic bonds.

  C hydrogen bonds.

  D van der Waals bonds.

3. Which of the following is NOT an organic molecule found in living organisms?

  A protein

  B nucleic acid

  C sodium chloride

  D lipid

4. Which combination of particle and charge is correct?

  A proton: positively charged

  B electron: positively charged

  C neutron: negatively charged

  D electron: no charge

5. In which of the following ways do isotopes of the same element differ?

  A in number of neutrons only

  B in number of protons only

  C in numbers of neutrons and protons

  D in number of neutrons and in mass

6. Which of the following molecules is made up of glycerol and fatty acids?

  A sugars   **C** lipids

  B starches   **D** nucleic acids

7. Nucleotides consist of a phosphate group, a nitrogenous base, and a

  A fatty acid.   **C** 5-carbon sugar.

  B lipid.   **D** 6-carbon sugar.

Questions 8–9

The enzyme catalase speeds up the chemical reaction that changes hydrogen peroxide into oxygen and water. The amount of oxygen given off is an indication of the rate of the reaction.

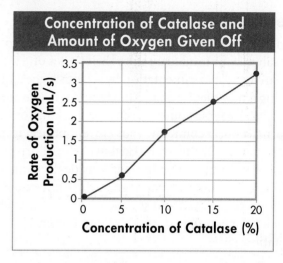

Concentration of Catalase and Amount of Oxygen Given Off

8. Based on the graph, what can you conclude about the relationship between enzyme concentration and reaction rate?

  A Reaction rate decreases with increasing enzyme concentration.

  B Reaction rate increases with decreasing enzyme concentration.

  C Reaction rate increases with increasing enzyme concentration.

  D The variables are indirectly proportional.

9. Which concentration of catalase will produce the fastest reaction rate?

  A 5%

  B 10%

  C 15%

  D 20%

Open-Ended Response

10. List some of the properties of water that make it such a unique substance.

If You Have Trouble With . . .

Question	1	2	3	4	5	6	7	8	9	10
See Lesson	2.4	2.1	2.3	2.1	2.1	2.3	2.3	2.4	2.4	2.2

Unit Project

Design the Experiment

Did you ever wonder how a medication goes from the lab to your local drug store shelf? A lot of research and experimentation by scientists goes into testing a new medication to make sure it is safe and effective. Imagine you are a scientist working for a pharmaceutical company. Your current project is to test a new medication for heartburn. Heartburn is a painful condition in which acid inside the stomach backs up into the esophagus—the connection between your throat and stomach. This new medication helps neutralize stomach acid to prevent irritation.

Your Task Design *three* possible experiments to test the safety and effectiveness of the new heartburn medication. Before you begin, think about how you will know if the medication actually neutralizes stomach acid. Once you've written your procedures, you will propose the experiments to your company's Executive Board for Research and Development.

For each experiment,

- identify a control and independent and dependent variables.
- form a hypothesis and predict the results.
- write a specific procedure that tests your hypothesis.
- Trade your procedure with a partner. Critique your partner's design, and recommend any necessary changes. Be sure to justify your suggestions.

Reflection Questions

1. Score your experimental designs using the rubric below. What score did you give yourself?
2. What did you do well in this project?
3. What about your designs needs improvement?
4. Are there any ethical dilemmas related to your experiments? Explain.

Assessment Rubric

Score	Scientific Content	Quality of Experiments
4	Correctly and extensively applies knowledge and understanding of unit concepts (i.e., pH scale) to experimental designs and predictions.	Experimental designs are clever and effectively test the hypotheses. Experimental conditions are carefully controlled and variables are correctly identified.
3	Applies relevant knowledge and understanding of unit concepts (i.e., pH scale) to experimental designs and predictions.	Experimental designs are logical and test the hypotheses. Experimental conditions are controlled and variables are correctly identified.
2	Applies relevant knowledge and understanding of unit concepts (i.e., pH scale) incompletely to experimental designs and predictions.	Experimental designs need some revisions—some parts are unclear or do not fully test the hypotheses. Variables and controls need corrections.
1	Does not correctly apply knowledge and understanding of unit concepts (i.e., pH scale) to experimental designs and predictions.	Experimental designs are unclear and do not test the hypotheses. Variables and controls listed are incorrect or absent.

Ecology

Chapters

3 The Biosphere

4 Ecosystems and Communities

5 Populations

6 Humans in the Biosphere

INTRODUCE the

Big ideas

- **Matter and Energy**
- **Interdependence in Nature**

❝Earth is a living planet on which all forms of life are linked to one another, and to land, water, and air. Through those links, energy flows and matter cycles in patterns that support life, including human society. We know enough about these patterns to realize that they are changing, due to human activity, in ways that we don't understand. Our challenge is to study our impact on the biosphere and plan for a healthy future.❞

Joe Levine

3 The Biosphere

Matter and Energy, Interdependence in Nature

Q: How do Earth's living and nonliving parts interact and affect the survival of organisms?

Great White Egret among some plants in the Florida Everglades

INSIDE:

- 3.1 What Is Ecology?
- 3.2 Energy, Producers, and Consumers
- 3.3 Energy Flow in Ecosystems
- 3.4 Cycles of Matter

CHAPTER MYSTERY

CHANGES IN THE BAY

Marine life in Rhode Island's Narragansett Bay is changing. One clue to those changes comes from fishing boat captains who boast about catching bluefish in November—a month after those fish used to head south for winter. Catches of winter flounder, however, are not as plentiful as they once were. These changes in fish populations coincide with the disappearance of the annual spring increase in plant and animal growth. Researchers working in the bay, meanwhile, report puzzling changes in the activities of bacteria living in mud on the bay floor. What's going on? Farms, towns, and cities surround the bay, but direct human influence on the bay has not changed much lately. So why are there so many changes to the bay's plant and animal populations? Could these changes be related to mud-dwelling bacteria? As you read the chapter, look for clues to help you understand the interactions of plants, animals, and bacteria in Narragansett Bay. Then, solve the mystery.

Never Stop Exploring Your World.
Finding out about Narragansett Bay is only the beginning. Take a video field trip with the ecogeeks of Untamed Science to see where this mystery leads.

● Untamed Science Video ● Chapter Mystery

What Is Ecology?

Key Questions

🔑 *What is ecology?*

🔑 *What are biotic and abiotic factors?*

🔑 *What methods are used in ecological studies?*

Vocabulary

biosphere • species • population • community • ecology • ecosystem • biome • biotic factor • abiotic factor

Taking Notes

Venn Diagram Make a Venn diagram that shows how the environment consists of biotic factors, abiotic factors, and some components that are truly a mixture of both. Use examples from the lesson.

THINK ABOUT IT Lewis Thomas, a twentieth-century science writer, was sufficiently inspired by astronauts' photographs of Earth to write: "Viewed from the distance of the moon, the astonishing thing about the earth … is that it is alive." Sounds good. But what does it mean? Was Thomas reacting to how green Earth is? Was he talking about how you can see moving clouds from space? How is Earth, in a scientific sense, a "living planet"? And how do we study it?

Studying Our Living Planet

🔑 *What is ecology?*

When biologists want to talk about life on a global scale, they use the term *biosphere*. The **biosphere** consists of all life on Earth and all parts of the Earth in which life exists, including land, water, and the atmosphere. The biosphere contains every organism, from bacteria living underground to giant trees in rain forests, whales in polar seas, mold spores drifting through the air—and, of course, humans. The biosphere extends from about 8 kilometers above Earth's surface to as far as 11 kilometers below the surface of the ocean.

Individual Organism
A **species** is a group of similar organisms that can breed and produce fertile offspring.

A **population** is a group of individuals that belong to the same species and live in the same area.

An assemblage of different populations that live together in a defined area is called a **community.**

The Science of Ecology Organisms in the biosphere interact with each other and with their surroundings, or environment. The study of these interactions is called **ecology.** 🔑 **Ecology is the scientific study of interactions among organisms and between organisms and their physical environment.** The root of the word *ecology* is the Greek word *oikos,* which means "house." So, ecology is the study of nature's "houses" and the organisms that live in those houses.

Interactions within the biosphere produce a web of interdependence between organisms and the environments in which they live. Organisms respond to their environments and can also change their environments, producing an ever-changing, or dynamic, biosphere.

Ecology and Economics The Greek word *oikos* is also the root of the word *economics.* Economics is concerned with human "houses" and human interactions based on money or trade. Interactions among nature's "houses" are based on energy and nutrients. As their common root implies, human economics and ecology are linked. Humans live within the biosphere and depend on ecological processes to provide such essentials as food and drinkable water that can be bought and sold or traded.

Levels of Organization Ecologists ask many questions about organisms and their environments. Some ecologists focus on the ecology of individual organisms. Others try to understand how interactions among organisms (including humans) influence our global environment. Ecological studies may focus on levels of organization that include those shown in **Figure 3–1.**

In Your Notebook *Draw a circle and label it "Me." Then, draw five concentric circles and label each of them with the appropriate level of organization. Describe your population, community, etc.*

FIGURE 3–1 Levels of Organization The kinds of questions that ecologists may ask about the living environment can vary, depending on the level at which the ecologist works. **Interpret Visuals** *What is the difference between a population and a community?*

All the organisms that live in a place, together with their physical environment, is known as an **ecosystem.**

A **biome** is a group of ecosystems that share similar climates and typical organisms.

Our entire planet, with all its organisms and physical environments, is known as the biosphere.

Biotic and Abiotic Factors

What are biotic and abiotic factors?

Ecologists use the word *environment* to refer to all conditions, or factors, surrounding an organism. Environmental conditions include biotic factors and abiotic factors, as shown in **Figure 3–2.**

Biotic Factors **The biological influences on organisms are called biotic factors.** A **biotic factor** is any living part of the environment with which an organism might interact, including animals, plants, mushrooms, and bacteria. Biotic factors relating to a bullfrog, for example, might include algae it eats as a tadpole, insects it eats as an adult, herons that eat bullfrogs, and other species that compete with bullfrogs for food or space.

Abiotic Factors **Physical components of an ecosystem are called abiotic factors.** An **abiotic factor** is any nonliving part of the environment, such as sunlight, heat, precipitation, humidity, wind or water currents, soil type, and so on. For example, a bullfrog could be affected by abiotic factors such as water availability, temperature, and humidity.

FIGURE 3–2 Biotic and Abiotic Factors Like all ecosystems, this pond is affected by a combination of biotic and abiotic factors. Some environmental factors, such as the "muck" around the edges of the pond, are a mix of biotic and abiotic components. Biotic and abiotic factors are dynamic, meaning that they constantly affect each other. **Classify** *What biotic factors are visible in this ecosystem?*

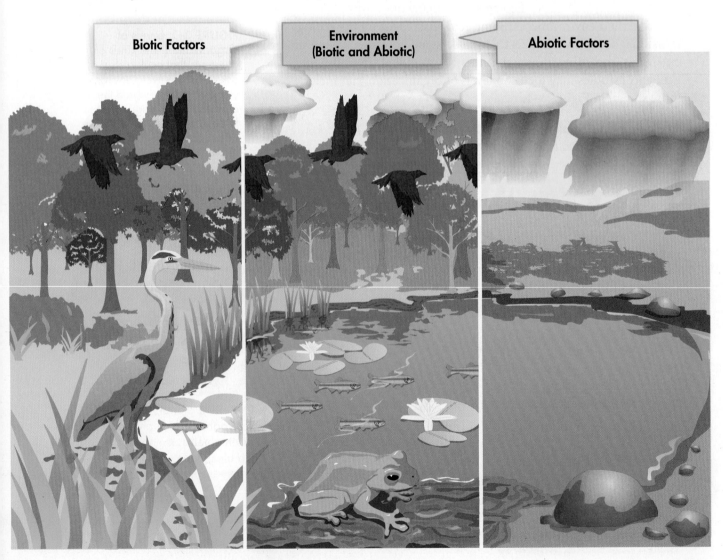

Biotic Factors

Environment (Biotic and Abiotic)

Abiotic Factors

Biotic and Abiotic Factors Together The difference between biotic and abiotic factors may seem to be clear and simple. But if you think carefully, you will realize that many physical factors can be strongly influenced by the activities of organisms. Bullfrogs hang out, for example, in soft "muck" along the shores of ponds. You might think that this muck is strictly part of the physical environment, because it contains nonliving particles of sand and mud. But typical pond muck also contains leaf mold and other decomposing plant material produced by trees and other plants around the pond. That material is decomposing because it serves as "food" for bacteria and fungi that live in the muck.

Taking a slightly wider view, the "abiotic" conditions around that mucky shoreline are strongly influenced by living organisms. A leafy canopy of trees and shrubs often shade the pond's shoreline from direct sun and protect it from strong winds. In this way, organisms living around the pond strongly affect the amount of sunlight the shoreline receives and the range of temperatures it experiences. A forest around a pond also affects the humidity of air close to the ground. The roots of trees and other plants determine how much soil is held in place and how much washes into the pond. Even certain chemical conditions in the soil around the pond are affected by living organisms. If most trees nearby are pines, their decomposing needles make the soil acidic. If the trees nearby are oaks, the soil will be more alkaline. This kind of dynamic mix of biotic and abiotic factors shapes every environment.

MYSTERY CLUE

What are three examples of abiotic factors that might affect life in Narragansett Bay?

 In Your Notebook *In your own words, explain the difference between biotic and abiotic factors. Give three examples of each.*

Quick Lab
GUIDED INQUIRY

How Do Abiotic Factors Affect Different Plant Species?

❶ Gather four paper cups. Use a pencil to punch three holes in the bottom of each cup. Fill two cups with equal amounts of sand and two cups with the same amount of potting soil. **CAUTION:** *Wash your hands well with soap and warm water after handling soil or plants.*

❷ Plant five rice seeds in one sand-filled cup and five rice seeds in one soil-filled cup. Plant five rye seeds in each of the other two cups. Label each cup with the type of seeds and soil it contains.

❸ Place all the cups in a warm, sunny location. Each day for two weeks, water the cups equally and record your observations of any plant growth.

Analyze and Conclude

1. Analyze Data In which medium did the rice grow better—sand or soil? Which was the better medium for the growth of rye?

2. Infer Soil retains more water than sand does, providing a moister environment. What can you infer from your observations about the kind of environment that favors the growth of rice? What kind of environment favors the growth of rye?

3. Draw Conclusions Which would compete more successfully in a dry environment—rice or rye? Which would be more successful in a moist environment?

Ecological Methods

⌐ What methods are used in ecological studies?

Some ecologists, like the one in **Figure 3–3**, use measuring tools to assess changes in plant and wildlife communities. Others use DNA studies to identify bacteria in marsh mud. Still others use data gathered by satellites to track ocean surface temperatures. ⌐ **Regardless of their tools, modern ecologists use three methods in their work: observation, experimentation, and modeling. Each of these approaches relies on scientific methodology to guide inquiry.**

Observation Observation is often the first step in asking ecological questions. Some observations are simple: Which species live here? How many individuals of each species are there? Other observations are more complex: How does an animal protect its young from predators? These types of questions may form the first step in designing experiments and models.

Experimentation Experiments can be used to test hypotheses. An ecologist may, for example, set up an artificial environment in a laboratory or greenhouse to see how growing plants react to different conditions of temperature, lighting, or carbon dioxide concentration. Other experiments carefully alter conditions in selected parts of natural ecosystems.

Modeling Many ecological events, such as effects of global warming on ecosystems, occur over such long periods of time or over such large distances that they are difficult to study directly. Ecologists make models to help them understand these phenomena. Many ecological models consist of mathematical formulas based on data collected through observation and experimentation. Further observations by ecologists can be used to test predictions based on those models.

FIGURE 3–3 Ecology Field Work
The three fundamental approaches to ecological research involve observing, experimenting, and modeling. This ecologist is measuring a giant *Rafflesia* flower in Borneo.

3.1 Assessment

Review Key Concepts ⌐

1. a. Review What are the six different major levels of organization, from smallest to largest, that ecologists commonly study?
   b. Apply Concepts Give an example of two objects or activities in your life that are interdependent. Explain your choice.

2. a. Review Is weather a biotic or abiotic factor?
   b. Compare and Contrast How are biotic and abiotic factors related? What is the difference between them?

3. a. Review Describe the three basic methods of ecological research.
   b. Apply Concepts Give an example of an ecological phenomenon that could be studied by modeling. Explain why modeling would be useful.

PRACTICE PROBLEM

4. Suppose you want to know if the water in a certain stream is safe to drink. Which ecological method(s) would you use in your investigation? Explain your reasoning and outline your procedure.

3.2 Energy, Producers, and Consumers

THINK ABOUT IT At the core of every organism's interaction with the environment is its need for energy to power life's processes. Ants use energy to carry objects many times their size. Birds use energy to migrate thousands of miles. You need energy to get out of bed in the morning! Where does energy in living systems come from? How is it transferred from one organism to another?

Primary Producers

🔑 What are primary producers?

Living systems operate by expending energy. Organisms need energy for growth, reproduction, and their own metabolic processes. In short, if there is no energy, there are no life functions! Yet, no organism can create energy—organisms can only use energy from other sources. You probably know that you get your energy from the plants and animals you eat. But where does the energy in your food come from? For most life on Earth, sunlight is the ultimate energy source. Over the last few decades, however, researchers have discovered that there are other energy sources for life. For some organisms, chemical energy stored in inorganic chemical compounds serves as the ultimate energy source for life processes.

Only algae, certain bacteria, and plants like the one in **Figure 3–4** can capture energy from sunlight or chemicals and convert it into forms that living cells can use. These organisms are called **autotrophs.** Autotrophs use solar or chemical energy to produce "food" by assembling inorganic compounds into complex organic molecules. But autotrophs do more than feed themselves. Autotrophs store energy in forms that make it available to other organisms that eat them. That's why autotrophs are also called **primary producers.** 🔑 **Primary producers are the first producers of energy-rich compounds that are later used by other organisms.** Primary producers are, therefore, essential to the flow of energy through the biosphere.

FIGURE 3–4 Primary Producers Plants obtain energy from sunlight and turn it into nutrients that can, in turn, be eaten and used for energy by animals such as this caterpillar.

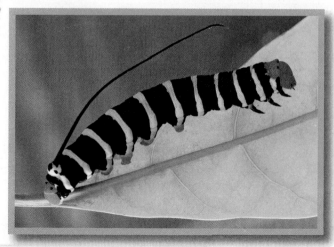

Key Questions

🔑 **What are primary producers?**

🔑 **How do consumers obtain energy and nutrients?**

Vocabulary

autotroph • primary producer • photosynthesis • chemosynthesis • heterotroph • consumer • carnivore • herbivore • scavenger • omnivore • decomposer • detritivore

Taking Notes

Concept Map As you read, use the highlighted vocabulary words to create a concept map that organizes the information in this lesson.

BUILD Vocabulary

PREFIXES The prefix *auto-* means "by itself." The Greek word *trophikos* means "to feed." An autotroph can, therefore, be described as a "self feeder," meaning that it does not need to eat other organisms for food.

Energy From the Sun The best-known and most common primary producers harness solar energy through the process of photosynthesis. **Photosynthesis** captures light energy and uses it to power chemical reactions that convert carbon dioxide and water into oxygen and energy-rich carbohydrates such as sugars and starches. This process, shown in **Figure 3–5** (below left), adds oxygen to the atmosphere and removes carbon dioxide. Without photosynthetic producers, the air would not contain enough oxygen for you to breathe! Plants are the main photosynthetic producers on land. Algae fill that role in freshwater ecosystems and in the sunlit upper layers of the ocean. Photosynthetic bacteria, most commonly cyanobacteria, are important primary producers in ecosystems such as tidal flats and salt marshes.

Life Without Light About 30 years ago, biologists discovered thriving ecosystems around volcanic vents in total darkness on the deep ocean floor. There was no light for photosynthesis, so who or what were the primary producers? Research revealed that these deep-sea ecosystems depended on primary producers that harness chemical energy from inorganic molecules such as hydrogen sulfide. These organisms carry out a process called **chemosynthesis** (kee moh SIN thuh sis) in which chemical energy is used to produce carbohydrates as shown in **Figure 3–5** (below right). Chemosynthetic organisms are not only found in the deepest, darkest ocean, however. Several types of chemosynthetic producers have since been discovered in more parts of the biosphere than anyone expected. Some chemosynthetic bacteria live in harsh environments, such as deep-sea volcanic vents or hot springs. Others live in tidal marshes along the coast.

FIGURE 3–5 Photosynthesis and Chemosynthesis Plants use the energy from sunlight to carry out the process of photosynthesis. Other autotrophs, such as sulfur bacteria, use the energy stored in chemical bonds in a process called chemosynthesis. In both cases, energy-rich carbohydrates are produced. **Compare and Contrast** *How are photosynthesis and chemosynthesis similar?*

In Your Notebook *In your own words, explain the differences and similarities between photosynthetic and chemosynthetic producers.*

Carbon dioxide
+
Water
+

Light Energy

Carbohydrates
+
Oxygen

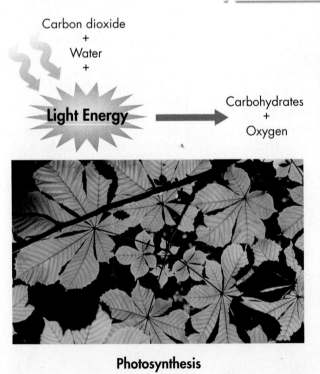

Photosynthesis

Chemical Energy

Carbon dioxide
+
Hydrogen sulfide
+
Oxygen

Carbohydrates
+
Sulfur compounds

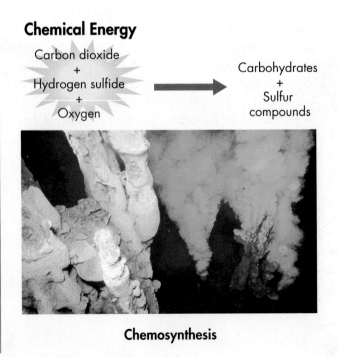

Chemosynthesis

Consumers

🔑 How do consumers obtain energy and nutrients?

Animals, fungi, and many bacteria cannot directly harness energy from the environment as primary producers do. These organisms, known as **heterotrophs** (HET uh roh trohfs) must acquire energy from other organisms—by ingesting them in one way or another. Heterotrophs are also called **consumers.** 🔑 **Organisms that rely on other organisms for energy and nutrients are called consumers.**

Types of Consumers Consumers are classified by the ways in which they acquire energy and nutrients, as shown in **Figure 3–6.** As you will see, the definition of *food* can vary quite a lot among consumers.

FIGURE 3–6 Consumers Consumers rely on other organisms for energy and nutrients. The Amazon rain forest shelters examples of each type of consumer as shown here.

Carnivores kill and eat other animals. Carnivores include snakes, dogs, cats, and this giant river otter. Catching and killing prey can be difficult and requires energy, but meat is generally rich in nutrients and energy and is easy to digest.

Herbivores like this military macaw obtain energy and nutrients by eating plant leaves, roots, seeds, or fruits. Common herbivores include cows, caterpillars, and deer.

Omnivores are animals whose diets naturally include a variety of different foods that usually include both plants and animals. Humans, bears, pigs, and this white-nosed coati are omnivores.

Scavengers are animals that consume the carcasses of other animals that have been killed by predators or have died of other causes. This king vulture is a scavenger.

Decomposers, such as bacteria and fungi (like this mushroom), "feed" by chemically breaking down organic matter. The decay caused by decomposers is part of the process that produces detritus—small pieces of dead and decaying plant and animal remains.

Detritivores (dee TRYT uh vawrz) like this giant earthworm feed on detritus particles, often chewing or grinding them into even smaller pieces. Many types of mites, snails, shrimp, and crabs are detritivores. Detritivores commonly digest decomposers that live on, and in, detritus particles.

Quick Lab
GUIDED INQUIRY

How Do Different Types of Consumers Interact?

❶ Place a potted bean seedling in each of two jars.

❷ Add 20 aphids to one jar and cover the jar with screening to prevent the aphids from escaping. Use a rubber band to attach the screening to the jar.

❸ Add 20 aphids and 4 ladybird beetles to the second jar. Cover the second jar as you did the first one.

❹ Place both jars in a sunny location. Observe the jars each day for one week and record your observations each day. Water the seedlings as needed.

Analyze and Conclude

1. Observe What happened to the aphids and the seedling in the jar without the ladybird beetles? What happened in the jar with the ladybird beetles? How can you explain this difference?

2. Classify Identify each organism in the jars as a producer or a consumer. If the organism is a consumer, what kind of consumer is it?

MYSTERY CLUE

Bacteria are important members of the living community in Narragansett Bay. How do you think the bacterial communities on the floor of the bay might be linked to its producers and consumers?

Beyond Consumer Categories Categorizing consumers is important, but these simple categories often don't express the real complexity of nature. Take herbivores, for instance. Seeds and fruits are usually rich in energy and nutrients, and they are often easy to digest. Leaves are generally poor in nutrients and are usually very difficult to digest. For that reason, herbivores that eat different plant parts often differ greatly in the ways they obtain and digest their food. In fact, only a handful of birds eat leaves, because the kind of digestive system needed to handle leaves efficiently is heavy and difficult to fly around with!

Moreover, organisms in nature often do not stay inside the tidy categories ecologists place them in. For example, some animals often described as carnivores, such as hyenas, will scavenge if they get a chance. Many aquatic animals eat a mixture of algae, bits of animal carcasses, and detritus particles—including the feces of other animals! So, these categories make a nice place to start talking about ecosystems, but it is important to expand on this topic by discussing the way that energy and nutrients move through ecosystems.

3.2 Assessment

Review Key Concepts 🔑

1. a. Review What are the two primary sources of energy that power living systems?

b. Pose Questions Propose a question that a scientist might ask about the variety of organisms found around deep-sea vents.

2. a. Review Explain how consumers obtain energy.

b. Compare and Contrast How are detritivores different from decomposers? Provide an example of each.

3.3 Energy Flow in Ecosystems

THINK ABOUT IT What happens to energy stored in body tissues when one organism eats another? That energy moves from the "eaten" to the "eater." You've learned that the flow of energy through an ecosystem always begins with either photosynthetic or chemosynthetic primary producers. Where it goes from there depends literally on who eats whom!

Food Chains and Food Webs

How does energy flow through ecosystems?

In every ecosystem, primary producers and consumers are linked through feeding relationships. Despite the great variety of feeding relationships in different ecosystems, energy always flows in similar ways. **Energy flows through an ecosystem in a one-way stream, from primary producers to various consumers.**

Food Chains You can think of energy as passing through an ecosystem along a food chain. A **food chain** is a series of steps in which organisms transfer energy by eating and being eaten. Food chains can vary in length. For example, in a prairie ecosystem, a primary producer, such as grass, is eaten by an herbivore, such as a grazing antelope. A carnivore, such as a coyote, in turn feeds upon the antelope. In this two-step chain, the carnivore is just two steps removed from the primary producer.

In some aquatic food chains, primary producers are a mixture of floating algae called **phytoplankton** and attached algae. As shown in **Figure 3–7**, these primary producers may be eaten by small fishes, such as flagfish. Larger fishes, like the largemouth bass, eat the small fishes. The bass are preyed upon by large wading birds, such as the anhinga, which may ultimately be eaten by an alligator. There are four steps in this food chain. The top carnivore is therefore four steps removed from the primary producer.

Key Questions

How does energy flow through ecosystems?

What do the three types of ecological pyramids illustrate?

Vocabulary

food chain • phytoplankton •
food web • zooplankton •
trophic level •
ecological pyramid •
biomass

Taking Notes

Preview Visuals Before you read, look at **Figure 3–7** and **Figure 3–9.** Note how they are similar and how they are different. Based on the figures, write definitions for *food chain* and *food web.*

FIGURE 3–7 Food Chains Food chains show the one-way flow of energy in an ecosystem. **Apply Concepts** *What is the ultimate source of energy for this food chain?*

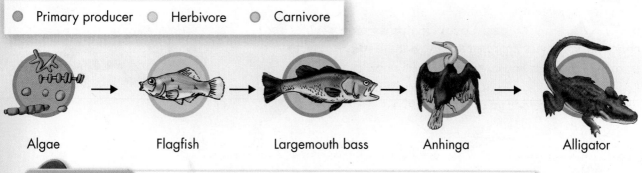

| ● Primary producer | ◐ Herbivore | ● Carnivore |

Algae — Flagfish — Largemouth bass — Anhinga — Alligator

Food Webs In most ecosystems, feeding relationships are much more complicated than the relationships described in a single, simple chain. One reason for this is that many animals eat more than one kind of food. For example, on Africa's Serengeti Plain, herbivores, such as zebras, gazelles, and buffaloes, often graze upon several different species of grasses. Several predators such as lions, hyenas, and leopards, in turn, often prey upon those herbivores! Ecologists call this network of feeding interactions a **food web.**

▶ *Food Chains Within Food Webs* The Everglades are a complex marshland ecosystem in southern Florida. Here, aquatic and terrestrial organisms interact in many overlapping feeding relationships that have been simplified and represented in **Figure 3–9.** Starting with a primary producer (algae or plants), see how many different routes you can take to reach the alligator, vulture, or anhinga. One path, from the algae to the alligator, is the same food chain you saw in **Figure 3–7.** In fact, each path you trace through the food web is a food chain. You can think of a food web, therefore, as linking together all of the food chains in an ecosystem. Realize, however, that this is a highly simplified representation of this food web, in which many species have been left out. Now, you can begin to appreciate how complicated food webs are!

▶ *Decomposers and Detritivores in Food Webs* Decomposers and detritivores are as important in most food webs as other consumers are. Look again at the Everglades web. Although white-tailed deer, moorhens, raccoons, grass shrimp, crayfish, and flagfish feed at least partly on primary producers, most producers die without being eaten. In the detritus pathway, decomposers convert that dead material to detritus, which is eaten by detritivores, such as crayfish, grass shrimp, and worms. At the same time, the decomposition process releases nutrients that can be used by primary producers. Thus, decomposers recycle nutrients in food webs as seen in **Figure 3–8.** Without decomposers, nutrients would remain locked within dead organisms.

In Your Notebook *Explain how food chains and food webs are related.*

BUILD Vocabulary

ACADEMIC WORDS The verb convert means "to change from one form to another." Decomposers convert, or change, dead plant matter into a form called detritus that is eaten by detritivores.

VISUAL ANALOGY

FIGURE 3–8 Earth's Recycling Center Decomposers break down dead and decaying matter and release nutrients that can be reused by primary producers. **Use Analogies** *How are decomposers like a city's recycling center?*

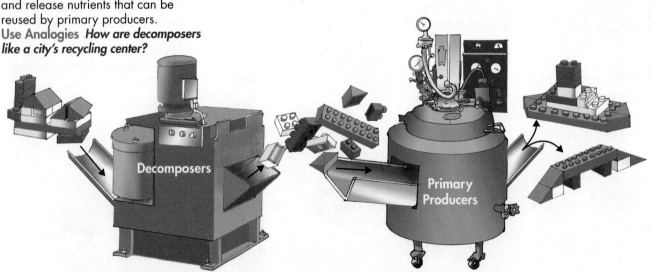

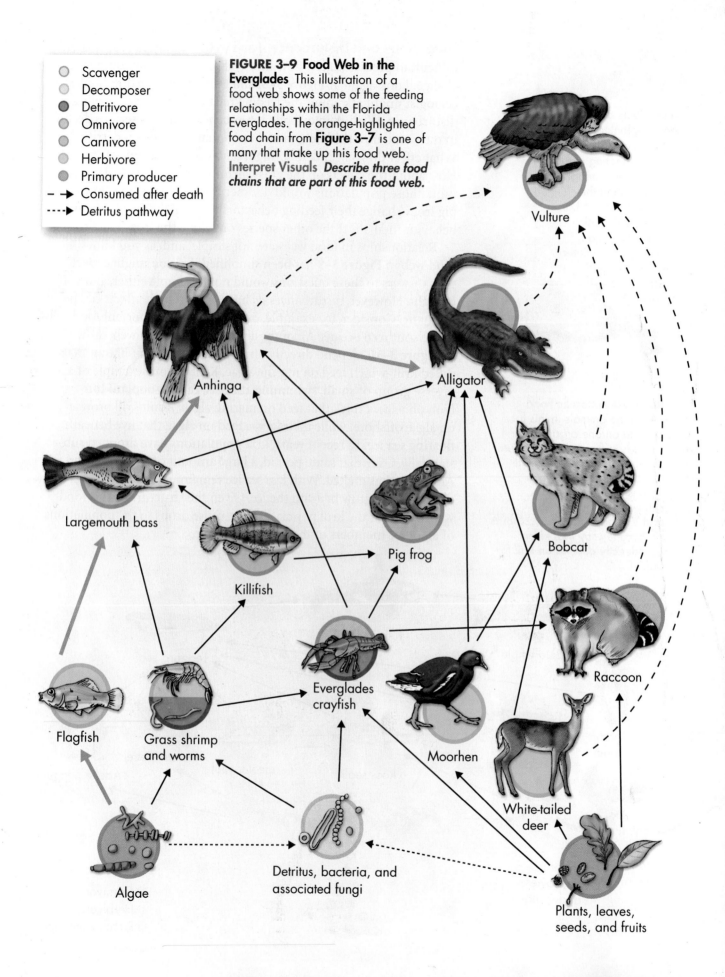

Scavenger
Decomposer
Detritivore
Omnivore
Carnivore
Herbivore
Primary producer
- → **Consumed after death**
···▶ **Detritus pathway**

FIGURE 3–9 Food Web in the Everglades This illustration of a food web shows some of the feeding relationships within the Florida Everglades. The orange-highlighted food chain from **Figure 3–7** is one of many that make up this food web. **Interpret Visuals** *Describe three food chains that are part of this food web.*

Vulture

Anhinga

Alligator

Largemouth bass

Bobcat

Killifish

Pig frog

Everglades crayfish

Raccoon

Flagfish

Grass shrimp and worms

Moorhen

White-tailed deer

Algae

Detritus, bacteria, and associated fungi

Plants, leaves, seeds, and fruits

MYSTERY CLUE

Researchers discovered that zooplankton in Narragansett Bay now graze on floating algae more actively through the winter than they ever did before. What effect do you think this might have on the annual late-winter "bloom" of algae that occurs in the water?

Food Webs and Disturbance Food webs are complex, so it is often difficult to predict exactly how they will respond to environmental change. Look again at **Figure 3–9,** and think about the questions an ecologist might ask about the feeding relationships in it following a disturbance. What if an oil spill, for example, caused a serious decline in the number of the bacteria and fungi that break down detritus? What effect do you think that might have on populations of crayfish? How about the effects on the grass shrimp and the worms? Do you think those populations would decline? If they did decline, how might pig frogs change their feeding behavior? How might the change in frog behavior then affect the other species on which the frog feeds?

Relationships in food webs are not simple, and, as you know, the food web in **Figure 3–9** has been simplified! So, you might expect that answers to these questions would not be simple either, and you'd be right. However, disturbances *do* happen, and their effects can be dramatic. Consider, for example, one of the most important food webs in the southern oceans. All of the animals in this food web, shown in **Figure 3–10,** depend directly or indirectly on shrimplike animals called krill, which feed on marine algae. Krill are one example of a diverse group of small, swimming animals, called **zooplankton** (zoh oh PLANK tun), that feed on marine algae. Adult krill browse on algae offshore, while their larvae feed on algae that live beneath floating sea ice. In recent years, krill populations have dropped substantially. Over that same period, a large amount of sea ice around Antarctica has melted. With less sea ice remaining, there are fewer of the algae that grow beneath the ice. Given the structure of this food web, a drop in the krill population can cause drops in the populations of all other members of the food web shown.

FIGURE 3–10 Antarctic Food Web All of the animals in this food web depend on one organism: krill. Disturbances to the krill's food source, marine algae, have the potential to cause changes in all of the populations connected to the algae through this food web. **Interpret Visuals** *What do ecologists mean when they say that killer whales indirectly depend on krill for survival?*

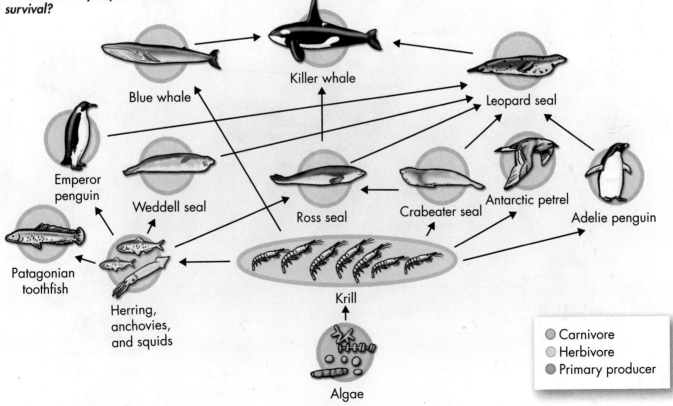

Blue whale · Killer whale · Leopard seal · Emperor penguin · Weddell seal · Ross seal · Crabeater seal · Antarctic petrel · Adelie penguin · Patagonian toothfish · Herring, anchovies, and squids · Krill · Algae

- ● Carnivore
- ○ Herbivore
- ● Primary producer

Trophic Levels and Ecological Pyramids

What do the three types of ecological pyramids illustrate?

Each step in a food chain or food web is called a **trophic level.** Primary producers always make up the first trophic level. Various consumers occupy every other level. One way to illustrate the trophic levels in an ecosystem is with an ecological pyramid. **Ecological pyramids** show the relative amount of energy or matter contained within each trophic level in a given food chain or food web. There are three different types of ecological pyramids: pyramids of energy, pyramids of biomass, and pyramids of numbers.

> **In Your Notebook** *Make a two-column chart to compare the three types of ecological pyramids.*

Pyramids of Energy Theoretically, there is no limit to the number of trophic levels in a food web or the number of organisms that live on each level. But there is one catch. Only a small portion of the energy that passes through any given trophic level is ultimately stored in the bodies of organisms at the next level. This is because organisms expend much of the energy they acquire on life processes, such as respiration, movement, growth, and reproduction. Most of the remaining energy is released into the environment as heat—a byproduct of these activities. **Pyramids of energy show the relative amount of energy available at each trophic level of a food chain or food web.**

The efficiency of energy transfer from one trophic level to another varies. On average, about 10 percent of the energy available within one trophic level is transferred to the next trophic level, as shown in **Figure 3–11.** For instance, one tenth of the solar energy captured and stored in the leaves of grasses ends up stored in the tissues of cows and other grazers. One tenth of *that* energy—10 percent of 10 percent, or 1 percent of the original amount—gets stored in the tissues of humans who eat cows. Thus, the more levels that exist between a producer and a given consumer, the smaller the percentage of the original energy from producers that is available to that consumer.

Analyzing Data

The 10 Percent Rule

As shown in **Figure 3–11,** an energy pyramid is a diagram that illustrates the transfer of energy through a food chain or food web. In general, only 10 percent of the energy available in one level is stored in the level above. Look at **Figure 3–11** and answer the questions below.

1. Calculate If there are 1000 units of energy available at the producer level of the energy pyramid, approximately how many units of energy are available to the third-level consumer? **MATH**

2. Interpret Diagrams What is the original source of the energy that flows through most ecosystems? Why must there be a continuous supply of energy into the ecosystem?

3. Infer Why are there usually fewer organisms in the top levels of an energy pyramid?

FIGURE 3–11 Pyramid of Energy Pyramids of energy show the relative amount of energy available at each trophic level. An ecosystem requires a constant supply of energy from photosynthetic or chemosynthetic producers. **Apply Concepts** *Explain how the amount of energy available at each trophic level often limits the number of organisms that each level can support.*

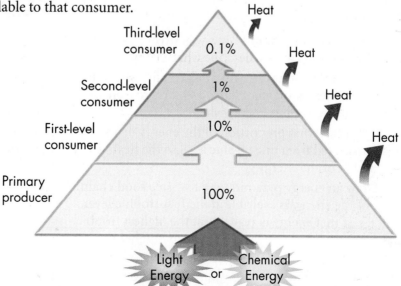

FIGURE 3–12 Pyramids of Biomass and Numbers
In most cases, pyramids of biomass and numbers follow the same general pattern. In the field modeled here, there are more individual primary producers than first-level consumers. Likewise, the primary producers collectively have more mass. The same patterns hold for the second and third-level consumers. With each step to a higher trophic level, biomass and numbers decrease.

Pyramids of Biomass and Numbers The total amount of living tissue within a given trophic level is called its **biomass.** Biomass is usually measured in grams of organic matter per unit area. The amount of biomass a given trophic level can support is determined, in part, by the amount of energy available. 🔑 **A pyramid of biomass illustrates the relative amount of living organic matter available at each trophic level in an ecosystem.**

Ecologists interested in the number of organisms at each trophic level uses a pyramid of numbers. 🔑 **A pyramid of numbers shows the relative number of individual organisms at each trophic level in an ecosystem.** In most ecosystems, the shape of the pyramid of numbers is similar to the shape of the pyramid of biomass for the same ecosystem. In this shape, the numbers of individuals on each level decrease from the level below it. To understand this point more clearly, imagine that an ecologist marked off several square meters in a field, and then weighed and counted every organism in that area. The result might look something like the pyramid in **Figure 3–12.**

In some cases, however, consumers are much less massive than organisms they feed upon. Thousands of insects may graze on a single tree, for example, and countless mosquitos can feed off a few deer. Both the tree and deer have a lot of biomass, but they each represent only one organism. In such cases, the pyramid of numbers may be turned upside down, but the pyramid of biomass usually has the normal orientation.

Review Key Concepts 🔑

1. a. Review Energy is said to flow in a "one-way stream" through an ecosystem. In your own words, describe what that means.

b. Form a Hypothesis Explain what you think might happen to the Everglades ecosystem shown in **Figure 3–9** if there were a sudden decrease in the number of crayfish.

2. a. Review On average, what proportion of the energy in an ecosystem is transferred from one trophic level to the next? Where does the rest of the energy go?

b. Calculate Draw an energy pyramid for a five-step food chain. If 100 percent of the energy is available at the first trophic level, what percentage of that energy is available at the highest trophic level? MATH

Apply the Big idea

Interdependence In Nature

3. Refer to **Figure 3–9,** which shows a food web in the Everglades. Choose one of the food chains within the web. Then, write a paragraph describing the feeding relationships among the organisms in the food chain.

3.4 Cycles of Matter

THINK ABOUT IT Living organisms are composed mostly of four elements: oxygen, carbon, hydrogen, and nitrogen. These four elements (and a few others, such as sulfur and phosphorus) are the basis of life's most important compounds: water, carbohydrates, lipids, nucleic acids, and proteins. In short, a handful of elements combine to form the building blocks of all known organisms. And yet, organisms cannot manufacture these elements and do not "use them up." So, where do essential elements come from? How does their availability affect ecosystems?

Recycling in the Biosphere

How does matter move through the biosphere?

Matter moves through the biosphere differently than the way in which energy moves. Solar and chemical energy are captured by primary producers and then pass in a one-way fashion from one trophic level to the next—dissipating in the environment as heat along the way. But while energy in the form of sunlight is constantly entering the biosphere, Earth doesn't receive a significant, steady supply of new matter from space. **Unlike the one-way flow of energy, matter is recycled within and between ecosystems.** Elements pass from one organism to another and among parts of the biosphere through closed loops called **biogeochemical cycles,** which are powered by the flow of energy as shown in **Figure 3–13.** As that word suggests, cycles of matter involve *bio*logical processes, *geo*logical processes, and *chem*ical processes. Human activity can also play an important role. As matter moves through these cycles, it is transformed. It is never created or destroyed—just changed.

Vocabulary

biogeochemical cycle • nutrient • nitrogen fixation • denitrification • limiting nutrient

Taking Notes

Outline Make an outline using the green and blue headings in this lesson. Fill in details as you read to help you organize the information.

VISUAL ANALOGY

THE MATTER MILL

FIGURE 3–13 Nutrients are recycled through biogeochemical cycles. These cycles are powered by the one-way flow of energy through the biosphere.
Use Analogies *How is the water flowing over the water wheel similar to the flow of energy in the biosphere?*

Energy

Cycles of Matter

Biological Processes

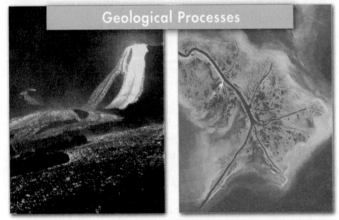

Geological Processes

Chemical and Physical Processes

Human Activity

There are many ways in which the processes involved in biogeochemical cycles can be classified. Here, we will use the following guidelines:

▶ *Biological Processes* Biological processes consist of any and all activities performed by living organisms. These processes include eating, breathing, "burning" food, and eliminating waste products.

▶ *Geological Processes* Geological processes include volcanic eruptions, the formation and breakdown of rock, and major movements of matter within and below the surface of the earth.

▶ *Chemical and Physical Processes* Chemical and physical processes include the formation of clouds and precipitation, the flow of running water, and the action of lightning.

▶ *Human Activity* Human activities that affect cycles of matter on a global scale include the mining and burning of fossil fuels, the clearing of land for building and farming, the burning of forests, and the manufacture and use of fertilizers.

These processes, shown in **Figure 3–14,** pass the same atoms and molecules around again and again. Imagine, for a moment, that you are a carbon atom in a molecule of carbon dioxide that has just been shot out of a volcano. The leaf of a blueberry bush in a nearby mountain range absorbs you during photosynthesis. You become part of a carbohydrate molecule in a blueberry. A caribou eats the fruit, and within a few hours, you pass out of the animal's body. You are soon swallowed by a dung beetle, which gets eaten by a hungry shrew. You are combined into the body tissues of the shrew, which is then eaten by an owl. You are released back into the atmosphere when the owl exhales carbon dioxide, dissolve in a drop of rainwater, and flow through a river into the ocean.

This could just be part of the never-ending cycle of a carbon atom through the biosphere. Carbon atoms in your body may once have been part of a rock on the ocean floor, the tail of a dinosaur, or even part of a historical figure such as Julius Caesar!

FIGURE 3–14 Biogeochemical Processes Cycles of matter involve biological, geological, chemical, and human factors.

The Water Cycle

How does water cycle through the biosphere?

Every time you see rain or snow, or watch a river flow, you are witnessing part of the water cycle. **Water continuously moves between the oceans, the atmosphere, and land—sometimes outside living organisms and sometimes inside them.** As **Figure 3–15** shows, water molecules typically enter the atmosphere as water vapor, a gas, when they evaporate from the ocean or other bodies of water. Water can also enter the atmosphere by evaporating from the leaves of plants in the process of transpiration (tran spuh RAY shun).

Water vapor may be transported by winds over great distances. If the air carrying it cools, water vapor condenses into tiny droplets that form clouds. When the droplets become large enough, they fall to Earth's surface as precipitation in the form of rain, snow, sleet, or hail. On land, some precipitation flows along the surface in what scientists call runoff, until it enters a river or stream that carries it to an ocean or lake. Precipitation can also be absorbed into the soil and is then called groundwater. Groundwater can enter plants through their roots, or flow into rivers, streams, lakes, or oceans. Some groundwater penetrates deeply enough into the ground to become part of underground reservoirs. Water that re-enters the atmosphere through transpiration or evaporation begins the cycle anew.

In Your Notebook *Define each of the following terms and describe how they relate to the water cycle:* evaporation, transpiration, precipitation, *and* runoff.

FIGURE 3–15 The Water Cycle This diagram shows the main processes involved in the water cycle. Scientists estimate that it can take a single water molecule as long as 4000 years to complete one cycle. **Interpret Visuals** *What are the two primary ways in which water that falls to Earth as precipitation passes through the water cycle?*

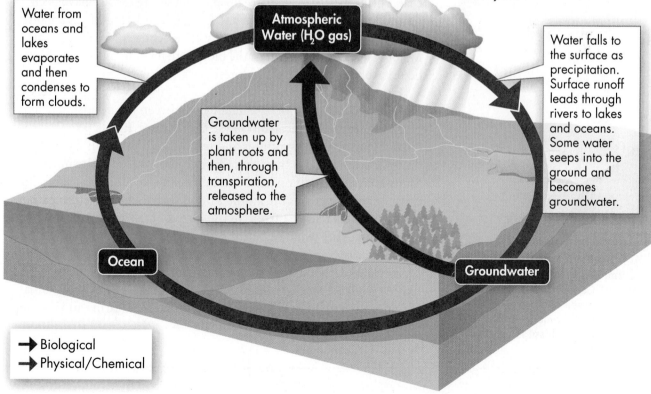

Water from oceans and lakes evaporates and then condenses to form clouds.

Atmospheric Water (H$_2$O gas)

Water falls to the surface as precipitation. Surface runoff leads through rivers to lakes and oceans. Some water seeps into the ground and becomes groundwater.

Groundwater is taken up by plant roots and then, through transpiration, released to the atmosphere.

Ocean

Groundwater

→ Biological
→ Physical/Chemical

Nutrient Cycles

🔑 *What is the importance of the main nutrient cycles?*

The chemical substances that an organism needs to sustain life are called **nutrients.** 🔑 **Every organism needs nutrients to build tissues and carry out life functions. Like water, nutrients pass through organisms and the environment through biogeochemical cycles. The three pathways, or cycles that move carbon, nitrogen, and phosphorus through the biosphere are especially critical for life.**

Another element, oxygen, participates in parts of the carbon, nitrogen, and phosphorus cycles by combining with these elements and cycling with them through parts of their journeys. Oxygen gas in the atmosphere is released by one of the most important of all biological activities: photosynthesis. Oxygen is used in respiration by all multicellular forms of life, and many single-celled organisms as well.

The Carbon Cycle Carbon is a major component of all organic compounds, including carbohydrates, lipids, proteins, and nucleic acids. In fact, carbon is such a key ingredient of living tissue and ecosystems that life on Earth is often described as "carbon-based life." Carbon in the form of calcium carbonate ($CaCO_3$) is an important component of many different kinds of animal skeletons and is also found in several kinds of rocks. Carbon and oxygen form carbon dioxide gas (CO_2), which is an important component of the atmosphere and is dissolved in oceans.

Some carbon-containing compounds that were once part of ancient forests have been buried and transformed by geological processes into coal. The bodies of marine organisms containing carbon have been transformed into oil or natural gas. Coal, oil, and natural gas are often referred to as fossil fuels because they are essentially "fossilized" carbon. Major reservoirs of carbon in the biosphere include the atmosphere, oceans, rocks, fossil fuels, and forests.

Figure 3–17 shows how carbon moves through the biosphere. Carbon dioxide is continuously exchanged between the atmosphere and oceans through chemical and physical processes. Plants take in carbon dioxide during photosynthesis and use the carbon to build carbohydrates. Carbohydrates then pass through food webs to consumers. Many animals—both on land and in the sea—combine carbon with calcium and oxygen as the animals build skeletons of calcium carbonate. Organisms release carbon in the form of carbon dioxide gas by respiration. Also, when organisms die, decomposers break down the bodies, releasing carbon to the environment. Geologic forces can turn accumulated carbon into carbon-containing rocks or fossil fuels. Carbon dioxide is released into the atmosphere by volcanic activity or by human activities, such as the burning of fossil fuels and the clearing and burning of forests.

FIGURE 3-16 Oxygen in the Biosphere The oxygen contained in the carbon dioxide exhaled by this bighorn sheep may be taken up by producers and re-released as oxygen gas. Together, respiration and photosynthesis contribute to oxygen's cycling through the biosphere.

BUILD Vocabulary

ACADEMIC WORDS The verb **accumulate** means "to collect or gather." Carbon accumulates, or collects, in soil and in the oceans where it cycles among organisms or is turned into fossil fuels.

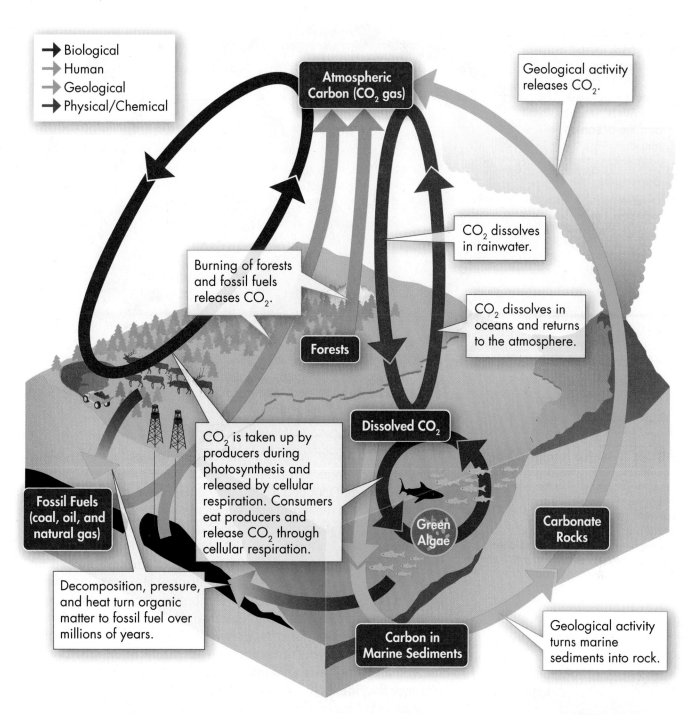

Legend:
→ Biological
→ Human
→ Geological
→ Physical/Chemical

Atmospheric Carbon (CO$_2$ gas)

Geological activity releases CO$_2$.

CO$_2$ dissolves in rainwater.

Burning of forests and fossil fuels releases CO$_2$.

CO$_2$ dissolves in oceans and returns to the atmosphere.

Forests

Dissolved CO$_2$

CO$_2$ is taken up by producers during photosynthesis and released by cellular respiration. Consumers eat producers and release CO$_2$ through cellular respiration.

Green Algae

Carbonate Rocks

Fossil Fuels (coal, oil, and natural gas)

Decomposition, pressure, and heat turn organic matter to fossil fuel over millions of years.

Carbon in Marine Sediments

Geological activity turns marine sediments into rock.

Scientists know a great deal about the biological, geological, chemical, and human processes that are involved in the carbon cycle, but important questions remain. How much carbon moves through each pathway? How do ecosystems respond to changes in atmospheric carbon dioxide concentration? How much carbon dioxide can the ocean absorb? Later in this unit, you will learn why answers to these questions are so important.

In Your Notebook *Describe one biological, one geological, one chemical, and one human activity that is involved in the carbon cycle.*

FIGURE 3–17 The Carbon Cycle
Carbon is found in several large reservoirs in the biosphere. In the atmosphere, it is found as carbon dioxide gas (CO$_2$); in the oceans, as dissolved carbon dioxide; on land, in organisms, rocks, and soil; and underground, as coal, petroleum, and calcium carbonate. **Interpret Visuals** *What is one of the processes that takes carbon dioxide out of the atmosphere?*

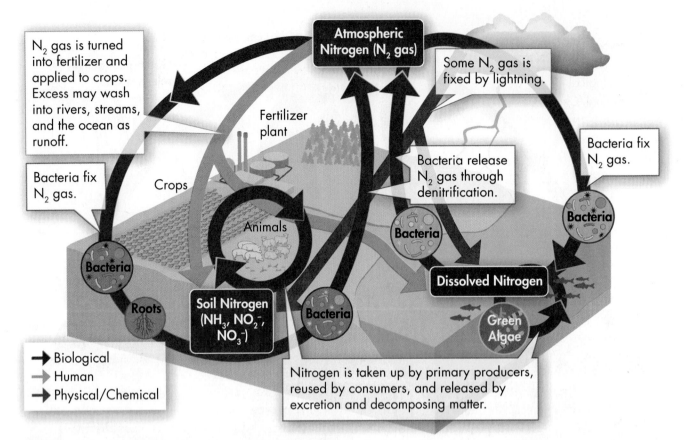

FIGURE 3–18 The Nitrogen Cycle
The atmosphere is the largest reservoir of nitrogen in the biosphere. Nitrogen also cycles through the soil and through the tissues of living organisms. **Interpret Visuals** *Through which two processes does nitrogen gas get converted into usable forms for organisms?*

Labels in figure:

- N₂ gas is turned into fertilizer and applied to crops. Excess may wash into rivers, streams, and the ocean as runoff.
- Atmospheric Nitrogen (N₂ gas)
- Some N₂ gas is fixed by lightning.
- Bacteria fix N₂ gas.
- Bacteria release N₂ gas through denitrification.
- Bacteria fix N₂ gas.
- Fertilizer plant
- Crops
- Animals
- Bacteria
- Bacteria
- Dissolved Nitrogen
- Bacteria
- Roots
- Soil Nitrogen (NH_3, NO_2^-, NO_3^-)
- Bacteria
- Green Algae
- → Biological
- → Human
- → Physical/Chemical
- Nitrogen is taken up by primary producers, reused by consumers, and released by excretion and decomposing matter.

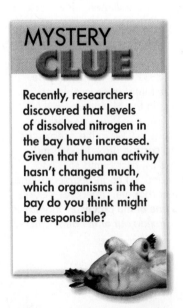

The Nitrogen Cycle All organisms require nitrogen to make amino acids, which combine to form proteins, and nucleic acids, which combine to form DNA and RNA. Many different forms of nitrogen occur naturally in the biosphere. Nitrogen gas (N_2) makes up 78 percent of Earth's atmosphere. Nitrogen-containing substances such as ammonia (NH_3), nitrate ions (NO_3^-), and nitrite ions (NO_2^-) are found in soil, in the wastes produced by many organisms, and in dead and decaying organic matter. Dissolved nitrogen also exists in several forms in the ocean and other large water bodies. **Figure 3–18** shows how different forms of nitrogen cycle through the biosphere.

Although nitrogen gas is the most abundant form of nitrogen on Earth, only certain types of bacteria can use this form directly. These bacteria convert nitrogen gas into ammonia, a process known as **nitrogen fixation.** Some of these nitrogen-fixing bacteria live in the soil and on the roots of certain plants, such as peanuts and peas, called legumes. Other bacteria convert that fixed nitrogen into nitrates and nitrites. Once these forms of nitrogen are available, primary producers can use them to make proteins and nucleic acids. Consumers eat the producers and reuse nitrogen to make their own nitrogen-containing compounds. Decomposers release nitrogen from waste and dead organisms as ammonia, nitrates, and nitrites that producers may take up again. Other bacteria obtain energy by converting nitrates into nitrogen gas, which is released into the atmosphere in a process called **denitrification.** A relatively small amount of nitrogen gas is converted to usable forms by lightning in a process called atmospheric nitrogen fixation. Humans add nitrogen to the biosphere through the manufacture and use of fertilizers. Excess fertilizer is often carried into surface water or groundwater by precipitation.

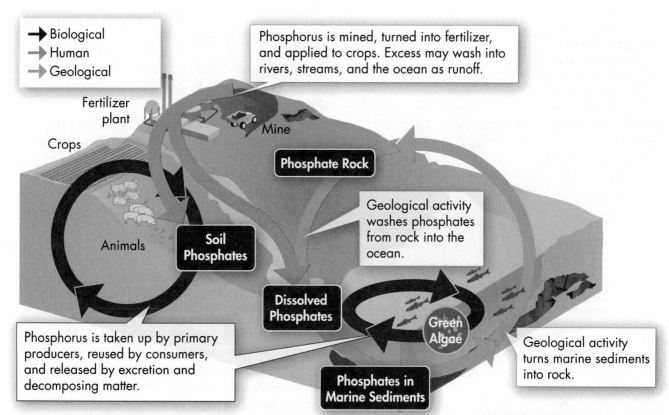

Biological
Human
Geological

Phosphorus is mined, turned into fertilizer, and applied to crops. Excess may wash into rivers, streams, and the ocean as runoff.

Fertilizer plant

Crops

Mine

Phosphate Rock

Geological activity washes phosphates from rock into the ocean.

Animals

Soil Phosphates

Dissolved Phosphates

Green Algae

Phosphorus is taken up by primary producers, reused by consumers, and released by excretion and decomposing matter.

Phosphates in Marine Sediments

Geological activity turns marine sediments into rock.

The Phosphorus Cycle Phosphorus is essential to living organisms because it forms a part of vital molecules such as DNA and RNA. Although phosphorus is of great biological importance, it is not abundant in the biosphere. Unlike carbon, oxygen, and nitrogen, phosphorus does not enter the atmosphere in significant amounts. Instead, phosphorus in the form of inorganic phosphate remains mostly on land, in the form of phosphate rock and soil minerals, and in the ocean, as dissolved phosphate and phosphate sediments, as seen in **Figure 3–19.**

As rocks and sediments gradually wear down, phosphate is released. Some phosphate stays on land and cycles between organisms and soil. Plants bind phosphate into organic compounds when they absorb it from soil or water. Organic phosphate moves through the food web, from producers to consumers, and to the rest of the ecosystem. Other phosphate washes into rivers and streams, where it dissolves. This phosphate may eventually makes its way to the ocean, where marine organisms process and incorporate it into biological compounds.

FIGURE 3–19 The Phosphorus Cycle Phosphorus in the biosphere cycles among the land, ocean sediments, and living organisms. Unlike other nutrients, phosphorus is not found in significant quantities in the atmosphere.

Nutrient Limitation

How does nutrient availability relate to the primary productivity of an ecosystem?

Ecologists are often interested in an ecosystem's primary productivity—the rate at which primary producers create organic material. **If ample sunlight and water are available, the primary productivity of an ecosystem may be limited by the availability of nutrients.** If even a single essential nutrient is in short supply, primary productivity will be limited. The nutrient whose supply limits productivity is called the **limiting nutrient.**

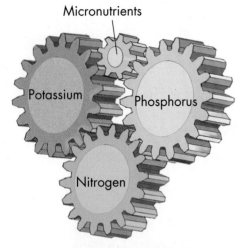

Micronutrients

Potassium

Phosphorus

Nitrogen

INTERLOCKING NUTRIENTS

FIGURE 3–20 The movement of each nutrient through ecosystems depends on the movements of all the others, because all are needed for living systems to function. **Use Analogies** *If these gears were modeling nutrient cycling in the ocean, which gear would typically determine how quickly—or slowly—all the other gears turn?*

Nutrient Limitation in Soil In all but the richest soil, the growth of crop plants is typically limited by one or more nutrients that must be taken up by plants through their roots. That's why farmers use fertilizers! Most fertilizers contain large amounts of nitrogen, phosphorus, and potassium, which help plants grow better in poor soil. Micronutrients such as calcium, magnesium, sulfur, iron, and manganese are necessary in relatively small amounts, and these elements are sometimes included in specialty fertilizers. (Carbon is not included in chemical fertilizers because plants acquire carbon dioxide from the atmosphere during photosynthesis.) All nutrient cycles work together like the gears in **Figure 3–20.** If any nutrient is in short supply—if any wheel "sticks"—the whole system slows down or stops altogether.

Nutrient Limitation in Aquatic Ecosystems The open oceans of the world are nutrient-poor compared to many land areas. Seawater typically contains only 0.00005 percent nitrogen, or 1/10,000 of the amount often found in soil. In the ocean and other saltwater environments, nitrogen is often the limiting nutrient. In streams, lakes, and freshwater environments, phosphorus is typically the limiting nutrient.

Sometimes, such as after heavy rains, an aquatic ecosystem receives a large input of a limiting nutrient—for example, runoff from heavily fertilized fields. When this happens, the result can be an algal bloom—a dramatic increase in the amount of algae and other primary producers. Why can runoff from fertilized fields produce algal blooms? More nutrients are available, so producers can grow and reproduce more quickly. If there are not enough consumers to eat the algae, an algal bloom can occur, in which case algae can cover the water's surface and disrupt the functioning of an ecosystem.

3.4 Assessment

Review Key Concepts

1. a. Review How does the way that matter flows through an ecosystem differ from the way that energy flows?

b. Apply Concepts What are the four types of processes that cycle matter through the biosphere? Give an example of each.

2. a. Review By what two processes is water cycled from land to the atmosphere?

b. Sequence Describe one way in which water from the ocean may make one complete cycle through the atmosphere and back to the ocean. Include the names of each process involved in your cycle.

3. a. Review Why do living organisms need nutrients?

b. Predict Based on your knowledge of the carbon cycle, what do you think might happen if humans were to continue to clear and burn vast areas of forests for building?

4. a. Review Explain how a nutrient can be a limiting factor in an ecosystem.

b. Apply Concepts Look back at the nitrogen and phosphorus cycles (**Figures 3–18** and **3–19**). How is fertilizer runoff related to algal blooms?

WRITE ABOUT SCIENCE

Explanation

5. Describe how oxygen, although it does not have an independent cycle, moves through the biosphere as part of the carbon cycle. Include a description of the various forms that oxygen takes.

Technology & BIOLOGY

Global Ecology From Space

Can ecologists track plant growth around the world? Can they follow temperature change in oceans from day to day, or the amount of polar ice from year to year? Yes! Satellites can provide these data, essential for understanding global ecology. Satellite sensors can be programmed to scan particular bands of the electromagnetic spectrum to reveal global patterns of temperature, rainfall, or the presence of plants on land or algae in the oceans. The resulting false-color images are both beautiful and filled with vital information.

Changes in Polar Ice Cover Sea ice around the North Pole has been melting more each summer since satellites began gathering data in 1979. The image below shows in white the amount of ice remaining at the end of the summer in 2007. The amount of ice at the same time of year for an average year between 1979 and 2007 is shown in green.

▲
2007 White areas show the average minimum amount of arctic ice cover at the end of the summer, 2007.
1979–2007 Green areas show the average minimum amount of ice cover between 1979 and 2007.

Plant and Algal Growth These data were gathered by NASA's Sea-viewing Wide Field-of-view Sensor (SeaWiFS), which is programmed to monitor the color of reflected light. In the image below, you can see how actively plants on land and algae in the oceans were harnessing solar energy for photosynthesis when these data were taken. A measurement of photosynthesis gives a measure of growth rates and the input of energy and nutrients into the ecosystem.

▲
On Land Dark green indicates active plant growth; yellow areas indicate barren deserts or mountains.
In the Sea Dark blue indicates very low active growth of algae. Red indicates the highest active growth.

WRITING Visit the Web site for the Goddard Space Flight Center Scientific Visualization service and select a set of satellite data to examine. Write a brief paragraph explaining what you learned from looking at those data.

Pre-Lab: The Effect of Fertilizer on Algae

Problem How do excess nutrients affect the growth of algae?

Materials test tubes, test-tube rack, glass-marking pencil, dropper pipettes, algae culture, 25-mL graduated cylinder, spring water, plant food, cotton balls, grow light

Lab Manual Chapter 3 Lab

Skills Predict, Compare and Contrast, Infer

Connect to the **Big idea** In a healthy ecosystem, nutrients cycle among primary producers, consumers, and decomposers. The growth of primary producers is limited by the availability of nutrients. Humans can intentionally increase the amount of nutrients in an ecosystem. For example, farmers may add fertilizer to the soil in which they grow crops. But the addition of nutrients to an ecosystem is not always planned. For example, runoff from soil that contains fertilizer may flow into coastal waters or freshwater ponds. In this lab, you will observe what happens when algae that live in those waters are provided with excess nutrients.

Background Questions

a. Review What is a limiting nutrient?

b. Explain Why do farmers use fertilizers?

c. Classify What role do algae play in freshwater ecosystems?

Pre-Lab Questions

Preview the procedure in the lab manual.

1. Design an Experiment What is the independent variable in this experiment?

2. Predict After four days, how will you be able to tell which test tube has more algae?

3. Control Variables Why will you grow *Chlorella* in spring water instead of pond water?

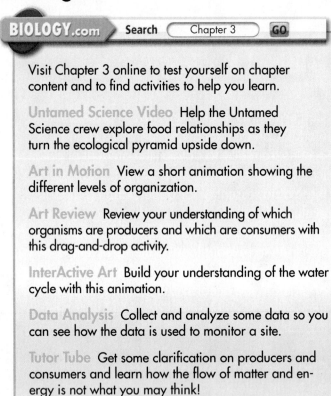

BIOLOGY.com   Search   Chapter 3   GO

Visit Chapter 3 online to test yourself on chapter content and to find activities to help you learn.

Untamed Science Video Help the Untamed Science crew explore food relationships as they turn the ecological pyramid upside down.

Art in Motion View a short animation showing the different levels of organization.

Art Review Review your understanding of which organisms are producers and which are consumers with this drag-and-drop activity.

InterActive Art Build your understanding of the water cycle with this animation.

Data Analysis Collect and analyze some data so you can see how the data is used to monitor a site.

Tutor Tube Get some clarification on producers and consumers and learn how the flow of matter and energy is not what you may think!

Visual Analogies Compare a recycling center to decomposers in this activity. Compare nutrient limitation to a series of cogs in this activity.

③ Study Guide

Big idea ▶ Matter and Energy, Interdependence in Nature

The biosphere is composed of an ever-changing mix of living and nonliving components. These components are constantly interacting to form the environments in which organisms struggle to survive and reproduce.

3.1 What Is Ecology?

🔑 Ecology is the scientific study of interactions among organisms and between organisms and their physical environment.

🔑 The biological influences on organisms are called biotic factors.

🔑 Physical components of an ecosystem are called abiotic factors.

🔑 Modern ecologists use three methods in their work: observation, experimentation, and modeling. Each of these approaches relies on scientific methodology to guide inquiry.

biosphere (64)	ecosystem (65)
species (64)	biome (65)
population (64)	biotic factor (66)
community (64)	abiotic factor (66)
ecology (65)	

3.2 Energy, Producers, and Consumers

🔑 Primary producers are the first producers of energy-rich compounds that are later used by other organisms.

🔑 Organisms that rely on other organisms for energy and nutrients are called consumers.

autotroph (69)	carnivore (71)
primary producer (69)	herbivore (71)
photosynthesis (70)	scavenger (71)
chemosynthesis (70)	omnivore (71)
heterotroph (71)	decomposer (71)
consumer (71)	detritivore (71)

3.3 Energy Flow in Ecosystems

🔑 Energy flows through an ecosystem in a one-way stream, from primary producers to various consumers.

🔑 Pyramids of energy show the relative amount of energy available at each trophic level of a food chain or food web. A pyramid of biomass illustrates the relative amount of living organic matter available at each trophic level of an ecosystem. A pyramid of numbers shows the relative number of individual organisms at each trophic level in an ecosystem.

food chain (73)	trophic level (77)
phytoplankton (73)	ecological pyramid (77)
food web (74)	biomass (78)
zooplankton (76)	

3.4 Cycles of Matter

🔑 Unlike the one-way flow of energy, matter is recycled within and between ecosystems.

🔑 Water continuously moves between the oceans, the atmosphere, and land—sometimes outside living organisms and sometimes inside them.

🔑 Every organism needs nutrients to build tissues and carry out life functions. Like water, nutrients pass through organisms and the environment through biogeochemical cycles. The carbon, nitrogen, and phosphorus cycles are especially critical for life.

🔑 If ample sunlight and water are available, the primary productivity of an ecosystem may be limited by the availability of nutrients.

biogeochemical cycle (79)	denitrification (84)
nutrient (82)	limiting nutrient (85)
nitrogen fixation (84)	

Think Visually Using information from this chapter, complete the following flowchart:

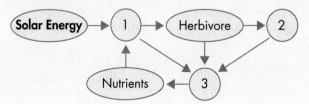

③ Assessment

3.1 What Is Ecology?

Understand Key Concepts

1. All of life on Earth exists in
   a. an ecosystem.   c. the biosphere.
   b. a biome.   d. ecology.

2. Which term describes a group of different species that live together in a defined area?
   a. a population   c. an ecosystem
   b. a community   d. a biosphere

3. Name the different levels of organization within the biosphere, from smallest to largest.

4. How do ecologists use modeling?

5. Give an example of how a biotic factor might influence the organisms in an ecosystem.

Think Critically

6. **Design an Experiment** Ecologists have discovered that the seeds of many plants that grow in forests cannot germinate unless they have been exposed to fire. Design an experiment to test whether a particular plant has seeds with this requirement. Include your hypothesis statement, a description of control and experimental groups, and an outline of your procedure.

7. **Pose Questions** You live near a pond that you have observed for years. One year you notice the water is choked with a massive overgrowth of green algae. What are some of the questions you might have about this unusual growth?

3.2 Energy, Producers, and Consumers

Understand Key Concepts

8. Primary producers are organisms that
   a. rely on other organisms for their energy and food supply.
   b. consume plant and animal remains and other dead matter.
   c. use energy they take in from the environment to convert inorganic molecules into complex organic molecules.
   d. obtain energy by eating only plants.

9. Which of the following organisms is a decomposer?

a.   c.

b.   d.

10. Which of the following describes how ALL consumers get their energy?
    a. directly from the sun
    b. from eating primary producers
    c. from inorganic chemicals like hydrogen sulfide
    d. from eating organisms that are living or were once living

11. What is chemosynthesis?

Think Critically

12. **Classify** Classify each of the following as an herbivore, a carnivore, an omnivore, or a detritivore: earthworm, bear, cow, snail, owl, human.

13. **Form a Hypothesis** People who explore caves where there is running water but no sunlight often find them populated with unique types of fishes and insects. What hypothesis can you make to explain the ultimate source of energy for these organisms?

3.3 Energy Flow in Ecosystems

Understand Key Concepts

14. The series of steps in which a large fish eats a small fish that has eaten algae is a
    a. food web.   c. pyramid of numbers.
    b. food chain.   d. pyramid of biomass.

15. The total amount of living tissue at each trophic level in an ecosystem can be shown in a(n)
    a. energy pyramid.   c. biomass pyramid.
    b. pyramid of numbers.   d. biogeochemical cycle.

Think Critically

16. Which group of organisms is always found at the base of a food chain or food web?

17. **Apply Concepts** Why is the transfer of energy in a food chain usually only about 10 percent efficient?

18. **Use Models** Describe a food chain of which you are a member. You may draw or use words to describe the chain.

19. **Use Models** Create flowcharts that show four different food chains in the food web shown below.

3.4 Cycles of Matter

Understand Key Concepts

20. Nutrients move through an ecosystem in
   a. biogeochemical cycles.
   b. water cycles.
   c. energy pyramids.
   d. ecological pyramids.

21. Which biogeochemical cycle does NOT include a major path in which the substance cycles through the atmosphere?
   a. water cycle   **c.** nitrogen cycle
   b. carbon cycle   **d.** phosphorus cycle

22. List two ways in which water enters the atmosphere in the water cycle.

23. Explain the process of nitrogen fixation.

24. What is meant by "nutrient limitation"?

solve the CHAPTER MYSTERY

CHANGES IN THE BAY

According to one hypothesis, rising water temperatures have caused most of the changes reported in Narragansett Bay. The bay's temperature has risen more than 1.5°C (3°F) since 1960. This warmth encourages bluefish to stay in the bay later in the fall. It also allows predatory warm-water shrimp to remain in the bay all winter, feeding on baby flounder. Warmer water also enables zooplankton to graze heavily on marine algae. This eliminates the late-winter algal bloom whose primary production used to provide organic carbon to the entire food web.

Those food web changes, in turn, seem to be driving unexpected shifts in the activities of bacteria that transform nitrogen. When the spring bloom provided organic carbon, bacteria denitrified the water, releasing nitrogen into the atmosphere. Now, the bacterial community has changed and actually fixes nitrogen, bringing more of it into the water. It is still not clear what this change means for the long-term health of the bay and adjacent coastal waters.

1. **Compare and Contrast** Compare the original situation in the bay with the current situation, taking note of changes in both the food web and the nitrogen cycle.

2. **Infer** Narragansett Bay harbors sea jellies that prefer warm water and have previously been present only in summer and early fall. These sea jellies eat fish eggs, fish larvae, and zooplankton. If the bay continues to warm, what do you think might happen to the population of sea jellies in the bay? What might that mean for the organisms the jellies feed on?

3. **Connect to the** Big idea Explain how the Narragansett Bay example demonstrates interconnections among members of a food web and abiotic environmental factors. Can you find similar studies in other aquatic habitats, such as Chesapeake Bay, the Everglades, or the Mississippi River delta? Explain.

Think Critically

25. Form a Hypothesis Ecologists discovered that trout were dying in a stream that ran through some farmland where nitrogen fertilizer was used on the crops. How might you explain what happened?

26. Apply Concepts Using a flowchart, trace the flow of energy in a simple marine food chain. Then, show where nitrogen is cycled through the chain when the top-level carnivore dies and is decomposed.

Connecting Concepts

Use Science Graphics

The graph below shows the effect of annual rainfall on the rate of primary productivity in an ecosystem. Use the graph to answer questions 27–29.

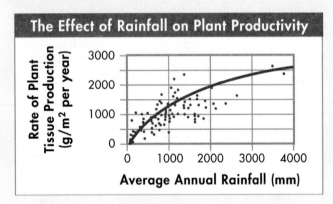

The Effect of Rainfall on Plant Productivity

Rate of Plant Tissue Production (g/m² per year) vs. Average Annual Rainfall (mm)

27. Interpret Graphs What happens to productivity as rainfall increases?

28. Predict What do you think the graph would look like if the *x*-axis were extended out to 6000 mm? Represent your prediction in a graph and explain your answer.

29. Apply Concepts What factors other than water might affect primary productivity?

Write About Science

30. Explanation Write a paragraph that (1) names and defines the levels of organization that an ecologist studies; (2) identifies the level that you would choose to study if you were an ecologist; (3) describes the method or methods you would use to study this level; and (4) gives a reason for your choice of method or methods.

31. Description Describe how biogeochemical cycles provide organisms with the raw materials necessary to synthesize complex organic compounds. Refer back to Chapter 2 for help in answering this question.

32. Assess the Big idea Explain how an element like carbon can be included in both the biotic and abiotic factors of an ecosystem.

Analyzing Data

Samples of ocean water are taken at different depths, and the amount of oxygen in the water at each depth is measured. The results are shown in the table.

Concentration of Oxygen

Depth of Sample (m)	Oxygen Concentration (ppm)
0	7.5
50	7.4
100	7.4
150	4.5
200	3.2
250	3.1
300	2.9

33. Interpret Tables Which of the following is the best description of what happens to the amount of available oxygen as you get deeper in the ocean?
  a. Available oxygen decreases at a constant rate.
  b. Available oxygen increases at a constant rate.
  c. Available oxygen remains steady until about 100 m, then drops rapidly.
  d. Oxygen is available at all ocean depths.

34. Draw Conclusions Light can penetrate to only a depth of between 50 and 100 m in most ocean water. What effect does this have on the water's oxygen concentration? Explain.

Standardized Test Prep

Multiple Choice

1. A group of individuals that belong to a single species and that live together in a defined area is termed a(n)
   A population.   C community.
   B ecosystem.   D biome.

2. Which of the following is NOT true about matter in the biosphere?
   A Matter is recycled in the biosphere.
   B Biogeochemical cycles transform and reuse molecules.
   C The total amount of matter decreases over time.
   D Water and nutrients pass between organisms and the environment.

3. Which is a source of energy for Earth's living things?
   A wind energy only
   B sunlight only
   C wind energy and sunlight
   D sunlight and chemical energy

4. Which of the following is a primary producer?
   A a producer, like algae
   B a carnivore, like a lion
   C an omnivore, like a human
   D a detritivore, like an earthworm

5. Human activities, such as the burning of fossil fuels, move carbon through the carbon cycle. Which other processes also participate in the carbon cycle?
   A biological processes only
   B geochemical processes only
   C chemical processes only
   D a combination of biological, geological, and chemical processes

6. What are the physical, or nonliving components of an ecosystem called?
   A abiotic factors
   B temperate conditions
   C biotic factors
   D antibiotic factors

Questions 7–8

The diagrams below represent the amount of biomass and the numbers of organisms in an ecosystem.

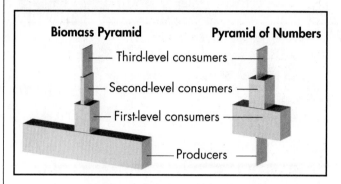

7. What can you conclude about the ecosystem from the pyramid of numbers shown?
   A There are more first-level consumers than producers.
   B There are more third-level consumers than second-level consumers.
   C There are more producers than first-level consumers.
   D There are more second-level consumers than first-level consumers.

8. What can you conclude about the producers in the ecosystem based on the two pyramids shown?
   A The producers in the ecosystem are probably very small organisms.
   B There are no producers in the ecosystem.
   C The producers in the ecosystem are probably large organisms.
   D Decomposers in the ecosystem outnumber the producers in the ecosystem.

Open-Ended Response

9. What ultimately happens to the bulk of matter in any trophic level of a biomass pyramid—that is, the matter that does not get passed to the trophic level above?

If You Have Trouble With . . .

Question	1	2	3	4	5	6	7	8	9
See Lesson	3.1	3.4	3.2	3.2	3.4	3.1	3.3	3.3	3.3

4 Ecosystems and Communities

 **Interdependence in Nature**

Q: How do abiotic and biotic factors shape ecosystems?

Cheetah looking out across the savanna at the Masai Mara National Reserve in Kenya

INSIDE:

- 4.1 Climate
- 4.2 Niches and Community Interactions
- 4.3 Succession
- 4.4 Biomes
- 4.5 Aquatic Ecosystems

CHAPTER
MYSTERY

THE WOLF EFFECT

During the 1920s, hunting and trapping eliminated wolves from Yellowstone National Park. For decades, ecologists hypothesized that the loss of wolves—important predators of elk and other large grazing animals—had changed the park ecosystem. But because there were no before-and-after data, it was impossible to test that hypothesis directly.

Then, in the mid-1990s, wolves were reintroduced to Yellowstone. Researchers watched park ecosystems carefully and sure enough, the number of elk in parts of the park began to fall just as predicted. But, unpredictably, forest and stream communities have changed, too. Could a "wolf effect" be affecting organisms in the park's woods and streams?

As you read this chapter, look for connections among Yellowstone's organisms and their environment. Then, solve the mystery.

Never Stop Exploring Your World.
The mystery of the Yellowstone wolves is just the beginning. Take a video field trip with the ecogeeks of Untamed Science to see where this mystery leads.

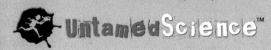

4.1 Climate

Key Questions

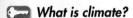 **What is climate?**

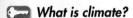 **What factors determine global climate?**

Vocabulary

weather
climate
microclimate
greenhouse effect

Taking Notes

Preview Visuals Before you read, look at **Figure 4–2.** What questions do you have about this diagram? Write a prediction that relates this figure to climate.

BUILD Vocabulary

PREFIXES The prefix *hemi-* in *hemisphere* means "half." The Northern Hemisphere encompasses the northern half of Earth.

THINK ABOUT IT When you think about climate, you might think of dramatic headlines: "Hurricane Katrina floods New Orleans!" or "Drought parches the Southeast!" But big storms and seasonal droughts are better described as *weather* rather than *climate*. So, what *is* climate, and how does it differ from weather? How do climate and weather affect organisms and ecosystems?

Weather and Climate

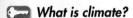 **What is climate?**

Weather and climate both involve variations in temperature, precipitation, and other environmental factors. **Weather** is the day-to-day condition of Earth's atmosphere. Weather where you live may be clear and sunny one day but rainy and cold the next. **Climate,** on the other hand, refers to average conditions over long periods. **A region's climate is defined by year-after-year patterns of temperature and precipitation.**

It is important to note that climate is rarely uniform even within a region. Environmental conditions can vary over small distances, creating **microclimates.** For example, in the Northern Hemisphere, south-facing sides of trees and buildings receive more sunlight, and are often warmer and drier, than north-facing sides. We may not notice these differences, but they can be very important to many organisms.

Factors That Affect Climate

 What factors determine global climate?

A person living in Orlando, Florida, may wear shorts and a T-shirt in December, while someone in Minneapolis, Minnesota, is still wearing a heavy coat in April. It rarely rains in Phoenix, Arizona, but it rains often in Mobile, Alabama. Clearly, these places all have different climates—but why? What causes differences in climate? **Global climate is shaped by many factors, including solar energy trapped in the biosphere, latitude, and the transport of heat by winds and ocean currents.**

In Your Notebook *Describe the climate where you live. What factors influence it?*

Solar Energy and the Greenhouse Effect The main force that shapes our climate is solar energy that arrives as sunlight and strikes Earth's surface. Some of that energy is reflected back into space, and some is absorbed and converted into heat. Some of that heat, in turn, radiates back into space, and some is trapped in the biosphere. The balance between heat that stays in the biosphere and heat lost to space determines Earth's average temperature. This balance is largely controlled by concentrations of three gases found in the atmosphere—carbon dioxide, methane, and water vapor.

As shown in **Figure 4–1**, these gases, called greenhouse gases, function like glass in a greenhouse, allowing visible light to enter but trapping heat. This phenomenon is called the **greenhouse effect.** If greenhouse gas concentrations rise, they trap more heat, so Earth warms. If their concentrations fall, more heat escapes, and Earth cools. Without the greenhouse effect, Earth would be about 30° Celsius cooler than it is today. Note that all three of these gases pass in and out of the atmosphere as part of nutrient cycles.

Latitude and Solar Energy Near the equator, solar energy is intense as the sun is almost directly overhead at noon all year. That's why equatorial regions are generally so warm. As **Figure 4–2** shows, the curvature of Earth causes the same amount of solar energy to spread out over a much larger area near the poles than near the equator. Thus, Earth's polar areas annually receive less intense solar energy, and therefore heat, from the sun. This difference in heat distribution creates three different climate zones: tropical, temperate, and polar.

The tropical zone, or tropics, which includes the equator, is located between 23.5° north and 23.5° south latitudes. This zone receives nearly direct sunlight all year. On either side of the tropical zone are the two temperate zones, between 23.5° and 66.5° north and south latitudes. Beyond the temperate zones are the polar zones, between 66.5° and 90° north and south latitudes. Temperate and polar zones receive very different amounts of solar energy at different times of the year because Earth's axis is tilted. As Earth revolves around the sun, solar radiation strikes different regions at angles that vary from summer to winter. During winter in the temperate and polar zones, the sun is much lower in the sky, days are shorter, and solar energy is less intense.

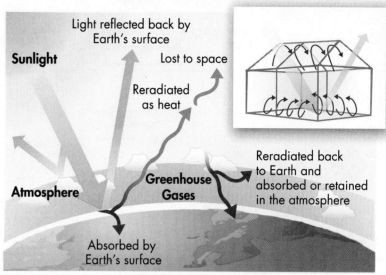

Light reflected back by Earth's surface

Sunlight

Lost to space

Reradiated as heat

Atmosphere

Greenhouse Gases

Reradiated back to Earth and absorbed or retained in the atmosphere

Absorbed by Earth's surface

THE GREENHOUSE EFFECT

FIGURE 4–1 Greenhouse gases in the atmosphere allow solar radiation to enter the biosphere but slow down the loss of reradiated heat to space. **Use Analogies** *What part of a greenhouse is analogous to the greenhouse gases in Earth's atmosphere?*

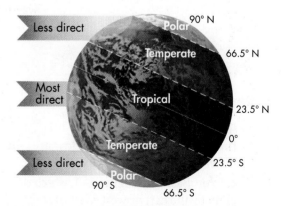

Less direct   90° N
Polar
Temperate   66.5° N
Most direct
Tropical   23.5° N
0°
Temperate   23.5° S
Less direct
Polar   66.5° S
90° S

FIGURE 4–2 Climate Zones Earth's climate zones are produced by unequal distribution of the sun's heat on Earth's surface. Polar regions receive less solar energy per unit area, and so less heat, than tropical regions do. The tilt of Earth's axis causes the distribution of sunlight to change over the course of the year.

66.5° N
23.5° N
0°
23.5° S
66.5° S

← Cold surface currents
← Warm surface currents
← Deep currents

Equator

← Polar easterlies
← Westerlies
← Northeast trade winds
← Southeast trade winds

FIGURE 4–3 Winds and Currents
Earth's winds (above left) and ocean currents (above right) interact to help produce climate patterns. The paths of winds and currents are the result of heating and cooling, Earth's rotation, and geographic features.
Interpret Visuals *In what direction do cold currents in the Northern Hemisphere generally move?*

Heat Transport in the Biosphere The unequal distribution of heat across the globe creates wind and ocean currents, which transport heat and moisture. Earth has winds because warm air is less dense and rises, and cool air is more dense and sinks. For this reason, air that is heated by a warm area of Earth's surface—such as air near the equator, for example—rises. As this warm air rises, it expands and spreads north and south, losing heat along the way. As it cools, the air sinks. At the same time, in cooler regions, near the poles, chilled air sinks toward Earth's surface, pushing air at the surface outward. This air warms as it travels over the surface. And as the air warms, it rises. These upward and downward movements of air create winds, as shown in **Figure 4–3** (above left). Winds transport heat from regions of rising warmer air to regions of sinking cooler air. Earth's rotation causes winds to blow generally from west to east over the temperate zones and from east to west over the tropics and the poles.

Similar patterns of heating and cooling occur in the oceans. Surface water is pushed by winds. These ocean currents transport enormous amounts of heat. Warm surface currents add moisture and heat to air that passes over them. Cool surface currents cool air that passes over them. In this way, surface currents affect the weather and climate of nearby landmasses. Deep ocean currents are caused by cold water near the poles sinking and flowing along the ocean floor. This water rises in warmer regions through a process called upwelling.

4.1 Assessment

Review Key Concepts 🔑

1. a. Review What is climate?

b. Compare and Contrast How are climate and weather different?

c. Infer Based on **Figure 4–3**, which do you think has a cooler climate: the east or west coast of southern Africa? Why?

2. a. Review What are the main factors that determine climate?

b. Relate Cause and Effect Explain what would likely happen to global climate if there was a dramatic decrease in greenhouse gases trapped in the atmosphere.

ANALYZING DATA

3. Research average monthly precipitation (in mm) and temperature (in °C) for Quito, Ecuador, a city on the equator. Create a bar graph for the precipitation data. Plot the temperature data in a line graph.

4.2 Niches and Community Interactions

THINK ABOUT IT If you ask someone where an organism lives, that person might answer "on a coral reef" or "in the desert." These answers are like saying that a person lives "in Miami" or "in Arizona." The answer gives the environment or location. But ecologists need more information to understand fully why an organism lives where it does and how it fits into its surroundings. What else do they need to know?

The Niche

🔑 What is a niche?

Organisms occupy different places in part because each species has a range of conditions under which it can grow and reproduce. These conditions help define where and how an organism lives.

Tolerance Every species has its own range of **tolerance,** the ability to survive and reproduce under a range of environmental circumstances, as shown in **Figure 4–4.** When an environmental condition, such as temperature, extends in either direction beyond an organism's optimum range, the organism experiences stress. Why? Because it must expend more energy to maintain homeostasis, and so has less energy left for growth and reproduction. Organisms have an upper and lower limit of tolerance for every environmental factor. Beyond those limits, the organism cannot survive. A species' tolerance for environmental conditions, then, helps determine its "address" or **habitat**—the general place where an organism lives.

Key Questions

🔑 What is a niche?

🔑 How does competition shape communities?

🔑 How do predation and herbivory shape communities?

🔑 What are the three primary ways that organisms depend on each other?

Vocabulary

tolerance • habitat • niche • resource • competitive exclusion principle • predation • herbivory • keystone species • symbiosis • mutualism • parasitism • commensalism

Taking Notes

Concept Map Use the highlighted vocabulary words to create a concept map that organizes the information in this lesson.

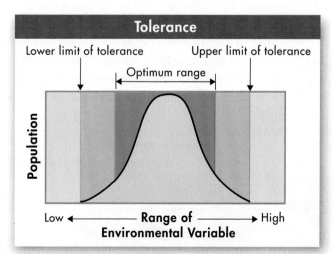

Tolerance

Lower limit of tolerance   Upper limit of tolerance

Optimum range

Population

Low ← **Range of** → High
Environmental Variable

FIGURE 4–4 Tolerance
This graph shows the response of a hypothetical organism to different values of a single environmental variable such as sunlight or temperature. At the center of the optimum range, organisms are likely to be most abundant. They become more rare in zones of physiological stress (medium blue), and are absent from zones of intolerance (light blue).

Defining the Niche Describing a species' "address" tells only part of its story. Ecologists also study a species' ecological "occupation"—where and how it "makes a living." This idea of occupation is encompassed in the idea of an organism's niche (nich). A **niche** describes not only what an organism does, but also how it interacts with biotic and abiotic factors in the environment. 🗝 **A niche is the range of physical and biological conditions in which a species lives and the way the species obtains what it needs to survive and reproduce.** Understanding niches is important to understanding how organisms interact to form a community.

▶ *Resources and the Niche* The term **resource** can refer to any necessity of life, such as water, nutrients, light, food, or space. For plants, resources can include sunlight, water, and soil nutrients—all of which are essential to survival. For animals, resources can include nesting space, shelter, types of food, and places to feed.

▶ *Physical Aspects of the Niche* Part of an organism's niche involves the abiotic factors it requires for survival. Most amphibians, for example, lose and absorb water through their skin, so they must live in moist places. If an area is too hot and dry, or too cold for too long, most amphibians cannot survive.

▶ *Biological Aspects of the Niche* Biological aspects of an organism's niche involve the biotic factors it requires for survival. When and how it reproduces, the food it eats, and the way in which it obtains that food are all examples of biological aspects of an organism's niche. Birds on Christmas Island, a small island in the Indian Ocean, for example, all live in the same habitat but they prey on fish of different sizes and feed in different places. Thus, each species occupies a distinct niche.

FIGURE 4–5 Competition Animals such as these two male stag beetles compete for limited resources. **Infer** *What resource do you think these two males are fighting over?*

Competition

🗝 *How does competition shape communities?*

If you look at any community, you will probably find more than one kind of organism attempting to use various essential resources. When organisms attempt to use the same limited ecological resource in the same place at the same time, competition occurs. In a forest, for example, plant roots compete for water and nutrients in the soil. Animals, such as the beetles in **Figure 4–5,** compete for resources such as food, mates, and places to live and raise their young. Competition can occur both among members of the same species (known as intraspecific competition) and between members of different species (known as interspecific competition).

In Your Notebook *Look at the beetles in **Figure 4–5.** Is this an example of intraspecific or interspecific competition? How do you know?*

The Competitive Exclusion Principle Direct competition between different species almost always produces a winner and a loser—and the losing species dies out. One series of experiments demonstrated this using two species of single-celled organisms. When the species were grown in separate cultures under the same conditions, each survived, as shown in **Figure 4–6.** But when both species were grown together in the same culture, one species outcompeted the other. The less competitive species did not survive.

Experiments like this one, along with observations in nature, led to the discovery of an important ecological rule. The **competitive exclusion principle** states that no two species can occupy exactly the same niche in exactly the same habitat at exactly the same time. If two species attempt to occupy the same niche, one species will be better at competing for limited resources and will eventually exclude the other species. As a result, if we look at natural communities, we rarely find species whose niches overlap significantly.

Dividing Resources Instead of competing for similar resources, species usually divide them. For instance, the three species of North American warblers shown in **Figure 4–7** all live in the same trees and feed on insects. But one species feeds on high branches, another feeds on low branches, and another feeds in the middle. The resources utilized by these species are similar yet different. Therefore, each species has its own niche. This division of resources was likely brought about by past competition among the birds. ⊙━ **By causing species to divide resources, competition helps determine the number and kinds of species in a community and the niche each species occupies.**

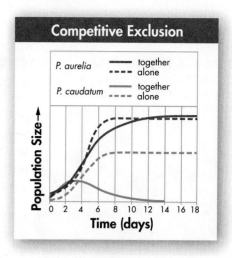

FIGURE 4–6 Competitive Exclusion
The two species of paramecia *P. aurelia* and *P. caudatum* have similar requirements. When grown in cultures separately (dashed lines), both populations grow quickly and then level off. When grown together under certain conditions (solid lines), however, *P. aurelia* outcompetes *P. caudatum* and drives it to extinction.

FIGURE 4–7 Resource Sharing
Each of these warbler species has a different niche in its spruce tree habitat. By feeding in different areas of the tree, the birds avoid competing directly with one another for food. *Infer What would happen if two of the warbler species tried to occupy the same niche in the same tree at the same time?*

Spruce Tree

Cape May Warbler

Bay-Breasted Warbler

Yellow-Rumped Warbler

FIGURE 4–8 Herbivory The ring-tailed lemur is an herbivore—meaning that it obtains its energy and nutrients from plants like the cactus it's eating here.

Predation, Herbivory, and Keystone Species

How do predation and herbivory shape communities?

Virtually all animals, because they are not primary producers, must eat other organisms to obtain energy and nutrients. Yet if a group of animals devours all available food in the area, they will no longer have anything to eat! That's why predator-prey and herbivore-plant interactions are very important in shaping communities.

Predator-Prey Relationships An interaction in which one animal (the predator) captures and feeds on another animal (the prey) is called **predation** (pree DAY shun). **Predators can affect the size of prey populations in a community and determine the places prey can live and feed.** Birds of prey, for example, can play an important role in regulating the population sizes of mice, voles, and other small mammals.

Herbivore-Plant Relationships Interactions between herbivores and plants, like the one shown in **Figure 4–8,** are as important as interactions between predators and prey. An interaction in which one animal (the herbivore) feeds on producers (such as plants) is called **herbivory.** **Herbivores can affect both the size and distribution of plant populations in a community and determine the places that certain plants can survive and grow.** Herbivores ranging from caterpillars to elk can have major effects on plant survival. For example, very dense populations of white-tailed deer are eliminating their favorite food plants from many places across the United States.

Analyzing Data

Predator-Prey Dynamics

The relationships between predator and prey are often tightly intertwined, particularly in an environment in which each prey has a single predator and vice versa. The graph here shows an idealized computer model of changes in predator and prey populations over time.

1. Predict Suppose a bacterial infection kills off most of the prey at point B on the graph. How would this affect the predator and prey growth curves at point C? At point D?

2. Predict Suppose a sudden extended cold spell destroys almost the entire predator population at point F on the graph. How would the next cycle of the prey population appear on the graph?

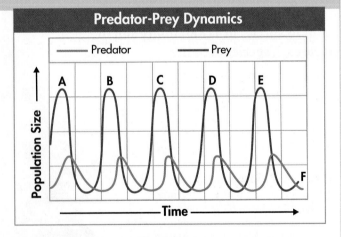

Predator-Prey Dynamics

Predator — Prey —

Population Size ↑

A   B   C   D   E

F

Time →

3. Relate Cause and Effect Suppose a viral infection kills all the prey at point D on the graph. What effect would this have on the predator and prey growth curves at point E? What will happen in future years to the predator population? How could ecologists ensure the continued survival of the predators in this ecosystem?

Keystone Species Sometimes changes in the population of a single species, often called a **keystone species,** can cause dramatic changes in the structure of a community. In the cold waters off the Pacific coast of North America, for example, sea otters devour large quantities of sea urchins. Urchins, in turn, are herbivores. Their favorite food is kelp, giant algae that grow in undersea "forests."

A century ago, sea otters were nearly eliminated by hunting. Unexpectedly, the kelp forest nearly vanished. What happened? Without otters as predators, the sea urchin population skyrocketed. Armies of urchins devoured kelp down to bare rock. Without kelp to provide habitat, many other animals, including seabirds, disappeared. Clearly, otters were a keystone species in this community. After otters were protected as an endangered species, their population began to recover. As otters returned, the urchin populations dropped, and kelp forests began to thrive again. Recently, however, the otter population has been falling again, and no one knows why.

> **In Your Notebook** *Not all keystone-species effects are due to predation. Describe the dramatic effects that the dam-building activities of beavers, a keystone species, might have on other types of organisms.*

MYSTERY CLUE

One of the favorite prey species of the wolves in Yellowstone is elk. How do you think this relationship could affect the ability of certain *plants* to grow in Yellowstone?

Symbioses

🔑 **What are the three primary ways that organisms depend on each other?**

Any relationship in which two species live closely together is called **symbiosis** (sim by OH sis), which means "living together." 🔑 **Biologists recognize three main classes of symbiotic relationships in nature: mutualism, parasitism, and commensalism.**

Mutualism The sea anemone's sting has two functions: to capture prey and to protect the anemone from predators. Even so, certain fish manage to snack on anemone tentacles. The clownfish, however, is immune to anemone stings. When threatened by a predator, clownfish seek shelter by snuggling deep into tentacles that would be deadly to most other fish, as seen in **Figure 4–9.** But if an anemone-eating species tries to attack their living home, the spunky clownfish dart out and fiercely chase away fish many times their size. This kind of relationship between species in which both benefit is known as **mutualism.**

FIGURE 4–9 Mutualism Clownfish live among the sea anemone's tentacles and protect the sea anemone by chasing away would-be attackers. The sea anemone, in turn, protects the clownfish from their predators. **Infer** *What could happen to the sea anemone if the clownfish died?*

FIGURE 4–10 Parasitism
This brown leech is feeding on the blood of its host, a human. In a parasitic relationship, the parasite benefits while the host is harmed.

Parasitism Tapeworms live in the intestines of mammals, where they absorb large amounts of their hosts' food. Fleas, ticks, lice, and leeches live on the bodies of mammals, feeding on their blood and skin, as seen in **Figure 4–10.** These are examples of **parasitism** (PAR uh sit iz um), relationships in which one organism lives inside or on another organism and harms it. The parasite obtains all or part of its nutritional needs from the host organism. Generally, parasites weaken but do not kill their host, which is usually larger than the parasite.

Commensalism Small marine animals called barnacles often attach themselves to a whale's skin, as seen in **Figure 4–11.** The barnacles perform no known service to the whale, nor do they harm it. Yet the barnacles benefit from the constant movement of water—that is full of food particles—past the swimming whale. This is an example of **commensalism** (kuh MEN sul iz um), a relationship in which one organism benefits and the other is neither helped nor harmed.

FIGURE 4–11 Commensalism
The barnacles attached to the skin of this grey whale are feeding on food in the water that passes over them as the whale swims. Although the barnacles clearly benefit from their relationship with the whale, they do not appear to affect the whale positively or negatively.

4.2 Assessment

Review Key Concepts 🔑

1. a. Review What is the difference between a habitat and a niche?

b. Use Analogies How is a niche like a profession? In ecological terms, describe your niche.

2. a. Review What is competition? Why can't two organisms compete if they live in different habitats?

b. Interpret Visuals Look at **Figure 4–7** and describe how the three species of warblers have divided their resources. Does each warbler have its own niche?

3. a. Review What is a keystone species?

b. Infer How might a dramatic decrease in vegetation lead to a decrease in a prey species? (*Hint:* Think of how the vegetation, prey, and predator could be connected in a food chain.)

4. a. Review What is symbiosis? What are the three major types of symbiosis?

b. Explain Bacteria living in a cow's stomach help the cow break down the cellulose in grass, gaining nutrients in the process. Is this an example of commensalism or mutualism? Explain your answer.

c. Apply Concepts What is the difference between a predator and a parasite? Explain your answer.

BUILD VOCABULARY

5. The suffix *-ism* means "the act, practice, or result of." Look up the meaning of *mutual*, and write a definition for *mutualism*.

Do you enjoy being outdoors? If you do, you might want to consider one of these careers.

MARINE BIOLOGIST

Ocean ecosystems cover over 70 percent of Earth's surface. Marine biologists study the incredible diversity of ocean life. Some marine biologists study organisms found in deep ocean trenches to understand how they survive in extreme conditions. Others work in aquariums, where they might conduct research, educate the public, or rehabilitate rescued marine wildlife.

PARK RANGER

For some people, camping and hiking aren't just recreational activities—they're work. Park rangers work in national, state, and local parks caring for the land and ensuring the safety of visitors. Park rangers perform a variety of tasks, including maintaining campsites and helping with search and rescue. Rangers are also responsible for looking after park wildlife.

WILDLIFE PHOTOGRAPHER

Wildlife photographers capture nature "in action." Their photographs can be used in books, magazines, and on the Internet to educate and entertain the public. Successful wildlife photographers need to be observant and adventurous. They also need to be patient enough to wait for the perfect shot.

CAREER CLOSE-UP

Dudley Edmondson, Wildlife Photographer

Dudley Edmondson began bird-watching at a young age. After high school, he began traveling and photographing the birds he observed. Mr. Edmondson has since been all over the United States taking pictures of everything from the landscapes and grizzly bears of Yellowstone Park to the butterflies that inhabit his own backyard. Through his work, he hopes to inspire people to travel and experience nature for themselves. This, he believes, will encourage a sense of responsibility to protect and preserve the environment.

> **What I like most about my work is the unique perspective it gives me on the world. Birds, insects, and plants are totally unaware of things like clocks, deadlines, and technology. When you work with living things, you work on their terms.**

WRITING Where have you seen nature photography used or displayed? How do those photos, or Mr. Edmondson's, help the public learn about the natural world?

4.3 Succession

Key Questions

🔑 How do communities change over time?

🔑 Do ecosystems return to "normal" following a disturbance?

Vocabulary
ecological succession
primary succession
pioneer species
secondary succession

Taking Notes

Compare/Contrast Table
As you read, create a table comparing primary and secondary succession.

FIGURE 4–12 Primary Succession
Primary succession occurs on newly exposed surfaces. In Glacier Bay, Alaska, a retreating glacier exposed barren rock. Over the course of more than 100 years, a series of changes has led to the hemlock and spruce forest currently found in the area. Changes in this community will continue for centuries.

THINK ABOUT IT In 1883, the volcanic island of Krakatau in the Indian Ocean was blown to pieces by an eruption. The tiny island that remained was completely barren. Within two years, grasses were growing. Fourteen years later, there were 49 plant species, along with lizards, birds, bats, and insects. By 1929, a forest containing 300 plant species had grown. Today, the island is blanketed by mature rain forest. How did the island ecosystem recover so quickly?

Primary and Secondary Succession

🔑 **How do communities change over time?**

The story of Krakatau after the eruption is an example of **ecological succession**—a series of more-or-less predictable changes that occur in a community over time. 🔑 **Ecosystems change over time, especially after disturbances, as some species die out and new species move in.** Over the course of succession, the number of different species present typically increases.

Primary Succession Volcanic explosions like the ones that destroyed Krakatau in 1883 and blew the top off Mount Saint Helens in Washington State in 1980 can create new land or sterilize existing areas. Retreating glaciers can have the same effect, leaving only exposed bare rock behind them. Succession that begins in an area with no remnants of an older community is called **primary succession.** An example of primary succession is shown in **Figure 4–12.**

——————————**Time**——————————▶

| 15 years | 35 years | 80 years | 115+ years |

The first species to colonize barren areas are called **pioneer species**—named after rugged human pioneers who first settled the wilderness. After pioneers created settlements, different kinds of people with varied skills and living requirements moved into the area. Pioneer species function in similar ways. One ecological pioneer that grows on bare rock is lichen—a mutualistic symbiosis between a fungus and an alga. Over time, lichens convert, or fix, atmospheric nitrogen into useful forms for other organisms, break down rock, and add organic material to form soil. Certain grasses, like those that colonized Krakatau early on, are also pioneer species.

Secondary Succession Sometimes, existing communities are not completely destroyed by disturbances. In these situations, where a disturbance affects the community without completely destroying it, **secondary succession** occurs. Secondary succession proceeds faster than primary succession, in part because soil survives the disturbance. As a result, new and surviving vegetation can regrow rapidly. Secondary succession often follows a wildfire, hurricane, or other natural disturbance. We think of these events as disasters, but many species are adapted to them. Although forest fires kill some trees, for example, other trees are spared, and fire can stimulate their seeds to germinate. Secondary succession can also follow human activities like logging and farming. An example of secondary succession is shown in **Figure 4–13.**

Why Succession Occurs Every organism changes the environment it lives in. One model of succession suggests that as one species alters its environment, other species find it easier to compete for resources and survive. As lichens add organic matter and form soil, for example, mosses and other plants can colonize and grow. As organic matter continues to accumulate, other species move in and change the environment further. For example, as trees grow, their branches and leaves produce shade and cooler temperatures nearer the ground. Over time, more and more species can find suitable niches and survive.

In Your Notebook *Summarize what happens in primary and secondary succession.*

BUILD Vocabulary
WORD ORIGINS The origin of the word *succession* is the Latin word *succedere,* meaning "to come after." **Ecological succession** involves changes that occur one after the other as species move into and out of a community.

FIGURE 4–13 Secondary Succession Secondary succession occurs in disturbed areas where remnants of previous ecosystems—soil and even plants—remain. This series shows changes taking place in abandoned fields of the Carolinas' Piedmont. Over the last century, these fields have passed through several stages and matured into oak forests. Changes will continue for years to come.

3 years   5 years   40+ years

Time

Successful Succession?

❶ Place a handful of dried plant material into a clean jar.

❷ Fill the jar with boiled pond water or sterile spring water. Determine the initial pH of the water with pH paper.

❸ Cover the jar and place it in an area that receives indirect light.

❹ Examine the jar every day for the next few days.

❺ When the water in the jar appears cloudy, prepare microscope slides of water from various levels of the jar. Use a pipette to collect the samples.

❻ Look at the slides under the low-power objective lens of a microscope and record your observations.

Analyze and Conclude

1. Infer Why did you use boiled or sterile water?

2. Infer Where did the organisms you saw come from?

3. Draw Conclusions Was ecological succession occurring? Give evidence to support your answer.

4. Evaluate and Revise Check your results against those of your classmates. Do they agree? How do you explain any differences?

Climax Communities

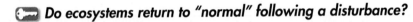

Do ecosystems return to "normal" following a disturbance?

Ecologists used to think that succession in a given area always proceeds through the same stages to produce a specific and stable climax community like the mature spruce and hemlock forest that is developing in Glacier Bay. Recent studies, however, have shown that succession doesn't always follow the same path, and that climax communities are not always uniform and stable.

Succession After Natural Disturbances Natural disturbances are common in many communities. Healthy coral reefs and tropical rain forests recover from storms, as shown in **Figure 4–14.** Healthy temperate forests and grasslands recover from wildfires. **Secondary succession in healthy ecosystems following natural disturbances often reproduces the original climax community.** But detailed studies show that some climax communities are not uniform. Often, they look more like patchwork quilts with areas in varying stages of secondary succession following multiple disturbances that took place at different times. Some climax communities are disturbed so often that they can't really be called stable.

FIGURE 4–14 Recovery From a Natural Disaster These photos show El Yunque Rain Forest in Puerto Rico, immediately following Tropical Storm Jeanne in September 2004, and then again in May, 2007.
Apply Concepts *What kind of succession occurred in this rain forest? How do you know?*

In Your Notebook *Describe what causes instability in some climax communities.*

Succession After Human-Caused Disturbances In North America, land cleared for farming and then abandoned often passes through succession that restores the original climax community. But this is not always the case. ⚷ **Ecosystems may or may not recover from extensive human-caused disturbances.** Clearing and farming of tropical rain forests, for example, can change the microclimate and soil enough to prevent regrowth of the original community.

Studying Patterns of Succession Ecologists, like the ones seen in **Figure 4–15,** study succession by comparing different cases and looking for similarities and differences. Researchers who swarmed over Mount Saint Helens as soon as it was safe might also have studied Krakatau, for example. In both places, primary succession proceeded through predictable stages. The first plants and animals that arrived had seeds, spores, or adult stages that traveled over long distances. Hardy pioneer species helped stabilize loose volcanic debris, enabling later species to take hold. Historical studies in Krakatau and ongoing studies on Mount Saint Helens confirm that early stages of primary succession are slow, and that chance can play a large role in determining which species colonize at different times.

FIGURE 4–15 Studying Succession
These Forest Service rangers are surveying some of the plants and animals that have returned to the area around Mount Saint Helens. The volcano erupted in 1980, leaving only barren land for miles.

4.3 Assessment

Review Key Concepts ⚷

1. a. Review What effects do pioneer species have on an environment undergoing primary succession?

b. Explain Why do communities change over time?

c. Apply Concepts When a whale or other large marine mammal dies and falls to the ocean floor, different waves of decomposers and scavengers feed off the carcass until nothing remains. Do you think this is an example of succession? Explain your reasoning.

2. a. Review What is a climax community?

b. Relate Cause and Effect What kinds of conditions might prevent a community from returning to its predisturbance state?

VISUAL THINKING

3. Look at the photo below. If you walked from this dune in a straight line away from the beach, what kinds of changes in vegetation would you expect to see? What sort of succession is this?

4.4 Biomes

Key Questions

🗝 **What abiotic and biotic factors characterize biomes?**

🗝 **What areas are not easily classified into a major biome?**

Vocabulary

canopy • understory • deciduous • coniferous • humus • taiga • permafrost

Taking Notes

Preview Visuals Before you read, preview **Figure 4–18.** Write down the names of the different biomes. As you read, examine the photographs and list the main characteristics of each biome.

FIGURE 4–16 The Effect of Coastal Mountains As moist ocean air rises over the upwind side of coastal mountains, it condenses, cools, and drops precipitation. As the air sinks on the downwind side of the mountain, it expands, warms, and absorbs moisture.

THINK ABOUT IT Why does the character of biological communities vary from one place to another? Why, for example, do temperate rain forests grow in the Pacific Northwest while areas to the east of the Rocky Mountains are much drier? How do similar conditions shape ecosystems elsewhere?

The Major Biomes

🗝 **What abiotic and biotic factors characterize biomes?**

In Lesson 1, you learned that latitude and the heat transported by winds are two factors that affect global climate. But Oregon, Montana, and Vermont have different climates and biological communities, even though those states are at similar latitudes and are all affected by prevailing winds that blow from west to east. Why? The reason is because other factors, among them an area's proximity to an ocean or mountain range, can influence climate.

Regional Climates Oregon, for example, borders the Pacific Ocean. Cold ocean currents that flow from north to south have the effect of making summers in the region cool relative to other places at the same latitude. Similarly, moist air carried by winds traveling west to east is pushed upward when it hits the Rocky Mountains. This air expands and cools, causing the moisture in the air to condense and form clouds. The clouds drop rain or snow, mainly on the upwind side of the mountains—the side that faces the winds, as seen in **Figure 4–16.** West and east Oregon, then, have very different regional climates, and different climates mean different plant and animal communities.

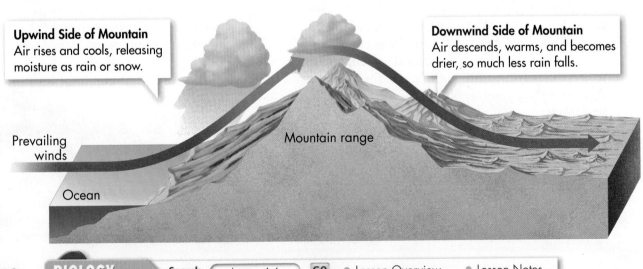

Upwind Side of Mountain
Air rises and cools, releasing moisture as rain or snow.

Downwind Side of Mountain
Air descends, warms, and becomes drier, so much less rain falls.

Prevailing winds

Mountain range

Ocean

Defining Biomes Ecologists classify Earth's terrestrial ecosystems into at least ten different groups of regional climate communities called biomes. 🔑 **Biomes are described in terms of abiotic factors like climate and soil type, and biotic factors like plant and animal life.** Major biomes include tropical rain forest, tropical dry forest, tropical grassland/savanna/shrubland, desert, temperate grassland, temperate woodland and shrubland, temperate forest, northwestern coniferous forest, boreal forest/taiga, and tundra. Each biome is associated with seasonal patterns of temperature and precipitation that can be summarized in a graph called a climate diagram, like the one in **Figure 4–17.** Organisms within each biome can be characterized by adaptations that enable them to live and reproduce successfully in the environment. The pages that follow discuss these adaptations and describe each biome's climate.

The distribution of major biomes is shown in **Figure 4–18.** Note that even within a defined biome, there is often considerable variation among plant and animal communities. These variations can be caused by differences in exposure, elevation, or local soil conditions. Local conditions also can change over time because of human activity or because of the community interactions described in this chapter and the next.

In Your Notebook *On the biome map in **Figure 4–18,** locate the place where you live. Which biome do you live in? Do your climate and environment seem to match the description of the biome on the following pages?*

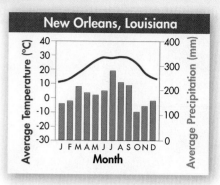

FIGURE 4–17 Climate Diagram
A climate diagram shows the average temperature and precipitation at a given location during each month of the year. In this graph, and those to follow, temperature is plotted as a red line, and precipitation is shown as vertical blue bars.

VISUAL SUMMARY

BIOMES

FIGURE 4–18 This map shows the locations of the world's major biomes. Each biome has a characteristic climate and community of organisms.

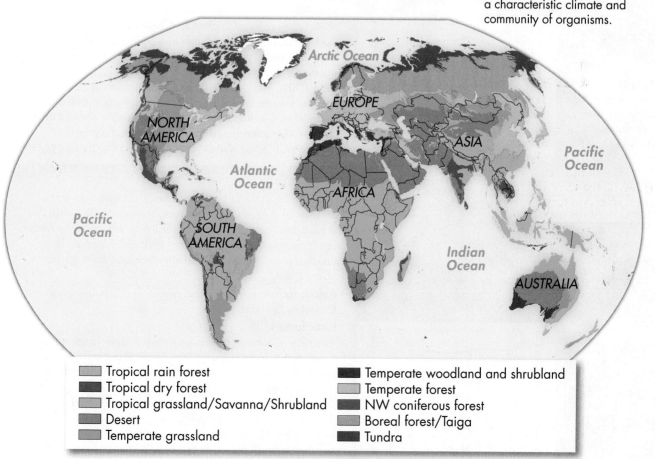

- Tropical rain forest
- Tropical dry forest
- Tropical grassland/Savanna/Shrubland
- Desert
- Temperate grassland
- Temperate woodland and shrubland
- Temperate forest
- NW coniferous forest
- Boreal forest/Taiga
- Tundra

TROPICAL RAIN FOREST

Tropical rain forests are home to more species than all other biomes combined. As the name suggests, rain forests get a lot of rain—at least 2 meters of it a year! Tall trees form a dense, leafy covering called a **canopy** from 50 to 80 meters above the forest floor. In the shade below the canopy, shorter trees and vines form a layer called the **understory.** Organic matter on the forest floor is recycled and reused so quickly that the soil in most tropical rain forests is not very rich in nutrients.

- **Abiotic factors** hot and wet year-round; thin, nutrient-poor soils subject to erosion
- **Biotic factors**
  Plant life: Understory plants compete for sunlight, so most have large leaves that maximize capture of limited light. Tall trees growing in poor shallow soil often have buttress roots for support. Epiphytic plants grow on the branches of tall plants as opposed to soil. This allows epiphytes to take advantage of available sunlight while obtaining nutrients through their host.
  Animal life: Animals are active all year. Many animals use camouflage to hide from predators; some can change color to match their surroundings. Animals that live in the canopy have adaptations for climbing, jumping, and/or flight.

Belem, Brazil

TROPICAL DRY FOREST

Tropical dry forests grow in areas where rainy seasons alternate with dry seasons. In most places, a period of rain is followed by a prolonged period of drought.

- **Abiotic factors** warm year-round; alternating wet and dry seasons; rich soils subject to erosion
- **Biotic factors**
  Plant life: Adaptations to survive the dry season include seasonal loss of leaves. A plant that sheds its leaves during a particular season is called **deciduous.** Some plants also have an extra thick waxy layer on their leaves to reduce water loss, or store water in their tissues.
  Animal life: Many animals reduce their need for water by entering long periods of inactivity called *estivation.* Estivation is similar to hibernation, but typically takes place during a dry season. Other animals, including many birds and primates, move to areas where water is available during the dry season.

Chennai, India

TROPICAL GRASSLAND/ SAVANNA/SHRUBLAND

This biome receives more seasonal rainfall than deserts but less than tropical dry forests. Grassy areas are spotted with isolated trees and small groves of trees and shrubs. Compacted soils, fairly frequent fires, and the action of large animals—for example, rhinoceroses and elephants—prevent some areas from turning into dry forest.

- **Abiotic factors** warm; seasonal rainfall; compact soils; frequent fires set by lightning
- **Biotic factors**
  Plant life: Plant adaptations are similar to those in the tropical dry forest, including waxy leaf coverings and seasonal leaf loss. Some grasses have a high silica content that makes them less appetizing to grazing herbivores. Also, unlike most plants, grasses grow from their bases, not their tips, so they can continue to grow after being grazed.
  Animal life: Many animals migrate during the dry season in search of water. Some smaller animals burrow and remain dormant during the dry season.

Mombasa, Kenya

DESERT

Deserts have less than 25 centimeters of precipitation annually, but otherwise vary greatly, depending on elevation and latitude. Many deserts undergo extreme daily temperature changes, alternating between hot and cold.

- **Abiotic factors** low precipitation; variable temperatures; soils rich in minerals but poor in organic material
- **Biotic factors**

 Plant life: Many plants, including cacti, store water in their tissues, and minimize leaf surface area to cut down on water loss. Cactus spines are actually modified leaves. Many desert plants employ special forms of photosynthesis that enable them to open their leaf pores only at night, allowing them to conserve moisture on hot, dry days.

 Animal life: Many desert animals get the water they need from the food they eat. To avoid the hottest parts of the day, many are nocturnal—active only at night. Large or elongated ears and other extremities are often supplied with many blood vessels close to the surface. These help the animal lose body heat and regulate body temperature.

Yuma, Arizona

TEMPERATE GRASSLAND

Plains and prairies, underlain by fertile soils, once covered vast areas of the midwestern and central United States. Periodic fires and heavy grazing by herbivores maintained plant communities dominated by grasses. Today, most have been converted for agriculture because their soil is so rich in nutrients and is ideal for growing crops.

- **Abiotic factors** warm to hot summers; cold winters; moderate seasonal precipitation; fertile soils; occasional fires
- **Biotic factors**

 Plant life: Grassland plants—especially grasses, which grow from their base—are resistant to grazing and fire. Dispersal of seeds by wind is common in this open environment. The root structure and growth habit of native grassland plants helps establish and retain deep, rich, fertile topsoil.

 Animal life: Because temperate grasslands are such open, exposed environments, predation is a constant threat for smaller animals. Camouflage and burrowing are two common protective adaptations.

Dallas, Texas

TEMPERATE WOODLAND AND SHRUBLAND

In open woodlands, large areas of grasses and wildflowers such as poppies are interspersed with oak and other trees. Communities that are more shrubland than forest are known as chaparral. Dense low plants that contain flammable oils make fire a constant threat.

- **Abiotic factors** hot dry summers; cool moist winters; thin, nutrient-poor soils; periodic fires
- **Biotic factors**

 Plant life: Plants in this biome have adapted to drought. Woody chaparral plants have tough waxy leaves that resist water loss. Fire resistance is also important, although the seeds of some plants need fire to germinate.

 Animal life: Animals tend to be browsers—meaning they eat varied diets of grasses, leaves, shrubs, and other vegetation. In exposed shrubland, camouflage is common.

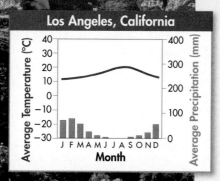

Los Angeles, California

TEMPERATE FOREST

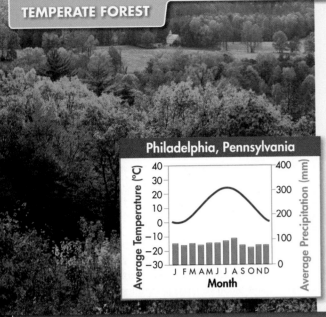

Philadelphia, Pennsylvania

Temperate forests are mostly made up of deciduous and evergreen coniferous (koh NIF ur us) trees. **Coniferous** trees, or conifers, produce seed-bearing cones, and most have leaves shaped like needles, which are coated in a waxy substance that helps reduce water loss. These forests have cold winters. In autumn, deciduous trees shed their leaves. In the spring, small plants burst from the ground and flower. Fertile soils are often rich in **humus,** a material formed from decaying leaves and other organic matter.

- **Abiotic factors** cold to moderate winters; warm summers; year-round precipitation; fertile soils
- **Biotic factors**

  Plant life: Deciduous trees drop their leaves and go into a state of dormancy in winter. Conifers have needlelike leaves that minimize water loss in dry winter air.

  Animal life: Animals must cope with changing weather. Some hibernate; others migrate to warmer climates. Animals that do not hibernate or migrate may be camouflaged to escape predation in the winter when bare trees leave them more exposed.

NORTHWESTERN CONIFEROUS FOREST

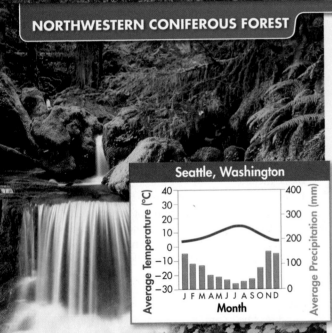

Seattle, Washington

Mild moist air from the Pacific Ocean influenced by the Rocky Mountains provides abundant rainfall to this biome. The forest includes a variety of conifers, from giant redwoods to spruce, fir, and hemlock, along with flowering trees and shrubs such as dogwood and rhododendron. Moss often covers tree trunks and the forest floor. Because of its lush vegetation, the northwestern coniferous forest is sometimes called a "temperate rain forest."

- **Abiotic factors** mild temperatures; abundant precipitation in fall, winter, and spring; cool dry summers; rocky acidic soils
- **Biotic factors**

  Plant life: Because of seasonal temperature variation, there is less diversity in this biome than in tropical rain forests. However, ample water and nutrients support lush, dense plant growth. Adaptations that enable plants to obtain sunlight are common. Trees here are among the world's tallest.

  Animal life: Camouflage helps insects and ground-dwelling mammals avoid predation. Many animals are browsers—they eat a varied diet—an advantage in an environment where vegetation changes seasonally.

BOREAL FOREST

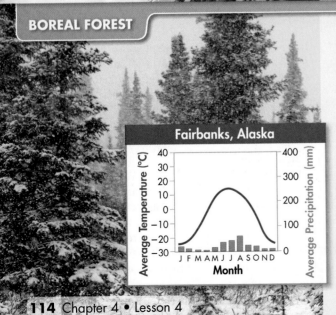

Fairbanks, Alaska

Dense forests of coniferous evergreens along the northern edge of the temperate zone are called boreal forests, or **taiga** (TY guh). Winters are bitterly cold, but summers are mild and long enough to allow the ground to thaw. The word *boreal* comes from the Greek word for "north," reflecting the fact that boreal forests occur mostly in the northern part of the Northern Hemisphere.

- **Abiotic factors** long cold winters; short mild summers; moderate precipitation; high humidity; acidic, nutrient-poor soils
- **Biotic factors**

  Plant life: Conifers are well suited to the boreal-forest environment. Their conical shape sheds snow, and their wax-covered needlelike leaves prevent excess water loss. In addition, the dark green color of most conifers absorbs heat energy.

  Animal life: Staying warm is the major challenge for animals. Most have small extremities and extra insulation in the form of fat or downy feathers. Some migrate to warmer areas in winter.

The tundra is characterized by **permafrost,** a layer of permanently frozen subsoil. During the short cool summer, the ground thaws to a depth of a few centimeters and becomes soggy. In winter, the top layer of soil freezes again. This cycle of thawing and freezing, which rips and crushes plant roots, is one reason that tundra plants are small and stunted. Cold temperatures, high winds, a short growing season, and humus-poor soils also limit plant height.

- **Abiotic factors** strong winds; low precipitation; short and soggy summers; long, cold, dark winters; poorly developed soils; permafrost
- **Biotic factors**
  Plant life: By hugging the ground, mosses and other low-growing plants avoid damage from frequent strong winds. Seed dispersal by wind is common. Many plants have adapted to growth in poor soil. Legumes, for example, have nitrogen-fixing bacteria on their roots.
  Animal life: Many animals migrate to avoid long harsh winters. Animals that live in the tundra year-round display adaptations, among them natural antifreeze, small extremities that limit heat loss, and a varied diet.

Analyzing Data

Which Biome?

An ecologist collected climate data from two locations. The graph shows the monthly average temperatures in the two locations. The total yearly precipitation in Location A is 273 cm. In Location B, the total yearly precipitation is 11 cm.

1. Interpret Graphs What variable is plotted on the horizontal axis? On the vertical axis?

2. Interpret Graphs How would you describe the temperature over the course of the year in Location A? In Location B?

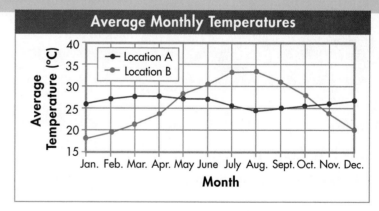

3. Draw Conclusions In which biome would you expect to find each location, given the precipitation and temperature data? Explain your answer.

4. Analyze Data Look up the average monthly temperature last year in the city you live in. Plot the data. Then look up the monthly rainfall for your city, and plot those data. Based on your results, which biome do you live in? Did the data predict the biome correctly?

MYSTERY CLUE

Yellowstone has high mountain slopes and valleys with streams. Can you think of any reason why moose and elk might prefer to graze in one of those places rather than the other? How do you think their preference might affect Yellowstone's plant communities?

Other Land Areas

🔑 **What areas are not easily classified into a major biome?**

Some land areas do not fall neatly into one of the major biomes. 🔑 **Because they are not easily defined in terms of a typical community of plants and animals, mountain ranges and polar ice caps are not usually classified into biomes.**

Mountain Ranges Mountain ranges exist on all continents and in many biomes. On mountains, conditions vary with elevation. From river valley to summit, temperature, precipitation, exposure to wind, and soil types all change, and so do organisms. If you climb the Rocky Mountains in Colorado, for example, you begin in a grassland. You then pass through pine woodland and then a forest of spruce and other conifers. Thickets of aspen and willow trees grow along streambeds in protected valleys. Higher up, soils are thin. Strong winds buffet open fields of wildflowers and stunted vegetation resembling tundra. Glaciers are found at the peaks of many ranges.

Polar Ice Caps Polar regions, like the one in **Figure 4–19**, border the tundra and are cold year-round. Plants are few, though some algae grow on snow and ice. Where rocks and ground are exposed seasonally, mosses and lichens may grow. Marine mammals, insects, and mites are the typical animals. In the north, where polar bears live, the Arctic Ocean is covered with sea ice, although more and more ice is melting each summer. In the south, the continent of Antarctica, inhabited by many species of penguins, is covered by ice nearly 5 kilometers thick in places.

FIGURE 4–19 Polar Ice Caps The polar ice caps do not fit neatly into a biome classification. At the poles, it is cold year-round, and land is usually covered with thick ice sheets.

4.4 Assessment

Review Key Concepts 🔑

1. a. Review List the major biomes, and describe one characteristic of each.

b. Explain How are biomes classified?

c. Compare and Contrast Choose two very different biomes. For each biome, select a common plant and animal. Compare how the plants and animals have adapted to their biomes.

2. a. Review Why aren't mountain ranges or polar ice caps classified as biomes?

b. Sequence Imagine that you are hiking up a mountain in the temperate forest biome. Describe how the plant life might change as you climb toward the summit.

Apply the Big idea

Interdependence in Nature

3. Choose one of the biomes discussed in this lesson. Then, sketch the biome. Include the biome's characteristic plant and animal life in your sketch. Add labels to identify the organisms, and write a caption describing the content of the sketch.

BIOLOGY.com > Search (Lesson 4.4) **GO**   • Self-Test   • Lesson Assessment

4.5 Aquatic Ecosystems

THINK ABOUT IT We call our planet "Earth," yet nearly three-fourths of Earth's surface is covered with water. Despite the vital roles aquatic ecosystems play in the biosphere, many of these ecosystems are only partly understood. What's life like underwater?

Conditions Underwater

What factors affect life in aquatic ecosystems?

Like organisms living on land, underwater organisms are affected by a variety of environmental factors. **Aquatic organisms are affected primarily by the water's depth, temperature, flow, and amount of dissolved nutrients.** Because runoff from land can affect some of these factors, distance from shore also shapes marine communities.

Water Depth Water depth strongly influences aquatic life because sunlight penetrates only a relatively short distance through water, as shown in **Figure 4–20.** The sunlit region near the surface in which photosynthesis can occur is known as the **photic zone.** The photic zone may be as deep as 200 meters in tropical seas, but just a few meters deep or less in rivers and swamps. Photosynthetic algae, called phytoplankton, live in the photic zone. Zooplankton—tiny free-floating animals—eat phytoplankton. This is the first step in many aquatic food webs. Below the photic zone is the dark **aphotic zone,** where photosynthesis cannot occur.

Many aquatic organisms live on, or in, rocks and sediments on the bottoms of lakes, streams, and oceans. These organisms are called the **benthos,** and their habitat is the benthic zone. Where water is shallow enough for the benthos to be within the photic zone, algae and rooted aquatic plants can grow. When the benthic zone is below the photic zone, chemosynthetic autotrophs are the only primary producers.

Key Questions

What factors affect life in aquatic ecosystems?

What are the major categories of freshwater ecosystems?

Why are estuaries so important?

How do ecologists usually classify marine ecosystems?

Vocabulary

photic zone • aphotic zone • benthos • plankton • wetland • estuary

Taking Notes

Compare/Contrast Table As you read, note the similarities and differences between the major freshwater and marine ecosystems in a compare/contrast table.

FIGURE 4–20 The Photic Zone Sunlight penetrates only a limited distance into aquatic ecosystems. Whatever the depth of this photic zone, it is the only area in which photosynthesis can occur. **Infer** *Why do you think some photic zones are only a few meters deep and others are as much as 200 meters deep?*

Temperature and Currents Aquatic habitats, like terrestrial habitats, are warmer near the equator and colder near the poles. Temperature in aquatic habitats also often varies with depth. The deepest parts of lakes and oceans are often colder than surface waters. Currents in lakes and oceans can dramatically affect water temperature because they can carry water that is significantly warmer or cooler than would be typical for any given latitude, depth, or distance from shore.

Nutrient Availability As you learned in Chapter 3, organisms need certain substances to live. These include oxygen, nitrogen, potassium, and phosphorus. The type and availability of these dissolved substances vary within and between bodies of water, greatly affecting the types of organisms that can survive there.

Freshwater Ecosystems

🔑 *What are the major categories of freshwater ecosystems?*

Only 3 percent of Earth's surface water is fresh water, but that small percentage provides terrestrial organisms with drinking water, food, and transportation. Often, a chain of streams, lakes, and rivers begins in the interior of a continent and flows through several biomes to the sea. 🔑 **Freshwater ecosystems can be divided into three main categories: rivers and streams, lakes and ponds, and freshwater wetlands.** Examples of these ecosystems are shown in **Figure 4–21.**

Rivers and Streams Rivers, streams, creeks, and brooks often originate from underground water sources in mountains or hills. Near a source, water has plenty of dissolved oxygen but little plant life. Downstream, sediments build up and plants establish themselves. Still farther downstream, water may meander slowly through flat areas. Animals in many rivers and streams depend on terrestrial plants and animals that live along their banks for food.

In Your Notebook *What kinds of adaptations would you expect in organisms living in a fast-flowing river or stream?*

MYSTERY CLUE

What is one way in which life in Yellowstone's streams might be affected by the presence or absence of plants along stream banks?

FIGURE 4–21 Freshwater Ecosystems and Estuaries Freshwater ecosystems include streams, lakes, and freshwater wetlands (bogs, swamps, and marshes). Salt marshes and mangrove swamps are estuaries—areas where fresh water from rivers meets salt water. **Interpret Visuals** *Based on these photos, what are two differences between streams and bogs?*

Stream

Lake

Freshwater Wetland: Bog

Lakes and Ponds The food webs in lakes and ponds often are based on a combination of plankton and attached algae and plants. **Plankton** is a general term that includes both phytoplankton and zooplankton. Water typically flows in and out of lakes and ponds and circulates between the surface and the benthos during at least some seasons. This circulation distributes heat, oxygen, and nutrients.

Freshwater Wetlands A **wetland** is an ecosystem in which water either covers the soil or is present at or near the surface for at least part of the year. Water may flow through freshwater wetlands or stay in place. Wetlands are often nutrient-rich and highly productive, and they serve as breeding grounds for many organisms. Freshwater wetlands have important environmental functions: They purify water by filtering pollutants and help to prevent flooding by absorbing large amounts of water and slowly releasing it. Three main types of freshwater wetlands are freshwater bogs, freshwater marshes, and freshwater swamps. Saltwater wetlands are called estuaries.

Estuaries

Why are estuaries so important?

An **estuary** (es tyoo er ee) is a special kind of wetland, formed where a river meets the sea. Estuaries contain a mixture of fresh water and salt water, and are affected by the rise and fall of ocean tides. Many are shallow, which means that enough sunlight reaches the benthos to power photosynthesis. Estuaries support an astonishing amount of biomass—although they usually contain fewer species than freshwater or marine ecosystems—which makes them commercially valuable. **Estuaries serve as spawning and nursery grounds for many ecologically and commercially important fish and shellfish species including bluefish, striped bass, shrimp, and crabs.**

Salt marshes are temperate estuaries characterized by salt-tolerant grasses above the low-tide line and seagrasses below water. One of the largest salt marshes in America surrounds the Chesapeake Bay in Maryland (shown below). Mangrove swamps are tropical estuaries characterized by several species of salt-tolerant trees, collectively called mangroves. The largest mangrove area in America is in Florida's Everglades National Park (shown below).

Freshwater Wetland: Marsh

Freshwater Wetland: Swamp

Estuary: Salt Marsh

Estuary: Mangrove Swamp

Marine Ecosystems

🔑 How do ecologists usually classify marine ecosystems?

Just as biomes typically occupy certain latitudes and longitudes, marine ecosystems may typically occupy specific areas within the ocean. 🔑 **Ecologists typically divide the ocean into zones based on depth and distance from shore.** Starting with the shallowest and closest to land, marine ecosystems include the intertidal zone, the coastal ocean, and the open ocean, as shown in **Figure 4–22.** Within these zones live a number of different communities.

> **In Your Notebook** *How would you expect communities of organisms in the open ocean to differ from those along the coast?*

Intertidal Zone Organisms in the intertidal zone are submerged in seawater at high tide and exposed to air and sunlight at low tide. These organisms, then, are subjected to regular and extreme changes in temperature. They also are often battered by waves and currents. There are many different types of intertidal communities. A typical rocky intertidal community exists in temperate regions where exposed rocks line the shore. There, barnacles and seaweed permanently attach themselves to the rocks.

BUILD Vocabulary

MULTIPLE MEANINGS The noun *subject* has many meanings, including "the main theme of a piece of work such as a novel" or "a course of study." The verb *subject,* however, means "to expose" or "to tend toward." Organisms are subjected, or exposed, to extreme conditions in the rocky intertidal zone.

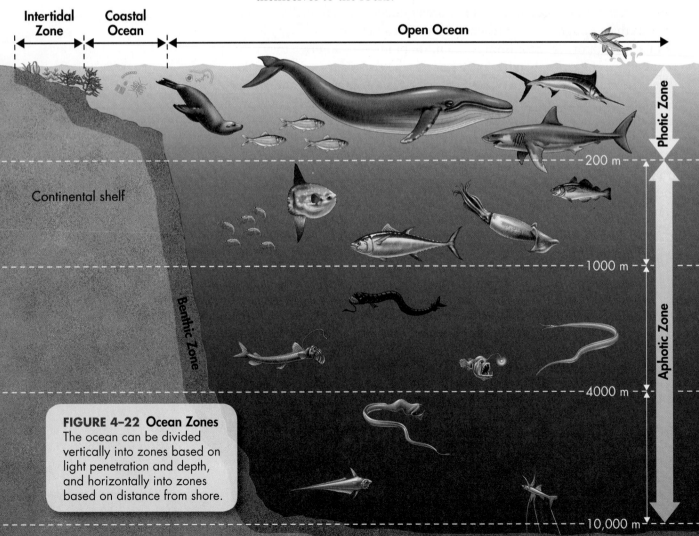

FIGURE 4–22 Ocean Zones The ocean can be divided vertically into zones based on light penetration and depth, and horizontally into zones based on distance from shore.

Coastal Ocean The coastal ocean extends from the low-tide mark to the outer edge of the continental shelf—the relatively shallow border that surrounds the continents. Water here is brightly lit, and is often supplied with nutrients by freshwater runoff from land. As a result, coastal oceans tend to be highly productive. Kelp forests and coral reefs are two exceptionally important coastal communities.

Open Ocean The open ocean begins at the edge of the continental shelf and extends outward. More than 90 percent of the world's ocean area is considered open ocean. Depth ranges from about 500 meters along continental slopes to more than 10,000 meters in deep ocean trenches. The open ocean can be divided into two main zones according to light penetration: the photic zone and the aphotic zone.

▶ *The Open Ocean Photic Zone* The open ocean typically has low nutrient levels and supports only the smallest species of phytoplankton. Still, because of its enormous area, most photosynthesis on Earth occurs in the sunlit top 100 meters of the open ocean.

▶ *The Open Ocean Aphotic Zone* The permanently dark aphotic zone includes the deepest parts of the ocean. Food webs here are based either on organisms that fall from the photic zone above, or on chemosynthetic organisms. Deep ocean organisms, like the fish in **Figure 4–23,** are exposed to high pressure, frigid temperatures, and total darkness. Benthic environments in the deep sea were once thought to be nearly devoid of life but are now known to have islands of high productivity. Deep-sea vents, where superheated water boils out of cracks on the ocean floor, support chemosynthetic primary producers.

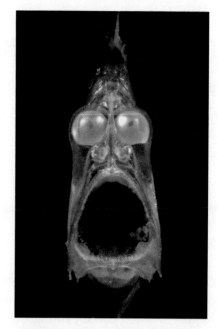

FIGURE 4–23 Creature From the Deep This silver hatchetfish lives in the aphotic zone of the Gulf of Mexico. **Apply Concepts** *What kinds of adaptations do you think this fish has that enable it to live in the harsh deep-ocean environment?*

4.5 Assessment

Review Key Concepts 🔑

1. a. Review What are the primary abiotic factors that affect life underwater?

b. Compare and Contrast What are some ways in which life in an aphotic zone might differ from life in a photic zone?

2. a. Review What are the major categories of freshwater ecosystems?

b. Apply Concepts What is a wetland? Why are wetlands important?

3. a. Review Where are estuaries found? Why is it important to protect estuaries?

b. Predict How might a dam upriver affect an estuary at the river's mouth?

4. a. Review List the three major marine ecological zones. Give two abiotic factors for each zone.

b. Apply Concepts Using **Figure 4–22** as a guide, draw a cross section of the ocean starting with a beach and ending with an ocean trench. Label the intertidal zone, coastal ocean, and open ocean. Subdivide the open ocean into photic and aphotic zones.

WRITE ABOUT SCIENCE

Explanation

5. Choose three different aquatic ecosystems. For each of these ecosystems, select a plant and an animal, and explain how the organisms have adapted to their environment.

Pre-Lab: Abiotic Factors and Plant Selection

Problem How can you decide which plants will thrive in a garden?

Materials plant hardiness zone map, plant catalogs, graph paper, tape measure

Lab Manual Chapter 4 Lab

Skills Focus Classify, Analyze Data, Use Models

Connect to the Big idea Why are white birch trees abundant in Minnesota, but not in the Florida Keys? Why do coconut palms grow in the Florida Keys, but not in Minnesota? Simply put, white birch trees could not tolerate the hot summers in the Keys and coconut palms could not tolerate the cold winters in Minnesota. A plant's habitat is determined by its range of tolerance for temperature and other abiotic factors. In other words, abiotic factors limit where a given plant can live.

In this lab, you will plan a garden for a specific location. You will select plants for the garden that can tolerate the abiotic factors in this location.

Background Questions

a. Review What is an abiotic factor? List three examples other than temperature.

b. Review What kinds of resources do plants need?

c. Relate Cause and Effect Give an example of an adaptation that helps a plant survive in a biome with low precipitation.

Pre-Lab Questions

Preview the procedure in the lab manual.

1. Predict How will knowing the plant hardiness zone for your area help you plan a garden?

2. Relate Cause and Effect What is the relationship between the last frost and the length of the growing season?

3. Form a Hypothesis A plant species grows well in one location in a small garden but does not grow as well in another location. Suggest one possible reason for this difference.

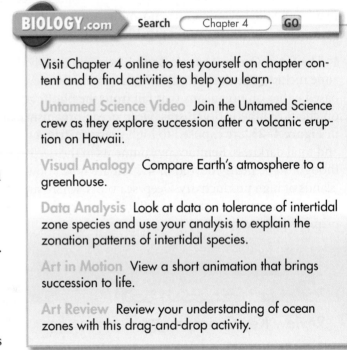

BIOLOGY.com   Search [Chapter 4] **GO**

Visit Chapter 4 online to test yourself on chapter content and to find activities to help you learn.

Untamed Science Video Join the Untamed Science crew as they explore succession after a volcanic eruption on Hawaii.

Visual Analogy Compare Earth's atmosphere to a greenhouse.

Data Analysis Look at data on tolerance of intertidal zone species and use your analysis to explain the zonation patterns of intertidal species.

Art in Motion View a short animation that brings succession to life.

Art Review Review your understanding of ocean zones with this drag-and-drop activity.

4 Study Guide

Big idea Interdependence in Nature

An organism's tolerance range for temperature, precipitation, and other abiotic factors helps determine where it lives. Biotic factors, such as competition, predation, and herbivory also help to determine an organism's potential habitat and niche.

4.1 Climate

🔑 A region's climate is defined by year-after-year patterns of temperature and precipitation.

🔑 Global climate is shaped by many factors, including solar energy trapped in the biosphere, latitude, and the transport of heat by winds and ocean currents.

weather (96)   microclimate (96)
climate (96)   greenhouse effect (97)

4.2 Niches and Community Interactions

🔑 A niche is the range of physical and biological conditions in which a species lives and the way the species obtains what it needs to survive and reproduce.

🔑 By causing species to divide resources, competition helps determine the number and kinds of species in a community and the niche each species occupies.

🔑 Predators can affect the size of prey populations in a community and determine the places prey can live and feed.

🔑 Herbivores can affect both the size and distribution of plant populations in a community and can determine the places that certain plants can survive and grow.

🔑 Biologists recognize three main classes of symbiotic relationships in nature: mutualism, parasitism, and commensalism.

tolerance (99)   herbivory (102)
habitat (99)   keystone species (103)
niche (100)   symbiosis (103)
resource (100)   mutualism (103)
competitive exclusion   parasitism (104)
  principle (101)   commensalism (104)
predation (102)

4.3 Succession

🔑 Ecosystems change over time, especially after disturbances, as some species die out and new species move in.

🔑 Secondary succession in healthy ecosystems following natural disturbances often reproduces the original climax community. Ecosystems may or may not recover from human-caused disturbances.

ecological succession (106) pioneer species (107)
primary succession (106)   secondary succession (107)

4.4 Biomes

🔑 Biomes are described in terms of abiotic factors like climate and soil type, and biotic factors like plant and animal life.

🔑 Mountain ranges and polar ice caps are not usually classified into biomes because they are not easily defined in terms of a typical community of plants and animals.

canopy (112)   coniferous (114)   permafrost (115)
understory (112)   humus (114)
deciduous (112)   taiga (114)

4.5 Aquatic Ecosystems

🔑 Aquatic organisms are affected primarily by the water's depth, temperature, flow, and amount of dissolved nutrients.

🔑 Freshwater ecosystems can be divided into three main categories: rivers and streams, lakes and ponds, and freshwater wetlands.

🔑 Estuaries serve as spawning and nursery grounds for many ecologically and commercially important fish and shellfish species.

🔑 Ecologists typically divide the ocean into zones based on depth and distance from shore.

photic zone (117)   benthos (117)   wetland (119)
aphotic zone (117) plankton (119)   estuary (119)

Think Visually Create a concept map that includes the following terms: *abiotic factors, biotic factors, community interactions, predation, competition, symbiosis, nutrients, ecosystems, light,* and *oxygen.*

4 Assessment

Understand Key Concepts

1. An increase in the greenhouse effect causes an increase in
   a. carbon dioxide.   **c.** oxygen.
   b. temperature.   **d.** water.

2. A small valley where the average temperature is usually higher than that of the surrounding countryside has its own
   a. weather.   **c.** rainfall.
   b. climate.   **d.** microclimate.

3. Distinguish between weather and climate.

4. Describe the three primary abiotic factors that produce Earth's major climate zones.

Think Critically

5. **Apply Concepts** Based on the relative positions of the sun and Earth, explain why Earth has climate zones and seasons.

6. **Infer** A plant grower has a greenhouse where she grows plants in the winter. The greenhouse is exposed to direct sunlight and often gets too hot for the plants. She paints the inside of the glass with a chalky white paint, and the temperature drops to comfortable levels. Explain why this procedure works.

4.2 Niches and Community Interactions

Understand Key Concepts

7. A relationship in which one organism is helped and another organism is neither helped nor hurt is called
   a. parasitism.   **c.** competition.
   b. mutualism.   **d.** commensalism.

8. The relationship between a tick and its host is an example of
   a. mutualism.
   b. parasitism.
   c. commensalism.
   d. succession.

9. What is the difference between an organism's habitat and its niche?

10. What is the competitive exclusion principle?

Think Critically

11. **Compare and Contrast** How are predation and parasitism similar? How are they different?

12. **Infer** Competition for resources in an area is usually more intense within a single species than between two different species. How would you explain this observation?

13. **Apply Concepts** Write a description of your niche in the environment. Include details about your ecosystem, and the biotic and abiotic factors around you. Be sure to describe your feeding habits as well as any interactions you have with members of other species.

4.3 Succession

Understand Key Concepts

14. Fires, hurricanes, and other natural disturbances can result in
   a. commensalism.   **c.** parasitism.
   b. competition.   **d.** succession.

15. The first organisms to repopulate an area affected by a volcanic eruption are called
   a. keystone species.   **c.** primary producers.
   b. climax species.   **d.** pioneer species.

16. What type of succession takes place after lava from a volcanic eruption covers an area?

17. Describe two major causes of ecological succession.

Think Critically

18. **Predict** A windstorm in a forest blows down the large trees in one part of the forest. Soon, sun-loving plants sprout in the new clearing. What type of succession is this? What do you think this area will look like in 5 years? In 50 years?

19. **Relate Cause and Effect** Explain why secondary succession usually proceeds faster than primary succession.

Understand Key Concepts

20. In a tropical rain forest, the dense covering formed by the leafy tops of tall trees is called the
   a. canopy.   **c.** niche.
   b. taiga.   **d.** understory.

21. Permafrost characterizes the biome called
   a. taiga.   **c.** savanna.
   b. boreal forest.   **d.** tundra.

22. What is a biome?

23. Why are plants generally few and far between in a desert?

Think Critically

24. **Apply Concepts** Although the amount of precipitation is low, most parts of the tundra are very wet during the summer. How would you explain this apparent contradiction?

25. **Infer** Deciduous trees in tropical dry forests lose water through their leaves every day. During summers with adequate rain, the leaves remain on the trees. During the cold dry season, the trees drop their leaves. In an especially dry summer, how might the adaptation of dropping leaves enable a tree to tolerate the drought?

26. **Infer** Consider these two biomes: (1) the temperate grassland and (2) the temperate woodland and shrubland. Coyotes live in both biomes. Describe two adaptations that might enable coyotes to tolerate conditions in both biomes.

4.5 Aquatic Ecosystems

Understand Key Concepts

27. Organisms that live near or on the ocean floor are called
   a. parasites.   **c.** plankton.
   b. benthos.   **d.** mangroves.

28. What is the meaning of the term *plankton*? Name the two types of plankton.

29. What are three types of freshwater wetlands?

30. How are salt marshes and mangrove swamps alike? How are they different?

solve the CHAPTER MYSTERY

THE WOLF EFFECT

Eliminating wolves from Yellowstone National Park contributed to an increase in the number of elk. These elk grazed so heavily, especially along streams, that the seedlings and shoots of aspens and willows, and other trees, could not grow. Fewer trees led to fewer dams being built by beavers and to an increase in runoff and erosion. Aquatic food webs broke down, affecting birds, fish, and other animals. The recent reintroduction of wolves has caused a decrease in the overall elk population and seems to have reduced elk grazing along certain streams. That may be in part because wolves are killing more elk and in part because elk have learned to stay away from places like stream banks and valleys, where wolves can attack them most easily.

In recent years, researchers have shown that streamside vegetation is exhibiting secondary succession and that aspen and willow trees are starting to grow back. There have been numerous other changes as well. Fewer elk mean more food for smaller animals. The increase in small prey, in turn, has brought diverse predators into the community. Carcasses abandoned by the wolves provide food for scavengers. In short, organisms from every trophic level have been affected by the Yellowstone wolves.

1. Predict The Yellowstone wolf and elk are linked through a predator-prey relationship. If a disease were to strike the elk population, how would the wolves be affected?

2. Form an Opinion Yellowstone is owned by the federal government. The reintroduction of wolves there angered nearby farmers because they feared their animals would be hunted. What level of responsibility do you think national parks should have toward their neighbors?

3. Connect to the **Big idea** Draw a food chain that connects Yellowstone's wolves, aspen and willow trees, and elk. Then write a paragraph that explains why the Yellowstone wolves are a keystone species.

Think Critically

31. Form a Hypothesis The deep ocean lies within the aphotic zone and is very cold. Suggest some of the unique characteristics that enable animals to live in the deep ocean.

32. Form an Opinion A developer has proposed filling in a salt marsh to create a coastal resort. What positive and negative effects do you think this proposal would have on wildlife and local residents? Would you support the proposal?

Connecting Concepts

Use Science Graphics

The following table presents primary productivity (measured in grams of organic matter produced per year per square meter) for several ecosystems. Use the table below to answer questions 33–36.

Productivity of Aquatic and Land Ecosystems	
Ecosystem	**Average Primary Productivity**
Aquatic Ecosystems	
Coral reef	2500
Estuary	1800
Open ocean	125
Land Ecosystems	
Tropical rain forest	2200
Tropical savanna	900
Tundra	90

33. Interpret Tables According to the table, which ecosystem is most productive? Use what you know to explain that fact.

34. Infer The open ocean is among the least productive ecosystems, yet it contributes greatly to the overall productivity of the biosphere. How do you explain this paradox?

35. Apply Concepts For each set of ecosystems, aquatic and land, explain how abiotic factors may account for the differences in primary productivity seen. Give two examples.

36. Infer Review the description of the Northwest coniferous forest on page 114. Do you think its average primary productivity is greater or less than that of the tropical savanna? Explain your answer.

Write About Science

37. Explanation Choose one of the ten major biomes, and write an overview of its characteristics. Explain how abiotic factors and common plants and wildlife are interrelated. Support your explanation with specific examples.

38. Assess the  How do abiotic factors influence what kinds of organisms are involved in the primary succession in an area following a volcanic eruption?

Analyzing Data

The graph here summarizes the changes in the total volume of ice in all the world's glaciers since 1960. Note that the volume changes on the y-axis are negative, meaning an overall loss of volume.

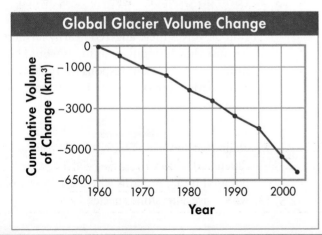

39. Interpret Graphs The greatest volume of glacial ice was lost
  a. between 1960 and 1970.
  b. between 1980 and 1990.
  c. between 1995 and 2000.
  d. before 1960.

40. Relate Cause and Effect The most reasonable explanation for the loss of glacier mass since 1960 is
  a. an increase in the total productivity of the world's oceans.
  b. a gradual rise in Earth's average temperature.
  c. an increase in the total amount of ice at Earth's poles.
  d. an increase in the sun's output of radiant energy.

Standardized Test Prep

Multiple Choice

1. The factor that generally has the greatest effect on determining a region's climate is its
   A longitude.
   B abundant plant species.
   C distance from the equator.
   D closeness to a river.

2. All of the following are abiotic factors that affect global climate EXCEPT
   A latitude.   C solar energy.
   B longitude.   D ocean currents.

3. The way an organism makes its living, including its interactions with biotic and abiotic factors of its environment, is called the organism's
   A habitat.   C lifestyle.
   B niche.   D biome.

4. If a newly introduced species fills a niche that is normally occupied by a native species, the two species compete. One of the species may die out as a result of
   A competitive exclusion.
   B predation.
   C commensalism.
   D mutualism.

5. Photosynthetic algae are MOST likely to be found in
   A the open-ocean benthic zone.
   B the aphotic zone.
   C the photic zone.
   D ocean trenches.

6. The water in an estuary is
   A salt water only.
   B poor in nutrients.
   C fresh water only.
   D a mixture of fresh water and salt water.

7. In which biome do organisms have the greatest tolerance to dry conditions?
   A tundra   C tropical savanna
   B desert   D boreal forest

Questions 8–9

Month-by-month climate data for the city of Lillehammer, Norway, is shown in the table below.

Climate Data for Lillehammer, Norway		
Month	Average Temperature (°C)	Average Precipitation (mm)
Jan.	−8.1	38.1
Feb.	−6.2	27.9
Mar.	−3.9	30.5
Apr.	3.3	35.6
May	8.9	45.7
June	13.9	63.5
July	16.4	81.3
Aug.	14.2	88.9
Sept.	9.5	58.4
Oct.	3.9	63.5
Nov.	−3.8	50.8
Dec.	−6.1	48.3

8. Which type of graph would be BEST suited to showing the precipitation data from the table?
   A bar graph   C pie chart
   B pictograph   D scatter plot

9. For a given set of data, the range is the difference between highest and lowest points. The average annual temperature range, in °C, for Lillehammer is approximately
   A −8.
   B 8.5.
   C 16.5.
   D 24.5.

Open-Ended Response

10. Why are lichens especially well adapted to play the role of pioneer organisms in an ecological succession?

If You Have Trouble With . . .										
Question	1	2	3	4	5	6	7	8	9	10
See Lesson	4.1	4.1	4.2	4.2	4.5	4.5	4.4	4.1	4.1	4.3

5 Populations

INSIDE:

- 5.1 How Populations Grow
- 5.2 Limits to Growth
- 5.3 Human Population Growth

928

Millions of red crabs live on Christmas Island in the Indian Ocean. Each year the entire adult crab population migrates from forest to sea to breed, making daily life a bit tricky for human residents!

CHAPTER
MYSTERY

A PLAGUE OF RABBITS

In 1859, an Australian farmer released 24 wild European rabbits from England on his ranch. "A few rabbits" he said, "could do little harm and might provide a touch of home, in addition to a spot of hunting."

Seven years later, he and his friends shot 14,253 rabbits. In ten years, more than 2 million rabbits were hunted on that farm alone! But hunters' glee turned into nationwide despair. That "touch of home" was soon covering the countryside like a great gray blanket. The millions of rabbits devoured native plants and pushed native animals to near extinction. They made life miserable for sheep and cattle ranchers.

These cute, fuzzy creatures weren't a problem in England. Why did they turn into a plague in Australia? Could they be stopped? How? As you read this chapter, look for clues on factors that affect population growth. Then, solve the mystery.

Never Stop Exploring Your World. Finding the solution to the rabbit population mystery is only the beginning. Take a video field trip with the ecogeeks of Untamed Science to see where this mystery leads.

UntamedScience™

5.1 How Populations Grow

Key Questions

🔑 How do ecologists study populations?

🔑 What factors affect population growth?

🔑 What happens during exponential growth?

🔑 What is logistic growth?

Vocabulary

population density •
age structure •
immigration • emigration •
exponential growth •
logistic growth •
carrying capacity

Taking Notes

Concept Map As you read, use the highlighted vocabulary words to create a concept map that organizes the information in this lesson.

THINK ABOUT IT In the 1950s, a fish farmer in Florida tossed a few plants called hydrilla into a canal. Hydrilla was imported from Asia for use in home aquariums because it is hardy and adaptable. The fish farmer assumed that hydrilla was harmless. But the few plants he tossed away reproduced quickly . . . and kept on reproducing. Today, their offspring strangle waterways across Florida and many other states. Tangled stems snag boats in rivers and overtake habitats; native water plants and animals are disappearing. Why did these plants get so out of control? Is there any way to get rid of them?

Meanwhile, people in New England who fish for a living face a different problem. Despite hard work and new equipment, their catch has dropped dramatically. The cod catch in one recent year was 3048 metric tons. Back in 1982, it was 57,200 metric tons—almost 19 times higher! Where did all the fish go? Can anything be done to increase their numbers?

Describing Populations

🔑 **How do ecologists study populations?**

At first glance, the stories of hydrilla and cod may seem unrelated. One is about plants growing out of control, and the other is about fish disappearing. Yet both involve dramatic changes in the size of a population. Recall that a population is a group of organisms of a single species that lives in a given area. 🔑 **Researchers study populations' geographic range, density and distribution, growth rate, and age structure.**

FIGURE 5–1 Invasive Hydrilla Hydrilla has spread through most of Florida in just a few decades. Efforts to control the waterweed cost millions of dollars a year.

Spread of Hydrilla Through Florida Watersheds
- 1950s
- 1960s
- 1970s
- 1980s
- 1990s

Atlantic Ocean

Florida

Gulf of Mexico

BIOLOGY.com ⟩ Search 〈 Lesson 5.1 〉 〈 GO 〉 • Lesson Overview • Lesson Notes

Geographic Range The area inhabited by a population is called its geographic range. A population's range can vary enormously in size, depending on the species. A bacterial population in a rotting pumpkin, for example, may have a range smaller than a cubic meter. The population of cod in the western Atlantic, on the other hand, covers a range that stretches from Greenland down to North Carolina. The natural range of one hydrilla population includes parts of southern India and Sri Lanka. The native range of another hydrilla population was in Korea. But humans have carried hydrilla to so many places that its range now includes every continent except Antarctica, and it is found in many places in the United States.

Density and Distribution **Population density** refers to the number of individuals per unit area. Populations of different species often have very different densities, even in the same environment. For example, a population of ducks in a pond may have a low density, while fish in the same pond community may have a higher density. *Distribution* refers to how individuals in a population are spaced out across the range of the population—randomly, uniformly, or mostly concentrated in clumps, as shown in **Figure 5–2.**

Growth Rate A population's growth rate determines whether the size of the population increases, decreases, or stays the same. Hydrilla populations in their native habitats tend to stay more or less the same size over time. These populations have a growth rate of around zero. In other words, they neither increase nor decrease in size. The hydrilla population in Florida, by contrast, has a high growth rate—which means that it increases in size. Populations can also decrease in size, as cod populations have been doing. The cod population has a negative growth rate.

Age Structure To fully understand a plant or animal population, researchers need to know more than just the number of individuals it contains. They also need to know the population's **age structure**—the number of males and females of each age a population contains. Why? Because most plants and animals cannot reproduce until they reach a certain age. Also, among animals, only females can produce offspring.

A. Random

B. Uniform

C. Clumped

FIGURE 5–2 Patterns of Distribution The dots in the inset illustrations represent individual members of a population. **A.** Purple lupines grow randomly in a field of wildflowers. **B.** King penguin populations show uniform spacing between individuals. **C.** Striped catfish form tight clumps.

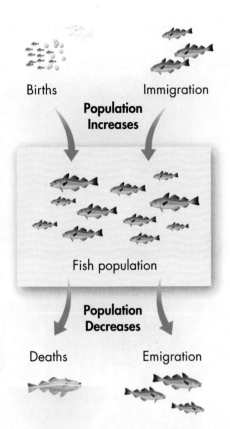

Births   Immigration

Population Increases

Fish population

Population Decreases

Deaths   Emigration

FIGURE 5–3 Natural Factors That Affect the Growth of a Fish Population The numbers of fish that hatch, die, enter, or leave the population affect the growth of the population. **Use Models** *How would you expand this model to include the effects of fishing?*

MYSTERY CLUE

What kind of growth does the rabbit population in Australia exhibit? Why does that present a problem?

Population Growth

What factors affect population growth?

What determines whether a population grows, shrinks, or stays the same size? A population will increase or decrease in size depending on how many individuals are added to it or removed from it, as shown in **Figure 5–3.** **The factors that can affect population size are the birthrate, death rate, and the rate at which individuals enter or leave the population.**

Birthrate and Death Rate Populations can grow if more individuals are born than die in any period of time. In other words, a population can grow when its birthrate is higher than its death rate. If the birthrate equals the death rate, the population may stay the same size. If the death rate is greater than the birthrate, the population is likely to shrink. Note that *birth* means different things in different species. Lions are born much like humans are born. Codfish, however, release eggs that hatch into new individuals.

Immigration and Emigration A population may grow if individuals move into its range from elsewhere, a process called **immigration** (im uh GRAY shun). Suppose, for example, that an oak grove in a forest produces a bumper crop of acorns one year. The squirrel population in that grove may increase as squirrels immigrate in search of food. On the other hand, a population may decrease in size if individuals move out of the population's range, a process called **emigration** (em uh GRAY shun). For example, a local food shortage or overcrowding can cause emigration. Young animals approaching maturity may emigrate from the area where they were born to find mates or establish new territories.

Exponential Growth

What happens during exponential growth?

If you provide a population with all the food and space it needs, protect it from predators and disease, and remove its waste products, the population will grow. Why? The population will increase because members of the population will be able to produce offspring. After a time, those offspring will produce their own offspring. Then, the offspring of *those* offspring will produce offspring. So, over time, the population will grow.

But notice that something interesting will happen: The size of each generation of offspring will be larger than the generation before it. This situation is called exponential (eks poh NEN shul) growth. In **exponential growth,** the larger a population gets, the faster it grows. **Under ideal conditions with unlimited resources, a population will grow exponentially.** Let's examine why this happens under different situations.

Organisms That Reproduce Rapidly We begin a hypothetical experiment with a single bacterium that divides to produce two cells every 20 minutes. We supply it with ideal conditions—and watch. After 20 minutes, the bacterium divides to produce two bacteria. After another 20 minutes, those two bacteria divide to produce four cells. At the end of the first hour, those four bacteria divide to produce eight cells.

Do you see what is happening here? After three 20-minute periods, we have $2 \times 2 \times 2$, or 8 cells. Another way to say this is to use an exponent: 2^3 cells. In another hour (six 20-minute periods), there will be 2^6, or 64 bacteria. In just one more hour, there will be 2^9, or 512. In one day, this bacterial population will grow to an astounding 4,720,000,000,000,000,000,000 individuals. What would happen if this growth continued without slowing down? In a few days, this bacterial population would cover the planet!

If you plot the size of this population on a graph over time, you get a J-shaped curve that rises slowly at first, and then rises faster and faster, as shown in **Figure 5–4.** If nothing interfered with this kind of growth, the population would become larger and larger, faster and faster, until it approached an infinitely large size.

Organisms That Reproduce Slowly Of course, many organisms grow and reproduce much more slowly than bacteria. For example, a female elephant can produce a single offspring only every 2 to 4 years. Newborn elephants take about 10 years to mature. But as you can see in **Figure 5–4,** if exponential growth continued, the result would be impossible. In the unlikely event that all descendants of a single elephant pair survived and reproduced, after 750 years there would be nearly 20 million elephants!

Organisms in New Environments Sometimes, when an organism is moved to a new environment, its population grows exponentially for a time. That's happening with hydrilla in the United States. It also happened when a few European gypsy moths were accidentally released from a laboratory near Boston. Within a few years, these plant-eating pests had spread across the northeastern United States. In peak years, they devoured the leaves of thousands of acres of forest. In some places, they formed a living blanket that covered the ground, sidewalks, and cars.

In Your Notebook Draw a growth curve for a *population of waterweed growing exponentially.*

Models of Exponential Growth

Growth of Bacterial Population

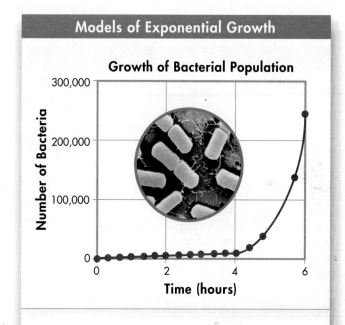

Growth of Elephant Population

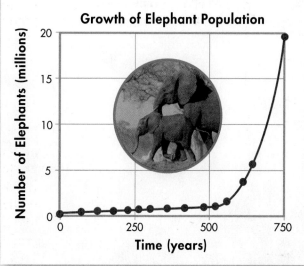

FIGURE 5–4 Exponential Growth In the presence of unlimited resources and in the absence of predation and disease, populations will grow exponentially. Bacteria, which reproduce rapidly, can produce huge populations in a matter of days. It would take elephants, which reproduce slowly, a few hundred years. Both hypothetical graphs show the characteristic J-shape of exponential growth.

Logistic Growth

🔑 What is logistic growth?

This ability of populations to grow exponentially presents a puzzle. Obviously, bacteria, elephants, hydrilla, and gypsy moths don't cover the Earth. This means that natural populations don't grow exponentially for long. Sooner or later, something—or several "somethings"—stops exponential growth. What happens?

Phases of Growth One way to begin answering this question is to watch how populations behave in nature. Suppose that a few individuals are introduced into a real-world environment. **Figure 5–5** traces the phases of growth that the population goes through.

▶ **Phase 1: Exponential Growth** After a short time, the population begins to grow exponentially. During this phase, resources are unlimited, so individuals grow and reproduce rapidly. Few individuals die, and many offspring are produced, so both the population size and the rate of growth increase more and more rapidly.

▶ **Phase 2: Growth Slows Down.** In real-world populations, exponential growth does not continue for long. At some point, the rate of population growth begins to slow down. This does not mean that the population size decreases. The population still grows, but the rate of growth slows down, so the population size increases more slowly.

▶ **Phase 3: Growth Stops.** At some point, the rate of population growth drops to zero. This means that the size of the population levels off. Under some conditions, the population will remain at or near this size indefinitely.

FIGURE 5–5 Real-world populations, such as those of the rhinoceros, show the characteristic S-shaped curve of logistic growth. As resources become limited, population growth slows or stops, leveling off at the carrying capacity.

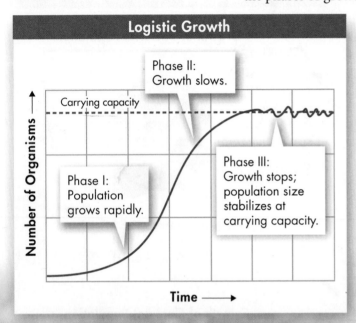

The Logistic Growth Curve The curve in **Figure 5–5** has an S-shape that represents what is called **logistic growth.** ⌐ Logistic growth occurs when a population's growth slows and then stops, following a period of exponential growth. Many familiar plant and animal populations follow a logistic growth curve.

What kinds of changes in a population's characteristics can produce logistic growth? Remember that a population grows when more organisms are born (or added to it) than die (or leave it). Thus, population growth may slow for several reasons. Growth may slow because the population's birthrate decreases. Growth may also slow if the death rate increases—or if births fall and deaths rise together. Similarly, population growth may slow if the rate of immigration decreases, the rate of emigration increases, or both. There are several reasons why these rates might change in a population, as you will see in the next lesson.

Carrying Capacity When the birthrate and the death rate are the same, and when immigration equals emigration, population growth stops. The population may still rise and fall somewhat, but the ups and downs average out around a certain population size. If you look again at **Figure 5–5,** you will see a broken, horizontal line through the region of the graph where population growth levels off. The point at which that line intersects the *y*-axis represents what ecologists call the carrying capacity. **Carrying capacity** is the maximum number of individuals of a particular species that a particular environment can support. Once a population reaches the carrying capacity of its environment, a variety of factors act to stabilize it at that size.

Analyzing Data

Multiplying Rabbits

Suppose that a pair of rabbits produces six offspring: three males and three females. Assume that no offspring die.

1. Calculate If each pair of rabbits breeds only once, how many offspring would be produced each year for five generations? **MATH**

2. Interpret Graphs Construct a graph of your data. Plot time on the *x*-axis and population on the *y*-axis. What type of growth is the rabbit population going through after 5 years?

5.1 Assessment

Review Key Concepts ⌐

1. a. Review List four characteristics that are used to describe a population.

b. Infer On your travels through eastern Canada and the United States, you notice gray squirrels everywhere. What can you infer about the squirrels' geographic range?

2. a. Review What natural factors can change a population's size?

b. Relate Cause and Effect More dandelion seedlings develop in a lawn than dandelion plants are removed. What is likely to happen to the lawn's dandelion population?

3. a. Review When do populations grow exponentially?

b. Apply Concepts Why does exponential growth show a characteristic J-shaped curve?

4. a. Review What is the characteristic shape of a logistic growth curve?

b. Explain Describe when logistic growth occurs.

c. Form a Hypothesis What factors might cause the carrying capacity of a population to change?

PRACTICE PROBLEM

5. Suppose you are studying a population of sunflowers growing in a small field. How would you determine the population density of sunflowers in a square meter of the field and in the entire field? Describe your procedure.

Biology & Society

What Can Be Done About Invasive Mussels?

It's hard to imagine that shellfish could cause millions of dollars worth of trouble every year. Meet the zebra mussel and the quagga mussel. Both species were carried to the Great Lakes in the mid-1980s from Eastern Europe in ships' ballast waters (water carried inside boats for balance). As adults, these mussels attach to almost any hard surface, including water pipes and boat hulls. After just a few years, both species colonized the entire Great Lakes region. Since then, they have been spread by recreational boaters who unknowingly carry mussels attached to their boats. By 2008, zebra mussels had been reported in 24 states; quagga mussels are already known in 14 states.

Why have these mussels become such pests? In American waterways, they escape whatever environmental factors keep their numbers in check in their native European habitats. As a result, these introduced species have become invasive species whose exponential growth produces huge populations at high densities—over 10,000 mussels per square meter of water in some places! These mussels grow in layers up to 20 centimeters thick, clogging water pipes that supply power plants and water treatment facilities. They also upset aquatic food webs, filtering so much plankton from the water that some native fishes and shellfish starve. What can be done to control such invasive species?

The Viewpoints

Invasive Species Should Be Destroyed A number of groups contend that zebra mussels should be removed completely. Some engineers are developing robotic submarines that can remove mussels from pipes. Some chemists are testing chemicals for the potential to destroy or disrupt the life cycle of zebra mussels. Other scientists are adding chemicals to paints and plastics to prevent mussels from attaching to new surfaces.

Zebra mussels clog water intake pipes.

Invasive Species Management Should Focus on Control and Prevention Others argue that efforts to physically remove or chemically poison invasive mussels offer only temporary control. The population bounces right back. These removal efforts are also incredibly expensive. In the Great Lakes alone, more than $200 million is spent each year in efforts to get rid of zebra and quagga mussels.

Therefore, many scientists believe that there is no way to remove these mussels and other established invasive species. Instead, these scientists attempt to control the growth of populations and prevent transfer of invasive species to new areas. One regulation, for example, could require boaters to filter and chemically clean all ballast water. Meanwhile, the search continues for some kind of control that naturally limits mussel numbers when they rise.

Research and Decide

1. Analyze the Viewpoints Research the current status of invasive mussel populations and the approaches being used to prevent the spread of these and other invasive aquatic species. What trends are zebra mussel populations showing?

2. Form an Opinion What kinds of natural population controls do you think would manage these invasive mussels most effectively? Why?

5.2 Limits to Growth

THINK ABOUT IT Now that you've seen *how* populations typically grow in nature, we can explore *why* they grow as they do. If populations tend to grow exponentially, why do they often follow logistic growth? In other words, what determines the carrying capacity of an environment for a particular species? Think again about hydrilla. In its native Asia, populations of hydrilla increase in size until they reach carrying capacity, and then population growth stops. But here in the United States, hydrilla grows out of control. The same is true of gypsy moths and many other introduced plant and animal species. Why does a species that is "well-behaved" in one environment grow out of control in another?

Limiting Factors

🔑 **What factors determine carrying capacity?**

Recall that the productivity of an ecosystem can be controlled by a limiting nutrient. A limiting nutrient is an example of a general ecological concept: a limiting factor. In the context of populations, a **limiting factor** is a factor that controls the growth of a population.

As shown in **Figure 5–6,** there are several kinds of limiting factors. Some—such as competition, predation, parasitism, and disease—depend on population density. Others—including natural disasters and unusual weather—do not depend on population density. 🔑 **Acting separately or together, limiting factors determine the carrying capacity of an environment for a species.** Limiting factors keep most natural populations somewhere between extinction and overrunning the planet.

Charles Darwin recognized the importance of limiting factors in shaping the history of life on Earth. As you will learn in Unit 5, the limiting factors we describe here produce the pressures of natural selection that stand at the heart of evolutionary theory.

Key Questions

🔑 *What factors determine carrying capacity?*

🔑 *What limiting factors depend on population density?*

🔑 *What limiting factors do not typically depend on population density?*

Vocabulary

limiting factor
density-dependent limiting factor
density-independent limiting factor

Taking Notes

Outline Make an outline using the green and blue headings in this lesson. Fill in details as you read to help you organize the information.

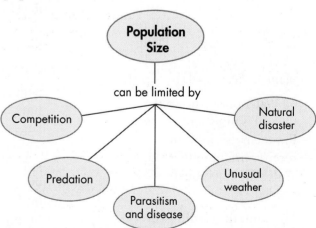

FIGURE 5–6 Limiting Factors Many different factors can limit population growth. Some of these factors depend on population density, while others do not. **Infer** *How might each of these factors increase the death rate in a population?*

FIGURE 5–7 **Competition** Male wolves may fight one another for territory or access to mates.

GUIDED INQUIRY

How Does Competition Affect Growth?

❶ Label two paper cups 3 and 15. Make several small holes in the bottom of each cup. Fill each cup two-thirds full with potting soil. Plant 3 bean seeds in cup 3, and plant 15 bean seeds in cup 15.

❷ Water both cups so that the soil is moist but not wet. Put them in a location that receives bright indirect light. Water the cups equally as needed.

❸ Count the seedlings every other day for two weeks.

Analyze and Conclude

1. Observe What differences did you observe between the two cups?

Density-Dependent Limiting Factors

🔑 *What limiting factors depend on population density?*

Density-dependent limiting factors operate strongly only when population density—the number of organisms per unit area—reaches a certain level. These factors do not affect small, scattered populations as much. 🔑 **Density-dependent limiting factors include competition, predation, herbivory, parasitism, disease, and stress from overcrowding.**

Competition When populations become crowded, individuals compete for food, water, space, sunlight, and other essentials. Some individuals obtain enough to survive and reproduce. Others may obtain just enough to live but not enough to enable them to raise offspring. Still others may starve to death or die from lack of shelter. Thus, competition can lower birthrates, increase death rates, or both.

Competition is a density-dependent limiting factor, because the more individuals living in an area, the sooner they use up the available resources. Often, space and food are related to one another. Many grazing animals compete for territories in which to breed and raise offspring. Individuals that do not succeed in establishing a territory find no mates and cannot breed.

Competition can also occur among members of different species that are attempting to use similar or overlapping resources. This type of competition is a major force behind evolutionary change.

Predation and Herbivory The effects of predators on prey and the effects of herbivores on plants are two very important density-dependent population controls. One classic study focuses on the relationship between wolves, moose, and plants on Isle Royale, an island in Lake Superior. The graph in **Figure 5–8** shows that populations of wolves and moose have fluctuated over the years. What drives these changes in population size?

▶ *Predator-Prey Relationships* In a predator-prey relationship, populations of predators and prey may cycle up and down over time. Sometimes, the moose population on Isle Royale grows large enough that moose become easy prey for wolves. When wolves have plenty to eat, their population grows. As the wolf population grows, the wolves begin to kill more moose than are born. This causes the moose death rate to rise higher than its birthrate, so the moose population falls. As the moose population drops, wolves begin to starve. Starvation raises the wolves' death rate and lowers their birthrate, so the wolf population also falls. When only a few predators are left, the moose death rate drops, and the cycle repeats.

In Your Notebook *Describe conditions that lead to competition in a population.*

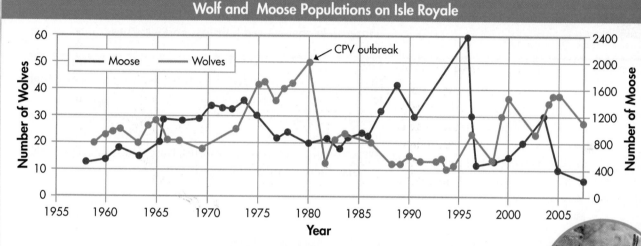

Wolf and Moose Populations on Isle Royale

Graph legend: — Moose — Wolves

Annotation on graph: CPV outbreak

Left axis: Number of Wolves (0, 10, 20, 30, 40, 50, 60)
Right axis: Number of Moose (0, 400, 800, 1200, 1600, 2000, 2400)
X-axis: Year (1955, 1960, 1965, 1970, 1975, 1980, 1985, 1990, 1995, 2000, 2005)

▶ **Herbivore Effects** Herbivory can also contribute to changes in population numbers. From a plant's perspective, herbivores are predators. So it isn't surprising that populations of herbivores and plants cycle up and down, just like populations of predators and prey. On parts of Isle Royale, large, dense moose populations can eat so much balsam fir that the population of these favorite food plants drops. When this happens, the moose may suffer from lack of food.

▶ **Humans as Predators** In some situations, human activity limits populations. For example, humans are major predators of codfish in New England. Fishing fleets, by catching more and more fish every year, have raised cod death rates so high that birthrates cannot keep up. As a result, the cod population has been dropping. Is there any way to solve the problem? Think of predator-prey interactions. The cod population can recover if we scale back fishing to lower the death rate sufficiently. Biologists are studying birthrates and the age structure of the cod population to determine how many fish can be taken without threatening the survival of the population.

FIGURE 5–8 Moose-Wolf Populations on Isle Royale The relationship between moose and wolves on Isle Royale illustrates how predation can affect population growth. In this case, the moose population was also affected by changes in food supply, and the wolf population was also impacted by a canine parvovirus (CPV) outbreak.

BUILD Vocabulary

ACADEMIC WORDS The verb **fluctuate** means to "rise and fall as if in waves." A population that fluctuates is unstable: Its numbers go up and down irregularly.

FIGURE 5–9 Parasitism The ticks feeding on the blood of this hedgehog can transmit bacteria that cause disease.

Parasitism and Disease Parasites and disease-causing organisms feed at the expense of their hosts, weakening them and often causing disease or death. The ticks on the hedgehog in **Figure 5–9**, for example, can carry diseases. Parasitism and disease are density-dependent effects because the denser the host population, the more easily parasites can spread from one host to another.

If you look back at the graph in **Figure 5–8**, you can see a sudden and dramatic drop in the wolf population around 1980. At that time, a viral disease of wolves was accidentally introduced to the island. This virus killed all but 13 wolves on the island—and only three of the survivors were females. The removal of wolves caused moose populations to skyrocket to 2400. The densely packed moose then became infested with winter ticks that caused hair loss and weakness.

Stress From Overcrowding Some species fight amongst themselves if overcrowded. Too much fighting can cause high levels of stress, which can weaken the body's ability to resist disease. In some species, stress from overcrowding can cause females to neglect, kill, or even eat their own offspring. Thus, stress from overcrowding can lower birthrates, raise death rates, or both. It can also increase rates of emigration.

Density-Independent Limiting Factors

🔑 *What limiting factors do not typically depend on population density?*

Density-independent limiting factors affect all populations in similar ways, regardless of population size and density. 🔑 **Unusual weather such as hurricanes, droughts, or floods, and natural disasters such as wildfires, can act as density-independent limiting factors.** In response to such factors, a population may "crash." After the crash, the population may build up again quickly, or it may stay low for some time.

For some species, storms can nearly extinguish local populations. For example, thrips, aphids, and other insects that feed on leaves can be washed out by a heavy rainstorm. Waves whipped up by hurricanes can devastate shallow coral reefs. Extremes of cold or hot weather also can take their toll, regardless of population density. A severe drought, for example, can kill off great numbers of fish in a river, as shown in **Figure 5–10**.

True Density Independence? Sometimes, however, the effects of so-called density-independent factors can actually vary with population density. On Isle Royale, for example, the moose population grew exponentially for a time after the wolf population crashed. Then, a bitterly cold winter with very heavy snowfall covered the plants that moose feed on, making it difficult for the moose to move around to find food.

MYSTERY CLUE

What factors do you think could limit the size of a rabbit population?

Because this was an island population, emigration was not possible; the moose weakened and many died. So, in this case, the effects of bad weather on the large, dense population were greater than they would have been on a small population. (In a smaller population, the moose would have had more food available because there would have been less competition.) This situation shows that it is sometimes difficult to say that a limiting factor acts *only* in a density-independent way.

Human activities can also place ecological communities under stress in ways that can hamper a population's ability to recover from natural disturbance. You will learn more about that situation in the next chapter.

Controlling Introduced Species In hydrilla's natural environment, density-dependent population limiting factors keep it under control. Perhaps plant-eating insects or fishes devour it. Or perhaps pests or diseases weaken it. Whatever the case, those limiting factors are not found in the United States. The result is runaway population growth!

Efforts at artificial density-independent control measures—such as herbicides and mechanical removal—offer only temporary solutions and are expensive. Researchers have spent decades looking for natural predators and pests of hydrilla. The best means of control so far seems to be an imported fish called grass carp, which view hydrilla as an especially tasty treat. These grass carp are not native to the United States. Only sterilized grass carp can be used to control hydrilla. Can you understand why?

FIGURE 5–10 Effects of a Severe Drought on a Population Dead fish lie rotting on the banks of the once-flowing Paraná de Manaquiri River in Brazil.

5.2 Assessment

Review Key Concepts 🔑

1. a. Review What is a limiting factor?

b. Apply Concepts How do limiting factors affect the growth of populations?

2. a. Review List three density-dependent limiting factors.

b. Relate Cause and Effect What is the relationship between competition and population size?

3. a. Review What is a density-independent limiting factor?

b. Apply Concepts Give three examples of density-independent factors that could severely limit the growth of a population of bats living in a cave.

Apply the Big idea

Interdependence in Nature

4. Study the factors that limit population growth shown in **Figure 5–6**. Classify each factor as biotic or abiotic. (*Hint:* Refer to Lesson 3.1 for information on biotic and abiotic factors.)

BIOLOGY.com > Search [Lesson 5.2] GO • Self-Test • Lesson Assessment

5.3 Human Population Growth

Key Questions

🔑 How has human population size changed over time?

🔑 Why do population growth rates differ among countries?

Vocabulary

demography
demographic transition

Taking Notes

Preview Visuals Before you read, preview the graphs in **Figures 5–11, 5–12,** and **5–13.** Make a list of questions about the graphs. Then, as you read, write down the answers to your questions.

BUILD Vocabulary

ACADEMIC WORDS The adverb **dramatically** means "forcefully" or "significantly." When something is described as having changed dramatically, it means it has changed in a striking way.

THINK ABOUT IT How quickly is the global human population growing? In the United States and other developed countries, the population growth rate is low. But in some developing countries, the population is growing very rapidly. Worldwide, there are more than four human births every second. At this birthrate, the human population is well on its way to reaching 9 billion in your lifetime. What do the present and future of human population growth mean for our species and its interactions with the rest of the biosphere?

Historical Overview

🔑 **How has human population size changed over time?**

🔑 **The human population, like populations of other organisms, tends to increase. The rate of that increase has changed dramatically over time.** For most of human existence, the population grew slowly because life was harsh. Food was hard to find. Predators and diseases were common and life-threatening. These limiting factors kept human death rates very high. Until fairly recently, only half the children in the world survived to adulthood. Because death rates were so high, families had many children, just to make sure that some would survive.

Exponential Human Population Growth As civilization advanced, life became easier, and the human population began to grow more rapidly. That trend continued through the Industrial Revolution in the 1800s. Food supplies became more reliable, and essential goods could be shipped around the globe. Several factors, including improved nutrition, sanitation, medicine, and healthcare, dramatically reduced death rates. Yet, birthrates in most parts of the world remained high. The combination of lower death rates and high birthrates led to exponential growth, as shown in **Figure 5–11.**

The Predictions of Malthus As you've learned, this kind of exponential growth cannot continue forever. Two centuries ago, this problem troubled English economist Thomas Malthus. Malthus suggested that only war, famine, and disease could limit human population growth. Can you see what Malthus was suggesting? He thought that human populations would be regulated by competition (war), limited resources (famine), parasitism (disease), and other density-dependent factors. Malthus's work was vitally important to the thinking of Charles Darwin.

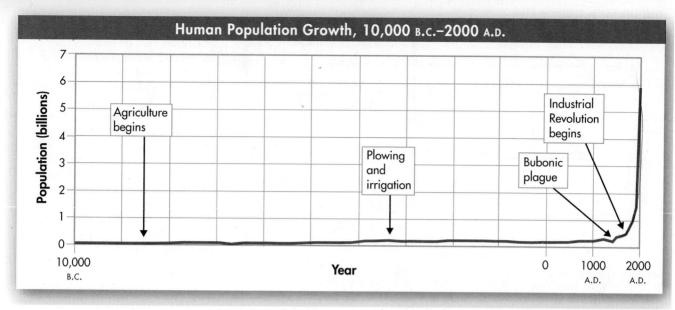

Human Population Growth, 10,000 B.C.–2000 A.D.

Agriculture begins

Plowing and irrigation

Bubonic plague

Industrial Revolution begins

Population (billions)

Year

10,000 B.C.

0 A.D.

1000 A.D.

2000 A.D.

World Population Growth Slows So what is happening to human population growth today? Exponential growth continued up to the second half of the twentieth century. The human population growth rate reached a peak around 1962–1963, and then it began to drop. The size of the global human population is still growing rapidly, but the rate of growth is slowing down.

It took 123 years for the human population to double from 1 billion in 1804 to 2 billion in 1927. Then it took just 33 years for it to grow by another billion people. The time it took for the population to increase each additional billion continued to fall until 1999, when it began, very slowly, to rise. It now takes longer for the global human population to grow by 1 billion than it did 20 years ago. What has been going on?

Patterns of Human Population Growth

🔑 Why do population growth rates differ among countries?

Scientists have identified several social and economic factors that affect human population growth. The scientific study of human populations is called **demography.** Demography examines characteristics of human populations and attempts to explain how those populations will change over time. 🔑 **Birthrates, death rates, and the age structure of a population help predict why some countries have high growth rates while other countries grow more slowly.**

In Your Notebook *Explain how the size of the global human population can increase while the rate of growth decreases.*

FIGURE 5–11 Human Population Growth Over Time After a slow start, the human population grew exponentially following advances in civilization. Change can be dramatic; these photos of Katmandu, Nepal, were taken from the same position in 1969 and 1999—just 30 years apart!

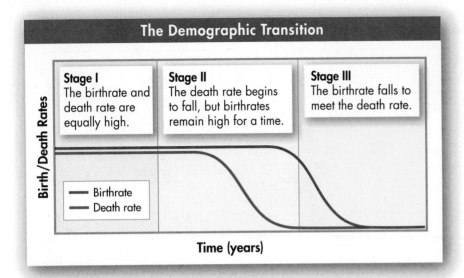

The Demographic Transition

Stage I
The birthrate and death rate are equally high.

Stage II
The death rate begins to fall, but birthrates remain high for a time.

Stage III
The birthrate falls to meet the death rate.

Birth/Death Rates

— Birthrate
— Death rate

Time (years)

FIGURE 5–12 The Demographic Transition Human birthrates and death rates are high for most of history (Stage I). Advances in nutrition, sanitation, and medicine lead to lower death rates. Birthrates remain high for a time, so births greatly exceed deaths (Stage II), and the population increases exponentially. As levels of education and living standards rise, families have fewer children and the birthrate falls (Stage III), and population growth slows. The demographic transition is complete when the birthrate meets the death rate, and population growth stops.

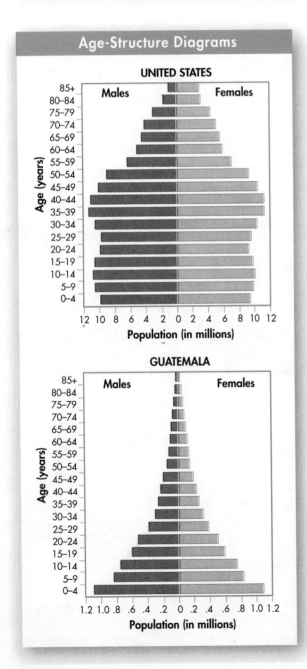

Age-Structure Diagrams

UNITED STATES

Males   Females

85+
80–84
75–79
70–74
65–69
60–64
55–59
50–54
45–49
40–44
35–39
30–34
25–29
20–24
15–19
10–14
5–9
0–4

Age (years)

12 10 8 6 4 2 0 2 4 6 8 10 12
Population (in millions)

GUATEMALA

Males   Females

85+
80–84
75–79
70–74
65–69
60–64
55–59
50–54
45–49
40–44
35–39
30–34
25–29
20–24
15–19
10–14
5–9
0–4

Age (years)

1.2 1.0 .8 .6 .4 .2 0 .2 .4 .6 .8 1.0 1.2
Population (in millions)

The Demographic Transition Human societies had equally high birthrates and death rates during most of history. But over the past century, population growth in the United States, Japan, and much of Europe slowed dramatically. Demographers developed a hypothesis to explain this shift. According to this hypothesis, these countries have completed the **demographic transition,** a dramatic change from high birthrates and death rates to low birthrates and death rates. The demographic transition is divided into three stages, as shown in **Figure 5–12.**

To date, the United States, Japan, and Europe have completed the demographic transition. Parts of South America, Africa, and Asia are passing through Stage II. (The United States passed through Stage II between 1790 and 1910.) A large part of ongoing human population growth is happening in only ten countries, with India and China in the lead. Globally, human population is still growing rapidly, but the rate of growth is slowing down. Our J-shaped growth curve may be changing into a logistic growth curve.

Age Structure and Population Growth To understand population growth in different countries, we turn to age-structure diagrams. **Figure 5–13** compares the age structure of the U.S. population with that of Guatemala, a country in Central America. In the United States, there are nearly equal numbers of people in each age group. This age structure predicts a slow but steady growth rate for the near future. In Guatemala, on the other hand, there are many more young children than teenagers, and many more teenagers than adults. This age structure predicts a population that will double in about 30 years.

FIGURE 5–13 Comparison of Age Structures These diagrams compare the populations of the United States and Guatemala. Notice the difference in their x-axis scales. **Analyze Data** *How do the two countries differ in the percentages of 10–14-year-olds in their populations?*

Future Population Growth To predict how the world's human population will grow, demographers consider many factors, including the age structure of each country and the effects of diseases on death rates—especially AIDS in Africa and parts of Asia. Current projections suggest that by 2050 the world population will reach 9 billion people. Will the human population level out to a logistic growth curve and become stable? This may happen if countries that are currently growing rapidly complete the demographic transition.

Current data suggest that global human population will grow more slowly over the next 50 years than it grew over the last 50 years. But because the growth rate will still be higher than zero in 2050, our population will continue to grow. In the next chapter, we will examine the effect of human population growth on the biosphere.

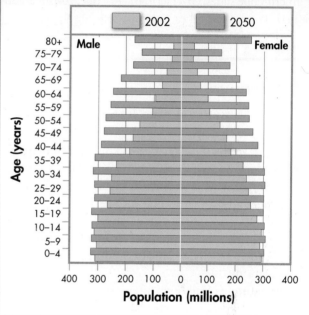

FIGURE 5–14 A Growing Population This graph (from the U.S. Census Bureau, International Database) shows the projected age structure of the world population in 2050. As population numbers climb, cities face various challenges, such as housing. The photo above shows a housing complex in Hong Kong; each apartment building is home to thousands of residents.

5.3 Assessment

Review Key Concepts

1. a. Review Describe the general trend of human population growth over time.

b. Relate Cause and Effect What factors contributed to the pattern of growth shown in **Figure 5–11**?

2. a. Review Why do populations in different countries grow at different rates?

b. Explain Describe the demographic transition and explain how it could affect a country's population growth rate.

c. Form an Opinion Are age-structure diagrams useful in predicting future population trends?

VISUAL THINKING

3. Describe the changes in human population predicted by **Figure 5–14**. How do you think those changes will affect society?

Skills Lab

Pre-Lab: The Growth Cycle of Yeast

Problem What type of population growth occurs in a yeast culture?

Materials yeast culture, stirring rod, dropper pipettes, microscope slides, coverslips, microscope, 10-mL graduated cylinder, test tubes, test-tube rack, graph paper

Lab Manual Chapter 5 Lab

Skills Measure, Calculate, Interpret Graphs

Connect to the Big idea Populations depend on, and are limited by, their environments. A population can grow when its members have the resources they need to survive and reproduce. Factors that can limit those resources include natural disasters, such as forest fires, and competition from other species. Predation and disease are also limiting factors for populations.

In nature, populations often experience cycles of growth and decline. In this lab, you will investigate whether such a cycle occurs in yeast populations.

Background Questions

a. Review What is the carrying capacity of a population?

b. Sequence Briefly describe the three phases of logistic growth.

c. Relate Cause and Effect Describe two different ways that a population might achieve a growth rate of zero.

d. Classify After two weeks of hot and sunny days with very little rain, the blades of grass in a backyard began to wither and die. Were any of the factors that caused the decline of the grass population dependent on density? Explain.

Pre-Lab Questions

Preview the procedure in the lab manual.

1. Infer Why was grape juice used to prepare the yeast cultures instead of plain water?

2. Form a Hypothesis Why will you locate the yeast cells under low power, but switch to high power to count the cells?

3. Calculate Suppose you have to do one dilution of your culture before you are able to count the yeast cells. If you count 21 yeast cells in the diluted sample, how many yeast cells were in the same area of the undiluted sample? MATH

4. Predict What do you think will happen to a yeast population between Day 3 and Day 7? Give reasons for your answer.

BIOLOGY.com   Search   Chapter 5   GO

Visit Chapter 5 online to test yourself on chapter content and to find activities to help you learn.

Untamed Science Join the Untamed Science crew as they learn the latest techniques for counting populations.

Art in Motion View a short animation that brings age-structure diagrams to life.

Art Review Review your understanding of limiting factors with this drag-and-drop activity.

InterActive Art Manipulate factors such as starting population size, birthrate, and death rate to see how they would impact moose and wolf populations over time.

Data Analysis Analyze logistic growth curves in order to make predictions about zebra mussel growth.

5 Study Guide

Big idea ▶ Interdependence in Nature

The way a population changes depends on many things, including its age structure, the rates at which individuals are added or removed from the population, and factors in the environment that limit its growth.

5.1 How Populations Grow

🔑 Researchers study populations' geographic range, density and distribution, growth rate, and age structure.

🔑 The factors that can affect population size are the birthrate, the death rate, and the rate at which individuals enter or leave the population.

🔑 Under ideal conditions with unlimited resources, a population will grow exponentially.

🔑 Logistic growth occurs when a population's growth slows and then stops, following a period of exponential growth.

population density (131)
age structure (131)
immigration (132)
emigration (132)

exponential growth (132)
logistic growth (135)
carrying capacity (135)

5.2 Limits to Growth

🔑 Acting separately or together, limiting factors determine the carrying capacity of an environment for a species.

🔑 Density-dependent limiting factors operate strongly when population density reaches a certain level. Density-dependent limiting factors include competition, predation, herbivory, parasitism, disease, and stress from overcrowding.

🔑 Density-independent limiting factors affect all populations in similar ways, regardless of population size and density. Unusual weather such as hurricanes, droughts, or floods, and natural disasters such as wild-fires, can act as density-independent limiting factors.

limiting factor (137)
density-dependent limiting factor (138)
density-independent limiting factor (140)

5.3 Human Population Growth

🔑 The human population, like populations of other organisms, tends to increase. The rate of that increase has changed dramatically over time.

🔑 Birthrates, death rates, and the age structure of a population help predict why some countries have high growth rates while other countries grow more slowly.

demography (143)   demographic transition (144)

Think Visually Create a table in which you describe the phases of logistic growth.

5 Assessment

Understand Key Concepts

1. The number of individuals of a single species per unit area is known as
   a. carrying capacity.
   b. logistic growth.
   c. population density.
   d. population growth rate.

2. The movement of individuals into an area is called
   a. demography.   c. immigration.
   b. carrying capacity. d. emigration.

3. The area inhabited by a population is known as its
   a. growth rate.
   b. geographic range.
   c. age structure.
   d. population density.

4. The graph below represents
   a. carrying capacity.   c. logistic growth.
   b. exponential growth. d. age structure.

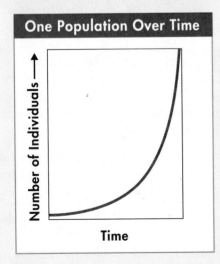

One Population Over Time

Number of Individuals →

Time

5. The maximum number of organisms of a particular species that can be supported by an environment is called
   a. logistic growth.   c. exponential growth.
   b. carrying capacity. d. population density.

6. What is the difference between immigration and emigration?

7. Sketch the exponential growth curve of a hypothetical population.

8. Describe the conditions under which logistic growth occurs.

9. What is carrying capacity? Give an example.

Think Critically

10. **Use Analogies** How is the carrying capacity of a city's roads similar to the carrying capacity of an ecosystem?

Understand Key Concepts

11. A limiting factor that depends on population size is called a
    a. density-dependent limiting factor.
    b. density-independent limiting factor.
    c. predator-prey relationship.
    d. parasitic relationship.

12. One example of a density-independent limiting factor is
    a. predation.   c. competition.
    b. hurricanes.   d. parasitism.

13. How might increasing the amount of a limiting nutrient in a pond affect the carrying capacity of the pond?

14. Describe the long-term effects of competition on populations of two different species competing for the same resources.

15. Describe how a predator-prey relationship can control both the predator population and the prey population.

16. How do parasites serve as a density-dependent limiting factor?

Think Critically

17. **Predict** What would happen to a population of predators if there was a sudden increase in food for the prey? Explain your answer.

18. **Apply Concepts** Why would a contagious virus that causes a fatal disease be considered a density-dependent limiting factor?

19. Infer Would a density-independent limiting factor have more of an effect on population size in a large ecosystem or in a small ecosystem?

20. Compare and Contrast How is the relationship between parasites and their hosts similar to a predator-prey relationship?

21. Apply Concepts How would a drop in the water level of a river affect a fish population living in that river?

5.3 Human Population Growth

Understand Key Concepts

22. The scientific study of human populations is called
   a. immigration.
   b. emigration.
   c. demographic transition.
   d. demography.

23. The demographic transition is considered complete when
   a. population growth stops.
   b. the birthrate is greater than the death rate.
   c. the death rate begins to fall.
   d. the death rate is greater than the birthrate.

24. How can you account for the fact that the human population has grown more rapidly during the past 500 years than it has at any other time in history?

25. What is the significance of the demographic transition in studies of human population around the world?

26. How does the age structure of a population affect its growth rate?

27. What factors did Thomas Malthus think would eventually limit the human population?

Think Critically

28. Compare and Contrast What shape population growth curve would you expect to see in a small town made up mainly of senior citizens? Compare this growth curve to that of a small town made up of newly married couples in their twenties.

29. Pose Questions What questions would a demographer need to answer to determine whether a country is approaching the demographic transition?

solve the CHAPTER MYSTERY

A PLAGUE OF RABBITS

Australia had no native rabbit population when the European rabbits arrived, so there were no density-dependent controls to keep their numbers in check. The rabbits' new environment provided many favorable conditions for survival, including fewer predators, parasites, and diseases. The initial small number of rabbits—which can reproduce rapidly—soon multiplied into millions.

High rabbit numbers caused serious environmental and agricultural damage. In an effort to manage the problem, many methods have been tried, including fencing, poisoning, the destruction of burrows, and the use of parasites and disease. In the 1950s, a rabbit virus that causes the fatal rabbit disease myxomatosis was deliberately introduced as a form of biological control. It killed countless rabbits. But the virus and rabbits soon reached an equilibrium that allowed host and parasite to coexist, and the rabbit population rose. Later, a new virus that causes rabbit hemorrhagic disease (RHD) was introduced, and the rabbit population dropped again. In several places, environmental recovery was dramatic: Native animals recovered, and native trees and shrubs thought to be locally extinct began to grow again. But the RHD virus and rabbits appear to have reached a new balance, and the rabbit population is rising again!

1. Predict Populations of wildcats and foxes (both also introduced to Australia) have come to depend on rabbits as prey. How do you think wildcats and foxes would be affected by a crash in the rabbit population?

2. Connect to the Big idea Why should people be cautious about introducing organisms into new environments?

Use Science Graphics

The following actual and projected data, from the United Nations Department of Economic and Social Affairs, Population Division, show when the global population reached or will reach an additional billion. Use the data table to answer questions 30 and 31.

World Population Milestones		
Population (billion)	Year	Time Interval (years)
1	1804	—
2	1927	123
3	1960	33
4	1974	14
5	1987	13
6	1999	12
7	2012	13
8	2027	15
8.9	2050	23

30. Observe When did the world population reach 1 billion people? When did it reach 6 billion?

31. Interpret Tables Describe the trend in population growth since the 1-billion-people mark.

Write About Science

32. Explanation Write a paragraph on the human population. Include the characteristics of a population, factors that affect its size, and changes in the size of the population from about 500 years ago to the present. Give a projection of how large the world population might be in the year 2050 and of how the growth rate in 2050 might compare to that in 2000. (*Hint*: Outline your ideas before you begin to write.)

33. Assess the Big idea Choose a specific organism and explain how the population of that organism depends on a number of factors that may cause it to increase, decrease, or remain stable in size.

Analyzing Data

The following graph shows the "boom-and-bust" pattern of regular rises and falls in the rabbit population in South Australia. The points at which various population control measures were introduced are indicated. Use the graph to answer questions 34 and 35.

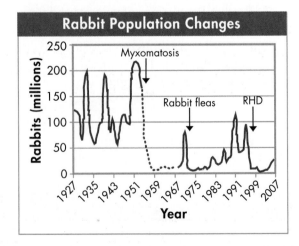

34. Interpret Graphs In which of the following years was the rabbit population density in South Australia most dense?
   a. 1936   **c.** 1975
   b. 1952   **d.** 2000

35. Infer European rabbit fleas were introduced in the late 1960s to help spread the effects of the rabbit disease myxomatosis. Based on the graph, what can you infer about the rabbit population after the fleas were introduced?
   a. The rabbit birthrate increased.
   b. The rabbit death rate increased.
   c. The rabbit death rate decreased.
   d. The fleas had no effect on the rabbit population.

Standardized Test Prep

Multiple Choice

1. The movement of individuals into an area is called
   A immigration.
   B emigration.
   C population growth rate.
   D population density.

2. All other things being equal, the size of a population will decrease if
   A birthrate exceeds the death rate.
   B immigration rate exceeds emigration rate.
   C death rate exceeds birthrate.
   D birthrate equals death rate.

3. Which of the following is NOT an example of a density-dependent limiting factor?
   A natural disaster   C competition
   B predator   D disease

4. A population like that of the United States with an age structure of roughly equal numbers in each of the age groups can be predicted to
   A grow rapidly over a 30-year-period and then stabilize.
   B grow little for a generation and then grow rapidly.
   C fall slowly and steadily over many decades.
   D show slow and steady growth for some time into the future.

5. In the presence of unlimited resources and in the absence of disease and predation, what would probably happen to a bacterial population?
   A logistic growth   C endangerment
   B exponential growth   D extinction

6. Which of the following statements best describes human population growth?
   A The growth rate has remained constant over time.
   B Growth continues to increase at the same rate.
   C Growth has been exponential in the last few hundred years.
   D Birthrate equals death rate.

7. Which of the following refers to when a population's birthrate equals its death rate?
   A limiting factor
   B carrying capacity
   C exponential growth
   D population density

Questions 8–9

Use the graph below to answer the following questions.

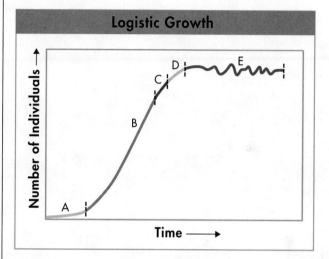

8. Which time interval(s) in the graph shows exponential growth?
   A D and E   C C and D
   B A and B   D E only

9. Which time interval(s) in the graph depicts the effects of limiting factors on the population?
   A A only   C C, D, and E
   B A and B   D C and D

Open-Ended Response

10. When a nonnative species is imported into a new ecosystem, the population sometimes runs wild. Explain why this might be the case.

If You Have Trouble With . . .

Question	1	2	3	4	5	6	7	8	9	10
See Lesson	5.1	5.1	5.2	5.3	5.1	5.3	5.1	5.1	5.2	5.2

6 Humans in the Biosphere

Big idea

Interdependence in Nature

Q: How have human activities shaped local and global ecology?

Viewed from space, the lights of human settlement are obvious. The brightest areas are the most developed but not necessarily the most populated. Development is one way in which humans, who today number over 6.5 billion, have affected the biosphere.

INSIDE:

- 6.1 A Changing Landscape
- 6.2 Using Resources Wisely
- 6.3 Biodiversity
- 6.4 Meeting Ecological Challenges

CHAPTER MYSTERY

MOVING THE *MOAI*

Easter Island is a tiny speck of land in the vast Pacific Ocean off the coast of Chile with a harsh tropical climate. The original islanders, who called themselves Rapa Nui, came from Polynesia. They carved hundreds of huge stone statues called *moai* (moh eye). Starting around 1200 A.D., the Rapa Nui somehow moved these mysterious statues, each of which weighed between 10 and 14 tons, from quarries to locations around the island. Nearly all theories about this process suggest that strong, large logs were necessary to move the *moai*. Yet by the time Europeans landed on the island in 1722, there was no sign of any trees large enough to provide such logs. What had happened? As you read this chapter, look for clues about the interactions of the Rapa Nui with their island environment. Then, solve the mystery.

Never Stop Exploring Your World.
The mystery of the moving *Moais* is just the beginning. Take a video field trip with the ecogeeks of Untamed Science to see where this mystery leads.

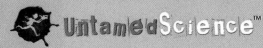
UntamedScience™

• Untamed Science Video   • Chapter Mystery

6.1 A Changing Landscape

Key Questions

🔑 How do our daily activities affect the environment?

🔑 What is the relationship between resource use and sustainable development?

Vocabulary

monoculture
renewable resource
nonrenewable resource
sustainable development

Taking Notes

Outline As you read, create an outline using the green and blue heads in this lesson. As you read, fill in key words, phrases, and ideas about each heading.

MYSTERY CLUE

Easter Island's first colonists brought with them banana trees, taro root, and chickens—and possibly some small mammalian "stowaways." What impact might these new organisms have had on the island's ecosystems?

THINK ABOUT IT The first humans to settle Hawaii came from Polynesia about 1600 years ago. These island people had customs that protected the natural resources of their new home. For example, they were prohibited from catching certain fish during spawning season and, for every coconut palm tree cut down, they had to plant two palms in its place. But Hawaiians did not treat their islands entirely like nature reserves. They cut trees to plant farms, and they introduced nonnative plants, pigs, chickens, dogs, and rats. This combination drove many native plant and animal species to extinction. Yet for centuries Hawaii's ecosystems provided enough fresh water, fertile soil, fish, and other resources to keep the society self-sufficient. What happened next is a lesson on managing limited resources—a lesson that is as important today as it was over 1000 years ago.

The Effect of Human Activity

🔑 **How do our daily activities affect the environment?**

Beginning in the late 1700s, new waves of settlers arrived in Hawaii. These people did not seem to understand the limits of island ecosystems. They imported dozens more plants and animals that became invasive pests. They cleared vast tracts of forest to grow sugar cane, pineapples, and other crops that required lots of water. And as the island's human population grew, they converted untouched land for other uses, including housing and tourism, as shown in **Figure 6–1**. The effect of these activities on Hawaii's ecosystems and its human inhabitants offers a window onto a globally important question: What happens when a growing human population does not adequately manage natural resources that are both vital and limited?

FIGURE 6–1 The Lesson of Hawaii Kalalau Valley along the Na Pali coast of Kauai looks almost untouched by humans. In contrast, Waikiki Beach on the island of Oahu is surrounded by built-up areas that support tourism.

Living on Island Earth Humans, like all forms of life, rely on Earth's life-support systems. And like all other organisms, we affect our environment when we obtain food, eliminate waste products, and build places to live. The effects of these activities can be most obvious on islands such as Hawaii because of their small size. Living on an island also can make people aware of limited resources and of an area's carrying capacity for humans because anything not available locally must be brought in from far away.

Most of us who live on large continents, however, probably don't think of land, food, and water as limited resources. In the past, environmental problems were local. There was always new land to settle and new sources of food and water. But today human activity has used or altered roughly half of all the land that's not covered with ice and snow. Some people suggest that as the global population reaches 7 billion people, we may be approaching the carrying capacity of the biosphere for humans. **Humans affect regional and global environments through agriculture, development, and industry in ways that have an impact on the quality of Earth's natural resources, including soil, water, and the atmosphere.**

In Your Notebook *Explain how Earth is like an island.*

Agriculture Agriculture is one of the most important inventions in human history. A dependable supply of food that can be stored for later use enabled humans to gather in settlements that grew into towns and cities. Settlements, in turn, encouraged the growth of modern civilization—government, laws, writing, and science. Modern agricultural practices have enabled farmers to double world food production over the last 50 years. **Monoculture,** for example, is the practice of clearing large areas of land to plant a single highly productive crop year after year, like the soybeans in **Figure 6–2.** Monoculture enables efficient sowing, tending, and harvesting of crops using machines. However, providing food for nearly 7 billion people impacts natural resources, including fresh water and fertile soil. Fertilizer production and farm machinery also consume large amounts of fossil fuels.

FIGURE 6–2 Monoculture This farmer is using a tractor to plow a large field of soybeans.
Apply Concepts *How has agriculture helped shape civilization?*

Quick Lab
GUIDED INQUIRY

Reduce, Reuse, Recycle

❶ Collect one day's worth of dry trash.

❷ Sort the trash into items that can be reused, recycled, or discarded because they can't be reused or recycled.

Analyze and Conclude

1. Analyze Data Look at the trash you've sorted. Roughly what percentage of the total does each type represent?

2. Predict What do you think happens to the trash you produce? Think of at least three ways trash can impact living things.

3. Evaluate List three ways you can reduce the amount of trash you produce.

BUILD Vocabulary

PREFIXES The prefix *mono-* in monoculture means "one, alone, single." Monoculture is the practice of planting a single productive crop, year after year.

Development As modern society developed, many people chose to live in cities. In the United States, as urban centers became crowded, people moved to, and built up, suburbs. The growth of cities and suburbs is tied to the high standard of living that Americans enjoy. Yet this development has environmental effects. Dense human communities produce lots of wastes. If these wastes are not disposed of properly, they affect air, water, and soil resources. In addition, development consumes farmland and divides natural habitats into fragments.

Industrial Growth Human society was transformed by the Industrial Revolution of the 1800s. Today, industry and scientific know-how provide us with the conveniences of modern life—from comfortable homes and clothes to electronic devices for work and play. Of course these conveniences require a lot of energy to produce and power. We obtain most of this energy by burning fossil fuels—coal, oil, and natural gas—and that affects the environment. In addition, industries have traditionally discarded wastes from manufacturing and energy production directly into the air, water, and soil.

Sustainable Development

🔑 **What is the relationship between resource use and sustainable development?**

In the language of economics, *goods* are things that can be bought and sold, that have value in terms of dollars and cents. *Services* are processes or actions that produce goods. Ecosystem goods and services are the goods and services produced by ecosystems that benefit the human economy.

Ecosystem Goods and Services Some ecosystem goods and services—like breathable air and drinkable water—are so basic that we often take them for granted. Healthy ecosystems provide many goods and services naturally and largely free of charge. But, if the environment can't provide these goods and services, society must spend money to produce them. In many places, for example, drinkable water is provided naturally by streams, rivers, and lakes, and filtered by wetlands like the one in **Figure 6–3.** But if water sources or wetlands are polluted or damaged, water quality may fall. In such cases, cities and towns must pay for mechanical or chemical treatment to provide safe drinking water.

FIGURE 6–3 Ecosystem Services The Hennepin and Hopper Lakes wetland is managed by The Wetlands Initiative—an organization dedicated to protecting and restoring Illinois's wetlands. The area, originally drained and leveed for farming in 1900, is shown in the inset before its 2003 restoration. **Apply Concepts** *What ecological services do wetlands provide?*

In Your Notebook *Describe three ecosystem goods and services you've used today.*

Renewable and Nonrenewable Resources Ecosystem goods and services are classified as either renewable or nonrenewable, as shown in **Figure 6–4**. A **renewable resource** can be produced or replaced by a healthy ecosystem. A single southern white pine is an example of a renewable resource because a new tree can grow in place of an old tree that dies or is cut down. But some resources are **nonrenewable resources** because natural processes cannot replenish them within a reasonable amount of time. Fossil fuels like coal, oil, and natural gas are nonrenewable resources formed from buried organic materials over millions of years. When existing deposits are depleted, they are essentially gone forever.

Sustainable Resource Use Ecological science can teach us how to use natural resources to meet our needs without causing long-term environmental harm. Using resources in such an environmentally conscious way is called **sustainable development.** 🔑 **Sustainable development provides for human needs while preserving the ecosystems that produce natural resources.**

What should sustainable development look like? It should cause no long-term harm to the soil, water, and climate on which it depends. It should consume as little energy and material as possible. Sustainable development must be flexible enough to survive environmental stresses like droughts, floods, and heat waves or cold snaps. Finally, sustainable development must take into account human economic systems as well as ecosystem goods and services. It must do more than just enable people to survive. It must help them improve their situation.

FIGURE 6–4 Natural Resources
Natural resources are classified as renewable or nonrenewable. Wind and coal are both natural resources that can provide energy. But wind is renewable, while coal—like other fossil fuels—is not.

6.1 Assessment

Review Key Concepts 🔑

1. a. Review List the three primary types of human activities that have affected regional and global environments. For each, give one benefit and one environmental cost.

b. Relate Cause and Effect How might more productive agricultural practices affect a developing nation's population? Its environmental health?

2. a. Review What is sustainable development? How can it help minimize the negative impacts of human activities?

b. Explain Explain why energy from the sun is a renewable resource but energy from oil is a nonrenewable resource.

c. Apply Concepts In addition to filtering water, wetlands provide flood control by absorbing excess water. Explain how society would provide these services (for a cost) if the ecosystem could not.

WRITE ABOUT SCIENCE

Description

3. What signs of growth do you see in your community? Write a paragraph telling how this growth might affect local ecosystems.

Key Questions

🔑 Why is soil important, and how do we protect it?

🔑 What are the primary sources of water pollution?

🔑 What are the major forms of air pollution?

Vocabulary

desertification
deforestation
pollutant
biological magnification
smog
acid rain

Taking Notes

Concept Map As you read, create a concept map to organize the information in this lesson.

THINK ABOUT IT Our economy is built on the use of natural resources, so leaving those resources untouched is not an option. Humans need to eat, for example, so we can't just stop cultivating land for farming. But the goods and services provided by healthy ecosystems are essential to life. We can't grow anything in soil that has lost its nutrients due to overfarming. If we don't properly manage agriculture, then, we may one day lose the natural resource on which it depends. So how do we find a balance? How do we obtain what we need from local and global environments without destroying those environments?

Soil Resources

🔑 **Why is soil important, and how do we protect it?**

When you think of natural resources, soil may not be something that comes to mind. But many objects you come into contact with daily rely on soil—from the grain in your breakfast cereal, to the wood in your home, to the pages of this textbook. 🔑 **Healthy soil supports both agriculture and forestry.** The mineral- and nutrient-rich portion of soil is called topsoil. Good topsoil absorbs and retains moisture yet allows water to drain. It is rich in organic matter and nutrients, but low in salts. Good topsoil is produced by long-term interactions between soil and the plants growing in it.

Topsoil can be a renewable resource if it is managed properly, but it can be damaged or lost if it is mismanaged. Healthy soil can take centuries to form but can be lost very quickly. And the loss of fertile soil can have dire consequences. Years of poorly managed farming in addition to severe drought in the 1930s badly eroded the once-fertile soil of the Great Plains. Thousands upon thousands of people lost their jobs and homes. The area essentially turned to desert, or, as it came to be known, a "dust bowl," as seen in **Figure 6–5.** What causes soil erosion, and how can we prevent it?

FIGURE 6–5 The Dust Bowl A ranch in Boise City, Idaho, is about to be hit by a cloud of dry soil on April 15, 1935.

Soil Erosion The dust bowl of the 1930s was caused, in part, by conversion of prairie land to cropland in ways that left soil vulnerable to erosion. Soil erosion is the removal of soil by water or wind. Soil erosion is often worse when land is plowed and left barren between plantings. When no roots are left to hold soil in place, it is easily washed away. And when soil is badly eroded, organic matter and minerals that make it fertile are often carried away with the soil. In parts of the world with dry climates, a combination of farming, overgrazing, seasonal drought, and climate change can turn farmland into desert. This process is called **desertification,** and it is what happened to the Great Plains in the 1930s. Roughly 40 percent of Earth's land is considered at risk for desertification. **Figure 6–6** shows vulnerable areas in North and South America.

Deforestation, or loss of forests, can also have a negative effect on soil quality. Healthy forests not only provide wood, but also hold soil in place, protect the quality of fresh water supplies, absorb carbon dioxide, and help moderate local climate. Unfortunately, more than half of the world's old-growth forests (forests that had never been cut) have already been lost to deforestation. In some temperate areas, such as the Eastern United States, forests can regrow after cutting. But it takes centuries for succession to produce mature, old-growth forests. In some places, such as in parts of the tropics, forests don't grow back at all after logging. This is why old-growth forests are usually considered nonrenewable resources.

Deforestation can lead to severe erosion, especially on mountainsides. Grazing or plowing after deforestation can permanently change local soils and microclimates in ways that prevent the regrowth of trees. Tropical rain forests, for example, look lush and rich, so you might assume they would grow back after logging. Unfortunately, topsoil in these forests is generally thin, and organic matter decomposes rapidly under high heat and humidity. When tropical rain forests are cleared for timber or for agriculture, their soil is typically useful for just a few years. After that the areas become wastelands, the harsh conditions there preventing regrowth.

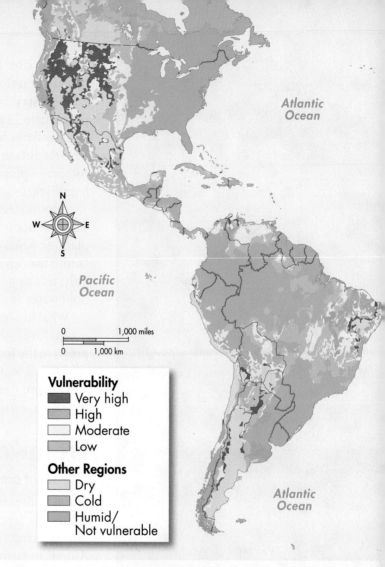

Vulnerability
- Very high
- High
- Moderate
- Low

Other Regions
- Dry
- Cold
- Humid/ Not vulnerable

FIGURE 6–6 Desertification Risk The U.S. Department of Agriculture assigns desertification risk categories based on soil type and climate. **Interpret Visuals** *Find your approximate location on the map. What category of desertification risk is your area in?*

MYSTERY CLUE

Forests of palm trees with strong, tall trunks and edible seeds once covered most of Easter Island. Why would the islanders have cut down these forests? What effect would deforestation have had?

In Your Notebook *Describe the relationship between agriculture and soil quality.*

Soil Use and Sustainability 🔑 **It is possible to minimize soil erosion through careful management of both agriculture and forestry.** Soil is most vulnerable to erosion when it is completely bare. Leaving stems and roots of the previous year's crop in the soil can help hold soil in place between plantings. And because different plants take different nutrients from the soil, crop rotation—planting different crops at different seasons or in different years—can help prevent both erosion and nutrient loss.

Altering the shape of the land is another way to limit erosion. The practice of contour plowing, shown in **Figure 6–7**, involves planting fields of crops across, instead of down, the slope of the land. This can reduce water runoff and therefore erosion. Similarly, terracing—shaping the land to create level "steps"—helps hold water and soil.

What are options for sustainable forestry? Selectively harvesting mature trees can promote the growth of younger trees and preserve the forest ecosystem, including its soil. In the southeastern United States, conditions enable foresters to plant, harvest, and replant tree farms. A well-managed tree farm both protects the soil and makes the trees themselves a renewable resource.

Freshwater Resources

🔑 *What are the primary sources of water pollution?*

Humans depend on fresh water and freshwater ecosystems for goods and services, including drinking water, industry, transportation, energy, and waste disposal. Some of the most productive American farmland relies heavily on irrigation, in which fresh water is brought in from other sources.

While fresh water is usually considered a renewable resource, some sources of fresh water are not renewable. The Ogallala aquifer, for example, spans eight states from South Dakota to Texas. The aquifer took more than a million years to collect and is not replenished by rainfall today. So much water is being pumped out of the Ogallala that it is expected to run dry in 20 to 40 years. In many places, freshwater supplies are limited. Only 3 percent of Earth's water is fresh water—and most of that is locked in ice at the poles. Since we can't infinitely expand our use of a finite resource, we must protect the ecosystems that collect and purify fresh water.

Water Pollution Freshwater sources can be affected by different kinds of pollution. A **pollutant** is a harmful material that can enter the biosphere. Sometimes pollutants enter water supplies from a single source—a factory or an oil spill, for example. This is called point source pollution. Often, however, pollutants enter water supplies from many smaller sources—the grease and oil washed off streets by rain or the chemicals released into the air by factories and automobiles. These pollutants are called nonpoint sources.

FIGURE 6–7 Contour Plowing Planting crops parallel to the land's natural contours can help reduce soil erosion.

Pollutants may enter both surface water and underground water supplies that we access with wells. Once contaminants are present, they can be extremely difficult to get rid of. 🔑 **The primary sources of water pollution are industrial and agricultural chemicals, residential sewage, and nonpoint sources.**

▶ *Industrial and Agricultural Chemicals* One industrial pollutant is a class of organic chemicals called PCBs that were widely used in industry until the 1970s. After several large-scale contamination events, PCBs were banned. However, because PCBs often enter mud and sand beneath bodies of water, they can be difficult, if not impossible, to eliminate. Parts of the Great Lakes and some coastal areas, for example, are still polluted with PCBs. Other harmful industrial pollutants are heavy metals like cadmium, lead, mercury, and zinc.

Large-scale monoculture has increased the use of pesticides and insecticides. These chemicals can enter the water supply in the form of runoff after heavy rains, or they can seep directly into groundwater. Pesticides can be very dangerous pollutants. DDT, which is both cheap and long lasting, effectively controls agricultural pests and disease-carrying mosquitoes. But when DDT gets into a water supply, it has disastrous effects on the organisms that directly and indirectly rely on that water—a function of a phenomenon called biological magnification.

Biological magnification occurs if a pollutant, such as DDT, mercury, or a PCB, is picked up by an organism and is not broken down or eliminated from its body. Instead, the pollutant collects in body tissues. Primary producers pick up a pollutant from the environment. Herbivores that eat those producers concentrate and store the compound. Pollutant concentrations in herbivores may be more than ten times the levels in producers. When carnivores eat the herbivores, the compound is still further concentrated. Thus, pollutant concentration increases at higher trophic levels. In the highest trophic levels, pollutant concentrations may reach 10 million times their original concentration in the environment, as shown in **Figure 6–8.**

These high concentrations can cause serious problems for wildlife and humans. Widespread DDT use in the 1950s threatened fish-eating birds like pelicans, osprey, falcons, and bald eagles. It caused females to lay eggs with thin, fragile shells, reducing hatching rates and causing a drop in bird populations. Since DDT was banned in the 1970s, bird populations have recovered. Still a concern is mercury, which accumulates in the bodies of certain marine fish such as tuna and swordfish.

In Your Notebook *In your own words, explain the process of biological magnification.*

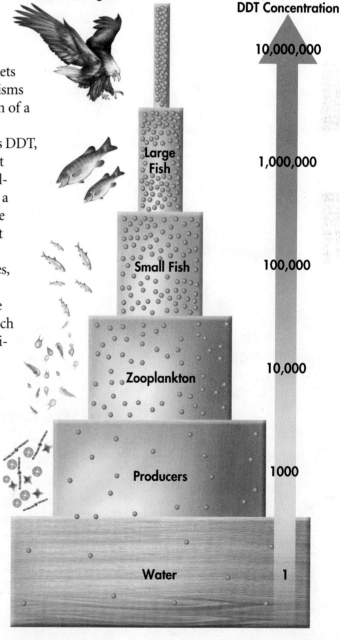

FIGURE 6–8 Biological Magnification In the process of biological magnification, the concentration of a pollutant like DDT—represented by the orange dots—is multiplied as it passes up the food chain from producers to consumers. **Calculate** *By what number is the concentration of DDT multiplied at each successive trophic level?* MATH

Fish-Eating Birds

Large Fish

Small Fish

Zooplankton

Producers

Water

Magnification of DDT Concentration

10,000,000

1,000,000

100,000

10,000

1000

1

▶ **Residential Sewage** Have you ever stopped to think what happens after you flush your toilet? Those wastes don't disappear! They become residential sewage. Sewage isn't poisonous, but it does contain lots of nitrogen and phosphorus. Reasonable amounts of these nutrients can be processed by and absorbed into healthy ecosystems. But large amounts of sewage can stimulate blooms of bacteria and algae that rob water of oxygen. Oxygen-poor areas called "dead zones" can appear in both fresh and salt water. Raw sewage also contains microorganisms that can spread disease.

Water Quality and Sustainability One key to sustainable water use is to protect the natural systems involved in the water cycle. For example, as water flows slowly through a wetland, densely growing plants absorb some excess nutrients and filter out certain pollutants. Similarly, forests and other vegetation help purify water that seeps into the ground or runs off into rivers and lakes. Protecting these ecosystems is a critical part of watershed conservation. A watershed includes all the land whose groundwater, streams, and rivers drain into the same place—such as a large lake or river. The idea behind watershed conservation is simple: Cleaning up the pollution in a local area can't do much good if the water running into it is polluted. You must consider the entire watershed to achieve long-lasting results.

Pollution control can have direct and positive effects on the water quality in a watershed. Sewage treatment can lower levels of sewage-associated bacteria and help prevent dead zones in bodies of water receiving the runoff. In some situations, agriculture can use integrated pest management (IPM) instead of pesticides. IPM techniques include biological control—using predators and parasites to regulate for pest insects—the use of less-poisonous sprays, and crop rotation.

Conserving water is, of course, also important. One example of water conservation in agriculture is drip irrigation, shown in **Figure 6–9,** which delivers water drop by drop directly to the roots of plants that need it.

BUILD Vocabulary

RELATED WORD FORMS The verb *purify* is related to the noun *pure*. *To purify* means "to make pure or clean." Wetlands purify water by removing pollutants.

FIGURE 6–9 Drip Irrigation These cabbages are supplied water directly to their roots through drip irrigation. Tiny holes in water hoses (inset) allow farmers to deliver water only where it's needed.

Atmospheric Resources

🔑 What are the major forms of air pollution?

The atmosphere is a common resource whose quality has direct effects on health. After all, the atmosphere provides the oxygen we breathe! In addition, ozone, a form of oxygen that is found naturally in the upper atmosphere, absorbs harmful ultraviolet radiation from sunlight before it reaches Earth's surface. It is the ozone layer that protects our skin from damage that can cause cancer.

The atmosphere provides many other services. For example, the atmosphere's greenhouse gases, including carbon dioxide, methane, and water vapor, regulate global temperature. As you've learned, without the greenhouse effect, Earth's average temperature would be about 30° Celsius cooler than it is today.

The atmosphere is never "used up." So, classifying it as a renewable or nonrenewable resource is not as important as understanding how human activities affect the quality of the atmosphere. For most of Earth's history, the quality of the atmosphere has been naturally maintained by biogeochemical cycles. However, if we disrupt those cycles, or if we overload the atmosphere with pollutants, the effects on its quality can last a very long time.

Air Pollution What happens when the quality of Earth's atmosphere is reduced? For one thing, respiratory illnesses such as asthma are made worse and skin diseases tend to increase. Globally, climate patterns may be affected. What causes poor air quality? Industrial processes and the burning of fossil fuels can release pollutants of several kinds. 🔑 **Common forms of air pollution include smog, acid rain, greenhouse gases, and particulates.**

▶ *Smog* If you live in a large city, you've probably seen **smog,** a gray-brown haze formed by chemical reactions among pollutants released into the air by industrial processes and automobile exhaust. Ozone is one product of these reactions. While ozone high up in the atmosphere helps protect life on Earth from ultraviolet radiation, at ground level, ozone and other pollutants threaten the health of people, especially those with respiratory conditions. Many athletes participating in the 2008 Summer Olympics in Beijing, China, expressed concern over how the intense smog, seen in **Figure 6–10,** would affect their performance and health.

FIGURE 6–10 Smog Despite closing factories and restricting vehicle access to the city, Beijing remained under a blanket of dense smog just days before the 2008 Summer Olympics. **Apply Concepts** *What component of smog is beneficial when part of the atmosphere, but harmful when at ground level?*

In Your Notebook *Compare and contrast the atmosphere as a resource with fresh water as a resource.*

American Air Pollution Trends

Each year, the U.S. Environmental Protection Agency (EPA) estimates emissions from a variety of sources. Look at the graph in **Figure 6–12.** The combined emissions of six common pollutants are plotted along with trends in energy consumption and automobile travel between 1980 and 2007. The values shown are the total percentage change. For example, in 1995, aggregate emissions had dropped about 30 percent from their level in 1980.

1. Interpret Data Describe the overall trend in emissions since 1980. Is this what you would expect given the trends in energy consumption and automobile travel? Explain your answer.

2. Interpret Data How does this graph differ from one that shows *absolute* values for emissions? Would that graph start at zero as this one does?

3. Infer What do you think has contributed to the trends you see in this graph? Why would the EPA be particularly interested in these data?

FIGURE 6–11 Acid Rain Acid rain results from the chemical transformation of nitrogen and sulfur products that come from human activities. These reactions can cause damage to stone statues and plant life.

▶ *Acid Rain* When we burn fossil fuels in our factories and homes, we release nitrogen and sulfur compounds. When those compounds combine with water vapor in the air, they form nitric and sulfuric acids. These airborne acids can drift for many kilometers before they fall as **acid rain.** Acidic water vapor can also affect ecosystems as fog or snow. In some areas, acid rain kills plants by damaging their leaves and changing the chemistry of soils and surface water. Examples of its effects are shown in **Figure 6–11.** Acid precipitation also can dissolve and release mercury and other toxic elements from soil, freeing those elements to enter other parts of the biosphere.

In Your Notebook *Create a flowchart that shows the steps in acid rain formation.*

▶ *Greenhouse Gases* Burning fossil fuels and forests releases stored carbon into the atmosphere as carbon dioxide, a greenhouse gas. Agricultural practices from raising cattle to farming rice release methane, another greenhouse gas. Although some greenhouse gases are necessary, when excess greenhouse gases accumulate in the atmosphere, they contribute to global warming and climate change.

▶ *Particulates* Particulates are microscopic particles of ash and dust released by certain industrial processes and certain kinds of diesel engines. Very small particulates can pass through the nose and mouth and enter the lungs, where they can cause serious health problems.

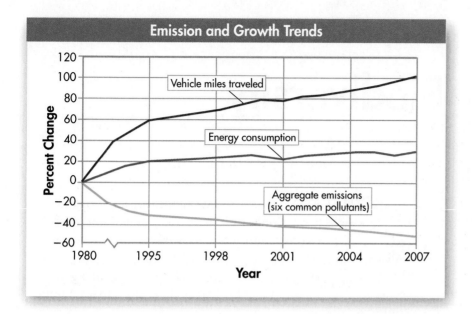

Emission and Growth Trends

Vehicle miles traveled

Energy consumption

Aggregate emissions (six common pollutants)

Year

Percent Change

FIGURE 6–12 Air Pollution Trends
This graph summarizes EPA findings of the total percentage change from 1980 to 2007 in vehicle miles traveled, energy consumption, and the combined emissions of six common pollutants—carbon monoxide, lead, nitrogen oxides, organic compounds, particulates, and sulfur dioxide. **Calculate** *In 1980, motorists in the Puget Sound region of Washington State traveled 36.4 million miles. Assuming that these motorists increased their miles traveled at the national rate, approximately how many miles did they travel in 2007?* MATH

Air Quality and Sustainability Improving air quality is difficult. Air doesn't stay in one place and doesn't "belong" to anyone. Automobile emission standards and clean-air regulations have improved air quality in some regions, however, and seem to be having a net positive effect, as shown in **Figure 6–12.** Efforts like these also have improved the atmosphere globally. At one time, for example, all gasoline was enriched with lead. But as leaded gasoline burned, lead was released in exhaust fumes and ultimately washed onto land and into rivers and streams. U.S. efforts to phase out leaded gasoline started in 1973 and were completed in 1996 when the sale of leaded gasoline was banned. Now that unleaded gasoline is used widely across the United States, lead levels in soils, rivers, and streams around the country have dropped significantly from earlier, higher levels.

6.2 Assessment

Review Key Concepts 🔑

1. a. Review What causes soil erosion? Why is soil erosion a problem?

b. Apply Concepts What are three ways in which the agriculture and forestry industries can improve the sustainability of soil?

2. a. Review How is fresh water both a renewable and a limited resource?

b. Explain Why are some pollutants more harmful to organisms at higher trophic levels?

c. Propose a Solution Pick one source of water pollution and describe a way in which we can reduce its effect.

3. a. Review What ecological goods and services does the atmosphere provide?

b. Relate Cause and Effect How does the use of fossil fuels negatively impact Earth's atmosphere?

ANALYZING DATA

4. Look at **Figure 6–8.** If the concentration of DDT in zooplankton measures 0.04 parts per million, what is the approximate concentration of DDT at each other trophic level shown? MATH

6.3 Biodiversity

Key Questions

🗝 *Why is biodiversity important?*

🗝 *What are the most significant threats to biodiversity?*

🗝 *How do we preserve biodiversity?*

Vocabulary

biodiversity
ecosystem diversity
species diversity
genetic diversity
habitat fragmentation
ecological hot spot

Taking Notes

Preview Visuals Before you read, look at **Figure 6–20.** Record three questions you have about the map. When you've finished reading, answer the questions.

THINK ABOUT IT Those of us who love nature are awed by the incredible variety of living things that share our planet. From multicolored coral reefs to moss-draped forests, *variety*, is "the spice of life." But variety in the biosphere gives us more than interesting things to look at. Our well-being is closely tied to the well-being of a great number of other organisms, including many that are neither majestic nor beautiful to our eyes.

The Value of Biodiversity

🗝 **Why is biodiversity important?**

Biological diversity, or **biodiversity,** is the total of all the genetically based variation in all organisms in the biosphere. To biologists, biodiversity is precious, worth preserving for its own sake. But what kinds of biodiversity exist, and what value do they offer society?

Types of Biodiversity Biodiversity exists on three levels: ecosystem diversity, species diversity, and genetic diversity. **Ecosystem diversity** refers to the variety of habitats, communities, and ecological processes in the biosphere. The number of different species in the biosphere, or in a particular area, is called **species diversity.** To date, biologists have identified and named more than 1.8 million species, and they estimate that at least 30 million more are yet be discovered. Much of this diversity exists among single-celled organisms. But new species of vertebrates, like the snake in **Figure 6–13,** are still being found.

Genetic diversity can refer to the sum total of all different forms of genetic information carried by a particular species, or by all organisms on Earth. Within each species, genetic diversity refers to the total of all different forms of genes present in that species. In many ways, genetic diversity is the most basic kind of biodiversity. It is also the hardest kind to see and appreciate. Yet, genetic diversity is vitally important to the survival and evolution of species in a changing world.

FIGURE 6–13 A New Species This tiny snake, native to the island of Barbados, is one of many recently discovered species. Photos of the snake were released in 2008. Infer *Why are you more likely to discover a new vertebrate species in a tropical area than in a desert?*

Valuing Biodiversity You can't touch, smell, or eat biodiversity, so many people don't think of it as a natural resource. But biodiversity is one of Earth's greatest natural resources. 🔑 **Biodiversity's benefits to society include contributions to medicine and agriculture, and the provision of ecosystem goods and services.** When biodiversity is lost, significant value to the biosphere and to humanity may be lost along with it.

▶ *Biodiversity and Medicine* Wild species are the original source of many medicines, including painkillers like aspirin and antibiotics like penicillin. The chemicals in wild species are used to treat diseases like depression and cancer. For example, the foxglove, shown in **Figure 6–14,** contains compounds called digitalins that are used to treat heart disease. These plant compounds are assembled according to instructions coded in genes. So the genetic information carried by diverse species is like a "natural library" from which we have a great deal to learn.

▶ *Biodiversity and Agriculture* Genetic diversity is also important in agriculture. Most crop plants have wild relatives, like the potatoes in **Figure 6–15.** These wild plants may carry genes we can use—through plant breeding or genetic engineering—to transfer disease or pest resistance, or other useful traits, to crop plants.

▶ *Biodiversity and Ecosystem Services* The number and variety of species in an ecosystem can influence that ecosystem's stability, productivity, and value to humans. Sometimes the presence or absence of a single keystone species, like the sea otter in **Figure 6–16,** can completely change the nature of life in an ecosystem. Also, healthy and diverse ecosystems play a vital role in maintaining soil, water, and air quality.

FIGURE 6–14 Medicinal Plants Digoxin, a drug derived from digitalin compounds in the foxglove plant, is used to treat heart disease.

FIGURE 6–15 Potato Diversity The genetic diversity of wild potatoes in South America can be seen in the colorful varieties shown here. The International Potato Center, based in Peru, houses a "library" of more than 4500 tuber varieties.

FIGURE 6–16 Keystone Species The sea otter is a keystone species. When the otter population falls, the population of its favorite prey, sea urchins, goes up. Population increases in sea urchins, in turn, cause a dramatic decrease in the population of sea kelp, the sea urchin's favorite food.

Threats to Biodiversity

🔑 What are the most significant threats to biodiversity?

Species have been evolving, changing, and dying out since life began. In fact scientists estimate that over 99 percent of the species that have ever lived are now extinct. So extinction is not new. But human activity today is causing the greatest wave of extinctions since dinosaurs disappeared. The current rate of species loss is approaching 1000 times the "typical" rate. And as species disappear, the potential contribution to human knowledge that is carried in their genes is lost.

Species diversity is related to genetic diversity. The more genetically diverse a species is, the greater its chances of surviving disturbances. So, as human activity reduces genetic diversity, species are put at a greater risk for extinction. Species diversity, in turn, is linked to ecosystem diversity. Therefore, as ecosystems are damaged, the organisms that inhabit them become more vulnerable to extinction.

How are humans influencing biodiversity? 🔑 **Humans reduce biodiversity by altering habitats, hunting, introducing invasive species, releasing pollution into food webs, and contributing to climate change.** Biologists compare loss of biodiversity to destroying a library before its books are ever read.

Altered Habitats When natural habitats are eliminated for agriculture or for urban development, the number of species in those habitats drops, and some species may become extinct. But, habitats don't need to be completely destroyed to put species at risk. Development often splits ecosystems into pieces, a process called **habitat fragmentation,** leaving habitat "islands." You probably think of islands as bits of land surrounded by water, but a biological island can be any patch of habitat surrounded by a different habitat, as shown in **Figure 6–17.** The smaller a habitat island, the fewer the species that can live there and the smaller their populations. Both changes make habitats and species more vulnerable to other disturbance.

MYSTERY CLUE

Easter Island probably never had the biological diversity of Hawaii and many other tropical islands. How would this affect its ability to rebound after a disturbance?

BUILD Vocabulary

ACADEMIC WORDS The adjective **vulnerable** means "open to attack or damage." Fragmented habitats are more vulnerable, or more apt to be damaged, than larger undisturbed habitats because they contain fewer species and smaller populations of organisms.

FIGURE 6–17 Habitat Fragmentation Deforestation for housing developments in Florida has led to the pattern of forest "islands" shown here. Habitat fragmentation limits biodiversity and the potential size of populations.

Hunting and the Demand for Wildlife Products Humans can push species to extinction by hunting. In the 1800s, hunting wiped out the Carolina parakeet and the passenger pigeon. Today endangered species in the United States are protected from hunting, but hunting still threatens rare animals in Africa, South America, and Southeast Asia. Some animals, like many birds, are hunted for meat. Others are hunted for their commercially valuable hides or skins or because people believe their body parts have medicinal properties. Still others, like the parrots in **Figure 6–18,** are hunted to be sold as pets. Hunted species are affected even more than other species by habitat fragmentation because fragmentation increases access for hunters and limits available hiding spaces for prey. The Convention on International Trade in Endangered Species (CITES) bans international trade in products from a list of endangered species. Unfortunately, it's difficult to enforce laws in remote wilderness areas.

Introduced Species Recall that organisms introduced to new habitats can become invasive and threaten biodiversity. For example, more than 130 introduced species live in the Great Lakes, where they have been changing aquatic ecosystems and driving native species close to extinction. One European weed, leafy spurge, infests millions of hectares across the Northern Great Plains. On rangelands, leafy spurge displaces grasses and other food plants, and its milky latex can sicken or kill cattle and horses. Each year, ranchers and farmers suffer losses of more than $120 million because of this single pest.

Pollution Many of the pollutants described in the last lesson also threaten biodiversity. DDT, for example, prevents birds from laying healthy eggs. In the United States, brown pelican, peregrine falcon, and other bird populations plummeted with widespread use of the chemical. Acid rain places stress on land and water organisms. Increased carbon dioxide in the atmosphere is dissolving in oceans, making them more acidic, which threatens biodiversity on coral reefs and in other marine ecosystems.

MYSTERY CLUE

Almost all the coconut shells found by researchers on Easter Island show signs of having been gnawed on by nonnative rats. Coconuts contain the seeds of the coconut palm. What effect do you think the rats had on the coconut palm population?

 In Your Notebook *Why is acidic water harmful to coral?*

Climate Change Climate change (a topic in the next lesson) is a major threat to biodiversity. Remember that organisms are adapted to their environments and have specific tolerance ranges to temperature and other abiotic conditions. If conditions change beyond an organism's tolerance, the organism must move to a more suitable location or face extinction. Species in fragmented habitats are particularly vulnerable to climate change because if conditions change they may not be able to move easily to a suitable habitat. Estimates vary regarding the effects of climate change on biodiversity. If global temperatures increase 1.5°C–2.5°C over late twentieth-century temperatures, 30 percent of species studied are likely to face increased risk of extinction. If the global temperature increase goes beyond 3.5°C, it is likely that 40–70 percent of species studied will face extinction.

Conserving Biodiversity

🔑 How do we preserve biodiversity?

What can we do to protect biodiversity? Should we focus on a particular organism like the scarlet macaw? Or should we try to save an entire ecosystem like the Amazon rain forest? We must do both. At the same time, conservation efforts must take human interests into account. 🔑 **To conserve biodiversity, we must protect individual species, preserve habitats and ecosystems, and make certain that human neighbors of protected areas benefit from participating in conservation efforts.**

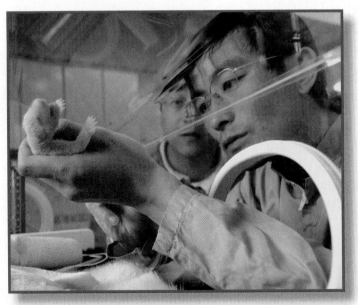

FIGURE 6–19 Saving an Individual Species Efforts to save the giant panda include a comprehensive captive breeding and reintroduction program. Here, a researcher examines an infant panda at China's Wolong Nature Reserve. **Apply Concepts** *How does captive breeding affect a population's genetic diversity?*

Protecting Individual Species In the past, most conservation efforts focused on individual species, and some of this work continues today. The Association of Zoos and Aquariums (AZA), for example, oversees species survival plans (SSPs) designed to protect threatened and endangered species. A key part of those plans is a captive breeding program. Members of the AZA carefully select and manage mating pairs of animals to ensure maximum genetic diversity. The ultimate goal of an SSP is to reintroduce individuals to the wild. Research, public education, and breeding programs all contribute to that goal. More than 180 species, including the giant panda shown in **Figure 6–19,** are currently covered by SSPs.

Preserving Habitats and Ecosystems The main thrust of global conservation efforts today is to protect not just individual species but entire ecosystems. The goal is to preserve the natural interactions of many species at once. To that end, governments and conservation groups work to set aside land as parks and reserves. The United States has national parks, forests, and other protected areas. Marine sanctuaries are being created to protect coral reefs and marine mammals.

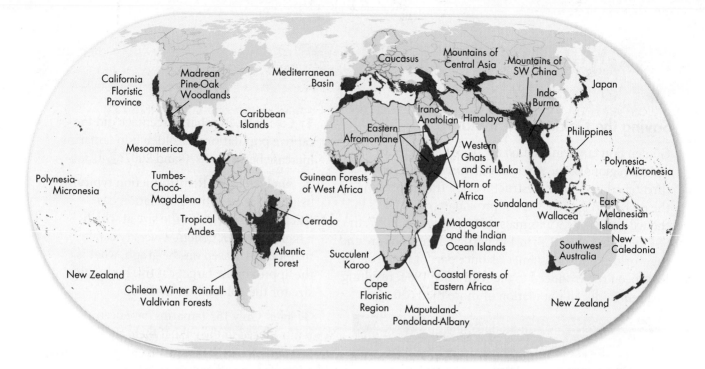

The challenge is protecting areas that are large enough and that contain the right resources to protect biodiversity. To make sure that conservation efforts are concentrated in the most important places, conservation biologists have identified ecological "hot spots," shown in red in **Figure 6–20.** An **ecological hot spot** is a place where significant numbers of species and habitats are in immediate danger of extinction. By identifying these areas, ecologists hope that scientists and governments can better target their efforts to save as many species as possible.

Considering Local Interests Protecting biodiversity often demands that individuals change their habits or the way they earn their living. In these cases it is helpful to offer some reward or incentive to the people or communities involved. The United States government, for example, has offered tax credits to people who've installed solar panels or bought hybrid cars. Similarly, many communities in Africa, Central America, and Southeast Asia have set aside land for national parks and nature reserves, like the park shown in **Figure 6–21,** to attract tourist dollars. In some Australian communities, farmers were paid to plant trees along rivers and streams as part of wildlife corridors connecting forest fragments. Not only did the trees help improve local water quality; they also improved the health of the farmers' cows, which were able to enjoy shade on hot days!

The use of carbon credits is one strategy aimed at encouraging industries to cut fossil fuels use. Companies are allowed to release a certain amount of carbon into the environment. Any unused carbon may be sold back at a set market value or traded to other companies. This strategy encourages industries to pay for lower-emission machinery and to adopt carbon-saving practices. In this way, pollution is capped or cut without adding a financial burden to the industry involved. This helps protect the economy while reducing biodiversity loss due to pollution. These examples show that conservation efforts work best when they are both informed by solid scientific information and benefit the communities affected by them.

FIGURE 6–20 Ecological Hot Spots Conservation International identifies biodiversity hot spots using two criteria. The area (1) must contain at least 1500 species of native vascular plants, and (2) it must have lost at least 70 percent of its original habitat. The 34 hot spots seen here cover just 2.3 percent of Earth's land surface, but they contain over 50 percent of the world's plant species and 42 percent of its terrestrial vertebrates.

FIGURE 6–21 Ecotourism A tourist gets an elephant-size kiss from one of the over 30 rescued elephants at Thailand's Elephant Nature Park.

Analyzing Data

Saving the Golden Lion Tamarin

Golden lion tamarins (GLTs) are primates native to the coastal regions of the Amazon rain forest. They have been threatened by habitat destruction and fragmentation. In the early 1970s, there were approximately 200 GLTs in the wild and only 91 animals in 26 zoos. As of 2007, the SSP included 496 GLTs in 145 participating zoos around the world. About 153 tamarins once part of the program have been reintroduced to the wild since 1984, resulting in a reintroduced population of more than 650.

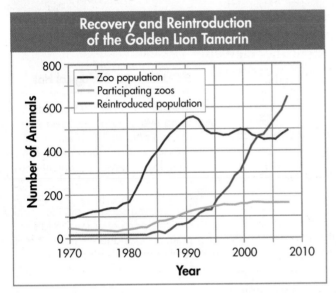

Recovery and Reintroduction of the Golden Lion Tamarin

- Zoo population
- Participating zoos
- Reintroduced population

Number of Animals (y-axis: 0, 200, 400, 600, 800)
Year (x-axis: 1970, 1980, 1990, 2000, 2010)

1. Calculate By what percentage did the captive population of golden lion tamarins increase between 1970 and 2007? **MATH**

2. Analyze Data Reintroduction typically begins once a captive population has reached a target size—the size at which a high degree of genetic diversity can be maintained. Based on the graph, what is the approximate target captive population size for the golden lion tamarin?

3. Infer Only 153 tamarins have been reintroduced to the wild. If there are now 650 tamarins in the reintroduced population, where did the other 497 come from?

4. Form an Opinion When populations of wild animals get very small, do you think they should be removed from the wild and brought into captivity? Why or why not?

Adapted from J. D. Ballou and J. Mickelberg, *International Studbook for Golden Lion Tamarins* (Washington, D.C.: National Zoological Park, Smithsonian Institution, 2007). B. Holst et al., *Lion Tamarin Population and Habitat Viability Assessment Workshop 2005, Final Report* (Apple Valley, MN: IUCN/SSC Conservation Breeding Specialist Group, 2006.)

6.3 Assessment

Review Key Concepts

1. a. Review Describe the different components of global biodiversity.
b. Apply Concepts What benefits does society get from biodiversity?

2. a. Review What are the major threats to biodiversity?
b. Relate Cause and Effect Explain the relationship between habitat size and species diversity.

3. a. Review What is the goal of a species survival plan?
b. Form an Opinion Do you think that the hot spot strategy is a good one? Explain your answer.

VISUAL THINKING

4. Look back at the biome map on page 111. Compare it to the map in **Figure 6–20**. Are there any similarities among the biomes the hot spots belong to? Using what you know about biomes, are you surprised by what you've found? Explain your answer.

6.4 Meeting Ecological Challenges

THINK ABOUT IT Every year, the EPA awards up to ten President's Environmental Youth Awards. Past winners have included an Eagle Scout from Massachusetts who encouraged people who fish to stop using lead weights that contaminate water and poison organisms, students from Washington State who reduced waste at their school and saved more than half a million dollars in the process, and a student from Florida who developed an outreach program to protect local sea turtles. What do these award winners have in common? They came up with ideas that protect the environment while satisfying both present and future needs. This kind of leadership is what will help us chart a new course for the future.

Ecological Footprints

🔑 **How does the average ecological footprint in America compare to the world's average?**

What is our impact on the biosphere today? To answer that question, think about the kind and amount of resources each of us uses. Ecologists refer to the human impact on the biosphere using a concept called the ecological footprint. The **ecological footprint** describes the total area of functioning land and water ecosystems needed both to provide the resources an individual or population uses and to absorb and make harmless the wastes that individual or population generates. Ecological footprints take into account the need to provide resources such as energy, food, water, and shelter, and to absorb such wastes as sewage and greenhouse gases. Ecologists use footprint calculations to estimate the biosphere's carrying capacity for humans. An artist's rendition of an ecological footprint is shown in **Figure 6–22.**

Footprint Limitations Ecologists talk about the ecological footprints of individuals, of countries, and of the world's population. Calculating actual numbers for ecological footprints, however, is complicated. The concept is so new that there is no universally accepted way to calculate footprint size. What's more, footprints give only a "snapshot" of the situation at a particular point in time.

Key Questions

🔑 *How does the average ecological footprint in America compare to the world's average?*

🔑 *How can ecology guide us toward a sustainable future?*

Vocabulary

ecological footprint
ozone layer
aquaculture
global warming

Taking Notes

Compare/Contrast Table As you read, create a table comparing the challenges associated with the ozone layer, fisheries, and global climate. Note the problem observed, the causes identified, and the solutions implemented.

VISUAL ANALOGY

ECOLOGICAL FOOTPRINTS

FIGURE 6–22 The food you eat, the miles you travel, and the electricity you use all contribute to your—and the population's—ecological footprint.

Comparing Footprints Although calculating *absolute* footprints is difficult, ecological footprints can be useful for making *comparisons* among different populations, as shown in **Figure 6–23.** 🔑 **According to one data set, the average American has an ecological footprint over four times larger than the global average.** The per person use of resources in America is almost twice that in England, more than twice that in Japan, and almost six times that in China. To determine the ecological footprint of an entire country, researchers calculate the footprint for a typical citizen and then multiply that by the size of the population.

> **In Your Notebook** *How have you contributed to your ecological footprint today? Give at least ten examples.*

FIGURE 6–23 Relative Footprints This world map shows each country in proportion to its ecological footprint. The United States has an ecological footprint about twice the world's average. By contrast, the African nation of Zambia has a footprint a little over one-fourth the global average. Compare each country's "footprint" size to its actual size on the smaller map below.

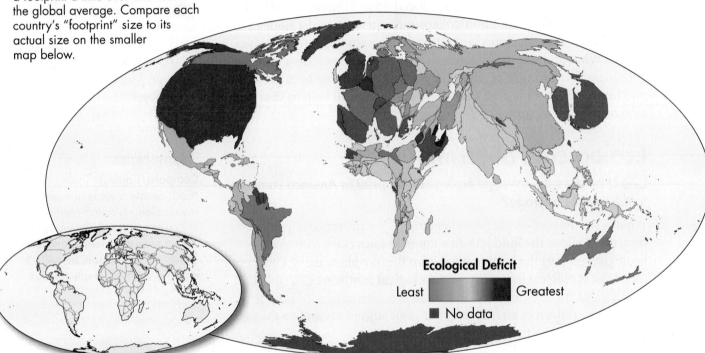

Ecological Deficit
Least   Greatest
■ No data

Ecology in Action

🔑 *How can ecology guide us toward a sustainable future?*

The future of the biosphere depends on our ecological footprints, global population growth, and technological development. Right now it's more common to hear stories of ecological challenges than successes. Given the size of those challenges, you might be tempted to give up, to feel that things are getting worse, and that there is nothing we can do about it. But ecological research, properly collected, analyzed, and applied, can help us make decisions that will produce profoundly positive effects on the human condition. The basic principles of ecology can guide us toward a sustainable future. 🔑 **By (1) recognizing a problem in the environment, (2) researching that problem to determine its cause, and then (3) using scientific understanding to change our behavior, we can have a positive impact on the global environment.** The following case studies illustrate the importance of the steps.

Case Study #1: Atmospheric Ozone

Between 20 and 50 kilometers above Earth's surface, the atmosphere contains a relatively high concentration of ozone called the **ozone layer.** Ozone at ground level is a pollutant, but the natural ozone layer absorbs harmful ultraviolet (UV) radiation from sunlight. Overexposure to UV radiation is the main cause of sunburn. It also can cause cancer, damage eyes, and lower resistance to disease. And intense UV radiation can damage plants and algae. By absorbing UV light, the ozone layer serves as a global sunscreen.

The following is an ecological success story. Over four decades, society has recognized a problem, identified its cause, and cooperated internationally to address a global issue.

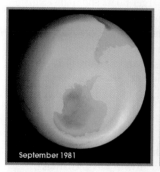 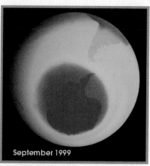

September 1981   September 1999

FIGURE 6–24 The Disappearing Ozone

FIGURE 6–25 CFC-Containing Refrigerators

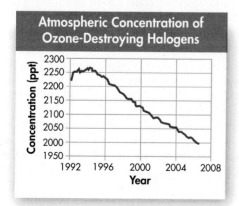

FIGURE 6–26 The Decline of CFCs

❶ Recognizing a Problem: "Hole" in the Ozone Layer Beginning in the 1970s, satellite data revealed that the ozone concentration over Antarctica was dropping during the southern winter. An area of lower ozone concentration is commonly called an ozone hole. It isn't really a "hole" in the atmosphere, of course, but an area where little ozone is present. For several years after the ozone hole was first discovered, it grew larger and lasted longer each year. **Figure 6–24** shows the progression from 1981 to 1999. The darker blue color in the later image indicates that the ozone layer had thinned since 1981.

❷ Researching the Cause: CFCs In 1974 a research team led by Mario Molina, F. Sherwood Rowland, and Paul J. Crutzen demonstrated that gases called chlorofluorocarbons (CFCs) could damage the ozone layer. This research earned the team a Nobel Prize in 1995. CFCs were once widely used as propellants in aerosol cans; as coolant in refrigerators, freezers, and air conditioners; and in the production of plastic foams.

❸ Changing Behavior: Regulation of CFCs Once the research on CFCs was published and accepted by the scientific community, the rest was up to policymakers—and in this case, their response was tremendous. Following the recommendations of ozone researchers, 191 countries signed a major agreement, the Montreal Protocol, which banned most uses of CFCs. Because CFCs can remain in the atmosphere for a century, their effects on the ozone layer are still visible. But ozone-destroying halogens from CFCs have been steadily decreasing since about 1994, as shown in **Figure 6–26,** evidence that the CFC ban has had positive long-term effects. In fact, current data predict that although the ozone hole will continue to fluctuate in size from year to year, it should disappear for good around the middle of this century.

Case Study #2: North Atlantic Fisheries

From 1950 to 1997, the annual world seafood catch grew from 19 million tons to more than 90 million tons. This growth led many to believe that the fish supply was an endless, renewable resource. However, recent dramatic declines in commercial fish populations have proved otherwise. This problem is one society is still working on.

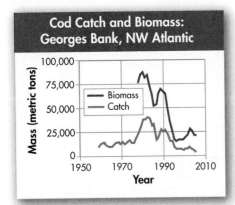

FIGURE 6–27 The Decline of Cod

FIGURE 6–28 Overfishing

FIGURE 6–29 Aquaculture

❶ Recognizing a Problem: More Work, Fewer Fish The cod catch has been rising and falling over the last century. Some of that fluctuation has been due to natural variations in ocean ecosystems. But often, low fish catches resulted when boats started taking too many fish. From the 1950s through the 1970s, larger boats and high-tech fish-finding equipment made the fishing effort both more intense and more efficient. Catches rose for a time but then began falling. The difference this time, was that fish catches continued to fall despite the most intense fishing effort in history. As shown in **Figure 6–27,** the total mass of cod caught has decreased significantly since the 1980s because of the sharp decrease of cod biomass in the ocean. You can't catch what isn't there.

❷ Researching the Cause: Overfishing Fishery ecologists gathered data including age structure and growth rates. Analysis of these data showed that fish populations were shrinking. By the 1990s, cod and haddock populations had dropped so low that researchers feared these fish might disappear for good. It has become clear that recent declines in fish catches were the result of overfishing, as seen in **Figure 6–28.** Fish were being caught faster than they could be replaced by reproduction. In other words, the death rates of commercial fish populations were exceeding birth rates.

❸ Changing Behavior: Regulation of Fisheries The U.S. National Marine Fisheries Service used its best data to create guidelines for commercial fishing. The guidelines specified how many fish of what size could be caught in U.S. waters. In 1996, the Sustainable Fisheries Act closed certain areas to fishing until stocks recover. Other areas are closed seasonally to allow fish to breed and spawn. These regulations are helping some fish populations recover, but not all. **Aquaculture**— the farming of aquatic animals—offers a good alternative to commercial fishing with limited environmental damage if properly managed.

Overall, however, progress in restoring fish populations has been slow. International cooperation on fisheries has not been as good as it was with ozone. Huge fleets from other countries continue to fish the ocean waters outside U.S. territorial waters. Some are reluctant to accept conservation efforts because regulations that protect fish populations for the future cause job and income losses today. Of course, if fish stocks disappear, the result will be even more devastating to the fishing industry than temporary fishing bans. The challenge is to come up with sustainable practices that ensure the long-term health of fisheries with minimal short-term impact on the fishing industry. Exactly how to meet that challenge is still up for debate.

Case Study #3: Climate Change

Global climate involves cycles of matter across the biosphere and everything modern humans do—from cutting and burning forests to manufacturing, driving cars, and generating electricity. The most reliable current information available on this subject comes from the 2007 report of the Intergovernmental Panel On Climate Change (IPCC). The IPCC is an international organization established in 1988 to provide the best possible scientific information on climate change. IPCC reports contain data and analyses that have been agreed upon and accepted by 2500 climate scientists from around the world and the governments participating in the study.

❶ Recognizing a Problem: Global Warming The IPCC report confirms earlier observations that global temperatures are rising. This increase in average temperature is called **global warming.** Remember that winds and ocean currents, which are driven by differences in temperature across the biosphere, shape climate. Given this link between temperature and climate, it isn't surprising that the IPCC report discusses more than warming. The report also discusses climate change—changes in patterns of temperature, rainfall, and other physical environmental factors that can result from global warming. There are many lines of evidence, both physical and biological, that have contributed to our current understanding of the climate change issue.

- **Physical Evidence** Physical evidence of global warming comes from several sources. The graphs in **Figure 6–30,** taken from data in the 2007 IPCC report, show that Earth's temperatures are getting warmer, its sea ice is melting, and its sea levels are rising. Eleven of the twelve years between 1995 and 2006 were among the warmest years since temperature recording began in 1850. Between 1906 and 2005, Earth's average global temperature rose 0.74°C. The largest changes are occurring in and near the Arctic Circle. Average temperatures in Alaska, for example, increased 2.4°C over the last 50 years. Sea level has risen since 1961 at a rate of 1.8 mm each year. This increase is caused by warmer water expanding and by melting glaciers, ice caps, and polar ice sheets. Satellite data confirm that arctic sea ice, glaciers, and snow cover are decreasing.

FIGURE 6–30 A Warming Earth

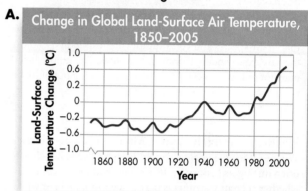

A. change from average 1961–1990 temperature

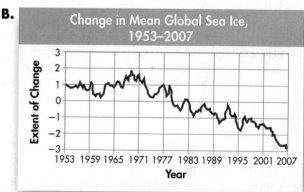

B. change from average 1953–2007 sea ice extent

C. change from average 1961–1991 sea level

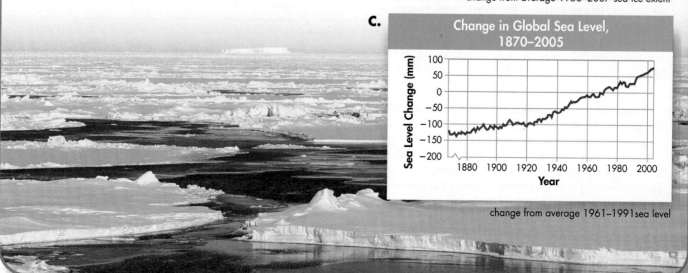

• **Biological Evidence** Small changes in climate that humans scarcely notice can be important to other organisms. Remember that each organism's range is determined by factors like temperature, humidity, and rainfall. If those conditions change, the organisms can be affected. If temperature rises, for example, organisms would usually move toward cooler places away from the equator and from warm lowlands to cooler, higher altitudes. In addition, plant flowering and animal breeding are often cued by seasonal changes. If warming is occurring, these organisms should respond as though spring begins earlier.

The IPCC report summarizes data from 75 studies covering 1700 species of plants and animals. These data confirm that many species and communities are responding as though they are experiencing rising temperatures. The yellow-bellied marmot in **Figure 6–31,** for example, is coming out of hibernation over a month earlier than it used to.

FIGURE 6–31
Waking Up Too Early

② **Researching the Cause: Models and Questions**
What is causing global warming? Earth's climate has changed often during its history. So researchers had to determine whether current warming is part of a natural cycle or whether it is caused by human activity or by astronomical and geological changes. As the IPCC report documents, concentrations of carbon dioxide and several other greenhouse gases have increased significantly over the last 200 years, as shown in **Figure 6–32.** Several kinds of data suggest this increase is due to the burning of fossil fuels, combined with the cutting and burning of forests worldwide. These activities add carbon dioxide to the atmosphere faster than the carbon cycle removes it. Most climate scientists agree that this added carbon dioxide is strengthening the natural greenhouse effect, causing the biosphere to retain more heat.

• **How Much Change?** How much warming is expected? For answers, researchers turn to computer models based on data. The models are complex and involve assumptions about climate and human activities. For these reasons, predictions are open to debate. The IPCC reports the result of six different models, which predict that average global temperatures will rise by the end of the twenty-first century from just under 2°C to as much as 6.4°C higher than they were in the year 2000.

• **Possible Effects of Climate Change** What does climate change mean? Some changes are likely to threaten ecosystems ranging from tundra and northern forests to coral reefs and the Amazon rain forest. The western United States is likely to get drier. The Sahara Desert, on the other hand, may become greener. Sea level may rise enough to flood some coastal ecosystems and human communities. And some models suggest that parts of North America may experience more droughts during the summer growing season.

FIGURE 6–32 Greenhouse Gases

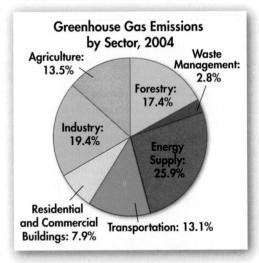

Greenhouse Gas Emissions by Sector, 2004

Agriculture: 13.5%
Waste Management: 2.8%
Forestry: 17.4%
Industry: 19.4%
Energy Supply: 25.9%
Residential and Commercial Buildings: 7.9%
Transportation: 13.1%

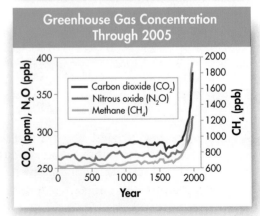

Greenhouse Gas Concentration Through 2005

Carbon dioxide (CO₂)
Nitrous oxide (N₂O)
Methane (CH₄)

③ Changing Behavior: The Challenges Ahead You have seen how research has led to actions that are preserving the ozone layer and attempting to restore fisheries. In terms of global climate, great challenges lie ahead of us. Scientists have been saying for more than two decades that the world needs to recognize the importance of climate change and take steps to minimize further warming. The changes in behavior needed to cut back on greenhouse gas emissions will be major and will require input from economics and many other fields beyond biology. Some changes will rely on new technology for renewable energy and more efficient energy use. Because changing our use of fossil fuels and other behaviors will be difficult, researchers continue to gather data as they try to make more accurate models. In the meantime, we have begun to see the emergence of electric cars, recycled products, and green buildings.

Nations of the world have begun holding international climate summits, at which they attempt to work out agreements to protect the atmosphere and climate—both of which are truly global issues. As the world, and our own government, tries to work through these challenges, remember that the purpose of ecology is not to predict disaster or to prevent people from enjoying modern life. The world is our island of life. Hopefully, humanity can work toward a day when scientific information and human ingenuity help us reach the common goal of preserving the quality of life on Earth.

FIGURE 6–33 Little Changes, Big Results

6.4 Assessment

Review Key Concepts 🔑

1. a. Review What are ecological footprints?

   b. Apply Concepts What are the limitations of the ecological footprint model, and how can ecologists best use it?

2. a. Review Why is the ozone layer important to living things?

   b. Explain What are the major types of physical and biological evidence for climate change?

   c. Propose a Solution Suggest one solution for the fisheries problem. Your solution can be at the international, national, regional, or individual level. Explain how it would help, and what challenges you see in implementing it.

Apply the Big idea

Interdependence in Nature

3. Refer to the carbon cycle on page 83. Describe how extensive burning of fossil fuels is affecting other reservoirs of carbon in the biosphere.

BIOLOGY.com   Search (Lesson 6.4) **GO** • Self-Test • Lesson Assessment

Pre-Lab: Acid Rain and Seeds

Problem How does acid rain affect seed germination?

Materials white vinegar, distilled water, large test tubes, test-tube rack, glass-marking pencil, 25-mL graduated cylinder, food coloring, pipette, pH paper, dried beans, paper towels, zip-close plastic bags, stick-on labels, hand lens

Lab Manual Chapter 6 Lab

Skills Focus Design an Experiment, Organize Data, Measure, Graph

Connect to the Big idea Every organism alters its environment in some way. Elephants uproot trees, prairie dogs dig tunnels, and corals build reefs. But no other organism has as much impact on the global environment as humans. One of the ways that humans affect global ecology is by burning fossil fuels. The burning produces carbon dioxide, which can accumulate in the atmosphere and cause climate change. Other products react with water to form nitric and sulfuric acids. Rain that contains these acids can damage many things, including stone statues and growing plants. In this lab, you will investigate the effect of acid rain on seeds.

Background Questions

a. Review What does a pH scale measure?

b. Review Which solution is more acidic, one with a pH of 4.0 or one with a pH of 5.0, and why?

c. Explain Use the water cycle to trace the path from acids in water vapor to plants.

Pre-Lab Questions

Preview the procedure in the lab manual.

1. Design an Experiment What do you think the purpose is of adding food coloring to the vinegar in Part A?

2. Infer How will you know that a seed has germinated?

3. Using Models In this lab, what do the solutions represent?

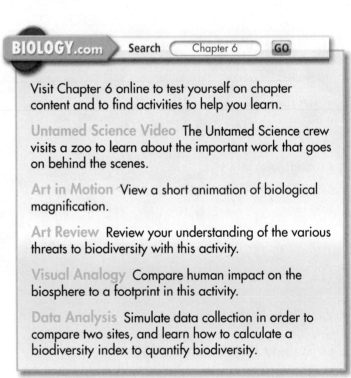

BIOLOGY.com Search Chapter 6 GO

Visit Chapter 6 online to test yourself on chapter content and to find activities to help you learn.

Untamed Science Video The Untamed Science crew visits a zoo to learn about the important work that goes on behind the scenes.

Art in Motion View a short animation of biological magnification.

Art Review Review your understanding of the various threats to biodiversity with this activity.

Visual Analogy Compare human impact on the biosphere to a footprint in this activity.

Data Analysis Simulate data collection in order to compare two sites, and learn how to calculate a biodiversity index to quantify biodiversity.

6 Study Guide

Big idea Interdependence in Nature

Humans affect natural ecological processes through agriculture, urban development, and industry. But ecological science gives us strategies for sustainable development, ways we can protect the environment without slowing human progress.

6.1 A Changing Landscape

🔑 Humans affect regional and global environments through agriculture, development, and industry in ways that have an impact on the quality of Earth's natural resources, including soil, water, and the atmosphere.

🔑 Sustainable development provides for human needs while preserving the ecosystems that produce natural resources.

monoculture (155) nonrenewable resource (157)
renewable resource (157) sustainable development (157)

6.2 Using Resources Wisely

🔑 Healthy soil supports both agriculture and forestry.

🔑 It is possible to minimize soil erosion through careful management of both agriculture and forestry.

🔑 The primary sources of water pollution are industrial and agricultural chemicals, residential sewage, and nonpoint sources.

🔑 Common forms of air pollution include smog, acid rain, greenhouse gases, and particulates.

desertification (159) biological
deforestation (159)   magnification (161)
pollutant (160)   smog (163)
                       acid rain (164)

6.3 Biodiversity

🔑 Biodiversity's benefits to society include contributions to medicine and agriculture, and the provision of ecosystem goods and services.

🔑 Humans reduce biodiversity by altering habitats, hunting, introducing invasive species, releasing pollution into food webs, and contributing to climate change.

🔑 To conserve biodiversity, we must protect individual species, preserve habitats and ecosystems, and make certain that human neighbors of protected areas benefit from participating in conservation efforts.

biodiversity (166)   genetic diversity (166)
ecosystem diversity (166) habitat fragmentation (168)
species diversity (166)   ecological hot spot (171)

6.4 Meeting Ecological Challenges

🔑 According to one data set, the average American has an ecological footprint over four times larger than the global average.

🔑 By (1) recognizing a problem in the environment, (2) researching that problem to determine its cause, and then (3) using scientific understanding to change our behavior we can have a positive impact on the global environment.

ecological footprint (173) aquaculture (176)
ozone layer (175)   global warming (177)

Think Visually

Create a flowchart that shows the steps in the biological magnification of DDT. Your flowchart should show how DDT enters the food web and what effects it has on organisms.

6 Assessment

6.1 A Changing Landscape

Understand Key Concepts

1. Which of the following human activities has NOT had an important role in transforming the biosphere to date?
   a. agriculture
   b. industry
   c. development
   d. aquaculture

2. A resource that cannot easily be replenished by natural processes is called
   a. common.
   b. renewable.
   c. nonrenewable.
   d. conserved.

3. Describe how Hawaiian settlers negatively affected the islands after the 1700s.

4. Name four services that ecosystems provide for the biosphere.

Think Critically

5. **Propose a Solution** Devise guidelines your biology class can use to dispose of its nonlab trash in a safe, "environmentally friendly" way.

6. **Compare and Contrast** How are renewable and nonrenewable resources alike? How are they different?

7. **Form a Hypothesis** Monoculture fields are usually very large and homogeneous. Do you think this makes them more or less vulnerable to disease and pests? Explain.

6.2 Using Resources Wisely

Understand Key Concepts

8. The conversion of a once soil-rich area to an area of little to no vegetation is called
   a. fragmentation.
   b. deforestation.
   c. desertification.
   d. acid rain.

9. The loss of fertile soils from an area through the action of water or wind is called
   a. acid rain.
   b. erosion.
   c. desertification.
   d. monoculture.

10. The concept of using natural resources at a rate that does not deplete them is called
    a. conservation.
    b. sustainable development.
    c. reforestation.
    d. successful use.

11. Examine the food web below. Which of the following organisms would accumulate the highest levels of a pesticide?
    a. hawk
    b. rabbit
    c. frog
    d. grasses

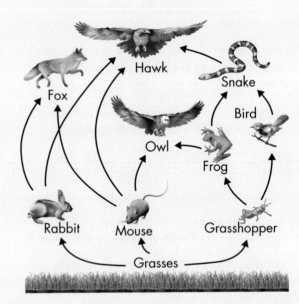

12. What is the difference between sustainable forestry and deforestation?

13. Identify some of the common sources of water pollution.

Think Critically

14. **Design an Experiment** Can covering soil with mulch or compost near the bases of plants help reduce soil erosion? Design an experiment to answer this question.

15. **Calculate** The concentration of a toxic chemical is magnified ten times at each trophic level. What will the concentration of the toxin be in organisms at the fifth trophic level if primary producers have concentrations of 40 parts per million? **MATH**

16. **Infer** Why are lakes that have been affected by acid rain often clear and blue?

6.3 Biodiversity

Understand Key Concepts

17. A species that is introduced to an environment where it has not lived before is described as
  a. native.
  c. threatened.
  b. nonnative.
  d. predatory.

18. What is a habitat fragment?

19. List three different kinds of biodiversity that might be described in a given biome.

Think Critically

20. Predict How do you think the loss of biodiversity would adversely affect humans?

21. Compare and Contrast Explain the difference between species diversity and ecosystem diversity.

6.4 Meeting Ecological Challenges

Understand Key Concepts

22. The burning of fossil fuels is a direct cause of each the following EXCEPT
  a. acid rain.
  c. smog.
  b. global warming.
  d. the ozone hole.

23. The total impact a person has on the biosphere can be represented by his or her
  a. contribution to climate change.
  b. ecological footprint.
  c. consumption of fossil fuel.
  d. production of carbon dioxide.

24. Cite three examples of physical evidence for global warming.

25. What are some of the biological effects of climate change?

Think Critically

26. Relate Cause and Effect Why hasn't the ozone layer repaired itself fully since the widespread ban of CFCs in 1987?

27. Apply Concepts Describe some of the steps taken to counter the effects of overfishing cod in the North Atlantic. Why is overfishing such a complex environmental issue?

solve the CHAPTER MYSTERY

MOVING THE *MOAI*

Easter Island's environment was not as biologically diverse, and not as resistant to ecological damage, as the Hawaiian Islands. The Rapa Nui cut palm trees for agriculture, for logs to move *moai*, and for wood to make fishing canoes. They mismanaged cleared fields, so fertile topsoil washed away.

Meanwhile, rats they brought to the island became invasive. Hordes of the rodents destroyed palm seedlings, ate coconuts, and digested palm seeds before they could germinate. Hawaiians also brought rats to their islands, and rats did serious damage to native Hawaiian plants. But in Hawaii's more diverse forests, some plant species were not as hard hit by rats and survived.

The combination of human activity and the effects of an invasive species led to the destruction of virtually all of Easter Island's forests. This combination, along with the effects of a harsh climate, limited the island's carrying capacity for humans from then on.

1. Relate Cause and Effect How did the small size of the island (about half the size of Long Island, New York) affect the outcome of deforestation and pest invasion?

2. Compare and Contrast Gather information on differences in geography, climate, and biological diversity between Hawaii and Easter Island. How do you think those differences made the islands respond differently to human settlement?

3. Connect to the Big idea All human cultures throughout history have interacted with their environments. Do you think that global human society has any lessons to learn from the experiences of the Rapa Nui, the Hawaiians, and other historic cultures?

Use Science Graphics

The graph shows the amount of bluefin tuna caught by the United States in the Atlantic Ocean between 2002 and 2006. Use the graph to answer questions 28 and 29.

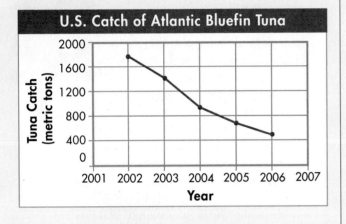

U.S. Catch of Atlantic Bluefin Tuna

28. Predict What trend would you expect to see in the annual catch from 2006 to 2007?

29. Propose a Solution What recommendations would you make to help the bluefin tuna population recover in the next decade or two?

Write About Science

30. Explanation Write a paragraph explaining the value of wetlands to human societies. In your paragraph, include the concept of biodiversity as well as the role of wetlands in maintaining water resources for human use.

31. Assess the  Why is it important to maintain species diversity in areas where humans live?

32. Assess the Big idea What environmental factors make high levels of biodiversity possible in most coastal waters? Refer to the discussion of abiotic and biotic factors in Chapter 4 if you need help answering this question.

Analyzing Data

The following graph shows the number of species introduced to new habitats in the United States in the last century. Some of the species were relocated to new habitats within the United States while others were imported from other countries.

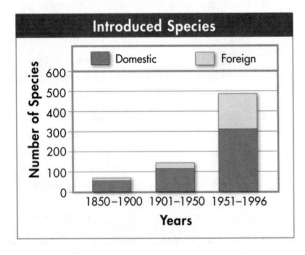

Introduced Species

33. Interpret Graphs Of domestic species and foreign species, which showed the greatest percentage increase between the 1901–1950 period and the 1951–1996 period?
 a. domestic species
 b. foreign species
 c. Both increased the same amount.
 d. There is not enough information to tell.

34. Draw Conclusions Which of the following statements about introduced species is most likely true based on the data shown?
 a. Species introduced from foreign countries are always more harmful than species relocated within the country.
 b. All introduced species are brought into this country by accident.
 c. It is likely that the increase in the number of introduced species is due to increased global travel, trade, and communication.
 d. The number of introduced species is likely to fall in the next half-century.

Standardized Test Prep

Multiple Choice

1. Which of the following statements about renewable resources is TRUE?
   A They are found only in tropical climates.
   B They can never be depleted.
   C They are replaceable by natural means.
   D They can never regenerate.

2. Which of the following is a nonrenewable resource?
   A wind   C coal
   B fresh water   D topsoil

3. Which of the following is NOT a direct effect of deforestation?
   A decreased productivity of the ecosystem
   B soil erosion
   C biological magnification
   D habitat destruction

4. The total variety of organisms in the biosphere is called
   A biodiversity.
   B species diversity.
   C ecosystem diversity.
   D genetic diversity.

5. Ozone is made up of
   A hydrogen.   C nitrogen.
   B oxygen.   D chlorine.

6. Ozone depletion in the atmosphere has been caused by
   A monoculture.
   B CFCs.
   C suburban sprawl.
   D soil erosion.

7. In a food chain, concentrations of harmful substances increase in higher trophic levels in a process is known as
   A biological magnification.
   B genetic drift.
   C biological succession.
   D pesticide resistance.

Questions 8 and 9

Fire ants first arrived in the United States in 1918, probably on a ship traveling from South America to Alabama. The maps below show the geographic location of the U.S. fire ant population in 1953 and 2001.

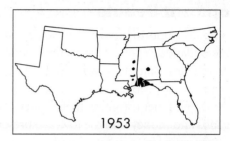

1953

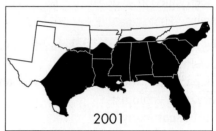

2001

8. Which of the following statements about fire ants in the United States is TRUE?
   A They reproduce slowly.
   B They are a native species of the United States.
   C They are an invasive species.
   D They do not compete with other ant species.

9. By 2010, fire ants are MOST likely to
   A have spread to a larger area.
   B have reached their carrying capacity.
   C die out.
   D return to South America.

Open-Response

10. Describe how ecologists use the ecological footprint concept.

If You Have Trouble With . . .

Question	1	2	3	4	5	6	7	8	9	10
See Lesson	6.1	6.2	6.2	6.3	6.2	6.4	6.2	6.3	6.3	6.4

Unit Project

Development Debate

A large company wants to build a new factory on your town's wetlands. Many people in the town are opposed to the idea, claiming it will disturb the local ecosystem and cause problems for residents. Others support the development, arguing that the new factory will bring jobs and money into the town. Representatives have been called in to debate the issue before the town council.

Your Task Take on one of the stakeholder roles listed below. Find evidence to support that point of view and debate the issue in class. The roles are

- Conservation ecologist
- CEO of the company
- Town mayor who supports the development
- Resident of the town who lives next to the wetlands

Be sure to
- justify your arguments with credible information.
- present your arguments in a clear and convincing manner.

Reflection Questions

1. Score your performance using the rubric below. What score did you give yourself?
2. What did you do well in this project?
3. What about your performance needs improvement?
4. After hearing various sides of the argument, meet with a partner and discuss which side you agree with the most. Justify your opinion.

Assessment Rubric

Score	Evidence Provided	Quality of Performance
4	Student justifies his/her argument with sophisticated and highly credible information.	Ideas are presented in a highly convincing and clear manner. Student shows a deep understanding of the issues involved.
3	Student justifies his/her argument with logical and credible information.	Ideas are presented in an effective and clear manner. Student shows a solid understanding of the issues involved.
2	Student provides some credible information, but other points are weak or inaccurate.	Some ideas are presented in an unclear manner. Student shows a limited understanding of the issues involved.
1	Student provides mostly illogical and invalid evidence to support his/her argument.	Most ideas are presented in an unclear manner. Student shows a very limited understanding of the issues involved.

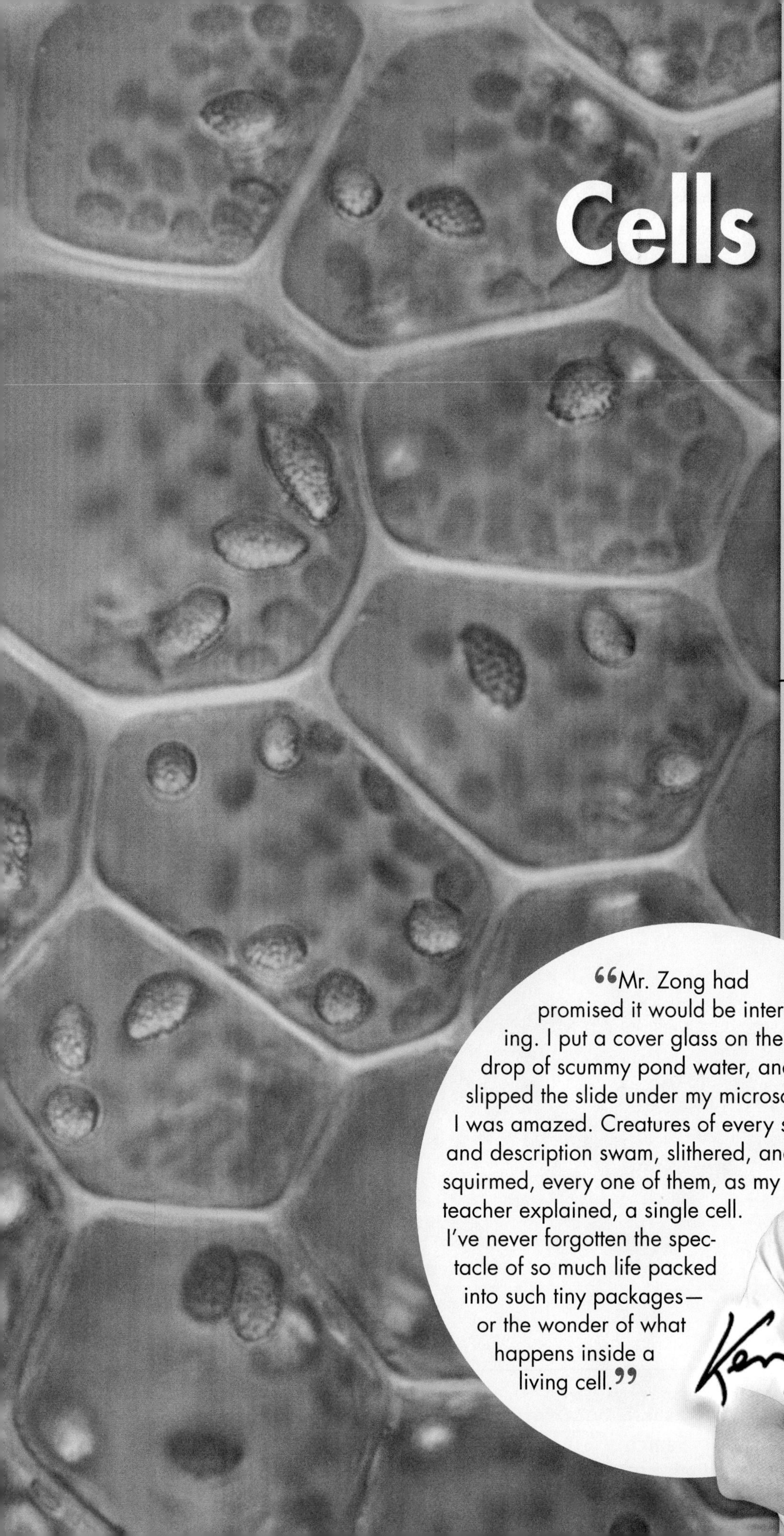

Cells

Chapters

7 Cell Structure
and Function

8 Photosynthesis

9 Cellular Respiration
and Fermentation

10 Cell Growth
and Division

─── **INTRODUCE the** ───

Big ideas

- **Cellular Basis of Life**
- **Homeostasis**
- **Growth, Development, and Reproduction**

"Mr. Zong had promised it would be interesting. I put a cover glass on the drop of scummy pond water, and slipped the slide under my microscope. I was amazed. Creatures of every shape and description swam, slithered, and squirmed, every one of them, as my teacher explained, a single cell. I've never forgotten the spectacle of so much life packed into such tiny packages— or the wonder of what happens inside a living cell."

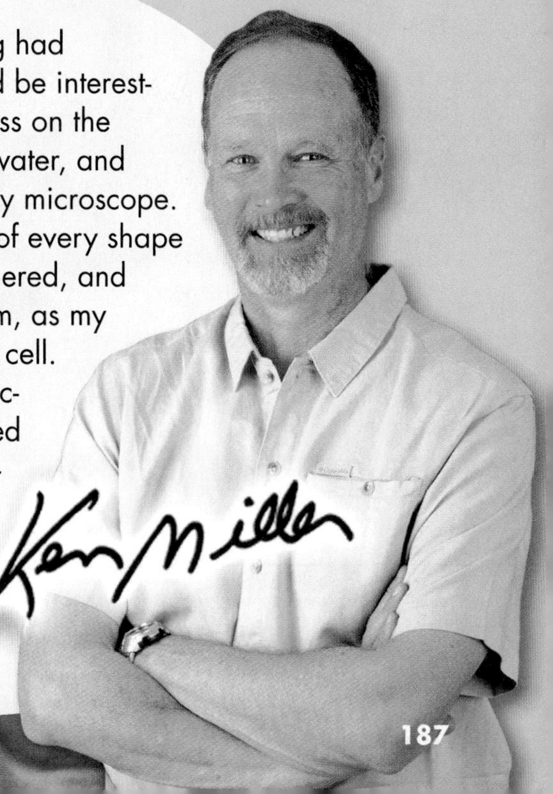

Ken Miller

7 Cell Structure and Function

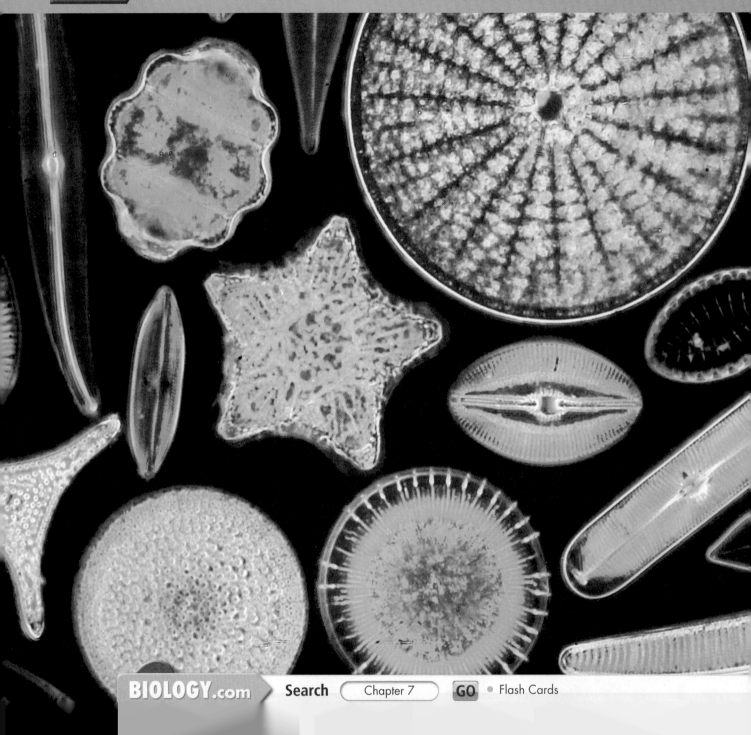

INSIDE:

- 7.1 Life Is Cellular
- 7.2 Cell Structure
- 7.3 Cell Transport
- 7.4 Homeostasis and Cells

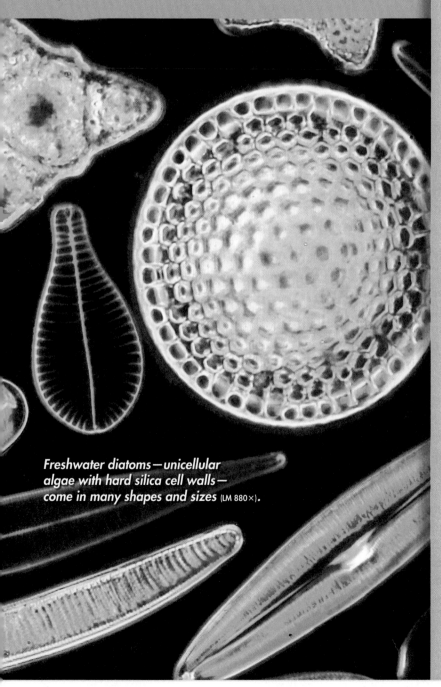

Freshwater diatoms—unicellular algae with hard silica cell walls— come in many shapes and sizes (LM 880×).

CHAPTER
MYSTERY

DEATH BY ... WATER?

Michelle was a healthy 25-year-old running in her first marathon. The hot and humid weather had made all the runners sweat profusely, so Michelle made sure she drank water at every opportunity. Gradually, she began to feel weak and confused. At the end of the marathon, Michelle staggered into a medical tent. Complaining of headache and nausea, she collapsed onto the floor. Volunteers quickly gave Michelle water for dehydration. Soon, her condition worsened and Michelle was rushed to the hospital, where she was gripped by a seizure and went into a coma. Why did treating Michelle with water make her condition worse? As you read this chapter, look for clues to help you predict how water made Michelle sick. Then, solve the mystery.

Never Stop Exploring Your World.
Michelle's mysterious illness is just the beginning. Take a video field trip with the ecogeeks of Untamed Science to see where this mystery leads.

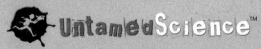
UntamedScience™

● Untamed Science Video ● Chapter Mystery

7.1 Life Is Cellular

Key Questions

🔑 What is the cell theory?

🔑 How do microscopes work?

🔑 How are prokaryotic and eukaryotic cells different?

Vocabulary

cell • cell theory • cell membrane • nucleus • eukaryote • prokaryote

Taking Notes

Outline Before you read, make an outline using the green and blue headings in the text. As you read, fill in notes under each heading.

THINK ABOUT IT What's the smallest part of any living thing that still counts as being "alive"? Is a leaf alive? How about your big toe? How about a drop of blood? Can we just keep dividing living things into smaller and smaller parts, or is there a point at which what's left is no longer alive? As you will see, there is such a limit, the smallest living unit of any organism—the cell.

The Discovery of the Cell

🔑 What is the cell theory?

"Seeing is believing," an old saying goes. It would be hard to find a better example of this than the discovery of the cell. Without the instruments to make them visible, cells remained out of sight and, therefore, out of mind for most of human history. All of this changed with a dramatic advance in technology—the invention of the microscope.

Early Microscopes In the late 1500s, eyeglass makers in Europe discovered that using several glass lenses in combination could magnify even the smallest objects to make them easy to see. Before long, they had built the first true microscopes from these lenses, opening the door to the study of biology as we know it today.

In 1665, Englishman Robert Hooke used an early compound microscope to look at a nonliving thin slice of cork, a plant material. Under the microscope, cork seemed to be made of thousands of tiny empty chambers. Hooke called these chambers "cells" because they reminded him of a monastery's tiny rooms, which were called cells. The term *cell* is used in biology to this day. Today we know that living cells are not empty chambers, that in fact they contain a huge array of working parts, each with its own function.

In Holland around the same time, Anton van Leeuwenhoek used a single-lens microscope to observe pond water and other things. To his amazement, the microscope revealed a fantastic world of tiny living organisms that seemed to be everywhere, in the water he and his neighbors drank, and even in his own mouth. Leeuwenhoek's illustrations of the organisms he found in the human mouth—which today we call bacteria—are shown in **Figure 7–1**.

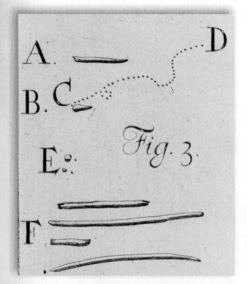

FIGURE 7–1 Early Microscope Images Using a simple microscope, Anton van Leeuwenhoek was the first to observe living microorganisms. These drawings, taken from one of his letters, show bacteria in the human mouth.

The Cell Theory Soon after van Leeuwenhoek, observations by scientists made it clear that **cells** are the basic units of life. In 1838, German botanist Matthias Schleiden concluded that all plants are made of cells. The next year, German biologist Theodor Schwann stated that all animals are made of cells. In 1855, German physician Rudolf Virchow concluded that new cells can be produced only from the division of existing cells, confirming a suggestion made by German Lorenz Oken 50 years earlier. These discoveries, confirmed by many biologists, are summarized in the **cell theory,** a fundamental concept of biology. 🔑 **The cell theory states:**

• **All living things are made up of cells.**
• **Cells are the basic units of structure and function in living things.**
• **New cells are produced from existing cells.**

Exploring the Cell

🔑 *How do microscopes work?*

A microscope, as you know, produces an enlarged image of something very small. 🔑 **Most microscopes use lenses to magnify the image of an object by focusing light or electrons.** Following in the footsteps of Hooke, Virchow, and others, modern biologists still use microscopes to explore the cell. But today's researchers use technology more powerful than the pioneers of biology could ever have imagined.

Light Microscopes and Cell Stains The type of microscope you are probably most familiar with is the compound light microscope. A typical light microscope allows light to pass through a specimen and uses two lenses to form an image. The first lens, called the objective lens, is located just above the specimen. This lens enlarges the image of the specimen. Most light microscopes have several objective lenses so that the power of magnification can be varied. The second lens, called the ocular lens, magnifies this image still further. Unfortunately, light itself limits the detail, or resolution, of images in a microscope. Like all forms of radiation, lightwaves are diffracted, or scattered, as they pass through matter. Because of this, light microscopes can produce clear images of objects only to a magnification of about 1000 times.

Another problem with light microscopy is that most living cells are nearly transparent. Using chemical stains or dyes, as in **Figure 7–2,** can usually solve this problem. Some of these stains are so specific that they reveal only certain compounds or structures within the cell. Many of the slides you'll examine in your biology class laboratory will be stained this way.

A powerful variation on these staining techniques uses dyes that give off light of a particular color when viewed under specific wavelengths of light, a property called fluorescence. Fluorescent dyes can be attached to specific molecules and can then be made visible using a special fluorescence microscope. New techniques, in fact, enable scientists to engineer cells that attach fluorescent labels of different colors to specific molecules as they are produced. Fluorescence microscopy makes it possible to see and identify the locations of these molecules and even allows scientists to watch them move around in a living cell.

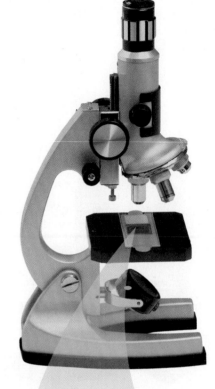

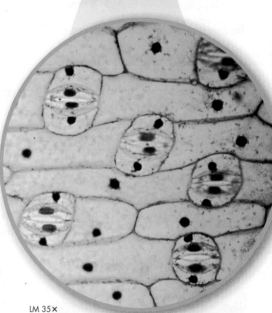

LM 35×

FIGURE 7–2 Light Microscope and Cell Stains This specimen of onion leaf skin has been stained with a compound called toluidine blue. The dye makes the cell boundaries and nuclei clearly visible.

Electron Microscopes Light microscopes can be used to see cells and cell structures as small as 1 millionth of a meter—certainly pretty small! But what if scientists want to study something smaller than that, such as a virus or a DNA molecule? For that, they need electron microscopes. Instead of using light, electron microscopes use beams of electrons that are focused by magnetic fields. Electron microscopes offer much higher resolution than light microscopes. Some types of electron microscopes can be used to study cellular structures that are 1 billionth of a meter in size.

There are two major types of electron microscopes: transmission and scanning. Transmission electron microscopes make it possible to explore cell structures and large protein molecules. But because beams of electrons can only pass through thin samples, cells and tissues must be cut into ultrathin slices before they can be examined. This is the reason that such images often appear flat and two dimensional.

In scanning electron microscopes, a pencil-like beam of electrons is scanned over the surface of a specimen. Because the image is formed at the specimen's surface, samples do not have to be cut into thin slices to be seen. The scanning electron microscope produces stunning three-dimensional images of the specimen's surface.

Electrons are easily scattered by molecules in the air, which means samples must be placed in a vacuum to be studied with an electron microscope. As a result, researchers must chemically preserve their samples. Electron microscopy, then, can only be used to examine nonliving cells and tissues.

Look at **Figure 7–3,** which shows yeast cells as they might look under a light microscope, transmission electron microscope, and scanning electron microscope. You may wonder why the cells appear to be different colors in each micrograph. (A micrograph is a photo of an object seen through a microscope.) The colors in light micrographs come from the cells themselves, or from the stains and dyes used to highlight them. Electron micrographs, however, are actually black and white. Electrons, unlike light, don't come in colors. So scientists often use computer techniques to add "false color" to make certain structures stand out.

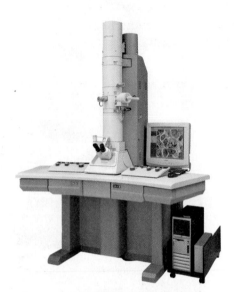

Transmission Electron Microscope

FIGURE 7–3 Micrographs Different types of microscopes can be used to examine cells. Here, yeast cells are shown in a light micrograph (LM 500×), transmission electron micrograph (TEM 4375×), and a scanning electron micrograph (SEM 3750×).
Infer *If scientists were studying a structure found on the surface of yeast, which kind of microscope would they likely use?*

In Your Notebook *You are presented with a specimen to examine. What are two questions you would ask to determine the best microscope to use?*

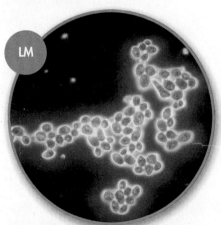

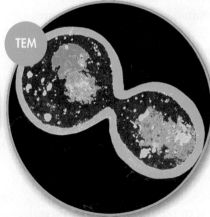

LM

TEM

SEM

What Is a Cell?

① Look through a microscope at a slide of a plant leaf or stem cross section. Sketch one or more cells. Record a description of their shape and internal parts.

② Repeat step 1 with slides of nerve cells, bacteria, and paramecia.

③ Compare the cells by listing the characteristics they have in common and some of the differences among them.

Analyze and Conclude

1. Classify Classify the cells you observed into two or more groups. Explain what characteristics you used to put each cell in a particular group.

Prokaryotes and Eukaryotes

🔑 *How are prokaryotic and eukaryotic cells different?*

Cells come in an amazing variety of shapes and sizes, some of which are shown in **Figure 7–4.** Although typical cells range from 5 to 50 micrometers in diameter, the smallest *Mycoplasma* bacteria are only 0.2 micrometer across, so small that they are difficult to see under even the best light microscopes. In contrast, the giant amoeba *Chaos chaos* can be 1000 micrometers (1 millimeter) in diameter, large enough to be seen with the unaided eye as a tiny speck in pond water. Despite their differences, all cells, at some point in their lives, contain DNA, the molecule that carries biological information. In addition, all cells are surrounded by a thin flexible barrier called a **cell membrane.** (The cell membrane is sometimes called the *plasma membrane* because many cells in the body are in direct contact with the fluid portion of the blood—the plasma.) There are other similarities as well, as you will learn in the next lesson.

Cells fall into two broad categories, depending on whether they contain a nucleus. The **nucleus** (plural: nuclei) is a large membrane-enclosed structure that contains genetic material in the form of DNA and controls many of the cell's activities. **Eukaryotes** (yoo KAR ee ohts) are cells that enclose their DNA in nuclei. **Prokaryotes** (pro KAR ee ohts) are cells that do not enclose DNA in nuclei.

MYSTERY CLUE

At the hospital, a sample of Michelle's blood was drawn and examined. The red blood cells appeared swollen. What kind of microscope was most likely used to study the blood sample?

FIGURE 7–4 Cell Size Is Relative The human eye can see objects larger than about 0.5 mm. Most of what interests cell biologists, however, is much smaller than that. Microscopes make seeing the cellular and subcellular world possible.

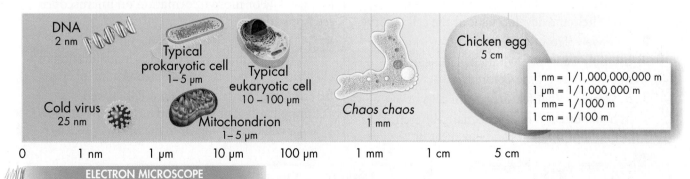

DNA 2 nm

Cold virus 25 nm

Typical prokaryotic cell 1–5 μm

Mitochondrion 1–5 μm

Typical eukaryotic cell 10 – 100 μm

Chaos chaos 1 mm

Chicken egg 5 cm

1 nm = 1/1,000,000,000 m
1 μm = 1/1,000,000 m
1 mm = 1/1000 m
1 cm = 1/100 m

0   1 nm   1 μm   10 μm   100 μm   1 mm   1 cm   5 cm

ELECTRON MICROSCOPE

LIGHT MICROSCOPE

UNAIDED HUMAN EYE

Prokaryotes As seen in **Figure 7–5,** prokaryotic cells are generally smaller and simpler than eukaryotic cells, although there are many exceptions to this rule. 🔑 **Prokaryotic cells do not separate their genetic material within a nucleus.** Despite their simplicity, prokaryotes carry out every activity associated with living things. They grow, reproduce, respond to the environment, and, in some cases, glide along surfaces or swim through liquids. The organisms we call bacteria are prokaryotes.

Eukaryotes Eukaryotic cells are generally larger and more complex than prokaryotic cells. Most eukaryotic cells contain dozens of structures and internal membranes, and many are highly specialized. 🔑 **In eukaryotic cells, the nucleus separates the genetic material from the rest of the cell.** Eukaryotes display great variety: some, like the ones commonly called "protists," live solitary lives as unicellular organisms; others form large, multicellular organisms—plants, animals, and fungi.

FIGURE 7–5 Cell Types In general, eukaryotic cells (including plant and animal cells) are more complex than prokaryotic cells.

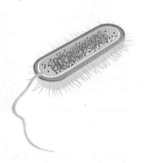

PROKARYOTIC CELL

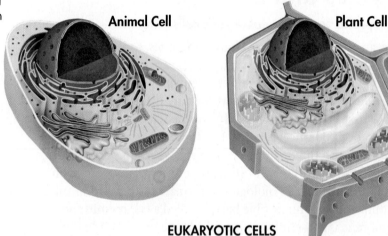

Animal Cell

Plant Cell

EUKARYOTIC CELLS

7.1 Assessment

Review Key Concepts 🔑

1. a. Review What is a cell?

  b. Explain What three statements make up the cell theory?

  c. Infer How did the invention of the microscope help the development of the cell theory?

2. a. Review How do microscopes work?

  b. Apply Concepts What does it mean if a micrograph is "false-colored?"

3. a. Review What features do all cells have?

  b. Summarize What is the main difference between prokaryotes and eukaryotes?

PRACTICE PROBLEMS | MATH

A light microscope can magnify images up to 1000 times. To calculate the total magnification of a specimen, multiply the magnification of the eyepiece lens by the magnification of the objective lens used. (For more information on microscopes, see Appendix B.)

4. Calculate What is the total magnification of a microscope that has an eyepiece magnification of 10× and an objective lens magnification of 50×.

5. Calculate A 10 micrometer cell is viewed through a 10× objective and a 10× eyepiece. How large will the cell appear to the microscope user?

Careers & BIOLOGY

Cells are the basic unit of all known life. If cells interest you, you might want to consider one of the following careers.

LABORATORY TECHNICIAN

Ever wonder what happens to the blood your doctor collects during your annual physical? It goes to a laboratory technician. Laboratory technicians perform routine procedures using microscopes, computers, and other equipment. Many laboratory technicians work in the medical field, evaluating and analyzing test results.

MICROSCOPIST

The images in **Figure 7–3** were captured by a microscopist. Microscopists make it possible to study structures too small to be seen without magnification. There are a variety of microscopy techniques, including staining and fluorescence, that microscopists can use to make images clear and informative for researchers. Some of these images are so striking that they have become a form of scientific art.

PATHOLOGIST

Pathologists are like detectives: They collect cellular information and tissue evidence to diagnose illness. Using a broad knowledge of disease characteristics and the best-available technology, pathologists analyze cells and tissues under a microscope and discuss their diagnoses with other doctors.

CAREER CLOSE-UP
Dr. Tanasa Osborne, Veterinary Pathologist

Dr. Tanasa Osborne studies osteosarcoma, the most common malignant bone tumor in children and adolescents. Her research with the National Institutes of Health and the National Cancer Institute is focused on improving outcomes for patients whose cancer has spread from one organ or system to another. Dr. Osborne is not a medical doctor, however—she is a veterinarian. Animals are often used as models to study human disease. Dr. Osborne's research, therefore, contributes to both animal and human health. Veterinary pathologists investigate many important issues in addition to cancer, including West Nile virus, avian flu, and other emerging infectious diseases that affect humans as well as animals.

“*My distinctive background allows me to approach science from a global (or cross-species) and systemic perspective.***”**

WRITING Explain how Dr. Osborne's research is an example of the effect science can have on society.

7.2 Cell Structure

Key Questions

🔑 **What is the role of the cell nucleus?**

🔑 **What are the functions of vacuoles, lysosomes, and the cytoskeleton?**

🔑 **What organelles help make and transport proteins?**

🔑 **What are the functions of chloroplasts and mitochondria?**

🔑 **What is the function of the cell membrane?**

Vocabulary

cytoplasm • organelle •
vacuole • lysosome •
cytoskeleton • centriole •
ribosome •
endoplasmic reticulum •
Golgi apparatus •
chloroplast • mitochondrion •
cell wall • lipid bilayer •
selectively permeable

Taking Notes

Venn Diagram Create a Venn diagram that illustrates the similarities and differences between prokaryotes and eukaryotes.

THINK ABOUT IT At first glance, a factory is a puzzling place. Machines buzz and clatter; people move quickly in different directions. So much activity can be confusing. However, if you take the time to watch carefully, what might at first seem like chaos begins to make sense. The same is true for the living cell.

Cell Organization

🔑 **What is the role of the cell nucleus?**

The eukaryotic cell is a complex and busy place. But if you look closely at eukaryotic cells, patterns begin to emerge. For example, it's easy to divide each cell into two major parts: the nucleus and the cytoplasm. The **cytoplasm** is the portion of the cell outside the nucleus. As you will see, the nucleus and cytoplasm work together in the business of life. Prokaryotic cells have cytoplasm too, even though they do not have a nucleus.

In our discussion of cell structure, we consider each major component of plant and animal eukaryotic cells—some of which are also found in prokaryotic cells—one by one. Because many of these structures act like specialized organs, they are known as **organelles,** literally "little organs." Understanding what each organelle does helps us understand the cell as a whole. A summary of cell structure can be found on pages 206–207.

VISUAL ANALOGY

THE CELL AS A LIVING FACTORY

FIGURE 7–6 The specialization and organization of work and workers contribute to the productivity of a factory. In much the same way, the specialized parts in a cell contribute to the cell's overall stability and survival.

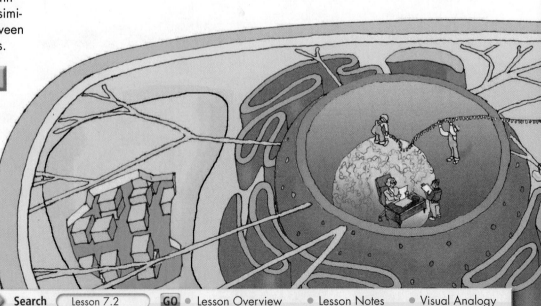

Comparing the Cell to a Factory In some respects, the eukaryotic cell is much like a living version of a modern factory (**Figure 7–6**). The different organelles of the cell can be compared to the specialized machines and assembly lines of the factory. In addition, cells, like factories, follow instructions and produce products. As we look through the organization of the cell, we'll find plenty of places in which the comparison works so well that it will help us understand how cells work.

The Nucleus In the same way that the main office controls a large factory, the nucleus is the control center of the cell. 🔑 **The nucleus contains nearly all the cell's DNA and, with it, the coded instructions for making proteins and other important molecules.** Prokaryotic cells lack a nucleus, but they do have DNA that contains the same kinds of instructions.

The nucleus, shown in **Figure 7–7**, is surrounded by a nuclear envelope composed of two membranes. The nuclear envelope is dotted with thousands of nuclear pores, which allow material to move into and out of the nucleus. Like messages, instructions, and blueprints moving in and out of a factory's main office, a steady stream of proteins, RNA, and other molecules move through the nuclear pores to and from the rest of the cell.

Chromosomes, which carry the cell's genetic information, are also found in the nucleus. Most of the time, the threadlike chromosomes are spread throughout the nucleus in the form of chromatin—a complex of DNA bound to proteins. When a cell divides, its chromosomes condense and can be seen under a microscope. You will learn more about chromosomes in later chapters.

Most nuclei also contain a small dense region known as the nucleolus (noo KLEE uh lus). The nucleolus is where the assembly of ribosomes begins.

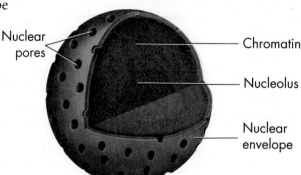

FIGURE 7-7 The Nucleus The nucleus controls most cell processes and contains DNA. The small, dense region in the nucleus is known as the nucleolus.

> **In Your Notebook** *Describe the structure of the nucleus. Include the words* nuclear envelope, nuclear pore, chromatin, chromosomes, *and* nucleolus *in your description.*

Organelles That Store, Clean Up, and Support

🔑 **What are the functions of vacuoles, lysosomes, and the cytoskeleton?**

Many of the organelles outside the nucleus of a eukaryotic cell have specific functions, or roles. Among them are structures called vacuoles, lysosomes, and cytoskeleton. These organelles represent the cellular factory's storage space, cleanup crew, and support structures.

Vacuoles and Vesicles Every factory needs a place to store things, and so does every cell. Many cells contain large, saclike, membrane-enclosed structures called **vacuoles**. 🔑 **Vacuoles store materials like water, salts, proteins, and carbohydrates.** In many plant cells, there is a single, large central vacuole filled with liquid. The pressure of the central vacuole in these cells increases their rigidity, making it possible for plants to support heavy structures, such as leaves and flowers. The image on the left in **Figure 7–8** shows a typical plant cell's large central vacuole.

Vacuoles are also found in some unicellular organisms and in some animals. The paramecium on the right in **Figure 7–8** contains an organelle called a contractile vacuole. By contracting rhythmically, this specialized vacuole pumps excess water out of the cell. In addition, nearly all eukaryotic cells contain smaller membrane-enclosed structures called vesicles. Vesicles store and move materials between cell organelles, as well as to and from the cell surface.

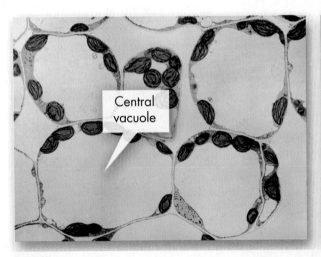

TEM 7000×

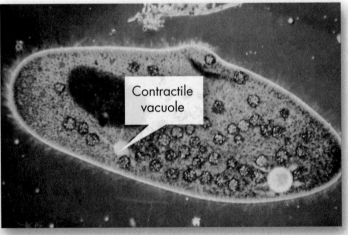

LM 500×

FIGURE 7–8 Vacuoles The central vacuole of plant cells stores salts, proteins, and carbohydrates. A paramecium's contractile vacuole controls the water content of the organism by pumping water out. **Apply Concepts** *How do vacuoles help support plant structures?*

Lysosomes Even the neatest, cleanest factory needs a cleanup crew, and that's where lysosomes come in. **Lysosomes** are small organelles filled with enzymes. 🔑 **Lysosomes break down lipids, carbohydrates, and proteins into small molecules that can be used by the rest of the cell. They are also involved in breaking down organelles that have outlived their usefulness.** Lysosomes perform the vital function of removing "junk" that might otherwise accumulate and clutter up the cell. A number of serious human diseases can be traced to lysosomes that fail to function properly. Biologists once thought that lysosomes were only found in animal cells, but it is now clear that lysosomes are also found in a few specialized types of plant cells as well.

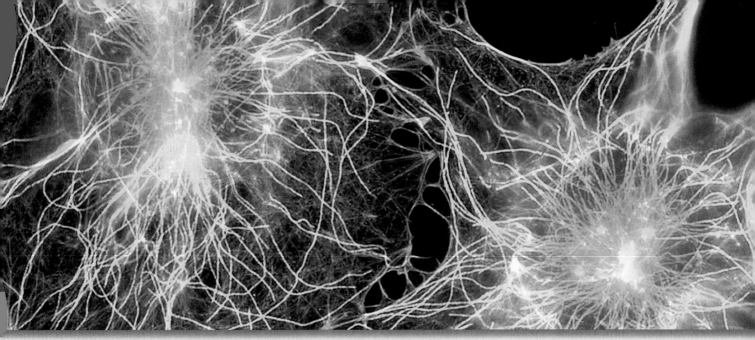

The Cytoskeleton As you know, a factory building is supported by steel or cement beams and by columns that hold up its walls and roof. Eukaryotic cells are given their shape and internal organization by a network of protein filaments known as the **cytoskeleton.** Certain parts of the cytoskeleton also help transport materials between different parts of the cell, much like the conveyor belts that carry materials from one part of a factory to another. Cytoskeletal components may also be involved in moving the entire cell as in cell flagella and cilia. 🔑 **The cytoskeleton helps the cell maintain its shape and is also involved in movement.** Fluorescence imaging, as seen in **Figure 7–9,** clearly shows the complexity of a cell's cytoskeletal network. Microfilaments (pale purple) and microtubules (yellow) are two of the principal protein filaments that make up the cytoskeleton.

▶ *Microfilaments* Microfilaments are threadlike structures made up of a protein called actin. They form extensive networks in some cells and produce a tough flexible framework that supports the cell. Microfilaments also help cells move. Microfilament assembly and disassembly are responsible for the cytoplasmic movements that allow amoebas and other cells to crawl along surfaces.

▶ *Microtubules* Microtubules are hollow structures made up of proteins known as tubulins. In many cells, they play critical roles in maintaining cell shape. Microtubules are also important in cell division, where they form a structure known as the mitotic spindle, which helps to separate chromosomes. In animal cells, organelles called centrioles are also formed from tubulins. **Centrioles** are located near the nucleus and help organize cell division. Centrioles are not found in plant cells.

Microtubules also help build projections from the cell surface—known as cilia (singular: cilium) and flagella (singular: flagellum)—that enable cells to swim rapidly through liquid. The microtubules in cilia and flagella are arranged in a "9 + 2" pattern, as shown in **Figure 7–10.** Small cross-bridges between the microtubules in these organelles use chemical energy to pull on, or slide along, the microtubules, producing controlled movements.

LM 1175×

FIGURE 7–9 Cytoskeleton The cytoskeleton supports and gives shape to the cell, and is involved in many forms of cell movement. These connective tissue fibroblast cells have been treated with fluorescent tags that bind to certain elements. Microfilaments are pale purple, microtubules are yellow, and the nuclei are green.

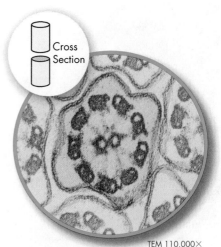

Cross Section

TEM 110,000×

FIGURE 7–10 The "9 + 2" Pattern of Microtubules In this micrograph showing the cross section of a cilium, you can clearly see the 9 + 2 arrangement of the red microtubules.
Apply Concepts *What is the function of cilia?*

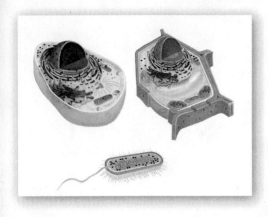

Organelles That Build Proteins

🔑 What organelles help make and transport proteins?

Life is a dynamic process, and living things are always working, building new molecules all the time, especially proteins, which catalyze chemical reactions and make up important structures in the cell. Because proteins carry out so many of the essential functions of living things, a big part of the cell is devoted to their production and distribution. Proteins are synthesized on ribosomes, sometimes in association with the rough endoplasmic reticulum in eukaryotes. The process of making proteins is summarized in **Figure 7–11.**

Ribosomes One of the most important jobs carried out in the cellular "factory" is making proteins. 🔑 **Proteins are assembled on ribosomes. Ribosomes** are small particles of RNA and protein found throughout the cytoplasm in all cells. Ribosomes produce proteins by following coded instructions that come from DNA. Each ribosome, in its own way, is like a small machine in a factory, turning out proteins on orders that come from its DNA "boss." Cells that are especially active in protein synthesis often contain large numbers of ribosomes.

Endoplasmic Reticulum Eukaryotic cells contain an internal membrane system known as the **endoplasmic reticulum** (en doh PLAZ mik rih TIK yuh lum), or ER. The endoplasmic reticulum is where lipid components of the cell membrane are assembled, along with proteins and other materials that are exported from the cell.

The portion of the ER involved in the synthesis of proteins is called rough endoplasmic reticulum, or rough ER. It is given this name because of the ribosomes found on its surface. Newly made proteins leave these ribosomes and are inserted into the rough ER, where they may be chemically modified.

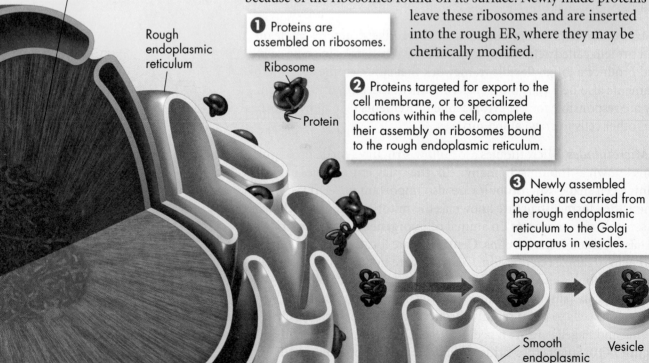

Nucleus

Rough endoplasmic reticulum

❶ Proteins are assembled on ribosomes.

Ribosome

Protein

❷ Proteins targeted for export to the cell membrane, or to specialized locations within the cell, complete their assembly on ribosomes bound to the rough endoplasmic reticulum.

❸ Newly assembled proteins are carried from the rough endoplasmic reticulum to the Golgi apparatus in vesicles.

Smooth endoplasmic reticulum

Vesicle

CYTOPLASM

🔑 Proteins made on the rough ER include those that will be released, or secreted, from the cell as well as many membrane proteins and proteins destined for lysosomes and other specialized locations within the cell. Rough ER is abundant in cells that produce large amounts of protein for export. Other cellular proteins are made on "free" ribosomes, which are not attached to membranes.

The other portion of the ER is known as smooth endoplasmic reticulum (smooth ER) because ribosomes are not found on its surface. In many cells, the smooth ER contains collections of enzymes that perform specialized tasks, including the synthesis of membrane lipids and the detoxification of drugs. Liver cells, which play a key role in detoxifying drugs, often contain large amounts of smooth ER.

Golgi Apparatus In eukaryotic cells, proteins produced in the rough ER move next into an organelle called the **Golgi apparatus,** which appears as a stack of flattened membranes. As proteins leave the rough ER, molecular "address tags" get them to the right destinations. As these tags are "read" by the cell, the proteins are bundled into tiny vesicles that bud from the ER and carry them to the Golgi apparatus. 🔑 **The Golgi apparatus modifies, sorts, and packages proteins and other materials from the endoplasmic reticulum for storage in the cell or release outside the cell.** The Golgi apparatus is somewhat like a customization shop, where the finishing touches are put on proteins before they are ready to leave the "factory." From the Golgi apparatus, proteins are "shipped" to their final destination inside or outside the cell.

In Your Notebook *Make a flowchart that shows how proteins are assembled in a cell.*

MAKING PROTEINS

FIGURE 7–11 Together, ribosomes, the endoplasmic reticulum, and the Golgi apparatus synthesize, modify, package, and ship proteins. **Infer** *What can you infer about a cell that is packed with more than the typical number of ribosomes?*

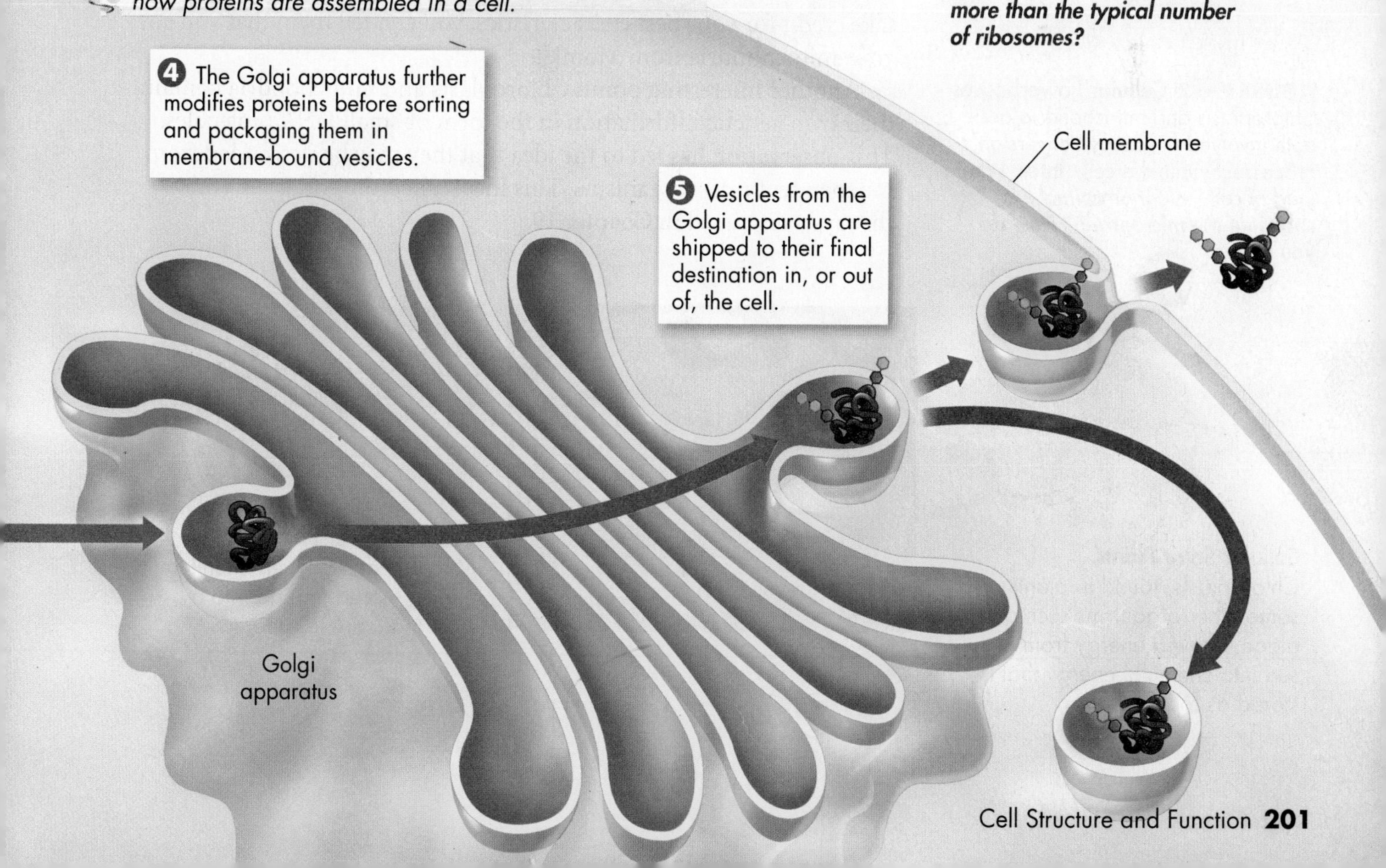

④ The Golgi apparatus further modifies proteins before sorting and packaging them in membrane-bound vesicles.

⑤ Vesicles from the Golgi apparatus are shipped to their final destination in, or out of, the cell.

Cell membrane

Golgi apparatus

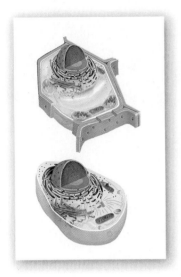

Organelles That Capture and Release Energy

🔑 **What are the functions of chloroplasts and mitochondria?**

All living things require a source of energy. Factories are hooked up to the local power company, but how do cells get energy? Most cells are powered by food molecules that are built using energy from the sun.

Chloroplasts Plants and some other organisms contain chloroplasts (KLAWR uh plasts). **Chloroplasts** are the biological equivalents of solar power plants. 🔑 **Chloroplasts capture the energy from sunlight and convert it into food that contains chemical energy in a process called photosynthesis.** Two membranes surround chloroplasts. Inside the organelle are large stacks of other membranes, which contain the green pigment chlorophyll.

Mitochondria Nearly all eukaryotic cells, including plants, contain mitochondria (myt oh KAHN dree uh; singular: mitochondrion). **Mitochondria** are the power plants of the cell. 🔑 **Mitochondria convert the chemical energy stored in food into compounds that are more convenient for the cell to use.** Like chloroplasts, two membranes—an outer membrane and an inner membrane—enclose mitochondria. The inner membrane is folded up inside the organelle, as shown in **Figure 7–12.**

One of the most interesting aspects of mitochondria is the way in which they are inherited. In humans, all or nearly all of our mitochondria come from the cytoplasm of the ovum, or egg cell. This means that when your relatives are discussing which side of the family should take credit for your best characteristics, you can tell them that you got your mitochondria from Mom!

Another interesting point: Chloroplasts and mitochondria contain their own genetic information in the form of small DNA molecules. This observation has led to the idea that they may be descended from independent microorganisms. This idea, called the endosymbiotic theory, is discussed in Chapter 19.

FIGURE 7–12 Cellular Powerhouses Chloroplasts and mitochondria are both involved in energy conversion processes within the cell. **Infer** *What kind of cell—plant or animal—is shown in the micrograph? How do you know?*

Cellular Solar Plants
Chloroplasts, found in plants and some other organisms such as algae, convert energy from the sun into chemical energy that is stored as food.

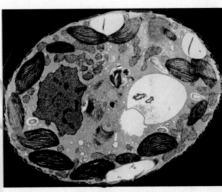

TEM 4500×

Cellular Power Plants
Mitochondria convert chemical energy stored in food into a form that can be used easily by the cell.

Making a Model of a Cell

❶ Your class is going to make a model of a plant cell using the whole classroom. Work with a partner or in a small group to decide what cell part or organelle you would like to model. (Use **Figure 7–14** on pages 206–207 as a starting point. It gives you an idea of the relative sizes of various cell parts and their possible positions.)

❷ Using materials of your choice, make a three-dimensional model of the cell part or organelle you chose. Make the model as complete and as accurate as you can.

❸ Label an index card with the name of your cell part or organelle, and list its main features and functions. Attach the card to your model.

❹ Attach your model to an appropriate place in the room. If possible, attach your model to another related cell part or organelle.

Analyze and Conclude

1. Calculate Assume that a typical plant cell is 50 micrometers wide (50×10^{-6} m). Calculate the scale of your classroom cell model. (*Hint:* Divide the width of the classroom by the width of a cell, making sure to use the same units.) MATH

2. Compare and Contrast How is your model cell part or organelle similar to the real cell part or organelle? How is it different?

3. Evaluate Based on your work with this model, describe how you could make a better model. What new information would your improved model demonstrate?

Cellular Boundaries

🔑 What is the function of the cell membrane?

A working factory needs walls and a roof to protect it from the environment outside, and also to serve as a barrier that keeps its products safe and secure until they are ready to be shipped out. Cells have similar needs, and they meet them in a similar way. As you have learned, all cells are surrounded by a barrier known as the cell membrane. Many cells, including most prokaryotes, also produce a strong supporting layer around the membrane known as a **cell wall.**

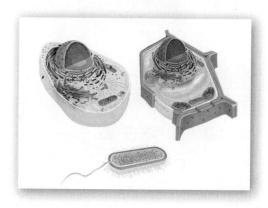

Cell Walls Many organisms have cell walls in addition to cell membranes. The main function of the cell wall is to support, shape, and protect the cell. Most prokaryotes and many eukaryotes have cell walls. Animal cells do not have cell walls. Cell walls lie outside the cell membrane. Most cell walls are porous enough to allow water, oxygen, carbon dioxide, and certain other substances to pass through easily.

Cell walls provide much of the strength needed for plants to stand against the force of gravity. In trees and other large plants, nearly all of the tissue we call wood is made up of cell walls. The cellulose fiber used for paper as well as the lumber used for building comes from these walls. So if you are reading these words off a sheet of paper from a book resting on a wooden desk, you've got cell walls all around you.

BUILD Vocabulary
ACADEMIC WORDS The adjective **porous** means "allowing materials to pass through." A porous cell wall allows substances like water and oxygen to pass through it.

Cell Membranes All cells contain cell membranes, which almost always are made up of a double-layered sheet called a lipid bilayer, as shown in **Figure 7–13.** The **lipid bilayer** gives cell membranes a flexible structure that forms a strong barrier between the cell and its surroundings. 🔑 **The cell membrane regulates what enters and leaves the cell and also protects and supports the cell.**

▶ *The Properties of Lipids* The layered structure of cell membranes reflects the chemical properties of the lipids that make them up. You may recall that many lipids have oily fatty acid chains attached to chemical groups that interact strongly with water. In the language of a chemist, the fatty acid portions of this kind of lipid are hydrophobic (hy druh FOH bik), or "water-hating," while the opposite end of the molecule is hydrophilic (hy druh FIL ik), or "water-loving." When these lipids, including the phospholipids that are common in animal cell membranes, are mixed with water, their hydrophobic fatty acid "tails" cluster together while their hydrophilic "heads" are attracted to water. A lipid bilayer is the result. As you can see in **Figure 7–13,** the head groups of lipids in a bilayer are exposed to the outside of the cell, while the fatty acid tails form an oily layer inside the membrane that keeps water out.

FIGURE 7–13 Every cell has a membrane that regulates the movement of materials. Nearly all cell membranes are made up of a lipid bilayer in which proteins and carbohydrates are embedded. **Apply Concepts** *Explain why lipids "self-assemble" into a bilayer when exposed to water.*

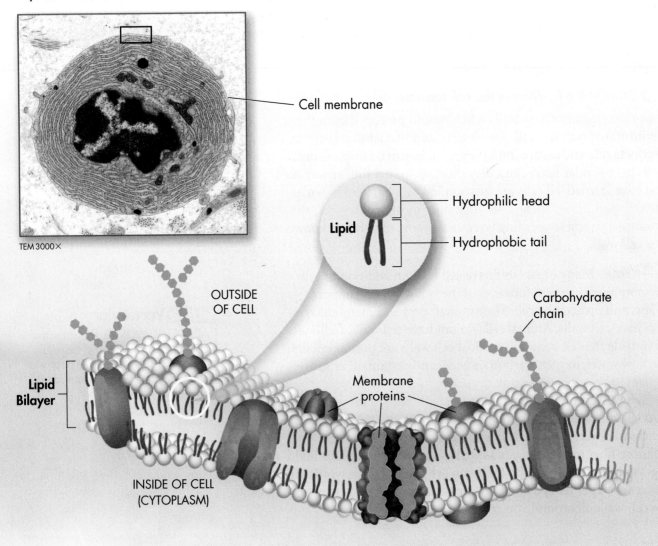

TEM 3000×

Cell membrane

Lipid

Hydrophilic head

Hydrophobic tail

OUTSIDE OF CELL

Carbohydrate chain

Lipid Bilayer

Membrane proteins

INSIDE OF CELL (CYTOPLASM)

▶ *The Fluid Mosaic Model* Embedded in the lipid bilayer of most cell membranes are protein molecules. Carbohydrate molecules are attached to many of these proteins. Because the proteins embedded in the lipid bilayer can move around and "float" among the lipids, and because so many different kinds of molecules make up the cell membrane, scientists describe the cell membrane as a "fluid mosaic." A mosaic is a kind of art that involves bits and pieces of different colors or materials. What are all these different molecules doing? As you will see, some of the proteins form channels and pumps that help to move material across the cell membrane. Many of the carbohydrate molecules act like chemical identification cards, allowing individual cells to identify one another. Some proteins attach directly to the cytoskeleton, enabling cells to respond to their environment by using their membranes to help move or change shape.

As you know, some things are allowed to enter and leave a factory, and some are not. The same is true for living cells. Although many substances can cross biological membranes, some are too large or too strongly charged to cross the lipid bilayer. If a substance is able to cross a membrane, the membrane is said to be permeable to it. A membrane is impermeable to substances that cannot pass across it. Most biological membranes are **selectively permeable,** meaning that some substances can pass across them and others cannot. Selectively permeable membranes are also called semipermeable membranes.

7.2 Assessment

Review Key Concepts 🔑

1. a. Review What are the two major parts of the cell?

b. Use Analogies How is the role of the nucleus in a cell similar to the role of the captain on a sports team?

2. a. Review What is the function of lysosomes?

b. Apply Concepts How do contractile vacuoles help maintain water balance?

3. a. Review What is the difference between rough and smooth ER?

b. Sequence Describe the steps involved in the synthesis, packaging, and export of a protein from a cell.

4. a. Review What is the function of mitochondria?

b. Infer You examine an unknown cell under a microscope and discover that the cell contains chloroplasts. From what type of organism does the cell likely come?

5. a. Review Why is the cell membrane sometimes referred to as a fluid mosaic? What part of the cell membrane acts like a fluid? And what makes it like a mosaic?

b. Explain How do the properties of lipids help explain the structure of a cell membrane?

c. Infer Why do you think it's important that cell membranes are *selectively* permeable?

VISUAL THINKING

6. Using the cells on the next page as a guide, draw your own models of a prokaryotic cell, a plant cell, and an animal cell. Then use each of the vocabulary words from this lesson to label your cells.

TYPICAL CELLS

FIGURE 7–14 Eukaryotic cells contain a variety of organelles, a few of which they have in common with prokaryotic cells. Note in the table on the facing page that while prokaryotic cells lack cytoskeleton and chloroplasts, they accomplish their functions in other ways as described. **Interpret Visuals** *What structures do prokaryotic cells have in common with animal cells? With plant cells?*

ANIMAL CELL

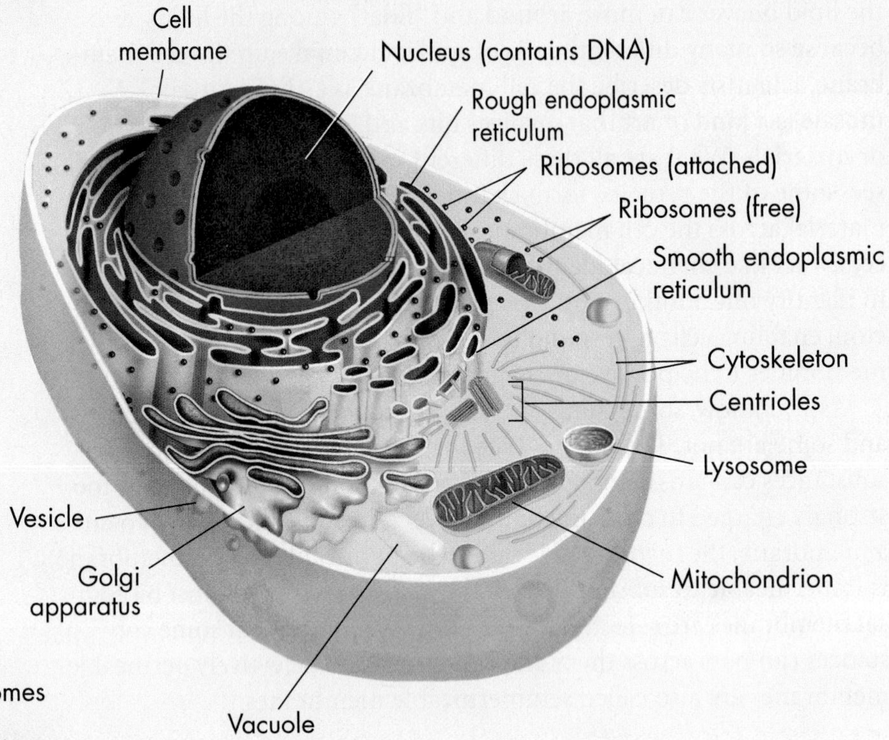

Cell membrane
Nucleus (contains DNA)
Rough endoplasmic reticulum
Ribosomes (attached)
Ribosomes (free)
Smooth endoplasmic reticulum
Cytoskeleton
Centrioles
Lysosome
Mitochondrion
Vesicle
Golgi apparatus
Vacuole

PROKARYOTIC CELL

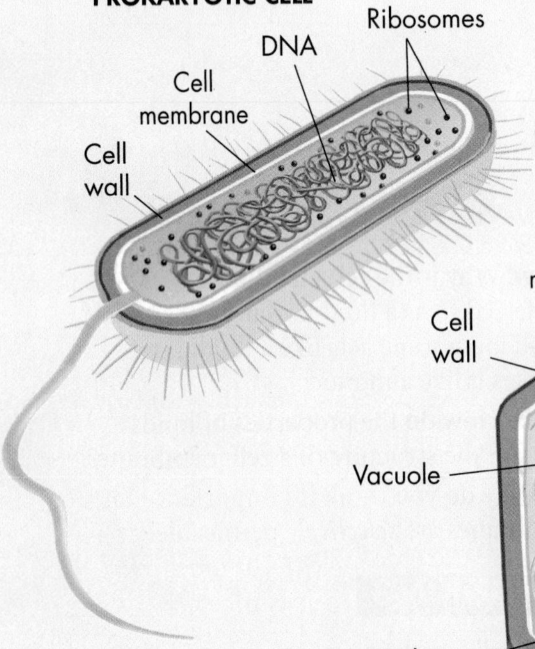

Ribosomes
DNA
Cell membrane
Cell wall

PLANT CELL

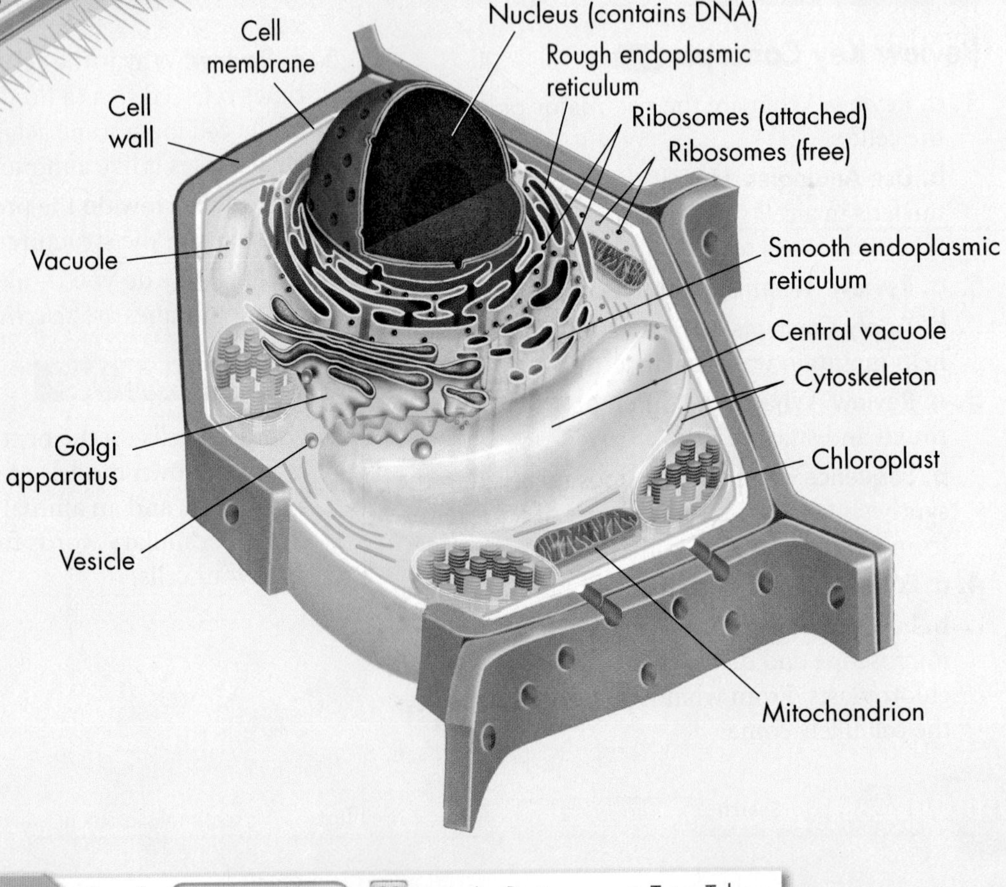

Cell membrane
Nucleus (contains DNA)
Rough endoplasmic reticulum
Ribosomes (attached)
Ribosomes (free)
Cell wall
Smooth endoplasmic reticulum
Central vacuole
Vacuole
Cytoskeleton
Chloroplast
Golgi apparatus
Vesicle
Mitochondrion

	Structure	Function	Prokaryote	Eukaryote: Animal	Plant
Cellular Control Center	Nucleus	Contains DNA	*Prokaryote DNA is found in cytoplasm.*	✓	✓
Organelles That Store, Clean-Up, and Support	Vacuoles and vesicles	Store materials		✓	✓
	Lysosomes	Break down and recycle macromolecules		✓	✓ (rare)
	Cytoskeleton	Maintains cell shape; moves cell parts; helps cells move	*Prokaryotic cells have protein filaments similar to actin and tubulin.*	✓	✓
	Centrioles	Organize cell division		✓	
Organelles That Build Proteins	Ribosomes	Synthesize proteins	✓	✓	✓
	Endoplasmic reticulum	Assembles proteins and lipids		✓	✓
	Golgi apparatus	Modifies, sorts, and packages proteins and lipids for storage or transport out of the cell		✓	✓
Organelles That Capture and Release Energy	Chloroplasts	Convert solar energy to chemical energy stored in food	*In some prokaryotic cells, photosynthesis occurs in association with internal photosynthetic membranes.*		✓
	Mitochondria	Convert chemical energy in food to usable compounds	*Prokaryotes carry out these reactions in the cytoplasm rather than in specialized organelles.*	✓	✓
Cellular Boundaries	Cell wall	Shapes, supports, and protects the cell	✓		✓
	Cell membrane	Regulates materials entering and leaving cell; protects and supports cell	✓	✓	✓

7.3 Cell Transport

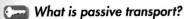

Key Questions

🔑 *What is passive transport?*

🔑 *What is active transport?*

Vocabulary

diffusion • facilitated diffusion • aquaporin • osmosis • isotonic • hypertonic • hypotonic • osmotic pressure

Taking Notes

Compare/Contrast Table As you read, create a compare/contrast table for passive and active transport.

MYSTERY CLUE

As Michelle ran, she perspired, losing salts from her bloodstream. And as she drank more and more water during the race, the concentration of dissolved salts and minerals in her bloodstream decreased. How do you think these phenomena contributed to Michelle's condition?

THINK ABOUT IT In the previous lesson, cell walls and cell membranes were compared to the roof and walls of a factory. When you think about how cells move materials in and out, it can be helpful to think of a cell as a nation. Before you can learn anything about a nation, it's important to understand where it begins and where it ends. The boundaries of a nation are its borders, and nearly every country tries to regulate and control the goods that move across those borders, like the shipping containers seen here entering and leaving

the port of Seattle. Each cell has its own border, which separates the cell from its surroundings and also determines what comes in and what goes out. How can a cell separate itself from its environment and still allow material to enter and leave? That's where transport across its border, the cell membrane, comes in.

Passive Transport

🔑 **What is passive transport?**

Every living cell exists in a liquid environment. One of the most important functions of the cell membrane is to keep the cell's internal conditions relatively constant. It does this by regulating the movement of molecules from one side of the membrane to the other.

Diffusion Cellular cytoplasm consists of many different substances dissolved in water. In any solution, solute particles move constantly. They collide with one another and tend to spread out randomly. As a result, the particles tend to move from an area where they are more concentrated to an area where they are less concentrated. When you add sugar to coffee or tea, for example, the sugar molecules move away from their original positions in the sugar crystals and disperse throughout the hot liquid. The process by which particles move from an area of high concentration to an area of lower concentration is known as **diffusion** (dih FYOO zhun). Diffusion is the driving force behind the movement of many substances across the cell membrane.

BIOLOGY.com 〉 Search (Lesson 7.3) **GO** • Lesson Overview • Lesson Notes • InterActive Art

What does diffusion have to do with the cell membrane? Suppose a substance is present in unequal concentrations on either side of a cell membrane, as shown in **Figure 7–15.** If the substance can cross the cell membrane, its particles will tend to move toward the area where it is less concentrated until it is evenly distributed. Once the concentration of the substance on both sides of the cell membrane is the same, equilibrium is reached.

Even when equilibrium is reached, particles of a solution continue to move across the membrane in both directions. However, because almost equal numbers of particles move in each direction, there is no further net change in the concentration on either side.

Diffusion depends on random particle movements. Therefore, substances diffuse across membranes without requiring the cell to use additional energy. ⬛ **The movement of materials across the cell membrane without using cellular energy is called passive transport.**

FIGURE 7–15 Diffusion Diffusion is the process by which molecules of a substance move from an area of higher concentration to an area of lower concentration. It does not require the cell to use energy. *Predict How would the movement of solute particles seen here be different if the initial area of high concentration had been on the inside of the cell instead of the outside?*

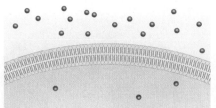

There is a higher concentration of solute on one side of the membrane than on the other.

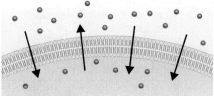

Diffusion causes a net movement of solute particles from the side of the membrane with the higher solute concentration to the side with the lower solute concentration.

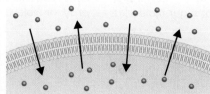

Once equilibrium is reached, solute particles continue to diffuse across the membrane in both directions but at approximately equal rates, so there is no net change in solute concentration.

Facilitated Diffusion Since cell membranes are built around lipid bilayers, the molecules that pass through them most easily are small and uncharged. These properties allow them to dissolve in the membrane's lipid environment. But many ions, like Cl^-, and large molecules, like the sugar glucose, seem to pass through cell membranes much more quickly than they should. It's almost as if they have a shortcut across the membrane.

How does this happen? Proteins in the cell membrane act as carriers, or channels, making it easy for certain molecules to cross. Red blood cells, for example, have protein carriers that allow glucose to pass through them in either direction. Only glucose can pass through these protein carriers. These cell membrane channels facilitate, or help, the diffusion of glucose across the membrane. This process, in which molecules that cannot directly diffuse across the membrane pass through special protein channels, is known as **facilitated diffusion.** Hundreds of different proteins have been found that allow particular substances to cross cell membranes. Although facilitated diffusion is fast and specific, it is still diffusion, so it does not require any additional use of the cell's energy.

In Your Notebook *Explain how you can demonstrate diffusion by spraying air freshener in a large room.*

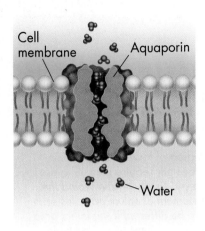

Cell membrane

Aquaporin

Water

FIGURE 7-16 An Aquaporin

Osmosis: An Example of Facilitated Diffusion Surprising new research has added water to the list of molecules that enter cells by facilitated diffusion. Recall that the inside of a cell's lipid bilayer is hydrophobic, or "water-hating." Because of this, water molecules have a tough time passing through the cell membrane. However, many cells contain water channel proteins, known as **aquaporins** (ak wuh PAWR inz), that allow water to pass right through them, as shown in **Figure 7–16.** The movement of water through cell membranes by facilitated diffusion is an extremely important biological process—the process of osmosis.

Osmosis is the diffusion of water through a selectively permeable membrane. In osmosis, as in other forms of diffusion, molecules move from an area of higher concentration to an area of lower concentration. The only difference is that the molecules that move in the case of osmosis are water molecules, not solute molecules. The process of osmosis is shown in **Figure 7–17.**

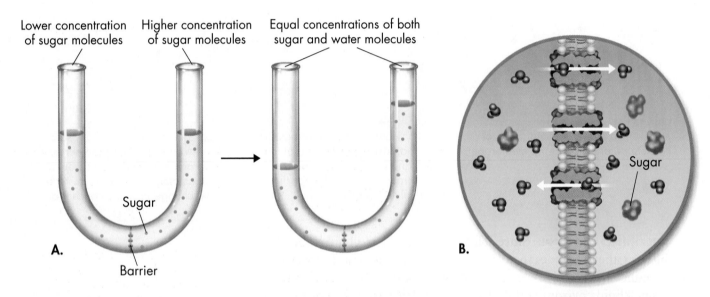

Lower concentration of sugar molecules

Higher concentration of sugar molecules

Equal concentrations of both sugar and water molecules

Sugar

A.

Barrier

B.

Sugar

FIGURE 7-17 Osmosis Osmosis is a form of facilitated diffusion. **A.** In a laboratory experiment, water moves through a selectively permeable barrier from an area of lower to higher solute concentration until equilibrium is reached. **B.** In the cell, water passes in through aquaporins embedded in the cell membrane. Although water moves in both directions through aquaporins, there is a net movement of water from an area of lower to higher sugar concentration. **Apply Concepts** *Does osmosis require the cell to use energy?*

▶ *How Osmosis Works* Look at the experimental setup in **Figure 7–17A.** The barrier is permeable to water but not to sugar. This means that water can cross the barrier in both directions, but sugar cannot. To start, there are more sugar molecules on the right side of the barrier than on the left side. Therefore, the concentration of water is lower on the right, where more of the solution is made of sugar. Although water molecules move in both directions across the membrane, there is a net movement of water toward the concentrated sugar solution.

Water will tend to move across the membrane until equilibrium is reached. At that point, the concentrations of water and sugar will be the same on both sides of the membrane. When this happens, the two solutions will be **isotonic,** which means "same strength." Note that "strength" refers to the amount of solute, not water. When the experiment began, the more concentrated sugar solution (right side of the tube) was **hypertonic,** or "above strength," compared to the left side. So the dilute sugar solution (left side of the tube) was **hypotonic,** or "below strength," compared to the right side. **Figure 7–17B** shows how osmosis works across a cell membrane.

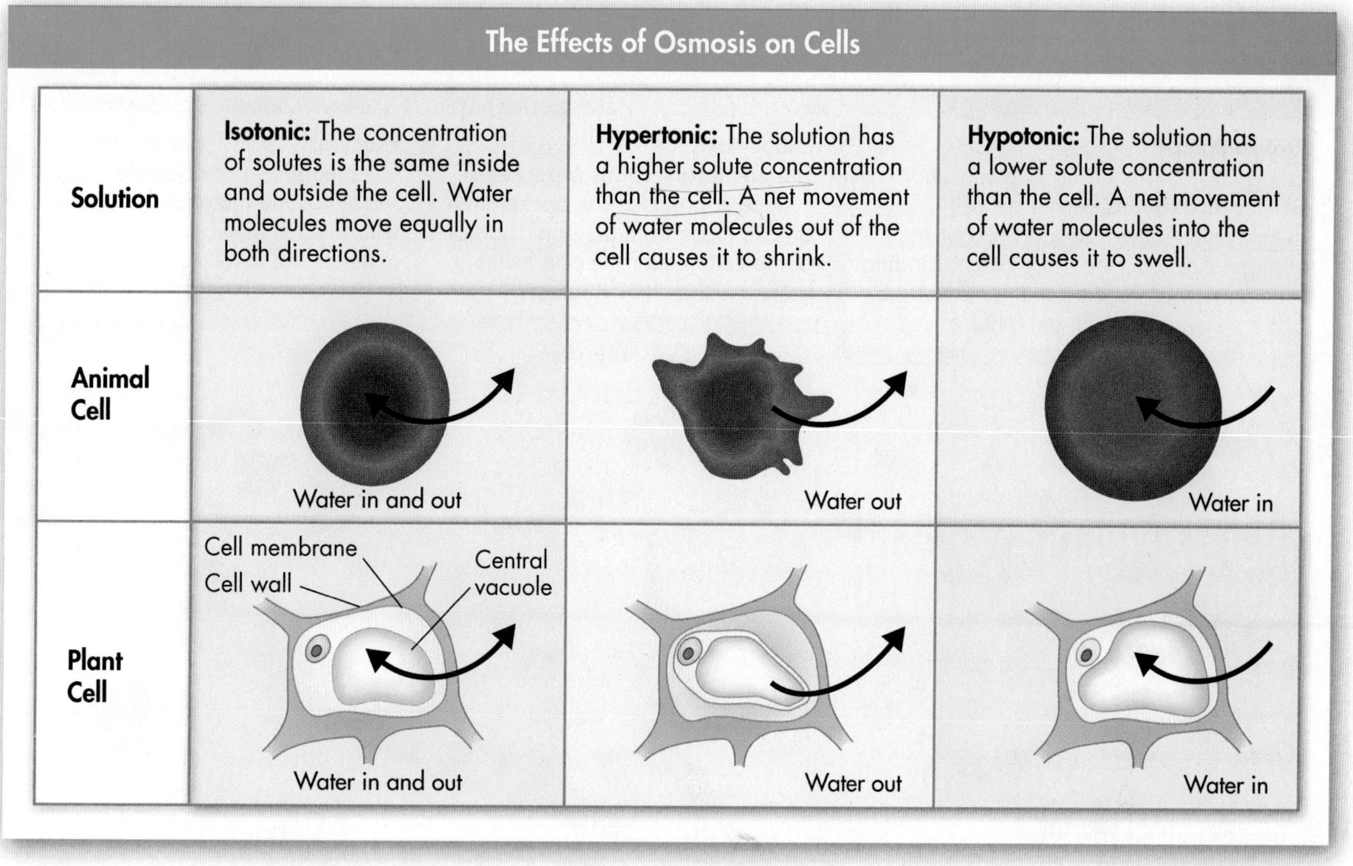

The Effects of Osmosis on Cells

	Isotonic: The concentration of solutes is the same inside and outside the cell. Water molecules move equally in both directions.	Hypertonic: The solution has a higher solute concentration than the cell. A net movement of water molecules out of the cell causes it to shrink.	Hypotonic: The solution has a lower solute concentration than the cell. A net movement of water molecules into the cell causes it to swell.
Solution			
Animal Cell	Water in and out	Water out	Water in
Plant Cell	Cell membrane / Cell wall / Central vacuole — Water in and out	Water out	Water in

▶ *Osmotic Pressure* Driven by differences in solute concentration, the net movement of water out of or into a cell produces a force known as **osmotic pressure.** As shown in **Figure 7–18,** osmotic pressure can cause an animal cell in a hypertonic solution to shrink, and one in a hypotonic solution to swell. Because cells contain salts, sugars, proteins, and other dissolved molecules, they are almost always hypertonic to fresh water. As a result, water tends to move quickly into a cell surrounded by fresh water, causing it to swell. Eventually, the cell may burst like an overinflated balloon. In plant cells, osmotic pressure can cause changes in the size of the central vacuole, which shrinks or swells as water moves into or out of the cell.

Fortunately cells in large organisms are not in danger of bursting because most of them do not come in contact with fresh water. Instead, the cells are bathed in blood or other isotonic fluids. The concentrations of dissolved materials in these isotonic fluids are roughly equal to those in the cells themselves.

What happens when cells do come in contact with fresh water? Some, like the eggs laid in fresh water by fish and frogs, lack water channels. As a result, water moves into them so slowly that osmotic pressure is not a problem. Others, including bacteria and plant cells, are surrounded by tough walls. The cell walls prevent the cells from expanding, even under tremendous osmotic pressure. Notice how the plant cell in **Figure 7–18** holds its shape in both hypertonic and hypotonic solutions while the animal red blood cell does not. However, increased osmotic pressure makes plant cells extremely vulnerable to cell wall injuries.

FIGURE 7–18 Osmotic Pressure Water molecules move equally into and out of cells placed in an isotonic solution. In a hypertonic solution, animal cells, like the red blood cell shown, shrink, and plant cell central vacuoles collapse. In a hypotonic solution, animal cells swell and burst. The central vacuoles of plant cells also swell, pushing the cell contents out against the cell wall. **Predict** *What would happen to the cells of a saltwater plant if the plant were placed in fresh water?*

In Your Notebook *In your own words, explain why osmosis is really just a special case of facilitated diffusion.*

Protein Pumps
Energy from ATP is used to pump small molecules and ions across the cell membrane. Active transport proteins change shape during the process, binding substances on one side of the membrane, and releasing them on the other.

Endocytosis
The membrane forms a pocket around a particle. The pocket then breaks loose from the outer portion of the cell membrane and forms a vesicle within the cytoplasm.

Exocytosis
The membrane of a vesicle surrounds the material then fuses with the cell membrane. The contents are forced out of the cell.

CYTOPLASM

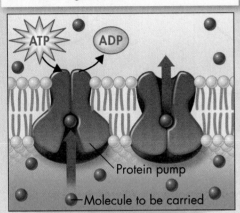

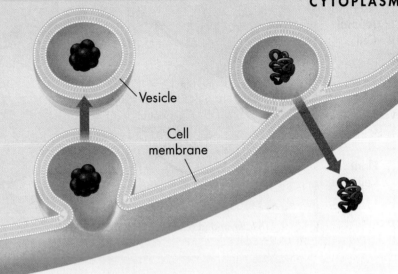

Vesicle

Cell membrane

VISUAL SUMMARY

ACTIVE TRANSPORT

FIGURE 7–19 Energy from the cell is required to move particles against a concentration gradient.
Compare and Contrast *What are the similarities and differences between facilitated diffusion and active transport by protein pump?*

Active Transport

What is active transport?

As powerful as diffusion is, cells sometimes must move materials against a concentration difference. **The movement of materials against a concentration difference is known as active transport. Active transport requires energy.** The active transport of small molecules or ions across a cell membrane is generally carried out by transport proteins—protein pumps—that are found in the membrane itself. Larger molecules and clumps of material can also be actively transported across the cell membrane by processes known as endocytosis and exocytosis. The transport of these larger materials sometimes involves changes in the shape of the cell membrane. The major types of active transport are shown in **Figure 7–19.**

Molecular Transport Small molecules and ions are carried across membranes by proteins in the membrane that act like pumps. Many cells use protein pumps to move calcium, potassium, and sodium ions across cell membranes. Changes in protein shape seem to play an important role in the pumping process. A considerable portion of the energy used by cells in their daily activities is spent providing the energy to keep this form of active transport working. The use of energy in these systems enables cells to concentrate substances in a particular location, even when the forces of diffusion might tend to move these substances in the opposite direction.

Bulk Transport Larger molecules and even solid clumps of material can be transported by movements of the cell membrane known as bulk transport. Bulk transport can take several forms, depending on the size and shape of the material moved into or out of the cell.

▶ **Endocytosis** Endocytosis (en doh sy TOH sis) is the process of taking material into the cell by means of infoldings, or pockets, of the cell membrane. The pocket that results breaks loose from the outer portion of the cell membrane and forms a vesicle or vacuole within the cytoplasm. Large molecules, clumps of food, even whole cells can be taken up in this way.

Phagocytosis (fag oh sy TOH sis) is a type of endocytosis, in which extensions of cytoplasm surround a particle and package it within a food vacuole. The cell then engulfs it. Amoebas use this method for taking in food, and white blood cells use phagocytosis to "eat" damaged cells, as shown in **Figure 7–20.** Engulfing material in this way requires a considerable amount of energy and is considered a form of active transport.

In a process similar to phagocytosis, many cells take up liquid from the surrounding environment. Tiny pockets form along the cell membrane, fill with liquid, and pinch off to form vacuoles within the cell. This type of endocytosis is known as pinocytosis (py nuh sy TOH sis).

▶ **Exocytosis** Many cells also release large amounts of material, a process known as exocytosis (ek soh sy TOH sis). During exocytosis, the membrane of the vacuole surrounding the material fuses with the cell membrane, forcing the contents out of the cell. The removal of water by means of a contractile vacuole is one example of this kind of active transport.

BUILD Vocabulary

PREFIXES The prefix *endo-* in *endocytosis* comes from a Greek word meaning "inside" or "within." The prefix *exo-* in *exocytosis* means "outside."

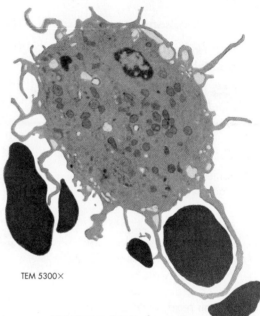

TEM 5300×

FIGURE 7–20 Endocytosis
The white blood cell seen here is engulfing a damaged red blood cell by phagocytosis—a form of endocytosis. Extensions, or "arms," of the white blood cell's cell membrane have completely surrounded the red blood cell.

7.3 Assessment

Review Key Concepts 🔑

1. a. Review What happens during diffusion?
   b. Explain Describe the process of osmosis.
   c. Compare and Contrast What is the difference between diffusion and facilitated diffusion?

2. a. Review How is active transport different from passive transport?
   b. Explain Describe the two major types of active transport.
   c. Compare and Contrast How is endocytosis different from exocytosis?

BUILD VOCABULARY

3. Based on the meanings of *isotonic, hypertonic,* and *hypotonic,* write definitions for the prefixes *iso-, hyper-,* and *hypo-*. Then come up with another set of words that uses these prefixes (the words do not need to have the same suffixes).

4. The prefix *phago-* means "to eat." The prefix *pino-* means "to drink." Look up the definition of *-cytosis,* and write definitions for *phagocytosis* and *pinocytosis.*

7.4 Homeostasis and Cells

Key Questions

🔑 *How do individual cells maintain homeostasis?*

🔑 *How do the cells of multi-cellular organisms work together to maintain homeostasis?*

Vocabulary

homeostasis • tissue • organ • organ system • receptor

Taking Notes

Preview Visuals Before you read, look at **Figures 7–22** and **7–23.** Then write two questions you have about the micrographs. As you read, write answers to your questions.

FIGURE 7–21 Unicellular Life Single-celled organisms, like this freshwater protozoan, must be able to carry out all of the functions necessary for life (SEM 600×).

THINK ABOUT IT From its simple beginnings, life has spread to every corner of our planet, penetrating deep into the earth and far beneath the surface of the seas. The diversity of life is so great that you might have to remind yourself that all living things are composed of cells, have the same basic chemical makeup, and even contain the same kinds of organelles. This does not mean that all living things are the same: Differences arise from the ways in which cells are specialized and the ways in which cells associate with one another to form multi-cellular organisms.

The Cell as an Organism

🔑 **How do individual cells maintain homeostasis?**

Cells are the basic living units of all organisms, but sometimes a single cell is the organism. In fact, in terms of their numbers, unicellular organisms dominate life on Earth. A single-celled organism does everything you would expect a living thing to do. Just like other living things, unicellular organisms must maintain **homeostasis,** relatively constant internal physical and chemical conditions. 🔑 **To maintain homeostasis, unicellular organisms grow, respond to the environment, transform energy, and reproduce.**

Unicellular organisms include both prokaryotes and eukaryotes. Prokaryotes, especially bacteria, are remarkably adaptable. Bacteria live almost everywhere—in the soil, on leaves, in the ocean, in the air, even within the human body.

Many eukaryotes, like the protozoan in **Figure 7–21,** also spend their lives as single cells. Some types of algae, which contain chloroplasts and are found in oceans, lakes, and streams around the world, are single celled. Yeasts, or unicellular fungi, are also widespread. Yeasts play an important role in breaking down complex nutrients, making them available for other organisms. People use yeasts to make bread and other foods.

Don't make the mistake of thinking that single-celled organisms are always simple. Prokaryote or eukaryote, homeostasis is still an issue for each unicellular organism. That tiny cell in a pond or on the surface of your pencil still needs to find sources of energy or food, to keep concentrations of water and minerals within certain levels, and to respond quickly to changes in its environment. The microscopic world around us is filled with unicellular organisms that are successfully maintaining that homeostatic balance.

Multicellular Life

🔑 *How do the cells of multicellular organisms work together to maintain homeostasis?*

Unlike most unicellular organisms, the cells of human beings and other multicellular organisms do not live on their own. They are interdependent; and like the members of a winning baseball team, they work together. In baseball, each player plays a particular position: pitcher, catcher, infielder, outfielder. And to play the game effectively, players and coaches communicate with one another, sending and receiving signals. Cells in a multicellular organism work the same way. 🔑 **The cells of multicellular organisms become specialized for particular tasks and communicate with one another to maintain homeostasis.**

Cell Specialization The cells of a multicellular organism are specialized, with different cell types playing different roles. Some cells are specialized to move; others, to react to the environment; still others, to produce substances that the organism needs. No matter what its role, each specialized cell, like the ones in **Figures 7–22** and **7–23,** contributes to homeostasis in the organism.

📝 **In Your Notebook** *Where in the human body do you think you would find cells that are specialized to produce digestive enzymes? Why?*

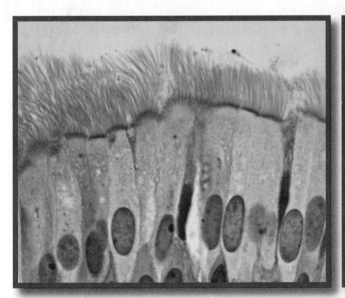

FIGURE 7–22 Specialized Animal Cells: Human Trachea Epithelium (LM 1000×)

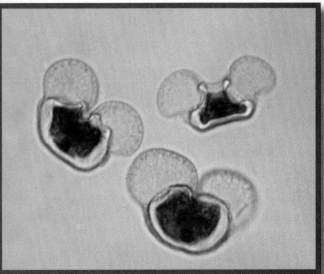

FIGURE 7–23 Specialized Plant Cells: Pine Pollen (LM 430×)

▶ *Specialized Animal Cells* Even the cleanest, freshest air is dirty, containing particles of dust, smoke, and bacteria. What keeps this bad stuff from getting into your lungs? That's the job of millions of cells that work like street sweepers. These cells line the upper air passages. As you breathe, they work night and day sweeping mucus, debris, and bacteria out of your lungs. These cells are filled with mitochondria, which produce a steady supply of the ATP that powers the cilia on their upper surfaces to keep your lungs clean.

▶ *Specialized Plant Cells* How can a pine tree, literally rooted in place, produce offspring with another tree hundreds of meters away? It releases pollen grains, some of the world's most specialized cells. Pollen grains are tiny and light, despite tough walls to protect the cells inside. In addition, pine pollen grains have two tiny wings that enable them to float in the slightest breeze. Pine trees release millions of pollen grains like these to scatter in the wind, land on seed cones, and begin the essential work of starting a new generation.

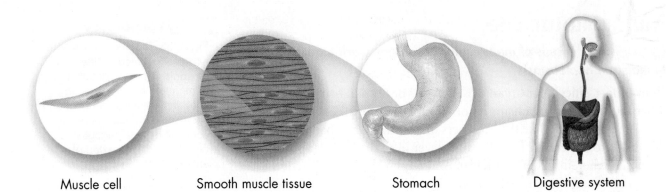

Muscle cell   Smooth muscle tissue   Stomach   Digestive system

FIGURE 7–24 Levels of Organization From least complex to most complex, the levels of organization in a multicellular organism include cells, tissues, organs, and organ systems.

Levels of Organization The specialized cells of multicellular organisms are organized into tissues, then into organs, and finally into organ systems, as shown in **Figure 7–24.** A **tissue** is a group of similar cells that performs a particular function. Many tasks in the body are too complicated to be carried out by just one type of tissue. In these cases, many groups of tissues work together as an **organ.** For example, each muscle in your body is an individual organ. Within a muscle, however, there is much more than muscle tissue. There are nervous tissues and connective tissues too. Each type of tissue performs an essential task to help the organ function. In most cases, an organ completes a series of specialized tasks. A group of organs that work together to perform a specific function is called an **organ system.** For example, the stomach, pancreas, and intestines work together as the digestive system.

Analyzing Data

Mitochondria Distribution in the Mouse

Scientists studied the composition of several organs in the mouse. They found that some organs and tissues contain more mitochondria than others. They described the amount of mitochondria present as a percentage of total cell volume. The higher the percentage volume made up of mitochondria, the more mitochondria present in the cells of the organ. The data are shown in the graph.

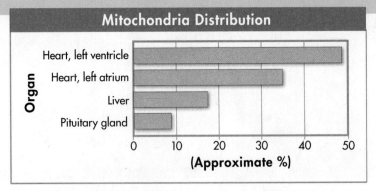

1. Interpret Graphs What approximate percentage of cell volume in the mouse liver is composed of mitochondria?

2. Calculate Approximately how much more cellular volume is composed of mitochondria in the left ventricle than in the pituitary gland? MATH

3. Infer There are four chambers in the mouse heart, the right and left ventricles, and the right and left atria. Based on the data given, which chamber, the left ventricle or left atrium, do you think pumps blood from the heart to the rest of the body? Explain your answer.

The organization of the body's cells into tissues, organs, and organ systems creates a division of labor among those cells that allows the organism to maintain homeostasis. Specialization and interdependence are two of the remarkable attributes of living things. Appreciating these characteristics is an important step in understanding the nature of living things.

Cellular Communication Cells in a large organism communicate by means of chemical signals that are passed from one cell to another. These cellular signals can speed up or slow down the activities of the cells that receive them and can even cause a cell to change what it is doing in a most dramatic way.

Certain cells, including those in the heart and liver, form connections, or cellular junctions, to neighboring cells. Some of these junctions, like those in **Figure 7–25,** hold cells together firmly. Others allow small molecules carrying chemical messages or signals to pass directly from one cell to the next. To respond to one of these chemical signals, a cell must have a **receptor** to which the signaling molecule can bind. Some receptors are on the cell membrane; receptors for other types of signals are inside the cytoplasm. The chemical signals sent by various types of cells can cause important changes in cellular activity. For example, the electrical signal that causes heart muscle cells to contract begins in a region of the muscle known as the pacemaker. Ions carry that electrical signal from cell to cell through a special connection known as a gap junction, enabling millions of heart muscle cells to contract as one in a single heartbeat. Other junctions hold the cells together, so the force of contraction does not tear the muscle tissue. Both types of junctions are essential for the heart to pump blood effectively.

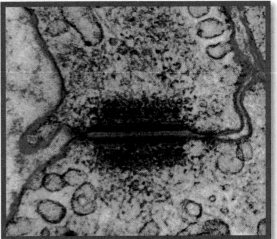

FIGURE 7–25 Cellular Junctions Some junctions, like the one seen in brown in this micrograph of capillary cells in the gas bladder of a toadfish, hold cells together in tight formations (TEM 21,600×).

7.4 Assessment

Review Key Concepts 🔑

1. a. Review What is homeostasis?

b. Explain What do unicellular organisms do to maintain homeostasis?

c. Apply Concepts The contractile vacuole is an organelle found in paramecia, a group of unicellular organisms. Contractile vacuoles pump out fresh water that accumulates in the organisms by osmosis. Explain how this is an example of the way paramecia maintain homeostasis.

2. a. Review What is cellular specialization?

b. Explain How do cellular junctions and receptors help an organism maintain homeostasis?

c. Predict Using what you know about the ways muscles move, predict which organelles would be most common in muscle cells.

WRITE ABOUT SCIENCE

Description

3. Use an area in your life—such as school, sports, or extracurricular activities—to construct an analogy that explains why specialization and communication are necessary for you to function well.

Pre-Lab: Detecting Diffusion

Problem How can you determine whether solutes are diffusing across a membrane?

Materials dialysis tubing, scissors, metric ruler, 250 mL beakers, twist ties, 10-mL graduated cylinders, 1% starch solution, iodine solution, forceps, 15% glucose solution, glucose test strip

Lab Manual Chapter 7 Lab

Skills Focus Use Models, Infer, Compare and Contrast

Connect to the Big idea The cell membrane forms a thin flexible barrier between a cell and its surroundings. The cell membrane controls what enters the cell and what leaves the cell. Diffusion is the process responsible for much of the movement across a cell membrane. During diffusion, solutes move from an area of high concentration to an area of lower concentration. When water is the molecule that is diffusing, the process is called osmosis. Proteins embedded in the membrane can facilitate the diffusion of many particles, including water. In this lab, you will use dialysis tubing to model the diffusion of small molecules.

Background Questions

a. **Review** What does it mean to say that a membrane is selectively permeable?

b. **Explain** Does the movement of molecules stop when the concentration of a solute is equal on both sides of a membrane? Explain.

c. **Compare and Contrast** What is the main difference between passive transport and active transport?

Pre-Lab Questions

Preview the procedure in the lab manual.

1. **Draw Conclusions** How will you know whether starch has diffused across the membrane in Part A? How will you know whether iodine has diffused across the membrane?

2. **Draw Conclusions** How will you be able to tell whether glucose has diffused across the membrane in Part B?

3. **Use Analogies** How is a window screen similar to a cell membrane?

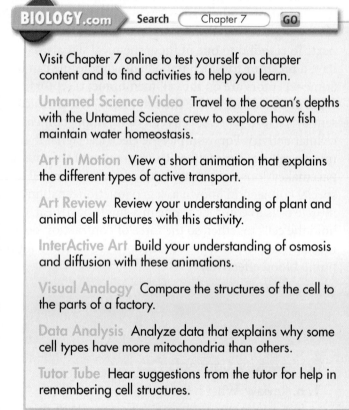

BIOLOGY.com   Search   Chapter 7   GO

Visit Chapter 7 online to test yourself on chapter content and to find activities to help you learn.

Untamed Science Video Travel to the ocean's depths with the Untamed Science crew to explore how fish maintain water homeostasis.

Art in Motion View a short animation that explains the different types of active transport.

Art Review Review your understanding of plant and animal cell structures with this activity.

InterActive Art Build your understanding of osmosis and diffusion with these animations.

Visual Analogy Compare the structures of the cell to the parts of a factory.

Data Analysis Analyze data that explains why some cell types have more mitochondria than others.

Tutor Tube Hear suggestions from the tutor for help in remembering cell structures.

7 Study Guide

Big ideas Cellular Basis of Life, Homeostasis

Cells are the basic units of life. Their structures are specifically adapted to their function and the overall goal of maintaining homeostasis. In multicellular organisms, cells may become specialized to carry out a particular function.

7.1 Life Is Cellular

🔑 The cell theory states that (1) all living things are made up of cells, (2) cells are the basic units of structure and function in living things, and (3) new cells are produced from existing cells.

🔑 Most microscopes use lenses to magnify the image of an object by focusing light or electrons.

🔑 Prokaryotic cells do not separate their genetic material within a nucleus. In eukaryotic cells, the nucleus separates the genetic material from the rest of the cell.

cell (191)	nucleus (193)
cell theory (191)	eukaryote (193)
cell membrane (193)	prokaryote (193)

7.2 Cell Structure

🔑 The nucleus contains nearly all the cell's DNA and, with it, the coded instructions for making proteins and other important molecules.

🔑 Vacuoles store materials like water, salts, proteins, and carbohydrates. Lysosomes break down large molecules into smaller ones that can be used by the cell. They are also involved in breaking down organelles that have outlived their usefulness. The cytoskeleton helps the cell maintain its shape and is also involved in movement.

🔑 Proteins are assembled on ribosomes.

🔑 Proteins made on the rough ER include those that will be released from the cell as well as many membrane proteins and proteins destined for specialized locations within the cell. The Golgi apparatus then modifies, sorts, and packages proteins and other materials for storage in the cell or release outside the cell.

🔑 Chloroplasts capture the energy from sunlight and convert it into food that contains chemical energy in a process called photosynthesis. Mitochondria convert the chemical energy stored in food into compounds that are more convenient for the cell to use.

🔑 The cell membrane regulates what enters and leaves the cell and also protects and supports the cell.

cytoplasm (196)	endoplasmic reticulum (200)
organelle (196)	Golgi apparatus (201)
vacuole (198)	chloroplast (202)
lysosome (198)	mitochondrion (202)
cytoskeleton (199)	cell wall (203)
centriole (199)	lipid bilayer (204)
ribosome (200)	selectively permeable (205)

7.3 Cell Transport

🔑 Passive transport (including diffusion and osmosis) is the movement of materials across the cell membrane without cellular energy.

🔑 The movement of materials against a concentration difference is known as active transport. Active transport requires energy.

diffusion (208)	isotonic (210)
facilitated diffusion (209)	hypertonic (210)
aquaporin (210)	hypotonic (210)
osmosis (210)	osmotic pressure (211)

7.4 Homeostasis and Cells

🔑 To maintain homeostasis, unicellular organisms grow, respond to the environment, transform energy, and reproduce.

🔑 The cells of multicellular organisms become specialized for particular tasks and communicate with one another to maintain homeostasis.

homeostasis (214)	organ system (216)
tissue (216)	receptor (217)
organ (216)	

Think Visually Use the terms *diffusion, facilitated diffusion, osmosis, active transport, endocytosis, phagocytosis, pinocytosis,* and *exocytosis* to create a concept map about the ways substances can move into and out of cells.

7 Assessment

Understand Key Concepts

1. In many cells, the structure that controls the cell's activities is the
   a. cell membrane.
   c. nucleolus.
   b. organelle.
   d. nucleus.

2. Despite differences in size and shape, at some point all cells have DNA and a
   a. cell wall.
   c. mitochondrion.
   b. cell membrane.
   d. nucleus.

3. What distinguishes a eukaryotic cell from a prokaryotic cell is the presence of
   a. a cell wall.
   c. DNA.
   b. a nucleus.
   d. ribosomes.

4. Create a table that summarizes the contributions made to the cell theory by Robert Hooke, Matthias Schleiden, Theodor Schwann, and Rudolf Virchow.

Think Critically

5. **Apply Concepts** If you wanted to observe a living organism—an amoeba, for example—which type of microscope would you use?

6. **Compare and Contrast** How are prokaryotic and eukaryotic cells alike? How do they differ?

Understand Key Concepts

7. In eukaryotic cells, chromosomes carrying genetic information are found in the
   a. ribosomes.
   c. nucleus.
   b. lysosomes.
   d. cell membrane.

8. The organelles that break down lipids, carbohydrates, and proteins into small molecules that can be used by the cell are called
   a. vacuoles.
   b. lysosomes.
   c. ribosomes.
   d. microfilaments.

9. Cell membranes consist mainly of
   a. lipid bilayers.
   c. carbohydrates.
   b. protein pumps.
   d. proteins.

10. Draw a cell nucleus. Label and give the function of the following structures: chromatin, nucleolus, and nuclear envelope.

11. What is the function of a ribosome?

12. Describe the role of the Golgi apparatus.

Think Critically

13. **Infer** The pancreas, an organ present in certain animals, produces enzymes used elsewhere in the animals' digestive systems. Which type of cell structure(s) might produce those enzymes? Explain your answer.

14. **Classify** For each of the following, indicate if the structure is found only in eukaryotes, or if it is found in eukaryotes and prokaryotes: cell membrane, mitochondria, ribosome, Golgi apparatus, nucleus, cytoplasm, and DNA.

Understand Key Concepts

15. The movement of water molecules across a selectively permeable membrane is known as
   a. exocytosis.
   c. endocytosis.
   b. phagocytosis.
   d. osmosis.

16. A substance that moves by passive transport tends to move
   a. away from the area of equilibrium.
   b. away from the area where it is less concentrated.
   c. away from the area where it is more concentrated.
   d. toward the area where it is more concentrated.

17. Describe the process of diffusion, including a detailed explanation of equilibrium.

18. What is the relationship between diffusion and osmosis? By definition, what's the only substance that undergoes osmosis?

19. What is the difference between passive transport and active transport?

Think Critically

20. Predict The beaker in the diagram below has a selectively permeable membrane separating two solutions. Assume that both water and salt can pass freely through the membrane. When equilibrium is reached, will the fluid levels be the same as they are now? Explain.

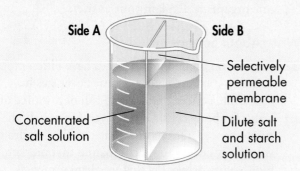

Side A   Side B

Selectively permeable membrane

Concentrated salt solution

Dilute salt and starch solution

21. Predict What would happen to a sample of your red blood cells if they were placed in a hypotonic solution? Explain.

22. Design Experiments You are given food coloring and three beakers. The first beaker contains water at room temperature, the second beaker contains ice water, and the third beaker contains hot water. Design a controlled experiment to determine the effects of temperature on the rate of diffusion. Be sure to state your hypothesis.

7.4 Homeostasis and Cells

Understand Key Concepts

23. Which of the following is true of ALL single-celled organisms?
a. They are all prokaryotes.
b. They are all bacteria.
c. They all reproduce.
d. They all have a nucleus.

24. A tissue is composed of a group of
a. similar cells.   c. organ systems.
b. related organelles.   d. related organs.

25. Explain the relationship among cell specialization, multicellular organisms, and homeostasis.

26. Describe the relationship among cells, tissues, organs, and organ systems.

solve the CHAPTER MYSTERY

DEATH BY ... WATER?

During the race, Michelle drank plenty of water, but she didn't replace the salts she lost due to sweating. As a result, her blood became hypotonic, and osmotic pressure led the cells in her brain (and throughout her body) to swell.

As Michelle's blood became more dilute, cells in her brain sent chemical signals to her kidneys to stop removing sodium chloride and other salts from her bloodstream. However, as she continued to sweat, she continued to lose salt through her skin.

By the end of the race, Michelle had lost a large quantity of salt and minerals and had taken in so much water that homeostasis had broken down, and her cells were damaged by unregulated osmotic pressure.

When Michelle was rushed to the hospital, the doctors discovered that she was suffering from hyponatremia, or water intoxication. Left untreated, this condition can lead to death.

1. Relate Cause and Effect When a person sweats, water and essential solutes called electrolytes are lost from body fluid. Michelle drank lots of water but did not replace lost electrolytes. What effect did this have on her cells?

2. Infer Had Michelle alternated between drinking water and a sports drink with electrolytes would her condition be the same?

3. Infer Do you think that hyponatremia results from osmosis or active transport? Explain your reasoning.

4. Connect to the Big idea Explain how hyponatremia disrupts homeostasis in the body.

Think Critically

27. **Infer** Would you expect skin cells to contain more or fewer mitochondria than muscle cells? Explain your answer.

28. **Infer** Pacemakers are devices that help keep heart muscle cells contracting at a steady rate. If a person needs a pacemaker, what does that suggest about his or her heart cells' ability to send and receive chemical messages?

Connecting Concepts

Use Science Graphics

Use the data table to answer questions 29–31.

Cell Sizes	
Cell	**Approximate Diameter**
Escherichia coli (bacterium)	0.5–0.8 μm
Human erythrocyte (red blood cell)	6–8 μm
Human ovum (egg cell)	100 μm
Saccharomyces cerevisiae (yeast)	5–10 μm
Streptococcus pneumoniae (bacterium)	0.5–1.3 μm

29. **Classify** Classify each of the cells listed as prokaryotic or eukaryotic.

30. **Compare and Contrast** Compare the sizes of the prokaryotic cells and eukaryotic cells.

31. **Infer** *Chlamydomonas reinhardtii* is a single-celled organism with an approximate diameter of 10 μm. Is it more likely a prokaryotic or eukaryotic organism? Explain your answer.

Write About Science

32. **Persuasion** Different beverages have different concentrations of solutes. Some beverages have low solute concentrations and can be a source of water for body cells. Other beverages have high solute concentrations and can actually dehydrate your body cells. Should companies that market high-solute drinks say that the drinks quench thirst?

33. **Assess the Big idea** What is the relationship between active transport and homeostasis? Give one example of active transport in an organism, and explain how the organism uses energy to maintain homeostasis.

Analyzing Data

Most materials entering the cell pass across the cell membrane by diffusion. In general, the larger the molecule, the slower the molecule diffuses across the membrane. The graph shows the sizes of several molecules that can diffuse across a lipid bilayer.

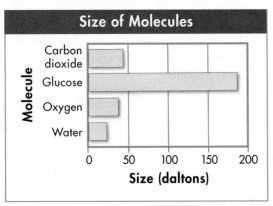

34. **Calculate** By approximately what percentage is a molecule of carbon dioxide smaller than a molecule of glucose? **MATH**
    a. 25% b. 50% c. 75% d. 100%

35. **Formulate Hypotheses** Which of the following is a logical hypothesis based on the graph shown?
    a. Cells contain more glucose than oxygen.
    b. Oxygen molecules diffuse across the cell membrane faster than water molecules.
    c. Glucose molecules must cross the cell membrane by active transport.
    d. Carbon dioxide crosses the cell membrane faster than glucose.

Standardized Test Prep

Multiple Choice

1. Animal cells have all of the following EXCEPT
   A mitochondria.
   B chloroplasts.
   C a nucleus.
   D a cell membrane.

2. The nucleus includes all of the following structures EXCEPT
   A cytoplasm.   C DNA.
   B a nuclear envelope.   D a nucleolus.

3. The human brain is an example of a(n)
   A cell.
   B tissue.
   C organ.
   D organ system.

4. Which cell structures are sometimes found attached to the endoplasmic reticulum?
   A chloroplasts
   B nuclei
   C mitochondria
   D ribosomes

5. Which process always involves the movement of materials from inside the cell to outside the cell?
   A phagocytosis
   B exocytosis
   C endocytosis
   D osmosis

6. Which of the following is an example of active transport?
   A facilitated diffusion
   B osmosis
   C diffusion
   D endocytosis

7. The difference between prokaryotic and eukaryotic cells involves the presence of
   A a nucleus.
   B genetic material in the form of DNA.
   C chloroplasts.
   D a cell membrane.

Questions 8–10

In an experiment, plant cells were placed in sucrose solutions of varying concentrations, and the rate at which they absorbed sucrose from the solution was measured. The results are shown in the graph below.

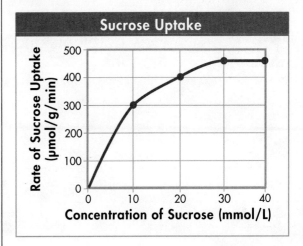

8. In this experiment, sucrose probably entered the cells by means of
   A endocytosis.   C osmosis.
   B phagocytosis.   D active transport.

9. The graph shows that as the concentration of sucrose increased from 10 to 30 mmol/L, the plant cells
   A took in sucrose more slowly.
   B took in sucrose more quickly.
   C failed to take in more sucrose.
   D secreted sucrose more slowly.

10. Based on the graph, the rate of sucrose uptake
    A increased at a constant rate from 0 to 30 mmol/L.
    B decreased at varying rates from 0 to 30 mmol/L.
    C was less at 25 mmol/L than at 5 mmol/L.
    D was constant between 30 and 40 mmol/L.

Open-Ended Response

11. What would you expect to happen if you placed a typical cell in fresh water?

If You Have Trouble With . . .											
Question	1	2	3	4	5	6	7	8	9	10	11
See Lesson	7.2	7.2	7.4	7.2	7.3	7.3	7.1	7.3	7.3	7.3	7.3

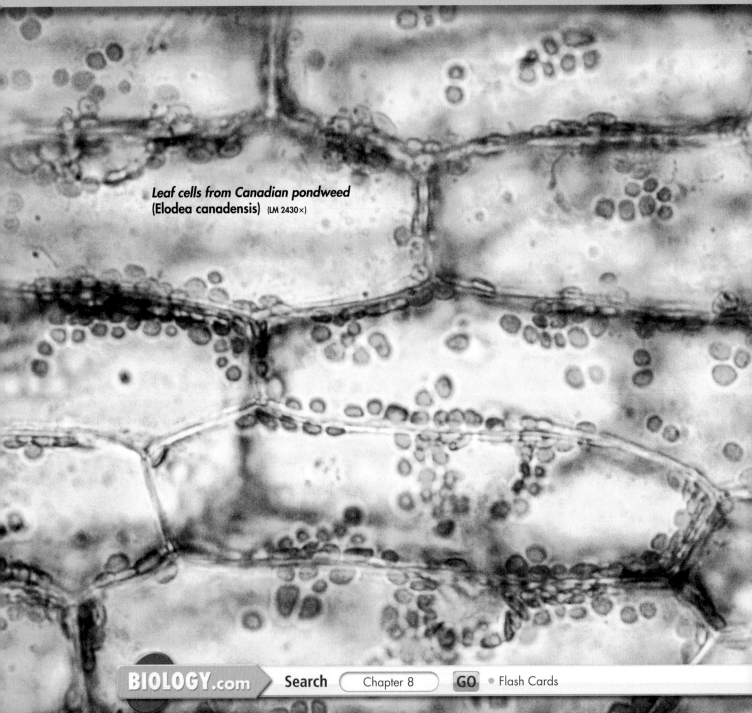

8 Photosynthesis

Big idea

Cellular Basis of Life

Q: How do plants and other organisms capture energy from the sun?

Leaf cells from Canadian pondweed (*Elodea canadensis*) (LM 2430×)

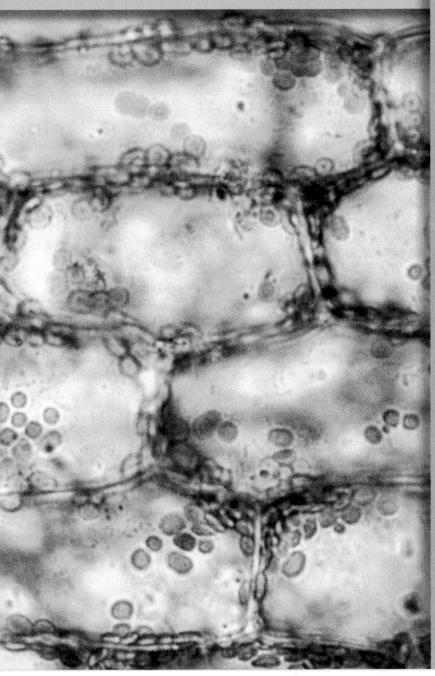

INSIDE:

- ## 8.1 Energy and Life
- ## 8.2 Photosynthesis: An Overview
- ## 8.3 The Process of Photosynthesis

CHAPTER
MYSTERY

OUT OF THIN AIR?

One of the earliest clues as to how photosynthesis works came from a simple study of plant growth. When a tiny seed grows into a massive tree, where does all its extra mass come from? More than 300 years ago, a Flemish physician named Jan van Helmont decided to find out. He planted a young willow tree, with a mass of just 2 kilograms, in a pot with 90 kilograms of dry soil. He watered the plant as needed and allowed it to grow in bright sunlight. Five years later, he carefully removed the tree from the pot and weighed it. It had a mass of about 77 kilograms. Where did the extra 75 kilograms come from? The soil, the water—or, maybe, right out of thin air? As you read this chapter, look for clues to help you discover where the willow tree's extra mass came from. Then, solve the mystery.

Never Stop Exploring Your World.
Understanding Jan van Helmont's experiments is just the beginning. Take a video field trip with the ecogeeks of Untamed Science to see where this mystery leads.

8.1 Energy and Life

Key Questions

🔑 Why is ATP useful to cells?

🔑 What happens during the process of photosynthesis?

Vocabulary
adenosine triphosphate (ATP) • heterotroph • autotroph • photosynthesis

Taking Notes

Compare/Contrast Table As you read, create a table that compares autotrophs and heterotrophs. Think about how they obtain energy, and include a few examples of each.

BUILD Vocabulary

ACADEMIC WORDS The verb **obtain** means "to get" or "to gain." Organisms must obtain energy in order to carry out life functions.

THINK ABOUT IT Homeostasis is hard work. Just to stay alive, organisms and the cells within them have to grow and develop, move materials around, build new molecules, and respond to environmental changes. Plenty of energy is needed to accomplish all this work. What powers so much activity, and where does that power come from?

Chemical Energy and ATP

🔑 Why is ATP useful to cells?

Energy is the ability to do work. Nearly every activity in modern society depends upon energy. When a car runs out of fuel—more precisely, out of the chemical energy in gasoline—it comes to a sputtering halt. Without electrical energy, lights, appliances, and computers stop working. Living things depend on energy, too. Sometimes the need for energy is easy to see. It takes plenty of energy to play soccer or other sports. However, there are times when that need is less obvious. Even when you are sleeping, your cells are quietly busy using energy to build new molecules, contract muscles, and carry out active transport. Simply put, without the ability to obtain and use energy, life would cease to exist.

Energy comes in many forms, including light, heat, and electricity. Energy can be stored in chemical compounds, too. For example, when you light a candle, the wax melts, soaks into the wick, and is burned. As the candle burns, chemical bonds between carbon and hydrogen atoms in the wax are broken. New bonds then form between these atoms and oxygen, producing CO_2 and H_2O (carbon dioxide and water). These new bonds are at a lower energy state than the original chemical bonds in the wax. The energy lost is released as heat and light in the glow of the candle's flame.

Living things use chemical fuels as well. One of the most important compounds that cells use to store and release energy is **adenosine triphosphate** (uh DEN uh seen try FAHS fayt), abbreviated **ATP.** As shown in **Figure 8–1,** ATP consists of adenine, a 5-carbon sugar called ribose, and three phosphate groups. As you'll see, those phosphate groups are the key to ATP's ability to store and release energy.

Adenine   Ribose   3 phosphate groups

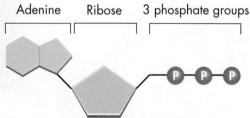

FIGURE 8–1 ATP ATP is the basic energy source used by all types of cells.

Storing Energy Adenosine diphosphate (ADP) is a compound that looks almost like ATP, except that it has two phosphate groups instead of three. This difference is the key to the way in which living things store energy. When a cell has energy available, it can store small amounts of it by adding phosphate groups to ADP molecules, producing ATP. As seen in **Figure 8–2**, ADP is like a rechargeable battery that powers the machinery of the cell.

Releasing Energy Cells can release the energy stored in ATP by the controlled breaking of the chemical bonds between the second and third phosphate groups. Because a cell can add or subtract these phosphate groups, it has an efficient way of storing and releasing energy as needed. ⚷ **ATP can easily release and store energy by breaking and re-forming the bonds between its phosphate groups. This characteristic of ATP makes it exceptionally useful as a basic energy source for all cells.**

Using Biochemical Energy One way cells use the energy provided by ATP is to carry out active transport. Many cell membranes contain sodium-potassium pumps, membrane proteins that pump sodium ions (Na^+) out of the cell and potassium ions (K^+) into it. ATP provides the energy that keeps this pump working, maintaining a carefully regulated balance of ions on both sides of the cell membrane. In addition, ATP powers movement, providing the energy for motor proteins that contract muscle and power the wavelike movement of cilia and flagella.

Energy from ATP powers other important events in the cell, including the synthesis of proteins and responses to chemical signals at the cell surface. The energy from ATP can even be used to produce light. In fact, the blink of a firefly on a summer night comes from an enzyme that is powered by ATP!

ATP is such a useful source of energy that you might think cells would be packed with ATP to get them through the day—but this is not the case. In fact, most cells have only a small amount of ATP—enough to last for a few seconds of activity. Why? Even though ATP is a great molecule for transferring energy, it is not a good one for storing large amounts of energy over the long term. A single molecule of the sugar glucose, for example, stores more than 90 times the energy required to add a phosphate group to ADP to produce ATP. Therefore, it is more efficient for cells to keep only a small supply of ATP on hand. Instead, cells can regenerate ATP from ADP as needed by using the energy in foods like glucose. As you will see, that's exactly what they do.

 In Your Notebook *With respect to energy, how are ATP and glucose similar? How are they different?*

FIGURE 8–2 When a phosphate group is added to an ADP molecule, ATP is produced. ADP contains some energy, but not as much as ATP. In this way, ADP is like a partially charged battery that can be fully charged by the addition of a phosphate group. **Use Analogies** *Explain the difference between the beams of light produced by the flashlight "powered" by ADP and the flashlight "powered" by ATP.*

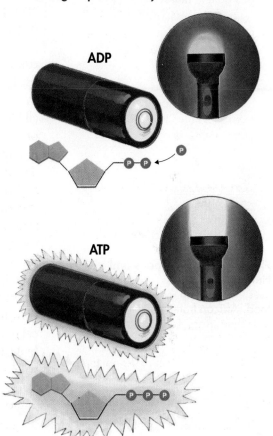

ADP

ATP

Like all plants, the willow tree van Helmont planted was an autotroph. What might its ability to harness the sun's energy and store it in food have to do with the tree's gain in mass?

Heterotrophs and Autotrophs

🔑 What happens during the process of photosynthesis?

Cells are not "born" with a supply of ATP—they must somehow produce it. So, where do living things get the energy they use to produce ATP? The simple answer is that it comes from the chemical compounds that we call food. Organisms that obtain food by consuming other living things are known as **heterotrophs.** Some heterotrophs get their food by eating plants such as grasses. Other heterotrophs, such as the leopard in **Figure 8–3,** obtain food from plants indirectly by feeding on plant-eating animals. Still other heterotrophs—mushrooms, for example—obtain food by absorbing nutrients from decomposing organisms in the environment.

Originally, however, the energy in nearly all food molecules comes from the sun. Plants, algae, and some bacteria are able to use light energy from the sun to produce food. Organisms that make their own food are called **autotrophs.** Ultimately, nearly all life on Earth, including ourselves, depends on the ability of autotrophs to capture the energy of sunlight and store it in the molecules that make up food. The process by which autotrophs use the energy of sunlight to produce high-energy carbohydrates—sugars and starches—that can be used as food is known as **photosynthesis.** *Photosynthesis* comes from the Greek words *photo,* meaning "light," and *synthesis,* meaning "putting together." Therefore, photosynthesis means "using light to put something together." 🔑 **In the process of photosynthesis, plants convert the energy of sunlight into chemical energy stored in the bonds of carbohydrates.** In the rest of this chapter, you will learn how this process works.

FIGURE 8–3 Autotrophs and Heterotrophs Grass, an autotroph, uses energy from the sun to produce food. African hares get their energy by eating grass. Leopards, in turn, get their energy by eating other organisms, like the hare.

8.1 Assessment

Review Key Concepts 🔑

1. a. Review What is ATP and what is its role in the cell?

b. Explain How does the structure of ATP make it an ideal source of energy for the cell?

c. Use Analogies Explain how ADP and ATP are each like a battery. Which one is "partially charged" and which one is "fully charged?" Why?

2. a. Review What is the ultimate source of energy for plants?

b. Explain How do heterotrophs obtain energy? How is this different from how autotrophs obtain energy?

c. Infer Why are decomposers, such as mushrooms, considered heterotrophs and not autotrophs?

Apply the Big idea

Interdependence in Nature

3. Recall that energy flows— and that nutrients cycle— through the biosphere. How does the process of photosynthesis impact both the flow of energy and the cycling of nutrients? You may wish to refer to Chapter 3 to help you answer this question.

BIOLOGY.com ▶ Search 〔 Lesson 8.1 〕 GO • Lesson Assessment • Self-Test

Biology & HISTORY

Understanding Photosynthesis Many scientists have contributed to understanding how plants carry out photosynthesis. Early research focused on the overall process. Later, researchers investigated the detailed chemical pathways.

1650   1700   1750   1800   1850   1900   1950   2000

JOHANNES BAPTISTA AB HELMONT

1643
▲ After analyzing his measurements of a willow tree's water intake and mass increase, Jan van Helmont concludes that trees gain most of their mass from water.

1779
Jan Ingenhousz finds that aquatic plants produce oxygen bubbles in the light but not in the dark. He concludes that plants need sunlight to produce oxygen. ▼

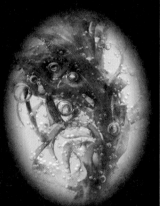

1771
Joseph Priestley experiments with a bell jar, a candle, and a plant and concludes that the plant releases oxygen. ▼

1845
Julius Robert Mayer proposes that plants convert light energy into chemical energy.

1948
Melvin Calvin traces the chemical path that carbon follows to form glucose. These reactions are also known as the Calvin cycle.

1992
Rudolph Marcus wins the Nobel Prize in chemistry for describing the process by which electrons are transferred from one molecule to another in the electron transport chain.

2004
▲ So Iwata and Jim Barber identify the precise mechanism by which water molecules are split in the process of photosynthesis. Their research may one day be applied to artificial photosynthesis technologies in order to produce a cheap supply of hydrogen gas that can be used as fuel.

WRITING Use the Internet or library resources to research the experiments conducted by one of these scientists. Then, write a summary describing how the scientist contributed to the modern understanding of photosynthesis.

8.2 Photosynthesis: An Overview

Key Questions

🔑 What role do pigments play in the process of photosynthesis?

🔑 What are electron carrier molecules?

🔑 What are the reactants and products of photosynthesis?

Vocabulary

pigment • chlorophyll • thylakoid • stroma • NADP+ • light-dependent reactions • light-independent reactions

Taking Notes

Outline Make an outline using the green and blue headings in this lesson. Fill in details as you read to help you organize the information.

THINK ABOUT IT How would you design a system to capture the energy of sunlight and convert it into a useful form? First, you'd have to collect that energy. Maybe you'd spread out lots of flat panels to catch the light. You might then coat the panels with light-absorbing compounds, but what then? How could you take the energy, trapped ever so briefly in these chemical compounds, and get it into a stable, useful, chemical form? Solving such problems may well be the key to making solar power a practical energy alternative. But plants have already solved all these issues on their own terms—and maybe we can learn a trick or two from them.

Chlorophyll and Chloroplasts

🔑 **What role do pigments play in the process of photosynthesis?**

Our lives, and the lives of nearly every living thing on the surface of Earth, are made possible by the sun and the process of photosynthesis. In order for photosynthesis to occur, light energy from the sun must somehow be captured.

Light Energy from the sun travels to Earth in the form of light. Sunlight, which our eyes perceive as "white" light, is actually a mixture of different wavelengths. Many of these wavelengths are visible to our eyes and make up what is known as the visible spectrum. Our eyes see the different wavelengths of the visible spectrum as different colors: shades of red, orange, yellow, green, blue, indigo, and violet.

FIGURE 8–4 Light Absorption

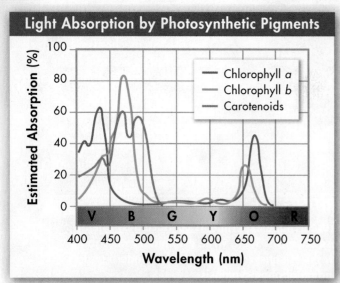

Light Absorption by Photosynthetic Pigments

— Chlorophyll *a*
— Chlorophyll *b*
— Carotenoids

(Estimated Absorption (%) vs Wavelength (nm))

V B G Y O R

400 450 500 550 600 650 700 750

Pigments Plants gather the sun's energy with light-absorbing molecules called **pigments.** 🔑 **Photosynthetic organisms capture energy from sunlight with pigments**. The plants' principal pigment is **chlorophyll** (KLAWR uh fil). The two types of chlorophyll found in plants, chlorophyll *a* and chlorophyll *b*, absorb light very well in the blue-violet and red regions of the visible spectrum. However, chlorophyll does not absorb light well in the green region of the spectrum, as shown in **Figure 8–4.**

230

Leaves reflect green light, which is why plants look green. Plants also contain red and orange pigments such as carotene that absorb light in other regions of the spectrum. Most of the time, the intense green color of chlorophyll overwhelms the accessory pigments, so we don't notice them. As temperatures drop late in the year, however, chlorophyll molecules break down first, leaving the reds and oranges of the accessory pigments for all to see. The beautiful colors of fall in some parts of the country are the result of this process.

Chloroplasts Recall from Chapter 7 that in plants and other photosynthetic eukaryotes, photosynthesis takes place inside organelles called chloroplasts. Chloroplasts contain an abundance of saclike photosynthetic membranes called **thylakoids** (THY luh koydz). Thylakoids are interconnected and arranged in stacks known as grana (singular: granum). Pigments such as chlorophyll are located in the thylakoid membranes. The fluid portion of the chloroplast, outside of the thylakoids, is known as the **stroma.** The structure of a typical chloroplast is shown in **Figure 8–5.**

Energy Collection What's so special about chlorophyll that makes it important for photosynthesis? Because light is a form of energy, any compound that absorbs light absorbs energy. Chlorophyll absorbs visible light especially well. In addition, when chlorophyll absorbs light, a large fraction of that light energy is transferred directly to electrons in the chlorophyll molecule itself. By raising the energy levels of these electrons, light energy can produce a steady supply of high-energy electrons, which is what makes photosynthesis work.

In Your Notebook *In your own words, explain why most plants will not grow well if kept under green light.*

ZOOMING IN

THE CHLOROPLAST

FIGURE 8–5 In plants, photosynthesis takes place inside chloroplasts. **Observe** *How are thylakoids arranged in the chloroplast?*

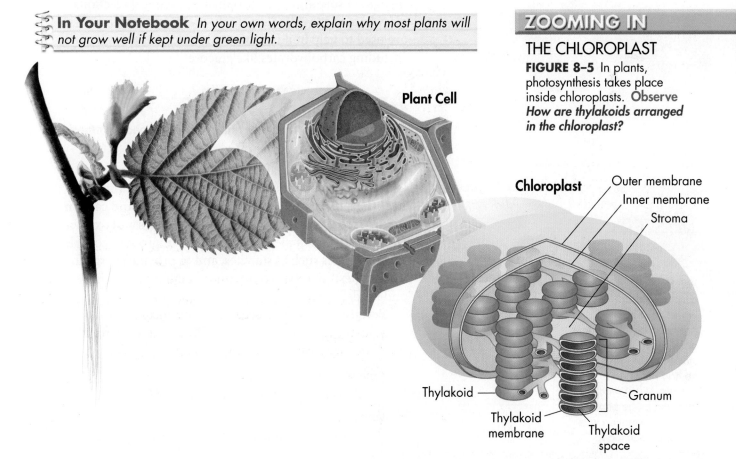

Plant Cell

Chloroplast

Outer membrane
Inner membrane
Stroma

Thylakoid

Thylakoid membrane

Granum

Thylakoid space

CARRYING ELECTRONS

FIGURE 8–6 NADP$^+$ is a carrier molecule that transports pairs of electrons (and an H$^+$ ion) in photosynthetic organisms, similar to how an oven mitt is used to transport a hot object such as a baked potato.

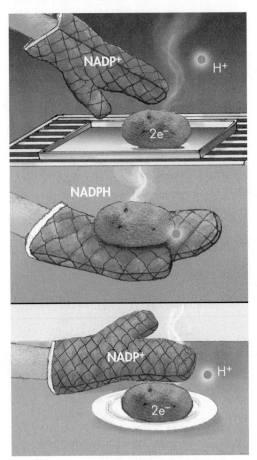

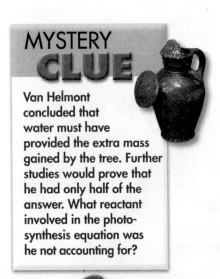

MYSTERY CLUE

Van Helmont concluded that water must have provided the extra mass gained by the tree. Further studies would prove that he had only half of the answer. What reactant involved in the photosynthesis equation was he not accounting for?

High-Energy Electrons

🔑 What are electron carrier molecules?

In a chemical sense, the high-energy electrons produced by chlorophyll are highly reactive and require a special "carrier." Think of a high-energy electron as being similar to a hot potato straight from the oven. If you wanted to move the potato from one place to another, you wouldn't pick it up in your hands. You would use an oven mitt—a carrier—to transport it, as shown in **Figure 8–6.** Plant cells treat high-energy electrons in the same way. Instead of an oven mitt, however, they use electron carriers to transport high-energy electrons from chlorophyll to other molecules. 🔑 **An electron carrier is a compound that can accept a pair of high-energy electrons and transfer them, along with most of their energy, to another molecule.**

One of these carrier molecules is a compound known as **NADP$^+$** (nicotinamide adenine dinucleotide phosphate). The name is complicated, but the job that NADP$^+$ has is simple. NADP$^+$ accepts and holds 2 high-energy electrons, along with a hydrogen ion (H$^+$). This converts the NADP$^+$ into NADPH. The conversion of NADP$^+$ into NADPH is one way in which some of the energy of sunlight can be trapped in chemical form. The NADPH can then carry the high-energy electrons that were produced by light absorption in chlorophyll to chemical reactions elsewhere in the cell. These high-energy electron carriers are used to help build a variety of molecules the cell needs, including carbohydrates like glucose.

An Overview of Photosynthesis

🔑 What are the reactants and products of photosynthesis?

Many steps are involved in the process of photosynthesis. However, the overall process of photosynthesis can be summarized in one sentence. 🔑 **Photosynthesis uses the energy of sunlight to convert water and carbon dioxide (reactants) into high-energy sugars and oxygen (products).** Plants then use the sugars to produce complex carbohydrates such as starches, and to provide energy for the synthesis of other compounds, including proteins and lipids.

Because photosynthesis usually produces 6-carbon sugars ($C_6H_{12}O_6$) as the final product, the overall reaction for photosynthesis can be shown as follows:

In Symbols:
$$6CO_2 + 6H_2O \xrightarrow{\text{light}} C_6H_{12}O_6 + 6O_2$$

In Words:
$$\text{Carbon dioxide} + \text{Water} \xrightarrow{\text{light}} \text{Sugars} + \text{Oxygen}$$

Light-Dependent Reactions Although the equation for photosynthesis looks simple, there are many steps to get from the reactants to the final products. In fact, photosynthesis actually involves two sets of reactions. The first set of reactions is known as the **light-dependent reactions** because they require the direct involvement of light and light-absorbing pigments. The light-dependent reactions use energy from sunlight to produce energy-rich compounds such as ATP. These reactions take place within the thylakoids—specifically, in the thylakoid membranes—of the chloroplast. Water is required in these reactions as a source of electrons and hydrogen ions. Oxygen is released as a byproduct.

Light-Independent Reactions Plants absorb carbon dioxide from the atmosphere and complete the process of photosynthesis by producing carbon-containing sugars and other carbohydrates. During the **light-independent reactions,** ATP and NADPH molecules produced in the light-dependent reactions are used to produce high-energy sugars from carbon dioxide. As the name implies, no light is required to power the light-independent reactions. The light-independent reactions take place outside the thylakoids, in the stroma.

The interdependent relationship between the light-dependent and light-independent reactions is shown in **Figure 8–7.** As you can see, the two sets of reactions work together to capture the energy of sunlight and transform it into energy-rich compounds such as carbohydrates.

In Your Notebook *Create a two-column compare/contrast table that shows the similarities and differences between the light-dependent and light-independent reactions of photosynthesis.*

BUILD Vocabulary
ACADEMIC WORDS The noun **byproduct** means "anything produced in the course of making another thing." Oxygen is considered a byproduct of the light-dependent reactions of photosynthesis because it is produced as a result of extracting electrons from water. Also, unlike ATP and NADPH, oxygen is not used in the second stage of the process, the light-independent reactions.

FIGURE 8–7 The Stages of Photosynthesis There are two stages of photosynthesis: light-dependent reactions and light-independent reactions. **Interpret Diagrams** *What happens to the ATP and NADPH produced in the light-dependent reactions?*

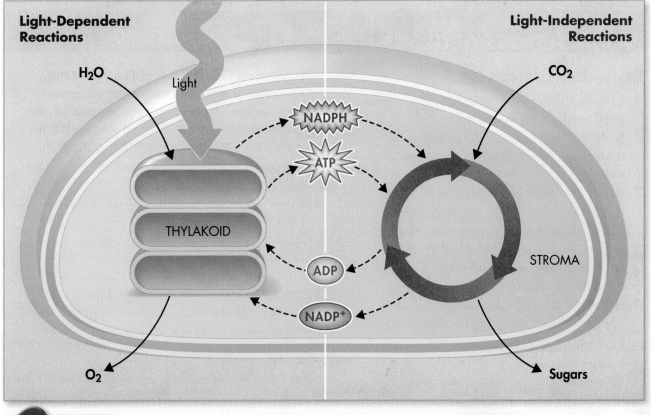

Light-Dependent Reactions

Light-Independent Reactions

H_2O Light NADPH ATP CO_2

THYLAKOID ADP NADP⁺ STROMA

O_2 Sugars

What Waste Material Is Produced During Photosynthesis?

❶ Fill a large, clear, plastic cup about halfway full with sodium bicarbonate solution. The sodium bicarbonate solution is a source of carbon dioxide.

❷ Place a freshly cut *Elodea* plant (with the cut stem at the bottom) in a large test tube. Fill the tube with sodium bicarbonate solution. **CAUTION:** *Handle the test tube carefully.*

❸ Hold your finger over the mouth of the test tube. Turn the test tube over, and lower it to the bottom of the cup. Make sure no air is trapped in the test tube.

❹ Place the cup in bright light.

❺ After no fewer than 20 minutes, look closely at the elodea leaves. Record your observations.

Analyze and Conclude

1. Observe What did you observe on the *Elodea* leaves?

2. Infer What substance accumulated on the leaves? Should that substance be considered a waste product? Explain.

3. Apply Concepts Which plant organelle carries out photosynthesis and produces the gas?

Elodea

Sodium bicarbonate solution

8.2 Assessment

Review Key Concepts 🔑

1. a. Review Why are pigments such as chlorophyll needed for photosynthesis?
b. Predict How well would a plant grow under pure yellow light? Explain your answer.

2. a. Review What is the function of NADPH?
b. Explain How is light energy converted into chemical energy during photosynthesis?
c. Infer How would photosynthesis be affected if there were a shortage of $NADP^+$ in the cells of plants?

3. a. Review Describe the overall process of photosynthesis, including the reactants and products.

b. Interpret Visuals Look at **Figure 8–7**. Into which set of reactions—light-dependent or light-independent—does each reactant of photosynthesis enter? From which set of reactions is each product of photosynthesis generated?

VISUAL THINKING

4. Create your own labeled diagram of a chloroplast. Using **Figure 8–5** as a guide, draw and label the thylakoids, grana, and stroma. Indicate on your drawing where the two sets of photosynthesis reactions take place.

5. Draw two leaves—one green and one orange. Using colored pencils, markers, or pens, show which colors of visible light are absorbed and reflected by each leaf.

The Process of Photosynthesis

THINK ABOUT IT Why membranes? Why do chloroplasts contain so many membranes? Is there something about biological membranes that makes them absolutely essential for the process of photosynthesis? As you'll see, there is. When most pigments absorb light, they eventually lose most of that energy as heat. In a sense, the "trade secret" of the chloroplast is how it avoids such losses, capturing light energy in the form of high-energy electrons—and membranes are the key. Without them, photosynthesis simply wouldn't work.

The Light-Dependent Reactions: Generating ATP and NADPH

What happens during the light-dependent reactions?

Recall that the process of photosynthesis involves two primary sets of reactions: the light-dependent and the light-independent reactions. The light-dependent reactions encompass the steps of photosynthesis that directly involve sunlight. These reactions explain why plants need light to grow. **The light-dependent reactions use energy from sunlight to produce oxygen and convert ADP and NADP$^+$ into the energy carriers ATP and NADPH.**

The light-dependent reactions occur in the thylakoids of chloroplasts. Thylakoids are saclike membranes containing most of the machinery needed to carry out these reactions. Thylakoids contain clusters of chlorophyll and proteins known as **photosystems.** The photosystems, which are surrounded by accessory pigments, are essential to the light-dependent reactions. Photosystems absorb sunlight and generate high-energy electrons that are then passed to a series of electron carriers embedded in the thylakoid membrane. Light absorption by the photosystems is just the beginning of this important process.

FIGURE 8–8 The Importance of Light Like most plants, this rice plant needs light to grow.
Apply Concepts *Which stage of photosynthesis requires light?*

Key Questions

What happens during the light-dependent reactions?

What happens during the light-independent reactions?

What factors affect photosynthesis?

Vocabulary

photosystem •
electron transport chain •
ATP synthase • Calvin cycle

Taking Notes

Flowchart As you read, create a flowchart that clearly shows the steps involved in the light-dependent reactions.

FIGURE 8-9 Why Green? The green color of most plants is caused by the reflection of green light by the pigment chlorophyll. Pigments capture light energy during the light-dependent reactions of photosynthesis.

Photosystem II The light-dependent reactions, shown in **Figure 8–10,** begin when pigments in photosystem II absorb light. (This first photosystem is called photosystem II simply because it was discovered after photosystem I.) Light energy is absorbed by electrons in the pigments found within photosystem II, increasing the electrons' energy level. These high-energy electrons (e^-) are passed to the electron transport chain. An **electron transport chain** is a series of electron carrier proteins that shuttle high-energy electrons during ATP-generating reactions.

As light continues to shine, more and more high-energy electrons are passed to the electron transport chain. Does this mean that chlorophyll eventually runs out of electrons? No, the thylakoid membrane contains a system that provides new electrons to chlorophyll to replace the ones it has lost. These new electrons come from water molecules (H_2O). Enzymes on the inner surface of the thylakoid break up each water molecule into 2 electrons, 2 H^+ ions, and 1 oxygen atom. The 2 electrons replace the high-energy electrons that have been lost to the electron transport chain. As plants remove electrons from water, oxygen is left behind and is released into the air. This reaction is the source of nearly all of the oxygen in Earth's atmosphere, and it is another way in which photosynthesis makes our lives possible. The hydrogen ions left behind when water is broken apart are released inside the thylakoid.

In Your Notebook *Explain in your own words why photosynthetic organisms need water and sunlight.*

Electron Transport Chain What happens to the electrons as they move down the electron transport chain? Energy from the electrons is used by the proteins in the chain to pump H^+ ions from the stroma into the thylakoid space. At the end of the electron transport chain, the electrons themselves pass to a second photosystem called photosystem I.

Photosystem I Because some energy has been used to pump H^+ ions across the thylakoid membrane, electrons do not contain as much energy as they used to when they reach photosystem I. Pigments in photosystem I use energy from light to reenergize the electrons. At the end of a short second electron transport chain, $NADP^+$ molecules in the stroma pick up the high-energy electrons, along with H^+ ions, at the outer surface of the thylakoid membrane, to become NADPH. This NADPH becomes very important, as you will see, in the light-independent reactions of photosynthesis.

Hydrogen Ion Movement and ATP Formation Recall that in photosystem II, hydrogen ions began to accumulate within the thylakoid space. Some were left behind from the splitting of water at the end of the electron transport chain. Other hydrogen ions were "pumped" in from the stroma. The buildup of hydrogen ions makes the stroma negatively charged relative to the space within the thylakoids. This gradient, the difference in both charge and H^+ ion concentration across the membrane, provides the energy to make ATP.

BUILD Vocabulary

ACADEMIC WORDS The noun **gradient** refers to "an area over which something changes." There is a charge gradient across the thylakoid membrane because there is a positive charge on one side and a negative charge on the other.

H⁺ ions cannot cross the membrane directly. However, the thylakoid membrane contains a protein called **ATP synthase** that spans the membrane and allows H⁺ ions to pass through it. Powered by the gradient, H⁺ ions pass through ATP synthase and force it to rotate, almost like a turbine being spun by water in a hydroelectric power plant. As it rotates, ATP synthase binds ADP and a phosphate group together to produce ATP. This process, which is known as chemiosmosis (kem ee ahz MOH sis), enables light-dependent electron transport to produce not only NADPH (at the end of the electron transport chain), but ATP as well.

Summary of Light-Dependent Reactions The light-dependent reactions produce oxygen gas and convert ADP and NADP⁺ into the energy carriers ATP and NADPH. What good are these compounds? As we will see, they have an important role to play in the cell: They provide the energy needed to build high-energy sugars from low-energy carbon dioxide.

LIGHT-DEPENDENT REACTIONS

FIGURE 8–10 The light-dependent reactions of photosynthesis take place in the thylakoids of the chloroplast. They use energy from sunlight to produce ATP, NADPH, and oxygen. **Interpret Visuals** *How many molecules of NADPH are produced per water molecule used in photosynthetic electron transport?*

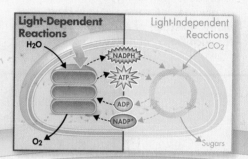

CYTOPLASM

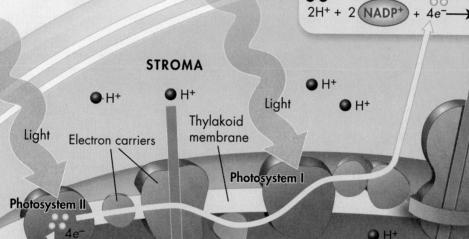

$2H^+ + 2$ NADP$^+$ $+ 4e^- \rightarrow 2$ NADPH → To Light-Independent Reactions

H⁺

ATP → To Light-Independent Reactions

ADP + Ⓟ

STROMA

Light   H⁺   H⁺

Light

Electron carriers

Thylakoid membrane

Photosystem I

ATP synthase

Photosystem II

4e⁻

H⁺

H⁺   H⁺   H⁺

THYLAKOID SPACE

H⁺

2 H₂O   4H⁺   O₂

Photosystem II
Light energy absorbed by photosystem II produces high-energy electrons. Water molecules are split to replace those electrons, releasing H⁺ ions and oxygen.

Electron Transport
High-energy electrons move down the electron transport chain, to photosystem I. Energy generated is used to pump H⁺ ions across the thylakoid membrane and into the thylakoid space.

Photosystem I
Electrons are reenergized in photosystem I. A second electron transport chain then transfers these electrons to NADP⁺, producing NADPH.

Hydrogen Ion Movement and ATP Formation
As the thylakoid space fills up with positively charged H⁺ ions, the inside of the thylakoid membrane becomes positively charged relative to the outside of the membrane. H⁺ ions pass back across the thylakoid membrane through ATP synthase. As the ions pass through, the ATP synthase molecule rotates and the energy produced is used to convert ADP to ATP.

The Light-Independent Reactions: Producing Sugars

🔑 What happens during the light-independent reactions?

The ATP and NADPH formed by the light-dependent reactions contain an abundance of chemical energy, but they are not stable enough to store that energy for more than a few minutes. During the light-independent reactions, commonly referred to as the **Calvin cycle,** plants use the energy that ATP and NADPH contain to build stable high-energy carbohydrate compounds that can be stored for a long time. 🔑 **During the light-independent reactions, ATP and NADPH from the light-dependent reactions are used to produce high-energy sugars.** The Calvin cycle is named after the American scientist Melvin Calvin, who worked out the details of this remarkable cycle. Follow **Figure 8–11** to see each step in this set of reactions.

ZOOMING IN

LIGHT-INDEPENDENT REACTIONS

FIGURE 8–11 The light-independent reactions of photosynthesis take place in the stroma of the chloroplast. The reactions use ATP and NADPH from the light-dependent reactions to produce high-energy sugars such as glucose. **Interpret Visuals** *How many molecules of ATP are needed for each "turn" of the Calvin cycle?*

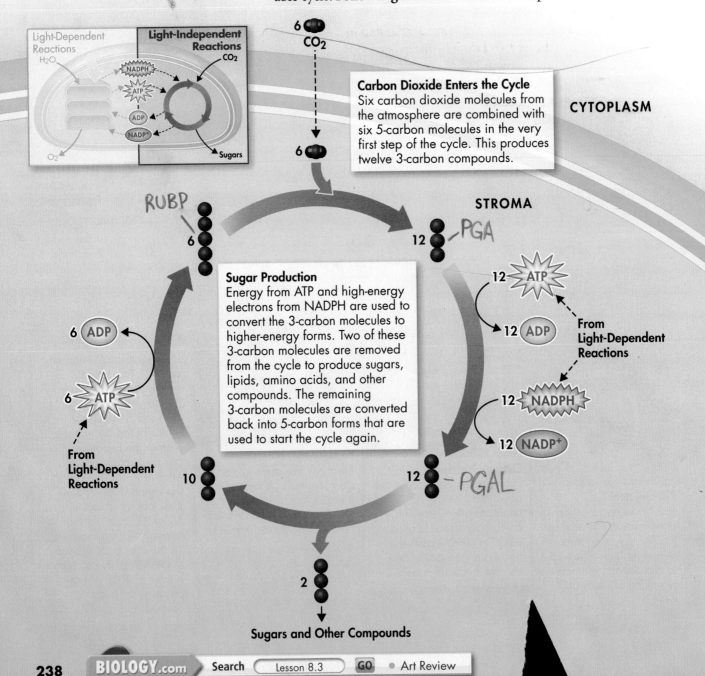

Carbon Dioxide Enters the Cycle
Six carbon dioxide molecules from the atmosphere are combined with six 5-carbon molecules in the very first step of the cycle. This produces twelve 3-carbon compounds.

Sugar Production
Energy from ATP and high-energy electrons from NADPH are used to convert the 3-carbon molecules to higher-energy forms. Two of these 3-carbon molecules are removed from the cycle to produce sugars, lipids, amino acids, and other compounds. The remaining 3-carbon molecules are converted back into 5-carbon forms that are used to start the cycle again.

CYTOPLASM

STROMA

RUBP

PGA

PGAL

From Light-Dependent Reactions

From Light-Dependent Reactions

Sugars and Other Compounds

BIOLOGY.com ▶ Search ⟨ Lesson 8.3 ⟩ **GO** • Art Review

Carbon Dioxide Enters the Cycle Carbon dioxide molecules enter the Calvin cycle from the atmosphere. An enzyme in the stroma of the chloroplast combines these carbon dioxide molecules with 5-carbon compounds that are already present in the organelle, producing 3-carbon compounds that continue into the cycle. For every 6 carbon dioxide molecules that enter the cycle, a total of twelve 3-carbon compounds are produced. Other enzymes in the chloroplast then convert these compounds into higher-energy forms in the rest of the cycle. The energy for these conversions comes from ATP and high-energy electrons from NADPH.

Sugar Production At midcycle, two of the twelve 3-carbon molecules are removed from the cycle. This is a very special step because these molecules become the building blocks that the plant cell uses to produce sugars, lipids, amino acids, and other compounds. In other words, this step in the Calvin cycle contributes to all of the products needed for plant metabolism and growth.

The remaining ten 3-carbon molecules are converted back into six 5-carbon molecules. These molecules combine with six new carbon dioxide molecules to begin the next cycle.

Summary of the Calvin Cycle The Calvin cycle uses 6 molecules of carbon dioxide to produce a single 6-carbon sugar molecule. The energy for the reactions that make this possible is supplied by compounds produced in the light-dependent reactions. As photosynthesis proceeds, the Calvin cycle works steadily, removing carbon dioxide from the atmosphere and turning out energy-rich sugars. The plant uses the sugars to meet its energy needs and to build macromolecules needed for growth and development, including lipids, proteins, and complex carbohydrates such as cellulose. When other organisms eat plants, they, too, can use the energy and raw materials stored in these compounds.

The End Results The two sets of photosynthetic reactions work together—the light-dependent reactions trap the energy of sunlight in chemical form, and the light-independent reactions use that chemical energy to produce stable, high-energy sugars from carbon dioxide and water. And, in the process, animals, including ourselves, get plenty of food and an atmosphere filled with oxygen. Not a bad deal at all!

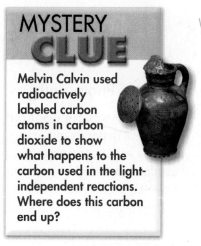

MYSTERY CLUE

Melvin Calvin used radioactively labeled carbon atoms in carbon dioxide to show what happens to the carbon used in the light-independent reactions. Where does this carbon end up?

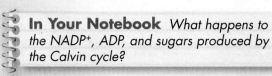

In Your Notebook *What happens to the NADP+, ADP, and sugars produced by the Calvin cycle?*

Rates of Photosynthesis

The rate at which a plant carries out photo-synthesis depends in part on environmental factors such as temperature, amount of water available, and light intensity. The graph shows how the average rates of photosynthesis between sun plants and shade plants changes with light intensity.

1. Use Tables and Graphs When light intensity is below 200 µmol photons/m^2/s, do sun plants or shade plants have a higher rate of photosynthesis?

2. Infer Light intensity in the Sonoran Desert averages about 400 µmol photons/m^2/s. According to the graph, what would be the approximate rate of photosynthesis for sun plants that grow in this environment?

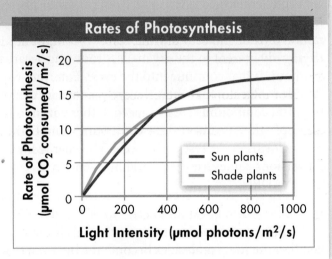

Rates of Photosynthesis

(graph: Rate of Photosynthesis (µmol CO_2 consumed/m^2/s) vs. Light Intensity (µmol photons/m^2/s), showing curves for Sun plants and Shade plants)

3. Form a Hypothesis Suppose you transplant a sun plant to a shaded forest floor that receives about 100 µmol photons/m^2/s. Do you think this plant will grow and thrive? Why or why not? How does the graph help you answer this question?

Factors Affecting Photosynthesis

🔑 *What factors affect photosynthesis?*

Temperature, Light, and Water Many factors influence the rate of photosynthesis. 🔑 **Among the most important factors that affect photosynthesis are temperature, light intensity, and the availability of water.** The reactions of photosynthesis are made possible by enzymes that function best between 0°C and 35°C. Temperatures above or below this range may affect those enzymes, slowing down the rate of photosynthesis. At very low temperatures, photosynthesis may stop entirely.

The intensity of light also affects the rate at which photosynthesis occurs. As you might expect, high light intensity increases the rate of photosynthesis. After the light intensity reaches a certain level, how-ever, the plant reaches its maximum rate of photosynthesis.

Because water is one of the raw materials of photosynthesis, a shortage of water can slow or even stop photosynthesis. Water loss can also damage plant tissues. To deal with these dangers, plants (such as desert plants and conifers) that live in dry conditions often have waxy coatings on their leaves that reduce water loss. They may also have biochemical adaptations that make photosynthesis more efficient under dry conditions.

BUILD Vocabulary

MULTIPLE MEANINGS The noun *intensity* is commonly used to refer to something or someone who is very emotional, focused, or active. In science, however, *intensity* refers to energy. Thus, light intensity is a measure of the amount of energy available in light. More intense light has more energy.

In Your Notebook *Explain in your own words what role enzymes play in chemical reactions such as photosynthesis.*

Photosynthesis Under Extreme Conditions In order to conserve water, most plants under bright, hot conditions (of the sorts often found in the tropics) close the small openings in their leaves that normally admit carbon dioxide. While this keeps the plants from drying out, it causes carbon dioxide within the leaves to fall to very low levels. When this happens to most plants, photosynthesis slows down or even stops. However, some plants have adapted to extremely bright, hot conditions. There are two major groups of these specialized plants: C4 plants and CAM plants. C4 and CAM plants have biochemical adaptations that minimize water loss while still allowing photosynthesis to take place in intense sunlight.

▶ *C4 Photosynthesis* C4 plants have a specialized chemical pathway that allows them to capture even very low levels of carbon dioxide and pass it to the Calvin cycle. The name "C4 plant" comes from the fact that the first compound formed in this pathway contains 4 carbon atoms. The C4 pathway enables photosynthesis to keep working under intense light and high temperatures, but it requires extra energy in the form of ATP to function. C4 organisms include important crop plants like corn, sugar cane, and sorghum.

▶ *CAM Plants* Other plants adapted to dry climates use a different strategy to obtain carbon dioxide while minimizing water loss. These include members of the family Crassulaceae. Because carbon dioxide becomes incorporated into organic acids during photosynthesis, the process is called Crassulacean Acid Metabolism (CAM). CAM plants admit air into their leaves only at night. In the cool darkness, carbon dioxide is combined with existing molecules to produce organic acids, "trapping" the carbon within the leaves. During the daytime, when leaves are tightly sealed to prevent the loss of water, these compounds release carbon dioxide, enabling carbohydrate production. CAM plants include pineapple trees, many desert cacti, and also the fleshy "ice plants" shown in **Figure 8–12,** which are frequently planted near freeways along the west coast to retard brush fires and prevent erosion.

FIGURE 8–12 CAM Plants Plants like this ice plant can survive in dry conditions due to their modified light-independent reactions. Air is allowed into the leaves only at night, minimizing water loss.

8.3 Assessment

Review Key Concepts 🔑

1. a. Review Summarize what happens during the light-dependent reactions of photosynthesis.
   b. Sequence Put the events of the light-dependent reactions in the order in which they occur and describe how each step is dependent on the step that comes before it.

2. a. Review What is the Calvin cycle?
   b. Compare and Contrast List at least three differences between the light-dependent and light-independent reactions of photosynthesis.

3. a. Review What are the three primary factors that affect the rate of photosynthesis?
   b. Interpret Graphs Look at the graph on page 240. What are the independent and dependent variables being tested?

BUILD VOCABULARY

4. The word *carbohydrate* comes from the prefix *carbo-*, meaning "carbon," and the word *hydrate*. Based on the reactants of the photosynthesis equation, what does *hydrate* mean?

Pre-Lab: Plant Pigments and Photosynthesis

Problem Do red leaves have the same pigments as green leaves?

Materials paper clips, one-hole rubber stoppers, chromatography paper strips, metric ruler, green and red leaves, coin, sheet of paper, large test tubes, test tube rack, glass-marking pencil, 10-mL graduated cylinder, isopropyl alcohol, colored pencils

Lab Manual Chapter 8 Lab

Skills Focus Predict, Analyze Data, Draw Conclusions

Connect to the Big idea Almost all life on Earth depends, directly or indirectly, on energy from sunlight. Photosynthesis is the process in which light energy is captured and converted to chemical energy. Many reactions are required for this conversion, which takes place in the chloroplasts of plant cells. Some of the reactions depend on light and some do not. Plant pigments play a major role in the light-dependent reactions. In this lab, you will use chromatography to compare the pigments in red leaves with those in green leaves.

Background Questions

a. **Compare and Contrast** What do all plant pigments have in common? How are they different?

b. **Review** Why do most leaves appear green?

c. **Review** What property makes chlorophyll so important for photosynthesis?

Pre-Lab Questions

Preview the procedure in the lab manual.

1. **Design an Experiment** What is the purpose of this lab?

2. **Control Variables** What is the control in this lab?

3. **Design an Experiment** Why must you place a leaf about 2 cm from the bottom of the paper before rubbing the leaf with the coin?

4. **Predict** Will red leaves contain the same amount of chlorophyll as green leaves? Why or why not?

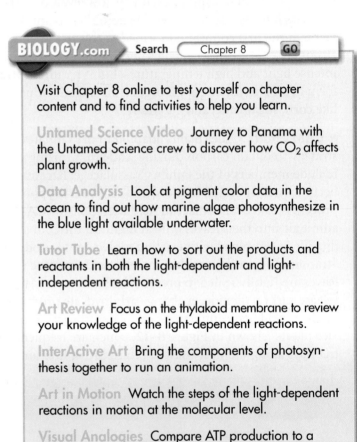

BIOLOGY.com   Search   [Chapter 8]   GO

Visit Chapter 8 online to test yourself on chapter content and to find activities to help you learn.

Untamed Science Video Journey to Panama with the Untamed Science crew to discover how CO_2 affects plant growth.

Data Analysis Look at pigment color data in the ocean to find out how marine algae photosynthesize in the blue light available underwater.

Tutor Tube Learn how to sort out the products and reactants in both the light-dependent and light-independent reactions.

Art Review Focus on the thylakoid membrane to review your knowledge of the light-dependent reactions.

InterActive Art Bring the components of photosynthesis together to run an animation.

Art in Motion Watch the steps of the light-dependent reactions in motion at the molecular level.

Visual Analogies Compare ATP production to a charged battery. See how the electron transport chain is like passing a hot potato.

8 Study Guide

Big idea Cellular Basis of Life

Photosynthesis is the process by which organisms convert light energy into chemical energy that all organisms can use directly, or indirectly, to carry out life functions.

8.1 Energy and Life

🔑 ATP can easily release and store energy by breaking and re-forming the bonds between its phosphate groups. This characteristic of ATP makes it exceptionally useful as a basic energy source for all cells.

🔑 In the process of photosynthesis, plants convert the energy of sunlight into chemical energy stored in the bonds of carbohydrates.

adenosine triphosphate   autotroph (228)
  (ATP) (226)   photosynthesis (228)
heterotroph (228)

8.2 Photosynthesis: An Overview

🔑 Photosynthetic organisms capture energy from sunlight with pigments.

🔑 An electron carrier is a compound that can accept a pair of high-energy electrons and transfer them, along with most of their energy, to another molecule.

🔑 Photosynthesis uses the energy of sunlight to convert water and carbon dioxide (reactants) into high-energy sugars and oxygen (products).

pigment (230)   light-dependent
chlorophyll (230)   reactions (233)
thylakoid (231)   light-independent
stroma (231)   reactions (233)
NADP$^+$ (232)

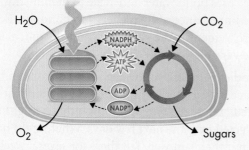

8.3 The Process of Photosynthesis

🔑 The light-dependent reactions use energy from sunlight to produce oxygen and convert ADP and NADP$^+$ into the energy carriers ATP and NADPH.

🔑 During the light-independent reactions, ATP and NADPH from the light-dependent reactions are used to produce high-energy sugars.

🔑 Among the most important factors that affect photosynthesis are temperature, light intensity, and the availability of water.

photosystem (235)   ATP synthase (237)
electron transport chain Calvin cycle (238)
  (236)

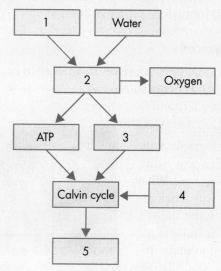

Think Visually
Using the information in this chapter, complete the following flowchart about photosynthesis.

8 Assessment

8.1 Energy and Life

Understand Key Concepts

1. Which of the following are autotrophs?
   a. deer
   c. leopards
   b. plants
   d. mushrooms

2. The principal chemical compound that living things use to store energy is
   a. DNA.
   c. H_2O.
   b. ATP.
   d. CO_2.

3. The amount of energy stored in a molecule of ATP compared to the amount stored in a molecule of glucose is
   a. greater.
   b. less.
   c. the same.
   d. variable, depending on conditions.

4. When a candle burns, energy is released in the form of
   a. carbon dioxide and water.
   b. the chemical substance ATP.
   c. light and heat.
   d. electricity and motion.

5. How do heterotrophs and autotrophs differ in the way they obtain energy?

6. Describe the three parts of an ATP molecule.

7. Compare the amounts of energy stored by ATP and glucose. Which compound is used by the cell as an immediate source of energy?

Think Critically

8. **Use Analogies** Develop an analogy to explain ATP and energy transfer to a classmate who does not understand the concept.

9. **Infer** Examine the photograph of the Indian pipe plant shown here. What can you conclude about the ability of the Indian pipe plant to make its own food? Explain your answer.

8.2 Photosynthesis: An Overview

Understand Key Concepts

10. In addition to light and chlorophyll, photosynthesis requires
    a. water and oxygen.
    b. water and sugars.
    c. oxygen and carbon dioxide.
    d. water and carbon dioxide.

11. The leaves of a plant appear green because chlorophyll
    a. reflects blue light.
    c. reflects green light.
    b. absorbs blue light.
    d. absorbs green light.

12. Write the basic equation for photosynthesis using the names of the starting and final substances of the process.

13. What role do plant pigments play in the process of photosynthesis?

14. Identify the chloroplast structures labeled A, B, and C. In which structure(s) do the light-dependent reactions occur? In which structure(s) do the light-independent reactions take place?

Think Critically

15. **Form a Hypothesis** Although they appear green, some plant leaves contain yellow and red pigments as well as chlorophyll. In the fall, those leaves may become red or yellow. Suggest an explanation for these color changes.

16. **Design an Experiment** Design an experiment that uses pond water and algae to demonstrate the importance of light energy to pond life. Be sure to identify the variables you will control and the variable you will change.

17. **Predict** Suppose you water a potted plant and place it by a window in a transparent, airtight jar. Predict how the rate of photosynthesis might be affected over the next few days. What might happen if the plant were left there for several weeks? Explain.

Understand Key Concepts

18. The first process in the light-dependent reactions of photosynthesis is
  a. light absorption. **c.** oxygen production.
  b. electron transport. **d.** ATP formation.

19. Which substance from the light-dependent reactions of photosynthesis is a source of energy for the Calvin cycle?
  a. ADP **c.** H_2O
  b. NADPH **d.** pyruvic acid

20. The light-independent reactions of photosynthesis are also known as the
  a. Calvin cycle. **c.** carbon cycle.
  b. sugar cycle. **d.** ATP cycle.

21. ATP synthase in the chloroplast membrane makes ATP, utilizing the energy of highly concentrated
  a. chlorophyll. **c.** hydrogen ions.
  b. electrons. **d.** NADPH.

22. CAM plants are specialized to survive under what conditions that would harm most other kinds of plants?
  a. low temperatures **c.** hot, dry conditions
  b. excess water **d.** long day lengths

23. Explain the role of $NADP^+$ as an energy carrier in photosynthesis.

24. Describe the role of ATP synthase and explain how it works.

25. Summarize the events of the Calvin cycle.

26. Discuss three factors that affect the rate at which photosynthesis occurs.

Think Critically

27. **Interpret Graphs** Study **Figure 8–11** on page 238 and give evidence to support the idea that the Calvin cycle does not depend on light.

28. **Apply Concepts** How do the events in the Calvin cycle depend on the light-dependent reactions of photosynthesis?

29. **Form a Hypothesis** Many of the sun's rays may be blocked by dust or clouds formed by volcanic eruptions or pollution. What are some possible short-term and long-term effects of this on photosynthesis? On other forms of life?

solve the CHAPTER MYSTERY

OUT OF THIN AIR?

Most plants grow out of the soil, of course, and you might hypothesize, as Jan van Helmont did, that soil contributes to plant mass. At the conclusion of his experiment with the willow tree, however, van Helmont discovered that the mass of the soil was essentially unchanged, but that the tree had increased in mass by nearly 75 kilograms. Van Helmont concluded that the mass must have come from water, because water was the only thing he had added throughout the experiment. What he didn't know, however, was that the increased bulk of the tree was built from carbon, as well as from the oxygen and hydrogen in water. We now know that most of that carbon comes from carbon dioxide in the air. Thus, mass accumulates from two sources: carbon dioxide and water. What form does the added mass take? Think about the origin of the word *carbohydrate*, from *carbo-*, meaning "carbon," and *hydrate*, meaning "to combine with water," and you have your answer.

1. Infer Although soil does not significantly contribute to plant mass, how might it help plants grow?

2. Infer If a scientist were able to measure the exact mass of carbon dioxide and water that entered a plant, and the exact mass of the sugars produced, would the masses be identical? Why or why not?

3. Apply Concepts What do plants do with all of the carbohydrates they produce by photosynthesis? (*Hint*: Plant cells have mitochondria in addition to chloroplasts. What do mitochondria do?)

4. Connect to the Big idea Explain how the experiments carried out by van Helmont and Calvin contributed to our understanding of how nutrients cycle in the biosphere.

Connecting Concepts

Use Science Graphics

A water plant placed under bright light gives off bubbles of oxygen. The table below contains the results of an experiment in which the distance from the light to the plant was varied. Use the data table to answer questions 30–33.

Oxygen Production	
Distance From Light (cm)	Bubbles Produced per Minute
10	39
20	22
30	8
40	5

30. **Graph** Use the data in the table to make a line graph.

31. **Interpret Graphs** Describe the observed trend. How many bubbles would you predict if the light was moved to 50 cm away? Explain.

32. **Draw Conclusions** What relationship exists between the plant's distance from the light and the number of bubbles produced? What process is occuring? Explain your answer.

33. **Apply Concepts** Based on the results of this experiment, explain why most aquatic primary producers live in the uppermost regions of deep oceans, lakes, and ponds.

Write About Science

34. **Creative Writing** Imagine that you are an oxygen atom and two of your friends are hydrogen atoms. Together, you make up a water molecule. Describe the events and changes that happen to you and your friends as you journey through the light-dependent reactions and the Calvin cycle of photosynthesis. Include illustrations with your description.

35. **Assess the** Big idea In eukaryotic plants, chlorophyll is found only in chloroplasts. Explain how the function of chlorophyll is related to its very specific location in the cell.

Analyzing Data

An experimenter subjected corn plants and bean plants to different concentrations of carbon dioxide and measured the amount of CO_2 taken up by the plants and used in photosynthesis. Data for the two plants are shown in the following graph.

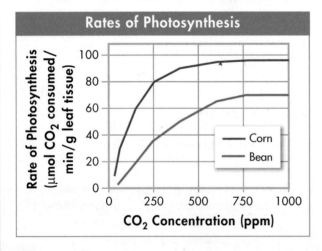

36. **Interpret Graphs** Bean plants reach their maximum rate of photosynthesis at what concentration of carbon dioxide?
   a. about 50 ppm
   b. about 200 ppm
   c. about 750 ppm
   d. 1000 ppm

37. **Draw Conclusions** From the data it is possible to conclude that
   a. beans contain more chlorophyll than corn contains.
   b. corn reaches its maximum photosynthetic rate at lower concentrations than beans do.
   c. beans reach their maximum photosynthetic rate at lower concentrations than corn does.
   d. beans use carbon dioxide more efficiently than corn does.

Standardized Test Prep

Multiple Choice

1. Autotrophs differ from heterotrophs because they
   A utilize oxygen to burn food.
   B do not require oxygen to live.
   C make carbon dioxide as a product of using food.
   D make their own food from carbon dioxide and water.

2. The principal pigment in plants is
   A chlorophyll.   C ATP.
   B oxygen.   D NADPH.

3. Which of the following is NOT produced in the light-dependent reactions of photosynthesis?
   A NADPH
   B sugars
   C hydrogen ions
   D ATP

4. Which of the following correctly summarizes the process of photosynthesis?
   A $H_2O + CO_2 \xrightarrow{\text{light}} \text{sugars} + O_2$
   B $\text{sugars} + O_2 \xrightarrow{\text{light}} H_2O + CO_2$
   C $H_2O + O_2 \xrightarrow{\text{light}} \text{sugars} + CO_2$
   D $\text{sugars} + CO_2 \xrightarrow{\text{light}} H_2O + O_2$

5. The color of light that is LEAST useful to a plant during photosynthesis is
   A red.   C green.
   B blue.   D violet.

6. The first step in photosynthesis is the
   A synthesis of water.
   B production of oxygen.
   C breakdown of carbon dioxide.
   D absorption of light energy.

7. In a typical plant, all of the following factors are necessary for photosynthesis EXCEPT
   A chlorophyll.
   B light.
   C oxygen.
   D water.

Questions 8–10

Several drops of concentrated pigment were extracted from spinach leaves. These drops were placed at the bottom of a strip of highly absorbent paper. After the extract dried, the paper was suspended in a test tube containing alcohol so that only the tip of the paper was in the alcohol. As the alcohol was absorbed and moved up the paper, the various pigments contained in the extract separated as shown in the diagram.

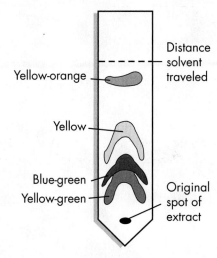

8. Which pigment traveled the shortest distance?
   A yellow-orange   C blue-green
   B yellow   D yellow-green

9. A valid conclusion that can be drawn from this information is that spinach leaves
   A use only chlorophyll during photosynthesis.
   B contain several pigments.
   C contain more orange pigment than yellow pigment.
   D are yellow-orange rather than green.

10. In which organelle would MOST of these pigments be found?
    A vacuoles   C mitochondria
    B centrioles   D chloroplasts

Open-Ended Response

11. Describe how high-energy electrons are ultimately responsible for driving the photosynthetic reactions.

If You Have Trouble With . . .

Question	1	2	3	4	5	6	7	8	9	10	11
See Lesson	8.1	8.2	8.2	8.2	8.2	8.3	8.3	8.2	8.2	8.2	8.3

9 Cellular Respiration and Fermentation

Big idea

Cellular Basis of Life

Q: How do organisms obtain energy?

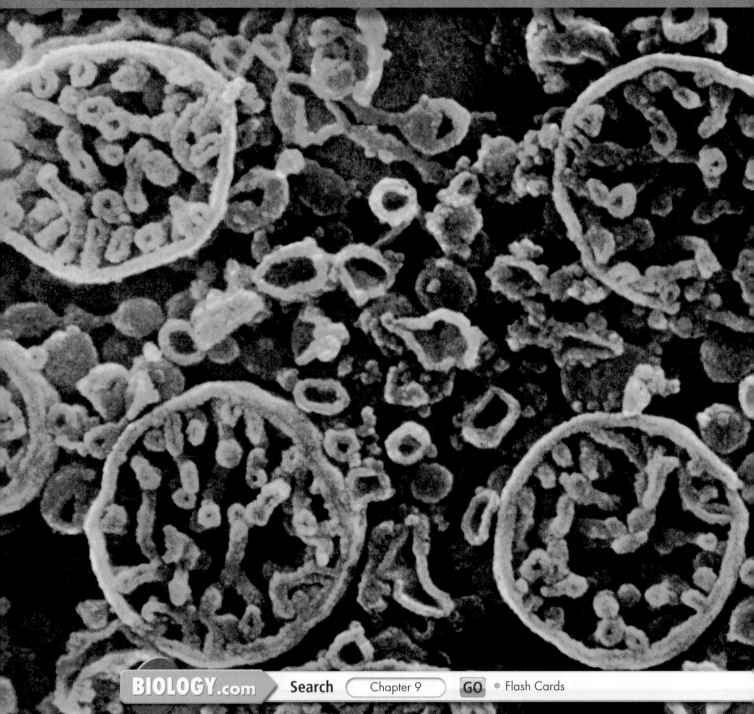

BIOLOGY.com   Search   (Chapter 9)   GO   • Flash Cards

INSIDE:

- 9.1 Cellular Respiration: An Overview
- 9.2 The Process of Cellular Respiration
- 9.3 Fermentation

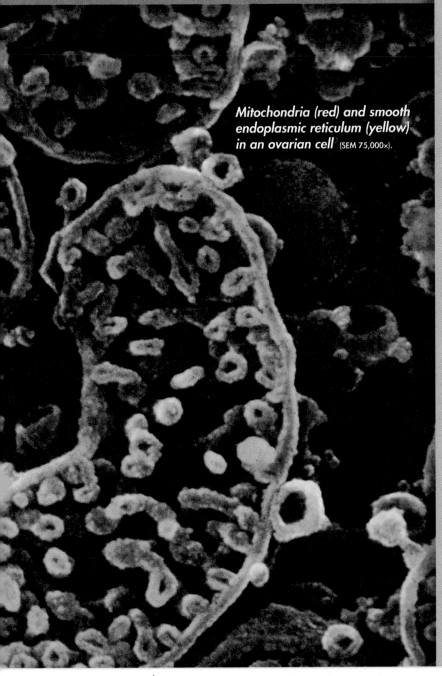

Mitochondria (red) and smooth endoplasmic reticulum (yellow) in an ovarian cell (SEM 75,000×).

CHAPTER
MYSTERY

DIVING WITHOUT A BREATH

Everyone is familiar with the sensation of being "out of breath." Just a few minutes of vigorous exercise can have humans huffing and puffing for air. But what if you couldn't get air? What if you were asked to hold your breath and exercise? Before too long, you'd pass out due to a lack of oxygen. This may seem like a silly thought experiment, but there are animals that exercise without breathing and without passing out all the time—whales. Unlike most animals that live their entire lives in water, whales still rely on oxygen obtained from air when they surface. Amazingly, sperm whales routinely stay underwater for 45 minutes or more when diving. Some scientists suspect that they can stay underwater for 90 minutes! How is that possible? Diving takes a lot of energy. How do whales stay active for so long on only one breath? As you read this chapter, look for clues. Then, solve the mystery.

Never Stop Exploring Your World. Learning about whales and their extraordinary ability to hold their breaths is just the beginning. Take a video field trip with the ecogeeks of Untamed Science to see where this mystery leads.

- Untamed Science Video   - Chapter Mystery

9.1 Cellular Respiration: An Overview

Key Questions

🔑 *Where do organisms get energy?*

🔑 *What is cellular respiration?*

🔑 *What is the relationship between photosynthesis and cellular respiration?*

Vocabulary

calorie • cellular respiration • aerobic • anaerobic

Taking Notes

Preview Visuals Before you read, study **Figure 9–2** on page 252. Make a list of questions that you have about the diagram. As you read, write down the answers to the questions.

BUILD Vocabulary

PREFIXES The prefix *macro-* means "large" or "elongated." Macromolecules are made up of many smaller molecular subunits. Carbohydrates, proteins, and lipids are important macromolecules found in living things.

THINK ABOUT IT When you are hungry, how do you feel? If you are like most people, you might feel sluggish, a little dizzy, and—above all—weak. Weakness is a feeling triggered by a lack of energy. You feel weak when you are hungry because food serves as a source of energy. Weakness is your body's way of telling you that your energy supplies are low. But how does food get converted into a usable form of energy? Car engines have to burn gasoline in order to release its energy. Do our bodies burn food the way a car burns gasoline, or is there something more to it?

Chemical Energy and Food

🔑 *Where do organisms get energy?*

Food provides living things with the chemical building blocks they need to grow and reproduce. Recall that some organisms, such as plants, are autotrophs, meaning that they make their own food through photosynthesis. Other organisms are heterotrophs, meaning that they rely on other organisms for food. For all organisms, food molecules contain chemical energy that is released when their chemical bonds are broken. 🔑 **Organisms get the energy they need from food.**

How much energy is actually present in food? Quite a lot, although it varies with the type of food. Energy stored in food is expressed in units of calories. A **calorie** is the amount of energy needed to raise the temperature of 1 gram of water 1 degree Celsius. The Calorie (capital *C*) that is used on food labels is a kilocalorie, or 1000 calories. Cells can use all sorts of molecules for food, including fats, proteins, and carbohydrates. The energy stored in each of these macromolecules varies because their chemical structures, and therefore their energy-storing bonds, differ. For example, 1 gram of the sugar glucose releases 3811 calories of heat energy when it is burned. By contrast, 1 gram of the triglyceride fats found in beef releases 8893 calories of heat energy when its bonds are broken. In general, carbohydrates and proteins contain approximately 4000 calories (4 Calories) of energy per gram, while fats contain approximately 9000 calories (9 Calories) per gram.

Cells, of course, don't simply burn food and release energy as heat. Instead, they break down food molecules gradually, capturing a little bit of chemical energy at key steps. This enables cells to use the energy stored in the chemical bonds of foods like glucose to produce compounds such as ATP that directly power the activities of the cell.

You Are What You Eat

Organisms get energy from the food they eat, but the energy contained in foods varies greatly. Most foods contain a combination of proteins, carbohydrates, and fats. One gram of protein or a carbohydrate such as glucose contains roughly 4 Calories. One gram of fat, however, contains about 9 Calories. The accompanying table shows the approximate composition of one serving of some common foods.

Composition of Some Common Foods			
Food	Protein (g)	Carbohydrate (g)	Fat (g)
Apple, 1 medium	0	22	0
Bacon, 2 slices	5	0	6
Chocolate, 1 bar	3	23	13
Eggs, 2 whole	12	0	9
2% milk, 1 cup	8	12	5
Potato chips, 15 chips	2	14	10
Skinless roasted turkey, 3 slices	11	3	1

1. Interpret Data Per serving, which of the foods included in the table has the most protein? Which has the most carbohydrates? Which has the most fat?

2. Calculate Approximately how many more Calories are there in 2 slices of bacon than there are in 3 slices of roasted turkey? Why is there a difference?

3. Calculate Walking at a moderate pace consumes around 300 Calories per hour. At that rate, how many minutes would you have to walk to burn the Calories in one chocolate bar? (*Hint:* Start by calculating the number of Calories consumed per minute by walking.)

Overview of Cellular Respiration

🔑 What is cellular respiration?

If oxygen is available, organisms can obtain energy from food by a process called **cellular respiration.** 🔑 **Cellular respiration is the process that releases energy from food in the presence of oxygen.** Although cellular respiration involves dozens of separate reactions, an overall chemical summary of the process is remarkably simple:

In Symbols:

$$6O_2 + C_6H_{12}O_6 \xrightarrow{enzymes} 6CO_2 + 6H_2O + Energy$$

In Words:

$$Oxygen + Glucose \longrightarrow Carbon\ dioxide + Water + Energy$$

As you can see, cellular respiration requires oxygen and a food molecule such as glucose, and it gives off carbon dioxide, water, and energy. Do not be misled, however, by the simplicity of this equation. If cellular respiration took place in just one step, all of the energy from glucose would be released at once, and most of it would be lost in the form of light and heat. Clearly, a living cell has to control that energy. It can't simply start a fire—the cell has to release the explosive chemical energy in food molecules a little bit at a time. The cell needs to find a way to trap those little bits of energy by using them to make ATP.

FIGURE 9–1 A Controlled Release Cellular respiration involves a series of controlled reactions that slowly release the energy stored in food. If the energy were to be released too suddenly, most of it would be lost in the forms of light and heat—just as it is when a marshmallow catches fire.

In Your Notebook *Do plants undergo cellular respiration? What organelle(s) do they have that helps you determine the answer?*

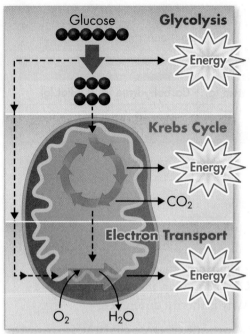

FIGURE 9–2 The Stages of Cellular Respiration There are three stages to cellular respiration: glycolysis, the Krebs cycle, and the electron transport chain. **Interpret Visuals** *Which stage(s) of cellular respiration occur in the mitochondrion?*

Stages of Cellular Respiration Cellular respiration captures the energy from food in three main stages—glycolysis, the Krebs cycle, and the electron transport chain. Although cells can use just about any food molecule for energy, we will concentrate on just one as an example—the simple sugar glucose. Glucose first enters a chemical pathway known as glycolysis (gly KAHL ih sis). Only a small amount of energy is captured to produce ATP during this stage. In fact, at the end of glycolysis, about 90 percent of the chemical energy that was available in glucose is still unused, locked in chemical bonds of a molecule called pyruvic (py ROO vik) acid.

How does the cell extract the rest of that energy? First, pyruvic acid enters the second stage of cellular respiration, the Krebs cycle, where a little more energy is generated. The bulk of the energy, however, comes from the final stage of cellular respiration, the electron transport chain. This stage requires reactants from the other two stages of the process, as shown by dashed lines in **Figure 9–2.** How does the electron transport chain extract so much energy from these reactants? It uses one of the world's most powerful electron acceptors—oxygen.

Oxygen and Energy Oxygen is required at the very end of the electron transport chain. Any time a cell's demand for energy increases, its use of oxygen increases, too. As you know, the word *respiration* is often used as a synonym for *breathing.* This is why we have used the term *cellular respiration* to refer to energy-releasing pathways within the cell. The double meaning of respiration points out a crucial connection between cells and organisms: Most of the energy-releasing pathways within cells require oxygen, and that is the reason we need to breathe, to respire.

Pathways of cellular respiration that require oxygen are said to be **aerobic** ("in air"). The Krebs cycle and electron transport chain are both aerobic processes. Even though the Krebs cycle does not *directly* require oxygen, it is classified as an aerobic process because it cannot run without the oxygen-requiring electron transport chain. Glycolysis, however, does not directly require oxygen, nor does it rely on an oxygen-requiring process to run. Glycolysis is therefore said to be **anaerobic** ("without air"). Even though glycolysis is anaerobic, it is considered part of cellular respiration because its final products are key reactants for the aerobic stages.

Recall that mitochondria are structures in the cell that convert chemical energy stored in food to usable energy for the cell. Glycolysis actually occurs in the cytoplasm of a cell, but the Krebs cycle and electron transport chain, which generate the majority of ATP during cellular respiration, take place inside the mitochondria. If oxygen is not present, another anaerobic pathway, known as fermentation, makes it possible for the cell to keep glycolysis running, generating ATP to power cellular activity. You will learn more about fermentation later in this chapter.

In Your Notebook *Make a flowchart that shows the different steps of cellular respiration.*

Comparing Photosynthesis and Cellular Respiration

🔑 **What is the relationship between photosynthesis and cellular respiration?**

If nearly all organisms break down food by the process of cellular respiration, why doesn't Earth run out of oxygen? Where does all of the carbon dioxide waste product go? How does the chemical energy stored in food get replaced? As it happens, cellular respiration is balanced by another process: photosynthesis. The energy in photosynthesis and cellular respiration flows in opposite directions. Look at **Figure 9–3** and think of the chemical energy in carbohydrates as money in the Earth's savings account. Photosynthesis is the process that "deposits" energy. Cellular respiration is the process that "withdraws" energy. As you might expect, the equations for photosynthesis and cellular respiration are the reverse of each other.

On a global level, photosynthesis and cellular respiration are also opposites. 🔑 **Photosynthesis removes carbon dioxide from the atmosphere, and cellular respiration puts it back. Photosynthesis releases oxygen into the atmosphere, and cellular respiration uses that oxygen to release energy from food.** The release of energy by cellular respiration takes place in nearly all life: plants, animals, fungi, protists, and most bacteria. Energy capture by photosynthesis, however, occurs only in plants, algae, and some bacteria.

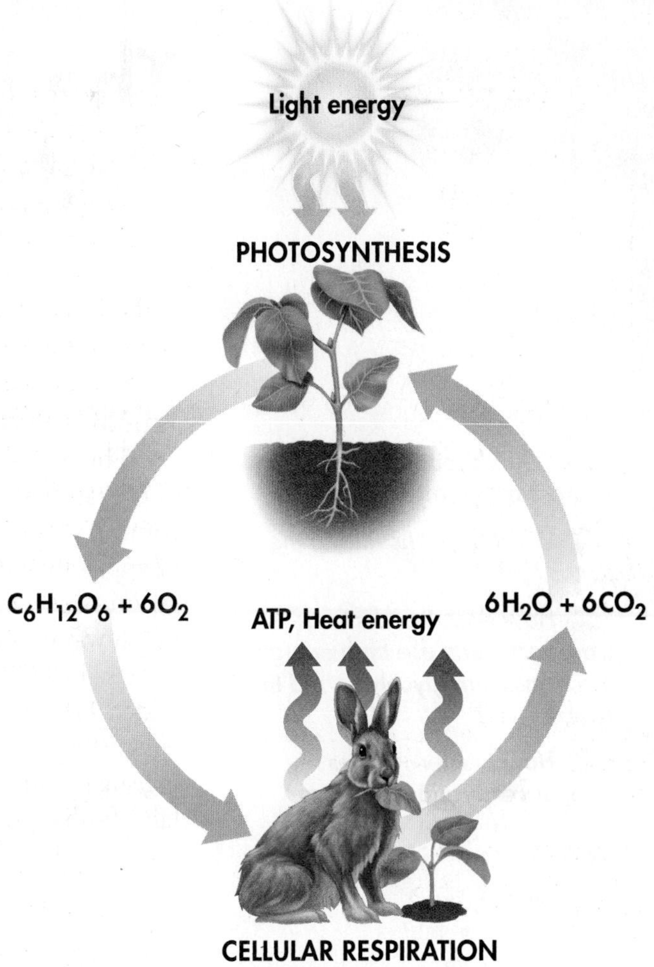

Light energy

PHOTOSYNTHESIS

$C_6H_{12}O_6 + 6O_2$

ATP, Heat energy

$6H_2O + 6CO_2$

CELLULAR RESPIRATION

FIGURE 9–3 Opposite Processes Photosynthesis and cellular respiration can be thought of as opposite processes. **Compare and Contrast** *Exactly how is the equation for photosynthesis different from the equation for cellular respiration?*

9.1 Assessment

Review Key Concepts 🔑

1. a. Review Why do all organisms need food?

b. Relate Cause and Effect Why do macromolecules differ in the amount of energy they contain?

2. a. Review Write the overall reaction for cellular respiration.

b. Apply Concepts How does the process of cellular respiration maintain homeostasis at the cellular level?

3. a. Review In what ways are cellular respiration and photosynthesis considered opposite processes?

b. Use Analogies How is the chemical energy in glucose similar to money in a savings account?

BUILD VOCABULARY

4. The Greek word *glukus* means "sweet," and the Latin word *lysis* refers to a process of loosening or decomposing. Based on this information, write a definition for the word *glycolysis*.

BIOLOGY.com | Search (Lesson 9.1) **GO** • Lesson Assessment • Self-Test • Art in Motion

The Process of Cellular Respiration

Key Questions

🔑 What happens during the process of glycolysis?

🔑 What happens during the Krebs cycle?

🔑 How does the electron transport chain use high-energy electrons from glycolysis and the Krebs cycle?

🔑 How much ATP does cellular respiration generate?

Vocabulary

glycolysis • NAD⁺ • Krebs cycle • matrix

Taking Notes

Compare/Contrast Table As you read, make a compare/contrast table showing the location, starting reactants, and end products of glycolysis, the Krebs cycle, and the electron transport chain. Also include how many molecules of ATP are produced in each step of the process.

THINK ABOUT IT

Food burns! It's true, of course, that many common foods (think of apples, bananas, and ground beef) have too much water in them to actually light with a match. However, foods with little water, including sugar and cooking oil, will indeed burn. In fact, flour, which contains both carbohydrates and protein, is so flammable that it has caused several explosions, including the one seen here at London's City Flour Mills in 1872 (which is why you're not supposed to store flour above a stove). So, plenty of energy is available in food, but how does a living cell extract that energy without setting a fire or blowing things up?

Glycolysis

🔑 **What happens during the process of glycolysis?**

The first set of reactions in cellular respiration is known as **glycolysis,** a word that literally means "sugar-breaking." Glycolysis involves many chemical steps that transform glucose. The end result is 2 molecules of a 3-carbon molecule called pyruvic acid. 🔑 **During glycolysis, 1 molecule of glucose, a 6-carbon compound, is transformed into 2 molecules of pyruvic acid, a 3-carbon compound.** As the bonds in glucose are broken and rearranged, energy is released. The process of glycolysis can be seen in **Figure 9–4.**

ATP Production Even though glycolysis is an energy-releasing process, the cell needs to put in a little energy to get things going. At the pathway's beginning, 2 ATP molecules are used up. Earlier in this chapter, photosynthesis and respiration were compared, respectively, to a deposit to and a withdrawal from a savings account. Similarly, the 2 ATP molecules used at the onset of glycolysis are like an investment that pays back interest. In order to earn interest from a bank, first you have to put money into an account. Although the cell puts 2 ATP molecules into its "account" to get glycolysis going, glycolysis produces 4 ATP molecules. This gives the cell a net gain of 2 ATP molecules for each molecule of glucose that enters glycolysis.

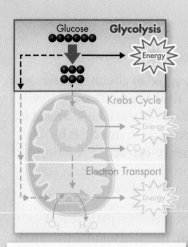

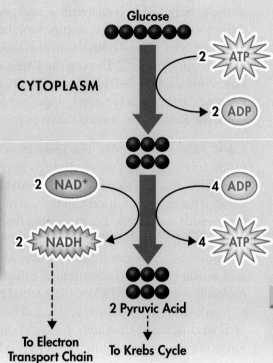

Glucose

CYTOPLASM

2 ATP

2 ADP

2 NAD⁺

4 ADP

2 NADH

4 ATP

2 Pyruvic Acid

To Electron Transport Chain

To Krebs Cycle

NADH Production
Four high-energy electrons are passed to the carrier NAD⁺ to produce NADH. NADH carries these electrons to the electron transport chain.

ATP Production
Two ATP molecules are "invested" to get the process of glycolysis going. Overall, 4 ATP molecules are produced, for a net gain of 2 ATP per molecule of glucose.

FIGURE 9–4 Glycolysis is the first stage of cellular respiration. During glycolysis, glucose is broken down into 2 molecules of pyruvic acid. ATP and NADH are produced as part of the process. **Interpret Visuals** *How many carbon atoms are there in glucose? How many carbon atoms are in each molecule of pyruvic acid?*

NADH Production One of the reactions of glycolysis removes 4 electrons, now in a high-energy state, and passes them to an electron carrier called **NAD⁺**, or nicotinamide adenine dinucleotide. Like NADP⁺ in photosynthesis, each NAD⁺ molecule accepts a pair of high-energy electrons. This molecule, now known as NADH, holds the electrons until they can be transferred to other molecules. As you will see, in the presence of oxygen, these high-energy electrons can be used to produce even more ATP molecules.

The Advantages of Glycolysis In the process of glycolysis, 4 ATP molecules are synthesized from 4 ADP molecules. Given that 2 ATP molecules are used to start the process, there is a net gain of just 2 ATP molecules. Although the energy yield from glycolysis is small, the process is so fast that cells can produce thousands of ATP molecules in just a few milliseconds. The speed of glycolysis can be a big advantage when the energy demands of a cell suddenly increase.

Besides speed, another advantage of glycolysis is that the process itself does not require oxygen. This means that glycolysis can quickly supply chemical energy to cells when oxygen is not available. When oxygen is available, however, the pyruvic acid and NADH "outputs" generated during glycolysis become the "inputs" for the other processes of cellular respiration.

BUILD Vocabulary

ACADEMIC WORDS The verb **synthesize** means "to bring together as a whole." Therefore, a molecule of ATP is synthesized when a phosphate group combines with the molecule ADP, forming a high-energy bond.

In Your Notebook *In your own words, describe the advantages of glycolysis to the cell in terms of energy production.*

The Krebs Cycle

What happens during the Krebs cycle?

In the presence of oxygen, pyruvic acid produced in glycolysis passes to the second stage of cellular respiration, the **Krebs cycle.** The Krebs cycle is named after Hans Krebs, the British biochemist who demonstrated its existence in 1937. **During the Krebs cycle, pyruvic acid is broken down into carbon dioxide in a series of energy-extracting reactions.** Because citric acid is the first compound formed in this series of reactions, the Krebs cycle is also known as the citric acid cycle.

Citric Acid Production The Krebs cycle begins when pyruvic acid produced by glycolysis passes through the two membranes of the mitochondrion and into the matrix. The **matrix** is the innermost compartment of the mitochondrion and the site of the Krebs cycle reactions. Once inside the matrix, 1 carbon atom from pyruvic acid becomes part of a molecule of carbon dioxide, which is eventually released into the air. The other 2 carbon atoms from pyruvic acid rearrange and form acetic acid, which is joined to a compound called coenzyme A. The resulting molecule is called acetyl-CoA. (The acetyl part of acetyl-CoA is made up of 2 carbon atoms, 1 oxygen atom, and 3 hydrogen atoms.) As the Krebs cycle begins, acetyl-CoA adds the 2-carbon acetyl group to a 4-carbon molecule already present in the cycle, producing a 6-carbon molecule called citric acid.

Energy Extraction As the cycle continues, citric acid is broken down into a 4-carbon molecule, more carbon dioxide is released, and electrons are transferred to energy carriers. Follow the reactions in **Figure 9–5** and you will see how this happens. First, look at the 6 carbon atoms in citric acid. One is removed, and then another, releasing 2 molecules of carbon dioxide and leaving a 4-carbon molecule. Why is the Krebs cycle a "cycle"? Because the 4-carbon molecule produced in the last step is the same molecule that accepts the acetyl-CoA in the first step. The molecule needed to start the reactions of the cycle is remade with every "turn."

Next, look for ATP. For each turn of the cycle, a molecule of ADP is converted to a molecule of ATP. Recall that glycolysis produces 2 molecules of pyruvic acid from 1 molecule of glucose. So, each starting molecule of glucose results in two complete turns of the Krebs cycle and, therefore, 2 ATP molecules. Finally, look at the electron carriers, NAD$^+$ and FAD (flavine adenine dinucleotide). At five places, electron carriers accept a pair of high-energy electrons, changing NAD$^+$ to NADH and FAD to FADH$_2$. FAD and FADH$_2$ are molecules similar to NAD$^+$ and NADH, respectively.

What happens to each of these Krebs cycle products—carbon dioxide, ATP, and electron carriers? Carbon dioxide is not useful to the cell and is expelled every time you exhale. The ATP molecules are *very* useful and become immediately available to power cellular activities. As for the carrier molecules like NADH, in the presence of oxygen, the electrons they hold are used to generate huge amounts of ATP.

In Your Notebook *List the electron carriers involved in the Krebs cycle. Include their names before and after they accept the electrons.*

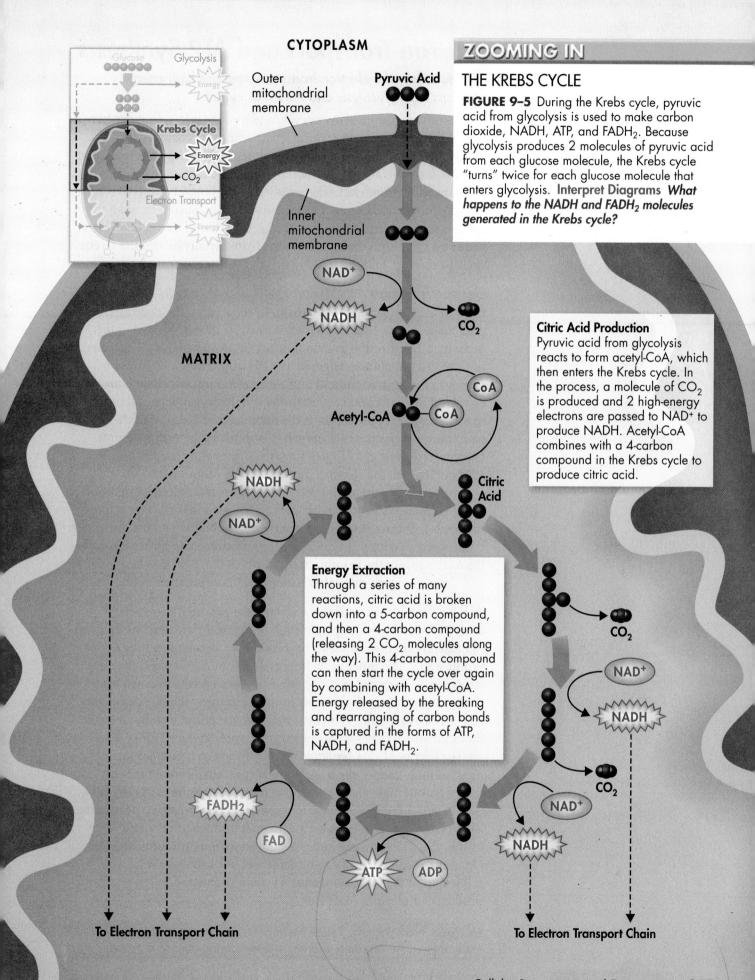

CYTOPLASM

Glucose Glycolysis

Krebs Cycle

Energy

CO₂

Electron Transport

Energy

O₂ H₂O

Outer mitochondrial membrane

Pyruvic Acid

Inner mitochondrial membrane

MATRIX

NAD⁺

NADH

CO₂

Acetyl-CoA CoA CoA

NADH

NAD⁺

Citric Acid

CO₂

NAD⁺

NADH

CO₂

NAD⁺

NADH

FADH₂

FAD

ATP ADP

To Electron Transport Chain

To Electron Transport Chain

ZOOMING IN

THE KREBS CYCLE

FIGURE 9–5 During the Krebs cycle, pyruvic acid from glycolysis is used to make carbon dioxide, NADH, ATP, and FADH₂. Because glycolysis produces 2 molecules of pyruvic acid from each glucose molecule, the Krebs cycle "turns" twice for each glucose molecule that enters glycolysis. **Interpret Diagrams** *What happens to the NADH and FADH₂ molecules generated in the Krebs cycle?*

Citric Acid Production
Pyruvic acid from glycolysis reacts to form acetyl-CoA, which then enters the Krebs cycle. In the process, a molecule of CO₂ is produced and 2 high-energy electrons are passed to NAD⁺ to produce NADH. Acetyl-CoA combines with a 4-carbon compound in the Krebs cycle to produce citric acid.

Energy Extraction
Through a series of many reactions, citric acid is broken down into a 5-carbon compound, and then a 4-carbon compound (releasing 2 CO₂ molecules along the way). This 4-carbon compound can then start the cycle over again by combining with acetyl-CoA. Energy released by the breaking and rearranging of carbon bonds is captured in the forms of ATP, NADH, and FADH₂.

Electron Transport and ATP Synthesis

🗝 *How does the electron transport chain use high-energy electrons from glycolysis and the Krebs cycle?*

Products from both the Krebs cycle and glycolysis feed into the last step of cellular respiration, the electron transport chain, as seen in **Figure 9–6.** Recall that glycolysis generates high-energy electrons that are passed to NAD^+, forming NADH. Those NADH molecules can enter the mitochondrion, where they join the NADH and $FADH_2$ generated by the Krebs cycle. The electrons are then passed from all those carriers to the electron transport chain. 🗝 **The electron transport chain uses the high-energy electrons from glycolysis and the Krebs cycle to convert ADP into ATP.**

Electron Transport NADH and $FADH_2$ pass their high-energy electrons to the electron transport chain. In eukaryotes, the electron transport chain is composed of a series of electron carriers located in the inner membrane of the mitochondrion. In prokaryotes, the same chain is in the cell membrane. High-energy electrons are passed from one carrier to the next. At the end of the electron transport chain is an enzyme that combines these electrons with hydrogen ions and oxygen to form water. Oxygen serves as the final electron acceptor of the electron transport chain. Thus, oxygen is essential for getting rid of low-energy electrons and hydrogen ions, the wastes of cellular respiration. Without oxygen, the electron transport chain cannot function.

Every time 2 high-energy electrons pass down the electron transport chain, their energy is used to transport hydrogen ions (H^+) across the membrane. During electron transport, H^+ ions build up in the intermembrane space, making it positively charged relative to the matrix. Similarly, the matrix side of the membrane, from which those H^+ ions have been taken, is now negatively charged compared to the intermembrane space.

ATP Production How does the cell use the potential energy from charge differences built up as a result of electron transport? As in photosynthesis, the cell uses a process known as chemiosmosis to produce ATP. The inner mitochondrial membrane contains enzymes known as ATP synthases. The charge difference across the membrane forces H^+ ions through channels in these enzymes, actually causing the ATP synthases to spin. With each rotation, the enzyme grabs an ADP molecule and attaches a phosphate group, producing ATP.

The beauty of this system is the way in which it couples the movement of high-energy electrons with the production of ATP. Every time a pair of high-energy electrons moves down the electron transport chain, the energy is used to move H^+ ions across the membrane. These ions then rush back across the membrane with enough force to spin the ATP synthase and generate enormous amounts of ATP. On average, each pair of high-energy electrons that moves down the full length of the electron transport chain provides enough energy to produce 3 molecules of ATP.

In Your Notebook *Relate the importance of oxygen in cellular respiration to the reason you breathe faster during intense exercise.*

BIOLOGY.com ▶ Search (Lesson 9.2) GO • Art Review • Tutor Tube

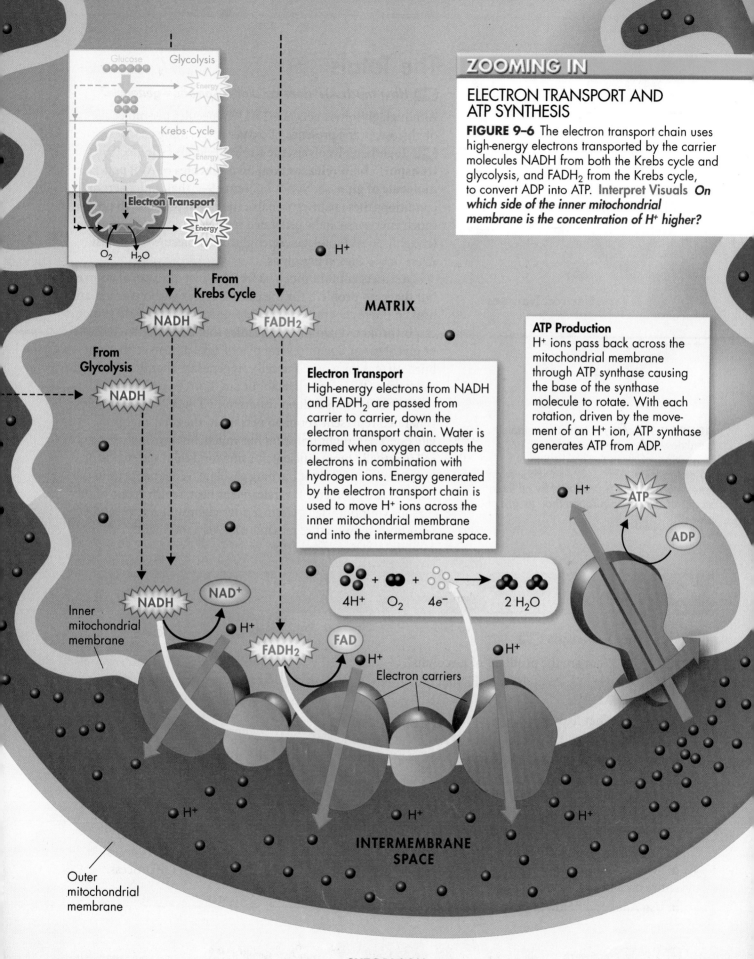

ELECTRON TRANSPORT AND ATP SYNTHESIS

FIGURE 9–6 The electron transport chain uses high-energy electrons transported by the carrier molecules NADH from both the Krebs cycle and glycolysis, and $FADH_2$ from the Krebs cycle, to convert ADP into ATP. **Interpret Visuals** *On which side of the inner mitochondrial membrane is the concentration of H+ higher?*

Glucose
Glycolysis
Energy

Krebs·Cycle
Energy
CO_2

Electron Transport
Energy
O_2 H_2O

H^+

From Krebs Cycle

NADH $FADH_2$

MATRIX

From Glycolysis

NADH

Electron Transport
High-energy electrons from NADH and $FADH_2$ are passed from carrier to carrier, down the electron transport chain. Water is formed when oxygen accepts the electrons in combination with hydrogen ions. Energy generated by the electron transport chain is used to move H+ ions across the inner mitochondrial membrane and into the intermembrane space.

ATP Production
H+ ions pass back across the mitochondrial membrane through ATP synthase causing the base of the synthase molecule to rotate. With each rotation, driven by the movement of an H+ ion, ATP synthase generates ATP from ADP.

H^+ ATP

$4H^+$ + O_2 + $4e^-$ → $2 H_2O$

ADP

NADH NAD^+

Inner mitochondrial membrane

H^+

$FADH_2$ FAD

H^+

H^+

Electron carriers

H^+

Outer mitochondrial membrane

H^+ H^+ H^+

INTERMEMBRANE SPACE

CYTOPLASM

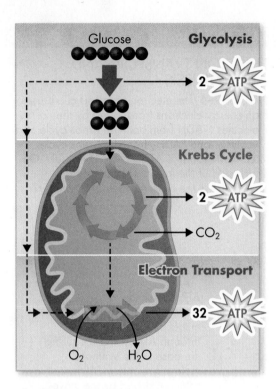

FIGURE 9–7 Energy Totals The complete breakdown of glucose through cellular respiration results in the production of 36 molecules of ATP. **Calculate** *How many times more energy is produced by all three stages of cellular respiration than by glycolysis alone?* MATH

The Totals

🔑 How much ATP does cellular respiration generate?

Although glycolysis nets just 2 ATP molecules per molecule of glucose, in the presence of oxygen, everything changes. 🔑 **Together, glycolysis, the Krebs cycle, and the electron transport chain release about 36 molecules of ATP per molecule of glucose.** Notice in **Figure 9–7** that under aerobic conditions these pathways enable the cell to produce 18 times as much energy as can be generated by anaerobic glycolysis alone (roughly 36 ATP molecules per glucose molecule versus just 2 ATP molecules in glycolysis).

Our diets contain much more than just glucose, of course, but that's no problem for the cell. Complex carbohydrates are broken down to simple sugars like glucose. Lipids and proteins can be broken down into molecules that enter the Krebs cycle or glycolysis at one of several places. Like a furnace that can burn oil, gas, or wood, the cell can generate chemical energy in the form of ATP from just about any source.

How efficient is cellular respiration? The 36 ATP molecules generated represent about 36 percent of the total energy of glucose. That might not seem like much, but it means that the cell is actually more efficient at using food than the engine of a typical automobile is at burning gasoline. What happens to the remaining 64 percent? It is released as heat, which is one of the reasons your body feels warmer after vigorous exercise, and why your body temperature remains 37°C day and night.

9.2 Assessment

Review Key Concepts 🔑

1. a. Review What are the products of glycolysis?

   b. Compare and Contrast How is the function of NAD^+ similar to that of $NADP^+$?

2. a. Review What happens to pyruvic acid in the Krebs cycle?

   b. Interpret Visuals Look at **Figure 9–5** and list the products of the Krebs cycle. What happens to each of these products?

3. a. Review How does the electron transport chain use the high-energy electrons from glycolysis and the Krebs cycle?

   b. Relate Cause and Effect How does the cell use the charge differences that build up across the inner mitochondrial membrane during cellular respiration?

4. a. Review How many molecules of ATP are produced in the entire breakdown of glucose?

   b. Use Analogies How is the cell like a furnace?

Apply the Big idea

Cellular Basis of Life

5. As you have learned, cellular respiration is a process by which cells transform energy stored in the bonds of food molecules into the bonds of ATP. What does the body do with all of the ATP this process generates? Review the characteristics of life in Chapter 1 and explain why ATP is necessary for each life process.

Biology & Society

Should Creatine Supplements Be Regulated?

ATP is the chemical compound that gives muscles the energy to contract, but the amount of ATP in most muscle cells is only enough for a few seconds of activity. Muscle cells have a chemical trick, however, that enables them to sustain maximum effort for several more seconds. They attach phosphate groups to a compound called creatine. As they contract, the cells quickly transfer phosphate from creatine to ADP, producing enough ATP to keep working. The creatine phosphate in skeletal muscles effectively doubles or triples the amount of ATP available for intense exercise.

If a little creatine is good, then more creatine would be even better, right? That's what many athletes think and that's why they take creatine supplements. Some studies do suggest that creatine may increase the body's capacity for strong, short-term muscle contractions. As a reason to regulate the use of creatine, however, critics point to potentially serious side effects—such as liver and kidney damage—when creatine is overused.

Because creatine occurs naturally in the body and in foods, testing for creatine use is nearly impossible; so, creatine is *not* banned in major sports leagues. However, due to a lack of long-term studies, the NCAA prohibits coaches from giving creatine to college athletes. Some schools argue that creatine should be banned altogether.

The Viewpoints

Creatine Supplements Should Not Be Regulated Taken in recommended doses, creatine helps build muscle strength and performance. Creatine supplements may help athletes train longer and build strength. No serious side effects have been reported in people who follow the instructions on container labels. Of course, anything can be harmful when abused, but creatine should not be treated any differently from other substances such as caffeine or sugar.

Creatine Supplements Should Be Regulated
Scientists know that creatine can cause severe health problems when abused. But even when used properly, creatine is known to cause some problems, such as dehydration and stomach upset. There have been no adequate studies on creatine use by people younger than 18, and there are no good studies of its long-term effects. For these reasons, creatine supplements should be regulated like cigarettes and alcohol—no one under the age of 18 should be allowed to buy them, and schools should have the right to regulate or prohibit their use by athletes.

Research and Decide

1. Analyze the Viewpoints Learn more about this issue by consulting library or Internet resources. Then, list the key arguments of the proponents and critics of creatine use.

2. Form an Opinion Should creatine be regulated? Research examples of high schools or colleges that have banned creatine use by athletes. What were the reasons for these decisions? Do you agree with them?

Fermentation

Key Questions

🔑 How do organisms generate energy when oxygen is not available?

🔑 How does the body produce ATP during different stages of exercise?

Vocabulary

fermentation

Taking Notes

Outline Before you read, make an outline using the green and blue headings in the text. As you read, fill in notes under each heading.

THINK ABOUT IT We are air-breathing organisms, and we use oxygen to release chemical energy from the food we eat. But what if oxygen is not around? What happens when you hold your breath and dive under water, or use up oxygen so quickly that you cannot replace it fast enough? Do your cells simply stop working? And, what about microorganisms that live in places where oxygen is not available? Is there a pathway that allows cells to extract energy from food in the absence of oxygen?

Fermentation

🔑 **How do organisms generate energy when oxygen is not available?**

Recall from earlier in this chapter that two benefits of glycolysis are that it can produce ATP quickly and that it does not require oxygen. However, when a cell generates large amounts of ATP from glycolysis, it runs into a problem. In just a few seconds, all of the cell's available NAD^+ molecules are filled up with electrons. Without oxygen, the electron transport chain does not run, so there is nowhere for the NADH molecules to deposit their electrons. Thus, NADH does not get converted back to NAD^+. Without NAD^+, the cell cannot keep glycolysis going, and ATP production stops. That's where a process called fermentation comes in.

When oxygen is not present, glycolysis is followed by a pathway that makes it possible to continue to produce ATP without oxygen. The combined process of this pathway and glycolysis is called **fermentation.** 🔑 **In the absence of oxygen, fermentation releases energy from food molecules by producing ATP.**

During fermentation, cells convert NADH to NAD^+ by passing high-energy electrons back to pyruvic acid. This action converts NADH back into the electron carrier NAD^+, allowing glycolysis to produce a steady supply of ATP. Fermentation is an anaerobic process that occurs in the cytoplasm of cells. Sometimes, glycolysis and fermentation are together referred to as anaerobic respiration. There are two slightly different forms of the process—alcoholic fermentation and lactic acid fermentation, as seen in **Figure 9–8.**

In Your Notebook *Make a compare/contrast table in which you compare alcoholic fermentation to lactic acid fermentation.*

Alcoholic Fermentation Yeasts and a few other microorganisms use alcoholic fermentation, which produces ethyl alcohol and carbon dioxide. A summary of alcoholic fermentation after glycolysis is

$$\text{Pyruvic acid} + \text{NADH} \longrightarrow \text{Alcohol} + CO_2 + NAD^+$$

Alcoholic fermentation is used to produce alcoholic beverages. It is also the process that causes bread dough to rise. When yeast cells in the dough run out of oxygen, the dough begins to ferment, giving off tiny bubbles of carbon dioxide. These bubbles form the air spaces you see in a slice of bread. The small amount of alcohol produced in the dough evaporates when the bread is baked.

Lactic Acid Fermentation Most organisms carry out fermentation using a chemical reaction that converts pyruvic acid to lactic acid. Unlike alcoholic fermentation, lactic acid fermentation does not give off carbon dioxide. However, like alcoholic fermentation, lactic acid fermentation also regenerates NAD^+ so that glycolysis can continue. Lactic acid fermentation after glycolysis can be summarized as

$$\text{Pyruvic acid} + \text{NADH} \longrightarrow \text{Lactic acid} + NAD^+$$

Certain bacteria that produce lactic acid as a waste product during fermentation are important to industry. For example, prokaryotes are used in the production of a wide variety of foods and beverages— such as cheese, yogurt, buttermilk, and sour cream—to which the acid contributes the familiar sour taste. Pickles, sauerkraut, and kimchi are also produced using lactic acid fermentation.

Humans are lactic acid fermenters. During brief periods without oxygen, many of the cells in our bodies are capable of producing ATP by lactic acid fermentation. The cells best adapted to doing that, however, are muscle cells, which often need very large supplies of ATP for rapid bursts of activity.

FIGURE 9–8 Fermentation In alcoholic fermentation, pyruvic acid produced by glycolysis is converted into alcohol and carbon dioxide. Lactic acid fermentation converts the pyruvic acid to lactic acid. **Compare and Contrast** *What reactants and products do the two types of fermentation have in common?*

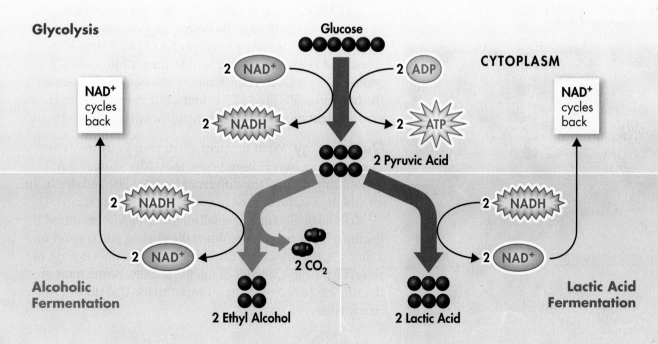

Quick Lab
GUIDED INQUIRY

How Does Exercise Affect Disposal of Wastes From Cellular Respiration?

① Label two test tubes A and B. Put 10 mL of water and a few drops of bromthymol blue solution in each test tube. Carbon dioxide causes bromthymol blue to turn yellow or green.

② Your partner will time you during this step. When your partner says "go," slowly blow air through a straw into the bottom of test tube A. **CAUTION:** *Do not inhale through the straw.*

③ When the solution changes color, your partner should say "stop" and then record how long the color change took.

④ Jog in place for 2 minutes. **CAUTION:** *Do not do this if you have a medical condition that interferes with exercise. If you feel faint or dizzy, stop immediately and sit down.*

⑤ Repeat steps 2–4 using test tube B.

⑥ Trade roles with your partner. Repeat steps 1 through 5.

Analyze and Conclude

1. Analyze Data How did exercise affect the time it took the solution to change color?

2. Infer What process in your body produces carbon dioxide? How does exercise affect this process?

FIGURE 9–9 Exercise and Energy
During a race, runners rely on the energy supplied by ATP to make it to the finish line. **Apply Concepts** *At the beginning of a race, what is the principal source of energy for the runners' muscles?*

Energy and Exercise

🔑 How does the body produce ATP during different stages of exercise?

Bang! The starter's pistol goes off, and the runners push off their starting blocks and sprint down the track, as seen in **Figure 9–9.** The initial burst of energy soon fades, and the runners settle down to a steady pace. After the runners hit the finish line, they walk around slowly and breathe deeply to catch their breath.

Let's look at what happens at each stage of the race in terms of the pathways the body uses to release energy. Humans have three main sources of ATP: ATP already in muscles, ATP made by lactic acid fermentation, and ATP produced by cellular respiration. At the beginning of a race, the body uses all three ATP sources, but stored ATP and lactic acid fermentation can supply energy only for a limited time.

Quick Energy What happens when your body needs lots of energy in a hurry? In response to sudden danger, quick actions might make the difference between life and death. To an athlete, a sudden burst of speed might win a race.

Cells normally contain small amounts of ATP produced during cellular respiration. When the starting gun goes off in a footrace, the muscles of the runners contain only enough of this ATP for a few seconds of intense activity. Before most of the runners have passed the 50-meter mark, that store of ATP is nearly gone.

At this point, the runners' muscle cells are producing most of their ATP by lactic acid fermentation, which can usually supply enough ATP to last about 90 seconds. In a 200- or 300-meter sprint, this may be just enough to reach the finish line.

Fermentation produces lactic acid as a byproduct. When the race is over, the only way to get rid of lactic acid is in a chemical pathway that requires extra oxygen. For that reason, you can think of a quick sprint as building up an oxygen debt that a runner has to repay with plenty of heavy breathing after the race. An intense effort that lasts just 10 or 20 seconds may produce an oxygen debt that requires several minutes of huffing and puffing to clear. ⚷ **For short, quick bursts of energy, the body uses ATP already in muscles as well as ATP made by lactic acid fermentation.**

Long-Term Energy What happens if a race is longer? How does your body generate the ATP it needs to run 2 kilometers or more, or to play in a soccer game that lasts more than an hour? ⚷ **For exercise longer than about 90 seconds, cellular respiration is the only way to continue generating a supply of ATP.** Cellular respiration releases energy more slowly than fermentation does, which is why even well-conditioned athletes have to pace themselves during a long race or over the course of a game. Your body stores energy in muscle and other tissues in the form of the carbohydrate glycogen. These stores of glycogen are usually enough to last for 15 or 20 minutes of activity. After that, your body begins to break down other stored molecules, including fats, for energy. This is one reason why aerobic forms of exercise such as running, dancing, and swimming are so beneficial for weight control. Some organisms, like the bear in **Figure 9–10,** count on energy stored in fat to get them through long periods without food.

MYSTERY CLUE

Whales rely on lactic acid fermentation for much of their energy requirements during a deep dive. If they can't inhale to repay their oxygen debt, what are they doing with all of the lactic acid produced by fermentation?

FIGURE 9–10 Energy Storage Hibernating animals like this brown bear in Alaska rely on stored fat for energy when they sleep through the winter. **Predict** *How will this bear look different when it wakes up from hibernation?*

9.3 Assessment

Review Key Concepts ⚷

1. a. Review Name the two main types of fermentation.

   b. Compare and Contrast How are alcoholic fermentation and lactic acid fermentation similar? How are they different?

2. a. Review Why do runners breathe heavily after a sprint race?

   b. Sequence List the body's sources of energy in the order in which they are used during a long-distance race.

PRACTICE PROBLEM

3. You have opened a bakery, selling bread made according to your family's secret recipe. Unfortunately, most customers find the bread too heavy. Review what you have learned about chemical reactions in Chapter 2 and make a list of factors such as temperature that might affect the enzyme-catalyzed fermentation reaction involved in baking bread. Predict how each factor will affect the rate of fermentation and propose a solution for making the bread lighter by adding more bubbles to your family bread recipe.

Real-World Lab

Pre-Lab: Comparing Fermentation Rates of Sugars

Problem How does the type of sugar affect the rate of fermentation?

Materials probe interface, gas pressure probe, hot plate, 400-mL beaker, thermometer, ring stand, test-tube clamp, medium test tube, test-tube rack, sugar solution, yeast suspension, pipettes, vegetable oil, 1-hole rubber stopper, plastic tubing with lock fitting

Lab Manual Chapter 9 Lab

Skills Focus Predict, Measure, Analyze Data, Infer

Connect to the **Big idea** In most cells, the pathways that release energy from food start with the conversion of glucose to pyruvic acid. This process does not require oxygen. When oxygen is present, however, pyruvic acid can react to form acetyl-CoA, which is used in the second stage of cellular respiration. When oxygen is not present, the pyruvic acid can be used in an anaerobic pathway. This alternate pathway from glucose to ATP is called fermentation. In this lab, you will use yeast to ferment sugars and compare the rates of fermentation.

Background Questions

a. Review What is the importance of the NAD^+ that is produced during the fermentation of pyruvic acid?

b. Review What other products are produced besides NAD^+ when yeast ferment sugar?

c. Compare and Contrast How are simple sugars different from disaccharides? (If needed, review Lesson 2.3 in your textbook.)

d. Use Analogies What do fermentation and a detour that drivers must use when roads are closed have in common?

Pre-Lab Questions

Preview the procedure in the lab manual.

1. Infer Why do you think you will add a layer of vegetable oil above the sugar and yeast mixture?

2. Relate Cause and Effect Explain why it is possible to compare the rates of fermentation by measuring gas pressure in the test tubes.

3. Predict Which of the sugars do you think will have the highest rate of fermentation, and why?

BIOLOGY.com   Search   Chapter 9   GO

Visit Chapter 9 online to test yourself on chapter content as well as find activities to help you learn.

Untamed Science Video Go underwater with the Untamed Science crew to discover why marine mammals can stay submerged for such a long time.

Data Analysis Analyze the role of lactic acid in exercise and learn about its effects on athletic performance.

Tutor Tube Improve your understanding of respiration by working "backward" from a breath of oxygen.

Art Review Review the components of electron transport and ATP synthesis.

InterActive Art See glycolysis and the Krebs cycle in action.

Art in Motion See how matter and energy cycle between photosynthesis and respiration.

9 Study Guide

Big idea Cellular Basis of Life

Organisms obtain the energy they need from the breakdown of food molecules by cellular respiration and fermentation.

9.1 Cellular Respiration: An Overview

🔑 Organisms get the energy they need from food.

🔑 Cellular respiration is the process that releases energy from food in the presence of oxygen.

🔑 Photosynthesis removes carbon dioxide from the atmosphere, and cellular respiration puts it back. Photosynthesis releases oxygen into the atmosphere, and cellular respiration uses that oxygen to release energy from food.

calorie (250)
cellular respiration (251)
aerobic (252)
anaerobic (252)

9.2 The Process of Cellular Respiration

🔑 During glycolysis, 1 molecule of glucose, a 6-carbon compound, is transformed into 2 molecules of pyruvic acid, a 3-carbon compound.

🔑 During the Krebs cycle, pyruvic acid is broken down into carbon dioxide in a series of energy-extracting reactions.

🔑 The electron transport chain uses the high-energy electrons from glycolysis and the Krebs cycle to convert ADP into ATP.

🔑 Together, glycolysis, the Krebs cycle, and the electron transport chain release about 36 molecules of ATP per molecule of glucose.

glycolysis (254)
NAD$^+$ (255)
Krebs cycle (256)
matrix (256)

9.3 Fermentation

🔑 In the absence of oxygen, fermentation releases energy from food molecules by producing ATP.

🔑 For short, quick bursts of energy, the body uses ATP already in muscles as well as ATP made by lactic acid fermentation.

🔑 For exercise longer than about 90 seconds, cellular respiration is the only way to continue generating a supply of ATP.

fermentation (262)

Think Visually Using the information in this chapter, complete the following compare/contrast table about cellular respiration and fermentation:

Comparing Cellular Respiration and Fermentation		
Characteristic	Cellular Respiration	Fermentation
Starting reactants	1	2
Pathways involved	3	4
End products	5	6
Number of ATP molecules produced	7	8

9 Assessment

9.1 Cellular Respiration: An Overview

Understand Key Concepts

1. Cells use the energy available in food to make a final energy-rich compound called
   - **a.** water.
   - **b.** glucose.
   - **c.** ATP.
   - **d.** ADP.

2. Each gram of glucose contains approximately how much energy?
   - **a.** 1 calorie
   - **b.** 1 Calorie
   - **c.** 4 calories
   - **d.** 4 Calories

3. The process that releases energy from food in the presence of oxygen is
   - **a.** synthesis.
   - **b.** cellular respiration.
   - **c.** ATP synthase.
   - **d.** photosynthesis.

4. The first step in releasing the energy of glucose in the cell is known as
   - **a.** fermentation.
   - **b.** glycolysis.
   - **c.** the Krebs cycle.
   - **d.** electron transport.

5. Which of the following organisms perform cellular respiration?

   A   B   C   D

   - **a.** only C
   - **b.** only A and C
   - **c.** only B and D
   - **d.** all of the above

6. What is a calorie? Briefly explain how cells use a high-calorie molecule such as glucose.

7. Write a chemical equation for cellular respiration. Label the molecules involved.

8. What percentage of the energy contained in a molecule of glucose is captured in the bonds of ATP at the end of glycolysis?

9. What does it mean if a process is "anaerobic"? Which part of cellular respiration is anaerobic?

Think Critically

10. **Use Analogies** Why is comparing cellular respiration to a burning fire a poor analogy?

11. **Compare and Contrast** Why are cellular respiration and photosynthesis considered opposite reactions?

9.2 The Process of Cellular Respiration

Understand Key Concepts

12. The net gain of energy from glycolysis is
    - **a.** 4 ATP molecules.
    - **b.** 2 ATP molecules.
    - **c.** 8 ADP molecules.
    - **d.** 3 pyruvic acid molecules.

13. The Krebs cycle takes place within the
    - **a.** chloroplast.
    - **b.** nucleus.
    - **c.** mitochondrion.
    - **d.** cytoplasm.

14. The electron transport chain uses the high-energy electrons from the Krebs cycle to
    - **a.** produce glucose.
    - **b.** move H^+ ions across the inner mitochondrial membrane.
    - **c.** convert acetyl-CoA to citric acid.
    - **d.** convert glucose to pyruvic acid.

15. How is glucose changed during glycolysis?

16. What is NAD^+? Why is it important?

17. Summarize what happens during the Krebs cycle. What happens to high-energy electrons generated during the Krebs cycle?

18. How is ATP synthase involved in making energy available to the cell?

Think Critically

19. **Compare and Contrast** How is the function of NAD^+ in cellular respiration similar to that of $NADP^+$ in photosynthesis?

20. **Compare and Contrast** Where is the electron transport chain found in a eukaryotic cell? Where is it found in a prokaryotic cell?

21. **Sequence** Explain how the products of glycolysis and the Krebs cycle are related to the electron transport chain. Draw a flowchart that shows the relationships between these products and the electron transport chain.

22. **Use Models** Draw and label a mitochondrion surrounded by cytoplasm. Indicate where glycolysis, the Krebs cycle, and the electron transport chain occur in a eukaryotic cell.

Understand Key Concepts

23. Because fermentation takes place in the absence of oxygen, it is said to be
    a. aerobic.
    b. anaerobic.
    c. cyclic.
    d. oxygen-rich.

24. The process carried out by yeast that causes bread dough to rise is
    a. alcoholic fermentation.
    b. lactic acid fermentation.
    c. cellular respiration.
    d. yeast mitosis.

25. During heavy exercise, the buildup of lactic acid in muscle cells results in
    a. cellular respiration.
    b. oxygen debt.
    c. fermentation.
    d. the Krebs cycle.

26. How are fermentation and cellular respiration similar?

27. Write equations to show how lactic acid fermentation compares with alcoholic fermentation. Which reactant(s) do they have in common?

Think Critically

28. **Infer** Certain types of bacteria thrive in conditions that lack oxygen. What does that fact indicate about the way they obtain energy?

29. **Infer** To function properly, heart muscle cells require a steady supply of oxygen. After a heart attack, small amounts of lactic acid are present. What does this evidence suggest about the nature of a heart attack?

30. **Predict** In certain cases, regular exercise causes an increase in the number of mitochondria in muscle cells. How might that situation improve an individual's ability to perform energy-requiring activities?

31. **Formulate Hypotheses** Yeast cells can carry out both fermentation and cellular respiration, depending on whether oxygen is present. In which case would you expect yeast cells to grow more rapidly? Explain.

32. **Apply Concepts** Carbon monoxide (CO) molecules bring the electron transport chain in a mitochondrion to a stop by binding to an electron carrier. Use this information to explain why carbon monoxide gas kills organisms.

solve the CHAPTER MYSTERY

DIVING WITHOUT A BREATH

To be able to sustain regular 45-minute intervals underwater, whales employ a number of special mechanisms. For example, whale blood is very tolerant of CO_2 buildup that results from the Krebs cycle. This allows whales to stay underwater for an extended period without triggering the reflex to surface. The Krebs cycle and electron transport rely on oxygen, of course. And once the oxygen is used—and it's used quickly!—whale muscles must rely on lactic acid fermentation to generate energy. In humans, lactic acid causes the pH of the blood to drop. If the blood gets too acidic, a dangerous condition called acidosis can occur. Whale muscles are extremely tolerant of lactic acid. The lactic acid remains in the muscles without causing acidosis. When whales resurface after a long dive, they inhale oxygen that clears away the lactic acid buildup.

1. **Relate Cause and Effect** Why must whales have blood that is tolerant of CO_2?

2. **Predict** Myoglobin, a molecule very similar to hemoglobin, stores oxygen in muscles. Would you expect to find more or less myoglobin than average in the muscle tissue of whales if you were to examine it under the microscope?

3. **Infer** How might being able to dive into very deep water be an advantage for whales such as the sperm whale?

4. **Connect to the Big idea** When swimming near the surface, whales breathe every time their heads break out of the water. How do you think the energy pathways used during this type of swimming differ from the ones used during long dives?

Connecting Concepts

Use Science Graphics

Use the nutritional information below to answer questions 33–35.

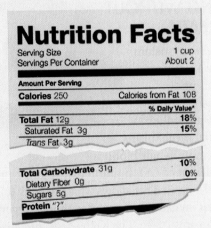

Nutrition Facts

Serving Size   1 cup
Servings Per Container   About 2

Amount Per Serving

Calories 250   Calories from Fat 108

                         % Daily Value*

Total Fat 12g   **18%**
   Saturated Fat 3g   **15%**
   Trans Fat 3g

Total Carbohydrate 31g   **10%**
   Dietary Fiber 0g   **0%**
   Sugars 5g
Protein "?"

33. Apply Concepts On average, how many Calories are there in 1 gram of a lipid, carbohydrate, and protein? Why the differences?

34. Calculate How many grams of protein must there be in order to account for the number of Calories per serving indicated? **MATH**

35. Calculate Look at the percent daily value column on the food label. The percent daily value represents the proportion of a typical day's Calories that, on average, should be contributed from the category listed. For example, 31 g of carbohydrates is approximately 10 percent of a daily value. So, a typical person's daily diet should contain about 310 g of carbohydrates. How many Calories does this represent? What percentage of a typical 2000-Calories-per-day diet should therefore come from carbohydrates? **MATH**

Write About Science

36. Explanation Expand the analogy of deposits and withdrawals of money that was used in the chapter to write a short paragraph that explains cellular respiration. (*Hint:* Think about what "inputs" or deposits are required and what "outputs" or returns are produced at each step.)

37. Assess the Big idea Draw a sketch that shows respiration (breathing) at the organismal, or whole animal, level. Draw another sketch that shows the overall process of cellular respiration. How do your sketches show breathing and cellular respiration as related processes?

Analyzing Data

The volume of oxygen uptake was measured in liters per minute (L/min). The scientist collecting the data was interested in how the volume of oxygen breathed in was affected as the difficulty level of the exercise (measured in watts) increased. The data are summarized in the accompanying graph.

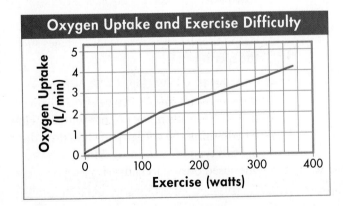

Oxygen Uptake and Exercise Difficulty

(y-axis: Oxygen Uptake (L/min), 0 to 5)
(x-axis: Exercise (watts), 0 to 400)

38. Interpret Graphs Based on the graph, at what level of exercise difficulty did oxygen uptake reach 3 L/min?
   a. approximately 100 watts
   b. approximately 200 watts
   c. between 200 and 300 watts
   d. between 300 and 400 watts

39. Formulate Hypotheses Which of the following is a valid hypothesis that explains the trend shown on the graph?
   a. As exercise becomes more difficult, the body relies more and more on lactic acid fermentation.
   b. Exercise below a level of 100 watts does not require increased oxygen uptake.
   c. Difficult exercise requires additional oxygen intake in order to generate extra ATP for muscle cells.
   d. The human body cannot maintain exercise levels above 500 watts.

Standardized Test Prep

Multiple Choice

1. What raw materials are needed for cellular respiration?
   A glucose and carbon dioxide
   B glucose and oxygen
   C carbon dioxide and oxygen
   D oxygen and lactic acid

2. During the Krebs cycle
   A hydrogen ions and oxygen form water.
   B the cell releases a small amount of energy through fermentation.
   C each glucose molecule is broken down into 2 molecules of pyruvic acid.
   D pyruvic acid is broken down into carbon dioxide in a series of reactions.

3. Which substance is needed to begin the process of glycolysis?
   A ATP   C pyruvic acid
   B NADP   D carbon dioxide

4. In eukaryotic cells, MOST of cellular respiration takes place in the
   A nuclei.   C mitochondria.
   B cytoplasm.   D cell walls.

5. Which substance is broken down during the process of glycolysis?
   A carbon   C glucose
   B NAD^+ D pyruvic acid

6. The human body can use all of the following as energy sources EXCEPT
   A ATP in muscles.
   B glycolysis.
   C lactic acid fermentation.
   D alcoholic fermentation.

7. During cellular respiration, which of the following are released as byproducts?
   A CO_2 and O_2
   B H_2O and O_2
   C O_2 and H_2O
   D CO_2 and H_2O

8. Which of the following is an aerobic process?
   A the Krebs cycle   C alcoholic fermentation
   B glycolysis   D lactic acid fermentation

Questions 9 and 10

The graph below shows the rate of alcoholic fermentation for yeast at different temperatures.

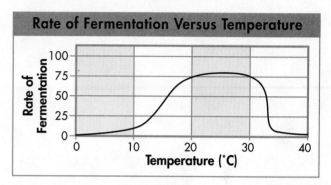

Rate of Fermentation Versus Temperature

9. According to the graph, what is the relationship between the rate of fermentation and temperature?
   A The rate of fermentation continually increases as temperature increases.
   B The rate of fermentation continually decreases as temperature increases.
   C The rate of fermentation increases with temperature at first, and then it rapidly decreases.
   D The rate of fermentation decreases with temperature at first, and then it rapidly increases.

10. Which statement could explain the data shown in the graph?
    A The molecules that regulate fermentation perform optimally at temperatures above 30°C.
    B The yeast begins releasing carbon dioxide at 30°C.
    C The yeast cannot survive above 30°C.
    D The molecules that regulate fermentation perform optimally at temperatures below 10°C.

Open-Ended Response

11. Explain how a sprinter gets energy during a 30-second race. Is the process aerobic or anaerobic? How does it compare to a long-distance runner getting energy during a 5-kilometer race?

If You Have Trouble With . . .										
Question	1	2	3	4	5	6	7	8	9	10	11
See Lesson	9.1	9.2	9.2	9.1	9.2	9.3	9.1	9.1	9.3	9.3	9.3

10 Cell Growth and Division

Growth, Development, and Reproduction

Q: How does a cell produce a new cell?

INSIDE:

- 10.1 Cell Growth, Division, and Reproduction
- 10.2 The Process of Cell Division
- 10.3 Regulating the Cell Cycle
- 10.4 Cell Differentiation

Embryonic cells from a whitefish blastula (LM 1250×)

CHAPTER MYSTERY

PET SHOP ACCIDENT

Julia stared into the salamander tank in horror. As an assistant in a pet shop, Julia had mistakenly put a small salamander in the same tank as a large one. Just as she realized her error, the large salamander attacked and bit off one of the small salamander's limbs.

Acting quickly, Julia scooped up the injured salamander and put it in its own tank. She was sure it would die before her shift ended. But she was wrong! Days passed...then weeks. Every time Julia checked on the salamander, she was more amazed at what she saw. How did the salamander's body react to losing a limb? As you read this chapter, look for clues to help you predict the salamander's fate. Think about the cell processes that would be involved. Then, solve the mystery.

Never Stop Exploring Your World.
Finding the solution to the Pet Shop mystery is only the beginning. Take a video field trip with the ecogeeks of Untamed Science to see where the mystery leads.

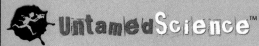

- Untamed Science Video   • Chapter Mystery

Cell Growth, Division, and Reproduction

Key Questions

🔑 What are some of the difficulties a cell faces as it increases in size?

🔑 How do asexual and sexual reproduction compare?

Vocabulary

cell division
asexual reproduction
sexual reproduction

Taking Notes

Outline As you read, create an outline about cell growth, division, and reproduction. As you read, fill in key phrases or sentences about each heading.

THINK ABOUT IT When a living thing grows, what happens to its cells? Does an organism get larger because each cell increases in size or because it produces more of them? In most cases, living things grow by producing more cells. What is there about growth that requires cells to divide and produce more of themselves?

Limits to Cell Size

🔑 What are some of the difficulties a cell faces as it increases in size?

Nearly all cells can grow by increasing in size, but eventually, most cells divide after growing to a certain point. There are two main reasons why cells divide rather than continuing to grow. 🔑 **The larger a cell becomes, the more demands the cell places on its DNA. In addition, a larger cell is less efficient in moving nutrients and waste materials across the cell membrane.**

Information "Overload" Living cells store critical information in a molecule known as DNA. As a cell grows, that information is used to build the molecules needed for cell growth. But as a cell increases in size, its DNA does not. If a cell were to grow too large, an "information crisis" would occur.

To get a better sense of information overload, compare a cell to a growing town. Suppose a small town has a library with a few thousand books. As more people move in, more people will borrow books. Sometimes, people may have to wait to borrow popular books. Similarly, a larger cell would make greater demands on its genetic "library." After a while, the DNA would no longer be able to serve the needs of the growing cell—it might be time to build a new library.

Exchanging Materials There is another critical reason why cell size is limited. Food, oxygen, and water enter a cell through its cell membrane. Waste products leave a cell in the same way. The rate at which this exchange takes place depends on the surface area of the cell, which is the total area of its cell membrane. The rate at which food and oxygen are used up and waste products are produced depends on the cell's volume. Understanding the relationship between a cell's surface area and its volume is the key to understanding why cells must divide rather than continue to grow.

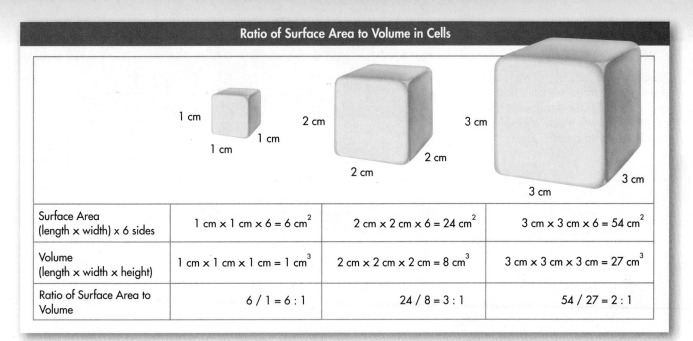

Ratio of Surface Area to Volume in Cells			
Surface Area (length × width) × 6 sides	1 cm × 1 cm × 6 = 6 cm^2	2 cm × 2 cm × 6 = 24 cm^2	3 cm × 3 cm × 6 = 54 cm^2
Volume (length × width × height)	1 cm × 1 cm × 1 cm = 1 cm^3	2 cm × 2 cm × 2 cm = 8 cm^3	3 cm × 3 cm × 3 cm = 27 cm^3
Ratio of Surface Area to Volume	6 / 1 = 6 : 1	24 / 8 = 3 : 1	54 / 27 = 2 : 1

▶ *Ratio of Surface Area to Volume* Imagine a cell that is shaped like a cube, like those shown in **Figure 10–1**. The formula for area ($l \times w$) is used to calculate the surface area. The formula for volume ($l \times w \times h$) is used to calculate the amount of space inside. By using a ratio of surface area to volume, you can see how the size of the cell's surface area grows compared to its volume.

Notice that for a cell with sides that measure 1 cm in length, the ratio of surface area to volume is 6/1 or 6 : 1. Increase the length of the cell's sides to 2 cm, and the ratio becomes 24/8 or 3 : 1. What if the length triples? The ratio of surface area to volume becomes 54/27 or 2 : 1. Notice that the surface area is not increasing as fast as the volume increases. For a growing cell, a decrease in the relative amount of cell membrane available creates serious problems.

FIGURE 10–1 Ratio of Surface Area to Volume As the length of the sides increases, the volume increases more than the surface area. **Interpret Tables** *What are the ratios comparing?*

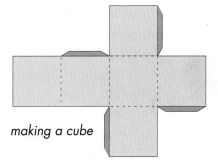

making a cube

Quick Lab
OPEN-ENDED INQUIRY

Modeling the Relationship Between Surface Area and Volume

❶ Use the drawing and grid paper to make patterns for a 6-cm cube, a 5-cm cube, a 4-cm cube, and a 3-cm cube.

❷ Cut out your patterns and fold them. Then use the tabs to tape or glue the sides together. Don't tape down the top side.

❸ Construct a data table to compare the volume, the surface area, and the ratio of surface area to volume of each cube.

❹ Use your data to calculate the number of 3-cm cubes that would fit in the same volume as the 6-cm cube. Also calculate the total surface area for the smaller cubes. MATH

Analyze and Conclude

1. Review Describe the function of a cell membrane and its relationship to what happens inside a cell.

2. Apply Concepts How does the surface area change when a large cell divides into smaller cells that have the same total volume?

GROWING PAINS

FIGURE 10–2 Lots of growth can mean lots of trouble—both in a town and in a cell. **Use Analogies** *How could cell growth create a problem that is similar to a traffic jam?*

▶ *Traffic Problems* To use the town analogy again, suppose the town has just a two-lane main street leading to the center of town. As the town grows, more and more traffic clogs the main street. It becomes increasingly difficult to move goods in and out.

A cell that continues to grow would experience similar problems. If a cell got too large, it would be more difficult to get sufficient amounts of oxygen and nutrients in and waste products out. This is another reason why cells do not continue to grow larger even if the organism does.

Division of the Cell Before it becomes too large, a growing cell divides, forming two "daughter" cells. The process by which a cell divides into two new daughter cells is called **cell division.**

Before cell division occurs, the cell replicates, or copies all of its DNA. This replication of DNA solves the problem of information overload because each daughter cell gets one complete copy of genetic information. Cell division also solves the problem of increasing size by reducing cell volume. Cell division results in an increase in the ratio of surface area to volume for each daughter cell. This allows for the efficient exchange of materials within a cell.

Cell Division and Reproduction

How do asexual and sexual reproduction compare?

Reproduction, the formation of new individuals, is one of the most important characteristics of living things. For an organism composed of just one cell, cell division can serve as a perfectly good form of reproduction. You don't have to meet someone else, conduct a courtship, or deal with rivals. All you have to do is to divide, and *presto*—there are two of you!

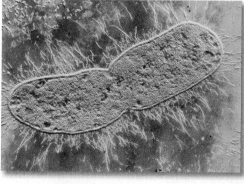

Bacterium
(TEM 32,800×)

Hydra
(LM 25×)

FIGURE 10–3 Asexual Reproduction Cell division leads to reproduction in single-celled organisms and some multicellular organisms. **Apply Concepts** *What do the offspring of each of these organisms have in common?*

Kalanchoe

Asexual Reproduction For many single-celled organisms, such as the bacterium in **Figure 10–3,** cell division is the only form of reproduction. The process can be relatively simple, efficient, and effective, enabling populations to increase in number very quickly. In most cases, the two cells produced by cell division are genetically identical to the cell that produced them. This kind of reproduction is called **asexual reproduction.** The production of genetically identical offspring from a single parent is known as asexual reproduction.

Asexual reproduction also occurs in many multicellular organisms. The small bud growing off the hydra will eventually break off and become an independent organism, an example of asexual reproduction in an animal. Each of the small shoots or plantlets on the tip of the kalanchoe leaf may also grow into a new plant.

Sexual Reproduction Unlike asexual reproduction, where cells separate to form a new individual, **sexual reproduction** involves the fusion of two separate parent cells. In sexual reproduction, offspring are produced by the fusion of special reproductive cells formed by each of two parents. Offspring produced by sexual reproduction inherit some of their genetic information from each parent. Most animals and plants reproduce sexually, and so do some single-celled organisms. You will learn more about the form of cell division that produces reproductive cells in Chapter 11.

BUILD Vocabulary

PREFIXES The prefix *a-* in *asexual* means "without." **Asexual reproduction** is reproduction without the fusion of reproductive cells.

In Your Notebook Use a Venn diagram to compare asexual and sexual reproduction.

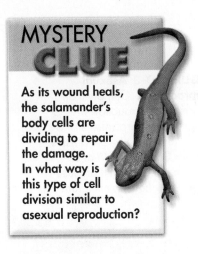

MYSTERY CLUE

As its wound heals, the salamander's body cells are dividing to repair the damage. In what way is this type of cell division similar to asexual reproduction?

Comparing Asexual and Sexual Reproduction You can see that each type of reproduction has its advantages and disadvantages when you look at each one as a strategy for survival. Species survive by reproducing. The better suited a species is to its environment, the greater its chance of survival.

For single-celled organisms, asexual reproduction is a survival strategy. When conditions are right, the faster they reproduce, the better their chance of survival over other organisms using the same resources. Having offspring that are genetically identical is also an advantage as long as conditions remain favorable. However, a lack of genetic diversity becomes a disadvantage when conditions change in ways that do not fit the characteristics of an organism.

Sexual reproduction is a different type of survival strategy. The process of finding a mate and the growth and development of offspring require more time. However, this can be an advantage for species that live in environments where seasonal changes affect weather conditions and food availability. Sexual reproduction also provides genetic diversity. If an environment changes, some offspring may have the right combination of characteristics needed to survive.

Some organisms reproduce both sexually and asexually. Yeasts, for example, are single-celled eukaryotes that use both strategies. They reproduce asexually most of the time. However, under certain conditions, they enter a sexual phase. The different advantages of each type of reproduction may help to explain why the living world includes organisms that reproduce sexually, those that reproduce asexually, and many organisms that do both.

10.1 Assessment

Review Key Concepts 🔑

1. a. Review Identify two reasons why a cell's growth is limited.

b. Explain As a cell's size increases, what happens to the ratio of its surface area to its volume?

c. Applying Concepts Why is a cell's surface area-to-volume ratio important?

2. a. Review What is asexual reproduction? What is sexual reproduction?

b. Explain What types of organisms reproduce sexually?

c. Summarize What are the advantages and disadvantages of both asexual and sexual reproduction?

VISUAL THINKING   MATH

3. The formula for finding the surface area of a sphere, such as a baseball or a basketball, is $A = 4\pi r^2$, where r is the radius. The formula for finding the volume of a sphere is $V = 4/3\pi r^3$.

a. Calculate Calculate the surface area and the volume of the baseball and the basketball. Then, write the ratio of surface area to volume for each sphere.

b. Infer If the baseball and basketball were cells, which would possess a larger ratio of area of cell membrane to cell volume?

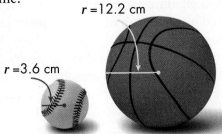

$r = 12.2$ cm

$r = 3.6$ cm

10.2 The Process of Cell Division

THINK ABOUT IT What role does cell division play in your life? You know from your own experience that living things grow, or increase in size, during particular stages of life or even throughout their lifetime. This growth clearly depends on the production of new cells through cell division. But what happens when you are finished growing? Does cell division simply stop? Think about what must happen when your body heals a cut or a broken bone. And finally, think about the every-day wear and tear on the cells of your skin, digestive system, and blood. Cell division has a role to play there, too.

Chromosomes

What is the role of chromosomes in cell division?

What do you think would happen if a cell were simply to split in two, without any advance preparation? The results might be disastrous, especially if some of the cell's essential genetic information wound up in one of the daughter cells, and not in the other. In order to make sure this doesn't happen, cells first make a complete copy of their genetic information before cell division begins.

Even a small cell like the bacterium *E. coli* has a tremendous amount of genetic information in the form of DNA. In fact, the total length of this bacterium's DNA molecule is 1.6 mm, roughly 1000 times longer than the cell itself. In terms of scale, imagine a 300-meter rope stuffed into a school backpack. Cells can handle such large molecules only by careful packaging. Genetic information is bundled into packages of DNA known as **chromosomes.**

Prokaryotic Chromosomes Prokaryotes lack nuclei and many of the organelles found in eukaryotes. Their DNA molecules are found in the cytoplasm along with most of the other contents of the cell. Most prokaryotes contain a single, circular DNA chromosome that contains all, or nearly all, of the cell's genetic information.

Key Questions

What is the role of chromosomes in cell division?

What are the main events of the cell cycle?

What events occur during each of the four phases of mitosis?

How do daughter cells split apart after mitosis?

Vocabulary

chromosome • chromatin • cell cycle • interphase • mitosis • cytokinesis • prophase • centromere • chromatid • centriole • metaphase • anaphase • telophase

Taking Notes

Two-Column Chart As you read, create a two-column chart. In the left column, make notes about what is happening in each stage of the cell cycle. In the right column, describe what the process looks like or draw pictures.

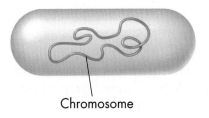

FIGURE 10–4 Prokaryotic Chromosome In most prokaryotes, a single chromosome holds most of the organism's DNA.

Chromosome

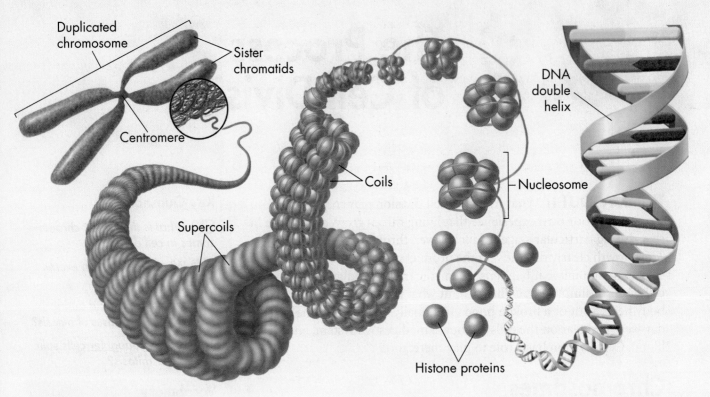

Duplicated chromosome

Sister chromatids

Centromere

Supercoils

Coils

Nucleosome

Histone proteins

DNA double helix

FIGURE 10–5 Eukaryotic Chromosome As a eukaryotic cell prepares for division, each chromosome coils more and more tightly to form a compact structure. **Interpret Visuals** *Which side of the diagram, left or right, shows the smallest structures, and which shows the largest?*

Eukaryotic Chromosomes Eukaryotic cells generally have much more DNA than prokaryotes have and, therefore, contain multiple chromosomes. Fruit flies, for example, have 8 chromosomes per cell, human cells have 46, and carrot cells have 18. The chromosomes in eukaryotic cells form a close association with histones, a type of protein. This complex of chromosome and protein is referred to as **chromatin.** DNA tightly coils around the histones, and together, the DNA and histone molecules form beadlike structures called nucleosomes. Nucleosomes pack together to form thick fibers, which condense even further during cell division. Usually the chromosome shape you see drawn is a duplicated chromosome with supercoiled chromatin, as shown in **Figure 10–5.**

Why do cells go to such lengths to package their DNA into chromosomes? One of the principal reasons is to ensure equal division of DNA when a cell divides. **Chromosomes make it possible to separate DNA precisely during cell division.**

In Your Notebook *Write instructions to build a eukaryotic chromosome.*

The Cell Cycle

What are the main events of the cell cycle?

Cells go through a series of events known as the **cell cycle** as they grow and divide. **During the cell cycle, a cell grows, prepares for division, and divides to form two daughter cells.** Each daughter cell then moves into a new cell cycle of activity, growth, and division.

The Prokaryotic Cell Cycle The prokaryotic cell cycle is a regular pattern of growth, DNA replication, and cell division that can take place very rapidly under ideal conditions. Researchers are only just beginning to understand how the cycle works in prokaryotes, and relatively little is known about its details. It is known that most prokaryotic cells begin to replicate, or copy, their DNA chromosomes once they have grown to a certain size. When DNA replication is complete, or nearly complete, the cell begins to divide.

The process of cell division in prokaryotes is a form of asexual reproduction known as binary fission. Once the chromosome has been replicated, the two DNA molecules attach to different regions of the cell membrane. A network of fibers forms between them, stretching from one side of the cell to the other. The fibers constrict and the cell is pinched inward, dividing the cytoplasm and chromosomes between two newly formed cells. Binary fission results in the production of two genetically identical cells.

The Eukaryotic Cell Cycle In contrast to prokaryotes, much more is known about the eukaryotic cell cycle. As you can see in **Figure 10–7,** the eukaryotic cell cycle consists of four phases: G_1, S, G_2, and M. The length of each part of the cell cycle—and the length of the entire cell cycle—varies depending on the type of cell.

At one time, biologists described the life of a cell as one cell division after another separated by an "in-between" period of growth called **interphase.** We now appreciate that a great deal happens in the time between cell divisions. Interphase is divided into three parts: G_1, S, and G_2.

▶ ***G_1 Phase: Cell Growth*** Cells do most of their growing during the G_1 phase. In this phase, cells increase in size and synthesize new proteins and organelles. The *G* in G_1 and G_2 stands for "gap," but the G_1 and G_2 phases are actually periods of intense growth and activity.

▶ ***S Phase: DNA Replication*** The G_1 phase is followed by the S phase. The *S* stands for "synthesis." During the S phase, new DNA is synthesized when the chromosomes are replicated. The cell at the end of the S phase contains twice as much DNA as it did at the beginning.

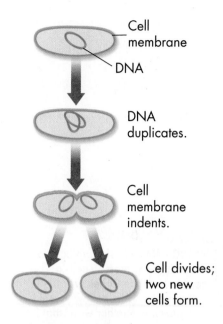

FIGURE 10–6 Binary Fission Cell division in a single-celled organism produces two genetically identical organisms.

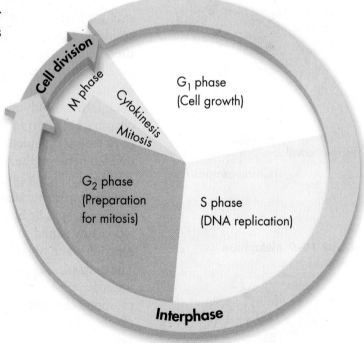

FIGURE 10–7 The Cell Cycle During the cell cycle, a cell grows, prepares for division, and divides to form two daughter cells. The cell cycle includes four phases—G_1, S, G_2, and M. **Infer** *During which phase or phases would you expect the amount of DNA in the cell to change?*

▶ **G₂ Phase: Preparing for Cell Division** When DNA replication is completed, the cell enters the G₂ phase. G₂ is usually the shortest of the three phases of interphase. During the G₂ phase, many of the organelles and molecules required for cell division are produced. When the events of the G₂ phase are completed, the cell is ready to enter the M phase and begin the process of cell division.

▶ **M Phase: Cell Division** The M phase of the cell cycle, which follows interphase, produces two daughter cells. The M phase takes its name from the process of mitosis. During the normal cell cycle, interphase can be quite long. In contrast, the process of cell division usually takes place quickly.

In eukaryotes, cell division occurs in two main stages. The first stage of the process, division of the cell nucleus, is called **mitosis** (my TOH sis). The second stage, the division of the cytoplasm, is called **cytokinesis** (sy toh kih NEE sis). In many cells, the two stages may overlap, so that cytokinesis begins while mitosis is still taking place.

Mitosis

🔑 *What events occur during each of the four phases of mitosis?*

Biologists divide the events of mitosis into four phases: prophase, metaphase, anaphase, and telophase. Depending on the type of cell, mitosis may last anywhere from a few minutes to several days. **Figure 10–8** through **Figure 10–11** show mitosis in an animal cell.

Prophase The first phase of mitosis, **prophase,** is usually the longest and may take up to half of the total time required to complete mitosis. 🔑 **During prophase, the genetic material inside the nucleus condenses and the duplicated chromosomes become visible. Outside the nucleus, a spindle starts to form.**

The duplicated strands of the DNA molecule can be seen to be attached along their length at an area called the **centromere.** Each DNA strand in the duplicated chromosome is referred to as a **chromatid** (KROH muh tid), or sister chromatid. When the process of mitosis is complete, the chromatids will have separated and been divided between the new daughter cells.

Also during prophase, the cell starts to build a spindle, a fanlike system of microtubules that will help to separate the duplicated chromosomes. Spindle fibers extend from a region called the centrosome, where tiny paired structures called **centrioles** are located. Plant cells lack centrioles, and organize spindles directly from their centrosome regions. The centrioles, which were duplicated during interphase, start to move toward opposite ends, or poles, of the cell. As prophase ends, the chromosomes coil more tightly, the nucleolus disappears, and the nuclear envelope breaks down.

Metaphase The second phase of mitosis, **metaphase,** is generally the shortest. 🔑 **During metaphase, the centromeres of the duplicated chromosomes line up across the center of the cell. Spindle fibers connect the centromere of each chromosome to the two poles of the spindle.**

BUILD Vocabulary

WORD ORIGINS The prefix *cyto-* in **cytokinesis** refers to cells and derives from the Greek word *kytos,* meaning "a hollow vessel." *Cytoplasm* is another word that has the same root.

FIGURE 10–8 Prophase

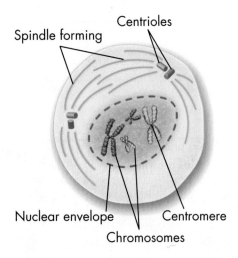

Spindle forming
Centrioles
Nuclear envelope
Centromere
Chromosomes

FIGURE 10–9 Metaphase

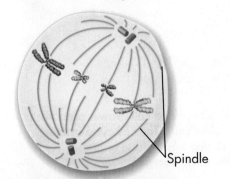

Spindle

Anaphase The third phase of mitosis, **anaphase,** begins when sister chromatids suddenly separate and begin to move apart. Once anaphase begins, each sister chromatid is now considered an individual chromosome. 🔑 **During anaphase, the chromosomes separate and move along spindle fibers to opposite ends of the cell.** Anaphase comes to an end when this movement stops and the chromosomes are completely separated into two groups.

Telophase Following anaphase is **telophase,** the fourth and final phase of mitosis. 🔑 **During telophase, the chromosomes, which were distinct and condensed, begin to spread out into a tangle of chromatin.** A nuclear envelope re-forms around each cluster of chromosomes. The spindle begins to break apart, and a nucleolus becomes visible in each daughter nucleus. Mitosis is complete. However, the process of cell division has one more step to go.

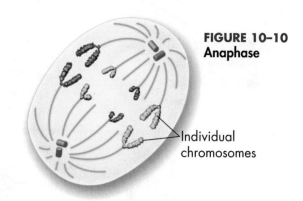

FIGURE 10–10
Anaphase

Individual chromosomes

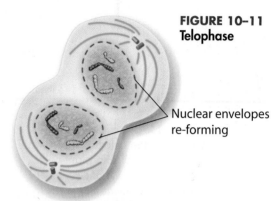

FIGURE 10–11
Telophase

Nuclear envelopes re-forming

> **In Your Notebook** *Create a chart that lists the important information about each phase of mitosis.*

Quick Lab
GUIDED INQUIRY

Mitosis in Action

❶ Examine a slide of a stained onion root tip under a microscope. Viewing the slide under low power, adjust the stage until you find the boxlike cells just above the root tip.

❷ Switch the microscope to high power and locate cells that are in the process of dividing.

❸ Find and sketch cells that are in each phase of mitosis. Label each sketch with the name of the appropriate phase.

Analyze and Conclude

1. Observe In which phase of the cell cycle were most of the cells you observed? Why do you think this is?

2. Draw Conclusions What evidence did you observe that shows mitosis is a continuous process, not a series of separate events?

3. Apply Concepts Cells in the root divide many times as the root grows longer and thicker. With each cell division, the chromosomes are divided between two daughter cells, yet the number of chromosomes in each cell does not change. What processes ensure that the normal number of chromosomes is restored after each cell division?

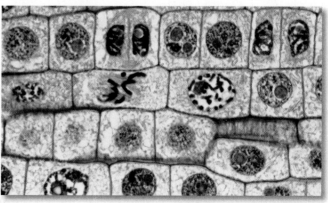

(LM 820×)

MYSTERY
CLUE

How would you expect
the salamander's
wound to affect
the cell cycle in the
cells around
the wound?

Cytokinesis

🔑 *How do daughter cells split apart after mitosis?*

As a result of mitosis, two nuclei—each with a duplicate set of chromosomes—are formed. All that remains to complete the M phase of the cycle is cytokinesis, the division of the cytoplasm itself. Cytokinesis usually occurs at the same time as telophase. 🔑 **Cytokinesis completes the process of cell division—it splits one cell into two.** The process of cytokinesis differs in animal and plant cells.

Cytokinesis in Animal Cells During cytokinesis in most animal cells, the cell membrane is drawn inward until the cytoplasm is pinched into two nearly equal parts. Each part contains its own nucleus and cytoplasmic organelles.

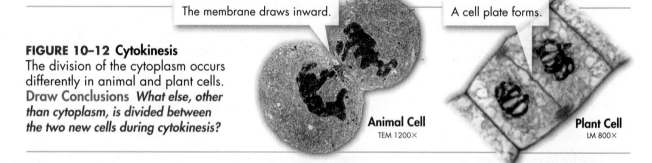

The membrane draws inward.

A cell plate forms.

FIGURE 10–12 Cytokinesis
The division of the cytoplasm occurs differently in animal and plant cells. **Draw Conclusions** *What else, other than cytoplasm, is divided between the two new cells during cytokinesis?*

Animal Cell
TEM 1200×

Plant Cell
LM 800×

Cytokinesis in Plant Cells Cytokinesis in plant cells proceeds differently. The cell membrane is not flexible enough to draw inward because of the rigid cell wall that surrounds it. Instead, a structure known as the cell plate forms halfway between the divided nuclei. The cell plate gradually develops into cell membranes that separate the two daughter cells. A cell wall then forms in between the two new membranes, completing the process.

10.2 Assessment

Review Key Concepts 🔑

1. a. Review What are chromosomes?
b. Compare and Contrast How does the structure of chromosomes differ in prokaryotes and eukaryotes?

2. a. Review What is the cell cycle?
b. Sequence During which phase of the cell cycle are chromosomes replicated?

3. a. Review What happens during each of the four phases of mitosis? Write one or two sentences for each phase.
b. Predict What do you predict would happen if the spindle fibers were disrupted during metaphase?

4. a. Review What is cytokinesis and when does it occur?
b. Compare and Contrast How does cytokinesis differ in animal and plant cells?

WRITE ABOUT SCIENCE

Summary
5. Summarize what happens during interphase. Be sure to include all three parts of interphase. *Hint:* Include all of the main details in your summary.

MITOSIS

FIGURE 10–13 The phases of mitosis shown here are typical of eukaryotic cells. These light micrographs are from a developing whitefish embryo (LM 415×). **Infer** *Why is the timing between what happens to the nuclear envelope and the activity of the mitotic spindle so critical?*

Interphase ▲
The cell grows and replicates its DNA and centrioles.

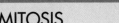

◄ Cytokinesis
The cytoplasm pinches in half. Each daughter cell has an identical set of duplicate chromosomes.

Prophase ►
The chromatin condenses into chromosomes. The centrioles separate, and a spindle begins to form. The nuclear envelope breaks down.

Metaphase ▼
The chromosomes line up across the center of the cell. Each chromosome is connected to spindle fibers at its centromere.

▼ Telophase
The chromosomes gather at opposite ends of the cell and lose their distinct shapes. Two new nuclear envelopes will form.

Anaphase ▼
The sister chromatids separate into individual chromosomes and are moved apart.

10.3 Regulating the Cell Cycle

Key Questions

🗝 How is the cell cycle regulated?

🗝 How do cancer cells differ from other cells?

Vocabulary

cyclin
growth factor
apoptosis
cancer
tumor

Taking Notes

Concept Map As you read, create a concept map to organize the information in this lesson.

THINK ABOUT IT How do cells know when to divide? One striking fact about cells in multicellular organisms is how carefully cell growth and cell division are controlled. Not all cells move through the cell cycle at the same rate.

In the human body, for example, most muscle cells and nerve cells do not divide at all once they have developed. In contrast, cells in the bone marrow that make blood cells and cells of the skin and digestive tract grow and divide rapidly throughout life. These cells may pass through a complete cycle every few hours. This process provides new cells to replace those that wear out or break down.

Controls on Cell Division

🗝 **How is the cell cycle regulated?**

When scientists grow cells in the laboratory, most cells will divide until they come into contact with each other. Once they do, they usually stop dividing and growing. What happens if those neighboring cells are suddenly scraped away in the culture dish? The remaining cells will begin dividing again until they once again make contact with other cells. This simple experiment shows that controls on cell growth and division can be turned on and off.

Something similar happens inside the body. Look at **Figure 10–14.** When an injury such as a cut in the skin or a break in a bone occurs, cells at the edges of the injury are stimulated to divide rapidly. New cells form, starting the process of healing. When the healing process nears completion, the rate of cell division slows, controls on growth are restored, and everything returns to normal.

The Discovery of Cyclins For many years, biologists searched for a signal that might regulate the cell cycle—something that would "tell" cells when it was time to divide, duplicate their chromosomes, or enter another phase of the cell cycle.

In the early 1980s, biologists discovered a protein in cells that were in mitosis. When they injected the protein into a nondividing cell, a mitotic spindle would form. They named this protein **cyclin** because it seemed to regulate the cell cycle. Investigators have since discovered a family of proteins known as cyclins that regulate the timing of the cell cycle in eukaryotic cells.

Regulatory Proteins The discovery of cyclins was just the start. Scientists have since identified dozens of other proteins that also help to regulate the cell cycle. 🔑 **The cell cycle is controlled by regulatory proteins both inside and outside the cell.**

▶ *Internal Regulators* One group of proteins, internal regulatory proteins, respond to events occurring inside a cell. Internal regulatory proteins allow the cell cycle to proceed only when certain events have occurred in the cell itself. For example, several regulatory proteins make sure a cell does not enter mitosis until its chromosomes have replicated. Another regulatory protein prevents a cell from entering anaphase until the spindle fibers have attached to the chromosomes.

▶ *External Regulators* Proteins that respond to events outside the cell are called external regulatory proteins. External regulatory proteins direct cells to speed up or slow down the cell cycle.

One important group of external regulatory proteins is the group made up of the growth factors. **Growth factors** stimulate the growth and division of cells. These proteins are especially important during embryonic development and wound healing. Other external regulatory proteins on the surface of neighboring cells often have an opposite effect. They cause cells to slow down or stop their cell cycles. This prevents excessive cell growth and keeps body tissues from disrupting one another.

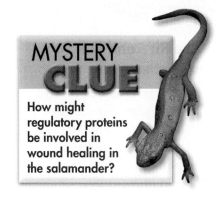

MYSTERY
CLUE

How might regulatory proteins be involved in wound healing in the salamander?

In Your Notebook *Use a cause-and-effect diagram to describe how internal and external regulators work together to control the cell cycle.*

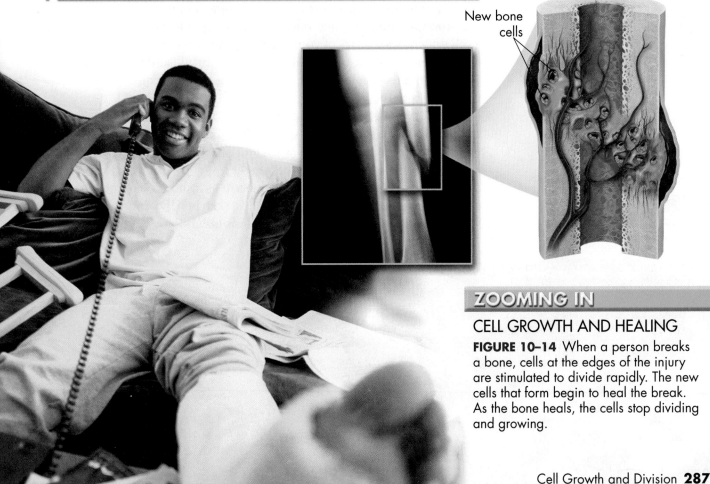

New bone cells

ZOOMING IN

CELL GROWTH AND HEALING

FIGURE 10–14 When a person breaks a bone, cells at the edges of the injury are stimulated to divide rapidly. The new cells that form begin to heal the break. As the bone heals, the cells stop dividing and growing.

Cell Growth and Division **287**

The Rise and Fall of Cyclins

Scientists measured cyclin levels in clam egg cells as the cells went through their first mitotic divisions after fertilization. The data are shown in the graph.

Cyclins are continually produced and destroyed within cells. Cyclin production signals cells to enter mitosis, while cyclin destruction signals cells to stop dividing and enter interphase.

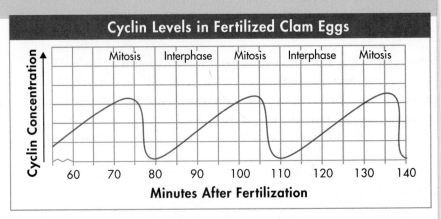

Cyclin Levels in Fertilized Clam Eggs

Mitosis | Interphase | Mitosis | Interphase | Mitosis

Cyclin Concentration (y-axis)

Minutes After Fertilization (x-axis): 60 70 80 90 100 110 120 130 140

1. Interpret Graphs How long does cyclin production last during a typical cell cycle in fertilized clam eggs?

2. Infer During which part of the cell cycle does cyclin production begin? How quickly is cyclin destroyed?

3. Predict Suppose that the regulators that control cyclin production are no longer produced. What are two possible outcomes?

Apoptosis Just as new cells are produced every day in a multicellular organism, many other cells die. Cells end their life cycle in one of two ways. A cell may die by accident due to damage or injury, or a cell may actually be "programmed" to die. **Apoptosis** (AYP up TOH sis) is a process of programmed cell death. Once apoptosis is triggered, a cell undergoes a series of controlled steps leading to its self-destruction. First, the cell and its chromatin shrink, and then parts of the cell's membranes break off. Neighboring cells then quickly clean up the cell's remains.

Apoptosis plays a key role in development by shaping the structure of tissues and organs in plants and animals. For example, look at the photos of a mouse foot in **Figure 10–15.** Each foot of a mouse is shaped the way it is partly because cells between the toes die by apoptosis during tissue development. When apoptosis does not occur as it should, a number of diseases can result. For example, the cell loss seen in AIDS and Parkinson's disease can result if too much apoptosis occurs.

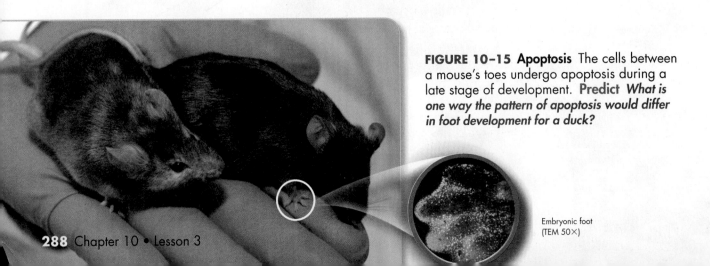

FIGURE 10-15 Apoptosis The cells between a mouse's toes undergo apoptosis during a late stage of development. **Predict** *What is one way the pattern of apoptosis would differ in foot development for a duck?*

Embryonic foot
(TEM 50×)

Cancer: Uncontrolled Cell Growth

How do cancer cells differ from other cells?

Why is cell growth regulated so carefully? The principal reason may be that the consequences of uncontrolled cell growth in a multicellular organism are very severe. **Cancer,** a disorder in which body cells lose the ability to control growth, is one such example.

Cancer cells do not respond to the signals that regulate the growth of most cells. As a result, the cells divide uncontrollably. Cancer cells form a mass of cells called a **tumor.** However, not all tumors are cancerous. Some tumors are benign, or noncancerous. A benign tumor does not spread to surrounding healthy tissue or to other parts of the body. Cancerous tumors, such as the one in **Figure 10–16,** are malignant. Malignant tumors invade and destroy surrounding healthy tissue.

As the cancer cells spread, they absorb the nutrients needed by other cells, block nerve connections, and prevent the organs they invade from functioning properly. Soon, the delicate balances that exist in the body are disrupted, and life-threatening illness results.

What Causes Cancer? Cancers are caused by defects in the genes that regulate cell growth and division. There are several sources of such defects, including: smoking or chewing tobacco, radiation exposure, other defective genes, and even viral infection. All cancers, however, have one thing in common: The control over the cell cycle has broken down. Some cancer cells will no longer respond to external growth regulators, while others fail to produce the internal regulators that ensure orderly growth.

An astonishing number of cancer cells have a defect in a gene called p53, which normally halts the cell cycle until all chromosomes have been properly replicated. Damaged or defective p53 genes cause cells to lose the information needed to respond to signals that normally control their growth.

In Your Notebook *Use a two-column chart to compare the controls that regulate normal cell growth to the lack of control seen in cancer cells.*

FIGURE 10–16 Growth of Cancer Cells Normal cells grow and divide in a carefully controlled fashion. Cells that are cancerous lose this control and continue to grow and divide, producing tumors.

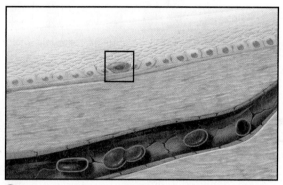

❶ A cell begins to divide abnormally.

❷ The cancer cells produce a tumor, which begins to displace normal cells and tissues.

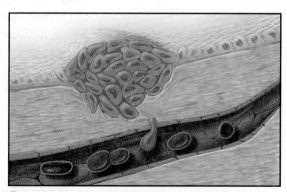

❸ Cancer cells are particularly dangerous because of their tendency to spread once they enter the bloodstream or lymph vessels. The cancer then moves into other parts of the body and forms secondary tumors, a process called metastasis.

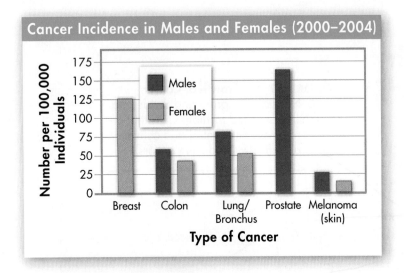

Cancer Incidence in Males and Females (2000–2004)

Number per 100,000 Individuals

175
150
125
100
75
50
25
0

Males
Females

Breast   Colon   Lung/   Prostate   Melanoma
                 Bronchus   (skin)

Type of Cancer

FIGURE 10–17 Cancer Incidence
Cancer can affect almost every organ in the body. **Interpret Graphs** *How many cases of breast cancer were reported compared to prostate cancer for the time period shown?*

Treatments for Cancer When a cancerous tumor is localized, it can often be removed by surgery. Skin cancer, the most common form of the disease, can usually be treated this way. Melanomas, the most serious form of skin cancer, can be removed surgically, but only if spotted very early.

Other forms of treatment make use of the fact that cancer cells grow rapidly and, therefore, need to copy their DNA more quickly than do most normal cells. This makes them especially vulnerable to damage from radiation. As a result, many tumors can be effectively treated with carefully targeted beams of radiation.

Medical researchers have worked for years to develop chemical compounds that would kill cancer cells, or at least slow their growth. The use of such compounds against cancer is known as chemotherapy. Great advances in chemotherapy have taken place in recent years and have even made it possible to cure some forms of cancer. However, because most chemotherapy compounds target rapidly dividing cells, they also interfere with cell division in normal, healthy cells. This produces serious side effects in many patients, and it is one of the reasons why scientists are so interested in gaining a better understanding of the role of cell cycle proteins in cancer. The goal of many researchers is to find highly specific ways in which cancer cells can be targeted for destruction while leaving healthy cells unaffected.

Cancer is a serious disease. Understanding and combating cancer remains a major scientific challenge, but scientists at least know where to start. Cancer is a disease of the cell cycle, and conquering cancer will require a much deeper understanding of the processes that control cell division.

10.3 Assessment

Review Key Concepts 🔑

1. a. Review Name the two types of proteins that regulate the cell cycle. How do these proteins work?

b. Form a Hypothesis Write a hypothesis about what you think would happen if cyclin were injected into a cell during mitosis. How could you test your hypothesis?

2. a. Review Why is cancer considered a disease of the cell cycle?

b. Compare and Contrast How are the growth of a tumor and the repair of a scrape on your knee similar? How are they different?

Apply the Big idea

Growth, Development, and Reproduction

3. Why do you think it is important that cells have a "control system" to regulate the timing of cell division?

Fluorescence Microscopy

Imagine being able to "see" proteins at work inside a cell, or to track proteins from where they are made to where they go. Scientists can now do all of these things, thanks to advances in fluorescence microscopy. One advance came from the discovery that Pacific jellyfish, properly known as *Aequorea victoria*, produce a protein that glows. By fusing the gene for this protein to other genes, scientists can label different parts of the cell with fluorescence. Other advances include the development of additional highly specific fluorescent labels and the invention of powerful laser microscopes. As the images on this page show, the view is clearly amazing.

WRITING Suppose you are a cell biologist studying cell division and cancer. What might you use a fluorescence microscope to study? Describe your ideas in a paragraph.

▲ **Viewing Labeled Specimens**
In fluorescence microscopy, a specimen is labeled with a molecule that glows under a specific wavelength of light. Different fluorescent labels give off different colors. This way, biologists can easily see exactly where a protein is located within a cell or tissue.

▼ **Normal Spindle**
Different fluorescent labels enable biologists to track how spindle fibers (green) form and how proteins help distribute chromosomes (red) evenly during mitosis.

▼ **Abnormal Spindle**
Cell cycle control has gone awry in this cell, causing an abnormal mitotic spindle to form.

10.4 Cell Differentiation

Key Questions

🔑 *How do cells become specialized for different functions?*

🔑 *What are stem cells?*

🔑 *What are some possible benefits and issues associated with stem cell research?*

Vocabulary

embryo • differentiation •
totipotent • blastocyst •
pluripotent • stem cell •
multipotent

Taking Notes

Compare/Contrast Table As you read, create a table comparing the ability of different cell types to differentiate.

THINK ABOUT IT The human body contains an estimated 100,000,000,000,000 (one hundred trillion) cells. That's a staggering number, but in one respect it's not quite as large as you might think. Why? Try to estimate how many times a single cell would have to divide through mitosis to produce that many cells. It may surprise you to learn that as few as 47 rounds of cell division can produce that many cells.

The results of those 47 cell cycles are truly amazing. The human body contains hundreds of distinctly different cell types, and every one of them develops from the single cell that starts the process. How do the cells get to be so different from each other?

From One Cell to Many

🔑 *How do cells become specialized for different functions?*

Each of us started life as just one cell. So, for that matter, did your pet dog, an earthworm, and the petunia on the windowsill. These living things pass through a developmental stage called an **embryo,** from which the adult organism is gradually produced. During the development process, an organism's cells become more and more differentiated and specialized for particular functions. **Figure 10–18** shows some of the specialized cells found in the roots, stems, and leaves of a plant.

Cells that
transport materials

FIGURE 10–18 Specialized Plant Cells

Cells that
store sugar

Cells that carry
out photosynthesis

Defining Differentiation The process by which cells become specialized is known as **differentiation** (dif ur en shee AY shun). 🔑 **During the development of an organism, cells differentiate into many types of cells.** A differentiated cell has become, quite literally, different from the embryonic cell that produced it, and specialized to perform certain tasks, such as contraction, photosynthesis, or protection. Our bodies, and the bodies of all multicellular organisms, contain highly differentiated cells that carry out the jobs we need to perform to stay alive.

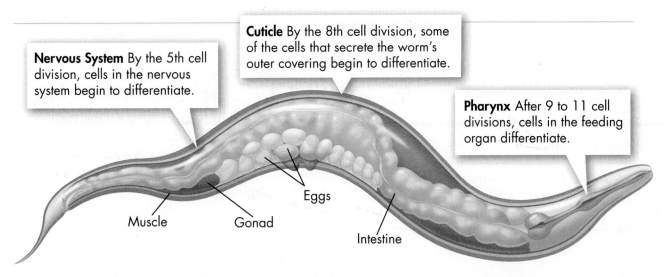

Nervous System By the 5th cell division, cells in the nervous system begin to differentiate.

Cuticle By the 8th cell division, some of the cells that secrete the worm's outer covering begin to differentiate.

Pharynx After 9 to 11 cell divisions, cells in the feeding organ differentiate.

Muscle   Gonad   Eggs   Intestine

FIGURE 10–19 Differentiation in *C. elegans* A fertilized egg develops into an adult worm after many cell divisions. Daughter cells from each cell division follow a specific path toward a role as a particular kind of cell.

Mapping Differentiation The process of differentiation determines a cell's ultimate identity, such as whether it will spend its life as a nerve cell or a muscle cell. In some organisms, a cell's role is rigidly determined at a specific point in the course of development. In the microscopic worm *Caenorhabditis elegans*, for example, biologists have mapped the outcome of each and every cell division from fertilized egg to adult.

The process of cell differentiation in *C. elegans* begins with the very first division and continues throughout embryonic development. **Figure 10–19** shows when some of the cells found in the adult begin to differentiate during development. Each and every time a new worm develops, the process is the same, resulting in 959 cells with precisely determined functions.

Differentiation in Mammals Other organisms, including mammals like us, go through a more flexible process in which cell differentiation is controlled by a number of interacting factors in the embryo, many of which are still not well understood. What is known, however, is that adult cells generally do reach a point at which their differentiation is complete—when they can no longer become other types of cells.

In Your Notebook *Starting with a single cell, calculate how many cells might result after 4, 8, and 10 cell divisions.*

Cellular Differentiation of *C. elegans*

The adult microscopic worm *C. elegans* contains 959 cells. The data table shows some of the different cell types in this worm. Copy the data table into your notebook and answer the following questions.

1. Calculate Calculate the percentage of the total cell number represented by each tissue or organ listed by using this formula:

$$\frac{\text{Number of cells in adult}}{\text{Total number of cells}} \times 100$$

2. Calculate Find both the number of cells and the percentage of the total represented by cells in tissues or organs not listed ("other"). The category includes cells from, among other organs, the intestine. Record the results in your table. MATH

Cell Type	Number of Cells in Adult	Percent of Total
Cuticle	213	22%
Gonad (excluding germ line cells)	143	
Mesoderm muscle	81	
Pharynx	80	
Other		

3. Infer Why does *C. elegans* make an ideal model for studying cellular differentiation?

4. Infer Why would it be more difficult to map the differentiation patterns in a different organism, such as a mammal?

Stem Cells and Development

🔑 *What are stem cells?*

One of the most important questions in biology is how all of the specialized, differentiated cell types in the body are formed from just a single cell. Biologists say that such a cell is **totipotent** (toh TIP uh tunt), literally able to do everything, to develop into any type of cell in the body (including the cells that make up the extraembryonic membranes and placenta). Only the fertilized egg and the cells produced by the first few cell divisions of embryonic development are truly totipotent. If there is a "secret" by which cells start the process of differentiation, these are the cells that know that secret.

Human Development After about four days of development, a human embryo forms into a **blastocyst,** a hollow ball of cells with a cluster of cells inside known as the inner cell mass. Even at this early stage, the cells of the blastocyst have begun to specialize. The outer cells form tissues that attach the embryo to its mother, while the inner cell mass becomes the embryo itself. The cells of the inner cell mass are said to be pluripotent (plu RIP uh tunt). Cells that are **pluripotent** can develop into most, but not all, of the body's cell types. They cannot form the tissues surrounding the embryo.

MYSTERY CLUE

Some adult salamander cells never completely differentiate. What ability do these cells retain?

📃 **In Your Notebook** *Look up the roots that form the words* totipotent, pluripotent, *and* multipotent. *How do the roots relate to each cell's ability to differentiate?*

Stem Cells

The unspecialized cells from which differentiated cells develop are known as stem cells. As the name implies, **stem cells** sit at the base of a branching "stem" of development from which different cell types form. Because of their potential to develop into other cell types, stem cells are the subject of intense interest by researchers around the world.

▶ *Embryonic Stem Cells* As you have seen, the pluripotent stem cells of the inner cell mass eventually produce all of the cells of the body. Embryonic stem cells are pluripotent cells found in the early embryo. In 1998, researchers at the University of Wisconsin found a way to grow these embryonic stem cells in culture. Their experiments confirmed that such cells did indeed have the capacity to produce just about any cell type in the human body. In fact, scientists have managed to coax mouse embryonic stem cells to differentiate into nerve cells, muscle cells, and even into sperm and egg cells. Recently, sperm made from embryonic stem cells were used to generate live mice.

▶ *Adult Stem Cells* For years, biologists have suspected that adult organisms might also contain some types of stem cells. Cells in the blood and skin, for example, have a limited life span and must be constantly replaced. This suggests that the body contains pools of stem cells from which new skin and blood cells can be produced.

Adult stem cells are groups of cells that differentiate to renew and replace cells in the adult body. Because of their more limited potential, adult stem cells are referred to as **multipotent** (muhl TIP uh tunt), meaning that they can develop into many types of differentiated cells. Typically, stem cells of a given organ or tissue produce only the types of cells that are unique to that tissue. For example, adult stem cells in the bone marrow can develop into several different types of blood cells, while stem cells in the brain can produce neurons, or nerve cells.

FIGURE 10–20 Embryonic Stem Cells After fertilization, the human embryo develops into a hollow ball of cells known as a blastocyst. The actual body of the embryo develops from the inner cell mass, a cluster of cells inside the blastocyst. Because of their ability to differentiate into each of the body's many cell types, these cells are known as embryonic stem cells.

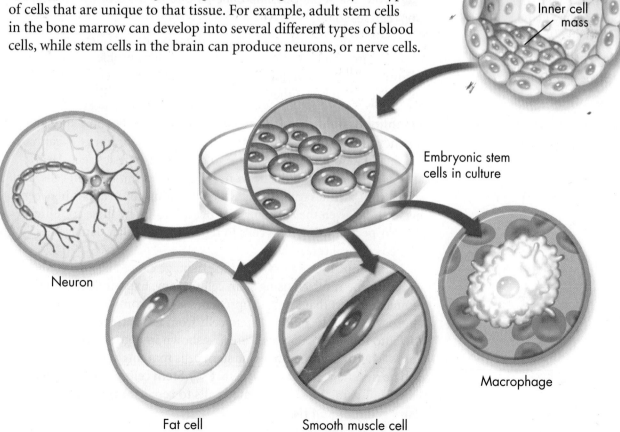

Blastocyst

Inner cell mass

Embryonic stem cells in culture

Neuron

Fat cell

Smooth muscle cell

Macrophage

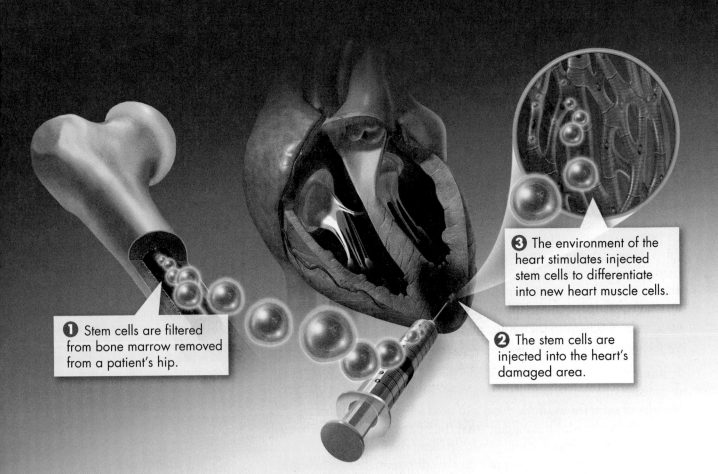

① Stem cells are filtered from bone marrow removed from a patient's hip.

② The stem cells are injected into the heart's damaged area.

③ The environment of the heart stimulates injected stem cells to differentiate into new heart muscle cells.

FIGURE 10–21 A Possible Future Treatment for Heart Disease? Stem cell research may lead to new ways to reverse the damage caused by a severe heart attack. The diagram shows one method currently being investigated. **Infer** *How would the fate of the stem cells change after they are moved from the bone marrow to the heart?*

Frontiers in Stem Cell Research

⊶ *What are some possible benefits and issues associated with stem cell research?*

Understanding how stem cells retain the capacity to differentiate into so many cell types is an important unsolved problem in biology. Scientists would like to learn exactly which signals tell a cell to become specialized, and how other cells remain multipotent.

Potential Benefits Basic research on stem cells takes on a special urgency in light of the importance it might have for human health. There are many causes of damage to particular types of cells. Heart attacks destroy cells in the heart muscle, strokes injure brain cells, and spinal cord injuries cause paralysis by breaking connections between nerve cells. Given the suffering and death caused by these conditions, the prospect of using stem cells to repair such cellular damage has excited medical researchers.

Many hope to see a day when the damage caused by a severe heart attack can be reversed using stem cell therapy. Experiments using animals suggest that several approaches show promise of success. One approach might be to inject stem cells from the patient's bone marrow into the heart's damaged area, as shown in **Figure 10–21**. Another approach is to inject embryonic stem cells that might eventually differentiate into new heart muscle cells. **⊶ Stem cells offer the potential benefit of using undifferentiated cells to repair or replace badly damaged cells and tissues.**

Ethical Issues Because adult stem cells can be obtained directly from the body of a willing donor, research with these cells has raised few ethical questions to date. This is not the case with embryonic stem cells, which are generally obtained from very early embryos.

Most techniques for harvesting embryonic stem cells cause the destruction of an embryo. For this reason, individuals who regard the embryo as entitled to the rights and protections of any human being object to such work. This concern has made government funding of embryonic stem cell research an important political issue. Groups seeking to protect embryos oppose such research as unethical. Other groups support such research as essential for saving human lives and argue that it would be unethical to restrict research. **Human embryonic stem cell research is controversial because the arguments for it and against it both involve ethical issues of life and death.**

It is possible, however, that in the not-too-distant future, both ethical concerns will be addressed with a technological solution. Some recent experiments have suggested that there may be ways to extract a small number of stem cells from an early embryo without damaging the embryo itself. Other experiments have shown that it is possible to switch "on" a small number of genes that reprogram adult cells to look and function like pluripotent embryonic stem cells. Such a technique would do away with the need to involve embryos at all. It also might make it possible to tailor specific therapies to the needs of each individual patient. Approaches like these, if successful, might allow potentially lifesaving research to go forward while avoiding any destruction of embryonic life.

In Your Notebook *Make a two-column chart that lists the benefits and issues related to stem cell research.*

10.4 Assessment

Review Key Concepts

1. a. Review What happens during differentiation?
b. Apply Concepts What does "mapping" refer to in the process of cell differentiation?
2. a. Review What are stem cells?
b. Compare and Contrast How are embryonic stem cells and adult stem cells alike? How are they different?
3. a. Review Summarize the potential benefits and issues of stem cell research.
b. Form an Opinion How might technological advances help address the ethical concerns surrounding stem cell research?

Apply the Big idea

Cellular Basis of Life
4. Use what you learned in this lesson to discuss how cells become specialized for different functions. Include an explanation of how the potential for specialization varies with cell type and how it varies over the life span of an organism.

BIOLOGY.com Search (Lesson 10.4) GO ● Self-Test ● Lesson Assessment

Design Your Own Lab

Pre-Lab: Regeneration in Planaria

Problem How potent are the stem cells in planaria?

Materials fresh water or spring water, planarians, petri dishes, glass-marking pencil, forceps, scalpel, dissecting microscope, glass microscope slide, lens paper, pipette, small paintbrush, clear ruler

Lab Manual Chapter 10 Lab

Skills Focus Form a Hypothesis, Design an Experiment, Draw Conclusions

Connect to the Big idea All cells come from existing cells. When most cells in a multicellular organism divide, they produce cells just like themselves. However, some cells can differentiate to form different types of cells. These cells enable an organism to repair tissue after an injury or in some cases to regenerate body parts. In this lab, you will investigate the ability of planarians to regenerate body parts.

Background Questions

a. Compare and Contrast What is the difference between totipotent stem cells and multipotent stem cells?

b. Apply Concepts What type of stem cell enables your body to produce cells, such as skin and blood cells that are constantly replaced by the body?

c. Apply Concepts What type of stem cell enables a salamander to regenerate its tail?

d. Compare and Contrast In what way is regeneration of a body part similar to asexual reproduction? In what way is it different?

Pre-Lab Questions

Preview the procedure in the lab manual.

1. Apply Concepts What would you expect to observe if the stem cells in planarians are totipotent? What would you expect to observe if the stem cells are multipotent?

2. Control Variables What will you use as a control in your experiment? Explain why you need this control.

3. Infer Two planarians are cut at different locations. Regeneration occurs in one planarian, but not in the other. Based on these results, what might you infer about stem cells in planarians?

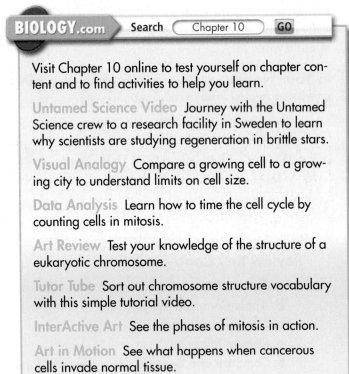

BIOLOGY.com   Search   Chapter 10   GO

Visit Chapter 10 online to test yourself on chapter content and to find activities to help you learn.

Untamed Science Video Journey with the Untamed Science crew to a research facility in Sweden to learn why scientists are studying regeneration in brittle stars.

Visual Analogy Compare a growing cell to a growing city to understand limits on cell size.

Data Analysis Learn how to time the cell cycle by counting cells in mitosis.

Art Review Test your knowledge of the structure of a eukaryotic chromosome.

Tutor Tube Sort out chromosome structure vocabulary with this simple tutorial video.

InterActive Art See the phases of mitosis in action.

Art in Motion See what happens when cancerous cells invade normal tissue.

10 Study Guide

Big idea ▶ Growth, Development, and Reproduction

Cells undergo cell division to produce new cells. In eukaryotic cells, cell division is part of a highly regulated cycle known as the cell cycle.

10.1 Cell Growth, Division, and Reproduction

🔑 The larger a cell becomes, the more demands the cell places on its DNA. In addition, a larger cell is less efficient in moving nutrients and waste materials across the cell membrane.

🔑 Asexual reproduction is the production of genetically identical offspring from a single parent.

🔑 Offspring produced by sexual reproduction inherit some of their genetic information from each parent.

cell division (276)
asexual reproduction (277)
sexual reproduction (277)

10.2 The Process of Cell Division

🔑 Chromosomes make it possible to separate DNA precisely during cell division.

🔑 During the cell cycle, a cell grows, prepares for division, and divides to form two daughter cells.

🔑 During prophase, the genetic material inside the nucleus condenses. During metaphase, the chromosomes line up across the center of the cell. During anaphase, the chromosomes separate and move along spindle fibers to opposite ends of the cell. During telophase, the chromosomes, which were distinct and condensed, begin to spread out into a tangle of chromatin.

🔑 Cytokinesis completes the process of cell division—it splits one cell into two.

chromosome (279)   centromere (282)
chromatin (280)   chromatid (282)
cell cycle (280)   centriole (282)
interphase (281)   metaphase (282)
mitosis (282)   anaphase (283)
cytokinesis (282)   telophase (283)
prophase (282)

10.3 Regulating the Cell Cycle

🔑 The cell cycle is controlled by regulatory proteins both inside and outside the cell.

🔑 Cancer cells do not respond to the signals that regulate the growth of most cells. As a result, the cells divide uncontrollably.

cyclin (286)   cancer (289)
growth factor (287)   tumor (289)
apoptosis (288)

10.4 Cell Differentiation

🔑 During the development of an organism, cells differentiate into many types of cells.

🔑 The unspecialized cells from which differentiated cells develop are known as stem cells.

🔑 Stem cells offer the potential benefit of using undifferentiated cells to repair or replace badly damaged cells and tissues.

🔑 Human embryonic stem cell research is controversial because the arguments for it and against it both involve ethical issues of life and death.

embryo (292)   pluripotent (294)
differentiation (293)   stem cell (295)
totipotent (294)   multipotent (295)
blastocyst (294)

Think Visually Using the information in this chapter, complete the following cycle diagram of the cell cycle.

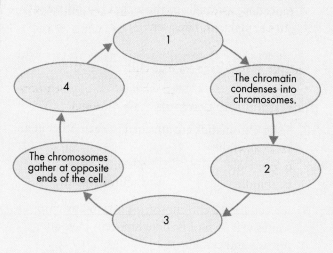

10 Assessment

10.1 Cell Growth, Division, and Reproduction

Understand Key Concepts

1. The rate at which materials enter and leave the cell depends on the cell's
   - **a.** volume.
   - **b.** weight.
   - **c.** speciation.
   - **d.** surface area.

2. In order for a cell to divide successfully, the cell must first
   - **a.** duplicate its genetic information.
   - **b.** decrease its volume.
   - **c.** increase its number of chromosomes.
   - **d.** decrease its number of organelles.

3. The process that increases genetic diversity within a population is
   - **a.** asexual reproduction. **c.** cell division.
   - **b.** sexual reproduction. **d.** binary fission.

4. Describe what is meant by each of the following terms: *cell volume, cell surface area, ratio of surface area to volume.*

5. Describe asexual and sexual reproduction as survival strategies.

Think Critically

6. **Calculate** Calculate the ratio of surface area to volume of an imaginary cubic cell measuring 4 mm long on each side. **MATH**

7. **Form a Hypothesis** In a changing environment, which organisms have an advantage—those that reproduce asexually or those that reproduce sexually? Explain your answer.

10.2 The Process of Cell Division

Understand Key Concepts

8. Sister chromatids are attached to each other at an area called the
   - **a.** centriole.
   - **b.** spindle.
   - **c.** centromere.
   - **d.** chromosome.

9. If a cell has 12 chromosomes, how many chromosomes will each of its daughter cells have after mitosis and cytokinesis?
   - **a.** 4   **b.** 6   **c.** 12   **d.** 24

10. Which of the illustrations below best represents metaphase of mitosis?

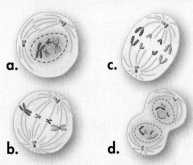

   a.   **c.**
   b.   **d.**

11. In plant cells, what forms midway between the divided nuclei during cytokinesis?
    - **a.** nuclear membrane **c.** cell membrane
    - **b.** centromere **d.** cell plate

12. Describe how a eukaryotic cell's chromosomes change as a cell prepares to divide.

13. What is the relationship between interphase and cell division?

14. List the following stages of mitosis in the correct sequence, and describe what happens during each stage: anaphase, metaphase, prophase, and telophase.

Think Critically

15. **Compare and Contrast** How is the process of cell division in prokaryotes different from cell division in eukaryotes?

16. **Form a Hypothesis** Some cells have several nuclei within their cytoplasm. Considering the events in a typical cell cycle, which phase of the cell cycle is not operating when such cells form?

17. **Compare and Contrast** Describe the differences between cell division in an animal cell and cell division in a plant cell.

18. **Relate Cause and Effect** The nerve cells in the human nervous system seldom undergo mitosis. Based on this information, explain why complete recovery from injuries to the nervous system usually does not occur.

19. **Apply Concepts** A scientist treats cells with a chemical that prevents DNA synthesis. In which stage of the cell cycle will these cells remain?

20. Interpret Visuals The diagram shows a phase of mitosis. Use the diagram to answer the following questions.

a. Identify the phase of mitosis shown in the diagram.
b. Is this a plant or animal cell? How do you know?
c. The four chromosomes shown in the center of this cell each have two connected strands. Explain how the two strands on the same chromosome compare with regard to the genetic information they carry. In your answer, be sure to explain why this is important to the cell.

10.3 Regulating the Cell Cycle

Understand Key Concepts

21. The timing in the cell cycle in eukaryotic cells is believed to be controlled by a group of closely related proteins known as
  a. chromatids.   **c.** centromeres.
  b. cyclins.   **d.** centrioles.

22. In the cell cycle, external regulatory proteins direct cells to
  a. speed up or slow down the cell cycle.
  b. remain unchanged.
  c. proceed and then stop the cell cycle.
  d. grow uncontrollably.

23. When some cells are removed from the center of a tissue culture, will new cells replace the cells that were removed? Explain.

24. Describe the role of cyclins.

Think Critically

25. Compare and Contrast How do cancer cells differ from noncancerous cells? How are they similar?

26. Predict A cell will usually undergo apoptosis if the cell experiences DNA damage that could lead to a tumor. Predict what may happen if a gene that controls apoptosis is damaged.

---

solve the CHAPTER MYSTERY

PET SHOP ACCIDENT

Julia kept a close eye on the injured salamander. About a month after the accident, Julia realized that a new limb was growing to replace the lost one! Salamanders are one of only a few vertebrates that can regenerate a complete limb. Examine the illustrations that show how a new limb develops. Then answer the questions.

Week 1: Dedifferentiation
At first, cells in the injured limb undergo dedifferentiation. During this process, cells such as muscle cells and nerve cells lose the characteristics that make them specialized.

Week 3: Blastema Formation
The dedifferentiated cells migrate to the wounded area and form a blastema—a growing mass of undifferentiated cells.

Week 5: Redifferentiation
Cells in the blastema then redifferentiate and form the tissues needed for a mature limb. The limb will continue to grow until it is full size.

1. Relate Cause and Effect Why is dedifferentiation of the salamander's limb cells necessary before regeneration can occur?

2. Classify What type of cells do you think are contained in the blastema? Explain.

3. Connect to the **Big idea** Unlike salamanders, planarians contain undifferentiated cells throughout their adult bodies. How might the regeneration process in salamanders and planarians differ?

10.4 Cell Differentiation

Understand Key Concepts

27. Bone marrow cells that produce blood cells are best categorized as
    a. embryonic stem cells.
    b. adult stem cells.
    c. pluripotent.
    d. totipotent cells.

28. Which type of cell has the potential to develop into any type of cell?
    a. totipotent
    b. pluripotent
    c. multipotent
    d. differentiated

29. What is a blastocyst?

30. What is cell differentiation and how is it important to an organism's development?

31. Describe two ways that technology may address the ethical concerns related to stem cell research.

Think Critically

32. **Relate Cause and Effect** When researchers discovered how to make skin stem cells pluripotent, how did they apply their discovery to the treatment for heart attack patients?

33. **Compare and Contrast** How does embryonic development and cell differentiation in *C. elegans* differ from how these processes work in mammals?

Connecting Concepts

Use Science Graphics

Use the data table to answer questions 34 and 35.

Life Spans of Various Human Cells		
Cell Type	**Life Span**	**Cell Division**
Red blood cells	<120 days	Cannot divide
Cardiac (heart) muscle	Long-lived	Cannot divide
Smooth muscle	Long-lived	Can divide
Neuron (nerve cell)	Long-lived	Most do not divide

34. **Compare and Contrast** Based on the data, in what ways might injuries to the heart and spinal cord be similar? How might they differ from injuries to smooth muscles?

35. **Predict** If cancer cells were added to the table, predict what would be written in the Life Span and Cell Division columns. Explain.

Write About Science

36. **Explanation** Recall what you learned about the characteristics of life in Chapter 1. Explain how cell division is related to two or more of those characteristics.

37. **Assess the** Big idea How is cancer an example of how changes to a single cell can affect the health of an entire organism?

Analyzing Data

A scientist performed an experiment to determine the effect of temperature on the length of the cell cycle in onion cells. His data are summarized in the table below.

Effect of Temperature on Length of Onion Cell Cycle	
Temperature (°C)	**Length of Cell Cycle (hours)**
10	54.6
15	29.8
20	18.8
25	13.3

38. **Interpret Tables** On the basis of the data in the table, how long would you expect the cell cycle to be at 5°C?
    a. less than 13.3 hours
    b. more than 54.6 hours
    c. between 29.8 and 54.6 hours
    d. about 20 hours

39. **Draw Conclusions** Given this set of data, what is one valid conclusion the scientist could state?

Standardized Test Prep

Multiple Choice

1. Which statement is true regarding a cell's surface area-to-volume ratio?
   A As the size of a cell increases, its volume decreases.
   B As the size of a cell decreases, its volume increases.
   C Larger cells will have a greater surface area-to-volume ratio.
   D Smaller cells will have a greater surface area-to-volume ratio.

2. Which of the following is NOT an advantage of asexual reproduction?
   A simple and efficient
   B produces large number of offspring quickly
   C increases genetic diversity
   D requires one parent

3. At the beginning of cell division, a chromosome consists of two
   A centromeres.   C chromatids.
   B centrioles.   D spindles.

4. What regulates the timing of the cell cycle in eukaryotes?
   A chromosomes   C nutrients
   B cyclins   D DNA and RNA

5. The period between cell divisions is called
   A interphase.   C G_3 phase.
   B prophase.   D cytokinesis.

6. Which of the following is TRUE about totipotent cells?
   A Embryonic stem cells are totipotent cells.
   B Totipotent cells are differentiated cells.
   C Totipotent cells can differentiate into any type of cell and tissue.
   D Adult stem cells are totipotent cells.

7. A cell enters anaphase before all of its chromosomes have attached to the spindle. This may indicate that the cell is not responding to
   A internal regulators.   C growth factors.
   B mitosis.   D apoptosis.

Questions 8–10

The spindle fibers of a dividing cell were labeled with a fluorescent dye. At the beginning of anaphase, a laser beam was used to mark a region of the spindle fibers about halfway between the centrioles and the chromosomes. The laser beam stopped the dye from glowing in this region, as shown in the second diagram. The laser did not inhibit the normal function of the fibers.

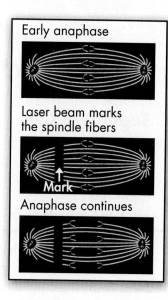

Early anaphase

Laser beam marks the spindle fibers

Mark

Anaphase continues

8. This experiment tests a hypothesis about
   A how chromosomes migrate during cell division.
   B how fluorescent dyes work in the cell.
   C the effect of lasers on cells.
   D why cells divide.

9. The diagrams show that chromosomes move to the poles of the cell as the spindle fibers
   A shorten on the chromosome side of the mark.
   B lengthen on the chromosome side of the mark.
   C shorten on the centriole side of the mark.
   D lengthen on the centriole side of the mark.

10. A valid conclusion that can be drawn from this experiment is that the spindle fibers break down
    A at the centrioles.
    B in the presence of dye.
    C when marked by lasers.
    D where they are attached to chromosomes.

Open-Ended Response

11. Explain why careful regulation of the cell cycle is important to multicellular organisms.

If You Have Trouble With . . .

Question	1	2	3	4	5	6	7	8	9	10	11
See Lesson	10.1	10.1	10.2	10.3	10.2	10.4	10.3	10.2	10.2	10.2	10.3

Unit Project

Superhero Cell

Do you like reading comics? Have you ever designed a comic book of your own? Here's your chance! A high school teacher has contacted you asking for a comic book on cells and cell processes. She has told you that her students are just about to start studying cells and need a good introduction to the topic. You've been tasked with developing the story line and visuals that will provide the students with a basic understanding of cell structure and function. Remember that sometimes a picture can be worth a thousand words—so be creative!

Your Task Write a comic book about a "superhero cell" for an audience of high school students.

Be sure to
- incorporate important concepts and details about the structure and function of various organelles and cell processes.
- provide insight into the ways cells work and interact with their environment.
- be entertaining and creative.

Reflection Questions

1. Score your project using the rubric below. What score did you give yourself?
2. What did you do well on this project?
3. What about your project needs improvement?
4. Exchange your comic book with a classmate and have him/her read it. What did your partner like about your comic book? What did he/she think could use improvement?

Assessment Rubric

Score	Scientific Content	Quality of Comic Book
4	The comic book includes accurate details about the structures and functions of several organelles and cell processes. It provides exceptional insight into how a cell works and interacts with its environment.	The comic book is thoughtfully and creatively written and illustrated.
3	The comic book includes mostly accurate details about the structure and functions of organelles and cell processes. It provides good insight into how a cell works and interacts with its environment.	The comic book is well written and includes some creativity. Illustrations are clear.
2	The comic book includes a few details about the structure and functions of organelles and cell processes, with some inaccuracies. It provides some insight into how a cell works and interacts with its environment.	The comic book needs some edits and could use more creativity. Some parts of the story line and illustrations are difficult to follow.
1	The comic book includes vague and inaccurate information about the structure and functions of organelles and cell processes. It provides little insight into how a cell works and interacts with its environment.	The comic book needs significant edits and includes very little creativity. Story line and illustrations are unclear.

Genetics

UNIT

4

Chapters

11 Introduction to Genetics

12 DNA

13 RNA and Protein Synthesis

14 Human Heredity

15 Genetic Engineering

── INTRODUCE the ──

Big ideas

- **Information and Heredity**
- **Cellular Basis of Life**
- **Science as a Way of Knowing**

❝Do you look more like mom or dad? I once ran my daughter's DNA on a finger-printing gel. It didn't settle whether she had her mother's eyes or mine, but half of the bands on that gel were identical to mine, and half, of course, to her mom's. It made me think just how remarkable human genetics really is. Our genes may come from our parents, but each of us gets a fresh shuffle and a brand-new deal of those genetic cards as we start our lives.❞

Ken Miller

11 Introduction to Genetics

Big idea > Information and Heredity

Q: How does biological information pass from one generation to another?

Genetics is the study of biological inheritance. The different coat colors of these Labrador retrievers are an example of the inherited characteristics that geneticists try to understand.

BIOLOGY.com > Search 〈 Chapter 11 〉 GO • Flash Cards

INSIDE:

- 11.1 The Work of Gregor Mendel
- 11.2 Applying Mendel's Principles
- 11.3 Other Patterns of Inheritance
- 11.4 Meiosis

CHAPTER
MYSTERY

GREEN PARAKEETS

Susan's birthday was coming up. Parakeets make great pets, so Susan's parents decided to give two birds to her as a birthday present. At the pet store, they selected two healthy green parakeets—one male and one female. They knew that green was Susan's favorite color.

Susan was delighted about her birthday present. She fed the birds and kept their cage clean. A few weeks later, Susan found three small eggs in the birds' nest. She couldn't wait to welcome three new green parakeets. When the eggs finally hatched, however, Susan was amazed. None of the chicks was green—one chick was white, one was blue, and one was yellow. Why weren't any of them green? What had happened to the green color of the birds' parents? As you read this chapter, look for clues to help you identify why the parakeet chicks were differently colored than their parents. Then, solve the mystery.

Never Stop Exploring Your World.
Finding the solution to the green parakeet mystery is only the beginning. Take a video field trip with the ecogeeks of Untamed Science to see where the mystery leads.

Untamed Science™

11.1 The Work of Gregor Mendel

Key Questions

🔑 Where does an organism get its unique characteristics?

🔑 How are different forms of a gene distributed to offspring?

Vocabulary

genetics • fertilization • trait • hybrid • gene • allele • principle of dominance • segregation • gamete

Taking Notes

Two-Column Chart Before you read, draw a line down the center of a sheet of paper. On the left side, write the main ideas in this lesson. On the right side, note the details and examples that support each of those ideas.

THINK ABOUT IT What is an inheritance? To many people, it is money or property left to them by relatives who have passed away. That kind of inheritance matters, of course, but there is another kind that matters even more. It is something we each receive from our parents—a contribution that determines our blood type, the color of our hair, and so much more. Most people leave their money and property behind by writing a will. But what kind of inheritance makes a person's face round or their hair curly?

The Experiments of Gregor Mendel

🔑 Where does an organism get its unique characteristics?

Every living thing—plant or animal, microbe or human being—has a set of characteristics inherited from its parent or parents. Since the beginning of recorded history, people have wanted to understand how that inheritance is passed from generation to generation. The delivery of characteristics from parent to offspring is called heredity. The scientific study of heredity, known as **genetics,** is the key to understanding what makes each organism unique.

The modern science of genetics was founded by an Austrian monk named Gregor Mendel. Mendel, shown in **Figure 11–1,** was born in 1822 in what is now the Czech Republic. After becoming a priest, Mendel spent several years studying science and mathematics at the University of Vienna. He spent the next 14 years working in a monastery and teaching high school. In addition to his teaching duties, Mendel was in charge of the monastery garden. In this simple garden, he was to do the work that changed biology forever.

Mendel carried out his work with ordinary garden peas, partly because peas are small and easy to grow. A single pea plant can produce hundreds of offspring. Today we call peas a "model system." Scientists use model systems because they are convenient to study and may tell us how other organisms, including humans, actually function. By using peas, Mendel was able to carry out, in just one or two growing seasons, experiments that would have been impossible to do with humans and that would have taken decades—if not centuries—to do with pigs, horses, or other large animals.

FIGURE 11–1 Gregor Mendel

  Search ⟨ Lesson 11.1 ⟩ GO • Lesson Overview • Lesson Notes

Pea Flower

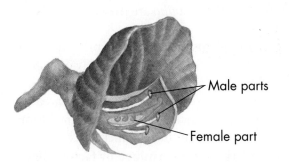

Male parts

Female part

Cross-Pollination

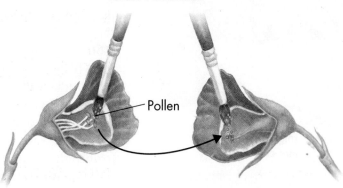

Pollen

The Role of Fertilization When Mendel began his experiments, he knew that the male part of each flower makes pollen, which contains the plant's male reproductive cells, called sperm. Similarly, Mendel knew that the female portion of each flower produces reproductive cells called eggs. During sexual reproduction, male and female reproductive cells join in a process known as **fertilization** to produce a new cell. In peas, this new cell develops into a tiny embryo encased within a seed.

Pea flowers are normally self-pollinating, which means that sperm cells fertilize egg cells from within the same flower. A plant grown from a seed produced by self-pollination inherits all of its characteristics from the single plant that bore it; it has a single parent.

Mendel's monastery garden had several stocks of pea plants. These plants were "true-breeding," meaning that they were self-pollinating, and would produce offspring identical to themselves. In other words, the traits of each successive generation would be the same. A **trait** is a specific characteristic, such as seed color or plant height, of an individual. Many traits vary from one individual to another. For instance, one stock of Mendel's seeds produced only tall plants, while another produced only short ones. One line produced only green seeds, another produced only yellow seeds.

To learn how these traits were determined, Mendel decided to "cross" his stocks of true-breeding plants—that is, he caused one plant to reproduce with another plant. To do this, he had to prevent self-pollination. He did so by cutting away the pollen-bearing male parts of a flower. He then dusted the pollen from a different plant onto the female part of that flower, as shown in **Figure 11–2.** This process, known as cross-pollination, produces a plant that has two different parents. Cross-pollination allowed Mendel to breed plants with traits different from those of their parents and then study the results.

Mendel studied seven different traits of pea plants. Each of these seven traits had two contrasting characteristics, such as green seed color or yellow seed color. Mendel crossed plants with each of the seven contrasting characteristics and then studied their offspring. The offspring of crosses between parents with different traits are called **hybrids.**

In Your Notebook *Explain, in your own words, what fertilization is.*

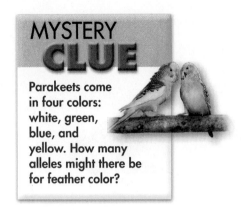
Genes and Alleles When doing genetic crosses, we call each original pair of plants the P, or parental, generation. Their offspring are called the F_1, or first filial, generation. (*Filius* and *filia* are the Latin words for "son" and "daughter.")

What were Mendel's F_1 hybrid plants like? To his surprise, for each trait studied, all the offspring had the characteristics of only one of its parents, as shown in **Figure 11–3.** In each cross, the nature of the other parent, with regard to each trait, seemed to have disappeared. From these results, Mendel drew two conclusions. His first conclusion formed the basis of our current understanding of inheritance. **An individual's characteristics are determined by factors that are passed from one parental generation to the next.** Today, scientists call the factors that are passed from parent to offspring **genes.**

Each of the traits Mendel studied was controlled by a single gene that occurred in two contrasting varieties. These variations produced different expressions, or forms, of each trait. For example, the gene for plant height occurred in one form that produced tall plants and in another form that produced short plants. The different forms of a gene are called **alleles** (uh LEELZ).

Dominant and Recessive Alleles Mendel's second conclusion is called the **principle of dominance.** This principle states that some alleles are dominant and others are recessive. An organism with at least one dominant allele for a particular form of a trait will exhibit that form of the trait. An organism with a recessive allele for a particular form of a trait will exhibit that form only when the dominant allele for the trait is not present. In Mendel's experiments, the allele for tall plants was dominant and the allele for short plants was recessive. Likewise, the allele for yellow seeds was dominant over the recessive allele for green seeds.

FIGURE 11–3 Mendel's F_1 Crosses When Mendel crossed plants with contrasting traits, the resulting hybrids had the traits of only one of the parents.

	Seed Shape	Seed Color	Seed Coat	Pod Shape	Pod Color	Flower Position	Plant Height
P	Round X Wrinkled	Yellow X Green	Gray X White	Smooth X Constricted	Green X Yellow	Axial X Terminal	Tall X Short
F_1	Round	Yellow	Gray	Smooth	Green	Axial	Tall

Mendel's Seven F_1 Crosses on Pea Plants

Classroom Variation

① Copy the data table into your notebook.

② Write a prediction of whether the traits listed in the table will be evenly distributed or if there will be more dominant than recessive traits.

③ Examine your features, using a mirror if necessary. Determine which traits you have for features A–E.

④ Interview at least 14 other students to find out which traits they have. Tally the numbers. Record the totals in each column.

Analyze and Conclude

1. Calculate Calculate the percentages of each trait in your total sample. How do these numbers compare to your prediction? MATH

Trait Survey				
Feature	Dominant Trait	Number	Recessive Trait	Number
A	Free ear lobes		Attached ear lobes	
B	Hair on fingers		No hair on fingers	
C	Widow's peak		No widow's peak	
D	Curly hair		Straight hair	
E	Cleft chin		Smooth chin	

2. Form a Hypothesis Why do you think recessive traits are more common in some cases?

In Your Notebook *Make a diagram that explains Mendel's principle of dominance.*

Segregation

🔑 **How are different forms of a gene distributed to offspring?**

Mendel didn't just stop after crossing the parent plants, because he had another question: Had the recessive alleles simply disappeared, or were they still present in the new plants? To find out, he allowed all seven kinds of F_1 hybrids to self-pollinate. The offspring of an F_1 cross are called the F_2 (second filial) generation. In effect, Mendel crossed the F_1 generation with itself to produce the F_2 offspring, as shown in **Figure 11–4.**

The F_1 Cross When Mendel compared the F_2 plants, he made a remarkable discovery: The traits controlled by the recessive alleles reappeared in the second generation. Roughly one fourth of the F_2 plants showed the trait controlled by the recessive allele. Why, then, did the recessive alleles seem to disappear in the F_1 generation, only to reappear in the F_2 generation?

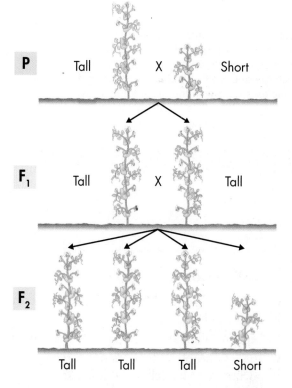

FIGURE 11–4 Results of the F_1 Cross When Mendel allowed the F_1 plants to reproduce by self-pollination, the traits controlled by recessive alleles reappeared in about one fourth of the F_2 plants in each cross.
Calculate *What proportion of the F_2 plants had a trait controlled by a dominant allele?* MATH

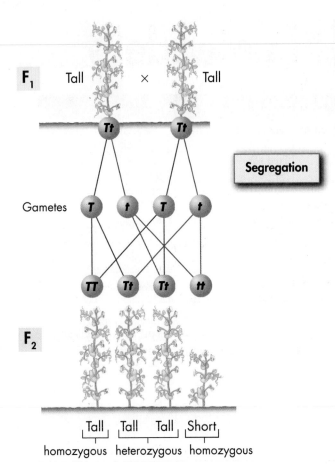

F₁ Tall × Tall

Segregation

Gametes

F₂

Tall | Tall | Tall | Short
homozygous | heterozygous | homozygous

FIGURE 11–5 Segregation During gamete formation, alleles segregate from each other so that each gamete carries only a single copy of each gene. Each F₁ plant makes two types of gametes—those with the allele for tallness and those with the allele for shortness. The alleles are paired up again when gametes fuse during fertilization.

Explaining the F₁ Cross To begin with, Mendel assumed that a dominant allele had masked the corresponding recessive allele in the F₁ generation. However, the trait controlled by the recessive allele did show up in some of the F₂ plants. This reappearance indicated that, at some point, the allele for shortness had separated from the allele for tallness. How did this separation, or **segregation,** of alleles occur? Mendel suggested that the alleles for tallness and shortness in the F₁ plants must have segregated from each other during the formation of the sex cells, or **gametes** (GAM eetz). Did that suggestion make sense?

The Formation of Gametes Let's assume, as Mendel might have, that all the F₁ plants inherited an allele for tallness from the tall parent and one for shortness from the short parent. Because the allele for tallness is dominant, all the F₁ plants are tall. ⊙ **During gamete formation, the alleles for each gene segregate from each other, so that each gamete carries only one allele for each gene.** Thus, each F₁ plant produces two kinds of gametes—those with the tall allele and those with the short allele.

Look at **Figure 11–5** to see how alleles separate during gamete formation and then pair up again in the F₂ generation. A capital letter represents a dominant allele. A lowercase letter represents a recessive allele. Now we can see why the recessive trait for height, *t*, reappeared in Mendel's F₂ generation. Each F₁ plant in Mendel's cross produced two kinds of gametes—those with the allele for tallness and those with the allele for shortness. Whenever a gamete that carried the *t* allele paired with the other gamete that carried the *t* allele to produce an F₂ plant, that plant was short. Every time one or both gametes of the pairing carried the *T* allele, a tall plant was produced. In other words, the F₂ generation had new combinations of alleles.

11.1 Assessment

Review Key Concepts ⚷

1. a. Review What did Mendel conclude determines biological inheritance?

b. Explain What are dominant and recessive alleles?

c. Apply Concepts Why were true-breeding pea plants important for Mendel's experiments?

2. a. Review What is segregation?

b. Explain What happens to alleles between the P generation and the F₂ generation?

c. Infer What evidence did Mendel use to explain how segregation occurs?

VISUAL THINKING

3. Use a diagram to explain Mendel's principles of dominance and segregation. Your diagram should show how alleles segregate during gamete formation.

11.2 Applying Mendel's Principles

THINK ABOUT IT *Nothing in life is certain.* There's a great deal of wisdom in that old saying, and genetics is a fine example. If a parent carries two different alleles for a certain gene, we can't be sure which of those alleles will be inherited by any one of the parent's offspring. However, think carefully about the nature of inheritance and you'll see that even if we can't predict the exact future, we can do something almost as useful—we can figure out the odds.

Probability and Punnett Squares

🔑 **How can we use probability to predict traits?**

Whenever Mendel performed a cross with pea plants, he carefully categorized and counted the offspring. Consequently, he had plenty of data to analyze. For example, whenever he crossed two plants that were hybrids for stem height (*Tt*), about three fourths of the resulting plants were tall and about one fourth were short.

Upon analyzing his data, Mendel realized that the principles of probability could be used to explain the results of his genetic crosses. **Probability** is a concept you may have learned about in math class. It is the likelihood that a particular event will occur. As an example, consider an ordinary event, such as flipping a coin. There are two possible outcomes of this event: The coin may land either heads up or tails up. The chance, or probability, of either outcome is equal. Therefore, the probability that a single coin flip will land heads up is 1 chance in 2. This amounts to 1/2, or 50 percent.

If you flip a coin three times in a row, what is the probability that it will land heads up every time? Each coin flip is an independent event with a 1/2 probability of landing heads up. Therefore, the probability of flipping three heads in a row is:

$$1/2 \times 1/2 \times 1/2 = 1/8$$

As you can see, you have 1 chance in 8 of flipping heads three times in a row. The multiplication of individual probabilities illustrates an important point: Past outcomes do not affect future ones. Just because you've flipped three heads in a row does not mean that you're more likely to have a coin land tails up on the next flip. The probability for that flip is still 1/2.

FIGURE 11–6 Probability Probability allows you to calculate the likelihood that a particular event will occur. The probability that the coin will land heads up is ½, or 50 percent.

Key Questions

🔑 *How can we use probability to predict traits?*

🔑 *How do alleles segregate when more than one gene is involved?*

🔑 *What did Mendel contribute to our understanding of genetics?*

Vocabulary

probability • homozygous • heterozygous • phenotype • genotype • Punnett square • independent assortment

Taking Notes

Preview Visuals Before you read, preview **Figure 11–7.** Try to infer the purpose of this diagram. As you read, compare your inference to the text. After you read, revise your statement if needed or write a new one about the diagram's purpose.

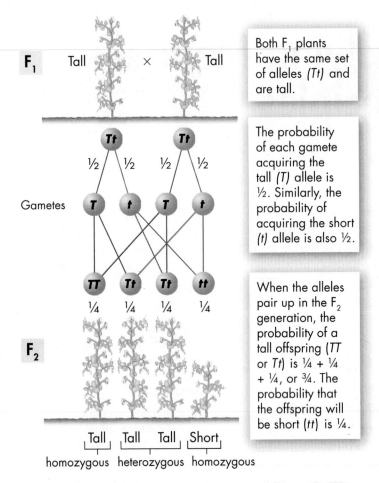

F₁ Tall × Tall

Both F₁ plants have the same set of alleles *(Tt)* and are tall.

Gametes

Tt   Tt
½   ½   ½   ½

T   t   T   t

The probability of each gamete acquiring the tall *(T)* allele is ½. Similarly, the probability of acquiring the short *(t)* allele is also ½.

TT   Tt   Tt   tt
¼   ¼   ¼   ¼

F₂

When the alleles pair up in the F₂ generation, the probability of a tall offspring *(TT* or *Tt)* is ¼ + ¼ + ¼, or ¾. The probability that the offspring will be short *(tt)* is ¼.

Tall | Tall | Tall | Short
homozygous heterozygous homozygous

FIGURE 11–7 Segregation and Probability In this cross, the *TT* and *Tt* allele combinations produced three tall pea plants, while the *tt* allele combination produced one short plant. These quantities follow the laws of probability. **Predict** *If you crossed a TT plant with a Tt plant, would the offspring be tall or short?*

Using Segregation to Predict Outcomes

The way in which alleles segregate during gamete formation is every bit as random as a coin flip. Therefore, the principles of probability can be used to predict the outcomes of genetic crosses.

Look again at Mendel's F₁ cross, shown in **Figure 11–7**. This cross produced a mixture of tall and short plants. Why were just 1/4 of the offspring short? Well, the F₁ plants were both tall. If each plant had one tall allele and one short allele (*Tt*), and if the alleles segregated as Mendel thought, then 1/2 of the gametes produced by the plants would carry the short allele (*t*). Yet, the *t* allele is recessive. The only way to produce a short (*tt*) plant is for two gametes, each carrying the *t* allele, to combine.

Like the coin toss, each F₂ gamete has a one in two, or 1/2, chance of carrying the *t* allele. There are two gametes, so the probability of both gametes carrying the *t* allele is $1/2 \times 1/2 = 1/4$. In other words, roughly one fourth of the F₂ offspring should be short, and the remaining three fourths should be tall. This predicted ratio—3 offspring exhibiting the dominant trait to 1 offspring exhibiting the recessive trait—showed up consistently in Mendel's experiments. For each of his seven crosses, about 3/4 of the plants showed the trait controlled by the dominant allele. About 1/4 showed the trait controlled by the recessive allele. Segregation did occur according to Mendel's model.

As you can see in the F₂ generation, not all organisms with the same characteristics have the same combinations of alleles. Both the *TT* and *Tt* allele combinations resulted in tall pea plants, but only one of these combinations contains identical alleles. Organisms that have two identical alleles for a particular gene—*TT* or *tt* in this example—are said to be **homozygous** (hoh moh zy gus). Organisms that have two different alleles for the same gene—such as *Tt*—are **heterozygous** (het ur oh zy gus).

Probabilities Predict Averages Probabilities predict the average outcome of a large number of events. If you flip a coin twice, you are likely to get one heads and one tails. However, you might also get two heads or two tails. To get the expected 50 : 50 ratio, you might have to flip the coin many times. The same is true of genetics.

The larger the number of offspring, the closer the results will be to the predicted values. If an F₂ generation contains just three or four offspring, it may not match Mendel's ratios. When an F₂ generation contains hundreds or thousands of individuals, the ratios usually come very close to matching predictions.

Genotype and Phenotype One of Mendel's most revolutionary insights followed directly from his observations of F_1 crosses: Every organism has a genetic makeup as well as a set of observable characteristics. All of the tall pea plants had the same **phenotype,** or physical traits. They did not, however, have the same **genotype,** or genetic makeup. Look again at **Figure 11–7** and you will find three different genotypes among the F_2 plants: *TT, Tt,* and *tt.* The genotype of an organism is inherited, and the phenotype is largely determined by the genotype. Two organisms may share the same phenotype but have different genotypes.

Using Punnett Squares One of the best ways to predict the outcome of a genetic cross is by drawing a simple diagram known as a **Punnett square.** ⚷ **Punnett squares use mathematical probability to help predict the genotype and phenotype combinations in genetic crosses.** Constructing a Punnett square is fairly easy. You begin with a square. Then, following the principle of segregation, all possible combinations of alleles in the gametes produced by one parent are written along the top edge of the square. The other parent's alleles are then segregated along the left edge. Next, every possible genotype is written into the boxes within the square, just as they might appear in the F_2 generation. **Figure 11–8** on the next page shows step-by-step instructions for constructing Punnett squares.

In Your Notebook *In your own words, write definitions for the terms* homozygous, heterozygous, phenotype, *and* genotype.

BUILD Vocabulary
PREFIXES The prefix *pheno-* in **phenotype** comes from the Greek word *phainein,* meaning "to show." *Geno-,* the prefix in **genotype,** is derived from the Greek word *genus,* meaning "race, kind."

Quick Lab
GUIDED INQUIRY

How Are Dimples Inherited?

❶ Write the last four digits of any telephone number. These four random digits represent the alleles of a gene that determines whether a person will have dimples. Odd digits represent the allele for the dominant trait of dimples. Even digits represent the allele for the recessive trait of no dimples.

❷ Use the first two digits to represent a father's genotype. Use the symbols *D* and *d* to write his genotype as shown in the example.

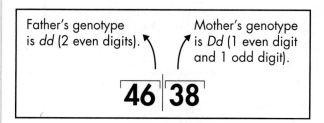
Father's genotype is *dd* (2 even digits). Mother's genotype is *Dd* (1 even digit and 1 odd digit).

46 | 38

❸ Use the last two digits the same way to find the mother's genotype. Write her genotype.

❹ Use **Figure 11–8** on the next page to construct a Punnett square for the cross of these parents. Then, using the Punnett square, determine the probability that their child will have dimples.

❺ Determine the class average of the percent of children with dimples.

Analyze and Conclude

1. Apply Concepts How does the class average compare with the result of a cross of two heterozygous parents?

2. Draw Conclusions What percentage of the children will be expected to have dimples if one parent is homozygous for dimples (*DD*) and the other is heterozygous (*Dd*)?

HOW TO MAKE A PUNNETT SQUARE

FIGURE 11–8 By drawing a Punnett square, you can determine the allele combinations that might result from a genetic cross.

One-Factor Cross		Two-Factor Cross

One-Factor Cross

Write the genotypes of the two organisms that will serve as parents in a cross. In this example we will cross a male and female osprey, or fish hawk, that are heterozygous for large beaks. They each have genotypes of *Bb*.

Bb and Bb

① Start With the Parents

Two-Factor Cross

In this example we will cross two pea plants that are heterozygous for size (tall and short alleles) and pod color (green and yellow alleles). The genotypes of the two parents are *TtGg* and *TtGg*.

TtGg and TtGg

Determine what alleles would be found in all of the possible gametes that each parent could produce.

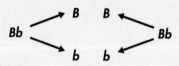

② Figure Out the Gametes

Determine what alleles would be found in all of the possible gametes that each parent could produce.

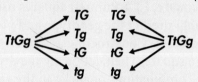

TtGg → TG, Tg, tG, tg ← TtGg

Draw a table with enough squares for each pair of gametes from each parent. In this case, each parent can make two different types of gametes, *B* and *b*. Enter the genotypes of the gametes produced by both parents on the top and left sides of the table.

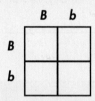

③ Line Them Up

In this case, each parent can make 4 different types of gametes, so the table needs to be 4 rows by 4 columns, or 16 squares.

	TG	tG	Tg	tg
TG				
tG				
Tg				
tg				

Fill in the table by combining the gametes' genotypes.

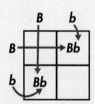

	B	b
B	BB	Bb
b	Bb	bb

④ Write Out the New Genotypes

Fill in the table by combining the gametes' genotypes.

	TG	tG	Tg	tg
TG				
tG			TtGg	
Tg				
tg		ttGg		

	TG	tG	Tg	tg
TG	TTGG	TtGG	TTGg	TtGg
tG	TtGG	ttGG	TtGg	ttGg
Tg	TTGg	TtGg	TTgg	Ttgg
tg	TtGg	ttGg	Ttgg	ttgg

Determine the genotype and phenotype of each offspring. Calculate the percentage of each. In this example, ³⁄₄ of the chicks will have large beaks, but only ½ will be heterozygous for this trait *(Bb)*.

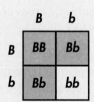

	B	b
B	BB	Bb
b	Bb	bb

⑤ Figure Out the Results

In this example, the color of the squares represents pod color. Alleles written in black indicate short plants, while alleles written in red indicate tall plants.

	TG	tG	Tg	tg
TG	TTGG	TtGG	TTGg	TtGg
tG	TtGG	ttGG	TtGg	ttGg
Tg	TTGg	TtGg	TTgg	Ttgg
tg	TtGg	ttGg	Ttgg	ttgg

BIOLOGY.com ▸ Search (Lesson 11.2) **GO** • InterActive Art

Independent Assortment

How do alleles segregate when more than one gene is involved?

After showing that alleles segregate during the formation of gametes, Mendel wondered if the segregation of one pair of alleles affects another pair. For example, does the gene that determines the shape of a seed affect the gene for seed color? To find out, Mendel followed two different genes as they passed from one generation to the next. Because it involves two different genes, Mendel's experiment is known as a two-factor, or "dihybrid," cross. (Single-gene crosses are "monohybrid" crosses.)

The Two-Factor Cross: F₁ First, Mendel crossed true-breeding plants that produced only round yellow peas with plants that produced wrinkled green peas. The round yellow peas had the genotype *RRYY*, and the wrinkled green peas had the genotype *rryy*. All of the F₁ offspring produced round yellow peas. These results showed that the alleles for yellow and round peas are dominant. As the Punnett square in **Figure 11–9** shows, the genotype in each of these F₁ plants is *RrYy*. In other words, the F₁ plants were all heterozygous for both seed shape and seed color. This cross did not indicate whether genes assort, or segregate independently. However, it provided the hybrid plants needed to breed the F₂ generation.

The Two-Factor Cross: F₂ In the second part of this experiment, Mendel crossed the F₁ plants to produce F₂ offspring. Remember, each F₁ plant was formed by the fusion of a gamete carrying the dominant *RY* alleles with another gamete carrying the recessive *ry* alleles. Did this mean that the two dominant alleles would always stay together, or would they segregate independently, so that any combination of alleles was possible?

In Mendel's experiment, the F₂ plants produced 556 seeds. Mendel compared their variation. He observed that 315 of the seeds were round and yellow, while another 32 seeds were wrinkled and green—the two parental phenotypes. However, 209 seeds had combinations of phenotypes, and therefore combinations of alleles, that were not found in either parent. This clearly meant that the alleles for seed shape segregated independently of those for seed color. Put another way, genes that segregate independently (such as the genes for seed shape and seed color in pea plants) do not influence each other's inheritance.

Mendel's experimental results were very close to the 9 : 3 : 3 : 1 ratio that the Punnett square shown in **Figure 11–10** predicts. Mendel had discovered the principle of **independent assortment.** **The principle of independent assortment states that genes for different traits can segregate independently during the formation of gametes.** Independent assortment helps account for the many genetic variations observed in plants, animals, and other organisms—even when they have the same parents.

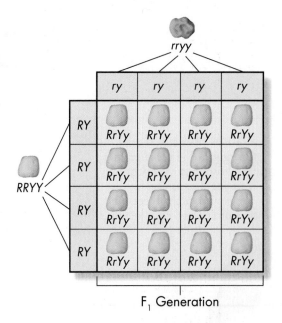

FIGURE 11–9 Two-Factor Cross: F₁ Mendel crossed plants that were homozygous dominant for round yellow peas with plants that were homozygous recessive for wrinkled green peas. All of the F₁ offspring were heterozygous dominant for round yellow peas. **Interpret Graphics** *How is the genotype of the offspring different from that of the homozygous dominant parent?*

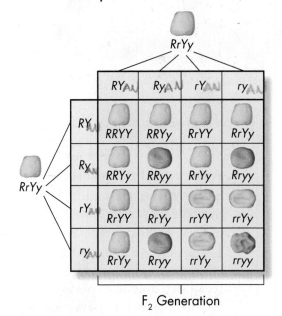

FIGURE 11–10 Two-Factor Cross: F₂ When Mendel crossed F₁ plants that were heterozygous dominant for round yellow peas, he found that the alleles segregated independently to produce the F₂ generation.

A Summary of Mendel's Principles

🔑 **What did Mendel contribute to our understanding of genetics?**

As you have seen, Mendel's principles of segregation and independent assortment can be observed through one- and two-factor crosses. 🔑 **Mendel's principles of heredity, observed through patterns of inheritance, form the basis of modern genetics.** These principles are as follows:

- The inheritance of biological characteristics is determined by individual units called genes, which are passed from parents to offspring.
- Where two or more forms (alleles) of the gene for a single trait exist, some alleles may be dominant and others may be recessive.
- In most sexually reproducing organisms, each adult has two copies of each gene—one from each parent. These genes segregate from each other when gametes are formed.
- Alleles for different genes usually segregate independently of each other.

Mendel's principles don't apply only to plants. At the beginning of the 1900s, the American geneticist Thomas Hunt Morgan wanted to use a model organism of another kind to advance the study of genetics. He decided to work on a tiny insect that kept showing up, uninvited, in his laboratory. The insect was the common fruit fly, *Drosophila melanogaster,* shown in **Figure 11–11.** *Drosophila* can produce plenty of offspring—a single pair can produce hundreds of young. Before long, Morgan and other biologists had tested all of Mendel's principles and learned that they applied to flies and other organisms as well. In fact, Mendel's basic principles can be used to study the inheritance of human traits and to calculate the probability of certain traits appearing in the next generation. You will learn more about human genetics in Chapter 14.

FIGURE 11–11 A Model Organism The common fruit fly, *Drosophila melanogaster,* is an ideal organism for genetic research. These fruit flies are poised on a lemon.

11.2 Assessment

Review Key Concepts 🔑

1. a. Review What is probability?

b. Use Models How are Punnett squares used to predict the outcomes of genetic crosses?

2. a. Review What is independent assortment?

b. Calculate An F_1 plant that is homozygous for shortness is crossed with a heterozygous F_1 plant. What is the probability that a seed from the cross will produce a tall plant? Use a Punnett square to explain your answer and to compare the probable genetic variations in the F_2 plants. **MATH**

3. a. Review How did Gregor Mendel contribute to our understanding of inherited traits?

b. Apply Concepts Why is the fruit fly an ideal organism for genetic research?

Apply the **Big** idea

Information and Heredity

4. Suppose you are an avid gardener. One day, you come across a plant with beautiful lavender flowers. Knowing that the plant is self-pollinating, you harvest its seeds and plant them. Of the 106 plants that grow from these seeds, 31 have white flowers. Using a Punnett square, draw conclusions about the nature of the allele for lavender flowers.

11.3 Other Patterns of Inheritance

THINK ABOUT IT Mendel's principles offer a tidy set of rules with which to predict various patterns of inheritance. Unfortunately, biology is not a tidy science. There are exceptions to every rule, and exceptions to the exceptions. What happens if one allele is not completely dominant over another? What if a gene has several alleles?

Beyond Dominant and Recessive Alleles

🔑 **What are some exceptions to Mendel's principles?**

Despite the importance of Mendel's work, there are important exceptions to most of his principles. For example, not all genes show simple patterns of inheritance. In most organisms, genetics is more complicated, because the majority of genes have more than two alleles. Also, many important traits are controlled by more than one gene. Understanding these exceptions allows geneticists to predict the ways in which more complex traits are inherited.

Incomplete Dominance A cross between two four o'clock (*Mirabilis jalapa*) plants shows a common exception to Mendel's principles. 🔑 **Some alleles are neither dominant nor recessive.** As shown in **Figure 11–12,** the F_1 generation produced by a cross between red-flowered (*RR*) and white-flowered (*WW*) *Mirabilis* plants consists of pink-colored flowers (*RW*). Which allele is dominant in this case? Neither one. Cases in which one allele is not completely dominant over another are called **incomplete dominance.** In incomplete dominance, the heterozygous phenotype lies somewhere between the two homozygous phenotypes.

Codominance A similar situation arises from **codominance,** in which the phenotypes produced by both alleles are clearly expressed. For example, in certain varieties of chicken, the allele for black feathers is codominant with the allele for white feathers. Heterozygous chickens have a color described as "erminette," speckled with black and white feathers. Unlike the blending of red and white colors in heterozygous four o'clocks, black and white colors appear separately in chickens. Many human genes, including one for a protein that controls cholesterol levels in the blood, show codominance, too. People with the heterozygous form of this gene produce two different forms of the protein, each with a different effect on cholesterol levels.

Key Questions

🔑 **What are some exceptions to Mendel's principles?**

🔑 **Does the environment have a role in how genes determine traits?**

Vocabulary
incomplete dominance • codominance • multiple allele • polygenic trait

Taking Notes
Outline Make an outline using the green and blue headings. As you read, write bulleted notes below each heading to summarize its topic.

FIGURE 11–12 Incomplete Dominance In four o'clock plants, the alleles for red and white flowers show incomplete dominance. Heterozygous (*RW*) plants have pink flowers—a mix of red and white coloring.

Analyzing Data

Human Blood Types

Red blood cells carry antigens, molecules that can trigger an immune reaction, on their surfaces. Human blood type A carries an A antigen, type B has a B antigen, type AB has both antigens, and type O carries neither antigen. The gene for these antigens has three alleles; A, B, and O.

For a transfusion to succeed, it must not introduce a new antigen into the body of the recipient. So, a person with type A blood may receive type O, but not vice versa.

Another gene controls a second type of antigen, known as Rh factor. Rh⁺ individuals carry this antigen, while Rh⁻ ones don't. This chart of the U.S. population shows the percentage of each blood type.

1. **Interpret Graphs** Which blood type makes up the greatest percentage of the U.S. population?
2. **Calculate** What percentage of the total U.S. population has a positive Rh factor? What percentage has a negative Rh factor?

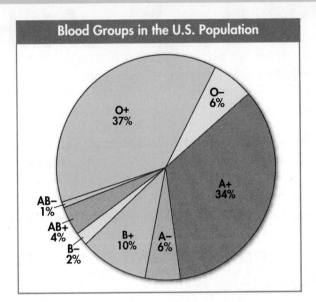

Blood Groups in the U.S. Population

O+ 37%
O− 6%
A+ 34%
A− 6%
B+ 10%
B− 2%
AB+ 4%
AB− 1%

3. **Infer** Which blood type can be used for transfusion into the largest percentage of individuals? Which type has the smallest percentage of possible donors available?

4. **Predict** Could a person with O⁺ blood have two parents with O⁻ blood? Could that person have a daughter with AB⁺ blood? Explain your answers.

MYSTERY CLUE

Green feathers don't actually contain green pigments. Rather, they contain a mixture of blue and yellow pigments. Could feather color be controlled by more than one gene?

Multiple Alleles So far, our examples have described genes for which there are only two alleles, such as *a* and *A*. In nature, such genes are the exception rather than the rule. 🔑 **Many genes exist in several different forms and are therefore said to have multiple alleles.** A gene with more than two alleles is said to have **multiple alleles.** An individual, of course, usually has only two copies of each gene, but many different alleles are often found within a population. One of the best-known examples is coat color in rabbits. A rabbit's coat color is determined by a single gene that has at least four different alleles. The four known alleles display a pattern of simple dominance that can produce four coat colors. Many other genes have multiple alleles, including the human genes for blood type.

Polygenic Traits 🔑 **Many traits are produced by the interaction of several genes.** Traits controlled by two or more genes are said to be **polygenic traits.** *Polygenic* means "many genes." For example, at least three genes are involved in making the reddish-brown pigment in the eyes of fruit flies. Polygenic traits often show a wide range of phenotypes. The variety of skin color in humans comes about partly because more than four different genes probably control this trait.

> **In Your Notebook** *In your own words, describe multiple alleles and polygenic traits. How are they similar? How are they different?*

Genes and the Environment

🔑 *Does the environment have a role in how genes determine traits?*

The characteristics of any organism—whether plant, fruit fly, or human being—are not determined solely by the genes that organism inherits. Genes provide a plan for development, but how that plan unfolds also depends on the environment. In other words, the phenotype of an organism is only partly determined by its genotype.

Consider the western white butterfly, *Pontia occidentalis*, shown in **Figure 11–13.** It is found throughout western North America. Butterfly enthusiasts had noted for years that western whites hatching in the summer (right) had different color patterns on their wings than those hatching in the spring (left). Scientific studies showed the reason— butterflies hatching in the shorter days of springtime had greater levels of pigment in their wings, making their markings appear darker than those hatching in the longer days of summer. In other words, the environment in which the butterflies develop influences the expression of their genes for wing coloration. 🔑 **Environmental conditions can affect gene expression and influence genetically determined traits.** An individual's actual phenotype is determined by its environment as well as its genes.

In the case of the western white butterfly, these changes in wing pigmentation are particularly important. In order to fly effectively, the body temperature of the butterfly must be 28°C–40°C (about 84°F–104°F). Since the spring months are cooler in the west, greater pigmentation helps them reach the body temperature needed for flight. Similarly, in the hot summer months, less pigmentation enables the moths to avoid overheating.

Environmental Temperature and Butterfly Needs		
Temp. Needed for Flight	Average Spring Temp.	Average Summer Temp.
28–40°C	26.5°C	34.8°C

FIGURE 11–13 Temperature and Wing Color Western white butterflies that hatch in the spring have darker wing patterns than those that hatch in summer. The dark wing color helps increase their body heat. This trait is important because the butterflies need to reach a certain temperature in order to fly. **Calculate** *What is the difference between the minimum temperature these butterflies need to fly and the average spring temperature? Would the same calculation apply to butterflies developing in the summer?* MATH

11.3 Assessment

Review Key Concepts 🔑

1. a. Review What does *incomplete dominance* mean? Give an example.

b. Design an Experiment Design an experiment to determine whether the pink flowers of petunia plants result from incomplete dominance.

2. a. Review What is the relationship between the environment and phenotype?

b. Infer What might be the result of an exceptionally hot spring on wing pigmentation in the western white butterfly?

PRACTICE PROBLEM

3. Construct a genetics problem to be given as an assignment to a classmate. The problem must test incomplete dominance, codominance, multiple alleles, or polygenic traits. Your problem must have an answer key that includes all of your work.

Careers & BIOLOGY

If you enjoy learning about genetics, you may want to pursue one of the careers listed below.

FORENSIC SCIENTIST

Do you enjoy solving puzzles? That's what forensic scientists do when they solve crimes. Local, state, and federal agencies employ forensic scientists to use scientific approaches that support criminal investigations. Criminalists are forensic scientists who specialize in the analysis of physical evidence, such as hair, fiber, DNA, fingerprints, and weapons. They are often called to testify in trials as expert witnesses.

PLANT BREEDER

Did you ever wonder how seedless watermelons become seedless? They are the product of a plant breeder. Plant breeders use genetic techniques to manipulate crops. Often, the goal is to make a crop more useful by increasing yield or nutritional value. Some breeders introduce new traits, such as pesticide resistance, to the plant's genetic makeup.

POPULATION GENETICIST

Why are certain populations more susceptible to particular diseases? This is the kind of question that population geneticists answer. Their goal is to figure out why specific traits of distinct groups of organisms occur in varying frequencies. The patterns they uncover can lead to an understanding of how gene expression changes as a population evolves.

CAREER CLOSE-UP:

Sophia Cleland, Population Geneticist and Immunologist

Sophia Cleland, a Ph.D. student in immunology at George Washington University, studies the molecular, cellular, and genetic mechanisms that contribute to autoimmune diseases. One of only a few Native Americans with an advanced degree in genetics, Ms. Cleland became interested in autoimmune diseases when she noticed that the frequencies of these illnesses, such as rheumatoid arthritis and lupus, were several times higher among her tribal communities (Lakota-Sioux and California Mission Indian) than among Caucasians. Furthermore, she observed that such diseases progressed more rapidly among these communities than in any other human group in the world. Because of the frequency and severity of these diseases among indigenous tribal groups, Ms. Cleland is spreading the word about the need for focused research in this area.

> *"A compromise is needed between the world views of indigenous tribal groups and modern scientific approaches to gathering knowledge. We will encounter difficulties, but by working together with an open mind to learn, balanced and just results are possible."*

WRITING How do you think a high frequency of genetic illness can affect a population? Explain.

11.4 Meiosis

THINK ABOUT IT As geneticists in the early 1900s applied Mendel's principles, they wondered where genes might be located. They expected genes to be carried on structures inside the cell, but *which* structures? What cellular processes could account for segregation and independent assortment, as Mendel had described?

Chromosome Number

🔑 **How many sets of genes are found in most adult organisms?**

To hold true, Mendel's principles require at least two events to occur. First, an organism with two parents must inherit a single copy of every gene from each parent. Second, when that organism produces gametes, those two sets of genes must be separated so that each gamete contains just one set of genes. As it turns out, chromosomes—those strands of DNA and protein inside the cell nucleus—are the carriers of genes. The genes are located in specific positions on chromosomes.

Diploid Cells Consider the fruit fly that Morgan used, *Drosophila.* A body cell in an adult fruit fly has eight chromosomes, as shown in **Figure 11–14.** Four of the chromosomes come from its male parent, and four come from its female parent. These two sets of chromosomes are **homologous** (hoh MAHL uh gus), meaning that each of the four chromosomes from the male parent has a corresponding chromosome from the female parent. A cell that contains both sets of homologous chromosomes is said to be **diploid,** meaning "two sets." 🔑 **The diploid cells of most adult organisms contain two complete sets of inherited chromosomes and two complete sets of genes.** The diploid number of chromosomes is sometimes represented by the symbol 2N. Thus, for *Drosophila,* the diploid number is 8, which can be written as $2N = 8$, where N represents the single set of chromosomes found in a sperm or egg cell.

Haploid Cells Some cells contain only a single set of chromosomes, and therefore a single set of genes. Such cells are **haploid,** meaning "one set." The gametes of sexually reproducing organisms, including fruit flies and peas, are haploid. For *Drosophila* gametes, the haploid number is 4, which can be written as $N = 4$.

Key Questions

🔑 How many sets of genes are found in most adult organisms?

🔑 What events occur during each phase of meiosis?

🔑 How is meiosis different from mitosis?

🔑 How can two alleles from different genes be inherited together?

Vocabulary

homologous • diploid • haploid • meiosis • tetrad • crossing-over • zygote

Taking Notes

Compare/Contrast Table Before you read, make a compare/contrast table to show the differences between mitosis and meiosis. As you read, complete the table.

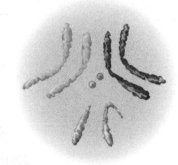

FIGURE 11–14 Fruit Fly Chromosomes These chromosomes are from a fruit fly. Each of the fruit fly's body cells is diploid, containing eight chromosomes.

FIGURE 11–15 Meiosis I During meiosis I, a diploid cell undergoes a series of events that results in the production of two daughter cells. Neither daughter cell has the same sets of chromosomes that the original diploid cell had. **Interpret Graphics** *How does crossing-over affect the alleles on a chromosome?*

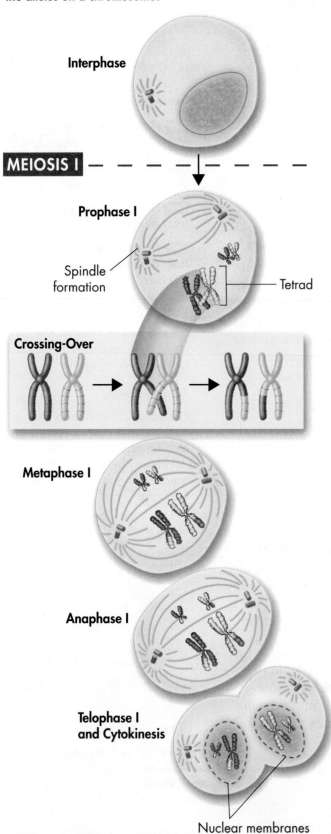

Interphase

MEIOSIS I — — — — —

Prophase I

Spindle formation

Tetrad

Crossing-Over

Metaphase I

Anaphase I

Telophase I and Cytokinesis

Nuclear membranes

Phases of Meiosis

🔑 *What events occur during each phases of meiosis?*

How are haploid (N) gamete cells produced from diploid (2N) cells? That's where meiosis (my OH sis) comes in. **Meiosis** is a process in which the number of chromosomes per cell is cut in half through the separation of homologous chromosomes in a diploid cell. Meiosis usually involves two distinct divisions, called meiosis I and meiosis II. By the end of meiosis II, the diploid cell becomes four haploid cells. Let's see how meiosis takes place in a cell that has a diploid number of 4 (2N = 4).

Meiosis I Just prior to meiosis I, the cell undergoes a round of chromosome replication during interphase. As in mitosis, which was discussed in Chapter 10, each replicated chromosome consists of two identical chromatids joined at the center. Follow the sequence in **Figure 11–15** as you read about meiosis I.

▶ *Prophase I* After interphase I, the cell begins to divide, and the chromosomes pair up. 🔑 **In prophase I of meiosis, each replicated chromosome pairs with its corresponding homologous chromosome.** This pairing forms a structure called a **tetrad,** which contains four chromatids. As the homologous chromosomes form tetrads, they undergo a process called **crossing-over.** First, the chromatids of the homologous chromosomes cross over one another. Then, the crossed sections of the chromatids—which contain alleles—are exchanged. Crossing-over therefore produces new combinations of alleles in the cell.

▶ *Metaphase I and Anaphase I* As prophase I ends, a spindle forms and attaches to each tetrad. 🔑 **During metaphase I of meiosis, paired homologous chromosomes line up across the center of the cell.** As the cell moves into anaphase I, the homologous pairs of chromosomes separate. 🔑 **During anaphase I, spindle fibers pull each homologous chromosome pair toward opposite ends of the cell.**

▶ *Telophase I and Cytokinesis* When anaphase I is complete, the separated chromosomes cluster at opposite ends of the cell. 🔑 **The next phase is telophase I, in which a nuclear membrane forms around each cluster of chromosomes. Cytokinesis follows telophase I, forming two new cells.**

Meiosis I results in two cells, called daughter cells. However, because each pair of homologous chromosomes was separated, neither daughter cell has the two complete sets of chromosomes that it would have in a diploid cell. Those two sets have been shuffled and sorted almost like a deck of cards. The two cells produced by meiosis I have sets of chromosomes and alleles that are different from each other and from the diploid cell that entered meiosis I.

Meiosis II The two cells now enter a second meiotic division. Unlike the first division, neither cell goes through a round of chromosome replication before entering meiosis II.

▶ *Prophase II* ⚷ **As the cells enter prophase II, their chromosomes—each consisting of two chromatids—become visible.** The chromosomes do not pair to form tetrads, because the homologous pairs were already separated during meiosis I.

▶ *Metaphase II, Anaphase II, Telophase II, and Cytokinesis* During metaphase of meiosis II, chromosomes line up in the center of each cell. As the cell enters anaphase, the paired chromatids separate. ⚷ **The final four phases of meiosis II are similar to those in meiosis I. However, the result is four haploid daughter cells.** In the example shown here, each of the four daughter cells produced in meiosis II receive two chromosomes. These four daughter cells now contain the haploid number (N)—just two chromosomes each.

Gametes to Zygotes The haploid cells produced by meiosis II are the gametes that are so important to heredity. In male animals, these gametes are called sperm. In some plants, pollen grains contain haploid sperm cells. In female animals, generally only one of the cells produced by meiosis is involved in reproduction. The female gamete is called an egg in animals and an egg cell in some plants. After it is fertilized, the egg is called a **zygote** (zy goht). The zygote undergoes cell division by mitosis and eventually forms a new organism.

In Your Notebook *Describe the difference between meiosis I and meiosis II. How are the end results different?*

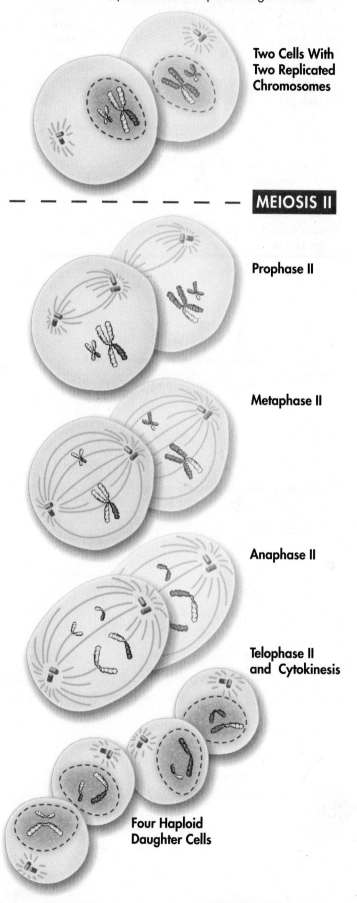

FIGURE 11–16 Meiosis II The second meiotic division, called meiosis II, produces four haploid daughter cells.

Two Cells With Two Replicated Chromosomes

MEIOSIS II

Prophase II

Metaphase II

Anaphase II

Telophase II and Cytokinesis

Four Haploid Daughter Cells

COMPARING MITOSIS AND MEIOSIS

FIGURE 11–17 Mitosis and meiosis both ensure that cells inherit genetic information. Both processes begin after interphase, when chromosome replication occurs. However, the two processes differ in the separation of chromosomes, the number of cells produced, and the number of chromosomes each cell contains.

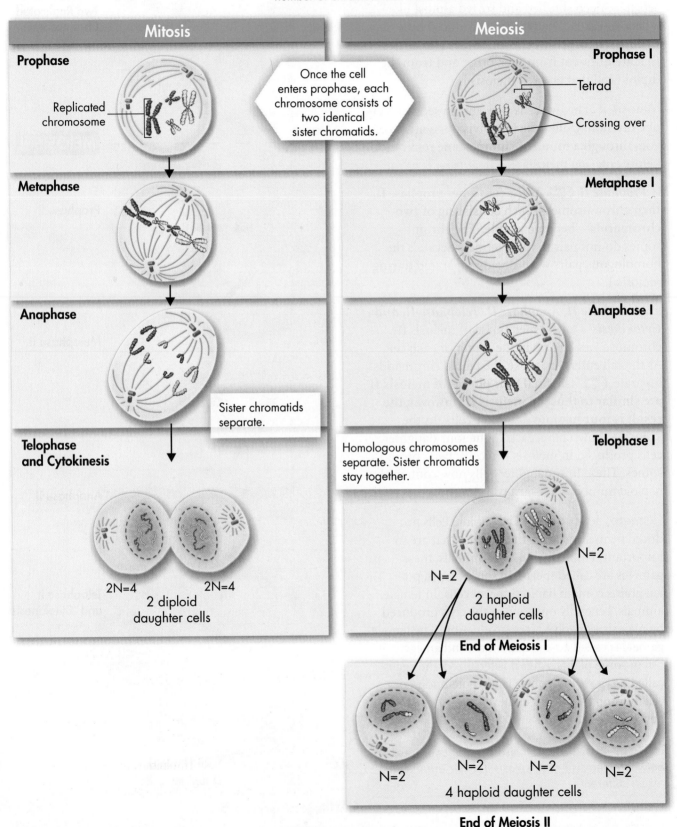

Mitosis

Prophase

Replicated chromosome

Metaphase

Anaphase

Telophase and Cytokinesis

2N=4   2N=4
2 diploid daughter cells

Once the cell enters prophase, each chromosome consists of two identical sister chromatids.

Sister chromatids separate.

Meiosis

Prophase I

Tetrad

Crossing over

Metaphase I

Anaphase I

Telophase I

Homologous chromosomes separate. Sister chromatids stay together.

N=2   N=2
2 haploid daughter cells

End of Meiosis I

N=2   N=2   N=2   N=2
4 haploid daughter cells

End of Meiosis II

Comparing Meiosis and Mitosis

How is meiosis different from mitosis?

The words *mitosis* and *meiosis* may sound similar, but the two processes are very different, as you can see in **Figure 11–17.** Mitosis can be a form of asexual reproduction, whereas meiosis is an early step in sexual reproduction. There are three other ways in which these two processes differ.

Replication and Separation of Genetic Material Mitosis and meiosis are both preceded by a complete copying, or replication, of the genetic material of chromosomes. However, the next steps differ dramatically. **In mitosis, when the two sets of genetic material separate, each daughter cell receives one complete set of chromosomes. In meiosis, homologous chromosomes line up and then move to separate daughter cells.** As a result, the two alleles for each gene are segregated, and end up in different cells. The sorting and recombination of genes in meiosis result in a greater variety of possible gene combinations than could result from mitosis.

Changes in Chromosome Number **Mitosis does not normally change the chromosome number of the original cell. This is not the case for meiosis, which reduces the chromosome number by half.** A diploid cell that enters mitosis with eight chromosomes will divide to produce two diploid daughter cells, each of which also has eight chromosomes. On the other hand, a diploid cell that enters meiosis with eight chromosomes will pass through two meiotic divisions to produce four haploid gamete cells, each with only four chromosomes.

Calculating Haploid and Diploid Numbers

Haploid and diploid numbers are designated by the algebraic notations N and 2N, respectively. Either number can be calculated when the other is known. For example, if the haploid number (N) is 3, the diploid number (2N) is 2 × 3, or 6. If the diploid number (2N) is 12, the haploid number (N) is 12/2, or 6.

The table shows haploid or diploid numbers of a variety of organisms. Copy the table into your notebook and complete it. Then, use the table to answer the questions that follow.

Trait Survey		
Organism	Haploid Number	Diploid Number
Amoeba	N=25	
Chimpanzee	N=24	
Earthworm	N=18	
Fern		2N=1010
Hamster	N=22	
Human		2N=46
Onion		2N=16

1. **Calculate** What are the haploid numbers for the fern and onion plants? **MATH**

2. **Interpret Data** In the table, which organisms' diploid numbers are closest to that of a human?

3. **Apply Concepts** Why is a diploid number always even?

4. **Evaluate** Which organism's haploid and diploid numbers do you find the most surprising? Why?

Number of Cell Divisions Mitosis is a single cell division, resulting in the production of two identical daughter cells. On the other hand, meiosis requires two rounds of cell division, and, in most organisms, produces a total of four daughter cells. ⚷ **Mitosis results in the production of two genetically identical diploid cells, whereas meiosis produces four genetically different haploid cells.**

Gene Linkage and Gene Maps

⚷ *How can two alleles from different genes be inherited together?*

If you think carefully about Mendel's principle of independent assortment in relation to meiosis, one question might bother you. Genes that are located on different chromosomes assort independently, but what about genes that are located on the same chromosome? Wouldn't they generally be inherited together?

Gene Linkage The answer to this question, as Thomas Hunt Morgan first realized in 1910, is yes. Morgan's research on fruit flies led him to the principle of gene linkage. After identifying more than 50 *Drosophila* genes, Morgan discovered that many of them appeared to be "linked" together in ways that, at first glance, seemed to violate the principle of independent assortment. For example, Morgan used a fly with reddish-orange eyes and miniature wings in a series of test crosses. His results showed that the genes for those two traits were almost always inherited together. Only rarely did the genes separate from each other. Morgan and his associates observed so many genes that were inherited together that, before long, they could group all of the fly's genes into four linkage groups. The linkage groups assorted independently, but all of the genes in one group were inherited together. As it turns out, *Drosophila* has four linkage groups and four pairs of chromosomes.

FIGURE 11–18 Gene Map This gene map shows the location of a variety of genes on chromosome 2 of the fruit fly. The genes are named after the problems that abnormal alleles cause, *not* after the normal structures. **Interpret Graphics** *Where on the chromosome is the "purple eye" gene located?*

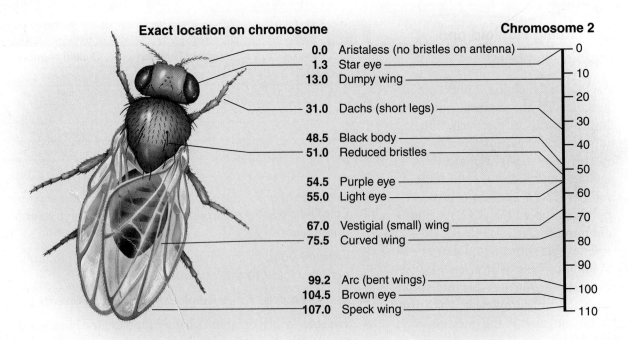

Exact location on chromosome

Chromosome 2

0.0	Aristaless (no bristles on antenna)
1.3	Star eye
13.0	Dumpy wing
31.0	Dachs (short legs)
48.5	Black body
51.0	Reduced bristles
54.5	Purple eye
55.0	Light eye
67.0	Vestigial (small) wing
75.5	Curved wing
99.2	Arc (bent wings)
104.5	Brown eye
107.0	Speck wing

Morgan's findings led to two remarkable conclusions. First, each chromosome is actually a group of linked genes. Second, Mendel's principle of independent assortment still holds true. It is the chromosomes, however, that assort independently, not individual genes. **Alleles of different genes tend to be inherited together from one generation to the next when those genes are located on the same chromosome.**

How did Mendel manage to miss gene linkage? By luck, or design, several of the genes he studied are on different chromosomes. Others are so far apart that they also assort independently.

Gene Mapping In 1911, a Columbia University student was working part time in Morgan's lab. This student, Alfred Sturtevant, wondered if the frequency of crossing-over between genes during meiosis might be a clue to the genes' locations. Sturtevant reasoned that the farther apart two genes were on a chromosome, the more likely it would be that crossing-over would occur between them. If two genes are close together, then crossovers between them should be rare. If two genes are far apart, then crossovers between them should be more common. By this reasoning, he could use the frequency of crossing-over between genes to determine their distances from each other.

Sturtevant gathered up several notebooks of lab data and took them back to his room. The next morning, he presented Morgan with a gene map showing the relative locations of each known gene on one of the *Drosophila* chromosomes. Sturtevant's method has been used to construct gene maps, like the one in **Figure 11–18,** ever since this discovery.

MYSTERY CLUE

White is the least common color found in parakeets. What does this fact suggest about the genotypes of both green parents?

11.4 Assessment

Review Key Concepts

1. a. Review Describe the main results of meiosis.

   b. Calculate In human cells, 2N = 46. How many chromosomes would you expect to find in a sperm cell? How many would you expect to find in an egg cell? **MATH**

2. a. Review Write a summary of each phase of meiosis.

   b. Use Analogies Compare the chromosomes of a diploid cell to a collection of shoes in a closet. How are they similar? What would make the shoe collection comparable to the chromosomes of a haploid cell?

3. a. Review What are the principal differences between mitosis and meiosis?

   b. Apply Concepts Is there any difference between sister chromatids and homologous pairs of chromosomes? Explain.

4. a. Review How does the principle of independent assortment apply to chromosomes?

   b. Infer If two genes are on the same chromosome but usually assort independently, what does that tell you about how close together they are?

Apply the Big idea

Information and Heredity

5. In asexual reproduction, mitosis occurs but meiosis does not occur. Which type of reproduction—sexual or asexual—results in offspring with greater genetic variation? Explain your answer.

Pre-Lab: Modeling Meiosis

Problem How does meiosis increase genetic variation?

Materials pop-it beads, magnetic centromeres, large sheet of paper, colored pencils, scissors

Lab Manual Chapter 11 Lab

Skills Use Models, Sequence, Draw Conclusions

Connect to the Big idea Inherited traits are passed from parents to offspring in the form of genes. Offspring produced by sexual reproduction receive one set of genes from each parent when the reproductive cells, or gametes, combine. Meiosis is the process by which gametes are produced. During meiosis, new combinations of genes form when genes cross over from one homologous chromosome to the other. Also, the sorting of chromatids among gametes is random. Both crossing-over and sorting lead to greater diversity in the genes of a population.

In this lab, you will model the steps of meiosis and track what happens to alleles as they move from diploid cells to haploid gametes.

Background Questions

a. Review What are alleles?

b. Sequence What happens during prophase I of meiosis? What happens during metaphase I? What happens during anaphase I?

c. Compare and Contrast In what ways does meiosis differ from mitosis?

Pre-Lab Questions

Preview the procedure in the lab manual.

1. Control Variables Why must you use the same number of beads when you construct the second chromosome in Step 1?

2. Infer Why is the longer chromosome pair used to model crossing-over?

3. Calculate A diploid cell has two pairs of homologous chromosomes. How many different combinations of chromosomes could there be in the gametes? MATH

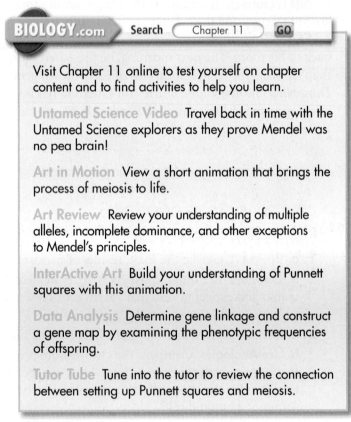

BIOLOGY.com   Search ⟨ Chapter 11 ⟩ GO

Visit Chapter 11 online to test yourself on chapter content and to find activities to help you learn.

Untamed Science Video Travel back in time with the Untamed Science explorers as they prove Mendel was no pea brain!

Art in Motion View a short animation that brings the process of meiosis to life.

Art Review Review your understanding of multiple alleles, incomplete dominance, and other exceptions to Mendel's principles.

InterActive Art Build your understanding of Punnett squares with this animation.

Data Analysis Determine gene linkage and construct a gene map by examining the phenotypic frequencies of offspring.

Tutor Tube Tune into the tutor to review the connection between setting up Punnett squares and meiosis.

11 Study Guide

Big idea ▶ Information and Heredity

Genetic information passes from parent to offspring during meiosis when gametes, each containing one representative from each chromosome pair, unite.

11.1 The Work of Gregor Mendel

🔑 An individual's characteristics are determined by factors that are passed from one parental generation to the next.

🔑 During gamete formation, the alleles for each gene segregate from each other so that each gamete carries only one allele for each gene.

genetics (308)   allele (310)
fertilization (309)   principle of dominance
trait (309)   (310)
hybrid (309)   segregation (312)
gene (310)   gamete (312)

11.2 Applying Mendel's Principles

🔑 Punnett squares use mathematical probability to help predict the genotype and phenotype combinations in genetic crosses.

🔑 The principle of independent assortment states that genes for different traits can segregate independently during the formation of gametes.

🔑 Mendel's principles of heredity, observed through patterns of inheritance, form the basis of modern genetics.

probability (313)   genotype (315)
homozygous (314)   Punnett square (315)
heterozygous (314)   independent
phenotype (315)   assortment (317)

11.3 Other Patterns of Inheritance

🔑 Some alleles are neither dominant nor recessive. Many genes exist in several different forms and are therefore said to have multiple alleles. Many traits are produced by the interaction of several genes.

🔑 Environmental conditions can affect gene expression and influence genetically determined traits.

incomplete dominance   multiple allele (320)
  (319)   polygenic trait (320)
codominance (319)

11.4 Meiosis

🔑 The diploid cells of most adult organisms contain two complete sets of inherited chromosomes and two complete sets of genes.

🔑 In prophase I, replicated chromosomes pair with corresponding homologous chromosomes. At metaphase I, paired chromosomes line up across the center of the cell. In anaphase I, chromosome pairs move toward opposite ends of the cell. In telophase I, a nuclear membrane forms around each cluster of chromosomes. Cytokinesis then forms two new cells. As the cells enter prophase II, their chromosomes become visible. The final four phases of meiosis II result in four haploid daughter cells.

🔑 In mitosis, when the two sets of genetic material separate, each daughter cell receives one complete set of chromosomes. In meiosis, homologous chromosomes line up and then move to separate daughter cells. Mitosis does not normally change the chromosome number of the original cell. Meiosis reduces the chromosome number by half. Mitosis results in the production of two genetically identical diploid cells, whereas meiosis produces four genetically different haploid cells.

🔑 Alleles of different genes tend to be inherited together from one generation from the next when those genes are located on the same chromosome.

homologous (323)   tetrad (324)
diploid (323)   crossing-over (324)
haploid (323)   zygote (325)
meiosis (324)

Think Visually Use the following terms to create a concept map: *alleles, genes, chromosomes, dominant, traits, recessive.*

11 Assessment

11.1 The Work of Gregor Mendel

Understand Key Concepts

1. Different forms of a gene are called
   a. hybrids.
   c. alleles.
   b. dominant factors.
   d. recessive factors.

2. Organisms that have two identical alleles for a particular trait are said to be
   a. hybrid.
   c. homozygous.
   b. heterozygous.
   d. dominant.

3. Mendel had many stocks of pea plants that were true-breeding. What is meant by this term?

4. Explain how Mendel kept his pea plants from self-pollinating.

Think Critically

5. **Design an Experiment** In sheep, the allele for white wool (*A*) is dominant over the allele for black wool (*a*). A ram is a male sheep. How would you determine the genotype of a white ram?

6. **Infer** Suppose Mendel crossed two pea plants and got both tall and short offspring. What could have been the genotypes of the two original plants? What genotype could *not* have been present?

11.2 Applying Mendel's Principles

Understand Key Concepts

7. A Punnett square is used to determine the
   a. probable outcome of a cross.
   b. actual outcome of a cross.
   c. result of incomplete dominance.
   d. result of meiosis.

8. The physical characteristics of an organism are called its
   a. genetics.
   c. phenotype.
   b. heredity.
   d. genotype.

9. The probability of flipping a coin twice and getting two heads is
   a. 1.
   c. 1/4.
   b. 1/2.
   d. 3/4.

10. List the four basic principles of genetics that Mendel discovered in his experiments. Briefly describe each of these principles.

11. In pea plants, the allele for yellow seeds is dominant over the allele for green seeds. Predict the genotypic ratio of offspring produced by crossing two parents that are heterozygous for this trait. Draw a Punnett square to illustrate your prediction.

Think Critically

12. **Apply Concepts** In guinea pigs, the allele for a rough coat (*R*) is dominant over the allele for a smooth coat (*r*). A heterozygous guinea pig (*Rr*) and a homozygous recessive guinea pig (*rr*) have a total of nine offspring. The Punnett square for this cross shows a 50 percent chance that any particular offspring will have a smooth coat. Explain how all nine offspring can have smooth coats.

	R	r
r	Rr	rr
r	Rr	rr

11.3 Other Patterns of Inheritance

Understand Key Concepts

13. A situation in which a gene has more than two alleles is known as
   a. complete dominance.
   b. codominance.
   c. polygenic dominance.
   d. multiple alleles.

14. A pink-flowered *Mirabilis* plant (*RW*) is crossed with a white-flowered *Mirabilis* (*WW*). What is the chance that a seed from this cross will produce a red-flowered plant?
   a. 0
   c. 1/2
   b. 1/4
   d. 1

15. What is the difference between multiple alleles and polygenic traits?

16. Why can multiple alleles result in many different phenotypes for a trait?

17. Are an organism's characteristics determined only by its genes? Explain.

Think Critically

18. **Interpret Visuals** Genes that control hair or feather color in some animals are expressed differently in the winter than in the summer. How might such a difference be beneficial to the ptarmigan shown here?

11.4 Meiosis

Understand Key Concepts

19. The illustration below represents what stage of meiosis?
    a. prophase I   **c.** telophase I
    b. anaphase II   **d.** metaphase I

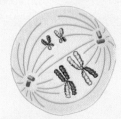

20. Unlike mitosis, meiosis in male mammals results in the formation of
    a. one haploid gamete.
    b. three diploid gametes.
    c. four diploid gametes.
    d. four haploid gametes.

21. A gene map shows
    a. the number of possible alleles for a gene.
    b. the relative locations of genes on a chromosome.
    c. where chromosomes are in a cell.
    d. how crossing-over occurs.

22. Suppose that an organism has the diploid number 2N = 8. How many chromosomes do this organism's gametes contain?

23. Describe the process of meiosis.

24. Explain why chromosomes, not individual genes, assort independently.

Think Critically

25. **Compare and Contrast** Compare the phases of meiosis I with the phases of meiosis II in terms of number and arrangement of the chromosomes.

solve the CHAPTER MYSTERY

GREEN PARAKEETS

After consulting with the owner of the pet store, Susan realized she had a rare gift. White parakeets are very uncommon. The pet shop owner told Susan that two genes control feather color. A dominant Y allele results in the production of a yellow pigment. The dominant B allele controls melanin production. If the genotype contains a capital Y (either YY or Yy) and a capital B, the offspring will be green. If the genotype contains two lowercase y alleles, and a capital B, the offspring will be blue. If the genotype contains two lowercase y's and two lowercase b's, the offspring will be white.

1. **Use Models** Draw a Punnett square that accounts for the inheritance of blue pigment.

2. **Use Models** Construct a Punnett square that explains the inheritance of a white pigment.

3. **Apply Concepts** Solve the mystery by determining the genotypes and phenotypes of the parents and offspring.

4. **Connect to the** **Big idea** What ratio of colored offspring would you expect if Susan breeds her original pair of parakeets in the years ahead? Would any offspring be green?

Connecting Concepts

Use Science Graphics

Seed coat was one trait that Mendel studied in pea plants. The coat, or covering, of the seed is either smooth or wrinkled. Suppose a researcher has two plants—one that makes smooth seeds and another that makes wrinkled seeds. The researcher crosses the wrinkled-seed plants and the smooth-seed plants, obtaining the following data. Use the data to answer questions 26–28.

Results of Seed Experiment		
Phenotype	**Number of Plants in the F_1 Generation**	
	Expected	**Observed**
Smooth seeds		60
Wrinkled seeds		72

26. Predict Mendel knew that the allele for smooth (R) seeds was dominant over the allele for wrinkled (r) seeds. If this cross was $Rr \times rr$, what numbers would fill the middle column?

27. Analyze Data Are the observed numbers consistent with the hypothesis that the cross is $Rr \times rr$? Explain your answer.

28. Draw Conclusions Are the data from this experiment alone sufficient to conclude that the allele for smooth seeds is dominant over the allele for wrinkled seeds? Why or why not?

Write About Science

29. Explain Write an explanation of dominant and recessive alleles that would be appropriate to give to an eighth-grade science class. You can assume that the eighth-grade students already know the meanings of *gene* and *allele*. (*Hint*: Use examples to make your explanation clear.)

30. Cause and Effect Explain why the alleles for reddish-orange eyes and miniature wings in *Drosophila* are usually inherited together. Describe the pattern of inheritance these alleles follow, and include the idea of gene linkage. (*Hint*: To organize your ideas, draw a cause-effect diagram that shows what happens to the two alleles during meiosis.)

31. Assess the Big idea Explain why the gene pairs described by Mendel behave in a way that is consistent with the behavior of chromosomes during gamete formation, fertilization, and reproduction.

A researcher studying fruit flies finds a mutant fly with brown-colored eyes. Almost all fruit flies in nature have bright red eyes. When the researcher crosses the mutant fly with a normal red-eyed fly, all of the F_1 offspring have red eyes. The researcher then crosses two of the F_1 red-eyed flies and obtains the following results in the F_2 generation.

Eye Color in the F_2 Generation	
Red eyes	37
Brown eyes	14

32. Calculate What is the ratio of red-eyed flies to brown-eyed flies? **MATH**
- **a.** 1 : 1
- **b.** 1 : 3
- **c.** 3 : 1
- **d.** 4 : 1

33. Draw Conclusions The allele for red eyes in fruit flies is
- **a.** dominant over brown eyes.
- **b.** recessive to brown eyes.
- **c.** codominant with the brown-eyed gene.
- **d.** a multiple allele with the brown-eyed gene and others.

Standardized Test Prep

Multiple Choice

1. What happens to the chromosome number during meiosis?
   A It doubles.
   B It stays the same.
   C It halves.
   D It becomes diploid.

2. Which ratio did Mendel find in his F_2 generation?
   A 3 : 1
   B 1 : 3 : 1
   C 1 : 2
   D 3 : 4

3. During which phase of meiosis is the chromosome number reduced?
   A anaphase I
   B metaphase I
   C telophase I
   D telophase II

4. Two pink-flowering plants are crossed. The offspring flower as follows: 25% red, 25% white, and 50% pink. What pattern of inheritance does flower color in these flowers follow?
   A dominance
   B multiple alleles
   C incomplete dominance
   D polygenic traits

5. Which of the following is used to construct a gene map?
   A chromosome number
   B mutation rate
   C rate of meiosis
   D recombination rate

6. Alleles for the same trait are separated from each other during the process of
   A cytokinesis.
   B meiosis I.
   C meiosis II.
   D metaphase II.

7. Which of the following is NOT one of Gregor Mendel's principles?
   A The alleles for different genes usually segregate independently.
   B Some forms of a gene may be dominant.
   C The inheritance of characteristics is determined by factors (genes).
   D Crossing-over occurs during meiosis.

Questions 8–9

Genes A, B, C, and D are located on the same chromosome. After calculating recombination frequencies, a student determines that these genes are separated by the following map units: C–D, 25 map units; A–B, 12 map units; B–D, 20 map units; A–C, 17 map units.

8. How many map units apart are genes A and D?
   A 5
   B 8
   C 10
   D 12.5

9. Which gene map best reflects the student's data?

   A
   A 5 B 12 C 8 D

   B
   A 8 B 20 C 5 D

   C
   A 8 B 17 C 12 D

   D
   C 5 B 12 A 8 D

Open-Ended Response

10. Explain why meiosis allows organisms to maintain their chromosome numbers from one generation to the next.

If You Have Trouble With . . .

Question	1	2	3	4	5	6	7	8	9	10
See Lesson	11.4	11.1	11.4	11.3	11.4	11.4	11.2	11.4	11.4	11.4

12 DNA

Information and Heredity, Cellular Basis of Life

Q: What is the structure of DNA, and how does it function in genetic inheritance?

INSIDE:

- **12.1 Identifying the Substance of Genes**
- **12.2 The Structure of DNA**
- **12.3 DNA Replication**

This sculpture, outside the Lawrence Hall of Science at the University of California at Berkeley, models the structure of DNA—the substance that genes are made of.

CHAPTER MYSTERY

UV LIGHT

"Put on your sunscreen!" This familiar phrase can be heard at most beaches on a sunny day. It's an important directive, though, because sunlight — for all its beneficial effects — can readily damage the skin. The most dangerous wavelengths of sunlight are the ones we can't see: the ultraviolet (UV) region of the electromagnetic spectrum. Not only can excess exposure to UV light damage skin cells, it can cause a deadly form of skin cancer that kills nearly 10,000 Americans each year. Why is UV light so dangerous? How can these particular wavelengths of light damage our cells to the point of causing cell death and cancer? As you read this chapter, look for clues to help you solve the question of why UV light is so damaging to skin cells. Then, solve the mystery.

Never Stop Exploring Your World.
Finding the connection between UV light and DNA is only the beginning. Take a video field trip with the ecogeeks of Untamed Science to see where the mystery leads.

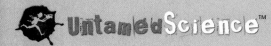

Identifying the Substance of Genes

Key Questions

🔑 **What clues did bacterial transformation yield about the gene?**

🔑 **What role did bacterial viruses play in identifying genetic material?**

🔑 **What is the role of DNA in heredity?**

Vocabulary

transformation
bacteriophage

Taking Notes

Flowchart As you read this section, make a flowchart that shows how scientists came to understand the molecule known as DNA.

THINK ABOUT IT How do genes work? To answer that question, the first thing you need to know is what genes are made of. After all, you couldn't understand how an automobile engine works without understanding what the engine is made of and how it's put together. So, how would you go about figuring out what molecule or molecules go into making a gene?

Bacterial Transformation

🔑 **What clues did bacterial transformation yield about the gene?**

In the first half of the twentieth century, biologists developed the field of genetics to the point where they began to wonder about the nature of the gene itself. To truly understand genetics, scientists realized they first had to discover the chemical nature of the gene. If the molecule that carries genetic information could be identified, it might be possible to understand how genes actually control the inherited characteristics of living things.

Like many stories in science, the discovery of the chemical nature of the gene began with an investigator who was actually looking for something else. In 1928, the British scientist Frederick Griffith was trying to figure out how bacteria make people sick. More specifically, Griffith wanted to learn how certain types of bacteria produce the serious lung disease known as pneumonia.

Griffith had isolated two very similar types of bacteria from mice. These were actually two different varieties, or strains, of the same bacterial species. Both strains grew very well in culture plates in Griffith's lab, but only one of them caused pneumonia. The disease-causing bacteria (S strain) grew into smooth colonies on culture plates, whereas the harmless bacteria (R strain) produced colonies with rough edges. The difference in appearance made the two strains easy to tell apart.

Griffith's Experiments When Griffith injected mice with disease-causing bacteria, the mice developed pneumonia and died. When he injected mice with harmless bacteria, the mice stayed healthy. Griffith wondered what made the first group of mice get pneumonia. Perhaps the S-strain bacteria produced a toxin that made the mice sick? To find out, he ran the series of experiments shown in **Figure 12–1.** First, Griffith took a culture of the S strain, heated the cells to kill them, then injected the heat-killed bacteria into laboratory mice. The mice survived, suggesting that the cause of pneumonia was not a toxin from these disease-causing bacteria.

In Griffith's next experiment, he mixed the heat-killed, S-strain bacteria with live, harmless bacteria from the R strain. This mixture he injected into laboratory mice. By themselves, neither type of bacteria should have made the mice sick. To Griffith's surprise, however, the injected mice developed pneumonia, and many died. When he examined the lungs of these mice, he found them to be filled not with the harmless bacteria, but with the disease-causing bacteria. How could that happen if the S-strain cells were dead?

Transformation Somehow, the heat-killed bacteria passed their disease-causing ability to the harmless bacteria. Griffith reasoned that, when he mixed the two types of bacteria together, some chemical factor transferred from the heat-killed cells of the S strain into the live cells of the R strain. This chemical compound, he hypothesized, must contain information that could change harmless bacteria into disease-causing ones. He called this process **transformation,** because one type of bacteria (the harmless form) had been changed permanently into another (the disease-causing form). Because the ability to cause disease was inherited by the offspring of the transformed bacteria, Griffith concluded that the transforming factor had to be a gene.

In Your Notebook *Write a summary of Griffith's experiments.*

FIGURE 12–1 Griffith's Experiments Griffith injected mice with four different samples of bacteria. When injected separately, neither heat-killed, disease-causing bacteria nor live, harmless bacteria killed the mice. The two strains injected together, however, caused fatal pneumonia. From this experiment, Griffith inferred that genetic information could be transferred from one bacterial strain to another. **Infer** *Why did Griffith test to see whether the bacteria recovered from the sick mice in his last experiment would produce smooth or rough colonies in a petri dish?*

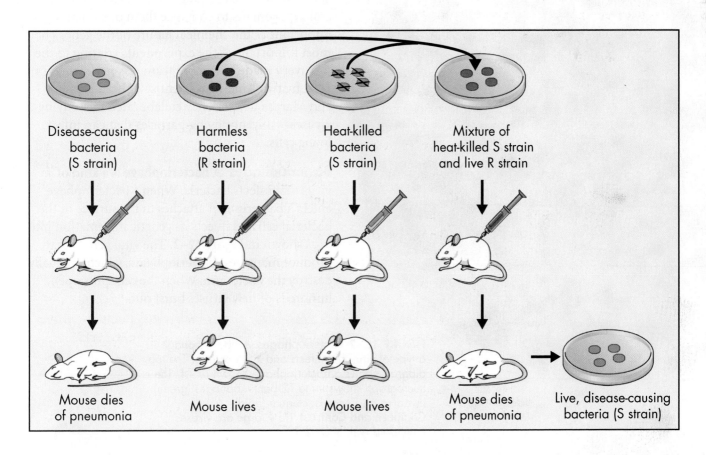

Disease-causing bacteria (S strain)

Harmless bacteria (R strain)

Heat-killed bacteria (S strain)

Mixture of heat-killed S strain and live R strain

Mouse dies of pneumonia

Mouse lives

Mouse lives

Mouse dies of pneumonia

Live, disease-causing bacteria (S strain)

The Molecular Cause of Transformation

In 1944, a group of scientists at the Rockefeller Institute in New York decided to repeat Griffith's work. Led by the Canadian biologist Oswald Avery, the scientists wanted to determine which molecule in the heat-killed bacteria was most important for transformation. They reasoned that if they could find this particular molecule, it might reveal the chemical nature of the gene.

Avery and his team extracted a mixture of various molecules from the heat-killed bacteria. They carefully treated this mixture with enzymes that destroyed proteins, lipids, carbohydrates, and some other molecules, including the nucleic acid RNA. Transformation still occurred. Clearly, since those molecules had been destroyed, none of them could have been responsible for transformation.

Avery's team repeated the experiment one more time. This time, they used enzymes that would break down a different nucleic acid—DNA. When they destroyed the DNA in the mixture, transformation did not occur. There was just one possible explanation for these results: *DNA was the transforming factor.* 🔑 **By observing bacterial transformation, Avery and other scientists discovered that the nucleic acid DNA stores and transmits genetic information from one generation of bacteria to the next.**

T4 Bacteriophage

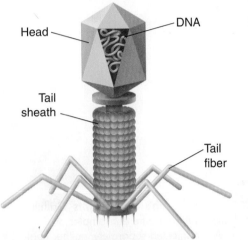

Head — DNA

Tail sheath

Tail fiber

TEM 200,000×

Bacterial Viruses

🔑 *What role did bacterial viruses play in identifying genetic material?*

Scientists are a skeptical group. It usually takes several experiments to convince them of something as important as the chemical nature of the gene. The most important of the experiments relating to the discovery made by Avery's team was performed in 1952 by two American scientists, Alfred Hershey and Martha Chase. They collaborated in studying viruses—tiny, nonliving particles that can infect living cells.

Bacteriophages A **bacteriophage** is a kind of virus that infects bacteria. When a bacteriophage enters a bacterium, it attaches to the surface of the bacterial cell and injects its genetic information into it, as shown in **Figure 12–2.** The viral genes act to produce many new bacteriophages, which gradually destroy the bacterium. When the cell splits open, hundreds of new viruses burst out.

FIGURE 12–2 Bacteriophages A bacteriophage is a type of virus that infects and kills bacteria. The top diagram shows a bacteriophage known as T4. The micrograph shows three T2 bacteriophages (green) invading an *E. coli* bacterium (gold).
Compare and Contrast *How large are viruses compared with bacteria?*

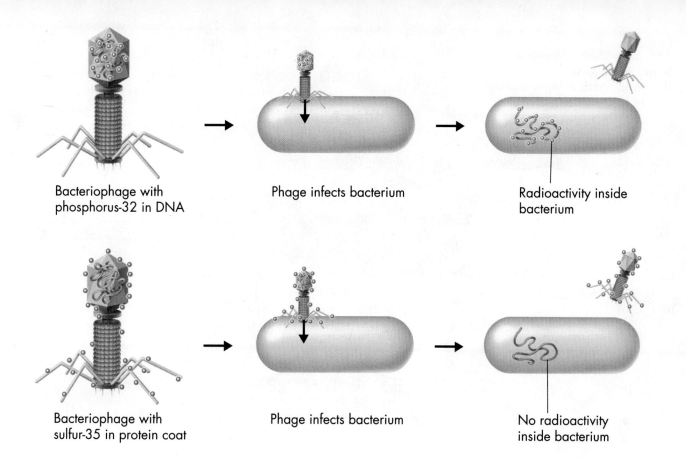

Bacteriophage with phosphorus-32 in DNA

Phage infects bacterium

Radioactivity inside bacterium

Bacteriophage with sulfur-35 in protein coat

Phage infects bacterium

No radioactivity inside bacterium

The Hershey-Chase Experiment Hershey and Chase studied a bacteriophage that was composed of a DNA core and a protein coat. They wanted to determine which part of the virus—the protein coat or the DNA core—entered the bacterial cell. Their results would either support or disprove Avery's finding that genes were made of DNA.

The pair grew viruses in cultures containing radioactive isotopes of phosphorus-32 (^{32}P) and sulfur-35 (^{35}S). This was a clever strategy, because proteins contain almost no phosphorus, and DNA contains no sulfur. Therefore, these radioactive substances could be used as markers, enabling the scientists to tell which molecules actually entered the bacteria, carrying the genetic information of the virus. If they found radioactivity from ^{35}S in the bacteria, it would mean that the virus's protein coat had been injected into the bacteria. If they found ^{32}P, then the DNA core had been injected.

The two scientists mixed the marked viruses with bacterial cells. They waited a few minutes for the viruses to inject their genetic material. Next, they separated the viruses from the bacteria and tested the bacteria for radioactivity. **Figure 12–3** shows the steps in this experiment. What were the results? Nearly all the radioactivity in the bacteria was from phosphorus (^{32}P), the marker found in DNA. Hershey and Chase concluded that the genetic material of the bacteriophage was indeed DNA, not protein. 🔑 **Hershey and Chase's experiment with bacteriophages confirmed Avery's results, convincing many scientists that DNA was the genetic material found in genes—not just in viruses and bacteria, but in all living cells.**

FIGURE 12–3 Hershey-Chase Experiment Alfred Hershey and Martha Chase used different radioactive markers to label the DNA and proteins of bacteriophages. The bacteriophages injected only DNA, not proteins, into bacterial cells.

In Your Notebook *Identify the independent and dependent variables in the Hershey-Chase experiment, and list some possible control variables.*

Storing Information
The genetic material stores information needed by every living cell.

HOW TO BE A CELL

How to Be a Cell

bestseller

ION TRANSPORT

RESPIRATION

MOVEMENT

CELL GROWTH

VISUAL ANALOGY

THE MAIN FUNCTIONS OF DNA

FIGURE 12–4 Like DNA, the book in this diagram contains coded instructions for a cell to carry out important biological processes, such as how to move or transport ions. The book, like DNA, can also be copied and passed along to the next generation. These three tasks— storing, copying, and transmitting information—are also the three main functions of DNA.

The Role of DNA

What is the role of DNA in heredity?

You might think that scientists would have been satisfied knowing that genes were made of DNA, but that was not the case at all. Instead, they wondered how DNA, or any molecule for that matter, could do the critical things that genes were known to do. The next era of study began with one crucial assumption. **The DNA that makes up genes must be capable of storing, copying, and transmitting the genetic information in a cell.** These three functions are analogous to the way in which you might share a treasured book, as pictured in **Figure 12–4.**

Storing Information The foremost job of DNA, as the molecule of heredity, is to store information. The genes that make a flower purple must somehow carry the information needed to produce purple pigment. Genes for blood type and eye color must have the information needed for their jobs as well, and other genes have to do even more. Genes control patterns of development, which means that the instructions that cause a single cell to develop into an oak tree, a sea urchin, or a dog must somehow be written into the DNA of each of these organisms.

Copying Information Before a cell divides, it must make a complete copy of every one of its genes. To many scientists, the most puzzling aspect of DNA was how it could be copied. The solution to this and other puzzles had to wait until the structure of the DNA molecule became known. Within a few weeks of this discovery, a copying mechanism for the genetic material was put forward. You will learn about this mechanism later in the chapter.

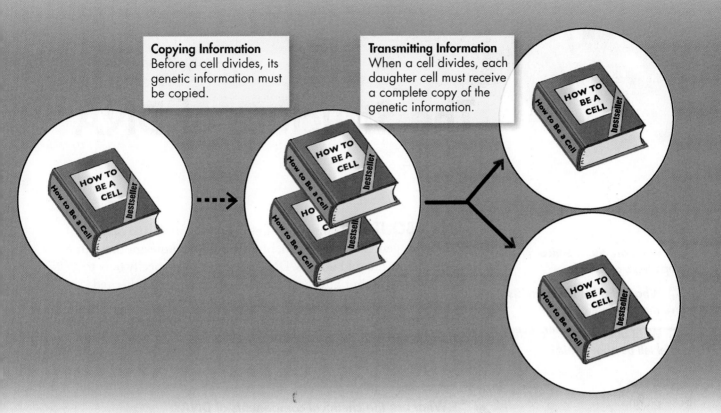

Copying Information
Before a cell divides, its genetic information must be copied.

Transmitting Information
When a cell divides, each daughter cell must receive a complete copy of the genetic information.

Transmitting Information As Mendel's work had shown, genes are transmitted from one generation to the next. Therefore, DNA molecules must be carefully sorted and passed along during cell division. Such careful sorting is especially important during the formation of reproductive cells in meiosis. Remember, the chromosomes of eukaryotic cells contain genes made of DNA. The loss of any DNA during meiosis might mean a loss of valuable genetic information from one generation to the next.

12.1 Assessment

Review Key Concepts 🔑

1. a. Review List the conclusions that Griffith and Avery drew from their experiments.

b. Identify Variables What was the experimental variable that Avery used when he repeated Griffith's work?

2. a. Review What conclusion did Hershey and Chase draw from their experiments?

b. Infer Why did Hershey and Chase grow viruses in cultures that contained both radioactive phosphorus and radioactive sulfur? What might have happened if they had used only one radioactive substance?

3. a. Review What are the three key roles of DNA?

b. Apply Concepts Why would the storage of genetic information in genes help explain why chromosomes are separated so carefully during mitosis?

Apply the **Big** idea

Science as a Way of Knowing

4. Choose either Griffith, Avery, or Hershey and Chase, and develop a flowchart that shows how that scientist or team of scientists used various scientific methods. Be sure to identify each method. You may use your flowchart from Taking Notes as a guide. If you need to, refer to the descriptions of scientific methods in Chapter 1.

The Structure of DNA

Key Questions

🔑 **What are the chemical components of DNA?**

🔑 **What clues helped scientists solve the structure of DNA?**

🔑 **What does the double-helix model tell us about DNA?**

Vocabulary

base pairing

Taking Notes

Outline As you read, find the key ideas for the text under each green heading. Write down a few key words from each main idea. Then, use these key words to summarize the information about DNA.

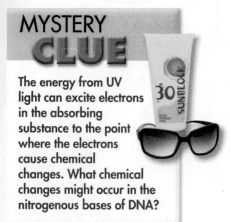

MYSTERY CLUE

The energy from UV light can excite electrons in the absorbing substance to the point where the electrons cause chemical changes. What chemical changes might occur in the nitrogenous bases of DNA?

THINK ABOUT IT It's one thing to say that the molecule called DNA carries genetic information, but it would be quite another thing to explain how it could do this. DNA must not only specify how to assemble proteins, but how genes can be replicated and inherited. DNA has to be a very special molecule, and it's got to have a very special structure. As we will see, understanding the structure of DNA has been the key to understanding how genes work.

The Components of DNA

🔑 **What are the chemical components of DNA?**

Deoxyribonucleic acid, or DNA, is a unique molecule indeed. 🔑 **DNA is a nucleic acid made up of nucleotides joined into long strands or chains by covalent bonds.** Let's examine each of these components more closely.

Nucleic Acids and Nucleotides As you may recall, nucleic acids are long, slightly acidic molecules originally identified in cell nuclei. Like many other macromolecules, nucleic acids are made up of smaller subunits, linked together to form long chains. Nucleotides are the building blocks of nucleic acids. **Figure 12–5** shows the nucleotides in DNA. These nucleotides are made up of three basic components: a 5-carbon sugar called deoxyribose, a phosphate group, and a nitrogenous base.

Nitrogenous Bases and Covalent Bonds Nitrogenous bases, simply put, are bases that contain nitrogen. DNA has four kinds of nitrogenous bases: adenine (AD uh neen), guanine (GWAH neen), cytosine (SY tuh zeen), and thymine (THY meen). Biologists often refer to the nucleotides in DNA by the first letters of their base names: A, G, C, and T. The nucleotides in a strand of DNA are joined by covalent bonds formed between the sugar of one nucleotide and the phosphate group of the next. The nitrogenous bases stick out sideways from the nucleotide chain. The nucleotides can be joined together in any order, meaning that any sequence of bases is possible. These bases, by the way, have a chemical structure that makes them especially good at absorbing ultraviolet (UV) light. In fact, we can determine the amount of DNA in a solution by measuring the amount of light it absorbs at a wavelength of 260 nanometers (nm), which is in the UV region of the electromagnetic spectrum.

If you don't see much in **Figure 12–5** that could explain the remarkable properties of DNA, don't be surprised. In the 1940s and early 1950s, the leading biologists in the world thought of DNA as little more than a string of nucleotides. They were baffled, too. The four different nucleotides, like the 26 letters of the alphabet, could be strung together in many different sequences, so it was possible they could carry coded genetic information. However, so could many other molecules, at least in principle. Biologists wondered if there were something more to the structure of DNA.

Solving the Structure of DNA

🔑 **What clues helped scientists solve the structure of DNA?**

Knowing that DNA is made from long chains of nucleotides was only the beginning of understanding the structure of this molecule. The next step required an understanding of the way in which those chains are arranged in three dimensions.

Chargaff's Rule One of the puzzling facts about DNA was a curious relationship between its nucleotides. Years earlier, Erwin Chargaff, an Austrian-American biochemist, had discovered that the percentages of adenine [A] and thymine [T] bases are almost equal in any sample of DNA. The same thing is true for the other two nucleotides, guanine [G] and cytosine [C]. The observation that [A] = [T] and [G] = [C] became known as "Chargaff's rule." Despite the fact that DNA samples from organisms as different as bacteria and humans obeyed this rule, neither Chargaff nor anyone else had the faintest idea why.

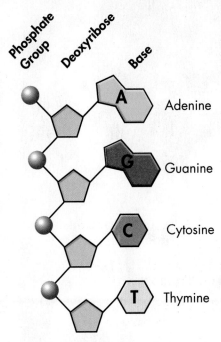

FIGURE 12–5 DNA Nucleotides DNA is made up of nucleotides, each with a deoxyribose molecule, a phosphate group, and a nitrogen-containing base. The four bases are adenine (A), guanine (G), cytosine (C), and thymine (T).
Interpret Visuals *How are these four nucleotides joined together to form part of a DNA chain?*

Analyzing Data

Base Percentages
In 1949, Erwin Chargaff discovered that the relative amounts of A and T, and of G and C, are almost always equal. The table shows a portion of the data that Chargaff collected.

1. Interpret Tables Which organism has the highest percentage of adenine?

2. Calculate If a species has 35 percent adenine in its DNA, what is the percentage of the other three bases? MATH

Percentages of Bases in Five Organisms				
Source of DNA	**A**	**T**	**G**	**C**
Streptococcus	29.8	31.6	20.5	18.0
Yeast	31.3	32.9	18.7	17.1
Herring	27.8	27.5	22.2	22.6
Human	30.9	29.4	19.9	19.8
E.coli	24.7	23.6	26.0	25.7

3. Draw Conclusions What did the fact that A and T, and G and C, occurred in equal amounts suggest about the relationship among these bases?

CLUES TO THE STRUCTURE OF DNA

FIGURE 12–6 Erwin Chargaff, Rosalind Franklin, James Watson, and Francis Crick were among the many scientists who helped solve the puzzle of DNA's molecular structure. Franklin's X-ray diffraction photograph shows the pattern that indicated the structure of DNA is helical.

Rosalind Franklin

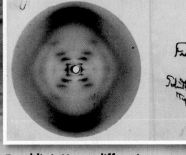

Erwin Chargaff

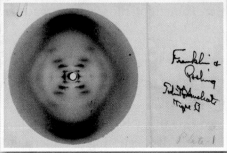

Franklin's X-ray diffraction photograph, May 1952

Franklin's X-Rays

In the early 1950s, the British scientist Rosalind Franklin began to study DNA. Franklin used a technique called X-ray diffraction to get information about the structure of the DNA molecule. First, she purified a large amount of DNA, then stretched the DNA fibers in a thin glass tube so that most of the strands were parallel. Next, she aimed a powerful X-ray beam at the concentrated DNA samples and recorded the scattering pattern of the X-rays on film. Franklin worked hard to obtain better and better patterns from DNA until the patterns became clear. The result of her work is the X-ray photograph shown in **Figure 12–6,** taken in the summer of 1952.

By itself, Franklin's X-ray pattern does not reveal the structure of DNA, but it does carry some very important clues. The X-shaped pattern shows that the strands in DNA are twisted around each other like the coils of a spring, a shape known as a helix. The angle of the X suggests that there are two strands in the structure. Other clues suggest that the nitrogenous bases are near the center of the DNA molecule.

The Work of Watson and Crick

While Franklin was continuing her research, James Watson, an American biologist, and Francis Crick, a British physicist, were also trying to understand the structure of DNA. They built three-dimensional models of the molecule that were made of cardboard and wire. They twisted and stretched the models in various ways, but their best efforts did nothing to explain DNA's properties.

Then, early in 1953, Watson was shown a copy of Franklin's remarkable X-ray pattern. The effect was immediate. In his book *The Double Helix,* Watson wrote: "The instant I saw the picture my mouth fell open and my pulse began to race."

BUILD Vocabulary

ACADEMIC WORDS In biochemistry, the noun **helix** refers to an extended spiral chain of units in a protein, nucleic acid, or other large molecule. The plural term is *helices.*

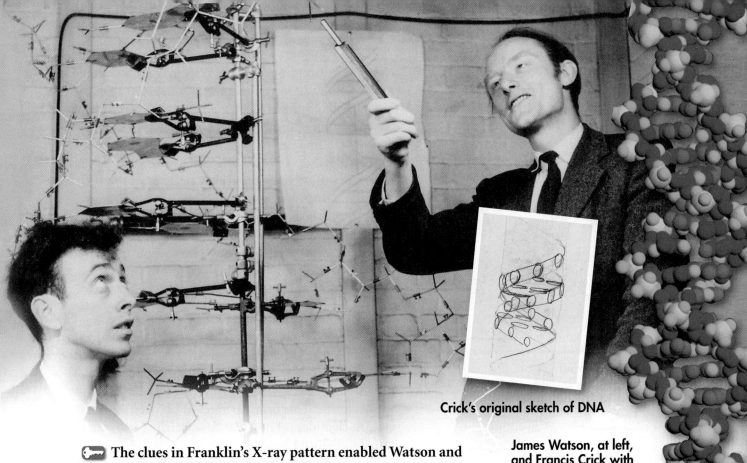

Crick's original sketch of DNA

James Watson, at left, and Francis Crick with their model of a DNA molecule in 1953

A computer model of DNA

🔑 **The clues in Franklin's X-ray pattern enabled Watson and Crick to build a model that explained the specific structure and properties of DNA.** The pair published their results in a historic one-page paper in April of 1953, when Franklin's paper describing her X-ray work was also published. Watson and Crick's breakthrough model of DNA was a double helix, in which two strands of nucleotide sequences were wound around each other.

The Double-Helix Model

🔑 *What does the double-helix model tell us about DNA?*

A double helix looks like a twisted ladder. In the double-helix model of DNA, the two strands twist around each other like spiral staircases. Watson and Crick realized that the double helix accounted for Franklin's X-ray pattern. Further still, it explained many of the most important properties of DNA. 🔑 **The double-helix model explains Chargaff's rule of base pairing and how the two strands of DNA are held together.** This model can even tell us how DNA can function as a carrier of genetic information.

Antiparallel Strands One of the surprising aspects of the double-helix model is that the two strands of DNA run in opposite directions. In the language of biochemistry, these strands are "antiparallel." This arrangement enables the nitrogenous bases on both strands to come into contact at the center of the molecule. It also allows each strand of the double helix to carry a sequence of nucleotides, arranged almost like letters in a four-letter alphabet.

In Your Notebook *Draw and label your own model of the DNA double-helix structure.*

MYSTERY CLUE

Our skin cells are exposed to UV light whenever they are in direct sunlight. How might this exposure affect base pairing in the DNA of our skin cells?

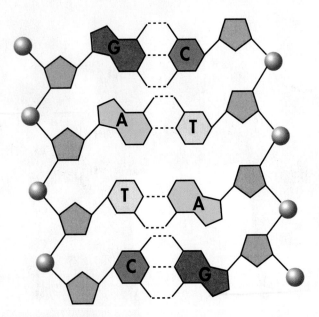

FIGURE 12–7 Base Pairing The two strands of DNA are held together by hydrogen bonds between the nitrogenous bases adenine and thymine, and between guanine and cytosine.

Hydrogen Bonding At first, Watson and Crick could not explain what forces held the two strands of DNA's double helix together. They then discovered that hydrogen bonds could form between certain nitrogenous bases, providing just enough force to hold the two strands together. As you may recall, hydrogen bonds are relatively weak chemical forces.

Does it make sense that a molecule as important as DNA should be held together by weak bonds? Indeed, it does. If the two strands of the helix were held together by strong bonds, it might well be impossible to separate them. As we will see, the ability of the two strands to separate is critical to DNA's functions.

Base Pairing Watson and Crick's model showed that hydrogen bonds could create a nearly perfect fit between nitrogenous bases along the center of the molecule. However, these bonds would form only between certain base pairs—adenine with thymine, and guanine with cytosine. This nearly perfect fit between A–T and G–C nucleotides is known as **base pairing**, and is illustrated in **Figure 12–7**.

Once they observed this process, Watson and Crick realized that base pairing explained Chargaff's rule. It gave a reason why [A] = [T] and [G] = [C]. For every adenine in a double-stranded DNA molecule, there has to be exactly one thymine. For each cytosine, there is one guanine. The ability of their model to explain Chargaff's observations increased Watson and Crick's confidence that they had come to the right conclusion, with the help of Rosalind Franklin.

12.2 Assessment

Review Key Concepts 🔑

1. a. Review List the chemical components of DNA.
   b. Relate Cause and Effect Why are hydrogen bonds so essential to the structure of DNA?

2. a. Review Describe the discoveries that led to the modeling of DNA.
   b. Infer Why did scientists have to use tools other than microscopes to solve the structure of DNA?

3. a. Review Describe Watson and Crick's model of the DNA molecule.
   b. Apply Concepts Did Watson and Crick's model account for the equal amounts of thymine and adenine in DNA? Explain.

VISUAL THINKING

4. Make a three-dimensional model showing the structure of a DNA molecule. Your model should include the four base pairs that help form the double helix.

Biology & HISTORY

Discovering the Role of DNA Genes and the principles of genetics were discovered before scientists identified the molecules that genes are made of. With the discovery of DNA, scientists have been able to explain how genes are replicated and how they function.

1860   1880   1900   1920   1940   1960   1980   2000

1865
Gregor Mendel shows that the characteristics of pea plants are passed along in a predictable way. His discovery begins the science of genetics.

1903

◄ **Walter Sutton** shows that chromosomes carry the cell's units of inheritance.

1911
Thomas Hunt Morgan ▲ demonstrates that genes are arranged in linear fashion on the chromosomes of the fruit fly.

1928
▼ **Frederick Griffith** discovers that bacteria contain a molecule that can transfer genetic information from cell to cell.

1944
Oswald Avery, Colin Macleod, and Maclyn McCarty show the substance that Griffith discovered is DNA.

1950
Erwin Chargaff analyzes the base composition of DNA in cells. He discovers that the amounts of adenine and thymine are almost always equal, as are the amounts of guanine and cytosine.

1952
Alfred Hershey and Martha Chase confirm that the genetic material of viruses is DNA, not protein. **Rosalind Franklin** records a critical X-ray diffraction pattern, demonstrating that DNA is in the form of a helix.

1953
James Watson and Francis Crick publish their model of the DNA double helix. The model was made possible by Franklin's work.

2000
▼ **Craig Venter and Francis Collins** announce the draft DNA sequence of the human genome at a White House ceremony in Washington, D.C. The final version is published in 2003.

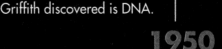

natur...

WRITING Use library or Internet resources to find out what James Watson or Francis Crick worked on after discovering the structure of DNA. Organize your findings about the scientist's work and make a multimedia presentation for the class.

DNA Replication

Key Questions

🔑 **What role does DNA polymerase play in copying DNA?**

🔑 **How does DNA replication differ in prokaryotic cells and eukaryotic cells?**

Vocabulary
replication
DNA polymerase
telomere

Taking Notes

Preview Visuals Before you read, study the diagram in **Figure 12–8.** Make a list of questions about the diagram. As you read, write down the answers to your questions.

BUILD Vocabulary

WORD ORIGINS The prefix *re-* means "back" or "again." *Plicare* is a Latin verb meaning "to fold." To replicate something is, in a sense, to repeat it, or to fold back again.

THINK ABOUT IT Before a cell divides, its DNA must first be copied. How might the double-helix structure of DNA make that possible? What might happen if one of the nucleotides were damaged or chemically altered just before the copying process? How might this affect the DNA inherited by each daughter cell after cell division?

Copying the Code

🔑 **What role does DNA polymerase play in copying DNA?**

When Watson and Crick discovered the structure of DNA, they immediately recognized one genuinely surprising aspect of the structure. Base pairing in the double helix explains how DNA can be copied, or replicated, because each base on one strand pairs with one—and only one—base on the opposite strand. Each strand of the double helix therefore has all the information needed to reconstruct the other half by the mechanism of base pairing. Because each strand can be used to make the other strand, the strands are said to be complementary.

The Replication Process Before a cell divides, it duplicates its DNA in a copying process called **replication.** This process, which occurs during late interphase of the cell cycle, ensures that each resulting cell has the same complete set of DNA molecules. During replication, the DNA molecule separates into two strands and then produces two new complementary strands following the rules of base pairing. Each strand of the double helix of DNA serves as a template, or model, for the new strand.

Figure 12–8 shows the process of DNA replication. The two strands of the double helix have separated, or "unzipped," allowing two replication forks to form. As each new strand forms, new bases are added following the rules of base pairing. If the base on the old strand is adenine, then thymine is added to the newly forming strand. Likewise, guanine is always paired to cytosine. For example, a strand that has the base sequence TACGTT produces a strand with the complementary base sequence ATGCAA. The result is two DNA molecules identical to each other and to the original molecule. Note that each DNA molecule resulting from replication has one original strand and one new strand.

In Your Notebook *In your own words, describe the process of DNA replication.*

350 BIOLOGY.com ⟩ Search (Lesson 12.3) GO ● Lesson Overview ● Lesson Notes ● InterActive Art

The Role of Enzymes DNA replication is carried out by a series of enzymes. These enzymes first "unzip" a molecule of DNA by breaking the hydrogen bonds between base pairs and unwinding the two strands of the molecule. Each strand then serves as a template for the attachment of complementary bases. You may recall that enzymes are proteins with highly specific functions. For this reason, they are often named for the reactions they catalyze. The principal enzyme involved in DNA replication is called **DNA polymerase** (PAHL ih mur ayz). 🔑 **DNA polymerase is an enzyme that joins individual nucleotides to produce a new strand of DNA.** Besides producing the sugar-phosphate bonds that join nucleotides together, DNA polymerase also "proofreads" each new DNA strand, so that each molecule is a near-perfect copy of the original.

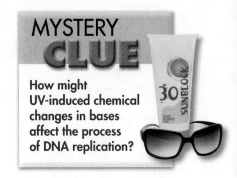

MYSTERY CLUE

How might UV-induced chemical changes in bases affect the process of DNA replication?

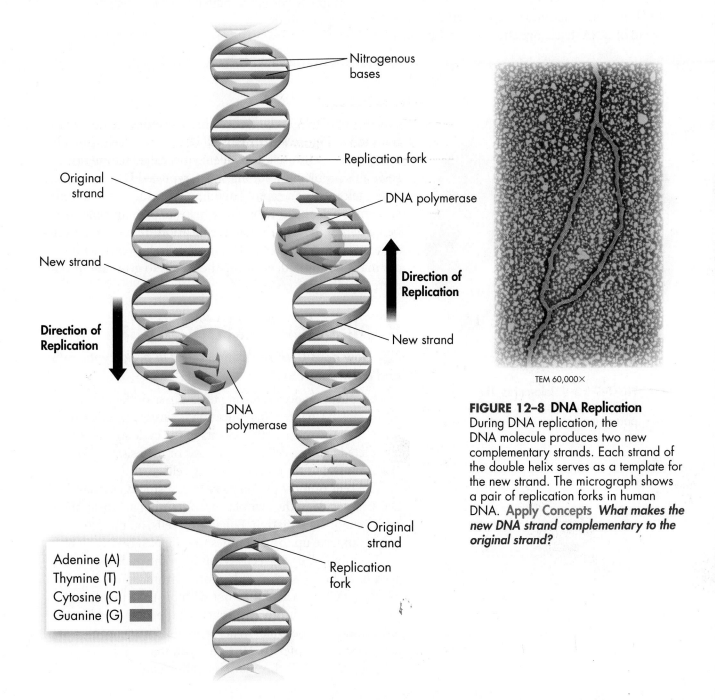

Nitrogenous bases

Replication fork

Original strand

DNA polymerase

New strand

Direction of Replication

Direction of Replication

New strand

DNA polymerase

Original strand

Replication fork

Adenine (A)
Thymine (T)
Cytosine (C)
Guanine (G)

TEM 60,000×

FIGURE 12–8 DNA Replication
During DNA replication, the DNA molecule produces two new complementary strands. Each strand of the double helix serves as a template for the new strand. The micrograph shows a pair of replication forks in human DNA. **Apply Concepts** *What makes the new DNA strand complementary to the original strand?*

Modeling DNA Replication

❶ Cut out small squares of white and yellow paper to represent phosphate and sugar molecules. Then, cut out small strips of blue, green, red, and orange paper to represent the four nitrogenous bases. Build a set of five nucleotides using your paper strips and tape. Look back at **Figure 12–5** if you need help.

❷ Using your nucleotides, tape together a single strand of DNA. Exchange strands with a partner.

❸ Model DNA replication by creating a strand that is complementary to your partner's original strand.

Analyze and Conclude

1. Use Models Taping together the nucleotides models the action of what enzyme?

2. Evaluate In what ways does this lab accurately represent DNA replication? How could you improve the lab to better show the steps of replication?

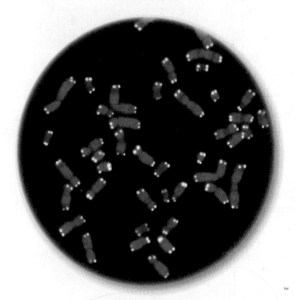

FIGURE 12–9 Telomeres The telomeres are the white (stained) part of the blue human chromosomes.

Telomeres DNA at the tips of chromosomes are known as **telomeres** (**Figure 12–9**). This DNA is particularly difficult to replicate. Cells use a special enzyme, called telomerase, to solve this problem by adding short, repeated DNA sequences to the telomeres. In rapidly dividing cells, such as stem cells and embryonic cells, telomerase helps to prevent genes from being damaged or lost during replication. Telomerase is often switched off in adult cells. In cancer cells, however, telomerase may be activated, enabling these cells to grow and proliferate rapidly.

Replication in Living Cells

🔑 *How does DNA replication differ in prokaryotic cells and eukaryotic cells?*

DNA replication occurs during the S phase of the cell cycle. As we saw in Chapter 10, replication is carefully regulated, along with the other critical events of the cycle so that it is completed before a cell enters mitosis or meiosis. But where, exactly, is DNA found inside a living cell?

The cells of most prokaryotes have a single, circular DNA molecule in the cytoplasm, containing nearly all the cell's genetic information. Eukaryotic cells, on the other hand, can have up to 1000 times more DNA. Nearly all of the DNA of eukaryotic cells is found in the nucleus, packaged into chromosomes. Eukaryotic chromosomes consist of DNA, tightly packed together with proteins to form a substance called chromatin. Together, the DNA and histone molecules form beadlike structures called nucleosomes, as described in Chapter 10. Histones, you may recall, are proteins around which chromatin is tightly coiled.

Prokaryotic DNA Replication In most prokaryotes, DNA replication does not start until regulatory proteins bind to a single starting point on the chromosome. These proteins then trigger the beginning of the S phase, and DNA replication begins. 🔑 **Replication in most prokaryotic cells starts from a single point and proceeds in two directions until the entire chromosome is copied.** This process is shown in **Figure 12–10.** Often, the two chromosomes produced by replication are attached to different points inside the cell membrane and are separated when the cell splits to form two new cells.

Eukaryotic DNA Replication Eukaryotic chromosomes are generally much bigger than those of prokaryotes. 🔑 **In eukaryotic cells, replication may begin at dozens or even hundreds of places on the DNA molecule, proceeding in both directions until each chromosome is completely copied.** Although a number of proteins check DNA for chemical damage or base pair mismatches prior to replication, the system is not foolproof. Damaged regions of DNA are sometimes replicated, resulting in changes to DNA base sequences that may alter certain genes and produce serious consequences.

The two copies of DNA produced by replication in each chromosome remain closely associated until the cell enters prophase of mitosis. At that point, the chromosomes condense, and the two chromatids in each chromosome become clearly visible. They separate from each other in anaphase of mitosis, as described in Chapter 10, producing two cells, each with a complete set of genes coded in DNA.

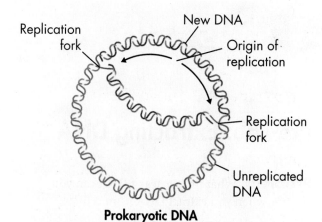

Prokaryotic DNA

Eukaryotic DNA

FIGURE 12–10 Differences in DNA Replication Replication in most prokaryotic cells (top) begins at a single starting point and proceeds in two directions until the entire chromosome is copied. In eukaryotic cells (bottom), replication proceeds from multiple starting points on individual chromosomes and ends when all the chromosomes are copied.

12.3 Assessment

Review Key Concepts 🔑

1. a. Review How is DNA replicated?
   b. Apply Concepts What is the role of DNA polymerase in DNA replication?
2. a. Review Where and in what form is prokaryotic DNA found? Where is eukaryotic DNA found?
   b. Infer What could be the result of damaged DNA being replicated?

VISUAL THINKING

3. Make a Venn diagram that compares the process of DNA replication in prokaryotes and eukaryotes. Compare the location, steps, and end products of the process in each kind of cell.

Pre-Lab: Extracting DNA

Problem What properties of DNA can you observe when you extract DNA from cells?

Materials self-sealing plastic freezer bag, ripe strawberry, detergent solution, 25-mL graduated cylinder, cheesecloth, funnel, test tube, test tube rack, chilled ethanol, stirring rod

Lab Manual Chapter 12 Lab

Skills Focus Predict, Observe, Draw Conclusions

Connect to the **Big idea** Not surprisingly, the molecules that store genetic information are long molecules. If the DNA from a human cell were unfolded, the double helix structure would be about one meter long. Yet, most of a cell's DNA can be folded and tightly packed inside the cell's tiny nucleus. How can scientists remove DNA from the nucleus so that it can be studied and analyzed? In this lab, you will learn that extracting DNA from living tissue is not as difficult as you might think.

Background Questions

a. Review Describe the structure of a DNA molecule.

b. Review What type of bond holds the strands of DNA together?

c. Apply Concepts How does the strength of those bonds affect how DNA functions?

Pre-Lab Questions

Preview the procedure in the lab manual.

1. Apply Concepts Why do strawberry cells need DNA?

2. Form a Hypothesis If you observe a cell nucleus under a compound microscope, you will not see a molecule of DNA. Why will you be able to see the DNA you extract?

3. Predict Use what you know about DNA to predict some of the physical properties of DNA.

4. Design an Experiment How could you determine what percentage of a strawberry's mass is DNA?

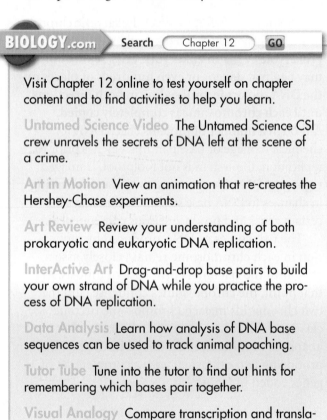

BIOLOGY.com Search Chapter 12 GO

Visit Chapter 12 online to test yourself on chapter content and to find activities to help you learn.

Untamed Science Video The Untamed Science CSI crew unravels the secrets of DNA left at the scene of a crime.

Art in Motion View an animation that re-creates the Hershey-Chase experiments.

Art Review Review your understanding of both prokaryotic and eukaryotic DNA replication.

InterActive Art Drag-and-drop base pairs to build your own strand of DNA while you practice the process of DNA replication.

Data Analysis Learn how analysis of DNA base sequences can be used to track animal poaching.

Tutor Tube Tune into the tutor to find out hints for remembering which bases pair together.

Visual Analogy Compare transcription and translation with the process of publishing a book.

12 Study Guide

Big ideas Information and Heredity, Cellular Basis of Life

DNA is a double-stranded protein molecule made up of nucleotide base pairs. DNA stores, copies, and transmits the genetic information in a cell.

12.1 Identifying the Substance of Genes

⚷ By observing bacterial transformation, Avery and other scientists discovered that the nucleic acid DNA stores and transmits genetic information from one generation of bacteria to the next.

⚷ Hershey and Chase's experiment with bacteriophages confirmed Avery's results, convincing many scientists that DNA was the genetic material found in genes—not just in viruses and bacteria, but in all living cells.

⚷ The DNA that makes up genes must be capable of storing, copying, and transmitting the genetic information in a cell.

transformation (339)   bacteriophage (340)

12.2 The Structure of DNA

⚷ DNA is a nucleic acid made up of nucleotides joined into long strands or chains by covalent bonds.

⚷ The clues in Franklin's X-ray pattern enabled Watson and Crick to build a model that explained the specific structure and properties of DNA.

⚷ The double-helix model explains Chargaff's rule of base pairing and how the two strands of DNA are held together.

base pairing (348)

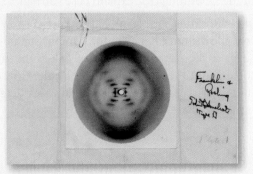

12.3 DNA Replication

⚷ DNA polymerase is an enzyme that joins individual nucleotides to produce a new strand of DNA.

⚷ Replication in most prokaryotic cells starts from a single point and proceeds in two directions until the entire chromosome is copied.

⚷ In eukaryotic cells, replication may begin at dozens or even hundreds of places on the DNA molecule, proceeding in both directions until each chromosome is completely copied.

replication (350)   telomere (352)
DNA polymerase (351)

Think Visually Using the information in this chapter, complete the following concept map about DNA replication:

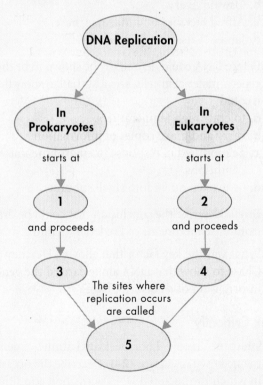

12 Assessment

12.1 Identifying the Substance of Genes

Understand Key Concepts

1. The process by which one strain of bacterium is apparently changed into another strain is called
   a. transcription.
   b. transformation.
   c. duplication.
   d. replication.

2. Bacteriophages are
   a. a form of bacteria.
   b. enzymes.
   c. coils of DNA.
   d. viruses.

3. Which of the following researchers used radioactive markers in experiments to show that DNA was the genetic material in cells?
   a. Frederick Griffith
   b. Oswald Avery
   c. Alfred Hershey and Martha Chase
   d. James Watson and Francis Crick

4. Before DNA could definitively be shown to be the genetic material in cells, scientists had to show that it could
   a. tolerate high temperatures.
   b. carry and make copies of information.
   c. be modified in response to environmental conditions.
   d. be broken down into small subunits.

5. Briefly describe the conclusion that could be drawn from the experiments of Frederick Griffith.

6. What was the key factor that allowed Hershey and Chase to show that DNA alone carried the genetic information of a bacteriophage?

Think Critically

7. **Interpret Visuals** Look back at Griffith's experiment shown in **Figure 12–1**. Describe the occasion in which the bacterial DNA withstood conditions that killed the bacteria. What happened to the DNA during the rest of the experiment?

8. **Evaluate** Avery and his team identified DNA as the molecule responsible for the transformation seen in Griffith's experiment. How did they control variables in their experiment to make sure that only DNA caused the effect?

12.2 The Structure of DNA

Understand Key Concepts

9. A nucleotide does NOT contain
   a. a 5-carbon sugar.
   b. an amino acid.
   c. a nitrogen base.
   d. a phosphate group.

10. According to Chargaff's rule of base pairing, which of the following is true about DNA?
    a. A = T, and C = G
    b. A = C, and T = G
    c. A = G, and T = C
    d. A = T = C = G

11. The bonds that hold the two strands of DNA together come from
    a. the attraction of phosphate groups for each other.
    b. strong bonds between nitrogenous bases and the sugar-phosphate backbone.
    c. weak hydrogen bonds between nitrogenous bases.
    d. carbon-to-carbon bonds in the sugar portion of the nucleotides.

12. Describe the components and structure of a DNA nucleotide.

13. Explain how Chargaff's rule of base pairing helped Watson and Crick model DNA.

14. What important clue from Rosalind Franklin's work helped Watson and Crick develop their model of DNA?

15. Why is it significant that the two strands of DNA are antiparallel?

Think Critically

16. **Use Models** How did Watson and Crick's model of the DNA molecule explain base pairing?

17. **Infer** Rosalind Franklin's X-ray pattern showed that the distance between the two phosphate-sugar backbones of a DNA molecule is the same throughout the length of the molecule. How did that information help Watson and Crick determine how bases are paired?

12.3 DNA Replication

Understand Key Concepts

18. In prokaryotes, DNA molecules are located in the
   a. nucleus. **c.** cytoplasm.
   b. ribosomes. **d.** histones.

19. In eukaryotes, nearly all the DNA is found in the
   a. nucleus. **c.** cytoplasm.
   b. ribosomes. **d.** histones.

20. The diagram below shows the process of DNA
   a. replication. **c.** transformation.
   b. digestion. **d.** transpiration.

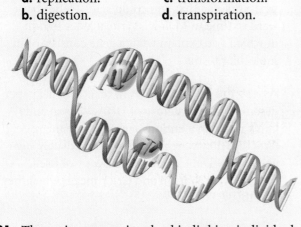

21. The main enzyme involved in linking individual nucleotides into DNA molecules is
   a. DNA protease. **c.** carbohydrase.
   b. ribose. **d.** DNA polymerase.

22. What is meant by the term *base pairing*? How is base pairing involved in DNA replication?

23. Describe the appearance of DNA in a typical prokaryotic cell.

24. Explain the process of replication. When a DNA molecule is replicated, how do the new molecules compare to the original molecule?

Think Critically

25. Use Analogies Is photocopying a document similar to DNA replication? Think of the original materials, the copying process, and the final products. Explain how the two processes are alike. Identify major differences.

26. Compare and Contrast Describe the similarities and differences between DNA replication in prokaryotic cells and in eukaryotic cells.

solve the CHAPTER MYSTERY

UV LIGHT

The nucleotides in DNA include the nitrogenous bases adenine, cytosine, guanine, and thymine (A, C, G, and T). The energy from UV light can produce chemical changes in these bases, damaging the DNA molecule and producing errors when DNA is replicated.

1. Predict Use your understanding of the structure of DNA to predict what sorts of problems excessive UV light might produce in the DNA molecule. How might these changes affect the functions of DNA?

2. Infer All cells have systems of enzymes that repair UV-induced damage to their DNA. Some cellular systems block DNA replication if there are base pairing problems in the double helix. Why are these systems important? How might they work?

3. Relate Cause and Effect Analyze the effects that UV light might have on skin cells. Why is UV light so dangerous? Why is the skin particularly vulnerable to it?

4. Connect to the Big idea Among humans who inherit genetic defects in their DNA-repair systems, the incidence of skin cancer is as much as 1000 times greater than average. Based on this information, what can you infer about the effect of UV light on DNA?

Use Science Graphics

A scientist studied the effect of exposing DNA to various wavelengths of ultraviolet light. The scientist determined the number of copying errors made after exposure to ultraviolet rays. The graph shows the results. Use the graph to answer questions 27 and 28.

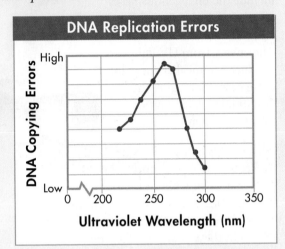

DNA Replication Errors

27. **Interpret Graphs** The most damaging effects of ultraviolet light on DNA replication occur at which wavelength?

28. **Infer** What conclusion would you draw from the graph about the effect of ultraviolet light on living organisms?

29. **Pose Questions** Ozone is a molecule that is very effective at absorbing ultraviolet light from the sun. Evidence indicates that human activities have contributed to the destruction of ozone in the atmosphere. What question would you ask about the effect of removing ozone from the atmosphere?

Write About Science

30. **Explanation** Recall that Gregor Mendel concluded that factors, which we now call genes, determine the traits that pass from one generation to the next. Imagine that you could send a letter backward in time to Mendel. Write a letter to him in which you explain what a gene consists of in molecular terms.

31. **Assess the Big idea** In their original paper describing the structure of DNA, Watson and Crick noted in a famous sentence that the structure they were proposing immediately suggested how DNA could make a copy of itself. Explain what Watson and Crick meant when they said this.

Analyzing Data

The following table shows the results of measuring the percentages of the four bases in the DNA of several different organisms. Some of the values are missing from the table.

Nitrogenous Bases (%)				
Organism	A	G	T	C
Human		19.9	29.4	
Chicken	28.8			21.5
Bacterium (*S. lutea*)	13.4			

32. **Predict** Based on Chargaff's rule, the percentage of adenine bases in human DNA should be around
   a. 30.9%.   **c.** 21.5%.
   b. 19.9%.   **d.** 13.4%.

33. **Calculate** The value for the percent of guanine bases in the bacterium would be expected to be about
   a. 13.4%.
   b. 28.8%.
   c. 36.6%.
   d. There is not enough information given.

34. **Predict** If the two DNA strands of the bacterium were separated and the base composition of just one of the strands was determined, you could expect
   a. the amount of A to equal the amount of T.
   b. the amount of C to equal the amount of G.
   c. the amount of A to equal the amounts of T, C, and G.
   d. the four nitrogenous bases to have any value.

Standardized Test Prep

Multiple Choice

1. During replication, which sequence of nucleotides would bond with the DNA sequence TATGA?
   A TATGA   C CACTA
   B ATACT   D AGTAT

2. The scientist(s) responsible for the discovery of bacterial transformation is (are)
   A Watson and Crick.   C Griffith.
   B Avery.   D Franklin.

3. Which of the following does NOT describe the structure of DNA?
   A double helix
   B nucleotide polymer
   C contains adenine-guanine pairs
   D sugar-phosphate backbone

4. What did Hershey and Chase's work show?
   A Genes are probably made of DNA.
   B Genes are probably made of protein.
   C Viruses contain DNA but not protein.
   D Bacteria contain DNA but not protein.

5. The two "backbones" of the DNA molecule consist of
   A adenines and sugars.
   B phosphates and sugars.
   C adenines and thymines.
   D thymines and sugars.

6. In eukaryotic chromosomes, DNA is tightly coiled around proteins called
   A DNA polymerase.
   B chromatin.
   C histones.
   D nucleotides.

7. When prokaryotic cells copy their DNA, replication begins at
   A one point on the DNA molecule.
   B two points on opposite ends of the DNA molecule.
   C dozens to hundreds of points along the molecule.
   D opposite ends of the molecule.

8. Compared to eukaryotic cells, prokaryotic cells contain
   A about 1000 times more DNA.
   B about one thousandth as much DNA.
   C twice as much DNA.
   D the same amount of DNA.

Questions 9–10

Under ideal conditions, a single bacterial cell can reproduce every 20 minutes. The graph shows how the total number of cells under ideal conditions can change over time.

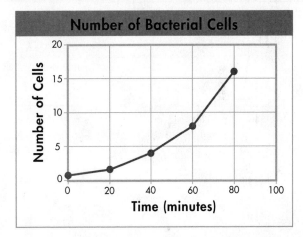

9. How many cells are present after 80 minutes?
   A 1   C 16
   B 2   D 32

10. If the DNA of this bacterium is 4 million base pairs in length, how many total molecules of A, T, C, and G are required for replication to be successful?
    A 2 million
    B 4 million
    C 8 million
    D 32 million

Open-Ended Response

11. Describe how eukaryotic cells are able to keep such large amounts of DNA in the small volume of the cell nucleus.

If You Have Trouble With . . .

Question	1	2	3	4	5	6	7	8	9	10	11
See Lesson	12.3	12.1	12.2	12.1	12.2	12.3	12.3	12.3	12.3	12.3	12.3

13 RNA and Protein Synthesis

Big idea

Information and Heredity

Q: How does information flow from DNA to RNA to direct the synthesis of proteins?

INSIDE:

- 13.1 RNA
- 13.2 Ribosomes and Protein Synthesis
- 13.3 Mutations
- 13.4 Gene Regulation and Expression

Two Bengal tigers—one with normal coloration and one with a genetic mutation that affects its coloring.

CHAPTER
MYSTERY

MOUSE-EYED FLY

It was definitely not a science fiction movie. The animal in the laboratory was real. Besides having two forward-looking eyes, it also had eyes on its knees and eyes on its hind legs. It even had eyes in the back of its head! Yet as strange as it looked, this animal was not a monster. It was simply a fruit fly with eyes in very strange places. These eyes looked like the fly's normal compound eyes, but a mouse gene transplanted into the fly's DNA had produced them. How could a mouse gene produce extra eyes in a fly?

As you read this chapter, look for clues to explain how a gene that normally controls the growth of eyes in mice could possibly cause a fly to grow extra eyes in unusual places. Then, solve the mystery.

Never Stop Exploring Your World.
Finding the solution to the mouse-eyed fly is only the beginning. Take a video field trip with the ecogeeks of Untamed Science to see where this mystery leads.

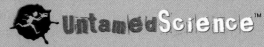

• Untamed Science Video   • Chapter Mystery

13.1 RNA

Key Questions

🔑 How does RNA differ from DNA?

🔑 How does the cell make RNA?

Vocabulary

RNA
messenger RNA
ribosomal RNA
transfer RNA
transcription
RNA polymerase
promoter
intron
exon

Taking Notes

Preview Visuals Before you read, look at **Figure 13–3.** Write a prediction of how you think a cell makes RNA based on the figure. Then as you read, take notes on how a cell makes RNA. After you read, compare your notes and your prediction.

THINK ABOUT IT We know that DNA is the genetic material, and we know that the sequence of nucleotide bases in its strands must carry some sort of code. For that code to work, the cell must be able to understand it. What exactly do those bases code for? Where is the cell's decoding system?

The Role of RNA

🔑 **How does RNA differ from DNA?**

When Watson and Crick solved the double-helix structure of DNA, they understood right away how DNA could be copied. All a cell had to do was to separate the two strands and then use base pairing to make a new complementary strand for each. But the structure of DNA by itself did not explain how a gene actually works. That question required a great deal more research. The answer came from the discovery that another nucleic acid—ribonucleic acid, or RNA—was involved in putting the genetic code into action. **RNA,** like DNA, is a nucleic acid that consists of a long chain of nucleotides.

In a general way, genes contain coded DNA instructions that tell cells how to build proteins. The first step in decoding these genetic instructions is to copy part of the base sequence from DNA into RNA. RNA then uses these instructions to direct the production of proteins, which help to determine an organisms's characteristics.

Comparing RNA and DNA Remember that each nucleotide in DNA is made up of a 5-carbon sugar, a phosphate group, and a nitrogenous base. This is true for RNA as well. 🔑 **But there are three important differences between RNA and DNA: (1) the sugar in RNA is ribose instead of deoxyribose, (2) RNA is generally single-stranded and not double-stranded, and (3) RNA contains uracil in place of thymine.** These chemical differences make it easy for enzymes in the cell to tell DNA and RNA apart.

You can compare the different roles played by DNA and RNA molecules in directing the production of proteins to the two type of plans builders use. A master plan has all the information needed to construct a building. But builders never bring a valuable master plan to the job site, where it might be damaged or lost. Instead, as **Figure 13–1** shows, they work from blueprints, inexpensive, disposable copies of the master plan.

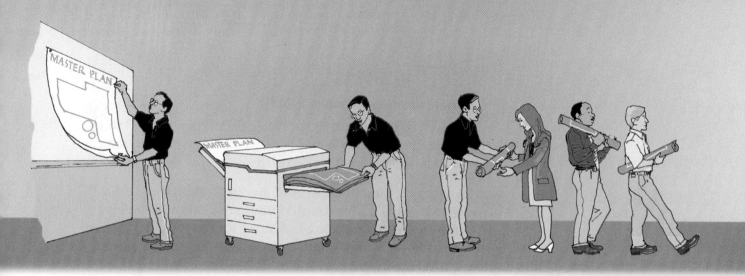

Similarly, the cell uses the vital DNA "master plan" to prepare RNA "blueprints." The DNA molecule stays safely in the cell's nucleus, while RNA molecules go to the protein-building sites in the cytoplasm—the ribosomes.

Functions of RNA You can think of an RNA molecule as a disposable copy of a segment of DNA, a working facsimile of a single gene. RNA has many functions, but most RNA molecules are involved in just one job—protein synthesis. RNA controls the assembly of amino acids into proteins. Like workers in a factory, each type of RNA molecule specializes in a different aspect of this job. **Figure 13–2** shows the three main types of RNA: messenger RNA, ribosomal RNA, and transfer RNA.

▶ *Messenger RNA* Most genes contain instructions for assembling amino acids into proteins. The RNA molecules that carry copies of these instructions are known as **messenger RNA** (mRNA). They carry information from DNA to other parts of the cell.

▶ *Ribosomal RNA* Proteins are assembled on ribosomes, small organelles composed of two subunits. These subunits are made up of several **ribosomal RNA** (rRNA) molecules and as many as 80 different proteins.

▶ *Transfer RNA* When a protein is built, a third type of RNA molecule transfers each amino acid to the ribosome as it is specified by the coded messages in mRNA. These molecules are known as **transfer RNA** (tRNA).

FIGURE 13–2 Types of RNA The three main types of RNA are messenger RNA, ribosomal RNA, and transfer RNA.

MASTER PLANS AND BLUEPRINTS

FIGURE 13–1 The different roles of DNA and RNA molecules in directing protein synthesis can be compared to the two types of plans used by builders: master plans and blueprints.

Messenger RNA
Carries instructions for polypeptide synthesis from nucleus to ribosomes in the cytoplasm.

Ribosome

Ribosomal RNA
Forms an important part of both subunits of the ribosome.

Amino acid

Transfer RNA
Carries amino acids to the ribosome and matches them to the coded mRNA message.

RNA Synthesis

⚿ How does the cell make RNA?

Cells invest large amounts of raw material and energy into making RNA molecules. Understanding how cells do this is essential to understanding how genes work.

Transcription Most of the work of making RNA takes place during **transcription.** ⚿ **In transcription, segments of DNA serve as templates to produce complementary RNA molecules.** The base sequences of the transcribed RNA complement the base sequences of the template DNA.

In prokaryotes, RNA synthesis and protein synthesis take place in the cytoplasm. In eukaryotes, RNA is produced in the cell's nucleus and then moves to the cytoplasm to play a role in the production of protein. Our focus here is on transcription in eukaryotic cells.

Transcription requires an enzyme, known as **RNA polymerase,** that is similar to DNA polymerase. RNA polymerase binds to DNA during transcription and separates the DNA strands. It then uses one strand of DNA as a template from which to assemble nucleotides into a complementary strand of RNA, as shown in **Figure 13–3.** The ability to copy a single DNA sequence into RNA makes it possible for a single gene to produce hundreds or even thousands of RNA molecules.

FIGURE 13–3 Transcribing DNA into RNA During transcription, the enzyme RNA polymerase uses one strand of DNA as a template to assemble complementary nucleotides into a strand of RNA.

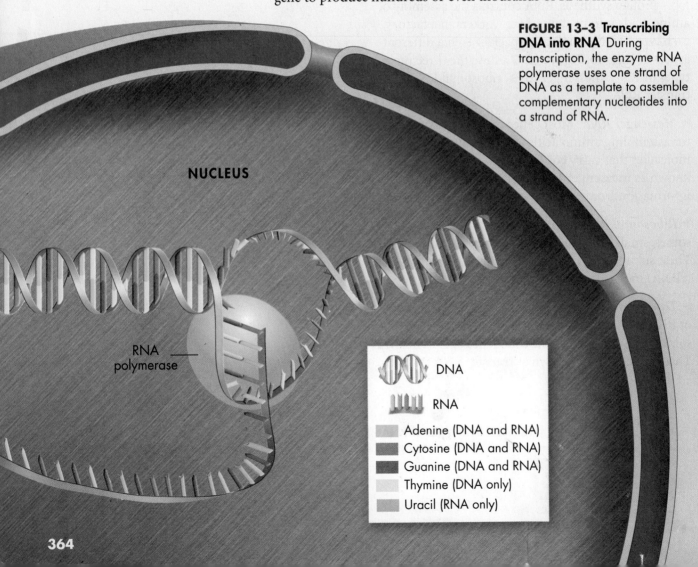

NUCLEUS

RNA polymerase

DNA

RNA

Adenine (DNA and RNA)
Cytosine (DNA and RNA)
Guanine (DNA and RNA)
Thymine (DNA only)
Uracil (RNA only)

Promoters How does RNA polymerase know where to start and stop making a strand of RNA? The answer is that RNA polymerase doesn't bind to DNA just anywhere. The enzyme binds only to **promoters,** regions of DNA that have specific base sequences. Promoters are signals in the DNA molecule that show RNA polymerase exactly where to begin making RNA. Similar signals in DNA cause transcription to stop when a new RNA molecule is completed.

RNA Editing Like a writer's first draft, RNA molecules sometimes require a bit of editing before they are ready to be read. These pre-mRNA molecules have bits and pieces cut out of them before they can go into action. The portions that are cut out and discarded are called **introns.** In eukaryotes, introns are taken out of pre-mRNA molecules while they are still in the nucleus. The remaining pieces, known as **exons,** are then spliced back together to form the final mRNA, as shown in **Figure 13–4.**

Why do cells use energy to make a large RNA molecule and then throw parts of that molecule away? That's a good question, and biologists still don't have a complete answer. Some pre-mRNA molecules may be cut and spliced in different ways in different tissues, making it possible for a single gene to produce several different forms of RNA. Introns and exons may also play a role in evolution, making it possible for very small changes in DNA sequences to have dramatic effects on how genes affect cellular function.

FIGURE 13–4 Introns and Exons Before many mRNA molecules can be read, sections called introns are "edited out." The remaining pieces, called exons, are spliced together. Then, an RNA cap and tail are added to form the final mRNA molecule.

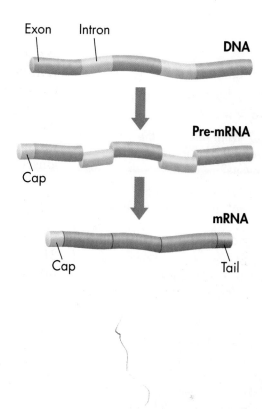

13.1 Assessment

Review Key Concepts

1. a. Review Describe three main differences between RNA and DNA.

   b. Explain List the three main types of RNA, and explain what they do.

   c. Infer Why is it important for a single gene to be able to produce hundreds or thousands of the same RNA molecules?

2. a. Review Describe what happens during transcription.

   b. Predict What do you think would happen if introns were not removed from pre-mRNA?

WRITE ABOUT SCIENCE

Creative Writing

3. An RNA molecule is looking for a job in a protein synthesis factory. It asks you to write its résumé. This RNA molecule is not yet specialized and could, with some structural changes, function as mRNA, rRNA, or tRNA. Write a résumé for this molecule that reflects the capabilities of each type of RNA.

13.2 Ribosomes and Protein Synthesis

Key Questions

🔑 **What is the genetic code, and how is it read?**

🔑 **What role does the ribosome play in assembling proteins?**

🔑 **What is the "central dogma" of molecular biology?**

Vocabulary

polypeptide • genetic code • codon • translation • anticodon • gene expression

Taking Notes

Outline Before you read, write down the green headings in this lesson. As you read, keep a list of the main points, and then write a summary for each heading.

THINK ABOUT IT How would you build a system to read the messages that are coded in genes and transcribed into RNA? Would you read the bases one at a time, as if the code were a language with just four words—one word per base? Perhaps you would read them, as we do in English, as individual letters that can be combined to spell longer words.

The Genetic Code

🔑 **What is the genetic code, and how is it read?**

The first step in decoding genetic messages is to transcribe a nucleotide base sequence from DNA to RNA. This transcribed information contains a code for making proteins. You learned in Chapter 2 that proteins are made by joining amino acids together into long chains, called **polypeptides.** As many as 20 different amino acids are commonly found in polypeptides.

The specific amino acids in a polypeptide, and the order in which they are joined, determine the properties of different proteins. The sequence of amino acids influences the shape of the protein, which in turn determines its function. How is the order of bases in DNA and RNA molecules translated into a particular order of amino acids in a polypeptide?

As you know from Lesson 13.1, RNA contains four different bases: adenine, cytosine, guanine, and uracil. In effect, these bases form a "language" with just four "letters": A, C, G, and U. We call this language the **genetic code.** How can a code with just four letters carry instructions for 20 different amino acids? 🔑 **The genetic code is read three "letters" at a time, so that each "word" is three bases long and corresponds to a single amino acid.** Each three-letter "word" in mRNA is known as a **codon.** As shown in **Figure 13–5,** a codon consists of three consecutive bases that specify a single amino acid to be added to the polypeptide chain.

FIGURE 13–5 Codons A codon is a group of three nucleotide bases in messenger RNA that specifies a particular amino acid. **Observe** *What are the three-letter groups of the codons shown here?*

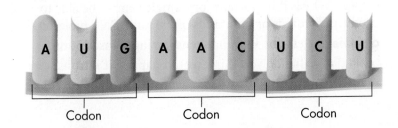

Codon   Codon   Codon

How to Read Codons Because there are four different bases in RNA, there are 64 possible three-base codons (4 × 4 × 4 = 64) in the genetic code. **Figure 13–6** shows these possible combinations. Most amino acids can be specified by more than one codon. For example, six different codons—UUA, UUG, CUU, CUC, CUA, and CUG—specify leucine. But only one codon—UGG—specifies the amino acid tryptophan.

Decoding codons is a task made simple by use of a genetic code table. Just start at the middle of the circle with the first letter of the codon, and move outward. Next, move out to the second ring to find the second letter of the codon. Find the third and final letter among the smallest set of letters in the third ring. Then read the amino acid in that sector.

Start and Stop Codons Any message, whether in a written language or the genetic code, needs punctuation marks. In English, punctuation tells us where to pause, when to sound excited, and where to start and stop a sentence. The genetic code has punctuation marks, too. The methionine codon AUG, for example, also serves as the initiation, or "start," codon for protein synthesis. Following the start codon, mRNA is read, three bases at a time, until it reaches one of three different "stop" codons, which end translation. At that point, the polypeptide is complete.

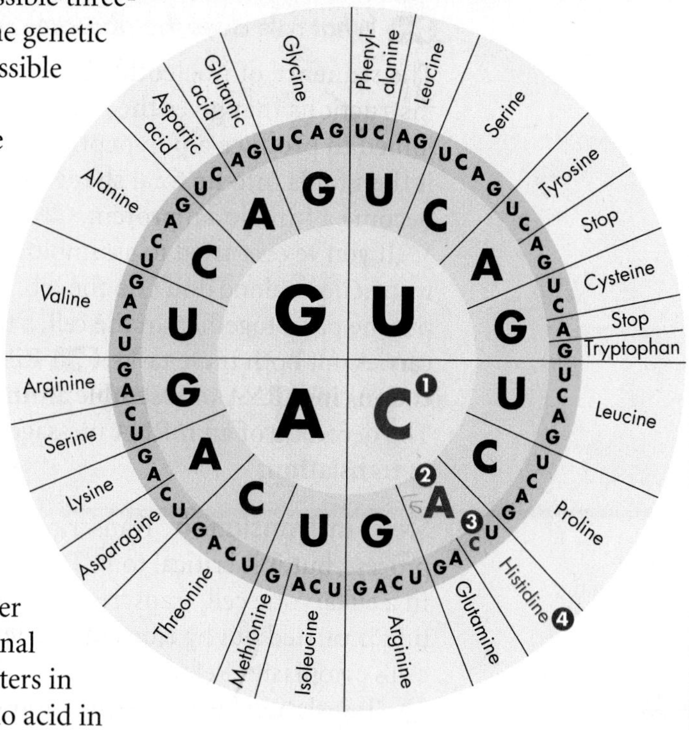

❶ To decode the codon CAC, find the first letter in the set of bases at the center of the circle.

❷ Find the second letter of the codon A, in the "C" quarter of the next ring.

❸ Find the third letter, C, in the next ring, in the "C-A" grouping.

❹ Read the name of the amino acid in that sector—in this case histidine.

FIGURE 13–6 Reading Codons
This circular table shows the amino acid to which each of the 64 codons corresponds. To read a codon, start at the middle of the circle and move outward.

Quick Lab
GUIDED INQUIRY

How Does a Cell Interpret Codons?

❶ A certain gene has the following base sequence:

GACAAGTCCACAATC

Write this sequence on a separate sheet of paper.

❷ From left to right, write the sequence of the mRNA molecule transcribed from this gene.

❸ Using **Figure 13–6,** read the mRNA codons from left to right. Then write the amino acid sequence of the polypeptide.

❹ Repeat step 2, reading the sequence of the mRNA molecule from right to left.

Analyze and Conclude

1. Apply Concepts Why did steps 3 and 4 produce different polypeptides?

2. Infer Do cells usually decode nucleotides in one direction only or in either direction?

Translation

🔑 What role does the ribosome play in assembling proteins?

The sequence of nucleotide bases in an mRNA molecule is a set of instructions that gives the order in which amino acids should be joined to produce a polypeptide. Once the polypeptide is complete, it then folds into its final shape or joins with other polypeptides to become a functional protein.

If you've ever tried to assemble a complex toy, you know that instructions alone don't do the job. You need to read them and then put the parts together. In the cell, a tiny factory—the ribosome—carries out both these tasks. 🔑 **Ribosomes use the sequence of codons in mRNA to assemble amino acids into polypeptide chains.** The decoding of an mRNA message into a protein is a process known as **translation.**

Steps in Translation Transcription isn't part of the translation process, but it is critical to it. Transcribed mRNA directs that process. In a eukaryotic cell, transcription goes on in the cell's nucleus; translation is carried out by ribosomes after the transcribed mRNA enters the cell's cytoplasm. Refer to **Figure 13–7** as you read about translation.

🅐 Translation begins when a ribosome attaches to an mRNA molecule in the cytoplasm. As each codon passes through the ribosome, tRNAs bring the proper amino acids into the ribosome. One at a time, the ribosome then attaches these amino acids to the growing chain.

VISUAL SUMMARY

TRANSLATION

FIGURE 13–7 During translation, or protein synthesis, the cell uses information from messenger RNA to produce proteins.

Messenger RNA

Messenger RNA is transcribed in the nucleus and then enters the cytoplasm.

🅐 Transfer RNA

Translation begins at AUG, the start codon. Each transfer RNA has an anticodon whose bases are complementary to the bases of a codon on the mRNA strand. The ribosome positions the start codon to attract its anticodon, which is part of the tRNA that binds methionine. The ribosome also binds the next codon and its anticodon.

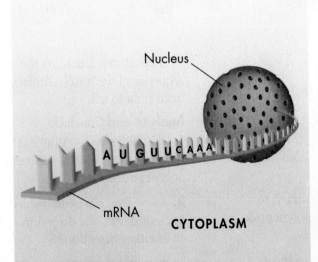

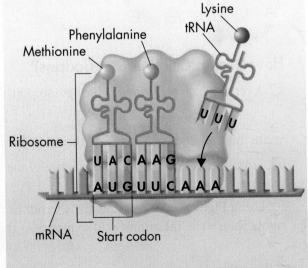

Each tRNA molecule carries just one kind of amino acid. In addition, each tRNA molecule has three unpaired bases, collectively called the **anticodon.** Each tRNA anticodon is complementary to one mRNA codon.

In the case of the tRNA molecule for methionine, the anticodon is UAC, which pairs with the methionine codon, AUG. The ribosome has a second binding site for a tRNA molecule for the next codon. If that next codon is UUC, a tRNA molecule with an AAG anticodon fits against the mRNA molecule held in the ribosome. That second tRNA molecule brings the amino acid phenylalanine into the ribosome.

B Like an assembly-line worker who attaches one part to another, the ribosome helps form a peptide bond between the first and second amino acids—methionine and phenylalanine. At the same time, the bond holding the first tRNA molecule to its amino acid is broken. That tRNA then moves into a third binding site, from which it exits the ribosome. The ribosome then moves to the third codon, where tRNA brings it the amino acid specified by the third codon.

C The polypeptide chain continues to grow until the ribosome reaches a "stop" codon on the mRNA molecule. When the ribosome reaches a stop codon, it releases both the newly formed polypeptide and the mRNA molecule, completing the process of translation.

In Your Notebook *Briefly summarize the three steps in translation.*

FIGURE 13–8 Molecular Model of a Ribosome This model shows ribosomal RNA and associated proteins as colored ribbons. The large subunit is blue, green, and purple. The small subunit is shown in yellow and orange. The three solid elements in the center are tRNA molecules.

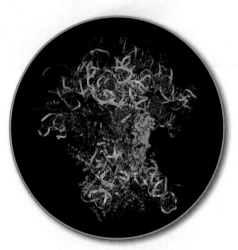

B The Polypeptide "Assembly Line"
The ribosome joins the two amino acids—methionine and phenylalanine—and breaks the bond between methionine and its tRNA. The tRNA floats away from the ribosome, allowing the ribosome to bind another tRNA. The ribosome moves along the mRNA, from right to left, binding new tRNA molecules and amino acids.

C Completing the Polypeptide
The process continues until the ribosome reaches one of the three stop codons. Once the polypeptide is complete, it and the mRNA are released from the ribosome.

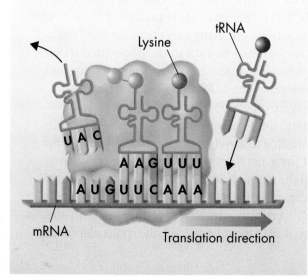

Lysine
tRNA
U A C
A A G U U U
A U G U U C A A A
mRNA
Translation direction

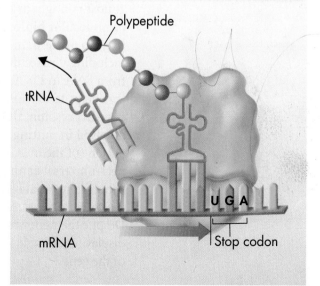

Polypeptide
tRNA
U G A
mRNA
Stop codon

The Roles of tRNA and rRNA in Translation All three major forms of RNA—mRNA, tRNA, and rRNA—come together in the ribosome during translation. The mRNA molecule, of course, carries the coded message that directs the process. The tRNA molecules deliver exactly the right amino acid called for by each codon on the mRNA. The tRNA molecules are, in effect, adaptors that enable the ribosome to "read" the mRNA's message accurately and to get the translation just right.

Ribosomes themselves are composed of roughly 80 proteins and three or four different rRNA molecules. These rRNA molecules help hold ribosomal proteins in place and help locate the beginning of the mRNA message. They may even carry out the chemical reaction that joins amino acids together.

The Molecular Basis of Heredity

What is the "central dogma" of molecular biology?

Gregor Mendel might have been surprised to learn that most genes contain nothing more than instructions for assembling proteins. He might have asked what proteins could possibly have to do with the color of a flower, the shape of a leaf, or the sex of a newborn baby. The answer is that proteins have everything to do with these traits. Remember that many proteins are enzymes, which catalyze and regulate chemical reactions. A gene that codes for an enzyme to produce pigment can control the color of a flower. Another gene produces proteins that regulate patterns of tissue growth in a leaf. Yet another may trigger the female or male pattern of development in an embryo. In short, proteins are microscopic tools, each specifically designed to build or operate a component of a living cell.

As you've seen, once scientists learned that genes were made of DNA, a series of other discoveries soon followed. Before long, with the genetic code in hand, a new scientific field called molecular biology had been established. Molecular biology seeks to explain living organisms by studying them at the molecular level, using molecules like DNA and RNA. One of the earliest findings came to be known, almost jokingly, as the field's "central dogma." **The central dogma of molecular biology is that information is transferred from DNA to RNA to protein.** In reality, there are many exceptions to this "dogma," including viruses that transfer information in the opposite direction, from RNA to DNA. Nonetheless, it serves as a useful generalization that helps to explain how genes work. **Figure 13–9** illustrates **gene expression,** the way in which DNA, RNA, and proteins are involved in putting genetic information into action in living cells.

One of the most interesting discoveries of molecular biology is the near-universal nature of the genetic code. Although some organisms show slight variations in the amino acids assigned to particular codons, the code is always read three bases at a time and in the same direction. Despite their enormous diversity in form and function, living organisms display remarkable unity at life's most basic level, the molecular biology of the gene.

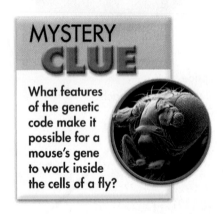

MYSTERY CLUE

What features of the genetic code make it possible for a mouse's gene to work inside the cells of a fly?

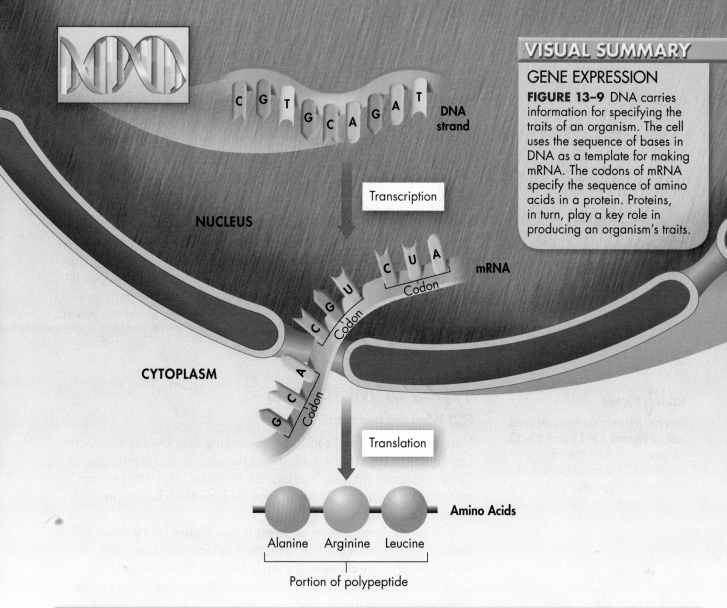

C G T T G C A G A T **DNA strand**

Transcription

NUCLEUS

CYTOPLASM

mRNA

Codon

Codon

Codon

Translation

Amino Acids

Alanine   Arginine   Leucine

Portion of polypeptide

VISUAL SUMMARY

GENE EXPRESSION

FIGURE 13-9 DNA carries information for specifying the traits of an organism. The cell uses the sequence of bases in DNA as a template for making mRNA. The codons of mRNA specify the sequence of amino acids in a protein. Proteins, in turn, play a key role in producing an organism's traits.

13.2 Assessment

Review Key Concepts 🔑

1. a. Review How does a cell interpret the genetic code?

b. Explain What are codons and anticodons?

c. Apply Concepts Using the table in **Figure 13–6,** identify the amino acids specified by codons: UGG, AAG, and UGC.

2. a. Review What happens during translation?

b. Compare and Contrast How is protein synthesis different from DNA replication? (*Hint*: Revisit Lesson 12.3.)

3. a. Review Why is the genetic code considered universal?

b. Explain What does the term *gene expression* mean?

c. Infer In what way does controlling the proteins in an organism control the organism's characteristics?

Apply the **Big** idea

Information and Heredity

4. Choose one component of translation to consider in depth. For instance, you might choose to consider one form of RNA or one step in the process. Then write a question or a series of questions about that component. Select one question, and use it to form a hypothesis that could be tested in an experiment.

BIOLOGY.com   Search   Lesson 13.2   GO   • Self-Test   • Lesson Assessment

13.3

Mutations

Key Questions

🔑 What are mutations?

🔑 How do mutations affect genes?

Vocabulary

mutation • point mutation • frameshift mutation • mutagen • polyploidy

Taking Notes

Preview Visuals Before you read, look at **Figures 13–11** and **13–12.** As you read, note the changes produced by various gene and chromosomal mutations.

THINK ABOUT IT The sequence of bases in DNA are like the letters of a coded message, as we've just seen. But what would happen if a few of those letters changed accidentally, altering the message? Could the cell still understand its meaning? Think about what might happen if someone changed at random a few lines of code in a computer program that you rely on. Knowing what you already do about the genetic code, what effects would you predict such changes to have on genes and the polypeptides for which they code?

Types of Mutations

🔑 **What are mutations?**

Now and then cells make mistakes in copying their own DNA, inserting the wrong base or even skipping a base as a strand is put together. These variations are called **mutations,** from the Latin word *mutare,* meaning "to change." 🔑 **Mutations are heritable changes in genetic information.**

Mutations come in many different forms. **Figure 13–10** shows two of the countless examples. But all mutations fall into two basic categories: Those that produce changes in a single gene are known as gene mutations. Those that produce changes in whole chromosomes are known as chromosomal mutations.

FIGURE 13–10 Plant and Animal Mutations

The elongated shape of this flower is caused by a mutation that affects the growing regions of the flower tissue.

A genetic condition called leucism leaves this lion without pigments in its hair, skin, and eyes.

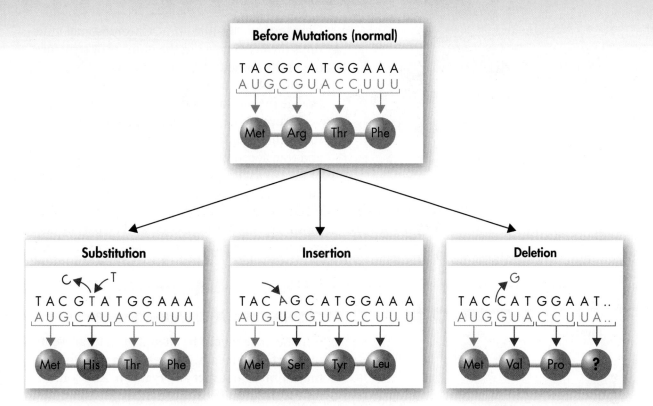

Before Mutations (normal)

```
T A C G C A T G G A A A
A U G C G U A C C U U U
```
Met Arg Thr Phe

Substitution

```
        C        T
T A C G T A T G G A A A
A U G C A U A C C U U U
```
Met His Thr Phe

Insertion

```
T A C A G C A T G G A A A
A U G U C G U A C C U U U
```
Met Ser Tyr Leu

Deletion

```
              G
T A C C A T G G A A T..
A U G G U A C C U U A..
```
Met Val Pro ?

Gene Mutations Gene mutations that involve changes in one or a few nucleotides are known as **point mutations** because they occur at a single point in the DNA sequence. Point mutations include substitutions, insertions, and deletions. They generally occur during replication. If a gene in one cell is altered, the alteration can be passed on to every cell that develops from the original one. Refer to **Figure 13–11** as you read about the different forms of point mutations.

▶ *Substitutions* In a substitution, one base is changed to a different base. Substitutions usually affect no more than a single amino acid, and sometimes they have no effect at all. For example, if a mutation changed one codon of mRNA from CCC to CCA, the codon would still specify the amino acid proline. But a change in the first base of the codon—changing CCC to ACC—would replace proline with the amino acid threonine.

▶ *Insertions and Deletions* Insertions and deletions are point mutations in which one base is inserted or removed from the DNA sequence. The effects of these changes can be dramatic. Remember that the genetic code is read three bases at a time. If a nucleotide is added or deleted, the bases are still read in groups of three, but now those groupings shift in every codon that follows the mutation.

Insertions and deletions are also called **frameshift mutations** because they shift the "reading frame" of the genetic message. By shifting the reading frame, frameshift mutations can change every amino acid that follows the point of the mutation. They can alter a protein so much that it is unable to perform its normal functions.

FIGURE 13–11 Point Mutations These diagrams show how changes in a single nucleotide can affect the amino acid sequence of proteins. **Analyze Data** *Which type of mutations affects only a single amino acid in a protein? Which can affect more than one?*

In Your Notebook *Use a cause/effect diagram to describe the different types of gene mutations.*

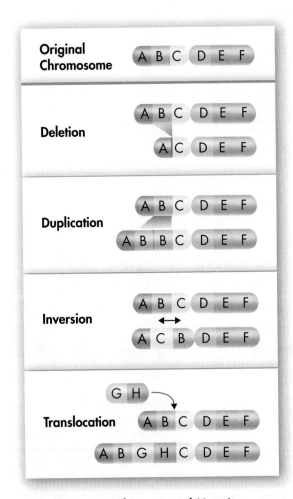

FIGURE 13-12 Chromosomal Mutations
Four types of mutations cause changes in whole chromosomes. **Use Diagrams** *What is the difference between inversion and translocation?*

Chromosomal Mutations Chromosomal mutations involve changes in the number or structure of chromosomes. These mutations can change the location of genes on chromosomes and can even change the number of copies of some genes.

Figure 13–12 shows four types of chromosomal mutations: deletion, duplication, inversion, and translocation. Deletion involves the loss of all or part of a chromosome; duplication produces an extra copy of all or part of a chromosome; and inversion reverses the direction of parts of a chromosome. Translocation occurs when part of one chromosome breaks off and attaches to another.

Effects of Mutations

How do mutations affect genes?

Genetic material can be altered by natural events or by artificial means. The resulting mutations may or may not affect an organism. And some mutations that affect individual organisms can also affect a species or even an entire ecosystem.

Many mutations are produced by errors in genetic processes. For example, some point mutations are caused by errors during DNA replication. The cellular machinery that replicates DNA inserts an incorrect base roughly once in every 10 million bases. But small changes in genes can gradually accumulate over time.

Quick Lab
GUIDED INQUIRY

Modeling Mutations

Small mutations in DNA can cause huge changes in the proteins that are synthesized. Similarly, small changes in a word can dramatically alter its meaning. Look at the following sequence of words:

milk   mile   wile   wise   wisp   wasp

Notice that each word differs from the previous word by just one letter and that none of the words is meaningless. Think of these changes as "point mutations" that affect word meaning.

Analyze and Conclude

1. Apply Concepts Start with the word *gene,* and change it letter by letter to make new words. Make sure each new word is an actual word but not a proper noun. Write at least four "point mutations" of the word *gene.*

2. Apply Concepts Show how you could use words to model a frameshift mutation. (*Hint:* You can use a sentence.)

3. Use Models Use the words in this sentence to model a substitution mutation.

Stressful environmental conditions may cause some bacteria to increase mutation rates. This can actually be helpful to the organism, since mutations may sometimes give such bacteria new traits, such as the ability to consume a new food source or to resist a poison in the environment.

Mutagens Some mutations arise from **mutagens,** chemical or physical agents in the environment. Chemical mutagens include certain pesticides, a few natural plant alkaloids, tobacco smoke, and environmental pollutants. Physical mutagens include some forms of electromagnetic radiation, such as X-rays and ultraviolet light. If these agents interact with DNA, they can produce mutations at high rates. Cells can sometimes repair the damage; but when they cannot, the DNA base sequence changes permanently. Some compounds interfere with base-pairing, increasing the error rate of DNA replication. Others weaken the DNA strand, causing breaks and inversions that produce chromosomal mutations.

In Your Notebook *Make a table to keep track of both the helpful and harmful results of mutations. As you read, fill it in.*

Harmful and Helpful Mutations As you've already seen, some mutations don't even change the amino acid specified by a codon, while others may alter a complete protein or even an entire chromosome. **The effects of mutations on genes vary widely. Some have little or no effect; and some produce beneficial variations. Some negatively disrupt gene function.** Many if not most mutations are neutral; they have little or no effect on the expression of genes or the function of the proteins for which they code. Whether a mutation is negative or beneficial depends on how its DNA changes relative to the organism's situation. Mutations are often thought of as negative, since they can disrupt the normal function of genes. However, without mutations, organisms could not evolve, because mutations are the source of genetic variability in a species.

▶*Harmful Effects* Some of the most harmful mutations are those that dramatically change protein structure or gene activity. The defective proteins produced by these mutations can disrupt normal biological activities, and result in genetic disorders. Some cancers, for example, are the product of mutations that cause the uncontrolled growth of cells. Sickle cell disease is a disorder associated with changes in the shape of red blood cells. You can see its effects in **Figure 13–13.** It is caused by a point mutation in one of the polypeptides found in hemoglobin, the blood's principal oxygen-carrying protein. Among the symptoms of the disease are anemia, severe pain, frequent infections, and stunted growth.

BUILD Vocabulary
WORD ORIGINS The word **mutagen** is a Latin word that means "origin of change." Mutagens change an organism's genetic information.

FIGURE 13–13 Effects of a Point Mutation Sickle cell disease affects the shape of red blood cells. The round cells in this false-colored SEM are normal red blood cells. The crescent and star-shaped cells are sickled cells. (SEM 1700×)

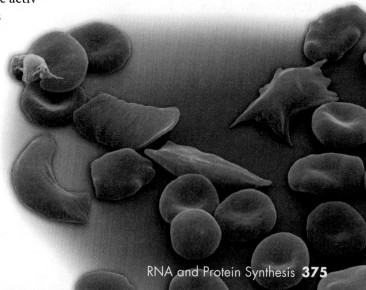

FIGURE 13–14 Polyploid Plants
The fruit of the Tahiti lime is seedless, a result of polyploidy. Changes to the ploidy number of citrus plants can affect the size and strength of the trees as well as the quality and seediness of their fruit.

▶ *Beneficial Effects* Some of the variation produced by mutations can be highly advantageous to an organism or species. **Mutations often produce proteins with new or altered functions that can be useful to organisms in different or changing environments.** For example, mutations have helped many insects resist chemical pesticides. And some have enabled microorganisms to adapt to new chemicals in the environment.

Over the past 20 years, mutations in the mosquito genome have made many African mosquitoes resistant to the chemical pesticides once used to control them. This may be bad news for humans, but it is highly beneficial to the insects themselves. Beneficial mutations occur in humans, too, including ones that increase bone strength and density, making fractures less likely, and mutations that increase resistance to HIV, the virus that causes AIDS.

Plant and animal breeders often make use of "good" mutations. For example, when a complete set of chromosomes fails to separate during meiosis, the gametes that result may produce triploid (3N) or tetraploid (4N) organisms. The condition in which an organism has extra sets of chromosomes is called **polyploidy.** Polyploid plants are often larger and stronger than diploid plants. Important crop plants—including bananas and the limes shown in **Figure 13–14**—have been produced this way. Polyploidy also occurs naturally in citrus plants, often through spontaneous mutations.

In Your Notebook *List five examples of mutations. Classify each as neutral, harmful, or helpful, and explain your reasoning.*

13.3 Assessment

Review Key Concepts

1. a. Review Describe the two main types of mutations.

b. Explain What is a frameshift mutation? Give an example.

c. Infer The effects of a mutation are not always visible. Choose a species, and explain how a biologist might determine whether a mutation has occurred and, if so, what type of mutation it is.

2. a. Review List three effects mutations can have on genes.

b. Apply Concepts What is the significance of mutations to living things?

VISUAL THINKING

3. Make a compare/contrast table to organize your ideas about gene mutations and chromosomal mutations. Then use your table to write a paragraph comparing and contrasting these two kinds of mutations.

13.4 Gene Regulation and Expression

THINK ABOUT IT Think of a library filled with how-to books. Would you ever need to use all of those books at the same time? Of course not. If you wanted to know how to fix a leaky faucet, you'd open a book about plumbing but would ignore the one on carpentry. Now picture a tiny bacterium like *E. coli*, which contains more than 4000 genes. Most of its genes code for proteins that do everything from building cell walls to breaking down food. Do you think *E. coli* uses all 4000-plus volumes in its genetic library at the same time?

Prokaryotic Gene Regulation

🔑 **How are prokaryotic genes regulated?**

As it turns out, bacteria and other prokaryotes do not need to transcribe all of their genes at the same time. To conserve energy and resources, prokaryotes regulate their activities, using only those genes necessary for the cell to function. For example, it would be wasteful for a bacterium to produce enzymes that are needed to make a molecule that is readily available from its environment. By regulating gene expression, bacteria can respond to changes in their environment—the presence or absence of nutrients, for example. How? 🔑 **DNA-binding proteins in prokaryotes regulate genes by controlling transcription.** Some of these regulatory proteins help switch genes on, while others turn genes off.

How does an organism know when to turn a gene on or off? One of the keys to gene transcription in bacteria is the organization of genes into operons. An **operon** is a group of genes that are regulated together. The genes in an operon usually have related functions. *E. coli*, shown in **Figure 13–15,** provides us with a clear example. The 4288 genes that code for proteins in *E. coli* include a cluster of 3 genes that must be turned on together before the bacterium can use the sugar lactose as a food. These three lactose genes in *E. coli* are called the *lac* operon.

FIGURE 13–15
Small Cell, Many Genes
This *E. coli* bacterium has been treated with an enzyme enabling its DNA, which contains more than 4000 genes, to spill out.

TEM 27,000×

Key Questions

🔑 How are prokaryotic genes regulated?

🔑 How are genes regulated in eukaryotic cells?

🔑 What controls the development of cells and tissues in multicellular organisms?

Vocabulary
operon
operator
RNA interference
differentiation
homeotic gene
homeobox gene
Hox gene

Taking Notes
Outline Before you read, use the headings in this lesson to make an outline. As you read, fill in the subtopics and smaller topics. Then add phrases or a sentence after each subtopic that provides key information.

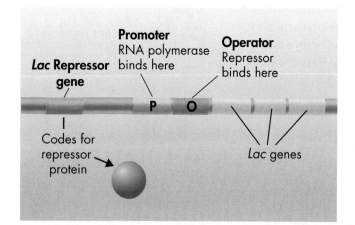

Promoter
RNA polymerase
binds here

Operator
Repressor
binds here

Lac Repressor
gene

|
Codes for
repressor
protein

P   O

Lac genes

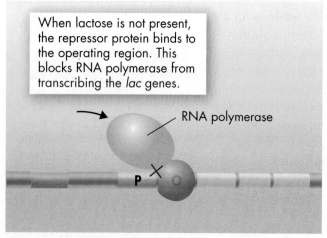

When lactose is not present, the repressor protein binds to the operating region. This blocks RNA polymerase from transcribing the *lac* genes.

RNA polymerase

P

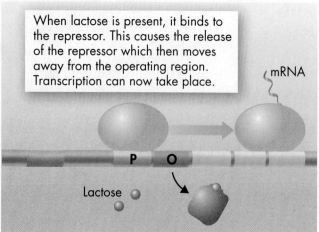

When lactose is present, it binds to the repressor. This causes the release of the repressor which then moves away from the operating region. Transcription can now take place.

mRNA

P   O

Lactose

The *Lac* Operon Why must *E. coli* be able to switch the *lac* genes on and off? Lactose is a compound made up of two simple sugars, galactose and glucose. To use lactose for food, the bacterium must transport lactose across its cell membrane and then break the bond between glucose and galactose. These tasks are performed by proteins coded for by the genes of the *lac* operon. This means, of course, that if the bacterium grows in a medium where lactose is the only food source, it must transcribe these genes and produce these proteins. If grown on another food source, such as glucose, it would have no need for these proteins.

Remarkably, the bacterium almost seems to "know" when the products of these genes are needed. When lactose is not present, the *lac* genes are turned off by proteins that bind to DNA and block transcription.

Promoters and Operators On one side of the operon's three genes are two regulatory regions. The first is a promoter (P), which is a site where RNA-polymerase can bind to begin transcription. The other region is called the **operator** (O). The O site is where a DNA-binding protein known as the *lac* repressor can bind to DNA.

▶ **The *Lac* Repressor Blocks Transcription** As **Figure 13–16** shows, when the *lac* repressor binds to the O region, RNA polymerase cannot reach the *lac* genes to begin transcription. In effect, the binding of the repressor protein switches the operon "off" by preventing the transcription of its genes.

▶ **Lactose Turns the Operon "On"** If the repressor protein is always present, how can the *lac* genes ever be switched on? Besides its DNA binding site, the *lac* repressor protein has a binding site for lactose itself. When lactose is added to the medium, it diffuses into the cell and attaches to the *lac* repressor. This changes the shape of the repressor protein in a way that causes it to fall off the operator. Now, with the repressor no longer bound to the O site, RNA polymerase can bind to the promoter and transcribe the genes of the operon. As a result, in the presence of lactose, the operon is automatically switched on.

FIGURE 13–16 Gene Expression in Prokaryotes
The *lac* genes in *E. coli* are turned off by *lac* repressors and turned on in the presence of lactose.
Use Analogies *How is the way lactose turns genes on and off similar to the way cold air signals a furnace to turn on or off?*

Eukaryotic Gene Regulation

How are genes regulated in eukaryotic cells?

The general principles of gene regulation in prokaryotes also apply to eukaryotes, although there are differences. Most eukaryotic genes are controlled individually and have more complex regulatory sequences than those of the *lac* repressor system.

Figure 13–17 shows several features of a typical eukaryotic gene. One of the most interesting is the TATA box, a short region of DNA, about 25 or 30 base pairs before the start of a gene, containing the sequence TATATA or TATAAA. The TATA box binds a protein that helps position RNA polymerase by marking a point just before the beginning of a gene.

Transcription Factors Gene expression in eukaryotic cells can be regulated at a number of levels. One of the most critical is the level of transcription, by means of DNA-binding proteins known as transcription factors. **By binding DNA sequences in the regulatory regions of eukaryotic genes, transcription factors control the expression of those genes.** Some transcription factors enhance transcription by opening up tightly packed chromatin. Others help attract RNA polymerase. Still others block access to certain genes, much like prokaryotic repressor proteins. In most cases, multiple transcription factors must bind before RNA polymerase is able to attach to the promoter region and start transcription.

Promoters have multiple binding sites for transcription factors, each of which can influence transcription. Certain factors activate scores of genes at once, dramatically changing patterns of gene expression in the cell. Other factors form only in response to chemical signals. Steroid hormones, for example, are chemical messengers that enter cells and bind to receptor proteins. These "receptor complexes" then act as transcription factors that bind to DNA, allowing a single chemical signal to activate multiple genes. Eukaryotic gene expression can also be regulated by many other factors, including the exit of mRNA molecules from the nucleus, the stability of mRNA, and even the breakdown of a gene's protein products.

In Your Notebook *Compare gene regulation in single-cell organisms and multicellular organisms.*

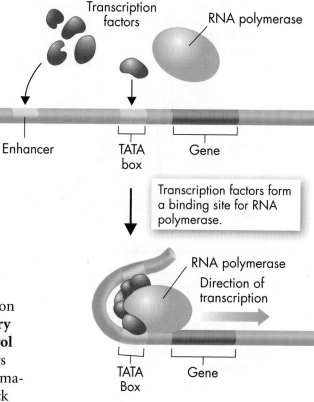

Transcription factors form a binding site for RNA polymerase.

RNA polymerase
Direction of transcription

TATA Box

Gene

FIGURE 13–17 The TATA Box and Transcription Many eukaryotic genes include a region called the TATA box that helps position RNA polymerase.

MYSTERY CLUE

To make the mouse gene work inside the cells of a fly, researchers attached a new promoter sequence to the gene. Why do you think they did that?

FIGURE 13–18 Blocking Gene Expression Like tiny pieces of sticky tape, microRNAs attach to certain mRNA molecules and stop them from passing on their protein-making instructions.
Interpret Visuals *What happens to the mRNA sequence that is complementary to the bound miRNA?*

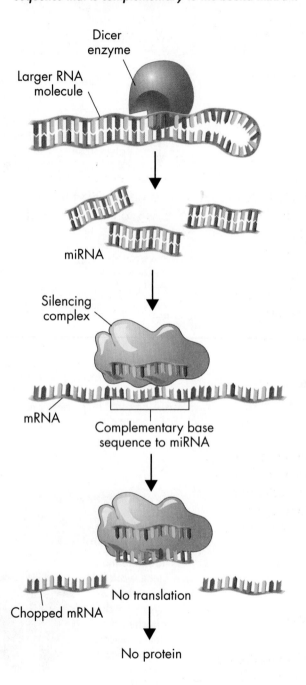

Dicer enzyme

Larger RNA molecule

miRNA

Silencing complex

mRNA

Complementary base sequence to miRNA

Chopped mRNA

No translation

No protein

Cell Specialization Why is gene regulation in eukaryotes more complex than in prokaryotes? Think for a moment about the way in which genes are expressed in a multicellular organism. The genes that code for liver enzymes, for example, are not expressed in nerve cells. Keratin, an important protein in skin cells, is not produced in blood cells. Cell specialization requires genetic specialization, yet all of the cells in a multicellular organism carry the same genetic code in their nucleus. Complex gene regulation in eukaryotes is what makes specialization possible.

RNA Interference For years biologists wondered why cells contain lots of small RNA molecules, only a few dozen bases long, that don't belong to any of the major groups of RNA (mRNA, tRNA, or rRNA). In the last decade, a series of important discoveries has shown that these small RNA molecules play a powerful role in regulating gene expression. And they do so by interfering with mRNA.

As **Figure 13–18** shows, after they are produced by transcription, the small interfering RNA molecules fold into double-stranded hairpin loops. An enzyme called the "Dicer" enzyme cuts, or dices, these double-stranded loops into microRNA (miRNA), each about 20 base pairs in length. The two strands of the loops then separate. Next, one of the miRNA pieces attaches to a cluster of proteins to form what is known as a silencing complex. The silencing complex binds to and destroys any mRNA containing a sequence that is complementary to the miRNA. In effect, miRNA sticks to certain mRNA molecules and stops them from passing on their protein-making instructions.

The silencing complex effectively shuts down the expression of the gene whose mRNA it destroys. Blocking gene expression by means of an miRNA silencing complex is known as **RNA interference.** At first, RNA interference (RNAi) seemed to be a rare event, found only in a few plants and other species. It's now clear that RNA interference is found throughout the living world and that it even plays a role in human growth and development.

Analyzing Data

The Discovery of RNA Interference

In 1998, Andrew Fire and Craig Mello carried out an experiment that helped explain the mechanism of RNA interference. They used RNA from a large gene called unc-22, which codes for a protein found in muscle cells. They prepared short mRNA fragments corresponding to two exon regions of the gene and injected them into egg cells of the worm *C. elegans.* Some of their results are shown in the table.

1. Draw Conclusions How did the adult worms' responses differ to injections of single-stranded mRNA (the "sense" strand), its complementary strand ("antisense"), and double-stranded RNA ("sense + antisense")?

Injections of mRNA into *C. elegans* Eggs		
Portion of Gene Used to Produce mRNA	Strand Injected	Result in Adult Worm
Unc-22 (exon 21–22)	Sense	Normal
	Antisense	Normal
	Sense + Antisense	Twitching
Unc-22 (exon 27)	Sense	Normal
	Antisense	Normal
	Sense + Antisense	Twitching

2. Form a Hypothesis Twitching results from the failure of muscle cells to control their contractions. What does this suggest about the unc-22 protein in some of the worms? How would you test your hypothesis?

3. Infer The injected fragments came from two different places in the gene and were only a few hundred bases long. The unc-22 mRNA is thousands of bases long. What does this suggest about the mechanism of RNA interference?

The Promise of RNAi Technology The discovery of RNAi has made it possible for researchers to switch genes on and off at will, simply by inserting double-stranded RNA into cells. The Dicer enzyme then cuts this RNA into miRNA, which activates silencing complexes. These complexes block the expression of genes producing mRNA complementary to the miRNA. Naturally this technology is a powerful way to study gene expression in the laboratory. However, RNAi technology also holds the promise of allowing medical scientists to turn off the expression of genes from viruses and cancer cells, and it may provide new ways to treat and perhaps even cure diseases.

Genetic Control of Development

What controls the development of cells and tissues in multicellular organisms?

Regulating gene expression is especially important in shaping the way a multicellular organism, like the mouse embryo in **Figure 13–19,** develops. Each of the specialized cell types found in the adult originates from the same fertilized egg cell. Cells don't just grow and divide during embryonic development. As the embryo develops, different sets of genes are regulated by transcription factors and repressors. Gene regulation helps cells undergo **differentiation,** becoming specialized in structure and function. The study of genes that control development and differentiation is one of the most exciting areas in biology today.

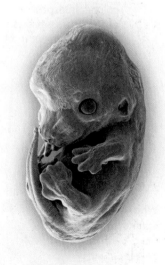

FIGURE 13–19 Differentiation This scanning electron micrograph shows a mouse embryo undergoing cell differentiation 23 days after conception.

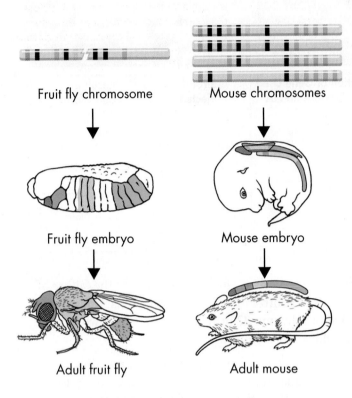

Fruit fly chromosome

Mouse chromosomes

Fruit fly embryo

Mouse embryo

Adult fruit fly

Adult mouse

FIGURE 13–20 Hox Genes and Body Development In fruit flies, a series of Hox genes along a chromosome determines the basic body structure. Mice have similar genes on four different chromosomes. The colored areas on the fly and mouse show the approximate body areas affected by genes of the corresponding colors. **Interpret Visuals** *What section of the bodies of flies and mice is coded by the genes shown in blue?*

MYSTERY
CLUE

What do you think controls the growth and development of eyes in flies and mice?

Homeotic Genes The American biologist Edward B. Lewis was the first to show that a specific group of genes controls the identities of body parts in the embryo of the common fruit fly. Lewis found that a mutation in one of these genes actually resulted in a fly with a leg growing out of its head in place of an antenna! From Lewis's work it became clear that a set of master control genes, known as **homeotic genes,** regulates organs that develop in specific parts of the body.

Homeobox and Hox Genes Molecular studies of homeotic genes show that they share a very similar 180-base DNA sequence, which was given the name homeobox. **Homeobox genes** code for transcription factors that activate other genes that are important in cell development and differentiation. Homeobox genes are expressed in certain regions of the body, and they determine factors like the presence of wings or legs.

In flies, a group of homeobox genes known as **Hox genes** are located side by side in a single cluster, as shown in **Figure 13–20.** Hox genes determine the identities of each segment of a fly's body. They are arranged in the exact order in which they are expressed, from anterior to posterior. A mutation in one of these genes can completely change the organs that develop in specific parts of the body.

Remarkably, clusters of Hox genes exist in the DNA of other animals, including humans. These genes are arranged in the same way—from head to tail. The function of Hox genes in humans seems to be almost the same as it is in fruit flies: They tell the cells of the body how to differentiate as the body grows. What this means, of course, is that nearly all animals, from flies to mammals, share the same basic tools for building the different parts of the body.

The striking similarity of master control genes—genes that control development—has a simple scientific explanation. Common patterns of genetic control exist because all these genes have descended from the genes of common ancestors. **Master control genes are like switches that trigger particular patterns of development and differentiation in cells and tissues.** The details can vary from one organism to another, but the switches are nearly identical. Recent studies have shown that the very same Hox gene that triggers the development of hands and feet is also active in the fins of certain fish.

Environmental Influences You've seen how cell differentiation is controlled at least in part by the regulation of gene expression. Conditions in an organism's environment play a role too. In prokaryotes and eukaryotes, environmental factors like temperature, salinity, and nutrient availability can influence gene expression. One example: The *lac* operon in *E. coli* is switched on only when lactose is the only food source in the bacteria's environment.

Metamorphosis is another well-studied example of how organisms can modify gene expression in response to change in their environment. Metamorphosis involves a series of transformations from one life stage to another. It is typically regulated by a number of external (environmental) and internal (hormonal) factors. As organisms move from larval to adult stages, their body cells differentiate to form new organs. At the same time, old organs are lost through cell death.

Consider the metamorphosis of a tadpole into a bullfrog, as shown in **Figure 13–21.** Under less than ideal conditions—a drying pond, a high density of predators, low amounts of food—tadpoles may speed up their metamorphosis. In other words, the speed of metamorphosis is determined by various environmental changes that are translated into hormonal changes, with the hormones functioning at the molecular level. Other environmental influences include temperature and population size.

FIGURE 13–21 Metamorphosis Environmental factors can affect gene regulation. If the bullfrog's environment changes for the worse, its genes will direct the production of hormones to speed the transformation of the tadpole (top photo) to the adult bullfrog (bottom photo).

13.4 Assessment

Review Key Concepts 🔑

1. a. Review How is the *lac* operon regulated?
 b. Explain What is a promoter?
 c. Use Analogies Write an analogy that demonstrates how the *lac* repressor functions.

2. a. Review Describe how most eukaryotic genes are controlled.
 b. Compare and Contrast How is gene regulation in prokaryotes and eukaryotes similar? How is it different?

3. a. Review What genes control cell differentiation during development?
 b. Compare and Contrast How is the way Hox genes are expressed in mice similar to the way they are expressed in fruit flies? How is it different?

PRACTICE PROBLEM

4. A hormone is a chemical that is produced in one part of the body, travels through the blood, and affects cells in other parts of the body. Many hormones are proteins. How might the production of a hormone affect the expression of genes in a eukaryotic cell? Write a hypothesis that could be tested to answer this question. (*Hint*: Include promoters in your hypothesis.)

Pre-Lab: From DNA to Protein Synthesis

Problem What are the steps involved in making a protein?

Lab Manual Chapter 13 Lab

Skills Focus Use Models, Sequence

Connect to the Big idea One of the most important tasks in a cell is the assembly of proteins from amino acids. This task always begins on ribosomes that are located throughout a cell's cytoplasm. The directions for the assembly of proteins are stored in DNA molecules. The information is carried to the ribosomes by a form of RNA called messenger RNA, or mRNA. In this lab, you will model the transcription of DNA and the translation of mRNA.

Background Questions

a. Review Is the following sequence from a DNA or mRNA molecule? How can you tell?

CUAAUGCCCUAGGGCACU

b. Compare and Contrast How are transcription and translation similar? How are they different?

c. Sequence List the following molecules in the order in which they take part in protein synthesis: amino acid, DNA, mRNA, tRNA.

Pre-Lab Questions

Preview the procedure in the lab manual.

1. Sequence Describe briefly the process you will use to decode the messages.

2. Compare and Contrast What role do stop codons play in protein synthesis? What are they used for in the coded messages?

3. Predict Which six letters will not appear in the coded messages? Give a reason for your answer.

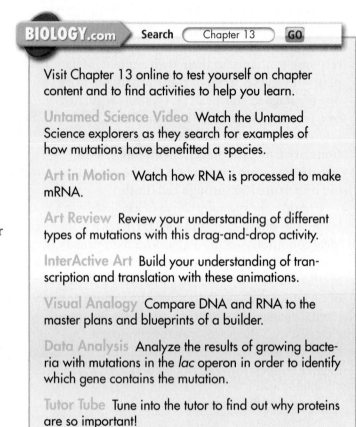

BIOLOGY.com Search Chapter 13 GO

Visit Chapter 13 online to test yourself on chapter content and to find activities to help you learn.

Untamed Science Video Watch the Untamed Science explorers as they search for examples of how mutations have benefitted a species.

Art in Motion Watch how RNA is processed to make mRNA.

Art Review Review your understanding of different types of mutations with this drag-and-drop activity.

InterActive Art Build your understanding of transcription and translation with these animations.

Visual Analogy Compare DNA and RNA to the master plans and blueprints of a builder.

Data Analysis Analyze the results of growing bacteria with mutations in the *lac* operon in order to identify which gene contains the mutation.

Tutor Tube Tune into the tutor to find out why proteins are so important!

13 Study Guide

Big idea ▶ Information and Heredity

Messenger RNA, transfer RNA, and ribosomal RNA work together in prokaryotic and eukaryotic cells to translate DNA's genetic code into functional proteins. These proteins, in turn, direct the expression of genes.

13.1 RNA

🔑 The main differences between RNA and DNA are that (1) the sugar in RNA is ribose instead of deoxyribose; (2) RNA is generally single-stranded, not double-stranded; and (3) RNA contains uracil in place of thymine.

🔑 In transcription, segments of DNA serve as templates to produce complementary RNA molecules.

RNA (362)   RNA polymerase (364)
messenger RNA (363)   promoter (365)
ribosomal RNA (363)   intron (365)
transfer RNA (363)   exon (365)
transcription (364)

13.2 Ribosomes and Protein Synthesis

🔑 The genetic code is read three "letters" at a time, so that each "word" is three bases long and corresponds to a single amino acid.

🔑 Ribosomes use the sequence of codons in mRNA to assemble amino acids into polypeptide chains.

🔑 The central dogma of molecular biology is that information is transferred from DNA to RNA to protein.

polypeptide (366)   translation (368)
genetic code (366)   anticodon (369)
codon (366)   gene expression (370)

13.3 Mutations

🔑 Mutations are heritable changes in genetic information.

🔑 The effects of mutations on genes vary widely. Some have little or no effect; some produce beneficial variations. Some negatively disrupt gene function.

🔑 Mutations often produce proteins with new or altered functions that can be useful to organisms in different or changing environments.

mutation (372)   mutagen (375)
point mutation (373)   polyploidy (376)
frameshift mutation (373)

13.4 Gene Regulation and Expression

🔑 DNA-binding proteins in prokaryotes regulate genes by controlling transcription.

🔑 By binding DNA sequences in the regulatory regions of eukaryotic genes, transcription factors control the expression of those genes.

🔑 Master control genes are like switches that trigger particular patterns of development and differentiation in cells and tissues.

operon (377)   homeotic gene (382)
operator (378)   homeobox gene (382)
RNA interference (380)   Hox gene (382)
differentiation (381)

Think Visually

Using the information in this chapter, complete the following flowchart about protein synthesis:

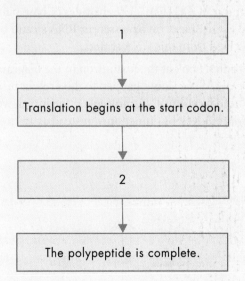

```
┌─────────────────────────────────┐
│                1                │
└─────────────────────────────────┘
                 │
                 ▼
┌─────────────────────────────────┐
│ Translation begins at the start │
│ codon.                          │
└─────────────────────────────────┘
                 │
                 ▼
┌─────────────────────────────────┐
│                2                │
└─────────────────────────────────┘
                 │
                 ▼
┌─────────────────────────────────┐
│  The polypeptide is complete.   │
└─────────────────────────────────┘
```

13 Assessment

13.1 RNA

Understand Key Concepts

1. The process by which the genetic code of DNA is copied into a strand of RNA is called
   a. translation.
   b. transcription.
   c. transformation.
   d. replication.

2. Which of the following describes RNA?
   a. RNA is usually double-stranded and contains the base thymine.
   b. RNA is usually single-stranded and contains the base uracil.
   c. RNA is longer than DNA and uses five bases to encode information.
   d. RNA is made in the nucleus of eukaryotic cells and stays there to carry out its functions.

3. Describe the function of each of the three types of RNA.

4. How does the enzyme that makes RNA know where to start transcribing the DNA?

5. Compare introns and exons.

Think Critically

6. **Apply Concepts** Suppose you start with the DNA strand ACCGTCAC. Use the rules of base pairing to list the bases on a messenger RNA strand transcribed from this DNA strand.

7. **Predict** Look at the first intron in the diagram below. What would happen to the protein produced by the mRNA molecule if the intron were not removed but functioned instead as an exon?

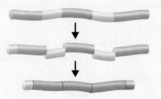

13.2 Ribosomes and Protein Synthesis

Understand Key Concepts

8. In messenger RNA, each codon specifies a particular
   a. nucleotide.
   b. enzyme.
   c. amino acid.
   d. promoter.

9. The number of codons in the genetic code is
   a. 3.   b. 4.   c. 20.   d. 64.

10. Which of the following statements about the genetic code is true?
    a. A codon can specify more than one amino acid.
    b. Every codon specifies a different amino acid.
    c. Some codons specify the same amino acid.
    d. Some codons have no function at all.

11. The process of making proteins on the ribosome based on instructions from messenger RNA is called
    a. transcription.
    b. transformation.
    c. translation.
    d. molecular biology.

12. What is a codon?

13. How do anticodons function?

14. If a code on a DNA molecule for a specific amino acid is CTA, what would the messenger RNA codon be? The transfer RNA codon?

15. Explain why controlling the proteins in an organism controls the organism's characteristics.

Think Critically

16. **Use Analogies** The word *transcribe* means "to write out." The word *translate* means "to express in another language." Review the meanings of *transcription* and *translation* in genetics. How do the technical meanings of these words relate to the everyday meanings of the words?

17. **Predict** A researcher identifies the nucleotide sequence AAC in a long strand of RNA inside a nucleus. In the genetic code, AAC codes for the amino acid asparagine. When that RNA becomes involved in protein synthesis, will asparagine necessarily appear in the protein? Explain your answer.

13.3 Mutations

Understand Key Concepts

18. Changes in DNA sequences that affect genetic information are known as
  a. replications.
  c. transformations.
  b. mutations.
  d. translations.

19. A single-base mutation in a messenger RNA molecule could transcribe the DNA sequence CAGTAT into
  a. GTCATA.
  c. GTCUTU.
  b. GUCAUA.
  d. GUAAUA.

20. A substance that can cause a change in the DNA code of an organism is called a
  a. toxin.
  c. nitrogenous base.
  b. mutagen.
  d. nucleotide.

21. Name and give examples of two major types of mutations. What do they have in common? How are they different?

22. How does a deletion mutation differ from a substitution mutation?

23. Can mutations have a positive effect?

Think Critically

24. **Compare and Contrast** How does the possible impact of a chromosomal mutation that occurs during meiosis differ from that of a similar event that occurs during mitosis of a body cell that is not involved in reproduction?

25. **Apply Concepts** A mutation in the DNA of an organism changes one base sequence in a protein-coding region from CAC to CAT. What is the effect of the mutation on the final protein? Explain your answer.

13.4 Gene Regulation and Expression

Understand Key Concepts

26. An expressed gene
  a. functions as a promoter.
  b. is transcribed into RNA.
  c. codes for just one amino acid.
  d. is made of mRNA.

solve the CHAPTER MYSTERY

MOUSE-EYED FLY

Years ago geneticists discovered a fly gene they called eyeless. Mutations that inactivate this gene cause flies to develop without eyes. Geneticists later discovered a mouse gene, called *Pax6*, that was homologous to eyeless. Transplanting an activated Pax6 gene into a fruit fly can cause the fly to grow eyes in odd places. This happens despite the fact that mouse eyes and fly eyes are very different. In fact the only reason we describe them as "eyes" is because they make vision possible.

How can the Pax6 gene perform the same role in such diverse animals? It probably began very early in the history of life, when eyes were just patches of light-sensitive cells on the skin of the common ancestors of all animals. As those organisms evolved and diversified, master control genes like Pax6 kept working, but with altered functions. Many genes like Pax6 are shared, not only by insects, but by all animals, including worms, sea urchins, and humans.

1. **Compare and Contrast** How are fly eyes and mouse eyes different? Similar?

2. **Infer** The Pax6 and eyeless genes code for transcription factors, not for parts of the actual eye. Why does this make sense in light of the effect of Pax6 when it is inserted into a fly?

3. **Connect to the** **Big idea** What feature of the genetic code makes it possible for a mouse gene to work inside the cell of a fly?

27. A group of genes that are regulated together is called a(n)

   a. promoter.   **c.** intron.

   b. operon.   **d.** allele.

28. To turn on the lactose-digesting enzymes of *E. coli*, the lactose must first

   a. bind to the repressor.

   b. bind to the DNA of the bacterium.

   c. separate from the repressor.

   d. initiate the synthesis of messenger RNA.

29. Blocking gene expression in eukaryotes with microRNA strands is called RNA

   a. transcription.   **c.** interference.

   b. translation.   **d.** digestion.

30. How is gene expression controlled in prokaryotes?

31. What is meant by the term *cell specialization*? How is cell specialization controlled?

32. Describe how a TATA box helps position RNA polymerase in a eukaryotic cell.

33. What is a homeobox gene?

Think Critically

34. **Apply Concepts** The number of promoter sequences, enhancer sites, and the TATA box in eukaryotes makes gene regulation in these organisms far more complex than regulation in prokaryotes. Why is regulation in eukaryotes so much more sophisticated?

Connecting Concepts

Use Science Graphics

Use the data table to answer questions 35 and 36.

Codon Translation	
Amino Acid	**mRNA Codons**
Alanine (Ala)	GCA, GCG, GCU, GCC
Valine (Val)	GUA, GUG, GUU, GUC
Leucine (Leu)	CUA, CUG, CUU, CUC, UUA, UUG

35. **Relate Cause and Effect** The table shows RNA codons for three amino acids. How would a substitution mutation in the third nucleotide position of the codons for alanine and valine affect the resulting protein?

36. **Infer** The three amino acids shown in the table have very similar—though not identical—properties. What substitution mutations could result in switching one of these amino acids for another? What might be the result?

Write About Science

37. **Explanation** Write a paragraph explaining why the effect of mutations can vary widely—from neutral to harmful to beneficial.

38. **Assess the Big idea** Explain the roles of the three types of RNA in taking the information in DNA and using it to make proteins.

Analyzing Data

RNA is the genetic material of many viruses. Scientists analyzed RNA from four different types of viruses. The content of the four nitrogenous bases is shown below.

Base Percentages in Four Viruses				
Virus	**A**	**U**	**C**	**G**
A	26.3	29.3	20.6	23.8
B	x	x	17.6	17.5
C	21.9	12.8	34.3	31.1
D	29.8	26.3	18.5	25.3

39. **Interpret Graphics** Which of the four types of viruses is most likely to use double-stranded RNA as its genetic material?

   a. Virus A   **c.** Virus C

   b. Virus B   **d.** Virus D

40. **Infer** The values in the two boxes labeled with an *x* would most likely be about

   a. 32.5 % A and 32.5% U.

   b. 17.5% A and 17.5% U.

   c. 26.3% A and 29.3% U.

   d. 32.5% A and 17.5% U.

Standardized Test Prep

Multiple Choice

1. How does RNA differ from DNA?
   - **A** RNA contains uracil and deoxyribose.
   - **B** RNA contains ribose and thymine.
   - **C** RNA contains uracil and ribose.
   - **D** RNA contains adenine and ribose.

2. How would the DNA sequence GCTATA be transcribed to mRNA?
   - **A** GCUAUA
   - **B** CGATAT
   - **C** CGAUAU
   - **D** GCUTUT

Questions 3–4

Use the chart below to answer the questions.

		Second Base in Code Word				
		A	**G**	**U**	**C**	
First Base in Code Word	**A**	Lys Lys Asn Asn	Arg Arg Ser Ser	Ile Met Ile Ile	Thr Thr Thr Thr	A G U C
	G	Glu Glu Asp Asp	Gly Gly Gly Gly	Val Val Val Val	Ala Ala Ala Ala	A G U C
	U	"Stop" "Stop" Tyr Tyr	"Stop" Trp Cys Cys	Leu Leu Phe Phe	Ser Ser Ser Ser	A G U C
	C	Gln Gln His His	Arg Arg Arg Arg	Leu Leu Leu Leu	Pro Pro Pro Pro	A G U C

Third Base in Code Word

3. Which of the following codons signifies the end of translation?
   - **A** CAA
   - **B** UGA
   - **C** AUC
   - **D** CCA

4. Which of the chains of amino acids corresponds to the nucleotide sequence UCAAGCGUA?
   - **A** glu-cys-pro
   - **B** glu-asp-"stop"
   - **C** thr-arg-met
   - **D** ser-ser-val

5. In eukaryotes, functional messenger RNA molecules are made from
   - **A** exons spliced together after introns are removed.
   - **B** introns spliced together after exons are removed.
   - **C** exons spliced together with introns.
   - **D** long pieces of RNA shortened by the Dicer enzyme.

6. Promoters are
   - **A** genes that code for individual proteins.
   - **B** proteins that bind with DNA and prevent transcription.
   - **C** DNA sequences near operons that regulate transcription.
   - **D** small molecules that bind with repressor proteins.

Questions 7–8

Use the diagrams below to answer the questions.

Normal Chromosome: (M)(N)(O)(P)(Q)(R)(S)

Mutant 1: (M)(P)(O)(N)(Q)(R)(S)

Mutant 2: (M)(N)(N)(O)(P)(Q)(R)(S)

7. Mutant 1 is a(n)
   - **A** deletion.
   - **B** translocation.
   - **C** inversion.
   - **D** duplication.

8. Mutant 2 is a(n)
   - **A** deletion.
   - **B** translocation.
   - **C** inversion.
   - **D** duplication.

Open-Ended Response

9. What is the function of the *lac* repressor system in *E. coli*?

If You Have Trouble With . . .

Question	1	2	3	4	5	6	7	8	9
See Lesson	13.1	13.1	13.2	13.2	13.1	13.1	13.3	13.3	13.4

14 Human Heredity

Information and Heredity

Q: How can we use genetics to study human inheritance?

INSIDE:

- 14.1 Human Chromosomes

- 14.2 Human Genetic Disorders

- 14.3 Studying the Human Genome

One thing to notice about this group of students is that none of them looks alike. The diversity of traits among the human race stems from one microscopic molecule—DNA.

CHAPTER MYSTERY

THE CROOKED CELL

When Ava visited her Uncle Eli in the hospital, he appeared tired and pale. He complained of sharp pains in his bones. "I've got sickle cell disease," Uncle Eli explained, short of breath. "I just hope it doesn't run in your side of the family."

That evening, Ava searched the Internet for information about her uncle's disease. She saw photos of red blood cells shaped like the letter *C*—a far cry from the healthy, round blood cells of a normal individual. Ava learned that these sickle-shaped cells are rigid and sticky. In blood vessels, they form clumps that can block blood flow and even cause organ damage. "Am I at risk?" Ava wondered. To find out, she would need to investigate her family history—and her own cells. As you read this chapter, look for clues that would help Ava discover whether she might carry sickle cell trait. Then, solve the mystery.

Never Stop Exploring Your World.
Finding out about Ava's risk of sickle cell disease is only the beginning. Take a video field trip with the ecogeeks of Untamed Science to see where the mystery leads.

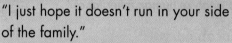

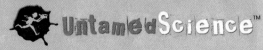

14.1

Human Chromosomes

Key Questions

🔑 **What is a karyotype?**

🔑 **What patterns of inheritance do human traits follow?**

🔑 **How can pedigrees be used to analyze human inheritance?**

Vocabulary

genome • karyotype • sex chromosome • autosome • sex-linked gene • pedigree

Taking Notes

Outline Before you read, make an outline of the major headings in the lesson. As you read, fill in main ideas and supporting details for each heading.

THINK ABOUT IT If you had to pick an ideal organism for the study of genetics, would you choose one that produced lots of offspring? How about one that was easy to grow in the lab? Would you select one with a short life span in order to do several crosses per month? How about all of the above? You certainly would not choose an organism that produced very few offspring, had a long life span, and could not be grown in a lab. Yet, when we study human genetics, this is exactly the sort of organism we deal with. Given all of these difficulties, it may seem a wonder that we know as much about human genetics as we do.

Karyotypes

🔑 **What is a karyotype?**

What makes us human? We might try to answer that question by looking under the microscope to see what is inside a human cell. Not surprisingly, human cells look much like the cells of other animals. To find what makes us uniquely human, we have to look deeper, into the genetic instructions that build each new individual. To begin this undertaking, we have to explore the human genome. A **genome** is the full set of genetic information that an organism carries in its DNA.

The study of any genome starts with chromosomes—those bundles of DNA and protein found in the nuclei of eukaryotic cells. To see human chromosomes clearly, cell biologists photograph cells in mitosis, when the chromosomes are fully condensed and easy to view. Scientists then cut out the chromosomes from the photographs and arrange them in a picture known as a **karyotype** (KAR ee uh typ). 🔑 **A karyotype shows the complete diploid set of chromosomes grouped together in pairs, arranged in order of decreasing size.**

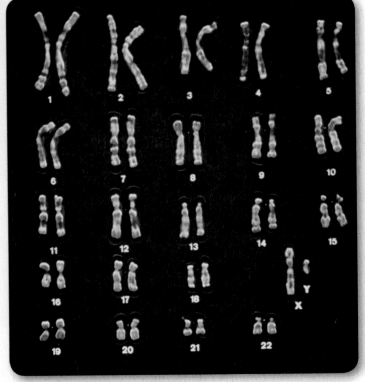

FIGURE 14–1 A Human Karyotype
A typical human cell has 23 pairs of chromosomes. These chromosomes have been cut out of a photograph and arranged to form a karyotype.

 BIOLOGY.com ▶ Search (Lesson 14.1) **GO** • Lesson Overview • Lesson Notes • Art Review

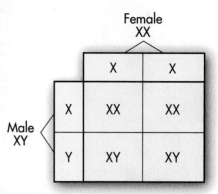

FIGURE 14–2 Sex Ratios Human egg cells contain a single X chromosome. Sperm cells contain either one X chromosome or one Y chromosome. **Interpret Tables** *What does this Punnett square suggest about the sex ratio of the human population?*

The karyotype in **Figure 14–1** is from a typical human cell, which contains 46 chromosomes, arranged in 23 pairs. Why do our chromosomes come in pairs? Remember that we begin life when a haploid sperm, carrying just 23 chromosomes, fertilizes a haploid egg, also with 23 chromosomes. The resulting diploid cell develops into a new individual and carries the full complement of 46 chromosomes—two sets of 23.

Sex Chromosomes
Two of the 46 chromosomes in the human genome are known as **sex chromosomes,** because they determine an individual's sex. Females have two copies of the X chromosome. Males have one X chromosome and one Y chromosome. As you can see in **Figure 14–2,** this is the reason why males and females are born in a roughly 50 : 50 ratio. All human egg cells carry a single X chromosome (23,X). However, half of all sperm cells carry an X chromosome (23,X) and half carry a Y chromosome (23,Y). This ensures that just about half the zygotes will be males and half will be females.

More than 1200 genes are found on the X chromosome, some of which are shown in **Figure 14–3.** Note that the human Y chromosome is much smaller than the X chromosome and contains only about 140 genes, most of which are associated with male sex determination and sperm development.

Autosomal Chromosomes
To distinguish them from the sex chromosomes, the remaining 44 human chromosomes are known as autosomal chromosomes, or **autosomes.** The complete human genome consists of 46 chromosomes, including 44 autosomes and 2 sex chromosomes. To quickly summarize the total number of chromosomes present in a human cell—both autosomes and sex chromosomes— biologists write 46,XX for females and 46,XY for males.

In Your Notebook *Describe what makes up a human karyotype.*

X Chromosome

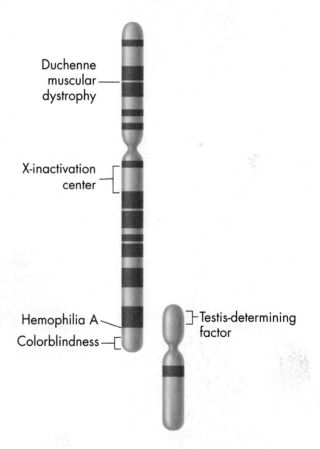

Duchenne muscular dystrophy

X-inactivation center

Hemophilia A

Colorblindness

Testis-determining factor

Y Chromosome

FIGURE 14–3 X and Y Chromosomes The human Y chromosome is smaller and carries fewer genes than the human X chromosome.

Transmission of Human Traits

🔑 *What patterns of inheritance do human traits follow?*

It has not been easy studying our species using traditional genetic techniques. Despite the difficulties, human genetics has progressed rapidly, especially in recent years, with the use of molecular techniques to study human DNA. What have these studies shown? Human genes follow the same Mendelian patterns of inheritance as the genes of other organisms.

Dominant and Recessive Alleles 🔑 **Many human traits follow a pattern of simple dominance.** For instance, a gene known as *MC1R* helps determine skin and hair color. Some of *MC1R*'s recessive alleles produce red hair. An individual with red hair usually has two of these recessive alleles, inheriting a copy from each parent. Dominant alleles for the *MC1R* gene help produce darker hair colors.

Another trait that displays simple dominance is the Rhesus, or Rh blood group. The allele for Rh factor comes in two forms: Rh⁺ and Rh⁻. Rh⁺ is dominant, so an individual with both alleles (Rh⁺/Rh⁻) is said to have Rh positive blood. Rh negative blood is found in individuals with two recessive alleles (Rh⁻/Rh⁻).

Codominant and Multiple Alleles 🔑 **The alleles for many human genes display codominant inheritance.** One example is the ABO blood group, determined by a gene with three alleles: I^A, I^B, and i. Alleles I^A and I^B are codominant. They produce molecules known as antigens on the surface of red blood cells. As **Figure 14–5** shows, individuals with alleles I^A and I^B produce both A and B antigens, making them blood type AB. The i allele is recessive. Individuals with alleles $I^A I^A$ or $I^A i$ produce only the A antigen, making them blood type A. Those with $I^B I^B$ or $I^B i$ alleles are type B. Those homozygous for the i allele (ii) produce no antigen and are said to have blood type O. If a patient has AB-negative blood, it means the individual has I^A and I^B alleles from the ABO gene and two Rh⁻ alleles from the Rh gene.

FIGURE 14–4 Recessive Alleles
Some of the recessive alleles of the *MC1R* gene cause red hair. An individual with red hair usually has two of these recessive alleles.

FIGURE 14–5 Human Blood Groups
This table shows the relationship between genotype and phenotype for the ABO blood group. It also shows which blood types can safely be transfused into people with other blood types. **Apply Concepts** *How can there be four different phenotypes even though there are six different genotypes?*

			Safe Transfusions	
Phenotype (Blood Type)	**Genotype**	**Antigen on Red Blood Cell**	**To**	**From**
A	$I^A I^A$ or $I^A i$	A	A, AB	A, O
B	$I^B I^B$ or $I^B i$	B	B, AB	B, O
AB	$I^A I^B$	A and B	AB	A, B, AB, O
O	ii	None	A, B, AB, O	O

Blood Groups

Sex-Linked Inheritance 🔑 Because the X and Y chromosomes determine sex, the genes located on them show a pattern of inheritance called sex-linkage. A **sex-linked gene** is a gene located on a sex chromosome. As you might expect, genes on the Y chromosome are found only in males and are passed directly from father to son. Genes located on the X chromosome are found in both sexes, but the fact that men have just one X chromosome leads to some interesting consequences.

For example, humans have three genes responsible for color vision, all located on the X chromosome. In males, a defective allele for any of these genes results in colorblindness, an inability to distinguish certain colors. The most common form, red-green colorblindness, occurs in about 1 in 12 males. Among females, however, colorblindness affects only about 1 in 200. Why is there such a difference? In order for a recessive allele, like colorblindness, to be expressed in females, it must be present in two copies—one on each of the X chromosomes. This means that the recessive phenotype of a sex-linked genetic disorder tends to be much more common among males than among females.

MYSTERY CLUE

The presence of two sickle cell alleles is needed to produce sickle cell disease. Males and females develop sickle cell disease in equal frequencies. What do these statements suggest about the location of the gene responsible for the disorder?

Quick Lab
GUIDED INQUIRY

How Is Colorblindness Transmitted?

❶ Make a data table with the column headings Trial, Colors, Sex of Individual, and Number of X-Linked Alleles. Draw ten rows under the headings and fill in the numbers 1 through 10 in the Trial column. Label one plastic cup Mother and a second plastic cup Father.

❷ The white beans represent X chromosomes. Use a black marker to make a dot on 1 white bean to represent the X-linked allele for colorblindness. Place this bean, plus 1 unmarked white bean, into the cup labeled Mother.

❸ Mark a black dot on 1 more white bean. Place this bean, plus 1 red bean, into the cup labeled Father. The red bean represents a Y chromosome.

❹ Close your eyes and pick one bean from each cup to represent how each parent contributes to a sex chromosome and a fertilized egg.

❺ In your data table, record the color of each bean and the sex of an individual who would carry this pair of sex chromosomes. Also record how many X-linked alleles the individual has. Put the beans back in the cups they came from.

❻ Determine whether the individual would have colorblindness.

❼ Repeat steps 4 to 6 for a total of 10 pairs of beans.

Analyze and Conclude

1. Draw Conclusions How do human sex chromosomes keep the numbers of males and females roughly equal?

2. Calculate Calculate the class totals for each data column. How many females were colorblind? How many males? Explain these results. MATH

3. Use Models Evaluate your model. How accurately does it represent the transmission of colorblindness in a population? Why?

FIGURE 14–6 X-Chromosome Inactivation Female calico cats are tri-colored. The color of spots on their fur is controlled by a gene on the X chromosome. Spots are either orange or black, depending on which X chromosome is inactivated in different patches of their skin.

BUILD Vocabulary

WORD ORIGINS The word **pedigree** combines the Latin words *pedem*, meaning "foot," and *gruem*, meaning "crane." A crane is a long-legged waterbird. On old manuscripts, a forked sign resembling a crane's footprint indicated a line of ancestral descent.

X-Chromosome Inactivation If just one X chromosome is enough for cells in males, how does the cell "adjust" to the extra X chromosome in female cells? The answer was discovered by the British geneticist Mary Lyon. In female cells, most of the genes in one of the X chromosomes are randomly switched off, forming a dense region in the nucleus known as a Barr body. Barr bodies are generally not found in males because their single X chromosome is still active.

The same process happens in other mammals. In cats, for example, a gene that controls the color of coat spots is located on the X chromosome. One X chromosome may have an allele for orange spots and the other X chromosome may have an allele for black spots. In cells in some parts of the body, one X chromosome is switched off. In other parts of the body, the other X chromosome is switched off. As a result, the cat's fur has a mixture of orange and black spots, like those in **Figure 14–6.** Male cats, which have just one X chromosome, can have spots of only one color. Therefore, if the cat's fur has three colors—white with orange and black spots, for example— you can almost be certain that the cat is female.

In Your Notebook *Write three quiz questions about the transmission of human traits and answer them.*

Human Pedigrees

 How can pedigrees be used to analyze human inheritance?

Given the complexities of genetics, how would you go about determining whether a trait is caused by a dominant or recessive allele and whether the gene for that trait is autosomal or sex-linked? The answers, not surprisingly, can be found by applying Mendel's basic principles of genetics.

To analyze the pattern of inheritance followed by a particular trait, you can use a chart that shows the relationships within a family. Such a chart is called a **pedigree.** A pedigree shows the presence or absence of a trait according to the relationships between parents, siblings, and offspring. It can be used for any species, not just humans.

The pedigree in **Figure 14–7** shows how one human trait—a white lock of hair just above the forehead— passes through three generations of a family. The allele for the white forelock trait is dominant. At the top of the chart is a grandfather who had the white forelock trait. Two of his three children inherited the trait. Three grandchildren have the trait, but two do not.

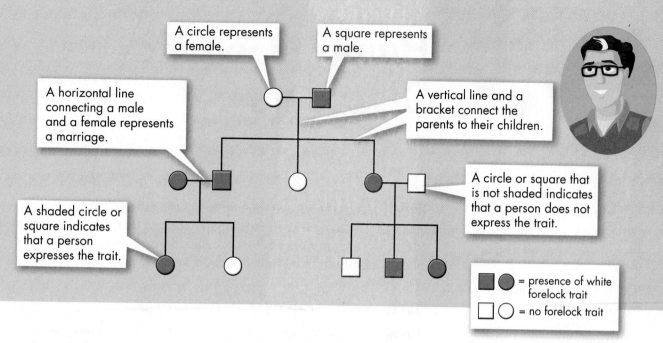

A circle represents a female.

A square represents a male.

A horizontal line connecting a male and a female represents a marriage.

A vertical line and a bracket connect the parents to their children.

A circle or square that is not shaded indicates that a person does not express the trait.

A shaded circle or square indicates that a person expresses the trait.

■ ● = presence of white forelock trait

□ ○ = no forelock trait

By analyzing a pedigree, we can often infer the genotypes of family members. For example, because the white forelock trait is dominant, all the family members in **Figure 14–7** lacking this trait must have homozygous recessive alleles. One of the grandfather's children lacks the white forelock trait, so the grandfather must be heterozygous for this trait.

With pedigree analysis, it is possible to apply the principles of Mendelian genetics to humans. 🔑 **The information gained from pedigree analysis makes it possible to determine the nature of genes and alleles associated with inherited human traits.** Based on a pedigree, you can often determine if an allele for a trait is dominant or recessive, autosomal or sex-linked.

FIGURE 14–7 Pedigree Example
This diagram shows what the symbols in a pedigree represent.
Interpret Visuals *What are the genotypes of both parents on the left in the second row? How do you know?*

14.1 Assessment

Review Key Concepts 🔑

1. a. Review What are autosomes?

b. Explain What determines whether a person is male or female?

c. Propose a Solution How can you use karyotypes to identify a species?

2. a. Review Explain how sex-linked traits are inherited.

b. Predict If a woman with type O blood and a man with type AB blood have children, what are the children's possible genotypes?

3. a. Review What does a pedigree show?

b. Infer Why would the Y chromosome be unlikely to contain any of the genes that are absolutely necessary for survival?

VISUAL THINKING

4. Choose a family and a trait, such as facial dimples, that you can trace through three generations. Find out who in the family has had the trait and who has not. Then, draw a pedigree to represent the family history of the trait.

14.2 Human Genetic Disorders

Key Questions

🔑 How do small changes in DNA molecules affect human traits?

🔑 What are the effects of errors in meiosis?

Vocabulary

nondisjunction

Taking Notes

Two-Column Chart Before you read, make a two-column chart. In the first column, write three questions you have about genetic disorders. As you read, fill in answers to your questions in the second column. When you have finished, research the answers to your remaining questions.

THINK ABOUT IT Have you ever heard the expression "It runs in the family"? Relatives or friends might have said that about your smile or the shape of your ears, but what could it mean when they talk of diseases and disorders? What, exactly, is a genetic disorder?

From Molecule to Phenotype

🔑 **How do small changes in DNA molecules affect human traits?**

We know that genes are made of DNA and that they interact with the environment to produce an individual organism's characteristics, or phenotype. However, when a gene fails to work or works improperly, serious problems can result.

Molecular research techniques have shown us a direct link between genotype and phenotype. For example, the wax that sometimes builds up in our ear canals can be one of two forms: wet or dry. People of African and European ancestry are more likely to have wet earwax—the dominant form. Those of Asian or Native American ancestry most often have the dry form, which is recessive. A single DNA base in the gene for a membrane-transport protein is the culprit. A simple base change from guanine (G) to adenine (A) causes this protein to produce dry earwax instead of wet earwax.

The connection between molecule and trait, and between genotype and phenotype, is often that simple, and just as direct. 🔑 **Changes in a gene's DNA sequence can change proteins by altering their amino acid sequences, which may directly affect one's phenotype.** In other words, there is a molecular basis for genetic disorders.

Disorders Caused by Individual Genes Thousands of genetic disorders are caused by changes in individual genes. These changes often affect specific proteins associated with important cellular functions.

▶ *Sickle Cell Disease* This disorder is caused by a defective allele for beta-globin, one of two polypeptides in hemoglobin, the oxygen-carrying protein in red blood cells. The defective polypeptide makes hemoglobin a bit less soluble, causing hemoglobin molecules to stick together when the blood's oxygen level decreases. The molecules clump into long fibers, forcing cells into a distinctive sickle shape, which gives the disorder its name.

Sickle-shaped cells are more rigid than normal red blood cells, and, therefore, they tend to get stuck in the capillaries—the narrowest blood vessels in the body. If the blood stops moving through the capillaries, damage to cells, tissues, and even organs can result.

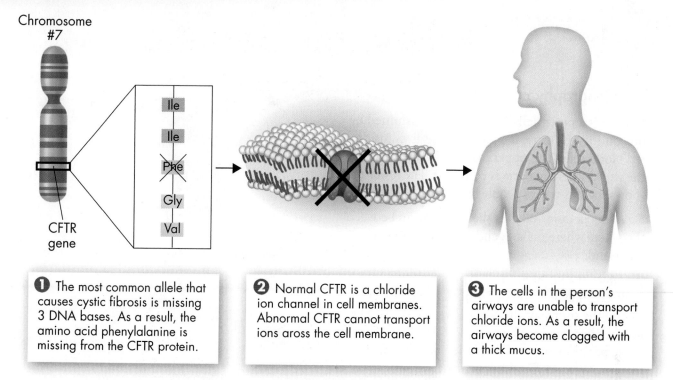

Chromosome #7

Ile
Ile
Phe
Gly
Val

CFTR gene

❶ The most common allele that causes cystic fibrosis is missing 3 DNA bases. As a result, the amino acid phenylalanine is missing from the CFTR protein.

❷ Normal CFTR is a chloride ion channel in cell membranes. Abnormal CFTR cannot transport ions aross the cell membrane.

❸ The cells in the person's airways are unable to transport chloride ions. As a result, the airways become clogged with a thick mucus.

▶ *Cystic Fibrosis* Known as CF for short, cystic fibrosis is most common among people of European ancestry. CF is caused by a genetic change almost as small as the earwax allele. Most cases result from the deletion of just three bases in the gene for a protein called cystic fibrosis transmembrane conductance regulator (CFTR). CFTR normally allows chloride ions (Cl^-) to pass across cell membranes. The loss of these bases removes a single amino acid—phenylalanine—from CFTR, causing the protein to fold improperly. The misfolded protein is then destroyed. With cell membranes unable to transport chloride ions, tissues throughout the body malfunction.

People with one normal copy of the CF allele are unaffected by CF, because they can produce enough CFTR to allow their cells to work properly. Two copies of the defective allele are needed to produce the disorder, which means the CF allele is recessive. Children with CF have serious digestive problems and produce thick, heavy mucus that clogs their lungs and breathing passageways.

▶ *Huntington's Disease* Huntington's disease is caused by a dominant allele for a protein found in brain cells. The allele for this disease contains a long string of bases in which the codon CAG—coding for the amino acid glutamine—repeats over and over again, more than 40 times. Despite intensive study, the reason why these long strings of glutamine cause disease is still not clear. The symptoms of Huntington's disease, namely mental deterioration and uncontrollable movements, usually do not appear until middle age. The greater the number of codon repeats, the earlier the disease appears, and the more severe are its symptoms.

FIGURE 14–8 Mutations Cause Cystic Fibrosis CF is usually caused by the deletion of three bases in the DNA of a single gene. As a result, the body does not produce normal CFTR, a protein needed to transport chloride ions. **Infer** *Why isn't the cause of CF considered a frameshift mutation?*

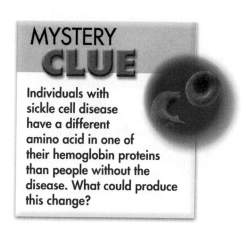

MYSTERY **CLUE**

Individuals with sickle cell disease have a different amino acid in one of their hemoglobin proteins than people without the disease. What could produce this change?

The Geography of Malaria

Malaria is a potentially fatal disease transmitted by mosquitoes. Its cause is a parasite that lives inside red blood cells. The upper map shows the parts of the world where malaria is common. The lower map shows regions where people have the sickle cell allele.

1. Analyze Data What is the relationship between the places where malaria and the sickle cell allele are found?

2. Infer In 1805, a Scottish explorer named Mungo Park led an expedition of European geographers to find the source of the Niger River in Africa. The journey began with a party of 45 Europeans. During the expedition, most of these men perished from malaria. Why do you think their native African guides survived?

3. Form a Hypothesis As the map shows, the sickle cell allele is not found in African populations that are native to southern Africa. Propose an explanation for this discrepancy.

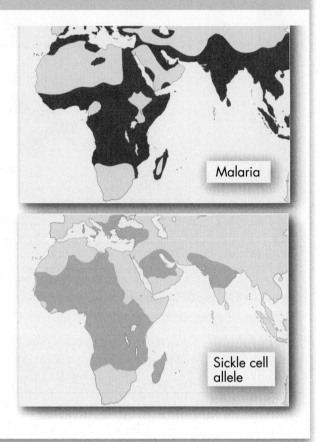

Malaria

Sickle cell allele

Genetic Advantages Disorders such as sickle cell disease and CF are still common in human populations. In the United States, the sickle cell allele is carried by approximately 1 person in 12 of African ancestry, and the CF allele is carried by roughly 1 person in 25 of European ancestry. Why are these alleles still around if they can be fatal for those who carry them? The answers may surprise you.

Most African Americans today are descended from populations that originally lived in west central Africa, where malaria is common. Malaria is a mosquito-borne infection caused by a parasite that lives inside red blood cells. Individuals with just one copy of the sickle cell allele are generally healthy and are also highly resistant to the parasite. This resistance gives them a great advantage against malaria, which even today claims more than a million lives every year.

More than 1000 years ago, the cities of medieval Europe were ravaged by epidemics of typhoid fever. Typhoid is caused by a bacterium that enters the body through cells in the digestive system. The protein produced by the CF allele helps block the entry of this bacterium. Individuals heterozygous for CF would have had an advantage when living in cities with poor sanitation and polluted water, and—because they also carried a normal allele—these individuals would not have suffered from cystic fibrosis.

Chromosomal Disorders

🔑 What are the effects of errors in meiosis?

Most of the time, the process of meiosis works perfectly and each human gamete gets exactly 23 chromosomes. Every now and then, however, something goes wrong. The most common error in meiosis occurs when homologous chromosomes fail to separate. This mistake is known as **nondisjunction,** which means "not coming apart." **Figure 14–9** illustrates the process.

🔑 **If nondisjunction occurs during meiosis, gametes with an abnormal number of chromosomes may result, leading to a disorder of chromosome numbers.** For example, if two copies of an autosomal chromosome fail to separate during meiosis, an individual may be born with three copies of that chromosome. This condition is known as a trisomy, meaning "three bodies." The most common form of trisomy, involving three copies of chromosome 21, is Down syndrome, which is often characterized by mild to severe mental retardation and a high frequency of certain birth defects.

Nondisjunction of the X chromosomes can lead to a disorder known as Turner's syndrome. A female with Turner's syndrome usually inherits only one X chromosome. Women with Turner's syndrome are sterile, which means that they are unable to reproduce. Their sex organs do not develop properly at puberty.

In males, nondisjunction may cause Klinefelter's syndrome, resulting from the inheritance of an extra X chromosome, which interferes with meiosis and usually prevents these individuals from reproducing. There have been no reported instances of babies being born without an X chromosome, indicating that this chromosome contains genes that are vital for the survival and development of the embryo.

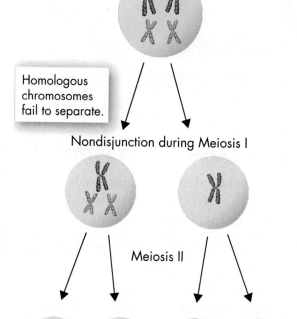

Homologous chromosomes fail to separate.

Nondisjunction during Meiosis I

Meiosis II

FIGURE 14–9 Nondisjunction This failure of meiosis causes gametes to have an abnormal number of chromosomes. **Apply Concepts** *Which phase of meiosis is shown in the first cell?*

14.2 Assessment

Review Key Concepts 🔑

1. a. Review How can a small change in a person's DNA cause a genetic disorder?

b. Infer How do genetic disorders such as CF support the theory of evolution?

2. a. Review Describe two sex chromosome disorders.

b. Apply Concepts How does nondisjunction cause chromosomal disorders?

WRITE ABOUT SCIENCE

Description

3. Write a paragraph explaining the process of nondisjunction. (*Hint:* To organize your writing, create a flowchart that shows the steps in the process.)

Biology & Society

Are Laws Protecting Genetic Privacy Necessary?

The rapid development of new tools and techniques to analyze DNA makes it possible to test for alleles related to thousands of medical conditions. In theory, the results of genetic testing should benefit everyone. Accurate genetic data helps physicians select the proper treatments for patients. It may allow people with genes that place them at risk of certain conditions to minimize those risks.

At issue, however, is individual privacy. Once a test is done, who has access to the data, and how can they use it? Could employers refuse to hire people who might drive up their medical costs? Might insurance companies refuse to renew the policies of individuals with genes for certain disorders? These are not hypothetical questions. In 2005, managers of a professional basketball team asked one of its players to be tested for a gene linked to heart ailments. When he refused, they traded the player to another team. Dr. Francis Collins, director of the National Human Genome Research Institute, worries that "the public is afraid of taking advantage of genetic testing." Is he correct? Should genetic data be protected by law, or should it be open to public view?

The Viewpoints

Genetic Privacy Does Not Need Legal Protection

Other laws already protect individuals from discrimination on the basis of medical disability. Employers and insurance companies are nonetheless allowed to ask individuals if they smoke, use alcohol, or have a history of medical problems. Having this information allows employers to make intelligent choices about whom to hire. It also helps insurance companies maintain lower rates for their healthiest clients. Free access to genetic data should be a public right.

Many commercial laboratories test human DNA for genetic disorders.

Genetic Privacy Should Be Protected by Law

The Genetic Information Nondiscrimination Act (GINA) went into effect in 2009, and it provides important protections to personal privacy. Individuals may not take advantage of today's advances in genetic medicine if they fear their personal information might be used to deny them employment or insurance. We need such laws to realize the full benefits of modern medicine and to protect otherwise healthy individuals from genetic discrimination.

Research and Decide

1. Analyze the Viewpoints To make an informed decision, learn more about genetic testing by consulting library or Internet resources. Then, list the key arguments expressed by the proponents and critics of both points of view. Find out if laws preventing genetic discrimination have been proposed or passed in your state.

2. Form an Opinion Should access and use of genetic data be regulated? Weigh both sides of the issue. Who will benefit from the sharing of genetic data? Will anyone suffer? Do some arguments outweigh others? If so, which ones? Explain your answers.

14.3 Studying the Human Genome

THINK ABOUT IT Just a few decades ago, computers were gigantic machines found only in laboratories and universities. Today, many of us carry small, powerful computers to school and work every day. Decades ago, the human genome was unknown. Today, we can see our entire genome on the Internet. How long will it be before having a copy of your own genome is as ordinary as carrying a cellphone in your pocket?

Manipulating DNA

🔑 **What techniques are used to study human DNA?**

Since discovering the genetic code, biologists have dreamed of a time when they could read the DNA sequences in the human genome. For a long time, it seemed impossible. DNA is a huge molecule—even the smallest human chromosome contains nearly 50 million base pairs. Manipulating such large molecules is extremely difficult. In the late 1960s, however, scientists found they could use natural enzymes in DNA analysis. From this discovery came many useful tools. 🔑 **By using tools that cut, separate, and then replicate DNA base by base, scientists can now read the base sequences in DNA from any cell.** Such techniques have revolutionized genetic studies of living organisms, including humans.

Cutting DNA Nucleic acids are chemically different from other macro-molecules such as proteins and carbohydrates. This difference makes DNA relatively easy to extract from cells and tissues. However, DNA molecules from most organisms are much too large to be analyzed, so they must first be cut into smaller pieces. Many bacteria produce enzymes that do exactly that. Known as **restriction enzymes,** these highly specific substances cut even the largest DNA molecule into precise pieces, called restriction fragments, that are several hundred bases in length. Of the hundreds of known restriction enzymes, each cuts DNA at a different sequence of nucleotides.

In Your Notebook *Make a flowchart that shows the processes scientists use to analyze DNA.*

Key Questions

🔑 What techniques are used to study human DNA?

🔑 What were the goals of the Human Genome Project, and what have we learned so far?

Vocabulary

restriction enzyme
gel electrophoresis
bioinformatics
genomics

Taking Notes

Preview Visuals Before you read, look at **Figure 14–10,** and write down three questions you have about the figure. As you read, find answers to your questions.

Separating DNA
Gel electrophoresis is used to separate DNA fragments. After being cut by restriction enzymes, the fragments are put into wells on a gel that is similar to a slice of gelatin. An electric voltage moves them across the gel. Shorter fragments move faster than longer fragments. Within an hour or two, the fragments all separate, each appearing as a band on the gel.

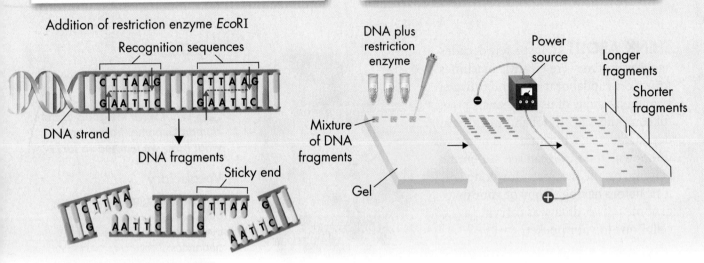

Addition of restriction enzyme *Eco*RI

Recognition sequences

DNA strand

DNA fragments

Sticky end

DNA plus restriction enzyme

Mixture of DNA fragments

Gel

Power source

Longer fragments

Shorter fragments

VISUAL SUMMARY

HOW SCIENTISTS MANIPULATE DNA

FIGURE 14–10 By using tools that cut, separate, and replicate DNA, scientists can read the base sequences in DNA from any cell. Knowing the sequence of an organism's DNA allows us to study specific genes.

Separating DNA Once DNA has been cut by restriction enzymes, scientists can use a technique known as **gel electrophoresis** to separate and analyze the differently sized fragments. **Figure 14–10** illustrates this simple, yet effective, method. A mixture of DNA fragments is placed at one end of a porous gel. When an electric voltage is applied to the gel, DNA molecules—which are negatively charged—move toward the positive end of the gel. The smaller the DNA fragment, the faster and farther it moves. The result is a pattern of bands based on fragment size. Specific stains that bind to DNA make these bands visible. Researchers can then remove individual restriction fragments from the gel and study them further.

Reading DNA After the DNA fragments have been separated, researchers use a clever chemical "trick" to read, or sequence, them. The single-stranded DNA fragments are placed in a test tube containing DNA polymerase—the enzyme that copies DNA—along with the four nucleotide bases, A, T, G, and C. As the enzyme goes to work, it uses the unknown strand as a template to make one new DNA strand after another. The tricky part is that researchers also add a small number of bases that have a chemical dye attached. Each time a dye-labeled base is added to a new DNA strand, the synthesis of that strand stops. When DNA synthesis is completed, the result is a series of color-coded DNA fragments of different lengths. Researchers can then separate these fragments, often by gel electrophoresis. The order of colored bands on the gel tells the exact sequence of bases in the DNA. The entire process can be automated and controlled by computers, so that DNA sequencing machines can read thousands of bases in a matter of seconds.

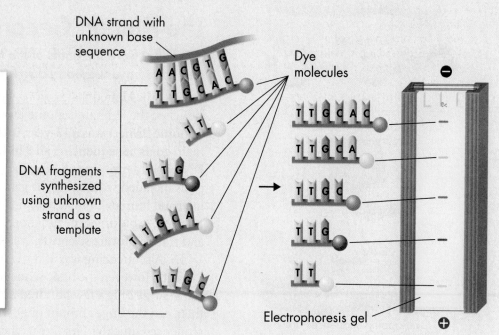

DNA strand with unknown base sequence

Dye molecules

Reading DNA

A small proportion of dye-labeled nucleotides are used to make a complementary DNA strand. Each time a labeled nucleotide is added to the strand, DNA replication stops. Because each base was labeled with a different color, the result is color-coded DNA fragments of different lengths. When gel electrophoresis is used to separate the fragments, scientists can "read" the DNA sequence directly from the gel.

DNA fragments synthesized using unknown strand as a template

Electrophoresis gel

Base sequence as "read" from the order of the bands on the gel from bottom to top: **T G C A C**

Quick Lab
GUIDED INQUIRY

Modeling Restriction Enzymes

❶ Write a 50-base, double-stranded DNA sequence using the bases A, C, G, and T in random order. Include each sequence shown below at least once in the sequence you write.

❷ Make three copies of your double-stranded sequence on three different-colored strips of paper.

❸ Use the drawings below to see how the restriction enzyme *Eco*RI would cut your DNA sequence. Use scissors to cut one copy of the sequence as *Eco*RI would.

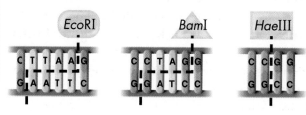

❹ Use the procedure in Step 3 to cut apart another copy of your sequence as the restriction enzyme *Bam*I would. Then, cut the third copy as the restriction enzyme *Hae*III would.

❺ Tape the single-stranded end of one of your DNA fragments to a complementary, single-stranded end of a classmate's fragment. This will form a single, double-stranded DNA molecule.

Analyze and Conclude

1. Observe Which restriction enzyme produced the most pieces? The fewest pieces?

2. Evaluate How well did your model represent the actual process of using restriction enzymes to cut DNA? (*Hint*: Contrast the length of your model DNA sequence to the actual length of a DNA molecule.)

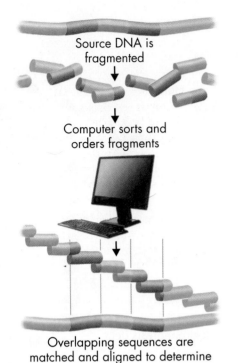

FIGURE 14–11 Shotgun Sequencing
This method rapidly sorts DNA fragments by overlapping base sequences.

```
GGGGCTGAGAGGGTGCCTGGGGGGCCAGGACGGAGCTGGGCCAGTGCACAGCTTCCCACACCTGCCCAC
CCCCAGAGTCCTGCCGCCACCCCCAGATCACACGGAAGATGAGGTCCGAGTGGCCTGCTGAGGACTTGC
TGCTTGTCCCCAGGTCCCCAGGTCATGCCCTCCTTCTGCCACCCTGGGGAGCTGAGGGCCTCAGCTGGG
GCTGCTGTCCTAAGGCAGGGTGGGAACTAGGCAGCCAGCAGGGAGGGGACCCCTCCCTCACTCCCACTC
TCCCACCCCCACCACCTTGGCCCATCCATGGCGGCATCTTTGGGCCATCCGGGACTGGGGACAGGGGTCC
TGGGGACAGGGGTCCCGGGGACAGGGTCCTGGGGACAGGGGTGTGAGGACAGGGGTCCCGGGGACAGGGG
TGTGGGGACAGGGGTCCCGGGGACAGGGGTGTGGGGACAGGGGTGTGGGGACAGGGGTGTGGGGACAGG
GGTGTGGGGACAGGGGTGTGGGGACAGGGGTGTGGGGACAGGGGTCCTGGGGACAGGGGTCCTGGGGACA
ACAGCAGCGCAAAGAGCCCCGCCCTGCAGCCTCCAGCTCTCCTGGTCTAATGTGGAAAGTGGCCCAGGT
GAGGGCTTTGCTCTCCTGGAGACATTTGCCCCCAGCTGTGAGCAGGACAGGTCTGGCCACCGGCCCCTG
TGGTTAAGACTCTAATGACCCGCTGGTCCTGAGGAAGAGGTGCTGACGACCAAGGAGATCTTCCCACAG
ACCCAGCACCAGGGAAATGGTCCGGAAATTGCAGCCTCAGCCCCCAGCCATCTGCCGACCCCCCCACCC
CAGGCCCTAATGGGCCAGGCGGCAGGGGTTGACAGGTAGGGGAGATGGGCTCTGAGACTATAAAGCCAG
CGGGGGCCCAGCAGCCCTCAGCCCTCCCAGGACAGGGTGCATCAGAAGAGGCCATCAAGCAGGTCTGTTC
CAAGGGCCTTTGCCTCAGGTGGGCTCAGGGTTCCAGGGTTGGGTGGCTGGACCCCAGGCCCCAGCTCTGCAGCA
GGGAGGACGTGGCTGGGCTCGTGAAGCATGTGGGGTGAGCCCAGGGGCCCAAGGCAGGGCACCTGGC
CTTCAGCCTGCCTCAGCCCTGCCTGTCACCCAAATCACTGTCCTTCTGCCATGGCCCTGTGGATGCGCC
TCCTGCCCCTGCTGGCGCTGCTGGCCCTCTGGGGACCTGACCCAGCCGCACCCTTTGTGAACCAACACC
TGTGCGGCTCACACCTGGTGGAAGCTCTCTACCTAGTGTGCGGGGAACGAGGCTTCTTCTACACACCCA
AGACCCGCCGGGAGGCAGAGGACCTGCAGGGTGAGCCAACCGCCCATTGCTGCCCCTGGCCGCCCCCAG
CCACCCCCTGCTCCTGGCGCTCCCACCCAGCATGGGCAGAAGGGGCAGGAGGCTGCCACCCAGCAGG
GGTCAGGTGCACTTTTTAAAAAGAAGTTCTCTTGGTCACGTCCTAAAGTGACCAGCTCCCTGTGGCC
CAGTCAGAATCTCAGCCTGAGGACGGTGTTGGCTTCGGCAGCCCGGAGATACATCAGAGGGTGGGCACG
CTCCTCCCTCCTCTCGCCCCTCAAACAAATGCCCCGAGCCCATTCTCCACCCTCATTTGATGACCGC
AGATTCAAGTGTTTTGTTAAGTAAAGTCCTGGGTGACCTGGGTTCACAGGGTGCCCACGCTGCCTGCC
TCTGGGCGAACACCCCATCACGCCCTGAGGAGGGCGTGGCTACCTGCCTGAGTGGGCCAGACCCCTGCT
GCCAGGCGCTCAGGCAGCTCCATAGTCAGGAGATGGGGAAGATGCTGGGGACAGGCCCTGGAGGAAGT
ACTGGGATCACGTCGTTCAGGCTCGTACTGTGACGCTGCCGGGGCGGGGGAAGGAGGTGGGACATGTG
GGCGTTGGGGCTGTAGGTCCACACCCACTGTGGGTGGCCTCCCTCTAACCTGGGTCCAGCCCGGCTG
GAGATGGGTGGAGTGCGACCTGGGCTGGCGGGGCAGCGGGGGCACTGTGTTCTCCCTGACTGTGTCCTCC
TGTGTCCCTGTGCCTCGCCGCGGTTCCGGAACCTGCTCTGCGCGGCACGTCCTGGCAGTGGGGCAGGTG
GAGCTGGGCGAGGGCCCTGGTGCAGGCAGCCTGCACCTGAGGAGTGTCCTTGGGGCTCCTGGGAGAGGT
GGCATTGTGCAACAATGCTGCACCAGCATCTGCCCCTCTACCAGCTGGAGAACTACTGCAACTAGACG
CAGCCCGCAGGCAGCCCCCACCCGCCGCCTCTGCACCGAGAGAGATGGAATAAAGCCCTTGCACCAGG
C
```

Insulin gene

Promoter — Intron — Start codon — Intron — Stop codon

FIGURE 14–12 Locating a Gene
A typical gene, such as that for insulin, has several DNA sequences that can serve as locators. These include the promoter, sequences between introns and exons, and start and stop codons.

The Human Genome Project

What were the goals of the Human Genome Project, and what have we learned so far?

In 1990, the United States, along with several other countries, launched the Human Genome Project. **The Human Genome Project was a 13-year, international effort with the main goals of sequencing all 3 billion base pairs of human DNA and identifying all human genes.** Other important goals included sequencing the genomes of model organisms to interpret human DNA, developing technology to support the research, exploring gene functions, studying human variation, and training future scientists.

DNA sequencing was at the center of the Human Genome Project. However, the basic sequencing method you saw earlier can analyze only a few hundred nucleotides at a time. How, then, can the huge amount of DNA in the human genome be sequenced quickly? First, researchers must break up the entire genome into manageable pieces. By determining the base sequences in widely separated regions of a DNA strand, they can use the regions as markers, not unlike the mile markers along a road that is thousands of miles long. The markers make it possible for researchers to locate and return to specific locations in the DNA.

Sequencing and Identifying Genes Once researchers have marked the DNA strands, they can use the technique of "shotgun sequencing." This rapid sequencing method involves cutting DNA into random fragments, then determining the base sequence in each fragment. Computer programs take the sequencing data, find areas of overlap between fragments, and put the fragments together by linking the overlapping areas. The computers then align these fragments relative to the known markers on each chromosome, as shown in **Figure 14–11.** The entire process is like putting a jigsaw puzzle together, but instead of matching shapes, the computer matches DNA base sequences.

Reading the DNA sequence of a genome is not the same as understanding it. Much of today's research explores the vast amount of data from the Human Genome Project to look for genes and the DNA sequences that control them. By locating sequences known to be promoters—binding sites for RNA polymerase—scientists can identify many genes. Shortly after a promoter, there is usually an area called an open reading frame, which is a sequence of DNA bases that will produce an mRNA sequence. Other sites that help to identify genes are the sequences that separate introns from exons, and stop codons located at the ends of open reading frames. **Figure 14–12** shows these sites on a typical gene.

Comparing Sequences If you were to compare the genomes of two unrelated individuals, you would find that most—but not all—of their DNA matches base-for-base with each other. On average, one base in 1200 will not match between two individuals. Biologists call these single base differences SNPs (pronounced "snips"), which stands for single nucleotide polymorphisms. Researchers have discovered that certain sets of closely linked SNPs occur together time and time again. These collections of linked SNPs are called haplotypes—short for haploid genotypes. To locate and identify as many haplotypes in the human population as possible, the International HapMap Project began in 2002. The aim of the project is to give scientists a rapid way to identify haplotypes associated with various diseases and conditions and to pave the way to more effective life-saving medical care in the future.

Sharing Data The Human Genome Project was completed in 2003. Copies of the human genome DNA sequence, and those of many other organisms, are now freely available on the Internet. Online computer access enables researchers and students to browse through databases of human DNA and study its sequence. More data from the human genome, and the genomes of other organisms, are added to these databases every day.

One of the key research areas of the Human Genome Project was a new field of study called **bioinformatics.** The root word, *informatics,* refers to the creation, development, and operation of databases and other computing tools to collect, organize, and interpret data. The prefix *bio-* refers to life sciences—specifically, molecular biology. Assembling the bits and pieces of the human genome would have been impossible without sophisticated computer programs that could recognize overlapping sequences and place them in the proper order, or immense databases where such information could be stored and retrieved. Without the tools of bioinformatics shown in **Figure 14–13,** the wealth of information gleaned from the Human Genome Project would hardly be useful. Bioinformatics also launched a more specialized field of study known as **genomics**—the study of whole genomes, including genes and their functions.

MYSTERY CLUE

Scientists can detect the sickle cell allele with a test for SNPs in the genes for the polypeptides that make up hemoglobin. What does this tell you about the sickle cell mutation?

FIGURE 14–13 Bioinformatics Bioinformatics is a new field that combines molecular biology with information science. It is critical to studying and understanding the human genome.

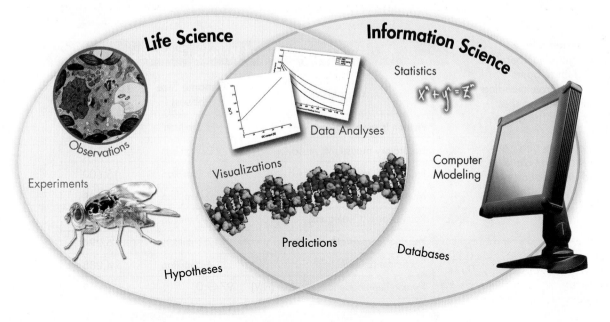

Life Science

Information Science

Observations

Experiments

Hypotheses

Visualizations

Data Analyses

Predictions

Statistics

$x^2 + y^2 = z^2$

Computer Modeling

Databases

FIGURE 14–14 Announcements
The first details of the human genome appeared in two well-known scientific journals in February 2001.

What We Have Learned In June 2000, scientists announced that a working copy of the human genome was complete. The first details appeared in the February 2001 issues of the journals *Nature* and *Science*. The full reference sequence was completed in April 2003, marking the end of the Human Genome Project—two years ahead of the original schedule. Coincidentally, that was also the fiftieth anniversary of Watson and Crick's publication of DNA structure that launched the era of molecular biology!

Besides finding that the human genome in its haploid form contains three billion nucleotide bases, the Human Genome Project uncovered a wealth of interesting, and sometimes surprising, information. For instance, only about 2 percent of our genome encodes instructions for the synthesis of proteins, and many chromosomes contain large areas with very few genes. As much as half of our genome is made up of DNA sequences from viruses and other genetic elements within human chromosomes. During the project, investigators completed the genomes of several other organisms, including unicellular ones. They found that more than 40 percent of the proteins coded for by our genome have strong similarity to proteins in many of those organisms, including fruit flies, worms, and even yeast. **Figure 14–15** compares the human genome with these and other model organisms.

By any standard, the Human Genome Project has been a great scientific success. **The Human Genome Project pinpointed genes and associated particular sequences in those genes with numerous diseases and disorders. It also identified about three million locations where single-base DNA differences occur in humans.** This information may help us find DNA sequences associated with diabetes, cancer, and other health problems. The Human Genome Project also transferred important new technologies to the private sector, including agriculture and medicine. By doing so, the project catalyzed the U.S. biotechnology industry and fostered the development of new medical applications.

FIGURE 14–15 Genome Size Comparisons The gene numbers in this table are not final. Some estimates include only protein-coding genes, while others include genes that code only for RNA. The discovery of small interfering RNAs (siRNAs) has complicated the definition of a gene. **Propose a Solution** *How could you find updated information on genome sizes?*

Size Comparison of Various Genomes		
Organism	**Genome Size (bases)**	**Estimated Genes**
Human (*Homo sapiens*)	3.2 billion	25,000
Laboratory mouse (*M. musculus*)	2.5 billion	24,174
Fruit fly (*D. melanogaster*)	165.0 million	13,600
Mustard weed (*A. thaliana*)	120.0 million	25,498
Roundworm (*C. elegans*)	97.0 million	19,000
Yeast (*S. cerevisiae*)	12.1 million	6,294
Bacterium (*E. coli*)	4.6 million	4,288
Human immunodeficiency virus (HIV)	9749.0	9

New Questions Throughout its duration, the Human Genome Project worked to identify and address ethical, legal, and social issues surrounding the availability of human genome data and its powerful new technologies. The issues, including privacy, fairness in the use of and access to genomic information, medical issues, and commercialization, are complex. For example, who owns and controls genetic information? Is genetic privacy different from medical privacy? Who should have access to personal genetic information, and how will it be used? Right now, these questions are hypothetical, but they may not be for long. In May 2008, President George Bush signed into law the Genetic Information Nondiscrimination Act, which prohibits U.S. insurance companies and employers from discriminating on the basis of information derived from genetic tests. Other protective laws may soon follow.

What's Next? Many more sequencing projects are underway, helped along by powerful new technologies. You can expect an ever-growing database of information from microbial, animal, and plant genomes in the years ahead. Each of these will have its own mysteries to be explored, not to mention the fact that we still don't fully understand the functions of as many as 50 percent of the human genes thus far discovered.

The 1000 Genomes Project, launched in 2008, will study the genomes of 1000 people in an effort to produce a detailed catalogue of human variation. Data from the project will be used in future studies of development and disease, and the information may hold the key to successful research on new drugs and therapies to save human lives and preserve health.

Perhaps the most important challenge that lies ahead is to understand how all the "parts" of cells—genes, proteins, and many other molecules—work together to create complex living organisms. Future efforts may provide a deeper understanding of the molecular processes underlying life and may influence how we view our own place in the global ecosystem.

14.3 Assessment

Review Key Concepts

1. a. Review How do molecular biologists identify genes in sequences of DNA?

b. Use Analogies How is shotgun sequencing similar to doing a jigsaw puzzle?

2. a. Review What is the Human Genome Project?

b. Form an Opinion Judge the potential impact of the Human Genome Project on both scientific thought and society. How might the project be used to benefit humankind? What potential problems might it create?

WRITE ABOUT SCIENCE

Persuasion

3. Scientists may one day be able to use genomics and molecular biology to alter a child's inherited traits. Under what circumstances, if any, should this ability be used? When should it not be used? Write a persuasive paragraph expressing your opinion. (*Hint:* Use specific examples of traits to support your ideas.)

Pre-Lab: Using DNA to Identify Human Remains

Problem How can pedigrees help scientists identify human remains?

Lab Manual Chapter 14 Lab

Skills Focus Analyze Data, Draw Conclusions

Connect to the Big idea The nucleus is not the only location in a cell where DNA can be found. DNA is also found in the mitochondria of cells. This mitochondrial DNA, or mtDNA, exists as small loops, rather than long strands. Unlike nuclear DNA, mtDNA is inherited only from the mother. Thus, except for mutations, the sequence of nucleotides in mtDNA remains constant over many generations.

Less than one percent of a cell's DNA is mtDNA, but in that percentage are many copies of the small mtDNA molecules. So when forensic scientists cannot collect a suitable sample of nuclear DNA, they look for mtDNA. Usable mtDNA can often be found even after a body decays or is burned. In this lab, you will explore how mtDNA was used to help confirm the identity of bones that scientists thought belonged to members of the Romanov family.

The Romanovs ruled Russia for 300 years until the Bolshevik Revolution of 1918 resulted in the execution of Tsar Nicholas II and his family.

3. Infer If two people have the same mtDNA, what can you infer about their biological relationship?

Background Questions

a. Review What is a pedigree?

b. Explain In a pedigree, what does a circle represent? What does a square represent?

c. Infer How do you know that mtDNA isn't sorted and recombined during meiosis?

Pre-Lab Questions

Preview the procedure in the lab manual.

1. Infer The tsar and tsarina had five children. Did all seven family members have the same mtDNA? Give a reason for your answer.

2. Predict To confirm that bones belonged to the tsar's children, which living relative would be more useful— a relative of the tsar or a relative of the tsarina? Why?

BIOLOGY.com Search [Chapter 14] **GO**

Visit Chapter 14 online to test yourself on chapter content and to find activities to help you learn.

Untamed Science Video The Untamed Science crew identifies the chromosomes that carry genes for colorblindness.

Art in Motion View a short animation that explains nondisjunction.

Art Review Review your understanding of karyotypes with this drag-and-drop activity.

InterActive Art Learn all about pedigrees and how to make them with this animation.

Data Analysis Analyze the connection between type O blood and an increased susceptibility to cholera.

Tutor Tube Why do traits sometimes "skip a generation"? Tune in to the tutor to find out.

14 Study Guide

Big idea ▸ Information and Heredity

Humans have 23 pairs of chromosomes, including one pair of sex chromosomes, that follow the same patterns of Mendelian inheritance as do other organisms. Scientists study human heredity using karyotypes, pedigrees, and Punnett squares, but they also use the tools of molecular biology and bioinformatics to study DNA and gene expression. The Human Genome Project has revolutionized the study of human heredity.

14.1 Human Chromosomes

🔑 A karyotype shows the complete diploid set of chromosomes grouped together in pairs, arranged in order of decreasing size.

🔑 Human genes follow the same Mendelian patterns of inheritance as the genes of other organisms. Many human traits follow a pattern of simple dominance. The alleles for other human genes display codominant inheritance. Because the X and Y chromosomes determine sex, the genes located on them show a pattern of inheritance called sex-linkage.

🔑 The information gained from pedigree analysis makes it possible to determine the nature of genes and alleles associated with inherited human traits.

genome (392)   autosome (393)
karyotype (392)   sex-linked gene (395)
sex chromosome (393)   pedigree (396)

14.2 Human Genetic Disorders

🔑 Changes in a gene's DNA sequence can change proteins by altering their amino acid sequences, which may directly affect one's phenotype.

🔑 If nondisjunction occurs during meiosis, gametes with an abnormal number of chromosomes may result, leading to a disorder of chromosome numbers.

nondisjunction (401)

14.3 Studying the Human Genome

🔑 By using tools that cut, separate, and then replicate DNA base by base, scientists can now read the base sequences in DNA from any cell.

🔑 The Human Genome Project was a 13-year, international effort with the main goals of sequencing all 3 billion base pairs of human DNA and identifying all human genes.

🔑 The Human Genome Project pinpointed genes and associated particular sequences in those genes with numerous diseases and disorders. It also identified about three million locations where single-base DNA differences occur in humans.

restriction enzyme (403)   bioinformatics (407)
gel electrophoresis (404) genomics (407)

Think Visually

Create a concept map using the following terms: nondisjunction, autosomes, sex chromosomes, Down syndrome, Turner's syndrome, and Klinefelter's syndrome.

14 Assessment

14.1 Human Chromosomes

Understand Key Concepts

1. A normal human diploid zygote contains
  a. 23 chromosomes.   **c.** 44 chromosomes.
  b. 46 chromosomes.   **d.** XXY chromosomes.

2. A chart that traces the inheritance of a trait in a family is called a(n)
  a. pedigree.   **c.** genome.
  b. karyotype.   **d.** autosome.

3. An example of a trait that is determined by multiple alleles is
  a. cystic fibrosis.   **c.** Down syndrome.
  b. ABO blood groups.   **d.** colorblindness.

4. What is the difference between autosomes and sex chromosomes?

5. Is it possible for a person with blood type alleles I^A and I^B to have blood type A? Explain your answer. (Refer to **Figure 14–5**).

Think Critically

6. Predict What are the possible genotypes of the parents of a male child who is colorblind?

7. Design an Experiment Fruit fly sex is determined by X and Y chromosomes, just as it is in humans. Researchers suspect that a certain disease is caused by a recessive allele in a gene located on the X chromosome in fruit flies. Design an experiment to test this hypothesis.

14.2 Human Genetic Disorders

Understand Key Concepts

8. A mutation involving a change in a single DNA base pair
  a. will definitely result in a genetic disease.
  b. will have no effect on the organism's phenotype.
  c. will produce a positive change.
  d. may have an effect on the organism's phenotype.

9. Cystic fibrosis is caused by
  a. nondisjunction of an autosome.
  b. a change of three base pairs in DNA.
  c. nondisjunction of a sex chromosome.
  d. deletion of an entire gene from a chromosome.

10. Malaria is a disease caused by a
  a. gene mutation.
  b. defect in red blood cells.
  c. bacterium found in water.
  d. parasite carried by mosquitoes.

11. Analyze the human karyotype below. Identify the chromosomal disorder that it shows.

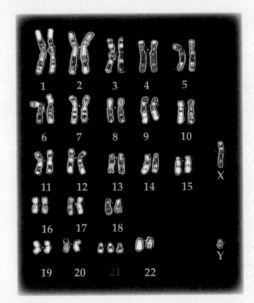

12. What is a chromosomal disorder?

13. Describe two sex-chromosome disorders.

Think Critically

14. Infer Can a genetic counselor use a karyotype to identify a carrier of cystic fibrosis? Explain.

15. Interpret Graphs What can you infer about the relationship between the age of the mother and the incidence of Down syndrome?

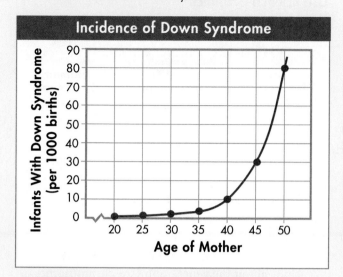

Incidence of Down Syndrome

Infants With Down Syndrome (per 1000 births) vs. Age of Mother

14.3 Studying the Human Genome

Understand Key Concepts

16. The human genome consists of approximately how many DNA base pairs?
  a. 30,000
  b. 3,000,000
  c. 300,000,000
  d. 3,000,000,000

17. The fraction of the human genome that actually codes for proteins is about
  a. 2%.
  b. 20%.
  c. 98%.
  d. 100%.

18. Cutting DNA into small pieces that can be sequenced is accomplished by
  a. restriction enzymes.
  b. DNA polymerase.
  c. gel electrophoresis.
  d. RNA polymerase.

19. If you sequence short pieces of DNA and then use a computer to find overlapping sequences that map to a much longer DNA fragment, you are using
  a. genomics.
  b. hapmaps.
  c. shotgun sequencing.
  d. open reading frame analysis.

20. Describe the tools and processes that scientists use to manipulate human DNA.

21. Explain why restriction enzymes are useful tools in sequencing DNA.

solve the CHAPTER MYSTERY

THE CROOKED CELL

When Ava inquired about her family's medical history, she found out that Uncle Eli's mother (Ava's grandmother) also had sickle cell disease, but Uncle Eli's father did not. One of her uncle's four children also had the disease. However, Ava's father, who is Eli's only sibling, did not have sickle cell disease, nor did Ava's mother. Ava's two siblings showed no signs of the disease, either.

1. Apply Concepts In general, what pattern of heredity does the sickle cell trait follow? Cite evidence from the chapter and its clues to support your conclusion.

2. Draw Conclusions Based on your answer to question 1, what can you conclude about the inheritance of sickle cell disease in Ava's family? What might be Ava's chances of being a carrier of the sickle cell trait?

3. Classify What kind of medical test could Ava request that would help determine whether or not she has the sickle cell trait? Explain your answer.

4. Infer The restriction enzyme *Mst* II, which cuts normal DNA at a particular site, will not recognize (and, therefore, will not cut) DNA that contains the sickle cell mutation. If Uncle Eli's DNA is cut with *Mst* II, will the restriction fragments be identical to those from his brother, Ava's father? Explain.

5. Focus on the Big idea Which technique(s) that you have read about in this chapter could be used to perform the kind of test described in question 4? Which technique could be used to analyze the results?

22. What is an SNP (single nucleotide polymorphism)?

23. What is bioinformatics?

Think Critically

24. Draw Conclusions Scientists have searched the human genome database to find possible promoter sequences. What is likely to be found near a promoter sequence?

25. Infer Why does DNA move toward the positive end of the gel during gel electrophoresis?

26. Observe The table below shows the DNA sequences that are recognized by five different restriction enzymes and the locations where those enzymes cut. Which enzymes produce DNA fragments with "sticky ends"? What is the common feature of the sequences cut by these enzymes?

DNA Sequences Cut by Enzymes

Enzyme	Recognition Sequence
*Alu*I	A G ↓ C T T C ↑ G A
*Hae*III	G G ↓ C C C C ↑ G G
*Bam*HI	G↓G A T C C C C T A G↑G
*Hind*III	A↓A G C T T T T C G A↑A
*Eco*RI	G↓A A T T C C T T A A↑G

Use Science Graphics

Use the data table to answer questions 27 and 28.

Chromosomes and Phenotypes

Sex Chromosomes	Fruit Fly Phenotype	Human Phenotype
XX	Female	Female
XY	Male	Male
X	Male	Female
XXY	Female	Male

27. Interpret Tables What differs in the sex-determining mechanism of the two organisms?

28. Draw Conclusions What can you logically conclude about the genes on the sex chromosomes of fruit flies and humans?

Write About Science

29. Explanation Write a paragraph that tells how colorblindness is inherited. Describe the condition and explain why it is much more common in males. (*Hint*: Begin your paragraph with a topic sentence that expresses the paragraph's main idea.)

30. Assess the Big idea Explain the relationship between meiosis and Down syndrome, Turner's syndrome, and Klinefelter's syndrome.

Analyzing Data

Hemophilia is an example of a sex-linked disorder. Two genes carried on the X chromosome help control blood clotting. A recessive allele in either of these two genes may produce hemophilia. The pedigree shows the transmission of hemophilia through three generations of a family.

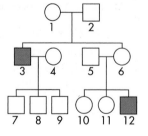

31. Interpret Diagrams Which mothers are definite carriers of the gene?

32. Apply Concepts Why did the sons of Person 3 not inherit the trait?

33. Apply Concepts How could Person 12 have hemophilia if neither of his parents had hemophilia?

Standardized Test Prep

Multiple Choice

1. Which of the following disorders can be observed in a human karyotype?
   A colorblindness
   B trisomy 21
   C cystic fibrosis
   D sickle cell disease

2. Which of the following disorders is a direct result of nondisjunction?
   A sickle cell disease
   B Turner's syndrome
   C Huntington's disease
   D cystic fibrosis

3. A woman is homozygous for A⁻ blood type. A man has AB⁻ blood type. What is the probability that the couple's child will have type B⁻ blood?
   A 0%   C 75%
   B 50%   D 100%

4. Cystic fibrosis is a genetic disorder caused by a
   A single base substitution in the gene for hemoglobin.
   B deletion of an amino acid from a chloride channel protein.
   C defective gene found on the X chromosome.
   D trisomy of chromosome 21.

5. The technique used to separate DNA strands of different lengths is
   A gel electrophoresis.
   B shotgun sequencing.
   C restriction enzyme digestion.
   D bioinformatics.

6. The study of whole genomes, including genes and their functions, is called
   A bioinformatics.
   B information science.
   C life science.
   D genomics.

7. DNA can be cut into shorter sequences by proteins known as
   A haplotypes.   C restriction enzymes.
   B polymerases.   D restriction fragments.

Questions 8–9

A student traced the recurrence of a widow's peak hairline in her family. Based on her interviews and observations, she drew the pedigree shown below.

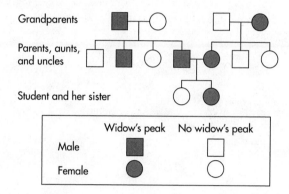

8. Which pattern of inheritance is consistent with the pedigree?
   A sex-linked inheritance
   B complete dominance
   C codominance
   D multiple alleles

9. What are the probable genotypes of the student's parents?
   A Mother—*Ww*; Father—*ww*
   B Mother—*ww*; Father—*ww*
   C Mother—*WW*; Father—*Ww*
   D Mother—*Ww*; Father—*Ww*

Open-Ended Response

10. Explain how the allele for sickle cell disease, which is a harmful allele when a person is homozygous, can be beneficial when a person is heterozygous.

If You Have Trouble With . . .

Question	1	2	3	4	5	6	7	8	9	10
See Lesson	14.1	14.2	14.1	14.2	14.3	14.3	14.3	14.1	14.1	14.2

15 Genetic Engineering

Big idea

Science as a Way of Knowing

Q: How and why do scientists manipulate DNA in living cells?

By cloning cells and modifying genes, scientists in Korea have developed cats that glow bright red in the dark. The cloned Turkish Angola on the left has a fluorescent protein in its skin cells. The protein gives off a red glow when exposed to ultraviolet light. The ordinary Turkish Angola on the right lacks the red fluorescent protein, so it appears green under ultraviolet light.

INSIDE:

- 15.1 Selective Breeding
- 15.2 Recombinant DNA
- 15.3 Applications of Genetic Engineering
- 15.4 Ethics and Impacts of Biotechnology

CHAPTER
MYSTERY

A CASE OF MISTAKEN IDENTITY

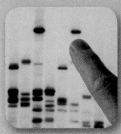

In the summer of 1998, an elderly Indiana woman was brutally assaulted. In the predawn darkness, she didn't get a look at her assailant's face.

At first light, police found a man only a few blocks from the victim's house. He was unconscious, his clothing was stained with blood, and there were scratches on his forearms. The man claimed that he had passed out following a drunken brawl. He couldn't remember what had happened afterward. The blood type of the stains on his clothing matched the victim's blood type. The police thought they had their man.

Hours later, the police knew they had the wrong suspect. They resumed their search for the real attacker, who was subsequently caught, tried, and convicted. As you read this chapter, look for clues to help you determine how the police knew they had the wrong suspect. Then, solve the mystery.

Never Stop Exploring Your World.
Finding the solution to the case of mistaken identity is only the beginning. Take a video field trip with the ecogeeks of Untamed Science to see where the mystery leads.

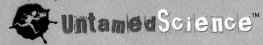

UntamedScience™

- Untamed Science Video   • Chapter Mystery

Genetic Engineering **417**

Key Questions

🔑 *What is selective breeding used for?*

🔑 *How do people increase genetic variation?*

Vocabulary

selective breeding
hybridization
inbreeding
biotechnology

Taking Notes

Outline Before you read this lesson, start an outline. Use the green headings in the lesson as first-level entries. Use the blue headings as second-level entries, leaving space after each entry. As you read, summarize the key ideas below your entries.

THINK ABOUT IT You've enjoyed popcorn at the movies, you've probably made it at home, and you've certainly seen it in stores. Where does it come from? Would you be surprised to learn that popcorn is one of the earliest examples of human efforts to select and improve living organisms for our benefit? Corn as we know it was domesticated at least 6000 years ago by Native Americans living in Mexico. A tiny kernel of popped corn found in a cave in New Mexico is more than 5000 years old!

Selective Breeding

🔑 *What is selective breeding used for?*

Visit a dog show, and what do you see? Striking contrasts are everywhere—from a tiny Chihuahua to a massive Great Dane, from the short coat of a Labrador retriever to the curly fur of a poodle, from the long muzzle of a wolfhound to the pug nose of a bulldog. The differences among breeds of dogs, like the ones in **Figure 15–1,** are so great that someone might think they are different species. They're not, of course, but where did these obvious differences come from?

The answer is that we did it. Humans have kept and bred dogs for thousands of years, always looking to produce animals that are better hunters, better retrievers, or better companions. We've done so by **selective breeding,** allowing only those animals with wanted characteristics to produce the next generation. 🔑 **Humans use selective breeding, which takes advantage of naturally occurring genetic variation, to pass wanted traits on to the next generation of organisms.**

FIGURE 15–1 Dog Breeds There are more than 150 dog breeds, and many new breeds are still being developed.

For thousands of years, we've produced new varieties of cultivated plants and nearly all domestic animals—including horses, cats, and cows—by selectively breeding for particular traits. Long before Europeans came to the New World, Native Americans had selectively bred teosinte (tee oh SIN tee), a wild grass native to central Mexico, to produce corn, a far more productive and nutritious plant. **Figure 15–2** shows both plants. Corn is now one of the world's most important crops. There are two common methods of selective breeding—hybridization and inbreeding.

Hybridization American botanist Luther Burbank may have been the greatest selective breeder of all time. During his lifetime (1849–1926), he developed more than 800 varieties of plants. As one of his tools, Burbank used **hybridization,** crossing dissimilar individuals to bring together the best of both organisms. Hybrids—the individuals produced by such crosses—are often hardier than either of the parents. Many of Burbank's hybrid crosses combined the disease resistance of one plant with the food-producing capacity of another. The result was a new line of plants that had the traits farmers needed to increase food production. **Figure 15–3** shows a type of peach developed using Burbank's methods.

Inbreeding To maintain desirable characteristics in a line of organisms, breeders often use a technique known as inbreeding. **Inbreeding** is the continued breeding of individuals with similar characteristics. The many breeds of dogs—from beagles to poodles—are maintained using this practice. Inbreeding helps ensure that the characteristics that make each breed unique are preserved. Although inbreeding is useful in preserving certain traits, it can be risky. Most of the members of a breed are genetically similar, which increases the chance that a cross between two individuals will bring together two recessive alleles for a genetic defect.

 In Your Notebook Compare and contrast hybridization and inbreeding.

FIGURE 15–2 Corn From Teosinte Modern corn was selectively bred from teosinte at least 6000 years ago. During its domestication, corn lost the ability to survive in the wild but gained valuable agricultural traits. For example, the hard case around the kernel disappeared over time, leaving the rows of soft corn kernels we enjoy today. **Observe** *What other differences can you see between the two plants?*

FIGURE 15–3 Selectively Bred Fruit Luther Burbank used hybridization— a form of selective breeding—to develop a variety of plants. These July Elberta peaches, *Prunus persica,* are among his most successful varieties.

Increasing Variation

🔑 *How do people increase genetic variation?*

Selective breeding would be nearly impossible without the wide variation found in natural populations of plants and animals. But sometimes breeders want more variation than exists in nature. 🔑 **Breeders can increase the genetic variation in a population by introducing mutations, which are the ultimate source of biological diversity.**

When scientists manipulate the genetic makeup of an organism, they are using biotechnology. **Biotechnology** is the application of a technological process, invention, or method to living organisms. Selective breeding is one form of biotechnology important in agriculture and medicine, but there are many others.

Polyploid Crops			
Plant	Probable Ancestral Haploid Number	Chromosome Number	Ploidy Level
Domestic oat	7	42	6N
Peanut	10	40	4N
Sugar cane	10	80	8N
Banana	11	22, 33	2N, 3N
Cotton	13	52	4N

FIGURE 15–4 Ploidy Numbers Because polyploid plants are often larger than other plants, many farmers deliberately grow polyploid varieties of crops like those listed above. **Interpret Tables** *Which plant has undergone the most dramatic changes in chromosome number?*

Bacterial Mutations Mutations—heritable changes in DNA—occur spontaneously, but breeders can increase the mutation rate of an organism by using radiation or chemicals. Many mutations are harmful to the organism. With luck and perseverance, however, breeders can often produce a few mutants—individuals with mutations— with useful characteristics that are not found in the original population. This technique has been particularly useful with bacteria. Because they are small, millions of bacteria can be treated with radiation or chemicals at the same time, which increases the chances of producing a useful mutant. This technique has allowed scientists to develop hundreds of useful bacterial strains. For instance, we have known for decades that certain strains of oil-digesting bacteria are effective for cleaning up oil spills. Today scientists are working to produce bacteria that can clean up radioactive substances and metal pollution in the environment.

Polyploid Plants Drugs that prevent the separation of chromosomes during meiosis are very useful in plant breeding. These drugs can produce cells that have many times the normal number of chromosomes. Plants grown from these cells are called polyploid because they have many sets of chromosomes. Polyploidy is usually fatal in animals. But, for reasons that are not clear, plants are much better at tolerating extra sets of chromosomes. Polyploidy can quickly produce new species of plants that are larger and stronger than their diploid relatives. A number of important crop plants, including bananas and many varieties of citrus fruits, have been produced in this way. **Figure 15–4** lists several examples of polyploid plants.

15.1 Assessment

Review Key Concepts 🔑

1. a. Review Give an example of selective breeding.

b. Compare and Contrast Suppose you are a geneticist trying to develop a sunflower with red petals and a short stem. As you compare the sunflowers you have on hand, what genetic variations would you look for? What kinds of plants would you select for crossing?

2. a. Review What is the relationship between genetic variations and mutations?

b. Explain How can breeders introduce mutations?

c. Draw Conclusions How is selective breeding a form of biotechnology?

WRITE ABOUT SCIENCE

Explanation

3. Write a paragraph in which you suggest ways that plants could be genetically altered to improve the world's food supply. (*Hint:* The first sentence in your paragraph should express the paragraph's main idea.)

Recombinant DNA

THINK ABOUT IT Suppose you have an electronic game you want to change. Knowing that the game depends on a coded program in a computer microchip, how would you set about rewriting the program? First you'd need a way to get the existing program out of the microchip. Then you'd have to read the program, make the changes you want, and put the modified code back into the microchip. What does this scenario have to do with genetic engineering? Just about everything.

Copying DNA

🔑 **How do scientists copy the DNA of living organisms?**

Until recently plant and animal breeders could only work with variations that already exist in nature. Even when breeders tried to add variation by introducing mutations, the changes they produced were unpredictable. Today genetic engineers can transfer certain genes at will from one organism to another, designing new living things to meet specific needs.

Recall from Chapter 14 that it is relatively easy to extract DNA from cells and tissues. The extracted DNA can be cut into fragments of manageable size using restriction enzymes. These restriction fragments can then be separated according to size using gel electrophoresis or another similar technique. That's the easy part. The tough part comes next: How do you find a specific gene?

The problem is huge. If we were to cut DNA from a bacterium like *E. coli* into restriction fragments averaging 1000 base pairs in length, we would have 4000 restriction fragments. In the human genome, we would have 3 million restriction fragments. How do we find the DNA of a single gene among millions of fragments? In some respects, it's the classic problem of finding a needle in a haystack—we have an enormous pile of hay and just one needle.

Actually, there is a way to find a needle in a haystack. We can toss the hay in front of a powerful magnet until something sticks. The hay won't stick, but a needle made of iron or steel will. Believe it or not, similar techniques can help scientists identify specific genes.

Key Questions

🔑 **How do scientists copy the DNA of living organisms?**

🔑 **How is recombinant DNA used?**

🔑 **How can genes from one organism be inserted into another organism?**

Vocabulary

polymerase chain reaction
recombinant DNA
plasmid
genetic marker
transgenic
clone

Taking Notes

Preview Visuals Before you read, preview **Figure 15–7** and write down any questions you may have about the figure. As you read, find answers to your questions.

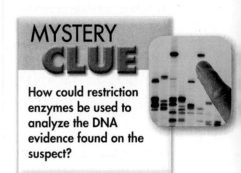

MYSTERY CLUE

How could restriction enzymes be used to analyze the DNA evidence found on the suspect?

FIGURE 15–5 A Fluorescent Gene The Pacific Ocean jellyfish, *Aequoria victoria*, emits a bluish glow. A protein in the jellyfish absorbs the blue light and produces green fluorescence. This protein, called GFP, is now widely used in genetic engineering.

FIGURE 15–6 Southern Blotting Southern blot analysis, named after its inventor Edwin Southern, is a research technique for finding specific DNA sequences, among dozens. A labeled piece of nucleic acid serves as a probe among the DNA fragments.

Finding Genes In 1987, Douglas Prasher, a biologist at Woods Hole Oceanographic Institute in Massachusetts, wanted to find a specific gene in a jellyfish. The gene he hoped to identify is the one that codes for a molecule called green fluorescent protein, or GFP. This natural protein, found in the jellyfish shown in **Figure 15–5,** absorbs energy from light and makes parts of the jellyfish glow. Prasher thought that GFP from the jellyfish could be used to report when a protein was being made in a cell. If he could somehow link GFP to a specific protein, it would be a bit like attaching a light bulb to that molecule.

To find the GFP gene, Prasher studied the amino acid sequence of part of the GFP protein. By comparing this sequence to a genetic code table, he was able to predict a probable mRNA base sequence that would have coded for this sequence of amino acids. Next, Prasher used a complementary base sequence to "attract" an mRNA that matched his prediction and would bind to that sequence by base pairing. After screening a genetic "library" with thousands of different mRNA sequences from the jellyfish, he found one that bound perfectly.

After Prasher located the mRNA that produced GFP, he set out to find the actual gene. Taking a gel in which restriction fragments from the jellyfish genome had been separated, he found that one of the fragments bound tightly to the mRNA. That fragment contained the actual gene for GFP, which is now widely used to label proteins in living cells. The method he used, shown in **Figure 15–6,** is called Southern blotting. Today it is often quicker and less expensive for scientists to search for genes in computer databases where the complete genomes of many organisms are available.

❶ Gel electrophoresis separates DNA fragments produced by restriction enzymes.

❷ Bands on the gel are immobilized by blotting onto nitrocellulose paper.

❸ Radioactive probes bind to fragments with complementary base sequences.

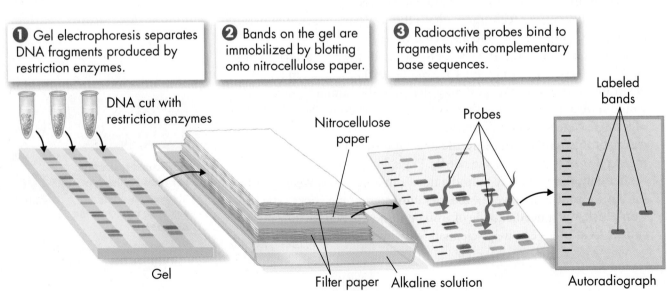

DNA cut with restriction enzymes

Nitrocellulose paper

Probes

Labeled bands

Gel

Filter paper   Alkaline solution

Autoradiograph

Polymerase Chain Reaction Once they find a gene, biologists often need to make many copies of it. A technique known as **polymerase chain reaction** (PCR) allows them to do exactly that. At one end of the original piece of DNA, a biologist adds a short piece of DNA that complements a portion of the sequence. At the other end, the biologist adds another short piece of complementary DNA. These short pieces are known as primers because they prepare, or prime, a place for DNA polymerase to start working.

As **Figure 15–7** suggests, the idea behind the use of PCR primers is surprisingly simple. **The first step in using the polymerase chain reaction method to copy a gene is to heat a piece of DNA, which separates its two strands. Then, as the DNA cools, primers bind to the single strands. Next, DNA polymerase starts copying the region between the primers. These copies can serve as templates to make still more copies.** In this way, just a few dozen cycles of replication can produce billions of copies of the DNA between the primers.

Where did Kary Mullis, the American scientist who invented PCR, find a DNA polymerase enzyme that could stand repeated cycles of heating and cooling? Mullis found it in bacteria from the hot springs of Yellowstone National Park in the northwestern United States—a powerful example of the importance of biodiversity to biotechnology!

In Your Notebook *List the steps in the PCR method.*

Changing DNA

How is recombinant DNA used?

Just as they were beginning to learn how to read and analyze DNA sequences, scientists began wondering if it might be possible to change the DNA of a living cell. As many of them realized, this feat had already been accomplished decades earlier. Do you remember Griffith's experiments on bacterial transformation? During transformation, a cell takes in DNA from outside the cell, and that added DNA becomes a component of the cell's own genome. Today biologists understand that Griffith's extract of heat-killed bacteria contained DNA fragments. When he mixed those fragments with live bacteria, a few of them took up the DNA molecules, transforming them and changing their characteristics. Griffith, of course, could only do this with DNA extracted from other bacteria.

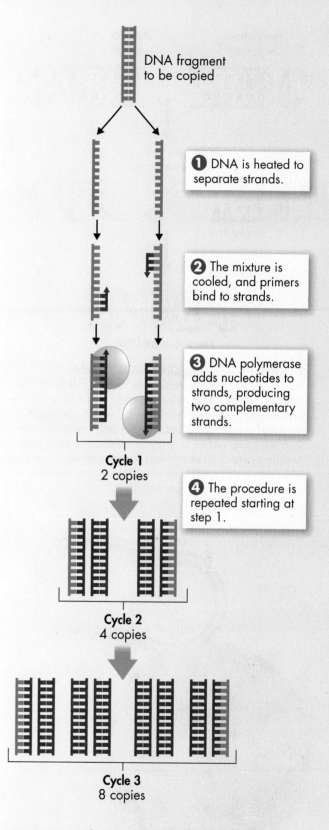

1 DNA is heated to separate strands.

2 The mixture is cooled, and primers bind to strands.

3 DNA polymerase adds nucleotides to strands, producing two complementary strands.

Cycle 1
2 copies

4 The procedure is repeated starting at step 1.

Cycle 2
4 copies

Cycle 3
8 copies

FIGURE 15–7 The PCR Method Polymerase chain reaction is used to make multiple copies of a gene. This method is particularly useful when only tiny amounts of DNA are available. **Calculate** *How many copies of the DNA fragment will there be after six PCR cycles?*
MATH

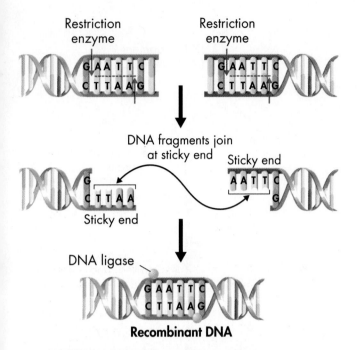

FIGURE 15–8 Joining DNA Pieces Together
Recombinant DNA molecules are made up of DNA from different sources. Restriction enzymes cut DNA at specific sequences, producing "sticky ends," which are single-stranded overhangs of DNA. If two DNA molecules are cut with the same restriction enzyme, their sticky ends will bond to a fragment of DNA that has the complementary sequence of bases. An enzyme known as DNA ligase can then be used to join the two fragments.

Labels in figure: Restriction enzyme, Restriction enzyme, DNA fragments join at sticky end, Sticky end, Sticky end, DNA ligase, Recombinant DNA. Sequences: GAATTC / CTTAAG

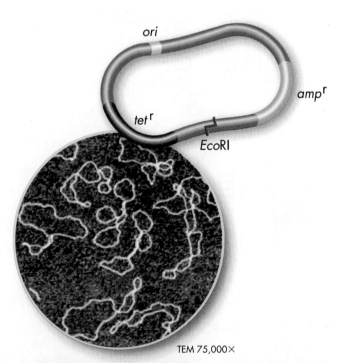

TEM 75,000×

FIGURE 15–9 A Plasmid Map Plasmids used for genetic engineering typically contain a replication start signal, called the origin of replication (*ori*), and a restriction enzyme cutting site, such as *Eco*RI. They also contain genetic markers, like the antibiotic resistance genes *tet*^{r} and *amp*^{r} shown here.

Labels in figure: ori, amp^r, tet^r, EcoRI

Combining DNA Fragments With today's technologies, scientists can produce custom-built DNA molecules in the lab and then insert those molecules—along with the genes they carry—into living cells. The first step in this sort of genetic engineering is to build a DNA sequence with the gene or genes you'd like to insert into a cell. Machines known as DNA synthesizers can produce short pieces of DNA, up to several hundred bases in length. These synthetic sequences can then be joined to natural sequences using DNA ligase or other enzymes that splice DNA together. These same enzymes make it possible to take a gene from one organism and attach it to the DNA of another organism, as shown in **Figure 15–8.** The resulting molecules are called **recombinant DNA.** This technology relies on the fact that any pair of complementary sequences tends to bond, even if each sequence comes from a different organism.
🔑 **Recombinant-DNA technology—joining together DNA from two or more sources—makes it possible to change the genetic composition of living organisms.** By manipulating DNA in this way, scientists can investigate the structure and functions of genes.

Plasmids and Genetic Markers Scientists working with recombinant DNA soon discovered that many of the DNA molecules they tried to insert into host cells simply vanished because the cells often did not copy, or replicate, the added DNA. Today scientists join recombinant DNA to another piece of DNA containing a replication "start" signal. This way, whenever the cell copies its own DNA, it copies the recombinant DNA too.

In addition to their own chromosomes, some bacteria contain small circular DNA molecules known as **plasmids.** Plasmids, like those shown in **Figure 15–9,** are widely used in recombinant DNA studies. Joining DNA to a plasmid, and then using the recombinant plasmid to transform bacteria, results in the replication of the newly added DNA along with the rest of the cell's genome.

Plasmids are also found in yeasts, which are single-celled eukaryotes that can be transformed with recombinant DNA as well. Biologists working with yeasts can construct artificial chromosomes containing centromeres, telomeres, and replication start sites. These artificial chromosomes greatly simplify the process of introducing recombinant DNA into the yeast genome.

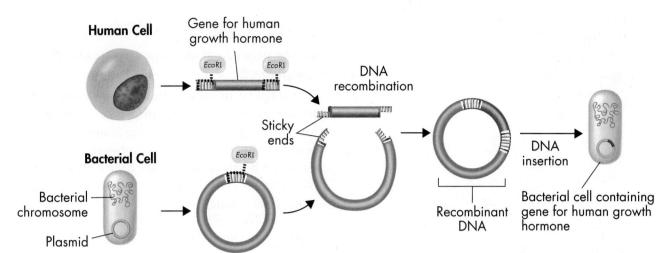

Human Cell

Gene for human growth hormone

EcoRI   EcoRI

DNA recombination

Sticky ends

Bacterial Cell

EcoRI

Bacterial chromosome

Plasmid

DNA insertion

Recombinant DNA

Bacterial cell containing gene for human growth hormone

FIGURE 15–10 Plasmid DNA Transformation
Scientists can insert a piece of DNA into a plasmid if both the plasmid and the target DNA have been cut by the same restriction enzymes to create sticky ends. With this method, bacteria can be used to produce human growth hormone. First, a human gene is inserted into bacterial DNA. Then, the new combination of genes is returned to a bacterial cell, which replicates the recombinant DNA over and over again. **Infer** *Why might scientists want to copy the gene for human growth hormone?*

Figure 15–10 shows how bacteria can be transformed using recombinant plasmids. First, the DNA being used for transformation is joined to a plasmid. The plasmid DNA contains a signal for replication, helping to ensure that if the DNA does get inside a bacterial cell, it will be replicated. In addition, the plasmid also has a genetic marker, such as a gene for antibiotic resistance. A **genetic marker** is a gene that makes it possible to distinguish bacteria that carry the plasmid from those that don't. Using genetic markers, researchers can mix recombinant plasmids with a culture of bacteria, add enough DNA to transform just one cell in a million, and still locate that one cell. After transformation, the culture is treated with an antibiotic. Only those rare cells that have been transformed survive, because only they carry the resistance gene.

 In Your Notebook *Write a summary of the process of plasmid DNA transformation.*

Quick Lab
GUIDED INQUIRY

Inserting Genetic Markers

❶ Write a random DNA sequence on a long strip of paper to represent an organism's genome.

❷ Have your partner write a short DNA sequence on a short strip of paper to represent a marker gene.

❸ Using the chart your teacher gives you, work with your partner to figure out how to insert the marker gene into the genome.

Analyze and Conclude

1. Apply Concepts Which restriction enzyme did you use? Why?

2. Use Models What kind of molecule did you and your partner develop?

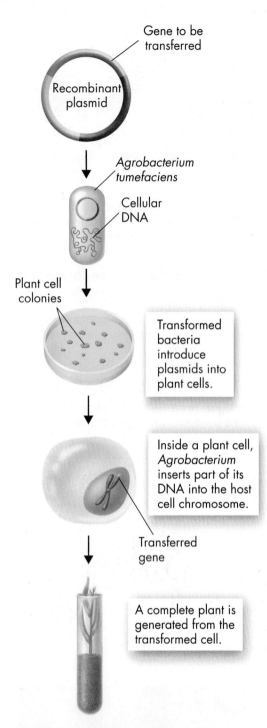

Gene to be transferred

Recombinant plasmid

Agrobacterium tumefaciens

Cellular DNA

Plant cell colonies

Transformed bacteria introduce plasmids into plant cells.

Inside a plant cell, *Agrobacterium* inserts part of its DNA into the host cell chromosome.

Transferred gene

A complete plant is generated from the transformed cell.

FIGURE 15–11 Transforming a Plant Cell *Agrobacterium* can be used to introduce bacterial DNA into a plant cell. The transformed cells can be cultured to produce adult plants.

Transgenic Organisms

How can genes from one organism be inserted into another organism?

The universal nature of the genetic code makes it possible to construct organisms that are **transgenic,** containing genes from other species. **Transgenic organisms can be produced by the insertion of recombinant DNA into the genome of a host organism.** Like bacterial plasmids, the DNA molecules used for transformation of plant and animal cells contain genetic markers that help scientists identify which cells have been transformed.

Transgenic technology was perfected using mice in the 1980s. Genetic engineers can now produce transgenic plants, animals, and microorganisms. By examining the traits of a genetically modified organism, it is possible to learn about the function of the transferred gene. This ability has contributed greatly to our understanding of gene regulation and expression.

Transgenic Plants Many plant cells can be transformed using *Agrobacterium.* In nature this bacterium inserts a small DNA plasmid that produces tumors in a plant's cells. Scientists can deactivate the plasmid's tumor-producing gene and replace it with a piece of recombinant DNA. The recombinant plasmid can then be used to infect and transform plant cells, as shown in **Figure 15–11.**

There are other ways to produce transgenic plants as well. When their cell walls are removed, plant cells in culture will sometimes take up DNA on their own. DNA can also be injected directly into some cells. If transformation is successful, the recombinant DNA is integrated into one of the plant cell's chromosomes.

Transgenic Animals Scientists can transform animal cells using some of the same techniques used for plant cells. The egg cells of many animals are large enough that DNA can be injected directly into the nucleus. Once the DNA is in the nucleus, enzymes that are normally responsible for DNA repair and recombination may help insert the foreign DNA into the chromosomes of the injected cell.

Recently it has become possible to eliminate particular genes by carefully engineering the DNA molecules that are used for transformation. The DNA molecules can be constructed with two ends that will sometimes recombine with specific sequences in the host chromosome. Once they do, the host gene normally found between those two sequences may be lost or specifically replaced with a new gene. This kind of gene replacement has made it possible to pinpoint the specific functions of genes in many organisms, including mice.

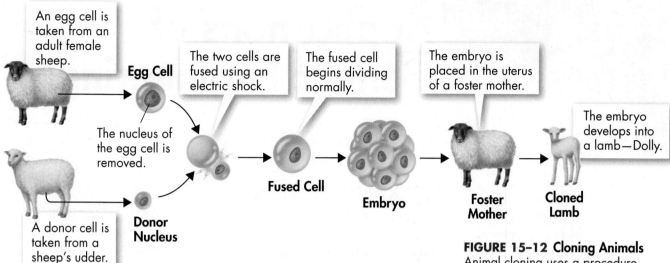

An egg cell is taken from an adult female sheep.

Egg Cell

The nucleus of the egg cell is removed.

A donor cell is taken from a sheep's udder.

Donor Nucleus

The two cells are fused using an electric shock.

The fused cell begins dividing normally.

Fused Cell

Embryo

The embryo is placed in the uterus of a foster mother.

Foster Mother

Cloned Lamb

The embryo develops into a lamb—Dolly.

FIGURE 15–12 Cloning Animals
Animal cloning uses a procedure called nuclear transplantation. The process combines an egg cell with a donor nucleus to produce an embryo. **Apply Concepts** *Why won't the cloned lamb resemble its foster mother?*

Cloning A **clone** is a member of a population of genetically identical cells produced from a single cell. The technique of cloning uses a single cell from an adult organism to grow an entirely new individual that is genetically identical to the organism from which the cell was taken.

Cloned colonies of bacteria and other microorganisms are easy to grow, but this is not always true of multicellular organisms, especially animals. Clones of animals were first produced in 1952 using amphibian tadpoles. In 1997, Scottish scientist Ian Wilmut stunned biologists by announcing that he had produced a sheep, called Dolly, by cloning.

Figure 15–12 shows the basic steps by which an animal can be cloned. First, the nucleus of an unfertilized egg cell is removed. Next, the egg cell is fused with a donor cell that contains a nucleus, taken from an adult. The resulting diploid egg develops into an embryo, which is then implanted in the uterine wall of a foster mother, where it develops until birth. Cloned cows, pigs, mice, and even cats have since been produced using similar techniques.

15.2 Assessment

Review Key Concepts 🔑

1. a. Review Describe the process scientists use to copy DNA.
 b. Infer Why would a scientist want to know the sequence of a DNA molecule?

2. a. Review How do scientists use recombinant DNA?
 b. Use Analogies How is genetic engineering like computer programming?

3. a. Review What is a transgenic organism?
 b. Compare and Contrast Compare the transformation of a plant cell with the transformation of an animal cell.

PRACTICE PROBLEM

4. Design an experiment to find a way to treat disorders caused by a single gene. State your hypothesis and list the steps you would follow. (*Hint*: Think about the uses of recombinant DNA.)

15.3 Applications of Genetic Engineering

Key Questions

🔑 How can genetic engineering benefit agriculture and industry?

🔑 How can recombinant-DNA technology improve human health?

🔑 How is DNA used to identify individuals?

Vocabulary

gene therapy
DNA microarray
DNA fingerprinting
forensics

Taking Notes

Outline Make an outline of this lesson by using the green and blue headings. As you read, take notes on the different applications of genetic engineering.

THINK ABOUT IT Have you eaten any genetically modified food lately? Don't worry if you're not sure how to answer that question. In the United States and many other countries, this kind of food doesn't have to be labeled in grocery stores or markets. But if you've eaten corn, potatoes, or soy products in any of your meals this week, chances are close to 100 percent that you've eaten foods modified in some way by genetic engineering.

Agriculture and Industry

🔑 **How can genetic engineering benefit agriculture and industry?**

Everything we eat and much of what we wear come from living organisms. Not surprisingly, then, researchers have used genetic engineering to try to improve the products we get from plants and animals. 🔑 **Ideally, genetic modification could lead to better, less expensive, and more nutritious food as well as less-harmful manufacturing processes.**

GM Crops Since their introduction in 1996, genetically modified (GM) plants, like the soybeans in **Figure 15–13,** have become an important component of our food supply. In 2007, GM crops made up 92 percent of soybeans, 86 percent of cotton, and 80 percent of corn grown in the United States. One type of modification, which has already proved particularly useful to agriculture, uses bacterial genes that produce a protein known as Bt toxin. While this toxin is harmless to humans and most other animals, enzymes in the digestive systems of insects convert Bt to a form that kills the insects. Plants with the Bt gene, then, do not have to be sprayed with pesticides. In addition, they produce higher yields of crops.

Resistance to insects is just one useful characteristic being engineered into crops. Others include resistance to herbicides, which are chemicals that destroy weeds, and resistance to viral infections. Some transgenic plants may soon produce foods that are resistant to rot and spoilage. And engineers are currently developing GM plants that may produce plastics for the manufacturing industry.

FIGURE 15–13 GM Soybeans Genetically modified soybeans are a popular crop in the United States.

Genetically Modified Crops in the United States

U.S. farmers have adopted GM crops widely since their introduction in 1996. Soybeans, cotton, and corn have been modified to tolerate herbicides and resist insect damage. The graph at the right summarizes the extent to which these crops were adopted between 1996 and 2007. The modified traits shown here include herbicide tolerance (HT) and insect resistance (Bt).

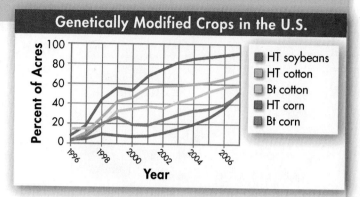

Genetically Modified Crops in the U.S.

- HT soybeans
- HT cotton
- Bt cotton
- HT corn
- Bt corn

Source: U.S. Department of Agriculture Economic Research Service Data Sets

1. Analyze Data Which two crops were most widely and rapidly adopted?

2. Draw Conclusions Why do you think the levels of adoption fell at certain points over the period?

3. Predict What do you think will happen to HT soybeans and HT corn over the next few years? Why? Use the graph to support your prediction.

4. Infer Why do you think an increasing number of farmers have chosen to grow crops with herbicide tolerance?

GM Animals Transgenic animals are also becoming more important to our food supply. For example, about 30 percent of the milk in U.S. markets comes from cows that have been injected with hormones made by recombinant-DNA techniques to increase milk production. Pigs can be genetically modified to produce more lean meat or high levels of healthy omega-3 acids. Using growth-hormone genes, scientists have developed transgenic salmon that grow much more quickly than wild salmon. This effort makes it practical to grow these nutritious fish in captive aquaculture facilities that do not threaten wild populations.

When scientists in Canada combined spider genes into the cells of lactating goats, the goats began to manufacture silk along with their milk. By extracting polymer strands from the milk and weaving them into thread, we can create a light, tough, and flexible material that could be used in such applications as military uniforms, medical sutures, and tennis racket strings. Scientists are now using human genes to develop antibacterial goat milk.

Researchers hope that cloning will enable them to make copies of transgenic animals, which would increase the food supply and could even help save endangered species. In 2008, the U.S. government approved the sale of meat and milk from cloned animals. Many farmers and ranchers hope that cloning technology will allow them to duplicate the best qualities of prize animals without the time and complications of traditional breeding.

In Your Notebook *Describe the ways in which GM organisms can benefit agriculture and industry.*

FIGURE 15–14 Antibacterial Goat Milk Scientists are working to combine a gene for lysozyme—an antibacterial protein found in human tears and breast milk—into the DNA of goats. Milk from these goats may help prevent infections in young children who drink it. **Apply Concepts** *What action do scientists hope the lysozyme gene will take in genetically modified goats?*

FIGURE 15–15 Vitamin-Rich Rice
Golden rice is a GM plant that contains increased amounts of provitamin A, or beta-carotene. Two genes engineered into the rice genome help the grains produce and accumulate beta-carotene. The intensity of the golden color indicates the concentration of beta-carotene in the edible part of the rice seed.

Health and Medicine

🔑 *How can recombinant-DNA technology improve human health?*

Biotechnology, in its broadest sense, has always been part of medicine. Early physicians extracted substances from plants and animals to cure their patients. Twentieth-century medicine saw the use of vaccination to save countless lives. 🔑 **Today, recombinant-DNA technology is the source of some of the most important and exciting advances in the prevention and treatment of disease.**

Preventing Disease One interesting development in transgenic technology is golden rice, shown in **Figure 15–15.** This rice contains increased amounts of provitamin A, also known as beta-carotene—a nutrient that is essential for human health. Provitamin A deficiencies produce serious medical problems, including infant blindness. There is hope that provitamin A-rich golden rice will help prevent these problems. Other scientists are developing transgenic plants and animals that produce human antibodies to fight disease.

In the future, transgenic animals may provide us with an ample supply of our own proteins. Several laboratories have engineered transgenic sheep and pigs that produce human proteins in their milk, making it easy to collect and refine the proteins. Many of these proteins can be used in disease prevention.

Medical Research Transgenic animals are often used as test subjects in medical research. In particular they can simulate human diseases in which defective genes play a role. Scientists use models based on these simulations to follow the onset and progression of diseases and to construct tests of new drugs that may be useful for treatment. This approach has been used to develop models for disorders like Alzheimer's disease and arthritis.

Treating Disease When recombinant-DNA techniques were developed for bacteria, biologists realized almost immediately that the technology held the promise to do something that had never been done before—to make important proteins that could prolong and even save human lives. For example, human growth hormone, which is used to treat patients suffering from pituitary dwarfism, was once scarce. Human growth hormone is now widely available because it is mass-produced by recombinant bacteria. Other products now made in genetically engineered bacteria include insulin to treat diabetes, blood-clotting factors for hemophiliacs, and potential cancer-fighting molecules such as interleukin-2 and interferon.

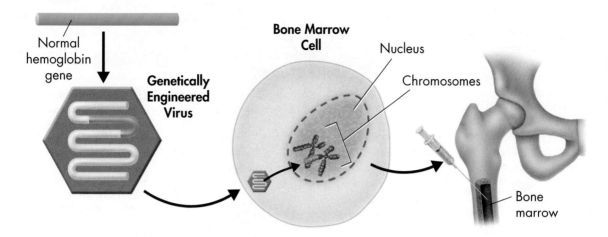

Normal hemoglobin gene

Genetically Engineered Virus

Bone Marrow Cell

Nucleus

Chromosomes

Bone marrow

If an individual is suffering from a missing or defective gene, can we replace that gene with a healthy one and fix the problem? The experimental field of gene therapy is attempting to answer that question. **Gene therapy** is the process of changing a gene to treat a medical disease or disorder. In gene therapy, an absent or faulty gene is replaced by a normal, working gene. This process allows the body to make the protein or enzyme it needs, which eliminates the cause of the disorder.

The idea of using gene therapy to cure disease arose from the major advances in molecular biology made in the past 20 years, including the Human Genome Project. **Figure 15–16** shows one of the ways in which researchers have attempted to carry out gene therapy. To deliver the correct, or therapeutic, gene to the affected, or target, cells, researchers first engineer a virus that cannot reproduce or cause harmful effects. They place DNA containing the therapeutic gene into the modified virus, and then they infect the patient's cells with it. In theory the virus will insert the healthy gene into the target cell and correct the defect. The challenge, however, is to deliver a gene that works correctly over the long term. For all the promise it holds, in most cases gene therapy remains a high-risk experimental procedure. For gene therapy to become an accepted treatment, we need more reliable ways to insert working genes and to ensure that the DNA used in the therapy does no harm.

Genetic Testing If two prospective parents suspect they are carrying the alleles for a genetic disorder such as cystic fibrosis (CF), how could they find out for sure? Because the CF allele has slightly different DNA sequences from its normal counterpart, genetic tests using labeled DNA probes can distinguish it. Like many genetic tests, the CF test uses specific DNA sequences that detect the complementary base sequences found in the disease-causing alleles. Other genetic tests search for changes in cutting sites of restriction enzymes. Some use PCR to detect differences between the lengths of normal and abnormal alleles. Genetic tests are now available for diagnosing hundreds of disorders.

FIGURE 15–16 How Gene Therapy Can Be Used Gene therapy uses normal genes to add to or replace defective genes or to boost a normal function like immunity. *Interpret Visuals How is the virus in this diagram being used?*

FIGURE 15–17 A Brave Volunteer Gene therapy can be risky. In 1999, 18-year-old Jesse Gelsinger volunteered for a gene therapy experiment designed to treat a genetic disorder of his liver. He suffered a massive reaction from the viruses used to carry genes into his liver cells, and he died a few days later. Jesse's case makes clear that experiments with gene therapy must be done with great caution.

❶ Preparing the cDNA Probe

ⓐ mRNA samples are isolated from two different types of cells or tissues, such as cancer cells and normal cells.

 mRNA from cancer cells
 mRNA from normal cells

ⓑ Enzymes are used to prepare complementary DNA molecules (cDNA) from both groups of mRNA. Contrasting fluorescent labels are attached to both groups of cDNA (red to one, green to the other).

 cDNA from cancer cells   cDNA from normal cells

❷ Preparing the Microarray

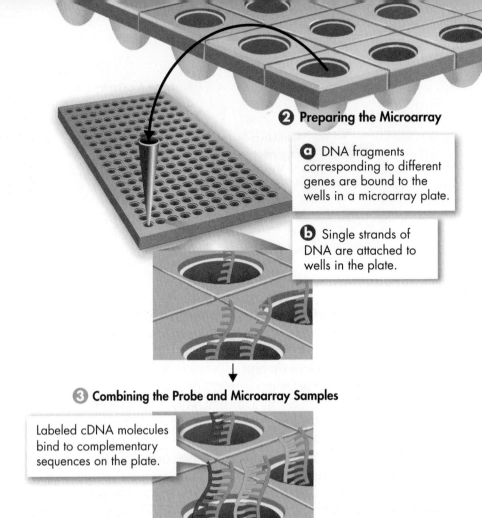

ⓐ DNA fragments corresponding to different genes are bound to the wells in a microarray plate.

ⓑ Single strands of DNA are attached to wells in the plate.

❸ Combining the Probe and Microarray Samples

Labeled cDNA molecules bind to complementary sequences on the plate.

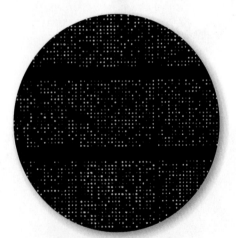

FIGURE 15–18 Analyzing Gene Activity DNA microarrays help researchers explore the underlying genetic causes of many human diseases.

Examining Active Genes Even though all of the cells in the human body contain identical genetic material, the same genes are not active in every cell. By studying which genes are active and which are inactive in different cells, scientists can understand how the cells function normally and what happens when genes don't work as they should. Today, scientists use **DNA microarray** technology to study hundreds or even thousands of genes at once to understand their activity levels. A DNA microarray is a glass slide or silicon chip to which spots of single-stranded DNA have been tightly attached. Typically each spot contains a different DNA fragment. Different colored tags are used to label the source of DNA.

Suppose, for example, that you want to compare the genes abnormally expressed in cancer cells with genes in normal cells from the same tissue. After isolating mRNA from both types of cells, you would use an enzyme to copy the mRNA base sequence into single-stranded DNA labeled with fluorescent colors—red for the cancer cell and green for the normal cell. Next you would mix both samples of labeled DNA together and let them compete for binding to the complementary DNA sequences already in the microarray. If the cancer cell produces more of a particular form of mRNA, then more red-labeled molecules will bind at the spot for that gene, turning it red. Where the normal cell produces more mRNA for another gene, that spot will be green. Where there is no difference between the two cell types, the spot will be yellow because it contains both colors. **Figure 15–18** shows how a DNA microarray is constructed and used.

① Chromosomes contain many regions with repeated DNA sequences that do not code for proteins. These vary from person to person. Here, one sample has 12 repeats between genes A and B, while the second sample has 9 repeats between the same genes.

② Restriction enzymes are used to cut the DNA into fragments containing genes and repeats. Note that the repeat fragments from these two samples are of different lengths.

③ The restriction fragments are separated according to size using gel electrophoresis. The DNA fragments containing repeats are then labeled using radioactive probes. This labeling produces a series of bands—the DNA fingerprint.

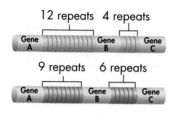

12 repeats   4 repeats

Gene A   Gene B   Gene C

9 repeats   6 repeats

Gene A   Gene B   Gene C

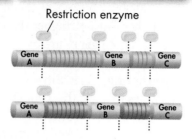

Restriction enzyme

Gene A   Gene B   Gene C

Gene A   Gene B   Gene C

Gel

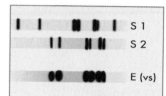

S 1
S 2
E (vs)

DNA fingerprint

Personal Identification

How is DNA used to identify individuals?

The complexity of the human genome ensures that no individual is exactly like any other genetically—except for identical twins, who share the same genome. Molecular biology has used this fact to develop a powerful tool called **DNA fingerprinting** for use in identifying individuals. **DNA fingerprinting analyzes sections of DNA that may have little or no function but that vary widely from one individual to another.** This method is shown in **Figure 15–19.** First, restriction enzymes cut a small sample of human DNA. Next, gel electrophoresis separates the restriction fragments by size. Then, a DNA probe detects the fragments that have highly variable regions, revealing a series of variously sized DNA bands. If enough combinations of enzymes and probes are used, the resulting pattern of bands can be distinguished statistically from that of any other individual in the world. DNA samples can be obtained from blood, sperm, or tissue—even from a hair strand if it has tissue at the root.

Forensic Science DNA fingerprinting has been used in the United States since the late 1980s. Its precision and reliability have revolutionized **forensics**—the scientific study of crime scene evidence. DNA fingerprinting has helped solve crimes, convict criminals, and even overturn wrongful convictions. To date, DNA evidence has saved more than 110 wrongfully convicted prisoners from death sentences.

DNA forensics is used in wildlife conservation as well. African elephants are a highly vulnerable species. Poachers, who slaughter the animals mainly for their precious tusks, have reduced their population dramatically. To stop the ivory trade, African officials now use DNA fingerprinting to identify the herds from which black-market ivory has been taken.

FIGURE 15–19 Identifying Individuals DNA fingerprinting can be used to determine a person's identity. It is especially useful in solving crimes. The diagram above shows how scientists match DNA evidence from a crime scene with two possible suspects. **Interpret Graphics** *Does the DNA fingerprint above match suspect 1 (S1) or suspect 2 (S2)? How can you tell?*

In Your Notebook *Describe the process of DNA fingerprinting.*

MYSTERY CLUE

What kind of evidence do you think investigators collected at the crime scene? What kinds of tests would they have run on this evidence? What would the tests have to show before the suspect was released?

Establishing Relationships In cases of disputed paternity, how does our justice system determine the rightful father of a child? DNA fingerprinting makes it easy to find alleles carried by the child that do not match those of the mother. Any such alleles must come from the child's biological father, and they will show up in his DNA fingerprint. The probability that those alleles will show up in a randomly picked male is less than 1 in 100,000. This means the likelihood that a given male is the child's father must be higher than 99.99 percent to confirm his paternity.

When genes are passed from parent to child, genetic recombination scrambles the molecular markers used for DNA fingerprinting, so ancestry can be difficult to trace. There are two ways to solve this problem. The Y chromosome never undergoes crossing over, and only males carry it. Therefore, Y chromosomes pass directly from father to son with few changes. The same is true of the small DNA molecules found in mitochondria. These are passed, with very few changes, from mother to child in the cytoplasm of the egg cell.

Because mitochondrial DNA (mtDNA) is passed directly from mother to child, your mtDNA is the same as your mother's mtDNA, which is the same as her mother's mtDNA. This means that if two people have an exact match in their mtDNA, then there is a very good chance that they share a common maternal ancestor. Y-chromosome analysis has been used in the same way and has helped researchers settle longstanding historical questions. One such question—did President Thomas Jefferson father the child of a slave?—may have been answered in 1998. DNA testing showed that descendants of the son of Sally Hemings, a slave on Jefferson's Virginia estate, carried his Y chromosome. This result suggests Jefferson was the child's father, although the Thomas Jefferson Foundation continues to challenge that conclusion.

15.3 Assessment

Review Key Concepts 🔑

1. a. Review Give two practical applications for transgenic plants and two for transgenic animals.

b. Infer What might happen if genetically modified fish were introduced into an aquaculture facility?

2. a. Review Name three uses for recombinant-DNA technology.

b. Apply Concepts Medicines in the body interact with the body's proteins. How might normal variations in your genes affect your response to different medicines?

3. a. Review List the steps in DNA fingerprinting.

b. Infer Why is DNA fingerprinting more accurate if the samples are cut with more than one restriction enzyme?

PRACTICE PROBLEM

4. Using restriction enzymes and gel electrophoresis, write the steps of a protocol in which you test for the allele of a gene that causes a genetic disorder.

Technology & BIOLOGY

Artificial Life?

In 2008, scientists at the J. Craig Venter Institute in Rockville, Maryland, produced a synthetic genome with more than half a million DNA base pairs. It may not be long before artificial cells containing similar genomes can be grown in the laboratory. How? First a complete DNA molecule, containing the minimum set of the genetic information needed to keep a cell alive, is produced in the laboratory. Then, that molecule is inserted into a living cell to replace the cell's DNA. The result is a cell whose genome is entirely synthetic. Scientists hope this technique can help them design cells for specific purposes, like capturing solar energy or manufacturing biofuels.

WRITING
How could ethical and societal factors affect the production of synthetic organisms? If you were a scientist working on the latest breakthroughs, how would you address those issues? Describe your ideas in an essay.

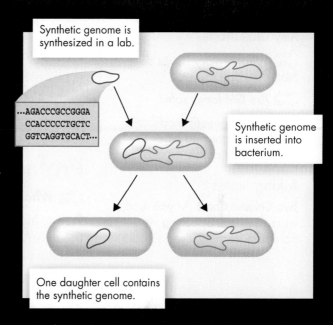

Synthetic genome is synthesized in a lab.

...AGACCCGCCGGGA CCACCCCCTGCTC GGTCAGGTGCACT...

Synthetic genome is inserted into bacterium.

One daughter cell contains the synthetic genome.

▲ Synthesizing a Genome
One way to synthesize life is to replace a cell's genome with an artificial DNA molecule. As a result, cell division may produce a daughter cell containing only the human-made genome.

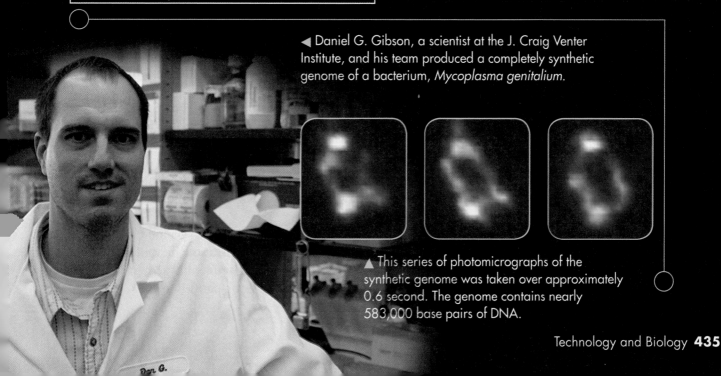

◄ Daniel G. Gibson, a scientist at the J. Craig Venter Institute, and his team produced a completely synthetic genome of a bacterium, *Mycoplasma genitalium*.

▲ This series of photomicrographs of the synthetic genome was taken over approximately 0.6 second. The genome contains nearly 583,000 base pairs of DNA.

15.4 Ethics and Impacts of Biotechnology

Key Questions

🔑 What privacy issues does biotechnology raise?

🔑 Are GM foods safe?

🔑 Should genetic modifications to humans and other organisms be closely regulated?

Taking Notes

Two-Column Chart As you read, write down the opposing viewpoints on each ethical issue.

THINK ABOUT IT Years ago a science fiction movie titled *Gattaca* speculated about a future world in which genetics determines people's ability to get ahead in life. In the movie, schooling, job prospects, and legal rights are rigidly determined by an analysis of the individual's DNA on the day he or she is born. Are we moving closer to this kind of society?

Profits and Privacy

🔑 **What privacy issues does biotechnology raise?**

Private biotechnology and pharmaceutical companies do much of the research involving GM plants and animals. Their goal is largely to develop profitable new crops, drugs, tests, or other products. Like most inventors, they protect their discoveries and innovations with patents. A patent is a legal tool that gives an individual or company the exclusive right to profit from its innovations for a number of years.

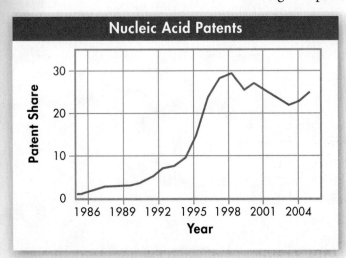

FIGURE 15–20 Patenting Nucleic Acids This graph shows the rise in the number of nucleic-acid patents between 1985 and 2005.

Patenting Life When you think about patents, you probably think about an inventor protecting a new machine or device. But molecules and DNA sequences can be patented, too. In fact, roughly one fifth of the known genes in the human genome are now patented commercially. Even laboratory techniques like PCR have been patented. When a scientist wants to run a PCR test, he or she must pay a fee for the license to use this process.

The ability to patent is meant to spur discovery and advancements in medicine and industry. After all, patent holders stand a good chance of reaping large financial rewards. Sometimes, though, patent holders demand high fees that block other scientists from exploring certain lines of research. That was the case in developing provitamin A-enriched golden rice, a GM plant described in Lesson 15.3. Even after the rice was developed, patent disputes kept it out of the hands of farmers for years.

Now consider the information held in your own genome. 🔑 **Do you have exclusive rights to your DNA? Should you, like patent holders, be able to keep your genetic information confidential?** When it comes to your own DNA, how much privacy are you entitled to?

Genetic Ownership One of the most hallowed sites in the United States is the one shown in **Figure 15–21.** It is the Tomb of the Unknowns in Arlington National Cemetery, near Washington, D.C. Buried here are the remains of unidentified American soldiers who fought our nation's wars. The tomb also serves as a focal point for the honor and remembrance of those service members lost in combat whose bodies have never been recovered.

Biotechnology offers hope that there will never be another unknown soldier. The U.S. military now requires all personnel to give a DNA sample when they begin their service. Those DNA samples are kept on file and used, if needed, to identify the remains of individuals who perish in the line of duty. In many ways, this practice is a comfort to military families, who can be assured that the remains of a loved one can be properly identified for burial.

But what if the government wants to use an individual's DNA sample for another purpose, in a criminal investigation or a paternity suit? What if health-insurance providers manage their healthcare policies based on a genetic predisposition to disease? For example, suppose that, years after giving a DNA sample, an individual is barred from employment or rejected for health insurance because of a genetic defect detected in the sample. Would this be a fair and reasonable use of genetic information?

After considering this issue for years, United States Congress passed the Genetic Information Nondiscrimination Act, which became law in 2008. This act protects Americans against discrimination based on their genetic information. Physicians and ethicists hope this will lead to more effective use of personal genetic information, without fear of prejudice in obtaining health insurance or employment.

Safety of Transgenics

🔑 **Are GM foods safe?**

Much controversy exists concerning foods that have had their DNA altered through genetic engineering. The majority of GM crops today are grown in the United States, although farmers around the world have begun to follow suit. Are the foods from GM crops the same as those prepared from traditionally bred crops?

Pros of GM Foods The companies producing seeds for GM crops would say that GM plants are actually better and safer than other crops. Farmers choose them because they produce higher yields, reducing the amount of land and energy that must be devoted to agriculture and lowering the cost of food for everyone.

Insect-resistant GM plants need little, if any, insecticide to grow successfully, reducing the chance that chemical residues will enter the food supply and lessening damage to the environment. In addition, GM foods have been widely available for more than a decade. 🔑 **Careful studies of such foods have provided no scientific support for concerns about their safety, and it does seem that foods made from GM plants are safe to eat.**

FIGURE 15–21 Unknown Identities The Tomb of the Unknowns in Arlington National Cemetery holds the remains of unknown American soldiers from World Wars I and II, the Korean War, and, until 1998, the Vietnam War. **Form an Opinion** *Should DNA testing be used to identify the remaining soldiers buried here? Why or why not?*

MYSTERY CLUE

What privacy considerations, if any, should investigators have taken into account when obtaining the DNA evidence?

Survey Biotechnology Opinions

❶ Select three safety, legal, or ethical issues related to genetic engineering.

❷ Design a survey to ask people their opinions on these issues.

❸ Find 15 people to answer your survey.

❹ Collect the surveys and tabulate the answers.

Analyze and Conclude

1. Analyze Data Did all respondents agree on any issue? If so, which one(s)?

2. Draw Conclusions If you had surveyed more people, do you think you would have found more or less agreement in the responses? Why or why not?

3. Evaluate How informed about biotechnology issues were the people you surveyed? If you were a politician or government official, how would you act on the results of your survey?

Cons of GM Foods Critics acknowledge some benefits of genetically modified foods, but they also point out that no long-term studies have been made of the hazards these foods might present. 🔑 **Even if GM food itself presents no hazards, there are many serious concerns about the unintended consequences that a shift to GM farming and ranching may have on agriculture.** Some worry that the insect resistance engineered into GM plants may threaten beneficial insects, killing them as well as crop pests. Others express concerns that use of plants resistant to chemical herbicides may lead to overuse of these weed-killing compounds.

Another concern is that the patents held on GM seeds by the companies that produce them may prove costly enough to force small farmers out of business, especially in the developing world. It is not clear whether any of these concerns should block the wider use of these new biotechnologies, but it is certain that they will continue to prove controversial in the years ahead.

In the United States, current federal regulations treat GM foods and non-GM foods equally. As a result, GM foods are not required to undergo special safety testing before entering the market. No additional labeling is required to identify a product as genetically modified unless its ingredients are significantly different from its conventional counterpart. The possibility that meat from GM animals may soon enter the food supply has heightened concerns about labeling. As a result, some states have begun to consider legislation to require the labeling of GM foods, thereby providing consumers with an informed choice.

In Your Notebook *List the pros and cons of GM foods.*

Ethics of the New Biology

 Should genetic modifications to humans and other organisms be closely regulated?

"Know yourself." The ancient Greeks carved this good advice in stone, and it has been guiding human behavior ever since. Biotechnology has given us the ability to know ourselves more and more. With this knowledge, however, comes responsibility.

You've seen how easy it is to move genes from one organism to another. For example, the GFP gene can be extracted from a jellyfish and spliced onto genes coding for important cellular proteins. This ability has led to significant new discoveries about how cells function.

The same GFP technology was used to create the fluorescent zebra fish shown in **Figure 15–22.** These fish—along with fluorescent mice, tadpoles, rabbits, and even cats—have all contributed to our understanding of cells and proteins. But the ability to alter life forms for any purpose, scientific or nonscientific, raises important questions. 🔑 **Just because we have the technology to modify an organism's characteristics, are we justified in doing so?**

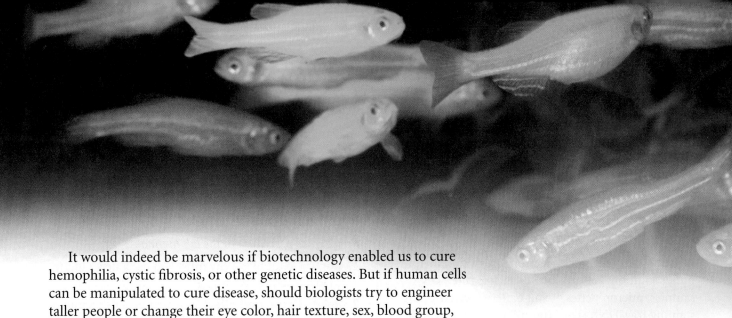

It would indeed be marvelous if biotechnology enabled us to cure hemophilia, cystic fibrosis, or other genetic diseases. But if human cells can be manipulated to cure disease, should biologists try to engineer taller people or change their eye color, hair texture, sex, blood group, or appearance? What will happen to the human species when we gain the opportunity to design our bodies or those of our children? What will be the consequences if biologists develop the ability to clone human beings by making identical copies of their cells? These are questions with which society must come to grips.

The goal of biology is to gain a better understanding of the nature of life. As our knowledge increases, however, so does our ability to manipulate the genetics of living things, including ourselves. In a democratic nation, all citizens—not just scientists—are responsible for ensuring that the tools science has given us are used wisely. This means that you should be prepared to help develop a thoughtful and ethical consensus of what should and should not be done with the human genome. To do anything less would be to lose control of two of our most precious gifts: our intellect and our humanity.

FIGURE 15–22 Gaining More Understanding These fluorescent zebra fish were originally bred to help scientists detect environmental pollutants. Today, studying fluorescent fish is helping us understand cancer and other diseases. The fish are also sold to the public at a profit.

15.4 Assessment

Review Key Concepts 🔑

1. a. Review What is a patent?

   b. Apply Concepts How could biotechnology affect your privacy?

2. a. Review What are genetically modified foods?

   b. Form an Opinion Should a vegetarian be concerned about eating a GM plant that contains DNA from a pig gene? Support your answer with details from the text.

3. a. Review What are the main concerns about genetic engineering discussed in this lesson or elsewhere in the chapter?

   b. Pose Questions Write three specific questions about the ethical, social, or legal implications of genetic engineering that do not appear in this lesson. For example, how does personal genetic information affect self-identity?

WRITE ABOUT SCIENCE

Persuasion

4. Biologists may one day be able to use genetic engineering to alter a child's inherited traits. Under what circumstances, if any, should this ability be used? Write a persuasive paragraph expressing your opinion.

Pre-Lab: Using DNA to Solve Crimes

Problem How can DNA samples be used to connect a suspect to a crime scene?

Materials gel block, electrophoresis chamber, buffer solution, 250-mL beaker, metric ruler, DNA samples, micropipettes, 9-volt batteries, electric cords, staining tray, DNA stain, 100-mL graduated cylinder, clock or timer

Lab Manual Chapter 15 Lab

Skills Focus Measure, Compare and Contrast, Draw Conclusions

Connect to the **Big idea** Scientists who worked on the Human Genome Project had to develop methods for sequencing and identifying genes. Those methods have since been used for many other applications. For example, genetically altered bacteria are used to produce large amounts of life-saving drugs. Another example is the use of DNA evidence to solve crimes. In this lab, you will prepare and compare DNA "fingerprints," or profiles.

Background Questions

a. Review What characteristic of the human genome makes DNA a powerful tool for solving crimes?

b. Review What do the segments of DNA that are used to make DNA profiles have in common?

c. Apply Concepts When forensic scientists want to determine whether two DNA samples come from the same person, they analyze more than one section of DNA. Why would the results be less reliable if the scientists compared only one section of DNA?

Pre-Lab Questions

Preview the procedure in the lab manual.

1. **Control Variables** Why must you use a new pipette to load each DNA sample?

2. **Relate Cause and Effect** Why will the DNA samples separate into bands as they move through the gel?

3. **Infer** Why is purple tracking dye added to the DNA samples?

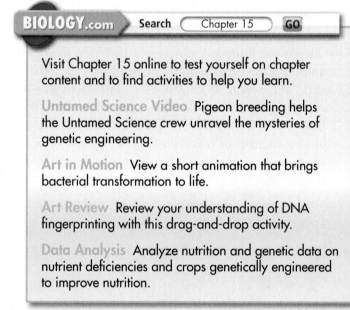

BIOLOGY.com Search (Chapter 15) GO

Visit Chapter 15 online to test yourself on chapter content and to find activities to help you learn.

Untamed Science Video Pigeon breeding helps the Untamed Science crew unravel the mysteries of genetic engineering.

Art in Motion View a short animation that brings bacterial transformation to life.

Art Review Review your understanding of DNA fingerprinting with this drag-and-drop activity.

Data Analysis Analyze nutrition and genetic data on nutrient deficiencies and crops genetically engineered to improve nutrition.

15 Study Guide

Big idea ▶ Science as a Way of Knowing

Genetic engineering allows scientists to manipulate the genomes of living things. Scientists can use bacteria to insert the DNA of one organism into another organism. Recombinant DNA has applications for agriculture, industry, medicine, and forensics. At the same time, there are ethical, legal, safety, and social issues surrounding the use of genetic engineering.

15.1 Selective Breeding

🔑 Humans use selective breeding, which takes advantage of naturally occurring genetic variation, to pass wanted traits on to the next generation of organisms.

🔑 Breeders can increase the genetic variation in a population by introducing mutations, which are the ultimate source of biological diversity.

selective breeding (418)   inbreeding (419)
hybridization (419)   biotechnology (419)

15.2 Recombinant DNA

🔑 The first step in using the polymerase chain reaction method to copy a gene is to heat a piece of DNA, which separates its two strands. Then, as the DNA cools, primers bind to the single strands. Next, DNA polymerase starts copying the region between the primers. These copies can serve as templates to make still more copies.

🔑 Recombinant-DNA technology—joining together DNA from two or more sources—makes it possible to change the genetic composition of living organisms.

🔑 Transgenic organisms can be produced by the insertion of recombinant DNA into the genome of a host organism.

polymerase chain   genetic marker (425)
  reaction (423)   transgenic (426)
recombinant DNA (424)   clone (427)
plasmid (424)

15.3 Applications of Genetic Engineering

🔑 Ideally, genetic modification could lead to better, less expensive, and more nutritious food as well as less-harmful manufacturing processes.

🔑 Recombinant-DNA technology is advancing the prevention and treatment of disease.

🔑 DNA fingerprinting analyzes sections of DNA that vary widely from one individual to another.

gene therapy (431)   DNA fingerprinting (433)
DNA microarray (432)   forensics (433)

15.4 Ethics and Impacts of Biotechnology

🔑 Should you, like patent holders, be able to keep your genetic information confidential?

🔑 Careful studies of GM foods have provided no scientific support for concerns about their safety.

🔑 There are many concerns about unintended consequences that a shift to GM farming and ranching may have on agriculture.

🔑 Just because we have the technology to modify an organism's characteristics, are we justified in doing so?

Think Visually
Complete the following concept map.

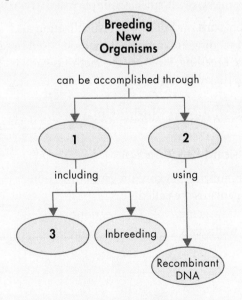

15 Assessment

Understand Key Concepts

1. Crossing dissimilar individuals to bring together their best characteristics is called
a. domestication.   **c.** hybridization.
b. inbreeding.   **d.** polyploidy.

2. Crossing individuals with similar characteristics so that those characteristics will appear in their offspring is called
a. inbreeding.   **c.** recombination.
b. hybridization.   **d.** polyploidy.

3. Taking advantage of naturally occurring variations in organisms to pass wanted traits on to future generations is called
a. selective breeding. **c.** hybridization.
b. inbreeding.   **d.** mutation.

4. How do breeders produce genetic variations that are not found in nature?

5. What is polyploidy? When is this condition useful?

Think Critically

6. **Propose a Solution** Suppose a plant breeder has a thornless rose bush with scentless pink flowers, a thorny rose bush with sweet-smelling yellow flowers, and a thorny rose bush with scentless purple flowers. How might this breeder develop a pure variety of thornless, sweet-smelling purple roses?

7. **Compare and Contrast** Hybridization and inbreeding are important methods used in selective breeding. How are the methods similar? How are they different?

Understand Key Concepts

8. Organisms that contain genes from other organisms are called
a. transgenic.   **c.** donors.
b. mutagenic.   **d.** clones.

9. What process is shown below?
a. cloning
b. transformation
c. hybridization
d. polymerase chain reaction

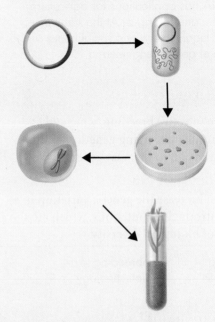

10. When cell transformation is successful, the recombinant DNA
a. undergoes mutation.
b. is treated with antibiotics.
c. becomes part of the transformed cell's genome.
d. becomes a nucleus.

11. Bacteria often contain small circular molecules of DNA known as
a. clones.   **c.** plasmids.
b. chromosomes.   **d.** hybrids.

12. A member of a population of genetically identical cells produced from a single cell is a
a. clone.   **c.** mutant.
b. plasmid.   **d.** sequence.

13. Describe what happens during a polymerase chain reaction.

14. Explain what genetic markers are and describe how scientists use them.

15. How does a transgenic plant differ from a hybrid plant?

Think Critically

16. Apply Concepts Describe one or more advantages of producing insulin and other proteins through genetic engineering.

17. Apply Concepts Bacteria and human beings are very different organisms. Why is it sometimes possible to combine their DNA and use a bacterium to make a human protein?

15.3 Applications of Genetic Engineering

Understand Key Concepts

18. Which of the following characteristics is often genetically engineered into crop plants?
 a. improved flavor
 b. resistance to herbicides
 c. shorter ripening times
 d. thicker stems

19. A substance that has been genetically engineered into transgenic rice has the potential to treat
 a. cancer.
 b. high blood pressure.
 c. vitamin A deficiency.
 d. malaria.

20. Physicians can screen for a genetic disorder using
 a. a DNA microarray.
 b. PCR.
 c. restriction enzyme analysis.
 d. DNA sequencing.

21. Describe how a DNA microarray might be used to distinguish normal cells from cancer cells.

22. Describe two important uses for DNA fingerprinting.

Think Critically

23. Infer If a human patient's bone marrow was removed, altered genetically, and reimplanted, would the change be passed on to the patient's children? Explain your answer.

solve the CHAPTER MYSTERY

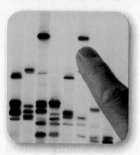

A CASE OF MISTAKEN IDENTITY

The first suspect was lucky: Twenty years earlier, it would have been an open-and-shut case. But by 1998, DNA fingerprinting was widely available. After the police took the suspect into custody, forensic scientists tested the DNA in the bloodstains on his shirt. Within a few hours, they knew they had the wrong suspect. Before long, the police caught the real attacker, who was subsequently tried and convicted of the crime.

1. Infer How did the investigators determine that the person they took into custody was not guilty of this crime?

2. Apply Concepts Did the DNA evidence from the bloodstains come from the red blood cells, the white blood cells, or both? Explain your answer.

3. Predict What if the initial suspect was related to the victim? Would that have changed the result? Why or why not?

4. Connect to the **Big idea** What might have happened if this crime were committed before DNA fingerprinting was discovered? Describe the series of events that might have taken place after police took in the first suspect.

Understand Key Concepts

24. The right to profit from a new genetic technology is protected by
   a. getting a copyright for the method.
   b. discovering a new gene.
   c. obtaining a patent.
   d. publishing its description in a journal.

25. Which of the following is most likely to be used in a court case to determine who the father of a particular child is?
   a. microarray analysis
   b. DNA fingerprinting
   c. gene therapy
   d. genetic engineering

26. Give an example of a disadvantage associated with patenting genes.

27. What is one argument used by critics of genetically modified foods?

Think Critically

28. Predict List three ways in which genetically engineered organisms might be used in the future.

29. Evaluate Your friend suggests that genetic engineering makes it possible for biologists to produce an organism with any combination of characteristics—an animal with the body of a frog and the wings of a bat, for example. Do you think this is a reasonable statement? Explain your answer.

Connecting Concepts

Use Science Graphics

Use the table below to answer question 30.

DNA Restriction Enzymes	
Enzyme	**Recognition Sequence**
*Bgl*III	A↓G A T C T T C T A G↑A
*Eco*RI	G↓A A T T C C T T A A↑G
*Hind*III	A↓A G C T T T T C G A↑A

30. Apply Concepts Copy the following DNA sequence and write its complementary strand.

ATGAGATCTACGGAATTCTCAAGCTTGAATCG

Where will each restriction enzyme in the table cut the DNA strand?

Write About Science

31. Explanation Your local newspaper has published an editorial against using genetic modification. It asserts that GM is still too new, and traditional selective breeding can accomplish the same things as GM. Write a letter to the editor supporting or opposing this position.

32. Assess the **Big idea** Briefly describe the major steps involved in inserting a human gene into a bacterium.

Analyzing Data

Questions 33–35 refer to the diagram, which shows the results of a criminal laboratory test.

33. Infer Briefly describe the biotechnological methods that would have been used to produce the results shown at the right.

34. Compare and Contrast How are the bands from the jeans and the shirt similar? How are they different?

35. Draw Conclusions Based on the results shown, what conclusions might a prosecutor present to a jury during a criminal trial?

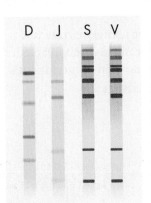

D = Defendant's blood

J = Blood from defendant's jeans

S = Blood from defendant's shirt

V = Victim's blood

Standardized Test Prep

Multiple Choice

1. Polyploidy may instantly produce new types of organisms that are larger and stronger than their diploid relatives in
   A animals.
   B plants.
   C bacteria.
   D fungi.

2. Which of the following characteristics does NOT apply to a plasmid?
   A made of DNA
   B found in bacterial cells
   C has circular loops
   D found in animal cells

3. To separate DNA fragments from one another, scientists use
   A polymerase chain reaction.
   B DNA microarrays.
   C gel electrophoresis.
   D restriction enzymes.

4. Restriction enzymes cut DNA molecules
   A into individual nucleotides.
   B at random locations.
   C at short sequences specific to each type of enzyme.
   D into equal-sized pieces.

5. The expression of thousands of genes at one time can be followed using
   A polymerase chain reaction.
   B plasmid transformation.
   C restriction enzymes.
   D DNA microarrays.

6. Genetically engineered crop plants can benefit farmers by
   A reducing the amount of land that is required to grow them.
   B introducing chemicals into the environment.
   C increasing an animal's resistance to antibiotics.
   D changing the genomes of other crop plants.

7. Genetic markers allow scientists to
   A clone animals.
   B separate strands of DNA.
   C synthesize antibiotics.
   D identify transformed cells.

Questions 8–9

The graph below shows the number of accurate copies of DNA produced by polymerase chain reaction.

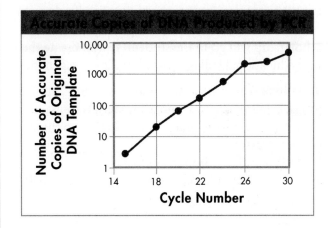

8. What can you conclude about cycles 18 through 26?
   A PCR produced accurate copies of template DNA at an exponential rate.
   B The amount of DNA produced by PCR doubled with each cycle.
   C The DNA copies produced by PCR were not accurate copies of the original DNA template.
   D The rate at which PCR produced accurate copies of template DNA fell in later cycles.

9. Based on the graph, which of the following might have happened between cycles 26 and 28?
   A PCR stopped producing accurate copies of the template.
   B The rate of reaction increased.
   C All of the template DNA was used up.
   D A mutation occurred.

Open-Ended Response

10. Why are bacteria able to make human proteins when a human gene is inserted in them with a plasmid?

If You Have Trouble With . . .

Question	1	2	3	4	5	6	7	8	9	10
See Lesson	15.1	15.2	15.2	15.2	15.3	15.4	15.2	15.2	15.2	15.3

Unit Project

Genetics Collage

Genetics is a fascinating field of study and is becoming increasingly important to society. A local genetics laboratory in your town wants to increase public awareness of the importance of genetics. To do so, it has decided to hold a scholarship competition. The scholarship will go to the student(s) who create the best educational collage related to topics in genetics.

Your Task Using magazine and newspaper clippings, Internet sources, and art materials to make a colorful collage. The images should relate to three central questions.

1) Why is DNA important to a cell?
2) Why is DNA important to you, as a human being?
3) Why is DNA important to society as a whole?

Be sure to
- communicate answers to the above questions in the images, words and phrases you choose.
- carefully design your collage so that it is clear and organized.

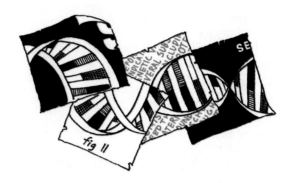

Reflection Questions

1. Score your collage using the rubric below. What score did you give yourself?
2. What did you do well in this project?
3. What about your collage needs improvement?
4. What could a person who didn't know much about DNA learn from your collage?

Assessment Rubric

Score	Scientific Content	Quality of Collage
4	Collage includes many important and thoughtful images related to the three central questions. Student demonstrates a deep understanding of genetics topics.	The collage is clear, organized, and creative.
3	Collage includes important images related to the three central questions. Student demonstrates an adequate understanding of genetics topics.	The collage is well designed and organized.
2	Collage is missing some important ideas and/or includes several insignificant ideas. Student demonstrates a limited level of understanding of genetics topics.	The collage could be better designed and organized.
1	Collage is missing several important ideas. Student demonstrates significant misunderstandings.	The collage is unclear and lacks a solid design.

Evolution

Chapters

16 Darwin's Theory of Evolution

17 Evolution of Populations

18 Classification

19 History of Life

INTRODUCE the
Big ideas

- **Evolution**
- **Unity and Diversity of Life**

"Darwin's theory of evolution by natural selection is often called 'the most important scientific idea that anyone has ever had.' Evolutionary theory provides the best scientific explanation for the unity and diversity of life. It unites all living things in a single tree of life and reminds us that humans are part of nature. As researchers explore evolutionary mysteries, they continue to marvel at Darwin's genius and his grand vision of the natural world."

Joe Levine

16 Darwin's Theory of Evolution

INSIDE:

- 16.1 Darwin's Voyage of Discovery
- 16.2 Ideas That Shaped Darwin's Thinking
- 16.3 Darwin Presents His Case
- 16.4 Evidence of Evolution

These Cuban tree snails show the variation that can exist within a species. That variation provides the raw material for evolution.

CHAPTER MYSTERY

SUCH VARIED HONEYCREEPERS

The misty rain forests on the Hawaiian island of Kauai are home to birds found nowhere else on Earth. Hiking at dawn, you hear them before you see them. Their songs fill the air with beautiful music. Then you spot a brilliant red bird with black wings called an 'i'iwi. As you watch, it uses its long, curved beak to probe for nectar deep in the flowers of 'ohi'a trees.

The 'i'iwi is just one of a number of species of Hawaiian honeycreepers, all of which are related to finches. Various honeycreeper species feed on nectar, insects, seeds, or fruits. Many Hawaiian honeycreepers, however, feed only on the seeds or nectar of unique Hawaiian plants.

How did all these birds get to Hawaii? How did some of them come to have such specialized diets? As you read the chapter, look for clues that help explain the number and diversity of Hawaiian honeycreepers. Then, solve the mystery.

Never Stop Exploring Your World.
Finding the solution to the honeycreepers mystery is only the beginning. Take a video field trip to Hawaii with the ecogeeks of Untamed Science to see where the mystery leads.

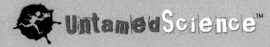

- Untamed Science Video   • Chapter Mystery

16.1 Darwin's Voyage of Discovery

Key Questions

🔑 **What was Charles Darwin's contribution to science?**

🔑 **What three patterns of biodiversity did Darwin note?**

Vocabulary
evolution
fossil

Taking Notes

Preview Visuals Before you read, look at **Figure 16–1.** Briefly summarize the route the *Beagle* took.

BUILD Vocabulary

RELATED WORD FORMS In biology, the noun **evolution** means "the process by which organisms have changed over time." The verb *evolve* means "to change over time."

THINK ABOUT IT If you'd met young Charles Darwin, you probably wouldn't have guessed that his ideas would change the way we look at the world. As a boy, Darwin wasn't a star student. He preferred bird-watching and reading for pleasure to studying. His father once complained, "You will be a disgrace to yourself and all your family." Yet Charles would one day come up with one of the most important scientific theories of all time—becoming far from the disgrace his father feared he would be.

Darwin's Epic Journey

🔑 **What was Charles Darwin's contribution to science?**

Charles Darwin was born in England on February 12, 1809—the same day as Abraham Lincoln. He grew up at a time when the scientific view of the natural world was shifting dramatically. Geologists were suggesting that Earth was ancient and had changed over time. Biologists were suggesting that life on Earth had also changed. The process of change over time is called **evolution.** 🔑 **Darwin developed a scientific theory of biological evolution that explains how modern organisms evolved over long periods of time through descent from common ancestors.**

Darwin's journey began in 1831, when he was invited to sail on the HMS *Beagle*'s five-year voyage along the route shown in **Figure 16–1.** The captain and his crew would be mapping the coastline of South America. Darwin planned to collect specimens of plants and animals. No one knew it, but this would be one of the most important scientific voyages in history. Why? Because the *Beagle* trip led Darwin to develop what has been called the single best idea anyone has ever had.

If you think evolution is just about explaining life's ancient history, you might wonder why it's so important. But Darwin's work offers vital insights into today's world by showing how the living world is constantly changing. That perspective helps us understand modern phenomena like drug-resistant bacteria and newly emerging diseases like avian flu.

In Your Notebook *Using what you know about ecology, explain how the ideas of a changing Earth and evolving life forms might be related.*

Observations Aboard the *Beagle*

🔑 **What three patterns of biodiversity did Darwin note?**

A collector of bugs and shells in his youth, Darwin had always been fascinated by biological diversity. On his voyage, the variety and number of different organisms he encountered dazzled him. In a single day's trip into the Brazilian forest, he collected 68 species of beetles, and he wasn't particularly looking for beetles!

Darwin filled his notebooks with observations about the characteristics and habitats of the different species he saw. But Darwin wasn't content just to describe biological diversity. He wanted to explain it in a scientific way. He kept his eyes and mind open to larger patterns into which his observations might fit. As he traveled, Darwin noticed three distinctive patterns of biological diversity: (1) Species vary globally, (2) species vary locally, and (3) species vary over time.

Species Vary Globally Darwin visited a wide range of habitats on the continents of South America, Australia, and Africa and recorded his observations. For example, Darwin found flightless, ground-dwelling birds called rheas living in the grasslands of South America. Rheas look and act a lot like ostriches. Yet rheas live only in South America, and ostriches live only in Africa. When Darwin visited Australia's grasslands, he found another large flightless bird, the emu.

🔑 **Darwin noticed that different, yet ecologically similar, animal species inhabited separated, but ecologically similar, habitats around the globe.**

Darwin also noticed that rabbits and other species living in European grasslands were missing from the grasslands of South America and Australia. What's more, Australia's grasslands were home to kangaroos and other animals that were found nowhere else. What did these patterns of geographic distribution mean? Why did different flightless birds live in similar grasslands across South America, Australia, and Africa, but not in the Northern Hemisphere? Why weren't there rabbits in Australian habitats that seemed ideal for them? And why didn't kangaroos live in England?

Quick Lab
GUIDED INQUIRY

Darwin's Voyage

❶ Using a world map and **Figure 16–1**, count the number of lines of 10° latitude the *Beagle* crossed.

❷ Using the biome map from Chapter 4 as a reference, identify three different biomes Darwin visited on his voyage.

Analyze and Conclude
1. Infer How did the geography of Darwin's voyage give him far greater exposure to species variability than his fellow scientists back home had?

FIGURE 16–1 Darwin's Voyage
On a five-year voyage aboard the *Beagle*, Charles Darwin visited several continents and many remote islands. **Draw Conclusions** *Why is it significant that many of the stops the Beagle made were in tropical regions?*

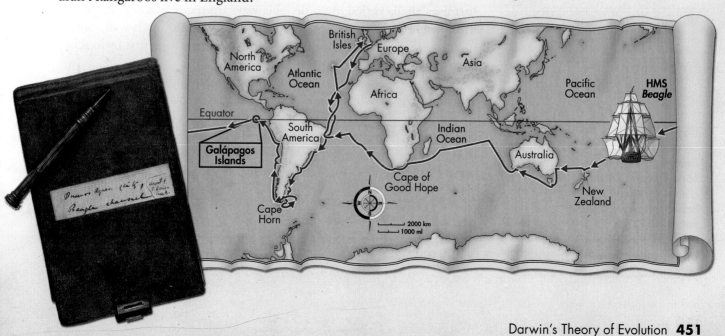

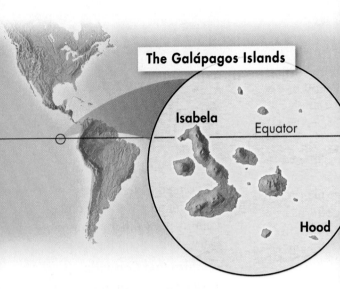

The Galápagos Islands

Isabela

Equator

Hood

Isabela Island Tortoise
Tortoises from Isabela Island have dome-shaped shells and short necks. Vegetation on this island is abundant and close to the ground.

Hood Island Tortoise
The shells of Hood Island tortoises are curved and open around their long necks and legs. This enables them to reach the island's sparse, high vegetation.

FIGURE 16–2 Tortoise Diversity
Among tortoises in the Galápagos Islands, shell shape corresponds to different habitats. Isabela Island has high peaks, is rainy, and has abundant vegetation. Hood Island, in contrast, is flat, dry, and has sparse vegetation.

MYSTERY CLUE

Like the small brown birds on the Galápagos, Hawaiian honeycreepers live on islands with slightly different habitats. How might these varied habitats have affected the evolution of honeycreeper species?

Species Vary Locally There were other puzzles, too. For example, Darwin found two species of rheas living in South America. One lived in Argentina's grasslands and the other in the colder, harsher grass and scrubland to the south. 🔑 **Darwin noticed that different, yet related, animal species often occupied different habitats within a local area.**

Other examples of local variation came from the Galápagos Islands, about 1000 km off the Pacific coast of South America. These islands are close to one another, yet they have different ecological conditions. Several islands were home to distinct forms of giant land tortoises. Darwin saw differences among the tortoises but didn't think much about them. In fact, like other travelers, Darwin ate several tortoises and tossed their remains overboard without studying them closely! Then Darwin learned from the islands' governor that the tortoises' shells varied in predictable ways from one island to another, as shown in **Figure 16–2.** Someone who knew the animals well could identify which island an individual tortoise came from, just by looking at its shell.

Darwin also observed that different islands had different varieties of mockingbirds, all which resembled mockingbirds that Darwin had seen in South America. Darwin also noticed several types of small brown birds on the islands with beaks of different shapes. He thought that some were wrens, some were warblers, and some were blackbirds. He didn't consider these smaller birds to be unusual or important—at first.

Species Vary Over Time In addition to collecting specimens of living species, Darwin also collected **fossils,** which scientists already knew to be the preserved remains or traces of ancient organisms. Some fossils didn't look anything like living organisms, but others did.

Darwin noticed that some fossils of extinct animals were similar to living species. One set of fossils unearthed by Darwin belonged to the long-extinct glyptodont, a giant armored animal. Currently living in the same area was a similar animal, the armadillo. You can see in **Figure 16–3** that the armadillo appears to be a smaller version of the glyptodont. Darwin said of the organisms: "This wonderful relationship in the same continent between the dead and the living, will, I do not doubt, hereafter throw more light on the appearance of organic beings on our earth, and their disappearance from it, than any other class of facts." So, why had glyptodonts disappeared? And why did they resemble armadillos?

Putting the Pieces of the Puzzle Together On the voyage home, Darwin thought about the patterns he'd seen. The plant and animal specimens he sent to experts for identification set the scientific community buzzing. The Galápagos mockingbirds turned out to belong to three separate species found nowhere else! And the little brown birds that Darwin thought were wrens, warblers, and blackbirds were actually all species of finches! They, too, were found nowhere else, though they resembled a South American finch species. The same was true of Galápagos tortoises, marine iguanas, and many plants that Darwin collected on the islands.

Darwin was stunned by these discoveries. He began to wonder whether different Galápagos species might have evolved from South American ancestors. He spent years actively researching and filling notebooks with ideas about species and evolution. The evidence suggested that species are not fixed and that they could change by some natural process.

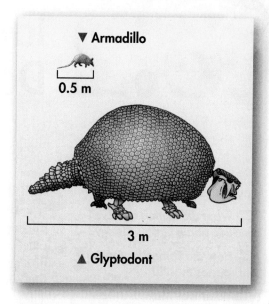

▼ Armadillo

0.5 m

3 m

▲ Glyptodont

FIGURE 16–3 Related Organisms? Despite their obvious differences, Darwin wondered if the armadillo might be related to the ancient glyptodont. **Compare and Contrast** *What similarities and differences do you see between these two animals?*

16.1 Assessment

Review Key Concepts 🔑

1. a. Review What is evolution?

b. Apply Concepts What ideas were changing in the scientific community at the time of Darwin's travels? How might those new ideas have influenced Darwin?

2. a. Review What three kinds of variations among organisms did Darwin observe during the voyage of the *Beagle*?

b. Infer Darwin found fossils of many organisms that did not resemble any living species. How might this finding have affected his understanding of life's diversity?

Apply the Big idea

Interdependence in Nature

3. You have learned that both biotic and abiotic factors affect ecosystems. Give some examples of each, and explain how biotic and abiotic factors could have affected the tortoises that Darwin observed on the Galápagos Islands.

16.2 Ideas That Shaped Darwin's Thinking

Key Questions

🔑 What did Hutton and Lyell conclude about Earth's history?

🔑 How did Lamarck propose that species evolve?

🔑 What was Malthus's view of population growth?

🔑 How is inherited variation used in artificial selection?

Vocabulary

artificial selection

Taking Notes

Outline Make an outline of this lesson using the green headings as main topics and the blue headings as subtopics. As you read, fill in details under each heading.

FIGURE 16–4 Ancient Rocks These rock layers in the Grand Canyon were laid down over millions of years and were then slowly washed away by the river, forming a channel.

THINK ABOUT IT All scientists are influenced by the work of other scientists, and Darwin was no exception. The *Beagle*'s voyage came during one of the most exciting periods in the history of science. Geologists, studying the structure and history of Earth, were making new observations about the forces that shape our planet. Naturalists were investigating connections between organisms and their environments. These and other new ways of thinking about the natural world provided the foundation on which Darwin built his ideas.

An Ancient, Changing Earth

🔑 **What did Hutton and Lyell conclude about Earth's history?**

Many Europeans in Darwin's day believed Earth was only a few thousand years old, and that it hadn't changed much. By Darwin's time, however, the relatively new science of geology was providing evidence to support different ideas about Earth's history. Most famously, geologists James Hutton and Charles Lyell formed important hypotheses based on the work of other researchers and on evidence they uncovered themselves. 🔑 **Hutton and Lyell concluded that Earth is extremely old and that the processes that changed Earth in the past are the same processes that operate in the present.** In 1785, Hutton presented his hypotheses about how geological processes have shaped the Earth. Lyell, who built on the work of Hutton and others, published the first volume of his great work, *Principles of Geology*, in 1830.

Hutton and Geological Change Hutton recognized the connections between a number of geological processes and geological features, like mountains, valleys, and layers of rock that seemed to be bent or folded. Hutton realized, for example, that certain kinds of rocks are formed from molten lava. He also realized that some other kinds of rocks, like those shown in **Figure 16–4,** form very slowly, as sediments build up and are squeezed into layers.

Hutton also proposed that forces beneath Earth's surface can push rock layers upward, tilting or twisting them in the process. Over long periods, those forces can build mountain ranges. Mountains, in turn, can be worn down by rain, wind, heat, and cold. Most of these processes operate very slowly. For these processes to have produced Earth as we know it, Hutton concluded that our planet must be much older than a few thousand years. He introduced a concept called *deep time*—the idea that our planet's history stretches back over a period of time so long that it is difficult for the human mind to imagine—to explain his reasoning.

Lyell's *Principles of Geology* Lyell argued that laws of nature are constant over time and that scientists must explain past events in terms of processes they can observe in the present. This way of thinking, called *uniformitarianism,* holds that the geological processes we see in action today must be the same ones that shaped Earth millions of years ago. Ancient volcanoes released lava and gases, just as volcanoes do now. Ancient rivers slowly dug channels, like the one in **Figure 16–5,** and carved canyons in the past, just as they do today. Lyell's theories, like those of Hutton before him, relied on there being enough time in Earth's history for these changes to take place. Like Hutton, Lyell argued that Earth was much, much older than a few thousand years. Otherwise, how would a river have enough time to carve out a valley?

Darwin had begun to read Lyell's books during the voyage of the *Beagle*, which was lucky. Lyell's work helped Darwin appreciate the significance of an earthquake he witnessed in South America. The quake was so strong that it threw Darwin onto the ground. It also lifted a stretch of rocky shoreline more than 3 meters out of the sea—with mussels and other sea animals clinging to it. Sometime later, Darwin observed fossils of marine animals in mountains thousands of feet above sea level.

Those experiences amazed Darwin and his companions. But only Darwin turned them into a startling scientific insight. He realized that he had seen evidence that Lyell was correct! Geological events like the earthquake, repeated many times over many years, could build South America's Andes Mountains—a few feet at a time. Rocks that had once been beneath the sea could be pushed up into mountains. Darwin asked himself, If Earth can change over time, could life change too?

BUILD Vocabulary

ACADEMIC WORDS The noun **process** means "a series of actions or changes that take place in a definite manner." The processes that shape Earth are the series of geological actions that do things such as build mountains and carve valleys.

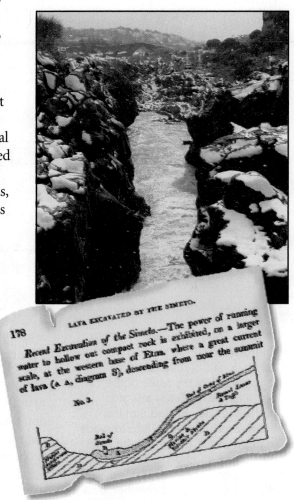

FIGURE 16–5 A woodcut from Lyell's *Principles of Geology* shows geological features near Italy's Mount Etna. Among them is a deep channel, labeled "B," carved into a bed of lava. The channel, shown in the photo, was formed gradually by the movement of water in the Simeto River.

Lamarck's Evolutionary Hypotheses

How did Lamarck propose that species evolve?

Darwin wasn't the first scientist to suggest that characteristics of species could change over time. Throughout the eighteenth century, a growing fossil record supported the idea that life somehow evolved. Ideas differed, however, about just *how* life evolved. The French naturalist Jean-Baptiste Lamarck proposed two of the first hypotheses. **Lamarck suggested that organisms could change during their lifetimes by selectively using or not using various parts of their bodies. He also suggested that individuals could pass these acquired traits on to their offspring, enabling species to change over time.** Lamarck published his ideas in 1809, the year Darwin was born.

Lamarck's Ideas Lamarck proposed that all organisms have an inborn urge to become more complex and perfect. As a result, organisms change and acquire features that help them live more successfully in their environments. He thought that organisms could change the size or shape of their organs by using their bodies in new ways. According to Lamarck, for example, a water bird could have acquired long legs because it began to wade in deeper water looking for food. As the bird tried to stay above the water's surface, its legs would grow a little longer. Structures of individual organisms could also change if they were not used. If a bird stopped using its wings to fly, for example, its wings would become smaller. Traits altered by an individual organism during its life are called *acquired characteristics.*

Lamarck also suggested that a bird that acquired a trait, like longer legs, during its lifetime could pass that trait on to its offspring, a principle referred to as *inheritance of acquired characteristics.* Thus, over a few generations, birds like the one in **Figure 16–6** could evolve longer and longer legs.

FIGURE 16–6 Acquired Characteristics? According to Lamarck, this black-necked stilt's long legs were the result of the bird's innate tendency toward perfection. He claimed that if a water bird needs long legs to wade in deep water, it can acquire them by making an effort to stretch and use its legs in new ways. He also claimed that the bird can then pass the trait on to its offspring.

Evaluating Lamarck's Hypotheses Today, we know that Lamarck's hypotheses were incorrect in several ways. For one thing, organisms don't have an inborn drive to become more perfect. Evolution does not mean that over time a species becomes "better" somehow, and evolution does not progress in a predetermined direction. We now also know that traits acquired by individuals during their lifetime cannot be passed on to offspring. However, Lamarck was one of the first naturalists to suggest that species are not fixed. He was among the first to try to explain evolution scientifically using natural processes. He also recognized that there is a link between an organism's environment and its body structures. So, although Lamarck's explanation of evolutionary change was wrong, his work paved the way for later biologists, including Darwin.

In Your Notebook *Why are Lamarck's ideas called scientific hypotheses and not scientific theories?*

Population Growth

🔑 What was Malthus's view of population growth?

In 1798, English economist Thomas Malthus noted that humans were being born faster than people were dying, causing overcrowding, as shown in **Figure 16–7.** 🔑 **Malthus reasoned that if the human population grew unchecked, there wouldn't be enough living space and food for everyone.** The forces that work against population growth, Malthus suggested, include war, famine, and disease.

Darwin realized that Malthus's reasoning applied even more to other organisms than it did to humans. A maple tree can produce thousands of seeds each summer. One oyster can produce millions of eggs each year. If all the descendants of almost any species survived for several generations, they would overrun the world. Obviously, this doesn't happen. Most offspring die before reaching maturity, and only a few of those that survive manage to reproduce.

Why was this realization so important? Darwin had become convinced that species evolved. But he needed a mechanism—a scientific explanation based on a natural process—to explain how and why evolution occurred. When Darwin realized that most organisms don't survive and reproduce, he wondered which individuals survive … and why.

Artificial Selection

🔑 How is inherited variation used in artificial selection?

To find an explanation for change in nature, Darwin studied change produced by plant and animal breeders. Those breeders knew that individual organisms vary—that some plants bear larger or smaller fruit than average for their species, that some cows give more or less milk than others in their herd. They told Darwin that some of this variation could be passed from parents to offspring and used to improve crops and livestock.

FIGURE 16–7 Overcrowding in London A nineteenth-century engraving shows the crowded conditions in London during Darwin's time. **Relate Cause and Effect** *According to Malthus, what would happen if the population of London continued to grow?*

Quick Lab
GUIDED INQUIRY

Variation in Peppers

❶ Obtain a green, yellow, red, or purple bell pepper.

❷ Slice open the pepper and count the number of seeds it contains.

❸ Compare your data with the data of other students who have peppers of a different color.

Analyze and Conclude

1. Calculate Find the average (mean) number of seeds in your class's peppers. Then determine by how much the number of seeds in each pepper differs from the mean number. **MATH**

2. Pose Questions Think of the kinds of variations among organisms that Darwin observed. If Darwin had seen your data, what questions might he have asked?

FIGURE 16–8 Artificial Selection
Darwin used artificial selection in breeding fancy pigeons at his home outside London.

Farmers would select for breeding only trees that produced the largest fruit or cows that produced the most milk. Over time, this selective breeding would produce more trees with even bigger fruit and cows that gave even more milk. Darwin called this process **artificial selection.** 🔑 **In artificial selection, nature provides the variations, and humans select those they find useful.** Darwin put artificial selection to the test by raising and breeding plants and fancy pigeon varieties, like those in **Figure 16–8.**

Darwin had no idea how heredity worked or what caused heritable variation. But he did know that variation occurs in wild species as well as in domesticated plants and animals. Before Darwin, scientists thought variations among individuals in nature were simply minor defects. Darwin's breakthrough was in recognizing that natural variation was very important because it provided the raw material for evolution. Darwin had all the information he needed. His scientific explanation for evolution was now formed—and when it was published, it would change the way people understood the living world.

16.2 Assessment

Review Key Concepts 🔑

1. a. Review What were Hutton's and Lyell's ideas about the age of Earth and the processes that shape the planet?

b. Apply Concepts How would Hutton and Lyell explain the formation of the Grand Canyon?

2. a. Review What is an acquired characteristic? What role did Lamarck think acquired characteristics played in evolution?

b. Evaluate What parts of Lamarck's hypotheses have been proved wrong? What did Lamarck get right?

3. a. Review According to Malthus, what factors limit human population growth?

b. Draw Conclusions How did Malthus influence Darwin?

4. a. Review What is artificial selection?

b. Infer Could artificial selection occur without inherited variation? Explain your answer.

WRITE ABOUT SCIENCE

Creative Writing

5. Imagine you are Thomas Malthus and the year is 1798. Write a newspaper article that explains your ideas about the impact of a growing population on society and the environment.

 **BIOLOGY**.com 〉 Search 〔 Lesson 16.2 〕 **GO** ● Self-Test ● Lesson Assessment

Biology & HISTORY

Origins of Evolutionary Thought The groundwork for the modern theory of evolution was laid during the 1700s and 1800s. Charles Darwin developed the central idea of evolution by natural selection, but others before and during his lifetime influenced his thinking.

| 1780 | 1790 | 1800 | 1810 | 1820 | 1830 | 1840 | 1850 | 1860 |

1785
▼ **James Hutton**
Hutton proposes that slow-acting geological forces shape the planet. He estimates Earth to be millions—not thousands—of years old.

1809
Jean-Baptiste Lamarck
Lamarck publishes his hypotheses of the inheritance of acquired traits. The ideas are flawed, but he is one of the first to propose a mechanism explaining how organisms change over time. ▼

1830–1833
Charles Lyell ▶
In his *Principles of Geology*, Lyell explains that over long periods, the same processes affecting Earth today have shaped Earth's ancient geological features.

1858
Alfred Russel Wallace
Wallace writes to Darwin, speculating on evolution by natural selection, based on his studies of the distribution of plants and animals.

1798
Thomas Malthus
In his *Essay on the Principle of Population*, Malthus predicts that left unchecked, the human population will grow beyond the space and food needed to sustain it.

1831
Charles Darwin
Darwin sets sail on the HMS *Beagle*, a voyage that will provide him with vast amounts of evidence to support his explanation of how evolution works. ▶

185?
Darwin publish
On the Orig
of Specie

WRITING Use the library or the Internet to find out more about Darwin and Wallace. Then write a dialogue between these two men, in which the conversation shows the similarities in their careers and theories.

16.3 Darwin Presents His Case

Key Questions

🔑 Under what conditions does natural selection occur?

🔑 What does Darwin's mechanism for evolution suggest about living and extinct species?

Vocabulary

adaptation
fitness
natural selection

Taking Notes

Preview Visuals Before you read this lesson, look at **Figure 16–10.** Read the information in the figure, and then write three questions you have about it. As you read, answer your questions.

THINK ABOUT IT Soon after reading Malthus and thinking about artificial selection, Darwin worked out the main points of his theory about natural selection. Most of his scientific friends considered Darwin's arguments to be brilliant, and they urged him to publish them. But although he wrote up a complete draft of his ideas, he put the work aside and didn't publish it for another 20 years. Why? Darwin knew that many scientists, including some of Darwin's own teachers, had ridiculed Lamarck's ideas. Darwin also knew that his own theory was just as radical, so he wanted to gather as much evidence as he could to support his ideas before he made them public.

Then, in 1858, Darwin reviewed an essay by Alfred Russel Wallace, an English naturalist working in Malaysia. Wallace's thoughts about evolution were almost identical to Darwin's! Not wanting to get "scooped," Darwin decided to move forward with his own work. Wallace's essay was presented together with some of Darwin's observations at a scientific meeting in 1858. The next year, Darwin published his first complete work on evolution: *On the Origin of Species.*

Evolution by Natural Selection

🔑 **Under what conditions does natural selection occur?**

Darwin's great contribution was to describe a process in nature—a scientific mechanism—that could operate like artificial selection. In *On the Origin of Species,* he combined his own thoughts with ideas from Malthus and Lamarck.

The Struggle for Existence After reading Malthus, Darwin realized that if more individuals are produced than can survive, members of a population must compete to obtain food, living space, and other limited necessities of life. Darwin described this as *the struggle for existence.* But which individuals come out on top in this struggle?

Variation and Adaptation Here's where individual variation plays a vital role. Darwin knew that individuals have natural variations among their heritable traits. He hypothesized that some of those variants are better suited to life in their environment than others. Members of a predatory species that are faster or have longer claws or sharper teeth can catch more prey. And members of a prey species that are faster or better camouflaged can avoid being caught.

Any heritable characteristic that increases an organism's ability to survive and reproduce in its environment is called an **adaptation.** Adaptations can involve body parts or structures, like a tiger's claws; colors, like those that make camouflage or mimicry possible; or physiological functions, like the way a plant carries out photosynthesis. Many adaptations also involve behaviors, such as the complex avoidance strategies prey species use. Examples of adaptations are shown in **Figure 16–9.**

Survival of the Fittest Darwin, like Lamarck, recognized that there must be a connection between the way an organism "makes a living" and the environment in which it lives. According to Darwin, differences in adaptations affect an individual's fitness. **Fitness** describes how well an organism can survive and reproduce in its environment.

Individuals with adaptations that are well suited to their environment can survive and reproduce and are said to have high fitness. Individuals with characteristics that are not well suited to their environment either die without reproducing or leave few offspring and are said to have low fitness. This difference in rates of survival and reproduction is called *survival of the fittest*. Note that *survival* here means more than just staying alive. In evolutionary terms, *survival* means reproducing and passing adaptations on to the next generation.

In Your Notebook *If an organism produces many offspring, but none of them reach maturity, do you think the organism has high or low fitness? Explain your answer.*

BUILD Vocabulary

RELATED WORD FORMS The verb *inherited* and the adjective *heritable* are related word forms. Inherited traits are passed on to offspring from their parents. They are described as *heritable* (or sometimes *inheritable*) characteristics.

VISUAL SUMMARY

ADAPTATIONS

FIGURE 16–9 Adaptations take many forms.

A. The scarlet king snake (bottom) is exhibiting mimicry—an adaptation in which an organism copies, or mimics, a more dangerous organism. Although the scarlet king snake is harmless, it looks like the poisonous eastern coral snake (top), so predators avoid it, too.

B. A scorpionfish's coloring is an example of camouflage—an adaptation that allows an organism to blend into its background and avoid predation. ▶

C. Adaptations often involve many systems and even behavior. Here, a crane is displaying defensive behavior in an effort to scare off the nearby fox.

NATURAL SELECTION

FIGURE 16-10 This hypothetical population of grasshoppers changes over time as a result of natural selection. **Interpret Visuals** *In the situation shown here, what characteristic is affecting the grasshoppers' fitness?*

❶ The Struggle for Existence Organisms produce more offspring than can survive. Grasshoppers can lay over 200 eggs at a time. Only a small fraction of these offspring survive to reproduce.

❷ Variation and Adaptation There is variation in nature, and certain heritable variations—called adaptations—increase an individual's chance of surviving and reproducing. In this population of grasshoppers, heritable variation includes yellow and green body color. Green coloration is an adaptation: Green grasshoppers blend into their environment and so are less visible to predators.

❸ Survival of the Fittest Because their green color serves to camouflage them from predators, green grasshoppers have a higher fitness than yellow grasshoppers. This means that green grasshoppers survive and reproduce more often than do yellow grasshoppers in this environment.

❹ Natural Selection Green grasshoppers become more common than yellow grasshoppers in this population over time because: (1) more grasshoppers are born than can survive, (2) individuals vary in color and color is a heritable trait, and (3) green individuals have a higher fitness in their current environment.

Natural Selection Darwin named his mechanism for evolution *natural selection* because of its similarities to artificial selection. **Natural selection** is the process by which organisms with variations most suited to their local environment survive and leave more off-spring. In both artificial and natural selection, only certain individuals in a population produce new individuals. But in natural selection, the environment—not a farmer or animal breeder—influences fitness.

When does natural selection occur? 🔑 **Natural selection occurs in any situation in which more individuals are born than can survive (the struggle for existence), there is natural heritable variation (variation and adaptation), and there is variable fitness among individuals (survival of the fittest).** Well-adapted individuals survive and reproduce. From generation to generation, populations continue to change as they become better adapted, or as their environment changes. **Figure 16–10** uses a hypothetical example to show the process of natural selection. Notice that natural selection acts only on inherited traits because those are the only characteristics that parents can pass on to their offspring.

Natural selection does not make organisms "better." Adaptations don't have to be perfect—just good enough to enable an organism to pass its genes to the next generation. Natural selection also doesn't move in a fixed direction. There is no one, perfect way of doing something, as demonstrated by **Figure 16–11.** Natural selection is simply a process that enables species to survive and reproduce in a local environment. If local environmental conditions change, some traits that were once adaptive may no longer be useful, and different traits may become adaptive. And if environmental conditions change faster than a species can adapt to those changes, the species may become extinct. Of course, natural selection is not the only mechanism driving evolution. You will learn about other evolutionary mechanisms in the next chapter.

> *In Your Notebook* Give at least two reasons why the following statement is NOT true: "The goal of natural selection is to produce perfect organisms."

MYSTERY CLUE

How might natural selection explain the history of the Hawaiian honeycreepers?

FIGURE 16–11 No Such Thing as Perfect Many different styles of pollination have evolved among flowering plants. Oak tree flowers (right) are pollinated by wind. Apple tree flowers (left) are pollinated by insects. Neither method is "better" than the other. Both kinds of pollination work well enough for these plants to survive and reproduce in their environments.

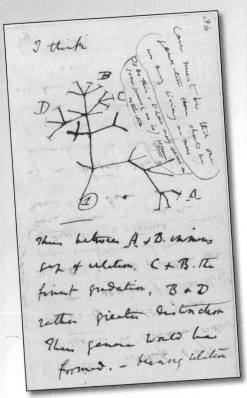

FIGURE 16–12 Descent With Modification This page from one of Darwin's notebooks shows the first evolutionary tree ever drawn. This sketch shows Darwin's explanation for how descent with modification could produce the diversity of life. Note that, just above the tree, Darwin wrote, "I think."

Common Descent

🔑 **What does Darwin's mechanism for evolution suggest about living and extinct species?**

Natural selection depends on the ability of organisms to reproduce, which means to leave descendants. Every organism alive today is descended from parents who survived and reproduced. Those parents descended from their parents, and so forth back through time.

Just as well-adapted individuals in a species survive and reproduce, well-adapted species survive over time. Darwin proposed that, over many generations, adaptation could cause successful species to evolve into new species. He also proposed that living species are descended, with modification, from common ancestors—an idea called *descent with modification.* Notice that this aspect of Darwin's theory implies that life has been on Earth for a very long time—enough time for all this descent with modification to occur! This is Hutton and Lyell's contribution to Darwin's theory: Deep time gave enough time for natural selection to act. For evidence of descent with modification over long periods of time, Darwin pointed to the fossil record.

Darwin based his explanation for the diversity of life on the idea that species change over time. To illustrate this idea, he drew the very first evolutionary tree, shown in **Figure 16–12.** This "tree-thinking" implies that all organisms are related. Look back in time, and you will find common ancestors shared by tigers, panthers, and cheetahs. Look farther back, and you will find ancestors that these felines share with dogs, then horses, and then bats. Farther back still is the common ancestor that all mammals share with birds, alligators, and fish. Far enough back are the common ancestors of all living things. 🔑 **According to the principle of common descent, all species—living and extinct—are descended from ancient common ancestors.** A single "tree of life" links all living things.

16.3 Assessment

Review Key Concepts 🔑

1. a. Review What happens in the process of natural selection?

b. Explain Why do organisms with greater fitness generally leave more offspring than organisms that are less fit?

c. Compare and Contrast How are natural selection and artificial selection similar? How are they different?

2. a. Review Why were Hutton's and Lyell's ideas important to Darwin?

b. Apply Concepts What do evolutionary trees show? What does a tree of life imply about all species living and extinct?

VISUAL THINKING

3. Look at the teeth in the lion's mouth. How is the structure of the lion's teeth an adaptation?

BIOLOGY.com   Search (Lesson 16.3) **GO**   • Self-Test   • Lesson Assessment

16.4 Evidence of Evolution

THINK ABOUT IT Darwin's theory depended on assumptions that involved many scientific fields. Scientists in some fields, including geology, physics, paleontology, chemistry, and embryology, did not have the technology or understanding to test Darwin's assumptions during his lifetime. And other fields, like genetics and molecular biology, didn't exist yet! In the 150 years since Darwin published *On the Origin of Species*, discoveries in all these fields have served as independent tests that could have supported or refuted Darwin's work. Astonishingly, every scientific test has supported Darwin's basic ideas about evolution.

Biogeography

🔑 **How does the geographic distribution of species today relate to their evolutionary history?**

Darwin recognized the importance of patterns in the distribution of life—the subject of the field called biogeography. **Biogeography** is the study of where organisms live now and where they and their ancestors lived in the past. 🔑 **Patterns in the distribution of living and fossil species tell us how modern organisms evolved from their ancestors.** Two biogeographical patterns are significant to Darwin's theory. The first is a pattern in which closely related species differentiate in slightly different climates. The second is a pattern in which very distantly related species develop similarities in similar environments.

Closely Related but Different To Darwin, the biogeography of Galápagos species suggested that populations on the island had evolved from mainland species. Over time, natural selection on the islands produced variations among populations that resulted in different, but closely related, island species.

Distantly Related but Similar On the other hand, similar habitats around the world are often home to animals and plants that are only distantly related. Darwin noted that similar ground-dwelling birds inhabit similar grasslands in Europe, Australia, and Africa. Differences in body structures among those animals provide evidence that they evolved from different ancestors. Similarities among those animals, however, provide evidence that similar selection pressures had caused distantly related species to develop similar adaptations.

Key Questions

🔑 How does the geographic distribution of species today relate to their evolutionary history?

🔑 How do fossils help to document the descent of modern species from ancient ancestors?

🔑 What do homologous structures and similarities in embryonic development suggest about the process of evolutionary change?

🔑 How can molecular biology be used to trace the process of evolution?

🔑 What does recent research on the Galápagos finches show about natural selection?

Vocabulary

biogeography
homologous structure
analogous structure
vestigial structure

Taking Notes

Concept Map Construct a concept map that shows the kinds of evidence that support the theory of evolution.

MYSTERY CLUE

How can biogeography help explain why some species of honeycreepers are found only on the Hawaiian Islands?

The Age of Earth and Fossils

How do fossils help to document the descent of modern species from ancient ancestors?

Two potential difficulties for Darwin's theory involved the age of Earth and gaps in the fossil record. Data collected since Darwin's time have answered those concerns and have provided dramatic support for an evolutionary view of life.

The Age of Earth Evolution takes a long time. If life has evolved, then Earth must be very old. Hutton and Lyell argued that Earth was indeed very old, but technology in their day couldn't determine just how old. Half a century after Darwin published his theory, however, physicists discovered radioactivity. Geologists now use radioactivity to establish the age of certain rocks and fossils. This kind of data could have shown that Earth is young. If that had happened, Darwin's ideas would have been refuted and abandoned. Instead, radioactive dating indicates that Earth is about 4.5 billion years old—plenty of time for evolution by natural selection to take place.

VISUAL SUMMARY

EVIDENCE FROM FOSSILS

FIGURE 16–13 Recently, researchers have found more than 20 related fossils that document the evolution of modern whales from ancestors that walked on land. Several reconstructions based on fossil evidence are shown below in addition to the modern mysticete and odontocete. **Infer** *Which of the animals shown was probably the most recent to live primarily on land?*

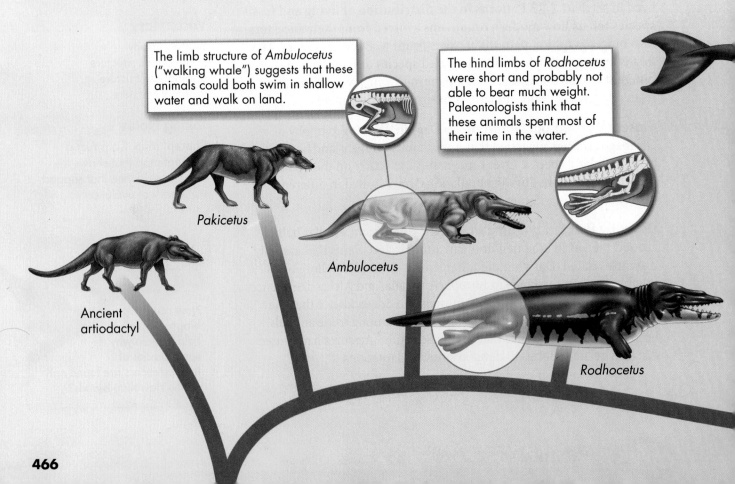

The limb structure of *Ambulocetus* ("walking whale") suggests that these animals could both swim in shallow water and walk on land.

The hind limbs of *Rodhocetus* were short and probably not able to bear much weight. Paleontologists think that these animals spent most of their time in the water.

Pakicetus

Ancient artiodactyl

Ambulocetus

Rodhocetus

Recent Fossil Finds Darwin also struggled with what he called the "imperfection of the geological record." Darwin's study of fossils had convinced him and other scientists that life evolved. But paleontologists in 1859 hadn't found enough fossils of intermediate forms of life to document the evolution of modern species from their ancestors. ☞ **Many recently discovered fossils form series that trace the evolution of modern species from extinct ancestors.**

Since Darwin, paleontologists have discovered hundreds of fossils that document intermediate stages in the evolution of many different groups of modern species. One recently discovered fossil series documents the evolution of whales from ancient land mammals, as shown in **Figure 16–13.** Other recent fossil finds connect the dots between dinosaurs and birds, and between fish and four-legged land animals. In fact, so many intermediate forms have been found that it is often hard to tell where one group begins and another ends. All historical records are incomplete, and the history of life is no exception. The evidence we do have, however, tells an unmistakable story of evolutionary change.

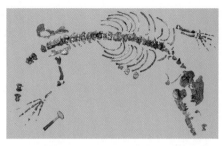

Fossil of the Eocene whale *Ambulocetus natans* (about 49 million years old)

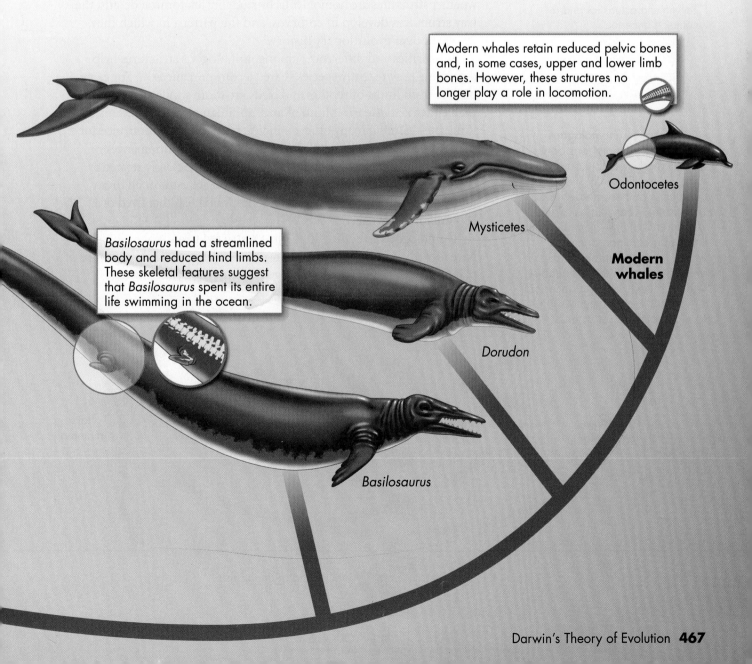

Modern whales retain reduced pelvic bones and, in some cases, upper and lower limb bones. However, these structures no longer play a role in locomotion.

Odontocetes

Mysticetes

Modern whales

Basilosaurus had a streamlined body and reduced hind limbs. These skeletal features suggest that *Basilosaurus* spent its entire life swimming in the ocean.

Dorudon

Basilosaurus

Comparing Anatomy and Embryology

🔑 *What do homologous structures and similarities in embryonic development suggest about the process of evolutionary change?*

By Darwin's time, scientists had noted that all vertebrate limbs had the same basic bone structure, as shown in **Figure 16–14.** Yet, some were used for crawling, some for climbing, some for running, and others for flying. Why should the same basic structures be used over and over again for such different purposes?

Homologous Structures Darwin proposed that animals with similar structures evolved from a common ancestor with a basic version of that structure. Structures that are shared by related species and that have been inherited from a common ancestor are called **homologous structures.** 🔑 **Evolutionary theory explains the existence of homologous structures adapted to different purposes as the result of descent with modification from a common ancestor.** Biologists test whether structures are homologous by studying anatomical details, the way structures develop in embryos, and the pattern in which they appeared over evolutionary history.

Similarities and differences among homologous structures help determine how recently species shared a common ancestor. For example, the front limbs of reptiles and birds are more similar to each other than either is to the front limb of an amphibian or mammal. This similarity—among many others—indicates that the common ancestor of reptiles and birds lived more recently than the common ancestor of reptiles, birds, and mammals. So birds are more closely related to crocodiles than they are to bats! The common ancestor of all these four-limbed animals was an ancient lobe-finned fish that lived over 380 million years ago.

Homologous structures aren't just restricted to animals. Biologists have identified homologies in many other organisms. Certain groups of plants, for example, share homologous stems, roots, and flowers.

BUILD Vocabulary

WORD ORIGINS The word homologous comes from the Greek word *homos*, meaning "same." Homologous structures may not look exactly the same, but they share certain characteristics and a common ancestor.

FIGURE 16–14 Homologous Limb Bones Homologous bones, as indicated by color-coding, support the differently shaped front limbs of these modern vertebrates. These limbs evolved, with modifications, from the front limbs of a common ancestor whose bones resembled those of an ancient fish. If these animals had no recent common ancestor, they would be unlikely to share so many common structures.

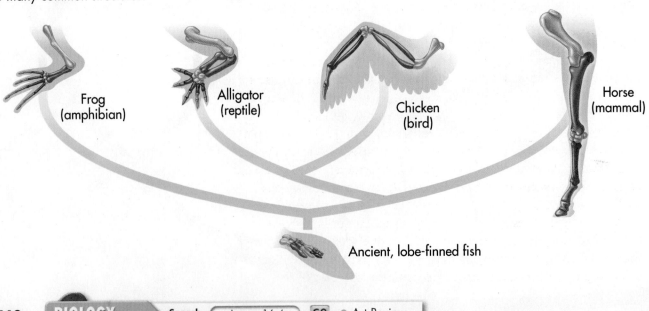

Frog (amphibian)

Alligator (reptile)

Chicken (bird)

Horse (mammal)

Ancient, lobe-finned fish

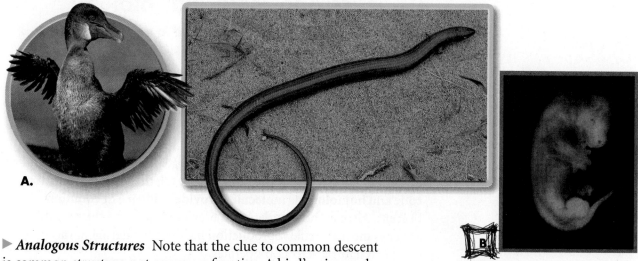

▶ **Analogous Structures** Note that the clue to common descent is common *structure*, not common *function*. A bird's wing and a horse's front limb have different functions but similar structures. Body parts that share common function, but not structure, are called **analogous structures.** The wing of a bee and the wing of a bird are analogous structures.

In Your Notebook *Do you think the shell of a clam and the shell of a lobster are homologous or analogous structures? Explain.*

▶ **Vestigial Structures** Not all homologous structures have important functions. **Vestigial structures** are inherited from ancestors but have lost much or all of their original function due to different selection pressures acting on the descendant. For example, the hipbones of the bottlenose dolphin, shown on page 467, are vestigial structures. In their ancestors, hipbones played a role in terrestrial locomotion. However, as the dolphin lineage adapted to life at sea, this function was lost. Why do dolphins and the organisms in **Figure 16–15** retain structures with little or no function? One possibility is that the presence of the structure does not affect an organism's fitness, and, therefore, natural selection does not act to eliminate it.

Embryology Researchers noticed a long time ago that the early developmental stages of many animals with backbones (called vertebrates) look very similar. Recent observations make clear that the same groups of embryonic cells develop in the same order and in similar patterns to produce many homologous tissues and organs in vertebrates. For example, despite the very different adult shapes and functions of the limb bones in **Figure 16–14,** all those bones develop from the same clumps of embryonic cells. Evolutionary theory offers the most logical explanation for these similarities in patterns of development. ☞ **Similar patterns of embryological development provide further evidence that organisms have descended from a common ancestor.**

Darwin realized that similar patterns of development offer important clues to the ancestry of living organisms. He could not have anticipated, however, the incredible amount of evidence for his theory that would come from studying the genes that control development—evidence from the fields of genetics and molecular biology.

FIGURE 16–15 Vestigial Organs and Embryology
A. The wings of the flightless cormorant and the legs of the Italian three-toed skink are vestigial structures. **B.** Because the early stages of development among vertebrates are so similar, it would take an expert to identify this as an opposum embryo. **Infer** *Looking at the legs of the skink, do you think its ancestors had functioning legs? Explain your answer.*

Genetics and Molecular Biology

How can molecular biology be used to trace the process of evolution?

The most troublesome "missing information" for Darwin had to do with heredity. Darwin had no idea how heredity worked, and he was deeply worried that this lack of knowledge might prove fatal to his theory. As it happens, some of the strongest evidence supporting evolutionary theory comes from genetics. A long series of discoveries, from Mendel to Watson and Crick to genomics, helps explain how evolution works. **At the molecular level, the universal genetic code and homologous molecules provide evidence of common descent.** Also, we now understand how mutation and the reshuffling of genes during sexual reproduction produce the heritable variation on which natural selection operates.

Life's Common Genetic Code One dramatic example of molecular evidence for evolution is so basic that by this point in your study of biology you might take it for granted. All living cells use information coded in DNA and RNA to carry information from one generation to the next and to direct protein synthesis. This genetic code is nearly identical in almost all organisms, including bacteria, yeasts, plants, fungi, and animals. This is powerful evidence that all organisms evolved from common ancestors that shared this code.

Molecular Homology in *Hoxc8*

Molecular homologies can be used to infer relationships among organisms. The diagram below shows a small portion of the DNA for the same gene, *Hoxc8,* in three animals—a mouse, a baleen whale, and a chicken.

1. Calculate What percentage of the nucleotides in the baleen whale's DNA are different from those of the mouse? (*Hint*: First count the number of DNA nucleotides in one entire sequence. Then count the nucleotides in the whale DNA that differ from those in the mouse DNA. Finally, divide the number of nucleotides that are different by the total number of nucleotides, and multiply the result by 100.) MATH

2. Calculate What percentage of the nucleotides in the chicken are different from those of the mouse? MATH

3. Draw Conclusions Do you think a mouse is more closely related to a baleen whale or to a chicken? Explain your answer.

4. Evaluate Do you think that scientists can use small sections of DNA, like the ones shown here, to infer evolutionary relationships? Why or why not?

Animal	Sequence of Bases in Section of *Hoxc8*
Mouse	C A G A A A T G C C A C T T T T A T G G C C C T G T T T G T C T C C C T G C T C
Baleen whale	C **C** G A A A T G C C **T** C T T T T A T G G C **G** C T G T T T G T C T C C C T G C **G** C
Chicken	**A** A **A** A A A T G C C **G** C T T T T A **C A** G C **T** C T G T T T G T C T C T **T** C T G C T **A**

Homologous Molecules In Darwin's day, biologists could only study similarities and differences in structures they could see. But physical body structures can't be used to compare mice with yeasts or bacteria. Today, we know that homology is not limited to physical structures. As shown in **Figure 16–16,** homologous proteins have been found in some surprising places. Homologous proteins share extensive structural and chemical similarities. One homologous protein is cytochrome c, which functions in cellular respiration. Remarkably similar versions of cytochrome c are found in almost all living cells, from cells in baker's yeast to cells in humans.

There are many other kinds of homologies at the molecular level. Genes can be homologous, too, which makes sense given the genetic code that all plants and animals share. One spectacular example is a set of ancient genes that determine the identities of body parts. Known as the Hox genes, they help to determine the head-to-tail axis in embryonic development. In vertebrates, sets of homologous Hox genes direct the growth of front and hind limbs. Small changes in these genes can produce dramatic changes in the structures they control. So, relatively minor changes in an organism's genome can produce major changes in an organism's structure and the structure of its descendants. At least some homologous Hox genes are found in almost all multicellular animals, from fruit flies to humans. Such profound biochemical similarities are best explained by Darwin's conclusion: Living organisms evolved through descent with modification from a common ancestor.

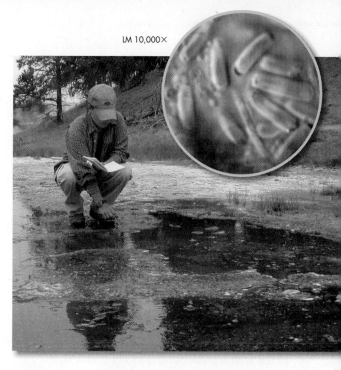

LM 10,000×

FIGURE 16–16 Similar Genes
Bacteria in this hot spring live in near-boiling water—an inhospitable environment to animals. Their cells even look different from animal cells. Yet many of their genes, and therefore the proteins coded by those genes, are similar to those of animals. This is more evidence that all organisms share an ancient common ancestor.

Testing Natural Selection

What does recent research on the Galápagos finches show about natural selection?

One way to gather evidence for evolutionary change is to observe natural selection in action. But most kinds of evolutionary change we've discussed so far took place over millions of years—which makes it tough to see change actually happening. Some kinds of evolutionary change, however, have been observed and studied repeatedly in labs and in controlled outdoor environments. Scientists have designed experiments involving organisms from bacteria to guppies to test Darwin's theories. Each time, the results have supported Darwin's basic ideas. But one of the best examples of natural selection in action comes from observations on animals living in their natural environment. Fittingly, those observations focused on Galápagos finches.

A Testable Hypothesis Remember that when Darwin first saw the Galápagos finches, he thought they were wrens, warblers, and blackbirds because they looked so different from one another. Once Darwin learned that the birds were all finches, he hypothesized that they had descended from a common ancestor.

FINCH BEAK TOOLS

FIGURE 16–17 Finches use their beaks as tools to pick up and handle food. Different types of foods are most easily handled with beaks of different sizes and shapes.

Tree Finches

Platyspiza

This vegetarian finch strips bark from woody plants with a beak designed to grip and hold tightly, like a pair of pliers.

Certhidea

This finch feeds on small, exposed insects that it picks off plant surfaces. Its thin, straight, narrow beak works like needle-nose pliers or forceps to firmly grasp small objects at the tip.

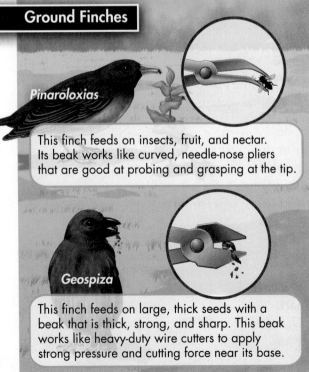

Ground Finches

Pinaroloxias

This finch feeds on insects, fruit, and nectar. Its beak works like curved, needle-nose pliers that are good at probing and grasping at the tip.

Geospiza

This finch feeds on large, thick seeds with a beak that is thick, strong, and sharp. This beak works like heavy-duty wire cutters to apply strong pressure and cutting force near its base.

Darwin noted that several finch species have beaks of very different sizes and shapes. Each species uses its beak like a specialized tool to pick up and handle its food, as shown in **Figure 16–17.** Darwin proposed that natural selection had shaped the beaks of different bird populations as they became adapted to eat different foods. That was a reasonable hypothesis. But was there any way to test it? No one thought there was a way until Peter and Rosemary Grant of Princeton University came along.

The Grants have spent more than 35 years studying Galápagos finches. They realized that Darwin's hypothesis rested on two testable assumptions. First, for beak size and shape to evolve, there must be enough heritable variation in those traits to provide raw material for natural selection. Second, differences in beak size and shape must produce differences in fitness.

The Grants have tested these hypotheses on the medium ground finch (*Geospiza*) on the island of Daphne Major. This island is large enough to support good-sized finch populations, yet small enough to allow the Grants to catch, tag, and identify nearly every bird of the species.

During their study, the Grants periodically recapture the birds. They record which individuals are alive and which have died, which have reproduced and which have not. For each individual, the Grants record anatomical characteristics like wing length, leg length, beak length, beak depth, beak color, feather colors, and total mass. The data the Grants have recorded show that there is indeed great variation of heritable traits among Galápagos finches.

Natural Selection The Grants' data have shown that individual finches with different-size beaks have better or worse chances of surviving both seasonal droughts and longer dry spells. When food becomes scarce during dry periods, birds with the largest beaks are more likely to survive, as shown in **Figure 16–18.** As a result, average beak size in this finch population has increased dramatically. **The Grants have documented that natural selection takes place in wild finch populations frequently, and sometimes rapidly.** Changes in food supply created selection pressure that caused finch populations to evolve within decades. This evolutionary change occurred much faster than many researchers thought possible.

Not only have the Grants documented natural selection in nature, their data also confirm that competition and environmental change drive natural selection. Traits that don't matter much under one set of environmental conditions became adaptive as the environment changes during a drought. **The Grants' work shows that variation within a species increases the likelihood of the species' adapting to and surviving environmental change.** Without heritable variation in beak sizes, the medium ground finch would not be able to adapt to feeding on larger, tougher seeds during a drought.

Evaluating Evolutionary Theory Advances in many fields of biology, along with other sciences, have confirmed and expanded most of Darwin's hypotheses. Today, evolutionary theory—which includes natural selection—offers insights that are vital to all branches of biology, from research on infectious disease to ecology. That's why evolution is often called the grand unifying theory of the life sciences.

Like any scientific theory, evolutionary theory is constantly reviewed as new data are gathered. Researchers still debate important questions such as precisely how new species arise and why species become extinct. And there is also significant uncertainty about exactly how life began. However, any questions that remain are about *how* evolution works—not *whether* evolution occurs. To scientists, evolution is the key to understanding the natural world.

Bird Survival Based on Beak Size

FIGURE 16–18 Survival and Beak Size This graph shows the survival rate of one species of ground finch, the medium ground finch, *Geospiza fortis*, during a drought period. **Interpret Graphs** *What trend does the graph show?*

16.4 Assessment

Review Key Concepts

1. a. Review What is biogeography?
 b. Relate Cause and Effect Why do distantly related species in very different places sometimes share similar traits?

2. a. Review Why are fossils important evidence for evolution?
 b. Interpret Visuals Use **Figure 16–13** to describe how a modern mysticete whale is different from *Ambulocetus*.

3. a. Review How do vestigial structures provide evidence for evolution?
 b. Compare and Contrast Explain the difference between homologous and analogous structures. Which are more important to evolutionary biologists? Why?

4. a. Explain What is the relationship between Hox genes and embryological development?
 b. Draw Conclusions Organisms A and B have very similar Hox genes, and their embryos, in the earliest stages of development, are also very similar. What do these similarities indicate about the ancestry of organisms A and B?

5. a. Explain What hypothesis have the Grants been testing?
 b. Draw Conclusions How do the Grants' data show that genetic variation is important in the survival of a species?

WRITE ABOUT SCIENCE

Explanation

6. In your own words, write a paragraph that explains how evidence since Darwin's time has strengthened his theories.

Pre Lab: Amino Acid Sequences: Indicators of Evolution

Problem How can you use proteins to determine how closely organisms are related?

Materials light-colored highlighting pen; graph paper

Lab Manual Chapter 16 Lab

Skills Analyze Data, Graph, Draw Conclusions

Connect to the Big idea For years, scientists who studied evolution had to rely on only visible differences among organisms. Then a new source of evidence emerged. Biochemists were able to unravel the sequences of bases in DNA and amino acids in proteins. Scientists are able to use these data to confirm relationships based on anatomy. They also use the data to show that some species that appear very different are in fact more closely related than had been thought.

Biologists can compare the sequences of amino acids in a protein for two species. In general, when the total number of differences is small, the species are closely related. When the total number of differences is large, the species are more distantly related.

In this lab, you will compare amino acid sequences for one protein and analyze the results of a similar comparison for another protein. You will use both sets of data to predict relatedness among organisms.

Background Questions

a. Review What are homologous molecules?

b. Explain Why might scientists use molecules instead of anatomy to figure out how closely rabbits and fruit flies are related?

c. Relate Cause and Effect Amino acid sequences in the proteins of two species are similar. What can you conclude about the DNA in those species, and why?

Pre-Lab Questions

Preview the procedure in the lab manual.

1. Predict Based only on their anatomy, rank gorillas, bears, chimpanzees, and mice from most recent common ancestor with humans to least recent.

2. Use Analogies You tell a story to a second person who tells it to a third person, and so on. As the story is retold, changes are introduced. Overtime, the number of changes increases. How is this process an analogy for what happens to DNA over time?

3. Infer Hemoglobin from two species is compared. On the long protein chains, there are three locations where the amino acids are different. Where would you place the common ancestor of the two species on the "tree of life," and why?

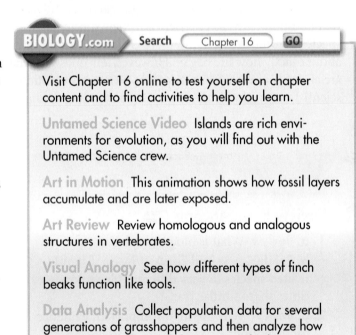

BIOLOGY.com Search Chapter 16 GO

Visit Chapter 16 online to test yourself on chapter content and to find activities to help you learn.

Untamed Science Video Islands are rich environments for evolution, as you will find out with the Untamed Science crew.

Art in Motion This animation shows how fossil layers accumulate and are later exposed.

Art Review Review homologous and analogous structures in vertebrates.

Visual Analogy See how different types of finch beaks function like tools.

Data Analysis Collect population data for several generations of grasshoppers and then analyze how the population changed due to natural selection.

16 Study Guide

Big idea ▶ Evolution

Natural selection is a natural process through which life evolves. It acts on populations whose individuals must struggle for existence and that have both heritable variation in traits and variable fitness among individuals.

16.1 Darwin's Voyage of Discovery

🔑 Darwin developed a scientific theory of biological evolution that explains how modern organisms evolved over long periods of time through descent from common ancestors.

🔑 Darwin noticed that (1) different, yet ecologically similar, animal species inhabited separated, but ecologically similar, habitats around the globe; (2) different, yet related, animal species often occupied different habitats within a local area; and (3) some fossils of extinct animals were similar to living species.

evolution (450)   fossil (452)

16.2 Ideas That Shaped Darwin's Thinking

🔑 Hutton and Lyell concluded that Earth is extremely old and that the processes that changed Earth in the past are the same processes that operate in the present.

🔑 Lamarck suggested that organisms could change during their lifetimes by selectively using or not using various parts of their bodies. He also suggested that individuals could pass these acquired traits on to their offspring, enabling species to change over time.

🔑 Malthus reasoned that if the human population grew unchecked, there wouldn't be enough living space and food for everyone.

🔑 In artificial selection, nature provides the variations, and humans select those they find useful.

artificial selection (458)

16.3 Darwin Presents His Case

🔑 Natural selection occurs in any situation in which more individuals are born than can survive, there is natural heritable variation, and there is variable fitness among individuals.

🔑 According to the principle of common descent, all species—living and extinct—are descended from ancient common ancestors.

adaptation (461)   natural selection (463)
fitness (461)

16.4 Evidence of Evolution

🔑 Patterns in the distribution of living and fossil species tell us how modern organisms evolved from their ancestors.

🔑 Many recently discovered fossils form series that trace the evolution of modern species from extinct ancestors.

🔑 Evolutionary theory explains the existence of homologous structures adapted to different purposes as the result of descent with modification from a common ancestor.

🔑 The universal genetic code and homologous molecules provide evidence of common descent.

🔑 The Grants have documented that natural selection takes place in wild Galápagos finch populations frequently, and sometimes rapidly, and that variation within a species increases the likelihood of the species adapting to and surviving environmental change.

biogeography (465)   analogous structure (469)
homologous   vestigial structure (469)
  structure (468)

Think Visually

Using the information in this chapter, create a concept map that links the following terms: *adaptation, artificial selection, biogeography, camouflage, Charles Darwin, Charles Lyell, evolution, fitness, fossil, homology, James Hutton, Jean-Baptiste Lamarck, mimicry, natural selection,* and *Thomas Malthus.*

Understand Key Concepts

1. Who observed variations in the characteristics of plants and animals on different islands of the Galápagos?
   a. James Hutton
   b. Charles Lyell
   c. Charles Darwin
   d. Thomas Malthus

2. In addition to observing living organisms, Darwin studied the preserved remains of ancient organisms called
   a. fossils.
   b. adaptations.
   c. homologies.
   d. vestigial structures.

3. What pattern of variation did Darwin observe among rheas, ostriches, and emus?

4. What connection did Darwin make between the Galápagos tortoises and their environments?

Think Critically

5. **Apply Concepts** Explain what the term *evolution* means, and give an example.

6. **Relate Cause and Effect** Why was Darwin's trip aboard the *Beagle* so important to his development of the theory of natural selection?

7. **Infer** Why was Darwin puzzled by the fact that there were no rabbits in Australia?

Understand Key Concepts

8. Which of the following ideas proposed by Lamarck was later found to be incorrect?
   a. Acquired characteristics can be inherited.
   b. All species are descended from other species.
   c. Living things change over time.
   d. There is a relationship between an organism and its environment.

9. Which of the following would an animal breeder use to increase the number of cows that give the most milk?
   a. overproduction
   b. genetic isolation
   c. acquired characteristics
   d. artificial selection

10. What accounts for the presence of marine fossils on mountaintops?

11. How did Lyell's *Principles of Geology* influence Darwin?

12. According to Malthus, what factors limit population growth? Why did Malthus's ideas apply to other organisms better than they did to humans?

13. What is artificial selection? How did this concept influence Darwin's thinking?

Think Critically

14. **Relate Cause and Effect** A sunflower produces many seeds. Will all the seeds grow into mature plants? Explain your answer.

15. **Evaluate** Explain why Lamarck made a significant contribution to science even though his explanation of evolution was wrong.

Understand Key Concepts

16. An inherited characteristic that increases an organism's ability to survive and reproduce in its specific environment is called a(n)
    a. vestigial structure.
    b. adaptation.
    c. speciation.
    d. analogous structure.

17. How well an organism survives and reproduces in its environment can be described as its
    a. fitness.
    b. homologies.
    c. common descent.
    d. analogies.

18. How does natural variation affect evolution?

19. Explain the following statement: "Descent with modification explains the diversity of life we see today."

20. Describe the conditions necessary for natural selection to occur.

Think Critically

21. **Apply Concepts** How would Darwin explain the long legs of the water bird in **Figure 16–6**? How would Darwin's explanation differ from Lamarck's explanation?

22. **Compare and Contrast** Distinguish between fitness and adaptation. How are the two concepts related?

23. **Infer** How does the process of natural selection account for the diversity of organisms that Darwin observed on the Galápagos Islands?

24. **Infer** Many species of birds build nests in which they lay eggs and raise the newly hatched birds. How might nest-building behavior be an adaptation that ensures reproductive fitness?

16.4 Evidence of Evolution

Understand Key Concepts

25. Structures that have different mature forms but develop from the same embryonic tissue are called
    a. analogous.   c. homologous.
    b. adaptations.   d. fossils.

26. Intermediate fossil forms are important evidence of evolution because they show
    a. how organisms changed over time.
    b. how animals behaved in their environments.
    c. how the embryos of organisms develop.
    d. molecular homologies.

27. How does the geographic distribution of organisms support the theory of evolution?

28. How do vestigial structures indicate that present-day organisms are different from their ancient ancestors?

29. How do DNA and RNA provide evidence for common descent?

solve the CHAPTER MYSTERY

SUCH VARIED HONEYCREEPERS

The 'i'iwi and other Hawaiian honeycreepers resemble Galápagos finches in a number of ways. They are species of small birds found nowhere else on Earth. They live on islands that are separated from one another by stretches of open sea and that are hundreds of miles from the nearest continent. They are also related to finches!

There are more than 20 known species of Hawaiian honeycreeper. Like the species of Galápagos finches, the honeycreeper species are closely related to one another. This is an indication that they are all descended, with modification, from a relatively recent common ancestor. Experts think the ancestor colonized the islands between 3 million and 4 million years ago. Many honeycreepers have specialized diets, evolutionary adaptations to life on the particular islands they call home. Today, habitat loss is endangering most of the honeycreepers. In fact, many species of honeycreeper are thought to have become extinct since humans settled on the islands.

1. **Infer** Suppose a small group of birds, not unlike the modern honeycreepers, landed on one of Hawaii's islands millions of years ago and then reproduced. Do you think all the descendants would have stayed on that one island? Explain your answer.

2. **Infer** Do you think that the climate and other environmental conditions are exactly the same everywhere on the Hawaiian Islands? How might environmental conditions have affected the evolution of honeycreeper species?

3. **Form a Hypothesis** Explain how the different species of honeycreepers in Hawaii today might have evolved from one ancestral species.

4. **Connect to the** Big idea Why are islands often home to species that exist nowhere else on Earth?

Think Critically

30. **Infer** Which animal—a cricket or a cat—would you expect to have cytochrome c more similar to that of a dog? Explain your answer.

31. **Infer** In all animals with backbones, oxygen is carried in blood by a molecule called hemoglobin. What could this physiological similarity indicate about the evolutionary history of vertebrates (animals with backbones)?

32. **Apply Concepts** Do you think some species of snake might have vestigial hip and leg bones? Explain your answer.

Connecting Concepts

Use Science Graphics

Use the illustration below to answer questions 33 and 34.

33. **Infer** Based on what you can see, which mice—white or brown—are better adapted to their environment? Explain your answer.

34. **Apply Concepts** In what way is the coloring of the brown mice an adaptation? What other adaptations besides coloring might affect the mice's ability to survive and reproduce?

Write About Science

35. **Explanation** Write a paragraph that explains how the age of Earth supports the theory of evolution.

36. **Summary** Summarize the conditions under which natural selection occurs. Then, describe three lines of evidence that support the theory of evolution by natural selection.

37. **Assess the** `Big idea` Write a newspaper article about the meeting at which Darwin's and Wallace's hypotheses of evolution were first presented. Explain the theory of evolution by natural selection for an audience that knows nothing about the subject.

38. **Assess the** `Big idea` Look back at **Figure 16–10** on page 462. Explain how conditions could change so that yellow coloring becomes adaptive. What would happen to the relative numbers of green and yellow grasshoppers in the population?

Analyzing Data

Cytochrome c is a small protein involved in cellular respiration. The table compares the cytochrome c of various organisms to that of chimpanzees. The left column indicates the organism, and the right column indicates the number of amino acids that are different from those in chimpanzee cytochrome c.

Organism	Number of Amino Acids That Are Different From Chimpanzee Cytochrome c
Dog	10
Moth	24
Penguin	11
Yeast	38

39. **Interpret Data** Which of these organisms probably shares the most recent common ancestor with chimpanzees?
    a. dog
    c. penguin
    b. moth
    d. yeast

40. **Calculate** The primary structure of cytochrome c contains 104 amino acids. Approximately how many of these amino acids are the same in the chimpanzee and moth? `MATH`
    a. 10
    c. 80
    b. 24
    d. 128

Standardized Test Prep

Multiple Choice

1. Which scientist formulated the theory of evolution through natural selection?
   - A Charles Darwin
   - B Thomas Malthus
   - C James Hutton
   - D Jean-Baptiste Lamarck

2. Lamarck's ideas about evolution were wrong because he proposed that
   - A species change over time.
   - B species descended from other species.
   - C acquired characteristics can be inherited.
   - D species are adapted to their environments.

3. Lyell's *Principles of Geology* influenced Darwin because it explained how
   - A organisms change over time.
   - B adaptations occur.
   - C the surface of Earth changes over time.
   - D the Galápagos Islands formed.

4. A farmer's use of the best livestock for breeding is an example of
   - A natural selection.
   - B artificial selection.
   - C extinction.
   - D adaptation.

5. The ability of an individual organism to survive and reproduce in its natural environment is called
   - A natural selection.
   - B evolution.
   - C descent with modification.
   - D fitness.

6. Which of the following is an important concept in Darwin's theory of evolution by natural selection?
   - A descent with modification
   - B homologous molecules
   - C processes that change the surface of Earth
   - D the tendency toward perfection

7. Which of the following does NOT provide evidence for evolution?
   - A fossil record
   - B natural variation within a species
   - C geographical distribution of living things
   - D homologous structures of living organisms

8. DNA and RNA provide evidence of evolution because
   - A all organisms have nearly identical DNA and RNA.
   - B no two organisms have exactly the same DNA.
   - C each RNA codon specifies just one amino acid.
   - D in most organisms, the same codons specify the same amino acids.

9. A bird's wings are homologous to a(n)
   - A fish's tailfin.
   - B alligator's claws.
   - C dog's front legs.
   - D mosquito's wings.

Questions 10 and 11

The birds shown below are 2 of the species of finches Darwin found on the Galápagos Islands.

Woodpecker Finch   **Large Ground Finch**

10. What process produced the two different types of beaks shown?
    - A artificial selection
    - B natural selection
    - C geographical distribution
    - D disuse of the beak

11. The large ground finch obtains food by cracking seeds. Its short, strong beak is an example of
    - A the struggle for existence.
    - B the tendency toward perfection.
    - C an adaptation.
    - D a vestigial organ.

Open-Ended Response

12. Compare and contrast the processes of artificial selection and natural selection.

If You Have Trouble With . . .

Question	1	2	3	4	5	6	7	8	9	10	11	12
See Lesson	16.1	16.2	16.2	16.2	16.3	16.3	16.4	16.4	16.4	16.3	16.3	16.3

17 Evolution of Populations

Poised on a flower, the two common blue butterflies (Polyommatus icarus) appear identical. However, if you look closely, you can see that the patterns on their wings are slightly different. Variations among individual members of a population provide the raw material for evolution and sometimes for the formation of new species.

BIOLOGY.com   Search   (Chapter 17)   **GO** • Flash Cards

INSIDE:

- **17.1 Genes and Variation**
- **17.2 Evolution as Genetic Change in Populations**
- **17.3 The Process of Speciation**
- **17.4 Molecular Evolution**

CHAPTER
MYSTERY

EPIDEMIC

In 1918, an epidemic began that would go on to kill more than 40 million people. A doctor wrote: "Dead bodies are stacked about the morgue like cordwood."

What was this terrible disease? It was a variety of the same influenza virus that causes "the flu" you catch again and again. How did this strain of a common virus become so deadly? And could that kind of deadly flu epidemic happen again?

The answers to those questions explain why we can't make a permanent vaccine against the flu, as we can against measles or smallpox. They also explain why public health officials worry so much about something you may have heard referred to as "bird flu." As you read this chapter, look for evolutionary processes that might help explain how new strains of influenza virus appear all the time. Then, solve the mystery.

Never Stop Exploring Your World.
Finding the solution to the epidemic mystery is only the beginning. Take a video field trip with the ecogeeks of Untamed Science to see where the mystery leads.

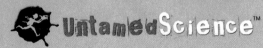

17.1 Genes and Variation

Key Questions

🔑 How is evolution defined in genetic terms?

🔑 What are the sources of genetic variation?

🔑 What determines the number of phenotypes for a given trait?

Vocabulary

gene pool
allele frequency
single-gene trait
polygenic trait

Taking Notes

Concept Map As you read about sources of genetic variation, construct a concept map to describe the sources.

THINK ABOUT IT Darwin developed his theory of natural selection without knowing how heredity worked. Mendel's studies on inheritance in peas were published during Darwin's lifetime, but no one (including Darwin) realized how important that work was. So Darwin had no idea how heritable traits pass from one generation to the next. What's more, although Darwin based his theory on heritable variation, he had no idea where that variation came from. What would happen when genetics answered those questions?

Genetics Joins Evolutionary Theory

🔑 How is evolution defined in genetic terms?

After Mendel's work was rediscovered around 1900, genetics took off like a rocket. Researchers discovered that heritable traits are controlled by genes that are carried on chromosomes. They learned how changes in genes and chromosomes generate variation.

All these discoveries in genetics fit perfectly into evolutionary theory. Variation is the raw material for natural selection, and finally scientists could study how and why variation occurs. Today, techniques of molecular genetics are used to form and test many hypotheses about heritable variation and natural selection. Modern genetics enables us to understand, better than Darwin ever could, how evolution works.

Genotype and Phenotype in Evolution Typical plants and animals contain two sets of genes, one contributed by each parent. Specific forms of a gene, called alleles, may vary from individual to individual. An organism's genotype is the particular combination of alleles it carries. An individual's genotype, together with environmental conditions, produces its phenotype. Phenotype includes all physical, physiological, and behavioral characteristics of an organism, such as eye color or height. Natural selection acts directly on phenotype, not genotype. In other words, natural selection acts on an organism's characteristics, not directly on its alleles.

FIGURE 17–1 Genes and Variation Why do biological family members resemble each other, yet also look so different? Similarities come from shared genes. Most differences come from gene shuffling during reproduction and environmental influences. A few differences may be caused by random mutations.

BIOLOGY.com ▶ Search (Lesson 17.1) **GO** ● Lesson Overview ● Lesson Notes

How does that work? In any population, some individuals have phenotypes that are better suited to their environment than are the phenotypes of other individuals. The better-suited individuals produce more offspring than the less fit individuals do. Therefore, organisms with higher fitness pass more copies of their genes to the next generation.

Natural selection never acts directly on genes. Why? Because it is an entire organism—not a single gene—that either survives and reproduces or dies without reproducing.

In Your Notebook *Describe how natural selection affects genotypes by acting on phenotypes.*

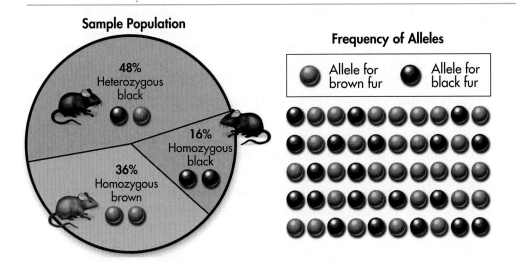

Sample Population

48% Heterozygous black

16% Homozygous black

36% Homozygous brown

Frequency of Alleles

Allele for brown fur

Allele for black fur

FIGURE 17–2 Alleles in a Population When scientists try to determine whether a population is evolving, they study its allele frequencies. This diagram shows allele frequencies for fur color in a mouse population. **Calculate** *Here, in a total of 50 alleles, 20 alleles are B (black) and 30 are b (brown). How many of each allele would be present in a total of 100 alleles?* MATH

Populations and Gene Pools Genetic variation and evolution are both studied in populations. A population is a group of individuals of the same species that mate and produce offspring. Because members of a population interbreed, they share a common group of genes called a gene pool. A **gene pool** consists of all the genes, including all the different alleles for each gene, that are present in a population.

Researchers study gene pools by examining the numbers of different alleles they contain. **Allele frequency** is the number of times an allele occurs in a gene pool, compared to the total number of alleles in that pool for the same gene. For example, in the mouse population in **Figure 17–2**, the allele frequency of the domiant *B* allele (black fur) is 40 percent, and the allele frequency of the recessive *b* allele (brown fur) is 60 percent. The allele frequency of an allele has nothing to do with whether the allele is dominant or recessive. In this mouse population, the recessive allele occurs more frequently than the dominant allele.

🔑 **Evolution, in genetic terms, involves a change in the frequency of alleles in a population over time.** For example, if the frequency of the *B* allele in **Figure 17–2** drops to 30 percent, the population is evolving. It's important to note that populations, not individuals, evolve. Natural selection operates on individual organisms, but the changes it causes in allele frequency show up in the population as a whole.

BUILD Vocabulary

MULTIPLE MEANINGS Perhaps the most common definition of the noun *pool* is a large man-made body of water in which you can swim. However, a *pool* can also refer to an available supply of a resource. In the case of a **gene pool**, the resource is genetic information.

Sources of Genetic Variation

🔑 *What are the sources of genetic variation?*

Genetics enables us to understand how heritable variation is produced. 🔑 **Three sources of genetic variation are mutation, genetic recombination during sexual reproduction, and lateral gene transfer.**

Mutations A mutation is any change in the genetic material of a cell. Some mutations involve changes within individual genes. Other mutations involve changes in larger pieces of chromosomes. Some mutations—called neutral mutations—do not change an organism's phenotype.

Mutations that produce changes in phenotype may or may not affect fitness. Some mutations, such as those that cause genetic diseases, may be lethal. Other mutations may lower fitness by decreasing an individual's ability to survive and reproduce. Still other mutations may improve an individual's ability to survive and reproduce.

How common are mutations? Recent estimates suggest that each of us is born with roughly 300 mutations that make parts of our DNA different from that of our parents. Most of those mutations are neutral. One or two are potentially harmful. A few may be beneficial.

Note that mutations matter in evolution only if they can be passed from generation to generation. For that to happen, mutations must occur in the germ line cells that produce either eggs or sperm. A mutation in skin cells that produces a nonlethal skin cancer, for example, will not be passed to the next generation.

Genetic Recombination in Sexual Reproduction Mutations are not the only source of heritable variation. You do not look exactly like your biological parents, even though they gave you all your genes. You probably look even less like any brothers or sisters you may have. Yet no matter how you feel about your relatives, mutant genes are not primarily what makes them look so different from you. Most heritable differences are due not to mutations, but to genetic recombination during sexual reproduction. Remember that each chromosome in a pair moves independently during meiosis. In humans, who have 23 pairs of chromosomes, this process can produce 8.4 million gene combinations!

Crossing-over is another way in which genes are recombined. Recall that crossing-over occurs during meiosis. In this process, paired chromosomes often swap lengths of DNA at random. Crossing-over further increases the number of new genotypes created in each generation. You can now understand why, in species that reproduce sexually, no two siblings (except identical twins) ever look exactly alike. With all that independent assortment and crossing-over, you can easily end up with your mother's eyes, your father's nose, and hair that combines qualities from both your parents. You can also now understand why, as Darwin noted, individual members of a species differ from one another.

FIGURE 17–3 Genetic Variation Genetic variation may produce visible variations in phenotype, such as the different-colored kernels in these ears of maize. Other kinds of genetic variation, such as resistance to disease, may not be visible, even though they are more important to evolutionary fitness.

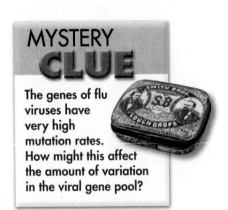

MYSTERY CLUE

The genes of flu viruses have very high mutation rates. How might this affect the amount of variation in the viral gene pool?

> **In Your Notebook** *Which source of variation brings more diversity into a gene pool—mutation or sexual reproduction? Explain.*

Lateral Gene Transfer Most of the time, in most eukaryotic organisms, genes are passed only from parents to offspring (during sexual or asexual reproduction). Some organisms, however, pass genes from one individual to another, or even from individuals of one species to another. Recall, for example, that many bacteria swap genes on plasmids as though the genes were trading cards. This passing of genes from one organism to another organism that is not its offspring is called lateral gene transfer. Lateral gene transfer can occur between organisms of the same species or organisms of different species.

Lateral gene transfer can increase genetic variation in any species that picks up the "new" genes. This process is important in the evolution of antibiotic resistance in bacteria. Lateral gene transfer has been common, and important, in single-celled organisms during the history of life.

Single-Gene and Polygenic Traits

🔑 *What determines the number of phenotypes for a given trait?*

Genes control phenotype in different ways. In some cases, a single gene controls a trait. Other times, several genes interact to control a trait. 🔑 **The number of phenotypes produced for a trait depends on how many genes control the trait.**

Single-Gene Traits In the species of snail shown below, some snails have dark bands on their shells, and other snails don't. The presence or absence of dark bands is a **single-gene trait**—a trait controlled by only one gene. The gene that controls shell banding has two alleles. The allele for a shell without bands is dominant over the allele for a shell with dark bands. All genotypes for this trait have one of two phenotypes—shells with bands or shells without bands. Single-gene traits may have just two or three distinct phenotypes.

The bar graph in **Figure 17–4** shows the relative frequency of phenotypes for this single gene in one population of snails. This graph shows that the presence of dark bands on the shells may be more common in a population than the absence of bands. This is true even though the allele for shells without bands is the dominant form. In populations, phenotypic ratios are determined by the frequency of alleles in the population as well as by whether the alleles are dominant or recessive.

FIGURE 17–4 Two Phenotypes In this species of snail, a single gene with two alleles controls whether or not a snail's shell has bands. The graph shows the percentages, in one population, of snails with bands and snails without bands.

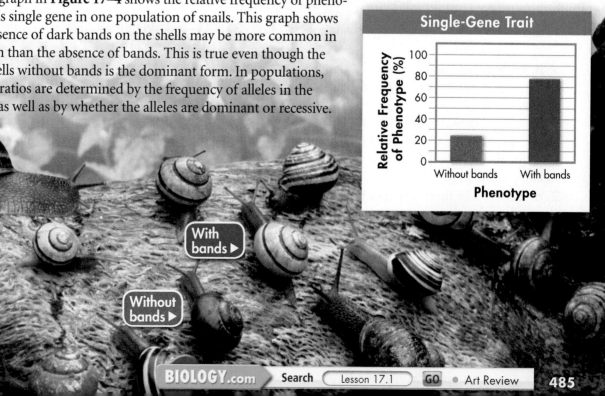

Single-Gene Trait

With bands ▶

Without bands ▶

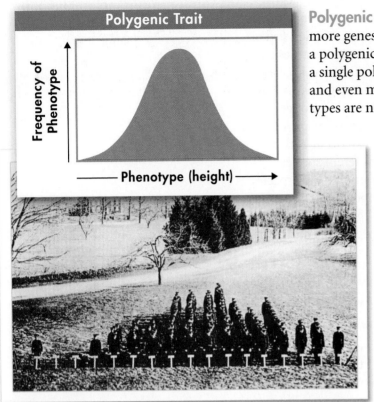

Polygenic Trait

Frequency of Phenotype

Phenotype (height) →

Polygenic Traits Many traits are controlled by two or more genes and are called **polygenic traits.** Each gene of a polygenic trait often has two or more alleles. As a result, a single polygenic trait often has many possible genotypes and even more different phenotypes. Often those phenotypes are not clearly distinct from one another.

Height in humans is one example of a polygenic trait. Height varies from very short to very tall and everywhere in between. You can sample phenotypic variation in this trait by measuring the height of all the students in your class. You can then calculate average height for this group. Many students will be just a little taller or shorter than average. Some, however, will be very tall or very short. If you graph the number of individuals of each height, you may get a graph similar to the one in **Figure 17–5.** The symmetrical bell-like shape of this curve is typical of polygenic traits. A bell-shaped curve is also called a normal distribution.

FIGURE 17–5 A Range ot Phenotypes The graph above shows the distribution of phenotypes that would be expected for a trait if many genes contributed to the trait. The photograph shows the actual distribution of heights in a group of young men. **Interpret Graphs** *What does the shape of the graph indicate about height in humans?*

17.1 Assessment

Review Key Concepts 🔑

1. a. Review Define the terms *gene pool* and *allele frequency*.

b. Explain In genetic terms, what indicates that evolution is occurring in a population?

c. Predict Suppose a dominant allele causes a plant disease that usually kills the plant before it can reproduce. Over time, what would probably happen to the frequency of that allele in the population?

2. a. Review List three sources of genetic variation.

b. Explain How does genetic recombination result in genetic variation?

c. Relate Cause and Effect Why does sexual reproduction provide more opportunities for genetic variation than asexual reproduction?

3. a. Review What is a single-gene trait? What is a polygenic trait?

b. Explain How does the range of phenotypes for single-gene traits differ from the range for polygenic traits?

c. Infer A black guinea pig and a white guinea pig mate and have offspring. All the offspring are black. Is the trait of coat color probably a single-gene trait or a polygenic trait? Explain.

WRITE ABOUT SCIENCE

Explanation

4. Explain how mutations are important in the process of biological evolution. (*Hint:* How does mutation affect genetic variation?)

17.2 Evolution as Genetic Change in Populations

THINK ABOUT IT Ever since humans began farming, they have battled insects that eat crops. Many farmers now use chemicals called pesticides to kill crop-destroying insects. When farmers first used modern pesticides such as DDT, the chemicals killed most insects. But after a few years, many pesticides stopped working. Today, farmers fight an ongoing "arms race" with insects. Scientists constantly search for new chemicals to control pests that old chemicals no longer control. How do insects fight back? By evolving.

At first, individual pesticides kill almost all insects exposed to them. But a few individual insects usually survive. Why? Because insect populations often contain enough genetic variation that a few individuals, just by chance, are resistant to a particular pesticide. By killing most of the susceptible individuals, farmers increase the relative fitness of the few individuals that can resist the poison. Those insects survive and reproduce, passing their resistance on to their offspring. After a few generations, the descendants of the original, resistant individuals dominate the population.

To understand completely how pesticide resistance develops, you need to know the relationship between natural selection and genetics.

Key Questions

🔑 **How does natural selection affect single-gene and polygenic traits?**

🔑 **What is genetic drift?**

🔑 **What conditions are required to maintain genetic equilibrium?**

Vocabulary

directional selection
stabilizing selection
disruptive selection
genetic drift
bottleneck effect
founder effect
genetic equilibrium
Hardy-Weinberg principle
sexual selection

Taking Notes

Preview Visuals Before you read, look at **Figure 17–6.** What evolutionary trend does it seem to show?

How Natural Selection Works

🔑 **How does natural selection affect single-gene and polygenic traits?**

Pesticide-resistant insects have a kind of fitness that protects them from a harmful chemical. In genetic terms, what does *fitness* mean? Each time an organism reproduces, it passes copies of its genes on to its offspring. We can, therefore, view evolutionary fitness as success in passing genes to the next generation. In the same way, we can view an evolutionary adaptation as any genetically controlled trait that increases an individual's ability to pass along its alleles.

Natural Selection on Single-Gene Traits Recall that evolution is any change over time in the allele frequency in a population. This process works somewhat differently for single-gene traits than for polygenic traits. 🔑 **Natural selection on single-gene traits can lead to changes in allele frequencies and, thus, to changes in phenotype frequencies.** For example, imagine that a population of lizards experiences mutations in one gene that determines body color. The normal color of the lizards is brown. The mutations produce red and black forms, as shown in **Figure 17–6.** What happens to the new alleles? If red lizards are more visible to predators, they might be less likely to survive and reproduce. Therefore, the allele for red coloring might not become common.

Black lizards, on the other hand, might absorb more sunlight and warm up faster on cold days. If high body temperature allows the lizards to move faster to feed and avoid predators, they might produce more offspring than brown forms produce. The allele for black color might increase in frequency. The black phenotype would then increase in frequency. If color change has no effect on fitness, the allele that produces it will not be under pressure from natural selection.

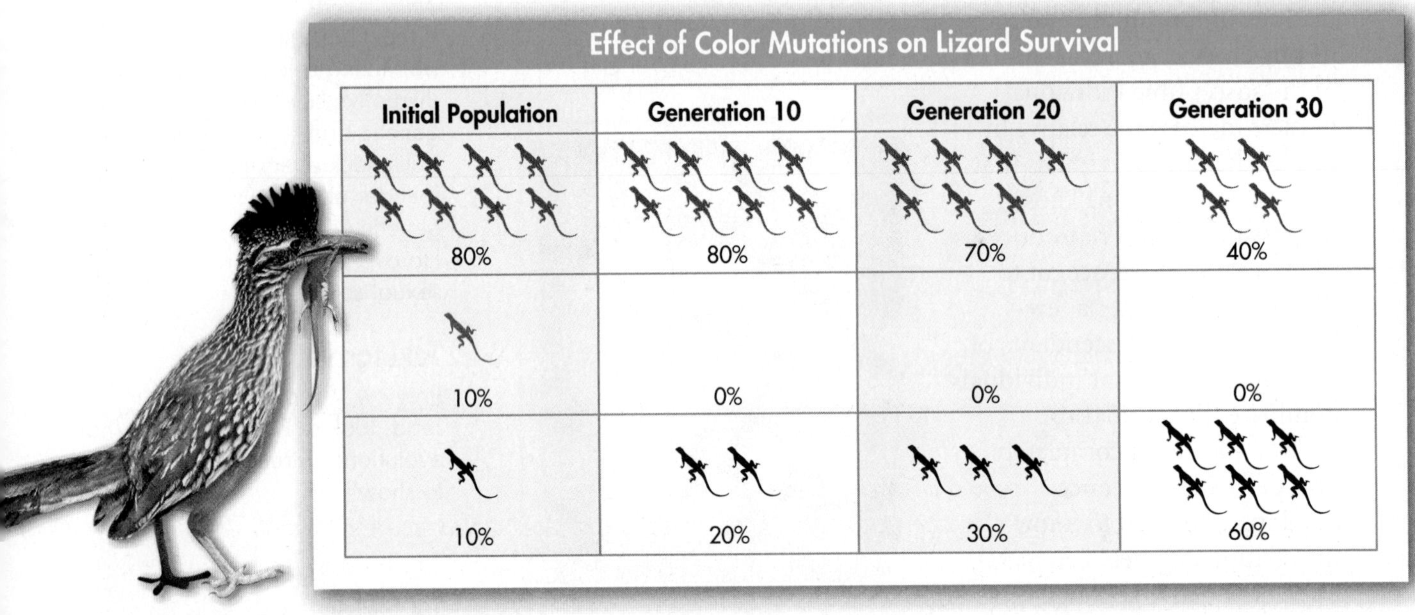

Effect of Color Mutations on Lizard Survival

Initial Population	Generation 10	Generation 20	Generation 30
80%	80%	70%	40%
10%	0%	0%	0%
10%	20%	30%	60%

FIGURE 17–6 Selection on a Single-Gene Trait Natural selection on a single-gene trait can lead to changes in allele frequencies and, thus, to evolution. **Interpret Visuals** *What has happened to produce the population shown in Generation 30?*

Natural Selection on Polygenic Traits When traits are controlled by more than one gene, the effects of natural selection are more complex. As you saw earlier, polygenic traits such as height often display a range of phenotypes that form a bell curve. The fitness of individuals may vary from one end of such a curve to the other. Where fitness varies, natural selection can act. 🔑 **Natural selection on polygenic traits can affect the relative fitness of phenotypes and thereby produce one of three types of selection: directional selection, stabilizing selection, or disruptive selection.** These types of selection are shown in **Figure 17–7.**

 In Your Notebook *As you read the text on the following page, summarize each of the three types of selection.*

▶ *Directional Selection* When individuals at one end of the curve have higher fitness than individuals in the middle or at the other end, **directional selection** occurs. The range of phenotypes shifts because some individuals are more successful at surviving and reproducing than are others.

Consider how limited resources, such as food, can affect individuals' fitness. Among seed-eating birds such as Darwin's finches, birds with bigger, thicker beaks can feed more easily on larger, harder, thicker-shelled seeds. Suppose the supply of small and medium-size seeds runs low, leaving only larger seeds. Birds with larger beaks would have an easier time feeding than would small-beaked birds. Big-beaked birds would therefore be more successful in surviving and passing genes to the next generation. Over time, the average beak size of the population would probably increase.

▶ *Stabilizing Selection* When individuals near the center of the curve have higher fitness than individuals at either end, **stabilizing selection** takes place. This situation keeps the center of the curve at its current position, but it narrows the curve overall.

For example, the mass of human infants at birth is under the influence of stabilizing selection. Very small babies are likely to be less healthy and, thus, less likely to survive. Babies who are much larger than average are likely to have difficulty being born. The fitness of these smaller or larger babies is, therefore, lower than that of more average-size individuals.

▶ *Disruptive Selection* When individuals at the outer ends of the curve have higher fitness than individuals near the middle of the curve, **disruptive selection** occurs. Disruptive selection acts against individuals of an intermediate type. If the pressure of natural selection is strong and lasts long enough, this situation can cause the single curve to split into two. In other words, disruptive selection creates two distinct phenotypes.

Suppose a bird population lives in an area where medium-size seeds become less common and large and small seeds become more common. Birds with unusually small or large beaks would have higher fitness. As shown in the graph, the population might split into two groups: one with smaller beaks and one with larger beaks.

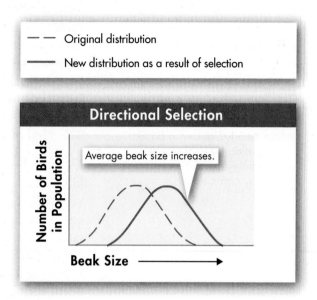

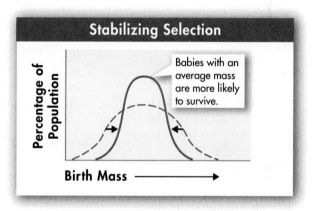

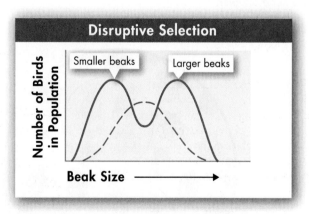

FIGURE 17–7 Selection on Polygenic Traits
Natural selection on polygenic traits has one of three patterns—directional selection, stabilizing selection, or disruptive selection.

Genetic Drift

What is genetic drift?

Natural selection is not the only source of evolutionary change. In small populations, an allele can become more or less common simply by chance. **In small populations, individuals that carry a particular allele may leave more descendants than other individuals leave, just by chance. Over time, a series of chance occurrences can cause an allele to become more or less common in a population.** This kind of random change in allele frequency is called **genetic drift.**

Genetic Bottlenecks Sometimes, a disaster, such as disease, can kill many individuals in a population. Just by chance, the smaller population's gene pool may have allele frequencies that are different from those of the original gene pool. If the reduced population later grows, its alleles will be different in frequency from the original population's. The **bottleneck effect** is a change in allele frequency following a dramatic reduction in the size of a population. A severe bottleneck effect can sharply reduce a population's genetic diversity.

The Founder Effect Genetic drift may also occur when a few individuals colonize a new habitat. These founding individuals may carry alleles that differ in relative frequencies from those of the main population, just by chance. The new gene pool may therefore start out with allele frequencies different from those of the parent gene pool, as shown in **Figure 17–8.** This situation, in which allele frequencies change as a result of the migration of a small subgroup of a population, is known as the **founder effect.**

One example of the founder effect is the evolution of several hundred species of fruit flies on different Hawaiian islands. All those species descended from the same mainland fruit fly population. However, species on different islands have allele frequencies that are different from those of the original species.

BUILD Vocabulary

ACADEMIC WORDS The adjective random means "lacking a pattern" or "happening by chance." A random change is a change that happens by chance.

FIGURE 17–8 Founder Effect
This illustration shows how two small groups from a large, diverse population could produce new populations that differ from the original group.
Compare and Contrast
Explain why the two populations of descendants are so different from one another.

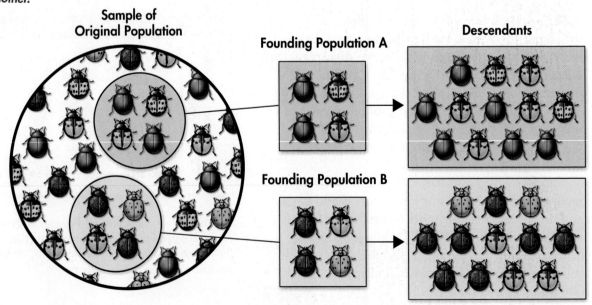

Sample of Original Population

Founding Population A

Founding Population B

Descendants

Allele Frequency

The Hardy-Weinberg principle can be used to predict the frequencies of certain genotypes if you know the frequency of other genotypes.

Imagine, for example, that you know of a genetic condition, controlled by two alleles S and s, which follow the rule of simple dominance at a single locus. The condition affects only homozygous recessive individuals. (The heterozygous phenotype shows no symptoms.) The population you are studying has a population size of 10,000 and there are 36 individuals affected by the condition ($q^2 = 0.0036$). Based on this information, use the Hardy-Weinberg equations to answer the following questions.

1. Calculate What are the frequencies of the S and s alleles?

2. Calculate What are the frequencies of the SS, Ss, and ss genotypes?

3. Calculate What percentage of people, in total, is likely to be carrying the s allele, whether or not they know it?

Evolution Versus Genetic Equilibrium

What conditions are required to maintain genetic equilibrium?

One way to understand how and why populations evolve is to imagine a model of a hypothetical population that does not evolve. If a population is not evolving, allele frequencies in its gene pool do not change, which means that the population is in **genetic equilibrium.**

Sexual Reproduction and Allele Frequency Gene shuffling during sexual reproduction produces many gene combinations. But a century ago, researchers realized that meiosis and fertilization, by themselves, do not change allele frequencies. So hypothetically, a population of sexually reproducing organisms could remain in genetic equilibrium.

The Hardy-Weinberg Principle The **Hardy-Weinberg principle** states that allele frequencies in a population should remain constant unless one or more factors cause those frequencies to change. The Hardy-Weinberg principle makes predictions like Punnett squares—but for populations, not individuals. Here's how it works. Suppose that there are two alleles for a gene: A (dominant) and a (recessive). A cross of these alleles can produce three possible genotypes: AA, Aa, and aa. The frequencies of genotypes in the population can be predicted by these equations, where p and q are the frequencies of the dominant and recessive alleles:

In symbols:

$$p^2 + 2pq + q^2 = 1 \text{ and } p + q = 1$$

In words:

(frequency of AA) + (frequency of Aa) + (frequency of aa)
= 100% and (frequency of A) + (frequency of a) = 100%

Suppose that, in one generation, the frequency of the A allele is 40 percent ($p = 0.40$) and the frequency of the a allele is 60 percent ($q = 0.60$).

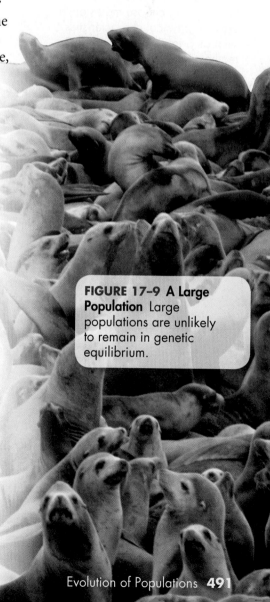

FIGURE 17–9 A Large Population Large populations are unlikely to remain in genetic equilibrium.

FIGURE 17–10 Choosing a Mate
Random mating is one condition required to maintain genetic equilibrium in a population. However, in many species, mating is not random. Female peacocks, for example, choose mates on the basis of physical characteristics such as brightly patterned tail feathers. This is a classic example of sexual selection.

If this population is in genetic equilibrium, chances of an individual in the next generation having genotype *AA* would be 16% ($p^2 = 0.40^2 = 0.16$ or 16%). The probability of genotype *aa* would be 36% ($q^2 = 0.60^2 = 0.36$). The probability of genotype *Aa* would be 48% ($2pq = 2 (0.40) (0.60) = 0.48$). If a population doesn't show these predicted phenotype frequencies, evolution is taking place. 🔑 **The Hardy-Weinberg principle predicts that five conditions can disturb genetic equilibrium and cause evolution to occur: (1) nonrandom mating; (2) small population size; and (3) immigration or emigration; (4) mutations; or (5) natural selection.**

▶ *Nonrandom Mating* In genetic equilibrium, individuals must mate with other individuals at random. But in many species, individuals select mates based on heritable traits, such as size, strength, or coloration, a practice known as **sexual selection.** When sexual selection is at work, genes for the traits selected for or against are not in equilibrium.

▶ *Small Population Size* Genetic drift does not usually have major effects in large populations, but can affect small populations strongly. Evolutionary change due to genetic drift thus happens more easily in small populations.

▶ *Immigration or Emigration* Individuals who join a population may introduce new alleles into the gene pool, and individuals who leave may remove alleles. Thus, any movement of individuals into (immigration) or out of (emigration) a population can disrupt genetic equilibrium, a process called *gene flow*.

▶ *Mutations* Mutations can introduce new alleles into a gene pool, thereby changing allele frequencies and causing evolution to occur.

▶ *Natural Selection* If different genotypes have different fitness, genetic equilibrium will be disrupted, and evolution will occur.

One or more of these conditions usually holds for real populations. So, most of the time, in most species, evolution happens.

17.2 Assessment

Review Key Concepts 🔑

1. a. Review How does natural selection affect a single-gene trait?
   b. Compare and Contrast Compare directional selection and disruptive selection.
2. a. Review Define genetic drift.
   b. Relate Cause and Effect How can the founder effect lead to changes in a gene pool?
3. a. Review What five conditions are necessary to maintain genetic equilibrium?

b. Infer Why is genetic equilibrium uncommon in actual populations?

Apply the Big idea

Evolution

4. Do you think populations stay in genetic equilibrium after the environment has changed significantly? Explain your answer.

Biology & Society

Should Antibiotic Use Be Restricted?

Natural selection and evolution aren't just about fossils and finches. Many disease-causing bacteria are evolving resistance to antibiotics—drugs intended to kill them or interfere with their growth.

During your lifetime, antibiotics have always been available and effective. So it is probably hard for you to imagine what life was like before antibiotics were discovered. It wasn't pleasant. During the 1930s, it was not unusual for half of all children in a family to die from bacterial infections that are considered trivial today.

When antibiotics were developed, they rapidly became one of medicine's greatest weapons. Antibiotics saved thousands of lives during World War II by controlling bacterial infections among wounded soldiers. Soon, many bacterial diseases, such as pneumonia, posed much less of a threat. That's why antibiotics were called "magic bullets" and "wonder drugs." But the magic is fading as bacteria evolve.

Bacterial populations have always contained a few individuals with mutations that enabled them to destroy, inactivate, or eliminate antibiotics. But those individuals didn't have higher fitness, so those mutant alleles didn't become common.

Then, doctors began prescribing antibiotics widely, and farmers started feeding antibiotics to farm animals to prevent infections. As a result, antibiotics have become a regular part of the environment for bacteria.

In this new environment, individuals with resistance alleles have higher fitness, so the resistance alleles increase in frequency. Also, resistance alleles can be transferred from one bacterial species to another on plasmids. Thus, disease-causing bacteria can pick up resistance from harmless strains.

Snort. Sniffle. Sneeze.
No Antibiotics Please.
Treat colds and flu with care.
Talk to your doctor.

GET SMART
CDC

Many bacteria, including those that cause tuberculosis and certain forms of staph infections, are evolving resistance to not just one antibiotic, but to almost all medicines known. Many doctors are terrified. They fear the loss of one of the vital weapons against bacterial disease. Given this problem, should government agencies restrict antibiotic use?

The Viewpoints

Restrict Antibiotic Use Some people think that the danger of an incurable bacterial epidemic is so high that the government must take action. Doctors overuse antibiotics because patients demand them. The livestock industry likes using antibiotics and will not change their practice unless forced to do so.

Don't Restrict Use Other people think that the doctors and the livestock industry need the freedom to find solutions that work best for them. Researchers are constantly developing new drugs. Some of these drugs can be reserved for human use only.

Research and Decide

1. Analyze the Viewpoints Learn more about this issue by consulting library and Internet resources. Then, list the advantages and disadvantages of restricting antibiotic use.

2. Form Your Opinion Should antibiotics be restricted? Would regulations be more appropriate in some situations than in others?

17.3 The Process of Speciation

Key Questions

🔑 What types of isolation lead to the formation of new species?

🔑 What is a current hypothesis about Galápagos finch speciation?

Vocabulary

species
speciation
reproductive isolation
behavioral isolation
geographic isolation
temporal isolation

Taking Notes

Compare/Contrast Table
In a compare/contrast table, describe the three mechanisms of reproductive isolation.

THINK ABOUT IT How does one species become two? Natural selection and genetic drift can change allele frequencies, causing a population to evolve. But a change in allele frequency by itself does not lead to the development of a new species.

Isolating Mechanisms

🔑 **What types of isolation lead to the formation of new species?**

Biologists define a **species** as a population or group of populations whose members can interbreed and produce fertile offspring. Given this genetic definition of species, what must happen for one species to divide or give rise to a new species? The formation of a new species is called **speciation.**

Interbreeding links members of a species genetically. Any genetic changes can spread throughout the population over time. But what happens if some members of a population stop breeding with other members? The gene pool can split. Once a population has thus split into two groups, changes in one of those gene pools cannot spread to the other. Because these two populations no longer interbreed, **reproductive isolation** has occurred. 🔑 **When populations become reproductively isolated, they can evolve into two separate species. Reproductive isolation can develop in a variety of ways, including behavioral isolation, geographic isolation, and temporal isolation.**

MYSTERY CLUE

A population of viruses inside a host's body is isolated from other viral populations. How might this isolation affect viral evolution?

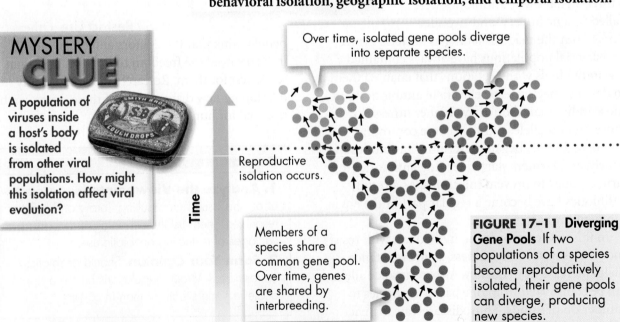

Over time, isolated gene pools diverge into separate species.

Reproductive isolation occurs.

Time

Members of a species share a common gene pool. Over time, genes are shared by interbreeding.

FIGURE 17–11 Diverging Gene Pools If two populations of a species become reproductively isolated, their gene pools can diverge, producing new species.

Behavioral Isolation Suppose two populations that are capable of interbreeding develop differences in courtship rituals or other behaviors. **Behavioral isolation** can then occur. For example, eastern and western meadowlarks are similar birds whose habitats overlap. But, members of the two species will not mate with each other, partly because they use different songs to attract mates. Eastern meadowlarks don't respond to western meadowlark songs, and vice versa.

Geographic Isolation When two populations are separated by geographic barriers such as rivers, mountains, or bodies of water, **geographic isolation** occurs. The Abert's squirrel in **Figure 17–12,** for example, lives in the Southwest. About 10,000 years ago, a small population became isolated on the north rim of the Grand Canyon. Separate gene pools formed. Genetic changes that appeared in one group were not passed to the other. Natural selection and genetic drift worked separately on each group and led to the formation of a distinct subspecies, the Kaibab squirrel. The Abert's and Kaibab squirrels are very similar, indicating that they are closely related. However, the Kaibab squirrel differs from the Abert's squirrel in significant ways, such as fur coloring.

Geographic barriers do not always guarantee isolation. Floods, for example, may link separate lakes, enabling their fish populations to mix. If those populations still interbreed, they remain a single species. Also, a geographic barrier may separate certain organisms but not others. A large river may keep squirrels and other small rodents apart but probably won't isolate bird populations.

Temporal Isolation A third isolating mechanism, known as **temporal isolation,** happens when two or more species reproduce at different times. For example, suppose three similar species of orchids live in the same rain forest. Each species has flowers that last only one day and must be pollinated on that day to produce seeds. Because the species bloom on different days, they cannot pollinate one another.

In Your Notebook *Explain how temporal isolation can lead to speciation.*

FIGURE 17–12 Geographic Isolation Abert's squirrel and the Kaibab squirrel are distinct subspecies within the same species. Their gene pools are separate. **Interpret Visuals** *What geographic barrier separates the two populations of squirrels?*

Speciation in Darwin's Finches

🔑 What is a current hypothesis about Galápagos finch speciation?

Recall that Peter and Rosemary Grant spent years on the Galápagos islands studying changes in finch populations. The Grants measured and recorded anatomical characteristics such as beak length of individual medium ground finches. Many of the characteristics appeared in bell-shaped distributions typical of polygenic traits. As environmental conditions changed, the Grants documented directional selection among the traits. When drought struck the island of Daphne Major, finches with larger beaks capable of cracking the thickest seeds survived and reproduced more often than others. Over many generations, the proportion of large-beaked finches increased.

We can now combine these studies by the Grants with evolutionary concepts to form a hypothesis that answers a question: How might the founder effect and natural selection have produced reproductive isolation that could have led to speciation among Galápagos finches? 🔑 **According to this hypothesis, speciation in Galápagos finches occurred by founding of a new population, geographic isolation, changes in the new population's gene pool, behavioral isolation, and ecological competition.**

Founders Arrive Many years ago, a few finches from South America—species M—arrived on one of the Galápagos islands, as shown in **Figure 17–13.** These birds may have gotten lost or been blown off course by a storm. Once on the island, they survived and reproduced. Because of the founder effect, allele frequencies of this founding finch population could have differed from allele frequencies in the original South American population.

Geographic Isolation The island's environment was different from the South American environment. Some combination of the founder effect, geographic isolation, and natural selection enabled the island finch population to evolve into a new species—species A. Later, a few birds from species A crossed to another island. Because these birds do not usually fly over open water, they move from island to island very rarely. Thus, finch populations on the two islands were geographically isolated from each other and no longer shared a common gene pool.

Changes in Gene Pools Over time, populations on each island adapted to local environments. Plants on the first island may have produced small, thin-shelled seeds, whereas plants on the second island may have produced larger, thick-shelled seeds. On the second island, directional selection would have favored individuals with larger, heavier beaks. These birds could crack open and eat the large seeds more easily. Thus, birds with large beaks would be better able to survive on the second island. Over time, natural selection would have caused that population to evolve larger beaks, forming a distinct population, B, characterized by a new phenotype.

FIGURE 17–13

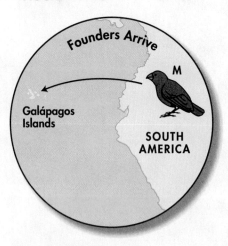

FIGURE 17–14

FIGURE 17–15

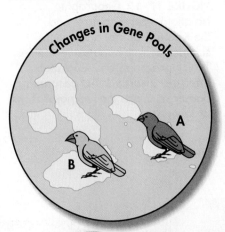

Behavioral Isolation Now, imagine that a few birds from the second island cross back to the first island. Will population-A birds breed with population-B birds? Probably not. These finches choose mates carefully. During courtship, they closely inspect a potential partner's beak. Finches prefer to mate with birds that have the same-size beak as they do. Big-beaked birds prefer to mate with other big-beaked birds, and smaller-beaked birds prefer to mate with other smaller-beaked birds. Because the populations on the two islands have evolved differently sized beaks, they would probably not mate with each other.

Thus, differences in beak size, combined with mating behavior, could lead to reproductive isolation. The gene pools of the two bird populations remain isolated—even when individuals live in the same place. The populations have now become two distinct species.

FIGURE 17–16

Competition and Continued Evolution As these two new species live together on the first island, they compete for seeds. During the dry season, birds that are most different from each other have the highest fitness. That is because the more specialized birds have less competition for certain kinds of seeds and other foods. Over time, species evolve in a way that increases the differences between them. The species-B birds on the first island may evolve into a new species, C.

The combined processes of geographic isolation on different islands, genetic change, and behavioral isolation could have repeated itself again and again across the Galápagos chain. Over many generations, the process could have produced the 13 different finch species found there today.

FIGURE 17–17

In Your Notebook *Explain how natural selection and behavioral isolation may have lead to reproductive isolation in Darwin's finches.*

17.3 Assessment

Review Key Concepts 🔑

1. a. Review What is geographic isolation?

b. Predict A newly formed lake divides a population of a beetle species into two groups. What other factors besides isolation might lead to the two groups becoming separate species?

2. a. Review What types of reproductive isolation may have been important in Galápagos finch speciation? Explain.

b. Apply Concepts Explain how the vegetarian tree finch, which feeds on fruit, might have evolved.

BUILD VOCABULARY

3. *Temporal* comes from the Latin word *tempus,* meaning "time." How is time a factor in temporal isolation?

4. *Isolation* is related to the Latin word *insula,* meaning "island." After reading about isolating mechanisms in this lesson, does the common origin of these two words make sense? Explain your answer.

17.4 Molecular Evolution

Key Questions

🔑 What are molecular clocks?

🔑 Where do new genes come from?

🔑 How may Hox genes be involved in evolutionary change?

Vocabulary
molecular clock

Taking Notes

Outline As you read, make an outline of this lesson. Use the green headings as the main topics and the blue headings as the subtopics.

THINK ABOUT IT Recall that an organism's genome is its complete set of genetic information. Thousands of ongoing projects are analyzing the genomes of organisms ranging from viruses to humans. The analysis of genomes enables us to study evolution at the molecular level. By comparing DNA sequences from all of these organisms, we can often solve important evolutionary puzzles. For example, DNA evidence may indicate how two species are related to one another, even if their body structures don't offer enough clues.

Timing Lineage Splits: Molecular Clocks

🔑 **What are molecular clocks?**

When researchers use a **molecular clock,** they compare stretches of DNA to mark the passage of evolutionary time. 🔑 **A molecular clock uses mutation rates in DNA to estimate the time that two species have been evolving independently.**

Neutral Mutations as "Ticks" To understand molecular clocks, think about old-fashioned pendulum clocks. They mark time with a swinging pendulum. A molecular clock also relies on a repeating process to mark time—mutation. As you've learned, simple mutations occur all the time, causing slight changes in the sequence of DNA. Some mutations have a major positive or negative effect on an organism's phenotype. These types of mutations are under powerful pressure from natural selection.

Many mutations, however, have no effect on phenotype. These neutral mutations tend to accumulate in the DNA of different species at about the same rate. Researchers can compare such DNA sequences in two species. The comparison can reveal how many mutations have occurred independently in each group, as shown in **Figure 17–18.** The more differences there are between the DNA sequences of the two species, the more time has elapsed since the two species shared a common ancestor.

In Your Notebook Which kind of mutation—neutral or negative—will most likely persist in a population over time? Explain.

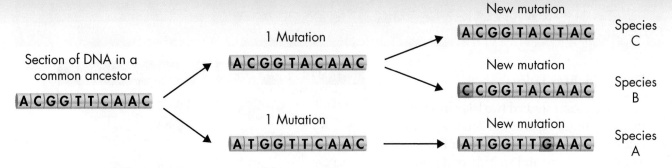

FIGURE 17–18 Molecular Clock
By comparing the DNA sequences of two or more species, biologists estimate how long the species have been separated. **Analyze Data** *What evidence indicates that species C is more closely related to species B than to species A?*

Calibrating the Clock The use of molecular clocks is not simple, because there is not just one molecular clock in a genome. There are many different clocks, each of which "ticks" at a different rate. This is because some genes accumulate mutations faster than others. These different clocks allow researchers to time different evolutionary events. Think of a conventional clock. If you want to time a brief event, you use the second hand. To time an event that lasts longer, you use the minute hand or the hour hand. In the same way, researchers choose a different molecular clock to compare great apes than to estimate when mammals and fishes shared a common ancestor.

Researchers check the accuracy of molecular clocks by trying to estimate how often mutations occur. In other words, they estimate how often the clock they have chosen "ticks." To do this, they compare the number of mutations in a particular gene in species whose age has been determined by other methods.

Gene Duplication

Where do new genes come from?

Where did the roughly 25,000 working genes in the human genome come from? Modern genes probably descended from a much smaller number of genes in the earliest life forms. But how could that have happened? **One way in which new genes evolve is through the duplication, and then modification, of existing genes.**

Copying Genes Most organisms carry several copies of various genes. Sometimes organisms carry two copies of the same gene. Other times there may be thousands of copies. Where do those extra copies come from, and what happens to them?

Remember that homologous chromosomes exchange DNA during meiosis in a process called crossing-over. Sometimes crossing-over involves an unequal swapping of DNA. In other words, one chromosome in the pair gets extra DNA. That extra DNA can carry part of a gene, a full gene, or a longer length of chromosome. Sometimes, in different ways, an entire genome can be duplicated.

Fishes in Two Lakes

A research team studied two lakes in an area that sometimes experiences flooding. Each lake contained two types of similar fishes: a dull brown form and an iridescent gold form. The team wondered how all the fishes were related, and they considered the two hypotheses diagrammed on the right.

1. Interpret Visuals Study the two diagrams. What does hypothesis A indicate about the ancestry of the fishes in Lake 1 and Lake 2? What does hypothesis B indicate?

2. Compare and Contrast According to the two hypotheses, what is the key difference in the way the brown and gold fish populations might have formed?

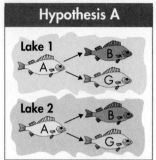
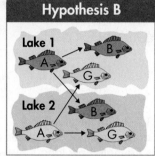

A = Possible ancestor
B = Contemporary brown form
G = Contemporary gold form
Shows possible line of descent

3. Draw Conclusions A DNA analysis showed that the brown and gold fishes from Lake 1 are the most closely related. Which hypothesis does this evidence support?

Duplicate Genes Evolve What's so important about gene duplication? Think about using a computer to write an essay for English class. You then want to submit a new version of the essay to your school newspaper. So, you make an extra copy of the original file and edit it for the newspaper.

Duplicate genes can work in similar ways. Sometimes, extra copies of a gene undergo mutations that change their function. The original gene is still around, just like the original copy of your English essay. So, the new genes can evolve without affecting the original gene function or product. **Figure 17–19** shows how this happens.

Gene Families Multiple copies of a duplicated gene can turn into a group of related genes called a gene family. Members of a gene family typically produce similar, yet slightly different, proteins. Your body, for example, produces a number of molecules that carry oxygen. Several of these compounds—called globins—are hemoglobins. The globin gene family that produces them evolved, after gene duplication, from a single ancestral globin gene. Some of the most important evolution research focuses on another gene family—Hox genes.

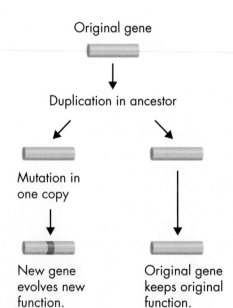

FIGURE 17–19 Gene Duplication In this diagram, a gene is first duplicated, and then one of the two resulting genes undergoes mutation.

Developmental Genes and Body Plans

🔑 *How may Hox genes be involved in evolutionary change?*

One exciting new research area is nicknamed "evo-devo" because it studies the relationship between evolution and embryological development. Darwin himself had a hunch that changes in the growth of embryos could transform adult body shape and size. Researchers now study how small changes in Hox gene activity could produce the kinds of evolutionary changes we see in the fossil record.

Hox Genes and Evolution As you read in Chapter 13, Hox genes determine which parts of an embryo develop arms, legs, or wings. Groups of Hox genes also control the size and shape of those structures. In fact, homologous Hox genes shape the bodies of animals as different as insects and humans—even though those animals last shared a common ancestor no fewer than 500 million years ago!

🔑 **Small changes in Hox gene activity during embryological development can produce large changes in adult animals.** For example, insects and crustaceans are related to ancient common ancestors that possessed dozens of legs. Today's crustaceans, including shrimp and lobsters, still have large numbers of paired legs, but insects have just 3 pairs of legs. What happened to those extra legs? Recent studies have shown that mutations in a single Hox gene, known as *Ubx*, turns off the growth of legs in the abdominal regions of insects. Thus, a change in one Hox gene accounts for a major evolutionary difference between two important animal groups.

Timing Is Everything Each part of an embryo starts to grow at a certain time, grows for a specific time, and stops growing at a specific time. Small changes in starting and stopping times can make a big difference in organisms. For example, small timing changes can make the difference between long, slender fingers and short, stubby toes. No wonder "evo-devo" is one of the hottest areas in evolutionary biology!

FIGURE 17–20 Change in a Hox Gene Insects such as fruit flies and crustaceans such as brine shrimp are descended from a common ancestor that had many legs. Due to mutations in the activity of a single Hox gene that happened millions of years ago, modern insects have fewer legs than do modern crustaceans. In the illustration, the legs of the fruit fly and the legs of the brine shrimp are the same color (red) because a variant of the same Hox gene, *Ubx*, directs the development of the legs of both animals.

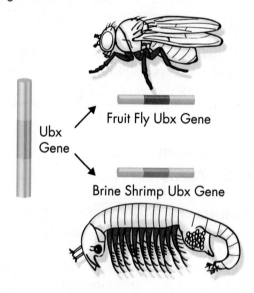

Ubx Gene

Fruit Fly Ubx Gene

Brine Shrimp Ubx Gene

17.4 Assessment

Review Key Concepts 🔑

1. a. Review What is a molecular clock?

 b. Explain Why do molecular clocks use mutations that have no effect on phenotype?

2. a. Review How can crossing-over result in gene duplication?

 b. Explain Describe how duplicate genes form.

 c. Relate Cause and Effect Why is gene duplication important in evolution?

3. a. Review Use the evolution of the insect body plan to explain the significance of Hox genes in evolution.

 b. Infer In evolution, why have small changes in Hox genes had a great impact?

VISUAL THINKING

4. The colored bands in the diagrams below represent mutations in a segment of DNA in species A, B, and C. Which two of the three species probably share the most recent common ancestor?

Species A	Species B	Species C
C	C	C
T	G	T
A	A	A
A	G	G
C	C	C
G	G	G
T	T	T
T	T	C
G	A	G
C	C	C

Skills Lab

Pre-Lab: Competing For Resources

Problem How can competition lead to speciation?

Materials assorted tools, large and small seeds, large and small paper plates, timer or clock with second hand

Lab Manual Chapter 17 Lab

Skills Focus Use Models, Predict, Apply Concepts

Connect to the **Big idea** Speciation is not easy to see in nature. Usually, new phenotypes take years to emerge or become common enough to be noticed. Also, new phenotypes can be difficult to track in a complex environment. For scientists who want to study speciation, islands can provide an ideal environment.

Peter and Rosemary Grant spent years studying finches on the Galápagos Islands. They measured and recorded the traits and diets of hundreds of birds. During a year with a severe drought, the Grants were able to observe natural selection in action as food became scarce. In this lab you will model variation in bird beaks and diet to demonstrate the impact of competition on survival and speciation.

Background Questions

a. Review What is speciation?

b. Relate Cause and Effect How did geographic isolation lead to speciation among the Galápagos finches?

c. Compare and Contrast How does an adaptation differ from other inherited traits?

Pre-Lab Questions

Preview the procedure in the lab manual.

1. Use Models In this lab, what do the different types of tools represent?

2. Predict Which tools do you think will work best for picking up small seeds? Which will work best for picking up large seeds?

3. Design an Experiment Why will the time you have to collect seeds be limited?

BIOLOGY.com   Search   Chapter 17   GO

Visit Chapter 17 online to test yourself on chapter content and to find activities to help you learn.

Untamed Science Video Climb the cliffs of Hawaii with the Untamed Science crew to discover how geographic isolation can result in a new species.

Data Analysis Find out what happened to Galápagos finches during a drought by comparing data on finches and their food sources.

Art Review Review your understanding of alleles and allele frequencies in a population.

Art in Motion Watch how different types of selection change the types of individuals that comprise a population.

Tutor Tube Learn more about the mechanisms of speciation from the tutor.

17 Study Guide

Big idea ▶ Evolution

A new species can form when a population splits into two groups that are isolated from one another. The gene pools of the two groups may become so different that the groups can no longer interbreed.

17.1 Genes and Variation

🔑 Evolution is a change in the frequency of alleles in a population over time.

🔑 Three sources of genetic variation are mutation, genetic recombination during sexual reproduction, and lateral gene transfer.

🔑 The number of phenotypes produced for a trait depends on how many genes control the trait.

gene pool (483)   single-gene trait (485)
allele frequency (483)   polygenic trait (486)

17.2 Evolution as Genetic Change in Populations

🔑 Natural selection on single-gene traits can lead to changes in allele frequencies and, thus, to changes in phenotype frequencies.

🔑 Natural selection on polygenic traits can affect the relative fitness of phenotypes and thereby produce one of three types of selection: directional selection, stabilizing selection, or disruptive selection.

🔑 In small populations, individuals that carry a particular allele may leave more descendants than other individuals leave, just by chance. Over time, a series of chance occurrences can cause an allele to become more or less common in a population.

🔑 The Hardy-Weinberg principle predicts that five conditions can disturb genetic equilibrium and cause evolution to occur: (1) nonrandom mating; (2) small population size; and (3) immigration or emigration; (4) mutations; or (5) natural selection.

directional selection (489)   founder effect (490)
stabilizing selection (489)   genetic equilibrium (491)
disruptive selection (489)   Hardy-Weinberg
genetic drift (490)   principle (491)
bottleneck effect (490)   sexual selection (492)

17.3 The Process of Speciation

🔑 When populations become reproductively isolated, they can evolve into two separate species. Reproductive isolation can develop in a variety of ways, including behavioral isolation, geographic isolation, and temporal isolation.

🔑 Speciation in Galápagos finches most likely occurred by founding of a new population, geographic isolation, changes in the new population's gene pool, behavioral isolation, and ecological competition.

species (494)   behavioral isolation (495)
speciation (494)   geographic isolation (495)
reproductive isolation (494) temporal isolation (495)

17.4 Molecular Evolution

🔑 A molecular clock uses mutation rates in DNA to estimate the time that two species have been evolving independently.

🔑 One way in which new genes evolve is through the duplication, and then modification, of existing genes.

🔑 Small changes in Hox gene activity during embryological development can produce large changes in adult animals.

molecular clock (498)

Think Visually

Construct a concept map explaining the sources of genetic variation.

17 Assessment

17.1 Genes and Variation

Understand Key Concepts

1. The combined genetic information of all members of a particular population forms a
   a. gene pool.
   b. niche.
   c. phenotype.
   d. population.

2. Mutations that improve an individual's ability to survive and reproduce are
   a. harmful.
   b. neutral.
   c. beneficial.
   d. chromosomal.

3. Traits, such as human height, that are controlled by more than one gene are known as
   a. single-gene traits.
   b. polygenic traits.
   c. recessive traits.
   d. dominant traits.

4. Explain what the term *allele frequency* means. Include an example illustrating your answer.

5. Explain why sexual reproduction is a source of genetic variation.

6. Explain what determines the number of phenotypes for a given trait.

7. What is *lateral gene transfer*?

8. Define evolution in genetic terms.

Think Critically

9. **Compare and Contrast** Which kind of mutation has the greater potential to affect the evolution of a population: a mutation to a body cell or a mutation in an egg cell? Explain.

10. **Apply Concepts** Explain how natural selection is related to phenotypes and genotypes.

11. **Apply Concepts** Explain how natural selection is related to individuals and populations.

12. **Relate Cause and Effect** How does genetic recombination affect genetic variation?

17.2 Evolution as Genetic Change in Populations

Understand Key Concepts

13. The type of selection in which individuals of average size have greater fitness than small or large individuals have is called
    a. disruptive selection.   c. directional selection.
    b. stabilizing selection.   d. neutral selection.

14. If coat color in a rabbit population is a polygenic trait, which process might have produced the graph below?

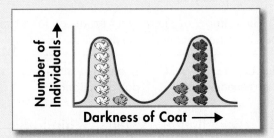

    a. disruptive selection   c. directional selection
    b. stabilizing selection   d. genetic equilibrium

15. A random change in a small population's allele frequency is known as
    a. a gene pool   c. variation
    b. genetic drift   d. fitness

16. What is *fitness* in genetic terms?

17. How do stabilizing selection and disruptive selection differ?

18. What is genetic equilibrium? In what kinds of situations is it likely to occur?

Think Critically

19. **Compare and Contrast** Distinguish between the ways in which natural selection affects single-gene traits and the ways in which it affects polygenic traits. How are phenotype frequencies altered in each case?

20. **Infer** In a certain population of plants, flower size is a polygenic trait. What kind of selection is likely to occur if environmental conditions favor small flowers?

21. **Infer** A road built through a forest splits a population of frogs into two large groups. The allele frequencies of the two groups are identical. Has genetic drift occurred? Why or why not?

22. **Form a Hypothesis** DDT is an insecticide that was first used in the 1940s to kill mosquitoes and stop the spread of malaria. As time passed, people began to notice that DDT became less effective. Explain, in genetic terms, how the insects became resistant to the pesticide.

17.3 The Process of Speciation

Understand Key Concepts

23. Temporal isolation occurs when two different populations
    a. develop different mating behaviors.
    b. become geographically separated.
    c. reproduce at different times.
    d. interbreed.

24. When two populations no longer interbreed, what is the result?
    a. genetic equilibrium   **c.** stabilizing selection
    b. reproductive isolation **d.** artificial selection

25. Explain how the different species of Galápagos finches may have evolved.

Think Critically

26. **Relate Cause and Effect** Explain why reproductive isolation usually must occur before a population splits into two distinct species.

27. **Form a Hypothesis** A botanist identifies two distinct species of violets growing in a field, as shown in the left of the illustration below. Also in the field are several other types of violets that, although somewhat similar to the two known species, appear to be new species. Develop a hypothesis explaining how the new species may have originated.

Viola pedatifida   *Viola sagittata*   Other violets

EPIDEMIC

The genes of flu viruses mutate often, and different strains can swap genes if they infect the same host at the same time. These characteristics produce genetic diversity that enables the virus to evolve.

Flu viruses also undergo natural selection. Think of our bodies as the environment for viruses. Our immune system attacks viruses by "recognizing" proteins on the surface of the viruses. Viruses whose proteins our bodies can recognize and destroy have low fitness. Viruses our bodies can't recognize have higher fitness.

Viral evolution regularly produces slightly different surface proteins that our immune systems can't recognize right away. These strains evade the immune system long enough to make people sick. That's

Influenza Virus

why you can catch the flu every winter, and why new flu vaccines must be made every year.

But now and then, influenza evolution produces radically new molecular "disguises" that our immune systems can't recognize *at all*. These can be deadly, like the 1918 strain. If a strain like that were to appear today, it could kill many people. That's why researchers are worried about "bird flu"—a strain of flu that can pass from birds, such as chickens, to humans.

1. **Connect to the Big idea** Explain why mutation and natural selection make developing new flu vaccines necessary every year.

2. **Infer** People do not need to receive a new measles vaccination every year. What does this suggest about a difference between flu viruses and the measles virus?

3. **Apply Concepts** Can you think of any other issues in public health that relate directly to evolutionary change?

Understand Key Concepts

28. A group of related genes that resulted from the duplication and modification of a single gene is called a

   a. gene pool.   **c.** lateral gene transfer.
   b. molecular clock.   **d.** gene family.

29. Each "tick" of a molecular clock is an occurrence of

   a. genetic drift.   **c.** DNA mutation.
   b. crossing-over.   **d.** mitosis.

30. How do chromosomes gain an extra copy of a gene during meiosis?

31. What are neutral mutations?

32. What is the study of "evo-devo," and how is it related to evolution?

Think Critically

33. Pose Questions What kinds of questions would scientists who are studying the evolution of Hox genes most likely be asking?

34. Apply Concepts Describe the relationship between evolutionary time and the similarity of genes in two species.

Connecting Concepts

Use Science Graphics

Use the data table to answer questions 35 and 36.

Frequency of Alleles		
Year	Frequency of Allele *B*	Frequency of Allele *b*
1910	0.81	0.19
1930	0.49	0.51
1950	0.25	0.75
1970	0.10	0.90

35. Interpret Tables Describe the trend shown by the data in the table.

36. Form a Hypothesis What might account for the trend shown by the data?

Write About Science

37. Explanation Explain the process that may have caused fruit flies to have fewer legs than their ancestors had.

38. Assess the Big idea Sometimes, biologists say, "Evolution is ecology over time." Explain that statement.

Analyzing Data

The graph shows data regarding the lengths of the beaks of three finch species. The percentage of individuals in each category of beak length is given.

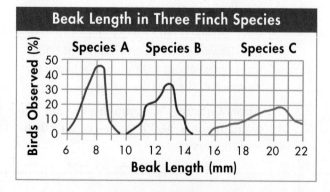

Beak Length in Three Finch Species

39. Interpret Graphs What is the shortest beak length observed in species A?

   a. 3 mm   **c.** 9 mm
   b. 6 mm   **d.** 12 mm

40. Analyze Data Which of the following is a logical interpretation of the data?

   a. Species B eats the smallest seeds.
   b. About 50 percent of species C eats seeds that are 20 mm long.
   c. Species C eats the largest seeds.
   d. All three species eat seeds of the same size.

Standardized Test Prep

Multiple Choice

1. Which of the following conditions is MOST likely to result in changes in allele frequencies in a population?
   A random mating
   B small population size
   C no migrations into or out of a population
   D absence of natural selection

2. Mutations and the genetic recombination that occurs during sexual reproduction are both sources of
   A genetic variation.
   B stabilizing selection.
   C genetic equilibrium.
   D genetic drift.

3. In a population of lizards, the smallest and largest lizards are more easily preyed upon than medium-size lizards. What kind of natural selection is MOST likely to occur in this situation?
   A genetic drift   C stabilizing selection
   B sexual selection   D directional selection

4. Populations of antibiotic-resistant bacteria are the result of the process of
   A natural selection.   C genetic drift.
   B temporal isolation.   D artificial selection.

5. If species A and B have very similar genes and proteins, what is probably true?
   A Species A and B share a relatively recent common ancestor.
   B Species A evolved independently of species B for a long period.
   C Species A is younger than species B.
   D Species A is older than species B.

6. When two species reproduce at different times, the situation is called
   A genetic drift.
   B temporal selection.
   C temporal isolation.
   D lateral gene transfer.

7. The length of time that two taxa have been evolving separately can be estimated using
   A genetic drift.   C a molecular clock.
   B gene duplication.   D Hox genes.

Questions 8–9

The graphs below show the changes in crab color at one beach.

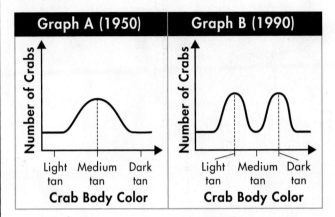

8. What process occurred over the 40-year period?
   A artificial selection   C stabilizing selection
   B directional selection   D disruptive selection

9. Which of the following is MOST likely to have caused the change in the distribution?
   A A new predator arrived that preferred dark-tan crabs.
   B A new predator arrived that preferred light-tan crabs.
   C A change in beach color made medium-tan crabs the least visible to predators.
   D A change in beach color made medium-tan crabs the most visible to predators.

Open-Ended Response

10. How does evolution change the relative frequency of alleles in a gene pool? Why does this happen?

If You Have Trouble With . . .

Question	1	2	3	4	5	6	7	8	9	10
See Lesson	17.3	17.1	17.2	17.2	17.4	17.3	17.4	17.2	17.2	17.1

18 Classification

The National Museum of Natural History houses one of the largest collections of bird species in the world. The collection represents about 80 percent of the world's diversity of birds.

INSIDE:

- **18.1 Finding Order in Diversity**
- **18.2 Modern Evolutionary Classification**
- **18.3 Building the Tree of Life**

CHAPTER
MYSTERY

GRIN AND BEAR IT

If you simply looked at a polar bear and brown bear, you would probably never doubt that they are members of different species. Polar bears grow much larger than brown bears, and their paws have adapted to swimming long distances and to walking on snow and ice. Their white fur camouflages them, but the coats on brown bears are, well, brown—and their paws aren't adapted to water.

Clearly polar bears and brown bears are very different physically. But do physical characteristics tell the whole story? Remember the definition of *species*: "a group of similar organisms that can breed and produce fertile offspring." Well, polar bears and brown bears can mate and produce fertile offspring. They must be members of the same species, then. But are they? As you read this chapter, look for clues to whether polar bears are a separate species. Then, solve the mystery.

Never Stop Exploring Your World.
Solving the mystery of scientific classification is only the beginning. Take a video field trip with the ecogeeks of Untamed Science to see where the mystery leads.

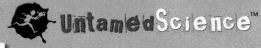

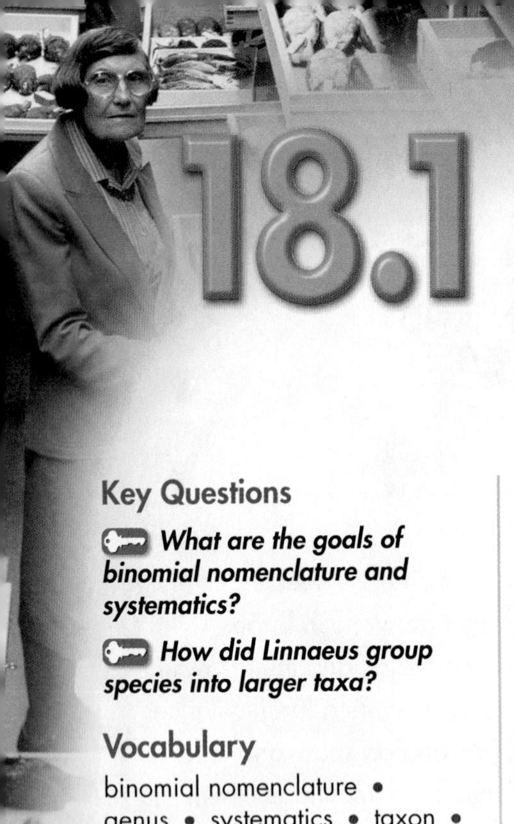

18.1 Finding Order in Diversity

Key Questions

🔑 What are the goals of binomial nomenclature and systematics?

🔑 How did Linnaeus group species into larger taxa?

Vocabulary

binomial nomenclature •
genus • systematics • taxon •
family • order • class •
phylum • kingdom

Taking Notes

Preview Visuals Before you read, look at **Figure 18–5.** Notice all the levels of classification. As you read, refer to the figure again.

THINK ABOUT IT Scientists have been trying to identify, name, and find order in the diversity of life for a long time. The first scientific system for naming and grouping organisms was set up long before Darwin. In recent decades, biologists have been completing a changeover from that older system of names and classification to a newer strategy that is based on evolutionary theory.

Assigning Scientific Names

🔑 **What are the goals of binomial nomenclature and systematics?**

The first step in understanding and studying diversity is to describe and name each species. To be useful, each scientific name must refer to one and only one species, and everyone must use the same name for that species. But what kind of name should be used? Common names can be confusing, because they vary among languages and from place to place. The animal in **Figure 18–1,** for example, can be called a cougar, a puma, a panther, or a mountain lion. Furthermore, different species may share a common name. In the United Kingdom, the word *buzzard* refers to a hawk, whereas in the United States, *buzzard* refers to a vulture.

Back in the eighteenth century, European scientists recognized that these kinds of common names were confusing, so they agreed to assign Latin or Greek names to each species. Unhappily, that didn't do much to clear up the confusion. Early scientific names often described species in great detail, so the names could be long. For example, the English translation of the scientific name of a tree might be "Oak with deeply divided leaves that have no hairs on their undersides and no teeth around their edges." It was also difficult to standardize these names, because different scientists focused on different characteristics. Many of these same characteristics can still be used to identify organisms when using dichotomous keys, as you can see in **Figure 18–2.**

FIGURE 18–1 Common Names You might recognize this as a cougar, a puma, a panther, or a mountain lion—all common names for the same animal. The scientific name for this animal is *Felis concolor.*

USING A DICHOTOMOUS KEY

FIGURE 18–2 A dichotomous key is used to identify organisms. It consists of a series of paired statements or questions that describe alternative possible characteristics of an organism. The paired statements usually describe the presence or absence of certain visible characteristics or structures. Each set of choices is arranged so that each step produces a smaller subset.

Suppose you found a leaf that you wanted to identify. The leaf looks like the one shown here. Use the key to identify this leaf.

Step	Leaf Characteristics	Tree
1a	Compound leaf (leaves divided into leaflets) . . . go to Step 2	
1b	Simple leaf (leaf not divided into leaflets) . . . go to Step 4	
2a	Leaflets all attached at a central point	Buckeye  ▶
2b	Leaflets attached at several points . . . go to Step 3	
3a	Leaflets tapered with pointed tips	 ◀ Pecan
3b	Leaflets oval with rounded tips	Locust  ▶
4a	Veins branched out from one central point . . . go to Step 5	
4b	Veins branched off main vein in middle of the leaf . . . go to Step 6	
5a	Heart-shaped leaf	Redbud  ▶
5b	Star-shaped leaf	 ◀ Sweet gum
6a	Leaf with jagged edges	Birch
6b	Leaf with smooth edges	Magnolia  ▶

Because your leaf is a simple leaf, you skip ahead to Step 4.

Continue reading the statements until you determine the identity of your leaf.

Because your leaf has jagged edges, you determine that it's from a birch tree.

Polar bears and
brown bears inter-
breed and produce
fertile hybrids in zoos,
but they very rarely
interbreed in nature.
What do you think
this means about the
relationship between
them?

Binomial Nomenclature In the 1730s, Swedish botanist Carolus Linnaeus, developed a two-word naming system called **binomial nomenclature.** **In binomial nomenclature, each species is assigned a two-part scientific name.** Scientific names are written in italic. The first word begins with a capital letter, and the second word is lowercased.

The polar bear in **Figure 18–3** is called *Ursus maritimus*. The first part of the name—*Ursus*—is the genus to which the organism belongs. A **genus** (plural: genera, JEN ur uh) is a group of similar species. The genus *Ursus* contains five other species of bears, including *Ursus arctos*, the brown bear or "grizzly."

The second part of a scientific name—in these examples, *maritimus* or *arctos*—is unique to each species. A species, remember, is generally defined as a group of individuals capable of interbreeding and producing fertile offspring. The species name is often a description of an important trait or the organism's habitat. The Latin word *maritimus*, refers to the sea, because polar bears often live on pack ice that floats in the sea.

In Your Notebook *The word* binomial *means "having two names." How does this meaning apply to binomial nomenclature?*

FIGURE 18–3 Binomial Nomenclature The scientific name of the polar bear is *Ursus maritimus*, which means "marine bear." The scientific name of the red maple is *Acer rubrum*. The genus *Acer* consists of all maple trees. The species *rubrum* describes the red maple's color.

Classifying Species Into Larger Groups In addition to naming organisms, biologists also try to organize, or classify, living and fossil species into larger groups that have biological meaning. In a useful classification system, organisms in a particular group are more similar to one another than they are to organisms in other groups. The science of naming and grouping organisms is called **systematics** (sis tuh MAT iks). **The goal of systematics is to organize living things into groups that have biological meaning.** Biologists often refer to these groups as **taxa** (singular: taxon).

Whether you realize it or not, you use classification systems all the time. You may, for example, talk about "teachers" or "mechanics." Sometimes you refer to a smaller, more specific group, such as "biology teachers" or "auto mechanics." When you do this, you refer to these groups using widely accepted names and characteristics that many people understand. In the same way, when you hear the word *bird*, you immediately think of an animal with wings and feathers.

Quick Lab
GUIDED INQUIRY

Classifying Fruits ✂️ ⚠️

❶ Obtain five different fruits.

❷ Use a knife to cut each fruit open and examine its structure. **CAUTION:** *Be careful with sharp instruments. Do not eat any of the cut fruits.*

❸ Construct a table with five rows and four columns. Label each row with the name of a different fruit.

❹ Examine the fruits, and choose four characteristics that help you tell the fruits apart. Label the columns in your table with the names of these characteristics.

❺ Record a description of each fruit in the table.

Analyze and Conclude

1. Classify Based on your table, which fruits most closely resemble one another?

The Linnaean Classification System

🔑 **How did Linnaeus group species into larger taxa?**

In addition to creating the system of binomial nomenclature, Linnaeus also developed a classification system that organized species into taxa that formed a hierarchy or set of ordered ranks. Linnaeus's original system had just four levels. 🔑 **Over time, Linnaeus's original classification system expanded to include seven hierarchical taxa: species, genus, family, order, class, phylum, and kingdom.**

We've already discussed the two smallest categories, species and genus. Now let's work our way up to the rank of kingdom by examining how camels are classified. The scientific name of a camel with two humps is *Camelus bactrianus.* (Bactria was an ancient country in Asia.) As you can see in **Figure 18–5,** the genus *Camelus* also includes another species, *Camelus dromedarius,* the dromedary, which has only one hump. In deciding how to place organisms into these larger taxa, Linnaeus grouped species according to anatomical similarities and differences.

▶ *Family* The South American llama bears some resemblance to Bactrian camels and dromedaries. But the llama is more similar to other South American species than it is to European and Asian camels. Therefore, llamas are placed in a different genus, *Lama;* their species name is *Lama glama.* Several genera that share many similarities, like *Camelus* and *Lama,* are grouped into a larger category, the **family**—in this case, Camelidae.

▶ *Order* Closely related families are grouped into the next larger rank—an **order.** Camels and llamas (family Camelidae) are grouped with several other animal families, including deer (family Cervidae) and cattle (family Bovidae), into the order Artiodactyla, hoofed animals with an even number of toes.

FIGURE 18–4 Carolus Linnaeus

BUILD Vocabulary

MULTIPLE MEANINGS The words **family, order, class,** and **kingdom** all have different meanings in biology than they do in common usage. For example, in systematics, a *family* is a group of genera. In everyday usage, a *family* is a group of people who are related to one another. Use a dictionary to find the common meanings of *order, class,* and *kingdom.*

Class Similar orders, in turn, are grouped into the next larger rank, a **class.** The order Artiodactyla is placed in the class Mammalia, which includes all animals that are warmblooded, have body hair, and produce milk for their young.

▶ **Phylum** Classes are grouped into a **phylum.** A phylum includes organisms that are different but share important characteristics. The class Mammalia is grouped with birds (class Aves), reptiles (class Reptilia), amphibians (class Amphibia), and all classes of fish into the phylum Chordata. These organisms share important body-plan features, among them a nerve cord along the back.

▶ **Kingdom** The largest and most inclusive of Linnaeus's taxonomic categories is the **kingdom.** All multicellular animals are placed in the kingdom Animalia.

FIGURE 18–5 From Species to Kingdom
This illustration shows how a Bactrian camel, *Camelus bactrianus,* is grouped within each taxonomic category. Only some representative organisms are illustrated for each taxon above the genus level. **Interpret Visuals** *What phylum does Camelus bactrianus belong to?*

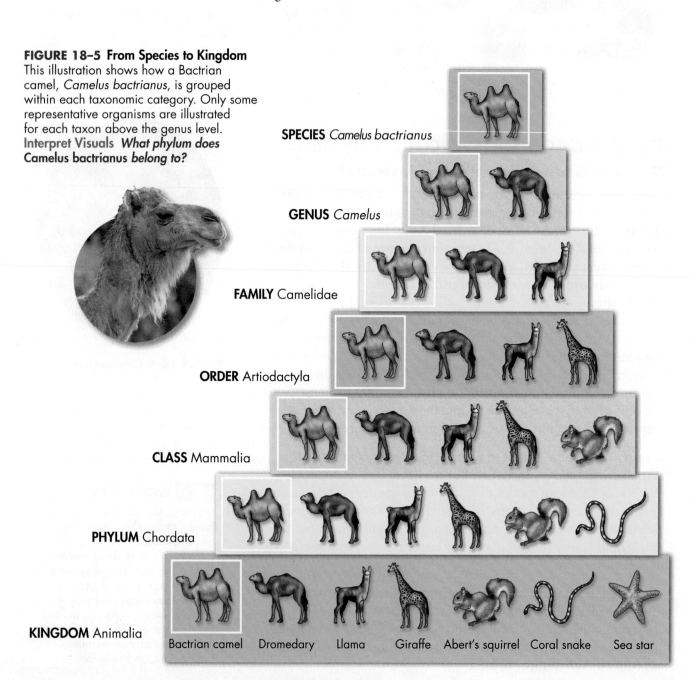

SPECIES *Camelus bactrianus*

GENUS *Camelus*

FAMILY Camelidae

ORDER Artiodactyla

CLASS Mammalia

PHYLUM Chordata

KINGDOM Animalia

Bactrian camel   Dromedary   Llama   Giraffe   Abert's squirrel   Coral snake   Sea star

Problems With Traditional Classification In a sense, members of a species determine which organisms belong to that species by deciding with whom they mate and produce fertile offspring. There is thus a "natural" definition of species. Researchers, on the other hand, define Linnaean ranks above the level of species. Because, over time, systematists have emphasized a variety of characteristics, some of these groups have been defined in different ways at different times.

For example, Linnaeus's strategy of classifying organisms according to visible similarities and differences seems simple at first. But how should scientists decide which similarities and differences are most important? If you lived in Linnaeus's time, for example, how would you have classified the animals shown in **Figure 18–6**? Adult barnacles and limpets live attached to rocks and have similar-looking shells. Adult crabs look quite unlike both barnacles and limpets. Based on these features, would you place limpets and barnacles together, and crabs in a different group? As biologists attempted to classify more organisms over time, these kinds of questions arose frequently.

Linnaeus was a good scientist, and he chose his characteristics carefully. Many of his groups are still valid under modern classification schemes. But Linnaeus worked more than a century before Darwin published his ideas about descent with modification. Modern systematists apply Darwin's ideas to classification and try look beyond simple similarities and differences to ask questions about evolutionary relationships. Linnaeus grouped organisms strictly according to similarities and differences. Scientists today try to assign species to a larger group in ways that reflect how closely members of those groups are related to each other.

FIGURE 18–6 Barnacles, Limpets, and Crabs Problems can arise when species are classified based on easily observed traits. Look closely at the barnacles (top), the limpets (bottom), and the crab (left). Notice their similarities and differences. **Compare and Contrast** *Which animals seem most alike? Why?*

18.1 Assessment

Review Key Concepts 🔑

1. a. Review Identify two goals of systematics.
 b. Explain Why do the common names of organisms—like *daisy* or *mountain lion*—often cause problems for scientists?
 c. Classify The scientific name of the sugar maple is *Acer saccharum.* What does each part of the name designate?
2. a. Review List the ranks in the Linnaean system of classification, beginning with the smallest.

b. Explain In which group of organisms are the members more closely associated—all of the organisms in the same kingdom or all of the organisms in the same order? Explain your answer.
c. Apply Concepts What do scientists mean when they say that species is the only "natural" rank in classification?

Apply the Big idea

Unity and Diversity of Life
3. Which category has more biological meaning— all brown birds or all birds descended from a hawklike ancestor? Why?

18.2 Modern Evolutionary Classification

Key Questions

🔑 What is the goal of evolutionary classification?

🔑 What is a cladogram?

🔑 How are DNA sequences used in classification?

Vocabulary

phylogeny
clade
monophyletic group
cladogram
derived character

Taking Notes

Outline Make an outline of this lesson using the green headings as the main topics and the blue headings as subtopics. As you read, fill in details under each heading.

THINK ABOUT IT Darwin's ideas about a "tree of life" suggests a new way to classify organisms—not just based on similarities and differences, but instead based on evolutionary relationships. Under this system, taxa are arranged according to how closely related they are. When organisms are rearranged in this way, some of the old Linnaean ranks fall apart. For example, the Linnaean class reptilia isn't valid unless birds are included—which means birds are reptiles! And not only are birds reptiles, they're also dinosaurs! Wondering why? To understand, we need to look at the way evolutionary classification works.

Evolutionary Classification

🔑 What is the goal of evolutionary classification?

The concept of descent with modification led to the study of **phylogeny** (fy LAHJ uh nee)—the evolutionary history of lineages. Advances in phylogeny, in turn, led to phylogenetic systematics. 🔑 **The goal of phylogenetic systematics, or evolutionary classification, is to group species into larger categories that reflect lines of evolutionary descent, rather than overall similarities and differences.**

Common Ancestors Phylogenetic systematics places organisms into higher taxa whose members are more closely related to one another than they are to members of any other group. The larger a taxon is, the farther back in time all of its members shared a common ancestor. This is true all the way up to the largest taxa.

Clades Classifying organisms according to these rules places them into groups called clades. A **clade** is a group of species that includes a single common ancestor and all descendants of that ancestor—living and extinct. How are clades different from Linnaean taxa? A clade must be a monophyletic (mahn oh fy LET ik) group. A **monophyletic group** includes a single common ancestor and *all* of its descendants.

Some groups of organisms defined before the advent of evolutionary classification are monophyletic. Some, however, are paraphyletic, meaning that the group includes a common ancestor but excludes one or more groups of descendants. These groups are invalid under evolutionary classification.

BUILD Vocabulary

WORD ORIGINS The word **cladogram** comes from two Greek words: *klados*, meaning "branch," and *gramma*, meaning "something that is written or drawn." A cladogram is an evolutionary diagram with a branching pattern.

> **In Your Notebook** In your own words, explain what makes a clade monophyletic or paraphyletic.

Cladograms

⚙ What is a cladogram?

Modern evolutionary classification uses a method called cladistic analysis. Cladistic analysis compares carefully selected traits to determine the order in which groups of organisms branched off from their common ancestors. This information is then used to link clades together into a diagram called a **cladogram.** ⚙ **A cladogram links groups of organisms by showing how evolutionary lines, or lineages, branched off from common ancestors.**

Building Cladograms

To understand how cladograms are constructed, think back to the process of speciation. A speciation event, in which one ancestral species splits into two new ones, is the basis of each branch point, or node, in a cladogram. That node represents the last point at which the two new lineages shared a common ancestor. As shown in part 1 of **Figure 18–7,** a node splits a lineage into two separate lines of evolutionary ancestry.

Each node represents the last point at which species in lineages above the node shared a common ancestor. The bottom, or "root" of a cladogram, represents the common ancestor shared by all of the organisms in the cladogram. A cladogram's branching patterns indicate degrees of relatedness among organisms. Look at part 2 of **Figure 18–7.** Because lineages 3 and 4 share a common ancestor more recently with each other than they do with lineage 2, you know that lineages 3 and 4 are more closely related to each other than either is to lineage 2. The same is true for lineages 2, 3, and 4. In terms of ancestry, they are more closely related to each other than any of them is to lineage 1. Look at the cladogram shown in part 3 of **Figure 18–7.** Does it surprise you that amphibians are more closely related to mammals than they are to ray-finned fish? In terms of ancestry, it's true!

FIGURE 18–7 Building a Cladogram A cladogram shows relative degrees of relatedness among lineages.

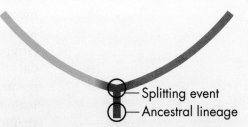

❶ Cladograms are diagrams showing how evolutionary lines, or lineages, split from each other over time. This diagram shows a single ancestral lineage splitting into two. The point of splitting is called a "node" in the cladogram.

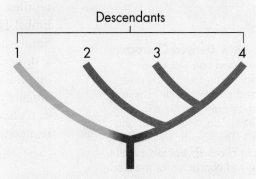

❷ How recently lineages share a common ancestor reflect how closely the lineages are related to one another. Here, lineages 3 and 4 are each more closely related to each other than any of them is to any other lineage.

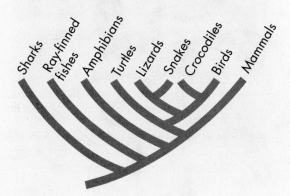

❸ This cladogram shows the evolutionary relationships among vertebrates, animals with backbones.

Derived Characters In contrast to Linnaean taxonomy, cladistic analysis focuses on certain kinds of characters, called derived characters, when assigning organisms into clades. A **derived character** is a trait that arose in the most recent common ancestor of a particular lineage and was passed along to its descendants.

Whether or not a character is derived depends on the level at which you're grouping organisms. Here's what we mean. **Figure 18–8** shows several traits that are shared by coyotes and lions, both members of the clade Carnivora. Four limbs is a derived character for the entire clade Tetrapoda because the common ancestor of all tetrapods had four limbs, and this trait was passed to its descendants. Hair is a derived character for the clade Mammalia. But for mammals, four limbs is *not* a derived character—if it were, only mammals would have that trait. Nor is four limbs or hair a derived character for clade Carnivora. Specialized shearing teeth, however, is. What about retractable claws? This trait is found in lions but not in coyotes. Thus, retractable claws is a derived character for the clade Felidae—also known as cats.

Losing Traits Notice above that four limbs is a derived character for clade Tetrapoda. But what about snakes? Snakes are definitely reptiles, which are tetrapods. But snakes certainly don't have four limbs! The *ancestors* of snakes, however, did have four limbs. Somewhere in the lineage leading to modern snakes, that trait was lost. Because distantly related groups of organisms can sometimes lose the same character, systematists are cautious about using the *absence* of a trait as a character in their analyses. After all, whales don't have four limbs either, but snakes are certainly more closely related to other reptiles than they are to whales.

FIGURE 18–8 Derived Characters
The coyote and lion share several characters—hair, four limbs, and specialized shearing teeth. These shared characters put them in the clades Tetrapoda, Mammalia, and Carnivora. The lion, however, has retractable claws. Retractable claws is the derived character for the clade Felidae.

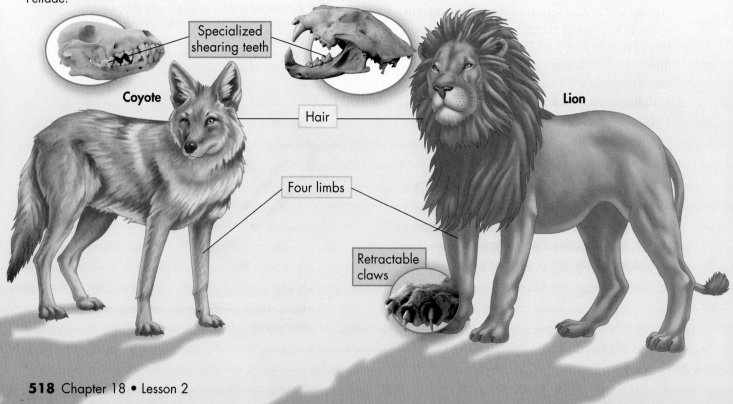

Coyote

Lion

Specialized shearing teeth

Hair

Four limbs

Retractable claws

INTERPRETING A CLADOGRAM

FIGURE 18–9 This cladogram shows the evolutionary history of cats. In a cladogram, all organisms in a clade share a set of derived characters. Notice that smaller clades are nested within larger clades. **Interpret Visuals** *For which clade in this cladogram is an amniotic egg a derived character?*

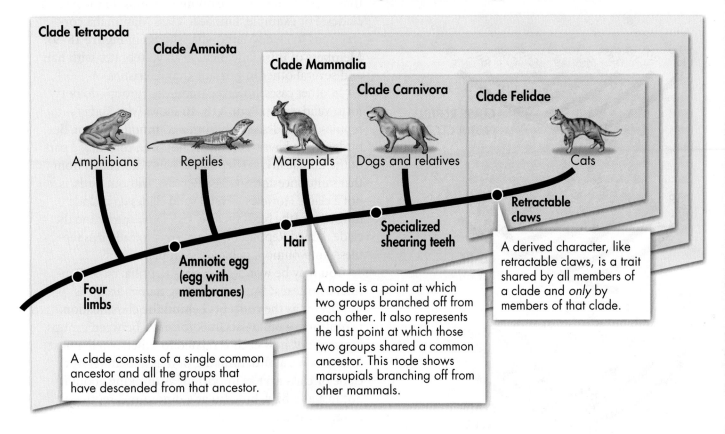

Clade Tetrapoda

Clade Amniota

Clade Mammalia

Clade Carnivora

Clade Felidae

Amphibians

Reptiles

Marsupials

Dogs and relatives

Cats

Retractable claws

Hair

Specialized shearing teeth

Amniotic egg (egg with membranes)

Four limbs

A clade consists of a single common ancestor and all the groups that have descended from that ancestor.

A node is a point at which two groups branched off from each other. It also represents the last point at which those two groups shared a common ancestor. This node shows marsupials branching off from other mammals.

A derived character, like retractable claws, is a trait shared by all members of a clade and *only* by members of that clade.

Interpreting Cladograms We can now put this information together to "read" a cladogram. **Figure 18–9** shows a simplified phylogeny of the cat family. The lowest node represents the last common ancestor of all four-limbed animals—members of the clade Tetrapoda. The forks in this cladogram show the order in which various groups branched off from the tetrapod lineage over the course of evolution. The positions of various characters in the cladogram reflect the order in which those characteristics arose in this lineage. In the lineage leading to cats, for example, specialized shearing teeth evolved before retractable claws. Furthermore, each derived character listed along the main trunk of the cladogram defines a clade. Hair, for example, is a defining character for the clade Mammalia. Retractable claws is a derived character shared only by the clade Felidae. Derived characters that occur "lower" on the cladogram than the branch point for a clade are not derived for that particular clade. Hair, for example, is not a derived character for the clade Carnivora.

In Your Notebook List the derived characters in *Figure 18–9* and explain which groups in the cladogram have those characters.

FIGURE 18–10 Clade or Not? A clade includes an ancestral species and all its descendants. Linnaean class Reptilia is not a clade because it does not include modern birds. Because it leaves this descendant group out, the class is paraphyletic. Clades Reptilia and Aves, however, are monophyletic and, therefore, valid clades. **Apply Concepts** *Would a group that included all of clade Reptilia plus amphibians be monophyletic or paraphyletic? Explain.*

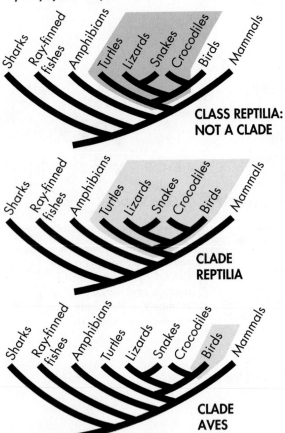

CLASS REPTILIA: NOT A CLADE

CLADE REPTILIA

CLADE AVES

Clades and Traditional Taxonomic Groups Which of the Linnaean groupings form clades, and which do not? Remember that a true clade must be monophyletic, which means that it contains an ancestral species and *all* of its descendants—it can't leave any out. It also cannot include any species which are not descendants of that original ancestor. Cladistic analysis shows that many traditional taxonomic groups do form valid clades. For example, Linnaean class Mammalia corresponds to clade Mammalia (shown in **Figure 18–9**). Members of this clade include all vertebrates with hair and several other important characteristics.

In other cases, however, traditional groups do not form valid clades. **Figure 18–10** shows why. Today's reptiles are all descended from a common ancestor. But birds, which have traditionally not been considered part of the Linnaean class Reptilia, are also descended from that same ancestor. So, class Reptilia, without birds, is not a clade. However, several valid clades *do* include birds: Aves (the birds themselves), Dinosauria, and the clade named Reptilia. So, is it correct to call birds reptiles? An evolutionary biologist would say yes!

You may be wondering: class Reptilia, clade Reptilia, who cares? But the resulting names aren't as important as the concepts behind the classification. Evolutionary biologists look for links between groups, figuring out how each is related to others. So the next time you see a bird, thinking of it as a member of a clade or class isn't as important as thinking about it not just as a bird, but also as a dinosaur, a reptile, a tetrapod, and a chordate.

Quick Lab
GUIDED INQUIRY

Constructing a Cladogram

❶ Identify the organism in the table that is least closely related to the others.

❷ Use the information in the table to construct a cladogram of these animals.

Analyze and Conclude

1. Interpret Tables What trait separates the least closely related animal from the other animals?

2. Apply Concepts Do you have enough information to determine where a frog should be placed on the cladogram? Explain your answer.

Derived Characters in Organisms			
Organism	**Derived Character**		
	Backbone	**Legs**	**Hair**
Earthworm	Absent	Absent	Absent
Trout	Present	Absent	Absent
Lizard	Present	Present	Absent
Human	Present	Present	Present

3. Draw Conclusions Does your cladogram indicate that lizards and humans share a more recent common ancestor than either does with an earthworm? Explain your answer.

DNA in Classification

How are DNA sequences used in classification?

The examples of cladistic analysis we've discussed so far are based largely on physical characteristics like skeletons and teeth. But the goal of modern systematics is to understand the evolutionary relationships of all life on Earth—from bacteria to plants, snails, and apes. How can we devise hypotheses about the common ancestors of organisms that appear to have no physical similarities?

Genes as Derived Characters Remember that all organisms carry genetic information in their DNA passed on from earlier generations. A wide range of organisms share a number of genes and show important homologies that can be used to determine evolutionary relationships. For example, all eukaryotic cells have mitochondria, and all mitochondria have their own genes. Because all genes mutate over time, shared genes contain differences that can be treated as derived characters in cladistic analysis. For that reason, similarities and differences in DNA can be used to develop hypotheses about evolutionary relationships. **In general, the more derived genetic characters two species share, the more recently they shared a common ancestor and the more closely they are related in evolutionary terms.**

New Techniques Suggest New Trees The use of DNA characters in cladistic analysis has helped to make evolutionary trees more accurate. Consider, for example, the birds in **Figure 18–11.** The African vulture in the top photograph looks a lot like the American vulture in the middle photograph. Both were traditionally classified in the falcon clade. But American vultures have a peculiar behavior: When they get overheated, they urinate on their legs, relying on evaporation to cool them down. Storks share this behavior, while African vultures do not. Could the behavior be a clue to the real relationships between these birds?

Biologists solved the puzzle by analyzing DNA from all three species. Molecular analysis showed that the DNA from American vultures is more similar to the DNA of storks than to the DNA of African vultures. DNA evidence therefore suggests that American vultures and storks share a more recent common ancestor than the American and African vultures do. Molecular analysis is a powerful tool that is now routinely used by taxonomists to supplement data from anatomy and answer questions like these.

FIGURE 18–11 DNA and Classification Scientists use similarities in the genetic makeup of organisms to help determine classification. Traditionally African vultures and American vultures were classified together in the falcon family. But DNA analysis suggests that American vultures are actually more closely related to storks.

MYSTERY CLUE

DNA comparisons show that some populations of brown bears are more closely related to polar bears than they are to other brown bears. What do you think this means for the classification of polar bears?

Often, scientists use DNA evidence when anatomical traits alone can't provide clear answers. Giant pandas and red pandas, for example, have given taxonomists a lot of trouble. These two species share anatomical similarities with both bears and raccoons, and both of them have peculiar wrist bones that work like a human thumb. DNA analysis revealed that the giant panda shares a more recent common ancestor with bears than with raccoons. DNA places red pandas, however, outside the bear clade. So pandas have been reclassified, placed with other bears in the clade Ursidae, as shown in **Figure 18–12.** What happened to the red panda? It is now placed in a different clade that also includes raccoons and other organisms such as seals and weasels.

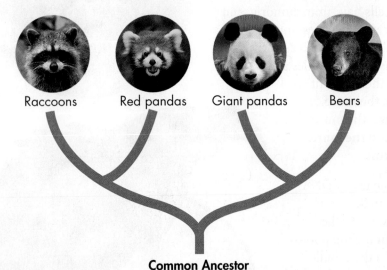

Raccoons   Red pandas   Giant pandas   Bears

Common Ancestor

FIGURE 18–12 Classification of Pandas Biologists used to classify the red panda and the giant panda together. However, cladistic analysis using DNA suggests that the giant panda shares a more recent common ancestor with bears than with either red pandas or raccoons.

18.2 Assessment

Review Key Concepts

1. a. Explain How does evolutionary classification differ from traditional classification?
b. Apply Concepts To an evolutionary taxonomist, what determines whether two species are in the same genus?

2. a. Explain What is a derived character?
b. Interpret Diagrams Along any one lineage, what do the locations of derived characters on a cladogram show? In your answer, use examples from **Figure 18–9.**

3. a. Review How do taxonomists use the DNA sequences of species to determine how closely two species are related?
b. Relate Cause and Effect Explain why the classification of American vultures has changed.

VISUAL THINKING

4. Examine the cladogram.
a. Interpret Diagrams Which groups—X and Y, or X , Y, and Z—have the most recent common ancestor?
b. Infer Which species—X and Y, or X and Z—share more derived characters?

X   Y   Z

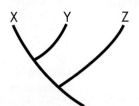

BIOLOGY.com   Search   Lesson 18.2   GO   • Self-Test   • Lesson Assessment

18.3 Building the Tree of Life

THINK ABOUT IT The process of identifying and naming all known organisms, living and extinct, is a huge first step toward the goal of systematics. Yet naming organisms is only part of the work. The real challenge is to group everything, from bacteria to dinosaurs to blue whales, in a way that reflects their evolutionary relationships. Over the years, new information and ways of studying organisms have produced major changes in Linnaeus's original scheme for organizing living things.

Changing Ideas About Kingdoms

🔑 **What are the six kingdoms of life as they are now identified?**

During Linnaeus's time, the only known differences among living things were the fundamental characteristics that separated animals from plants. Animals were organisms that moved from place to place and used food for energy. Plants were green organisms that generally did not move and got their energy from the sun.

As biologists learned more about the natural world, they realized that Linnaeus's two kingdoms—Animalia and Plantae—did not reflect the full diversity of life. Classification systems have changed dramatically since Linnaeus's time, as shown in **Figure 18–13.** And hypotheses about relationships among organisms are still changing today as new data are gathered.

Key Questions

🔑 *What are the six kingdoms of life as they are now identified?*

🔑 *What does the tree of life show?*

Vocabulary

domain • Bacteria • Archaea • Eukarya

Taking Notes

Concept Map As you read, construct a concept map describing the characteristics of the three domains.

Kingdoms of Life, 1700s–1990s

First Introduced	Names of Kingdoms					
1700s	Plantae					Animalia
Late 1800s	Protista			Plantae		Animalia
1950s	Monera		Protista	Fungi	Plantae	Animalia
1990s	Eubacteria	Archaebacteria	Protista	Fungi	Plantae	Animalia

FIGURE 18–13 From Two to Six Kingdoms This diagram shows some of the ways in which organisms have been classified into kingdoms since the 1700s.

Comparing the Domains

The table in **Figure 18–14** compares the three domains and six kingdoms. Use the information in the table to answer the following questions.

1. Interpret Tables Which kingdom has cells that lack cell walls?

2. Interpret Tables Which domain contains multicellular organisms?

3. Compare and Contrast On the basis of information in the table, how are the members of domain Archaea similar to those of domain Bacteria? How are organisms in domain Archaea similar to those in domain Eukarya?

Five Kingdoms As researchers began to study microorganisms, they discovered that single-celled organisms were significantly different from plants and animals. At first all microorganisms were placed in their own kingdom, named Protista. Then yeasts and molds, along with mushrooms, were placed in their own kingdom, Fungi.

Later still, scientists realized that bacteria lack the nuclei, mitochondria, and chloroplasts found in other forms of life. All prokaryotes (bacteria) were placed in yet another new kingdom, Monera. Single-celled eukaryotic organisms remained in the kingdom Protista. This process produced five kingdoms: Monera, Protista, Fungi, Plantae, and Animalia.

Six Kingdoms By the 1990s, researchers had learned a great deal about the genetics and biochemistry of bacteria. That knowledge made clear that the organisms in kingdom Monera were actually two genetically and biochemically different groups. As a result, the monerans were separated into two kingdoms, Eubacteria and Archaebacteria, bringing the total number of kingdoms to six. 🔑 **The six-kingdom system of classification includes the kingdoms Eubacteria, Archaebacteria, Protista, Fungi, Plantae, and Animalia.** This system of classification is shown in the bottom row of **Figure 18–13** on the previous page.

FIGURE 18–14 Three Domains Today organisms are grouped into three domains and six kingdoms. This table summarizes the key characteristics used to classify organisms into these major taxonomic groups.

Classification of Living Things

DOMAIN	Bacteria	Archaea	Eukarya			
KINGDOM	Eubacteria	Archaebacteria	"Protista"	Fungi	Plantae	Animalia
CELL TYPE	Prokaryote	Prokaryote	Eukaryote	Eukaryote	Eukaryote	Eukaryote
CELL STRUCTURES	Cell walls with peptidoglycan	Cell walls without peptidoglycan	Cell walls of cellulose in some; some have chloroplasts	Cell walls of chitin	Cell walls of cellulose; chloroplasts	No cell walls or chloroplasts
NUMBER OF CELLS	Unicellular	Unicellular	Most unicellular; some colonial; some multicellular	Most multicellular; some unicellular	Most multicellular: some green algae unicellular	Multicellular
MODE OF NUTRITION	Autotroph or heterotroph	Autotroph or heterotroph	Autotroph or heterotroph	Heterotroph	Autotroph	Heterotroph
EXAMPLES	*Streptococcus, Escherichia coli*	Methanogens, halophiles	*Amoeba, Paramecium,* slime molds, giant kelp	Mushrooms, yeasts	Mosses, ferns, flowering plants	Sponges, worms, insects, fishes, mammals

Three Domains Genomic analysis has revealed that the two main prokaryotic groups are even more different from each other, and from eukaryotes, than previously thought. So biologists established a new taxonomic category—the domain. A **domain** is a larger, more inclusive category than a kingdom. Under this system, there are three domains—domain Bacteria (corresponding to the kingdom Eubacteria); domain Archaea (which corresponds to the kingdom Archaebacteria); and domain Eukarya (kingdoms Fungi, Plantae, and Animalia, and the "Protista").

Why do we put quotations around about the old kingdom Protista? Well, scientists now recognize that this is a paraphyletic group. This means that there is no way to put all unicellular eukaryotes into a clade that contains a single common ancestor, all of its descendants, and only those descendants. Since only monophyletic groups are valid under evolutionary classification, we use quotations to show that this is not a true clade. A summary of the three-domain system is shown in **Figure 18–14.**

The Tree of All Life

🔑 *What does the tree of life show?*

Remember that modern evolutionary classification is a rapidly changing science with a difficult goal—to present all life on a single evolutionary tree. As evolutionary biologists study relationships among taxa, they regularly change not only the way organisms are grouped, but also sometimes the names of groups. Remember that cladograms are visual presentations of hypotheses about relationships, and not hard and fast facts. 🔑 **The tree of life shows current hypotheses regarding evolutionary relationships among the taxa within the three domains of life.**

Domain Bacteria Members of the domain **Bacteria** are unicellular and prokaryotic. Their cells have thick, rigid walls that surround a cell membrane. The cell walls contain a substance known as peptidoglycan (PEP tih doh gly kun). These bacteria are ecologically diverse, ranging from free-living soil organisms to deadly parasites. Some photosynthesize, while others do not. Some need oxygen to survive, while others are killed by oxygen. This domain corresponds to the kingdom Eubacteria.

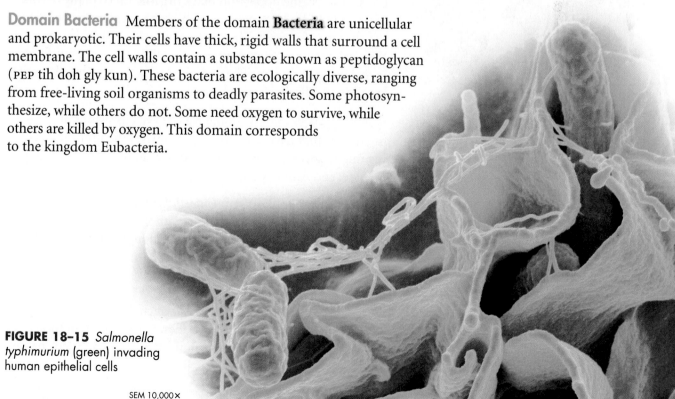

FIGURE 18–15 *Salmonella typhimurium* (green) invading human epithelial cells

SEM 10,000×

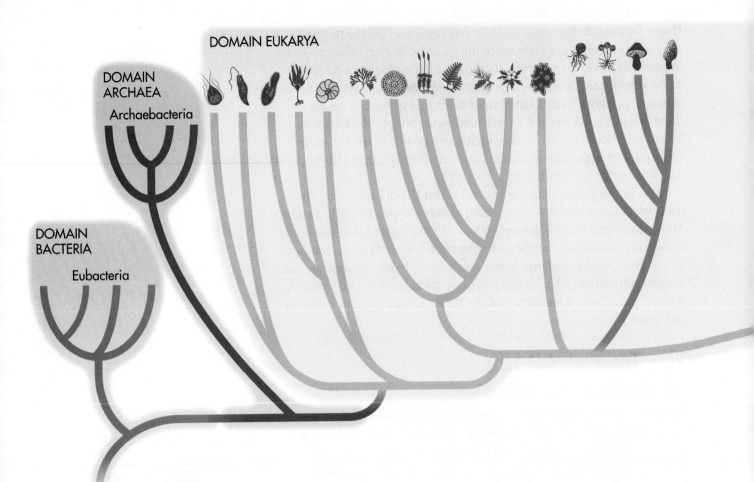

DOMAIN EUKARYA

DOMAIN
ARCHAEA

Archaebacteria

DOMAIN
BACTERIA

Eubacteria

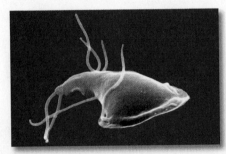

SEM 13,000×

FIGURE 18–16 *Sulfolobus* This member of the domain Archaea is found in hot springs and thrives in acidic and sulfur-rich environments.

LM 900×

FIGURE 18–17 "Protists" "Protists" can live just about anywhere. *Giardia* is a parasitic freshwater ciliate.

Domain Archaea Also unicellular and prokaryotic, members of the domain **Archaea** (ahr KEE uh) live in some of the most extreme environments you can imagine—in volcanic hot springs, brine pools, and black organic mud totally devoid of oxygen. Indeed, many of these bacteria can survive only in the absence of oxygen. Their cell walls lack peptidoglycan, and their cell membranes contain unusual lipids that are not found in any other organism. The domain Archaea corresponds to the kingdom Archaebacteria.

Domain Eukarya The domain **Eukarya** consists of all organisms that have a nucleus. It comprises the four remaining major groups of the six-kingdom system: "Protista," Fungi, Plantae, and Animalia.

▶ *The "Protists": Unicellular Eukaryotes* Recall that we are using quotations with this group to indicate that it is a paraphyletic group. Although some people still use the name "protists" to refer to these organisms, scientists who work with them have known for years that they do not form a valid clade. **Figure 18–18** reflects current cladistic analysis, which divides these organisms into at least five clades. The positions of these groups on the cladogram reflect its paraphyletic nature.

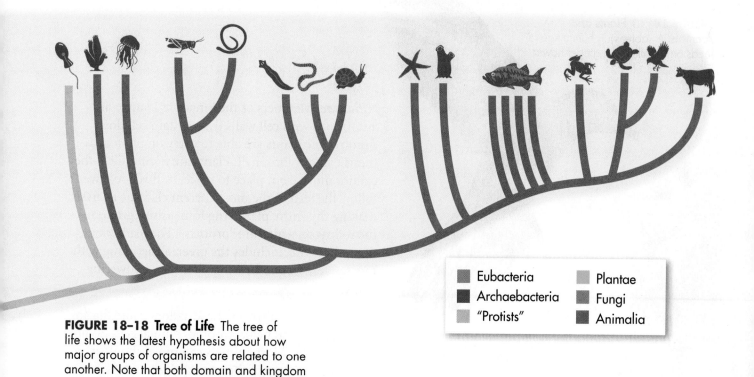

FIGURE 18-18 Tree of Life The tree of life shows the latest hypothesis about how major groups of organisms are related to one another. Note that both domain and kingdom designations are shown. **Classify** *Which of the six kingdoms contains organisms that are not all in the same clade?*

Each group of "the eukaryotes formerly known as protists" is separate, and each shares closest common ancestors with other groups, rather than with each other. Most are unicellular, but one group, the brown algae, is multicellular. Some are photosynthetic, while others are heterotrophic. Some display characters that most closely resemble those of plants, fungi, or animals.

▶ **Fungi** Members of the kingdom Fungi are heterotrophs with cell walls containing chitin. Most feed on dead or decaying organic matter. Unlike other heterotrophs, fungi secrete digestive enzymes into their food source. After the digestive enzymes have broken down the food into smaller molecules, the fungi absorb the small molecules into their bodies. Mushrooms and other recognizable fungi are multicellular. Some fungi—yeasts, for example—are unicellular.

In Your Notebook *Explain why kingdom Protista is not valid under evolutionary classification.*

FIGURE 18-19 Ghost Fungus

FIGURE 18-20 Plants and Animals A sabre-wing hummingbird feeds on a pollinating ginger flower.

▶ **Plantae** Members of the kingdom Plantae are autotrophs with cell walls that contain cellulose. Autotrophic plants are able to carry on photosynthesis using chlorophyll. Plants are nonmotile—they cannot move from place to place. In this book, we follow the lead of the most current cladistic analysis, making the entire plant kingdom a sister group to the red algae, which are "protists." The plant kingdom, therefore, includes the green algae, along with mosses, ferns, cone-bearing plants, and flowering plants.

▶ **Animalia** Members of the kingdom Animalia are multicellular and heterotrophic. Animal cells do not have cell walls. Most animals can move about, at least for some part of their life cycle. As you will see in later chapters, there is incredible diversity within the animal kingdom, and many species of animals exist in nearly every part of the planet.

18.3 Assessment

Review Key Concepts 🔑

1. a. Review What are the six kingdoms of life as they are now identified?

b. Explain Why did systematists establish the domain?

c. Classify What were the monerans? Why did systematists split them into two kingdoms?

2. a. Review What are the three domains of life?

b. Explain Why are quotes used when describing the kingdom "Protista"?

c. Predict Do you think the tree of life cladogram will always stay the same as it is in **Figure 18–18?** Explain your answer.

ANALYZING DATA

3. The table compares some molecular characteristics of organisms in the three domains.

a. Interpret Tables Which domains have unbranched lipids in their cell membranes?

b. Interpret Tables Which domain has just one type of RNA polymerase?

c. Analyze Data On the basis of this table, how are archaea different from bacteria?

Molecular Characteristic	Domain		
	Bacteria	Archaea	Eukarya
Introns (parts of genes that do not code)	Rare	Sometimes present	Present
RNA polymerase	One type	Several types	Several types
Histones found with DNA	Not present	Present	Present
Lipids in cell membrane	Unbranched	Some branched	Unbranched

Technology & BIOLOGY

Bar-Coding Life

Until recently, classification has been a time-consuming process. A new project hopes to make identifying species as simple as scanning a supermarket bar code. It combines DNA sequencing with miniature computers, data processing, and the Internet.

To make this work, researchers picked a segment of DNA that all animals carry, the mitochondrial cytochrome oxidase (CO1) gene. (A chloroplast gene will probably be used for plants). Each base in the DNA sequence of CO1 is shown as a color-coded stripe, making it easy to spot differences between the barcodes of two specimens. The results are stored in a database.

> **WRITING** Learn more about DNA bar-coding on the Internet. Then write a paragraph describing another possible use for the DNA bar-coding technology.

▶ **Hermit Thrush**

Closely related species have similar bar codes. Species that are not closely related have bar codes that are very different from one another.

In the future, a researcher will be able to take a tiny sample of tissue or hair, analyze it using a portable device, and get a report on closest matches. Recent versions of this software even use maps to show where similar specimens have been collected before.

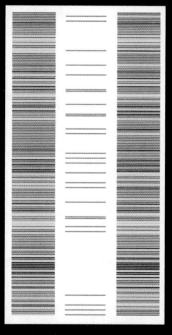

▶ The bar code on the left belongs to the hermit thrush and the bar code on the right belongs to the American robin. Differences between the two bar codes, shown as lines in the middle column, show the genetic distance between the two species.

▶ **American Robin**

Pre-Lab: Dichotomous Keys

Problem Can you construct a dichotomous key that can be used to identify organisms?

Materials reference materials

Lab Manual Chapter 18 Lab

Skills Focus Observe, Classify, Compare and Contrast, Sequence

Connect to the Big idea   Given the enormous variety of life on Earth, not even experts can identify every organism they observe. Both experts and amateurs use dichotomous keys to identify organisms. These keys are based on the appearance of organisms. A key is a series of paired statements. Readers select the statement that best describes an organism at each step until the organism is identified and named. In this lab, you will practice using a dichotomous key. Then you will construct your own key for a group of organisms.

Background Questions

a. Review Why do biologists prefer to identify an organism by its scientific name?

b. Compare and Contrast Explain how the way modern biologists group species into larger categories is different from the system that Linnaeus used.

c. Review How many choices does a dichotomous key provide at each step?

Pre-Lab Questions

Preview the procedure in the lab manual.

1. Observe Name three different physical traits that are used in the shark dichotomous key.

2. Classify Do all the sharks you will try to identify belong to the same genus? Explain your answer.

3. Apply Concepts After you make a list of physical traits that you can use in your dichotomous key, how will you decide which trait to pick for the first step?

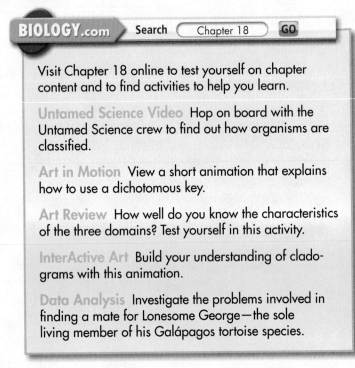

BIOLOGY.com   Search (Chapter 18) GO

Visit Chapter 18 online to test yourself on chapter content and to find activities to help you learn.

Untamed Science Video Hop on board with the Untamed Science crew to find out how organisms are classified.

Art in Motion View a short animation that explains how to use a dichotomous key.

Art Review How well do you know the characteristics of the three domains? Test yourself in this activity.

InterActive Art Build your understanding of cladograms with this animation.

Data Analysis Investigate the problems involved in finding a mate for Lonesome George—the sole living member of his Galápagos tortoise species.

18 Study Guide

Big idea ▶ Unity and Diversity of Life

The goal of biologists who classify organisms is to construct a tree of life that shows how all organisms are related to one another.

18.1 Finding Order in Diversity

🔑 In binomial nomenclature, each species is assigned a two-part scientific name.

🔑 The goal of systematics is to organize living things into groups that have biological meaning.

🔑 Over time, Linnaeus's original classification system expanded to include seven hierarchical taxa: species, genus, family, order, class, phylum, and kingdom.

binomial nomenclature (512)   order (513)
genus (512)   class (514)
systematics (512)   phylum (514)
taxon (512)   kingdom (514)
family (513)

18.2 Modern Evolutionary Classification

🔑 The goal of phylogenetic systematics, or evolutionary classification, is to group species into larger categories that reflect lines of evolutionary descent, rather than overall similarities and differences.

🔑 A cladogram links groups of organisms by showing how evolutionary lines, or lineages, branched off from common ancestors.

🔑 In general, the more derived genetic characters two species share, the more recently they shared a common ancestor and the more closely they are related in evolutionary terms.

phylogeny (516)   cladogram (517)
clade (516)   derived character (518)
monophyletic group (516)

18.3 Building the Tree of Life

🔑 The six-kingdom system of classification includes the kingdoms Eubacteria, Archaebacteria, Protista, Fungi, Plantae, and Animalia.

🔑 The tree of life shows current hypotheses regarding evolutionary relationships among the taxa within the three domains of life.

domain (525)   Archaea (526)
Bacteria (525)   Eukarya (526)

Think Visually Using the information in this chapter, complete the following Venn diagram comparing members of kingdom Plantae and kingdom Fungi.

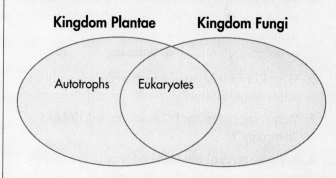

Kingdom Plantae   Kingdom Fungi

Autotrophs   Eukaryotes

18 Assessment

18.1 Finding Order in Diversity

Understand Key Concepts

1. The science of naming and grouping organisms is called
   - **a.** anatomy.
   - **b.** systematics.
   - **c.** botany.
   - **d.** paleontology.

2. Solely from its name, you know that *Rhizopus nigricans* must be
   - **a.** a plant.
   - **b.** an animal.
   - **c.** in the genus *Nigricans*.
   - **d.** in the genus *Rhizopus*.

3. A useful classification system does NOT
   - **a.** show relationships.
   - **b.** reveal evolutionary trends.
   - **c.** use different scientific names for the same organism.
   - **d.** change the taxon of an organism based on new data.

4. In Linnaeus's system of classifying organisms, orders are grouped together into
   - **a.** classes.
   - **b.** species.
   - **c.** families.
   - **d.** genera.

5. The largest and most inclusive of the Linnaean taxonomic ranks is the
   - **a.** kingdom.
   - **b.** order.
   - **c.** phylum.
   - **d.** domain.

6. Why do biologists assign each organism a universally accepted name?

7. Why is species the only Linnaean rank defined "naturally"?

8. What features of binomial nomenclature make it useful for scientists of all nations?

9. What is a taxon?

Think Critically

10. **Apply Concepts** What is a major problem with traditional classification? Give an example that demonstrates this problem.

11. **Use Analogies** Why is it important for a supermarket to have a classification scheme for displaying the foods that it sells?

12. **Classify** Venn diagrams can be used to make models of hierarchical classification schemes. A Venn diagram is shown below. Four groups are represented by circular regions—A, B, C, and D. Each region represents a collection of organisms or members of a taxonomic level. Regions that overlap, or intersect, share common members. Regions that do not overlap do not have members in common. Use the following terms to label the regions shown in the diagram: *kingdom Animalia*, *phylum Chordata*, *class Insecta*, and *class Mammalia*.

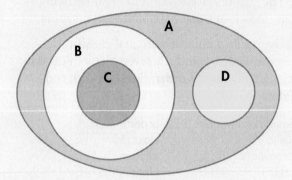

18.2 Modern Evolutionary Classification

Understand Key Concepts

13. A group that is limited to a common ancestor and all of its descendants is called a
    - **a.** taxon.
    - **b.** phylogeny.
    - **c.** tree of life.
    - **d.** monophyletic group.

14. A specific trait that is used to construct a cladogram is called a
    - **a.** taxon.
    - **b.** structural feature.
    - **c.** clade.
    - **d.** derived character.

15. A branch of a cladogram that consists of a single common ancestor and all the descendants of that ancestor is called
    - **a.** cladistics.
    - **b.** a kingdom.
    - **c.** a clade.
    - **d.** a class.

16. What does each individual node in a cladogram represent?

17. Why can differences in mitochondrial DNA be used as derived characters?

18. What is phylogeny?

Think Critically

19. **Apply Concepts** Both snakes and worms are tubular, with no legs. How could you determine whether their similarity in shape means that they share a recent common ancestor?

20. **Pose Questions** What questions would Linnaeus ask to determine a classification? What questions would a modern systematist ask?

21. **Apply Concepts** You are a biologist who is searching for new species in the Amazon jungle. You find two new species of beetles, beetle A and beetle B, that resemble each other closely but have somewhat different markings on their wings. In addition, both beetle A and beetle B resemble beetle C, a species that has already been identified. How could DNA similarities be used to help determine whether beetle A and beetle B are more closely related to each other or to beetle C?

22. **Infer** What is the relationship between natural selection and phylogeny?

23. **Apply Concepts** Explain why hair is a derived character for clade Mammalia but having four limbs is not. For which clade is four limbs a derived character?

18.3 Building the Tree of Life

Understand Key Concepts

24. The three domains are
    a. Animalia, Plantae, and Archaebacteria.
    b. Plantae, Fungi, and Eubacteria.
    c. Bacteria, Archaea, and Eukarya.
    d. Protista, Bacteria, and Animalia.

25. Which of the following kingdoms includes only heterotrophs?
    a. Protista
    b. Fungi
    c. Plantae
    d. Eubacteria

26. How do domains and kingdoms differ?

27. What characteristics are used to place an organism in the domain Bacteria?

solve the CHAPTER MYSTERY

GRIN AND BEAR IT

Most biologists classify the polar bear, *Ursus maritimus*, as a separate species from the brown bear, *Ursus arctos*. The teeth, body shape, metabolism, and behavior of polar bears are very different from those of brown bears. But some systematists are now questioning that classification.

Are polar bears and brown bears two distinct species? The answer depends on what a species is. The usual definition of *species* is "a group of similar organisms that can breed and produce fertile offspring." Polar bears and brown bears can, in fact, mate and produce offspring that are fertile. However, in the natural environment, polar bears and brown bears almost never mate.

The question is complicated by DNA analysis. There are different populations of brown bears, and these different populations have somewhat different genetic makeups. DNA analysis has shown that some populations of brown bears are more closely related to polar bears than they are to other populations of brown bears. According to DNA analysis, if polar bears are indeed a separate species, brown bears by themselves do not form a single clade.

1. **Classify** List the evidence that supports classifying polar bears and brown bears into two different species. Then list the evidence that indicates that polar bears and brown bears belong to the same species.

2. **Infer** What evidence indicates that different populations of brown bears belong to different clades?

3. **Connect to the** Big idea Do you think that the classic definition of *species*—"a group of similar organisms that can breed and produce fertile offspring"—is still adequate? Why or why not?

28. Which domain consists of prokaryotes whose cell walls lack peptidoglycan?

29. Describe the four kingdoms that make up the domain Eukarya.

30. What characteristic(s) differentiate the kingdom Fungi from the kingdom Eubacteria?

31. What do the branches of the tree of life try to show?

Think Critically

32. Classify In terms of cladistic analysis, what is the problem with placing all members of kingdom Protista into the same clade?

33. Classify Study the descriptions of the following organisms, and place them in the correct kingdom.
Organism A: Multicellular eukaryote without cell walls
Organism B: Its cell walls lack peptidoglycan, and its cell membranes contain certain lipids that are not found in other organisms. It lives in an extreme environment and can survive only in the absence of oxygen.
Organism C: Unicellular eukaryote with cell walls of chitin

Use Science Graphics

The cladogram below shows the relationships among three imaginary groups of organisms—groups A, B, and C. Use the cladogram to answer questions 34–36.

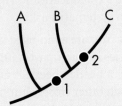

34. Interpret Visuals Which groups share derived character 1?

35. Apply Concepts What does the node, or fork, between groups B and C represent?

36. Apply Concepts Which group split off from the other groups first?

Write About Science

37. Explanation Write a short explanation of the way in which taxonomists use similarities and differences in DNA to help classify organisms and infer evolutionary relationships. (*Hint:* Use a specific example to help clarify your explanation.)

38. Assess the Big idea Explain what the tree of life is and what its various parts represent. Also explain why the tree of life probably will change. (*Hint*: When you explain what the various parts represent, use the terms *base* and *branches*.)

Use the table to answer questions 39–41.

	Turtle	Lamprey	Frog	Fish	Cat
Hair	No	No	No	No	Yes
Amniotic egg	Yes	No	No	No	Yes
Four legs	Yes	No	Yes	No	Yes
Jaw	Yes	No	Yes	Yes	Yes
Vertebrae	Yes	Yes	Yes	Yes	Yes

39. Interpret Tables The first column lists derived characters that can be used to make a cladogram of vertebrates. Which characteristic is shared by the most organisms? Which by the fewest?

40. Sequence From the information given, place the animals in sequence from the most recently evolved to the most ancient.

41. Draw Conclusions Of the following pairs—lamprey-turtle, fish-cat, and frog-turtle—which are probably most closely related?

Standardized Test Prep

Multiple Choice

1. Which of the following is NOT a characteristic of Linnaeus's system for naming organisms?
   A two-part name
   B multipart name describing several traits
   C name that identifies the organism's genus
   D name that includes the organism's species identifier

2. In which of the following are the Linnaean ranks in correct order?
   A phylum, kingdom, species
   B genus, order, family
   C kingdom, phylum, class
   D order, class, family

3. In the six-kingdom system of classifying living things, which kingdoms contain unicellular organisms?
   A Eubacteria only
   B Eubacteria and "Protista" only
   C Archaebacteria only
   D Eubacteria, Archaebacteria, Plantae, and "Protista"

4. If species A and B have very similar genes, which of the following statements is probably true?
   A Species A and B shared a relatively recent common ancestor.
   B Species A evolved independently of species B for a long period.
   C Species A and species B are the same species.
   D Species A is older than species B.

5. The taxon called Eukarya is a(n)
   A order.   C kingdom.
   B phylum.   D domain.

6. Members of the kingdom "Protista" are classified into
   A two domains.   C three species.
   B three domains. D three kingdoms.

Questions 7–9

The cladogram below shows the evolutionary relationships among four groups of plants.

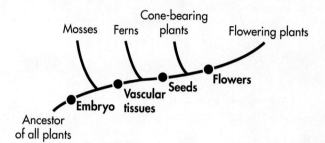

7. Which of the following groups, taken by themselves, do NOT form a clade?
   A cone-bearing plants and flowering plants
   B ferns, cone-bearing plants, and flowering plants
   C mosses and ferns
   D mosses, ferns, cone-bearing plants, and flowering plants

8. Which of the following groups share the most recent common ancestor?
   A cone-bearing plants and flowering plants
   B mosses and ferns
   C mosses and cone-bearing plants
   D ferns and flowering plants

9. Which derived character appeared first during the course of the plants' evolution?
   A seeds
   B flowers
   C embryo
   D vascular tissues

Open-Ended Response

10. Why have biologists changed many of Linnaeus's original classifications of organisms?

Question	1	2	3	4	5	6	7	8	9	10
If You Have Trouble With . . .										
See Lesson	18.1	18.1	18.3	18.2	18.3	18.3	18.2	18.2	18.2	18.2

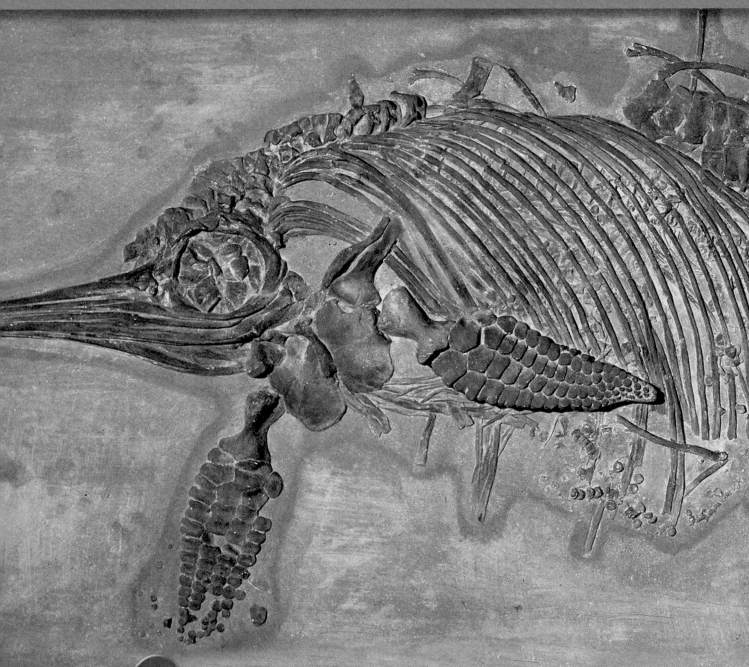

19 History of Life

Evolution

Q: How do fossils help biologists understand the history of life on Earth?

INSIDE:

- 19.1 The Fossil Record
- 19.2 Patterns and Processes of Evolution
- 19.3 Earth's Early History

Ichthyosaurs were dolphinlike marine reptiles that prowled the seas in the Mesozoic. This ichthyosaur died around the time of giving birth.

CHAPTER
MYSTERY

MURDER IN THE PERMIAN

Just over 250 million years ago, during the Permian Period, life on Earth came as close as it has ever come to being wiped out. The Permian extinction may be the greatest murder mystery in the history of the world. Whatever happened back then killed off over 55 percent of all families on Earth, including about 96 percent of marine species and 70 percent of terrestrial vertebrate species. Ancient ecosystems were so completely disrupted that it took millions of years for them to be restored.

Researchers once thought that this "great dying" took place over a long time. But new fossil data suggest that it took no more than 200,000 years and possibly less. In geological terms, that's a short time. As you read this chapter, look for clues as to what could have killed so many different forms of life. Then, solve the mystery.

Never Stop Exploring Your World.
Finding the solution to this mystery is only the beginning. Take a video field trip with the ecogeeks of Untamed Science to see where the mystery leads.

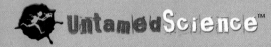

19.1 The Fossil Record

Key Questions

🔑 What do fossils reveal about ancient life?

🔑 How do we date events in Earth's history?

🔑 How was the geologic time scale established, and what are its major divisions?

🔑 How have our planet's environment and living things affected each other to shape the history of life on Earth?

Vocabulary

extinct • paleontologist • relative dating • index fossil • radiometric dating • half-life • geologic time scale • era • period • plate tectonics

Taking Notes

Outline Make an outline using the green and blue headings in this lesson. Fill in details as you read to help you organize the information in the lesson.

THINK ABOUT IT Fossils, the preserved remains or traces of ancient life, are priceless treasures. They tell of life-and-death struggles and of mysterious worlds lost in the mists of time. Taken together, the fossils of ancient organisms make up the history of life on Earth called the fossil record. How can fossils help us understand life's history?

Fossils and Ancient Life

🔑 What do fossils reveal about ancient life?

Fossils are the most important source of information about extinct species. An **extinct** species is one that has died out. Fossils vary enormously in size, type, and degree of preservation, and they form only under certain conditions. For every organism preserved as a fossil, many died without leaving a trace, so the fossil record is not complete.

Types of Fossils Fossils can be as large and perfectly preserved as an entire animal, complete with skin, hair, scales, or feathers. They can also be as tiny as bacteria, developing embryos, or pollen grains. Many fossils are just fragments of an organism—teeth, pieces of a jawbone, or bits of leaf. Sometimes an organism leaves behind trace fossils—casts of footprints, burrows, tracks, or even droppings. Although most fossils are preserved in sedimentary rocks, some are preserved in other ways, like the insect shown in **Figure 19–1.**

FIGURE 19–1 Diversity of Fossils There are all different types of fossils. A fossil can be a single bone, some footprints, or entire organisms.

▲ Dimetrodon footprints

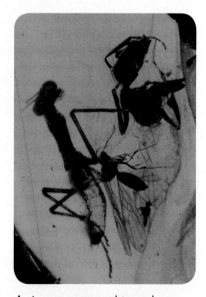
▲ Insect preserved in amber

Fossils in Sedimentary Rock Most fossils are preserved in sedimentary rock. **Figure 19–2** shows how. ❶ Sedimentary rock usually forms when small particles of sand, silt, clay, or lime muds settle to the bottom of a river, lake, ocean, or other body of water. Sedimentary rock can also form from compacted desert sands. ❷ As sediments build up, they bury dead organisms that have sunk to the bottom. If the remains of these organisms are buried relatively quickly, they may not be scattered by scavengers. Usually, soft body structures decay quickly after death, so only wood, shells, bones, or teeth remain. These hard structures can be preserved if they are saturated or replaced with mineral compounds. Sometimes, however, organisms are buried so quickly that soft tissues are protected from aerobic decay. When this happens, fossils may preserve incredibly detailed imprints of soft-bodied animals and structures like skin or feathers.

❸ As layers of sediment continue to build up over time, the remains are buried deeper and deeper. Over many years, water pressure gradually compresses the lower layers. This pressure, along with chemical activity, can turn the sediments into rock.

What Fossils Can Reveal Although the fossil record is incomplete, it contains an enormous amount of information for **paleontologists** (pay lee un TAHL uh jists), researchers who study fossils to learn about ancient life. 🔑 **From the fossil record, paleontologists learn about the structure of ancient organisms, their environment, and the ways in which they lived.** By comparing body structures in fossils—a backbone, for example—to body structures in living organisms, researchers can infer evolutionary relationships and form hypotheses about how body structures and species have evolved. Bone structure and footprints can indicate how animals moved. Fossilized plant leaves and pollen suggest whether an area was a swamp, a lake, a forest, or a desert. Also, when different kinds of fossils are found together, researchers can sometimes reconstruct entire ancient ecosystems.

In Your Notebook *Construct a flowchart to explain how the remains of a snail might become fossilized in sedimentary rock.*

Fossil fish *Diplomystus dentatus* (about 50 million years old)

BUILD Vocabulary
WORD ORIGINS The words paleontology and **paleontologist** come from the Greek word *palaios*, meaning "ancient." A paleontologist studies the remains of ancient life.

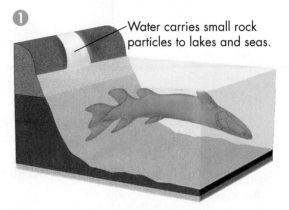
❶ Water carries small rock particles to lakes and seas.

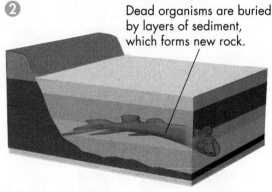
❷ Dead organisms are buried by layers of sediment, which forms new rock.

❸ The preserved remains may later be discovered and studied.

FIGURE 19–2 Fossil Formation Most fossils, like the fish shown here, form in sedimentary rock. **Interpret Photos** *What part of the fish has been preserved as a fossil?*

Dating Earth's History

🔑 How do we date events in Earth's history?

The fossil record wouldn't be as useful without a time scale to tell us what happened when. Researchers use several techniques to date rocks and fossils.

Relative Dating Since sedimentary rock is formed as layers of sediment are laid on top of existing sediments, lower layers of sedimentary rock, and fossils they contain, are generally older than upper layers. **Relative dating** places rock layers and their fossils in a temporal sequence, as shown in **Figure 19–3**. 🔑 **Relative dating allows paleontologists to determine whether a fossil is older or younger than other fossils.**

To help establish the relative ages of rock layers and their fossils, scientists use index fossils. **Index fossils** are distinctive fossils used to establish and compare the relative ages of rock layers and the fossils they contain. A useful index fossil must be easily recognized and will occur only in a few rock layers (meaning the organism lived only for a short time), but these layers will be found in many places (meaning the organism was widely distributed). Trilobites, a large group of distinctive marine organisms, are often used as index fossils. There are more than 15,000 recognized species of trilobite. Together, they can be used to establish the relative dates of rock layers spanning nearly 300 million years.

Radiometric Dating Relative dating is important, but provides no information about a fossil's absolute age in years. One way to date rocks and fossils is radiometric dating. **Radiometric dating** relies on radioactive isotopes, which decay, or break down, into stable isotopes at a steady rate. A **half-life** is the time required for half of the radioactive atoms in a sample to decay. After one half-life, half of the original radioactive atoms have decayed, as shown in **Figure 19–4.**

FIGURE 19–3 Index Fossils Each of these fossils is an index fossil. If the same index fossil is found in two widely separated rock layers, the rock layers are probably similar in age. **Draw Conclusions** *Using the index fossils shown, determine which layers are "missing" from each location. Layers may be missing because they were never formed, or because they were eroded.*

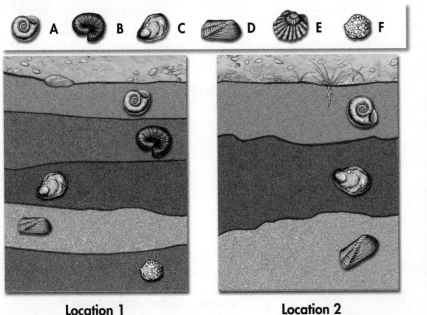

A   B   C   D   E   F

Location 1   Location 2   Location 3

After another half-life, another half of the remaining radioactive atoms will have decayed. 🔑 **Radiometric dating uses the proportion of radioactive to stable isotopes to calculate the age of a sample.**

Different radioactive isotopes decay at different rates, so they have different half-lives. Elements with short half-lives are used to date recent fossils. Elements with long half-lives are used for dating older fossils. To understand this, think of timing sports events. For a 50-yard dash, a coach depends on the fast-moving second hand of a stopwatch. To time a marathon, slower-moving hour and minute hands are also important.

A number of radioactive isotopes are used to determine the ages of rocks and fossils. An isotope known as carbon-14 is particularly useful for directly dating organisms that lived in the recent past. Carbon-14 is produced at a steady rate in the upper atmosphere, so air generally contains a tiny amount of it, in addition to the much more common stable, nonradioactive form, carbon-12. Plants take carbon-14 in when they absorb carbon dioxide during photosynthesis, and animals acquire it when they eat plants or other animals. Once an organism dies, it no longer takes in this isotope, so its age can be determined by the amount of carbon-14 still remaining in tissues such as bone, hair, or wood. Carbon-14 has a half-life of roughly 5730 years, so its use is limited to organisms that lived in the last 60,000 years.

Older fossils can be dated indirectly by dating the rock layers in which they are found. Isotopes with much longer half-lives are used for this purpose, including potassium-40 (half-life: 1.26 billion years, shown in **Figure 19–4**), uranium-238 (4.5 billion years), and rubidium-87 (48.8 billion years). Over many years, geologists have combined the use of these and other isotope methods to make increasingly accurate estimates of the ages of geological formations. These studies have provided direct physical evidence for the ages of the index fossils used to identify periods of Earth history.

In Your Notebook *Explain why carbon-14 can't be used to estimate the age of very old fossils.*

Modeling Half-Life

❶ Construct a data table or spreadsheet with two columns and five rows. Label the columns Spill Number and Number of Squares Returned. Take a sheet of paper, and cut out 100 1-cm squares. Place an *X* on each square, and put all the squares in a cup.

❷ Mix the squares in the cup, and spill them out.

❸ Remove all the squares that have an *X* showing. Count the squares left, record the number, and return the remaining squares to the cup.

❹ Repeat steps 2 and 3 until there are five or fewer squares left. Make a graph of your results with the number of spills on the *x*-axis and the number of squares remaining after each spill on the *y*-axis.

Analyze and Conclude

1. Analyze Data How many spills did you need to remove half the squares? To remove three fourths?

2. Calculate If each spill represents one year, what is the half-life of the squares?
MATH

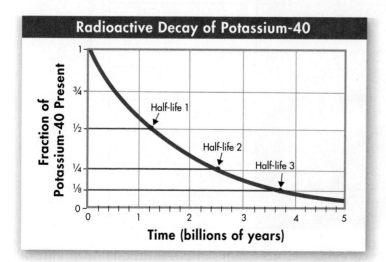

FIGURE 19–4 Radioactive Decay
A half-life is the time it takes half the radioactive atoms in a sample to decay. The half-life of potassium-40 is 1.26 billion years.

Geologic Time Scale

🔑 How was the geologic time scale established, and what are its major divisions?

Geologists and paleontologists have built a time line of Earth's history called the **geologic time scale.** The most recent version is shown in Figure 19–5. 🔑 **The geologic time scale is based on both relative and absolute dating. The major divisions of the geologic time scale are eons, eras, and periods.**

FIGURE 19–5 Geologic Time Scale The basic divisions of the geologic time scale are eons, eras, and periods. Precambrian time was the name originally given to all of Earth's history before the Phanerozoic Eon. Note that the Paleogene and Neogene are sometimes called the Tertiary period. However, this term is generally considered outdated.

Establishing the Time Scale By studying rock layers and index fossils, early paleontologists placed Earth's rocks and fossils in order according to their relative age. As they worked, they noticed major changes in the fossil record at boundaries between certain rock layers. Geologists used these boundaries to determine where one division of geologic time ended and the next began. Years later, radiometric dating techniques were used to assign specific ages to the various rock layers. This time scale is constantly being tested, verified, and adjusted.

Geologic Time Scale

Eon	Era	Period	Time (millions of years ago)
Phanerozoic	Cenozoic	Quaternary	1.8–present
		Neogene	23–1.8
		Paleogene	65.5–23
	Mesozoic	Cretaceous	146–65.5
		Jurassic	200–146
		Triassic	251–200
	Paleozoic	Permian	299–251
		Carboniferous	359–299
		Devonian	416–359
		Silurian	444–416
		Ordovician	488–444
		Cambrian	542–488
Precambrian Time	Proterozoic		2500–542
	Archean		4000–2500
	Hadean		About 4600–4000

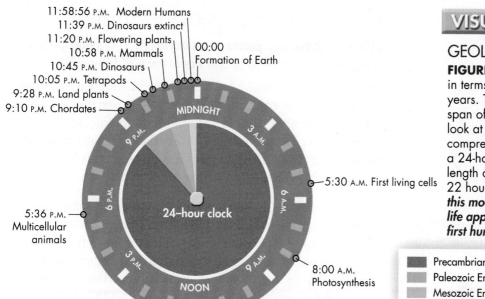

11:58:56 P.M. Modern Humans
11:39 P.M. Dinosaurs extinct
11:20 P.M. Flowering plants
10:58 P.M. Mammals
10:45 P.M. Dinosaurs
10:05 P.M. Tetrapods
9:28 P.M. Land plants
9:10 P.M. Chordates

00:00 Formation of Earth

MIDNIGHT

9 P.M.   3 A.M.

6 P.M.   6 A.M.

24-hour clock

5:30 A.M. First living cells

5:36 P.M.
Multicellular
animals

3 P.M.   9 A.M.

NOON

8:00 A.M.
Photosynthesis

12:48 P.M. Eukaryotic cells

GEOLOGIC TIME AS A CLOCK

FIGURE 19–6 It can be hard to think in terms of billions or even millions of years. To help visualize the enormous span of time since Earth formed, look at the 24-hour clock here. It compresses the history of Earth into a 24-hour period. Notice the relative length of Precambrian Time—almost 22 hours. **Use Analogies** *Using this model, about what time did life appear? The first plants? The first humans?*

■	Precambrian 00:00–9:07 P.M.
■	Paleozoic Era 9:07–10:40 P.M.
■	Mesozoic Era 10:40–11:39 P.M.
■	Cenozoic Era 11:39–00:00 P.M.

Divisions of the Geologic Time Scale Divisions of geologic time have different lengths. The Cambrian Period, for example, began 542 million years ago and continued until 488 million years ago, which makes it 54 million years long. The Cretaceous Period was 80 million years long.

Geologists now recognize four eons. The Hadean Eon, during which the first rocks formed, spans the time from Earth's formation to about 4 billion years ago. The Archean Eon, during which life first appeared, followed the Hadean. The Proterozoic Eon began 2.5 billion years ago and lasted until 542 million years ago. The Phanerozoic (fan ur uh ZOH ic) Eon began at the end of the Proterozoic and continues to the present.

Eons are divided into **eras.** The Phanerozoic Eon, for example, is divided into the Paleozoic, Mesozoic, and Cenozoic Eras. And eras are subdivided into **periods,** which range in length from nearly 100 million years to just under 2 million years. The Paleozoic Era, for example, is divided into six periods, including the Permian Period.

Naming the Divisions Divisions of the geologic time scale were named in different ways. The Cambrian Period, for example, was named after Cambria—an old name for Wales, where rocks from that time were first identified. The Carboniferous ("carbon-bearing") Period is named for large coal deposits that formed during that time.

Geologists started to name divisions of the time scale before any rocks older than the Cambrian Period had been identified. For this reason, all of geologic time before the Cambrian was simply called Precambrian Time. Precambrian Time, however, actually covers about 90 percent of Earth's history, as shown in **Figure 19–6.**

MYSTERY CLUE

Paleontologists discovered dramatic changes in the fossil record at the end of the Permian Period. What methods do you think they used to date that change at 251 million years ago?

FIGURE 19–7 The Changing Face of Earth Over the last 225 million years, the face of the Earth has changed dramatically.

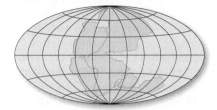

End of Permian Period At the end of the Permian Period, Earth's continents collided to form one giant landmass called Pangaea.

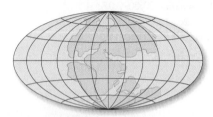

Triassic Period During the Triassic Period, Pangaea started to break apart and form separate land masses.

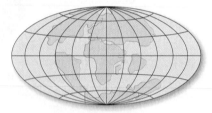

End of Cretaceous Period By the end of the Cretaceous Period, the continents as we know them began to drift apart.

Present Day

Life on a Changing Planet

How have our planet's environment and living things affected each other to shape the history of life on Earth?

Today, it's easy to think of places on Earth where the environment is relatively constant from year to year. Arizona is dry, coastal Washington State is wet, Antarctica is cold, and the Sahara is hot. But this was not always the case. Earth's physical environment has undergone striking changes in its history, and many of these changes have affected life in dramatic ways.

Physical Forces Climate is one of the most important aspects of the physical environment, and Earth's climate has been anything but constant over the history of life. Many of these changes were triggered by fairly small shifts in global temperature. For example, during the global "heat wave" of the Mesozoic era, average global temperatures were only 6°C to 12°C higher than they were in the twentieth century. During the great ice ages, which swept across the globe as recently as 10,000 years ago, temperatures were only about 5°C cooler than they are now. Yet, these temperature shifts had far-reaching effects on living things.

Geological forces have also transformed life on Earth, building mountains and even moving whole continents. Remember that local climates are influenced by the interactions of wind and ocean currents with geological features like mountains and plains. Volcanic forces have altered landscapes over much of Earth, even producing entire islands that provide new habitats. The Hawaiian Islands, home to scores of unique plant and animal species, are a perfect example of how volcanic islands can alter the course of evolution. **Building mountains, opening coastlines, changing climates, and geological forces have altered habitats of living organisms repeatedly throughout Earth history.**

Over the long term, the process of continental drift has produced even more dramatic changes in Earth's biological landscape. As shown in **Figure 19–7,** continents have collided to form "super continents," and then drifted apart again, profoundly changing the flow of ocean currents. Continental drift has also affected the distribution of fossils and living organisms worldwide. For example, the continents of Africa and South America are now separated by the Atlantic Ocean. But fossils of *Mesosaurus*, an aquatic reptile, have been found in Africa and South America. The presence of these fossils on both continents reflects the fact that both were joined at one time. The theory of **plate tectonics** explains these movements as the result of solid "plates" moving slowly, as little as 3 cm a year, over Earth's mantle.

Forces from space have even altered Earth's physical environment. There is strong evidence that comets and large meteors have crashed into Earth many times in the past. Some of these impacts may have been so violent that they kicked enough dust and debris in the atmosphere to cause, or contribute to, worldwide extinctions of organisms on land and in the water.

Biological Forces Although we think of life as reacting to Earth's physical environment, in many cases life actually plays a major role in shaping that environment. Iron deposits in ancient sedimentary rock indicate that Earth's early oceans contained large amounts of soluble iron and little oxygen. The first photosynthetic organisms began absorbing carbon dioxide and releasing large amounts of oxygen. Our planet has never been the same since then. Earth cooled as carbon dioxide levels dropped. The iron content of the oceans fell, as iron ions reacted with oxygen to form insoluble compounds that settled to the ocean floor. These changes affected climate and ocean chemistry in many ways. **The actions of living organisms over time have changed conditions in the land, water, and atmosphere of planet Earth.**

Even today, organisms shape the landscape as they build soil from rock and sand. Plants, animals, and microorganisms are active players in global cycles of key elements, including carbon, nitrogen, and oxygen. Earth is a living planet, and its physical environment reflects that fact.

19.1 Assessment

Review Key Concepts

1. a. Explain What can a paleontologist learn from fossils?
b. Relate Cause and Effect Why have so few organisms become fossilized?

2. a. Review What are the two ways in which geologists determine the age of fossils?
b. Draw Conclusions Many more fossils have been found since Darwin's day, giving us a more complete record of life's history. How would this information make relative dating more accurate?

3. a. Explain How are eras and periods related?
b. Interpret Visuals Use **Figure 19–5** to determine when the Silurian Period began and how long it lasted.

4. a. Review Describe three processes that have affected the history of life on Earth.
b. Relate Cause and Effect Describe two ways in which continental drift has affected organisms.

VISUAL THINKING

5. Look at the fossil bat in the photograph below. Describe the fossil. What can you infer about how the organism moved? Explain your answer.

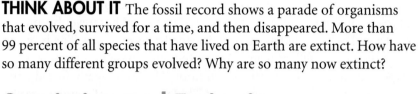

Key Questions

🔑 *What processes influence whether species and clades survive or become extinct?*

🔑 *How fast does evolution take place?*

🔑 *What are two patterns of macroevolution?*

🔑 *What evolutionary characteristics are typical of coevolving species?*

Vocabulary

macroevolutionary patterns
background extinction
mass extinction
gradualism
punctuated equilibrium
adaptive radiation
convergent evolution
coevolution

Taking Notes

Concept Map Construct a concept map that includes the patterns of macroevolution shown in this lesson.

FIGURE 19–8 Paleontologists at Work The white covering protects the fossils until they can reach a museum.

THINK ABOUT IT The fossil record shows a parade of organisms that evolved, survived for a time, and then disappeared. More than 99 percent of all species that have lived on Earth are extinct. How have so many different groups evolved? Why are so many now extinct?

Speciation and Extinction

🔑 *What processes influence whether species and clades survive or become extinct?*

The study of life's history leaves no doubt that life has changed over time. Many of those changes occurred within species, but others occurred in larger clades and over longer periods of time. These grand transformations in anatomy, phylogeny, ecology, and behavior, which usually take place in clades larger than a single species, are known as **macroevolutionary patterns.** The ways new species emerge through speciation, and the ways species disappear through extinction, are among the simplest macroevolutionary patterns. The emergence, growth, and extinction of larger clades, such as dinosaurs, mammals, or flowering plants are examples of larger macroevolutionary patterns.

Macroevolution and Cladistics Paleontologists study fossils to learn about patterns of macroevolution and the history of life. Part of this process involves classifying fossils. Fossils are classified using the same cladistic techniques, based on shared derived characters, that are used to classify living species. In some cases, fossils are placed in clades that contain only extinct organisms. In other cases, fossils are classified into clades that include living organisms.

Remember that cladograms illustrate hypotheses about how closely related organisms are. Hypothesizing that a fossil species is *related* to a living species is not the same thing as claiming that the extinct organism is a direct *ancestor* of that (or any other) living species. For example, **Figure 19–9** does not suggest that any of the extinct species shown are direct ancestors of modern birds. Instead, those extinct species are shown as a series of species that descended, over time, from a line of common ancestors.

> **In Your Notebook** *Explain what macroevolution is and how fossils can show macroevolutionary trends.*

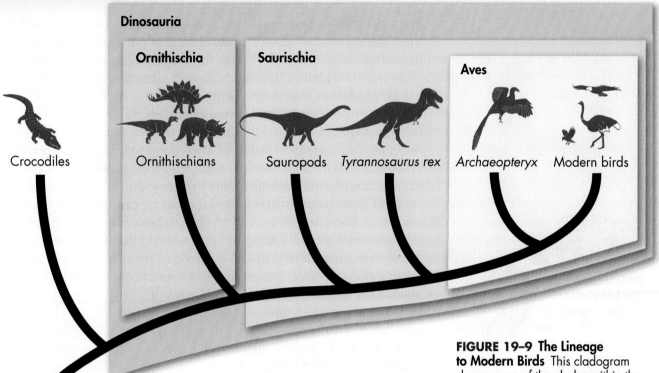

Dinosauria

Ornithischia

Saurischia

Aves

Crocodiles

Ornithischians

Sauropods   *Tyrannosaurus rex*

Archaeopteryx   Modern birds

FIGURE 19–9 The Lineage to Modern Birds This cladogram shows some of the clades within the large clade Reptilia. Notice that clade Dinosauria is represented today by modern birds. **Classify** *What are the two major clades of dinosaurs?*

Adaptation and Extinction Throughout the history of life, organisms have faced changing environments. When environmental conditions change, processes of evolutionary change enable some species to adapt to new conditions and thrive. Species that fail to adapt eventually become extinct. Interestingly, the rates at which species appear, adapt, and become extinct vary among clades, and from one period of geologic time to another.

Why have some clades produced many successful species that survived over long periods of time, while other clades gave rise to only a few species that vanished due to extinction? Paleontologists have tried to answer this question by studying macroevolutionary patterns of speciation and extinction in different clades over time.

One way to think about this process is in terms of species diversity. The emergence of new species with different characteristics can serve as the "raw material" for macroevolutionary change within a clade over long periods. In some cases, the more varied the species in a particular clade are, the more likely the clade is to survive environmental change. This is similar to the way in which genetic variation serves as raw material for evolutionary change for populations within a species. **If the rate of speciation in a clade is equal to or greater than the rate of extinction, the clade will continue to exist. If the rate of extinction in a clade is greater than the rate of speciation, the clade will eventually become extinct.**

The clade Reptilia (part of which is shown in **Figure 19–9**) is one example of a highly successful clade. It not only includes living organisms like snakes, lizards, turtles and crocodiles, but also dinosaurs that thrived for tens of millions of years. As you know, most species in the clade Dinosauria are now extinct. But the clade itself survived, because it produced groups of new species that successfully adapted to changing conditions. One of those groups survives and thrives today—we call them birds.

Patterns of Extinction Species are always evolving and competing—and some species become extinct because of the slow but steady process of natural selection. Paleontologists use the term **background extinction** to describe this kind of "business as usual" extinction. In contrast, a **mass extinction** is an event during which many species become extinct over a relatively short period of time. A mass extinction isn't just a small increase in background extinction. In a mass extinction, entire ecosystems vanish, and whole food webs collapse. Species become extinct because their environment breaks down and the ordinary process of natural selection can't compensate quickly enough.

Until recently researchers looked for a single cause for each mass extinction. For example, geologic evidence shows that at the end of the Cretaceous Period, a huge asteroid crashed into Earth. The impact threw huge amounts of dust and water vapor into the atmosphere, causing global climate change. At about the same time, dinosaurs and many other species became extinct. It is reasonable to infer, then, that the asteroid played a significant role in this mass extinction. Many mass extinctions, however, were probably caused by several factors, working in combination: volcanic eruptions, moving continents, *and* changing sea levels, for example.

After a mass extinction, biodiversity is dramatically reduced. But this is not bad for all organisms. Extinction offers new opportunities to survivors. And as speciation and adaptation produce new species to fill empty niches, biodiversity recovers. But this recovery takes a long time—typically between 5 and 10 million years. Some groups of organisms survive a mass extinction, while other groups do not.

MYSTERY CLUE

Evidence indicates that before the Permian extinction, the oceans lost most of their oxygen. What effect do you think the loss of oxygen had on most organisms?

Analyzing Data

Extinctions Through Time

The graph shows how the rate of extinction has changed over time. Study the graph, and then answer the questions.

1. Interpret Graphs What is plotted on the *y*-axis?

2. Analyze Data Which mass extinction killed off the highest percentage of genera?

3. Draw Conclusions Describe the overall pattern of extinction shown on the graph.

4. Infer What evidence is this graph probably based on?

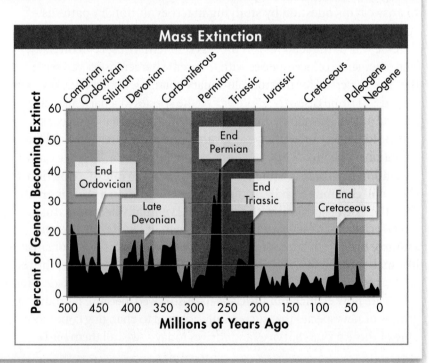

Rate of Evolution

How fast does evolution take place?

How quickly does evolution operate? Does it always take place at the same speed? **Evidence shows that evolution has often proceeded at different rates for different organisms at different times over the long history of life on Earth.** Two models of evolution—gradualism and punctuated equilibrium—are shown in **Figure 19–10.**

Gradualism Darwin was impressed by the slow, steady pace of geologic change. He suggested that evolution also needed to be slow and steady, an idea known as **gradualism.** The fossil record shows that many organisms have indeed changed gradually over time.

Punctuated Equilibrium However, numerous examples in the fossil record indicate that the pattern of slow, steady change does not always hold. Horseshoe crabs, for example, have changed little in structure from the time they first appeared in the fossil record. Much of the time, these species are said to be in a state of equilibrium. This means that their structures do not change much even though they continue to evolve genetically.

Every now and then something happens to upset this equilibrium for some species. **Punctuated equilibrium** is the term used to describe equilibrium that is interrupted by brief periods of more rapid change. (Remember that we use *rapid* here relative to the geologic time scale. For geologists, rapid change can take thousands of years!) The fossil record does reveal periods of relatively rapid change in particular groups of organisms. In fact, some biologists suggest that most new species are produced during periods of rapid change.

Rapid Evolution After Equilibrium There are several reasons why evolution may proceed at different rates for different organisms at different times. Rapid evolution may occur after a small population becomes isolated from the main population. This small population can evolve faster than the larger one because genetic changes spread more quickly among fewer individuals. Rapid evolution may also occur when a small group of organisms migrates to a new environment. That's what happened with the Galápagos finches. In addition, mass extinctions open many ecological niches, creating new opportunities for those organisms that survive. It's not surprising, then, that groups of organisms that survive mass extinctions evolve rapidly in the several million years after the extinction.

> **In Your Notebook** *In your own words, describe gradualism and punctuated equilibrium.*

FIGURE 19–10 Models of Evolution
Biologists have considered two different patterns for the rate of evolution, gradualism and punctuated equilibrium. These illustrations are simplified to show the general trend of each model.
Interpret Visuals *How do the diagrams illustrate these two models?*

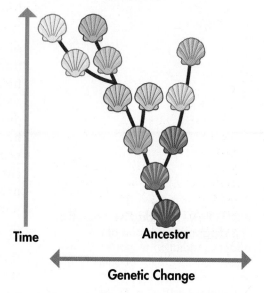

Gradualism involves a slow, steady change in a particular line of descent.

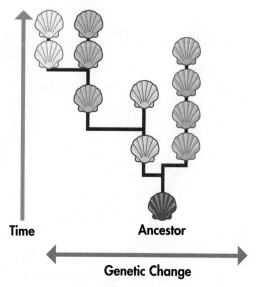

Punctuated equilibrium involves stable periods interrupted by rapid changes.

Adaptive Radiation and Convergent Evolution

🔑 *What are two patterns of macroevolution?*

As paleontologists study the fossil record, they look for patterns. 🔑 **Two important patterns of macroevolution are adaptive radiation and convergent evolution.** As you'll see, Darwin noted both patterns while aboard the *Beagle.*

Adaptive Radiation Studies of fossils and living organisms often show that a single species or small group of species has diversified over time into a clade containing many species. These species display variations on the group's ancestral body plan, and often occupy different ecological niches. These differences are the product of an evolutionary process called adaptive radiation. **Adaptive radiation** is the process by which a single species or a small group of species evolves over a relatively short time into several different forms that live in different ways. An adaptive radiation may occur when species migrate to a new environment or when extinction clears an environment of a large number of inhabitants. In addition, a species may evolve a new feature that enables it to take advantage of a previously unused environment.

▶ *Adaptive Radiations in the Fossil Record* Dinosaurs—one of several spectacular adaptive radiations of reptiles—flourished for about 150 million years during the Mesozoic. The fossil record documents that in the dinosaurs' heyday, mammals diversified but remained small. After most dinosaurs became extinct, however, an adaptive radiation of mammals began. That radiation, part of which is shown in **Figure 19–11,** produced the great diversity of mammals of the Cenozoic Era.

FIGURE 19–11 Adaptive Radiation This diagram shows part of the adaptive radiation of mammals. Note how the groups of animals shown have adapted to many different ways of life—including two groups which have become aquatic. **Interpret Visuals** *According to this diagram, which mammal group is most closely related to elephants? Does this surprise you? Explain.*

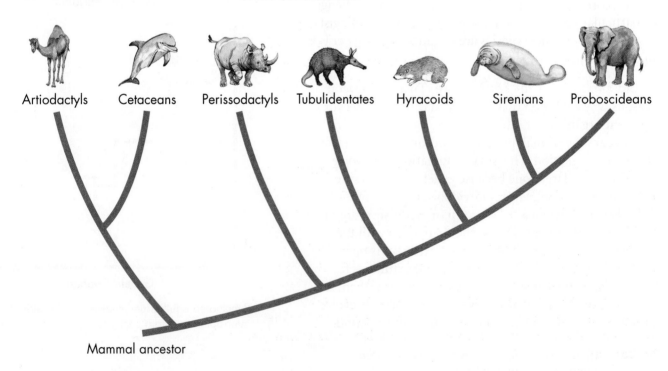

Artiodactyls Cetaceans Perissodactyls Tubulidentates Hyracoids Sirenians Proboscideans

Mammal ancestor

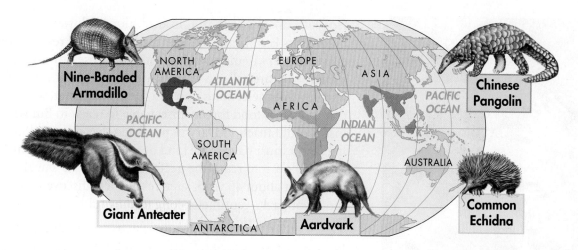

FIGURE 19–12 Convergent Evolution Mammals that feed on ants and termites evolved independently five times. Although each species is unique, each has evolved powerful front claws, a long hairless snout, and a tongue covered with sticky saliva. These adaptations are useful for hunting and eating insects.

▶ *Modern Adaptive Radiations* Galápagos finches and Hawaiian honeycreepers are two examples of adaptive radiations in modern organisms. In each of these cases, numerous species evolved from a single founding species. Both finches and honeycreepers evolved different beaks and behaviors that enable each of them to eat different kinds of food.

Convergent Evolution Sometimes, groups of organisms evolve in different places or at different times, but in similar environments. These organisms start out with different structures on which natural selection can operate. But they face similar selection pressures. In these situations, natural selection may mold different body structures in ways that perform similar functions. Because they perform similar functions, these body structures may look similar. Evolution produces similar structures and characteristics in distantly related organisms through the process of **convergent evolution.** Convergent evolution has occurred often in both plants and animals. For example, mammals that feed on ants and termites evolved not once, but five times, in different regions as shown in **Figure 19–12.** Remember how Darwin noted striking similarities among large, distantly related grassland birds? Emus, rheas, and ostriches are another example of convergent evolution.

Coevolution

🔑 **What evolutionary characteristics are typical of coevolving species?**

Sometimes the life histories of two or more species are so closely connected that they evolve together. Many flowering plants, for example, can reproduce only if their flowers attract a specific pollinator species. Pollinators, in turn, may depend on the flowers of certain plants for food in the form of pollen or nectar. The process by which two species evolve in response to changes in each other over time is called **coevolution.**
🔑 **The relationship between two coevolving organisms often becomes so specific that neither organism can survive without the other. Thus, an evolutionary change in one organism is usually followed by a change in the other organism.**

FIGURE 19–13 Plants and Herbivorous Insects Milkweed plants produce toxic chemicals. But monarch caterpillars not only can tolerate this toxin, they also can store it in their body tissues to use as a defense against *their* predators.

Flowers and Pollinators Coevolution of flowers and pollinators is common and can lead to unusual results. For example, Darwin discovered an orchid whose flowers had a long structure called a spur. Way down at the bottom of that 40-centimeter-long spur is a supply of nectar, which could serve as food for any insect able to reach it. But what insect could reach it? Darwin predicted that some pollinating insect must have some kind of feeding structure that would allow it to reach the nectar. Darwin never saw that insect. But about 40 years later, researchers discovered a moth with a 40-centimeter-long feeding tube that matched Darwin's prediction!

Plants and Herbivorous Insects Plants and herbivorous insects also demonstrate close, albeit less "friendly," coevolutionary relationships. Insects have been feeding on flowering plants since both groups emerged. Over time, many plants evolved bad-tasting or poisonous compounds that discourage insects from eating them. Some of the most powerful natural poisons are compounds developed by plants in response to insect attacks. But once plants began to produce poisons, natural selection on herbivorous insects favored any variants that could alter, inactivate, or eliminate those poisons. Time and again, a group of insects, like the caterpillar in **Figure 19–13,** evolved a way to deal with the particular poisons produced by a certain group of plants.

19.2 Assessment

Review Key Concepts 🔑

1. a. Review How does variation within a clade affect the clade's chance of surviving environmental change?

b. Compare and Contrast How is mass extinction different from background extinction?

2. a. Review Explain how punctuated equilibrium is different from gradualism.

b. Relate Cause and Effect Why would evolution speed up when a small group of organisms migrates to a new environment?

3. a. Review What is adaptive radiation?

b. Relate Cause and Effect When might adaptive radiation result in convergent evolution?

4. a. Review What is coevolution?

b. Apply Concepts Describe an example of coevolution.

Apply the Big idea

Evolution

5. What role does the environment play in convergent evolution?

19.3 Earth's Early History

THINK ABOUT IT How did life on Earth begin? What were the earliest forms of life? How did life and the biosphere interact? Origin-of-life research is a dynamic field. But even though some current hypotheses likely will change, our understanding of other aspects of the story is growing.

The Mysteries of Life's Origins

🔑 **What do scientists hypothesize about early Earth and the origin of life?**

Geological and astronomical evidence suggests that Earth formed as pieces of cosmic debris collided with one another. While the planet was young, it was struck by one or more huge objects, and the entire globe melted. For millions of years, violent volcanic activity shook Earth's crust. Comets and asteroids bombarded its surface. About 4.2 billion years ago, Earth cooled enough to allow solid rocks to form and water to condense and fall as rain. Earth's surface became stable enough for permanent oceans to form.

This infant planet was very different from Earth today. 🔑 **Earth's early atmosphere contained little or no oxygen. It was principally composed of carbon dioxide, water vapor, and nitrogen, with lesser amounts of carbon monoxide, hydrogen sulfide, and hydrogen cyanide.** If you had been there, a few deep breaths would have killed you! Because of the gases in the atmosphere, the sky was probably pinkish-orange. And because the oceans contained lots of dissolved iron, they were probably brown. This was the Earth on which life began.

Key Questions

🔑 **What do scientists hypothesize about early Earth and the origin of life?**

🔑 **What theory explains the origin of eukaryotic cells?**

🔑 **What is the evolutionary significance of sexual reproduction?**

Vocabulary
endosymbiotic theory

Taking Notes

Flowchart Construct a flowchart that shows what scientists hypothesize are the major steps from the origin of Earth to the appearance of eukaryotic cells.

FIGURE 19–14 Early Earth
Violent volcanic eruptions helped shape Earth's early history.

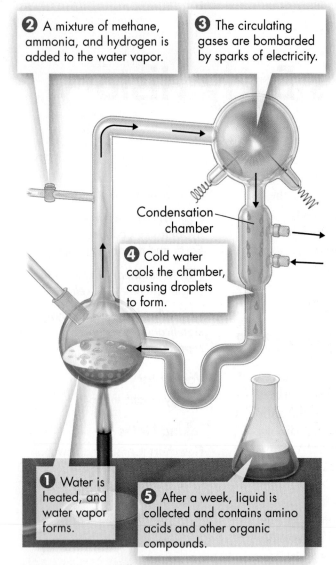

❷ A mixture of methane, ammonia, and hydrogen is added to the water vapor.

❸ The circulating gases are bombarded by sparks of electricity.

Condensation chamber

❹ Cold water cools the chamber, causing droplets to form.

❶ Water is heated, and water vapor forms.

❺ After a week, liquid is collected and contains amino acids and other organic compounds.

FIGURE 19–15 Miller-Urey Experiment Miller and Urey produced amino acids, which are needed to make proteins, by passing sparks through a mixture of hydrogen, methane, ammonia, and water vapor. Evidence now suggests that the composition of Earth's early atmosphere was different from their 1953 experiment. However, more recent experiments with different mixtures of gases have produced similar results.

The First Organic Molecules Could organic molecules assemble under conditions on early Earth? In 1953, chemists Stanley Miller and Harold Urey tried to answer that question. They filled a sterile flask with water, to simulate the oceans, and boiled it. To the water vapor, they added methane, ammonia, and hydrogen, to simulate what they thought had been the composition of Earth's early atmosphere. Then, as shown in **Figure 19–15,** they passed the gases through electrodes, to simulate lightning. Next, they passed the gases through a condensation chamber, where cold water cooled them, causing drops to form. The liquid circulated through the experimental apparatus for a week. The results were spectacular: They produced 21 amino acids—building blocks of proteins. 🔑 **Miller and Urey's experiment suggested how mixtures of the organic compounds necessary for life could have arisen from simpler compounds on a primitive Earth.**

We now know that Miller and Urey's ideas on the composition of the early atmosphere were incorrect. But new experiments based on current ideas of the early atmosphere have also produced organic compounds. In fact, in 1995, one of Miller's more accurate mixtures produced cytosine and uracil, two bases found in RNA.

Formation of Microspheres A stew of organic molecules is a long way from a living cell, and the leap from nonlife to life is the greatest gap in scientific hypotheses of life's early history. Geological evidence suggests that during the Archean Eon, 200 to 300 million years after Earth cooled enough to carry liquid water, cells similar to bacteria were common. How might these cells have originated?

Large organic molecules form tiny bubbles called proteinoid microspheres under certain conditions. Microspheres are not cells, but they have some characteristics of living systems. Like cells, they have selectively permeable membranes through which water molecules can pass. Microspheres also have a simple means of storing and releasing energy. Several hypotheses suggest that structures similar to proteinoid microspheres acquired the characteristics of living cells as early as 3.8 billion years ago.

Evolution of RNA and DNA Another unanswered question is the origin of RNA and DNA. Remember that cells are controlled by information stored in DNA, which is transcribed into RNA and then translated into proteins. How could this complex biochemical machinery have evolved?

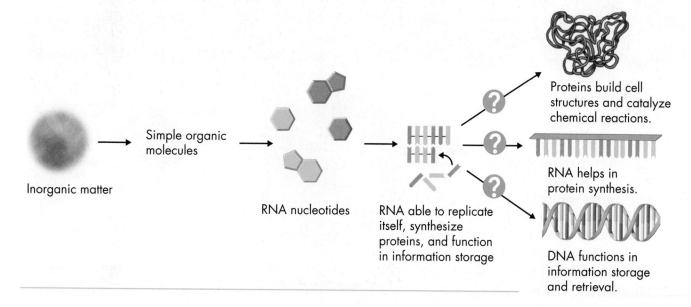

| Inorganic matter | Simple organic molecules | RNA nucleotides | RNA able to replicate itself, synthesize proteins, and function in information storage |

Proteins build cell structures and catalyze chemical reactions.

RNA helps in protein synthesis.

DNA functions in information storage and retrieval.

Scientists haven't solved this puzzle, but molecular biologists have generated intriguing hypotheses. A number of experiments that simulated conditions on early Earth suggest that small sequences of RNA could have formed from simpler molecules. Why is that interesting? It is interesting because we now know that, under the right conditions, some RNA sequences help DNA replicate. Other RNA sequences process messenger RNA after transcription. Still other RNA sequences catalyze chemical reactions, and some RNA molecules even grow and replicate on their own. **The "RNA world" hypothesis proposes that RNA existed by itself before DNA. From this simple RNA-based system, several steps could have led to DNA-directed protein synthesis.** This hypothesis, shown in **Figure 19–16,** is still being tested.

Production of Free Oxygen Microscopic fossils, or microfossils, of prokaryotes that resemble bacteria have been found in Archean rocks more than 3.5 billion years old. Those first life forms evolved in the absence of oxygen because at that time Earth's atmosphere contained very little of that highly reactive gas.

During the early Proterozoic Eon, photosynthetic bacteria became common. By 2.2 billion years ago, these organisms were churning out oxygen. At first, the oxygen combined with iron in the oceans, producing iron oxide, or rust. Iron oxide, which is not soluble in water, sank to the ocean floor, forming great bands of iron that are the source of most iron ore mined today. Without iron, the oceans changed color from brown to blue-green.

Next, oxygen gas began to accumulate in the atmosphere. The ozone layer began to form, and the skies turned their present shade of blue. Over several hundred million years, oxygen concentrations rose until they reached today's levels. In a sense, this increase in oxygen created the first global "pollution" crisis. To the first cells, which evolved in the absence of oxygen, this reactive gas was a deadly poison! The rise of oxygen in the atmosphere drove some early life forms to extinction. Some organisms, however, evolved new metabolic pathways that used oxygen for respiration. These organisms also evolved ways to protect themselves from oxygen's powerful reactive abilities.

FIGURE 19–16 Origin of RNA and DNA The "RNA world" hypothesis about the origin of life suggests that RNA evolved before DNA. Scientists have not yet demonstrated the later stages of this process in a laboratory setting. **Interpret Visuals** *How would RNA have stored genetic information?*

SEM 11,500×

FIGURE 19–17 Fossilized Bacteria Fossilized bacteria are the earliest evidence of life on Earth. These rod-shaped bacterial cells (red) are seen calcified on the shell of a single-celled protozoan.

Comparing Atmospheres

Many scientists think that Earth's early atmosphere may have been similar to the gases released by a volcano today. The graphs show the composition of the atmosphere today and the composition of gases released by a volcano.

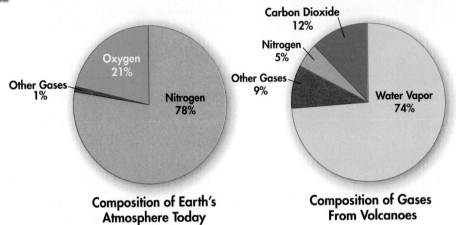

Composition of Earth's Atmosphere Today

Other Gases 1%
Oxygen 21%
Nitrogen 78%

Composition of Gases From Volcanoes

Carbon Dioxide 12%
Nitrogen 5%
Other Gases 9%
Water Vapor 74%

1. Interpret Graphs Which gas is most abundant in Earth's atmosphere today? What percentage of that gas may have been present in the early atmosphere?

2. Interpret Graphs Which gas was probably most abundant in the early atmosphere?

3. Infer Where did the water in today's oceans probably come from?

Origin of Eukaryotic Cells

🔑 *What theory explains the origin of eukaryotic cells?*

One of the most important events in the history of life was the evolution of eukaryotic cells from prokaryotic cells. Remember that eukaryotic cells have nuclei, but prokaryotic cells do not. Eukaryotic cells also have complex organelles. Virtually all eukaryotes have mitochondria, and both plants and algae also have chloroplasts. How did these complex cells evolve?

Endosymbiotic Theory Researchers hypothesize that about 2 billion years ago, some ancient prokaryotes began evolving internal cell membranes. These prokaryotes were the ancestors of eukaryotic organisms. Then, according to **endosymbiotic** (en doh sim by AHT ik) **theory,** prokaryotic cells entered those ancestral eukaryotes. These intruders didn't infect their hosts, as parasites would have done, and the host cells didn't digest them, as they would have digested prey. Instead, the small prokaryotes began living inside the larger cells, as shown in **Figure 19–18.**

🔑 **The endosymbiotic theory proposes that a symbiotic relationship evolved over time, between primitive eukaryotic cells and the prokaryotic cells within them.** This idea was proposed more than a century ago. At that time, microscopists saw that the membranes of mitochondria and chloroplasts resembled the cell membranes of free-living prokaryotes. This observation led to two related hypotheses.

BUILD Vocabulary

PREFIXES The prefix *endo-* in **endosymbiotic theory** means "within" or "inner." The endosymbiotic theory involves a symbiotic relationship between eukaryotic cells and the prokaryotes within them.

One hypothesis proposes that mitochondria evolved from endo-symbiotic prokaryotes that were able to use oxygen to generate energy-rich ATP. Inside primitive eukaryotic cells, these energy-generating prokaryotes evolved into mitochondria that now power the cells of all multicellular organisms. Mitochondria enabled cells to metabolize oxygen. Without this ability, cells would have been killed by the free oxygen in the atmosphere.

Another hypothesis proposes that chloroplasts evolved from endo-symbiotic prokaryotes that had the ability to photosynthesize. Over time, these photosynthetic prokaryotes evolved within eukaryotic cells into the chloroplasts of plants and algae.

Modern Evidence During the 1960s, Lynn Margulis of Boston University gathered evidence that supported the endosymbiotic theory. Margulis noted first that mitochondria and chloroplasts contain DNA similar to bacterial DNA. Second, she noted that mitochondria and chloroplasts have ribosomes whose size and structure closely resemble those of bacteria. Third, she found that mitochondria and chloroplasts, like bacteria, reproduce by binary fission when cells containing them divide by mitosis. Mitochondria and chloroplasts, then, share many features of free-living bacteria. These similarities provide strong evidence of a common ancestry between free-living bacteria and the organelles of living eukaryotic cells.

In Your Notebook *Describe two hypotheses relating to the endosymbiotic theory.*

FIGURE 19–18 The Endosymbiotic Theory
The endosymbiotic theory proposes that eukaryotic cells arose from living communities formed by prokaryotic organisms. Ancient prokaryotes may have entered primitive eukaryotic cells, remained there, and evolved into organelles. **Infer** *Is it likely that nonphotosynthetic prokaryotes could have evolved into chloroplasts? Explain your answer.*

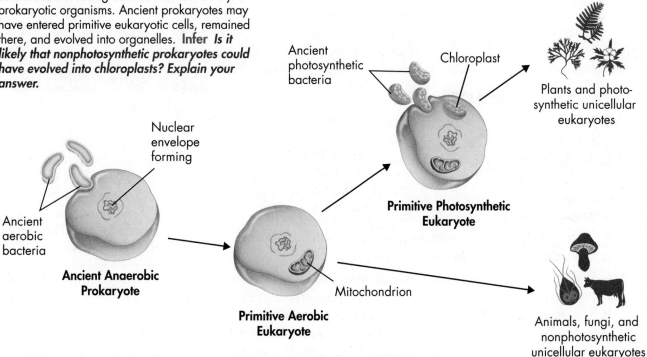

Ancient photosynthetic bacteria

Chloroplast

Plants and photo-synthetic unicellular eukaryotes

Nuclear envelope forming

Ancient aerobic bacteria

Ancient Anaerobic Prokaryote

Primitive Photosynthetic Eukaryote

Mitochondrion

Primitive Aerobic Eukaryote

Animals, fungi, and nonphotosynthetic unicellular eukaryotes

Sexual Reproduction and Multicellularity

What is the evolutionary significance of sexual reproduction?

Sometime after eukaryotic cells arose, they began to reproduce sexually. **The development of sexual reproduction sped up evolutionary change because sexual reproduction increases genetic variation.**

Significance of Sexual Reproduction When prokaryotes reproduce asexually, they duplicate their genetic material and pass it on to daughter cells. This process is efficient, but it yields daughter cells whose genomes duplicate their parent's genome. Genetic variation is basically restricted to mutations in DNA.

In contrast, when eukaryotes reproduce sexually, offspring receive genetic material from two parents. Meiosis and fertilization shuffle and reshuffle genes, generating lots of genetic diversity. That's why the offspring of sexually reproducing organisms are never identical to either their parents or their siblings (except for identical twins). The more heritable variation, the more "raw material" natural selection has to work on. Genetic variation increases the likelihood of a population's adapting to new or changing environmental conditions.

Multicellularity Multicellular organisms evolved a few hundred million years after the evolution of sexual reproduction. Early multicellular organisms underwent a series of adaptive radiations, resulting in great diversity.

19.3 Assessment

Review Key Concepts

1. a. Review What was Earth's early atmosphere like?

b. Explain What does Miller and Urey's experiment tell us about the organic compounds needed for life?

c. Predict You just read that life arose from nonlife billions of years ago. Could life arise from nonlife today? Why or why not?

2. a. Review What does the endosymbiotic theory propose?

b. Explain According to this theory, how did mitochondria evolve?

c. Apply Concepts What evidence supports the theory?

3. a. Review Why is the development of sexual reproduction so important in the history of life?

b. Sequence Put the following events in the order in which they occurred: *sexual reproduction, development of eukaryotic cells, free oxygen in the atmosphere,* and *development of photosynthesis.*

WRITE ABOUT SCIENCE

Explanation

4. Write a paragraph explaining the "RNA world" hypothesis. What parts of the hypothesis have yet to be proved? Is it possible that we will never know the origins of RNA and DNA? Explain your answer.

More than 99 percent of the species that ever lived are now extinct. If studying past life interests you, you might consider one of the following careers.

FOSSIL PREPARATOR

If you believe what you see in the movies, fossils are usually found perfectly preserved and intact. But the truth is that fossils are almost always found jumbled and encased in rock. Using microscopes and delicate hand tools, fossil preparators remove fossils from the surrounding rock. Preparators carefully reconstruct damaged pieces and record information about fossil position and rock composition.

MUSEUM GUIDE

Museum guides are educators. But instead of using books to teach, they use museum exhibits. A museum guide at a natural history museum, for example, might have fossils that visitors can touch and manipulate. Museum guides also perform demonstrations and give informal talks.

PALEONTOLOGIST

Paleontologists study extinct and ancient life. It is not all about fossils, however. Today paleontolgists use everything from biochemistry to computer modeling to understand the evolutionary relationships among organisms. Living animals are also sometimes used to study movement, behavior, or development.

CAREER CLOSE-UP:

Dr. Kristi Curry Rogers, Curator of Paleontology, Science Museum of Minnesota

Dr. Curry Rogers' work is big—very big. Dr. Curry Rogers is a paleontologist who studies how the giant long-necked sauropod dinosaurs grew. How can you study how an extinct animal grew over 65 million years ago? By studying microscopic bone structure, Dr. Curry Rogers can estimate how long it took the animal to reach full size. This kind of research can help scientists understand how dinosaurs regulated their body temperature. In addition to questions about sauropod growth, Dr. Curry Rogers is also investigating how different sauropods are related.

"Unlike many kids who go through a 'fossil phase,' I never grew out of it!"

WRITING Choose one of the careers described here. Explain why this career is important to understanding the history of life.

PALEOZOIC ERA

Cambrian Period	Ordovician Period	Silurian Period

Cambrian Period

During the Cambrian Period, multicellular life experienced its greatest adaptive radiation in what is called the Cambrian Explosion. Many species were fossilized during this period because many organisms evolved hard body parts, including shells and outer skeletons. Landmasses moved in ways that created vast shallow marine habitats. Jawless fishes first appeared. The Cambrian ended with a large mass extinction in which nearly 30 percent of all animal groups died.

▲ *Elrathia*

Silurian Period

During the Silurian Period, land areas rose, draining shallow seas and creating moist tropical habitats. Jawless fishes underwent an extensive radiation, and the first fish with true jaws appeared. The first multicellular land plants evolved from aquatic ancestors. Arthropods became the first animals to live on land.

▲ Sea Lily Fossil

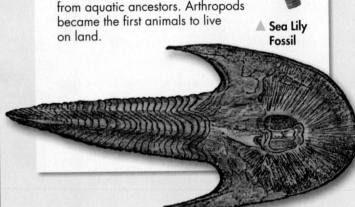
▲ *Cephalaspis* (raylike jawless fish)

▼ *Stenaster* (early sea star)

Pleurocysities (early echinoderms) ▼

Ordovician Period

Oceans flooded large land areas, creating more shallow marine habitats. Animal groups that survived the Cambrian extinction experienced dramatic adaptive radiations. These radiations generated great diversity in major animal phyla. Invertebrates dominated the seas. Early vertebrates evolved bony coverings.

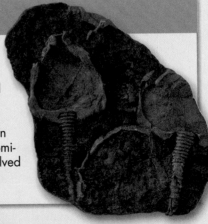

Permian Period

During the Permian Period, invertebrates, vertebrates, and land plants continued to expand over Earth's continents. Reptiles experienced the first of several major adaptive radiations, which produced the ancestors of modern reptiles, dinosaurs, and mammals. The Permian Period ended with the biggest mass extinction of all time. More than 50 percent of terrestrial animal families and more than 95 percent of marine species became extinct.

▲ Crinoid

Devonian Period

During the Devonian Period, invertebrates and vertebrates thrived in the seas. Fishes evolved jaws, bony skeletons, and scales. Sharks began their adaptive radiation. Certain groups of fishes evolved leglike fins, and some of these evolved into the first amphibians. Some land plants, such as ferns, adapted to drier areas. Insects began to radiate on land.

Early Amphibian ▼

◀ Fossil Fern From Carboniferous Period

Carboniferous Period

During the Carboniferous Period, mountain building created a wide range of habitats, from swampy lowlands to drier upland areas. Giant ferns, club mosses, and horsetails formed vast swampy forests. Amphibians, insects, and land plants experienced major adaptive radiations. Winged insects evolved into many forms, including huge dragonflies and cockroaches. For early vertebrates, insects were food; for plants, insects were predators. The first reptiles evolved from ancient amphibians.

Triassic Period	Jurassic Period	Cretaceous Period

Triassic Period

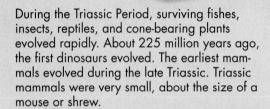

During the Triassic Period, surviving fishes, insects, reptiles, and cone-bearing plants evolved rapidly. About 225 million years ago, the first dinosaurs evolved. The earliest mammals evolved during the late Triassic. Triassic mammals were very small, about the size of a mouse or shrew.

▲ **Living Horsetails**   ▲ **Horsetail Fossil**

Cretaceous Period

During the Cretaceous Period, *Tyrannosaurus rex* roamed the land, while   ▲ **T. rex**
flying reptiles and birds soared in the sky. Turtles, crocodiles, and other, now-extinct reptiles like plesiosaurs swam among fishes and invertebrates in the seas. Leafy trees, shrubs, and flowering plants emerged and experienced adaptive radiations. The Cretaceous ended with another mass extinction. More than half of all plant and animal groups were wiped out, including all dinosaurs except the ancestors of modern birds.

Jurassic Period

During the Jurassic Period, dinosaurs became the most diverse land animals. They "ruled" for about 150 million years, but different types lived at different times. One lineage of dinosaurs evolved feathers and ultimately led to modern birds. *Archaeopteryx*, the first feathered fossil to be discovered, evolved during this time.

◄ **Pterodactyl Fossil**

▼ *Maiasaura* **Nest**

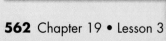

Paleogene Period	Neogene Period	Quaternary Period

Paleogene Period

During the Paleogene Period, climates changed from warm and moist to cool and dry. Flowering plants, grasses, and insects flourished. After the dinosaurs and giant marine reptiles went extinct, mammals underwent a major adaptive radiation. As climates changed, forests were replaced by open woods and grasslands. Large mammals—ancestors of cattle, deer, and sheep and other grazers—evolved and spread across the grasslands. In the sea, the first whales evolved.

▲ Early Mammal

Neogene Period

During the Neogene Period, colliding continents pushed up modern mountain ranges, including the Alps in Europe and the Rockies, Cascades, and Sierra Nevadas in North America. As mountains rose, ice and snow built up at high elevations and in the Arctic. Falling sea levels and colliding continents created connections between North and South America, and between Africa, Europe, and Asia. Those connections led to great movements of land animals between continents. Climates continued a cooling and drying trend, and grasslands continued to expand. Modern grazing animals continued to coevolve with grasses, evolving specialized digestive tracts to deal with tough, low-nutrient grass tissue.

◀ Neanderthal Skull

Quaternary Period

During the Quaternary Period, Earth cooled. A series of ice ages saw thick glaciers advance and retreat over parts of Europe and North America. So much water was frozen in glaciers that sea levels fell by more than 100 meters. Then, about 20,000 years ago, Earth's climate began to warm. Over thousands of years, glaciers melted, and sea levels rose. In the oceans, algae, coral, mollusks, fishes, and mammals thrived. Insects and birds shared the skies. Land mammals—among them bats, cats, dogs, cattle, and mammoths—became common. Between 6 and 7 million years ago, one group of mammals began an adaptive radiation that led to the ancestors and close relatives of modern humans.

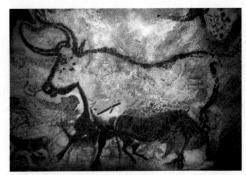

▲ Cave paintings

Pre-Lab: Using Index Fossils

Problem How can fossils be used to determine the relative ages of rock layers?

Materials scissors

Lab Manual Chapter 19 Lab

Skills Focus Interpret Visuals, Sequence, Draw Conclusions

Connect to the **Big idea**   When detectives work on a case, they may look for items with a time stamp, such as parking tickets and credit card slips. Such items can help detectives piece together a sequence of events. Events related to a crime usually occur within a relatively short period of time. In contrast, the events that paleontologists study will have occurred over millions of years. Placing these events in their proper order can be challenging. The clues that a paleontologist uses to sequence events in the history of life are fossils buried in rock layers. In this lab, you will use fossils to place rock layers in order from oldest to youngest.

Background Questions

a. Review What is a fossil? What are the characteristics of a good index fossil?

b. Explain What characteristic of radioactive decay allows scientists to assign specific ages to rock layers?

c. Classify How do fossils help geologists decide where one division of geologic time should end and another division begin?

Pre-Lab Questions

Preview the procedure in the lab manual.

1. Organize Data After you cut out the drawings of the rock layers, how will you begin the process of sorting the layers by age?

2. Infer *Desmatosuchus* was a crocodile relative that lived only during the Triassic Period. Horsetails are plants that first appeared in the Triassic Period and still exist. Which of these organisms would be more useful as an index fossil for the Triassic Period? Why?

3. Use Analogies Luke found a box of photos labeled 1970–1995. Each photo shows his entire extended family. No dates appear on the photos. Luke knows that his grandmother died in 1985 and his uncle was born in 1975. Luke's sister was born in 1990. How can Luke use this information to sort the photos into four batches? How are Luke's relatives similar to index fossils?

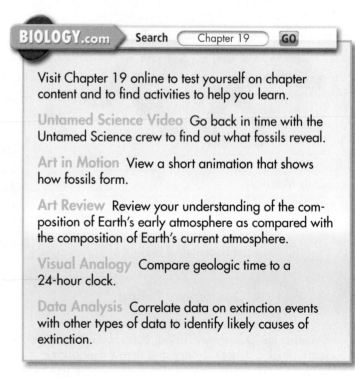

BIOLOGY.com   Search (Chapter 19)   **GO**

Visit Chapter 19 online to test yourself on chapter content and to find activities to help you learn.

Untamed Science Video Go back in time with the Untamed Science crew to find out what fossils reveal.

Art in Motion View a short animation that shows how fossils form.

Art Review Review your understanding of the composition of Earth's early atmosphere as compared with the composition of Earth's current atmosphere.

Visual Analogy Compare geologic time to a 24-hour clock.

Data Analysis Correlate data on extinction events with other types of data to identify likely causes of extinction.

19 Study Guide

Big idea ▸ Evolution

Paleontologists use fossils to learn about the structure and environments of ancient organisms. Fossils also give clues to events that happened during Earth's history.

19.1 The Fossil Record

🔑 From the fossil record, paleontologists learn about the structure of ancient organisms, their environment, and the ways in which they lived.

🔑 Relative dating allows paleontologists to determine whether a fossil is older or younger than other fossils. Radiometric dating uses the proportion of radioactive to stable isotopes to calculate the age of a sample.

🔑 The geologic time scale is based on both relative and absolute dating. The major divisions of the geologic time scale are eons, eras, and periods.

🔑 Building mountains, opening coastlines, changing climates, and geological forces have altered habitats of living organisms repeatedly throughout Earth history. In turn, the actions of living organisms over time have changed conditions in the land, water, and atmosphere of planet Earth.

extinct (538)
paleontologist (539)
relative dating (540)
index fossil (540)
radiometric dating (540)

half-life (540)
geologic time scale (542)
era (543)
period (543)
plate tectonics (544)

19.2 Patterns and Processes of Evolution

🔑 If the rate of speciation in a clade is equal to or greater than the rate of extinction, the clade will continue to exist. If the rate of extinction in a clade is greater than the rate of speciation, the clade will eventually become extinct.

🔑 Evidence shows that evolution has often proceeded at different rates for different organisms at different times over the long history of life on Earth.

🔑 Two important patterns of macroevolution are adaptive radiation and convergent evolution. Adaptive radiation occurs when a single species or a small group of species evolves over a relatively short time into several different forms that live in different ways. Convergent evolution occurs when unrelated organisms evolve into similar forms.

🔑 The relationship between two coevolving organisms often becomes so specific that neither organism can survive without the other. Thus, an evolutionary change in one organism is usually followed by a change in the other organism.

macroevolutionary
  patterns (546)
background extinction (548)
mass extinction (548)
gradualism (549)

punctuated equilibrium (549)
adaptive radiation (550)
convergent evolution (551)
coevolution (551)

19.3 Earth's Early History

🔑 Earth's early atmosphere contained little or no oxygen. It was principally composed of carbon dioxide, water vapor, and nitrogen, with lesser amounts of carbon monoxide, hydrogen sulfide, and hydrogen cyanide.

🔑 Miller and Urey's experiment suggested how mixtures of the organic compounds necessary for life could have arisen from simpler compounds on a primitive Earth.

🔑 The "RNA world" hypothesis proposes that RNA existed by itself before DNA. From this simple RNA-based system, several steps could have led to DNA-directed protein synthesis.

🔑 The endosymbiotic theory proposes that a symbiotic relationship evolved over time between primitive eukaryotic cells and the prokaryotic cells within them.

🔑 The development of sexual reproduction sped up evolutionary change because sexual reproduction increases genetic variation.

endosymbiotic theory (556)

Think Visually Construct a table comparing the Paleozoic, Mesozoic, and Cenozoic eras. Include the approximate time periods for each era and identify the characteristic organisms.

19 Assessment

Understand Key Concepts

1. Scientists who specialize in the study of fossils are called
   a. biologists.
   c. zoologists.
   b. paleontologists.
   d. geologists.

2. Sedimentary rocks usually form when layers of small particles are compressed
   a. in the atmosphere.
   c. in mountains.
   b. in a snow field.
   d. under water.

3. Using C–14 to analyze rock layers
   a. is a method of estimating absolute age.
   b. is a method of estimating relative age.
   c. can only be used on extremely ancient rock layers.
   d. is impossible because rock layers do not contain carbon.

4. Half-life is the time required for half the atoms in a radioactive sample to
   a. decay.
   c. expand.
   b. double.
   d. be created.

5. According to the theory of plate tectonics,
   a. Earth's climate has changed many times.
   b. Earth's continents move very slowly.
   c. evolution occurs at different rates.
   d. giant asteroids crashed into Earth in the past.

6. How does relative dating enable paleontologists to estimate a fossil's age?

7. Explain how radioactivity is used to date rocks.

8. What is the geologic time scale, and how was it developed?

9. How have the activities of organisms affected Earth's environment?

Think Critically

10. **Calculate** The half-life of carbon-14 is 5730 years. What is the age of a fossil containing 1/16 the amount of carbon-14 of living organisms? Explain your calculation. MATH

11. **Apply Concepts** Evolutionary biologists say that there is a good reason for gaps in the fossil record.

Can you explain why some extinct animals and plants were never fossilized?

Understand Key Concepts

12. The process that produces similar-looking structures in unrelated groups of organisms is
    a. adaptive radiation.
    c. convergent evolution.
    b. coevolution.
    d. mass extinction.

13. The general term for large-scale evolutionary changes that take place over long periods of time is called
    a. macroevolution.
    b. coevolution.
    c. convergent evolution.
    d. geologic time.

14. Cladograms that are based on the fossil record always show
    a. which organisms are direct ancestors of the others.
    b. relationships based on shared derived characteristics.
    c. that clades are made up only of extinct species.
    d. relative ages of organisms in the clade.

15. Explain and give an example of the process of adaptive radiation.

16. Explain the model of evolution known as punctuated equilibrium.

17. Use an example to explain the concept of coevolution.

Think Critically

18. **Infer** Major geologic changes often go hand in hand with mass extinctions. Why do you think this is true?

19. **Apply Concepts** Why is rapid evolution especially likely to occur in a small population that has been separated from the main population?

20. **Apply Concepts** What is the role of natural selection in adaptive radiation? How do these processes lead to diversity?

Understand Key Concepts

21. Earth's early atmosphere contained little or no
   a. water vapor.   **c.** nitrogen.
   b. carbon dioxide.   **d.** oxygen.

22. In their experiment that modeled conditions on ancient Earth, Miller and Urey used electric sparks to simulate
   a. temperature.
   b. sunlight.
   c. atmospheric gases.
   d. lightning.

23. Outlines of ancient cells that are preserved well enough to identify them as prokaryotes are
   a. microfossils.   **c.** autotrophs.
   b. heterotrophs.   **d.** phototrophic.

24. What hypotheses have scientists proposed to explain Earth's early atmosphere and the way the oceans formed?

25. The diagram below shows the apparatus that Miller and Urey used in their experiment. Explain both what water and gases were meant to represent and what Miller and Urey were hoping to accomplish.

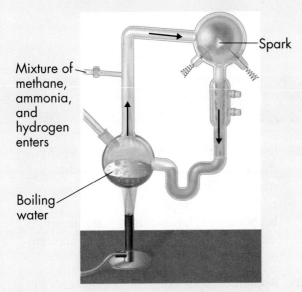

Mixture of methane, ammonia, and hydrogen enters

Spark

Boiling water

26. How are proteinoid microspheres similar to living cells?

27. How did the addition of oxygen to Earth's atmosphere affect the evolution of life?

28. According to the endosymbiotic theory, how did mitochondria originate?

solve the CHAPTER MYSTERY

MURDER IN THE PERMIAN

Solving a 250-million-year-old murder mystery isn't easy! In recent years, scientists have studied the chemistry of Permian rocks and changes in the fossil record. Some researchers determined that enormous and long-lasting volcanic eruptions in Siberia vented carbon dioxide into the atmosphere, causing a massive change in global climate. This put species and ecosystems under great environmental stress.

Other researchers used geochemical analyses to show that atmospheric oxygen levels dropped to roughly half of what they are today. Huge parts of the oceans lost all oxygen. Because of the reduction in available oxygen, land animals near sea level might have been gasping for breath as you would on top of Mount Everest.

Finally, there is evidence that an asteroid hit Earth! To this day, paleontologists are testing competing hypotheses that try to explain which of the events that occurred at this time caused the mass extinction. However, these hypotheses are constantly changing and have probably changed since this book was written.

1. Compare and Contrast How do current hypotheses about the Permian extinction compare with the predominant theory about the Cretaceous extinction?

2. Form a Hypothesis From the information in this book, suggest an explanation for the Permian mass extinction.

3. Pose Questions What questions could you ask to find out whether your hypothesis is correct? What evidence would answer those questions?

4. Connect to the **Big idea** What role have mass extinctions played in the history of life?

Think Critically

29. **Use Models** What part of Miller and Urey's apparatus represents rain? What important role would rain play in chemical evolution?

30. **Relate Cause and Effect** How do you think the cells that took in the ancestors of mitochondria and chloroplasts benefited from the relationship?

Connecting Concepts

Use Science Graphics

The diagram shows rock layers in two different places. Use the diagram to answer questions 31 and 32.

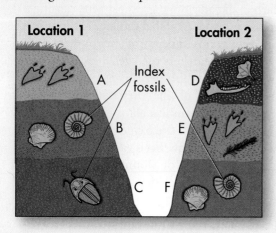

31. Which fossils are probably older—those in layer A or those in layer C? How do you know?

32. Which rock layer in location 2 is probably about the same age as layer C in location 1? How do you know?

33. What are the characteristics of a useful index fossil?

Write About Science

34. **Explanation** Write a paragraph comparing conditions on early Earth with those on modern Earth.

35. **Description** Use the example of body shape in sharks, dolphins, and penguins to explain convergent evolution.

36. **Assess the** **Big idea** Explain how the formation of sedimentary rock gives paleontologists information about the sequence in which life forms appeared on Earth.

37. **Assess the** **Big idea** When describing their theory of punctuated equilibrium, Stephen Jay Gould and Niles Eldredge often used the motto "stasis is data." Stasis is another word for equilibrium. Explain what Gould and Eldredge meant.

Analyzing Data

The table below compares the half-life of several radioactive atoms. Use the table to answer questions 38 and 39.

Isotope and Decay Product		Half-Life (years)
Rubidium-87 →	Strontium-87	48.8 billion
Thorium-232 →	Lead-208	14.0 billion
Uranium-235 →	Lead-207	704.0 million
Uranium-238 →	Lead-206	4.5 billion

38. **Interpret Data** Which atoms have half-lives that are longer than the age of the oldest microfossils?
    a. uranium-235 only
    b. thorium-232, rubidium-87, and uranium-235
    c. rubidium-87, thorium-232, and uranium-238
    d. uranium-235 and rubidium-87

39. **Apply Concepts** Lead-207 is found only in rocks that also contain uranium-235. Analysis of a sample shows that it has three times as many atoms of lead-207 as there are atoms of uranium-235. How many half-lives have passed since this rock formed?
    a. one   b. two   c. three   d. four

Standardized Test Prep

Multiple Choice

1. Useful index fossils are found
   A in a small area for a short time.
   B in a small area for a long time.
   C over a large area for a short time.
   D over a large area for a long time.

2. What happens if the rate of extinction in a clade is greater than the rate of speciation?
   A The clade will eventually become extinct.
   B The clade will continue to exist.
   C The species in the clade will become more varied.
   D The number of species in the clade will stay the same.

3. Which of the following is evidence for the endo-symbiotic theory?
   A Mitochondria and chloroplasts contain DNA similar to bacterial DNA.
   B Mitochondria and chloroplasts have similar functions in the cell.
   C Mitochondria and chloroplasts have no DNA of their own.
   D Mitochondria and chloroplasts can live independently when removed from the eukaryotic cell.

4. Carbon–14 is NOT useful for dating most fossils because
   A it has a very long half-life.
   B it has a very short half-life.
   C most organisms contain more potassium than carbon.
   D it is found only in certain rock layers.

5. The movement of continents has played a significant role in evolution because
   A continents move rapidly and some organisms cannot adjust.
   B without the movement of continents, there would be no water on Earth.
   C the movement of continents has caused environments to change.
   D all mass extinctions are the result of continental drift.

Questions 6 and 7

The graph shows the decay of radioactive isotopes. Use the information in the graph to answer the questions that follow.

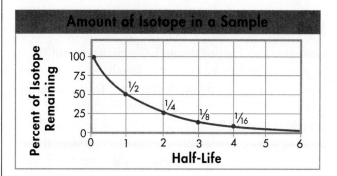

6. The half-life of thorium-230 is 75,000 years. How long will it take for $\frac{7}{8}$ of the original amount of thorium-230 in a sample to decay?
   A 75,000 years
   B 225,000 years
   C 25,000 years
   D 150,000 years

7. The half-life of potassium-40 is about 1.3 billion years. After four half-lives have passed, how much of the original sample will be left?
   A $\frac{1}{16}$
   B $\frac{1}{16} \times 1300$ million grams
   C $\frac{1}{4}$
   D $\frac{1}{4} \times 1300$ million grams

Open-Ended Response

8. How does the process by which sedimentary rock forms allow scientists to determine the relative ages of fossils?

If You Have Trouble With . . .

Question	1	2	3	4	5	6	7	8
See Lesson	19.1	19.2	19.3	19.1	19.1	19.1	19.1	19.1

Unit Project

Evolution Documentary

Have you ever flipped through the channels and stopped on a documentary that caught your eye? And before you knew it an hour had passed? Documentaries can be a great way to learn about fascinating topics. Imagine you are a TV producer and have been hired to produce a documentary on evolution for a public television station. Your target audience is the general public.

Your Task Write a script for a 5–10 minute segment of an evolution documentary and present it to your class.

Be sure to
- discuss evidence for evolution by bringing in specific examples.
- present the information clearly and in an engaging manner.
- explain why the misconceptions listed below are *not* true:
    1) Evolution causes organisms to improve— life has gotten better over time.
    2) Evolution is not observable or testable.
    3) Gaps in the fossil record disprove evolution.
    4) Natural selection involves organisms "trying" to adapt.
    5) Natural selection is the only way that populations can change over time.

Reflection Questions
1. Score your documentary using the rubric below. What score did you give yourself?
2. What did you do well in this project?
3. What needs improvement?
4. What do you think a member of the general public would learn from your documentary?

Assessment Rubric

Score	Scientific Content	Quality of Documentary Script
4	Documentary provides accurate evidence for evolution and clearly corrects several misconceptions.	Information is presented in a clear, organized, and engaging manner.
3	Documentary provides some accurate evidence for evolution and attempts to correct misconceptions.	Information is presented in a clear and organized manner, but it could be more engaging.
2	Documentary provides little evidence for evolution and does not correct misconceptions well.	Information could be presented in a clearer manner. The script needs editing.
1	Documentary does not provide evidence for evolution and does not attempt to correct misconceptions.	Information is presented in a disorganized and confusing manner. The script needs a lot of editing.

A Visual Guide to
The Diversity of Life

▲ The Chambered Nautilus, found today in the Pacific Ocean, is one of the few living representatives of a group that once flourished in ancient seas 265 million years before the dinosaurs evolved. This Visual Guide will give you a glimpse of life's great variety and evolutionary history.

A Visual Guide to
The Diversity of Life

CONTENTS

How to Use This Guide	**DOL•3**
The Tree of Life	**DOL•4**
Bacteria	**DOL•6**
• Proteobacteria	DOL•7
• Spirochaetes	DOL•7
• Actinobacteria	DOL•7
• Cyanobacteria	DOL•7
Archaea	**DOL•8**
• Crenarchaeotes	DOL•9
• Euryarchaeotes	DOL•9
• Korarchaeotes	DOL•9
• Nanoarchaeotes	DOL•9
Protists	**DOL•10**
• Excavates	DOL•11
• Chromalveolates	DOL•12
• Cercozoa, Foraminiferans, and Radiolarians	DOL•14
• Rhodophytes	DOL•15
• Amoebozoa	DOL•15
• Choanozoa	DOL•15
Fungi	**DOL•16**
• Basidiomycetes	DOL•17
• Ascomycetes	DOL•18
• Zygomycetes	DOL•19
• Chytrids	DOL•19
Plants	**DOL•20**
• Green Algae	DOL•21
• Bryophytes	DOL•22
• Seedless Vascular Plants	DOL•23
• Gymnosperms	DOL•24
• Angiosperms	DOL•26
Animals	**DOL•30**
• Porifera (Sponges)	DOL•31
• Cnidarians	DOL•32
• Arthropods	DOL•34
• Nematodes (Roundworms)	DOL•38
• Platyhelminthes (Flatworms)	DOL•39
• Annelids (Segmented Worms)	DOL•40
• Mollusks	DOL•42
• Echinoderms	DOL•44
• Nonvertebrate Chordates	DOL•46
• Fishes	DOL•48
• Amphibians	DOL•52
• Reptiles	DOL•54
• Birds	DOL•56
• Mammals	DOL•60

HOW TO USE THIS GUIDE

Use this visual reference tool to explore the classification and characteristics of organisms, including their habitats, ecology, behavior, and other important facts. This guide reflects the latest understandings about phylogenetic relationships within the three domains of life. Divided into six color-coded sections, the Visual Guide begins with a brief survey through the Bacteria and Archaea domains. It next discusses the major groups of protists, fungi, and plants. The final section provides information on nine animal phyla.

❶ See how the group of organisms relates to others on the tree of life.

❷ Learn about the general characteristics that all members of the group share.

❸ Discover the members of the group and learn about their traits.

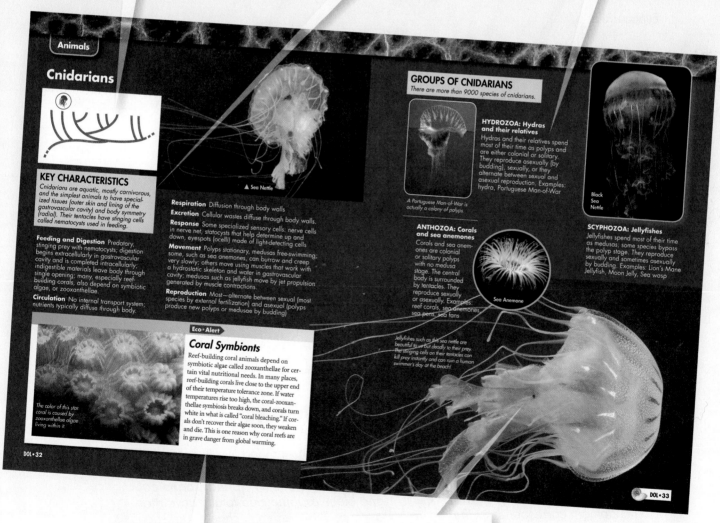

Animals

Cnidarians

KEY CHARACTERISTICS
Cnidarians are aquatic, mostly carnivorous, and the simplest animals to have specialized tissues (outer skin and lining of the gastrovascular cavity) and body symmetry (radial). Their tentacles have stinging cells called nematocysts used in feeding.

Feeding and Digestion Predatory, stinging prey with nematocysts; digestion begins extracellularly in gastrovascular cavity and is completed intracellularly; indigestible materials leave body through single opening; many, especially reef-building corals, also depend on symbiotic algae, or zooxanthellae.

Circulation No internal transport system; nutrients typically diffuse through body.

Respiration Diffusion through body walls

Excretion Cellular wastes diffuse through body walls.

Response Some specialized sensory cells: nerve cells in nerve net, statocysts that help determine up and down, eyespots (ocelli) made of light-detecting cells

Movement Polyps stationary, medusas free-swimming; some, such as sea anemones, can burrow and creep very slowly; others move using muscles that work with a hydrostatic skeleton and water in gastrovascular cavity; medusas such as jellyfish move by jet propulsion generated by muscle contractions.

Reproduction Most—alternate between sexual (most species by external fertilization) and asexual (polyps produce new polyps or medusae by budding)

▲ Sea Nettle

Eco•Alert

Coral Symbionts
Reef-building coral animals depend on symbiotic algae called zooxanthellae for certain vital nutritional needs. In many places, reef-building corals live close to the upper end of their temperature tolerance zone. If water temperatures rise too high, the coral-zooxanthellae symbiosis breaks down, and corals turn white in what is called "coral bleaching." If corals don't recover their algae soon, they weaken and die. This is one reason why coral reefs are in grave danger from global warming.

The color of this star coral is caused by zooxanthellae algae living within it.

GROUPS OF CNIDARIANS
There are more than 9000 species of cnidarians.

HYDROZOA: Hydras and their relatives
Hydras and their relatives spend most of their time as polyps and are either colonial or solitary. They reproduce asexually (by budding), sexually, or they alternate between sexual and asexual reproduction. Examples: hydra, Portuguese Man-of-War

A Portuguese Man-of-War is actually a colony of polyps.

ANTHOZOA: Corals and sea anemones
Corals and sea anemones are colonial or solitary polyps with no medusa stage. The central body is surrounded by tentacles. They reproduce sexually or asexually. Examples: reef corals, sea anemones, sea pens, sea fans

Sea Anemone

SCYPHOZOA: Jellyfishes
Jellyfishes spend most of their time as medusas; some species bypass the polyp stage. They reproduce sexually and sometimes asexually by budding. Examples: Lion's Mane Jellyfish, Moon Jelly, Sea wasp

Black Sea Nettle

Jellyfishes such as this sea nettle are beautiful to us but deadly to their prey. The stinging cells on their tentacles can kill prey instantly and can ruin a human swimmer's day at the beach!

DOL•32

DOL•33

❹ Investigate current news and interesting facts about the group.

❺ See photographs of representative animals within each group.

THE TREE OF LIFE

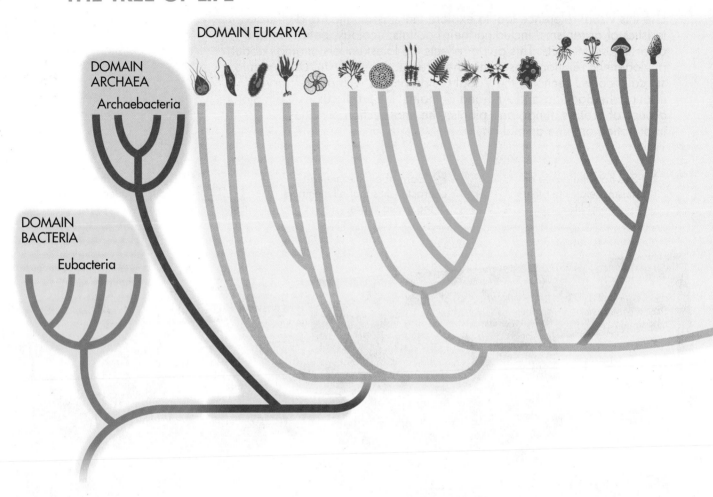

Before you begin your tour through the kingdoms of life, review this big picture from Chapter 18. The pages that follow will give you a glimpse of the incredible diversity found within each of the "branches" shown here.

DOMAIN BACTERIA

Members of the domain Bacteria are unicellular and prokaryotic. The bacteria are ecologically diverse, ranging from free-living soil organisms to deadly parasites. This domain corresponds to the kingdom Eubacteria.

DOMAIN ARCHAEA

Also unicellular and prokaryotic, members of the domain Archaea live in some of the most extreme environments you can imagine, including volcanic hot springs, brine pools, and black organic mud totally devoid of oxygen. The domain Archaea corresponds to the kingdom Archaebacteria.

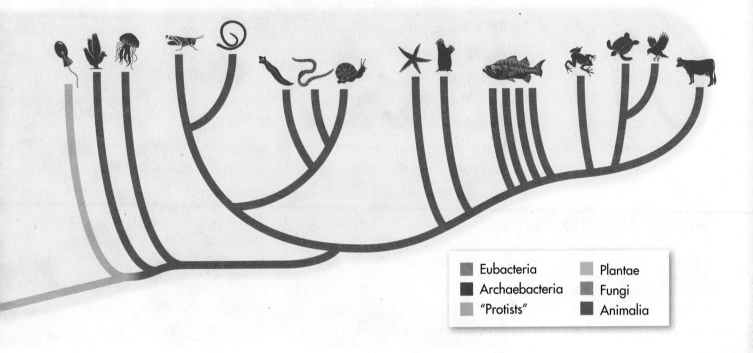

Eubacteria	Plantae
Archaebacteria	Fungi
"Protists"	Animalia

DOMAIN EUKARYA

The domain Eukarya consists of all organisms that have cells with nuclei. It is organized into the four remaining kingdoms of the six-kingdom system: Protista, Fungi, Plantae, and Animalia.

THE "PROTISTS"

Notice that the branches for the kingdom Protista are not together in one area, as is the case with the other kingdoms. In fact, recent molecular studies and cladistic analyses have shown that "eukaryotes formerly known as Protista" do not form a single clade. Current cladistic analysis divides these organisms into at least six clades. They cannot, therefore, be properly placed into a single taxon.

FUNGI

Members of the kingdom Fungi are heterotrophs. Most feed on dead or decaying organic matter. The most recognizable fungi, including mushrooms, are multicellular. Some fungi, such as yeasts, are unicellular.

PLANTS

Members of the kingdom Plantae are autotrophs that carry out photosynthesis. Plants have cell walls that contain cellulose. Plants are nonmotile—they cannot move from place to place.

ANIMALS

Members of the kingdom Animalia are multicellular and heterotrophic. Animal cells do not have cell walls. Most animals can move about, at least for some part of their life cycle.

Bacteria

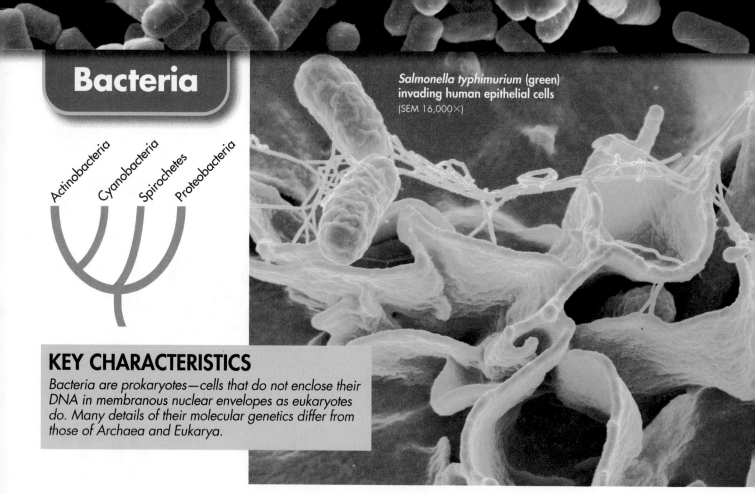

Actinobacteria Cyanobacteria Spirochetes Proteobacteria

Salmonella typhimurium (green) invading human epithelial cells (SEM 16,000×)

KEY CHARACTERISTICS

Bacteria are prokaryotes—cells that do not enclose their DNA in membranous nuclear envelopes as eukaryotes do. Many details of their molecular genetics differ from those of Archaea and Eukarya.

Cell Structure Variety of cell shapes, including spherical, rodlike, and spiral; most have cell walls containing peptidoglycan. Few if any have internal organelles. Some have external flagella for cell movement.

Genetic Organization All essential genes are in one large DNA double helix that has its ends joined to form a closed loop. Smaller loops of DNA (plasmids) may carry nonessential genes. Simultaneous transcription and translation; introns generally not present; histone proteins absent

Reproduction By binary fission; no true sexual reproduction; some achieve recombination by conjugation.

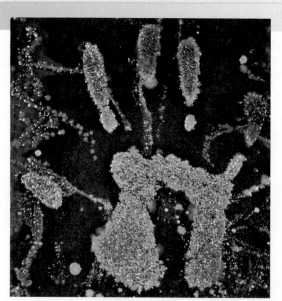

▸**Did You Know?**▸

A World of Bacteria

Putting Bacteria in Proper Perspective

"Planet of the Bacteria" was the title of an essay by the late Stephen Jay Gould. He pointed out that the dominant life forms on planet Earth aren't humans, or animals, or plants. They are bacteria. They were here first, and they inhabit more places on the planet than any other form of life. In fact, bacteria make up roughly 10 percent of our own dry body weight! In terms of biomass and importance to the planet, bacteria truly do rule this planet. They, not we, are number one.

◂ *The bacterial colonies shown here are growing in the print of a human hand on agar gel.*

GROUPS OF BACTERIA

There is no generally agreed phylogeny for the bacteria. Included here are some of the major groups within the domain.

PROTEOBACTERIA

This large and diverse clade of bacteria includes *Escherichia* (*E. coli*), *Salmonella*, *Helicobacter*, and the nitrogen-fixing soil bacterium *Rhizobium*.

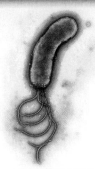

Helicobacter pylori is rod-shaped and has several flagella used for movement. This bacterium infects the stomach lining and causes ulcers in some people. (TEM 7100×)

SPIROCHAETES

The spiral-shaped bacterium that causes syphilis is Treponema pallidum. *(SEM 10,000×)* ▼

The spirochaetes (SPY roh keets) are named for their distinctive spiral shape. They move in a corkscrew-like fashion, twisting along as they are propelled by flagella on both ends of the cell. Most are free-living, but a few cause serious diseases, including syphilis, Lyme disease, and leptospirosis.

ACTINOBACTERIA

A large number of soil bacteria belong to this group. Some form long filaments. Members include the *Streptomyces* and *Actinomyces*, which are natural producers of many antibiotics, including streptomycin. A related group is the *Firmicutes*. The *Firmicutes* include *Bacillus anthracis* (anthrax), *Clostridia* (tetanus and botulism), and *Bacillus thuringiensis*, which produces a powerful insecticide used for genetic engineering in plants.

▲ *Chains of spores of soil bacteria, genus* Streptomyces *(SEM 3400×)*

CYANOBACTERIA

The cyanobacteria are photosynthetic prokaryotes that were once called "blue-green algae." They are among the oldest organisms on Earth, having been identified in rocks dating to more than 3 billion years ago. They are found in salt water and fresh water, in the soil, and even on the surfaces of damp rocks. They are the only organisms on Earth that are able to fix carbon and nitrogen under aerobic conditions, and this enables them to play critical roles in the global ecosystem, where they serve as key sources of carbon and nitrogen.

▼ *Many cyanobacteria form long filaments of attached cells, like those shown here (genus* Lyngbya, *SEM 540×).*

•A Closer Look ▶

The Gram Stain
A Microbiologist's Quick Diagnostic

Gram-positive bacteria appear purple after staining, while gram-negative bacteria appear pink. (LM 1000×) ▶

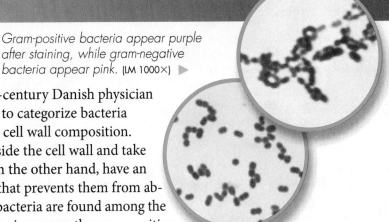

The Gram stain, developed by the nineteenth-century Danish physician Hans Christian Gram, allows microbiologists to categorize bacteria quickly into one of two groups based on their cell wall composition. Gram-positive bacteria lack a membrane outside the cell wall and take up the stain easily. Gram-negative bacteria, on the other hand, have an outer membrane of lipids and carbohydrates that prevents them from absorbing the gram stain. Many gram-negative bacteria are found among the proteobacteria. On the other hand, actinobacteria are mostly gram-positive.

Archaea

Korarchaeotes
Crenarchaeotes
Euryarchaeotes
Nanoarchaeotes

KEY CHARACTERISTICS

Archaea are prokaryotes that differ from bacteria in so many details of structure and metabolism that they are viewed as a different domain than bacteria. Genetically, they have more in common with eukaryotes than with bacteria. Their cell walls do not contain peptidoglycan.

▲ The volcano Solfatara, near Naples, Italy, is home to many archaea in the genus Sulfolobus.

Cell Structure Cells similar to those of bacteria in appearance; many have flagella that are different in structure and biochemical composition from bacterial flagella. Cell membrane lipids also different from those of bacteria; few internal organelles

Genetic Organization As in bacteria, all essential genes are in one large DNA double helix that has its ends joined to form a closed loop. Proteins responsible for transcription and translation are similar to those of eukaryotes. Also like eukaryotes, most species contain introns, and all species contain DNA-binding histone proteins.

Reproduction By binary fission; no true sexual reproduction, but some achieve recombination by conjugation.

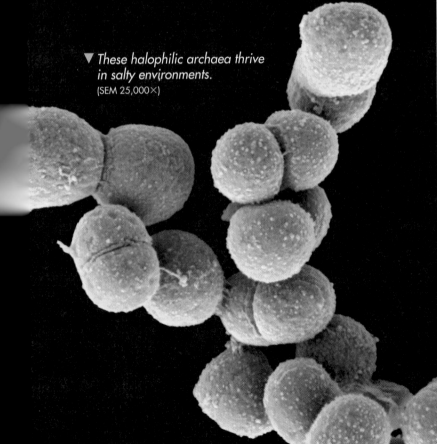

▼ These halophilic archaea thrive in salty environments.
(SEM 25,000×)

• Did You Know?

Hot Enough for You?
The Original Extremists

Way before extreme sports and extreme reality TV shows came the archaea—the original and ultimate extremists. When archaea were first discovered, biologists called them *extremophiles*, a term that literally means "lovers of the extreme." For many archaea, the name still fits. In fact, they have proven especially difficult to grow in the lab, since they require such extreme temperatures and dangerous chemical conditions to thrive. One species will grow only in sulfuric acid! Archaea found in deep-sea ocean vents thrive in temperatures exceeding 100° Celsius, while others enjoy life in the frigid waters of the Arctic.

GROUPS OF ARCHAEA

To date, four major clades of archaea have been identified. Biologists continue to debate how these clades are related to one another.

CRENARCHAEOTES

The crenarchaeotes (kren AHR kee ohts) include organisms that live in the hottest and most acidic environments known. Most of the known species have been isolated from thermal vents and hot springs—the prefix *cren-* means "spring." Some species grow using organic compounds as energy sources, but others fix carbon from carbon dioxide, using hydrogen or sulfur to provide chemical energy.

▶ Sulfolobus archaea *thrives in acidic and sulfur-rich environments and experiences optimal growth at 80° Celsius.* (SEM 33,200×)

KORARCHAEOTES

Scientists recently discovered the korarchaeote (kawr AHR kee oht) lineage in Obsidian Pool, Yellowstone National Park, and have since discovered more species in Iceland. Their DNA sequences place them apart from other archaea. The korarchaeotes may in fact be one of the least-evolved lineages of modern life that has been detected in nature so far.

▲ *Korarchaeotes from Obsidian Pool are shown in a lab culture with other microbes from their community.*
(SEM 6000×)

NANOARCHAEOTES

Only a single species of this group has been discovered, in 2002, attached to a much larger crenarchaeote! Nanoarchaeotes (na noh AHR kee ohts) grow in hot vents near the coastal regions of the ocean and show definite molecular differences from other archaea. More research is needed to characterize this group, but what is known is that they have the smallest known genome of any organism.

▼ *The newly discovered* Nanoarchaeum equitans *(smaller cells) is shown attached to its host, genus* Ignicoccus *(larger cells).*
(LM 2000×)

▼ Colony of *Methanosarcina* archaea (SEM 40,000×)

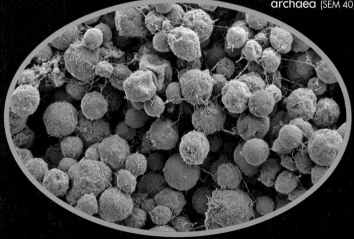

EURYARCHAEOTES

The euryarchaeotes (yoor ee AHR kee ohts) are a very diverse group of archaea, living in a broad range of habitats. The prefix *eury-* comes from a Greek word meaning "broad." The methanogens are a major group of euryarchaeotes that play essential roles in the environment. They help to break down organic compounds in oxygen-poor environments, releasing methane gas in the process. Another group, the *Halobacteria*, are found in salt ponds, where the concentration of sodium chloride approaches saturation.

Protists

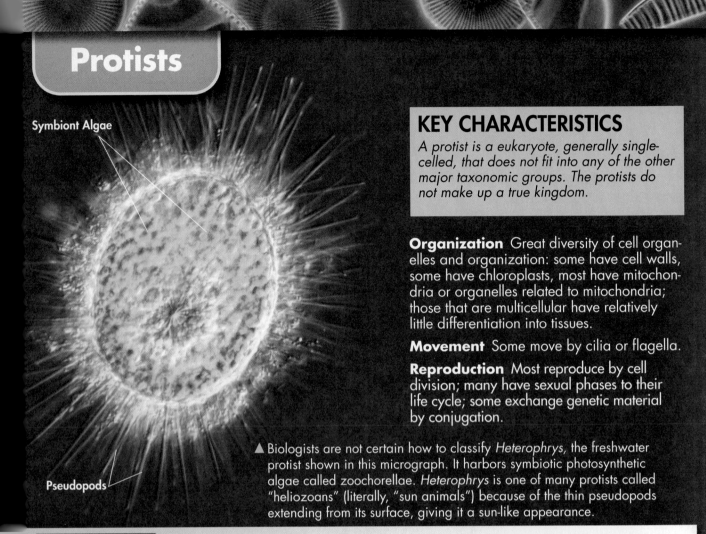

Symbiont Algae

Pseudopods

KEY CHARACTERISTICS

A protist is a eukaryote, generally single-celled, that does not fit into any of the other major taxonomic groups. The protists do not make up a true kingdom.

Organization Great diversity of cell organelles and organization: some have cell walls, some have chloroplasts, most have mitochondria or organelles related to mitochondria; those that are multicellular have relatively little differentiation into tissues.

Movement Some move by cilia or flagella.

Reproduction Most reproduce by cell division; many have sexual phases to their life cycle; some exchange genetic material by conjugation.

▲ Biologists are not certain how to classify *Heterophrys*, the freshwater protist shown in this micrograph. It harbors symbiotic photosynthetic algae called zoochorellae. *Heterophrys* is one of many protists called "heliozoans" (literally, "sun animals") because of the thin pseudopods extending from its surface, giving it a sun-like appearance.

•Did You Know?

The Kingdom That Isn't
The Challenges of Classifying Protists

Biologists traditionally classified protists by splitting them into funguslike, plantlike, and animal-like groups. This seemed to work for a while, but when they studied protists more carefully with new research tools, including genome-level molecular analysis, this traditional system simply fell apart.

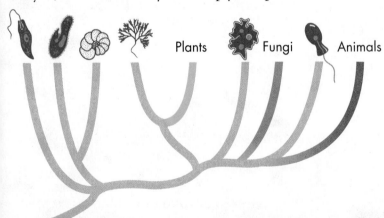

Plants   Fungi   Animals

Biologists now think that protists shouldn't be classified as a kingdom at all. In fact, when scientists look for the deepest and most fundamental divisions among eukaryotes, they find that all of those divisions are within the protists themselves, not between protists and other eukaryotes. Starting over, biologists could simply use those divisions to define newer, more accurate "kingdoms," but that might cause new problems. For one thing, it would lump two of the traditional kingdoms (animals and fungi) together, and it would leave a handful of kingdoms that contain only unicellular organisms. There is no perfect solution to this problem. Here, "protists" are considered a kingdom for the sake of convenience, but keep in mind that their differences are really too great for any single kingdom to contain.

Excavates

KEY CHARACTERISTICS

Excavates (EKS kuh vayts) have a characteristic feeding groove, usually supported by microtubules. Most have flagella. A few lack mitochondria and are unable to carry out oxidative phosphorylation, although they do possess remnants of the organelle.

GROUPS OF EXCAVATES

The excavates include a wide diversity of protists, from free-living photosynthesizers to some of humankind's most notorious pathogens.

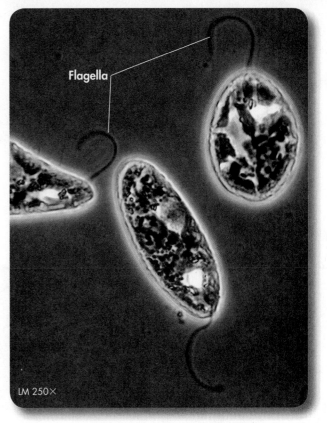

Flagella

LM 250×

▲ Photosynthetic Euglena gracilis is commonly found in lakes and ponds.

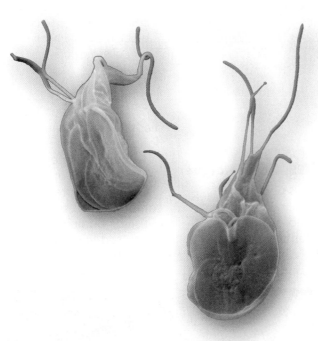

▲ The diplomonad Giardia is a dangerous intestinal parasite that frequently contaminates freshwater streams. Giardia infections are common in wildlife and pet dogs and cats. (SEM 1800×)

DIPLOMONADS

These organisms get their name from the fact that they possess two distinct and different nuclei (from Greek, diplo = double). The double nuclei probably derived from an ancient symbiotic event in which one species was engulfed by another. Cells contain multiple flagella, usually arranged around the body of the cell. Most species of diplomonads are parasitic.

DISCICRISTATES

Discicristates (disk ee KRIS tayts) are named for the disc-shaped cristae present in their mitochondria. Some species are photosynthetic and free-living, such as *Euglena*, while others are dangerous parasites.

▼ The ribbonlike cells of Trypanosoma brucei *cause African sleeping sickness. The parasitic protist is transmitted by tsetse flies to humans, where it infects the blood, lymph, and spinal fluid. Severe nervous system damage and death are the usual result.* (SEM 6700×)

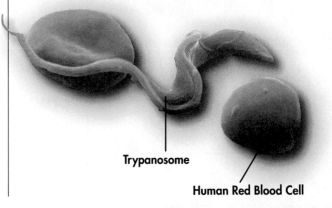

Trypanosome

Human Red Blood Cell

Chromalveolates

SEM 280×

KEY CHARACTERISTICS

Chromalveolates (krohm AL vee uh layts) get their name from alveoli, flattened vesicles that line the cell membrane. The prefix chromo-, meaning "pigment," reflects evidence that members of this clade share a common ancestor that had accessory pigments used in photosynthesis.

GROUPS OF CHROMALVEOLATES

The chromalveolates are one of the largest and most diverse groups of eukaryotes.

PHAEOPHYTES: Brown algae

Phaeophytes (FAY uh fyts) are mostly found in salt water. They are some of the most abundant and visible of the algae. Most species contain fucoxanthin, a greenish-brown pigment from which the group gets its common name. The multicellular brown alga known as giant kelp can grow as large as 60 meters in length.

▼ Brown algae in genus Fucus are commonly found in tidepools and on rocky shorelines of the United States.

LM 200×

▲ This species, in genus Synura, is a colonial alga.

CHRYSOPHYTES: Golden algae

Chrysophytes (KRIS oh fyts) are known for colorful accessory pigments in their chloroplasts. Most are found in fresh water and are photosynthetic.

SEM 1000×

▲ Diatoms often produce intricate shells made from silicon dioxide that persist long after they die.

DIATOMS

Diatoms are mostly found in salt water. When they die, they sink to the ocean floor, and their shells pile up in large deposits. Diatomaceous earth, as these deposits are known, can be used to screen out small particles, and is often used in swimming pool filters.

▲ Water molds growing on a dead goldfish

OOMYCETES: Water molds

These nonphotosynthetic organisms are often confused with fungi. Oomycetes (oh uh MY seed eez) typically produce fuzzy mats of material on dead or decaying animals and plants. Oomycetes are also responsible for a number of serious plant diseases, including potato blight, sudden oak death, and ink disease, which infects the American chestnut tree.

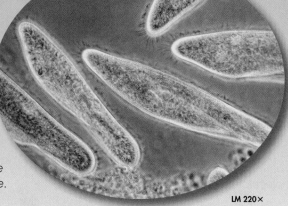

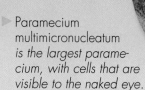

▶ *Paramecium multimicronucleatum is the largest paramecium, with cells that are visible to the naked eye.*

LM 220×

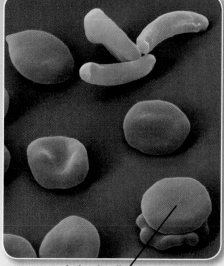

Human Red Blood Cell   SEM 5000×

CILIATES

These common organisms may contain hundreds or even thousands of short cilia extending from the surface of the cell. The cilia propel the ciliate through the water, and may sweep food particles into a gullet. Ciliates are large compared to other protists, with some cells exceeding 1 mm in length.

DINOFLAGELLATES

Dinoflagellates are photosynthetic protists found in both fresh and salt water. Their name comes from their two distinct flagella, usually oriented at right angles to each other. Roughly half of dinoflagellate species are photosynthetic; the other half live as heterotrophs. Many dinoflagellate species are luminescent, and when agitated by sudden movement in the water, give off light.

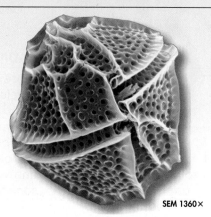

SEM 1360×

▲ *The two flagella of dinoflagellates originate in grooves within thick plates of cellulose that resemble a cross shape, as shown here (genus Protoperidinium).*

▲ *Apicomplexans in genus Plasmodium are mosquito-borne parasites. Shown in green are the remnants of a red blood cell that burst when plasmodia reproduced inside.*

APICOMPLEXANS

The apicomplexans (AYP ih kum plek sunz) are named for a unique organelle near one end of the cell known as the apical complex. This structure contains vesicles with enzymes that allow apicomplexans to enter other cells and take up residence as parasites.

Eco•Alert

Toxic Blooms
Dangerous Dinoflagellates

Great blooms of the dinoflagellates *Gonyaulax* and *Karenia* have occurred in recent years on the East Coast of the United States, although scientists are not sure of the reason. These blooms are known as "red tides." *Gonyaulax* and *Karenia* produce a toxin that can become amplified in the food chain when filter-feeding shellfish such as oysters contentrate it in their tissues. Eating shellfish from water affected by red tide can cause serious illness, paralysis, and even death.

▲ *A red tide containing toxic dinoflagellates*

Cercozoa, Foraminiferans, and Radiolarians

There is no single morphological characteristic that unites this diverse trio, but many have extensions of cytoplasm called pseudopods and many produce protective shells. The grouping together of Cercozoa, Foraminifera, and Radiolaria is based almost entirely on molecular analyses and not on morphology.

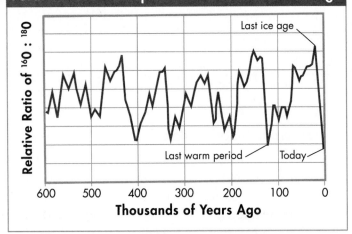

SEM 175×

FORAMINIFERANS

Foraminifera (fawr uh min IF uh ra) produce intricate and beautiful shells that differ from species to species. Slender pseudopods that emerge through tiny holes in the shell enable them to capture food, including bacteria. As many as 4000 species exist.

▼ *Peneroplis pertusus has a spiral-shaped shell.*

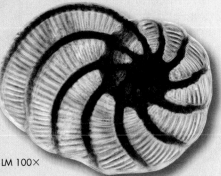

LM 100×

▲ *Radiolarian shells are composed of silica or strontium sulfate.*

RADIOLARIANS

These organisms have an intricate structure in which the nucleus is found in an inner region of the cell known as the endoplasm. The outer portion of the cell, known as the ectoplasm, contains lipid droplets and vacuoles. These organisms sometimes form symbiotic relationships with photosynthetic algae, from which they obtain food.

CERCOZOA

Members of this clade are common in soil, where they feed on bacteria as well as decaying organic matter. Many have flagella, and some produce scales made of silica that protect their surfaces.

▶ A Look Back in Time

Foraminiferan Fossils

Ancient Climates Revealed

Abundant fossils of foraminiferans have been found in sediments dating to the Cambrian period (560 million years ago). For decades, oil companies have taken advantage of these ancient fossils to locate the sediments most likely to contain oil, but now there is another use for them—measuring the sea temperature of ancient Earth. Foraminiferans take dissolved oxygen from seawater to make the calcium carbonate ($CaCO_3$) in their shells, and when they do so, they take up two isotopes of oxygen, ^{16}O and ^{18}O. Because water made from ^{16}O is less dense, more of it evaporates into the atmosphere when the seas are warm—increasing the amount of ^{18}O in

Foraminiferan Isotope Ratios and Climate Change

Graph: Relative Ratio of ^{16}O : ^{18}O (y-axis) versus Thousands of Years Ago (x-axis, from 600 to 0). Labels indicate "Last ice age," "Last warm period," and "Today."

the remaining seawater, and in the fossil shells. The ratio between ^{16}O and ^{18}O in these fossils allows scientists to study the history of seawater temperature, as shown in the graph above.

Rhodophytes

Also known as the red algae, these organisms get their name (from Greek, *rhodo* = red and *phyte* = plant) from reddish accessory pigments called phycobilins (fy koh BIL inz). These highly efficient pigments enable red algae to grow anywhere from the ocean's surface to depths as great as 268 meters. Most species are multicellular. Rhodophytes are the sister group to kingdom Plantae.

▼ Some things that we call seaweeds, such as this rhodophyte, are actually protists. (LM 35×)

Amoebozoa

Members of the Amoebozoa (uh MEE boh zoh ah) are amoebalike organisms that move by means of cytoplasmic streaming, also called amoeboid movement, using pseudopods.

▼ *Slime molds live as single microscopic amoebas in the soil, but aggregate into a colony when conditions are right, forming a multicellular fruiting body. In this image, some of the fruiting bodies have burst, releasing spores.*

Fruiting Body

SEM 85×

▼ *This solitary amoeba, Penardia mutabilis, has very slender pseudopods.*

Pseudopods

LM 300×

Choanozoa

Members of the clade Choanozoa (koh AN uh zoh uh) can be solitary or colonial and are found in aquatic environments around the world. This clade is the sister group to kingdom Animalia.

Choanoflagellates are a major group in the clade Choanozoa. They get their name from a collar of cytoplasm that surrounds their single flagellum (form Greek, *choano* = collar.) Many species trap food within the collar and ingest it.

Fungi

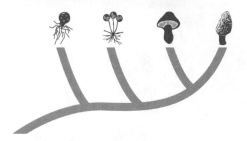

KEY CHARACTERISTICS

Fungi are heterotrophic eukaryotes with cell walls that contain chitin. Fungi were once thought to be plants that had lost their chloroplasts. It is now clear, however, that they are much more closely related to animals than to plants. More than 100,000 species of fungi are known. Distinctions among the phyla are made on the basis of DNA comparisons, cell structure, reproductive structures, and life cycles.

▲ *Stinkhorn fungus (genus* Dictyophora*)*

Organization Some are unicellular yeasts, but most have a multicellular body called a mycelium that consists of one or more slender, branching cells called hyphae.

Feeding and Digestion Obtain food by extracellular digestion and absorption

Reproduction Most have sexual phases to their life cycle and are haploid at most points during the cycle. Most produce tough, asexual spores, which are easily dispersed and able to endure harsh environmental conditions. Asexual reproduction by budding and splitting is also common.

> • **A Closer Look**

Consumers Beware!
Edible and Inedible Mushrooms

Many types of fungi have long been considered delicacies, and several different species of mushrooms are cultivated for food. You may have already tasted sliced mushrooms on pizza, feasted on delicious sautéed portobello mushrooms, or eaten shiitake mushrooms. When properly cooked and prepared, domestic mushrooms are tasty and nutritious.

Wild mushrooms are a different story: Although some are edible, many are poisonous. Because many species of poisonous mushrooms look almost identical to edible mushrooms, you should never pick or eat any mushrooms found in the wild. Instead, mushroom gathering should be left to experts who can positively identify each mushroom they collect. The result of eating a poisonous mushroom can be severe illness, or even death.

▲ *Fly Agaric (*Amanita muscaria*) is poisonous to humans.*

Basidiomycetes

The basidiomycetes, or club fungi, are named for the basidium (buh SID ee um; plural: basidia). The basidium is a reproductive cell that resembles a club.

Life Cycle Basidiomycetes undergo what is probably the most elaborate life cycle of all the fungi, shown below.

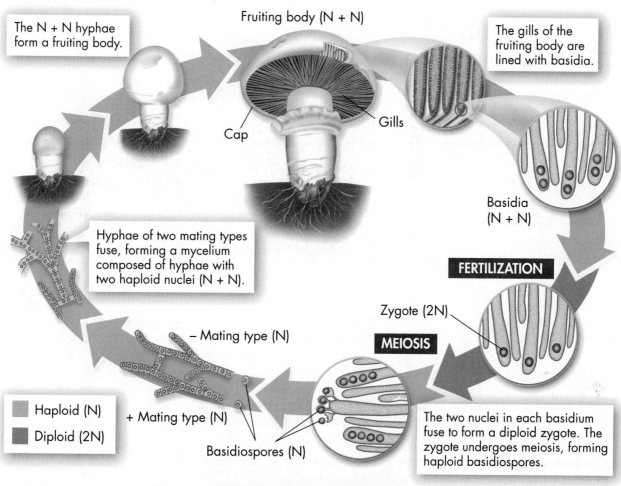

The N + N hyphae form a fruiting body.

Fruiting body (N + N)

The gills of the fruiting body are lined with basidia.

Cap

Gills

Basidia (N + N)

Hyphae of two mating types fuse, forming a mycelium composed of hyphae with two haploid nuclei (N + N).

FERTILIZATION

Zygote (2N)

– Mating type (N)

MEIOSIS

Haploid (N)

Diploid (2N)

+ Mating type (N)

Basidiospores (N)

The two nuclei in each basidium fuse to form a diploid zygote. The zygote undergoes meiosis, forming haploid basidiospores.

Diversity More than 26,000 species of basidiomycetes have been described, roughly a third of all known fungal species. Examples include the stinkhorn and fly agaric mushrooms shown on the previous page, and the shelf fungus and puffball at right.

▶ Shelf fungi (Polypore family) often grow on the sides of dead or dying trees.

▼ A puffball releases its spores.

Ascomycetes

The ascomycetes, or sac fungi, are named for the ascus (AS kus), a saclike reproductive structure that contains spores.

Life Cycle The ascomycete life cycle includes an asexual phase, in which haploid spores are released from structures called conidiophores, and a sexual phase.

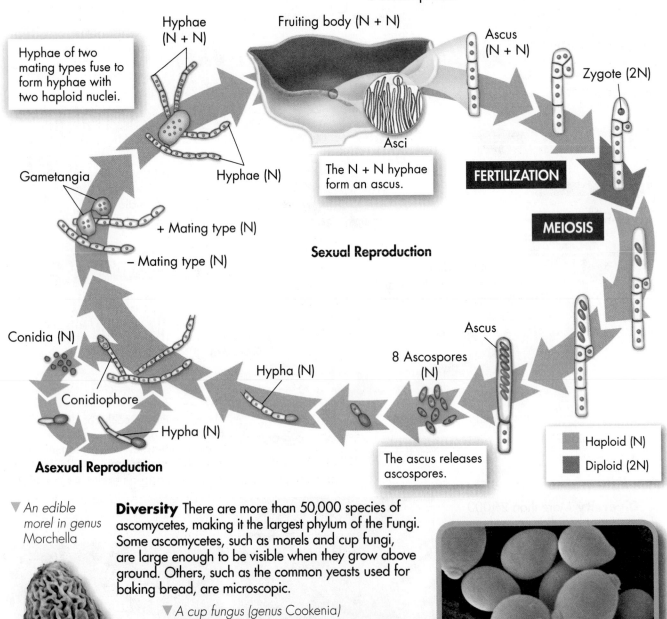

Hyphae (N + N)

Fruiting body (N + N)

Ascus (N + N)

Hyphae of two mating types fuse to form hyphae with two haploid nuclei.

Zygote (2N)

Gametangia

Hyphae (N)

Asci

The N + N hyphae form an ascus.

FERTILIZATION

+ Mating type (N)

− Mating type (N)

Sexual Reproduction

MEIOSIS

Conidia (N)

Ascus

8 Ascospores (N)

Conidiophore

Hypha (N)

Hypha (N)

Hypha (N)

The ascus releases ascospores.

	Haploid (N)
	Diploid (2N)

Asexual Reproduction

▼ An edible morel in genus Morchella

Diversity There are more than 50,000 species of ascomycetes, making it the largest phylum of the Fungi. Some ascomycetes, such as morels and cup fungi, are large enough to be visible when they grow above ground. Others, such as the common yeasts used for baking bread, are microscopic.

▼ A cup fungus (genus Cookenia)

SEM 4900×

▲ Saccharomyces cerevisiae, *the yeast used to raise bread dough, is a unicellular ascomycete that reproduces asexually by budding.*

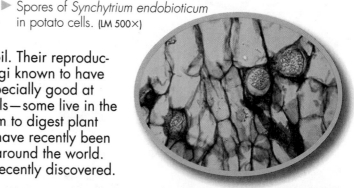

Zygomycetes

The hyphae of zygomycetes generally lack cross walls between cells. Zygomycetes get their name from the sexual phase of their reproductive cycle, which involves a structure called a zygosporangium that forms between the hyphae of two different mating types. One group within the zygomycetes, the Glomales, form symbiotic mycorrhizae (my koh RY zee) with plant roots.

◄ The fruiting body of the common black bread mold, Rhizopus stolonifer (SEM 450×)

◄ This micrograph shows mycorrhizal fungi in symbiosis with soybean roots. The soybean plant provides nutrient sugars to the fungus, while the fungus provides water and essential minerals to the plant. (SEM 200×)

Chytrids

► Spores of *Synchytrium endobioticum* in potato cells. (LM 500×)

Members of this phylum live in water or moist soil. Their reproductive cells have flagella, making them the only fungi known to have a motile stage to their life cycle. Chytrids are especially good at digesting cellulose, the material of plant cell walls—some live in the digestive systems of cows and deer, helping them to digest plant matter. Others are pathogens—certain chytrids have recently been associated with the decline of frog populations around the world. About 1000 species are known, many of them recently discovered.

▲ Lichen-covered oak trees in Shenandoah National Park, Virginia

Eco•Alert

Look to the Lichens

Lichens as Bio-Indicators

Lichens are mutualistic associations between a fungus, usually an ascomycete, and a photosynthetic organism, usually an alga. They are incredibly durable, and have even been reported to survive in the vacuum of space. However, they are also incredibly sensitive indicators of the state of the atmosphere. In particular, when sulfur dioxide is released into the atmosphere, it often reacts with water to form acids (including sulfuric acid) that pollute rainfall. Lichens can be severely damaged by acidic rainfall, although the degree of damage depends on the substrate upon which they grow. Lichens disappear first from the bark of pine and fir trees, which are themselves somewhat acidic. Lichens on elms, which have alkaline bark, are the last to go. By careful monitoring of the health of lichen populations of various trees, scientists can uses these remarkable organisms as low-tech monitors for the health of the environment.

Plants

KEY CHARACTERISTICS

Plants are eukaryotes with cell walls composed of cellulose. Plants carry out photosynthesis using the green pigments chlorophyll a and b, and they store the products of photosynthesis as starch.

▶ *A banana plant in bloom*

▼ *A typical plant life cycle*

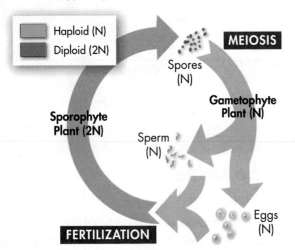

▮ Haploid (N)	
▮ Diploid (2N)	

MEIOSIS

Spores (N)

Gametophyte Plant (N)

Sporophyte Plant (2N)

Sperm (N)

Eggs (N)

FERTILIZATION

• A Closer Look

Prokaryotes Within
The Origins of Chloroplasts

Chloroplasts, which contain their own DNA, are found in all green plants, but where did they come from? In 1905, the Russian botanist Konstantin Mereschkowsky, noticing the similarities between chloroplasts and cyanobacteria, proposed that these organelles originated from a symbiotic relationship formed with the ancestors of today's plants.

This hypothesis still holds up very well today. New DNA studies suggest that all chloroplasts are descended from a single photosynthetic prokaryote, closely related to today's cyanobacteria.

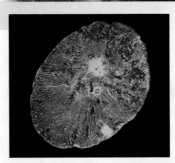

The photosynthetic membranes (shown in green) visible in this thin section of a cyanobacterium resemble the thylakoid membranes of plant cell chloroplasts. (TEM 14,000×)

Green Algae

KEY CHARACTERISTICS

The green algae are plants that do not make embryos. All other plants form embryos as part of their life cycle. The green algae include both unicellular and multicellular species, and they are primarily aquatic.

Organization Single cells, colonies, and a few truly multicellular species

Movement Many swim using whiplike flagella.

Water Transport Water diffuses in from the environment.

Reproduction Asexual and sexual, with gametes and spores; some species show alternation of generations.

GROUPS OF GREEN ALGAE

The three most diverse groups of green algae are profiled below.

▲ Clumps of Spirogyra, a filamentous green alga, are commonly called water silk or mermaid's tresses.

CHLOROPHYTES: Classic green algae

These algae usually live as single cells, like *Chlamydomonas*, or in colonies, like *Volvox*. They are found in both fresh and salt water, and some species are even known to live in arctic snowbanks.

▶ Chlamydomonas *is a unicellular green alga. Each cell has two flagella, which are used in movement.* (SEM 3000×)

ULVOPHYTES: Sea lettuces

The ulvophytes are large organisms composed of hundreds or thousands of cells. Most form large, flattened green sheets and are often simply called seaweed. They show both haploid and diploid phases in their life cycle, but in many species, such as the common sea lettuce, *Ulva*, it is difficult to tell the two phases apart.

▽ Ulva lactuca

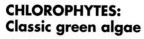
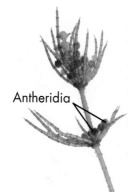

CHAROPHYTES: Stoneworts

Among the green algae, the charophytes (KAHR uh fyts) are the closest relatives of more complicated plants. They are mostly freshwater species. Their branching filaments may be anchored to the substrate by thin rhizoids.

Antheridia

◀ Chara *with antheridia (sperm-producing structures) visible*

Bryophytes

KEY CHARACTERISTICS

Bryophytes (BRY oh fyts), found mostly on land, are multicellular plants that lack true vascular tissue. This lack of vascular tissue limits their height to just a few centimeters and restricts them to moist soils.

Organization Complex and specialized tissues, including protective external layers and rhizoids

Movement Adults stationary; male gametes swim to egg cells using flagella.

Water Transport Diffusion from cell to cell; in some mosses, water flows through specialized tissue.

Reproduction All reproduce sexually with alternation of generations, producing gametes and spores. Most reproduce asexually, too. The gametophyte stage is dominant, with the sporophyte stage dependent on the gametophyte.

▲ *Mosses thrive in shady, damp locations, such as along the banks of this Oregon creek.*

GROUPS OF BRYOPHYTES

Although they are listed together here, the three major groups of bryophytes are now considered to have evolved independently from each other.

MOSSES:
Classic bryophytes

Mosses are found on damp, well-shaded soil, and occasionally along the sides of tree trunks.

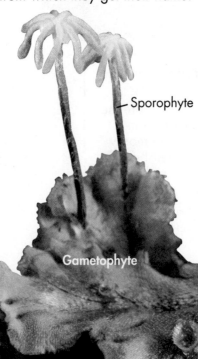

Sporophyte

Mat of gametophytes

LIVERWORTS

Liverworts are flat, almost leaf-like plants that grow on the damp forest floor. Some species are shaped almost like the liver, from which they get their name.

Sporophyte

Gametophyte

HORNWORTS

Hornworts get their name from their sporophytes, tiny green structures resembling horns. Like other bryophytes, hornworts are found mostly in damp, well-shaded areas. Only about 100 species are known.

Sporophytes

Gametophyte

Seedless Vascular Plants

KEY CHARACTERISTICS

This informal grouping lumps together all the plants that have true vascular tissue but lack seeds. Vascular tissue is a key adaptation to life on land. By carrying water and food throughout plant structures, vascular tissue permitted the evolution of roots and tree-size plants, and it allowed plants to spread into dry areas of land.

Organization Complex and specialized tissues, including true roots, stems, and leaves

Movement Adults stationary; male gametes swim to egg cells using flagella.

Water Transport Through vascular tissue

Reproduction Alternation of generations, producing spores, eggs, and swimming sperm; the sporophyte stage is dominant, but the sporophyte is not dependent on the gametophyte as it is in bryophytes.

GROUPS OF SEEDLESS VASCULAR PLANTS

Besides the flowering plants, these organisms make up the most diverse collection of land plants, with more than 10,000 known species.

FERNS

Ferns are common and abundant. Because they need standing water to reproduce, ferns are generally found in areas that are damp at least part of the year. The sporophyte phase of the life cycle is dominant. Spores are produced in prominent clusters known as sori (SOH ry) on the undersides of leaves.

▼ Polypodium vulgare

Sori

CLUB MOSSES

Not really mosses, these vascular plants are also called lycopods (LY koh pahdz). These plants were especially abundant during the Carboniferous Period 360 to 290 million years ago, when they grew as large as trees. Today, their remains make up a large part of coal deposits mined for fuel.

▼ The small club moss known as Lycopodium can be found growing on the forest floor throughout the temperate regions of North America. They look like tiny pine trees at first glance, but they are, in fact, small, seedless plants.

HORSETAILS

Only a single living genus of horsetails is known, *Equisetum* (ek wi SEET um). These plants were thought to resemble horses' tails; their name is derived from this perception. Today, only 25 species are known, confined to wet areas of soil. But horsetails were once much more diverse, larger in size, and abundant. Abrasive silica, found in many horsetails, was used in colonial times as a scouring powder to help clean pots and pans.

▼ Equisetum

Gymnosperms

KEY CHARACTERISTICS

Gymnosperms are seed-bearing vascular plants whose seeds are exposed to the environment, rather than being enclosed in a fruit. The seeds are usually located on the scales of cones.

Organization True roots, stems, and leaves

Movement Adults stationary; within pollen grains, male gametophytes drift in air or are carried by animals to female structures, where they release sperm that move to eggs.

Water Transport Through vascular tissue

Reproduction Sexual; alternation of generations; the sporophyte stage is dominant. Female gametophytes live within the parent sporophyte. Pollen grains carry sperm to eggs, so open water is not needed for fertilization.

▶ *Some bristlecone pines are thousands of years old, like this one growing in Nevada.*

Rising From the Ashes
Fire's Role in Seed Germination

We generally think of forest fires as being natural disasters, and that's typically true. Some gymnosperm species, however, are so well adapted to the arid conditions of the American West that they actually depend upon such fires to spread their seeds.

The best-known example is the Jack Pine, *Pinus banksiana*. Its seed cones are thick and heat resistant. When engulfed in a fire, its seeds escape damage. The fire's high heat helps to open the outer coat of the cone, enabling the seeds to pop out afterward. As a result, Jack Pines are among the very first plants to repopulate a forest that has been damaged by fire.

▲ *The high heat of a forest fire opens the cones of the Jack Pines, releasing their seeds. The inset shows a Jack Pine seedling growing in the charred remains of the fire.*

GROUPS OF GYMNOSPERMS

There are four groups of gymnosperms, representing about 800 species in total.

CONIFERS

Conifers are by far the most diverse group of living gymnosperms, represented by nearly 700 species worldwide. They include the common pine, spruce, fir, and redwood trees that make up a large share of the forests in the temperate regions of the world. Conifers have enormous economic importance. Their wood is used for residential building, to manufacture paper, and as a source of heat. Compounds from their resins are used for a variety of industrial purposes.

▲ *Most conifers retain their leaves year-round.*

CYCADS

Cycads (SY kads) are beautiful palmlike plants that have large cones. Cycads first appeared in the fossil record during the Triassic Period, 225 million years ago. Huge forests of cycads thrived when dinosaurs roamed Earth. Today, only nine genera of cycads exist. Cycads can be found growing naturally in tropical and subtropical places such as Mexico, the West Indies, Florida, and parts of Asia, Africa, and Australia.

▶ *A Sago Palm, Cycas revoluta*

▲ *Ginkgoes are often planted in urban settings, where their toughness and resistance to air pollution make them popular shade trees.*

GINKGOES

Ginkgoes (GING kohs) were common when dinosaurs were alive, but today the group contains only one species, *Ginkgo biloba*. The living *Ginkgo* species looks similar to its fossil ancestors—in fact, *G. biloba* may be one of the oldest seed plant species alive today.

GNETOPHYTES

About 70 present-day species of gnetophytes (NET oh fyts) are known, placed in just three genera. The reproductive scales of these plants are clustered in cones.

▶ *Welwitschia mirabilis, an inhabitant of the Namibian desert in southwestern Africa, is one of the most remarkable gnetophytes. Its huge leathery leaves grow continuously and spread across the ground.*

Cones

Angiosperms

KEY CHARACTERISTICS

Angiosperms are plants that bear seeds in a closed ovary. The ovary is part of a reproductive organ known as a flower. Seeds are formed in a double fertilization event, which forms a diploid embryo and a triploid endosperm tissue. As seeds mature, ovaries develop into fruits that help to disperse the seeds.

Organization True roots, stems, and leaves

Movement Adults stationary; within pollen grains, male gametophytes drift in air or are carried by animals to female structures, where they release sperm that move to eggs.

Water Transport Through vascular tissue

Reproduction Sexual, with alternation of generations; also asexual. The sporophyte stage is dominant. Female gametophytes live within the parent sporophyte. Pollen carries sperm to eggs, so open water is not needed for fertilization.

▶ *A Southern Long-Nosed Bat pollinates the Saguaro Cactus,* Carnegia gigantea, *while collecting nectar from its blossoms.*

▸A Closer Look ▸

Whatever Happened to Monocots and Dicots?

Traditionally, flowering plants have been divided into just two groups, monocots and dicots, based on the number of seed leaves in their embryos. Today, however, molecular studies have shown that the dicots aren't really one group. Some of the most primitive flowering plants (like *Amborella*) are dicots, and so are some of the most advanced flowering plants, while the monocots fall right in between. So, while monocots are indeed a single group, the term *dicots* is now just an informal, though still useful, grouping.

Amborella   Water lilies   Monocots   Magnoliids   Eudicots

Ancestral Angiosperm

GROUPS OF ANGIOSPERMS

The great majority of plant species—over 260,000—are angiosperms.

▲ *Water lilies are aquatic plants that produce flowers and leaves, which float on the surface of the water.*

NYMPHAEACEAE: Water lilies

About 50 species of water lilies are known, and they are of special interest to plant taxonomists. Their DNA and flower structure suggest that they are, along with *Amborella*, one of the earliest groups to have split off from the main line of flowering plant evolution. Examples of water lilies are found throughout the world.

MAGNOLIIDS:
Magnolia trees and others

The most famous genus of these plants is *Magnolia*, which includes nearly 200 species. Laurels and tulip poplars are also magnoliids (mag NOH lee ids). Because of their flower structure, magnoliids were once thought to be nearly as primitive as water lilies. Genetic studies now suggest that they split off from the rest of the angiosperm line after monocots and, therefore, do not represent the earliest flowering plants.

▼ *The Tulip Poplar is a long, straight tree often used as wood for telephone poles. Its flowers are greenish and shaped like tulips.*

AMBORELLA

Amborella does not represent a group of plants but instead just a single species found only on the island of New Caledonia in the South Pacific Ocean. DNA studies show that *Amborella* is equally separated from all other flowering plants living today, suggesting that it is descended from plants that split off from the main line of flowering plant evolution as long ago as 100 million years.

▲ *The flowers of Amborella trichopoda are simpler than those of most other plants, and the species has a number of features that place it at the very base of flowering plant evolution.*

▶ *Magnolia trees produce conspicuous flowers, which contain multiple stamens and multiple pistils.*

GROUPS OF ANGIOSPERMS CONTINUED...

MONOCOTS

The monocots include an estimated 65,000 species, roughly 20 percent of all flowering plants. They get their name from the single seed leaf found in monocot embryos, and they include some of the plants that are most important to human cultures. Monocots grown as crops account for a majority of the food produced by agriculture. These crops include wheat, rice, barley, corn, and sugar cane. Common grasses are monocots, as are onions, bananas, orchids, coconut palms, tulips, and irises.

Aerial roots

▲ Many orchid species are grown by enthusiasts for their rare beauty. Notice the aerial roots on this specimen, which grows as an epiphyte in its natural environment.

▲ Onions are just one of many examples of monocot crop species.

▲ This African hillside is dotted with clumps of Wild Pampas Grass.

◄ This sugar cane in Vietnam has been bundled for sale.

Eco•Alert

Coevolution: Losing the Pollinators

The successes of flowering plants are clearly due to coevolution with their insect pollinators. Common honey bees are among the most important of these, gathering nectar from the flowers of hundreds of plant species and spreading pollen from plant to plant as they go.

Unfortunately, beekeepers around the world, including the United States, are facing a serious crisis. "Colony collapse disorder," as beekeepers describe it, causes bees to fly away from the hive and either never return, or return only to weaken and die. The disease threatens to affect scores of important crops, which depend upon bees to produce fruit and seeds. Suspicion has centered on a fungus or a virus that might spread from colony to colony, but at this point there is no definitive cause or cure.

EUDICOTS: "TRUE DICOTS"

Eudicots (YOO dy kahts) account for about 75 percent of all angiosperm species. The name means "true dicots," and these plants are the ones usually given as examples of dicot stem, leaf, and flower structure. Eudicots have distinctive pollen grains with three grooves on their surfaces, and DNA studies strongly support their classification in a single group. They include a number of important subgroups, five of which are described here.

Ranunculales

The ranunculales subgroup (ruh NUNH kyu lay les) includes, and is named after, buttercups (genus *Ranunculus*). Also included in this subgroup are a number of well-known flowers such as columbines, poppies, barberries, and moonseed.

▶ Rocky Mountain Columbine

▲ Clusterhead Pinks

Caryophyllales

Cacti are probably the most well-known plants in the caryophyllales subgroup (KAR ee oh fy lay les). Pinks and carnations, spinach, rhubarb, and insect-eating plants, such as sundews and pitcher plants, are also members.

Saxifragales

Plants in the saxifragales (SAK suh frij ay les) subgroup include peonies, witch hazel, gooseberries, and coral bells.

Rosids

The rosids include, as you might expect, the roses. However, this subgroup also includes many popular fruits, such as oranges, raspberries, strawberries, and apples. Some of the best-known trees, including poplars, willows, and maples, are also members.

▲ Orange

◀ Peony

Asterids

The nearly 80,000 asterid species include sunflowers, azaleas, snapdragons, blueberries, tomatoes, and potatoes.

▼ The flower heads in a field of sunflowers all track the sun as it moves across the sky; thus, they all face the same direction.

Animals

Snow Leopard

KEY CHARACTERISTICS
Animals are multicellular, heterotrophic, eukaryotic organisms whose cells lack cell walls.

• A Closer Look

A Common Ancestor

Recent molecular studies and cladistic analyses recognize the clade Choanozoa to be the true sister group to all Metazoa—multicellular animals. Choanozoa is one group of organisms formerly called "protists" and is named for choanoflagellates (art and photo right), single-celled, colonial organisms that look like certain cells of sponges and flatworms. Current thinking suggests that the choanoflagellates alive today are the best living examples of what the last common ancestor of metazoans looked like.

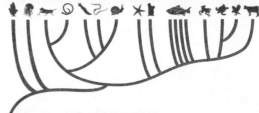

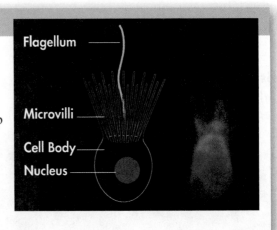

Flagellum

Microvilli

Cell Body

Nucleus

Porifera (Sponges)

KEY CHARACTERISTICS

Sponges are the simplest animals. They are classified as animals because they are multicellular, heterotrophic, lack cell walls, and have some specialized cells. They are aquatic, lack true tissues and organs, and have internal skeletons of spongin and/or spicules of calcium carbonate or silica. Sponges have no body symmetry.

Feeding and Digestion Filter feeders; intracellular digestion.

Circulation Via flow of water through body

Respiration Oxygen diffuses from water into cells as water flows through body.

Excretion Wastes diffuse from cells into water as water flows through body.

Response No nervous system; little capacity to respond to environmental changes.

Movement Juveniles drift or swim freely; adults are stationary.

Reproduction Most—sexual with internal fertilization; water flowing out of sponge disperses sperm, which fertilizes eggs inside sponge(s); may reproduce asexually by budding or producing gemmules.

GROUPS OF SPONGES

There are more than 5000 species of sponges; most are marine. Three major groups are described below.

DEMOSPONGIAE: Typical sponges

More than 90 percent of all living sponge species are in this group, including the few freshwater species. They have skeletons made of spongin, a flexible protein. Some species have silica spicules. Examples: Yellow Sponge, bath sponges, Carnivorous Mediterranean Sponge, tube sponges

HEXACTINELLIDA: Glass sponges

Glass sponges live in the deep ocean and are especially abundant in the Antarctic. They are called "glass" sponges because their skeletons are made of glasslike silica spicules. Examples: Venus's Flower Basket, Cloud Sponge

◄ Glass Sponge

CALCAREA: Calcareous sponges

Calcareous sponges live in shallow, tropical marine waters and are the only sponges with calcium carbonate spicules. Example: *Clathrina*

▼ **Orange Elephant Ear Sponge**

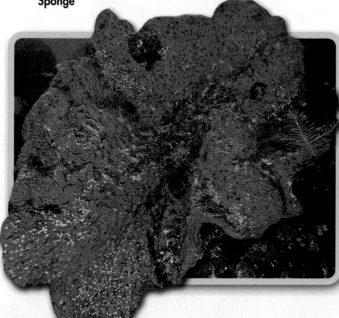

Yellow Tubular Sponge ▶

Cnidarians

▲ Sea Nettle

KEY CHARACTERISTICS

Cnidarians are aquatic, mostly carnivorous, and the simplest animals to have specialized tissues (outer skin and lining of the gastrovascular cavity) and body symmetry (radial). Their tentacles have stinging cells called nematocysts used in feeding.

Feeding and Digestion Predatory, stinging prey with nematocysts; digestion begins extracellularly in gastrovascular cavity and is completed intracellulary; indigestible materials leave body through single opening; many, especially reef-building corals, also depend on symbiotic algae, or zooxanthellae.

Circulation No internal transport system; nutrients typically diffuse through body.

Respiration Diffusion through body walls

Excretion Cellular wastes diffuse through body walls.

Response Some specialized sensory cells: nerve cells in nerve net, statocysts that help determine up and down, eyespots (ocelli) made of light-detecting cells

Movement Polyps stationary, medusas free-swimming; some, such as sea anemones, can burrow and creep very slowly; others move using muscles that work with a hydrostatic skeleton and water in gastrovascular cavity; medusas such as jellyfish move by jet propulsion generated by muscle contractions.

Reproduction Most—alternate between sexual (most species by external fertilization) and asexual (polyps produce new polyps or medusae by budding)

Eco•Alert

Coral Symbionts

The color of this star coral is caused by zooxanthellae algae living within it.

Reef-building coral animals depend on symbiotic algae called zooxanthellae for certain vital nutritional needs. In many places, reef-building corals live close to the upper end of their temperature tolerance zone. If water temperatures rise too high, the coral-zooxanthellae symbiosis breaks down, and corals turn white in what is called "coral bleaching." If corals don't recover their algae soon, they weaken and die. This is one reason why coral reefs are in grave danger from global warming.

GROUPS OF CNIDARIANS
There are more than 9000 species of cnidarians.

HYDROZOA: Hydras and their relatives

Hydras and their relatives spend most of their time as polyps and are either colonial or solitary. They reproduce asexually (by budding), sexually, or they alternate between sexual and asexual reproduction. Examples: hydra, Portuguese Man-of-War

A Portuguese Man-of-War is actually a colony of polyps.

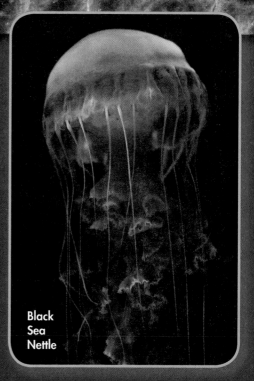

Black Sea Nettle

ANTHOZOA: Corals and sea anemones

Corals and sea anemones are colonial or solitary polyps with no medusa stage. The central body is surrounded by tentacles. They reproduce sexually or asexually. Examples: reef corals, sea anemones, sea pens, sea fans

Sea Anemone

SCYPHOZOA: Jellyfishes

Jellyfishes spend most of their time as medusas; some species bypass the polyp stage. They reproduce sexually and sometimes asexually by budding. Examples: Lion's Mane Jellyfish, Moon Jelly, Sea wasp

Jellyfishes such as this sea nettle are beautiful to us but deadly to their prey. The stinging cells on their tentacles can kill prey instantly and can ruin a human swimmer's day at the beach!

Arthropods

KEY CHARACTERISTICS

Arthropods are the most diverse of all multicellular organisms. They have segmented bodies and jointed appendages. They are supported by tough exoskeletons made of chitin, which they periodically shed as they grow. Arthropods are coelomate protostomes with bilateral symmetry.

Eco•Alert

Beetle Damage

You probably know that some insects can seriously damage crop plants. But insects affect plants in natural habitats, too. One example is the mountain pine beetle, which is dramatically extending its range. Global warming appears to be enabling the beetle to survive farther north, and at higher altitudes, than it used to. The new beetle infestation is causing extensive damage to northern and high-altitude forests in North America. The death of millions of acres of trees has resulted in the release of large amounts of carbon dioxide, a greenhouse gas, into the atmosphere. You can see the sort of damage the beetles cause in the photo at right.

▲ *Mountain pine beetle damage to pine trees in White River National Forest, Colorado*

Feeding and Digestion Extremely diverse: herbivores, carnivores, detritivores, parasites, bloodsuckers, scavengers, filter feeders; digestive system with two openings; many feeding specializations in different groups

Circulation Open circulatory system with heart and arteries

Respiration Terrestrial—tracheal tubes or book lungs; aquatic—gills or book gills (horseshoe crabs)

Excretion Terrestrial—Malpighian tubules; aquatic—diffusion into water

Response Well-developed nervous system with brain; sophisticated sense organs

Movement Muscles attached internally to jointed exoskeletons

Reproduction Usually sexual, although some species may reproduce asexually under certain circumstances; many undergo metamorphosis during development

Most animals, including this land crab, are arthropods.

GROUPS OF ARTHROPODS

Phylum Arthropoda contains more known species than any other phylum. Scientists have identified more than 1,000,000 arthropod species, and some scientists expect there are millions yet to be identified. Arthropods are classified based on the number and structure of body segments and appendages.

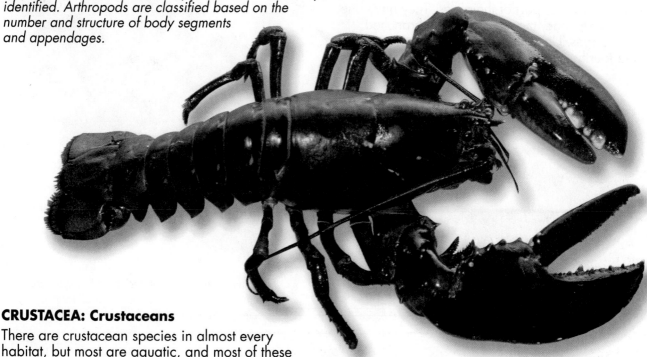

▲ Lobster

CRUSTACEA: Crustaceans

There are crustacean species in almost every habitat, but most are aquatic, and most of these are marine. They have two or three body sections, two pairs of antennae, and chewing mouthparts called mandibles. Many have a carapace, or "shell," that covers part or all of the body. Examples: crabs, lobsters, crayfish, pill bugs, water fleas, barnacles

CHELICERATA: Chelicerates

▲ Red Velvet Mite

Living chelicerates include horseshoe crabs and arachnids. (Their extinct relatives include trilobites and giant "sea-scorpions.") Most living chelicerates are terrestrial. The body is composed of two parts—the cephalothorax and abdomen. The first pair of appendages are specialized feeding structures called chelicerae. Chelicerates have no antennae.

Horseshoe crabs are actually more closely related to spiders than to crabs!

Merostomata: Horseshoe crabs

The class Merostomata once included many species, but only four species of horseshoe crab survive today. All are marine. They have five pairs of walking legs and a long, spinelike tail.

Arachnida: Arachnids

The vast majority of arachnids are terrestrial. They have four pairs of walking legs and no tail. Examples: spiders, ticks, mites, scorpions, daddy longlegs

▲ Mexican Beauty Tarantula

Animals

UNIRAMIA: Uniramians

Most uniramians are terrestrial, although some are aquatic for all or part of their lives. They have one pair of antennae, mandibles, and unbranched appendages. Uniramians include at least three fourths of all known animal species!

Uniramians include centipedes, millipedes, and insects—more than three fourths of all known animal species, including this Elephant Hawk Moth.

Insecta: Insects

There are more than 1,000,000 insect species in more than 25 orders. An insect body is divided into three parts—head, thorax, and abdomen. Insects have three pairs of legs and usually one or two pairs of wings attached to the thorax. Some insects undergo complete metamorphosis. Examples: termites, ants, beetles, dragonflies, flies, moths, grasshoppers

The Death's-Head Hawk Moth is named for the skull-like shape on the adult's head (above). Like many insects, this moth undergoes complete metamorphosis, during which the larva (below), or caterpillar, turns into a pupa, and, eventually, an adult.

Praying Mantis

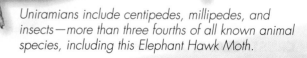

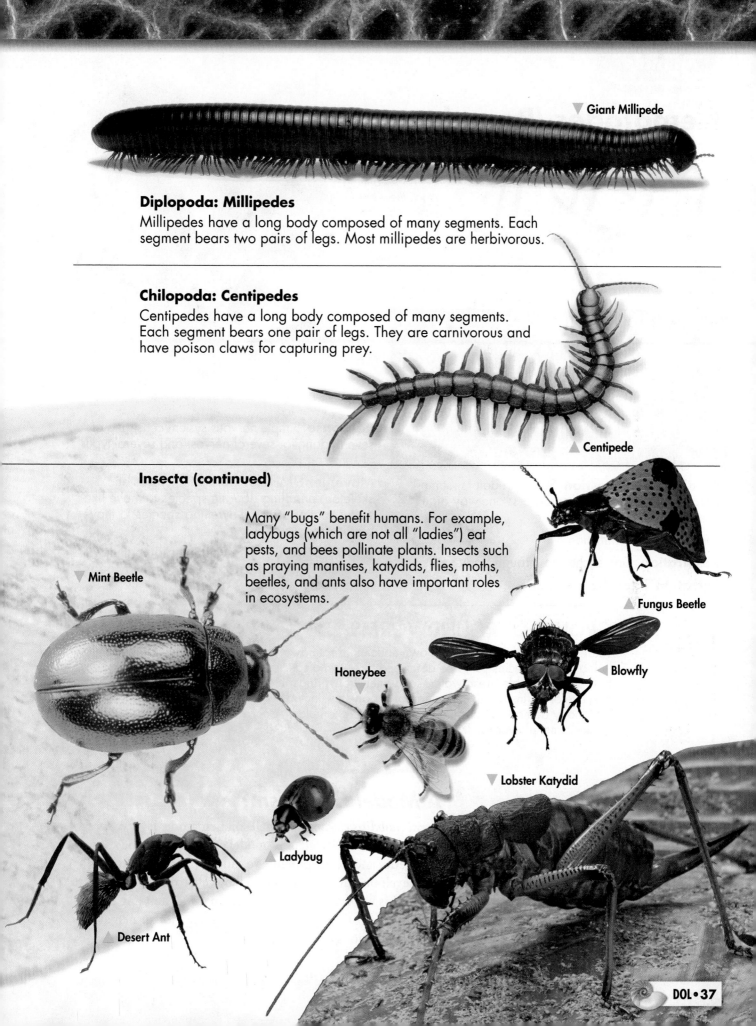

Giant Millipede

Diplopoda: Millipedes

Millipedes have a long body composed of many segments. Each segment bears two pairs of legs. Most millipedes are herbivorous.

Chilopoda: Centipedes

Centipedes have a long body composed of many segments. Each segment bears one pair of legs. They are carnivorous and have poison claws for capturing prey.

Centipede

Insecta (continued)

Many "bugs" benefit humans. For example, ladybugs (which are not all "ladies") eat pests, and bees pollinate plants. Insects such as praying mantises, katydids, flies, moths, beetles, and ants also have important roles in ecosystems.

Fungus Beetle

Mint Beetle

Blowfly

Honeybee

Lobster Katydid

Ladybug

Desert Ant

Nematodes (Roundworms)

"Hooks" in the mouth of a hookworm attach the worms to their hosts so that they can drink the host's blood or ingest their digested foods.

▲ **Foleyella**
(SEM 130×)

KEY CHARACTERISTICS

Nematodes, or roundworms, are unsegmented worms with a tough outer cuticle, which they shed as they grow. This "molting" is one reason that nematodes are now considered more closely related to arthropods than to other wormlike animals. Nematodes are the simplest animals to have a "one-way" digestive system through which food passes from mouth to anus. They are protostomes and have a pseudocoelom.

Feeding and Digestion Some predators, some parasites, and some decomposers; one-way digestive tract with mouth and anus

Circulation By diffusion

Respiration Gas exchange through body walls

Excretion Through body walls

Response Simple nervous system consisting of several ganglia, several nerves, and several types of sense organs

Movement Muscles work with hydrostatic skeleton, enabling aquatic species to move like water snakes and soil-dwelling species to move by thrashing around.

Reproduction Sexual with internal fertilization; separate sexes; parasitic species may lay eggs in several hosts or host organs.

GROUPS OF ROUNDWORMS

There are more than 15,000 known species of roundworms, and there may be half a million species yet to be described. Free-living species live in almost every habitat imaginable: fresh water, salt water, hot springs, ice, soil. Parasitic species live on or inside a wide range of organisms, including insects, humans, and many domesticated animals and plants. Examples: *Ascaris lumbricoides,* hookworms, pinworms, *Trichinella, C. elegans*

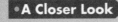
• **A Closer Look** ▶

A Model Organism?

Caenorhabditis elegans is a small soil nematode. Fifty years ago, this species was selected as a "model organism" for the study of genetics and development. We can now chart the growth and development of *C. elegans,* cell by cell, from fertilization to adult. This information is invaluable in understanding the development in other species—including many other nematodes that cause serious disease.

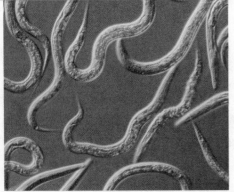

◀ *C. elegans* (LM 64×)

Platyhelminthes (Flatworms)

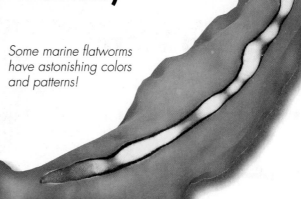

Some marine flatworms have astonishing colors and patterns!

▲ Blue Pseudoceros Flatworm

KEY CHARACTERISTICS

Flatworms are soft worms with tissues and internal organ systems. They are the simplest animals to have three embryonic germ layers, bilateral symmetry, and cephalization. They are acoelomates.

Feeding and Digestion Free-living—predators or scavengers that suck food in through a pharynx and digest it in a system that has one opening. Parasitic—feed on blood, tissue fluids, or cell pieces of the host, using simpler digestive systems than free-living species have. Tapeworms, which absorb nutrients from food that the host has already digested, have no digestive system.

Circulation By diffusion

Respiration Gas exchange by diffusion

Excretion Some—flame cells remove excess water and may remove metabolic wastes such as ammonia and urea. Many flame cells are connected to tubules that release substances through pores in the skin.

Response Free-living—several ganglia connected by nerve cords that run through the body, along with eye-spots and other specialized sensory cells; parasitic—simpler nervous system than free-living forms have

Movement Free-living—using cilia and muscle cells.

Reproduction Free-living—most are hermaphrodites that reproduce sexually with internal fertilization; parasitic—commonly reproduce asexually by fission but also often reproduce sexually

GROUPS OF FLATWORMS

Flatworms are an amazingly diverse group of worms that include more than 20,000 species. They have historically been placed into three classes, but these taxa now appear not to be true clades, and will probably change.

TREMATODA: Flukes

Most flukes are parasites that infect internal organs of their hosts, but some infect external parts such as skin or gills. The life cycle typically involves more than one host or organ. Examples: *Schistosoma*, liver fluke

TURBELLARIA: Turbellarians

Turbellarians are free-living aquatic and terrestrial predators and scavengers. Many are colorful marine species. Examples: planarians, polyclad flatworm

CESTODA: Tapeworms

Tapeworms are very long intestinal parasites that lack a digestive system and absorb nutrients directly through their body walls. The tapeworm body is composed of many repeated sections (proglottids) that contain both male and female reproductive organs.

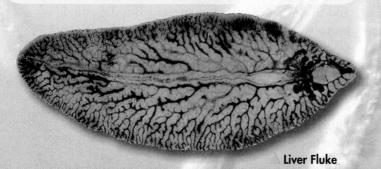

Liver Fluke

Annelids (Segmented Worms)

KEY CHARACTERISTICS

Annelids are coelomate protostome worms whose bodies are composed of segments separated by internal partitions. The annelid digestive system has two openings.

Peacock worms, whose feather-shaped gills look somewhat like peacock feathers, are marine annelids, or polychaetes.

Feeding and Digestion Filter feeders, carnivores, or parasites; many obtain food using a muscular pharynx, often equipped with "teeth"; widely varied digestive systems—some, such as earthworms, have complex digestive tracts.

Circulation Closed circulatory system with dorsal and ventral blood vessels; dorsal vessel pumps blood like a heart.

Respiration Aquatic—gills; terrestrial—skin

Excretion Digestive waste exits through anus; nitrogenous wastes eliminated by nephridia

Response Nervous system includes a rudimentary brain and several nerve cords; sense organs best-developed in free-living saltwater species

Movement Hydrostatic skeleton based on sealed body segments surrounded by longitudinal and circular muscles; many annelids have appendages that enable movement.

Reproduction Most—sexual, some through external fertilization with separate sexes, but others are simultaneous hermaphrodites that exchange sperm; most have a trochophore larval stage

•Did You Know?

Not-So-Modern Medicine

You may have heard that medieval healers used leeches to remove "excess" blood from patients and to clean wounds after surgery. But did you know that leeches—or at least compounds from leech saliva—have a place in modern medicine? Leech saliva contains the protein hirudin, which prevents blood from clotting. Some surgeons use leeches to relieve pressure caused by blood that pools in tissues after plastic surgery. Hirudin is also used to prevent unwanted blood clots.

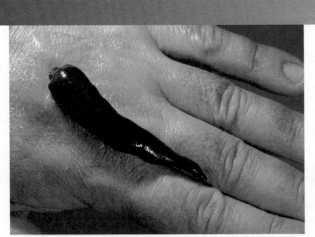

▲ *Leech* (Hirudo medicinalis) *drawing blood from a hand*

▼ Feather-Duster Worms

◀ Giant Earthworm

GROUPS OF ANNELIDS
There are more than 15,000 species of annelids.

HIRUDINEA: Leeches

Most leeches live in fresh water. They lack appendages. Leeches may be carnivores or blood-sucking external parasites. Example: medicinal leech (*Hirudo medicinalis*)

POLYCHAETA: Polychaetes

Polychaetes live in salt water; many move with paddle-like appendages called parapodia tipped with bristle-like setae. Examples: sandworms, blood-worms, fanworms, feather-duster worms

The white, bristle-like structures on the sides of this bearded fireworm are setae.

OLIGOCHAETA: Oligochaetes

Oligochaetes live in soil or fresh water. They lack appendages. Some use setae for movement but have fewer than polychaetes.
Examples: *Tubifex*, earthworms

Mollusks

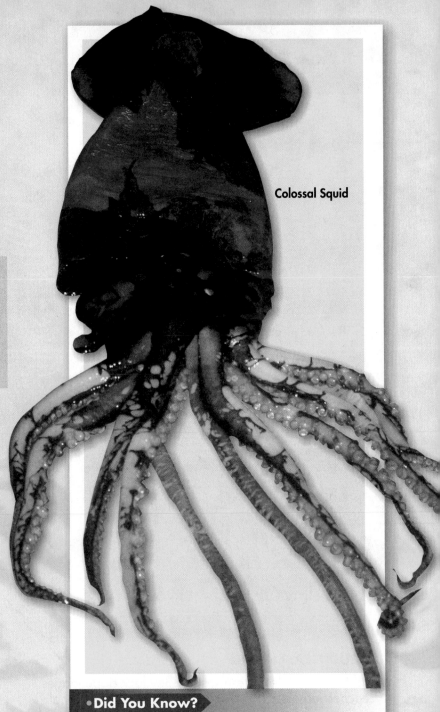

Colossal Squid

KEY CHARACTERISTICS

Mollusks have soft bodies that typically include a muscular foot. Body forms vary greatly. Many mollusks possess a hard shell secreted by the mantle, but in some, the only hard structure is internal. Mollusks are coelomate protostomes with bilateral symmetry.

Feeding and Digestion Digestive system with two openings; diverse feeding styles—mollusks can be herbivores, carnivores, filter feeders, detritivores, or parasites

Circulation Snails and clams—open circulatory system; octopi and squid—closed circulatory system

Respiration Aquatic mollusks—gills inside the mantle cavity; land mollusks—a saclike mantle cavity whose large, moist surface area is lined with blood vessels.

Excretion Body cells release ammonia into the blood, which nephridia remove and release outside the body.

Response Complexity of nervous system varies greatly; extremely simple in clams, but complex in some octopi.

Movement Varies greatly, by group. Some never move as adults, while others are very fast swimmers.

Reproduction Sexual; many aquatic species have free-swimming trochophore larval stage.

•Did You Know?

The Colossal Squid

The Colossal Squid, the largest of all mollusks, has the largest eyes of any known animal. One 8-meter-long, 450-kilogram specimen of the species *Mesonychoteuthis hamiltoni* had eyes 28 centimeters across—larger than most dinner plates! The lens of this huge eye was the size of an orange.

GROUPS OF MOLLUSKS

Mollusks are traditionally divided into several classes based on characteristics of the foot and the shell; specialists estimate that there are somewhere between 50,000 and 200,000 species of mollusks alive today.

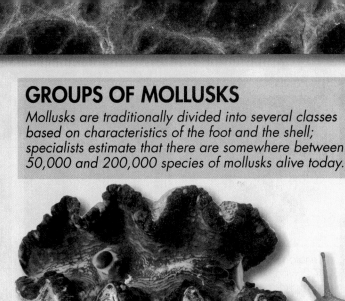

▲ Giant Clam

Garden Snail ▲

▲ Chambered Nautilus

BIVALVIA: Bivalves

Bivalves are aquatic. They have a two-part hinged shell and a wedge-shaped foot. They are mostly stationary as adults. Some burrow in mud or sand; others attach to rocks. Most are filter feeders that use gill siphons to take in water that carries food. Clams have open circulatory systems. Bivalves have the simplest nervous systems among mollusks. Examples: clams, oysters, scallops, mussels

GASTROPODA: Gastropods

There are both terrestrial and aquatic gastropods. Most have a single spiral, chambered shell. Gastropods use a broad, muscular foot to move and have a distinct head region. Snails and slugs feed with a structure called a radula that usually works like sandpaper. Some species are predators whose harpoon-shaped radula carries deadly venom. They have open circulatory systems. Many gastropod species are cross-fertilizing hermaphrodites. Examples: snails, slugs, nudibranchs, sea hares

CEPHALOPODA: Cephalopods

Cephalopods live in salt water. The cephalopod has a highly developed brain and sense organs. The head is attached to a single foot, which is divided into tentacles. They have closed circulatory systems. Octopi use beaklike jaws for feeding; a few are venomous. Cephalopods have the most complex nervous systems among mollusks; octopi have complex behavior and have shown the ability to learn in laboratory settings. Examples: octopi, squids, nautilus, cuttlefish

Nudibranchs, such as this Hypseiodoris species, are marine gastropods without shells. They breathe through gills (the orange structures) on their backs.

Echinoderms

KEY CHARACTERISTICS

Echinoderms are marine animals that have spiny skin surrounding an endoskeleton. Their unique water vascular system includes tube feet with suction-cuplike ends used in moving and feeding. The water vascular system also plays a role in respiration, circulation, and excretion. Echinoderms are coelomate deuterostomes. Adults exhibit 5-part radial symmetry.

Feeding and Digestion Method varies by group—echinoderms can be filter feeders, detritivores, herbivores, or carnivores.

Circulation Via fluid in the coelom, a rudimentary system of vessels, and the water vascular system

Respiration Gas exchange is carried out by surfaces of tube feet, and, in many species, by skin gills.

Crinoid fossil, about 400 million years old

Living modern crinoid (feather star)

• A Look Back in Time

Crinoids Then and Now

Echinoderms have a long fossil record that dates all the way back to the Cambrian Period. Although these animals have been evolving for millions of years, some fossil crinoids look a great deal like living crinoids.

Excretion Digestive wastes released through anus; nitrogenous cellular wastes excreted as ammonia through tube feet and skin gills.

Response Minimal nervous system; nerve ring is connected to body sections by radial nerves; most have scattered sensory cells that detect light, gravity, and chemicals secreted by prey.

Movement In most, tube feet work with endoskeleton to enable locomotion.

Reproduction Sexual, with external fertilization; larvae have bilateral symmetry, unlike adults.

You can't miss the 5-part radial symmetry of this red mesh sea star moving across a coral reef.

GROUPS OF ECHINODERMS

There are more than 7000 species of echinoderms.

◀ Sea star

CRINOIDEA: Crinoids

Crinoids are filter feeders; some use tube feet along feathery arms to capture plankton. The mouth and anus are on the upper surface of the body disk. Some are stationary as adults while others can "walk" using short "arms" on the lower body surface. Examples: sea lily, feather star

▶ Feeding crinoid

ASTEROIDEA: Sea stars

Sea stars are bottom dwellers whose star-shaped bodies have flexible joints. They are carnivorous—the stomach pushes through the mouth onto the body tissues of prey and pours out digestive enzymes. The stomach then retracts with the partially digested prey; digestion is completed inside the body. Examples: crown-of-thorns sea star, sunstar

▼ Basket star feeding on Orange Finger Sponge

ECHINOIDEA

Echinoids lack arms. Their endoskeleton is rigid and boxlike and covered with movable spines. Most echinoids are herbivores or detritivores that use five-part jawlike structures to scrape algae from rocks. Examples: sea urchin, sand dollar, sea biscuit

▼ *Sea urchins grazing on kelp*

OPHIUROIDEA: Ophiuroids

Ophiuroids have small body disks, long, armored arms, and flexible joints. Most are filter feeders or detritivores. Examples: brittle star, basket star

▼ Sea cucumber

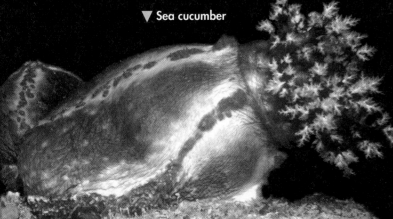

HOLOTHUROIDEA: Sea cucumbers

Sea cucumbers have a cylindrical, rubbery body with a reduced endoskeleton and no arms. They typically lie on their side and move along the ocean floor by the combined action of tube feet and body-wall muscles. These filter feeders or detritivores use a set of retractable feeding tentacles on one end to take in sand and detritus, from which they glean food.

Nonvertebrate Chordates

Tunicates are chordates named for the colorful tunic-like covering the adults have. As larvae, tunicates have all the characteristics of chordates, as well as bilateral symmetry, but as adults, they look very, very different.

KEY CHARACTERISTICS

The nonvertebrate chordates are the only chordates that lack a backbone. Like other chordates, they have a nerve cord, notochord, pharyngeal pouches, and a tail at some point during development. They are coelomate deuterostomes. The two subphyla, tunicates and lancelets, differ significantly.

Feeding and Digestion Filter feeders; tunicates—in most, water carrying food particles enters through an incurrent siphon; food is strained out in the pharynx and passed to the digestive system; lancelets—mucus in the pharynx catches food particles carried in by water, which are then carried into digestive tract

Circulation Closed; tunicates—heart pumps blood by "wringing out," and flow periodically reverses direction; lancelets—no heart, but blood vessels pump blood through body in one direction

Respiration Tunicates—gas exchange occurs in the gills and across other body surfaces; lancelets—through pharynx and body surfaces

Excretion Tunicates—most through excurrent siphon; lancelets—flame cells in nephridia release water and nitrogenous wastes into the atrium and out through an opening called an atriopore

Response Cerebral ganglion, few specialized sensory organs; tunicates—sensory cells in and on the siphons and other internal surfaces help control the amount of water passing through the pharynx; lancelets—a pair of eyespots detect light

Movement Tunicates—free-swimming larvae, but most are stationary as adults; lancelets—no appendages: they move by contracting muscles paired on either side of the body

Reproduction Tunicates—most sexual and hermaphroditic with external fertilization, but some reproduce by budding; most have free-swimming tadpole-like larvae that metamorphose into adults; lancelets—sexual with external fertilization

Eco Alert

Out-of-Control Tunicates

Asian Stalked Tunicate

You've never heard of them, but Asian stalked tunicates are disrupting marine ecosystems in Washington State; Prince Edward Island, Canada; and elsewhere. Tunicate larvae are carried in the ballast water of freight ships and discharged wherever the ships make port. There, away from their usual predators, the tunicates grow out of control, smothering shellfish beds and covering boats, docks, and underwater equipment. Researchers are still trying to figure out how to control them.

GROUPS OF NONVERTEBRATE CHORDATES

There are two major groups of nonvertebrate chordates: tunicates and lancelets (sometimes called amphioxus).

Two lancelets, Branchiostoma lanceolatum, poking out of sand.

CEPHALOCHORDATA: Lancelets

Lancelets are fishlike animals that have bilateral symmetry and live in salt water. They are filter feeders and have no internal skeleton. Example: *Branchiostoma*

UROCHORDATA: Tunicates

Tunicates are filter feeders that live in salt water. Most adults have a tough outer covering ("tunic") and no body symmetry; most display chordate features and bilateral symmetry only during larval stages. Many adults are stationary; some are free-swimming. Examples: sea squirts, sea peaches, salps

▼ Pastel Sea Squirt

Sea Squirts

Fishes

KEY CHARACTERISTICS

The word fish is used informally to describe aquatic vertebrates that look similar even though they belong to several different clades, because all are adapted to life in water. Most vertebrates we call fishes have paired fins, scales, and gills.

Feeding and Digestion Varies widely, both within and between groups: herbivores, carnivores, parasites, filter feeders, detritivores; digestive organs often include specialized teeth and jaws, crop, esophagus, stomach, liver, pancreas

Circulation Closed, single-loop circulatory system; two-chambered heart

Respiration Gills; some have specialized lungs or other adaptations that enable them to obtain oxygen from air.

Excretion Diffusion across gill membranes; kidneys

Response Brain with many parts; highly developed sense organs, including lateral line system

Movement Paired muscles on either side of backbone; many have highly maneuverable fins; the largest groups have two sets of paired fins; some have a gas-filled swim bladder that regulates buoyancy.

Reproduction Methods vary within and between groups: external or internal fertilization; oviparous, ovoviviparous, or viviparous

• A Look Back in Time ▶

Live Birth in Devonian Seas

You might think that live birth is a recent addition to chordate diversity. Guess again. Recent fossil finds of fishes from the Devonian Period show that at least one group of fishes was already bearing live young 380 million years ago. Two incredibly well preserved fossils, including that of the fish *Materpiscis*, show the remains of young with umbilical cords still attached to their mother's bodies. This is the earliest fossil evidence of viviparity in vertebrates.

▲ *Artist's conception of Materpiscis giving birth*

GROUPS OF FISHES

Fishes are the largest group of vertebrates, including more than 30,000 species. Evolutionary classification of these animals is still a work in progress; many traditional groups are now known not to be clades. "Fishes" actually represent several ancient clades, one of which includes tetrapods, or four-limbed vertebrates. Fishes, as we treat them here, include two groups of jawless fishes (hagfishes and lampreys), cartilaginous fishes, and bony fishes.

Sweetlips are, despite their funny faces, easily recognizable as fish.

"JAWLESS FISHES"

Hagfishes and lampreys make up separate clades, but their bodies share common features that distinguish them from other fishes. They have no jaws, lack vertebrae, and their skeletons are made of fiber and cartilage.

PETROMYZONTIDA: Lampreys

Lampreys are mostly filter feeders as larvae and parasites as adults. The head of an adult lamprey is taken up almost completely by a circular, tooth-bearing, sucking disk with a round mouth. Adult lampreys typically attach themselves to fishes. They hold on to their hosts using the teeth in their sucking disk and then scrape away at the skin with a rasping tongue. Lampreys then suck up their host's tissues and body fluids. Because lampreys feed mostly on blood, they are called "vampires of the sea."

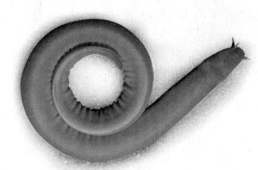

▲ Pacific Hagfish

MYXINI: Hagfishes

Hagfishes have pinkish gray wormlike bodies and four or six short tentacles around their mouths. They retain notochords as adults. Hagfishes lack image-forming eyes, but have light-detecting sensors scattered around their bodies. They feed on dead and dying animals using a rasping tongue that scrapes away layers of flesh.

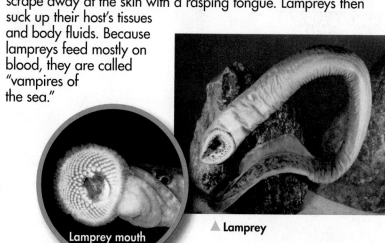

Lamprey mouth

▲ Lamprey

Tiger Shark

CHONDRICHTHYES: Cartilaginous Fishes

Members of this clade are considered "cartilaginous" because they lack true bone; their skeletons are built entirely of cartilage. Most cartilaginous fishes also have tough, scales, which make their skin as rough as sandpaper.

Holocephalans: Chimaeras

Chimaeras have smooth skin that lacks scales. Most have just a few platelike, grinding teeth and a venomous spine located in front of the dorsal fin. Examples: ghostfish, ratfish, rabbitfish

Elephant Fish

Elasmobranchii: Sharks, skates, and rays

Sharks, skates, and rays are very diverse, but all have skin covered with toothlike scales known as dermal denticles. Elasmobranchii make up the vast majority of living cartilaginous fish species.

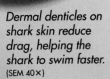

Dermal denticles on shark skin reduce drag, helping the shark to swim faster. (SEM 40×)

Galeomorphi: Sharks

Most of the 350 or so shark species have large, curved asymmetrical tails, torpedo-shaped bodies, and pointed snouts with a mouth underneath. Predatory sharks, such as the great white, have many teeth arranged in rows. As teeth in the front rows are worn out or lost, new teeth replace them. Some sharks go through 20,000 teeth in their lifetime! Other sharks are filter feeders, and some species have flat teeth for crushing mollusk and crustacean shells. Examples: Great White Shark, Whale Shark, Hammerhead Shark

Squalomorphi: Skates and rays

Skates and rays have diverse feeding habits. Some feed on bottom-dwelling invertebrates by using their mouths as powerful vacuums. Others filter-feed on plankton. When not feeding or swimming, many skates and rays cover themselves with a thin layer of sand and rest on the ocean floor. Example: stingray

Hammerhead Shark

Blue-Spotted Ribbon-Tailed Ray

OSTEICHTHYES: Bony fishes

The skeletons of these vertebrates are made of true bone. This clade includes the ancestors and living members of all "higher" vertebrate groups—including tetrapods.

Rainbow Trout

Actinopterygii: Ray-finned fishes

Almost all living bony fishes belong to a huge group called ray-finned fishes. The name *ray-finned* refers to the slender bony rays that are connected to one another by a layer of skin to form fins.

Coelacanth

Sarcopterygii: Lobe-finned fishes

Seven living species of bony fishes, including lungfishes and coelacanths, are classified as lobe-finned fishes. Lungfishes live in fresh water, but coelacanths are marine. The fleshy fins of lobe-finned fishes are supported by strong bones rather than rays. Some of these bones are homologous to the limb bones of land vertebrates. Examples: lungfish, coelacanths

This clade includes the ancestors of tetrapods, so, technically, all living tetrapods (including us!) are Sarcopterygians! As a result, the bony-fish clade includes almost half of all chordate species!

Amphibians

Marsupial Frog

KEY CHARACTERISTICS

The word amphibian means "double life," an apt name for these vertebrates, most of which live in water as larvae and on land as adults. Most adult amphibians breathe with lungs, lack scales and claws, and have moist skin that contains mucous glands.

Feeding and Digestion Tadpoles—usually filter feeders or herbivores with long, coiled intestines to digest plant material; adults—carnivores with shorter intestines for processing meat

Circulation Double-loop system with three-chambered heart

Respiration Larvae breathe through skin and gills; most adult species have lungs, though a few use gills; lungless salamanders breathe through their mouth-cavity lining and skin.

Excretion Kidneys produce urine.

Response Well-developed nervous and sensory systems; organs include protective nictitating membrane over moveable eyes, tympanic membranes, lateral line system

Movement Larvae have tails; adults have limbs (except caecilians); some have specialized toes for climbing.

Reproduction Most lay eggs without shells that are fertilized externally; most undergo metamorphosis from aquatic tadpole larvae that breathe with gills to land-dwelling adults, which usually have lungs and limbs.

Eco•Alert

Red-Eyed Treefrog

The Frogs Are Disappearing!

For several decades, scientists have noticed that amphibian populations worldwide have been decreasing, and a number of species have become extinct. Scientists have not yet pinpointed a single cause for this problem. It is, however, becoming clear that amphibians are susceptible to a variety of environmental threats, including habitat loss, ozone depletion, acid rain, water pollution, fungal infections, and introduced aquatic predators.

To better understand this decline, biologists worldwide have been focusing their efforts and sharing data about amphibian populations. One amphibian-monitoring program covers all of North America.

Red Eft

GROUPS OF AMPHIBIANS

The three orders of amphibians include more than 6000 species, roughly 5000 of which are frogs and toads.

URODELA: Salamanders and newts

Salamanders and newts have long bodies and tails. Most also have four legs. All are carnivores. Adults usually live in moist woods, where they tunnel under rocks and rotting logs. Some salamanders, such as the mud puppy, keep their gills as adults and live in water all their lives. Examples: Barred Tiger Salamander, Red Eft

American Toad

ANURA: Frogs and toads

Adult frogs and toads are amphibians without tails that can jump. Frogs tend to have long legs and make long jumps, whereas toads have shorter legs that limit them to shorter hops. Frogs are generally more dependent on bodies of fresh water than toads, which may live in moist woods or even deserts. Examples: treefrogs, Leopard Frog, American Toad, spadefoot toads

APODA: Caecilians

The least-known and most unusual amphibians are the legless caecilians. They have tentacles, and many have fishlike scales embedded in their skin—which shows that not all amphibians fit the general definition. Caecilians live in water or burrow in moist soil or sediment, feeding on small invertebrates such as termites. Examples: Ringed Caecilian, Yellow-Striped Caecilian

Ringed Caecilian

▶ Because amphibian eggs must develop in water, most live in moist climates. Some, such as this Alpine Newt, live on cool, rainy mountain slopes.

Reptiles

Saltwater crocodiles, such as this young one, are the largest living reptiles and sometime reach 6 meters long. But that's still only half as long as their famous dinosaur ancestor, T. rex!

KEY CHARACTERISTICS OF REPTILES

Living reptiles, traditionally classified in the class Reptilia, are ectothermic vertebrates with dry, scaly skin; lungs; and amniotic eggs. Modern evolutionary classification now recognizes a larger clade Reptilia that includes living reptiles, extinct dinosaurs, and birds—the living descendants of one dinosaur group.

Feeding and Digestion Feeding methods vary by group; digestive systems—herbivores have long digestive systems to break down plant materials; carnivores may swallow prey whole

Circulation Two loops; heart with two atria and one or two ventricles

Respiration Spongy lungs provide large surface area for gas exchange; lungs operated by muscles and moveable ribs

Excretion Kidneys; urine contains ammonia or uric acid

Response Brain; well-developed senses including, in some species, infrared detectors that can spot warm-bodied prey in the dark

Movement Strong limbs (except snakes)

Reproduction Internal fertilization via cloaca; amniotic egg with leathery shell

Eco•Alert

Calling Doctor 'Gator!

You might think of alligators mostly as killing machines, but their blood may soon provide medicines that can save lives. An alligator's immune system works quite differently from our own. Proteins in their white blood cells can kill multidrug resistant bacteria, disease-causing yeasts, and even HIV. Remarkably, these proteins work against pathogens to which the animals have never been exposed. Researchers are currently sequencing the genes for these proteins and hope to develop them into human medicines in the near future.

GROUPS OF REPTILES

There are nearly 9000 species of reptiles (not including birds).

SPHENODONTA: Tuataras

The tuatara, found only on a few small islands off the coast of New Zealand, is the only living member of this group. Tuataras resemble lizards in some ways, but they lack external ears and retain primitive scales.

Tuatara

SQUAMATA: Lizards, snakes, and relatives

There are more than 8000 species of lizards and snakes. Most lizards have legs, clawed toes, and external ears. Some lizards have evolved highly specialized structures, such as glands in the lower jaw that produce venom. Snakes are legless; they have lost both pairs of legs through evolution. Examples: iguanas, Milk Snake, Coral Snake

Leopard Gecko

ARCHOSAURS: Crocodilians; pterosaurs and dinosaurs (extinct); and birds

This clade includes some of the most spectacular animals that have ever lived. The extinct dinosaurs and pterosaurs (flying reptiles), whose adaptive radiations produced some of the largest animals ever to walk Earth or fly above it, are the closest relatives of birds. Living crocodilians are short-legged and have long and typically broad snouts. They are fierce carnivorous predators, but the females are attentive mothers. Crocodilians live only in regions where the climate remains warm year-round. We discuss birds separately. Examples: extinct types: *Tyrannosaurus, Pteranodon*; living types: alligators, crocodiles, caimans, and birds (see following pages)

Paraguay Caiman

Leopard Tortoise

TESTUDINE: Turtles and tortoises

Turtles and tortoises have a shell built into their skeleton. Most can pull their heads and legs into the shell for protection. Instead of teeth, these reptiles have hornlike ridges covering their jaws equipped with sharp beaklike tips. Strong limbs can lift their body off the ground when walking or, in the case of sea turtles, can drag their body across a sandy shore to lay eggs. Examples: snapping turtles, green sea turtles, Galápagos tortoise

Birds

Today, only birds have feathers. These delicate, intricately interlocking and beautiful structures keep birds warm and cool and enable most to fly.

Common Kingfisher

KEY CHARACTERISTICS OF BIRDS

Birds, once placed in a class of their own, are now recognized as endothermic reptiles with feathers and hard-shelled, amniotic eggs that are descended from dinosaurs. Birds have two scaly legs and front limbs modified into wings, which enable most species to fly.

Feeding and Digestion No teeth; bills adapted to widely varied foods, including insects, seeds, fruits, nectar, fish, meat; organs of the digestive system include crop, gizzard, cloaca

Circulation Two loops with four-chambered heart; separation of oxygen-rich and oxygen-poor blood

Respiration Constant, one-way flow of air through lungs and air sacs increases the efficiency of gas exchange and supports high metabolic rate

Excretion Kidneys remove nitrogenous wastes from blood, converting them to uric acid, which is excreted through cloaca

Response Brain with large optic lobes and enlarged cerebellum; highly evolved sense organs including, in some species, eyes that can see ultraviolet light

Movement Skeleton made up of lightweight, hollow bones with internal struts for strength; powerful muscles; most fly

Reproduction Internal fertilization via cloaca; amniotic egg with hard, brittle shell; depending on species, newly hatched young may be precocial—downy-feathered chicks able to move around and feed themselves, or altricial—bare-skinned and totally dependent on their parents

---

• A Look Back in Time ▶

Birds of a Feather

Fossils recently discovered in lake beds in China have greatly expanded our understanding of bird evolution. One exciting discovery was that of a four-winged dinosaur named *Microraptor gui* from about 125 million years ago. *Microraptor gui*, which was related to *Tyrannosaurus rex*, had feathers on both its wings *and* its legs, so some researchers hypothesize that it flew like a biplane! This and other fossils show that several lineages of dinosaurs and ancient birds evolved various kinds of feathers over millions of years.

Artist's conception of *Microraptor gui*

GROUPS OF BIRDS

Evolutionary classification of living birds is still a work in progress, as different techniques and analyses produce different results. There are about 10,000 species. The groups described below illustrate some of the diversity of birds.

Ostrich

PALEOGNATHAE: Ostriches, emus, kiwis, and relatives

This group represents an early branch of the bird family tree that is separate from all other living birds. This clade includes the largest birds alive today. Ostriches can be 2.5 meters tall and weigh 130 kilograms! Kiwis, however, are only about the size of chickens. Roughly a dozen living species are scattered throughout the Southern Hemisphere. All are flightless, but the larger species can run very fast. They generally eat a variety of plant material, insects, and other small invertebrates. Examples: Ostrich, emus, Brown Kiwi, Greater Rhea, Dwarf Cassowary

SPHENISCIDAE: Penguins

These flightless birds of the Southern Hemisphere are adapted to extreme cold and hunting in water. Though they cannot fly, they use their wings as flippers when they swim. Penguins have more feathers per square centimeter than any other bird; this density allows them to repel water and conserve heat effectively. Some species form large colonies. Examples: Emperor Penguin, Chinstrap Penguin, King Penguin

Redhead

ANATIDAE: Ducks, geese, and swans

These birds spend much of their time feeding in bodies of water. Webbed feet enable them to paddle efficiently across the surface of the water. Most fly well, however, and many species migrate thousands of kilometers between breeding and resting locations.
Examples: Redhead, Ross's goose, Trumpeter Swan

King Penguins

Galápagos Hawk

FALCONIDAE AND ACCIPITRIDAE:
Falcons, eagles, and hawks

These fierce predators, often called raptors, typically have powerful hooked bills, large wingspans, and sharp talons. Raptors have powerful flight muscles and keen eyesight, enabling them to see prey at a distance. Examples: Eurasian Kestrel, Golden Eagle, Galápagos Hawk

PICIDAE AND RAMPHASTIDAE:
Woodpeckers and toucans

Woodpeckers are tree-dwelling birds with two toes in front and two in back. (Most birds have three in front and one in back; the two-and-two arrangement makes moving up and down tree trunks easier.) Woodpeckers are typically carnivores that eat insects and their larvae. Toucans usually use their huge, often colorful bills to eat fruit. Examples: Black Woodpecker, Keel-Billed Toucan

Black Woodpecker with chicks

Keel-Billed Toucan

PASSERIFORMES: Passerines

Also called perching birds, this is by far the largest and most diverse group of birds, with about 5000 species. Most are songbirds. Examples: flycatchers, mockingbirds, cardinals, crows, chickadees, and finches.

Summer Tanager

Great Crested Flycatcher

Mountain Bluebird

Hooded Warbler

Lark Sparrow

Blue Grosbeak

Mammals

Feeding and Digestion Diet varies with group; foods range from seeds, fruits, and leaves to insects, fish, meat, and even blood; teeth, jaws, and digestive organs are adapted to diet

Circulation Two loops; four-chambered heart; separation of oxygen-rich and oxygen-poor blood

Respiration Lungs controlled by two sets of muscles.

Excretion Highly evolved kidneys filter urea from blood and produce urine.

Response Most highly evolved brain of all animals; keen senses

KEY CHARACTERISTICS

Mammals are endothermic vertebrates with hair and mammary glands that produce milk to nourish their young.

Movement Flexible backbone; variations in limb bones and muscles enable wide range of movement across groups: from burrowing and crawling to walking, running, hopping, and flying

Reproduction Internal fertilization; developmental process varies with group (monotreme, marsupial, placental)

▸**Did You Know?**

Platypus: Mix-and-Match Genome

The duckbill platypus has such an odd mix of reptile and mammal features that some scientists thought the first specimens were hoaxes produced by sticking parts of different animals together! Recent genome studies have revealed an equally odd mix of reptilian and mammalian genes. Genes for reptile-like vision, the production of egg yolk, and the production of venom link the platypus to reptiles. Genes for the production of milk link it to other mammals. The evidence provides confirmation that this monotreme represents a truly ancient lineage, one from the time close to that at which mammals branched off from reptiles.

GROUPS OF MAMMALS

The three living groups of mammals are the monotremes, the marsupials, and the placentals. There are about 5000 species of mammals, usually divided into about 26 orders, most of which are placentals. There is only one order of monotremes.

This black-backed jackal pup is enjoying a moment of independence from its family group. Mammals provide intensive parental care to their young.

Short-Beaked Echidna (Albino)

MONOTREMATA: Monotremes

Monotremes—egg-laying mammals—share two important characteristics with reptiles. First, the digestive, reproductive, and urinary systems of monotremes all open into a cloaca similar to that of reptiles. Second, monotreme development is similar to that of reptiles. Like a reptile, a female monotreme lays soft-shelled eggs incubated outside her body. The eggs hatch in about ten days. Unlike reptiles, however, young monotremes are nourished by mother's milk, which they lick from pores on the surface of her abdomen. Only five monotreme species exist today, all in Australia and New Guinea. Examples: Duckbill Platypus, echidnas

MARSUPIALIA: Marsupials

Marsupials bear live young at an extremely early stage of development. A fertilized egg develops into an embryo inside the mother's reproductive tract. The embryo is then "born" in what would be an embryonic stage for more familiar mammals. It crawls across its mother's fur and attaches to a nipple that, in most species, is located in a pouch called the marsupium. The embryo spends several months attached to the nipple. It continues to nurse until it can survive on its own. Examples: kangaroos, wallabies, wombats, opossums

Wombat

PLACENTALIA: Placental Mammals

Placental mammals are the mammals with which you are most familiar. This group gets its name from a structure called the placenta, which is formed when the embryo's tissues join with tissues within the mother's body. Nutrients, gases, and wastes are exchanged between embryo and mother through the placenta. The placenta allows the embryo to develop inside the mother longer so that placental young are born at a later stage of development than other mammals are. Development may take as little as a few weeks (mice), to as long as two years (elephants). After birth, most placental mammals care for their young and provide them with nourishment by nursing. Examples: Mice, cats, dogs, seals, whales, elephants, humans

Chiroptera: Bats

These are the only mammals capable of true flight. There are more than 900 species of bats! They eat mostly insects or fruit and nectar, although a few species feed on the blood of other vertebrates. Examples: fruit bats, Little Brown Myotis, Vampire Bat

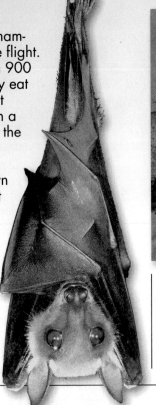

Epauletted Bat, roosting

Lioness attacking Greater Kudu

Carnivora: Carnivores

Many members of this group, such as tigers and hyenas, chase or stalk prey by running or pouncing, then kill with sharp teeth and claws. Dogs, bears, and other members of this group may eat plants as well as meat. Examples: dogs, cats, skunks, seals, bears

Sirenia: Sirenians

Sirenians are herbivores that live in rivers, bays, and warm, coastal waters scattered throughout the world. These large, slow-moving mammals lead fully aquatic lives. Examples: manatees, dugongs

Manatee mother and nursing calf

African Hedgehog mother and baby

Insectivora: Insectivores

These insect eaters have long, narrow snouts and sharp claws that are well suited for digging. Examples: shrews, moles, hedgehogs

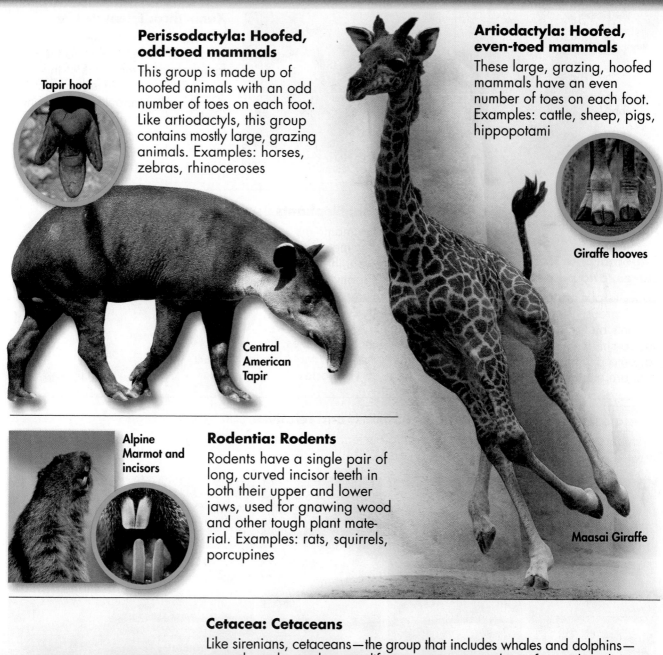

Perissodactyla: Hoofed, odd-toed mammals

This group is made up of hoofed animals with an odd number of toes on each foot. Like artiodactyls, this group contains mostly large, grazing animals. Examples: horses, zebras, rhinoceroses

Tapir hoof

Central American Tapir

Artiodactyla: Hoofed, even-toed mammals

These large, grazing, hoofed mammals have an even number of toes on each foot. Examples: cattle, sheep, pigs, hippopotami

Giraffe hooves

Maasai Giraffe

Rodentia: Rodents

Rodents have a single pair of long, curved incisor teeth in both their upper and lower jaws, used for gnawing wood and other tough plant material. Examples: rats, squirrels, porcupines

Alpine Marmot and incisors

Cetacea: Cetaceans

Like sirenians, cetaceans—the group that includes whales and dolphins—are adapted to underwater life, yet must come to the surface to breathe. Most cetaceans live and breed in the ocean. Examples: whales, dolphins

Atlantic Spotted Dolphin

Animals

Xenarthra: Edentates

The word *edentate* means "toothless," which refers to the fact that some members of this group (sloths and anteaters) have simple teeth without enamel or no teeth at all. Armadillos, however, have more teeth than most other mammals! Examples: sloths, anteaters, armadillos

Northern Tamandua

Black-Tailed Jackrabbit

Lagomorpha: Rabbit, hares, and pikas

Lagomorphs are entirely herbivorous. They differ from rodents by having two pairs of incisors in the upper jaw. Most lagomorphs have hind legs that are adapted for leaping.

Proboscidea: Elephants

These are the mammals with trunks. Some time ago, this group went through an extensive adaptive radiation that produced many species, including mastodons and mammoths, which are now extinct. Only two species, the Asian Elephant and the African elephant, survive today.

Asian Elephant and calf

Primates: Lemurs, monkeys, apes, humans, and relatives

Members of this group are closely related to ancient insectivores but have a highly developed cerebrum and complex behaviors.

Sifaka

Tarsier

Langur

Baboon and baby

Orangutan

Gorilla

Chimpanzee

Data Tables and Graphs

How can you make sense of the data from a science experiment? The first step is to organize the data. You can organize data in data tables and graphs to help you interpret them.

Data Tables

You have gathered your materials and set up your experiment. But before you start, you need to plan a way to record what happens during the experiment. By creating a data table, you can record your observations and measurements in an orderly way.

Suppose, for example, that a scientist conducted an experiment to find out how many kilocalories people of different body masses burned while performing various activities for 30 minutes. The data table below shows the results.

Notice in this data table that the independent variable (body mass) is the heading of the first column. The dependent variable (for Experiment 1, the number of kilocalories burned while bicycling for 30 minutes) is the heading of the next column. Additional columns were added for related experiments.

Bar Graphs

A bar graph is useful for comparing data from two or more distinct categories. In this example, pancreatic secretions in the small intestine are shown.

To create a bar graph, follow these steps.

1. On graph paper, draw a horizontal, or *x*-axis, and a vertical, or *y*-axis.

2. Write the names of the categories (the independent variable) along one axis, usually the horizontal axis. You may put the categories on the vertical axis if that graph shape better fits on your page. Label the axis.

3. Label the other axis with the name of the dependent variable and the unit of measurement. Then, create a scale along that axis by marking off equally spaced numbers that cover the range of the data values.

4. For each category, draw a solid bar at the appropriate value. Then, fill in the space from the bar to the axis representing the independent variable. Make all the bars the same width.

5. Add a title that describes the graph.

Calories Burned in 30 Minutes			
Body Mass	Experiment 1: Bicycling	Experiment 2: Playing Basketball	Experiment 3: Watching Television
30 kg	60 Calories	120 Calories	21 Calories
40 kg	77 Calories	164 Calories	27 Calories
50 kg	95 Calories	206 Calories	33 Calories
60 kg	114 Calories	248 Calories	38 Calories

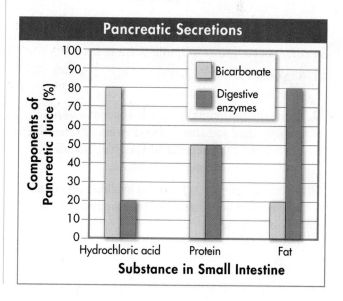

Line Graphs

A line graph is used to display data that show how the dependent variable changes in response to manipulations of the independent variable. You can use a line graph when your independent variable is continuous, that is, when there are other points between the ones that you tested. For example, the graph below shows how the growth of a bacterial population is related to time. The graph shows that the number of bacteria approximately doubles every 20 minutes. Line graphs are powerful tools because they also allow you to estimate values for conditions that you did not test in the experiment.

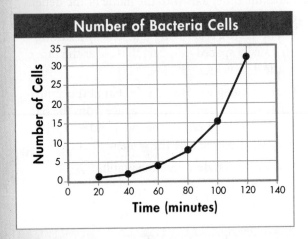

To construct a line graph, follow these steps.

1. On graph paper, draw a horizontal, or *x*-axis, and a vertical, or *y*-axis.

2. Label the horizontal axis with the name of the independent variable. Label the vertical axis with the name of the dependent variable. Include the units of measurement on both axes.

3. Create a scale on each axis by marking off equally spaced numbers that cover the range of the data values collected.

4. Plot a point on the graph for each data value. To do this, follow an imaginary vertical line extending up from the horizontal axis for an independent variable value. Then, follow an imaginary horizontal line extending across from the vertical axis at the value of the associated dependent variable. Plot a point where the two lines intersect. Repeat until all your data values are plotted.

5. Connect the plotted points with a solid line. Not all graphs are linear, so you may discover that it is more appropriate to draw a curve to connect the points.

The data in the graph at the left fit neatly on a smooth curve. But if you were to connect each data point on the graph below, you would have a mess that yielded little useful information. In some cases, it may be most useful to draw a line that shows the general trend of the plotted points. This type of line is often called a line of best fit. Such a line runs as closely as possible to all the points and allows you to make generalizations or predictions based on the data. Some points will fall above or below a line of best fit.

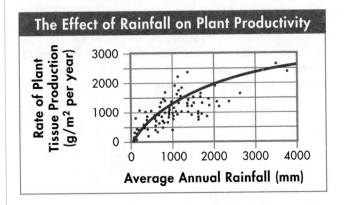

Circle Graphs

Circle graphs, or pie charts, display data as parts of a whole. Like bar graphs, circle graphs can be used to display data that fall into separate categories. Unlike bar graphs, however, circle graphs can only be used when you have data for all the categories that make up a given group. The circle, or "pie," represents 100 percent of a group, while the sectors, or slices, represent the percentages of each category that make up that group. The example below compares the different blood groups found in the U.S. population.

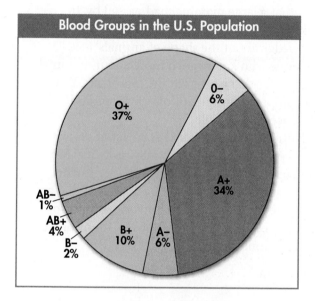

Blood Groups in the U.S. Population

O+ 37%
O– 6%
A+ 34%
A– 6%
B+ 10%
B– 2%
AB+ 4%
AB– 1%

To construct a circle graph, follow these steps.

1. Draw a circle and mark the center. Then, draw a radius line from the center to the circle's edge.

2. Determine the size of a sector of the graph by calculating the number of degrees that correspond to a percentage you wish to represent. For example, in the graph shown, B⁺ makes up 10 percent of all blood groups; 360 degrees × 0.10 = 36 degrees.

3. With a protractor fixed at the center of the circle, measure the angle—in this example, 36 degrees—from the existing radius, and draw a second radius at that point. Label the sector with its category and the percentage of the whole it represents. Repeat for each of the other categories, measuring each sector from the previous radius so the sectors don't overlap.

4. For easier reading, shade each sector differently.

5. Add a title that describes the graph.

Reading Diagrams

In scientific figures showing a cut-away of a structure, the diagram or photograph is showing the structure from a particular angle. Look for clues throughout this book that will help you interpret the view being shown.

Cross Sections

A cross section shows a horizontal cut through the middle of a structure. This icon will help you locate cross sections.

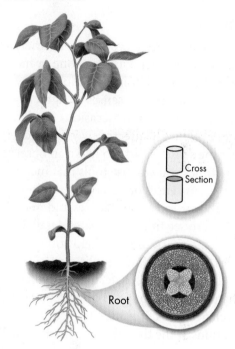

Cross Section

Root

Longitudinal Sections

A longitudinal section shows a vertical cut through the middle of a structure. This icon will help you locate longitudinal sections.

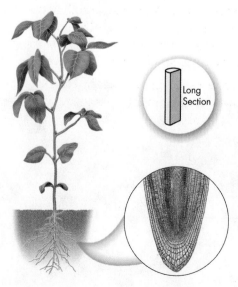

Long Section

Basic Process Skills

During a biology course, you often carry out short lab activities as well as lengthier experiments. Here are some skills that you will use.

Observing

In every science activity, you make a variety of observations. Observing is using one or more of the five senses to gather information. Many observations involve the senses of sight, hearing, touch, and smell. On rare occasions in a lab—but only when explicitly directed by your teacher—you may use the sense of taste to make an observation.

Sometimes you will use tools that increase the power of your senses or make observations more precise. For example, hand lenses and microscopes enable you to see things in greater detail. Rulers, balances, and thermometers help you measure key variables. Besides expanding the senses or making observations more accurate, tools may help eliminate personal opinions or preferences.

In science, it is customary to record your observations at the time they are made, usually by writing or drawing in a notebook. You may also make records by using computers, cameras, videotapes, and other tools. As a rule, scientists keep complete accounts of their observations, often using tables to organize their observations.

Inferring

In science, as in daily life, observations are usually followed by inferences. Inferring is interpreting an observation or statement based on prior knowledge.

For example, suppose you're on a mountain hike and you see footprints like the ones illustrated below. Based on their size and shape, you might infer that a large mammal had passed by. In making that inference, you would use your knowledge about the shape of animals' feet. Someone who knew much more about mammals might infer that a bear left the footprints. You can compare examples of observations and inferences in the table.

Notice that an inference is an act of reasoning, not a fact. An inference may be logical but not true. It is often necessary to gather further information before you can be confident that an inference is correct. For scientists, that information may come from further observations or from research done by others.

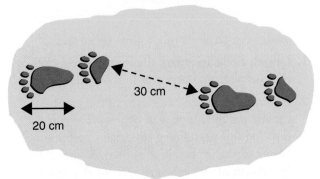

30 cm

20 cm

Comparing Observations and Inferences	
Sample Observations	**Sample Inferences**
The footprints in the soil each have five toes.	An animal made the footprints.
The larger footprints are about 20 cm long.	A bear made the footprints.
The space between each pair of footprints is about 30 cm.	The animal was walking, not running.

As you study biology, you may make different types of inferences. For example, you may generalize about all cases based on information about some cases: *All the plant roots I've observed grow downward, so I infer that all roots grow downward.* You may determine that one factor or event was caused by another factor or event: *The bacteria died after I applied bleach, so I infer that bleach kills bacteria.* Predictions may be another type of inference.

Predicting

People often make predictions, but their statements about the future could be either guesses or inferences. In science, a prediction is an inference about a future event based on evidence, experience, or knowledge. For example, you can say, *On the first day of next month, it will be sunny.* If your statement is based on evidence of weather patterns in the area, then the prediction is scientific. If the statement was made without considering any evidence, it's just a guess.

Predictions play a major role in science because they provide a way to test ideas. If scientists understand an event or the properties of a particular object, they should be able to make accurate predictions about that event or object. Some predictions can be tested simply by making observations. At other times, carefully designed experiments are needed.

Classifying

If you have ever heard people debate whether a tomato is a fruit or a vegetable, you've heard an argument about classification. Classifying is the process of grouping items that are alike according to some organizing idea or system. Classifying occurs in every branch of science, but it is especially important in biology because living things are so numerous and diverse.

You may have the chance to practice classifying in different ways. Sometimes you will place objects into groups using an established system. At other times, you may create a system of your own by examining a variety of objects and identifying their properties.

Classification can have different purposes. Sometimes it's done just to keep things organized, to make lab supplies easy to find, for example.

More often, though, classification helps scientists understand living things better and discover relationships among them. For example, one way biologists determine how groups of vertebrates are related is to compare their bones. Biologists classify certain animal parts as bone or muscle and then investigate how they work together.

Using Models

Some cities refuse to approve any new buildings that could cast shadows on a popular park. As architects plan buildings in such locations, they use models that can show where a proposed building's shadow will fall at any time of day in any season of the year. A model is a mental or physical representation of an object, process, or event. In science, models are usually made to help people understand natural objects and processes.

Models can be varied. Mental models, such as mathematical equations, can represent some kinds of ideas or processes. For example, the equation for the surface area of a sphere can model the surface of Earth, enabling scientists to determine its size. Physical models can be made of a huge variety of materials; they can be two dimensional (flat) or three dimensional (having depth). In biology, a drawing of a molecule or a cell is a typical two-dimensional model. Common three-dimensional models include a representation of a DNA molecule and a plastic skeleton of an animal.

Physical models can also be made "to scale," which means they are in proportion to the actual object. Something very large, such as an area of land being studied, can be shown at 1/100 of its actual size. A tiny organism can be shown at 100 times its size.

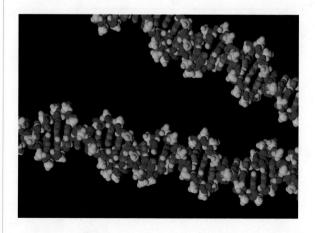

Organizing Information

When you study or want to communicate facts and ideas, you may find it helpful to organize information visually. Here are some common graphic organizers you can use. Notice that each type of organizer is useful for specific types of information.

Flowcharts

A flowchart can help you represent the order in which a set of events has occurred or should occur. Flowcharts are useful for outlining the steps in a procedure or stages in a process with a definite beginning and end.

To make a flowchart, list the steps in the process you want to represent and count the steps. Then, create the appropriate number of boxes, starting at the top of a page or on the left. Write a brief description of the first event in the first box, and then fill in the other steps, box by box. Link each box to the next event in the process with an arrow.

Concept Maps

Concept maps can help you organize a topic that has many subtopics. A concept map begins with a main idea and shows how it can be broken down into specific topics. It makes the ideas easier to understand by presenting their relationships visually.

You construct a concept map by placing the concept words (usually nouns) in ovals and connecting the ovals with linking words. The most general concept usually is placed at the top of the map or in the center. The content of the other ovals becomes more specific as you move away from the main concept. The linking words, which describe the relationship between the linked concepts, are written on a line between two ovals. If you follow any string of concepts and linking words down through a map, they should sound almost like a sentence.

Some concept maps may also include linking words that connect a concept in one branch to another branch. Such connections, called cross-linkages, show more complex interrelationships.

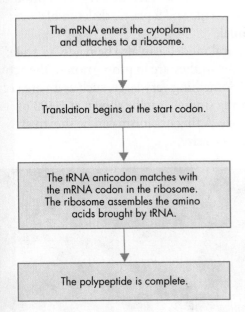

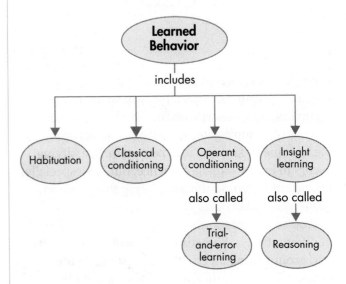

Compare/Contrast Tables

Compare/contrast tables are useful for showing the similarities and differences between two or more objects or processes. The table provides an organized framework for making comparisons based on specific characteristics.

To create a compare/contrast table, list the items to be compared across the top of the table. List the characteristics that will form the basis of your comparison in the column on the left. Complete the table by filling in information for each item.

Comparing Fermentation and Cellular Respiration		
Characteristic	**Fermentation**	**Cellular Respiration**
Starting reactants	Glucose	Glucose, oxygen
Pathways involved	Glycolysis, several others	Glycolysis, Krebs cycle, electron transport
End products	CO_2 and alcohol *or* CO_2 and lactic acid	CO_2, H_2O
Number of ATP molecules produced	2	36

Venn Diagrams

Another way to show similarities and differences between items is with a Venn diagram. A Venn diagram consists of two or more ovals that partially overlap. Each oval represents a particular object or idea. Characteristics that the objects share are written in the area of overlap. Differences or unique characteristics are written in the areas that do not overlap.

To create a Venn diagram, draw two overlapping ovals. Label them with the names of the objects or the ideas they represent. Write the unique characteristics in the part of each oval that does not overlap. Write the shared characteristics within the area of overlap.

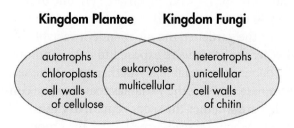

Kingdom Plantae   **Kingdom Fungi**

autotrophs	eukaryotes	heterotrophs
chloroplasts	multicellular	unicellular
cell walls of cellulose		cell walls of chitin

Cycle Diagrams

A cycle diagram shows a sequence of events that is continuous, or cyclical. A continuous sequence does not have a beginning or an end; instead, each event in the process leads to another event. The diagram shows the order of the events.

To create a cycle diagram, list the events in the process and count them. Draw one box for each event, placing the boxes around an imaginary circle. Write one of the events in an oval, and then draw an arrow to the next oval, moving clockwise. Continue to fill in the boxes and link them with arrows until the descriptions form a continuous circle.

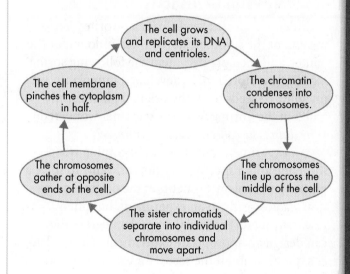

The cell grows and replicates its DNA and centrioles.

The chromatin condenses into chromosomes.

The chromosomes line up across the middle of the cell.

The sister chromatids separate into individual chromosomes and move apart.

The chromosomes gather at opposite ends of the cell.

The cell membrane pinches the cytoplasm in half.

Conducting an Experiment

A science experiment is a procedure designed to test a prediction. Some types of experiments are fairly simple to design. Others may require ingenious problem solving.

Starting With Questions or Problems

A gardener collected seeds from a favorite plant at the end of the summer, stored them indoors for the winter, and then planted them the following spring. None of the stored seeds developed into plants, yet uncollected seeds from the original plant germinated in the normal way. The gardener wondered: *Why didn't the collected seeds germinate?*

An experiment may have its beginning when someone asks a specific question or wants to solve a particular problem. Sometimes the original question leads directly to an experiment, but often researchers must restate the problem before they can design an appropriate experiment. The gardener's question about the seeds, for example, is too broad to be tested by an experiment, because there are so many possible answers. To narrow the topic, the gardener might think about related questions: *Were the seeds I collected different from the uncollected seeds? Did I try to germinate them in poor soil or with insufficient light or water? Did storing the seeds indoors ruin them in some way?*

Developing a Hypothesis

In science, a question about an object or event is answered by developing a possible explanation called a hypothesis. The hypothesis may be developed after long thought and research, or it may come to a scientist "in a flash." How a hypothesis is formed doesn't matter; it can be useful as long as it leads to predictions that can be tested.

The gardener decided to focus on the fact that the nongerminating seeds were stored in the warm conditions of a heated house. That premise led the person to propose this hypothesis: *Seeds require a period of low temperatures in order to germinate.*

The next step is to make a prediction based on the hypothesis, for example: *If seeds are stored indoors in cold conditions, they will germinate in the same way as seeds left outdoors during the winter.* Notice that the prediction suggests the basic idea for an experiment.

Designing an Experiment

A carefully designed experiment can test a prediction in a reliable way, ruling out other possible explanations. As scientists plan their experimental procedures, they pay particular attention to the factors that must be controlled.

The gardener decided to study three groups of seeds: (1) some that would be left outdoors throughout the winter, (2) some that would be brought indoors and kept at room temperature, and (3) some that would be brought indoors and kept cold.

Controlling Variables

As researchers design an experiment, they identify the variables, factors that can change. Some common variables include mass, volume, time, temperature, light, and the presence or absence of specific materials. An experiment involves three categories of variables. The factor that scientists purposely change is called the independent variable. An independent variable is also known as a manipulated variable. The factor that may change because of the independent variable and that scientists want to observe is called the dependent variable. A dependent variable is also known as a responding variable. Factors that scientists purposely keep the same are called controlled variables. Controlling variables enables researchers to conclude that the changes in the dependent variable are due exclusively to changes in the independent variable.

For the gardener, the independent variable is whether the seeds were exposed to cold conditions. The dependent variable is whether or not the seeds germinate. Among the variables that must be controlled are whether the seeds remain dry during storage, when the seeds are planted, the amount of water the seeds receive, and the type of soil used.

Interpreting Data

The observations and measurements that are made in an experiment are called data. Scientists usually record data in an orderly way. When an experiment is finished, the researcher analyzes the data for trends or patterns, often by doing calculations or making graphs, to determine whether the results support the hypothesis.

For example, after planting the seeds in the spring, the gardener counted the seeds that germinated and found these results: None of the seeds kept at room temperature germinated, 80 percent of the seeds kept in the freezer germinated, and 85 percent of the seeds left outdoors during the winter germinated. The trend was clear: The gardener's prediction appeared to be correct.

To be sure that the results of an experiment are correct, scientists review their data critically, looking for possible sources of error. Here, *error* refers to differences between the observed results and the true values. Experimental error can result from human mistakes or problems with equipment. It can also occur when the small group of objects studied does not accurately represent the whole group. For example, if some of the gardener's seeds had been exposed to a herbicide, the data might not reflect the true seed germination pattern.

Drawing Conclusions

If researchers are confident that their data are reliable, they make a final statement summarizing their results. That statement, called the conclusion, indicates whether the data support or refute the hypothesis. The gardener's conclusion was this: *Some seeds must undergo a period of freezing in order to germinate.* A conclusion is considered valid if it is a logical interpretation of reliable data.

Following Up an Experiment

When an experiment has been completed, one or more events often follow. Researchers may repeat the experiment to verify the results. They may publish the experiment so that others can evaluate and replicate their procedures. They may compare their conclusion with the discoveries made by other scientists. And they may raise new questions that lead to new experiments. For example, *Are the spores of fungi affected by temperature as these seeds were?*

Researching other discoveries about seeds would show that some other types of plants in temperate zones require periods of freezing before they germinate. Biologists infer that this pattern makes it less likely the seeds will germinate before winter, thus increasing the chances that the young plants will survive.

The Metric System

The standard system of measurement used by scientists throughout the world is known as the International System of Units, abbreviated as SI (Système International d'Unités, in French). It is based on units of 10. Each unit is 10 times larger or 10 times smaller than the next unit. The table lists the prefixes used to name the most common SI units.

Common SI Prefixes		
Prefix	Symbol	Meaning
kilo-	k	1000
hecto-	h	100
deka-	da	10
deci-	d	0.1 (one tenth)
centi-	c	0.01 (one hundredth)
milli-	m	0.001 (one thousandth)

Commonly Used Metric Units

Length To measure length, or distance from one point to another, the unit of measure is a meter (m). A meter is slightly longer than a yard.

Useful equivalents:

1 meter = 1000 millimeters (mm)
1 meter = 100 centimeters (cm)
1000 meters = 1 kilometer (km)

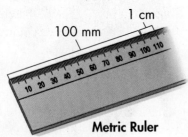

Metric Ruler

Volume To measure the volume of a liquid, or the amount of space an object takes up, the unit of measure is a liter (L). A liter is slightly more than a quart.

Useful equivalents:

1 liter = 1000 milliliters (mL)

Mass To measure the mass, or the amount of matter in an object, the unit of measure is the gram (g). A paper clip has a mass equal to about one gram.

Useful equivalents:

1000 grams = 1 kilogram (kg)

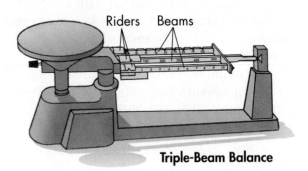

Triple-Beam Balance

Temperature To measure the hotness or coldness of an item, or its temperature, you use the unit degrees. The freezing point of water is 0°C (Celsius). The boiling point of water is 100°C.

Metric-English Equivalents

2.54 centimeters (cm) = 1 inch (in.)
1 meter (m) = 39.37 inches (in.)
1 kilometer (km) = 0.62 miles (mi)
1 liter (L) = 1.06 quarts (qt)
236 milliliters (mL) = 1 cup (c)
1 kilogram (kg) = 2.2 pounds (lb)
28.3 grams (g) = 1 ounce (oz)
$°C = 5/9 \times (°F - 32)$

Safety Symbols

These symbols appear in laboratory activities to alert you to possible dangers and to remind you to work carefully.

Safety Goggles Always wear safety goggles to protect your eyes during any activity involving chemicals, flames or heating, or the possibility of flying objects, particles, or substances.

Lab Apron Wear a laboratory apron to protect your skin and clothing from injury.

Plastic Gloves Wear disposable plastic gloves to protect yourself from contact with chemicals or organisms that could be harmful. Keep your hands away from your face, and dispose of the gloves according to your teacher's instructions at the end of the activity.

Breakage Handle breakable materials such as thermometers and glassware with care. Do not touch broken glass.

Heat-Resistant Gloves Use an oven mitt or other hand protection when handling hot materials. Hot plates, hot water, and glassware can cause burns. Never touch hot objects with your bare hands.

Heating Use a clamp or tongs to hold hot objects. Do not touch hot objects with your bare hands.

Sharp Object Scissors, scalpels, pins, and knives are sharp. They can cut or puncture your skin. Always direct sharp edges and points away from yourself and others. Use sharp instruments only as directed.

Electric Shock Avoid the possibility of electric shock. Never use electrical equipment around water or when the equipment or your hands are wet. Be sure cords are untangled and cannot trip anyone. Disconnect equipment when it is not in use.

Corrosive Chemical This symbol indicates the presence of an acid or other corrosive chemical. Avoid getting the chemical on your skin or clothing, or in your eyes. Do not inhale the vapors. Wash your hands when you are finished with the activity.

Poison Do not let any poisonous chemical get on your skin, and do not inhale its vapor. Wash your hands when you are finished with the activity.

Flames Tie back loose hair and clothing, and put on safety goggles before working with fire. Follow instructions from your teacher about lighting and extinguishing flames.

No Flames Flammable materials may be present. Make sure there are no flames, sparks, or exposed sources of heat present.

Fumes Poisonous or unpleasant vapors may be produced. Work in a ventilated area or, if available, in a fume hood. Avoid inhaling a vapor directly. Test an odor only when directed to do so by your teacher, using a wafting motion to direct the vapor toward your nose.

Physical Safety This activity involves physical movement. Use caution to avoid injuring yourself or others. Follow instructions from your teacher. Alert your teacher if there is any reason that you should not participate in the activity.

Animal Safety Treat live animals with care to avoid injuring the animals or yourself. Working with animal parts or preserved animals may also require caution. Wash your hands when you are finished with the activity.

Plant Safety Handle plants only as your teacher directs. If you are allergic to any plants used in an activity, tell your teacher before the activity begins. Avoid touching poisonous plants and plants with thorns.

Disposal Chemicals and other materials used in the activity must be disposed of safely. Follow the instructions from your teacher.

Hand Washing Wash your hands thoroughly when finished with the activity. Use soap and warm water. Lather both sides of your hands and between your fingers. Rinse well.

General Safety Awareness You may see this symbol when none of the symbols described earlier applies. In this case, follow the specific instructions provided. You may also see this symbol when you are asked to design your own experiment. Do not start your experiment until your teacher has approved your plan.

Science Safety Rules

Working in the laboratory can be an exciting experience, but it can also be dangerous if proper safety rules are not followed at all times. To prepare yourself for a safe year in the laboratory, read the following safety rules. Make sure that you understand each rule. Ask your teacher to explain any rules you don't understand.

Dress Code

1. Many materials in the laboratory can cause eye injury. To protect yourself from possible injury, wear safety goggles whenever you are working with chemicals, burners, or any substance that might get into your eyes. Avoid wearing contact lenses in the laboratory. Tell your teacher if you need to wear contact lenses to see clearly, and ask if there are any safety precautions you should observe.

2. Wear a laboratory apron or coat whenever you are working with chemicals or heated substances.

3. Tie back long hair to keep it away from any chemicals, burners, candles, or other laboratory equipment.

4. Before working in the laboratory, remove or tie back any article of clothing or jewelry that can hang down and touch chemicals and flames.

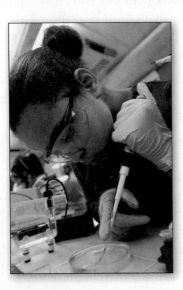

General Safety Rules and First Aid

5. Read all directions for an experiment several times. Follow the directions exactly as they are written. If you are in doubt about any part of the experiment, ask your teacher for assistance.

6. Never perform investigations your teacher has not authorized. Do not use any equipment unless your teacher is in the lab.

7. Never handle equipment unless you have specific permission.

8. Take care not to spill any material in the laboratory. If spills occur, ask your teacher immediately about the proper cleanup procedure. Never pour chemicals or other substances into the sink or trash container.

9. Never eat or drink in, or bring food into, the laboratory.

10. Immediately report all accidents, no matter how minor, to your teacher.

11. Learn what to do in case of specific accidents, such as getting acid in your eyes or on your skin. (Rinse acids off your body with lots of water.)

12. Be aware of the location of the first-aid kit. Your teacher should administer any required first aid due to injury. Your teacher may send you to the school nurse or call a physician.

13. Know where and how to report an accident or fire. Find out the location of the fire extinguisher, fire alarm, and phone. Report any fires to your teacher at once.

Heating and Fire Safety

14. Never use a heat source such as a candle or burner without wearing safety goggles.

15. Never heat a chemical you are not instructed to heat. A chemical that is harmless when cool can be dangerous when heated.

16. Maintain a clean work area and keep all materials away from flames. Be sure that there are no open containers of flammable liquids in the laboratory when flames are being used.

17. Never reach across a flame.

18. Make sure you know how to light a Bunsen burner. (Your teacher will demonstrate the proper procedure for lighting a burner.) If the flame leaps out of a burner toward you, turn the gas off immediately. Do not touch the burner. It may be hot. Never leave a lighted burner unattended!

19. When you are heating a test tube or bottle, point the opening away from yourself and others. Chemicals can splash or boil out of a heated test tube.

20. Never heat a closed container. The expanding hot air, vapors, or other gases inside may blow the container apart, causing it to injure you or others.

21. Never pick up a container that has been heated without first holding the back of your hand near it. If you can feel the heat on the back of your hand, the container may be too hot to handle. Use a clamp or tongs when handling hot containers or wear heat-resistant gloves if appropriate.

Using Chemicals Safely

22. Never mix chemicals for "the fun of it." You might produce a dangerous, possibly explosive substance.

23. Many chemicals are poisonous. Never touch, taste, or smell a chemical that you do not know for certain is harmless. If you are instructed to smell fumes in an experiment, gently wave your hand over the opening of the container and direct the fumes toward your nose. Do not inhale the fumes directly from the container.

24. Use only those chemicals needed in the investigation. Keep all container lids closed when a chemical is not being used. Notify your teacher whenever chemicals are spilled.

25. Dispose of all chemicals as instructed by your teacher. To avoid contamination, never return chemicals to their original containers.

26. Be extra careful when working with acids or bases. Pour such chemicals from one container to another over the sink, not over your work area.

27. When diluting an acid, pour the acid into water. Never pour water into the acid.

28. If any acids or bases get on your skin or clothing, rinse them with water. Immediately notify your teacher of any acid or base spill.

Using Glassware Safely

29. Never heat glassware that is not thoroughly dry. Use a wire screen to protect glassware from any flame.

30. Keep in mind that hot glassware will not appear hot. Never pick up glassware without first checking to see if it is hot.

31. Never use broken or chipped glassware. If glassware breaks, notify your teacher and dispose of the glassware in the proper trash container.

32. Never eat or drink from laboratory glassware. Thoroughly clean glassware before putting it away.

Using Sharp Instruments

33. Handle scalpels or razor blades with extreme care. Never cut material toward you; cut away from you.

34. Notify your teacher immediately if you cut yourself when in the laboratory.

Working With Live Organisms

35. No experiments that will cause pain, discomfort, or harm to animals should be done in the classroom or at home.

36. Your teacher will instruct you how to handle each species that is brought into the classroom. Animals should be handled only if necessary. Special handling is required if an animal is excited or frightened, pregnant, feeding, or with its young.

37. Clean your hands thoroughly after handling any organisms or materials, including animals or cages containing animals.

End-of-Experiment Rules

38. When an experiment is completed, clean up your work area and return all equipment to its proper place.

39. Wash your hands with soap and warm water before and after every experiment.

40. Turn off all burners before leaving the laboratory. Check that the gas line leading to the burner is off as well.

Use of the Microscope

The microscope used in most biology classes, the compound microscope, contains a combination of lenses. The eyepiece lens is located in the top portion of the microscope. This lens usually has a magnification of 10×. Other lenses, called objective lenses, are at the bottom of the body tube on the revolving nosepiece. By rotating the nosepiece, you can select the objective through which you will view your specimen.

The shortest objective is a low-power magnifier, usually 10×. The longer ones are of high power, usually up to 40× or 43×. The magnification is marked on the objective. To determine the total magnification, multiply the magnifying power of the eyepiece by the magnifying power of the objective. For example, with a 10× eyepiece and a 40× objective, the total magnification is 10 × 40 = 400×.

Learning the name, function, and location of each of the microscope's parts is necessary for proper use. Use the following procedures when working with the microscope.

1. Carry the microscope by placing one hand beneath the base and grasping the arm of the microscope with the other hand.

2. Gently place the microscope on the lab table with the arm facing you. The microscope's base should be resting evenly on the table, approximately 10 cm from the table's edge.

3. Raise the body tube by turning the coarse adjustment knob until the objective lens is about 2 cm above the opening of the stage.

4. Rotate the nosepiece so that the low-power objective (10×) is directly in line with the body tube. A click indicates that the lens is in line with the opening of the stage.

5. Look through the eyepiece and switch on the lamp or adjust the mirror so that a circle of light can be seen. This is the field of view. Moving the lever of the diaphragm permits a greater or smaller amount of light to come through the opening of the stage.

6. Place a prepared slide on the stage so that the specimen is over the center of the opening. Use the stage clips to hold the slide in place.

7. Look at the microscope from the side. Carefully turn the coarse adjustment knob to lower the body tube until the low-power objective almost touches the slide or until the body tube can no longer be moved. Do not allow the objective to touch the slide.

8. Look through the eyepiece and observe the specimen. If the field of view is out of focus, use the coarse adjustment knob to raise the body tube while looking through the eyepiece. **CAUTION:** *To prevent damage to the slide and the objective, do not lower the body tube using the coarse adjustment while looking through the eyepiece.* Focus the image as best you can with the coarse adjustment knob. Then, use the fine adjustment knob to focus the image more sharply. Keep both eyes open when viewing a specimen. This helps prevent eyestrain.

1. **Eyepiece:** Contains a magnifying lens.
2. **Arm:** Supports the body tube.
3. **Low-power objective:** Provides a magnification of 10x.
4. **Stage:** Supports the slide being observed.
5. **Opening of the stage:** Permits light to pass up to the eyepiece.
6. **Fine adjustment knob:** Moves the body tube slightly to adjust the image.
7. **Coarse adjustment knob:** Moves the body tube to focus the image.
8. **Base:** Supports the microscope.
9. **Illuminator:** Produces light or reflects light up toward the eyepiece.
10. **Diaphragm:** Regulates the amount of light passing up toward the eyepiece.
11. **Stageclips:** Hold the slide in place.
12. **High-power objective:** Provides a magnification of 40x.
13. **Nosepiece:** Holds the objectives and can be rotated to change the magnification.
14. **Body tube:** Maintains the proper distance between the eyepiece and the objectives.

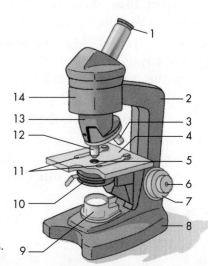

9. Adjust the lever of the diaphragm to allow the right amount of light to enter.

10. To change the magnification, rotate the nosepiece until the desired objective is in line with the body tube and clicks into place.

11. Look through the eyepiece and use the fine adjustment knob to bring the image into focus.

12. After every use, remove the slide. Return the low-power objective into place in line with the body tube. Clean the stage of the microscope and the lenses with lens paper. Do not use other types of paper to clean the lenses; they may scratch the lenses.

Preparing a Wet-Mount Slide

1. Obtain a clean microscope slide and a coverslip. A coverslip is very thin, permitting the objective lens to be lowered very close to the specimen.

2. Place the specimen in the middle of the microscope slide. The specimen must be thin enough for light to pass through it.

3. Using a dropper pipette, place a drop of water on the specimen.

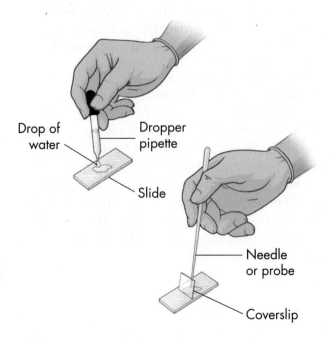

Drop of water — Dropper pipette

Slide

Needle or probe

Coverslip

4. Lower one edge of the coverslip so that it touches the side of the drop of water at about a 45° angle. The water will spread evenly along the edge of the coverslip. Using a dissecting needle or probe, slowly lower the coverslip over the specimen and water as shown in the drawing. Try not to trap any air bubbles under the coverslip. If air bubbles are present, gently tap the surface of the coverslip over the air bubble with a pencil eraser.

5. Remove any excess water around the edge of the coverslip with a paper towel. If the specimen begins to dry out, add a drop of water at the edge of the coverslip.

Staining Techniques

1. Obtain a clean microscope slide and coverslip.

2. Place the specimen in the middle of the microscope slide.

3. Using a dropper pipette, place a drop of water on the specimen. Place the coverslip so that its edge touches the drop of water at a 45° angle. After the water spreads along the edge of the coverslip, use a dissecting needle or probe to lower the coverslip over the specimen.

4. Add a drop of stain at the edge of the coverslip. Using forceps, touch a small piece of lens paper or paper towel to the opposite edge of the coverslip, as shown in the drawing. The paper causes the stain to be drawn under the coverslip and to stain the cells in the specimen.

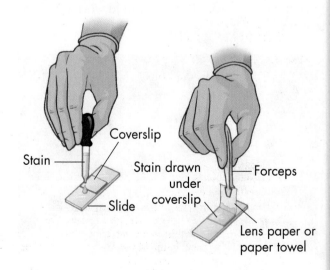

Stain — Coverslip

Stain drawn under coverslip — Forceps

Slide

Lens paper or paper towel

Engineers are people who use scientific and technological knowledge to solve practical problems. To design new products, engineers usually follow the process described here, even though they may not follow these steps in the exact order.

Identify a Need

Before engineers begin designing a new product, they must first identify the need they are trying to meet. For example, suppose you are a member of a design team in a company that makes toys. Your team has identified a need: a toy boat that is inexpensive and easy to assemble.

Research the Problem

Engineers often begin by gathering information that will help them with their new design. This research may include finding articles in books, in magazines, or on the Internet. It may also include talking to other engineers who have solved similar problems. Engineers also often perform experiments related to the product they want to design.

For your toy boat, you could look at toys that are similar to the one you want to design. You might do research on the Internet. You could also test some materials to see whether they would work well in a toy boat.

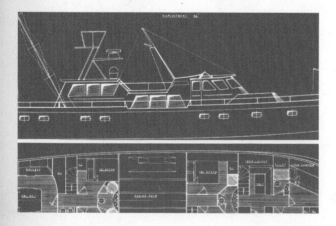

Design a Solution

Research gives engineers information that helps them design a product. When engineers design new products, they usually work in teams.

Generating Ideas Often, design teams hold brainstorming meetings in which any team member can contribute ideas. Brainstorming is a creative process in which one team member's suggestions can spark ideas in other group members. Brainstorming can lead to new approaches to solving a design problem.

Evaluating Constraints During brainstorming, a design team will often come up with several possible designs. The team must then evaluate each one.

As part of their evaluation, engineers consider constraints. Constraints are factors that limit or restrict a product design. Physical characteristics, such as the properties of materials used to make your toy boat, are constraints. Cost and time are also constraints. If the materials in a design cost a lot, or if the design takes a long time to make, it may be impractical.

Making Trade-offs Design teams usually need to make trade-offs. A trade-off is the acceptance of the benefits of one design aspect at the cost of another. In designing your toy boat, you will have to make trade-offs. For example, suppose one material is sturdy but not fully waterproof. Another material is more waterproof, but breakable. You may decide to give up the benefit of sturdiness in order to obtain the benefit of waterproofing.

Build and Evaluate a Prototype

Once the team has chosen a design plan, the engineers build a prototype of the product. A prototype is a working model used to test a design. Engineers evaluate the prototype to see whether it works well, is easy to operate, is safe to use, and holds up to repeated use.

Think of your toy boat. What would the prototype be like? Of what materials would it be made? How would you test it?

Troubleshoot and Redesign

Few prototypes work perfectly, which is why they need to be tested. Once a design team has tested a prototype, the members analyze the results and identify any problems. The team then tries to troubleshoot, or fix the weaknesses in the design. For example, if your toy boat leaks or wobbles, the boat should be redesigned to eliminate those problems.

Communicate the Solution

A team needs to communicate the final design to the people who will manufacture the product. To do this, teams may use sketches, detailed drawings, computer simulations, and written descriptions.

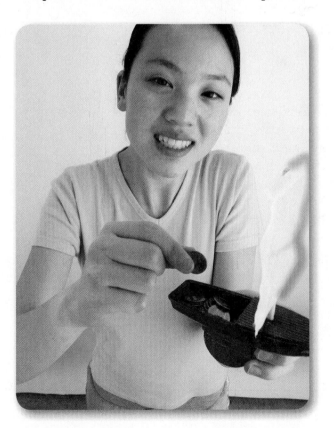

Activity

You can use the technology design process to design and build a toy boat.

Research and Investigate

1. Visit the library or go online to research toy boats.

2. Investigate how a toy boat can be powered, including wind, rubber bands, or baking soda and vinegar.

3. Brainstorm materials, shapes, and steering methods for your boat.

Design and Build

4. Based on your research, design a toy boat that
   - is made of readily available materials
   - is no larger than 15 cm long and 10 cm wide
   - includes a power system, a rudder, and a cargo area
   - travels 2 meters in a straight line while carrying a load of 20 pennies

5. Sketch your design and write a step-by-step plan for building your boat. After your teacher approves your plan, build your boat.

Evaluate and Redesign

6. Test your boat, evaluate the results, and identify any technological design problems in your boat.

7. Based on your evaluation, redesign your toy boat so it performs better.

8. As a class, compare the test results for each boat. Choose the model that best meets the needs of the toy company.

Scientists use math to organize, analyze, and present data. This appendix will help you review some basic math skills.

Formulas and Equations

Formulas and equations are used in many areas of science. Both formulas and equations show the relationships between quantities. Any numerical sentence that contains at least one variable and at least one mathematical operator is called an equation. A formula is a type of equation that states the relationship between unknown quantities represented by variables.

For example, Speed = Distance ÷ Time is a formula, because no matter what values are inserted, speed is always equal to distance divided by time. The relationship between the variables does not change.

Example
Follow these steps to convert a temperature measurement of 50°F to Celsius.

1. Determine the formula that shows the relationship between these quantities.
   °F = (9/5 × °C) + 32°F

2. Insert values you know into the formula.
   50°F = (9/5 × °C) + 32°F

3. Solve the resulting equation.
   50°F − 32°F = (9/5 × °C)
   18°F = 9/5 × °C
   18°F × 5/9 = 10°C

Applying Formulas and Equations

There are many applications of formulas in science. The example described below uses a formula to calculate density.

Example
Follow these steps to calculate the density of an object that has a mass of 45 g and a volume of 30 cm^3.

1. Determine the formula that shows the relationship between these quantities.
   Density = Mass/Volume

2. Insert values you know into the formula.
   Density = 45 g/30 cm^3

3. Solve the resulting equation.
   Density = 1.5 g/cm^3

Mean, Median, and Mode

The mean is the average, or the sum of the data divided by the number of data items. The middle number in a set of ordered data is called the median. The mode is the number that appears most often in a set of data.

Example
A scientist counted the number of distinct songs sung by seven different male birds and collected the data shown below.

Male Bird Songs							
Bird	A	B	C	D	E	F	G
Number of Songs	36	29	40	35	28	36	27

To determine the mean number of songs, find the sum of the songs sung by all the male birds and divide by the number of male birds.

$$\text{Mean} = 231/7 = 33 \text{ songs}$$

To find the median number of songs, arrange the data items in numerical order and identify the number in the middle.

$$27 \quad 28 \quad 29 \quad 35 \quad 36 \quad 36 \quad 40$$

The number in the middle is 35, so the median number of songs is 35.

The mode is the value that appears most frequently. In the data, 36 appears twice, while every other item appears only once. Therefore, 36 is the mode.

Estimation

An estimate is a reasonable approximation of a numerical value. Estimates are made based on careful assumptions and known information.

Scientists use estimates in biology for two primary reasons: when an exact count or calculation cannot be made or is impractical to make, and to make reasonable approximations of answers that will be calculated or measured later.

One method for estimation used in biology is sampling. In sampling, the number of organisms in a small area (a sample) is multiplied to estimate the number of organisms in a larger area.

Example
Follow these steps to use sampling to estimate the total number of birds in the photo.

1. Count the birds in the highlighted area of the photo. In the highlighted area of the photo, there are 36 birds.

2. Determine the portion of the entire photo represented by the highlighted area. In this case, the highlighted area is 1/6 of the total area.

3. Calculate your estimate by multiplying the number of birds in the sample area by 6 (because the entire photo is 6 times as large as the sample area). A reasonable estimate of the total number of birds is 36 × 6, or 216 birds.

HINT: Estimates and calculated answers are rarely exactly the same. However, a large difference between an estimated answer and a calculated answer indicates there may be a problem with the estimate or calculation.

Using Measurements in Calculations

Density is an example of a value that is calculated using two measurements. Density represents the amount of mass in a particular volume of a substance. The units used for density are grams per milliliter (g/mL) or grams per cubic centimeter (g/cm³). Density is calculated by dividing an object's mass by its volume.

Example
Follow these steps to calculate the density of an object.

1. Measure and record the mass of an object in grams.

2. Measure and record the volume of an object in mL or cm³.

3. Use the following formula to calculate density:

$$\text{Density} = \text{Mass/Volume}$$

Effects of Measurement Errors

Density is calculated using two measured values. An error in the measurement of either mass or volume will result in the calculation of an incorrect density.

Example
A student measured the mass of an object as 2.5 g and its volume as 2.0 cm³. The actual mass of the object is 3.5 g; the actual volume is 2.0 cm³. What is the effect of the measurement error on the calculation of density?

Follow these steps to determine the effect of a measurement error on calculation.

1. Determine the density using the student's measurements.
   Density = Mass/Volume
   Density = 2.5 g/2.0 cm³
   Density = 1.25 g/cm³

2. Determine the density using the actual values.
   Density = Mass/Volume
   Density = 3.5 g/2.0 cm³
   Density = 1.75 g/cm³

3. Compare the calculated and the actual values.

In this case, a measurement of mass that was less than the actual value resulted in a calculated value for the density that was less than the actual density.

Accuracy

The accuracy of a measurement is its closeness to the actual value. Measurements that are accurate are close to the actual value.

Both clocks on this page show a time of 3:00. Suppose, though, that these clocks had not been changed to reflect daylight savings time. The time shown on the clocks would be inaccurate. On the other hand, if the actual time is 3:00, these clocks would be accurate.

Precision

Precision describes the exactness of a measurement. The clocks shown on this page differ in precision. The analog clock measures time to the nearest minute. The digital clock measures time to the nearest second. Time is measured more precisely by the digital clock than by the analog clock.

Comparing Accuracy and Precision

There is a difference between accuracy and precision. Measurements can be accurate (close to the actual value) but not precise. Measurements can also be precise but not accurate. When making scientific measurements, both accuracy and precision are important. Accurate and precise measurements result from the careful use of high-quality measuring tools.

Significant Figures

Significant figures are all of the digits that are known in a measurement, plus one additional digit, which is an estimate. In the figure below, the length of a turtle's shell is being measured using a centimeter ruler. The ruler has unnumbered divisions representing millimeters. In this case, two numbers can be determined exactly: the number of centimeters and the number of millimeters. One additional digit can be estimated. So, the measurement of this turtle's shell can be recorded with three significant figures as 8.80 centimeters.

Rules for Significant Digits
Follow these rules to determine the number of significant figures in a number.

All nonzero numbers are significant.
    Example: 3217 has four significant digits.

Zeros are significant if
• They are between nonzero digits. Example: 509
• They follow a decimal point and a nonzero digit. Example: 7.00

Zeros are not significant if
• They follow nonzero digits in a number without a decimal. Example: 7000
• They precede nonzero digits in a number with a decimal. Example: 0.0098

Calculating With Significant Figures

When measurements are added or subtracted, the precision of the result is determined by the precision of the least-precise measurement. The result may need to be rounded so the number of digits after the decimal is the same as the least-precise measurement.

Example
Follow these steps to determine the correct number of significant figures when adding 4.51 g, 3.27 g, and 6.0 g.

1. Determine which measurement is reported with the least degree of precision. In this case, the least-precise measurement, 6.0 g, has one digit after the decimal point.

2. The result must be rounded so that it also has one digit after the decimal point. After rounding, the result of this calculation is 13.8 g.

When measurements are multiplied or divided, the answer must have the same number of significant figures as the measurement with the fewest number of significant figures.

Example
Follow these steps to determine the correct number of significant figures when multiplying 120 m by 6.32 m.

1. Determine the number of significant figures in each of the measurements. In this case, the measurement 120 m has two significant figures; the measurement 6.32 m has three significant figures.

2. The result must be rounded to have only two significant figures. After rounding, the result of this calculation is 760 m^2.

Scientific Notation

In science, measurements are often very large or very small. Using scientific notation makes these large and small numbers easier to work with.

Using scientific notation requires an understanding of exponents and bases. When a number is expressed as a base and an exponent, the base is the number that is used as a factor. The exponent tells how many times the base is multiplied by itself. For example, the number 25 can be expressed as a base and an exponent in the following way:

$$25 = 5 \times 5 = 5^2$$

In the example above, 5 is the base and 2 is the exponent. In scientific notation, the base is always the number 10. The exponent tells how many times the number 10 is multiplied by itself.

A number written in scientific notation is expressed as the product of two factors, a number between 1 and 10 and the number 10 with an exponent. For example, the number 51,000 can be expressed in scientific notation. To find the first factor, move the decimal to obtain a number between 1 and 10. In this case, the number is 5.1. The exponent can be determined by counting the number of places the decimal point was moved. The decimal point was moved four places to the left. So, 51,000 expressed in scientific notation is 5.1×10^4.

Numbers that are less than one can also be expressed in scientific notation. In the case of numbers less than one, the decimal point must be moved to the right to obtain a number between 1 and 10. For example, in the number 0.000098, the decimal point must move five places to the right to obtain the number 9.8. When the decimal point is moved to the right, the exponent is negative. So, 0.000098 expressed in scientific notation is 9.8×10^{-5}.

Calculating With Scientific Notation

Numbers expressed in scientific notation can be used in calculations. When adding or subtracting numbers expressed in scientific notation, the first factors must be rewritten so the exponents are the same.

Example
Follow these steps to add $(4.30 \times 10^4) + (2.1 \times 10^3)$.

1. Move the decimal point in one of the expressions so the exponents are the same.
   $(43.0 \times 10^3) + (2.1 \times 10^3)$

2. Add the first factors, keeping the value of the exponents the same.
   $(43.0 \times 10^3) + (2.1 \times 10^3) = 45.1 \times 10^3$

3. Move the decimal point so the first factor is expressed as the product of a number between and 1 and 10 and an exponent with base 10.
   $45.1 \times 10^3 = 4.51 \times 10^4$

When numbers expressed in scientific notation are multiplied, the exponents are added. When numbers expressed in scientific notation are divided, the exponents are subtracted.

Example
Use the following steps to determine the area of a rectangular field that has a length of 1.5×10^3 meters and a width of 3.2×10^2 meters.

1. Write down the expressions to be multiplied.
   $(1.5 \times 10^3 \text{ m})(3.2 \times 10^2 \text{ m})$

2. Multiply the first factors, add the exponents, and multiply any units.
   $= (1.5 \times 3.2)(10^{3+2}) \text{ m} \times \text{m}$
   $= 4.8 \times 10^5 \text{ m}^2$

Dimensional Analysis

Scientific problems and calculations often involve unit conversions, or changes from one unit to another. Dimensional analysis is a method of unit conversion.

Suppose you were counting a pile of pennies. If there were 197 pennies in the pile, how many dollars would the pennies be worth? To determine the answer, you need to know the conversion factor between pennies and dollars. A conversion factor simply shows how two units are related. In this case, the conversion factor is 100 pennies = 1 dollar. Determining that 197 pennies is equal to $1.97 is an example of a unit conversion.

In dimensional analysis, the conversion factor is usually expressed as a fraction. Remember that the two values in any conversion factor are equal to one another. So, the two values form a fraction with the value of 1. Look at the example below to see how dimensional analysis can be applied to an everyday problem.

Example
A student walked 1.5 kilometers as part of a school fitness program. How many meters did the student walk?

1. 1.5 km = _?_ m

2. 1 km = 1000 m

3. 1000 m/1 km

4. 1.5 km × 1000 m/1 km = 1500 m (cross out "km" in two places); 1.5 km = 1500 m

Applying Dimensional Analysis

There are many applications of dimensional analysis in science. The example below demonstrates the use of dimensional analysis to convert units.

Example
The average teenage girl needs about 2200 kilocalories of energy from food each day. How many calories is this equivalent to?

Use the following steps to convert kilocalories to calories.

1. Determine the conversion factor that relates the two units.
   1 kilocalorie = 1000 calories

2. Write the conversion factor in the form of a fraction.
   1000 calories/1 kilocalorie

3. Multiply the measurement by the conversion factor.
   2200 kilocalories × 1000 calories/1 kilocalorie = 2,200,000 calories

Periodic Table of the Elements

Representative Elements
- Alkali Metals
- Alkaline Earth Metals
- Other Metals
- Metalloids
- Nonmetals
- Noble Gases

Transition Elements
- Transition Metals
- Inner transition metals

C	Solid	
Br	Liquid	
He	Gas	
Tc	Not found in nature	

Key:
- Atomic number
- Electrons in each energy level
- Element symbol
- Element name
- Average atomic mass

14
Si
2 8 4
Silicon
28.086
*

*The atomic masses in parentheses are the mass numbers of the longest-lived isotope of elements for which a standard atomic mass cannot be defined.

*Name not officially assigned.

Elements 104–114 are the transactinide elements.

Group 1 / 1A
- 1 H Hydrogen 1.0079
- 3 Li Lithium 6.941
- 11 Na Sodium 22.990
- 19 K Potassium 39.098
- 37 Rb Rubidium 85.468
- 55 Cs Cesium 132.91
- 87 Fr Francium (223)

Group 2 / 2A
- 4 Be Beryllium 9.0122
- 12 Mg Magnesium 24.305
- 20 Ca Calcium 40.08
- 38 Sr Strontium 87.62
- 56 Ba Barium 137.33
- 88 Ra Radium (226)

Group 3 / 3B
- 21 Sc Scandium 44.956
- 39 Y Yttrium 88.906
- 71 Lu Lutetium 174.97
- 103 Lr Lawrencium (262)

Group 4 / 4B
- 22 Ti Titanium 47.90
- 40 Zr Zirconium 91.22
- 72 Hf Hafnium 178.49
- 104 Rf Rutherfordium (261)

Group 5 / 5B
- 23 V Vanadium 50.941
- 41 Nb Niobium 92.906
- 73 Ta Tantalum 180.95
- 105 Db Dubnium (262)

Group 6 / 6B
- 24 Cr Chromium 51.996
- 42 Mo Molybdenum 95.94
- 74 W Tungsten 183.85
- 106 Sg Seaborgium (263)

Group 7 / 7B
- 25 Mn Manganese 54.938
- 43 Tc Technetium (98)
- 75 Re Rhenium 186.21
- 107 Bh Bohrium (264)

Group 8 / 8B
- 26 Fe Iron 55.847
- 44 Ru Ruthenium 101.07
- 76 Os Osmium 190.2
- 108 Hs Hassium (265)

Group 9 / 8B
- 27 Co Cobalt 58.933
- 45 Rh Rhodium 102.91
- 77 Ir Iridium 192.22
- 109 Mt Meitnerium (268)

Group 10 / 8B
- 28 Ni Nickel 58.71
- 46 Pd Palladium 106.4
- 78 Pt Platinum 195.09
- 110 Ds Darmstadtium (269)

Group 11 / 1B
- 29 Cu Copper 63.546
- 47 Ag Silver 107.87
- 79 Au Gold 196.97
- 111 Rg Roentgenium (272)

Group 12 / 2B
- 30 Zn Zinc 65.38
- 48 Cd Cadmium 112.41
- 80 Hg Mercury 200.59
- 112 Uub Ununbium (277)

Group 13 / 3A
- 5 B Boron 10.81
- 13 Al Aluminum 26.982
- 31 Ga Gallium 69.72
- 49 In Indium 114.82
- 81 Tl Thallium 204.37

Group 14 / 4A
- 6 C Carbon 12.011
- 14 Si Silicon 28.086
- 32 Ge Germanium 72.59
- 50 Sn Tin 118.69
- 82 Pb Lead 207.2
- 114 Uuq Ununquadium

Group 15 / 5A
- 7 N Nitrogen 14.007
- 15 P Phosphorus 30.974
- 33 As Arsenic 74.922
- 51 Sb Antimony 121.75
- 83 Bi Bismuth 208.98

Group 16 / 6A
- 8 O Oxygen 15.999
- 16 S Sulfur 32.06
- 34 Se Selenium 78.96
- 52 Te Tellurium 127.60
- 84 Po Polonium (209)

Group 17 / 7A
- 9 F Fluorine 18.998
- 17 Cl Chlorine 35.453
- 35 Br Bromine 79.904
- 53 I Iodine 126.90
- 85 At Astatine (210)

Group 18 / 8A
- 2 He Helium 4.0026
- 10 Ne Neon 20.179
- 18 Ar Argon 39.948
- 36 Kr Krypton 83.80
- 54 Xe Xenon 131.30
- 86 Rn Radon (222)

Lanthanide Series
- 57 La Lanthanum 138.91
- 58 Ce Cerium 140.12
- 59 Pr Praseodymium 140.91
- 60 Nd Neodymium 144.24
- 61 Pm Promethium (145)
- 62 Sm Samarium 150.4
- 63 Eu Europium 151.96
- 64 Gd Gadolinium 157.25
- 65 Tb Terbium 158.93
- 66 Dy Dysprosium 162.50
- 67 Ho Holmium 164.93
- 68 Er Erbium 167.26
- 69 Tm Thulium 168.93
- 70 Yb Ytterbium 173.04

Actinide Series
- 89 Ac Actinium (227)
- 90 Th Thorium 232.04
- 91 Pa Protactinium 231.04
- 92 U Uranium 238.03
- 93 Np Neptunium (237)
- 94 Pu Plutonium (244)
- 95 Am Americium (243)
- 96 Cm Curium (247)
- 97 Bk Berkelium (247)
- 98 Cf Californium (251)
- 99 Es Einsteinium (252)
- 100 Fm Fermium (257)
- 101 Md Mendelevium (258)
- 102 No Nobelium (259)

Glossary

A

abiotic factor: physical, or nonliving, factor that shapes an ecosystem (66)
factor abiótico: factor físico, o inanimado, que da forma a un ecosistema

acid: compound that forms hydrogen ions (H⁺) in solution; a solution with a pH of less than 7 (44)
ácido: compuesto que en una solución produce iones hidrógeno (H⁺); una solución con un pH inferior a 7

acid rain: rain containing nitric and sulfuric acids (164)
lluvia ácida: lluvia que contiene ácido nítrico y ácido sulfúrico

activation energy: energy that is needed to get a reaction started (51)
energía de activación: energía necesaria para que comience una reacción

adaptation: heritable characteristic that increases an organism's ability to survive and reproduce in an environment (461)
adaptación: característica heredable que aumenta la capacidad de un organismo de sobrevivir y reproducirse en un medio ambiente

adaptive radiation: process by which a single species or a small group of species evolves into several different forms that live in different ways (550)
radiación adaptativa: proceso mediante el cual una sola especie o un grupo pequeño de especies evoluciona y da lugar a diferentes seres que viven de diversas maneras

adenosine triphosphate (ATP): compound used by cells to store and release energy (226)
trifosfato de adenosina (ATP): compuesto utilizado por las células para almacenar y liberar energía

adhesion: force of attraction between different kinds of molecules (41)
adhesión: fuerza de atracción entre diferentes tipos de moléculas

aerobic: process that requires oxygen (252)
aeróbico: proceso que requiere oxígeno

age structure: number of males and females of each age in a population (131)
estructura etaria: número de machos y de hembras de cada edad en una población

allele: one of a number of different forms of a gene (310)
alelo: cada una de las diversas formas de un gen

allele frequency: number of times that an allele occurs in a gene pool compared with the number of alleles in that pool for the same gene (483)
frecuencia alélica: número de veces que aparece un alelo en un caudal genético, comparado con la cantidad de alelos en ese caudal para el mismo gen

amino acid: compound with an amino group on one end and a carboxyl group on the other end (48)
aminoácido: compuesto que contiene un grupo amino en un extremo y un grupo carboxilo en el otro extremo

anaerobic: process that does not require oxygen (252)
anaeróbico: proceso que no requiere oxígeno

analogous structures: body parts that share a common function, but not structure (469)
estructuras análogas: partes del cuerpo que tienen la misma función, mas no la misma estructura

anaphase: phase of mitosis in which the chromosomes separate and move to opposite ends of the cell (283)
anafase: fase de la mitosis en la cual los cromosomas se separan y se desplazan hacia los extremos opuestos de la célula

anticodon: group of three bases on a tRNA molecule that are complementary to the three bases of a codon of mRNA (369)
anticodón: grupo de tres bases en una molécula de ARN de transferencia que son complementarias a las tres bases de un codón de ARN mensajero

aphotic zone: dark layer of the oceans below the photic zone where sunlight does not penetrate (117)
zona afótica: sección oscura de los océanos donde no penetra la luz solar, situada debajo de la zona fótica

apoptosis: process of programmed cell death (288)
apoptosis: proceso de muerte celular programada

aquaculture: raising of aquatic organisms for human consumption (176)
acuicultura: cría de organismos acuáticos para el consumo humano

aquaporin: water channel protein in a cell (210)
acuaporina: proteína que canaliza el agua en una célula

Archaea: domain consisting of unicellular prokaryotes that have cell walls that do not contain peptidoglycan; corresponds to the kingdom Archeabacteria (526)
Arqueas: dominio formado por procariotas unicelulares cuyas paredes celulares no contienen peptidoglicano; corresponden al reino de las Arqueabacterias

artificial selection: selective breeding of plants and animals to promote the occurrence of desirable traits in offspring (458)
selección artificial: cría selectiva de plantas y animales para fomentar la ocurrencia de rasgos deseados en la progenie

asexual reproduction: process of reproduction involving a single parent that results in offspring that are genetically identical to the parent (19, 277)
reproducción asexual: proceso de reproducción que involucra a un único progenitor y da por resultado descendencia genéticamente idéntica a ese progenitor

atom: the basic unit of matter (34)

  átomo: unidad básica de la materia

ATP synthase: cluster of proteins that span the cell membrane and allow hydrogen ions (H^+) to pass through it (237)

  ATP sintasa: complejo de proteínas unidas a la membrana celular que permiten el paso de los iones de hidrógeno (H^+) a través de ella

autosome: chromosome that is not a sex chromosome; also called autosomal chromosome (393)

  autosoma: cromosoma que no es un cromosoma sexual; también llamado cromosoma autosómico

autotroph: organism that is able to capture energy from sunlight or chemicals and use it to produce its own food from inorganic compounds; also called a producer (69, 228)

  autótrofo: organismo capaz de atrapar la energía de la luz solar o de las sustancias químicas y utilizarla para producir su propio alimento a partir de compuestos inorgánicos; también llamado productor

B

background extinction: extinction caused by slow and steady process of natural selection (548)

  extinción de fondo: extinción causada por un proceso lento y continuo de selección natural

Bacteria: domain of unicellular prokaryotes that have cell walls containing peptidoglycan; corresponds to the kingdom eubacteria (525)

  Bacteria: pertenece al dominio de los unicelulares procariota cuyas paredes celulares contienen peptidoglicano; corresponde al reino de las Eubacterias

bacteriophage: kind of virus that infects bacteria (340)

  bacteriófago: clase de virus que infecta a las bacterias

base: compound that produces hydroxide ions (OH^-) in solution; solution with a pH of more than 7 (44)

  base: compuesto que en una solución produce iones hidróxido (OH^-); una solución con un pH superior a 7

base pairing: principle that bonds in DNA can form only between adenine and thymine and between guanine and cytosine (348)

  apareamiento de bases: principio que establece que los enlaces en el ADN sólo pueden formarse entre adenina y timina y entre guanina y citocina

behavioral isolation: form of reproductive isolation in which two populations develop differences in courtship rituals or other behaviors that prevent them from breeding (495)

  aislamiento conductual: forma de aislamiento reproductivo en la cual dos poblaciones desarrollan diferencias en sus rituales de cortejo o en otros comportamientos que evitan que se apareen

benthos: organisms that live attached to or near the bottom of lakes, streams, or oceans (117)

  bentos: organismos que viven adheridos al fondo, o cerca del fondo, de lagos, arroyos u océanos

bias: particular preference or point of view that is personal, rather than scientific (14)

  parcialidad: preferencia especial o punto de vista que es personal en lugar de ser científico

binomial nomenclature: classification system in which each species is assigned a two-part scientific name (512)

  nomenclatura binaria: sistema de clasificación en el cual a cada especie se le asigna un nombre científico que consta de dos partes

biodiversity: total of the variety of organisms in the biosphere; also called biological diversity (166)

  biodiversidad: totalidad de los distintos organismos que se hallan en la biósfera; también denominada diversidad biológica

biogeochemical cycle: process in which elements, chemical compounds, and other forms of matter are passed from one organism to another and from one part of the biosphere to another (79)

  ciclo biogeoquímico: proceso en el cual los elementos, los compuestos químicos y otras formas de materia pasan de un organismo a otro y de una parte de la biósfera a otra

biogeography: study of past and present distribution of organisms (465)

  biogeografía: estudio de la distribución pasada y presente de los organismos

bioinformatics: application of mathematics and computer science to store, retrieve, and analyze biological data (407)

  bioinformática: aplicación de las matemáticas y de la informática para almacenar, recuperar y analizar información biológica

biological magnification: increasing concentration of a harmful substance in organisms at higher trophic levels in a food chain or food web (161)

  bioacumulación: concentración creciente de sustancias perjudiciales en los organismos de los niveles tróficos más elevados de una cadena o red alimentaria

biology: scientific study of life (17)

  biología: estudio científico de la vida

biomass: total amount of living tissue within a given trophic level (78)

  biomasa: cantidad total de tejido vivo dentro de un nivel trófico dado

biome: a group of ecosystems that share similar climates and typical organisms (65)

    bioma: un grupo de ecosistemas que comparten climas similares y organismos típicos

biosphere: part of Earth in which life exists including land, water, and air or atmosphere (21, 64)

    biósfera: parte de la Tierra en la cual existe vida, y que incluye el suelo, el agua y el aire o atmósfera

biotechnology: process of manipulating organisms, cells, or molecules, to produce specific products (419)

    biotecnología: proceso de manipular organismos, células o moléculas con el fin de obtener productos específicos

biotic factor: any living part of the environment with which an organism might interact (66)

    factor biótico: cualquier parte viva del medio ambiente con la cual un organismo podría interaccionar

blastocyst: stage of early development in mammals that consists of a hollow ball of cells (294)

    blastocisto: etapa temprana del desarrollo de los mamíferos que consiste en una bola hueca formada por una capa de células

bottleneck effect: a change in allele frequency following a dramatic reduction in the size of a population (490)

    efecto cuello de botella: un cambio en la frecuencia alélica que resulta cuando el tamaño de una población reduce drásticamente

buffer: compound that prevents sharp, sudden changes in pH (44)

    solución amortiguadora: compuesto que evita cambios bruscos y repentinos en el pH

C

calorie: amount of energy needed to raise the temperature of 1 gram of water by 1 degree Celsius (250)

    caloría: cantidad de energía necesaria para elevar la temperatura de 1 gramo de agua en 1 grado Celsius

Calvin cycle: light-independent reactions of photosynthesis in which energy from ATP and NADPH is used to build high-energy compounds such as sugar (238)

    ciclo de Calvin: reacciones de la fotosíntesis independientes de la luz en las cuales se utiliza la energía del ATP y del NADPH para elaborar compuestos con alto contenido energético, como el azúcar

cancer: disorder in which some of the body's cells lose the ability to control growth (289)

    cáncer: enfermedad en la cual algunas de las células del cuerpo pierden la capacidad de controlar su crecimiento

canopy: dense covering formed by the leafy tops of tall rain forest trees (112)

    dosel forestal: cubierta densa formada por las copas de los árboles altos del bosque tropical

carbohydrate: compound made up of carbon, hydrogen, and oxygen atoms; type of nutrient that is the major source of energy for the body (46)

    hidrato de carbono: compuesto formado por átomos de carbono, hidrógeno y oxígeno; tipo de nutriente que es la fuente principal de energía para el cuerpo

carnivore: organism that obtains energy by eating animals (71)

    carnívoro: organismo que obtiene energía al comer otros animales

carrying capacity: largest number of individuals of a particular species that a particular environment can support (135)

    capacidad de carga: mayor cantidad de individuos de una especie en particular que un medio ambiente específico puede mantener

catalyst: substance that speeds up the rate of a chemical reaction (52)

    catalizador: sustancia que acelera la velocidad de una reacción química

cell: basic unit of all forms of life (191)

    célula: unidad básica de todas las formas de vida

cell cycle: series of events in which a cell grows, prepares for division, and divides to form two daughter cells (280)

    ciclo celular: serie de sucesos en los cuales una célula crece, se prepara para dividirse y se divide para formar dos células hijas

cell division: process by which a cell divides into two new daughter cells (276)

    división celular: proceso por el cual una célula se divide en dos células hijas nuevas

cell membrane: thin, flexible barrier that surrounds all cells; regulates what enters and leaves the cell (193)

    membrana celular: barrera flexible y delgada que rodea a todas las células; regula lo que entra y sale de la célula

cell theory: fundamental concept of biology that states that all living things are composed of cells; that cells are the basic units of structure and function in living things; and that new cells are produced from existing cells (191)

    teoría celular: concepto fundamental de la Biología que establece que todos los seres vivos están compuestos por células; que las células son las unidades básicas estructurales y funcionales de los seres vivos; y que las células nuevas se producen a partir de células existentes

cell wall: strong, supporting layer around the cell membrane in some cells (203)

    pared celular: capa resistente que sirve de sostén y está situada alrededor de la membrana celular de algunas células

cellular respiration: process that releases energy by breaking down glucose and other food molecules in the presence of oxygen (281)

    respiración celular: proceso que libera energía al descomponer la glucosa y otras moléculas de los alimentos en presencia de oxígeno

Glossary (continued)

centriole: structure in an animal cell that helps to organize cell division (199, 282)

    centríolo: estructura de una célula animal que contribuye a organizar la división celular

centromere: region of a chromosome where the two sister chromatids attach (282)

    centrómero: región de un cromosoma donde se unen las dos cromátidas hermanas

chemical reaction: process that changes, or transforms, one set of chemicals into another set of chemicals (50)

    reacción química: proceso que cambia, o transforma, un grupo de sustancias químicas en otro grupo de sustancias químicas

chemosynthesis: process in which chemical energy is used to produce carbohydrates (70)

    quimiosíntesis: proceso en el cual la energía química se utiliza para producir hidratos de carbono

chlorophyll: principal pigment of plants and other photosynthetic organisms (230)

    clorofila: pigmento fundamental de las plantas y de otros organismos fotosintéticos

chloroplast: organelle found in cells of plants and some other organisms that captures the energy from sunlight and converts it into chemical energy (202)

    cloroplasto: orgánulo de las células de las plantas y de otros organismos que captura la energía de la luz solar y la convierte en energía química

chromatid: one of two identical "sister" parts of a duplicated chromosome (282)

    cromátida: una de las dos partes "hermanas" idénticas de un cromosoma duplicado

chromatin: substance found in eukaryotic chromosomes that consists of DNA tightly coiled around histones (280)

    cromatina: sustancia que se halla en los cromosomas eucarióticos y que consiste en ADN enrollado apretadamente alrededor de las histonas

chromosome: threadlike structure of DNA and protein that contains genetic information; in eukaryotes, chromosomes are found in the nucleus; in prokaryotes, they are found in the cytoplasm (279)

    cromosoma: estructura larga de ADN y proteína, con forma de hilo, que posee información genética; en los eucariotas, los cromosomas están dentro del núcleo; en los procariotas, los cromosomas están en el citoplasma

clade: evolutionary branch of a cladogram that includes a single ancestor and all its descendants (516)

    clado: rama evolutiva de un cladograma que incluye a un único ancestro y a todos sus descendientes

cladogram: diagram depicting patterns of shared characteristics among species (517)

    cladograma: diagrama que representa patrones de características compartidas entre especies

class: in classification, a group of closely related orders (514)

    clase: en la clasificación, un grupo de varios órdenes relacionados estrechamente

climate: average year-to-year conditions of temperature and precipitation in an area over a long period of time (96)

    clima: promedio anual de las condiciones de temperatura y precipitación en un área durante un largo período de tiempo

clone: member of a population of genetically identical cells produced from a single cell (427)

    clon: miembro de una población de células genéticamente idénticas producidas a partir de una célula única

codominance: situation in which the phenotypes produced by both alleles are completely expressed (319)

    codominancia: situación en la cual los fenotipos producidos por ambos alelos están expresados completamente

codon: group of three nucleotide bases in mRNA that specify a particular amino acid to be incorporated into a protein (366)

    codón: grupo de tres bases de nucleótidos en el RNA mensajero que especifican la incorporación de un aminoácido en particular en una proteína

coevolution: process by which two species evolve in response to changes in each other over time (551)

    coevolución: proceso por el cual dos especies evolucionan en respuesta a cambios mutuos en el transcurso del tiempo

cohesion: attraction between molecules of the same substance (41)

    cohesión: atracción entre moléculas de la misma sustancia

commensalism: symbiotic relationship in which one organism benefits and the other is neither helped nor harmed (104)

    comensalismo: relación simbiótica en la cual un organismo se beneficia y el otro ni se beneficia ni sufre daño

community: assemblage of different populations that live together in a defined area (64)

    comunidad: conjunto de varias poblaciones que viven juntas en un área definida

competitive exclusion principle: principle that states that no two species can occupy the same niche in the same habitat at the same time (101)

    principio de exclusión competitiva: principio que afirma que dos especies no pueden ocupar el mismo nicho en el mismo hábitat al mismo tiempo

compound: substance formed by the chemical combination of two or more elements in definite proportions (36)

    compuesto: sustancia formada por la combinación química de dos o más elementos en proporciones definidas

coniferous: term used to refer to trees that produce seed-bearing cones and have thin leaves shaped like needles (114)

coníferas: término utilizado para referirse a los árboles que producen conos portadores de semillas y que tienen hojas delgadas con forma de aguja

consumer: organism that relies on other organisms for its energy and food supply; also called a heterotroph (71)

consumidor: organismo que depende de otros organismos para obtener su energía y su provisión de alimentos; también llamado heterótrofo

control group: group in an experiment that is exposed to the same conditions as the experimental group except for one independent variable (7)

grupo de control: en un experimento, grupo que está expuesto a las mismas condiciones que el grupo experimental, excepto por una variable independiente

controlled experiment: experiment in which only one variable is changed (7)

experimento controlado: experimento en el cual sólo se cambia una variable

convergent evolution: process by which unrelated organisms independently evolve similarities when adapting to similar environments (551)

evolución convergente: proceso mediante el cual organismos no relacionados evolucionan independientemente hacia caracteres similares cuando se adaptan a ambientes parecidos

covalent bond: type of bond between atoms in which the electrons are shared (37)

enlace covalente: tipo de enlace entre átomos en el cual se comparten los electrones

crossing-over: process in which homologous chromosomes exchange portions of their chromatids during meiosis (324)

entrecruzamiento: proceso por el cual los cromosomas homólogos intercambian partes de sus cromátidas durante la meiosis

cyclin: one of a family of proteins that regulates the cell cycle in eukaryotic cells (286)

ciclina: un componente de la familia de proteínas que regulan el ciclo celular de las células eucariotas

cytokinesis: division of the cytoplasm to form two separate daughter cells (282)

citocinesis: división del citoplasma para formar dos células hijas separadas

cytoplasm: in eukaryotic cells, all cellular contents outside the nucleus; in prokaryotic cells, all of the cells' contents (196)

citoplasma: en una célula eucariota, todo el contenido celular fuera del núcleo; en las células procariotas, todo el contenido de las células

cytoskeleton: network of protein filaments in a eukaryotic cell that gives the cell its shape and internal organization and is involved in movement (199)

citoesqueleto: en una célula eucariota, red de filamentos proteínicos que otorga a la célula su forma y su organización interna y participa en el movimiento

D

data: evidence; information gathered from observations (8)

datos: evidencia; información reunida a partir de observaciones

deciduous: term used to refer to a type of tree that sheds its leaves during a particular season each year (112)

caduco: término utilizado para referirse a un tipo de árbol que pierde sus hojas cada año durante una estación en particular

decomposer: organism that breaks down and obtains energy from dead organic matter (71)

descomponedor: organismo que descompone y obtiene energía de la materia orgánica muerta

deforestation: destruction of forests (159)

deforestación: destrucción de los bosques

demographic transition: change in a population from high birth and death rates to low birth and death rates (144)

transición demográfica: en una población, cambio de índices de nacimiento y mortalidad altos a índices de nacimiento y mortalidad bajos

demography: scientific study of human populations (143)

demografía: estudio científico de las poblaciones humanas

denitrification: process by which bacteria convert nitrates into nitrogen gas (84)

desnitrificación: proceso por el cual las bacterias del suelo convierten los nitratos en gas nitrógeno

density-dependent limiting factor: limiting factor that depends on population density (138)

factor limitante dependiente de la densidad: factor limitante que depende de la densidad de la población

density-independent limiting factor: limiting factor that affects all populations in similar ways, regardless of the population density (140)

factor limitante independiente de la densidad: factor limitante que afecta a todas las poblaciones de manera similar, sin importar la densidad de la población

deoxyribonucleic acid (DNA): genetic material that organisms inherit from their parents (18)

ácido desoxirribonucleico (ADN): material genético que los organismos heredan de sus padres

dependent variable: variable that is observed and that changes in response to the independent variable; also called the responding variable (7)

variable dependiente: variable que está siendo observada y cambia en respuesta a la variable independiente; también llamada variable de respuesta

derived character: trait that appears in recent parts of a lineage, but not in its older members (518)

carácter derivado: rasgo que aparece en los descendientes recientes de un linaje, pero no en sus miembros más viejos

Glossary (continued)

desertification: lower land productivity caused by over-farming, overgrazing, seasonal drought, and climate change (159)

  desertificación: disminución de la productividad de la tierra debido al cultivo y al pastoreo excesivo, a la sequía estacional y al cambio climático

detritivore: organism that feeds on plant and animal remains and other dead matter (71)

  detritívoro: organismo que se alimenta de restos animales y vegetales y demás materia orgánica muerta

differentiation: process in which cells become specialized in structure and function (293, 381)

  diferenciación: proceso en el cual las células se especializan en estructura y función

diffusion: process by which particles tend to move from an area where they are more concentrated to an area where they are less concentrated (208)

  difusión: proceso por el cual las partículas tienden a desplazarse desde un área donde están más concentradas hacia un área donde están menos concentradas

diploid: term used to refer to a cell that contains two sets of homologous chromosomes (323)

  diploide: término utilizado para referirse a una célula que contiene dos series de cromosomas homólogos

directional selection: form of natural selection in which individuals at one end of a distribution curve have higher fitness than individuals in the middle or at the other end of the curve (489)

  selección direccional: forma de selección natural en la cual los individuos que se hallan en un extremo de la curva de distribución poseen una mayor capacidad de adaptación que los individuos que se hallan en el centro o en el otro extremo de la curva

disruptive selection: natural selection in which individuals at the upper and lower ends of the curve have higher fitness than individuals near the middle of the curve (489)

  selección disruptiva: forma de selección natural en la cual los individuos que se hallan en los extremos superior e inferior de la curva poseen una mayor capacidad de adaptación que los individuos que se hallan cerca del centro de la curva

DNA fingerprinting: tool used by biologists that analyzes an individual's unique collection of DNA restriction fragments; used to determine whether two samples of genetic material are from the same person (433)

  prueba de ADN: herramienta utilizada por los biólogos mediante la cual se analiza el conjunto de los fragmentos de restricción de ADN exclusivo de cada individuo; utilizada para determinar si dos muestras de material genético pertenecen a la misma persona; también llamada huella genética o análisis de ADN

DNA microarray: glass slide or silicon chip that carries thousands of different kinds of single-stranded DNA fragments arranged in a grid. A DNA microarray is used to detect and measure the expression of thousands of genes at one time (432)

  chip de ADN: superficie de vidrio o chip de silicona que contiene miles de diferentes tipos de fragmentos de ADN de una sola cadena dispuestos en una cuadrícula. Un chip de ADN se utiliza para detectar y medir la expresión de miles de genes a la vez

DNA polymerase: principal enzyme involved in DNA replication (351)

  ADN polimerasa: enzima fundamental involucrada en la replicación del ADN

domain: larger, more inclusive taxonomic category than a kingdom (525)

  dominio: categoría taxonómica más amplia e inclusiva que un reino

E

ecological footprint: total amount of functioning ecosystem needed both to provide the resources a human population uses and to absorb the wastes that population generates (173)

  huella ecológica: cantidad total de ecosistema en funcionamiento necesaria para proporcionar los recursos que utiliza una población humana y para absorber los residuos que genera esa población

ecological hot spot: small geographic area where significant numbers of habitats and species are in immediate danger of extinction (171)

  zona de conflicto ecológico: área geográfica pequeña donde cantidades importantes de hábitats y especies se hallan en peligro de extinción inmediato

ecological pyramid: illustration of the relative amounts of energy or matter contained within each trophic level in a given food chain ōr food web (77)

  pirámide ecológica: ilustración de las cantidades relativas de energía o materia contenidas dentro de cada nivel trófico en una cadena o red alimenticia dada

ecological succession: series of gradual changes that occur in a community following a disturbance (106)

  sucesión ecológica: serie de cambios graduales que ocurren en una comunidad después de una alteración

ecology: scientific study of interactions among organisms and between organisms and their environment (65)

    ecología: estudio científico de las interacciones entre organismos y entre los organismos y su medio ambiente

ecosystem: all the organisms that live in a place, together with their nonliving environment (65)

    ecosistema: todos los organismos que viven en un lugar, junto con su medio ambiente inanimado

ecosystem diversity: variety of habitats, communities, and ecological processes in the biosphere (166)

    diversidad de ecosistemas: variedad de hábitats, comunidades y procesos ecológicos que existen en la biósfera

electron: negatively charged particle; located in the space surrounding the nucleus (34)

    electrón: partícula con carga negativa; ubicada en el espacio que rodea al núcleo

electron transport chain: series of electron carrier proteins that shuttle high-energy electrons during ATP-generating reactions (236)

    cadena de transporte de electrones: serie de proteínas transportadoras que llevan electrones de alta energía, durante las reacciones generadoras de ATP

element: pure substance that consists entirely of one type of atom (35)

    elemento: sustancia pura que consiste íntegramente en un tipo de átomo

embryo: developing stage of a multicellular organism (292)

    embrión: una de las etapas de desarrollo de un organismo multicelular

emigration: movement of individuals out of an area (132)

    emigración: desplazamiento de individuos fuera de un área

endoplasmic reticulum: internal membrane system found in eukaryotic cells; place where lipid components of the cell membrane are assembled (200)

    retículo endoplasmático: sistema de membranas internas de las células eucariotas; lugar donde se reúnen los componentes lipídicos de la membrana celular

endosymbiotic theory: theory that proposes that eukaryotic cells formed from a symbiotic relationship among several different prokaryotic cells (556)

    teoría endosimbiótica: teoría que propone que las células eucariotas se formaron a partir de una relación simbiótica entre varias células procariotas distintas

enzyme: protein catalyst that speeds up the rate of specific biological reactions (52)

    enzima: proteína catalizadora que acelera la velocidad de reacciones biológicas específicas

era: major division of geologic time; usually divided into two or more periods (543)

    era: división principal del tiempo geológico; usualmente dividida en dos o más períodos

estuary: kind of wetland formed where a river meets the ocean (119)

    estuario: tipo de humedal que se forma donde un río se une al océano

Eukarya: domain consisting of all organisms that have a nucleus; includes protists, plants, fungi, and animals (526)

    Eukarya (eucariontes): dominio compuesto por todos los organismos que tienen un núcleo; incluye a los protistas, las plantas, los hongos y los animales

eukaryote: organism whose cells contain a nucleus (193)

    eucariota: organismo cuyas células contienen un núcleo

evolution: change over time; the process by which modern organisms have descended from ancient organisms (450)

    evolución: cambio en el transcurso del tiempo; el proceso por el cual los organismos actuales se derivaron de los organismos antiguos

exon: expressed sequence of DNA; codes for a protein (365)

    exón: secuencia expresada de ADN; codifica una porción específica de una proteína

exponential growth: growth pattern in which the individuals in a population reproduce at a constant rate (132)

    crecimiento exponencial: patrón de crecimiento en el cual los individuos de una población se reproducen a una tasa constante

extinct: term used to refer to a species that has died out and has no living members (538)

    extinto: término utilizado para referirse a una especie que ha desaparecido y de la que ninguno de sus miembros está vivo

F

facilitated diffusion: process of diffusion in which molecules pass across the membrane through cell membrane channels (209)

    difusión facilitada: proceso de difusión en el cual las moléculas atraviesan la membrana a través de los canales de la membrana celular

family: in classification, group of similar genera (513)

    familia: en la clasificación, grupo de géneros similares

fermentation: process by which cells release energy in the absence of oxygen (262)

    fermentación: proceso por el cual las células liberan energía en ausencia de oxígeno

fertilization: process in sexual reproduction in which male and female reproductive cells join to form a new cell (309)

    fecundación: proceso de la reproducción sexual en el cual las células reproductoras masculinas y femeninas se unen para formar una célula nueva

fitness: how well an organism can survive and reproduce in its environment (461)

    aptitud: capacidad de un organismo para sobrevivir y reproducirse en su medio ambiente

food chain: series of steps in an ecosystem in which organisms transfer energy by eating and being eaten (73)

cadena alimenticia: serie de pasos en un ecosistema, en que los organismos transfieren energía al alimentarse y al servir de alimento

food web: network of complex interactions formed by the feeding relationships among the various organisms in an ecosystem (74)

red alimenticia: red de interacciones complejas constituida por las relaciones alimenticias entre los varios organismos de un ecosistema

forensics: scientific study of crime scene evidence (433)

ciencias forenses: estudio científico de las pruebas en la escena del crimen

fossil: preserved remains or traces of ancient organisms (452)

fósil: restos conservados o vestigios de organismos antiguos

founder effect: change in allele frequencies as a result of the migration of a small subgroup of a population (490)

efecto fundador: cambio en las frecuencias alélicas como consecuencia de la migración de un subgrupo pequeño de una población

frameshift mutation: mutation that shifts the "reading frame" of the genetic message by inserting or deleting a nucleotide (373)

mutación de corrimiento de estructura: mutación que cambia el "marco de lectura" del mensaje genético insertando o eliminando un nucleótido

G

gamete: sex cell (312)

gameto: célula sexual

gel electrophoresis: procedure used to separate and analyze DNA fragments by placing a mixture of DNA fragments at one end of a porous gel and applying an electrical voltage to the gel (404)

electroforesis en gel: procedimiento utilizado para separar y analizar fragmentos de ADN colocando una mezcla de fragmentos de ADN en un extremo de un gel poroso y aplicando al gel un voltaje eléctrico

gene: sequence of DNA that codes for a protein and thus determines a trait; factor that is passed from parent to offspring (310)

gen: secuencia de ADN que contiene el código de una proteína y por lo tanto determina un rasgo; factor que se transmite de un progenitor a su descendencia

gene expression: process by which a gene produces its product and the product carries out its function (370)

expresión génica: proceso por el cual un gen produce su producto y el producto lleva a cabo su función

gene pool: all the genes, including all the different alleles for each gene, that are present in a population at any one time (483)

caudal de genes: todos los genes, incluidos todos los alelos diferentes para cada gen, que están presentes en una población en un momento dado

gene therapy: process of changing a gene to treat a medical disease or disorder. An absent or faulty gene is replaced by a normal working gene. (431)

terapia genética o génica: proceso en el cual se cambia un gen para tratar una enfermedad o una afección médica. Se reemplaza un gen ausente o defectuoso con un gen de funcionamiento normal.

genetic code: collection of codons of mRNA, each of which directs the incorporation of a particular amino acid into a protein during protein synthesis (366)

código genético: conjunto de codones del ARN mensajero, cada uno de los cuales dirige la incorporación de un aminoácido en particular a una proteína durante la síntesis proteica

genetic diversity: sum total of all the different forms of genetic information carried by a particular species, or by all organisms on Earth (166)

diversidad genética: suma de todas las distintas formas de información genética portadas por una especie en particular, o por todos los organismos de la Tierra

genetic drift: random change in allele frequency caused by a series of chance occurrences that cause an allele to become more or less common in a population (490)

tendencia genética: alteración al azar de la frecuencia alélica causada por una serie de acontecimientos aleatorios que hacen que un alelo se vuelva más o menos común en una población

genetic equilibrium: situation in which allele frequencies in a population remain the same (491)

equilibrio genético: situación en la cual las frecuencias alélicas de una población se mantienen iguales

genetic marker: alleles that produce detectable phenotypic differences useful in genetic analysis (425)

marcador genético: alelos que producen diferencias fenotípicas detectables, útiles en el análisis genético

genetics: scientific study of heredity (308)

genética: estudio científico de la herencia

genome: entire set of genetic information that an organism carries in its DNA (392)

genoma: todo el conjunto de información genética que un organismo transporta en su ADN

genomics: study of whole genomes, including genes and their functions (407)

genómica: estudio integral de los genomas, incluyendo los genes y sus funciones

genotype: genetic makeup of an organism (315)

   genotipo: composición genética de un organismo

genus: group of closely related species; the first part of the scientific name in binomial nomenclature (512)

   género: grupo de especies relacionadas estrechamente; la primera parte del nombre científico en la nomenclatura binaria

geographic isolation: form of reproductive isolation in which two populations are separated by geographic barriers such as rivers, mountains, or bodies of water, leading to the formation of two separate subspecies (495)

   aislamiento geográfico: forma de aislamiento reproductivo en el cual dos poblaciones están separadas por barreras geográficas como ríos, montañas o masas de agua, dando lugar a la formación de dos subespecies distintas

geologic time scale: timeline used to represent Earth's history (542)

   escala de tiempo geológico: línea cronológica utilizada para representar la historia de la Tierra

global warming: increase in the average temperatures on Earth (177)

   calentamiento global: aumento del promedio de temperatura en la tierra

glycolysis: first set of reactions in cellular respiration in which a molecule of glucose is broken into two molecules of pyruvic acid (254)

   glicólisis: primer conjunto de reacciones en la respiración celular, en las cuales una molécula de glucosa se descompone en dos moléculas de ácido pirúvico

Golgi apparatus: organelle in cells that modifies, sorts, and packages proteins and other materials from the endoplasmic reticulum for storage in the cell or release outside the cell (201)

   aparato de Golgi: orgánulo de las células que modifica, clasifica y agrupa las proteínas y otras sustancias provenientes del retículo endoplasmático para almacenarlas en la célula o enviarlas fuera de la célula

gradualism: the evolution of a species by gradual accumulation of small genetic changes over long periods of time (549)

   gradualismo: evolución de una especie por la acumulación gradual de pequeños cambios genéticos ocurridos en el transcurso de largos períodos de tiempo

greenhouse effect: process in which certain gases (carbon dioxide, methane, and water vapor) trap sunlight energy in Earth's atmosphere as heat (97)

   efecto invernadero: proceso mediante el cual ciertos gases (dióxido de carbono, metano y vapor de agua) atrapan la energía de la luz solar en la atmósfera terrestre en forma de calor

growth factor: one of a group of external regulatory proteins that stimulate the growth and division of cells (287)

   factor de crecimiento: una de las proteínas del grupo de proteínas reguladoras externas que estimulan el crecimiento y la división de las células

H

habitat: area where an organism lives, including the biotic and abiotic factors that affect it (99)

   hábitat: área donde vive un organismo, incluidos los factores bióticos y abióticos que lo afectan

habitat fragmentation: splitting of ecosystems into pieces (168)

   fragmentación del hábitat: la ruptura, o separación en partes, de los ecosistemas

half life: length of time required for half of the radioactive atoms in a sample to decay (540)

   vida media: período de tiempo requerido para que se desintegre la mitad de los átomos radiactivos de una muestra

haploid: term used to refer to a cell that contains only a single set of genes (323)

   haploide: tipo de célula que posee un solo juego de cromosomas

Hardy-Weinberg principle: principle that states that allele frequencies in a population remain constant unless one or more factors cause those frequencies to change (491)

   principio de Hardy-Weinberg: el principio que afirma que las frecuencias alélicas de una población permanecen constantes a menos que uno o más factores ocasionen que esas frecuencias cambien

herbivore: organism that obtains energy by eating only plants (71)

   herbívoro: organismo que obtiene energía alimentándose solo de plantas

herbivory: interaction in which one animal (the herbivore) feeds on producers (such as plants) (102)

   herbivorismo: interacción en la cual un animal (el herbívoro) se alimenta de productores (como las plantas)

heterotroph: organism that obtains food by consuming other living things; also called a consumer (71, 228)

   heterótrofo: organismo que obtiene su alimento consumiendo otros seres vivos; también llamado consumidor

heterozygous: having two different alleles for a particular gene (314)

   heterocigota: que tiene dos alelos diferentes para un gen dado

homeobox gene: The homeobox is a DNA sequence of approximately 130 base pairs, found in many homeotic genes that regulate development. Genes containing this sequence are known as homeobox genes, and they code for transcription factors, proteins that bind to DNA, and they also regulate the expression of other genes. (382)

   gen homeobox: el homeobox es una secuencia de ADN de aproximadamente 130 pares de bases, presente en muchos genes homeóticos que regulan el desarrollo. Los genes que contienen esta secuencia se denominan genes homeobox y codifican los factores de transcripción, las proteínas que se adhieren al ADN y regulan la expresión de otros genes

homeostasis: relatively constant internal physical and chemical conditions that organisms maintain (19, 214)

homeostasis: las condiciones internas, químicas y físicas, que los organismos mantienen relativamente constantes

homeotic gene: a class of regulatory genes that determine the identity of body parts and regions in an animal embryo. Mutations in these genes can transform one body part into another (382)

gen homeótico: tipo de genes reguladores que determinan la identidad de las partes y regiones del cuerpo en un embrión animal. Las mutaciones de estos genes pueden transformar una parte del cuerpo en otra

homologous: term used to refer to chromosomes in which one set comes from the male parent and one set comes from the female parent (323)

homólogos: término utilizado para referirse a los cromosomas en los que un juego proviene del progenitor masculino y un juego proviene del progenitor femenino

homologous structures: structures that are similar in different species of common ancestry (468)

estructuras homólogas: estructuras que son similares en distintas especies que tienen un ancestro común

homozygous: having two identical alleles for a particular gene (314)

homocigota: que tiene dos alelos idénticos para un gen dado

Hox gene: a group of homeotic genes clustered together that determine the head to tail identity of body parts in animals. All hox genes contain the homeobox DNA sequence. (382)

gen Hox: grupo de genes homeóticos agrupados en un conjunto que determinan la identidad posicional de las partes del cuerpo de los animales. Todos los genes Hox contienen la secuencia de ADN homeobox

humus: material formed from decaying leaves and other organic matter (114)

humus: material formado a partir de hojas en descomposición y otros materiales orgánicos

hybrid: offspring of crosses between parents with different traits (309)

híbrido: descendencia del cruce entre progenitores que tienen rasgos diferentes

hybridization: breeding technique that involves crossing dissimilar individuals to bring together the best traits of both organisms (419)

hibridación: técnica de cría que consiste en cruzar individuos diferentes para reunir los mejores rasgos de ambos organismos

hydrogen bond: weak attraction between a hydrogen atom and another atom (41)

enlace de hidrógeno: atracción débil entre un átomo de hidrógeno y otro átomo

hypertonic: when comparing two solutions, the solution with the greater concentration of solutes (210)

hipertónica: al comparar dos soluciones, la solución que tiene la mayor concentración de solutos

hypothesis: possible explanation for a set of observations or possible answer to a scientific question (7)

hipótesis: explicación posible para un conjunto de observaciones o respuesta posible a una pregunta científica

hypotonic: when comparing two solutions, the solution with the lesser concentration of solutes (210)

hipotónica: al comparar dos soluciones, la solución que tiene la menor concentración de solutos

I

immigration: movement of individuals into an area occupied by an existing population (132)

inmigración: desplazamiento de individuos a un área ocupada por una población ya existente

inbreeding: continued breeding of individuals with similar characteristics to maintain the derived characteristics of a kind of organism (419)

endogamia: la cría continua de individuos con características semejantes para mantener las características derivadas de un tipo de organismo

incomplete dominance: situation in which one allele is not completely dominant over another allele (319)

dominancia incompleta: situación en la cual un alelo no es completamente dominante sobre otro alelo

independent assortment: one of Mendel's principles that states that genes for different traits can segregate independently during the formation of gametes (317)

distribución independiente: uno de los principios de Mendel que establece que los genes para rasgos diferentes pueden segregarse independientemente durante la formación de los gametos

independent variable: factor in a controlled experiment that is deliberately changed; also called manipulated variable (7)

variable independiente: en un experimento controlado, el factor que se modifica a propósito; también llamada variable manipulada

index fossil: distinctive fossil that is used to compare the relative ages of fossils (540)

fósil guía: fósil distintivo usado para comparar las edades relativas de los fósiles

inference: a logical interpretation based on prior knowledge and experience (7)

inferencia: interpretación lógica basada en la experiencia y en conocimientos previos

interphase: period of the cell cycle between cell divisions (281)

interfase: período del ciclo celular entre las divisiones celulares

intron: sequence of DNA that is not involved in coding for a protein (365)

intrón: secuencia de ADN que no participa en la codificación de una proteína

ion: atom that has a positive or negative charge (37)

ion: átomo que tiene una carga positiva o negativa

ionic bond: chemical bond formed when one or more electrons are transferred from one atom to another (37)

enlace iónico: enlace químico que se forma cuando uno o más electrones se transfieren de un átomo a otro

isotonic: when the concentration of two solutions is the same (210)

isotónica: cuando la concentración de dos soluciones es la misma

isotope: one of several forms of a single element, which contains the same number of protons but different numbers of neutrons (35)

isótopo: cada una de las diferentes formas de un único elemento, que contiene la misma cantidad de protones pero cantidades distintas de neutrones

J, K

karyotype: micrograph of the complete diploid set of chromosomes grouped together in pairs, arranged in order of decreasing size (392)

cariotipo: micrografía de la totalidad del conjunto diploide de cromosomas agrupados en pares, ordenados por tamaño decreciente

keystone species: single species that is not usually abundant in a community yet exerts strong control on the structure of a community (103)

especie clave: especie que habitualmente no es abundante en una comunidad y sin embargo ejerce un fuerte control sobre la estructura de esa comunidad

kingdom: largest and most inclusive group in Linnean classification (514)

reino: grupo más grande e inclusivo del sistema de clasificación inventado por Linneo

Krebs cycle: second stage of cellular respiration in which pyruvic acid is broken down into carbon dioxide in a series of energy-extracting reactions (256)

ciclo de Krebs: segunda fase de la respiración celular en la cual el ácido pirúvico se descompone en dióxido de carbono en una serie de reacciones que liberan energía

L

light-dependent reactions: set of reactions in photosynthesis that use energy from light to produce ATP and NADPH (233)

reacciones dependientes de la luz: en la fotosíntesis, conjunto de reacciones que emplean la energía proveniente de la luz para producir ATP y NADPH

light-independent reactions: set of reactions in photosynthesis that do not require light; energy from ATP and NADPH is used to build high-energy compounds such as sugar; also called the Calvin cycle (233)

reacciones independientes de la luz: en la fotosíntesis, conjunto de reacciones que no necesitan luz; la energía proveniente del ATP y del NADPH se emplea para construir compuestos con gran contenido energético, como el azúcar; también llamado ciclo de Calvin

limiting factor: factor that causes population growth to decrease (137)

factor limitante: un factor que hace disminuir el crecimiento de la población

limiting nutrient: single essential nutrient that limits productivity in an ecosystem (85)

nutriente limitante: un solo nutriente esencial que limita la productividad de un ecosistema

lipid: macromolecule made mostly from carbon and hydrogen atoms; includes fats, oils, and waxes (47)

lípido: macromolécula compuesta principalmente por átomos de carbono e hidrógeno; incluye las grasas, los aceites y las ceras

lipid bilayer: flexible double-layered sheet that makes up the cell membrane and forms a barrier between the cell and its surroundings (204)

bicapa lipídica: lámina flexible de dos capas que constituye la membrana celular y forma una barrera entre la célula y su entorno

logistic growth: growth pattern in which a population's growth slows and then stops following a period of exponential growth (135)

crecimiento logístico: patrón de crecimiento en el cual el desarrollo de una población se reduce y luego se detiene después de un período de crecimiento exponencial

lysosome: cell organelle that breaks down lipids, carbohydrates, and proteins into small molecules that can used by the rest of the cell (198)

lisosoma: orgánulo celular que descompone los lípidos, los hidratos de carbono y las proteínas en moléculas pequeñas que pueden ser utilizadas por el resto de la célula

Glossary *(continued)*

M

macroevolutionary patterns: changes in anatomy, phylogeny, ecology, and behavior that take place in clades larger than a single species (546)

    patrones de macroevolución: cambios que ocurren en la anatomía, filogenia, ecología y comportamiento de clados que abarcan a más de una especie

mass extinction: event during which many species become extinct during a relatively short period of time (548)

    extinción masiva: suceso durante el cual se extinguen muchas especies durante un período de tiempo relativamente corto

matrix: innermost compartment of the mitochondrion (256)

    matriz: compartimento más interno de la mitocondria

meiosis: process in which the number of chromosomes per cell is cut in half through the separation of homologous chromosomes in a diploid cell (324)

    meiosis: proceso por el cual el número de cromosomas por célula se reduce a la mitad mediante la separación de los cromosomas homólogos de una célula diploide

messenger RNA (mRNA): type of RNA that carries copies of instructions for the assembly of amino acids into proteins from DNA to the rest of the cell (363)

    ARN mensajero: tipo de ARN que transporta copias de las instrucciones para el ensamblaje de los aminoácidos en proteínas, desde el ADN al resto de la célula

metabolism: the combination of chemical reactions through which an organism builds up or breaks down materials (19)

    metabolismo: la combinación de reacciones químicas a través de las cuales un organismo acumula o desintegra materiales

metaphase: phase of mitosis in which the chromosomes line up across the center of the cell (282)

    metafase: fase de la mitosis en la cual los cromosomas se alinean a través del centro de la célula

microclimate: environmental conditions within a small area that differs significantly from the climate of the surrounding area (96)

    microclima: condiciones medioambientales de un área pequeña que difieren significativamente del clima del área circundante

mitochondrion: cell organelle that converts the chemical energy stored in food into compounds that are more convenient for the cell to use (202)

    mitocondria: orgánulo celular que convierte la energía química almacenada en los alimentos en compuestos más apropiados para que la célula los use

mitosis: part of eukaryotic cell division during which the cell nucleus divides (282)

    mitosis: fase de la división de las células eucariotas durante la cual se divide el núcleo celular

mixture: material composed of two or more elements or compounds that are physically mixed together but not chemically combined (42)

    mezcla: material compuesto por dos o más elementos o compuestos que están mezclados físicamente pero no están combinados químicamente

molecular clock: method used by researchers that uses mutation rates in DNA to estimate the length of time that two species have been evolving independently (498)

    reloj molecular: método de investigación que emplea las tasas de mutación del ADN para estimar el lapso de tiempo en que dos especies han evolucionado independientemente

molecule: smallest unit of most compounds that displays all the properties of that compound (37)

    molécula: la unidad más pequeña de la mayoría de los compuestos que exhibe todas las propiedades de ese compuesto

monoculture: farming strategy of planting a single, highly productive crop year after year (155)

    monocultivo: estrategia agrícola que consiste en plantar año tras año un único cultivo altamente productivo

monomer: small chemical unit that makes up a polymer (46)

    monómero: pequeña unidad química que forma un polímero

monophyletic group: group that consists of a single ancestral species and all its descendants and excludes any organisms that are not descended from that common ancestor (516)

    grupo monofilético: grupo que consiste en una especie con un único ancestro y todos sus descendientes y excluye a todos los organismos que no descienden de ese ancestro común

monosaccharide: simple sugar molecule (46)

    monosacárido: molécula de azúcar simple

multiple alleles: a gene that has more than two alleles (320)

    alelos múltiples: un gen que tiene más de dos alelos

multipotent: cell with limited potential to develop into many types of differentiated cells (295)

    multipotentes: células con potencial limitado para generar muchos tipos de células diferenciadas

mutagen: chemical or physical agents in the environment that interact with DNA and may cause a mutation (375)

    mutágeno: agentes físicos o químicos del medioambiente que interaccionan con el ADN y pueden causar una mutación

mutation: change in the genetic material of a cell (372)

    mutación: cambio en el material genético de una célula

mutualism: symbiotic relationship in which both species benefit from the relationship (103)

  mutualismo: relación simbiótica en la cual ambas especies se benefician

N

NAD⁺ (nicotinamide adenine dinucleotide): electron carrier involved in glycolysis (255)

  NAD⁺ (dinucleótido de nicotinamida adenina): transportador de electrones que participa en la glucólisis

NADP⁺ (nicotinamide adenine dinucleotide phosphate): carrier molecule that transfers high-energy electrons from chlorophyll to other molecules (232)

  NADP⁺ (fosfato de dinucleótido de nicotinamida adenina): molécula transportadora de electrones que transfiere electrones de alta energía desde la clorofila a otras moléculas

natural selection: process by which organisms that are most suited to their environment survive and reproduce most successfully; also called survival of the fittest (463)

  selección natural: proceso por el cual los organismos más adaptados a su medioambiente sobreviven y se reproducen más exitosamente; también llamada supervivencia del más apto

niche: full range of physical and biological conditions in which an organism lives and the way in which the organism uses those conditions (100)

  nicho: toda la variedad de condiciones biológicas y físicas en las que vive un organismo y la manera en la que dicho organismo utiliza esas condiciones

nitrogen fixation: process of converting nitrogen gas into nitrogen compounds that plants can absorb and use (84)

  fijación de nitrógeno: el proceso por el cual el gas nitrógeno se convierte en los compuestos nitrogenados que las plantas pueden absorber y utilizar

nondisjunction: error in meiosis in which the homologous chromosomes fail to separate properly (401)

  no disyunción: error que ocurre durante la meiosis, en el que cromosomas homólogos no logran separarse adecuadamente

nonrenewable resource: resource that cannot be replenished by a natural process within a reasonable amount of time (157)

  recurso no renovable: recurso que no se puede reponer mediante un proceso natural dentro de un período de tiempo razonable

nucleic acid: macromolecules containing hydrogen, oxygen, nitrogen, carbon, and phosphorus (48)

  ácido nucleico: macromoléculas que contienen hidrógeno, oxígeno, nitrógeno, carbono y fósforo

nucleotide: subunit of which nucleic acids are composed; made up of a 5-carbon sugar, a phosphate group, and a nitrogenous base (48)

  nucleótido: subunidad que constituye los ácidos nucleicos; compuesta de un azúcar de 5 carbonos, un grupo fosfato y una base nitrogenada

nucleus: the center of an atom, which contains the protons and neutrons (34); in cells, structure that contains the cell's genetic material in the form of DNA (193)

  núcleo: el centro de un átomo, contiene los protones y los neutrones; en las células, la estructura que contiene el material genético de la célula en forma de ADN

nutrient: chemical substance that an organism needs to sustain life (82)

  nutriente: sustancia química que un organismo necesita para continuar con vida

O

observation: process of noticing and describing events or processes in a careful, orderly way (6)

  observación: el método de percibir y describir sucesos o procesos de manera atenta y ordenada

omnivore: organism that obtains energy by eating both plants and animals (71)

  omnívoro: organismo que obtiene energía alimentándose de plantas y animales

operator: short DNA region, adjacent to the promoter of a prokaryotic operon, that binds repressor proteins responsible for controlling the rate of transcription of the operon (378)

  operador: pequeña región de ADN, adyacente al promotor del operón de una procariota, que une las proteínas represoras responsables de controlar la tasa de transcripción del operón

operon: in prokaryotes, a group of adjacent genes that share a common operator and promoter and are transcribed into a single mRNA (377)

  operón: en las procariotas, grupo de genes adyacentes que comparten un operador y un promotor en común y que son transcritas a un solo ARN mensajero

order: in classification, a group of closely related families (513)

  orden: en la clasificación, un grupo de familias relacionadas estrechamente

organ: group of tissues that work together to perform closely related functions (216)

  órgano: grupo de tejidos que trabajan juntos para realizar funciones estrechamente relacionadas

organ system: group of organs that work together to perform a specific function (216)

  sistema de órganos: grupo de órganos que trabajan juntos para realizar una función específica

organelle: specialized structure that performs important cellular functions within a cell (196)

 orgánulo: estructura especializada que realiza funciones celulares importantes dentro de una célula

osmosis: diffusion of water through a selectively permeable membrane (210)

 ósmosis: la difusión de agua a través de una membrana de permeabilidad selectiva

osmotic pressure: pressure that must be applied to prevent osmotic movement across a selectively permeable membrane (211)

 presión osmótica: la presión que debe aplicarse para evitar el movimiento osmótico a través de una membrana de permeabilidad selectiva

ozone layer: atmospheric layer in which ozone gas is relatively concentrated; protects life on Earth from harmful ultraviolet rays in sunlight (175)

 capa de ozono: capa atmosférica en la cual el gas ozono se encuentra relativamente concentrado; protege a los seres vivos de la Tierra de los perjudiciales rayos ultravioletas de la luz solar

P

paleontologist: scientist who studies fossils (539)

 paleontólogo: científico que estudia los fósiles

parasitism: symbiotic relationship in which one organism lives on or inside another organism and harms it (104)

 parasitismo: relación simbiótica en la cual un organismo vive sobre otro organismo o en su interior y lo perjudica

pedigree: chart that shows the presence or absence of a trait according to the relationships within a family across several generations (396)

 árbol genealógico: diagrama que muestra la presencia o ausencia de un rasgo de acuerdo con las relaciones intrafamiliares a través de varias generaciones

period: division of geologic time into which eras are subdivided (543)

 período: división del tiempo geológico en la que se subdividen las eras

permafrost: layer of permanently frozen subsoil found in the tundra (115)

 permacongelamiento: capa de subsuelo congelado en forma permanente que se halla en la tundra

pH scale: scale with values from 0 to 14, used to measure the concentration of H^+ ions in a solution; a pH of 0 to 7 is acidic, a pH of 7 is neutral, and a pH of 7 to 14 is basic (43)

 escala del pH: escala con valores de 0 a 14, utilizada para medir la concentración de iones H^+ en una solución; un pH de 0 a 7 es ácido, un pH de 7 es neutro y un pH de 7 a 14 es básico

phenotype: physical characteristics of an organism (315)

 fenotipo: características físicas de un organismo

photic zone: sunlight region near the surface of water (117)

 zona fótica: región cerca de la superficie del mar en la que penetra la luz solar

photosynthesis: process used by plants and other autotrophs to capture light energy and use it to power chemical reactions that convert carbon dioxide and water into oxygen and energy-rich carbohydrates such as sugars and starches (70, 228)

 fotosíntesis: proceso empleado por las plantas y otros organismos autótrofos para atrapar la energía luminosa y utilizarla para impulsar reacciones químicas que convierten el dióxido de carbono y el agua en oxígeno e hidratos de carbono de gran contenido energético, como azúcares y almidones

photosystem: cluster of chlorophyll and proteins found in thylakoids (235)

 fotosistema: conjunto de clorofila y proteínas que se hallan en los tilacoides

phylogeny: the evolutionary history of a lineage (516)

 filogenia: historia evolutiva del linaje

phylum (pl. phyla): in classification, a group of closely related classes (514)

 filo: en la clasificación, un grupo de clases estrechamente relacionadas

phytoplankton: photosynthetic algae found near the surface of the ocean (73)

 fitoplancton: algas fotosintéticas que se hallan cerca de la superficie del océano

pigment: light-absorbing molecule used by plants to gather the sun's energy (230)

 pigmento: moléculas que absorben la luz, empleadas por las plantas para recolectar la energía solar

pioneer species: first species to populate an area during succession (107)

 especies pioneras: las primeras especies en poblar un área durante la sucesión ecológica

plankton: microscopic organisms that live in aquatic environments; includes both phytoplankton and zooplankton (119)

 plancton: organismos microscópicos que viven en medios ambientes acuáticos; incluye el fitoplancton y el zooplancton

plasmid: small, circular piece of DNA located in the cyto-plasm of many bacteria (424)

  plásmido: pequeña porción circular de ADN ubicada en el citoplasma de muchas bacterias

plate tectonics: geologic processes, such as continental drift, volcanoes, and earthquakes, resulting from plate movement (544)

  tectónica de placas: procesos geológicos, como la deriva continental, los volcanes y los terremotos, que son conse-cuencia de los movimientos de las placas

pluripotent: cells that are capable of developing into most, but not all, of the body's cell types (294)

  pluripotentes: células capaces de convertirse en la mayo-ría de células del cuerpo, pero no en todas

point mutation: gene mutation in which a single base pair in DNA has been changed (373)

  mutación puntual: mutación genética en la cual se ha modificado un único par de bases en el ADN

pollutant: harmful material that can enter the biosphere through the land, air, or water (160)

  contaminante: material nocivo que puede ingresar en la biósfera a través de la tierra, el aire o el agua

polygenic trait: trait controlled by two or more genes (320, 486)

  rasgo poligénico: rasgo controlado por dos o más genes

polymer: molecules composed of many monomers; makes up macromolecules (46)

  polímero: molécula compuesta por muchos monómeros; forma macromoléculas

polymerase chain reaction (PCR): the technique used by biologists to make many copies of a particular gene (423)

  reacción en cadena de la polímerasa (PCR): técnica usada por los biólogos para hacer muchas copias de un gen específico

polypeptide: long chain of amino acids that makes pro-teins (366)

  polipéptido: cadena larga de aminoácidos que constituye las proteínas

polyploidy: condition in which an organism has extra sets of chromosomes (376)

  poliploidía: condición en la cual un organismo tiene grupos adicionales de cromosomas

population: group of individuals of the same species that live in the same area (64)

  población: grupo de individuos de la misma especie que viven en la misma área

population density: number of individuals per unit area (131)

  densidad de población: número de individuos que viven por unidad de superficie

predation: interaction in which one organism (the preda-tor) captures and feeds on another organism (the prey) (102)

  depredación: interacción en la cual un organismo (el predador) captura y come a otro organismo (la presa)

primary producer: first producer of energy-rich com-pounds that are later used by other organisms (69)

  productor primario: los primeros productores de compuestos ricos en energía que luego son utilizados por otros organismos

primary succession: succession that occurs in an area in which no trace of a previous community is present (106)

  sucesión primaria: sucesión que ocurre en un área en la cual no hay rastros de la presencia de una comunidad anterior

principle of dominance: Mendel's second conclusion, which states that some alleles are dominant and others are recessive (310)

  principio de dominancia: segunda conclusión de Men-del, que establece que algunos alelos son dominantes y otros son recesivos

probability: likelihood that a particular event will occur (313)

  probabilidad: la posibilidad de que ocurra un suceso dado

product: elements or compounds produced by a chemical reaction (50)

  producto: elemento o compuesto producido por una reacción química

prokaryote: unicellular organism that lacks a nucleus (193)

  procariota: organismo unicelular que carece de núcleo

promoter: specific region of a gene where RNA polymerase can bind and begin transcription (365)

  promotor: región específica de un gen en donde la ARN polimerasa puede unirse e iniciar la transcripción

prophase: first and longest phase of mitosis in which the genetic material inside the nucleus condenses and the chro-mosomes become visible (282)

  profase: primera y más prolongada fase de la mitosis, en la cual el material genético dentro del interior del núcleo se condensa y los cromosomas se hacen visibles

protein: macromolecule that contains carbon, hydrogen, oxygen, and nitrogen; needed by the body for growth and repair (48)

  proteína: macromolécula que contiene carbono, hidrógeno, oxígeno y nitrógeno; necesaria para el creci-miento y reparación del cuerpo

punctuated equilibrium: pattern of evolution in which long stable periods are interrupted by brief periods of more rapid change (549)

  equilibrio interrumpido: patrón de evolución en el cual los largos períodos de estabilidad se ven interrumpidos por breves períodos de cambio más rápido

Punnett square: diagram that can be used to predict the genotype and phenotype combinations of a genetic cross (315)

  cuadro de Punnett: un diagrama que puede utilizarse para predecir las combinaciones de genotipos y fenotipos en un cruce genético

Q, R

radiometric dating: method for determining the age of a sample from the amount of a radioactive isotope to the non-radioactive isotope of the same element in a sample (540)

datación radiométrica: método para determinar la edad de una muestra a partir de la cantidad de isótopo radioactivo en relación a la de isótopo no radiactivo del mismo elemento en dicha muestra

reactant: elements or compounds that enter into a chemical reaction (50)

reactante: elemento o compuesto que participa en una reacción química

receptor: on or in a cell, a specific protein to whose shape fits that of a specific molecular messenger, such as a hormone (217)

receptor: proteína específica que puede encontrarse en la membrana celular o dentro de la célula, cuya forma se corresponde con la de un mensajero molecular específico, por ejemplo una hormona

recombinant DNA: DNA produced by combining DNA from different sources (424)

ADN recombinante: ADN producido por la combinación de ADN de orígenes diferentes

relative dating: method of determining the age of a fossil by comparing its placement with that of fossils in other rock layers (540)

datación relativa: método para determinar la edad de un fósil comparando su ubicación con la de los fósiles hallados en otras capas de roca

renewable resource: resource that can be produced or replaced by healthy ecosystem functions (157)

recurso renovable: recurso que se puede producir o reemplazar mediante el funcionamiento saludable del ecosistema

replication: process of copying DNA prior to cell division (350)

replicación: proceso de copia de ADN previo a la división celular

reproductive isolation: separation of a species or population so that they no longer interbreed and evolve into two separate species (494)

aislamiento reproductor: separación de una especie o de una población de tal manera que ya no pueden aparearse y evolucionan hasta formar dos especies separadas

resource: any necessity of life, such as water, nutrients, light, food, or space (100)

recurso: todo lo necesario para la vida, como agua, nutrientes, luz, alimento o espacio

restriction enzyme: enzyme that cuts DNA at a sequence of nucleotides (403)

enzima restrictiva: enzima que corta el ADN en una secuencia de nucleótidos

ribonucleic acid (RNA): single-stranded nucleic acid that contains the sugar ribose (362)

ácido ribonucleico (ARN): hebra única de ácido nucleico que contiene el azúcar ribose

ribosomal RNA (rRNA): type of RNA that combines with proteins to form ribosomes (363)

ARN ribosomal: tipo de ARN que se combina con proteínas para formar los ribosomas

ribosome: cell organelle consisting of RNA and protein found throughout the cytoplasm in a cell; the site of protein synthesis (200)

ribosoma: orgánulo celular formado por ARN y proteína que se halla en el citoplasma de una célula; lugar donde se sintetizan las proteínas

RNA interference (RNAi): introduction of double-stranded RNA into a cell to inhibit gene expression (380)

ARN de interferencia: introducción de un ARN de doble hebra en una célula para inhibir la expresión de genes específicos

RNA polymerase: enzyme that links together the growing chain of RNA nucleotides during transcription using a DNA strand as a template (364)

ARN polimerasa: enzima que enlaza los nucleótidos de la cadena de ARN en crecimiento durante la transcripción, usando una secuencia de ADN como patrón o molde

S

scavenger: animal that consumes the carcasses of other animals (71)

carroñero: animal que consume los cadáveres de otros animales

science: organized way of gathering and analyzing evidence about the natural world (5)

ciencia: manera organizada de reunir y analizar la información sobre el mundo natural

secondary succession: type of succession that occurs in an area that was only partially destroyed by disturbances (107)

sucesión secundaria: tipo de sucesión que ocurre en un área destruida sólo parcialmente por alteraciones

segregation: separation of alleles during gamete formation (312)

segregación: separación de los alelos durante la formación de gametos

selective breeding: method of breeding that allows only those organisms with desired characteristics to produce the next generation (418)

    reproducción selectiva o selección artificial: método de reproducción que sólo permite la producción de una nueva generación a aquellos organismos con características deseadas

selectively permeable: property of biological membranes that allows some substances to pass across it while others cannot; also called semipermeable membrane (205)

    permeabilidad selectiva: propiedad de las membranas biológicas que permite que algunas sustancias pasen a través de ellas mientras que otras no pueden hacerlo; también llamada membrana semipermeable

sex chromosome: one of two chromosomes that determines an individual's sex (393)

    cromosoma sexual: uno de los pares de cromosomas que determina el sexo de un individuo

sex-linked gene: gene located on a sex chromosome (395)

    gen ligado al sexo: gen situado en un cromosoma sexual

sexual reproduction: type of reproduction in which cells from two parents unite to form the first cell of a new organism (19, 277)

    reproducción sexual: tipo de reproducción en la cual las células de dos progenitores se unen para formar la primera célula de un nuevo organismo

sexual selection: when individuals select mates based on heritable traits (492)

    selección sexual: cuando un individuo elige a su pareja sexual atraído por sus rasgos heredables

single-gene trait: trait controlled by one gene that has two alleles (485)

    rasgo de un único gen (monogénico): rasgo controlado por un gen que tiene dos alelos

smog: gray-brown haze formed by a mixture of chemicals (163)

    esmog: neblina marrón grisácea formada por una mezcla de compuestos químicos

solute: substance that is dissolved in a solution (42)

    soluto: sustancia que está disuelta en una solución

solution: type of mixture in which all the components are evenly distributed (42)

    solución: tipo de mezcla en la cual todos los compuestos están distribuidos de forma homogénea

solvent: dissolving substance in a solution (42)

    disolvente: sustancia que disuelve una solución

speciation: formation of a new species (494)

    especiación: formación de una nueva especie

species: a group of similar organisms that can breed and produce fertile offspring (64, 494)

    especie: un grupo de organismos similares que pueden reproducirse y producir una descendencia fértil

species diversity: number of different species that make up a particular area (166)

    diversidad de especies: número de especies diferentes que forman un área determinada

stabilizing selection: form of natural selection in which individuals near the center of a distribution curve have higher fitness than individuals at either end of the curve (489)

    selección estabilizadora: forma de selección natural en la cual los individuos situados cerca del centro de una curva de distribución tienen mayor aptitud que los individuos que se hallan en cualquiera de los extremos de la curva

stem cell: unspecialized cell that can give rise to one or more types of specialized cells (295)

    célula troncal: célula no especializada que puede originar uno o más tipos de células especializadas

stimulus (pl. stimuli): signal to which an organism responds (18)

    estímulo: señal a la cual responde un organismo

stroma: fluid portion of the chloroplast; outside of the thylakoids (231)

    estroma: parte fluida del cloroplasto; en el exterior de los tilacoides

substrate: reactant of an enzyme-catalyzed reaction (52)

    sustrato: reactante de una reacción catalizada por enzimas

suspension: mixture of water and nondissolved material (42)

    suspensión: mezcla de agua y material no disuelto

sustainable development: strategy for using natural resources without depleting them and for providing human needs without causing long-term environmental harm (157)

    desarrollo sostenible: estrategia para utilizar los recursos naturales sin agotarlos y para satisfacer las necesidades humanas sin causar daños ambientales a largo plazo

symbiosis: relationship in which two species live close together (103)

    simbiosis: relación en la cual dos especies viven en estrecha asociación

systematics: study of the diversity of life and the evolutionary relationships between organisms (512)

    sistemática: estudio de la diversidad de la vida y de las relaciones evolutivas entre los organismos

T

taiga: biome with long cold winters and a few months of warm weather; dominated by coniferous evergreens; also called boreal forest (114)

    taiga: bioma con inviernos largos y fríos y pocos meses de tiempo cálido; dominado por coníferas de hojas perennes; también llamada bosque boreal

taxon (pl. taxa): group or level of organization into which organisms are classified (512)

taxón: grupo o nivel de organización en que se clasifican los organismos

telomere: repetitive DNA at the end of a eukaryotic chromosome (352)

telómero: ADN repetitivo situado en el extremo de un cromosoma eucariota

telophase: phase of mitosis in which the distinct individual chromosomes begin to spread out into a tangle of chromatin (283)

telofase: fase de la mitosis en la cual los distintos cromosomas individuales comienzan a separarse y a formar hebras de cromatina

temporal isolation: form of reproductive isolation in which two or more species reproduces at different times (495)

aislamiento temporal: forma de aislamiento reproductivo en la cual dos o más especies se reproducen en épocas diferentes

tetrad: structure containing four chromatids that forms during meiosis (324)

tétrada: estructura con cuatro cromátidas que se forma durante la meiosis

theory: well-tested explanation that unifies a broad range of observations and hypotheses, and enables scientists to make accurate predications about new situations (13)

teoría: explicación basada en pruebas que unifica una amplia gama de observaciones e hipótesis; permite que los científicos hagan predicciones exactas ante situaciones nuevas

thylakoid: saclike photosynthetic membranes found in chloroplasts (231)

tilacoide: membranas fotosintéticas con forma de bolsa situadas en los cloroplastos

tissue: group of similar cells that perform a particular function (216)

tejido: grupo de células similares que realizan una función en particular

tolerance: ability of an organism to survive and reproduce under circumstances that differ from their optimal conditions (99)

tolerancia: capacidad de un organismo de sobrevivir y reproducirse en circunstancias que difieren de sus condiciones óptimas

totipotent: cells that are able to develop into any type of cell found in the body (including the cells that make up the extraembryonic membranes and placenta) (294)

totipotentes: células capaces de convertirse en cualquier tipo de célula del cuerpo (incluidas las células que forman las membranas situadas fuera del embrión y la placenta)

trait: specific characteristic of an individual (309)

rasgo: característica específica de un individuo

transcription: synthesis of an RNA molecule from a DNA template (364)

transcripción: síntesis de una molécula de ARN a partir de una secuencia de ADN

transfer RNA (tRNA): type of RNA that carries each amino acid to a ribosome during protein synthesis (363)

ARN de transferencia: tipo de ARN que transporta a cada aminoácido hasta un ribosoma durante la síntesis de proteínas

transformation: process in which one strain of bacteria is changed by a gene or genes from another strain of bacteria (339)

transformación: proceso en el cual una cepa de bacterias es transformada por uno o más genes provenientes de otra cepa de bacterias

transgenic: term used to refer to an organism that contains genes from other organisms (426)

transgénico: término utilizado para referirse a un organismo que contiene genes provenientes de otros organismos

translation: process by which the sequence of bases of an mRNA is converted into the sequence of amino acids of a protein (368)

traducción (genética): proceso por el cual la secuencia de bases de un ARN mensajero se convierte en la secuencia de aminoácidos de una proteína

trophic level: each step in a food chain or food web (77)

nivel trófico: cada paso en una cadena o red alimenticia

tumor: mass of rapidly dividing cells that can damage surrounding tissue (289)

tumor: masa de células que se dividen rápidamente y pueden dañar al tejido circundante

U

understory: layer in a rain forest found underneath the canopy formed by shorter trees and vines (112)

sotobosque: en un bosque tropical, la capa de vegetación que se halla bajo el dosel forestal, formada por árboles más bajos y enredaderas

V

vacuole: cell organelle that stores materials such as water, salts, proteins, and carbohydrates (198)

vacuola: orgánulo celular que almacena sustancias como agua, sales, proteínas e hidratos de carbono

van der Waals force: slight attraction that develops between oppositely charged regions of nearby molecules (38)

fuerzas de van der Waals: atracción leve que se desarrolla entre las regiones con cargas opuestas de moléculas cercanas

vestigial structure: structure that is inherited from ancestors but has lost much or all of its original function (469)

estructura vestigial: estructura heredada de los ancestros que ha perdido su función original en gran parte o por completo

W

weather: day-to-day conditions of the atmosphere, including temperature, precipitation, and other factors (96)

tiempo: condiciones diarias de la atmósfera, entre las que se incluyen la temperatura, la precipitación y otros factores

wetland: ecosystem in which water either covers the soil or is present at or near the surface for at least part of the year (119)

humedal: ecosistema en el cual el agua cubre el suelo o está presente en la superficie durante al menos una parte del año

X, Y, Z

zooplankton: small free-floating animals that form part of plankton (76)

zooplancton: pequeños animales que flotan libremente y forman parte del plancton

zygote: fertilized egg (325)

cigoto: huevo fertilizado

Index

A

Abiotic factors, **66**–67, 100, 111
Acetyl-CoA, 256
Acid rain, **164,** 180
Acids, **44**
  amino, **48**–49, 84, 366
  fatty, 47–48
  nucleic, **48,** 344, 403, 436
Acquired characteristics, 456
Actin, 199
Activation energy, **51**–52
Active site, 53
Active transport, **212**–213, 227
Adaptations, **461**
  to biomes, 112–115
  evolutionary, 487
  and natural selection, 461–464
Adaptive radiation, **550**–551
Adenine, 344–345, 348, 366
Adenosine diphosphate (ADP), 227, 235
Adenosine triphosphate (ATP), 48, **226**–227
  ATP synthase, **237,** 258
  and cellular respiration, 252, 254–260
  and exercise, 264–265
  and fermentation, 262–263
  and photosynthesis, 235–239
Adhesion, **41**
Adult stem cells, 295, 297
Aerobic respiration, **252**
Age structure of populations, **131,** 144
Agriculture, 155
Air pollution, 163–165
Alcoholic fermentation, 263
Algae
  in food chains and webs, 73–74
  green, 528
  and photosynthesis, 70
  phytoplankton, 73, 117
  red, 528
  unicellular, 214
Alkaline solution, 44
Alleles, **310,** 482. *See also* Genetics
  allele frequencies, **483,** 490–492
  dominant and recessive, 310–312, 318, 394
  and gene linkage, 328–329
  multiple and codominant, **320,** 394

  and phenotypes, 488
  segregation of, **312,** 314, 318
  and traits, 397, 485–486
Amino acids, **48**–49
  and genetic code, 366
  in nitrogen cycle, 84
Amniota, 518–519
Amoebas, 213
Anaerobic respiration, **252,** 262
Animal behavior
  and climate change, 178
Animalia, 514, 523–524, 528
Animals. *See also* Chordates;
  Invertebrates; Vertebrates
  asexual reproduction in, 277
  cell differentiation in, 293
  cells of, 203, 206–207, 211, 215
  cloned, 427, 429
  cytokinesis, 284
  genetically modified, 429–430
  transgenic, 426, 429–430
Antigens, 394
Antiparallel strands, 347
Aphotic zone, **117,** 121
Apoptosis, **288**
Aquaculture, **176**
Aquaporins, **210**
Aquatic ecosystems, 117–121
  biotic and abiotic factors in, 66–67
  changes in, 63
  energy production in, 70
  estuaries, **119**
  food chains and webs in, 73–76
  freshwater, 118–119
  marine, 120–121
  nutrient limitation in, 86
  underwater conditions in, 117–118
Archaea, 524, **526**
Archaebacteria, 524, 526
Archean Eon, 542
Artificial selection, 457–**458,** 461
Asexual reproduction, **19,** 277–278
  in plants, 277
  in prokaryotes, 281
Association of Zoos and Aquariums
  (AZA), 170
Atmospheric resources, 163–165
Atomic number, 35
Atoms, **34**–38
ATP. *See* Adenosine triphosphate
  (ATP)
ATP synthase, **237,** 258
Autosomes, **393**
Autotrophs, **69,** 117, **228,** 250
Avery, Oswald, 340, 349

B

Background extinction, 548
Bacteria, 214
  and cell organelles, 557
  chemosynthetic, 70
  classification of, 524–526
  early images of, 190
  gene expression in, 377
  growth of, 133, 146
  lateral gene transfer in, 485
  and mutations, 375, 420
  photosynthetic, 70, 545, 555
  and recombinant DNA, 424–425
  viral infections of, 340–341
Bacteria, domain, 524–**525**
Bacterial transformation, **339**–340
Bacteriophages, **340**–341
Bar coding, DNA, 529
Barr body, 396
Base pairing, **348,** 350
Bases, **44**
Beagle, 450–451
Beak size, 473, 502
Behavioral isolation, **495,** 497
Benign tumors, 289
Benthic zone, 117, 121
Benthos, **117**
Beta-carotene, 430
Beta-globin, 398
Bias, **14**
Binary fission, 281
Binomial nomenclature, **511**
Biodiversity, **166**–171. *See also*
  Diversity
  conservation, 170–171
  patterns of, 451–453, 465
  threats to, 168–170
  types of, 166–167
Biogeochemical cycles, **79,** 163
Biogeography, **465**
Bioinformatics, **407,** 422
Biological magnification, **161**
Biology, 17–25, 80
  defined, **17**
  fields of, 22–23
  measurement in, 24
  molecular, **23,** 370
  and safety, 25
  themes of, 20–21
Biomass, **78**
Biomes, **65,** 110–116, 122
Biosphere, **21, 64.** *See also* Ecology;
  Ecosystems
Biotechnology, **23, 419,** 436–439.
  See also Genetic engineering
Biotic factors, **66**–67, 100

Birds
  behavioral isolation in, 495
  evolution of, 520, 547
  and natural selection, 472–473, 489, 496–497
  and resource sharing, 101
Birthrate, 132, 142–143
Bisphenol-A (BPA), 16
Blastocyst, **294**
Blastula, 272–273
Blood, 42
  carbon dioxide removal from, 50, 52
  groups, 394
  pH of, 44
  types, 320
Bonds, chemical, 36–38
  carbon, 45
  covalent, **37,** 344
  hydrogen, **41,** 348
  ionic, **37**
Boreal forests, 114
Botanical illustrator, 655
Bottleneck effect, **490**
Breeding
  artificial selection, 457–**458**
  inbreeding, **419**
  selective, **418**–420
Brown algae, 527
Bt toxin, 428
Buffers, **44**
Bulk transport, 213
Burbank, Luther, 419

C

C. elegans, 293–294, 381
Calcium, 82
Calorie, **250**
Calvin, Melvin, 229, 238
Calvin cycle, **238**–239
Cambrian Period, 542, 543, 560
Camouflage, 113–114
CAM plants, 241
Cancer, **289**–290
  skin, 337, 357
Canopy, **112**
Capillary action, 41
Carbohydrates, **46**–47, 250–251
Carbon, 35, 45
Carbon credits, 171
Carbon cycle, 82–83
Carbon dating, 541
Carbon dioxide
  atmospheric, 164, 169, 178
  in blood, 52
  and cellular respiration, 253
  and climate, 545

  and nutrient cycles, 82–83
  and photosynthesis, 239, 241, 253
  removal from bloodstream, 50, 52
Carbonic anhydrase, 52
Carboniferous Period, 543, 561
Carnivores, **71**
Carrying capacity
  of biosphere, 155
  of species, **135**
Catalysts, **52**
Cell, 20, **191**
  active transport, **212**–213, 227
  animal, 203, 206–207, 211, 215
  artificial, 435
  cell membranes, **193,** 203–204, 209–213
  cell plate, 284
  cell stains, 191
  cell theory, **191**
  daughter, 276, 280, 325, 327–328
  diploid and haploid, **323**–328
  discovery of, 190–191
  and food molecules, 250
  and homeostasis, **214**–217
  human, 392–393
  and microscopes, 190–192
  multipotent, **295**
  mutations of, 375
  organelles, **196,** 198–202
  passive transport, **209**–211
  plant, 203, 206–207, 211, 215
  plasma, 1017
  pluripotent, **294**
  RNA synthesis in, 364–365
  size of, 193, 274–276
  specialization of, 215, 380
  stem, **294**–297
  structure of, 196–207
  totipotent, **294**
  tumors, **289**
  walls of, **203**
Cell cycle, **280**–282
  and apoptosis, **288**
  eukaryotic, 281
  growth factors, **287**
  phases of, 281–282
  prokaryotic, 281
  regulating, 286–290
Cell differentiation, 215, 292–297, 380–381
  defined, **293**
  and environment, 383
  and Hox genes, 382
  in plants, 292
  stem cells, 294–297
Cell division, 191, 274–290. *See also* Cell cycle; Meiosis

  and cancer, 290
  and cell size, 274–276
  and chromosomes, **279**–280, 282–283
  controls on, 286–288
  cytokinesis, **282,** 284
  defined, **276**
  and interphase, **281**
  mitosis, **282**–285, 328
  and reproduction, 277–278
Cellular junctions, 217
Cellular respiration, 250–260
  aerobic and anaerobic, **252,** 260
  defined, **251**
  efficiency of, 256
  and electron transport, 258
  and exercise, 265
  glycolysis, 252, **254**–255
  Krebs cycle, 252, **256**–260
  overview of, 251–252
  and photosynthesis, 253
  stages of, 251
Cellulose, 47
Cenozoic Era, 563
Centrioles, **199, 282**
Centromere, **282**
Chargaff, Erwin, 344, 348–349
Chase, Martha, 340–341, 349
Chemical reactions, **50**–51, 80
Chemiosmosis, 237, 258
Chemistry of life, 34–53
  atoms, **34**
  bonding, 36–38
  carbon compounds, 45–49
  chemical reactions, 50–51, 80
  compounds, **36**–38
  elements and isotopes, **35**
  enzymes, **52**–54
Chemosynthesis, **70**
Chemosynthetic organisms, 117, 121
Chemotherapy, 290
Chesapeake Bay, 119
Chlorine, 35, 37
Chlorofluorocarbons (CFCs), 175
Chlorophyll, 202, 230–232
Chloroplasts, **202,** 231, 557
Cholesterol, 319
Chordata, 513
Chromatid, **282**
Chromatin, 197, **280,** 352
Chromosomes, 197, **279**–280
  artificial, 424
  autosomal, **393**
  and cell division, 282–283
  chromosomal mutations, 372, 374–375

Chromosomes (cont'd)
  disorders of, 401
  eukaryotic, 280, 343, 352–353
  and gene linkage, 328–329
  homologous, **323**–325, 327
  human, 392–397
  karyotypes, **392**–393
  and polyploid plants, 376, 420
  polyploidy, 376
  prokaryotic, 279
  sex, **393**
  telomeres, **352**
  X and Y chromosomes, 393–396,
    401, 434
Cilia, 199
Citric acid cycle, 256
Clades, **516**–520, 546–547
Cladograms, **517**–520
Class, **514**
Classification, 510–528
  binomial nomenclature, **512**
  clades, **516**–520, 546–547
  class, **514**
  and DNA, 521–522
  domains, **525**–528
  evolutionary, 516–520
  family, **513**
  of fossils, 546
  genus, **512**
  kingdoms, **514**, 523–525
  Linnaean system, **513**–515
  order, **513**
  phylum, **514**
  systematics, **512**–513, 516–517
  three-domain system, 524–528
Climate, **96**–98, 110
  and biomes, **65**, 110–116, 122
  change, 170, **177**–179
  diagram, 111
  evolution of, 544
Climax communities, 108–109
Clone, **427**, 429
Codominance, **319**, 394
Codons, **366**–367
Coenzyme A, 256
Coevolution, **551**–552
Cohesion, **41**
Collins, Francis, 349, 402
Colorblindness, 395
Commensalism, **104**
Common ancestors, **464**, 468–469,
  516–521

Communities, **64**, 100–102, 108–109
Competition, ecological
  and communities, 100–102
  and natural selection, 473, 497
  and population density, 138
Competitive exclusion principle, **101**
Complementary strands, 350
Complex carbohydrates, 47
Compound microscope, 26
Compounds, chemical, **36**–38
Coniferous forests, 114
Conifers, **114**
Conservation, 162, 170–171, 176.
    See also Resources, natural
Consumers, **71**–72
Continental drift, 544–545
Continental shelf, 121
Contour plowing, 160
Contractile vacuole, 198
Control group, **7**
Controlled experiment, **7**, 9
Convergent evolution, **551**
Coral reefs, 121
Cork, 190
Covalent bonds, **37**, 344
C4 plants, 241
Crassulacean Acid Metabolism
    (CAM), 241
Creatine supplements, 261
Creativity, 10
Cretaceous Period, 548, 562
Crick, Francis, 346–350, 362
Crop plants, 428–429, 437–438
Crop rotation, 160
Crossing-over, **324**, 329, 484, 499
Cross-pollination, 309
Crustaceans, 501
Crutzen, Paul J., 175
Currents, ocean, 98, 118
Cyanobacteria, 70
Cycles
  carbon, 82–83
  cell, **280**–282, 286–290
  matter, 79–86
  nitrogen, 82–83
  nutrients, 82–86
  phosphorous, 85
  water, 81
Cyclins, **286**, 288
Cystic fibrosis (CF), 399–400, 431
Cytochrome *c*, 471
Cytokinesis, **282**, 284, 324
Cytoplasm, **196**
Cytosine, 344–345, 348, 366
Cytoskeleton, **199**

D

Darwin, Charles, 13, 137, 143,
    450–473, 482, 549, 552
Data, **8**
Dating techniques, 466, 540–541
Daughter cells, 276, 280, 325, 327–328
Death rate, 132, 142–143
Deciduous plants, **112**
Decomposers, **71**, 74
Deforestation, **159**
Dehydration, 189
Democritus, 34
Demographic transition, **144**
Demography, **143**. *See also* Population
  growth
Denitrification, **84**
Density-dependent limiting factors,
    137–141
Density-independent limiting factors,
    137, 140–141
Deoxyribonucleic acid. *See* DNA
Deoxyribose, 344, 362
Dependent variable, **7**
Derived characters, **518**–519, 521
Descent with modification, 464, 516
Desertification, **159**
Deserts, 113
Detritivores, **71**, 74
Devonian Period, 561
Dicer enzyme, 380–381
Dichloro diphenyl trichloroethane
    (DDT), 161, 169
Dichotomous key, **511**
Differentiation, **381**–382. *See also* Cell
  differentiation
Diffusion, **208**–211, 218
Dihybrid cross, 317
Dinosaurs, 520, 548, 550
Diploid cells, **323**–328
Directional selection, **489**
Disaccharides, 46
Disruptive selection, **489**
Distribution of populations, 131
Diversity, 21. *See also* Biodiversity
  ecosystem, **166**
  and extinction, 548
  genetic, **166**–168, 820
  species, **166**, 168
Djimdoumalbaye, Ahounta, 773
DNA, 18, 23, 48, 340–354. *See also*
    Human heredity
  and cell size, 274, 276
  chromosomes, **279**–280
  and classification, 521–522, 529
  components of, **344**–345
  crossing-over, 484, 499

DNA (cont'd)
   DNA fingerprinting, **433**–434, 440, 443
   DNA microarray, **432**
   DNA polymerase, **351**, 404, 423
   DNA replication, 281, **350**–353, 374–375, 424–425
   double-helix model of, **347**–348
   in eukaryotic cells, 193, 352–353
   evolution of, 554–555
   extraction, 354, 403
   functions of, 342–343
   and genetic disorders, 398
   as genetic material, 340–341
   manipulating, 403–405
   mtDNA, 434
   mutation rates in, 498–499
   and privacy, 437
   in prokaryotic cells, 193, 352–353
   recombinant, 421–425, 430
   and RNA, 362–365
   sequencing, 404–409
Domains, **525**–528
Dominance
   codominance, **319**
   incomplete, **319**
   principle of, **310**, 318
Dominant alleles, 310–312, 318, 394
Double Helix, The, 346
Double-helix model, **347**–348
Down syndrome, 401
Drip irrigation, 162
Drosophila melanogaster, 318, 323, 328, 361, 382, 387, 490, 501
Dry forests, 112
Dwarfism, 430
Dynamic interaction. *See* Interdependence

E

E. coli, 377, 383, 421
Earth
   age of, 454–455, 467
   early history of, 553–555
   evolution of, 544–545
   geologic time scale, **542**–543
Ecological pyramids, **77**–78
Ecology, **23,** 64–65
   case studies, 175–179
   defined, **65**
   disturbance of, 76, 80, 106–109
   ecological footprint **173**–174
   ecological hot spot, **171**
   ecological succession, **106**–109
   global, **22**
   methods of studying, 68
   and sustainability, 157, 174

Ecosystems, **65.** *See also* Aquatic ecosystems
   biomes, **65,** 110–116, 122
   and climate, **96**–98
   competition in, 100–103
   diversity of, **166**
   goods and services, 156–157
   limiting factors in, 137
   niches in, 99–**100**
   preserving, 170–171
   recycling within, 79–86
   succession in, **106**–109
   symbioses in, 103–104
Electron, **34,** 36–38
Electron carriers, **232,** 236
Electron microscopes, 192
Electron transport chain
   and cellular respiration, 258
   and photosynthesis, **236,** 252
Elements, **35**
Embryological development, 469, 500–501
Embryonic stem cells, 272–273, 295–297
Embryos, **292**
   and gene regulation, 380–382
Emigration, **132**
Endangered species, 169–170
Endocytosis, 212–213
Endoplastic reticulum, **200**–201, 248–249
Endosymbiotic theory, 202, **556**–557
Energy, 20
   activation, **51**–52
   and ATP, 226–227
   from autotrophs, 71
   and carbohydrates, 46
   and cellular respiration, 260
   in chemical reactions, 51
   from chemosynthesis, 70
   and chlorophyll, 230–231
   consumers of, 71
   ecological pyramids of, 77
   and exercise, 264–265
   and food, 250
   in food chains and webs, 73–76
   heat, 41
   and oxygen, 252
   from photosynthesis, 70
   producers of, 69–70
   solar, 97
Environment. *See also* Adaptations; Ecology; Ecosystems
   biotic and abiotic, 66–67
   disturbance of, 76, 80, 106–109
   and evolution, 544–545, 547–548

   and gene expression, 321, 383
   and human activity, 154–156, 173–174, 183
   and mutations, 375
   and survival, 278, 473, 491
Environmental Protection Agency (EPA), 173
Enzymes, **52**–54
   DNA polymerase, **351**
   restriction, **403**–405, 421
Epiphytic plants, 112
Era, geologic, **543**
Escherichia coli, 377, 383, 421
Estivation, 112
Estuary, **119**
Ethics, 14, 297, 438–439
Eubacteria, 524–525
Eukarya, 524, **526**
Eukaryotes, **193**–194, 521
   cell cycle of, 281
   cell structure of, 196–207
   DNA replication in, 352–353
   electron transport chain in, 258
   eukaryotic chromosomes, 280, 343, 352–353
   gene regulation in, 379–381
   and genetic variation, 557
   origin of, 556–557
   single-celled, 523
   transcription in, 364
   unicellular, 214, 526–527
Everglades, 119
"Evo-devo," 500
Evolution, 13, 19, 21, **450.** *See also* Natural selection
   adaptive radiation, **550**–551
   and artificial selection, 457–**458**
   and classification, 516–522
   coevolution, **551**–552
   common ancestors, 464, 468–469, 516–521, 546
   convergent, **551**
   descent with modification, 464, 516
   of DNA and RNA, 554–555
   of Earth, 544–545
   and environment, 544–544, 547–548
   of eukaryotic cells, 556–557
   and fossil record, 466–467
   and gene pools, 482–483
   and genetic drift, **490**
   and genetic equilibrium, 491–492
   and Hox genes, 500–501
   of infectious diseases, 23
   of insects, 487
   macroevolution, 546–547
   of mammals, 468

Evolution (cont'd)
  of mitochondria, 557
  molecular, 498–501
  of multicellular organisms, 558
  of organic molecules, 554
  of populations, 483–492
  of prokaryotic cells, 556–557
  rate of, 549
  and sexual reproduction, 558
  and speciation, **494**–497, 517,
    546–547
Exercise and energy, 264–265
Exocytosis, 212–213
Exons, **365**
Experiment, controlled, **7, 9**
Experimentation, ecological, 68
Exponential growth, **132**–133
Extinction, 168–170, **538**, 546–548

F
Facilitated diffusion, **209**–211
FAD (flavine adenine dinucleotide),
    256
FADH₂, 256
Family, **513**
Fats, 250–251
Fatty acids, 47–48
Fermentation, 252, **262**–263, 265–266
  alcoholic, 263
  lactic acid, 263, 265, 269
Fertilization, 325
  of pea plants, **309**
Fertilizers, 84, 86
Fish, 500
Fitness, **461**. *See also* Natural selection
Flagella, 199
Flavine adenine dinucleotide (FAD),
    256
Flowers
  and pollinators, 552
Fluid mosaic model, 205
Fluorescence microscopy, 191, 291
Food
  chains, **73**–76
  and energy, 250
  and fats, 250–251
  genetically modified, 437–438
  webs, **74**–76
Forensics, **433**
Forensic scientist, 322
Forests, 109, 112, 114, 159
Fossil fuels, 82, 178

Fossil preparator, 559
Fossils, 453, 538–545
  adaptive radiations in, 550
  classification of, 546
  and continental drift, 545
  dating, 541
  and evolutionary theory, 466–467
  index, **540**
  microfossils, 555
  types of, 538–539
Founder effect, **490**, 496
Frameshift mutations, **373**
Franklin, Rosalind, 346–349
Freshwater ecosystems, 118–119
Freshwater resources, 160–162
Frogs, 383
Fructose, 46
Fruit flies, 318, 323, 328, 361, 382,
    387, 490
Fungi, 523–524, 527

G
Galactose, 46, 378
Galápagos finches, 453, 471–473,
    496–497
Galápagos islands, 452
Gametes, **312**, 325
  and gene sets, 323
Gel electrophoresis, **404**–405, 422
Gene flow, 492
Genes, 18, **310**
  alleles of, **310**, 482
  and cancers, 289
  and chromosomes, 323
  as derived characters, 521
  and DNA, 340–341
  and DNA microarrays, 432
  gene duplication, 499–500
  gene expression, **370**–371, 377–383
  gene families, 500
  gene pools, **483**, 490
  gene regulation, 377–383
  gene therapy, **431**
  homeobox, **382**
  homeotic, **382**
  homologous, 471
  Hox, **382**, 471, 500–501
  identifying, 406
  lateral gene transfer, 485
  linkage, 328–329
  mapping, 328–329
  MC1R, 394
  mutations of, 372–376, 484
  and phenotypes, 485–486
  and proteins, 370
  sex-linked, **395**
  Ubx, 501

Genetic engineering, 418–439
  in agriculture and industry,
    428–429
  ethics of, 438–439
  in health and medicine, 430–432
  personal identification, 433–434
  and privacy, 402, 436–437
  recombinant DNA, 421–425
  and safety, 437–438
  selective breeding, **418**–420
  transgenic organisms, 426–427
Genetic Information Non-
  discrimination Act, 402, 409, 437
Genetics, **308**–329. *See also* Alleles;
    Meiosis
  codominance, **319**, 394
  dominant and recessive alleles,
    310–312, 318
  genetic code, **366**–367, 370, 470
  genetic disorders, 395, 398–401
  genetic diversity, **166**–168
  genetic drift, **490**
  genetic equilibrium, **491**–492
  genetic marker, **425**
  genetic recombination, 484
  genetic testing, 402, 431
  genetic variation, 419–420,
    482–486, 558
  incomplete dominance, **319**
  multiple alleles, **320**
  principle of dominance, **310**, 318
  principle of independent
    assortment, 317–318, 328–329
  segregation of alleles, **312**, 314, 318
  traits, **309, 320**
Genome, human, **392**–393, 403–409,
    436
Genomics, **23, 407**, 435
Genotypes, **315**, 321, 397–398, 407, 482
Genus, **511**, 516
Geographic isolation, **495**, 496
Geological processes, 80
Geologic time scale, **542**–543
Gibson, Daniel G., 435
Global ecology, **22**
Global warming, **177**
Globins, 500
Glucose, 46–47, 209, 251, 378
Glycogen, 47
Glycolysis, 252, **254**–255, 262
Golgi apparatus, **201**
Gradualism, **549**
Grana, 231
Grant, Peter and Rosemary, 472–473,
    496
Grassland, 112–113
Great Plains, 158–159

Green algae, 528
Green fluorescent protein (GFP), 422
Greenhouse effect, **97,** 163–164, 178, 545
Griffith, Frederick, 338–340, 349, 423
Guanine, 344–345, 348, 366

H

Habitat, **99**
Habitat fragmentation, **168**
Hair
color, 394, 396–397
Half-life, **540**–541
Haploid cells, **323**–328
Haplotypes, 407
Hardy-Weinberg principle, **491**
Heart disease, 167
Heat
absorption, 122
capacity, 41
greenhouse effect, 97
transport, 98
Helix, 346
Helmont, Jan van, 225, 229, 245
Hemoglobin, 49, 57, 375, 398
Herbicides, 428, 438
Herbivores, **71**
Herbivory, **102,** 138–139
Heredity, 20, 308, 318. *See also*
Genetics; Human heredity
Hershey, Alfred, 340–341, 349
Heterotrophs, **71, 228,** 250, 527
Heterozygous organisms, **314**
Histones, 280, 352
Homeobox genes, **382**
Homeostasis, **19**–20
and cells, **214**–217
and pH, 44
Homeotic genes, **382**
Homologous chromosomes, **323**–325, 327
Homologous proteins, 471
Homologous structures, **468**–469
Homozygous organisms, **314**
Hooke, Robert, 190
Hormones
steroid and nonsteroid, 379
Hoxc8, 470
Hox genes, **382,** 471, 500–501
Human activity, 154–156, 173–174, 183. *See also* Resources, natural
Human Genome Project, **406**–409, 430
Human growth hormone (HGH), 3, 29, 430
Human heredity, 392–409
genetic disorders, 395, 398–401
and genome, **392**–393, 403–409

karyotypes, **392**–393
pedigrees, **396**–397, 410
transmission of traits, 394–396
Human populations. *See also*
Populations
growth patterns of, 143–145
history of, 142–143
impact of, 80, 84, 109, 139, 141
Huntington's disease, 399
Hutton, James, 454–455, 459, 467
Hybridization, **419**
Hybrids, **309**
Hydrochloric acid, 44
Hydrogen, 35, 51
Hydrogen bonds, **41,** 348
Hydrogen ions, 43–44
and cellular respiration, 258
and photosynthesis, 236–237
Hydrophilic molecules, 204
Hydrophobic molecules, 204
Hypertonic solutions, **210**–211
Hyponatremia, 221
Hypothesis, **7,** 9
Hypotonic solutions, **210**–211

I

Ichthyosaur, 536–537
Immigration, **132**
Inbreeding, **419**
Incomplete dominance, **319**
Independent assortment, principle of, **317**–318, 328–329
Independent variable, **7**
Index fossils, **540**
Infectious diseases, **23**
Inference, **7**
Ingenhousz, Jan, 229
Inheritance, 308, 310, 318, 456, 461. *See also* Genetics; Human heredity
Inorganic chemistry, 45
Insecticides, 161, 428, 438
Insects
and Hox genes, 501
mutations in, 376
and plant evolution, 552
Integrated pest management (IPM), 162
Interdependence, 21
of biosphere, 64–65
in food chains and webs, 73–76
Intergovernmental Panel on Climate Change (IPCC), 177–178
International HapMap Project, 407
International System of Units (SI), 24
Interphase, **281,** 324
Intertidal zone, 120
Introduced species, 169

Introns, **365**
Invasive species, 136
Ionic bonds, **37**
Ions, **37,** 43–44
Isolation, reproductive, **494**–495
Isotonic solutions, **210**–211
Isotopes, **35**
Iwata, So, 229

J

Jellyfish, 422
Jurassic Period, 562

K

Karyotypes, **392**–393
Keystone species, **103,** 167
Kilocalorie, 250
Kingdoms, **514,** 523–525
Klinefelter's syndrome, 401
Krebs, Hans, 256
Krebs cycle, 252, **256**–260

L

Laboratory technician, 195
Lac operon, 377–378, 383
Lac repressor, 378
Lactic acid fermentation, 263, 265, 269
Lactose, 378, 383
Lamarck, Jean-Baptiste, 456, 459, 460
Lateral gene transfer, 485
Leeches, 104
Leucine, 367
Levels of organization
ecological, 65
multicellular organisms, 216–217
proteins, 49
Lewis, Edward B., 382
Lichens, 107
Light. *See also* Sunlight
absorption, 230
and photosynthesis, 240
Light-dependent reactions, **233,** 235–237
Light-independent reactions, **233,** 238–239
Light microscopes, 191–192
Limb formation, 468–469
Limiting nutrient, **85**
Linnaean classification system, 512–514
Linnaeus, Carolus, 510–513, 515, 516
Lipid bilayer, **204**–205
Lipids, **47,** 204
Liver, 201
Living things, 17–19
Logistic growth, 134–**135**

Lyell, Charles, 454–455, 459
Lyon, Mary, 396
Lysosomes, **198**
Lysozyme, 429

M

Macleod, Colin, 349
Macroevolution, **546**–547
Macromolecules, 46–49, 250, 344
Malaria, 400
Malignant tumors, 289
Malthus, Thomas, 142, 457, 459, 460
Mammalia, 518–519, 520
Mangrove swamps, 12, 119
Manipulated variable, **7**
Marcus, Rudolph, 229
Margulis, Lynn, 557
Marine biologist, 105
Marine ecosystems, 120–121
Mass extinction, **548**
Mass number, 35
Matrix, **256**
Matter, cycles of, 20, 79–86
Mayer, Julius Robert, 229
McCarty, Maclyn, 349
MC1R gene, 394
Measurement, scientific, 24
Medicine, 430–432
Meiosis, **324**–329. *See also* Sexual
   reproduction
   crossing-over, **324**, 329, 484, 499
   meiosis I, 324–325
   meiosis II, 325
   and mitosis, 326–328
   modeling, 330
   nondisjunction in, 401
Mello, Craig, 381
Membranes
   cell, **193**, 203–204, 209–213
   thylakoid, 236–237
Mendel, Gregor, 308–318, 329, 349,
   370, 482
Mercury, 161
Mesozoic Era, 544, 562
Messenger RNA (mRNA), **363**,
   368–370
Metabolism, **19**
Metamorphosis, 383
Methionine, 369
Metric system, **24**
Microclimates, **96**
Microfilaments, 199

Microfossils, 555
Micrographs, 192
MicroRNA (miRNA), 380–381
Microscopes, 190–192
Microscopist, 195
Microspheres, 554
Microtubules, 199
Miller, Stanley, 554
Mitochondria, **202**, 216, 248–249,
   252, 521
   evolution of, 557
   matrix of, **256**
Mitochondrial DNA (mtDNA), 434
Mitosis, **282**–285. *See also* Asexual
   reproduction
   DNA replication, 353
   and meiosis, 326–328
Mitotic spindle, 199
Mixture, **42**
Modeling, ecological, 68
Model systems, 308
Molecular biology, **23**, 370
Molecular clocks, **498**–499
Molecular evolution, 498–501
Molecular transport, 212
Molecules, **37**
   electron carrier, **232**
   evolution of, 554
   homologous, 470–471
   hydrophilic/hydrophobic, 204
   macromolecules, 46–49, 250, 344
   polar, 40–41
   water, 37, 40–41
Molina, Mario, 175
Monera, 523–524
Monoculture, **155**
Monohybrid cross, 317
Monomers, **46**
Monophyletic group, **516**
Monosaccharides, **46**
Montreal Protocol, 175
Morgan, Thomas Hunt, 318, 323,
   328–329, 349
Mountain ranges, 116
Mount Saint Helens, 106, 109
Mullis, Kary, 423
Multicellular organisms, 527–528
   cells of, 215–217
   evolution of, 558
Multiple alleles, **320**
Multipotent cells, **295**
Museum guide, 559
Mutagens, **375**
Mutant, 420
Mutations, **372**–376, 484, 491
   bacterial, 420
   chromosomal, 372, 374–375

   effects of, 374–376
   gene, 372–376, 484
   and genetic variation, 419–420
   and molecular clocks, 498–499
   neutral, 484, 498
Mutualism, **103**

N

NAD⁺, **255**–256, 262–263
NADH, 255–256, 262–263
NADP⁺, **232**–233, 235–237
NADPH, 232, 235–239
Natural resources. *See* Resources,
   natural
Natural selection, 460–464. *See also*
   Evolution
   and adaptations, 461–464
   and beak size, 472–473, 496–497
   and competition, 473, 497
   defined, 462
   directional, **489**
   disruptive, **489**
   and extinction, 548
   and phenotypes, 482–483, 488–489
   on polygenic traits, 488–489
   on single-gene traits, 488
Neogene Period, 563
Neutral mutations, 484, 498
Neutrons, **34**–35
Niches, **99**–100
Nicotinamide adenine dinucleotide
   (NAD⁺), **255**
Nicotinamide adenine dinucleotide
   phosphate (NADP⁺), **232**–233,
   235–237
Nitrogen cycle, 84
Nitrogen fixation, **84**, 585
Nitrogenous bases, 344–345
Nondisjunction, **401**
Nonpoint source pollution, 160
Nonrenewable resources, **157**
Northwestern coniferous forests,
   114
Nucleic acids, **48**, 344, 403, 436
Nucleolus, 197
Nucleosomes, 280, 352
Nucleotides, **48**, 344–345, 357
Nucleus, **34**, **193**–194, **197**
Nutrient cycles, 82–86
   carbon, 82–83
   limitations of, 85–86
   nitrogen, 82–83
   phosphorous, 82–83
Nutrients, **82**, **869**
   limiting, **85**
   and plant growth, 160

O

Observation
 ecological, 68
 scientific, **6**
Occupation of organism, 100
Ocean currents, 98, 118
Oceans, 120–121. *See also* Aquatic
  ecosystems
Oken, Lorenz, 191
Omnivores, **71**
1000 Genomes Project, 409
On the Origin of Species, 460
Operator (O), **378**
Operon, **377**–378
Order, **513**
Ordovician Period, 560
Organelles, **196,** 198–202
Organic chemistry, 45. *See also*
  Chemistry of life
Organic molecules, 554
Organisms, interactions of, **65**
Organs
 cellular, **216**
Organ systems
 cellular, **216**
Osmosis, **210**–211, 218
Osmotic pressure, **211**
Ova, 202
Overfishing, 176
Oxygen, 35
 accumulation of, 555
 and electron transport, 258
 in glycolysis, 255
 molecules of, 37
 and photosynthesis, 236, 253
 and respiration, 249,
  251–253
Ozone, 163
Ozone layer, **175**

P

Paleontologist, 538, **539,** 559
Paleozoic Era, 560–561
Paramecium, 198
Parasitism, **104,** 140
Park ranger, 105
Particulates, 164
Passive transport, **209**–211
Pathologist, 195
Pax6 gene, 387
Pedigrees, **396**–397, 410
Peer review, 12
Pepsin, 53
Peptidoglycan, 525
Period, geologic, **543**

Periodic Table, 35
Permafrost, **115**
Permian Period, 561
Pesticides, 161, 487
Phagocytosis, 213
Phanerozoic Eon, 542–543, 560–563
Phenotypes, **315**
 alleles and, 488
 and genes, 485–486
 and genotypes, 321, 398
 and natural selection, 482–483,
  488–489
Phenylalanine, 369, 399
Phosphorus cycle, 85
Photic zone, **117,** 121
Photosynthesis, **70,** 224–241
 and adenosine triphosphate (ATP),
  226–227, 235–239
 and autotrophs, **228**
 C4 and CAM plants, 113, 241
 and carbon dioxide, 239, 241, 253
 and cellular respiration, 253
 and chlorophyll, **230**–232
 and chloroplasts, 202, 231
 defined, **228**
 factors affecting, 240–241
 and light-dependent reactions, 233,
  235–237
 and light-independent reactions,
  233, 238–239
 and mesophyll, 681
 overview of, 232–233
 and plants, 70, 113, 230–231
 rate of, 240
Photosynthetic bacteria, 70, 555
Photosystems, **235**–236
pH, **43**–44, 53
Phylogenetic systematics, 516–517
Phylogeny, **516**
Phylum, **514**
Phytoplankton, **73,** 117
Pigments, **230**–231
Pinocytosis, 213
Pioneer species, **107**
Plankton, **118**
Plantae, 523–524, 528
Plant breeder, 322
Plants
 and acid rain, 180
 asexual reproduction in, 277
 and cell differentiation, 292
 cells of, 203, 206–207, 211, 215
 crop, 428–429, 437–438
 cytokinesis, 284
 epiphytic, 112
 genetically modified, 428, 430
 and herbivory, **102,** 138–139, 552

 and nutrients, 160
 and photosynthesis, 70, 113, 230–231
 polyploidy in, **376,** 420
 and polysaccharides, 47
 temporal isolation in, 495
 transgenic, 426, 428, 430
 vacuoles in, 198
Plasma membrane, 193
Plasmids, **424**–425
Plate tectonics, **544**–545
Pluripotent cells, **294**
Point mutations, **373**
Point source pollution, 160
Polar molecules, 40–41
Polar zones, 97
Pollen grain, 215, 325
Pollination, 309, 552
Pollutants, **160**–165, 169
Polychlorinated biphenyls (PCBs), 161
Polygenic traits, **320, 486,** 488–489
Polymerase chain reaction (PCR), **423**
Polymerization, 46
Polymers, **46**
Polypeptides, 48, **366**
Polyploidy, **376,** 420
Polysaccharides, 47
Polyunsaturated fats, 47
Population geneticist, 322
Population growth, 130–145
 exponential, **132**–133
 factors affecting, 132
 human, 142–145
 limiting factors, **137**–141
 logistic, 134–**135**
 rate of, 131
Populations, **64**
 age structure of, **131,** 144
 alleles in, 483
 density of, **131,** 138–140
 describing, 130–131
 distribution of, 131
 evolution of, 483–492
 frequency of phenotypes in,
  485–486, 488–489
 and gene pools, 483, 490
 and genetic drift, **490**
 and genetic equilibrium, **491**–492
 geographic range of, 131
 overcrowding in, 140
Prasher, Douglas, 422
Precambrian Time, 543
Precipitation, 112
Predation, **102,** 138–139
Priestly, Jacob, 229
Primary producers, **69**
Primary succession, **106**–107
Principle of dominance, **310,** 318

Principle of independent assortment, **317**–318, 328–329
Principles of Geology, 454–455
Probability, **313**–314
Products, **50**
Prokaryotes, **193**–194, 197, 523. *See also* Bacteria
  archaea, 524, **526**
  asexual reproduction in, 281
  cell cycle of, 281
  DNA replication in, 352–353
  electron transport chain in, 258
  evolution of, 556–557
  in food production, 263
  gene regulation in, 377–378
  microfossils of, 555
  prokaryotic chromosomes, 279
  transcription in, 364
  unicellular, 214, 525–526
Promoters, **365**
Proteinoid microspheres, 554
Proteins, **48**–49
  cell production of, 200–201
  cyclins, **286,** 288
  food value of, 250–251
  and genes, 370
  histones, 280
  homologous, 471
  levels of organization, 49
  protein carriers, 209
  protein pumps, 212
  protein synthesis, 363, 366–370, 384
  regulatory, 287
  and ribosomes, **200**
Proterozoic Eon, 542, 543
Protista, 523–524, 526–527
Protists, 526–527
Protons, **34**–35
Protozoan, 214
Punctuated equilibrium, **549**
Punnett squares, **315**–316
Pyramids of biomass, 78
Pyramids of energy, 77
Pyramids of numbers, 78
Pyruvic acid, 252, 254, 256

Q

Qualitative data, 8
Quantitative data, 8
Quaternary Period, 542, 563

R

Radioactive isotopes, **35**
Radioactivity, 466
Radiometric dating, **540**–541
Rain forests, 109, 112
Random mating, 492
Reactants, **50**
Receptors, **217**
Recessive alleles, 310–312, 318, 394
Recombinant DNA, 421–**424,** 430
Regional climates, 110
Regulatory proteins, 287
Relative dating, **540**
Renewable resources, **157**
Replication, DNA, **350**–353
Reproduction, 19–20. *See also* Asexual reproduction; Sexual reproduction
  in animals, 277
  and cell division, 277–278
Reproductive isolation, **494**–495, 497
Reptiles, 468
Resources, natural, **100**–101, 158–165. *See also* Biodiversity
  atmospheric, 163–165
  freshwater, 160–162
  renewable/nonrenewable, **157**
  soil, 158–160
Respiration, 249, 251–253. *See also* Cellular respiration
Responding variable, **7**
Restriction enzymes, **403**–405, 421
Rh blood group, 394
Ribonucleic acid (RNA). *See* RNA
Ribose, 362
Ribosomal RNA (rRNA), **363, 370**
Ribosomes, **200,** 363, 368–370
RNA, 48, **362**–371
  and DNA, 362–365
  evolution of, 554–555
  miRNA, 380–381
  mRNA, **363,** 368–370
  RNA interference, **380**–381
  RNA polymerase, **364**–365
  transcription, **364,** 368, 377–379
  translation, **368**–370
  tRNA, **363,** 368–370
Rowland, F. Sherwood, 175

S

Safety studies, 16
Salt, 36–37, 42
Salt marshes, 6–8, 11–12, 119
Saturated fats, 47
Scavengers, **71**
Schleiden, Matthias, 191
Schopenhauer, Arthur, 6
Schwann, Theodor, 191
Science, 4–15
  attitudes of, 10
  defined, **5**
  goals of, 5
  as knowing, 21
  measurement in, 24
  methodology of, 6–9
  peer review, 12
  scientific theories, **13**
  and society, 14–15
Secondary succession, **106**–107
Sedimentary rock, 539–540
Segregation of alleles, **312,** 314, 318
Selection. *See* Natural selection
Selective breeding, **418**–420
Selectively permeable membranes, **205**
Self-pollination, 309
Sewage, 162
Sex chromosomes, **393**
Sex-linked gene, **395**
Sexual reproduction, **19, 277**–278
  and allele frequency, 492
  and evolution, 558
  genetic recombination in, 484
Shrubland, 112–113
Sickle cell disease, 375, 391, 398, 400, 413
Silencing complex, 380–381
Single-celled eukaryotes, 523. *See also* Protists
Single-gene traits, **485,** 488
Single nucleotide polymorphisms (SNPs), 407
Sister chromatid, 282
Skepticism, 10
Skin. *See also* Integumentary system
  cancer, 337, 357
  color, 394
Smog, **163**
Sodium, 35, 37
Sodium chloride, 36–37, 42
Soil
  erosion, **159**–160
  resources, 158–160
Soil ecosystems
  nitrogen cycle in, 84
  nutrient limitation in, 86
Solar energy. *See also* Sunlight
  and climate, 97
  and photosynthesis, 70
Solute, **42**
Solution, **42**–43
Solvent, **42**
Southern, Edward, 422
Southern blotting, 422

Speciation, **494**–497, 517, 546–547
    Galapágos finches, 496–497
    and reproductive isolation, 494–495
Species, **64, 494,** 509, 533
    and acquired characteristics, 456
    carrying capacity of, **135**
    diversity, **166,** 168
    endangered, 169–170
    and genus, 516
    introduced, 169
    invasive, 136
    keystone, **103,** 167
    naming, 510–511
    and niches, 100–101
    pioneer, **107**
    tolerance of, **99**
Species survival plans (SSPs), 170
Spectrum, visible, 230
Sperm, 325
Stabilizing selection, **489**
Staining, cell, 191
Starches, 46
Start codon, 367
Stem cells, **295**–297
Steroid hormones, 379
Steroids, 47
Stimulus, **18**
Stop codon, 367
Stroma, **231**
Struggle for existence, 460, 462–463
Sturtevant, Alfred, 329
Subatomic particles, 34
Substrates, **52**–53
Succession, ecological, **106**–109
Sucrose, 46
Sugars
    carbohydrates, 46
    and photosynthesis, 239
Sunlight, 230. *See also* Light
    and aquatic ecosystems, 117
    and plants, 635
    and skin, 337, 357
Surface tension, 41
Survival of the fittest, 461–463
Survival strategies, 278
Suspension, **42**
Sustainable development, 156–**157,**
    160, 174, 176
Sutton, Walter, 349
Symbiosis, **103**–104
Synthetic genome, 435
Systematics, **512,** 516–517

T

Taiga, **114**
TATA box, 379

Taxon, **511,** 516
Taxonomy, 510
Technology, 11
Telomerase, 352
Telomeres, **352**
Temperate forests, 114
Temperate zones, 97
Temperature
    and butterfly wing color, 321
    and enzymes, 53
    and extinction, 170
    global warming, **177**
    and photosynthesis, 240
    and water depth, 118
Temporal isolation, **495**
Terracing, 160
Tertiary Period, 563
Tetrad, **324**
Tetrapoda, 518–519
Theory, **13**
Thomas, Lewis, 64
Thylakoid membranes, 236–237
Thylakoids, **231,** 233, 235
Thymine, 344–345, 348, 362
Tissues
    cell, **216**
Tolerance of species, **99**
Topsoil, 158
Totipotent cells, **294**
Trachea epithelium, 215
Traits, **309**
    and alleles, 397, 485–486
    and environment, 321
    polygenic, **320, 486,** 488–489
    single–gene, **485,** 488
    transmission of, 394–396
Transcription, **364,** 368, 377–378
Transcription factors, 379
Transfer RNA (tRNA), **363,** 368–370
Transformation, bacterial, **339**–340
Transgenic organisms, **426**–430
Translation, **368**–370
Transport
    active, **212**–213, 227
    passive, **209**–211
Tree of life, **23**
Triassic Period, 562
Trilobites, 540
Trisomy, 401
Trophic levels, **77**–78
Tropical rain forests, 109, 112
Tropical zone, 97
Tryptophan, 367
Tubulins, 199
Tumors, **289**
Tundra, 115
Turkish Angola, 416–417

Turner's syndrome, 401
Two-factor cross, 317
Typhoid, 400

U

Ubx gene, 501
Ultraviolet (UV) light, 337, 344,
    357
Understory, **112**
Unicellular organisms, 214, 525–527
Unsaturated fats, 47
Uracil, 362, 366
Urey, Harold, 554

V

Vacuoles, **198**
Valence electrons, 36
Van der Waals forces, **38**
Van Leeuwenhoek, Anton, 190
Variation, 419–420, 457–458, 460,
    462–463, 482–486. *See also*
    Natural selection
Venter, Craig, 349
Vesicles, 198
Vestigial structures, **469**
Virchow, Rudolf, 191
Viruses
    bacterial, 340–341
    and cells, 579
Visible spectrum, 230

W

Wallace, Alfred Russel, 459, 460
Water
    atomic composition of, 36
    cycle, 81
    dehydration, 189
    intoxication, 221
    molecules of, 37, 40–41
    osmosis, **210**–211, 218
    and photosynthesis, 240
    properties of, 40–43
    quality and pollution, 156,
        160–162
    solutions and suspensions, **42**
Watershed, 162
Watson, James, 349–350, 362
Weather, **96**
Wetlands, **119,** 156
Wildlife photographer, 105
Wilmut, Ian, 427
Wind
    and heat transport, 98
Woodland, 113

Index cont'd

X
X chromosomes, 393–396, 401
X-ray diffraction, 346

Y
Y chromosomes, 393–395, 434
Yeasts, 192, 214, 263, 278, 424

Z
Zooplankton, **76,** 117
Zygote, **325**

Credits

Staff Credits
Jennifer Angel, Amy C. Austin, Laura Baselice, Neil Benjamin, Peggy Bliss, Diane Braff, Daniel Clem, Glen Dixon, Alicia Franke, Julia Gecha, Ellen Granter, Anne Jones, Stephanie Keep, Beth Kun, George Lychock, Ranida Touranont McKneally, Anne McLaughlin, Rich McMahon, Laura Morgenthau, Debbie Munson, Deborah Nicholls, Michelle Reyes, Rashid Ross, Laurel Smith, Lisa Smith-Ruvalcaba, Ted Smykal, Amanda M. Watters, Berkley Wilson

Additional Credits
Bryan Cholfin, Lisa Furtado Clark, Sharon Donahue, Amy Hamel, Courtenay Kelley, Hilary L. Maybaum, Anakin S. Michele, Jan Van Aarsen, Rachel Youdelman

Front Cover, Spine, and Title Page: ©Ralph A. Clevenger/Corbis. **Back Cover:** ©Pete Oxford/Minden Pictures.

iii: Stew Milne. **viii:** L, Courtesy of Grant Wiggins; R, Jen-Yi Wu. **xi:** ©Pete Oxford/Minden Pictures. **xii:** T, Piotr Naskrecki, Minden Pictures; B, ©Ed Rescheke/Peter Arnold, Inc. **xiv:** Andrew Syred/Photo Researchers, Inc. **xvi:** T, Colin Keates/DK Images. **xvii:** Colin Keates ©Dorling Kindersley, Courtesy of the Natural History Museum, London. **xix:** ©Fred Bavendam/Minden Pictures. **xxi:** Courtesy of Beng Chiak Tan. **xxii:** Stew Milne. **1:** ©Keren Su/CORBIS. **2–3:** ©Steve Wursta/Photopress Washington/Corbis. **3:** TR, Comstock/Jupiter Images. **4:** B, Flip Nicklin/Minden Pictures/Getty Images; ©Photopress Washington/Corbis Sygma. **5:** Flip Nicklin/Minden Pictures. **6–7:** Michael Melford/National Geographic/Getty Images. **8:** Bkgrnd, Michael Melford/NationalGeographic/Getty Images; Inset, Comstock/Jupiter Images. **10:** ©Photopress Washington/Corbis Sygma. **11:** B, Ron Chapple Stock/PhotoLibrary; T, Comstock/Jupiter Images. **12:** Dani Yeske/Peter Arnold. **14:** Pascal Goetgheluck/Photo Researchers, Inc. **15:** Romeo Gocad/AFP/Getty Images. **16:** RM, ©SuperStock, Inc.; L, ©Digital Vision Ltd./SuperStock; R, ©fStop/SuperStock; LM, ©Digital Vision Ltd./SuperStock. **17:** B, Masa Ushioda/Image Quest Marine; T, ©Photopress Washington/Corbis Sygma. **18–19:** Bkgrnd, Martin Rugner/Age Fotostock. **18:** BR, Cathy Keifer/Shutterstock; BL, Dwight Kuhn. **19:** T, John Marshall/Corbis; BL, Biophoto Associates/Photo Researchers, Inc.; BR, ©G. Thomas Bishop/Custom Medical Stock; Lower M, Dwight Kuhn; Upper M, Biophoto Associates/Photo Researchers, Inc. **21:** T, Comstock/Jupiter Images; B, Klein/Peter Arnold, Inc. **22–23:** Mark Moffett/Minden Pictures/Getty Images. **23:** Lower M, Michael Nichols/National Geographic/Getty Images; B, Tek Image/Photo Researchers, Inc.; T, Jim Richardson/Corbis; Upper M, Joseph Nettis/Photo Researchers, Inc. **24:** B, Daniel J. Cox/Corbis. **25:** Brand X/Jupiter Images. **28:** ©Anthony Bannister/Corbis. **29:** Comstock/Jupiter Images. **32–33:** Image by ©Hans Strand/CORBIS. **33:** TR, Flip Nicklin/Minden Pictures. **34:** Image by ©Hans Strand/CORBIS. **35:** Mediacolors/Alamy. **37:** Flip Nicklin/Minden Pictures. **38:** M, Ingo Arndt/FotoNatura/Minden Pictures; R, Andrew Syred/Photo Researchers, Inc.; L, Martin Harvey/Corbis. **39:** R, Juniors Bildarchiv/Alamy; L, Courtesy, Draper Labs. **40:** Image by ©Hans Strand/CORBIS. **41:** T, Piet Munsterman/Foto Natura/Minden Pictures; B, ©Richard Megna/Fundamental Photos. **42:** Flip Nicklin/Minden Pictures. **43:** B, ©Noam Armonn/istockphoto.com; MB, ©fanelie rosier/istockphoto.com; MT, ©Milos Luzanin/istockphoto.com; T, ©Nancy Louie/istockphoto.com. **45:** Image by ©Hans Strand/CORBIS. **47:** Michael Rosenfeld/Getty Images. **50:** Image by ©Hans Strand/CORBIS. **53:** TR, Flip Nicklin/Minden Pictures; L, Thomas A. Steitz, Howard Hughes Medial Institute, Yale University. **57:** Flip Nicklin/Minden Pictures. **61:** ©Pete Oxford/Minden Pictures. **62–63:** Stan Osolinski/Oxford Scientific/Jupiter Images. **63:** TR, ©Jeff Rotman/www.jeffrotman.com. **64:** BL, Tim Graham/Getty Images; BM, Arnold Streifengnu Shah/Peter Arnold Inc.; BR, Yva Momatiuk & John Eastcott/Minden Pictures; T, Stan Osolinski/Oxford Scientific/Jupiter Images. **65:** R, NASA; L, Dmitri Kessel/Time Life Pictures/Getty Images; M, Planetary Visions Ltd./Photo Researchers, Inc. **67:** ©Jeff Rotman/www.jeffrotman.com. **68:** Frans Lanting/Minden Pictures. **69:** B, Piotr Naskrecki, Minden Pictures; T, Stan Osolinski/Oxford Scientific/Jupiter Images. **70:** L, Vincenzo Lombardo/Photodisc/Getty Images; R, IFREMER French Research Institute for Exploration of the Sea. **71:** TR, Pete Oxford/MINDEN PICTURES/Getty Images; TL, Kevin Schafer/Peter Arnold; RM, Roy Toft/National Geographic Creative/Getty Images; BR, Devon Graham/Project Amazonas, Inc.; BL, Wolfgang Kaehler/Alamy; Bkgrnd, Will & Deni McIntyre/Stone/Getty Images; ML, Carol Farneti Foster/Oxford Scientific/PhotoLibrary. **72:** B, ©Jeff Rotman/www.jeffrotman.com; T, Woodt Stock/Alamy. **73:** T, Stan Osolinski/Oxford Scientific/Jupiter Images. **76:** ©Jeff Rotman/www.jeffrotman.com. **79:** Stan Osolinski/Oxford Scientific/Jupiter Images. **80:** TL, Joel Sartore/Getty Images; Upper MR, NASA; Lower MR, Kalish Dimaggio/Flirt Collection/PhotoLibrary; BL, Jim Wark/Peter Arnold; TR, Image Source/PhotoLibrary; Upper ML, Francesco Ruggeri/Getty Images; Lower ML, Adrian Dorst/Peter Arnold; BR, Corbis/PhotoLibrary. **82:** Jeff Foott/Discovery Channel Image/Getty Images. **84:** ©Jeff Rotman/Jeffrotman.com. **87:** T, NASA/Goddard Space Flight Center, The Sea/WIFS Project and GeoEye, Scientific Visualization Studio; B, NASA/Goddard Space Flight Center, Scientific Visualization Studio. **91:** ©Jeff Rotman/www.jeffrotman.com. **94–95:** Anup Shah/npl/Minden Pictures. **95:** T, ©George McCarthy/Nature Picture Library. **96:** R, ©NOAA/ZUMA/Corbis; L, Anup Shah/npl/Minden Pictures. **99:** Anup Shah/npl/Minden Pictures. **100:** ©Mitsuhiko Imamori/Minden Pictures. **102:** ©Cyril Ruoso/Minden Pictures. **103:** T, ©George McCarthy/Nature Picture Library; B, ©Hal Beral/Corbis. **104:** B, ©Todd Pusser/Nature Picture Library; T, ©Mark Taylor/Nature Picture Library. **105:** ©Stan Tekiela. **106:** Anup Shah/npl/Minden Pictures. **108:** T, Orlando Carrasquillo, El Yunque National Forest, Ecosystem Management Team; B, Orlando Carrasquillo, El Yunque National Forest, Ecosystem Management Team. **109:** Inset, L, ©Macduff Everton/CORBIS; B, ©Hallmark Institute/Photolibrary Group; Inset, R, ©Reuters/CORBIS; T, ©Gary Braasch/CORBIS. **110:** Anup Shah/npl/Minden Pictures. **112:** T, Juan Carlos Muñoz/AGE Fotostock; M, ©Staffan Widstrand/Nature Picture Library; B, ©Michele Burgess/SuperStock. **113:** T, ©Darrell Gulin/CORBIS; M, ©Jim Brandenburg/Minden Pictures; B, ©Debra Behr/Alamy. **114:** T, ©Natural Selection Jerry Whaley/Design Pics/Corbis; M, ©Stuart Westmorland/CORBIS; B, ©age fotostock/SuperStock. **115:** ©2008 Jim D. Barr/AlaskaStock.com. **116:** T, ©George McCarthy/Nature Picture Library; B, Thomas Mangelsen/Minden Pictures. **117:** B, ©Corbis/SuperStock; T, Anup Shah/npl/Minden Pictures. **118:** BL, ©Pacific Stock/SuperStock; BM, David Noton/Nature Picture Library; BR, Philippe Clement/Nature Picture Library; T, ©George McCarthy/Nature Picture Library. **119:** L, ©MICHAEL GADOMSKI/Animals Animals - Earth Scenes; RM, ©Cindy Ruggieri; R, ©age fotostock/SuperStock; MR, ©GORDON & CATHY ILLG/Animals Animals - Earth Scenes. **121:** Dante Fenolio/Photo Researchers, Inc. **124:** ©Anthony Bannister; Gallo Images/CORBIS. **125:** ©George McCarthy/Nature Picture Library. **128–129:** ©Jean-Paul Ferrero/Auscape/Minden Pictures. **129:** TR, Eric Wanders/Foto Natura/Minden Pictures. **130:** T, ©Jean-Paul Ferrero/Auscape/Minden Pictures; B, Agricultural Research Service, USDA/Stephen Ausmus. **131:** T, ©Photographers Choice RF/SuperStock; M, Copyright ©JOHNNY JOHNSON/Animals Animals/Earth Scenes; B, ©Fred Bavendam/Minden Pictures. **132:** Eric Wanders/Foto Natura/Minden Pictures. **133:** T, ©SciMAT/Photo Researchers, Inc.; B, ©Pete Oxford/Minden Pictures. **134:** ©Ingo Arndt/Minden Pictures. **136:** B, I-R/S/GRANT HEILMAN PHOTOGRAPHY, INC; TL, ©Digital Vision Ltd./SuperStock; TR, ©fStop/SuperStock; TML, ©Digital Vision Ltd./SuperStock; TMR, ©SuperStock, Inc. **137:** B, ©Joke Stuurman-Huitema/Foto Natura/Minden Pictures; T, ©Jean-Paul Ferrero/Auscape/Minden Pictures. **138:** ©John Conrad/CORBIS. **139:** B, ©WILDLIFE/Peter Arnold Inc.; T, ©D. Robert & Lorri Franz/CORBIS. **140:** T, ©Les Stocker/Photolibrary Group; B, Eric Wanders/Foto Natura/Minden Pictures. **141:** ©(AP Photo/Xinhua Photo, Jiang Yi. **142:** ©Jean-Paul Ferrero/Auscape/Minden Pictures. **143:** T, FOTOGRAF/Still Pictures/Peter Arnold, Inc.; B, FOTOGRAF/Still Pictures/Peter Arnold, Inc. **145:** ©image100/Photolibrary. **147:** R, ©(AP Photo/Xinhua Photo, Jiang Yi; L, ©Fred Bavendam/Minden Pictures. **149:** Eric Wanders/Foto Natura/Minden Pictures. **152–153:** NASA/NSSDC. **153:** TR, ©SIME s.a.s/eStock Photo. **154:** ML, ©SIME s.a.s/eStock Photo; BL, ©Douglas Peebles/eStockPhoto; BR, ©Douglas Peebles/eStockPhoto; TL, NASA/NSSDC. **155:** Patrick Bennett/Superstock. **156:** Inset, ©The Wetlands Initiative Archives; Bkgrnd, By Gary Sullivan, The Wetlands Initiative. **157:** T, ©Maurizio Borgese/Hemis/Corbis; B, ©Bobby Model/Getty Images. **158:** B, ©AP Photo; T, NASA/NSSDC. **159:** ©SIME s.a.s/eStock Photo. **160:** ©Jim Richardson/CORBIS. **162:** Bkgrnd, ©Maxphotos/Newscom; Inset, ©Richard T. Nowitz/CORBIS. **163:** ©Jason Lee/Reuters Pictures. **164:** Inset, ©Adam Hart-Davis/Photo Researchers, Inc.; Bkgrnd, ©Superstock. **166:** B, ©AP Photo/Penn State University, S. Blair Hedges); T, NASA/NSSDC. **167:** BM, ©(c) Noel Hendrickson/GETTY IMAGES; Bkgrnd, ©Marcos G. Meider/Superstock; BL, ©Paolo Aguilar/epa/Corbis. **168:** T, ©SIME s.a.s/eStock Photo; B, ©Creatas/Photolibrary Group. **169:** B, ©SIME s.a.s/eStock Photo; T, MARIANA BAZO/Reuters/Landov LLC. **170:** ©Katherine Feng/Globio/Minden Pictures. **171:** ©Barbara Walton/epa/Corbis. **173:** NASA/NSSDC. **175:** T, Images by Greg Shirah, NASA Goddard Space Flight Center Scientific Visualization Studio; B, ©Jerry Mason/Photo Researchers, Inc. **176:** T, ©Jeffrey L. Rotman/CORBIS; B, BRIAN J. SKERRY/National Geographic Image Collection. **177:** ©Armin Rose/Shutterstock. **178:** ©Sumio Harada/Minden Pictures. **179:** Inset, T, ©UPPA/Photoshot/Newscom; Inset, Lower, ©Realimage/Alamy; Bkgrnd, Charmagne Leung/California Academy of Sciences. **181:** Patrick Bennett/Superstock. **183:** ©SIME s.a.s/eStock Photo. **187:** ©Clouds Hill Imaging Ltd./CORBIS. **188–189:** Dr. Robert Berdan. **189:** TR, ©simple stock shots/Age Fotostock. **190:** B, Science Museum Library/Science & Society Picture Library; T, Dr. Robert Berdan. **191:** T, ©Grafissimo/iStockphoto.com; B, ©Dwight Kuhn; T, istockphoto.com. **192:** TL, Courtesy Hitachi High-Technologies; BL, Michael Abbey/Photo Researchers, Inc.; BR, SciMAT/Photo Researchers, Inc.; BM, Dr. Gopal Murti/Photo Researchers, Inc. **193:** ©simple stock shots/Age Fotostock.**195:** Courtesy, Dr. Tanasa Osborne. **196:** T, Dr. Robert Berdan. **198:** L, Biophoto Associates/Photo Researchers, Inc.; R, Eric Grave/Science Photo Library/Photo Researchers, Inc. **199:** T, Dr. Torsten Wittmann/Photo Researchers, Inc; B, Omikron/Photo Researchers, Inc. **202:** Biophoto Associates/Photo Researchers, Inc. **204:** Science Photo Library/Custom Medical Stock Photo. **208:** BL, ©simple stock shots/Age Fotostock; TR, Vince Streano/Stone/Getty Images; T, Dr. Robert Berdan. **213:** NIBSC/Photo Researchers, Inc. **214:** B, Volker Steger/Christian Bardele/Photo Researchers, Inc.; T, Dr. Robert Berdan. **215:** R, Ed Reschke/Peter Arnold; L, Ed Reschke/Peter Arnold. **217:** Don W. Fawcett/Photo Researchers, Inc. **221:** Alan Bailey/Rubberball/Getty Images. **224–225:** Perennou Nuridsany/Photo Researchers, Inc. **225:** TR, Watering can (earthenware), English School, (16th century)/©Museum of London, UK,/The Bridgeman Art Library International. **226:** Perennou Nuridsany/Photo Researchers, Inc. **228:** R, Anup Shah/Minden Pictures; L, Watering can (earthenware), English School, (16th century)/©Museum of London, UK,/The Bridgeman Art Library International. **229:** TL, The Granger Collection, New York; BL, American Chemical Society; ML, Biophoto Associates/Photo Researchers; MR, Imperial College London; R, James Barber, The Royal Society. **230:** Perennou Nuridsany/Photo Researchers, Inc. **231:** Andy Small/GAP Photos/Getty Images. **232:** Watering can (earthenware), English School, (16th century)/©Museum of London, UK,/The Bridgeman Art Library International. **235:** B, Doable/A. Collection/Getty Images; Perennou Nuridsany/Photo Researchers, Inc. **236:** Imagewerks/Getty Images. **239:** Watering can (earthenware), English School, (16th century)/©Museum of London, UK,/The Bridgeman Art Library International. **241:** Richard Cummins/Corbis. **243:** Imagewerks/Getty Images. **244:** John T. Fowler/Alamy. **245:** Watering can (earthenware), English School, (16th century)/©Museum of London, UK,/The Bridgeman Art Library International. **248–249:** Professor Pietro M. Motta/Photo Researchers, Inc. **249:** T, Flip Nicklin/Minden Pictures. **250:** Professor Pietro M. Motta/Photo Researchers, Inc. **251:** Stock Food Creative/Getty Images. **252:** Flip Nicklin/Minden Pictures. **254:** R, City of London Libraries and Guildhall Art Gallery/Heritage Images; L, Professor Pietro M. Motta/Photo Researchers, Inc. **256:** Flip Nicklin/Minden Pictures. **261:** B, Photos.Inc/Jupiter Images; TML, ©SuperStock, Inc.; TL, ©Digital Vision Ltd./SuperStock; TR, ©fStop/SuperStock; TMR, ©Digital Vision Ltd./SuperStock. **262:** Professor Pietro M. Motta/Photo Researchers, Inc. **264:** Brand X Pictures/Photo Library. **265:** T, Flip Nicklin/Minden Pictures; B, Matthias Breiter/Minden Pictures/Getty Images. **267:** Brand X Pictures/Photo Library. **269:** Michael Nolan/Peter Arnold. **272–273:** ©Michael Abbey/Photo Researchers, Inc. **273:** TR, ©Joe McDonald/CORBIS. **274:** R, Art Wolfe/Photo Researchers, Inc.; L, (c) Michael Abbey/Photo Researchers, Inc. **277:** L, ©CNRI/Photo Researchers, Inc.; R, Ed Reschke/PhotoLibrary Group, Inc.; M, ©Oxford Scientific Films/Photolibrary. **278:** BL, ©Martin Paul Ltd. Inc./Index Stock Imagery; BR, ©Ingram Publishing/Index Stock Imagery; T, ©Joe McDonald/CORBIS. **279:** (c) Michael Abbey/Photo Researchers, Inc. **283:** ©Ed Reschke/Peter Arnold, Inc. **284:** BL, ©DR GOPAL MURTI/SCIENCE PHOTO LIBRARY/Photo Researchers; BR, Wood/Custom Medical Stock Photo; TL, ©Joe McDonald/CORBIS. **285:** T, ©Ed Rescheke/Peter Arnold, Inc; RT, ©Ed Rescheke/Peter Arnold, Inc; RB, ©Ed Rescheke/Peter Arnold, Inc; B, ©Ed Reschke/Peter Arnold, Inc.; BL, ©Ed Rescheke/Peter Arnold, Inc; TL, ©Ed Reschke/Peter Arnold, Inc. **286:** (c) Michael Abbey/Photo Researchers, Inc. **287:** BL, ©Paul Aresu/Getty Images; BR, ©Scott Camazine/Photo Researchers, Inc.; T, ©Joe McDonald/CORBIS. **288:** L, National Institutes of Health; R, Paul Martin/Wellcome Images. **291:** TR, ©Peter Arnold, Inc./Alamy; BR, ©Max Planck Institute for Molecular Genetics; BL, ©Max Planck Institute for Molecular Genetics; TL, Hiroya Minakuchi/Minden Pictures. **292:** BL, Professor Ray F. Evert/University of Wisconsin; BML, ©Jim Haseloff/The Wellcome Trust Medical Photographic Library; BMR, ©John Durham/Photo Researchers, Inc.; BR, Neil Fletcher ©Dorling Kindersley; TL, ©Michael Abbey/Photo Researchers, Inc. **294:** ©Joe McDonald/CORBIS. **301:** ©Joe McDonald/CORBIS. **305:** BSIP LAURENT/PhotoResearchers Inc. **306–307:** ©Biosphoto/Labat J.-M. & Rouquette F./Peter Arnold Inc. **307:** RT, blickwinkel/Alamy. **308:** B, ©Bettmann/CORBIS; T, ©Biosphoto/Labat J.-M. & Rouquette F./Peter Arnold Inc. **310:** blickwinkel/Alamy. **313:** RB, Brand X/Jupiter Images; T, ©Biosphoto/Labat J.-M. & Rouquette F./Peter Arnold Inc. **318:** Maximilian Weinzier/Alamy. **319:** BL, Christopher Burrows/Alamy; BL, Christopher Burrows/Alamy; BL, Cubo Images/Alamy; TL, ©Biosphoto/Labat J.-M. & Rouquette F./Peter Arnold Inc. **320:** blickwinkel/Alamy. **321:** L, Stepan Bartos/Photo Researchers, Inc.; R, Stepan Bartos/Photo Researchers, Inc. **322:** Photo courtesy Sofia Cleland. **323:** ©Biosphoto/Labat J.-M. & Rouquette F./Peter Arnold Inc. **329:** blickwinkel/Alamy. **333:** R, blickwinkel/Alamy; L, Michael Quinton/Minden Pictures. **336–337:** Charles C. Benton/Kite Aerial Photography. **337:** TR, ©Pearson Education. Photo by Heather Wright; BR, ©aliciahh/istockphoto.com. **338:** Charles C. Benton/Kite Aerial Photography. **340:** Eye of Science/Photo Researchers, Inc. **344:** M, ©Pearson Education. Photo by Heather Wright; B, ©aliciahh/istockphoto.com; T, Charles C. Benton/Kite Aerial Photography. **346:** Bkgrnd, by Courtesy of the National Portrait Gallery, London; R, Courtesy Ava Helen & Linus Pauling Papers/Special Collections/Oregon State University; M, With permission of the University Archives, Columbia University in the City of New York. **347:** Bkgrnd, A. Barrington Brown/Photo Researchers, Inc.; RT, Kenneth Eward/BioGrafx/Photo Researchers, Inc.; RB, ©aliciahh/istockphoto.com; TM, Wellcome Library, London. RM, ©Pearson Education. Photo by Heather Wright. **349:** ML, Biophoto Associates/Photo Researchers, Inc.; M, ©arlindo71/istockphoto.com; BL, ©GlobalP/istockphoto.com; BR, Reprinted by permission from Macmillan Publishers Ltd: Nature, February 15, 2001, Volume 409, Number 6822. Copyright ©2001. **350:** Charles C. Benton/Kite Aerial Photography. **351:** T, ©Pearson Education. Photo by Heather Wright; M, ©aliciahh/istockphoto.com; B, ©Dr. Gopal Murti/Science Photo Library/Photo Researchers, Inc. **352:** Dr. Hesed Padilla-Nash/National Cancer Institute. **355:** Courtesy Ava Helen & Linus Pauling Papers/Special Collections/Oregon State University. **357:** T, ©Pearson Education. Photo by Heather Wright; B, ©aliciahh/istockphoto.com. **360–361:** Konrad Wothe/Minden Pictures. **361:** TR, EYE OF SCIENCE/SPL/Photo Researchers, Inc. **362:** Konrad Wothe/Minden Pictures. **366:** Konrad Wothe/Minden Pictures. **369:** ©MRC Lab of Molecular Biology. Wellcome Images. **370:** EYE OF SCIENCE/SPL/Photo Researchers, Inc. **372:** BL, ©Bob Gibbons/Photo Researchers, Inc.; T, Konrad Wothe/Minden Pictures; BR, Tony Camacho/Photo Researchers, Inc. **375:** B, ©Eye of Science/Photo Researchers, Inc.; **376:** ©travismanley/istockphoto.com. **377:** B, G. Murti/Photo Researchers, Inc.; T, Konrad Wothe/Minden Pictures. **379:** EYE OF SCIENCE/SPL/Photo Researchers, Inc. **381:** Steve Gschmeissner/Photo Researchers, Inc. **382:** EYE OF SCIENCE/SPL/Photo Researchers, Inc. **383:** T, ©Randy M. Ury/CORBIS; M, ©BRECK P. KENT/Animals Animals - Earth Scenes; B, ©Randy M. Ury/Corbis. **387:** EYE OF SCIENCE/SPL/Photo Researchers, Inc. **390–391:** Digital Vision. **391:** TR, ©Dr. Stanley Flegler/Visuals Unlimited. **392:** T, Digital Vision; B, CNRI/Photo Researchers, Inc. **393:** Image Source/Getty Images. **394:** CMCD Visual Symbols Library/drr.net. **395:** T, ©Dr. Stanley Flegler/Visuals Unlimited; B, ©Pearson; **396:** Dave King ©Dorling Kindersley. **398:** Digital Vision. **399:** ©Dr. Stanley Flegler/Visuals Unlimited. **402:** B, Phanie/Photo Researchers, Inc.; TMR, ©SuperStock, Inc.; TML, ©Digital Vision Ltd./SuperStock; TR, ©fStop/SuperStock; TL, ©Digital Vision Ltd./SuperStock. **403:** B, Barry Rosenthal/Getty Images; T, Digital Vision. **407:** T, ©Dr. Stanley Flegler/Visuals Unlimited; Lower BL, ©arlindo71/istockphoto.com; BM, Kenneth Eward/BioGrafx/Photo Researchers, Inc.; BR, PR NEWSWIRE; Upper BL, Biophoto Associates/Photo Researchers, Inc. **408:** R, Reprinted by permission from Macmillan Publishers Ltd: Nature, February 15, 2001, Volume 409, Number 6822. Copyright ©2001; L, From Science, Volume 291, No. 5507, February 16 2001. Reprinted with permission from AAAS. Image ©Ann Cutting. **410:** AP Images. **411:** Phanie/Photo Researchers, Inc. **412:** PHANIE/Photo Researchers, Inc. **413:** ©Dr. Stanley Flegler/Visuals Unlimited. **416–417:** Gyeongsang National University/HO/epa/Corbis. **417:** TR, ©David Parker/Photo Researchers, Inc. **418:** TR, Thinkstock/Jupiter Images; B, Corbis Royalty Free/Jupiter Images. **419:** Jim Strawser/Alamy. **420:** Jose F. Poblete/Corbis. **421:** M, Andrew Syred/Photo Researchers, Inc.; T, ©Gyeongsang National University/HO/epa/Corbis; ©Gyeongsang National University/HO/epa/Corbis; B, ©David Parker/Photo Researchers, Inc. **422:** Wernher Krutein/Photovault. **424:** Torunn Berge/Photo Researchers, Inc. **427:** AP Photo/PA/Files. **428:** B, AGStock/Alamy; T, ©Gyeongsang National University/HO/epa/Corbis. **429:** Goat, Jan L. Carson/University of California at Davis; Girl, ©istockphoto.com/Katrina Brown. **430:** UPI/Digital Railroad.net. **431:** Mickie Gelsinger. **432:** Dr. Malcolm Campbell and the GCAT Program of Davidson College. **433:** Index Stock/SuperStock. **434:** ©David